FILM HISTORY

AN INTRODUCTION

FILM HISTORY

AN INTRODUCTION

KRISTIN THOMPSON
DAVID BORDWELL

University of Wisconsin–Madison

McGRAW-HILL, INC.

New York / St. Louis / San Francisco / Auckland / Bogotá / Caracas
Lisbon / London / Madrid / Mexico City / Milan / Montreal / New Delhi
San Juan / Singapore / Sydney / Tokyo / Toronto

FILM HISTORY:
AN INTRODUCTION

Photo Credits appear on page 825, and on this
page by reference.

This book is printed on acid-free paper.

1 2 3 4 5 6 7 8 9 0 DOW   DOW 9 0 9 8 7 6 5 4

ISBN 0-07-006449-0 (hard cover)
ISBN 0-07-006445-8 (soft cover)

This book was set in Bodoni Book by Ruttle,
Shaw & Wetherill, Inc.
The editors were Peter Labella,
Cynthia Ward, and Curt Berkowitz;
the designer was Joan E. O'Connor;
the production supervisor was Louise Karam.
R. R. Donnelley & Sons Company was printer
and binder.

Cover photos (top to bottom):

Yeelen © October Films, 1993;
Sergei Eisenstein's *Potemkin;* An unidentified
Pathé film, c. 1905; Marcel Carné's
Le Jour se lève; The Godfather,
copyright © 1993 by Paramount Pictures.
All rights reserved.

Library of Congress Cataloging-in-Publication Data

Thompson, Kristin, (date).
    Film history: an introduction / Kristin Thompson, David Bordwell.
        p.   cm.
    Includes bibliographical references and index.
    ISBN 0-07-006449-0—ISBN 0-07-006445-8 (softcover)
    1. Motion pictures—History.   I. Bordwell, David.   II. Title.
PN1993.5.A1T45   1994
791.43'09—dc20   93-42486

ABOUT THE AUTHORS

Kristin Thompson and David Bordwell are married and live in Madison, Wisconsin.

Kristin Thompson is an Honorary Fellow in the Department of Communication Arts at the University of Wisconsin—Madison. She holds a master's degree in film from the University of Iowa and a doctorate in film from the University of Wisconsin—Madison. She has published *Eisenstein's Ivan the Terrible* (Princeton University Press, 1981), *Exporting Entertainment: America's Place in World Film Markets,1907–1934* (British Film Institute, 1985), *Breaking the Glass Armor: Neoformalist Film Analysis* (Princeton University Press, 1988), and *Wooster Proposes, Jeeves Disposes; or, Le Mot Juste* (James H. Heinemann, 1992), a study of P. G. Wodehouse. She is currently at work on a history of European avant-garde film styles of the 1920s. In her spare time she studies Egyptology.

David Bordwell is Jacques Ledoux Professor of Film Studies in the Department of Communication Arts at the University of Wisconsin—Madison. He holds a master's degree and a doctorate in film from the University of Iowa. His books include *The Films of Carl-Theodor Dreyer* (University of California Press, 1981), *Narration in the Fiction Film* (University of Wisconsin Press, 1985), *Ozu and the Poetics of Cinema* (Princeton University Press, 1988), *Making Meaning: Inference and Rhetoric in the Interpretation of Cinema* (Harvard University Press, 1989), and *The Cinema of Einstein* (Harvard University Press, 1993). He has won a University Distinguished Teaching Award.

The authors have previously collaborated on *Film Art: An Introduction* (McGraw-Hill, 4th ed., 1993) and, with Janet Staiger, on *The Classical Hollywood Cinema: Film Style and Mode of Production to 1960* (Columbia University Press, 1985).

TO GABRIELLE

Chez Léon tout est bon

CONTENTS

PART THREE: THE DEVELOPMENT OF SOUND CINEMA, 1926–1945

10 THE HOLLYWOOD STUDIO SYSTEM, 1930–1945

PREFACE

S umming up a hundred years in the development of a major mass medium is a daunting task. We have tried, within the compass of a single volume, to construct a readable history of the principal trends within mainstream fictional filmmaking, documentary filmmaking, and experimental cinema. Our Introduction and the essay which follows it, "History, Historiography, and Film History," lay out in more detail the assumptions and frame of reference which have guided our work. We hope that this book will prove a useful initiation to an endlessly fascinating subject.

We have been studying film history for twenty-five years, and we are well aware of how much a historian owes to archives, libraries, and individuals. Many archivists helped us gain access to films and photographs. We thank Elaine Burroughs, Jackie Morris, Julie Rigg, and the staff of the National Film Archive of the British Film Institute; Paul Spehr, Kathy Loughney, Patrick Loughney, Cooper Graham, and the staff of the Motion Picture, Television, and Recorded Sound Division of the Library of Congress; Mark-Paul Meyer, Eric de Kuyper, and the staff of the Nederlands Filmmuseum; Eileen Bowser, Charles Silver, Mary Corliss, and the staff of the Film Study Center of the Museum of Modern Art; Ib Monty, Marguerite Engberg, and the staff of the Danish Film Museum; Vincent Pinel and the staff of the Cinémathèque Française of Paris; Robert Rosen, Eddie Richmond, and the staff of the UCLA Film Archive; Bruce Jenkins, Mike Maggiore, and the staff of the Walker Art Center Film Department; Robert A. Haller, Carol Pipolo, and the staff of Anthology Film Archives; and Edith Kramer and the staff of the Pacific Film Archive. We owe special thanks to Jan-Christopher Horak and Paolo Cherchai Usai of the Motion Picture Division of George Eastman House, who assisted our work "beyond the call of duty." Finally, this book could not have been as comprehensive and detailed as it has become without the generosity of the late Jacques Ledoux and his successor Gabrielle Claes. Along with their staff at the Cinémathèque Royale de Belgique, they kindly supported our work in innumerable ways.

In addition, we wish to thank others who shared information and films with us: Jacques Aumont, John Belton, Edward Branigan, Carlos Bustamente,

Chen Mei, David Desser, Michael Drozewski, Michael Friend, André Gaudreault, Kevin Heffernan, Richard Hincha, Kyoko Hirano, Donald Kirihara, Hiroshi Komatsu, Richard Maltby, Albert Moran, Charles Musser, Peter Parshall, William Paul, Richard Peña, Tony Rayns, Donald Richie, David Rodowick, Phil Rosen, Barbara Scharres, Alex Sesonske, Alissa Simon, Cecille Starr, Yuri Tsivian, Alan Upchurch, Ruth Vasey, Marc Vernet, and Chuck Wolfe. Jerry Carlson went out of his way to assist our work on Eastern European and Latin American topics, while Diane and Kewal Verma helped us get access to obscure Hindi films. Tom Gunning waded through the entire manuscript and offered many valuable suggestions.

Our coverage of silent cinema was enhanced by the annual "Giornate del cinema muto" events at Pordenone, Italy. These gatherings have revolutionized the study of silent cinema, and we are grateful to Davide Turconi, Lorenzo Codelli, Paolo Cherchi Usai, and their associates for inviting us to participate in them.

We are also grateful to our readers in the discipline, who provided helpful criticism and suggestions: Jonathan Buchsbaum, Queens College; Jeremy Butler, University of Alabama; Diane Carson, St. Louis Community College; Thomas D. Cooke, University of Missouri; David A. Daly, Southwest Missouri State University; Peter Haggart, University of Idaho; Brian Henderson, State University of New York at Buffalo; Scott L. Jensen, Weber State College; Kathryn Kalinak, Rhode Island College; Jay B. Korinek, Henry Ford Community College; Sue Lawrence, Marist College; Karen B. Mann, Western Illinois University; Charles R. Myers, Humboldt State University; John W. Ravage, University of Wyoming; Jere Real, Lynchburg College; Lucille Rhodes, Long Island University; H. Wayne Schuth, University of North Orleans; J. P. Telotte, Georgia Tech University; Charles C. Werberig, Rochester Institute of Technology; and Ken White, Diablo Valley College.

This project could not have come into being without the resources and people of the University of Wisconsin–Madison. Much of this volume derives from our teaching and scholarly work, activities which have been generously supported by the Department of Communication Arts, the Graduate School, and the Institute for Research in the Humanities. Moreover, we have come to rely on the Wisconsin Center for Film and Theater Research, its collections and its staff supervised by our Archivist, the ever-cooperative Maxine Fleckner Ducey.

In addition, our Madison colleagues lent their expertise to this book. Tino Balio's suggestions improved our coverage of the film industry; Ben Brewster scrutinized our chapters on early cinema; Noël Carroll offered detailed comments on experimental cinema and Hollywood film; Don Crafton supplied suggestions and photographic materials on animation and early French cinema; Lea Jacobs improved our understanding of Hollywood film and women's cinema; Vance Kepley advised us on Russian and Soviet film; J. J. Murphy informed our discussion of the avant-garde; Marc Silberman helped us nuance our treatment of German film history. Our intellectual debts to these colleagues are deepened by our admiration and affection.

Kristin Thompson
David Bordwell

INTRODUCTION

Around the world, at any instant, millions of people are watching movies. They watch mainstream entertainment, serious "art films," documentaries, cartoons, experimental films, educational shorts. They sit in air-conditioned theaters, in village squares, in art museums, in college classrooms, or in their homes before a television screen. The world's film theatres attract around fifteen billion customers each year. With the availability of films on video—broadcast, fed from cable or satellites, or played back from cassette or laserdisc—the audience has multiplied far beyond that.

Nobody needs to be convinced that film is one of the century's most influential media. Not only can you recall your most exciting or tearful moments at the movies. You can also probably remember moments in ordinary life when you tried to be as graceful, as selfless, as tough, or as compassionate as those larger-than-life figures on the screen. The way we dress and cut our hair, the way we talk and act, the things we believe or doubt—all these aspects of our lives are shaped by films. Films also provide us with powerful aesthetic experiences, insights into cultures, and glimpses of new ways of thinking.

So we aren't surprised that people rush to the latest hit or rent a cult favorite from the video store. Why, though, should anybody care about *old* movies?

For one thing, they offer the same sort of insights that we get from watching contemporary movies. Some offer intense artistic experiences or penetrating visions of human life in other times and places. Some are documents of everyday existence, or of extraordinary historical events which continue to reverberate in our times. Still other old movies are resolutely strange. They refuse to assimilate themselves to our current habits of thought. They force us to acknowledge that films can be radically different from what we are used to and that we must adjust our own field of view to accommodate what was, astonishingly, taken for granted by others.

Film history includes more than just films. By studying how films were made and received, we discover the range of options available to filmmakers and film viewers. By studying the social and cultural influences on films, we come to understand better the ways in which films may bear the traces of the societies that make and consume them. Film history opens up a range of issues in the history of politics, of culture, and of the arts (both "high" and "popular").

Yet another answer to our question is this: studying old movies and the times in which they were made is intrinsically fun. As a relatively new field of academic research (no more than thirty years old), film history has the excitement of a young discipline. There are more questions than answers, more uncertainties than absolutes. There is still so much to be discovered— so many unseen films, so many unexplored genres and directors and national industries, so many new perspectives on key issues—that we can confidently say that historical research into film is one of the most energetic areas of humanistic study today.

This book aims to introduce the history of film as it is understood now. It assumes no specialized knowledge of film aesthetics or theory, although some acquaintance with these areas would certainly benefit the reader.[1] We have tried, in the space of one volume, to sum up the history of film as it is presently conceived, written, and taught by its most accomplished scholars.

Our purview has been limited to those realms of filmmaking which are most frequently studied. We consider theatrical fiction films, documentary films, experimental or avant-garde filmmaking, and animation. There are other types of cinema—most notably educational, industrial, and scientific-information films—but whatever their intrinsic interest, for the moment they play secondary roles in most historians' concerns.

Film History: An Introduction is not, however, exactly a distillation of an "essential" film history. Researchers are fond of saying that there is no film *history*, only film *histories*. Sometimes this means that there can be no intelligible, coherent "grand narrative" that puts all the facts into place. The history of avant-garde film does not fit neatly into the history of color technology or the development of the Western or the life of John Ford. At other times, the slogan means that historians work from various perspectives and within the ambit of different interests and purposes.

We agree with both points. There is no single narrative of film history that accounts for all events, causes, and consequences. And the variety of historical approaches guarantees that historians will draw diverse and dissenting conclusions. We also think that film history is more aptly thought of as a set of film histo*ries* because research into film history involves asking a series of *questions* and searching for *evidence* in order to answer them in the course of an *argument*. When historians focus on different questions, turn up different evidence, and formulate different arguments, we have not a single history but a diverse set of historical arguments.

We discuss these principles in more detail in the following section, "History, Historiography, and Film History." That section can be thought of as an introduction to the intricacies of such issues. For now, we should simply indicate the sorts of questions and evidence we have chosen to concentrate on.

We have been guided by three principal questions.

1. *How have uses of the film medium changed or become normalized over time?* Within "uses of the medium" we include matters of film form: the part/whole organization of the film. Often this involves telling a story, but a film's overall form might also be based on an argument or a more conceptual pattern. The term "uses of the medium" also includes matters of film style, the patterned uses of film techniques (*mise-en-scene,* or staging, lighting, setting, and costume; camerawork; editing; and sound). In addition, any balanced conception of how the medium has been used must also consider film modes (documentary, avant-garde, fiction, animation) and genres (the Western, the thriller, the musical, and so on), so we also examine these phenomena. All such matters are central to most college and university survey courses in film history.

A central purpose of *Film History: An Introduction* is to survey the uses of the medium in different times and places. Sometimes we dwell on the creation of stable norms of form and style, as when we examine how Hollywood standardized certain editing options in the first two decades of filmmaking. At other times, we examine how filmmakers have proposed innovative ways of structuring form or using film technique.

2. *How have the conditions of the film industry—production, distribution, and exhibition—affected the uses of the medium?* Films are made within modes of production—habitual ways of organizing the labor and materials involved in creating a movie. Some modes of production are industrial. In these circumstances films are business ventures by companies whose purpose is to produce them for consumption. The classic instance of industrial production is the *studio* system, in which firms are organized in order to make films for large audiences through fairly detailed division of labor. Another sort of industrial production might be called the *artisanal,* or *one-off,* approach, in which a production company makes one film at a time (and perhaps only one film at all). Other modes of production are less highly organized, involving small groups or individuals who make films for specific purposes. In any event, the ways in which films are made have had particular effects on the look and sound of the finished product.

So have the ways in which films are shown and consumed. For example, the major technological innovations associated with the early 1950s—widescreen, stereophonic sound, increased use of color—were actually available decades earlier. Each could have been developed before the 1950s, but the U.S. film industry had no pressing need to do so, since film attendance was so high that spending money on new attractions would not have significantly increased profits. Only when attendance dropped precipitously in the late

1940s were producers and exhibitors impelled to introduce new technologies to lure audiences back into theaters.

3. *How have international trends emerged in the uses of the film medium and in the film market?* In this book we try to balance consideration of important national contributions with a sense of how international and cross-cultural influences were operating. Directors and films migrate, shaping cinema in many countries. Influences seep across borders, not least because in every country films from outside the country occupy space on the screen. Genres are vagabond as well. The Hollywood Western influenced the Japanese samurai film and the Italian Western, genres which in turn influenced the Hong Kong kung-fu film of the 1970s; interestingly, Hollywood films then began incorporating elements of the martial arts movie.

Just as important, the film industry itself is significantly transnational. At certain periods, circumstances closed off countries from the flow of films, but most often there has been a global film market, and we understand it best by tracing trends across cultures and regions. We have paid particular attention to conditions which allowed people to see films made outside their own country.

Each of these "How?" questions includes a great many "Why?" questions. For any part of the processes we focus on, we can ask what conditions caused them to operate as they did. Why, for instance, did Soviet filmmakers of the 1920s originate a form of editing distinctly opposed to the continuity system developed in Hollywood? Why did Surrealist filmmakers undertake their experiments in disturbing, aggressive narrative? Why did Hollywood's studio system begin to fragment in the late 1940s? Why did "new waves" and "young cinemas" arise in Europe, the Soviet Union, and Japan all around 1960? Why are more films produced now with international investment than in the 1930s or 1940s? Historians are keen to know what factors made a change occur, and our general questions include a host of subquestions about causes and effects.

A great many other questions could be asked, and thus other histories could be written. But questions about the use of the medium, the activities of national film industries, and the international implications of both processes have governed the organization of this book.

We divide film history into five large periods—early cinema (to about 1918), the late silent era (1919–1929), the development of sound cinema (1926–1945), the period after World War II (1946–1960s), and the contemporary era (1960s to the present). These divisions reflect developments in film form and style; major changes in film production, distribution, and exhibition; and significant international trends. The periodization cannot be exactly synchronized for all three factors, but it does indicate approximate boundaries for the changes we try to plot.

In our attempt to answer the three questions in a systematic way, we have relied on secondary sources, principally the writings of other historians on the matters we consider. We have also used primary sources: trade papers, the writings of filmmakers, and films. Since films constitute our major primary source, we need to say a word about how they serve as evidence in writing film history.

Although the cinema is a relatively young medium, invented only about a century ago, many films have already been lost or destroyed. For decades, movies were seen as products with temporary commercial value, and companies did little to ensure their preservation. Even when film archives were founded, beginning in the 1930s, they faced a daunting task in attempting to collect and shelter the thousands of films which had already been made. Moreover, the nitrate film stock, upon which most films up to the early 1950s were printed, was highly flammable and deteriorated over time. Deliberate destruction of films, archive and warehouse fires, and the gradual decomposition of nitrate stored in bad conditions have led to the loss of many titles. (See the frame below, where severe nitrate deterioration has all but obliterated the figures.) According to rough estimates, only about twenty-five percent of silent films survive. Many of these are still sitting in vaults, unidentified or unpreserved due to lack of funds.

Even more recent films may be inaccessible to the researcher. Films made in some small countries, particularly in the Third World, do not circulate widely. Small archives may not have the facilities to preserve films or show them to researchers. In some cases political regimes may choose to suppress certain films and promote others. We have attempted to examine a great range of types of international films, but lack of availability inevitably means that no historical account can be complete. In addition, many films have been recut or otherwise altered, and researchers may encounter difficulties in determining whether a version is original.

Although we have been selective, and have not been able to see, or scrutinize, as many films as we would like, we offer this book as both an overview of the history of cinema and an attempt to see it in a somewhat new light. Film history, for us, is less an inert body of knowledge than an *activity* of inquiry. After a researcher has made a serious argument in an attempt to answer a question, "film history" is no longer quite what it was before. The reader gains not only new information and a new point of view. New patterns emerge which can make even familiar facts stand out with a fresh force.

If film history is a generative, self-renewing activity, then we cannot simply be offering a condensation here. We are, in a sense, casting what we find into a new form. Throughout the years spent researching and writing this book, we have come to believe that it offers a fairly novel version of the shape

A frame from *Willy Reilly and his Colleen Bawn* (Film Company of Ireland, 1918).

of film history in both its overall contour and its specific detail. We have relied on the research of a great many scholars in gathering the information and arguments presented here, but we are chiefly responsible for the particular story we tell.

That story will be modified in the light of further research. Part of the excitement of film history as an activity of inquiry is that every attempt to make sense of it is open to continuous revision and renewal. We thank not only the scholars and students whose research has made it possible for us to reconceive the history of the medium we love. We also thank, in advance, those scholars and students who will challenge us to rethink the ideas we offer here.

◆ REFERENCES

1. The survey of film aesthetics most appropriate to our undertaking here is David Bordwell and Kristin Thompson, *Film Art: An Introduction*, 4th ed. (New York: McGraw-Hill, 1992).

HISTORY, HISTORIOGRAPHY, AND FILM HISTORY

AN ADVANCED INTRODUCTION

While millions are watching movies at this moment, a few thousand are studying the films of the past. One person is trying to discover whether a certain film was made in 1904 or 1905. Another is tracing the fortunes of a short-lived Scandinavian production company. Another is poring over a 1927 Japanese film shot by shot to find out how it tells its story. Some researchers are comparing prints of obscure films to determine which one can be considered the original. Other scholars are studying a group of films signed by the same director, or set designer, or producer. Some are scrutinizing patent records and technical diagrams, legal testimony and production files. And still others are interviewing retired employees to discover how the Bijou Theater in their hometown was run during the 1940s.

Why?

HISTORY AS PROGRAMMATIC RESEARCH

One reason is evident. Most film historians—teachers, archivists, journalists, and free-lancers—are "cinephiles," lovers of cinema. Like bird-watchers, stamp collectors, art historians, and other devotees, they enjoy acquiring knowledge about the object of their affection.

Movie fans may stop there, regarding the accumulating of facts about their passion as an end in itself. But great as the pleasure of knowing the names of all the Three Stooges' wives might be, most film historians are not trivia buffs.

Film historians mount *research programs,* systematic inquiries into film's past. A historian's research program is organized around *questions* that require answering. A research program also consists of *assumptions* and *background knowledge.* For a film historian, a fact takes on significance only in the context of a research program.

Consider the image at the top of the page, from a film of the silent era. If you are a film archivist—that is, someone who works in a library devoted to collecting and preserving motion pictures—you often find a film which you cannot identify. Perhaps the title credit is missing, or the print carries a title which is not that of the original. Your research program is, broadly, identification. The film presents you with a series of questions. What is the date of production or of release? In what country was it made? What individuals or group made the film? Who are the players in the shot?

Our mysterious film carries only the title *Wanda l'espione* ("Wanda the Spy")—most likely a title given to it by a distributor. It was probably imported rather than made in the small country in which the print was discovered. Fortunately its lead actress is a famous star, Francesca Bertini. Identifying her makes it most likely that the film is Italian, made during the height of her career in the 1910s. The film's style allows the researcher to narrow the range of dates even more. The camera frames straight on into the sets, and the actors seldom come close enough to the camera to cut off more than their feet. The editing pace is slow, and the action is staged so that performers exit and enter through a rear doorway. All these stylistic features are typical of European filmmaking around 1915. Such clues can be followed up by referring to a filmography (that is, a list of films) of Bertini's career. A plot description of a 1915 film in which she starred, *Diana l'affascinatrice* ("Diana the Seductress"), matches the action of the unidentified print.

Note that the identification depended on certain assumptions. For example, the researcher assumed that it is extremely unlikely, if not impossible, for a 1977 filmmaker to scheme to bedevil archivists and make a fake 1915 Italian film. (Film historians seldom need worry about forgeries, as art historians must.) Note, too, that background knowledge was indispensable. The researcher had reason to believe that films staged and cut a certain way are characteristic of the mid-1910s, and the researcher recognized a star from other films of the period.

Consider another possibility. A number of films have been identified as all having been made by the same production company. And we have other information documenting the company's production process. We have scripts in various drafts; we have memos passed among writers, directors, producers, and other staff; we have sketches for sets and costumes. This is a rich lode of data—too rich, in fact. The historian's problem is now selecting relevant data and salient facts.

What makes a datum relevant, a fact salient? The historian's *research program* and its *questions*. One scholar might be interested in tracing common features of the company's production process; she is asking, in effect: "In general, how did this firm typically go about making movies?" Another historian's research program might concentrate on the films of a certain director who worked for the company. He might ask: "What aspects of visual style distinguish the director's films, and what influence might they have had on other films made by the firm?"

Some facts would be central to one program but peripheral to another. The historian of the company's production routines might not particularly care about a daring stylistic innovation introduced by the director who is the very center of another historian's inquiry. Conversely, that historian might be uninterested in how the company's producers promoted certain stars.

Again, assumptions exert pressure on the researcher's framing of questions and pursuit of information. The company historian assumes that one can trace general tendencies of production organization, largely because film companies tend to make films by following fairly set routines. The director-centered researcher assumes—perhaps initially only as a hunch—that his director's films do have a distinct style. And both historians would mobilize background knowledge, about how companies work and how directors direct, to guide their research.

Historians in any discipline do more than accumulate facts. No facts speak for themselves. Facts are interesting and important only as part of research programs. Then they help us ask and answer questions.

FILM HISTORY AS DESCRIPTION AND EXPLANATION

Inevitably, a historian needs at least a little information to prod her to ask questions. But the historian does not necessarily sift through mountains of facts and then judiciously ask a question. A historian may begin with a question, and sometimes that question might be better described as a hunch or an intuition or even just an itch.

For example, one young historian saw a few of the "anarchic" American comedies of the 1930s and noticed that their vulgar gags and absurd situations were very different from the more sophisticated comedy of the period. On the assumption that stage comedy might have been a source, he framed a question: "Might vaudeville and its performance style have shaped the comedies of the early 1930s?" He began to gather information. He examined films, read coverage of the comedians in the Hollywood trade papers, and studied shifts in American taste in humor. The process of research led him to refine his question and to mount a detailed account of how comedians introduced a vaudeville aesthetic into sound films but then muted it in accord with Hollywood's own standards of taste.[1]

Nonhistorians often visualize the historical researcher as a cousin to Indiana Jones, braving library stacks and crawling through attics in quest of the treasure-lode of documents that overturn received opinion. Certainly new documentation has a key role to play in historical research. One scholar gained entry to the long-inaccessible files of Hollywood's censorship agency, the Hays Office, and she was able to put forth a new account of the office's procedures and functions.[2] Similarly, the increasing availability of films from cinema's earliest era has created an entire subfield of cinema history.[3]

Still, many research projects rely more on asking new questions than on unearthing new data. In some cases, the research question seems to have been answered by previous historians, but another researcher comes along and suggests a more complete or complex answer.

For example, no historian disputes the fact that Warner Bros. was quick to invest in talking pictures in the late 1920s. For a long time most historians believed that the firm took the risk because it was on the verge of bankruptcy and was desperate to save itself. But then another historian suggested that publicly available evidence, accessible to any researcher who cared to look, strongly indicated that Warners was not bankrupt and that investment in sound films was a carefully planned attempt to break into the ranks of the big studios.[4]

Our examples all indicate that the historian's research program aims to do at least one of two things.

1. The historian tries to *describe* a process or state of affairs. He asks, "What?" and "Who?" and "Where?" and "When?" What is this film, and who made it, and when and where? In what ways does this director's work differ from that of others? What was the vaudeville comedic style? What evidence is there that a studio is bankrupt? Who is the actor in this shot, or who was responsible for scripts at this company? Where was this film shown, and who might have seen it? Here the historian's problem is largely one of finding information that will answer such questions.

Accurate description is indispensable for all historical research. No researcher can start from scratch, and every scholar is indebted to descriptive work for identifying films, collating versions, compiling filmographies, establishing timelines, and creating reference works that supply names, dates, and the like. The more sophisticated and long-lived a historical discipline is, the richer and more complete is its battery of descriptive reference material.

2. The historian also tries to *explain* a process or state of affairs. She asks, "How does this work?" and "Why did this happen?" How did this company assign tasks, lay out responsibilities, carry a project to completion? How did this director's work influence other films from the company? Why did Warners pursue talkies when larger companies were reluctant? Why did some sound comedians adopt the vaudeville comedic style while others did not?

Much of the most interesting historical research is explanatory. "How?" questions typically address fairly stable or long-lived states of affairs, such as the work routines of our hypothetical movie studio. Answers to "How?" questions are often called *functional* explanations because they offer an account of the workings of a process and the role some factor plays in that process.

By contrast, "Why?" questions typically center on change over time: Why did this situation come to be different from what preceded it? Warners' pursuit of talkies represents a change from the industry policy of the moment, so the historian asks what conditions led to this development. This is usually called *causal* explanation. The historian looks for circumstances and events which could make something else happen later.

The film historian, like a historian of art or politics, proposes an *explanatory argument*. Having asked a "How?" or "Why?" question, he puts forward an answer, based on an examination of evidence in the light of assumptions and background knowledge. In reading historical writing, we need to recognize that the essay or book is not just a mass of facts but an argument. The historian's argument consists of evidence marshaled to create a plausible explanation for an event or state of affairs. The argument, that is, aims to answer some historical question.

EVIDENCE

Most arguments about empirical matters—and the history of film is principally an empirical matter—rely on evidence. Evidence consists of information which gives grounds for believing that the argument is sound. Evidence is part of the reason for believing that the historian has found a plausible answer to the question she is asking.

Film historians work with evidence of many sorts. For most researchers, copies of the films they study furnish central pieces of evidence. Historians also rely on print sources, both published (books, magazines, trade journals, newspapers) and unpublished (memoirs, letters, notes, production files, scripts, court testimony, etc.). Historians of film technology study film stock, cameras, sound recorders, and other materials and equipment. A film studio or an important location might also serve as a source of evidence.

Usually historians must verify their sources of evidence. Often this depends on the sort of descriptive research we have already mentioned. The problem is particularly acute with film prints. Films have always circulated in differing versions. In the 1920s, Hollywood films were shot in two versions, one for the United States and one for export. These could differ considerably in length, content, and even visual style. To this day, many Hollywood films are released in Europe in more erotic or violent versions than are screened in the United States. In addition, films have deteriorated and been subject to cutting and revision. Many current video versions of films have been trimmed, expanded, or otherwise altered from their theatrical release format.

Often, then, the historian does not always know whether the print she is seeing represents anything like an original, if indeed there can be said to be an "original" version. Historians try to be aware of the differences among the versions of the films they are studying and try to account for them; indeed, the fact that there are different versions can itself be a source of questions.

Historians generally distinguish between *primary* and *secondary* sources. Usually these terms refer to more immediate and less immediate evidence. For example, if you are studying Japanese cinema of the 1920s, films and printed matter from that period would be primary. Later discussions of the period, usually by someone else who was studying it, would count as secondary.

Often, though, one scholar's secondary source is another's primary source because the researchers are asking different questions. A critic's 1960 essay about a 1925 film would be a secondary source if your question centers on the 1925 film. If, however, you are writing a history of film criticism, the critic's 1960 essay would be a primary source.

EXPLANATORY FRAMEWORKS

Any particular piece of historical research may involve both description and explanation, in different mixtures. The techniques of descriptive research are very specialized and involve a wide range of background knowledge. For example, some experts on early silent cinema can date a film copy by examining the photographic stock on which it is printed. The number and shape of the sprocket holes, along with the manner in which a manufacturer's name is printed along the edges of the film strip, can help date the print. Knowing the date of the stock on which a film has been printed can in turn help narrow down a film's date and country of origin.

Historical explanation involves particular bodies of knowledge and concepts as well. Here are some of them.

CHRONOLOGY

Chronology is essential to historical explanation, and descriptive research is an indispensable aid to establishing the sequence of events. The historian needs to know that this film was made before that one, or event B took place after A. But history is not merely chronology. A chronicle of events is no more an explanation of them than a record of high and low tides is an account of why tides change. History, as we've already mentioned, centrally involves explanation.

CAUSALITY

Much historical explanation involves cause and effect. Historians work with conceptions of various kinds of causes.

Individual Causes. People have beliefs and desires, and they act in the light of them. In acting, they make things happen. It is thus often reasonable to explain a historical change or a past state of affairs in the light of the attitudes and behavior of individuals. This is not to say that individuals make everything happen, or that things happen as people originally intended, or that people always understand just why they did what they did. It is simply to say that historians may justifiably appeal to what people think and feel and do as part of an explanation.

Some historians believe that *all* historical explanation must appeal to person-based causes sooner or later. (This position is usually called *methodological individualism*.) A different, and even stronger, assumption is that only individuals, and exceptional individuals at that, have the power to create historical change. This view is sometimes called the "Great Man" theory of history (even though it is applied to women as well).

Group Causes. People often act in groups, and at times we speak of the group as having a kind of existence over and above the individuals who comprise it. Groups have rules and roles, structures and routines, and often these factors make things happen. We speak of a government's declaring war, and this act may not be reducible to more detailed statements about what all the individuals involved believed and did.

When we say that "Warner Bros. decided to adopt sound," we are making a meaningful claim even if we have no information about the beliefs and desires of the individual decision-makers at the company; we may not even fully know who they are. Some historians assert that any historical explanation must, sooner or later, ground itself in group-based causes. This position is usually called *holism* or *methodological collectivism,* as opposed to methodological individualism.

Several sorts of groups are important to the history of cinema. Throughout this book we will be talking of *institutions*—government agencies, film studios, distribution firms, and other fairly formal, organized groups. We will also be talking about more informal affiliations of filmmakers. These are usually called *movements* or *schools*: small assemblies of filmmakers and critics who share the same interests, beliefs about cinema, conceptions of film form and style, and the like. (Movements are discussed in more detail in the introduction to Part Two, pp. 83–84.)

INFLUENCE

Most historians use some notion of influence to explain change. Influence is a way of identifying the power of an individual, or a group, or even a film over other historical factors. Members of a movement can influence a director to make a film a certain way, but just seeing a film can also influence a director.

"Influence" does not mean simple copying. You may have been influenced by a parent or a teacher, but you have not necessarily mimicked the person's behavior. In the arts, influence is often a matter of one artist getting ideas from other artists' work but then pursuing those ideas in a fairly idiosyncratic way. The result may be quite different from the initial artwork. The contemporary director Jean-Luc Godard was influenced by Jean Renoir, although their films are markedly different. Sometimes we can detect the influence by examining the films; sometimes we rely on the testimony of the filmmaker.

A body of work by a group of directors may also influence film history. Soviet films of the 1920s influenced the documentary director John Grierson. The Hollywood cinema, as a set of films, has been enormously influential throughout film history, although all the directors influenced by it certainly did not see the same films. Influences are particular kinds of causes, so it is not surprising that influences may involve both individual activity and group activity.

TRENDS AND GENERALIZATIONS

Any historical question opens up a body of data for investigation. Once the historian starts to look closely at the data—go through the studio records, examine the films, page through the trade press—she discovers that there is much, much more going on than the question addresses. It is like looking into a microscope and discovering that a drop of water teems with organisms of a confounding variety of types, all going about very different business.

No historian can avoid leaving material out. For one thing, the historical record is already incomplete. Many events go unrecorded, and many documents are lost forever. Further, historians inevitably select. They reduce the messy complications of history to a more coherent, cogent story. Historians simplify and streamline.

One principal way they go about this is by postulating *trends.* Lots of things are going on, they say, but "by and large," or "on the whole," or "for the most part" we can identify a general tendency. Not all Hollywood films of the 1940s were made in black and white, but most were; not all Hollywood films today are in color, but nearly all are. This is a change, and we can see a trend toward increasing use of color film stock between the 1940s and the 1960s. Our task is to explain how and why this trend occurred.

By positing trends, historians generalize. They necessarily set aside interesting exceptions and aberrations. But this is no sin, since the answer to a question is necessarily pitched at a certain level of generality. All historical explanations pull back from the palpitating texture of reality. Recognizing that tendencies are "for-the-most-part" generalizations allows the scholar to acknowledge that there is more going on than she is going to explain.

PERIODS

Historical chronology and causation are without beginning or end. The child who incessantly asks what came before that or what made that happen has discovered that we can trace out a sequence of events indefinitely. Historians necessarily limit the stretch of time they will explore, and they go on to break that stretch into meaningful phases or segments.

For example, the historian studying American silent cinema already assumes that this is a period within film history, usualy held to run from about 1894 to around 1929. The historian will probably further segment this stretch of time. It might be broken up by decade (the 1900s, the 1910s, the

1920s), by changes external to film (say, pre–World War I, World War I, post–World War I), or by stages or phases in the development of storytelling style (say, 1894–1907, 1908–1917, etc.).

Every historian periodizes according to the research program he adopts and the questions he asks. Historians recognize that periodization can't be rigid: trends do not follow in neat order. It is illuminating to think of the American "structural" film of the early 1970s as a kind of response to the "underground" film of the 1960s, but underground films were still being made well into the 1970s. Histories of genres often mark periods by innovative films, but this is not to deny that there may be a great deal of continuity in less innovative works across periods.

Similarly, we ought not to expect that the history of technology or styles or genres will necessarily march in step with political or social history. It is significant to speak of the period after World War II as a distinctive one because this global conflict had major effects on film industries and filmmakers in most countries; but other political events do not create distinct periods in relation to changes in film form or the film market. Here, as ever, the historian's research program and central questions will shape her sense of the relevant periods and parallel events. (This is one reason that scholars often speak of film *histories* rather than a single film history.)

SIGNIFICANCE

In mounting explanations, historians of all arts make assumptions about the historical significance of the artworks they discuss. We might treat a work as a "monument," studying it because it is a highly valued accomplishment. Alternatively, we might study a work as a "document" because it records some historical activity that is worth knowing about, such as the state of a society at a given moment or a process within the art form itself.

In this book, we assume that the films we discuss have significance on any or all of the following three criteria:

Intrinsic Excellence. Some films are, simply, outstanding by artistic criteria. They are rich, moving, complex, thought-provoking, intricate, meaningful, or the like. At least partly because of their quality, such films have played a key role in the history of cinema.

Influence. A film may be historically significant by virtue of its impact on other films. It may create or change a genre, inspire filmmakers to try something new, or gain such a wide popularity that it spawns imitations and tributes. Since influence is an important part of historical explanations, this sort of film plays a role in this book.

Typicality. Some films are significant because they vividly represent instances or trends. They stand in for many other films of the same type.

A particular film might be significant on two or even all three of these counts. A highly accomplished genre film, such as *Singin' in the Rain* or *Rio*

Bravo, is often considered both excellent and highly typical. Many acclaimed masterworks, such as *The Birth of a Nation* or *Citizen Kane,* were also highly influential, and some also typify broader tendencies.

TYPES OF EXPLANATORY FRAMEWORKS

Some historians believe that there are distinct types of explanation in film history. A fairly standard list would include:

> *Biographical history:* focusing on an individual's life history
>
> *Industrial or economic history:* focusing on business practices
>
> *Aesthetic history:* focusing on film art (form, style, genre)
>
> *Technological history:* focusing on the materials and machines of film
>
> *Social/cultural/political history:* focusing on the role of cinema in the larger society

This sort of inventory helps us understand that there is not *one* history of film but several possible histories, each adopting a different perspective.[5]

Nevertheless, such typologies can be misleading if they are taken too strictly. If film history is an attempt to answer questions, then not all questions will fall neatly into one of these pigeonholes. If you want to know *why* a film looks the way it does, this may not be a purely aesthetic question; it might be linked to the biography of the filmmaker or to broader industrial, technical, or social factors. A study of film genres might involve cultural factors, and a person's life cannot easily be separated from her or his work conditions (the film industry) or the political context.

We propose that the student of film history think rather in terms of questions. These might well cut across any typological boundaries; indeed, one could argue that the most interesting questions will.

If we had to squeeze our book into a pigeonhole, we could say that it is predominantly aesthetic and industrial. It examines how types of films, film styles, and film forms have changed in relation to the conditions of film production, distribution, and exhibition within certain countries and within the international flow of films. But this is too confining, as even a cursory look at what follows will indicate. Sometimes we invoke the individual—a powerful producer, an innovative filmmaker, an imaginative critic. Sometimes we consider technology. And we often frame our account with discussions of the political, social, and cultural context of a period.

Recall our first central question: How have uses of the film medium changed or become normalized over time? This is a question about aesthetic matters, but it also impinges on factors of technology. For instance, conceptions of "realistic" filmmaking changed with the introduction of portable cameras and sound equipment in the late 1950s. Similarly, our second question—How have the conditions of the film industry affected the uses of the medium?—is at once economic, technological, and aesthetic. Finally, asking how international trends have emerged in the uses of the film medium and in the film market concerns both economic and social/cultural/political factors. In the early era of cinema, films circulated freely among countries, and viewers often did not know the nationality of a film they were seeing. In the 1910s, however, war and nationalism blocked certain films from circulating. At the same time, the growth of particular film industries, notably Hollywood, depended upon access to other markets, so the degree to which films could circulate boosted some nations' output and damaged that of others. In addition, the circulation of U.S. films abroad served to spread American cultural values, which in turn created both admiration and hostility.

In sum, we have been guided, as we think most historians are, by research questions rather than rigid conceptions of the "kind" of history we are writing. And what we take to be the most plausible answer to a given question will depend upon the strength of the evidence and the argument we can make for it, not on a prior commitment to writing only a certain kind of history.

HISTORY AS STORY

Our answers to historical questions are, however, not simply given in a list or summary. Like most historical arguments, ours takes a narrative form.

Historians use language to communicate their arguments and evidence to others. Descriptive research programs can do this through a summary of findings: This film is *Diana l'affascinatrice,* made by Caesar-Film in 1915, directed by Gustavo Serena, and so on. But historical explanations require a more complicated linguistic crafting.

Sometimes historians frame their explanations as persuasive arguments. To take an example already cited, a historian investigating the development of sound by Warner Bros. might start by considering the various explanations already offered and taken for granted. Then he might set forth the reasons for believing his alternative interpretation.[6] This is a familiar form of rhetorical argument, eliminating unsatisfactory beliefs before settling on a more plausible one.

More often, historians' explanations take the form of stories. Narrative history, as it is called, seeks to answer "How?" and "Why?" questions by tracing the relevant circumstances and conditions over time. It produces a chain of causes and effects, or it shows how a process works, by telling a story about them. For instance, if we are trying to answer the question, "How did the Hays Office negotiate with firms to arrive at an agreement about an acceptable film?" we can frame a step-by-step narrative of the censorship process. Or, if you are seeking to explain what led the Hays Office to be created, you may wish to lay out the causal factors in a story. As these examples indicate, the story's "players" might be individuals or groups, institutions or even films; the "plot" consists of the situations in which the players operate and the changes which they initiate and undergo.

Narratives are one of the basic ways in which humans make sense of the world, and so it is not surprising that historians use stories to make past events intelligible. We have accordingly framed this book as a large-scale narrative, one which includes several stories within it. This is partly because of custom: virtually all introductory historical works take this perspective, and readers are comfortable with it. But we also believe that there are advantages of working on a wide canvas. New patterns of information may leap to the eye, and fresh causal and functional connections may become more visible when we consider history as a dynamic, ongoing process.

Our account synthesizes several histories and leaves others to other scholars. Recognizing that there are many stories to be told about cinema, we have appended to each chapter a section of Notes and Queries. Here we raise side issues, explore bypaths, and trace some more specialized historiographic matters. More broadly, we recognize that any historical account must be constantly tested and revised, and we offer *Film History: An Introduction* as one such account.

◆ REFERENCES

1. The result may be read in Henry Jenkins, *What Made Pistachio Nuts? Early Sound Comedy and the Vaudeville Aesthetic* (New York: Columbia University Press, 1992).
2. See Lea Jacobs, *The Wages of Sin: Censorship and the Fallen Woman Film, 1928–1942* (Madison: University of Wisconsin Press, 1991).
3. See, for example, Yuri Tsivian, ed., *Silent Witnesses: Russian Films 1908–1919* (Pordenone: Giornate del Cinema Muto, 1989); Charles Musser, *Before the Nickelodeon: Edwin S. Porter and the Edison Manufacturing Company* (Berkeley: University of California Press, 1991); Tom Gunning, *D. W. Griffith and the Origins of American Narrative Film: The Early Years at Biograph* (Urbana: University of Illinois Press, 1991).
4. Douglas Gomery, "The Coming of Sound: Technological Change in the American Film Industry," in Tino Balio, ed., *The American Film Industry*, rev. ed. (Madison: University of Wisconsin Press, 1985), pp. 229–251.
5. See Robert C. Allen and Douglas Gomery, *Film History: Theory and Practice* (New York: Knopf, 1985).
6. This is, by and large, the strategy followed by Douglas Gomery in "Writing the History of the American Film Industry: Warner Bros and Sound," *Screen* 17, 1 (Spring 1976): 40–53.

A NOTE
ON FORMAT

In the text, film titles are given in the form in which they are best known to English-language viewers. Sometimes this means they are in translation (*Voyage to Italy*), sometimes this means that the original language is used (*Hiroshima mon amour*). When a film is better known by an original-language title, we have supplied a parenthetical English translation on the first mention. Films with no generally accepted English title have had their titles translated into English.

We have adopted this policy in order to save space in the text and to make for smoother reading. The original titles of all non-English-language films are, however, given in the index.

We have tried to define specialized terms on their first appearance. We have also provided a Glossary for the most important items. Further details on many specialized terms can be found in David Bordwell and Kristin Thompson, *Film Art: An Introduction*, 4th ed. (New York: McGraw-Hill, 1993).

Whenever possible, dates of films are given as the dates of initial release. In some cases, such as experimental films, release dates may be fairly meaningless; we therefore rely upon the date attributed by the filmmaker or film scholars in the area. This is often the date of production.

Virtually all the images illustrating particular films are frame enlargements. *Frame enlargements* are photographic blow-ups of single images taken directly from a copy of the film. They are to be distinguished from *production stills,* which are posed shots taken by photographers during the filming. Many film history textbooks rely upon production stills, but such photos usually bear little similarity to the images in the actual film. For our purposes, frame enlargements function as indispensable evidence for our claims about film style.

Similarly, all our color illustrations of film shots are frame enlargements. Here production stills are particularly misleading, since the color process used in making the still photograph is very seldom faithful to the photographic process used in shooting the movie. In particular, production stills do not fully convey the richness of the Technicolor motion-picture image.

Each chapter offers both a running narrative and a conceptual argument about major trends in film history. Sometimes, however, we develop arguments or lay out information which would disrupt or digress from the chapter's organization. We have therefore inserted occasional Boxes which provide sidelights and in-depth discussion on important issues.

We have also appended to each chapter a set of Notes and Queries. These offer comments on specialized topics, suggestions for further reading, and illustrative examples of how historians have made discoveries and reinterpreted the past.

FILM HISTORY

AN INTRODUCTION

PART ONE

EARLY CINEMA

The medium of cinema appeared in the mid-1890s, an era when the United States was still expanding into one of the world's major colonialist powers. The Spanish-American War of 1898 resulted in the United States' gaining control of Puerto Rico, the Philippines, Guam, Hawaii, and part of Samoa. The United States itself was still in the process of formation. Idaho, Montana, and North and South Dakota had become states in 1889, and Arizona and New Mexico would not enter the Union until 1912. During the late nineteenth century, railroading, oil, tobacco, and other industries were expanding rapidly, and in 1890, the Sherman Antitrust Act was passed in an attempt to limit the growth of monopolies.

Due to hard times in southern and eastern Europe, a new wave of immigrants arrived on American shores after 1890. Living mostly in ethnic communities within large cities, these non-English speakers would form a sizable audience for the largely visual entertainment medium of silent cinema.

The first decade of the new century saw a progressivist impulse in America, under the presidency of Theodore Roosevelt. There were movements to give women the vote, to prohibit child labor, to enforce antitrust laws, and in general to institute government regulations to protect consumers. This era was also one of virulent racism, scarred by many lynch-

ings. African-American progressives formed the National Association for the Advancement of Colored People in 1909.

American expansion came at a time when the major European powers had already established far-flung empires and were engaged in an intricate game of jockeying for further power in such unstable areas as the Balkan States and the decaying Ottoman Empire. Tensions over such maneuvering, as well as mutual distrust, especially between France and Germany, led to the outbreak of World War I in 1914. This conflict gradually drew countries from all over the globe into the fighting. Despite widespread popular resistance, the United States entered the fray in 1917 and broke the stalemate that had developed. The balance shifted in favor of Britain and France, and Germany surrendered in 1918.

The global balance of power had permanently shifted. Germany lost many of its colonies, and the United States emerged as the world's leading financial force. President Woodrow Wilson tried to expand progressivist principles on an international scale, proposing a League of Nations to foster world unity. The League, formed in 1919, helped build a spirit of international cooperation during the 1920s, but it proved too weak to prevent lingering tensions from eventually causing a second international conflict.

During the three decades before World War I, the cinema was invented and grew from a small amusement-arcade business to an international industry. Films began as brief moving views presented as novelties, and by the late 1910s, the lengthy narrative feature film was fast becoming established as the basis for cinema programs.

The invention of the cinema was a lengthy process, involving engineers and entrepreneurs in several countries. Struggles among patent holders in the United States slowed the development of the industry there, while French companies quickly seized the lead in markets throughout the world (Chapter 1).

From 1905 on, a rapid expansion in demand for motion-picture entertainment in the United States led to the spread of small movie theaters called nickelodeons. This demand was fueled in part by the rising immigrant population and in part by the shorter work hours gained by the increasingly militant labor-union movement. In a short time America was far and away the world's largest market for films—a situation that would soon allow it to increase its selling power abroad as well.

During the period of the "nickelodeon boom," the story film became the main type of fare offered on programs. Films made in France, Italy, Denmark, the United Kingdom, the United States, and elsewhere circulated widely around the world. Narrative traits and stylistic techniques changed rapidly as influences passed back and forth among countries. Movies grew longer, employed more editing, added explanatory intertitles, and contained a greater variety of camera distances. Adaptations from literature and lavish historical spectacles added prestige to the new art form (Chapter 2).

World War I had an enormous impact on the cinema. The outbreak of hostilities triggered a severe cutback in French production, and the country lost its leading position in world markets. Italy soon encountered similar problems. The growing Hollywood film industry stepped in to fill the gap in supply, expanding its distribution system abroad. By the war's end, American films had an international grip that other countries would struggle, usually with limited success, to loosen.

During this era, exploration of film form went on in many countries. Film editing grew subtle and complex, acting styles became enormously varied, and directors explored possibilities of long takes, of realistic decor, and of camera movement. By the end of World War I, many of the conventions that are familiar to us in the cinema today had already been established (Chapter 3).

I

THE INVENTION
AND EARLY YEARS
OF THE CINEMA,
1880s–1904

The nineteenth century saw a vast proliferation of visual forms of popular culture. The industrial era offered ways of easily duplicating large numbers of lantern slides, books of photographs, and cheap illustrated fiction. The middle and working classes of many countries could visit elaborate dioramas—painted backdrops with three-dimensional figures depicting famous historical events. Circuses, "freak" shows, amusement parks, and music halls provided other forms of inexpensive entertainment. In the United States, numerous dramatic troupes toured, performing in the theaters and opera houses which at that time existed even in small towns.

Hauling entire theater productions from town to town, however, was expensive. Similarly, most people had to travel long distances to visit major dioramas or amusement parks. In the days before airplane travel, few could hope to see for themselves the exotic lands they glimpsed in static view in their stereopticon viewers or in books of travel photographs.

The cinema was to offer a cheaper way of providing visual sorts of entertainment to the masses. Actors would be able to record performances which then could easily be shown to audiences around the world. Travelogues would bring the sights of far-flung places, with movement, directly to spectators' hometowns. Movies would become the popular visual art form of the late Victorian age.

The cinema was invented during the 1890s. It appeared in the wake of the industrial revolution, as did the telephone (invented in 1876), the phonograph (1877), and the automobile (developed during the 1880s and 1890s). Like them, it was a technological device that became the basis of a large industry. It was also a new form of entertainment and a new artistic medium. During the first decade of the cinema's existence, inventors were working to improve the machines for making and showing films. Filmmakers also had to explore what sorts of images they could record, and exhibitors had to figure out how to present those images to audiences.

THE INVENTION OF THE CINEMA

The cinema is a complicated medium, and before it could be invented, several technological requirements had to be met.

PRECONDITIONS FOR MOTION PICTURES

First, scientists had to realize that the human eye will perceive motion if a series of slightly different images is placed before it in rapid succession—minimally around sixteen per second. During the nineteenth century, scientists explored this property of vision. A number of optical toys were marketed that gave an illusion of movement by using a small number of drawings, each altered somewhat. In 1832, Belgian physicist Joseph Plateau and Austrian geometry professor Simon Stampfer independently created the device that came to be called the Phenakistoscope (Fig. 1.1). The Zoetrope, invented in 1833, contained a series of drawings on a narrow strip of paper inside a revolving drum (Fig. 1.2). The Zoetrope was widely sold after 1867, along with other optical toys. Similar principles were later used in films, but in these toys, the same motion was simply repeated over and over.

A second technological requirement for the cinema was the capacity to project a rapid series of images on a surface. Since the seventeenth century, entertainers and educators had been using "magic lanterns" to project glass lantern slides, but there had been no way to flash large numbers of images fast enough to create the illusion of motion.

A third prerequisite for the invention of the cinema was the ability to use photography to make successive pictures on a clear surface. The exposure time would have to be short enough to take sixteen or more frames in a single second. Such techniques came about slowly. The first still photograph was made on a glass plate in 1826 by Claude Niépce, but it required an exposure time of eight hours. For years photography was done on glass or metal, without the use of negatives, so only one copy of each image was possible; exposures took several minutes each. In 1839, Henry Fox Talbot introduced negatives made on paper. At about this same time, it became possible to print photographic images on glass lantern slides and project them. Not until 1878, however, did split-second exposure times become feasible.

Fig. 1.1 A Phenakistoscope, with a spinning disc of figures which the user views through a slot to perceive the illusion of movement.

Fourth, the cinema would require that photographs be printed on a base flexible enough to be passed through a camera rapidly. Strips or discs of glass could be used, but only a short series of images could be registered on them. In 1888, George Eastman devised a still camera that made photographs on rolls of sensitized paper. This camera, which he named the Kodak, simplified photography so that unskilled amateurs could take pictures. The next year Eastman introduced transparent celluloid roll film, creating a breakthrough in the move toward cinema. The film was intended for still cameras, but inventors could use the same flexible material in designing machines to take and project motion pictures (though it was apparently about a year before the stock was improved enough to be practical).

Fifth, and finally, experimenters needed to find a suitable intermittent mechanism for their cameras and projectors. A strip of film sliding continuously past the gate would create a blur unless the light source was quite dim. The film had to be repeatedly stopped for a split-second exposure and then covered with a shutter as the next frame moved into place. Fortunately, other inventions of the century also needed intermittent mechanisms to stop their movement many times per second. For example, the sewing machine (invented in 1846) held cloth still several times per second while a needle pierced it.

By the 1890s, all the technical conditions necessary for the cinema existed. The question was, who would bring the necessary elements together in a way that could be successfully exploited on a wide basis?

Fig. 1.2 Looking through the slots in a revolving Zoetrope, the viewer receives an impression of movement.

MAJOR PRECURSORS OF MOTION PICTURES

Some inventors made important contributions without themselves achieving moving photographic images. Among these men were several interested in analyzing motion. In 1878, photographer Eadweard Muybridge was asked by ex-governor of California Leland Stanford to find a way of photographing running horses so as to facilitate the study of their gaits. Muybridge set up a row of twelve cameras, each making an exposure in one-thousandth of a second. The photos recorded one-half-second intervals of movement (Fig. 1.3). Muybridge later made a lantern to project moving images of horses, but these were drawings copied from his photographs onto a revolving disc. Muybridge did not go on to invent motion pictures, but he made a major contribution to anatomical science through the thousands of motion studies in still photographs that he made using his multiple-camera setup.

In 1882, inspired by Muybridge's work, French physiologist Étienne Jules Marey studied the flight of birds and other rapid animal movements by means of a photographic gun. Shaped like a rifle, it exposed twelve images around the edge of a circular glass plate that made a single revolution in one second. In 1888, Marey built a box-type camera that used an intermittent mechanism to expose a series of photographs on a strip of paper film, at speeds of up to 120 frames per second. Marey was the first to combine flexible film stock and an intermittent mechanism in photographing motion. He was

Fig. 1.3 One of Muybridge's earliest motion studies, photographed on June 19, 1878.

interested in analyzing movements rather than in reproducing them on a screen, but his work inspired other inventors. During this same period, many other scientists used various devices to record and analyze movement.

A fascinating and isolated figure in the history of the invention of the cinema was Frenchman Émile Reynaud. In 1877, he had built an optical toy, the Projecting Praxinoscope. This was a spinning drum, rather like the Zoetrope, but one in which viewers saw the moving images in a series of mirrors rather than through slots. Around 1882, he devised a way of using mirrors and a lantern to project a brief series of drawings on a screen. In 1889, Reynaud exhibited a much larger version of the Praxinoscope. From 1892 on, he regularly gave public performances using long, broad strips of hand-painted frames (Fig. 1.4). These were the first public exhibitions of moving images, though the effect on the screen was jerky and slow. The labor involved in the making of the bands meant that Reynaud's films could not easily be reproduced. Strips of photographs were more practical, and in 1895 Reynaud started using a camera to make his Praxinoscope films. By 1900 he was out of business, however, due to competition from other, simpler motion-picture projection systems. In despair, he destroyed his machines, though copies have recently been reconstructed.

Another Frenchman came close to inventing the cinema as early as 1888—six years before the first commercial showings of moving photographs. That year, Augustin Le Prince, working in England, was able to make some brief films, shot at about sixteen frames per second, using Kodak's recently introduced paper roll film. To be projected, however, the frames needed to

Fig. 1.4 Using long flexible bands of drawings, Reynaud's Praxinoscope rear-projected cartoon figures onto a screen upon which the scenery was painted.

be printed on a transparent strip; lacking flexible celluloid, Le Prince apparently was unable to devise a satisfactory projector. In 1890, while traveling in France, he disappeared, along with his valise of patent applications, creating a mystery that has never been solved. Thus his camera was never exploited commercially and had virtually no impact on the subsequent invention of the cinema.

AN INTERNATIONAL PROCESS OF INVENTION

It is difficult to attribute the invention of the cinema to a single source. There was no one moment when the cinema emerged. Rather, the technology of the motion picture came about through an accumulation of contributions. These came primarily from the United States, Germany, England, and France.

In 1888, Thomas Edison, already the successful inventor of the phonograph and the electric light bulb, decided to design machines for making and showing moving photographs. Much of the work was done by his assistant, W. K. L. Dickson. Since Edison's phonograph worked by recording sound on cylinders, the pair tried fruitlessly to make rows of tiny photographs around similar cylinders. In 1889, Edison went to Paris and saw Marey's camera, which used strips of flexible film. Dickson then obtained some Eastman Kodak film stock and began working on a new type of machine. By 1891, the Kinetograph camera and Kinetoscope viewing box (Fig. 1.5) were ready to be patented and demonstrated. Dickson cut the Eastman film into 1-inch-wide strips (roughly 35 millimeters) and punched four holes on either side of each frame so that toothed gears could pull the film through the camera and Kinetoscope. These early decisions influenced the entire history of the

Fig. 1.5 The Kinetoscope was a peephole device that ran the film around a series of rollers. Viewers activated it by putting a coin in a slot.

Fig. 1.6 Edison's studio was named after the police paddy wagons, or "Black Marias," that it resembled. The slanted portion of the roof opened to admit sunlight for filming, and the whole building revolved on a track to catch the optimal sunlight.

cinema, for 35mm film stock with four perforations per frame has remained the norm. (Amazingly, an original Kinetoscope film can be shown on a modern projector.) Initially, however, the film was exposed at about forty-six frames per second—much faster than the average speed later adopted for silent filmmaking.

Edison and Dickson needed films for their machines before they could exploit them commercially. They built a small studio, called the "Black Maria," on the grounds of Edison's New Jersey laboratory and were ready for production by January 1893 (Fig. 1.6). The films lasted only twenty seconds or so—the longest run of film that the Kinetoscope could hold. Most films were brief excerpts from the acts of noted vaudeville and sports figures. Dancers and acrobats performed (Fig. 1.7). Annie Oakley displayed her shooting ability, and a bodybuilder flexed his muscles. A few Kinetoscope shorts were knockabout comic skits, forerunners of the story film.

Edison had exploited his phonograph by leasing it to special phonograph parlors, where the public paid a nickel to hear records through earphones. (Only in 1895 did phonographs become available for home use.) He did the same with the Kinetoscope. On April 14, 1894, the first Kinetoscope parlor opened in New York. Soon other parlors, both in the United States and abroad, exhibited the machines (Fig. 1.8). For about two years the Kinetoscope was highly profitable, but it was eclipsed when other inventors, inspired by Edison's new device, found ways to project films on a screen.

Another early system for taking and projecting films was invented by Max and Emil Skladanowsky. Their Bioscop held two strips of film, each $3\frac{1}{2}$ inches wide, running side by side; frames of each were projected alternately. The Skladanowsky brothers showed a fifteen-minute program at a large vaudeville theater in Berlin on November 1, 1895—nearly two months

Fig. 1.7 Amy Muller danced in the Black Maria on March 24, 1896. The black background and patch of sunlight from the opening in the roof were standard traits of Kinetoscope films.

Fig. 1.8 A typical entertainment parlor, with phonographs (note the dangling earphones) at left and center, and a row of Kinetoscopes at the right.

Fig. 1.9 Unlike many other early cameras, the Lumière Cinématographe was small and portable. This 1930 photo shows Francis Doublier, one of the firm's representatives who toured the world showing and making films during the 1890s, posing with his Cinématographe.

before the famous Lumière screening at the Grand Café. The Bioscop system was too cumbersome, however, and the Skladanowskys eventually adopted the standard 35mm, single-strip film used by more influential inventors. The brothers toured Europe through 1897, but they did not establish a stable production company.

The Lumière brothers, Louis and Auguste, invented a projection system that helped make the cinema a commercially viable enterprise internationally. Their family was the biggest European manufacturer of photographic plates. In 1894, a local Kinetoscope exhibitor asked them to make films that would be cheaper than the ones sold by Edison. Soon they had designed an elegant little camera, the Cinématographe, which used 35mm film and an intermittent mechanism modeled on that of the sewing machine (Fig. 1.9). The camera could serve as a printer when the positive copies were made. Then, mounted in front of a magic lantern, it formed part of the projector as well. One important decision that the Lumières made was to shoot their films at sixteen frames per second (rather than the forty-six frames per second used by Edison); this rate became the standard international average film speed for about twenty-five years. The first film made with this system was *Workers Leaving the Factory*, apparently shot in March 1895 (Fig. 1.10). It was shown in public at a meeting of the Société d'Encouragement à l'Industrie Nationale in Paris on March 22. Six further showings to scientific and commercial groups followed, including additional films shot by Louis.

On December 28, 1895, one of the most famous film screenings in history took place. The location was a room in the Grand Café in Paris. In those days, cafés were gathering spots where people sipped coffee, read newspapers, and were entertained by singers and other performers. That

Fig. 1.10 The Lumière brothers' first film, *Workers Leaving the Factory*, was a single shot made outside their photographic factory. It embodied the essential appeal of the first films: realistic movement of actual people.

evening, fashionable patrons paid a franc to see a twenty-five minute program of ten films, about a minute each. Among the films shown were a close view of Auguste Lumière and his wife feeding their baby, a staged comic scene of a boy stepping on a hose to cause a puzzled gardener to squirt himself (later named *Arroseur arrosé*, or "The Waterer Watered"), and a view of the sea.

Although the first shows did moderate business, within weeks the Lumières were offering twenty shows a day, with long lines of spectators waiting to get in. They moved quickly to exploit this success, sending representatives all over the world to show and make more short films.

At the same time that the Lumière brothers were developing their system, a parallel process of invention was going on in England. The Edison Kinetoscope had premiered in London in October 1894, and the parlor that displayed the machines did so well that it asked R. W. Paul, a maker of photographic equipment, to make some extra machines for it. For reasons that are still not clear, Edison had not patented the Kinetoscope outside the United States, so Paul was free to sell copies to anyone who wanted them. Since Edison would supply films only to exhibitors who had leased his own machines, Paul also had to invent a camera and make films to go with his duplicate Kinetoscopes.

By March 1895, Paul and his partner, Birt Acres, had a functional camera, which they based partly on the one Marey had made seven years earlier for analyzing motion. Acres shot thirteen films during the first half of the year, but the partnership broke up. Paul went on improving the camera, aiming to serve the Kinetoscope market, while Acres concentrated on creating a projector. On January 14, 1896, Acres showed some of his films to the Royal Photographic Society. Among these was *Rough Sea at Dover* (Fig. 1.11), which would become one of the most popular very early films. Seeing such one-shot films of simple actions or landscapes today, we can hardly grasp how impressive they were to audiences who had never seen moving photographic images. A contemporary review of Acres's Royal Photographic Society program hints, however, at their appeal:

> The most successful effect, and one which called forth rounds of applause from the usually placid members of the "Royal," was a reproduction of a number of breaking waves, which may be seen to roll in from the sea, curl over against a jetty, and break into clouds of snowy spray that seemed to start from the screen.[1]

Acres presented other demonstrations, but he did not attempt to exploit his projector and films systematically.

Projected films were soon shown regularly in England, however. The Lumière brothers sent a representative who opened a successful run of the Cinématographe in London on February 20, 1896, about a month after Acres's first screening. Paul went on improving his camera and invented a projector, which he used in several theaters to show copies of the films Acres had shot the year before. Unlike other inventors, Paul sold his machines rather than leasing them. By doing so, he not only speeded up the spread of the film industry in Great Britain but also supplied filmmakers and exhibitors abroad

Fig. 1.11 Birt Acres's *Rough Sea at Dover*, one of the first films projected on a screen in both England and the United States. It showed large waves crashing against a seawall.

who were unable to get other machines. These included one of the most important early directors, Georges Méliès.

During this period, projection systems and cameras were also being devised in the United States. Three important rival groups competed to introduce a commercially successful system.

Woodville Latham and his sons Otway and Gray began work on a camera and projector during 1894 and were able to show one film to reporters on April 21, 1895. They even opened a small storefront theater in May, where their program ran for years. The projector did not attract much attention, because it cast only a dim image. The Latham group did make one considerable contribution to film technology, however. Most cameras and projectors could use only a short stretch of film, lasting less than three minutes, since the tension created by a longer, heavier roll would break the film. The Lathams added a simple, but effective, loop to relieve the tension, allowing much longer films to be made. The Latham loop has been used in most cameras and projectors ever since. Indeed, so important was the technique that a patent involving it was to shake up the entire American film industry in 1912. An improved Latham projector was used by some exhibitors, but other systems able to cast brighter images gained greater success.

A second group of entrepreneurs, the partnership of C. Francis Jenkins and Thomas Armat, first exhibited their Phantoscope projector at a commercial exposition in Atlanta in October 1895, showing Kinetoscope films. Partly due to competition from the Latham group and a Kinetoscope exhibitor, who also showed films at the exposition, and partly due to dim, unsteady projection, the Phantoscope attracted skimpy audiences. Later that year, Jenkins and Armat split up. Armat improved the projector, renamed it the Vitascope, and obtained backing from the entrepreneurial team of Norman Raff and Frank Gammon. Raff and Gammon were nervous about offending Edison, so in February they displayed the machine for him. Since the Kinetoscope's big initial popularity was fading, Edison agreed to manufacture Armat's projector and supply films for it. For publicity purposes, it was marketed as "Edison's Vitascope," even though he had had no hand in devising it.

The Vitascope's public premiere was at Koster and Bial's Music Hall on April 23, 1896. Six films were shown, five of them originally shot for the Kinetoscope; the sixth was Acres's *Rough Sea at Dover*, which again was singled out for praise. The showing was a triumph, and although it was not the first time films had been projected commercially in the United States, it marked the beginning of projected movies as a viable industry there.

The third major early invention in the United States began as another peepshow device. In late 1894, Herman Casler patented the Mutoscope, a flip-card device (Fig. 1.12). He needed a camera, however, and turned to his friend W. K. L. Dickson for advice; the latter, unhappy with his situation at Edison, cooperated. With other partners, they formed the American Mutoscope Company. By early 1896, Casler and Dickson (who left Edison) had their camera, but the market for peepshow movies had declined, and they decided to concentrate on projection. Using several films made during that year, the American Mutoscope Company soon had programs playing theaters around the country and touring with vaudeville shows.

Fig. 1.12 At the right, a Mutoscope, a penny-in-the-slot machine with a crank that the viewer turned in order to turn a drum containing a series of photographs. The stand at the left shows the circular arrangement of the cards, each of which was briefly held still and then flipped down to create the illusion of movement.

The camera and projector were unusual, employing 70mm film that yielded larger, clearer images. By 1897, American Mutoscope was the most popular film company in the country. That year the firm also begin showing its films in penny arcades and other entertainment spots, using the Mutoscope. The simple card holder of the Mutoscope was less likely to break down than was the Kinetoscope, and American Mutoscope soon dominated the peepshow side of film exhibition as well. (Some Mutoscopes remained in use for decades.)

By 1897, the invention of the cinema was largely completed. There were two principal means of exhibition: peepshow devices for individual viewers and projection systems for audiences. Typically, projectors used 35mm film with sprocket holes of similar shape and placement, so most films could be shown on different brands of projector. But what kinds of films were being made? Who was making them? How and where were people seeing them?

EARLY FILMMAKING AND EXHIBITION

The cinema may have been an amazing novelty in the 1890s, but it came into being within a larger and varied context of Victorian-era leisure-time activities.

During the late nineteenth century, many homes had optical toys like the Zoetrope. Families often owned stereoscopes, hand-held viewers that created three-dimensional effects by using rectangular cards with two photographs printed side by side. Sets of cards depicted exotic locales or staged narratives. Many middle-class families also owned pianos, around which they gathered to sing. Increased literacy led to the spread of cheap popular fiction. The newfound ability to print photographs led to the publication of travel books that took the reader on vicarious tours of distant lands.

A great assortment of public entertainments was also available. All but the tiniest towns had theaters, and traveling shows crisscrossed the country. These might be dramatic troupes putting on plays, or lecturers using magic-lantern slides to illustrate their talks, or even concerts using the newly invented phonograph to bring the sounds of big-city orchestras to a wide public. Vaudeville offered middle-class audiences a variety of acts on a single program, ranging from performing animals to plate-spinning jugglers to slapstick comedians. Burlesque offered a similar potpourri of acts, though less family-oriented in their vulgar comedy and occasional nudity. People living in large cities also could go to amusement parks, like Coney Island in New York, which offered such attractions as roller coasters and elephant rides.

The new medium of film moved smoothly into this spectrum of popular entertainment. As the early films that we have already mentioned suggest, most subjects were nonfiction, or "actualities." These might be "scenics," or short travelogues, offering views of distant lands. News events might be depicted in brief "topicals." Radio and television journalism was still decades in the future, and even newspapers usually published drawings rather than photographs.

In many cases, cinematographers covered news events in the locations where they occurred. Often, however, filmmakers re-created current events in the studio—both to save money and to make up for the fact that cameramen had not been on the scene. In 1898, for example, both American and European producers used model ships in miniature landscapes to re-create the sinking of the battleship "Maine" and other key occurrences relating to the Spanish-American War. Audiences probably did not actually believe that these faked scenes were records of real incidents. Instead, they accepted them as representations of those incidents, comparable to engravings in news magazines.

From the beginning, fiction films were also important. Typically these were brief staged scenes. The Lumières' *Arroseur arrosé*, presented in their first program in 1895, showed a boy tricking a gardener by stepping on his hose. Such simple jokes formed a major genre of early filmmaking. Some of these fiction films were shot outdoors, but simple painted backdrops were quickly adopted and remained common for decades.

Looking at very early films, we may find them so alien that we wonder what sort of appeal they held for audiences. With a little imagination, though, we can see that people were probably interested in films for much the same reasons that we are. Every type of early film has some equivalent in contemporary media. The glimpses of news events, for example, may seem crude, yet they are comparable to the short clips shown on television news programs. Early scenics gave viewers glimpses of faraway lands, just as today travel lectures in colleges and churches utilize films, and televised documentaries show similar exotic views. Television variety shows offer a mix of acts that is somewhat comparable to early film programs. As we shall see, however, fiction films gradually became the most popular attraction in early theaters—a position they have held ever since.

Most films in this early period consisted of a single shot. The camera was set up in one position, and the action unfolded during a continuous take. In some cases, filmmakers did make a series of shots of the same subject. The resulting shots were then treated as a series of separate films. Exhibitors had the option of buying the whole series of shots and running them together, thus approximating a multishot film. They might also, however, choose to buy only a few of the shots, combining them with other films or lantern slides to create a unique program. During this early period, exhibitors had considerable control over the shape of their programs—a control that would disappear from about 1899, as producers began making longer films consisting of multiple shots.

Quite a few of these early exhibitors had experience running lantern-slide programs or other forms of public entertainment. Many strove for great variety, mixing scenics, topicals, and fiction films in a single program. The typical program had musical accompaniment. In the more modest presentations, a pianist might play; in vaudeville theaters, the house orchestra provided music. In some cases, exhibitors had noises synchronized with the actions on the screen. The exhibitor might lecture during part of the program, describing the exotic landscapes, the current events, and the brief stories passing across the screen. At the least, the exhibitor would announce the titles, since early films had no credits at the beginning or intertitles to explain the action. Some showmen mixed films with lantern slides or provided musical interludes using a phonograph. During these early years, the audience's response depended on the exhibitor's skill in organizing and presenting the program.

During the first decade of cinema, films were shown in many countries around the world. But the making of films was concentrated largely in the three principal countries where the motion-picture camera had originated: France, England, and the United States.

THE GROWTH OF THE FRENCH FILM INDUSTRY

The Lumières' early screenings were successful, but the brothers believed that film would be a short-lived fad. They moved quickly to exploit the Cinématographe. They initially avoided selling their machines, instead sending operators to tour abroad, showing films in rented theaters and cafés. These operators also made one-shot scenics of local points of interest. From 1896 on, the Lumière catalogue rapidly expanded to include hundreds of views of Spain, Egypt, Italy, Japan, and many other countries. Although the Lumière brothers are usually remembered for their scenics and topicals, they also produced many staged films, usually brief comic scenes.

Some of the Lumière operators' films were technically innovative. Eugène Promio, for example, is usually credited with originating the moving camera. The earliest cameras were supported by rigid tripods that did not allow the camera to swivel and make "panorama," or panning, shots. In 1896, Promio introduced movement into a view of Venice by placing the tripod and camera in a gondola. Promio and other filmmakers continued this practice, placing their cameras in boats and on trains (Fig. 1.13). Traveling shots of this type (and soon panning movements as well) were associated mainly with scenics and topicals during this era.

Because the Lumières quickly began exhibiting their films abroad, the first showings of projected motion pictures in many countries were put on by their operators. Thus the history of the cinema in many nations begins with the arrival of the Cinématographe. This is apparent from the accompanying chronology, which samples the earliest known public screenings in several countries.

Of course, the Lumières and their rivals concentrated on the more lucrative markets and avoided some smaller countries. No screenings are known to have taken place in Bolivia, for example, until 1909, when two Italian entrepreneurs took films there. Ideological pressures kept the cinema out of some markets. In 1900, Iran's royal family obtained a camera and projector in Europe and began making home movies. A theater that opened in Tehran in 1905, however, was soon forced by religious leaders to close.

On the whole, though, the Lumières and a few other firms made the cinema an international phenomenon. The Lumières further aided the spread of cinema when, in 1897, they began selling their Cinématographes.

Fig. 1.13 Lumière operator Eugène Promio influenced many filmmakers by placing his camera in moving boats to make several of his films, including *Egypte: Panorama des rives du Nil* ("Egypt: Panorama of the Banks of the Nile," 1896).

THE SPREAD OF THE CINEMA AROUND THE WORLD: SOME REPRESENTATIVE EXAMPLES

1896

March 1	Lumière program premieres in Brussels, Belgium.
May 11	A magician, Carl Hertz, shows R. W. Paul films at the Empire Theatre in Johannesburg, South Africa, using a projector purchased from Paul.
May 15	Lumière program begins a run in Madrid, Spain.
May 17	A Lumière operator shows films in St. Petersburg, Russia.
July 7	Lumière operators show films in a rented room in Watson's Hotel, Bombay, India.
July 8	A Lumière program opens in a fashionable district of Rio de Janeiro, Brazil.
July 15	The first Lumière screening in Czechoslovakia takes place in the Casino in Karlovy Vary.
August	Carl Hertz shows his R. W. Paul program at the Melbourne Opera House, Australia. (The first Lumière program in Australia begins in Sydney on September 28.)
Aug. 11	An unidentified operator shows films as part of a vaudeville program in Shanghai, China. (In July 1897, an Edison representative tours teahouses and amusement parks in China.)
Aug. 15	At a rented hall in Mexico City, a highly successful run of Lumière films begins.
December	A Lumière program shows at a café in Alexandria, Egypt.

1897

Jan. 28	Lumière films are shown in a fashionable theater in Maracaibo, Venezuela.
Feb. 15	Under the supervision of a Lumière representative, a Japanese entrepreneur premieres the Cinématographe in a theater in Osaka. (Edison's Vitascope was shown a week later, also in Osaka.)
Late February	A Lumière program premieres in Ruse, Bulgaria.

That same year saw a setback for their firm, however. On May 4, 1897, during a film screening at the Charity Bazaar in Paris, a curtain was ignited by the ether being used to fuel the lamp of the projector (which was not a Cinématographe). The resulting blaze was one of the worst tragedies in the history of the cinema, killing about 125 people, most of them from the upper class. As a result, the cinema lost some of its attraction for fashionable city dwellers. In France, for several years, films were mainly exhibited in less lucrative traveling fairground shows *(fêtes forains)*. The Lumières continued producing films, but gradually more innovative rivals made their films seem old-fashioned. Their firm ceased production in 1905, though Louis and Auguste remained innovators in the area of still photography.

Following the initial success of the Lumière Cinématographe in 1895, other film production firms appeared in France. Among these was a small company started by a man who was perhaps the most important single filmmaker of the cinema's early years, Georges Méliès. (See Box.)

Two other firms that were to dominate the French film industry were formed shortly after the invention of the cinema. Charles Pathé was a phonograph seller and exhibitor in the early 1890s. In 1895, he purchased some of R. W. Paul's imitation Kinetoscopes, and the following year formed Pathé Frères, which initially made most of its money on phonographs. From 1901, however, Pathé concentrated more on film production, and profits soared. The firm expanded rapidly. In 1902, it built a glass-sided studio and began selling the Pathé camera, which became the world's most widely used camera until the end of the 1910s.

At first Pathé's production was somewhat derivative, borrowing ideas from Méliès and from American and English films. For example, in 1901,

GEORGES MÉLIÈS, MAGICIAN OF THE CINEMA

Méliès was a magician who owned the Théâtre Robert-Houdin, named for the foremost French conjuror. After seeing the Lumière Cinématographe in 1895, he decided to add films to his program, but the Lumière brothers were not yet selling machines. In early 1896, he obtained a projector from English inventor R. W. Paul and by studying it was able to build his own camera. He was soon showing films at the Robert-Houdin.

Although Méliès is remembered mainly for his delightful fantasy movies, replete with camera tricks and painted scenery, he made films in all the genres of the day. His earliest work, most of which is lost, included many Lumière-style scenics and brief comedies, filmed outdoors. During his first year of production, he made 78 films, including his first trick film, *The Vanishing Lady* (1896). In it, Méliès appeared as a magician who transforms a woman into a skeleton. The trick was accomplished by stopping the camera and substituting the skeleton for the woman. Later, Méliès used stop-motion and other special effects to create more complex magic and fantasy scenes. These tricks had to be accomplished in the camera, while filming; prior to the mid-1920s, few laboratory manipulations were possible. Méliès also acted in many of his films, recognizable as a dapper and spry figure with a bald head, moustache, and pointed beard.

In order to be able to control the mise-en-scene and cinematography of his films, Méliès built a small glass-enclosed studio. Finished by early 1897, the studio permitted Méliès to design and construct sets painted on canvas flats (Fig. 1.14). Even working in this studio, however, Méliès continued

Fig. 1.15 One of many reconstructed documentaries relating to the sinking of the American battleship "Maine," which began the Spanish-American War, Georges Méliès's *Divers at Work on the Wreck of the "Maine"* used a painted set with actors playing the divers. A fish tank in front of the camera suggested an undersea scene.

to create various kinds of films. In 1898, for example, he filmed some reconstructed topicals, such as *Divers at Work on the Wreck of the "Maine"* (Fig. 1.15). His 1899 film, *The Dreyfus Affair,* told the story of the Jewish officer convicted of treason in 1894 on the basis of false evidence put forth through anti-Semitic motives. The controversy was still raging when Méliès made his pro-Dreyfus picture. As was customary at the time, he released each of the ten shots as a separate film. When shown together, the shots combined into one of the most complex works of the cinema's early years. (Modern prints of *The Dreyfus Affair* typically combine all the shots in a single reel.) With his next work, *Cinderella* (1899), Méliès began joining multiple shots and selling them as one film.

Méliès's films, and especially his fantasies, were extremely popular in France and abroad, and they were widely imitated. They were also commonly pirated, and Méliès had to open a sales office in the United States in 1903 to protect his interests. Among the most celebrated of his fims was *A Trip to the Moon* (1902), a comic science-fiction story of a group of scientists traveling to the moon in a space capsule and escaping after being taken prisoner by a race of subterranean creatures (Fig. 1.16). Méliès often enhanced the beauty of his elaborately designed mise-en-scene by using hand-applied tinting (Color Plate 1.1).

Except in Méliès's first years of production, many of his films involved sophisticated stop-motion effects. Devils burst out of a cloud of smoke, pretty women vanish, and leaping

Fig. 1.14 The interior of the Star studio, with Méliès on the balcony lifting a rolled backdrop while assistants arrange a large painted shell and trapdoors. Painted theater-style flats and smaller set elements are stored at the right rear or hang on the back wall.

Fig. 1.16 The space capsule lands in the Man in the Moon's eye in Méliès's fantasy, *A Trip to the Moon.*

men change into demons in midair. Some historians have criticized Méliès for depending on static theatrical sets instead of editing. Yet recent research has shown that in fact his stop-motion effects also utilized editing. He would cut the film in order to match the movement of one object perfectly with that of the thing into which it was transformed. Such cuts were designed to be unnoticeable, but clearly Méliès was a master of one type of editing.

For a time Méliès's films continued to be widely successful. After 1905, however, his fortunes slowly declined. His tiny firm was hard put to supply the burgeoning demand for films, especially in the face of competition from bigger companies. He continued to produce quality films, including his late masterpiece, *Conquest of the Pole* (1912), but eventually these came to seem old-fashioned as filmmaking conventions changed. In 1912, deep in debt, Méliès stopped producing, having made just over 500 films (fewer than two-thirds of which survive). He died in 1938, after decades of working in his wife's candy and toy shop.

Ferdinand Zecca, the company's most important director, made *Scenes from My Balcony*. It picked up on the vogue, recently started in England, for shots presenting things as if seen through telescopes or microscopes (Figs. 1.17, 1.18). Pathé's films were extremely well liked. While it only took a sale of fifteen copies of a given film to break even, actual sales averaged 350 prints. Pathé expanded abroad, opening sales offices in London, New York, Moscow, Berlin, and St. Petersburg in 1904 and 1905 and others in later years. Selling both projectors and films, Pathé encouraged people to get into the business of exhibition, thus creating more demand for Pathé films. As we shall see in the next chapter, within a few years, Pathé Frères would be the single largest film company in the world.

Its main rival in France was a smaller firm formed by inventor Léon Gaumont. Like Lumière Frères, Gaumont initially dealt in still photographic equipment. The firm began producing films in 1897. These were mostly actualities made by Alice Guy, the first female filmmaker. Gaumont's involvement in film production remained limited in this era, since Léon was more concerned with technical innovations in film equipment. Building a production studio in 1905 made Gaumont more prominent, largely through the work of director Louis Feuillade.

ENGLAND AND THE "BRIGHTON SCHOOL"

After the first public film screenings in early 1896, film exhibition spread quickly in England, largely because R. W. Paul was willing to sell projectors. At first, most films were grouped together to be shown as a single act on the program of a music hall (the British equivalent of American vaudeville

Fig. 1.17

Fig. 1.18

Figs. 1.17 and 1.18 One of many mildly risqué films made in this early period, Zecca's *Scenes from My Balcony* shows a man looking through a telescope, followed by shots of what he sees, including a woman undressing.

Fig. 1.19 A typical fairground film show in England, about 1900. Behind the elaborate painted façades, the auditoriums were simple tents. Note here the picture of Thomas Edison in the center and the use of a drum to attract spectators.

theaters). Beginning in 1897, short, cheap film shows were also widely presented in fairgrounds, appealing to working-class audiences (Fig. 1.19).

At first, most English films followed the usual pattern of offering simple novelty subjects. For example, in 1896, Paul made *Twins' Tea Party* (Fig. 1.20). Filmmakers also concentrated on important news events. Topicals showing the annual Derby were popular, and both the parade celebrating Queen Victoria's Jubilee in 1897 and events relating to the Boer War in South Africa were widely circulated. Some of these early newsreels included more than one shot. The operator might simply stop and restart the camera to capture only highlights of the action, or he might actually splice bits of film together to hurry the action along. Similarly, some scenics were influenced by the Lumière films' placement of the camera on moving vehicles. "Phantom rides," designed to give the spectator the illusion of traveling, became popular in England and other countries (Fig. 1.21). As was common, British exhibitors gathered many types of films into a varied program.

Early English films became famous for their imaginative special-effects cinematography. For example, Cecil Hepworth began producing on a small scale in 1899. At first he concentrated on actualities, but he soon directed trick films as well (Fig. 1.22). Hepworth went on to become the most important British producer in the era from 1905 to 1914.

There were other producers scattered around England, but the most notable were those in the small, but influential, group later dubbed the "Brighton School" because they worked in or near that resort town. Chief among them were G. A. Smith and James Williamson, both of whom were still photographers who branched into filmmaking in 1897. Both also built small studios that opened at one side to admit sunlight. Both explored special effects and editing in ways that influenced filmmakers in other countries.

Williamson's 1900 film, *The Big Swallow*, is a good example of the ingenuity of the Brighton filmmakers. It begins with a view of a man, seen against a blank background, gesturing angrily because he does not want his picture taken. He walks forward until his wide-open mouth blots out the view

Fig. 1.20 Paul's *Twins' Tea Party* appealed to audiences by showing two cute toddlers squabbling and then kissing and making up. It was typical of many films of this era: a single shot taken on an open-air stage in direct sunlight, against a neutral backdrop.

Fig. 1.21

Fig. 1.22

Fig. 1.23

Fig. 1.24

Fig. 1.21 *View from an Engine Front— Barnstaple,* made by the Warwick Trading Company in 1898, was typical of a popular genre, the "phantom ride."

Fig. 1.22 In Hepworth's *Explosion of a Motor Car* (1900), stop-motion changes a real car into a fake one, which promptly blows up. A passing bobbie dutifully inventories the body parts that rain in from above, creating a grim but amusing film.

Figs. 1.23 and 1.24 Two stages of Williamson's *The Big Swallow,* as the irritated subject "eats" the cinematographer and camera.

Fig. 1.25

Fig. 1.26

Figs. 1.25 and 1.26 In *Mary Jane's Mishap,* close views alternate with long shots to show such details as the maid accidentally smearing a "moustache" on her face while shining some shoes.

(Fig. 1.23). An imperceptible cut then substitutes a black backdrop for his mouth, and we see the cinematographer and his camera pitch forward into this void. Another concealed cut returns us to the open mouth, and the man backs away from the camera, laughing and chewing triumphantly (Fig. 1.24).

Smith's 1903 grotesque comedy, *Mary Jane's Mishap,* uses editing in a remarkably sophisticated way. One basic distant framing of a slovenly maid in a kitchen is interrupted by several cut-ins to medium shots that show her amusing facial expressions (Figs. 1.25, 1.26). Although the actor's position is usually not matched well at the cuts, there is a general attempt to create a continuous action while using closer shots to guide our attention. This principle would become one basis for the dominant continuity style of film-making that developed over approximately the next fifteen years.

The English cinema was innovative and internationally popular for several years early in the history of motion pictures, though it would soon weaken in the face of French, Italian, American, and Danish competition.

THE UNITED STATES: COMPETITION AND THE RESURGENCE OF EDISON

The United States was far and away the largest market for motion pictures, since it had more theaters per capita than any other country. For over fifteen years American and foreign firms competed vigorously there. Although American films were sold abroad, U.S. firms concentrated on the domestic market. This competition was one reason why France and Italy were soon to move

Fig. 1.27 "The Messiah's Entry into Jerusalem," one of the single-shot tableaux that made up *The Passion Play of Oberammergau*, produced by the Eden Musée, an important New York entertainment establishment.

Fig. 1.28 Eugène Lauste, an American Mutoscope Company employee who had helped invent the Biograph camera, by the camera booth in the Casino de Paris, where he showed films during 1897–1898. The hall, with its potted palms and chandeliers, indicates the sort of elegant venue in which some early film screenings were held.

ahead of the United States and control the international film trade until the mid-1910s.

After the first New York presentation of Edison's Vitascope in April 1896, film exhibition spread rapidly across the country. The Vitascope was not for sale, but individual entrepreneurs bought the rights to exploit it in different states. During 1896–1897, however, many small companies marketed their own projectors, all designed to show 35mm prints. Since films were not yet copyrighted, and prints were sold rather than rented, it was difficult to control the circulation of films. Edison's pictures were often duplicated and sold, while Edison profited by duping films imported from France and England. Firms also frequently made direct imitations of each other's movies.

Soon hundreds of projectors were in use, and films were shown in vaudeville houses, amusement parks, small storefront theaters, summer resorts, fairs, even churches and opera houses. The years 1895–1897 were the novelty period of the cinema, because the primary appeal was simply the astonishment of seeing movement and unusual sights reproduced on the screen. By early 1898, however, films' novelty had worn off. As attendance declined, many exhibitors went out of business. One event that helped revive the industry was the Spanish-American War of 1898. Patriotic fervor made audiences eager to see anything relating to the conflict, and companies in the United States and abroad profited by making authentic and even staged films.

Another type of film that helped revive the industry was the Passion Play. Beginning in 1897, filmmakers made series of single-shot scenes from Jesus' life—views that resembled illustrations in Bibles or magic-lantern slides. One such series of shots was released in February 1898 as *The Passion Play of Oberammergau* (Fig. 1.27). (The title lent the film respectability, though it in fact had no connection with the traditional German spectacle.) As with many of the more elaborate films of the day, the exhibitor had the option of buying some or all of the shots and combining them, along with lantern slides and other religious material, to make a lengthy program. Boxing films were also popular, especially since they could often be shown in places where live bouts were prohibited.

From 1898, then, the American film industry enjoyed a certain stability, with most films being shown in vaudeville theaters. Production increased during this period to meet the high demand.

The American Mutoscope Company did particularly well during the late 1890s, partly because of its clear 70mm images, displayed by the company's own touring operators in vaudeville houses. By 1897 American Mutoscope was the most popular film company in America, and it attracted audiences abroad as well (Fig. 1.28). American Mutoscope began filming in a new rooftop studio (Fig. 1.29). The firm changed its name in 1899 to American Mutoscope and Biograph (AM&B), reflecting its double specialization in peepshow Mutoscope reels and projected films. Over the next several years, AM&B was hampered by a lawsuit brought against it by Edison, who consistently took competitors to court for infringing patents and copyrights. In 1902, however, AM&B won the suit, and its prosperity grew. In 1903 it began to make and sell films in 35mm rather than 70mm, a change that boosted sales.

Fig. 1.29 Officials of the American Mutoscope Company (including W. K. L. Dickson, second from right) in the firm's new rooftop studio. Like the Black Maria, the studio rotated on rails to catch the sun. The camera was sheltered in the metal booth, and simple painted sets were built against the framework.

Fig. 1.30 At the City Hall in New York, Vitagraph personnel (J. Stuart Blackton to the right of the central camera, Albert E. Smith second from left) ready to film an important topical event: the triumphal return of Admiral George Dewey after the Battle of Manila, 1898.

Beginning in 1908, it employed one of the most important silent-era directors, D. W. Griffith.

Another important company that got its start during the early years of the cinema was American Vitagraph, founded in 1897 by J. Stuart Blackton and Albert E. Smith as an advertising firm. Vitagraph got its start in production by making popular films relating to the Spanish-American War (Fig. 1.30). Like other production companies of this period, Vitagraph was threatened with patent- and copyright-infringement lawsuits by Edison, who hoped to control the American market. Vitagraph survived by agreeing to cooperate with Edison, making films for the Edison firm and in turn dealing in Edison films itself. After AM&B's 1902 legal triumph over Edison briefly reduced the risk of lawsuits throughout the industry, Vitagraph expanded production. Within a few years, it would emerge as an important firm making stylistically innovative films. Blackton would also make some of the earliest animated films.

The rise in production at AM&B and Vitagraph in the wake of Edison's failed lawsuit obliged Edison's company to make more films to counter their competition. One tactic the Edison firm tried with success was making longer films shot in the studio. In this endeavor, it had the assistance of the most important American filmmaker of this early period, Edwin S. Porter.

Porter was a film projectionist who was also an expert at making photographic equipment. In late 1900 he went to work for Edison, whom he greatly admired. He was assigned to improve the firm's cameras and projectors. That year the Edison Company built a new glass-enclosed rooftop studio in New York, where films could be shot using the typical painted stage-style scenery of the era. In early 1901, Porter began operating a camera there. At this stage of cinema history the cameraman was effectively the film's director, and soon Porter was responsible for many of the company's most popular films.

Porter has often been credited with virtually all the innovations of the pre-1908 period, including making the first story film *(Life of an American Fireman)* and inventing editing as we know it. In fact, he often drew upon techniques already used by Méliès, Smith, and Williamson. He imaginatively developed his models, however, and he undoubtedly introduced some original techniques. His position as the foremost filmmaker of the preeminent American production company gave his works wide exposure and made them popular and influential.

There had been many, indeed hundreds, of staged fictional films made before *Life of an American Fireman* (1903). Porter himself had done several, including a version of *Jack and the Beanstalk* in 1902. He had access to all the foreign films that the Edison Company was duping, so he could study the latest innovations. He examined Méliès's *A Trip to the Moon* closely and decided to copy its manner of telling a story in a series of shots. From 1902 on, many of his films contained several shots, with significant efforts to match time and space across cuts.

Porter's *Life of an American Fireman* is a notable attempt at such storytelling. It begins with a long shot of a dozing fireman dreaming of a woman and child threatened by fire; the dream is rendered as a sort of "thought balloon," a circular vignette superimposed in the upper part of the screen. A cut to a close-up shows a hand pulling a public fire alarm. Several shots, mixing studio and location filming, show the firemen racing to the scene. The film ends with two lengthy shots that show the same action from two vantage points. The first shot shows a fireman coming in a bedroom window to rescue a mother and then returning to save her baby. In the second shot, we see both rescues again, from a camera position outside the house. To a modern audience, this repetition of events may seem strange, but such displays of the same event from different viewpoints were not uncommon in the early cinema. [In Méliès's *A Trip to the Moon,* we see the explorers'

Fig. 1.31

Fig. 1.32

Figs. 1.31 and 1.32 Porter's *Uncle Tom's Cabin* used an intertitle to introduce each shot. Here "The Escape of Eliza" leads to a single shot of the famous episode in the novel in which Eliza flees across the ice floes on a river.

capsule land in the Man in the Moon's eye (Fig. 1.16) and then see the landing again from a camera position on the moon's surface.] *Life of an American Fireman* was based on earlier films and lantern slides depicting fire-fighting techniques. Brighton School director James Williamson had made a similar film, *Fire!*, in 1901.

Porter made several significant films in 1903, among them an adaptation of the popular stage version of the novel *Uncle Tom's Cabin*. Porter's film was a series of one-shot scenes of famous episodes in the novel, linked by printed intertitles—the first known to have been used in an American film (Figs. 1.31, 1.32). (Porter derived this technique from a G. A. Smith film.) His most important film, *The Great Train Robbery*, was also made in 1903. It used eleven shots to tell the story of a gang of bandits who hold up a train. A telegraph operator whom they tie up at the beginning alerts authorities, and a posse ambushes the thieves as they divide the loot. Porter edits together shots depicting the telegraph office, the robbery on the train, and the local townspeople at a dance. Although he does not cut back and forth to show simultaneous action, a few years later other filmmakers would begin alternating shots presenting different locales, thus creating a technique called "intercutting." Porter's film was, nonetheless, gripping in its depiction of violent action (Fig. 1.33). Indeed, a novel extra shot, showing one of the robbers in a close view firing a gun toward the camera, was included; exhibitors had the option of placing it at the beginning or end of the film. Perhaps no film of the pre-1905 period was as popular as *The Great Train Robbery*.

Porter worked for Edison for several more years. In 1905 he directed *The Kleptomaniac*, a social critique that contrasted the situations of two women who commit theft. The first part shows a rich kleptomaniac stealing goods at a department store; we then see shots of a poor woman impulsively taking a loaf of bread. The final courtroom scene shows the poor woman being sentenced, while the rich one is let off. In Porter's 1906 film, *The Dream of a Rarebit Fiend*, superimposition and a rocking camera depict a drunkard's dizziness, while Méliès-style special effects show his dream of flying above a city. In 1909, Porter left Edison to become an independent producer, but he was soon outshone by others who were just entering the field.

From 1902 to 1905, Porter was one of many filmmakers who contributed to an industrywide concentration on fiction filmmaking. Unlike topicals, which were dependent on unpredictable news events, fiction films could be carefully planned in advance. While scenics involved expensive travel to

Fig. 1.33 To make this shot for *The Great Train Robbery*, Porter exposed the film twice, showing most of the action of the holdup staged in the studio, with the view of the train as seen through the window filmed separately.

distant locales, fiction films allowed their makers to stay at or near the studio. Both of these factors facilitated steady, predictable releases of films. Moreover, audiences seemed to prefer story films. Some of these were still one-shot views, but increasingly filmmakers used a series of shots to depict comic chases, lavish fantasies, and intense dramas.

By 1904, major changes were taking place in the new medium and art form of the cinema. Fiction films were becoming the industry's main product. Increasingly, movies were rented to exhibitors, a practice that established the division among production, distribution, and exhibition that was to shape the expansion of the film industry. Exhibition was spreading internationally, so films would soon be seen in most countries.

Although we have stressed production in France, England, and the United States, small-scale production also occurred in other parts of the world from an early date. Enterprising exhibitors made scenics and topicals of local interest to mix into their programs of imported films. In Spain, for instance, the first films were taken by Eugène Promio when he brought the Lumière Cinématographe to Madrid in 1896. By October of the same year, however, Eduardo Jimeno shot the first Spanish-made film, *Worshippers Leaving the Noon Mass at Pilar de Zaragoza;* similar imitations of Lumière actualities and even fiction films were produced in 1897. In India, exhibitor Harishchandra Sakharam Bhatwadekar ordered a Lumière camera and filmed wrestling matches, circus monkeys, and local events, showing these actualities in his program of imported films beginning in 1899. Entrepreneurs in other countries made similar films, but, since only one or a few prints were made, hardly any survive.

During the first ten years of the commercial exploitation of the cinema, conditions were established for international growth of the industry. Moreover, filmmakers had begun to explore the creative possibilities of the new medium. These activities were to intensify in the next decade.

◆ NOTES AND QUERIES

IDENTIFICATION AND PRESERVATION OF EARLY FILMS

In the silent era, there were no libraries or archives to preserve films. The great majority of films from the first decade of the cinema are lost or incomplete, and even those that survive are often difficult to identify. Many had no title at the beginning, and there were seldom stars or other distinctive traits that would provide even a slight clue as to the source.

Fortunately, however, some segments of this era of film history have been preserved. In the United States, there was a method of copyrighting films by printing every frame on a long roll of paper. This practice lasted from 1894 to 1912, although only a small proportion of films produced were copyrighted in this fashion. These "paper prints" were discovered in the 1940s at the Library of Congress and rephotographed onto film. In France, many negatives of the Lumière company were preserved, and even now hundreds have not been printed as positive viewing prints. In some cases, release copies of early films were stored away and found later, so archivists can duplicate them.

Historians have also combed catalogues of early sales and distribution companies, trying to create lists *(filmographies)* of the movies made in a country or by a single studio. For a description of the paper prints, see Kemp Niver, *Motion Pictures from the Library of Congress Paper Print Collection 1894–1912* (Berkeley: University of California Press, 1967). Niver's *Biograph Bulletins 1896–1908* (Los Angeles: Locare Research Group, 1971) reproduces the American Mutoscope and Biograph catalogues for this era; it provides a good example of the type of material historians work with. Denis Gifford's *The British Film Catalogue 1895–1985: A Reference Guide* (London: David & Charles, 1986) represents one of the most ambitious attempts to document a country's entire fiction-film production.

REVIVING INTEREST IN EARLY CINEMA: THE BRIGHTON CONFERENCE

For many years, the earliest period of the cinema was treated as relatively unimportant. Historians dealt with the invention of cameras and projectors but dismissed early films as crude. Overgeneralizations abounded. Edwin S. Porter, for example, was credited with being virtually the only stylistic forerunner of the American cinema's system of editing.

A major event in 1978 helped change many notions about the early cinema. The Fédération International des Archives du Film (FIAF, the International Federation of Film Archives) held its annual conference in Brighton, as a salute to the Brighton School. Many film historians were invited, and nearly six hundred pre-1907 films were screened. The result was a new appreciation of the variety and fascination of early films. To this day, the study of the silent cinema remains one of the liveliest research areas of film history.

The proceedings of the Brighton Conference, along with a tentative filmography of surviving prints, have been published as *Cinema 1900/1906: An Analytical Study*, 2 vols., ed. Roger Holman (Brussels: FIAF, 1982). For a description of the Brighton Conference and its effects on historians' work, see Jon Gartenberg, "The Brighton Project: Archives and Historians," *Iris* **2**, 1 (1984): 5–16. *Early Cinema: Space, Frame, Narrative*, ed. Thomas Elsaesser, with Adam Barker (London: British Film Institute, 1990) contains several essays influenced by the Brighton event and written by historians who participated, including Charles Musser, Tom Gunning, André Gaudreault, Noël Burch, and Barry Salt.

◆ REFERENCE

1. From *The Photogram,* quoted in John Barnes, *The Beginnings of the Cinema in England* (New York: Barnes & Noble, 1976), p. 64.

2

THE INTERNATIONAL EXPANSION OF THE CINEMA, 1905–1912

Before 1904, the cinema led a somewhat vagrant existence. Since producers sold film prints, exhibitors showed them in vaudeville houses, music halls, rented theaters, and fairground tents. Around 1905, however, the film industry expanded and stabilized. Permanent theaters were devoted especially to film, and production expanded to meet increased demand. Italy and Denmark joined the ranks of important producing countries, and filmmaking on a smaller scale emerged in many other lands.

After 1905, films grew longer, using more shots and telling more complex stories. Filmmakers explored new techniques for conveying narrative information. Perhaps no other era has seen such extensive changes in films' formal and stylistic traits.

FILM PRODUCTION IN EUROPE

FRANCE

During this period, the French film industry was still the largest, and its movies were the ones most frequently seen around the world. The two main firms, Pathé Frères and Gaumont, continued to expand, and other companies were formed in response to an increased demand from exhibitors. As in many western countries, workers were winning a shorter workweek and thus had more leisure time for inexpensive entertainments. The French firms also courted a wider middle-class audience.

In 1905–1906, the French film industry was growing rapidly. Pathé was already a large company, with three separate studios. It was also one of the earliest film companies to become *vertically integrated.* Vertical integration means most basically that a firm controls the production, distribution, and exhibition of a film. As we shall see time and again in this book, vertical integration has been a major strategy pursued by film companies and often a measure of their strength. Pathé made its own cameras and projectors, produced films, and manufactured the film stock for release prints. In 1906, Pathé also began buying theaters. The following year, the firm began to distribute its own films by renting rather than selling them to exhibitors. By then, it was the largest film company in the world. Over the next few years, it started distributing films made by other companies as well.

By 1905, Pathé had six filmmakers, still overseen by Ferdinand Zecca, each making a film a week. The films were in a variety of genres: actualities, historical films, trick films, dramas, vaudeville acts, and chases. During 1903–1904, Pathé created an elaborate system for hand-stenciling color onto release prints. Stencils were painstakingly cut from a copy of the film itself, with a different stencil for each color. Assembly lines of women workers then painted the colors on each separate release print. Pathé reserved color for trick films and films displaying flowers or elegantly dressed women (Color Plate 2.1). Such hand-coloring was used until the early sound era.

Among Pathé's most profitable films were series starring popular comics: the "Boireau" series (with André Deed), the "Rigadin" films (with the music-hall star Prince), and, above all, the Max Linder series. Linder's films reflected the industry's growing bid for respectability by being set in a middle-class milieu (Fig. 2.1). Max typically suffered embarrassment in social situations, such as wearing painfully tight shoes to an elegant dinner. He was often thwarted in love; in *Une ruse de Max* ("Max's Ruse"), he unsuccessfully tries to commit suicide in various ways, calling upon his valet to fetch a knife, a gun, and so on. Linder's films were enormously influential. Charles Chaplin once referred to Linder as his "professor" and himself as Linder's "disciple."[1] Linder worked in both the United States and France from 1909 until his death in 1925.

Aside from being a vertically integrated firm, Pathé also used the strategy of *horizontal integration.* This term means that a firm expands within one sector of the film industry, as when a distributor opens additional offices in new towns. Pathé enlarged its film production by opening studios in such places as Italy, Russia, and the United States. During 1909–1911, its Moscow branch was making about half the films produced in Russia.

Pathé's main French rival, Gaumont, also expanded rapidly. After finishing its new studio in 1905, the firm took on additional filmmakers. Alice Guy trained this staff and turned to making longer films herself (Fig. 2.2). Among the new filmmakers was scriptwriter and director Louis Feuillade, who took over the supervision of Gaumont's films when Guy left in 1908. He became one of the silent cinema's most important artists, and his career paralleled Gaumont's fortunes until the 1920s. Feuillade was extraordinarily

Fig. 2.1 Max Linder in *Une ruse de Max* ("Max's Ruse," directed by Linder in 1913). Linder's distinctive appearance— elegant clothes, top hat, and dapper moustache—influenced other comics to adopt "trademark" outfits.

Fig. 2.2 Alice Guy collaborated with designer Victorin Jasset on *La Naissance, la vie et la mort de Notre-Seigneur Jésus-Christ* ("The Birth, Life and Death of Our Lord Jesus Christ," 1906). This scene of the scourging of Christ indicates the elaborate staging and sets used for some prestige films of this period.

Figs. 2.3 and 2.4 The sets and acting in *The Assassination of the Duc de Guise* derived from the theater. Its shots, however, showed characters moving smoothly from one space to another, as when the Duc de Guise walks through a curtained doorway to confront his enemies.

Fig. 2.3   Fig. 2.4

versatile, making comedies, historical films (Color Plate 2.2), thrillers, and melodramas.

Following Pathé's lead, other companies and entrepreneurs opened film theaters, aiming at affluent consumers. Such theaters often showed longer and more prestigious films. Prosperity in the French industry and in film exports led to the formation of several smaller firms during this period.

One of these had a significant impact. As its name suggests, the Film d'Art company, founded in 1908, identified itself with elite tastes. One of its first efforts was *The Assassination of the Duc de Guise* (1908, Charles Le Bargy and Albert Lambert). Using stage stars, a script by a famous dramatist, and an original score by classical composer Camille Saint-Saëns, the film told the story of a famous incident in French history (Figs. 2.3, 2.4). It was widely shown, gaining a successful release in the United States. *The Assassination of the Duc de Guise* and similar works created a certain notion of what "art films" should be like. The Film d'Art company, however, lost money on most of its productions and was sold in 1911.

By and large, however, the French industry prospered. By 1910, the traveling *fêtes foraines* had dwindled, and larger film theaters were the rule. During the same era, however, French firms were facing challenges in the lucrative American market.

ITALY

Italy came somewhat late to the film production scene, but beginning in 1905 its industry grew rapidly. Within a few years, Italy's film industry somewhat resembled that of France.

Although films were produced in several cities, Rome's Cines firm (founded 1905) and Turin's Ambrosio (1905) and Itala (1906) soon emerged as the principal companies. The new firms were handicapped by a lack of experienced personnel, and some lured artists away from French firms. For example, Cines hired one of Pathé's main filmmakers, Gaston Velle, as its artistic director. As a result, some Italian films were imitations, even remakes, of French movies.

Exhibition also expanded rapidly. Italy depended less than other European countries on films being shown in traveling fairs and other temporary

Fig. 2.5

Fig. 2.6

Fig. 2.5 The large sets, crowd scenes, and lavish historical costumes of *The Fall of Troy* were typical of Italian epics.

Fig. 2.6 French-born clown Ferdinand Guillaume as the popular Polidor in *Polidor coi baffi* ("Polidor's Moustache," 1914).

venues. Instead, many permanent theaters opened. Thus, in Italy, cinema won respect as a new art form earlier than in other countries. Italian producers moved toward "art films" at about the same time that Film d'Art was making *The Assassination of the Duc de Guise.* In 1908, the Ambrosio company made *The Last Days of Pompeii,* the first of many adaptations of Bulwer-Lytton's historical novel. As a result of this film's popularity, the Italian cinema became identified with historical spectacle.

By 1910, Italy was probably second only to France in the number of films it sent around the world. Partly because Italian producers catered to permanent film theaters, they were among the first who consistently made films of more than one reel (that is, longer than fifteen minutes). For example, in 1910, a major director of the period, Giovanni Pastrone, made *Il Caduta de Troia* (*The Fall of Troy;* Fig. 2.5) in three reels. The triumph of this and similar films encouraged Italian producers to make longer, more lavish epics, a trend that culminated in the mid-1910s.

Not all Italian films were epics, however. For example, beginning in 1909, producers again imitated the French by creating several comic series. Itala hired Pathé's André Deed, who briefly abandoned his "Boireau" character to become Cretinetti ("Little Cretin"). Other companies found French or Italian comics to build series around, such as Ambrosio's Robinet and Cines's Polidor (Fig. 2.6). These films were much cheaper than epics. They were also livelier and more spontaneous, and they became internationally popular. Hundreds of such films were made, but the fad gradually declined during the 1910s.

DENMARK

That a small country like Denmark became a significant player in world cinema was largely due to entrepreneur Ole Olsen. He had been an exhibitor, initially using a peepshow machine and later running one of the first movie theaters in Copenhagen. In 1906, he formed a production company, Nordisk, and immediately began opening distribution offices abroad. Nordisk's breakthrough came in 1907 with *Lion Hunt,* a fiction film about a safari. Because two lions were actually shot during the production, the film was banned in

Fig. 2.7 Nordisk's second studio was typical of such buildings in many countries during the silent era. Glass walls and roof permitted sunlight to illuminate scenes.

Denmark, but the publicity generated huge sales abroad. The company's New York branch, established in 1908, sold Nordisk films under the brand name Great Northern. In the same year, Olsen completed the first of four glass studios for indoor production (Fig. 2.7).

Nordisk films quickly established an international reputation for excellent acting and production values. It specialized in crime thrillers, dramas, and somewhat sensationalistic melodramas, including "white-slave" (prostitution) stories. Nordisk had a circus set permanently installed, and some of the firm's major films were melodramas of circus life, such as *The Four Devils* (1911, Robert Dineson and Alfred Lind) and *Dødespringet til Hest frå Cirkus-Kuplen* ("Death Jump on Horseback from the Circus Dome," 1912, Eduard Schnedler-Sørensen). The latter film concerns a count who loses his fortune through covering the gambling debts of a friend. His skill at riding horses allows him to work in a circus, where he becomes romantically involved with two women (Fig. 2.8). One of them jealously tries to kill him by causing his horse to plunge from a high platform; the second nurses him back to health. Rival producers admired such films for compressing abrupt plot twists and highly emotional situations into two or three reels.

Although a few smaller companies started up during this period, Olsen eventually managed either to buy them or to drive them out of business. Nevertheless, it was one of these short-lived small firms that made the film *The Abyss* (1910, Urban Gad), which brought instant fame to actress Asta Nielsen. Indeed, like Max Linder, she was one of the first international film stars. Dark and thin, with large, intense eyes, she possessed an unconventional beauty. She often played women destroyed by love: seduced and abandoned, or sacrificing themselves for the happiness of the men they love (Fig. 2.9). Nielsen was equally adept at comedy, however, and although she had trained in the theater, she was one of the earliest screen performers whose

Fig. 2.8 A dramatic staging in depth in *Dødespringet til Hest frå Cirkus-Kuplen:* the heroine watches from the foreground as the hero demonstrates his equestrian skills in the circus ring.

style seemed to owe nothing to the stage. Nielsen went to work in Germany, where she became one of the mainstays of the industry.

The Danish industry remained healthy until World War I cut off many of its export markets.

OTHER COUNTRIES

Led by Cecil Hepworth's production company, England remained a significant force in world film markets. Filmmaking spread to other countries as well. The earliest systematic production in Japan, for example, was launched in 1908. Most films made there were apparently records of Kabuki plays, filmed in static long shots. A few German production companies started up, though the industry did not begin to flourish until 1913. Pathé dominated Russian filmmaking, but several domestic firms also established themselves. In other countries, small production companies appeared, produced a few films, and disappeared.

In general, the years before World War I saw the emergence of France, Italy, and the United States as the main centers of film industries competing on the international scene.

Fig. 2.9 The arrest of the heroine at the end of *The Abyss*.

THE STRUGGLE FOR THE EXPANDING AMERICAN FILM INDUSTRY

Today Hollywood dominates the international market in entertainment media. Before World War I, however, the United States was not yet the most economically important country. Great Britain still ruled the waves: its ships carried more goods than did those of any other country, and London was the globe's financial center.

Moreover, the American firms concentrated on meeting the swiftly expanding domestic demand for films, not on invading foreign markets. The companies were also competing for power in the new industry. The period 1905–1912 saw American producers, distributors, and exhibitors trying to bring some stability to the shifting and confused film business.

THE NICKELODEON BOOM

By 1905, films were showing in most of the available vaudeville houses, local theaters, and other venues. The main trend in the American film industry during the years 1905–1907 was the huge multiplication of film theaters. They were typically small stores, installed with fewer than two hundred seats. Admission was usually a nickel (hence the term "nickelodeon") or a dime for a program running fifteen to sixty minutes. Most nickelodeons had only one projector. During reel changes a singer would perform a current song, accompanied by lantern slides.

Fig. 2.10 A drawing from a 1909 Gaumont catalogue, showing how sound effects could be produced behind the screen. The hanging sheet of metal at the left, when shaken, created the sound of thunder.

Nickelodeons spread for several reasons. When production companies turned away from actualities toward story films, moviegoing became less a novelty and more a regular entertainment. Many people were gaining shorter workweeks and had more time for entertainment. In addition, film producers took to renting rather than selling films. Since exhibitors no longer had to keep running the same films until they made back their purchase price, they could change their programs two, three, even seven times a week. As a result, some of their patrons returned regularly. Nickelodeons could run the same brief programs over and over continuously, from late morning to midnight. Many exhibitors made huge profits.

Nickelodeons had advantages over earlier forms of exhibition. Unlike amusement parks, they were not seasonal. They were cheaper than vaudeville houses and more regularly available than traveling exhibitors. Expenses were low. Spectators typically sat on benches or in simple wooden seats. There were seldom newspaper advertisements to alert patrons in advance concerning programs. Patrons usually either attended on a regular basis or simply dropped in. The front of the theater displayed hand-painted signs with the names of the films, and there might be a phonograph or barker attracting the attention of passersby.

There was almost always some sound accompaniment. The exhibitor might lecture along with the film, but piano or phonograph accompaniment was probably more common. In some cases, actors stood behind the screen and spoke dialogue in synchronization with the action on the screen. More frequently, people used noisemakers to create sound effects appropriate to the action (Fig. 2.10).

In the days before 1905, when films had mainly been shown in vaudeville theaters or by touring lecturer-exhibitors, admission prices were often twenty-five cents or more—too much for most blue-collar workers. Nickel theaters, however, opened films to a mass audience, many of them immigrants. Nickelodeons clustered in business districts and working-class neighborhoods in cities. Blue-collar workers could attend theaters near their homes, while secretaries and office boys caught a show during the lunch hour or before taking public transport home after work. Women and children made up a significant proportion of city audiences, stopping in for a break during shopping. In small towns, a nickelodeon might be the only place showing films, and people from all strata of society would watch movies together.

Although films continued to be shown in vaudeville houses and by a few touring exhibitors, by 1908, nickelodeons had become the main form of exhibition. As a result, many more movies were needed by the new distributors, or "film exchanges," which bought prints from the producers. A single nickelodeon, using three films in a program that changed three times a week, would rent about 450 titles a year!

During the nickelodeon boom, most films came from abroad. Pathé, Gaumont, Hepworth, Cines, Nordisk, and other European firms flooded the weekly release schedules. Since there were far more theaters in the United States than in any other country, a huge number of copies of a film could be sold to exchanges there. Such sales helped keep the English industry healthy and allowed the Italian and Danish industries to expand quickly.

The nickelodeons also launched the careers of several important businessmen. The Warner brothers got their start as nickelodeon exhibitors (Fig. 2.11). Carl Laemmle, later the founder of Universal, opened his first nickelodeon in Chicago in 1906. Louis B. Mayer, who became the second "M" of MGM (Metro-Goldwyn-Mayer), ran a small theater in Haverhill, Massachusetts. Other studio executives who started out running nickelodeons included Adolph Zukor (later head of Paramount), William Fox (who formed the company that became 20th Century-Fox), and Marcus Loew (whose Loew's was the parent company of MGM). These men would help create the basic structure of the Hollywood studio system during the 1910s.

Fig. 2.11 The Cascade Theater in Newcastle, Pennsylvania: the first nickelodeon acquired by Jack, Albert, Sam, and Harry Warner. A sign promises "Refined Entertainment for Ladies, Gentlemen, and Children." The Warners went on to careers in exhibition and production, eventually establishing Warner Bros.

THE MOTION PICTURE PATENTS COMPANY VS. THE INDEPENDENTS

In the meantime, hostilities broke out. The more established leaders of the industry consolidated power among themselves and tried to exclude newcomers. The nickelodeon boom spurred this struggle, since control of the burgeoning film industry would be highly profitable.

Since 1897, the Edison company had tried to force its competitors out of business by suing them for patent infringement. Edison claimed to own the basic patents on motion-picture cameras, projectors, and film stock. Some companies, like Vitagraph, paid Edison a license fee in order to be able to go on producing. After a court decision went in Edison's favor in 1904, other companies joined in paying such fees. American Mutoscope & Biograph (AM&B), however, refused to cooperate with Edison, since its Biograph camera had a different mechanism and separate patents.

In early 1907, an appeals court handed down an important decision. Edison had again sued AM&B for infringement of its camera patent. The decision reaffirmed that AM&B's camera was sufficiently different and did not infringe Edison's patent. The decision also stated, however, that other camera designs currently in use *did* infringe that patent. As a result, all production companies and importers assumed they had to pay either AM&B or Edison in order to stay in business.

The rivalry between Edison and AM&B became more intense in 1908. Edison decided to sue AM&B yet again, this time claiming that the latter company had infringed its patents on film stock. AM&B countered by buying the patent for the Latham loop and suing Edison for using this device in its cameras and projectors. The two firms set up rival licensing arrangements in early 1908: members of the Association of Edison Licensees paid Edison in order to be able to go on making films, and the Biograph Association of Licensees collected money mostly from foreign companies and importers who wanted to bring films into the American market.

The film market approached chaos. Exhibitors needed a great many films, but producers were so busy fighting each other that they could not release enough titles. During this same period, however, Edison and AM&B negotiated to create a separate company that would control all competitors by owning and charging licensing fees on all the existing patents. In December 1908, the Motion Picture Patents Company (MPPC), headed by Edison and AM&B, was created. Several other production companies belonged to the MPPC: Vitagraph, Selig, Essanay, Lubin, and Kalem. To keep operating, each had to pay fees to the two main companies (though Vitagraph, which had contributed a patent to the arrangement, got back a portion of the license fees).

In an attempt to gain a larger share of the U.S. market, the American members of the MPPC strictly limited the number of foreign firms which could join and import films. Pathé, the largest importer, and Méliès were allowed into the MPPC, as was George Kleine, a major Chicago firm that imported European films by Gaumont and Urban-Eclipse (an English-French company). Several European companies, such as Great Northern (Nordisk) and all Italian firms, were shut out of this arrangement. Although foreign companies continued to operate in the United States, both in the MPPC and as independents, they never regained the large share of the market that they had enjoyed before 1908. France and Italy continued to be the leaders in markets outside the United States until World War I.

The MPPC hoped to control all three phases of the industry: production, distribution, and exhibition. Only licensed companies could make films, only licensed distribution firms could release them, and all theaters that wanted to rent films made by members of the MPPC had to pay a weekly fee for the privilege. Eastman Kodak agreed to sell film stock only to members of the MPPC, and in return they would buy no stock except from Kodak.

This arrangement set the stage for control over the entire U.S. film market by an *oligopoly*. When one company dominates its market, that firm has a monopoly. In an oligopoly, a small number of firms cooperate to control the market and block the entry of new companies. Members of the MPPC's oligopoly tried to eliminate all other firms by threatening to sue for patent infringement. A producer who used a film camera without paying the MPPC risked being taken to court. The same was true for exhibitors, since the MPPC claimed to control the patents covering their projectors.

During 1909, the American film industry stabilized somewhat. MPPC members set up a regular schedule of weekly releases. Newer films cost more and declined in value after they had been shown for a while (a situation which has survived to the present in a system of "first runs," "second runs," and so on). One reel became the standard film length. Each reel rented for the same price, whatever the film was, since producers viewed films as standard products, like sausages.

Still, the MPPC encountered challenges. Not all producers, distributors, and exhibitors were willing to pay fees to Edison and AM&B. Exhibitors who had purchased their projectors outright were particularly annoyed. It is estimated that about 6000 theaters agreed to pay the weekly fee, but another 2000 refused. The unlicensed theaters provided a market that unlicensed producers and distributors could serve. This portion of the industry was soon identified as "the independents."

In April 1909, the first effective blow against the MPPC was dealt when Carl Laemmle, who ran the largest American distribution firm, turned in his license. He started the Independent Motion Picture (IMP) Corporation, a small firm that would later form the basis for the Universal studio. Within the next few years, more than a dozen other independent companies started up across the country, including Thanhouser, Solax (headed by Alice Guy Blaché, formerly of Gaumont in France), and the New York Motion Picture Company, headed by Thomas H. Ince, who would become one of the most important producers of the 1910s. Independent theaters could rent films from the European companies shut out of the MPPC arrangement. Trying to avoid patent-infringement suits by the MPPC, independent companies claimed to be using cameras that employed a different mechanism.

The MPPC responded to the independent movement. In 1910 the MPPC created the General Film Company as an attempt to monopolize distribution. The General Film Company was to release all the films made by MPPC producers. The MPPC also hired detectives to gain evidence that producers were using cameras with the Latham loop and other devices patented by the MPPC. Between 1909 and 1911, the MPPC brought lawsuits against nearly all the independent producers for using patent-infringing cameras. One such suit, against Laemmle's IMP, was based on the Latham-loop patent. In 1912, the courts ruled against the MPPC, on the grounds that the technique of the Latham loop had been anticipated in earlier patents. This meant that independent companies could use any camera without fearing litigation. This court decision was a severe blow to the MPPC.

Also in 1912, the American government began proceedings against the MPPC as a trust (a group of companies acting in unfair constraint of trade). The case was decided against the MPPC in 1915. By that point, however, a number of the independent firms had wisely allied themselves with national distributors and opted for the new feature-film format. In contrast, some former members of the MPPC had become victims of mismanagement. As a result, several members of the independent sector of the industry began to create the new, more stable oligopoly that formed the Hollywood film industry.

SOCIAL PRESSURES AND SELF-CENSORSHIP

The quick spread of nickelodeons led to social pressures aimed at reforming the cinema. Many religious groups and social workers considered the nickel theaters sinister places where young people cold be led astray. The movies were seen as a training ground for prostitution and robbery. French films were criticized for treating adultery in a comic fashion. Violent subject matter such as reenacted executions and murders were common fare early in the nickelodeon boom.

In late 1908, the mayor of New York briefly succeeded in closing down all the city's nickelodeons, and local censorship boards were formed in several towns. A concerned group of New York citizens formed the Board of Censorship in March 1909. This was a private body, aimed at improving the movies and thus forestalling the federal government from passing a national censorship law. Producers were to submit films voluntarily, and films that passed could include a notice of approval. As a way of gaining respectability, MPPC members allowed their films to be examined, and they even supported the board financially. This cooperation led the group to change its name to the National Board of Censorship (and, in 1915, to the National Board of Review). Although censorship boards continued to be formed on the municipal and state levels, no national censorship law was ever passed. Variants of this policy of voluntary self-censorship have existed in the American film industry ever since.

Both the MPPC and the independents also tried to improve the public image of the movies by releasing more prestigious films that would appeal to middle- and upper-class spectators. Films became longer and more complex in their narratives. Stories derived from celebrated literature or portraying important historical events counterbalanced the popular slapstick chases and crime films. Some of these prestigious films, such as *The Assassination of the Duc de Guise* and *The Fall of Troy,* came from abroad. American producers increasingly turned to similar source material. In 1909, D. W. Griffith filmed Robert Browning's verse play, *Pippa Passes,* quoting lines from the original as intertitles. Adaptations of Shakespeare's plays condensed to one or two reels became common.

Along with this move to appeal to refined audiences came a change in the theaters where films were shown. Some nickelodeons were still functioning after 1915, but from 1908 on, exhibitors also began to build or convert larger theaters for showing films. These establishments might charge ten or twenty-five cents, or even more, for longer programs. Some theaters combined films and live vaudeville acts. Popular song slides, which were perceived as lower class, gradually disappeared as the better-class theaters began to use two projectors—and hence had no need for a song to cover the change of reels. Musical accompaniment by orchestras or pipe organs, ornate decorations, and occasional educational lectures accompanying the films were all designed to create an atmosphere very different from that of the nickel movie houses.

THE RISE OF THE FEATURE FILM

Part of the move toward longer programs and more prestigious films involved increasing the length of the films. In the early years of the century, "feature" simply meant an unusual film that could be featured in the advertising. During the nickelodeon boom, when the one-reel length became standard, "feature" still had the same meaning. But the term also came to be associated with longer films. Before 1909, these were typically prize-fight films or religious epics and were often shown in legitimate theaters rather than nickelodeons.

By 1909, some American producers started making multireel films. Because the MPPC's rigid release system allowed only for single reels, such films had to be released in one part per week. In late 1909 and early 1910, for example, Vitagraph sold *The Life of Moses* as five separate reels. Once all five were out, however, some exhibitors chose to show them together. Longer films continued to be shown in weekly portions.

In Europe, the exhibition system was more flexible, and multireel films were common there. When these were imported into the United States, they were typically shown in their entirety in legitimate theaters, at higher admission prices. As we have seen, Itala's three-reel *The Fall of Troy* (Fig. 2.5) had a great success in 1911. In 1912, Adolph Zukor triumphantly imported *Queen Elizabeth* and *Camille*, French productions starring the famous stage actress Sarah Bernhardt. Such pressure from imports led American firms to release longer films as a unit. In 1911, Vitagraph brought out its three-reel *Vanity Fair* as one film. By the mid-1910s, the feature film would become the standard basis for programming in more prestigious theaters, and the mixture of short films preferred by nickelodeon managers was declining.

THE STAR SYSTEM

In the earliest years of the cinema, films were advertised as novelties. Once the nickelodeon boom and the formation of the MPPC had regularized the American industry, companies sold films by brand name. Spectators knew that they were seeing an Edison or a Vitagraph or a Pathé picture, but filmmakers and actors received no screen credit. In vaudeville, the legitimate theater, and the opera, the star system was well established. Film actors' names, however, were not publicized—in part because fame would allow them to demand higher wages.

Indeed, before 1908–1909, few actors worked regularly enough in films to be recognized. At about that point, however, producers started signing actors to longer contracts, and audiences began to see the same faces in film after film. By 1909, viewers were spontaneously demonstrating interest in their favorites, asking theater managers the actors' names or writing to the studios for photographs. Fans made up names for the most popular stars: Florence Lawrence, who regularly appeared in Griffith's films, became "the Biograph Girl"; Florence Turner was "the Vitagraph Girl"; and Vitagraph's

Fig. 2.12 An advertisement from October 1911 names Owen Moore and Mary Pickford as the stars of an upcoming release by an independent producer, Majestic.

heartthrob, Maurice Costello, was dubbed "Dimples." Reviewers recognized that certain actors were now anonymous stars. Of Griffith's 1909 film *Lady Helen's Escapade*, a commentator remarked: "Of course, the chief honors of the picture are borne by the now famous Biograph girl, who must be gratified by the silent celebrity she has achieved. This lady combines with very great personal attractions very fine dramatic abilities indeed."[2]

By 1910, some companies responded to audience demand and began exploiting their popular actors for publicity purposes. Kalem supplied theaters with photographs to display in their lobbies. Personal appearances by stars in theaters became an institution. In 1911, the first fan magazine, *The Motion Picture Story Magazine*, appeared. That same year, an enterprising firm began selling photo postcards of popular players. Stars were named in advertisements aimed at exhibitors (Fig. 2.12). Still, until 1914, films seldom included credits.

THE MOVE TO HOLLYWOOD

The first American film companies were located in New Jersey and New York. Other producers emerged in Chicago (Selig, Essanay), Philadelphia (Lubin), and elsewhere in the East and the Midwest. Because filmmakers filmed outdoors or in sunlit glass studios, poor weather could hamper production. After the formation of the MPPC in 1908, some film companies sent production units to sunnier climes for the winter: New York–based firms might head to Florida, while Chicago companies tended to go west.

As early as 1908, a producing unit from the Selig company filmed on location in the Los Angeles area. It returned there to set up a makeshift studio in 1909 and a more substantial one in 1910. In 1909, Ince's New York Motion Picture Co. also established operations there. Several other firms began working around Los Angeles in 1910. American Biograph began sending Griffith there during the winter season.

During the early 1910s, the Los Angeles area emerged as the major production center for the United States. It had several advantages. Its clear, dry weather permitted filming outdoors most days of the year. Southern California offered a variety of landscapes, including ocean, desert, mountain, forest, and hillside. The Western had emerged as one of the most popular American genres. Such films looked more authentic when filmed in the real West rather than in New Jersey.

The small suburb of Hollywood was one of several where studios were established, and its name eventually came to stand for the entire American filmmaking industry—despite the fact that many decisions were still made in New York, in the head offices of the companies. Studios in the Hollywood area soon grew from small open-air stages to sizable complexes with large enclosed studios and numerous departments.

In 1904, the American film industry had consisted of several small companies trying to put each other out of business. By 1912, it had gone through an unsuccessful attempt by one group, the MPPC, to monopolize the market. Now more film firms were in existence, and they were on the brink of building the business into something much larger and more stable.

FURTHER EXPLORATIONS OF FILM STYLE

Beginning in 1904, American commercial filmmaking became increasingly oriented toward narrative. Moreover, with the new emphasis on one-reel films, narratives became longer and necessitated a series of shots. Filmmakers sought ways of making narrative films that would be comprehensible to audiences. How could techniques of editing, camerawork, acting, and lighting be combined so as to clarify what was happening in a film? How could the spectator grasp where and when the action was occurring?

Filmmakers solved such problems over the span of several years. Sometimes they influenced each other, while at other times two filmmakers might happen upon the same technique. Some devices were tried and abandoned. By 1917, filmmakers had worked out a system of formal principles that were standard in American filmmaking. That system has come to be called the *classical Hollywood cinema.* Despite this name, many of the basic principles of the system were being worked out before filmmaking was centered in Hollywood, and indeed, many of those principles were first applied in other countries. In this period before World War I, film style was still largely international, since films circulated widely outside their countries of origin.

The basic problem that confronted filmmakers early in the nickelodeon era was that audiences could not understand the causal, spatial, and temporal relations in many films. If the editing repeated actions, the spectator might not grasp that the same event was being shown twice. An actor's elaborate pantomime might fail to convey the meaning of a crucial action. A review of a 1906 Edison film lays out the problem:

> Regardless of the fact that there are a number of good motion pictures brought out, it is true that there are some which, although photographically good, are poor because the manufacturer, being familiar with the picture and the plot, does not take into consideration that the film was not made for him but for the audience. A subject recently seen was very good photographically, and the plot also seemed to be good, but could not be understood by the audience.[3]

In some theaters, a lecturer might explain the plot as the film unrolled, but producers could not rely on such aids.

Filmmakers came to assume that a film should guide the spectator's attention, making every aspect of the story on the screen as clear as possible. In particular, films increasingly set up a chain of narrative causes and effects. One event would plainly lead to an effect, which would in turn cause another effect, and so on. Moreover, an event was typically caused by a character's beliefs or desires. Character psychology had not been particularly important in early films. Slapstick chases or melodramas depended more on physical action or familiar situations than on character traits. Increasingly after 1907, however, character psychology motivated actions. By following a series of characters' goals and resulting conflicts, the spectator could comprehend the action.

Some of the most important innovations of this period came in the use of many shots within the film. In one sense, editing was a boon to the filmmaker, permitting instant movement from one space to another or cuts to closer views to reveal details. But if the spectator could not keep track of the temporal and spatial relations between one shot and the next, editing might only increase confusion. In some cases, intertitles could help. Editing also came to emphasize *continuity* among shots. Certain cues indicated that time was flowing uninterruptedly across cuts. Between scenes, other cues might suggest how much time had been skipped over. When a cut moved from one space to another, the director needed to orient the viewer.

Clarity also demanded that the camera frame the action in such a way as to guide the viewer's eye to the most salient actions. Every aspect of silent filmmaking—intertitles, editing, camera framing, acting, and set and costume design—came to be used for narrative clarity.

INTERTITLES

Before 1905, most films had no intertitles. Their main titles often gave information concerning the basic situations in the simple narratives to come. In 1904, for example, the Lubin company released *A Policeman's Love Affair,* a six-shot comedy about a rich woman who catches a policeman wooing her maid and throws a bucket of water on him. In Chapter 1, we saw that Edwin S. Porter's 1903 *Uncle Tom's Cabin* used a separate intertitle to introduce the situation of each shot (see Figs. 1.31, 1.32). The longer film length standardized during the nickelodeon era led to an increasing number of intertitles.

There were two types of intertitles. *Expository* titles were initially more common. Their texts were in the third person, summarizing the upcoming action or simply setting up the situation. A typical one-reeler of 1911, *Her Mother's Fiancé* (made by Yankee, a small independent), introduced one scene with this title: "Home from School. The Widow's daughter comes home unexpectedly and surprises her mother." Other expository intertitles were more laconic, like the chapter titles in a book. In a 1911 Vitagraph film, *The Inherited Taint,* a scene begins with the title "An engagement broken." Intertitles could also signal time gaps between scenes; titles such as "The following day" and "One month later" became common.

Filmmakers also sought a type of intertitle that could convey narrative information less baldly. Information presented in *dialogue* titles seemed to come from within the story action. Moreover, because films increasingly focused on character psychology, dialogue titles could suggest characters' thoughts in a more precise way than gestures could. At first filmmakers were not quite sure where to insert dialogue titles. Some put the title before the shot in which the character delivered the line. Other filmmakers placed the dialogue title in the middle of the shot, just after the character had begun to speak. The latter placement became the norm by 1914, as filmmakers realized that the spectator could better understand the scene if the title closely coincided with the speech in the image.

THE BEGINNINGS
OF THE CONTINUITY SYSTEM

When editing links a series of shots, narrative clarity will be enhanced if the spectator understands how the shots relate to each other spatially and temporally. Is time continuing uninterruptedly, or has some time been skipped (creating an ellipsis)? Are we still seeing the same space, or has the scene shifted to a new locale? As Alfred Capus, a scriptwriter for the French firm Film d'Art, put it in 1908, "If we wish to retain the attention of the public, we have to maintain unbroken connection with each preceding [shot]."[4] During this period, filmmakers developed techniques for maintaining this "unbroken connection." By 1917, these techniques would come together into the continuity system of editing. This system involved three basic ways of joining shots: intercutting, analytical editing, and contiguity editing.

Intercutting. Before 1906, narrative films did not move back and forth between actions in separate spaces. In most cases, one continuous action formed the whole story. The popular chase genre provides the best example. Here an event triggers the chase, and the characters keep running through one shot after another until the culprit is caught. If several actions were involved, the film would concentrate on one in its entirety and then move on to the next.

One of the earliest known cases where the action moves back and forth between locales, with at least two shots in each place, occurs in *The 100-to-One Shot* (1906, Vitagraph). The situation is a last-minute race to pay the mortgage before the landlord evicts a family. The last four shots show the hero speeding toward and arriving at the house:

Shot 29. A street, with a car driving forward.
Shot 30. Inside the house, the landlord starts to force the old father to leave.
Shot 31. The street in front of the house, with the hero pulling up in the car.
Shot 32. Inside the house, the hero pays the landlord and tears up the eviction notice. General rejoicing.

Presumably the filmmakers realized that when cutting moved back and forth between two different spaces, the spectator would understand that the actions were taking place simultaneously.

Early intercutting could be used for actions other than rescues. French films, especially Pathé's, were influential in developing this technique. A clever chase film of 1907, *The Runaway Horse*, for example, shows a cart horse eating a bag of oats outside a shop while his driver delivers laundry inside an apartment building. In the first shot, the horse is scrawny and the bag full (Fig. 2.13). In the next shot, we see the driver inside the building

Fig. 2.13

Fig. 2.14

Fig. 2.15

Figs. 2.13–2.15 Intercutting in *The Runaway Horse* allowed the filmmakers to give the impression that the horse grows healthy and fat by eating a whole bag of oats.

(Fig. 2.14). Four more shots of the horse are interspersed with six of the driver inside. The filmmakers substituted successively more robust animals, so the cart horse seems to get fatter as the sack empties (Fig. 2.15). By the end of the scene, the horse is very lively, and a chase ensues.

D. W. Griffith is the early director most often associated with the development of intercutting (see Notes and Queries). After working as a minor stage and film actor, Griffith started making films at AM&B in 1908. He soon began creating films that used various techniques in extraordinarily original ways. Despite the fact that filmmakers were not credited, viewers soon recognized that films from American Biograph (the name which the company assumed in 1909) were consistently among the best made by American studios.

Griffith was undoubtedly influenced by earlier films, including *The Runaway Horse*, but of all directors of the period, he explored the possibilities of intercutting most daringly. One of his most extended and suspenseful early uses of the technique came in *The Lonely Villa* (1909). The plot involves thieves who lure a man away from his isolated country home by sending a false message. Griffith cuts among the man, the thieves, and the family inside the house. Having car trouble, the man stops, calls home, and learns that the thieves are breaking into a room where his wife and daughters are barricaded. He hires a gypsy wagon, and a series of shots continues to connect the husband's rescue group, the thieves, and the terrified family (Figs. 2.16–2.18). *The Lonely Villa* contains over fifty shots, most of which involve intercutting. A contemporary reviewer described the electrifying effect of the film's suspense sequence:

> "Thank God, they're saved!" said a woman behind us at the conclusion of the Biograph film bearing the above name. Just like this woman, the entire audience were in a state of intense excitement as this picture was being shown. And no wonder, for it is one of the most adroitly managed bits of bloodless film drama that we have seen.[5]

Griffith experimented with intercutting, especially in rescue scenes, for several years. By 1912, intercutting was a common technique in American films.

Analytical Editing.　This term refers to editing that breaks a single space down into separate framings. One simple way of doing this was to cut in

Fig. 2.16

Fig. 2.17

Fig. 2.18

closer to the action. Thus a long shot would show the entire space, and a closer one would enlarge small objects or facial expressions. Cut-ins in the period before 1905 were rare (see Figs. 1.25, 1.26).

During the nickelodeon era, filmmakers began inserting closer views into the middles of scenes. Often these were notes or photographs that the characters examine. These were called "inserts" and were usually seen from the character's point of view in order to make the action comprehensible to the viewer.

Between 1907 and 1911, simple cut-ins to small gestures or objects were occasionally used (Figs. 2.19, 2.20). Cut-ins did not become common until the mid-1910s, however. As we shall see in Chapter 3, longer features led to longer individual scenes, with filmmakers cutting more freely within a single space.

Contiguity Editing. In some scenes, characters move out of the space of one shot and reappear in a nearby locale. Such movements were crucial to the chase genre. Typically, a group of characters would run through the shot and then out of sight; we then cut to an adjacent locale, where the process is repeated as they run through again. A series of such shots made up most of the film. A similar pattern occurs in an early model of clear storytelling, *Rescued by Rover* (produced in 1905 by Cecil Hepworth in England, and probably directed by Lewin Fitzhamon). After a baby is kidnapped, the family dog races from the house and through the town, finds the baby, runs back to fetch the father, and leads him to the kidnapper's lair. In all the shots of

Figs. 2.16–2.18 Successive shots from near the end of the intercut rescue scene in *The Lonely Villa* show simultaneous action in three locales.

Fig. 2.19

Fig. 2.20

Figs. 2.19 and 2.20 In *After One Hundred Years* (1911, Selig), a cut-in to a closer view shows a man discovering a bullet hole in a mantelpiece, a detail that would not be visible in the initial distant framing.

Fig. 2.21

Fig. 2.22

Figs. 2.21 and 2.22 *Rescued by Rover:* Running consistently toward the left foreground, Rover leads its master through a clearly defined series of contiguous spaces to reach the kidnapper's hideout.

Rover running toward the lair, the dog moves forward through the space of one shot, exits to the left of the camera, and comes into the space of the next shot, still running forward and exiting left (Figs. 2.21, 2.22).

Not all films of this early period show the characters moving in consistent directions in the contiguous spaces. By the teens, however, many filmmakers seem to have realized that keeping the direction of movement constant helped the audience keep track of spatial relations. In 1911, a reviewer complained about inconsistencies:

> Attention has been called frequently in *Mirror* film reviews to apparent errors of direction or management as to exits and entrances in motion picture production. . . . A player will be seen leaving a room or locality in a certain direction, and in the very next connecting [shot], a sixteenth of a second later, he will enter in exactly the opposite direction. . . . Any one who has watched pictures knows how often his sense of reality has been shocked by this very thing. To him it is as if the player had turned abruptly around in a fraction of a second and was moving the other way.[6]

Within the next few years, filmmakers frequently kept characters moving in the same direction (Figs. 2.23, 2.24). As we shall see, during the mid-1910s the idea of keeping screen direction consistent became an implicit rule in Hollywood-style editing.

Another way of indicating that two contiguous spaces are near each other is to show a character looking offscreen in one direction and then cut to what that character sees. In the earliest cases where characters' viewpoints were used to motivate a cut, we would see exactly what the character saw, from his or her optical *point of view*. The earliest point-of-view shots simulated views through microscopes, telescopes, and binoculars to show that we are seeing what characters see (Figs. 2.25, 2.26). By the early teens, a new type of point-of-view shot was becoming common. A character simply looks offscreen, and we know from the camera's position in the second shot that we are seeing what the character sees (Figs. 2.27, 2.28).

The second shot might, however, reveal what the character is looking at but not show it from his or her exact point of view. Such a cut is called an *eyeline match* (Figs. 2.29, 2.30). Such editing was an excellent way of showing that one space was near another, thus clarifying the dramatic action (Figs. 2.31, 2.32). During the early 1910s, the eyeline match became a standard way of showing the relationship between successive shots. The eyeline match

Figs. 2.23 and 2.24 In *Alma's Champion* (1912, Vitagraph), the first shot shows the hero exiting leftward. In the next shot, he moves into a nearby space along the tracks. His continued leftward movement, plus the presence of the train in the background, help the spectator understand where the actions are taking place.

Fig. 2.23

Fig. 2.24

Fig. 2.25

Fig. 2.26

Figs. 2.25 and 2.26 In the 1905 Pathé comedy *The Scholar's Breakfast,* a shot of the scientist looking through his microscope leads to a point-of-view shot.

Fig. 2.27

Fig. 2.28

Figs. 2.27 and 2.28 Two shots from *A Friendly Marriage* (1911, Vitagraph). When the wife looks offscreen in the first shot, we understand that the framing through the window in the second represents her point of view.

Fig. 2.29

Fig. 2.30

Figs. 2.29 and 2.30 In Griffith's *A Corner in Wheat* (1909, American Biograph), visitors touring the wheat warehouse glance down into a bin. The next shot shows what they see—the bin—but not from their point of view.

Fig. 2.31

Fig. 2.32

Figs. 2.31 and 2.32 In *The Gambler's Charm* (1910, Lubin), the gambler shoots through the door of a bar. He and the other characters look off toward the right, and it is clear that they are looking at the wounded man in the second shot.

also depended upon the 180-degree rule. For example, if a character glances off to the right, he or she is assumed to be offscreen left in the next shot.

At about the same time that the eyeline match came into occasional use, filmmakers also used a double eyeline match: one character looking offscreen and then a cut to another character looking in the opposite direction

Figs. 2.33 and 2.34 In *The Loafer* (1911, Essanay), two characters argue in a field. The cutting employs a shot/reverse-shot technique: one character looks off left, shouting at the other, and then we see his opponent reacting, looking off right.

Fig. 2.33

Fig. 2.34

at the first. This type of cutting, with some further elaboration, has come to be known as the *shot/reverse shot*. It is used in conversations, fights, and other situations in which characters interact with each other. One of the earliest known shot/reverse shots occurs in an Essanay Western (Figs. 2.33, 2.34). The shot/reverse-shot technique became more common over the next decade. Today it remains the principal way of constructing conversation scenes in narrative films.

CAMERA POSITION AND ACTING

Decisions about where to place the camera were important for ensuring that the action would be comprehensible to the viewer. The edges of the image created a "frame" for the events depicted. Objects or figures at the center tended to be more noticeable. Methods of framing the action changed after 1908.

In order to convey the psychology of the characters, for example, filmmakers began to put the camera slightly closer to the actors so that their facial expressions would be more visible. This trend seems to have started about 1909, when the "9-foot" line was introduced. This meant that the camera, instead of being 12 or 16 feet back and showing the actors from head to toe, was placed only 9 feet away, cutting off the actors just below the knee. Some reviewers complained that this looked unnatural and inartistic, but others praised the acting in films by Vitagraph, which pioneered this technique.

Griffith, in particular, explored the possibilities of enlarging facial expressions. In early 1912, he began training his talented group of young actresses, including Lillian Gish, Blanche Sweet, Mae Marsh, and Mary Pickford, to register a lengthy series of emotions using only slight gestures and facial changes. An early result of these experiments was *The Painted Lady*, in 1912, a tragic story of a demure young woman who is courted by a man who turns out to be a thief. After she shoots him during a robbery attempt, she goes mad and relives their romance in fantasy. Throughout much of *The Painted Lady*, Griffith places the camera relatively close to the heroine, framing her from the waist up, so that her slightest expressions and movements are visible (Fig. 2.35). During the early teens, conventional pantomime gestures continued to be used, but they were more restrained and were increasingly used in combination with facial expressions.

Fig. 2.35 Griffith's *The Painted Lady* was an early instance of a film that concentrated on the virtuosic acting of its star, Blanche Sweet. Here she portrays the heroine's madness.

Another technique of framing that changed during this period was the use of high and low camera angles. In early fiction films, the camera usually viewed the action at a level angle, about chest- or waist-high. By about 1911, however, filmmakers began occasionally to frame the action from above or below when doing so provided a more effective vantage point on the scene (Fig. 2.36). Danish films, in particular, used dramatic high and low angles and were influential in fostering this technique.

During these same years, camera tripods were equipped with heads that swiveled. With such tripods, the camera could be turned from side to side to make *pan* shots or swiveled up and down to create *tilts*. Tilts and pans were often used to make slight adjustments, or *reframings,* when the figures moved about. This ability to keep the action centered also enhanced the comprehensibility of scenes.

Fig. 2.36 A camera framing from a slightly high angle enhances the drama of the final guillotine scene in Vitagraph's 1911 three-reel feature, *A Tale of Two Cities.*

COLOR

Although most of the prints of silent films that we see today are black and white, many were colored in some fashion when they first appeared.

Color might enhance realism. After Pathé introduced its stencil system, other companies used similar techniques (Color Plate 2.3). Color could also provide information about the narrative situation and hence make the story clearer to the spectator. Two techniques for coloring release prints became common during this period. *Tinting* involved dipping an already-developed positive print into a dye bath that colored the lighter portions of the images, while the dark ones remained black. In *toning,* the already-developed positive print was placed in a different chemical solution which saturated the dark areas of the frame, while the lighter areas remained nearly white. Vitagraph's *Jephtah's Daughter* uses tinting for a miracle scene by firelight. The pink color suggests the light of the flames (Color Plate 2.4). Blue tinting was frequently used to indicate scenes taking place at night (Color Plate 2.2). Amber tints were common for night interiors, green for scenes in nature, and so on. Similar color codes held for toning. For ordinary daylight scenes, toning in sepia or purple was common (Color Plate 2.5).

SET DESIGN AND LIGHTING

During the period 1905–1912, as production companies were making more money from their films, some built larger studio buildings to replace the earlier open-air stages and cramped interior studios. Most of these had glass walls to admit sunlight but also included some type of electric lighting. As a result, many films used deeper, more three-dimensional settings, and some used artificial light.

At the beginning of the nickelodeon era, many fiction films were still using painted theatrical-style backdrops or flats, with some real furniture or props mixed in (Fig. 2.37; see also Figs. 1.15, 1.25, 1.32, and 2.14). Over the next several years, however, more three-dimensional sets, without painted furniture, windows, and so on, came into use. (See Figs. 2.5, 2.18, and 2.31.)

Fig. 2.37 In this scene from *The 100-to-One Shot* (1906, Vitagraph), the table and chairs are real, but the fireplace, wall, door frame, window, flowerpots— even the sunlight coming in through the window—are painted on a backdrop. Note also the stark shadows cast on the floor by the sunlight used to illuminate the scene.

Fig. 2.38 In *Shamus O'Brien* (1912, IMP), much of the scene is dark, while an arc lamp low and offscreen right simulates the light from a fire. (Contrast the set design and lighting of this scene with those of Fig. 2.37.)

The set in *The Lonely Villa* (Fig. 2.18), with its two sidewalls, gives a greater sense of depth than does the one in Figure 2.37.

Most lighting in early films was even and flat, provided by sunshine or banks of electric lights (Figs. 2.14, 2.17, and 2.31). During this era, however, filmmakers sometimes used a single arc lamp to cast a strong light from one direction. Such lamps could be placed in a fireplace to suggest a fire (Fig. 2.38). The control of artificial studio lighting would be an important development in American film style of the late 1910s.

By 1912, American filmmakers had established many basic techniques for telling a clear story. Spectators could usually see the characters clearly and understand where they were in relation to each other, what they could see, and what they were saying. These techniques would be elaborated and polished over the next decade, until the Hollywood narrative system was sophisticated indeed.

AN INTERNATIONAL STYLE

Many aspects of film style were used in similar ways internationally. French, Italian, Danish, English, and American films and, to a lesser extent, films of other countries circulated widely outside the countries in which they were made. Two examples from very different places should suffice to suggest how widely standard techniques were disseminated.

The chase film, so typical of the years 1904–1908, was an international genre. In the Netherlands, where production was miniscule, a chase film called *De Mesavonture van een fransch Heertje zonder Pantalon aan het Strand te Zandvoort* ("The Misadventures of a Frenchman without Pants on the Beach of Zandvoort," c. 1905, Alberts Frères) followed the standard pattern: a man falls asleep on the beach, the tide rises to wet his trousers, he removes them, and indignant bystanders and police chase him through a series of adjacent locales (Figs. 2.39, 2.40).

The classical continuity style developed later in this period also was widely influential. The earliest Indian fiction feature film, *Raja Harischandra*, was made in 1912 and released in 1913; its director was the first major Indian filmmaker, D. G. Phalke. Like many of Phalke's later films, its subject matter was derived from traditional Indian mythology. Only the first two of

Figs. 2.39 and 2.40 In *De Mesavonture van een fransch Heertje zonder Pantalon aan het Strand te Zandvoort*, a pair of shots show the unfortunate hero being chased along the beach.

Fig. 2.39

Fig. 2.40

Fig. 2.41

Fig. 2.42

Fig. 2.43

the film's four reels survives, but it indicates that Phalke had grasped the 9-foot line, contiguity cutting, and other current principles of western filmmaking (Figs. 2.41–2.43).

After 1912, filmmakers continued to explore techniques for telling stories clearly. As we shall see in the next chapter, however, World War I interrupted the circulation of films among countries, and some nations developed distinctive film styles.

Fig. 2.41 In the Indian fantasy film, *Raja Harischandra*, the King explains to his Queen that he has given his kingdom to an old sage whom he had offended. The framing uses the 9-foot line of western filmmaking. (Following Indian theatrical tradition, the Queen and her women are played by boys.)

Figs. 2.42 and 2.43 In *Raja Harischandra*, D. G. Phalke uses consistent screen direction as the King walks rightward through the forest and, in a cut to a contiguous space, arrives at the hut of the villainous sage.

THE BEGINNINGS OF FILM ANIMATION

ilms using some aspects of animation existed from the beginnings of the cinema. Emile Reynaud's drawn images for his projecting Praxinoscope formed an important forerunner for cinematic animation (pp. 6–7). Quick-draw artists from vaudeville—among them J. Stuart Blackton, one of the founders of Vitagraph—performed in several early films. There is some evidence that in 1890s' advertising films and films made for toy projectors, filmmakers created movement of objects or drawings by photographing them one frame at a time.

Animation within the film industry seems to have begun in 1906, when Blackton made *Humorous Phases of Funny Faces* for Vitagraph. It consisted mostly of drawings of faces that developed frame by frame, as Blackton added bits of lines. Thus the drawings gradually appeared but did not move—until the end, when the faces roll their eyes. That same year, Pathé produced *Le Théâtre de Petit Bob* (*Little Bob's Theater*), for which Spanish filmmaker Segundo de Chomón patiently moved objects between single-frame exposures to

make the contents of a boy's toybox appear to "come to life." Such animation of objects is called *pixillation*.

Creating animated films took a great deal of time and effort. In this early period, they usually were the painstaking creations of individual artists, working alone or with an assistant. Animation involved either making objects seem to move or bringing many separate drawings to life.

The earliest major film animating objects was Vitagraph's *The Haunted Hotel* (1907), directed by J. Stuart Blackton. Here the "magical" movement occurred within a live-action film. A hotel patron is plagued by supernatural forces, rendered onscreen through double exposures, wires, stop-motion, and other tricks. In one scene, we see a close view of objects on a table. A knife moves on its own to cut and butter bread (Fig. 2.44). *The Haunted Hotel* was one of the first releases by Vitagraph's new Paris office, and it was widely imitated abroad.

Emile Cohl, who worked primarily for Gaumont from 1908 to 1910, was the first person to devote his energies to

Fig. 2.44 In J. Stuart Blackton's *The Haunted Hotel* (1907), a meal prepares itself through frame-by-frame animation.

Fig. 2.46 In *Little Nemo*, the characters move about, but there is no story line. The lack of scenery saved McCay from having to fill up each sheet of paper.

Fig. 2.45 Emile Cohl's *Fantasmagorie* (1908) was drawn in black ink on white paper and then printed in negative to give the impression of moving chalk figures on a blackboard.

Fig. 2.47 The grasshopper hero of *The Revenge of a Kinematograph Camerman* films the adulterous activities of a beetle who has insulted him. Later the beetle and his wife see the film in a movie program, whereupon she thrashes him with her umbrella.

drawn animation. His first cartoon was *Fantasmagorie* (1908; Fig. 2.45). In order to create steady movement, Cohl placed each drawing on a plate of glass illuminated from beneath, and then he traced the image onto the next sheet of paper, making slight changes in the figures. His many films were often based on bizarre, stream-of-consciousness transformations of a series of shapes, one into another. Cohl also made live-action films, often incorporating some animated sequences. Like Méliès, Cohl retired from filmmaking in the teens and lived a life of poverty until his death in 1938.

In the United States, eminent comic-strip artist and vaudevillian, Windsor McCay also began making drawn animated films, initially to project in his stage act. His first film was *Little Nemo*, completed in 1911; it featured characters from his famous newspaper strip, "Little Nemo in Slumberland" (Fig. 2.46). The film contains a live-action prologue which shows how the enormous number of drawings necessary for the animation were made. McCay made a second cartoon, *The Story of a Mosquito*, in 1912, and a third, *Gertie*, in 1914. (Commonly seen prints of these films today contain live-action shots that were added after their use in McCay's stage act.) *Mosquito* and *Gertie* contain sketchy background settings, which an assistant traced on every page. McCay made a few more films, utilizing new labor-saving techniques created after 1912.

In 1910, perhaps the greatest puppet animator of all time began work. In Russia, Polish-born Ladislav Starevicz made some fiction shorts "acted" by insects. The realistic movements in these films baffled audiences and reviewers:

What is so amazing about this film is that the beetles portray the situation with such plausibility. When angry they shake their feelers and raise their horns, they march just like people. . . . How is it all done? Not one of the viewers could explain it. If the beetles were performing then their trainer must be a man of magical endurance and patience. That the actors were indeed beetles is clear from careful examination of their appearance.[7]

Like other animators, Starevicz was indeed a man of "magical patience," but he was manipulating plastic puppets with wire joints, changing their positions from frame to frame. His most famous early film is *The Revenge of a Kinematograph Cameraman* (1912; Fig. 2.47). Its witty story and detailed movements of the insect puppets remain engrossing today. Starevicz made many more animated and live-action films in Russia; then he fled to Paris in the wake of the 1917 Bolshevik Revolution. There he remained active for many decades.

After 1912, animation was to become a more regular part of filmmaking as labor-saving techniques were invented and patented. The early individual animators largely gave way to staffs of people who worked together to make cartoons. Even so, to this day there are still animators who work alone, following the tradition of Cohl, McCay, Starevicz, and others.

◆ NOTES AND QUERIES

GRIFFITH'S IMPORTANCE IN THE DEVELOPMENT OF FILM STYLE

If this book had been written several years earlier, this chapter's discussion of changing film style would probably have dealt primarily with D. W. Griffith. Griffith himself helped to create the myth that he had "invented" virtually every important technique for film storytelling. In late 1913, just after he had left American Biograph, he ran a newspaper advertisement claiming to have created the close-up, intercutting, fade-outs, and restrained acting. Early historians, unable to see many films from the pre-1913 period, took him at his word, and Griffith became the "father" of the cinema.

More recent research, especially since the 1978 Brighton Conference (see Notes and Queries, Chapter 1) has brought many other films to light, and historians have realized that numerous filmmakers were simultaneously exploring similar film techniques. Griffith's importance has come to be seen in terms of his ability to combine these techniques in daring ways (as when he extends the number of shots in the intercutting in *The Lonely Villa*). Most historians now agree that Griffith's imagination, ambition, and skill made him the foremost American filmmaker of this era.

Traditional accounts of Griffith as the inventor of the modern cinema appear in some of the earliest film histories, including Terry Ramsaye's *A Million and One Nights* (1926; rep., New York: Simon & Schuster, 1964), Chap. 50, "Griffith Evolves Screen Syntax," and Lewis Jacobs's *The Rise of the American Film* (1939; rep., New York: Teachers College Press, 1968), Chap. 7, "D. W. Griffith: New Discoveries."

Two more recent accounts of the early development of film style stress typical films rather than highlighting those by masters like Griffith: Barry Salt, *Film Style & Technology: History and Analysis* (London: Starword, 1983), Chaps. 7–8, and David Bordwell, Janet Staiger, and Kristin Thompson, *The Classical Hollywood Cinema: Film Style and Mode of Production to 1960*

(New York: Columbia University Press, 1985), Chaps. 14, 16–17. Salt's *"The Physician of the Castle," Sight & Sound* **54,** 4 (Autumn 1985): 284–285, revealed that the intercutting in this Pathé film probably influenced Griffith (the article also provides an interesting insight into how historians make such discoveries). Tom Gunning's *D. W. Griffith and the Origins of American Narrative Film* (Urbana: University of Illinois Press, 1991) balances a detailed examination of Griffith's first two years of filmmaking with a look at the larger context within which he worked. See also Joyce E. Jesionowski, *Thinking in Pictures: Dramatic Structure in D. W. Griffith's Biograph Films* (Berkeley: University of California Press, 1987), which suggests (especially in the Introduction) that the discovery of other filmmakers' contributions may have led historians to deemphasize Griffith too much.

◆ REFERENCES

1. Inscription on a photograph reproduced in Charles Ford, *Max Linder* (Paris: Éditions Seghers, 1966), opposite p. 65.
2. Quoted in Tom Gunning, *D. W. Griffith and the Origins of American Narrative Film: The Early Years at Biograph* (Urbana: University of Illinois Press, 1991), pp. 219–220.
3. Quoted in Charles Musser, *Before the Nickelodeon: Edwin S. Porter and the Edison Manufacturing Company* (Berkeley: University of California Press, 1991), p. 360.
4. Quoted in Eileen Bowser, *The Transformation of Cinema, 1907–1915* (New York: Scribners, 1990), p. 57. The original word used by Capus was "scene," which was the term used during that period to mean "shot."
5. Quoted in Gunning, *D. W. Griffith,* p. 204. The word "bloodless" refers to the fact that no actual violence is committed in the film.
6. "Spectator" [Frank Woods], "Spectator's Comments," *New York Dramatic Mirror* **65,** 1681 (8 Mar. 1911): 29.
7. Quoted in Yuri Tsivian et al., *Silent Witnesses: Russian Films 1908–1919* (London: British Film Institute, 1989), p. 586.

3

NATIONAL CINEMAS, HOLLYWOOD CLASSICISM, AND WORLD WAR I, 1913–1919

The period around the beginning of World War I marked a turning point in the history of the cinema. In 1913 alone, an extraordinary array of important feature films were made in Europe: in France, Léonce Perret's *L'Enfant de Paris;* in Germany, Paul von Woringen's *Die Landstrasse* and Stellan Rye's *The Student of Prague;* in Denmark, August Blom's *Atlantis* and Benjamin Christensen's *The Mysterious X;* in Sweden, Victor Sjöström's *Ingeborg Holm;* in Italy, Giovanni Pastrone's *Cabiria* (released in early 1914). Also in 1913, the serial emerged as a major film form, and labor-saving techniques were introduced into animation. During the mid-teens, the feature film was becoming standardized internationally. A few directors brought Swedish cinema into a "golden age" that would last into the 1920s. Some countries saw the creation and consolidation of major firms and studios that would dominate film history for decades. Most crucially, the Hollywood industry was taking shape. In some other countries, problems caused the decline of major industries: the war forced both France and Italy to reduce their high levels of production.

During this period, filmmakers around the world were exploring the *expressive* possibilities of film style. In its first decade or so, cinema relied upon the display of action for its novelty value. Then, during the nickelodeon era, filmmakers tested ways of telling stories clearly. From about 1912 on, some directors increasingly realized that distinctive lighting, editing, acting, set design, and other film techniques could not only clarify the unfolding of the action but also heighten the film's impact. Time and again in this chapter, we will see filmmakers creating striking compositions by shooting with the light behind the subjects, or using lengthy takes to create a realistic sense of ordinary time passing, or cutting among widely disparate elements to make a conceptual point. Such techniques could enhance the narrative by lending atmosphere, meaning, and suspense.

In the midst of these important changes, World War I began during August 1914. The war had profound effects on the international cinema, some of which are still being felt today. The war effort severely curtailed filmmaking in the two leading producing countries, France and Italy. American companies stepped in to fill the vacuum. As of 1916, the United States became the leading supplier of films to the world market, and it has held that position ever since. Much of the history of world cinema has been bound up with the struggles of various national industries to compete with Hollywood's domination. The war also isolated several producing countries. For the first time, distinctive national cinemas arose—as opposed to the open flow of films and influences that had previously been the rule.

THE AMERICAN TAKEOVER OF WORLD MARKETS

As we saw in the previous chapter, up to 1912, American film companies were largely taken up in the competition for their own domestic market. They were hard put to satisfy the huge demand for films created by the nickelodeon boom. Edison, American Biograph, and the other Patents Company members also hoped to limit competition from French, Italian, and other imported films.

Still, it was obvious that a great deal of money was to be made in exporting films. The first American company to open its own distribution offices in Europe was Vitagraph, which had a branch in London in 1906 and soon a second in Paris. By 1909, other American firms were moving into foreign markets as well. This expansion of American distribution abroad continued until the mid-1920s. Initially most companies except for Vitagraph sold their films indirectly. Inexperienced with overseas trading, they simply sold the foreign rights to their films to export agents or foreign distribution firms. London became a center for the international circulation of U.S. films. Many British firms profited by acting as the agents for this business—though in doing so they weakened British production by turning over a large share of the U.K. market to American films.

France, Italy, and other producing countries still provided stiff competition around the world. Nonetheless, even before the war began, U.S. films were becoming very popular in some countries. By 1911, for example, an estimated 60 to 70 percent of films imported into Great Britain were American. The United States was also doing well in Germany, Australia, and New Zealand. In most other markets, however, the American share was much smaller. Without the war, Hollywood might not have gained a preeminent global position.

The beginning of the war caused a near cessation of French filmmaking. Many industry personnel were immediately sent to the front. Pathé's raw-stock factory switched to manufacturing munitions, and studios were converted into barracks. Once it became apparent that the fighting would drag on for years, the French industry gradually resumed production but never on the scale of the prewar era. A less extreme cutback in production affected Italy once it entered the war in 1916.

Hollywood firms seized the opportunity to corner foreign markets. Cut off from European films, many countries found a new source in the United States. By 1916, American exports had risen dramatically. Over the next few years, American firms sold fewer films through London agents. They began to market their own products directly, opening distribution branches in South America, Australia, the Far East, and European countries not isolated by the hostilities. In this way, American companies collected all the profits themselves and were soon in a strong position in many countries. About 60 percent of Argentina's imports during 1916, for example, were American films, and in subsequent years South American nations bought more and more Hollywood films. The U.S. shares of even the French and Italian markets were rising. About 95 percent of screenings in Australia and New Zealand consisted of American films.

After the war, the U.S. industry maintained its lead abroad partly because of certain economic factors. A film's production budget was based on how much it could be expected to earn. Up to the mid-1910s, when most of

Fig. 3.1 The Elphinstone Picture Palace in Colombo, Ceylon, shows Paramount's big-budget adaptation of *Beau Geste* (1926), starring Ronald Colman. Native drivers wait for their colonialist employers, who are enjoying the film.

an American film's income came from the domestic market, budgets were modest. Once a film could predictably earn more money abroad, its budget could be higher. It could then recover its costs in the United States and be sold cheaply abroad, undercutting local national production. By 1917, Hollywood firms estimated costs based on both domestic and foreign sales. Accordingly, producers invested in big sets, lavish costumes, and more lighting equipment. Highly paid stars like Mary Pickford and William S. Hart were soon idolized around the world (Fig. 3.1).

Other countries found it hard to compete against such sumptuous production values. Low budgets led to low sales, which in turn perpetuated the low budgets. Moreover, it was usually cheaper to buy an American film than to finance a local production. Some countries have managed to counter these disadvantages, at least temporarily. Throughout this book, we shall see how a number of alternatives to Hollywood cinema have arisen. Basically, however, Hollywood has had two advantages since the mid-1910s: the average production budget has remained higher in Hollywood than anywhere else in the world, and importing an American film is still often cheaper than producing one locally.

THE RISE OF NATIONAL CINEMAS

Before World War I, the cinema was largely an international affair. Technical and stylistic discoveries made in one country were quickly seen and assimilated elsewhere. The war, however, disrupted the free flow of films across borders. Some national industries benefited from this disruption. A few countries were partially or wholly cut off from imports, yet the demand for films remained. Hence domestic production rose in such countries, especially Sweden, Russia, and Germany. Other countries, such as France, Denmark, and Italy, suffered a decline from prewar levels but managed to continue and develop on prewar traditions. In many cases, stylistic influences could not circulate so freely across borders. For example, the singular filmmaking practice that developed in Russia during the war had virtually no impact abroad and remained almost entirely unknown in the West for over seventy years. Many intriguing discoveries are still being made about the 1910s, perhaps the most underresearched period of cinema history. (See Notes and Queries.)

GERMANY

Before 1912, the German film industry was relatively insignificant. Its films were not widely exported, and imports dominated its domestic market. The cinema also had a low reputation in Germany. During the early 1910s, reformers and censors attacked the cinema as immoral. Theatrical and arts journals portrayed the cinema as a lowbrow form of entertainment, primarily because competition from films had caused theater attendance to decline. In May 1912, organizations of playwrights, directors, and actors went so far as to boycott the cinema.

By late 1912, however, the boycott was broken, as film producers competed to sign those same playwrights, directors, and actors to exclusive contracts. Similarly, film firms sought to adapt prestigious literary works and to have established authors write original screenplays. During 1913 there arose the *Autorenfilm*, or "authors' film." The term "author" did not mean then what *auteur* means today—the director of the film. Rather, the *Autorenfilm* was publicized largely on the basis of a famous writer who had written the film script or the original literary work from which the film was adapted. The director of the film was seldom mentioned. The *Autorenfilm* was, in effect, Germany's equivalent of the Film d'Art in France (p. 28) and other attempts at creating an art cinema. Similarly, stage stars were hired and featured prominently in the publicity for such films. A few leading theatrical directors, most notably Max Reinhardt, worked briefly in the cinema.

Fig. 3.2 The climactic scene of *Die Landstrasse* consists primarily of a lengthy take concentrating on gradual changes in the characters' expressions rather than on action.

The *Autorenfilm* was established with *Der Andere* ("The Other," 1913, Max Mack). This film was adapted from a drama by the established playwright Paul Lindau and starred a major theatrical performer, Albert Basserman. *Der Andere* was reviewed favorably by theater journals. Another important *Autorenfilm* was *Die Landstrasse* ("The Country Road," 1913, Paul von Woringen). This time Lindau wrote an original script, dealing with an escaped convict who commits a murder in a small village. The murder is blamed on a passing beggar, who is finally cleared by the convict's deathbed confession. From a modern perspective, *Die Landstrasse* seems an unusually sophisticated film. It proceeds at a slow pace, carefully setting up parallelisms between the convict and the beggar. There are a number of very long takes that de-emphasize action in favor of concentration on minute details—an early exploration of expressive cinematic techniques. One framing simply shows a forest setting, with the beggar wandering in from the background and sitting by a bush in the foreground to eat the scraps of food he has obtained in the village. More dramatically, the revelation of the dying convict's guilt comes in a minutes-long shot that encompasses the beggar's anguished reaction and the reactions of the onlookers (Fig. 3.2).

The most successful and famous *Autorenfilm* is *The Student of Prague* (1913, Stellan Rye). It was based on an original screenplay by the popular writer Hanns Heinz Ewers and marked the entry of theater star Paul Wegener into the cinema. For decades, Wegener was to remain a major force in German filmmaking. *The Student of Prague* was a Faust-like story of a student who gives his mirror image to a demonic character in exchange for wealth. The image dogs the hero and finally provokes a fatal duel. Aided by the great cameraman Guido Seeber, Rye and Wegener used special effects to create scenes of the student and his double confronting each other (Fig. 3.3). The fantasy elements of this film would become a prominent trait of German cinema, culminating in the German Expressionist movement of the 1920s (Chapter 5).

Fig. 3.3 In *The Student of Prague*, exposure of separate portions of the same shot during filming allowed two characters, both played by Paul Wegener, to confront each other.

The *Autorenfilm* lent respectability to the cinema, but most of the films were not successful with the public, and the notion of basing films on works by famous authors declined during 1914.

During the same period, however, the German industry was expanding. Domestic films were gaining popular success, largely due to the rise of the star system. Two very different female stars became widely known. The

Fig. 3.4 Part of a complex shot in Urban Gad's last film with Asta Nielsen, *Weisse Rosen* ("White Roses," 1916), filmed into a mirror. Characters enter and exit from offscreen, seen directly or as reflections, as the plot develops.

Fig. 3.5 The large interior of the temple in *Cabiria.*

blonde Henny Porten was the ideal of German womanhood; her films were soon export successes, and she was on the verge of becoming internationally famous as the war began. Her worldwide fame would finally come during the 1920s. The Danish actress Asta Nielsen had quickly caught on in Germany after moving there in 1911. Her Danish husband, Urban Gad, directed her in many short films until their separation in 1915. These were notable for Nielsen's varied portrayals, ranging from comic adolescents to betrayed lovers (Fig. 3.4), and she had a great impact on acting styles in other countries.

During the early years of the war, Germany continued to import films, especially from Denmark. Officials soon concluded, however, that the anti-German content of some of these films was hurting the war effort. In 1916, Germany banned film imports. This ban would later stimulate the domestic film industry, helping it to become powerful internationally during the war.

ITALY

Italian cinema flourished in the first half of the teens. The success of exported films and the establishment of the feature film by 1913 attracted talented people to the industry and led producing companies to compete energetically.

Historical epics continued to have the most conspicuous triumphs abroad. In 1913, Enrico Guazzoni's *Quo Vadis?* was an enormous hit and confirmed the epic as the main Italian genre. *Quo Vadis?* was followed in 1914 by one of the most internationally popular films of the era, Giovanni Pastrone's *Cabiria.* Set in the Roman Empire of the third century B.C., *Cabiria* involved kidnapping and human sacrifice, as the hero Fulvio and his strong-man slave Maciste try to rescue the heroine. Mammoth scenes showed a palace destroyed by an erupting volcano and a huge temple within which children are thrown into a fiery figure of the pagan god Moloch (Fig. 3.5). *Cabiria* also consistently used innovative slow tracking shots toward or away from static action. Camera movement had appeared in the early years of the cinema, particularly in scenics (pp. 14, 18). Filmmakers had also occasionally used mobile framing for expressive purposes in narrative films, as when D. W. Griffith begins and ends *The Country Doctor* (1909) with pans across a rural landscape. *Cabiria*'s tracking shots were more influential, however, and the "Cabiria movement" became a common element in films of the mid-1910s.

A second distinctively Italian genre resulted from the rise of the star system. Several beautiful female stars became wildly popular. These were the *divas* ("goddesses"). They typically starred in what are sometimes known as "frock-coat" films—stories of passion and intrigue in upper-middle-class and aristocratic settings. The situations were unrealistic and often tragic, usually featuring eroticism and death, and were initially influenced by the importation of Asta Nielsen's German films.

The *diva* films played up luxurious settings, fashionable costumes, and the heightened acting of the performers. *Ma l'amor mio non muore!* ("But My Love Does Not Die," 1913, Mario Caserini) established the genre. It made Lyda Borelli an instant star, and she remained one of the most celebrated *divas.* Borelli's main rival was Francesca Bertini, whose 1915 *Assunta Spina* (Gustavo Serena) inaugurated a series of films centered on her star persona

(Fig. 3.6). *Diva* films remained popular during the second half of the 1910s and then quickly declined in the 1920s.

The male equivalent of the *diva* was the strongman. The characters of Ursus in *Quo Vadis?* and of the slave Maciste in *Cabiria* started this trend. Maciste was played by a muscular dockworker, Bartolomeo Pagano (Fig. 3.7). His character so fascinated audiences that Pagano went on to star in a series of Maciste films that lasted into the 1920s. Unlike *Cabiria*, these, and other strongman films, were set in the present rather than the historical past. This genre declined temporarily after 1923, as Italian filmmaking sank into crisis. The *peplum* film, or the heroic historical epic, often involving brawny heroes, resurfaced decades later with such films as *Hercules* (1957).

After the war, Italy tried to regain its place on world markets but could not make inroads against American films. In 1919, a large new firm called the Unione Cinematografica Italiana attempted to revive Italian production. Its dependence on formulaic filmmaking exacerbated the industry's decline during the 1920s.

Fig. 3.6 *Diana l'affascinatrice* ("Diana, the Seductress," 1915, Gustavo Serena), a spy melodrama that displayed the histrionic talents and elegant costumes of Francesca Bertini.

RUSSIA

Like Germany, Russia developed a distinctive national cinema in near isolation as a result of World War I. Before the war, Russian production had been largely dominated by Pathé, which opened a studio in Russia in 1908, and Gaumont, which followed suit in 1909. The first Russian-owned filmmaking company, started in 1907 by photographer A. O. Drankov, was able to compete reasonably well. A second Russian firm, Khanzhonkov, appeared in 1908. During the early 1910s, exhibition expanded, and other, smaller Russian producers opened companies.

Fig. 3.7 The faithful Maciste, seen here in a shot from *Cabiria*, inspired the strongman genre in Italian cinema.

As in other European countries, during 1912–1913, the cinema was gaining respectability, with famous authors writing scenarios. Since Tsar Nikolai II and his family were ardent film fans, fashionable audiences as well as the masses went to the cinema. Although most audiences favored imported films, by 1914, Russia had a small, but healthy, film industry.

When Russia entered World War I in July 1914, the borders were immediately closed, and many foreign distribution firms—primarily the German ones—closed their Moscow offices. With competition reduced, new companies were formed, including the third of the three important Russian producers, Yermoliev. In 1916, when Italy entered the war, its films also dwindled in the Russian market, and the domestic industry continued to grow.

During this era, Russian filmmakers innovated a unique approach to the new art. One trait of this approach was subject matter with a melancholy tone. Even before the war, Russian audiences favored tragic endings. As one film trade paper put it: " 'All's well that ends well!' This is the guiding principle of foreign cinema. But Russian cinema stubbornly refuses to accept this and goes its own way. Here it's 'All's well that ends badly'—we need tragic endings."[1] The pace of many Russian films was slow, with frequent pauses and deliberate gestures enabling the players to linger over each action.

This slow pace derived from a fascination with psychology. One appeal

Fig. 3.8 In *Child of the Big City* (1914), Evgenii Bauer places a gauzy curtain in the foreground as the *femme fatale* dines with her friends; this curtain is subsequently drawn aside and the camera tracks back as the characters move forward.

Fig. 3.9 In *Father Sergius*, Protazanov uses sidelighting and staging in depth to enhance the tragic atmosphere as the protagonist resists an attempted seduction by a jaded society woman.

of these films was the display of intense, virtuosic acting. In this, Russian filmmaking was heavily influenced by Italian, German, and Danish films. Russian producers consciously sought actors and actresses who could duplicate Asta Nielsen's popularity. Many Russian films of this period were also somewhat comparable to the Italian *diva* films, which made intensity of acting the main appeal. Russian acting, however, was less flamboyant and more concerned with subtleties of character.

The two most important Russian directors of the war period, Evgenii Bauer and Yakov Protazanov, were masters of the brooding melodrama. From a training in art, Bauer entered the cinema in 1912 as a set designer and soon became a director. His mise-en-scène was characterized by deep, detailed sets (Fig. 3.8) and an unusually strong sidelighting; he also occasionally used complex tracking shots. Several of Bauer's films carried the Russian love for melancholy to extremes, centering on morbid subject matter. In *The Dying Swan* (1917), an obsessed artist tries to capture death in his painting of a melancholy ballerina; when she is suddenly transformed by love, he strangles her in order to finish his masterpiece. Bauer was the main director at the Khanzhonkov company, where he was given a free rein.

Protazanov began directing in 1912, and he worked mostly for Yermoliev. Several of his main films of this period were prestigious adaptations from Pushkin and Tolstoy. They starred Ivan Mozhukhin, a stage actor who had become immensely popular in films. Mozhukhin was the epitome of the Russian ideal in acting: tall and handsome, with hypnotic eyes, he cultivated a slow, fervent style. He starred in the title role of Protazanov's adaptation of Tolstoy's novel *Father Sergius*, made in 1917 between the February and October Revolutions and released in early 1918 (Fig. 3.9). After a brief self-exile in Paris, Protazanov returned to become one of the most successful directors in the USSR when filmmaking revived there during the 1920s.

By 1916, the Russian film industry had grown, and there were thirty production firms in existence. The 1917 Bolshevik Revolution brought filmmaking to a near standstill, however, and the slow, intense style that had developed in Russia during the war soon became old-fashioned. Since the Revolution's principal impact on the cinema was felt during the 1920s, we shall examine the events of the late 1910s in a later chapter.

FRANCE

During the early 1910s, the French film industry was still thriving. Many new theaters were being built, and demand was high. Although imported American films were beginning to encroach on the market, French production remained robust.

In 1913, however, the largest company, Pathé Frères, took the first of several steps that ultimately would harm the French industry. It cut back on the increasingly costly production side of the business to concentrate on the profitable areas of distribution and exhibition. In the United States, French films were being squeezed out by the growth of independent firms. Pathé dropped its membership in the Motion Picture Patents Company, forming an independent distribution firm in 1913. This firm released several widely

THE BRIEF HEYDAY OF THE SERIAL

Today the serial is usually remembered as a trivial form of cinema, consisting largely of low-budget thrillers aimed at the youthful matinee audience in the period from the 1930s to the 1950s. Yet the serial originated as the main attraction in many theaters during the 1910s. Serial episodes can be seen as a kind of transitional form between the one-reeler and the feature film. Though some early serial episodes were quite short, others lasted forty-five minutes or more. They would be shown with other short films—newsreels, cartoons, comic or dramatic narratives—but they would be the featured item on the program. Serials were usually action-oriented, offering thrilling elements like master criminals, lost treasures, exotic locales, and daring rescues.

The true serial carried a story line over all its episodes. Typically, each episode ended at a high point, with the main characters in danger. These "cliffhangers" (so called because characters often ended up suspended from cliffs or buildings) lured the spectator back for the next installment.

Serials originated at almost the same time in the United States and France. The earliest American serial was *The Adventures of Kathlyn* (1914), made by the Selig company and starring Kathlyn Williams. Its episodes, set in India, were self-contained, but there was also an overall plot line. The same was true of *The Perils of Pauline*, made by Pathé in 1914. This hugely successful serial made a star of Pearl White and inspired other firms to make similar films. Williams and White established the pattern of the "serial queen," a heroine (often described as "plucky") who survived numerous outlandish plots against her life (Fig. 3.10). By late 1915, American

Fig. 3.11 The first episode of *Fantomas* ends as Juve sees a vision of the escaped Fantomas, in his famous evening clothes and mask, tauntingly holding out his hands to be handcuffed.

serials were highly profitable and were technically on a par with feature films of the era.

The greatest filmmaker associated with this form was Louis Feuillade. This prolific Gaumont director made around eighty films a year between 1907 and 1913, working in various genres. A turning point in his career, however, was the "Fantomas" crime serial, beginning in 1913 with *Fantomas* and continuing through 1914 with four additional feature-length episodes. (Even after this point, however, he continued to direct comedies as well.) The "Fantomas" serial adapted the successful writings of Pierre Souvestre and Marcel Allain, whose books have become classics.

Fantomas was the ultimate criminal, master of many disguises, who constantly eludes his determined rival, the detective Juve (Fig. 3.11). Feuillade filmed this crime story in the streets of Paris and in conventional studio sets, creating a bizarre juxtaposition of an everyday milieu and fantastic, nightmarish events. His subsequent thriller serials, including *Juve contra Fantomas* ("Juve versus Fantomas," 1913), *Les Vampires* (1915), and *Judex* (1916), continued this style. Feuillade was extremely popular with the general public, but he was also embraced by the Surrealists for the (perhaps unconscious) poetic quality of his work. This side of Feuillade's films makes them seem highly modern today.

Serials also became significant in Germany during the 1910s. *Homunculus* (1916, Otto Rippert) told the story of a laboratory-created humanoid who manipulated stock markets and ultimately tried to control the world. After the war, pro-

Fig. 3.10 Near the end of the first episode of *The Perils of Pauline*, the heroine shinnies down a rope from a balloon which has been set adrift by the villain.

ducer-director Joe May specialized in lavish serials starring his wife, Mia May, Germany's serial queen. His eight-part epic, *The Mistress of the World* (1919–1920), was perhaps the most expensive German project in the immediate postwar years. During seven episodes, the heroine undergoes ordeals in Chinese, Mayan, and African locales (Fig. 3.12). In the seventh installment she is rescued; the eighth wittily depicts the making of a sensationalistic film about her adventures.

Serial production continued to be important in France and some other countries into the 1920s, but in the United States it became a way of creating inexpensive programs in smaller theaters and of attracting children. During the sound era in the 1930s, the action serial played the same roles.

Fig. 3.12 One of the many large, exotic sets constructed for *The Mistress of the World.*

Fig. 3.13 Filming inside a real building without using artificial light, Léonce Perret created dramatic silhouette effects in *L'Enfant de Paris.*

successful serials during the 1910s, including *The Perils of Pauline* (see Box). By 1919, however, Pathé's concentration on serials and shorts put it on the margins of the American industry, which was dominated by big firms making features.

Unlike Pathé, Gaumont expanded production in the years just before the war. Two important Gaumont directors, Léonce Perret and Louis Feuillade, did some of their best work during this period. Perret had come to fame in 1909 as a comic actor, directing his own series of "Léonce" films. During the mid-1910s, he also made some major features. *L'Enfant de Paris* ("Child of Paris," 1913) and *Roman d'un mousse* ("Tale of a Cabin Boy," 1914) were intensely melodramatic narratives of abducted children. They were notable for their beautiful cinematography, including skillful location filming and an unusual use of backlighting (Fig. 3.13). Perret also varied his camera angles considerably and broke scenes down into more shots than was then typical. He thus helped expand the cinema's expressive possibilities. Perret's style became more formulaic later on, when he worked in Hollywood in the second half of the decade and returned to France to make historical epics in the 1920s.

Feuillade continued to work in a variety of genres, including comedies and a naturalistic series, "La vie telle qu'elle est" ("Life as it is"). His main achievements, however, were in the new serial form (see Box).

Despite Pathé's and Gaumont's dominance of French production, they made no attempt to monopolize the industry, and smaller companies coexisted peacefully with them, staying in business by specializing in certain types of films.

All this activity came to an abrupt halt when World War I began. By the end of 1914, it had become apparent that the fighting would continue for a considerable period, and some theaters reopened. In early 1915, production resumed on a limited basis. Newsreels became more important, and all the firms made highly patriotic fiction films, such as *Mères français* ("French Mothers," 1917, René Hervil and Louis Mercanton).

Pathé's response to the war was to focus its efforts on its American distribution wing, releasing films made by independent producers in the United States. With the huge success of *The Perils of Pauline* and subsequent serials, Pathé remained profitable. It was, however, no longer providing a stable leadership for French film production. Through its distribution, Pathé was also helping American films gain a greater share of the French market. French intellectuals and the general public alike adored the new American stars: Charlie Chaplin, Douglas Fairbanks, William S. Hart, and Lillian Gish. Writer Philippe Soupault suggests how suddenly and intensely American films affected Parisian viewers:

> Then one day we saw hanging on the walls great posters as long as serpents. At every street-corner a man, his face covered with a red handkerchief, leveled a revolver at the peaceful passersby. We imagined that we heard galloping hoofs, the roar of motors, explosions, and cries of death. We rushed into the cinema, and realized immediately that everything had changed. On the screen appeared the smile of Pearl White—that almost ferocious smile which announced the revolution, the beginning of a new world.[2]

Serial queen Pearl White was idolized in France after the release of *Les Mystères de New York*, the French title of her second Pathé serial, *The Exploits of Elaine* (1915). During 1917, American films passed the 50 percent mark in French exhibition.

The real impact of American films in France was not apparent until after the war. In 1918–1919, French firms attempting to bring production back up to its old levels found it virtually impossible to reduce the American share of their market. The next chapter will examine how the French industry reacted, trying to create competitive alternatives to Hollywood cinema.

SCANDINAVIA

In Denmark, Ole Olsen's Nordisk films continued to dominate production, though a small number of other firms operated during the 1910s. During 1913–1914, Nordisk and other companies were moving toward longer films of two, three, even four reels. One historian has summarized the typical style of Nordisk's films: "The lighting effects, the stories, the realism of interior settings, the extraordinary use of natural and urban locations, the intensity of the naturalistic acting style, the emphasis on fate and the passions."[3]

The work of August Blom, Nordisk's top director of the early teens, typifies this style. His most important film was *Atlantis* (1913), at eight reels the longest Danish film to date. Its plot offered a fairly conventional psychological melodrama, but the film dwelt on beautifully designed sets (Fig. 3.14) and spectacular scenes, such as the sinking of an ocean liner (inspired by the *Titanic* disaster of the previous year). *Atlantis* was triumphantly successful abroad.

Another Nordisk director, Forest Holger-Madsen, made an outstanding film, *The Evangelist* (1914). The narrative involves a frame story and lengthy flashback, as a preacher tells a young man about his time in prison as a

Fig. 3.14 A set depicting a hallway in a sculptor's house attracts the eye in August Blom's *Atlantis*.

Fig. 3.15 An elaborate, realistic model of a cityscape, combined with strong backlighting, makes this scene in *The Evangelist* unusual for its period.

Fig. 3.16 Shooting into the sun creates a dramatic silhouette effect on an old mill, whose blades form part of the "X" motif in Benjamin Christensen's *The Mysterious X.*

Fig. 3.15

Fig. 3.16

Figs. 3.17 and 3.18 A suspenseful tracking shot in *Night of Revenge*, beginning on the frightened heroine as she sees something outside her window and moving back rapidly to reveal an intruder forcing his way in and rushing to her.

Fig. 3.17

Fig. 3.18

result of being wrongfully convicted of murder. His tale saves the young man from a life of crime. The preacher's dark, grim room, in which he relates his story, exemplifies the use of setting to create mood (Fig. 3.15).

One of the most original and eccentric directors of the silent cinema also began working in the Danish industry. Benjamin Christensen started as an actor at the small Dansk Biografkompagni in 1911 and soon became president of the firm. His impressive debut as a director was *The Mysterious X* (1913), in which he also starred. It was a melodramatic story of spies and false accusations of treason, shot in a particularly bold visual style. Stark side- and backlighting create silhouette effects (Fig. 3.16); few films of this period contain such striking compositions. Christensen went on to make an equally virtuosic drama, *Night of Revenge* (1916). Here he added tracking shots that intensify the suspense and shock as a convict terrorizes a family (Figs. 3.17, 3.18).

Christensen did not complete another film until the 1920s, when his *Witchcraft Through the Ages* (1922) was made in Sweden. It was a bizarre, episodic quasi-documentary tracing the history of witchcraft. After censorship difficulties with this film, Christensen moved into more conventional film-making, directing dramas and thrillers in Germany and Hollywood during the 1920s.

World War I had a mixed effect on the Danish cinema. Initially Denmark benefited, since, as a neutral northern country, it was in a unique position to furnish films to markets like Germany and Russia, which were cut off from their normal suppliers. But in 1916 Germany banned film imports. In 1917, the United States cut back on its dealings with Denmark, and the Russian Revolution eliminated that market. During the 1910s, many top Danish directors and actors were also lured away, mainly to Germany and Sweden.

By the war's end, Denmark was no longer a significant force in international distribution.

In 1912, Sweden suddenly and unexpectedly began producing a string of innovative, distinctive films. This development was all the more impressive because most of these films were made by only three directors: Georg af Klercker, Maurice Stiller, and Victor Sjöström. Moreover, the Swedish cinema initially had little impact abroad, and so its filmmakers were working without the larger budgets made possible by export. Sweden was among the first countries to create a major cinema by drawing deliberately upon the particular traits of its national culture. Swedish films were characterized by their dependence on northern landscapes and by their use of local literature, costumes, customs, and the like. After the war's end, their specifically Swedish qualities made these films novel and popular in other countries.

The success of Nordisk in Denmark had been one inspiration for the formation of a small Swedish firm in 1907, the Svenska Biografteatern. It eventually would form the basis of the leading Swedish film firm, still in existence. Located in the small provincial city of Kristianstad, the firm was initially a theater chain. In 1909, Charles Magnusson took over its management and built it into the country's main production company. In 1910, Julius Jaenzon, a cinematographer who had mainly made topicals, joined the firm. He was to photograph most of Stiller's and Sjöström's films of the 1910s. Under Magnusson and Jaenzon's guidance, the firm produced films on a small scale in a tiny studio above its main cinema in Kristianstad. (This building is one of the few early glass-sided studios that can still be visited; it houses a small cinema museum.)

In 1912, Svenska moved to a larger studio in Stockholm. The first director it hired was Georg af Klercker, who became head of production. That same year, actors Maurice Stiller and Victor Sjöström were hired to boost Svenska's production. All three directed, wrote scripts, and acted. They made many short films with modest budgets during the next few years.

After the beginning of the war, Germany was blocking film imports to several northern European countries. Since few films got past this blockade, Swedish production was boosted and filmmakers were relatively free of foreign influence for a few years.

Until recently, the work of Georg af Klercker was largely overshadowed by the contributions of Stiller and Sjöström. In the mid-1980s, however, several of his films were restored and shown in retrospectives. They revealed a skillful and versatile director with a strong sense of pictorial beauty. Af Klercker had begun as an actor, and he also did set designs when he first joined Svenska. He was soon directing but did not get on well with Magnusson and quit in 1913. He worked at smaller production firms, primarily Hasselbladfilm (founded in 1915). There he was the undisputed leader, directing most of the firm's output.

Af Klercker made comedies, crime thrillers, war films, and melodramas, usually with fairly conventional stories. In all of them, however, he displays a distinctive eye for landscape, light, and variety of framing within scenes. His films contain some of the most beautiful sets of this period, defined by simple lines but richly furnished with details. Af Klercker skillfully suggests offscreen space: background rooms are often just visible through beaded curtains, and mirrors reveal action occurring outside the frame. He also

Fig. 3.19

Fig. 3.20

Fig. 3.21

Fig. 3.19 The careful placement of real plants in both foreground and background of this shot from *Dödsritten under Cirkus-Kuplen* ("Death Ride under the Circus Dome," 1912) typify Georg af Klercker's emphasis on elegant settings.

Fig. 3.20 The heroine of *Thomas Graal's Best Film* finds out she is to star in a film and practices acting—in a flamboyant style that parodies contemporary Italian *diva* films.

Fig. 3.21 The heroine's body is borne past the icebound ship on which the mercenaries had hoped to escape at the end of *Sir Arne's Treasure*.

elicited subtle, restrained performances from his actors (Fig. 3.19). In 1918–1919, Hasselblad went through mergers that made it a part of Svenska Bio, which then became Svenska Filmindustri (the name it has kept ever since). At that point af Klercker gave up filmmaking to go into business.

Af Klercker's more famous colleagues, Stiller and Sjöström, both stayed at Svenska, directing, acting, and writing scripts. They were extremely prolific until both went to Hollywood, Sjöström in 1923, Stiller in 1925. Unfortunately, however, most of the negatives of the films made by Svenska were destroyed in a fire in 1941. This disaster, one of the most tragic losses among many nitrate fires, means that few of Svenska's early films have survived. Most existing prints of Stiller and Sjöström films have been copied from early positive release prints; hence their visual quality is often mediocre. Still, even such prints indicate the high artistic merit of these films.

So many of Maurice Stiller's early films are lost that it is difficult to judge his career before the mid-1910s. He is mainly remembered for the urbane wit of several films he made between 1916 and 1920, as well as for his adaptations of the works of Nobel prize–winning Swedish novelist Selma Lagerlöf.

The wit was well displayed in the comedy *Thomas Graal's Best Film* (1917). In it, an eccentric scriptwriter-actor (played delightfully by Victor Sjöström) glimpses and falls in love with a young woman, Bessie, and refuses to finish his overdue scenario unless she can be found and persuaded to star in it. Meanwhile, the free-spirited Bessie rejects her wealthy parents' choice of a fiancé and decides to accept the movie role (Fig. 3.20). The film alternates between the two main characters, including fantasy scenes representing the scenario the hero writes, showing how he imagines the love story between himself and Bessie might turn out. Eventually the two actually meet and become engaged. The result was one of the cleverest films about filmmaking made in the silent era. It was so successful that a sequel was made: *Thomas Graal's Best Child* (1918), in which the pair marry and have a baby.

Stiller's most famous film was the antithesis of these comedies. A tragedy set in Renaissance-period Sweden, *Sir Arne's Treasure* (1919) was adapted from a Lagerlöf story. Three fugitive mercenaries pillage the castle of Sir Arne, trying to escape with his treasure. The town's harbor is icebound, however, trapping them until spring. The young woman Elsalill, the sole survivor of the massacre, falls in love with Sir Archie, not realizing that he is one of the killers. Despite his love for Elsalill, Sir Archie ends by using her as a shield in a vain escape attempt. The final scene shows the towns-people bearing her coffin across the ice as spring approaches (Fig. 3.21).

Stiller continued making both comedies and dramas. In 1920, he directed *Erotikon*, often credited as the first sophisticated sex comedy. It treated romantic relations casually, as a neglected young wife flirts with and finally starts an affair with a handsome suitor, while her middle-aged husband, an absentminded professor, pairs off with his pretty niece. *Erotikon* may well have influenced German director Ernst Lubitsch, who later became famous for clever sexual innuendo in his films in Hollywood in the 1920s. Stiller also adapted another Lagerlöf novel in his two-part epic, *The Story of Gösta Berling* (1924; available in the United States only in an abridged version). This story of a defrocked minister torn between a dissolute life and the love of an unhappily married countess contains several remarkable scenes and performances; among these is the first major role of the young Greta Garbo, as the countess. She was discovered by Stiller, and they both soon went to Hollywood, where her career was more successful than his.

Victor Sjöström was one of the most important directors of the entire silent era. His style was austere and naturalistic. He used restrained acting and staged scenes in considerable depth, both in location shots and in sets. His narratives frequently traced in great detail the grim consequences of a single action. Sjöström's early masterpiece, *Ingeborg Holm* (1913), for example, begins with a happy middle-class family; the father suddenly falls ill and dies, and the plot follows the wife's descent into poverty and madness as she struggles vainly to keep her children. The film consists primarily of lengthy shots that hold on a series of actions that unfold within deep sets (Figs. 3.22–3.26). The slow, steady pace conveys a remarkable impression

Figs. 3.22–3.26 In *Ingeborg Holm*, a long-shot framing shows the heroine parting from her son. Reluctant to leave her, he returns to hug her again as the gatekeeper opens the gate (Fig. 3.22). As the boy moves away again with his foster mother, Ingeborg quickly ducks into the doorway (Fig. 3.23). The boy turns back once more (Fig. 3.24) and, not seeing his mother, sadly follows his foster mother (Fig. 3.25). Once the pair has gone, the gatekeeper locks the gate and returns just in time to catch Ingeborg as she emerges again and begins to faint (Fig. 3.26). The staging with the heroine's back to the camera displays Sjöström's refusal to overemphasize her emotions.

Fig. 3.22

Fig. 3.23

Fig. 3.24

Fig. 3.25

Fig. 3.26

Fig. 3.27 Years after the death of his family, the vengeful protagonist rages against the tempestuous sea in *Terje Vigen*.

Fig. 3.28 The fugitive hero wandering in the vast countryside in *The Outlaw and His Wife*.

of the heroine's decades of misfortune, despite the fact that *Ingeborg Holm* lasts only about seventy minutes.

Terje Vigen (1916) demonstrates Sjöström's mastery of landscape as an expressive element in the action. During wartime, Terje Vigen, a sailor, attempts to fetch food in his rowboat but is captured by the enemy. During his lengthy imprisonment, his wife and child die of starvation. Years later, the embittered protagonist gains power over the family of the man who captured him and must decide whether to wreak his revenge by killing them. Again the narrative traces out the long-term results of an event, suggesting an implacable fate guiding the characters. Sjöström heightens the effect of his narrative by using the sea as a prominent backdrop for much of the action, seeming to reflect the hero's anger (Fig. 3.27).

Landscapes were also prominent in *The Outlaw and His Wife* (1917). Again a single desperate action, the hero's theft of a sheep to feed his family, affects his entire life. Fleeing arrest (Fig. 3.28), Berg-Ejvind finds temporary safety working on the farm of a rich widow, Halla. They fall in love, but he is again pursued by the authorities. Abandoning her estate, Halla follows Berg-Ejvind into the mountains, where they live together for many years before dying in each other's arms in a blizzard. Sjöström daringly undercut the intense romanticism of this story by making the final scene in a snowbound cabin involve an ugly, petty quarrel between the couple; they reconcile at the end, just before they die.

The war had restricted exports of Swedish films, and *The Outlaw and His Wife* was the first to burst onto the international scene. The French, reeling from the recent flood of American films, reacted with delight. Critic and future filmmaker Louis Delluc praised *The Outlaw and His Wife:*

> And the public is swept away with emotion. For the public is awestruck by the barren landscapes, the mountains, the rustic costumes, both the austere ugliness and the acute lyricism of such closely observed feelings, the truthfulness of the long scenes which focus exclusively on the couple, the violent struggles, the high tragic end of the two aged lovers who escape life through a final embrace in a desertlike snowscape.[4]

In general, the Swedish cinema was recognized as the first major alternative to Hollywood to emerge after the war.

Even more successful was Sjöström's 1920 film, *The Phantom Chariot*, again adapted from Lagerlöf. It uses remarkably complex means to tell the story of a drunken lout who nearly dies in a cemetery at midnight on New Year's Eve. He is given a chance to ride a ghostly carriage driven by death and witness how his behavior has ruined the lives of two women who love him. The ghostly superimpositions (accomplished entirely in the camera during filming) were some of the most elaborate yet attempted. Similarly, the story was told in an intricately interwoven set of flashbacks that became highly influential in European cinema of the 1920s. *The Phantom Chariot* quickly came to be considered a classic and was often revived.

Ironically, the very success of the Swedish cinema abroad contributed to its decline. After about 1920, Svenska concentrated on expensive prestige pictures designed for export. Only a few of these, like *The Story of Gösta*

Berling, were artistic successes. Sjöström's and Stiller's growing reputations led Hollywood firms to lure them away from Svenska. Moreover, other countries were entering the international marketplace, and the small Swedish cinema could not compete. After 1921, film production in Sweden fell precipitously.

Fig. 3.29 A row of open-air filmmaking stages at Universal City, c. 1915. A series of films could be made simultaneously on sets built side by side. The overhead framework held sheets of translucent material to diffuse the strong California sunlight.

THE CLASSICAL HOLLYWOOD CINEMA

The Motion Picture Patents Company dominated the American film industry between 1908 and 1911, but it lost much of its power after a 1912 court decision rendered the Latham-loop patent (p. 35) void. Independent firms soon regrouped and expanded into a studio system that would form the basis for American filmmaking for decades. Certain filmmaking roles—chiefly the role of the producer—became central. In addition, the star system gained full strength, as celebrities came to command enormous salaries and even began producing in their own right.

THE MOVE TO THE STUDIO SYSTEM

The process of building the Hollywood studio system often involved the combination of two or more small production or distribution firms. In 1912, independent producer Carl Laemmle, who had doggedly fought the MPPC, was pivotal in forming the Universal Film Manufacturing Company, a distribution firm to release the output of his own IMP Company and several other independent and foreign firms. By 1913 Laemmle had gained control of the new company, and in 1915 he opened Universal City, a studio north of Hollywood (Fig. 3.29), forming the basis of a complex that still exists. By that point, Universal was well on the way to being vertically integrated, combining production and distribution in the same firm.

Also in 1912, Adolph Zukor scored a tremendous success by importing and distributing *Queen Elizabeth,* a French feature starring Sarah Bernhardt.

Zukor then formed Famous Players in Famous Plays to exploit the star system and prestigious literary adaptations. Famous Players would soon become part of the most powerful studio in Hollywood. Another step toward the studio system came in 1914, when W. W. Hodkinson banded eleven local distributors together into Paramount, the first national distributor devoted solely to features. Zukor was soon distributing his Famous Players films through Paramount.

Another feature-film company originated in 1914. The Jesse L. Lasky Feature Play Company was centered primarily around the films of former playwright Cecil B. De Mille. Lasky also distributed through Paramount. In 1916, Zukor took over Paramount, merged Famous Players in Famous Plays and the Jesse L. Lasky Feature Play Company into Famous Players–Lasky, and made Paramount this new firm's distribution subsidiary. This was another key move in fusing smaller American producers and distributors into larger, vertically integrated firms. Paramount soon controlled many of the most popular silent stars, including Gloria Swanson, Mary Pickford, and Douglas Fairbanks, as well as top directors like D. W. Griffith, Mack Sennett, and De Mille.

Other firms formed during the 1910s would be crucial in the industry. Sam, Jack, and Harry Warner moved from exhibiting to distributing, founding Warner Bros. in 1913. By 1918 they began producing but remained a relatively small firm until the 1920s. Similarly, William Fox formed the Fox Film Co. in 1914. Three smaller firms that would merge into MGM in 1924 all began during this era: Metro in 1914, and Goldwyn and Mayer in 1917.

A major challenge to Paramount's growing power soon arose. Paramount was releasing 102 features a year and requiring that theaters had to show all of them (with two programs per week) in order to get any. This was an early instance of "block booking," a practice that later repeatedly drew charges of monopolistic practices. In 1917, a group of exhibitors resisted this tactic by banding together to finance and distribute independent features. They formed the First National Exhibitors Circuit, which soon was supplying films to hundreds of theaters nationwide. Zukor responded by beginning to buy up theaters for his own company in 1919, preparing the way for one of the main trends in the industry during the 1920s: increasing vertical integration through the growth of national theater chains.

Vertical integration was an important factor that contributed to Hollywood's international power. During this same period, Germany was just beginning to develop a vertically integrated film industry (Chapter 5). France's leading firm, Pathé, was backing away from vertical integration by moving out of production. No other country had a studio system as strong as that of the United States.

The Hollywood studios have often been referred to as "factories," turning out strings of similar films as if on assembly lines. This characterization is only partly true. Each film was different and so required specific planning and execution. The studios did, however, develop methods of making films as efficiently as possible. By 1914, most big firms had differentiated between the director, who was responsible for shooting the film, and the producer, who oversaw the entire production.

The labor of filmmaking was increasingly divided among expert practitioners. There were separate scenario departments, for example, and writers

Fig. 3.30 Producer Thomas H. Ince in his studio at Inceville. The glass roof and walls are covered with cloth to permit the use of artificial light. Later studios had no windows.

specializing in plotting, dialogue, or intertitles might all contribute to a single script. The version used during filming was the "continuity" script, and it broke the action down into individual, numbered shots. The script allowed the producer to estimate how much a given film would cost. The continuity script also allowed people working on the film to coordinate their efforts, even though they might never communicate directly with each other. In the planning stage, the set designer would use the script to determine what types of sets were necessary. After the shooting was done, the editor put the film together, guided by the numbers shown on a slate at the beginning of each shot, which corresponded to the numbers in the script. These shots were designed to match at each cut, creating a continuity of narrative action.

The big film companies also built studio facilities during the 1910s, mostly in the Los Angeles area. Initially these primarily involved outdoor filming on covered stages (see Fig. 3.29). By the late 1910s, however, large "dark" studios were also constructed, either by covering the glass walls or building windowless enclosures (Fig. 3.30). Here filmmakers controlled lighting with electric lamps. These studios also had extensive *backlots*, where large outdoor sets could be constructed; to save money, the production firms often kept some of these standing, using them over and over.

Again, no other country could match Hollywood's approach. Few firms employed so many different film specialists, and only a small number of studios outside the United States could boast of facilities as extensive as those of the big companies like Paramount.

FILMMAKING IN HOLLYWOOD DURING THE 1910s

During the late 1910s, foreign audiences, many of whom had been cut off from the Hollywood product during the war, marveled at how American films

Figs. 3.31 and 3.32 A conversation between the hero, played by Douglas Fairbanks, and the villain of *Manhattan Madness* (1916, Allan Dwan), edited in shot/reverse shot.

Fig. 3.31

Fig. 3.32

Figs. 3.33 and 3.34 A cut from a man looking downward to a high angle shows us his point of view on the characters at the bottom of the staircase in *The On-the-Square Girl* (1917, Frederick J. Ireland).

Fig. 3.33

Fig. 3.34

had changed. Aside from having appealing stars and lavish sets, they were fast-paced and stylistically polished. One reason for this appeal was that American filmmakers had gone on exploring the classical Hollywood style, linking technique to clear storytelling. (See pp. 41–48.)

Filmmakers continued to use intercutting in increasingly complex ways. By the mid-1910s, individual scenes within a single space were also likely to be broken into several shots, beginning with an establishing shot, followed by one or more cut-ins to show portions of the action. Directors and cinematographers were expected to match the positions and movements of actors and objects at each cut so that the shift in framing would be less noticeable. Point-of-view shots were used more commonly and with greater flexibility. The use of shot/reverse-shot editing for conversation situations had been rare in the early 1910s (p. 46), but by 1917 it occurred at least once in virtually every film (Figs. 3.31, 3.32). Similarly, cuts from people looking to point-of-view shots of what they see were common by then (Figs. 3.33, 3.34). Indeed, by 1917, the fundamental techniques of continuity editing, including adherence to the 180° line, or axis of action, had been worked out. Filmmakers would typically break even a simple scene into several shots, cutting to closer views and placing the camera at various vantage points within the action itself (Figs. 3.35–3.37).

The look of individual shots also changed. As we have seen in previous chapters, most early films were shot using flat, overall light, from either the sun or artificial lights or from a combination of both sources. During the mid-1910s, filmmakers experimented with "effects" lighting, that is, selective lighting over only part of the scene, motivated as coming from a specific

Fig. 3.35

Fig. 3.36

Fig. 3.37

source. The most influential film to include this technique was Cecil B. De Mille's *The Cheat* (1915; Figs. 3.38–3.40), which utilized arc lamps derived from the theater. By the end of the 1910s and the early 1920s, large film studios boasted a great array of different types of lamps for every purpose.

As feature films became standardized, Hollywood filmmakers established firmer guidelines for creating intelligible plots. These guidelines have changed little ever since. Hollywood plots consist of clear chains of causes and effects, and most of these involve character psychology (as opposed to social or natural forces). Each major character is given a set of comprehensible, consistent traits. The Hollywood protagonist is typically goal-oriented, trying to achieve success in work, sports, or some other activity. The hero's goal conflicts with the desires of other characters, creating a struggle that is resolved only at the end—which is typically a happy one. Hollywood films usually intensify interest by presenting not one but two interdependent plot lines. Almost inevitably one of these involves romance, which gets woven in with the protagonist's quest to achieve a goal. The plot will also arouse suspense through deadlines, escalating conflicts, and last-minute rescues. These principles of storytelling contributed to the enduring international success of American films.

Figs. 3.35–3.37 A typical continuity editing pattern in *Her Code of Honor* (1919, John Stahl). An establishing shot of a tea party (not shown) leads to a closer view of a young man and woman conversing and then an eyeline match to a medium shot of her stepfather, delighted at their courtship. Finally, a more distant framing reestablishes the space by showing all three characters.

FILMS AND FILMMAKERS

During this period, the big Hollywood firms grew enormously. Feature-length films (running on average about 75 minutes) dominated exhibition by 1915. The studios competed to sign up the most popular actors to long-term con-

Figs. 3.38–3.40 Light from a single, powerful spotlight offscreen left creates a dramatic silhouette on a translucent wall after the villain is shot in *The Cheat*.

Fig. 3.38

Fig. 3.39

Fig. 3.40

Fig. 3.41 The figure of Christ superimposed on a battlefield in the pacifist drama *Civilization*.

Fig. 3.42 The southern son's return home is filmed at an oblique angle so that the doorway conceals his mother as she embraces him in *The Birth of a Nation*. Such understatement enhances the emotional power of the moment.

Fig. 3.43 Griffith mounted his camera on a car to create fast tracking shots before the galloping Klan members in the climactic rescue sequence.

tracts. Some stars, like Mary Pickford and Charles Chaplin, were making thousands, even tens of thousands, of dollars a week by the end of the decade. Studios also bought the rights to many famous literary works and adapted them as vehicles for their stars.

The huge expansion of American production required many directors. Some of these had begun working earlier, but a younger generation also entered the cinema.

Thomas H. Ince had started by directing many short films in the early 1910s, but he also became a producer in the ranks of the independents. As the decade progressed, he focused more on producing. Today he is remembered primarily for having contributed to the move toward efficiency in studio filmmaking, particularly the use of the continuity script to control production. He still directed occasionally, however. His 1916 *Civilization* (co-directed with Raymond B. West and Reginald Barker) is notable as one of a number of pacifist films made in the years before America entered World War I. The story takes place in a mythical kingdom ruled by a warmongering king. Christ enters the resurrected body of a young pacifist who dies in battle and converts the king with a message of peace (Fig. 3.41). This was Ince's last directorial effort, however, and he concentrated on producing—including most of the Westerns of William S. Hart—until his death in 1924.

In 1913, D. W. Griffith left the Biograph Company, where he had made over four hundred short films since 1908. Biograph was reluctant to allow Griffith to make films longer than two reels. Despite the firm's resistance, he completed a four-reel historical epic, *Judith of Bethulia* (1913), in the wake of the success of the Italian import *Quo Vadis?*, but it was his last film for Biograph. During 1914 he made four feature films for the independent distribution firm which he managed, Mutual, including *The Avenging Conscience*, an imaginative adaptation of Poe that employs fantasy scenes.

That same year, however, he was at work on a far more ambitious project. Independently financed from various sources, the twelve-reel *The Birth of a Nation* told an epic tale of the American Civil War by centering on two families who befriend each other but are on opposite sides in the conflict. The father of the northern family, Stoneman, pushes through legislation that gives rights to freed slaves after the war, while the elder son of the southern family helps start the Ku Klux Klan in response to outrages committed in his town. This bigoted account of African-Americans' role in southern history aroused great controversy when it was released, but it was enormously successful and influential for its dynamic and original style. Using many actors from his days at Biograph, Griffith created subtle portrayals of the members of the two families (Fig. 3.42). His regular cinematographer, Billy Bitzer, created shots ranging from large-scale views of battles to intimate details of the characters' lives. Later scenes build up excitement by cutting among two different last-minute rescue situations, as renegade ex-slaves attack a group in a cabin and elsewhere the heroine's virtue is menaced by the villainous mulatto leader (Fig. 3.43).

In his next film, Griffith tried to outdo himself. *Intolerance*, released in 1916, was even longer (fourteen reels, or roughly three and a half hours). Griffith uses an abstract theme, the idea of intolerance through the ages, to link four separate stories set in different historical epochs: the fall of Babylon,

Fig. 3.44

Fig. 3.45

Figs. 3.44 and 3.45 In *Intolerance*, Griffith boldly cuts directly from galloping chariots in the Babylonian era to a speeding train in the modern story.

the last part of Christ's life, the St. Bartholomew's Day Massacre in France, and a tale of a labor strike and gangster activity in modern-day America. To stress the unchanging nature of intolerance, Griffith intercuts these stories rather than telling them one after the other. Through most of the film, intertitles and an allegorical figure of a woman rocking a cradle announce the shifts from one story to the next. In the final section, however, as four separate rescues are attempted, Griffith suddenly cuts among them without such signals. The result is a daring experiment in the use of editing to join disparate spaces and times (Figs. 3.44, 3.45). *Intolerance* was also innovative in its cinematography, as when Bitzer mounted the camera on a movable elevator to create swooping movements over the huge set of the Babylonian court.

Intolerance was not as successful as *The Birth of a Nation,* and Griffith's subsequent features of the 1910s were less experimental. Griffith went on location to film war footage for *Hearts of the World* (1918), a story set in a French village during World War I. He made delightful country romances with *A Romance of Happy Valley* and *True Heart Susie* (both 1919) and a drama that used unusual hazy soft-focus cinematography, *Broken Blossoms* (1919).

Griffith was the most famous director of this era. He quickly came to be credited with innovating most of the major film techniques—something he encouraged in publicizing himself. Some modern historians have treated *The Birth of a Nation* and *Intolerance* as almost the only important American films of this period. Without detracting from Griffith's prestige, however, we should realize that many excellent filmmakers worked during this era, some of whose work is only beginning to be explored. (See Notes and Queries.)

Griffith managed to keep considerable control over his productions, despite the growing supervision of the studio producers. Other directors who began working in this era also became powerful creative figures. In 1914, Maurice Tourneur emigrated from France and became known as a distinctive filmmaker with a strong sense of pictorial beauty. One of his first American films, *The Wishing Ring* (1914), was subtitled "An Idyll of Old England," and it is a fanciful story of a poor girl who naively believes that a ring a gypsy has given her is magical. She tries to use it to reconcile a local earl and his estranged son and does so simply by befriending both. Tourneur managed to create a remarkable atmosphere of a rustic English village, even though the entire film was made in New Jersey. Tourneur was one of the many filmmakers testing the expressive possibilities of the film medium

Fig. 3.46 Maurice Tourneur uses a tent opening to create a dynamic composition for a dramatic moment in *The Last of the Mohicans.*

Fig. 3.47 Keystone comedies often parodied conventional melodramas, as when villain Ford Sterling threatens to saw Mabel Normand in half in *Mabel's Awful Mistake* (1915, Mack Sennett). The white streaks at the sides are nitrate deterioration.

Fig. 3.48 In *His New Job* (1915, Essanay, Charles Chaplin), Chaplin provided a look behind the scenes of comic filmmaking at the "Lockstone" film company, a reference to his beginnings at Keystone.

during this era. In 1918, he experimented with using modernist theatrical set design in *The Blue Bird* and *Prunella,* though these were less popular than most of his films of the 1910s. He also made some highly intelligent literary adaptations, including *Victory* (1919, from Joseph Conrad's novel) and *The Last of the Mohicans* (1920, from James Fenimore Cooper). The latter, often considered his finest film, fully displays Tourneur's visual style, including his characteristic use of foreground shapes silhouetted against a landscape, often framed in a cave or doorway (Fig. 3.46). During the 1920s, Tourneur increasingly had trouble retaining control over his productions as the studio system grew, and he returned to Europe in 1926.

Unlike Tourneur, Cecil B. De Mille survived within the studio system and managed to control many of his own productions throughout a long and prolific career. De Mille is often thought of today primarily for his historical epics of the sound era, but during his early career, he made many innovative films in various genres. *The Cheat* and several other pictures he made in 1915 were influential in popularizing directional, selective lighting (Figs. 3.38–3.40). De Mille made a number of unpretentious, well-acted period films during the mid-1910s, including *The Warrens of Virginia* (1915) and *The Girl of the Golden West* (1916). In 1918, he made *Male and Female,* adapted from J. M. Barrie's play *The Admirable Crichton* and starring Gloria Swanson. The enormous success of this film led De Mille to concentrate on romantic comedies, often set in sophisticated society. His films of the 1920s became more extravagant, exploiting elaborate sets and fashionable costumes.

Other major Hollywood directors also began their careers in the 1910s. Actor Raoul Walsh, who had directed several two-reel films, made an impressive feature debut in 1915 with *The Regeneration,* a realistic story set in a slum milieu. John Ford began making low-budget Westerns in 1917 and directed dozens of them over the next few years. Unfortunately, nearly all are lost, but two surviving films, *Straight Shooting* (1917) and *Hell Bent* (1918), indicate that Ford had a rare feeling for landscape and a flexible understanding of the continuity system from the beginning.

Some of the most popular directors and stars of this era were associated with the genre of slapstick comedy. Once feature films were standardized, they were typically shown on a program that included shorts, such as comedies, newsreels, and brief dramas. Among the most popular shorts were the films of producer-director Mack Sennett. Sennett headed the Keystone company, which specialized in slapstick comedy. Sennett used a great deal of fast action, including chases with the bumbling "Keystone Kops." His small stable of comic stars, who often directed their own pictures, included Charlie Chaplin, Ben Turpin, and Mabel Normand (Fig. 3.47).

Chaplin, an English music-hall performer, became an international star with Keystone, going on to direct his own films at Essanay, Mutual, and First National in the course of the 1910s (Fig. 3.48). Chaplin's style was notable for his comically inappropriate use of objects, as in *The Pawnshop* (1916), where he gauges the value of a clock by listening to its ticking with a stethoscope. His dexterity led to many elaborately choreographed fights, chases, and mix-ups, such as the breakneck shenanigans on roller skates in *The Rink* (1916). In a few of his films, such as *The Vagabond* (1916) and *The Immigrant,* Chaplin also introduced an element of pathos unheard-of in slapstick films. Chaplin's "Little Tramp," with his bowler, cane, and oversized shoes, was soon one of the most widely recognized figures in the world.

One of Sennett's rivals was Hal Roach, who produced films with the young Harold Lloyd. Although Lloyd's initial series character, "Lonesome Luke," was basically an imitation of Chaplin, he soon donned a pair of dark-rimmed glasses and developed his own persona (Fig. 3.49). Other comics of the period included Roscoe "Fatty" Arbuckle and his sidekick Buster Keaton, who would come into his own as a star in the 1920s.

The Western also continued to be popular during the 1910s. One of its most prominent stars was William S. Hart. Hart had been a stage actor and did not enter films until he was nearly fifty. His age, plus his long, lean face, allowed him to play weather-beaten, world-weary roles. His characters were often criminals or men with shady pasts; the plots frequently involved his redemption by love. As a result, Hart's persona became known as the "good-badman," an approach taken up by many subsequent Western stars (Fig. 3.50). His worn clothing and other realistic touches gave Hart's Westerns a sense of historical authenticity, despite their often conventional plots.

Another cowboy star of this period was in many ways Hart's opposite. Tom Mix came out of a background of rodeos and wild-West shows. His films were less realistic than Hart's and emphasized fast action, fancy riding, and stunts. After years of making low-budget shorts for Selig, Mix moved to Fox in 1917 and soon became the most popular cowboy star of the silent era.

One event at the end of this decade indicates the importance that major stars and directors had assumed by this time. In 1919, three of the most popular actors—Mary Pickford, Douglas Fairbanks, and Charles Chaplin—joined the leading director, D. W. Griffith, in establishing a new firm, United Artists. This was a prestigious distribution company, dealing only in films that these four produced independently. (Later other independent producers and stars, such as Samuel Goldwyn and Buster Keaton, also distributed through United Artists.) Although Griffith had to drop out a few years later, the new firm did give some stars and producers a high degree of control that was quite unlike the experiences of filmmakers working for the big studios. We shall see some of its results in Chapter 7.

The development of the Hollywood studio system during the 1910s and the accompanying American takeover of world film markets were among the most influential changes in cinema history. In essence, the events of these

Fig. 3.49

Fig. 3.50

Fig. 3.49 *The City Slicker* (1918) displays Harold Lloyd's typical persona, a brash young fellow in spectacles and a straw hat.

Fig. 3.50 The protagonist of *Hell's Hinges* (1916, William S. Hart and Charles Swickard) epitomizes Hart's "good-badman" character, as he reads the Bible given him by the heroine—with a bottle of whiskey at his elbow.

Fig. 3.51 In *The Artist's Dream* (1913, John Bray), the animated dog is painted onto a background setting printed on a series of sheets of paper.

Fig. 3.52 A frame from *Bobby Bumps and His Goatmobile* (1917), in which the moving figures are drawn on transparent celluloid sheets placed over a single painting of the setting.

Fig. 3.53 An Edison cartoon of 1915, *Cartoons in the Hotel*, animated by Raoul Barré. The head of the cow has been "slashed" off its body, which remains static, while separate drawings allow the head to move.

years defined standard commercial filmmaking. Some of the companies that began in this era are still making films. The division of labor into specialized tasks has continued to the present day. The star system is still one of the primary means of appealing to audiences, and directors continue to coordinate the process of filmmaking. The basic principles of the classical Hollywood style of filmmaking have changed remarkably little. Finally, for better or worse, during this era, "Hollywood" and "the movies" became almost synonymous for many audiences around the world.

ANIMATION

Just as the labor involved in live-action filmmaking was being divided, animated films were becoming standardized within the American industry. Several filmmakers realized that cartoons could be made more economically and quickly if the work could be broken down on an assembly-line system. The main animator could design and supervise the work, while subsidiary workers drew most of the pictures needed for the film's movement. In addition, during the 1910s, a small number of technical innovations speeded up the process of animation: the mechanical printing of background settings, the use of transparent cels, and the slash technique of drawing action.

Early animators like Emile Cohl and Windsor McCay worked by making huge numbers of drawings. McCay had an assistant to trace the background settings onto sheets of paper. In 1913, John Randolph Bray devised a method of mechanizing the process of animation: he printed the same background on many sheets of paper, then animated painted shapes on top of that background to create *The Artist's Dream* (Fig. 3.51).

In December 1914, Bray started his own animation studio, hiring a young man named Earl Hurd. That same month, Hurd applied for a patent on the idea of drawing the moving figures in animated cartoons on sheets of transparent celluloid. (The individual sheets are called *cels*, giving rise to the term "cel animation.") This technique meant that each moving portion could be redrawn bit by bit on separate cels, while the background remained constant. Hurd's "Bobby Bumps" series were among the most popular cartoons of the decade (Fig. 3.52).

During this same period, Raoul Barré developed the *slash system* of animation. A figure would be drawn on paper, and then the portion of the body that moved would be cut away and redrawn on the sheet of paper below the remaining portion of the figure. In order to keep the shapes steady on the screen when moving portions were redrawn, Barré proposed steadying the sheets of paper on a pair of pegs at the top of the drawing. This peg system of registration has remained central to animation ever since, because it allows cels drawn by several different animators to fit together smoothly. During 1915, Barré used the slash system to create a brief series of "Animated Grouch Chasers" for the Edison Company. These were live-action shorts with embedded animated sequences (Fig. 3.53).

During the 1910s, animation was done by independent firms that sold the rights to their short films to distributors. Cartoons were sometimes among the short films shown on programs before features. During the 1920s, thanks in part to the labor-saving devices developed during the 1910s, animated shorts would become a much more popular and regular element of movie programs.

SMALLER PRODUCING COUNTRIES

During the 1910s, many countries began producing fiction films. These films and the circumstances of their making were extremely varied. Unfortunately, it is presently impossible to write adequate histories of such filmmaking practices, since few films from these smaller producing countries survive. The production companies, usually small and often short-lived, seldom could preserve the negatives of their films. In many cases only a small number of prints were distributed, so the chances of one surviving were slim. Many countries, such as Mexico, India, Colombia, and New Zealand, only relatively recently have established archives to save their cinematic heritage. Even the few films that do survive are usually hard to see today except in large cities where archives schedule historical retrospectives.

Despite such problems, most countries have managed to salvage at least a few silent films. On the basis of these, we can make some generalizations about filmmaking in the less prominent producing countries in the silent era.

Producers in such countries had little hope of exporting their films. This meant that they could afford only small budgets, so production values were usually relatively low. Filmmakers concentrated on movies that would appeal primarily to audiences within their own countries.

Films made in the smaller producing nations share two general traits. First, many were shot on location. Since production was sporadic, large studio facilities simply did not exist, and filmmakers made a virtue of necessity, exploiting distinctive natural landscapes and local historical buildings for interesting mise-en-scene. Those studio facilities that did exist were small and technologically limited. Little artificial lighting was available, and many interior scenes of this period were shot in simple open-air stages, in sunlight.

Second, filmmakers frequently sought to differentiate their low-budget films from the more polished imported works by using national literature and history as sources for their stories. In many cases, such local appeal worked, since audiences wanted at least occasionally to see films that reflected their own culture. In some cases these films were novel enough to be exported.

A good example of a film which used these tactics is *The Sentimental Bloke*, perhaps the most important Australian silent film (1919, Raymond Longford). Based upon a popular book of dialect verses by Australian author C. J. Dennis, the film presented a working-class romance. The intertitles quoted passages from the poem, and the scenes were shot in the inner-city Woolloomooloo district of Sydney (Fig. 3.54). The film was very popular in Australia. "It is a blessed relief and refreshment," wrote one reviewer, "after much of the twaddlesome picturing and camouflaged lechery of the films that come to us from America."[5] *The Sentimental Bloke* received some distribution in Great Britain, the United States, and other markets—though the local dialect in the intertitles had to be revised so that foreign viewers could understand the story.

Fig. 3.54 A meeting between the hero and heroine of *The Sentimental Bloke*, staged in a Sydney street with ordinary working-class activities occurring in the background.

Fig. 3.55 The staging of a historical battle on location gives a nearly documentary quality to some scenes of *Ul Ultimo Malon.*

Fig. 3.56 A set representing the interior of a tenant cottage, shot on an open-air stage in full daylight, in *Willy Reilly and His Colleen Bawn.*

Other films of the era drew upon similar appeals. In Argentina, Alcides Greca directed *Ul Ultimo Malon* ("The Last Indian Attack," 1917), based on a historical incident of 1904 (Fig. 3.55). Similarly, a 1919 production by the small, newly formed Film Company of Ireland, *Willy Reilly and His Colleen Bawn* (released 1920, John MacDonagh), was based on an Irish novel by William Carleton, which in turn was based on traditional ballads and events of the Catholic-Protestant conflicts of the 1745 period. Many of the film's scenes were filmed outdoors in the countryside of Ireland. Some interior scenes were also shot outdoors (Fig. 3.56). In 1919, the Canadian producer Ernest Shipman made a film called *Back to God's Country* (director, David M. Hartford). The screenplay was written by Nell Shipman, the film's star, who in the 1920s became a notable independent producer and director. Much of the film was made in the Canadian wilderness, and the story stressed the heroine's love of animals and natural landscapes (Fig. 3.57). Again, the distinctive Canadian subject matter and scenery made the film successful abroad.

The strategies of using national subject matter and shooting on location have remained common in countries with limited production to the present day.

The 1910s, then, were a crucial transitional period for the cinema. International explorations of storytelling techniques and stylistic expressivity led to a cinema that was surprisingly close to what we know today. Indeed, in many ways, early as they are, the films of the mid- to late 1910s are more like modern movies than they are like the novelty-oriented short subjects made only a decade or so earlier.

Similarly, by 1919, the postwar international situation in the film industry would have long-range consequences. Hollywood dominated world markets, and most countries had to struggle to compete with it, either by imitating its films or by finding alternatives to them. The Swedish filmmakers had created a powerful national cinema, but it was too small to make real headway against the Americans after the war. Russia's distinctive film style was cut off by the 1917 Revolution. The struggle against Hollywood domination would shape much of what happened within national film industries for decades to come. The next three chapters will examine some important styles of filmmaking that arose shortly after World War I. Chapter 7 will then describe Hollywood in the late silent period.

◆ NOTES AND QUERIES

THE ONGOING REDISCOVERY OF THE 1910s

The work of understanding film history continues. Perhaps no era remains so little known today as the 1910s. For many years, this period was dismissed as important for only a few events. It was widely known that World War I strangled European production, permitting Hollywood's worldwide dominance. Griffith and Ince were studied as major American producer-directors;

silent comedies, particularly those of Mack Sennett, were also discussed. Among foreign filmmakers, a few films by Stiller and Sjöström were considered classics.

The widespread revision of film history that has occurred in recent decades initially concentrated on very early cinema. During the 1980s, however, increasing attention was paid to the 1910s. One contribution to this rediscovery has been the annual festival of silent film, "Le Giornate del Cinema Muto" ("The Days of the Silent Cinema"), held in Pordenone, Italy, since 1982. Although the Pordenone festival screens films from the entire silent period, some of its most dramatic revelations have come during its retrospectives concentrating on the 1910s. In 1986, an extensive program of pre-1919 Scandinavian films was shown. Among other revelations, this was the occasion for the international revival of interest in Georg af Klercker. Ironically, af Klercker's departure from Svenska meant that the negatives of his films were not among those in the tragic Svenska fire of 1941; Hasselblad kept the negatives in its own vault, and twenty of his twenty-eight films for Hasselblad survive, many in nearly pristine condition. Similar Pordenone programs have dealt with Hollywood cinema of the 1910s (1988), pre-Revolutionary Russian films (1989), and German cinema of the pre-1920 era (1990). Important catalogues containing collections of essays on these subjects have been published (in Italian and English). See Paolo Cherchi Usai and Lorenzo Codelli, eds., *Sulla via di Hollywood 1911–1920* (Pordenone: Edizioni Biblioteca dell'Immagine, 1988); Yuri Tsivian, ed., *Silent Witnesses: Russian Films 1908–1919* (London: British Film Institute, 1989); and Paolo Cherchi Usai and Lorenzo Codelli, eds., *Before Caligari: German Cinema, 1895–1920* (Madison: University of Wisconsin Press, 1990).

Le Giornate del Cinema Muto has helped emphasize how crucial the preservation and availability of early films are to our knowledge of cinema history. Early synoptic histories were based on the few masterpieces available in film archives. While important in themselves, these films did not necessarily give an accurate indication of national cinemas as wholes. Moreover, some important filmmakers have been virtually forgotten. The Pordenone festival has been crucial in bringing such directors as Georg af Klercker and Evgenii Bauer to historians' attention. Similarly, masterpieces like *Die Landstrasse* have been all but forgotten until a discovery (in this case by the Filmmuseum of the Netherlands) of a single copy. Today many national archives take the opportunity of the Pordenone festival to display prints of newly discovered or restored films, and these are then shown in other archives and museums around the world. Undoubtedly some unknown directors and lost films will resurface and modify our view of film history. Such rediscoveries can happen for any period of film history, as we shall see in subsequent chapters, but the 1910s still offer a wide field for exploration.

Fig. 3.57 Nell Shipman and a bear on location in the Canadian wilderness in *Back to God's Country.*

◆ REFERENCES

1. Quoted in Yuri Tsivian, "Some Preparatory Remarks on Russian Cinema," in Tsivian, ed., *Silent Witnesses: Russian Films 1908–1919* (London: British Film Institute, 1989), p. 24.

2. Quoted in Richard Abel, *French Cinema: The First Wave, 1915–1929* (Princeton, N.J.: Princeton University Press, 1984), p. 10.
3. Ron Mottram, *The Danish Cinema Before Dreyer* (Metuchen, N.J.: Scarecrow, 1988), p. 117.
4. Louis Delluc, "Cinema: *The Outlaw and His Wife*," (1919) in Richard Abel, ed., *French Film Theory and Criticism 1907–1939*, vol. 1 (Princeton, N.J.: Princeton University Press, 1988), p. 188.
5. Quoted in Graham Shirley and Brian Adams, *Australian Cinema: The First Eighty Years* (Australia: Angus & Robertson Publishers and Currency Press, 1983), p. 56.

PART TWO

THE LATE SILENT ERA, 1919–1929

Although classical Hollywood form and style have been pervasive since the 1910s, we shall find many alternative approaches to filmmaking in different periods and places. So far we have looked at styles associated with a single filmmaker (such as Georges Méliès or D. W. Griffith), with a company (Pathé), or with a national industry (the huge classical Hollywood cinema or the small Swedish production). Some groups of films belong to a unified *movement*. A movement involves several filmmakers, working for a limited period and usually in a single country, whose films share significant formal traits.

Because film movements arise as distinctive alternatives to the style of the ordinary filmmaking of their day, they often employ unusual techniques. Since few commercial film industries encourage the use of techniques that might alienate the broad audience, we might wonder how such movements can arise. For each movement, the reasons are different, and for each one that we study, we shall look briefly at the conditions in the film industry and the country as a whole that permitted the movement to exist for a limited period.

The years 1918–1933 saw an astonishing variety of explorations in alternative film styles. No fewer than three avant-garde movements arose within commercial industries and flourished briefly: French Impressionism (1918–1929), German Expressionism (1920–1927), and Soviet Montage (1925–1933). Moreover, the 1920s saw the beginnings of an independent experimental cinema—including Surrealism, Dadaism, and abstract films.

There are many reasons for such intense, varied activity in this period. One of the most important involves the new prominence of the Hollywood cinema as a stylistic and commercial force. Chapters 2 and 3 described the establishment of the narrative and stylistic premises of the classical Hollywood cinema during the 1910s. We also saw how the wartime decline in European production allowed American firms to expand into world markets.

After the war, widely differing situations existed in other producing nations, but all faced one common factor: a need to compete with Hollywood. In some countries, like Great Britain, such competition usually involved imitating Hollywood films. Other national cinemas followed this strategy but also encouraged filmmakers to experiment, in the hope that innovative films could compete with the Hollywood product. Some postwar avant-garde films became successful, partly on the basis of their novelty.

Since the invention of the cinema, virtually everyone thought of the new medium primarily as a form of entertainment and as a commercial product. Although some filmmakers, like Maurice Tourneur and Victor Sjöström, took the cinema seriously as an art form, few observers conceived that filmmakers could experiment with modernist styles derived from the other arts. In the late 1910s and 1920s, however, this idea caught on in a number of European countries.

Many of the institutions we now consider integral parts of the film world first came into being then. For example, the specialized film journal, publishing theoretical and analytical articles, arose in France in the 1910s and proliferated internationally over the next decade. Similarly, the earliest groups of enthusiasts devoted to alternative cinema were formed—taking their name, the "ciné-club," from French groups that started the trend. Until the mid-1920s, there were no theaters devoted to the showing of art films. Whether a theater was large or small, first-run or second-run, it showed ordinary commercial films. Gradually, however, the "little cinema" movement spread, again beginning in France. Such theaters catered to a small but loyal portion of the public interested in foreign and avant-garde films. Finally, the first conferences and exhibitions devoted to the cinema as an art were held during the 1920s.

Many of the circumstances that allow any film movement to come into being, however, are unique to its time and place. No single set of circumstances will predictably give rise to a movement. Indeed, as we shall see in the next three chapters, the conditions in France, Germany, and the Soviet Union differed vastly in the postwar era.

We shall go on to examine Hollywood in the 1920s, a period during which it continued to expand and to polish the new classical narrative style developed during the previous decade (Chapter 7). Finally, we will look at international trends of this period, including efforts to resist Hollywood competition and attempts to create an international experimental cinema (Chapter 8).

4

FRANCE
IN THE 1920s

THE FRENCH FILM INDUSTRY AFTER WORLD WAR I

French film production declined during World War I, as many resources were drained away to support the fighting. Moreover, American films increasingly entered France. In the years immediately following the war's end, French screenings consisted of only 20 to 30 percent French films, with Hollywood supplying most of the rest.

French producers faced an uphill struggle in trying to regain their prewar strength. Throughout the silent era, industry experts believed that French production was in a crisis. In 1929, for instance, France made 68 features, while Germany produced 220 and the United States 562. Even in 1926, the worst pre-Depression year for European production, Germany had managed 202 films to France's 55, while Hollywood outstripped both with about 725. In 1928, one of the best years for the Europeans, France made 94 films, compared with 221 for Germany and 641 for the United States.

As such figures suggest, France's "crisis" fluctuated in its severity, but the struggle to boost production gained little ground in the postwar decade. The industry's problems, however, probably benefited the fledgling French Impressionist movement. Companies were apparently willing to experiment, seeking a successful alternative to the Hollywood cinema. Several directors central to the movement—Abel Gance, Marcel L'Herbier, Germaine Dulac, and Jean Epstein—made their early films for large firms.

The problems confronting French film production in the period 1918–1928 are traceable to several factors. For one thing, imported films continued to pour into France in the 1920s. American films were the most numerous, especially early in the decade. Even though America's share declined steadily throughout the mid- to late 1920s, other countries, primarily Germany and Great Britain, gained ground faster than did France itself.

The situation for exports was little better. Foreign films were difficult to place in the lucrative American market, and only a tiny number of French films had any success there during this period. And with American films dominating most other markets, the French could count on only limited export—primarily to areas that already had a regular cultural exchange with France, such as Belgium, Switzerland, and French colonies in Africa and Southeast Asia. The French market itself was relatively small, and films seldom could make back their costs without wider exportation. Thus there was a continuous call for a distinctively French cinema that might help counter foreign competition, both at home and abroad. For several years after the war, it seemed as though the new French style that came to be known as Impressionism might help create that national cinema.

French production was also hampered by disunity. Before World War I two big companies, Pathé and Gaumont, had controlled the French film industry. After the war, both cut back severely on the riskiest sector of the industry, production, concentrating on surer profits from distribution and exhibition. Thus the largest French firms backed off from vertical integration just as vertically integrated firms were strengthening the Hollywood industry. France's production sector consisted of a few large and medium-size firms and of many small companies. The latter often made only one or a few films each and then disappeared. This artisanal production strategy offered little hope for successful competition with America.

Why were there so many small companies in France? The answer lies partly in domestic business traditions. In the 1920s, French business was still dominated by small companies; the move toward mergers and big corporations in other industrialized countries had not yet caught hold. During this decade, between 80 and 90 percent of French cinemas were owned by individuals. Similarly, many distribution and production firms were small and privately owned.

Because it was easier to make money in distribution and exhibition, people investing in the film industry usually put their money into one of these areas, avoiding the risks of production. As a result, the French tendency toward small production companies persisted. Someone, often a director or star, would raise money for a film. If it failed, the company went out of business or struggled along for another film or two. Many films of this era also had low budgets. Even by the late twenties, when the film industry was slightly better off, one expert estimated the average cost of a French feature at $30,000 (in 1927) to $40,000 (in 1928). (During the late 1920s, budgets for Hollywood features averaged more than $400,000.)

As a result, the interests of the three sectors of the industry—production, distribution, and exhibition—often conflicted. Most importantly, small exhibitors had no stake in French production. They wanted to show whatever would bring them the most money—usually American imports. Responding to the demands of theater owners, distributors provided Hollywood films. Moreover, it was often cheaper to purchase a foreign film than to produce a French film. Hence imported films undercut French ones.

Producers repeatedly called for the government to limit imported films. Inevitably, however, the more powerful distributors and exhibitors, who made most of their money on imports, opposed any quota, and they typically won out. Despite some minor measures to limit importation in the late 1920s, a strong quota was not passed until the 1930s.

Not only did the government fail to protect producers from foreign competition, it also assailed the industry with high taxes on movie tickets. During the 1920s, these taxes ran anywhere from 6 to 40 percent, depending on a theater's size and income. Such taxes hurt every level of the industry, since exhibitors could not risk losing patrons by raising admission prices, and hence they could not pay as much to the distributors and producers of the films.

To make matters still worse, technical facilities were outdated. As in other European countries, French producers depended on the glass studios built before the war. The lack of capital investment hampered companies in reequipping these studios to catch up with the technological innovations American firms had made during the 1910s, particularly in lighting (pp. 71–73).

Moreover, French filmmakers were unaccustomed to using artificial lighting extensively. In the late teens, French visitors to Hollywood were awed by the vast lighting systems. As director Henri Diamant-Berger observed in early 1918, "Lighting effects are sought and achieved in America by the addition of strong light sources, and not, as in France, by the suppression of other sources. In America, lighting effects are created; in France, shadow effects are created."[1] That is, French filmmakers would typically start with sunlight and block off parts of the light to create dark patches within the set. American filmmakers had more flexibility, eliminating sunlight altogether and creating exactly the effects they wanted with artificial light.

There were some attempts to bring this kind of control to French filmmaking. In 1919 director Louis Mercanton rigged up portable lighting equipment to take on location for his realist filmmaking. For the epic *The Three Musketeers* (1921–1922), Diamant-Berger installed American-style overhead lighting in a studio at Vincennes, which thus became one of the earliest studios in France to be so equipped. Modern lighting technology increasingly became available during the 1920s, but it remained too expensive for universal use.

Similarly, although some new studios were built, few had extensive backlots of the sort owned by the larger American and German producers. Most studios were in the Parisian suburbs, surrounded by houses rather than by open space. Large sets often had to be constructed in rented studios. Partly as a result of this and partly through a desire for realism, French filmmakers went on location more often than did their counterparts in other major producing countries. French chateaux, palaces, and other historic landmarks appear as the backdrops of many silent films; similarly, filmmakers made a virtue of necessity by using natural landscapes and scenes shot in French villages.

MAJOR POSTWAR GENRES

Despite foreign competition, industry disunity, lack of capital, government indifference, and limited technical resources, the French industry produced a variety of films. In most countries, serials declined in prestige during the late teens, but in France, they remained among the most lucrative films well into the 1920s. Big firms like Pathé and Gaumont found that a high-budget costume drama or literary adaptation could make a profit only when shown in several parts. Because moviegoers regularly attended their local theater, they were willing to return for all the episodes.

Some French serials of the postwar era followed the established pattern, with cliffhanger endings, master criminals, and exotic locales, as in Louis Feuillade's *Tih-Minh* (1919). But social pressures against the glorification of crime and perhaps also a sense that the formula was becoming stale led to changes. Feuillade, whose films were now virtually Gaumont's sole output, turned to serials based on popular sentimental novels with *Les Deux gamines* ("The Two Kids," 1921) and continued in this vein until his death in 1925. Diamant-Berger's epic adaptation of *The Three Musketeers* was among the decade's most successful films. Henri Fescourt directed *Mandrin* (1924), whose twelve episodes continued the traditions of kidnaps, disguises, and rescues—but presented them as swashbuckling feats in an eighteenth-century setting.

Whether made in serial format or not, many prestigious and expensive productions were historical epics. In many cases film companies economized by using French monuments as settings (Fig. 4.1). Such films were often intended for export. *The Miracle of the Wolves* (1924, Raymond Bernard) was the most lavish French historical film yet made; while its interiors used sets, many scenes were shot in the medieval town of Carcassone. The film's producer, the Société des Films Historiques, gave it a gala New York run, but, as often happened with such attempts, no American distributor purchased *The Miracle of the Wolves*.

A modest genre was the fantasy film, and its most prominent practitioner was René Clair. His first film, *Paris qui dort* ("Sleeping Paris," aka *The Crazy Ray*, 1924), was a comic story of a mysterious ray that paralyzes Paris. Clair used freeze-frame techniques and unmoving actors to create the sense of an immobile city. Several characters flying above the city escape the ray and proceed to live luxuriously by taking whatever they want; soon they track down the source of the problem and set things moving again. In Clair's *Le Voyage imaginaire* ("The Imaginary Journey," 1926), the hero dreams that he is transported by a witch to a fairyland, created with fancifully painted sets (Fig. 4.2). Such fantasies revived a popular tradition of the early cinema in France, drawing upon camera tricks and stylized sets somewhat as Méliès and Gaston Velle had done.

Comedies continued to be popular after the war. Max Linder, who had been lured briefly to Hollywood, returned to make comedies in France, including one of the earliest comic features, *Le Petit café* (1919, Raymond Bernard). Linder played a waiter who inherits a large sum of money but must go on working to fulfill his contract; comic scenes follow as he tries to get

Fig. 4.1 Some scenes in *L'Agonie des aigles* ("The Agony of the Eagles," 1921), a Pathé film about Napoléon, were shot on location outside Fontainebleau.

Fig. 4.2 Among the supernatural events in *Le Voyage imaginaire* is a scene in which a waxworks museum comes to life—including figures of Charlie Chaplin and Jackie Coogan as they appeared in Chaplin's 1921 film *The Kid.*

himself fired. The film's witty touches (Fig. 4.3) made it a surprise hit and helped give the comic genre more respectability in France. Other important comedies were made by Clair, whose *The Italian Straw Hat* (1928) brought him an international fame that would grow in the sound era.

THE FRENCH IMPRESSIONIST MOVEMENT

Between 1918 and 1923, a new generation of filmmakers sought to explore the cinema as an art. These directors considered French filmmaking stodgy and preferred the lively Hollywood films that had flooded into France during the war. Their films displayed a fascination with pictorial beauty and an interest in intense psychological exploration.

Fig. 4.3 Max Linder's comic feature *Le Petit café* combines intertitles with live action.

THE IMPRESSIONISTS' RELATION TO THE INDUSTRY

These filmmakers were aided by the crises that plagued the French industry. Because companies would often shift their policies or reorganize, filmmakers had various ways of obtaining financing. Some Impressionist directors also divided their time between avant-garde projects and more profit-oriented films. Germaine Dulac made some important Impressionist films, including *The Smiling Madame Beudet* and *Gossette* (both 1923), but she spent much of her career making more conventional dramas. Similarly, Jean Epstein directed costume pictures in between some of his most experimental works. Jacques Feyder was among the more commercially successful of French directors in the 1920s, making a huge hit, *L'Atlantide*, in 1921; yet he made Impressionist films from 1923 to 1926. Few Impressionists had the luxury of working full-time in their preferred style, yet they kept the movement going for over a decade.

Despite their avant-garde proclivities, these directors had to make their way within the regular commercial firms. The first to depart from established stylistic traditions was Abel Gance, who had entered filmmaking in 1911 as a scenarist and then began directing. Aside from making an unreleased Méliès-like fantasy, *La Folie du Dr. Tube* ("Dr. Tube's Madness," 1915), he had worked on commercial projects. With a passion for Romantic literature and art, however, Gance aspired to make more personal works. His *La Dixième symphonie* is the first major film of the Impressionist movement. It concerns a composer who writes a symphony so powerful that his friends consider it a successor to Beethoven's nine symphonies. Gance suggests the listeners' emotional reactions to the score by a series of visual devices (Fig. 4.4). Such attempts to convey sensations and emotional "impressions" would become central to the Impressionist movement.

Fig. 4.4 In *La Dixième symphonie*, Gance juxtaposes a dancer and piano keys to suggest the subjective impact of a musical passage.

La Dixième symphonie was produced by Charles Pathé, who continued to finance and distribute Gance's films after the director formed his own production company. This was a risk for Pathé, since some Gance films like *J'Accuse* and *La Roue* were lengthy and expensive. Yet Gance was the most

A CHRONOLOGY OF FRENCH IMPRESSIONIST CINEMA

1918 November: Germany and Austria surrender, ending World War I.

La Dixième symphonie ("The Tenth Symphony"), Abel Gance

1919 Summer: Independent company, Films Abel Gance, is formed.

J'Accuse ("I Accuse"), Abel Gance

Rose-France, Marcel L'Herbier

1920 January: Louis Delluc publishes *Le Journal du Ciné-Club,* then starts *Cinéa* in April.

Le Carnival des vérités ("Carnival of Truths"), Marcel L'Herbier

L'Homme du large ("The Man of the Open Sea"), Marcel L'Herbier

1921 *Fièvre* ("Fever"), Louis Delluc

El Dorado, Marcel L'Herbier

1922 Yermoliev's emigré company becomes Films Albatros.

La Femme de nulle part ("The Woman from Nowhere"), Louis Delluc

La Roue ("The Wheel"), Abel Gance

1923 *L'Auberge rouge* ("The Red Inn"), Jean Epstein

Don Juan et Faust ("Don Juan and Faust"), Marcel L'Herbier

La Souriante Madame Beudet (The Smiling Madame Beudet), Germaine Dulac

Coeur fidèle ("Faithful Heart"), Jean Epstein

Crainquebille, Jacques Feyder

Le Marchand de plaisir ("The Seller of Pleasure"), Jaque Catelain

Gossette ("The Little Kid"), Germaine Dulac

Le Brasier ardent ("The Burning Brazier"), Ivan Mosjoukine and Alexandre Volkoff

1924 March: Louis Delluc dies.

La Galérie des monstres ("The Freak Show"), Jaque Catelain

L'Inondation ("The Flood"), Louis Delluc

L'Inhumaine ("The Inhuman One"), Marcel L'Herbier

Kean, Alexandre Volkoff

Catherine, Albert Dieudonné (script by Jean Renoir)

La Belle Nivernaise ("The Beautiful Nivernaise"), Jean Epstein

L'Ironie du destin ("The Irony of Destiny"), Dimitri Kirsanoff

1925 *L'Affiche* ("The Poster"), Jean Epstein

Visages d'enfants ("Children's Faces"), Jacques Feyder

Feu Mathias Pascal ("The Late Mathias Pascal"), Marcel L'Herbier

La Fille de l'eau ("The Daughter of the Water"), Jean Renoir

1926 Les Films Jean Epstein is formed.

Gribiche, Jacques Feyder

Menilmontant, Dimitri Kirsanoff

1927 *6½ × 11*, Jean Epstein

La Glace à trois faces ("The Three-Sided Mirror"), Jean Epstein

Napoléon vu par Abel Gance ("Napoléon as Seen by Abel Gance"), Abel Gance

1928 Les Films Jean Epstein goes out of business.

L'Herbier's company, Cinégraphics, is absorbed by Cinéromans.

Brumes d'automne ("Autumn Mists"), Dimitri Kirsanoff

La Chute de la maison Usher (The Fall of the House of Usher), Jean Epstein

La Petite marchande d'allumettes (The Little Match Girl), Jean Renoir

1929 *L'Argent* ("Money"), Marcel L'Herbier

Finis Terrae ("The End of the Earth"), Jean Epstein

popular of the Impressionists. In a 1920 poll ranking the public's favorite films, the only French productions near the top were by Gance.

The other major firm, Gaumont, was making most of its money from Feuillade serials. It invested some of the profits in a group of films by Marcel L'Herbier, whose debut work, *Rose-France,* was the second Impressionist film. This allegory of war-battered France was so symbolic as to be nearly incomprehensible, and it was not widely seen. Still, L'Herbier made two more Impressionist films, *L'Homme du large* and *El Dorado,* for Gaumont, and by 1920 critics began to notice that France had a cinematic avant-garde.

Even Jean Epstein, who was to make some of the most experimental of the Impressionist films, began with a quasi-documentary, *Pasteur* (1923), for Pathé. Germaine Dulac was hired to direct her avant-garde character study, *The Smiling Madame Beudet,* by the Film d'Art company, which originated the project as an adaptation of a recent successful play.

Indeed, in these early years, the only Impressionist filmmaker who remained at the periphery of the industry was critic and theorist Louis Delluc. Using inherited money and assistance from other filmmakers, he supported the tiny companies that produced his low-budget films like *Fièvre.* A few years later, Jean Renoir, son of painter Auguste Renoir, ventured into different types of avant-garde filmmaking, including Impressionism, supported by his own money (derived in part from selling some of his father's paintings). Another Impressionist filmmaker, Dimitri Kirsanoff, worked with the most limited means of all, scraping together funds without any production company and making inexpensive films like *L'Ironie du destin* and *Menilmontant.*

One other firm made major contributions to Impressionism in its early years. The Russian production group, Yermoliev (p. 000), fleeing the Soviet government's nationalization of the film industry, settled in Paris in 1920 and reorganized as Albatros in 1922. At first this firm made popular fantasies, melodramas, and the like. The company's lead actor, Ivan Mosjoukine (who had changed his name from the Russian Mozhukhin), quickly became a major French star. In 1923, however, Albatros produced one of the most daring of the Impressionist films, *Le Brasier ardent,* co-directed by Mosjoukine and Alexandre Volkoff. In 1924 it made *Kean,* directed by Volkoff and starring Mosjoukine. Though a small company, Albatros was profitable, and it also produced Impressionist films by French directors: Epstein worked there in the mid-1920s, and L'Herbier's company co-produced *Feu Mathias Pascal* with Albatros.

The most prolific and successful directors of the movement were able to start their own companies. After his early successes for Pathé, Gance formed Films Abel Gance in 1919 (though it did not become financially independent of Pathé until 1924). After a disagreement with Gaumont over *Don Juan et Faust* in 1923, L'Herbier formed Cinégraphic. This firm produced most of L'Herbier's subsequent 1920s work and also financed Delluc's *L'Inondation* and two Impressionist films directed by one of L'Herbier's main actors, Jaque Catelain. Epstein formed Les Films Jean Epstein in 1926 and kept it going for two years, during which he made some of the Impressionist movement's most daring films. Such independent production fostered the Impressionist movement. As we shall see, after the filmmakers lost their small companies in quick succession, the movement faded.

IMPRESSIONIST THEORY

The style of the Impressionist movement derived partly from the directors' beliefs about the cinema as an art form. They expressed these beliefs in poetic, often abstruse essays and manifestos which helped define them as a distinct group.

The Impressionists saw art as a form of expression, conveying the personal vision of the artist. Art does not yield truth; instead, it creates an experience, and that experience leads to emotions for the spectator. Art creates these feelings not by making direct statements but by evoking or suggesting them. In short, artworks create fleeting feelings, or impressions. By the 1920s, this view of art was a bit old-fashioned, being rooted in nineteenth-century Romantic and Symbolist aesthetics.

Sometimes Impressionist theorists claimed that the cinema is a synthesis of the other arts. It creates spatial relationships, as architecture, painting, and sculpture do. Because cinema is also a temporal art, however, it combines its spatial qualities with rhythmic relationships comparable to those of music, poetry, and dance. On the other hand, Impressionist theorists also treated the cinema as a pure medium, presenting unique possibilities to the artist. This claim led some filmmakers to advocate making only *cinéma pur* ("pure cinema"), abstract films which concentrated on graphic and temporal form, often with no narrative (Chapter 8). Most Impressionists took a less radical course, making narrative films that explore the medium of cinema.

Whether a given writer claimed that films synthesized the older arts or created a totally new art form, all theorists agreed that film is the opposite of theater. Much French production was condemned as mere imitation of the stage. Most Impressionists believed that in order to avoid theatricality, films should display naturalistic acting. And indeed, the acting in many Impressionist films is strikingly restrained. For example, as the heroine of *Menilmontant*, Nadia Sibirskaia provides a model of the Impressionists' ideal of subtle, expressive acting. (See Fig. 4.8.) Similarly, the Impressionists advocated location shooting, and their films contain many evocative landscapes and authentic village scenes.

In trying to define the nature of the film image, the Impressionists often referred to the concept of *photogénie*, a term that indicates something more complex than an object's simply being "photogenic." For them, *photogénie* was the basis of cinema. Louis Delluc popularized the term around 1918, using it to define that quality which distinguishes a film shot from the original object photographed. The process of filming, according to Delluc, lends an object a new expressiveness by giving the viewer a fresh perception of it.

Kirsanoff wrote: "Each thing existing in the world knows another existence on the screen."[2] As this sentence suggests, *photogénie* could become a mystical concept. If we pin it down a bit, we can say that *photogénie* is created by the properties of the camera: framing isolates objects from their environment, black-and-white film stock transforms their appearance, special optical effects further change them, and so on. By such means, Impressionist theorists believed, the cinema gives us access to a realm beyond everyday experience. It shows us the souls of people and the essences of objects.

With respect to film form, the Impressionists insisted that cinema should not imitate theatrical or literary narratives. They also argued that film form should be based on "visual rhythm." This idea stems from the Impressionists' belief that emotions, rather than stories, should be the basis for films. It is hard to imagine a narrative film that depends solely on visual rhythm and eliminates causes and effects. Still, the Impressionists insisted that their attention to rhythm put their films closer to music than to any other art form.

FORMAL TRAITS OF IMPRESSIONISM

These assumptions about the nature of cinema had a considerable impact on the Impressionist films' style and narrative structure. Most importantly, filmic techniques often function to convey character subjectivity. This subjectivity includes mental images, such as visions, dreams, or memories; optical point-of-view (POV) shots; and characters' perceptions of events rendered without POV shots. While it is true that films in all countries had used such devices as superimpositions and flashbacks to show characters' thoughts or feelings, the Impressionists went much further in this direction.

As we have just seen, the Impressionists were also concerned about enhancing the *photogénie* of their films. Because of this, and because of their interest in character subjectivity, many of the Impressionists' innovations involve camerawork. Most obviously, Impressionist films frequently contain *optical devices* that affect the look of the photographic image.

Such optical devices might be present to enhance the image by making it more beautiful or striking (Figs. 4.5, 4.6). More often, though, optical tricks convey characters' impressions. *Superimpositions* may convey a character's thoughts or memories (Figs. 4.7, 4.8). A *filter* placed over the lens may

Fig. 4.5

Fig. 4.6

Fig. 4.5 Gance's *La Roue* contains many oval and round masks to change the rectangular shape of the image.

Fig. 4.6 In L'Herbier's *Rose-France*, an elaborate mask divides the frame into three images, centering the heroine as if in a traditional triptych painting.

Fig. 4.7

Fig. 4.8

Fig. 4.7 As the hero of L'Herbier's *Feu Mathias Pascal* sits in a moving train, we see what he is thinking through a series of images of his village and family, superimposed over the moving train tracks.

Fig. 4.8 When the heroine of *Menilmontant* stands on a bridge and contemplates suicide, the superimposition of the river over her face suggests her mental turmoil.

Fig. 4.9

Fig. 4.10

Fig. 4.11

Figs. 4.9 and 4.10 A filter creates a subjective effect in *El Dorado*.

Fig. 4.11 Filters for subjective effect in the wedding-night scene in *Napoléon*.

function to suggest subjectivity, usually without the shot's being taken from the character's optical POV. In L'Herbier's *El Dorado,* the heroine is a performer in a Spanish cabaret. While onstage, she worries about her sick son, and her distraction is suggested by a filter that blurs her figure but not the women around her (Fig. 4.9). As the other women snap her out of her reverie, the filter disappears and she comes into sharp view (Fig. 4.10). Here the feelings conveyed are those of the heroine, and the shot is not taken from anyone's POV. In *Napoléon,* the passion of Napoléon and Josephine as they kiss on their wedding night is conveyed by a series of gauze filters that drop one by one between the couple and the lens, gradually blurring the screen to gray (Fig. 4.11).

Occasionally the Impressionists would shoot into a curved mirror to distort the image. Such distortions could create a POV shot, as in Dulac's *The Smiling Madame Beudet;* this film contains many optical devices which convey the heroine's unhappiness with her boorish husband. In a point-of-view shot of M. Beudet, his wife's dislike leads her to see him as grotesque (Fig. 4.12). L'Herbier uses a similar mirror shot in *El Dorado* (Fig. 4.13), but here the framing is not from anyone's POV; it simply conveys the man's drunkenness subjectively.

Throwing the lens out of focus could also convey subjectivity, whether we see the characters or see through their eyes. In *Le Brasier ardent,* the heroine and her husband have just agreed to divorce, and she sadly stands thinking (Figs. 4.14, 4.15). After the hero of Renoir's *La Fille de l'eau* has been in a fight, he sits groggily as a POV shot conveys his mental state (Figs.

Fig. 4.12 Madame Beudet's view of her husband in *The Smiling Madame Beudet.*

Fig. 4.13 A shot made using a curved mirror, from L'Herbier's *El Dorado.*

Fig. 4.12

Fig. 4.13

Fig. 4.14

Fig. 4.15

Fig. 4.16

Fig. 4.17

Fig. 4.18

Fig. 4.19

Fig. 4.20

Fig. 4.21

Figs. 4.14 and 4.15 In *Le Brasier ardent,* the image goes out of focus to suggest the heroine's mental abstraction.

Figs. 4.16 and 4.17 A point-of-view shot in *La Fille de l'eau* shows the hero's vision blurred as a result of a beating.

Fig. 4.18 In Jacques Feyder's *Visages d'enfants,* a low camera height and slightly low angle show the optical POV of a child being scolded.

Fig. 4.19 A drunken woman's dizziness is conveyed in *Feu Mathias Pascal* through a canted framing as she staggers along a hallway.

Fig. 4.20 In *Feu Mathias Pascal,* Mathias dreams of leaping on his enemy.

Fig. 4.21 In a split-screen process he called Polyvision, Gance conveys the chaos of a pillow fight in *Napoléon.*

4.16, 4.17). Similarly, the framing of a shot may suggest characters' POVs or inner states (Figs. 4.18, 4.19).

Virtually any manipulation of the camera could be used subjectively. Slow motion was common in rendering mental images (Fig. 4.20). In *Napoléon,* Gance divided the frame into a grid of smaller, distinct images (Fig. 4.21). He also used three cameras side by side to create an extremely wide format called a *triptych* (Fig. 4.22). This functioned to create wide vistas, symbolic juxtapositions of images, and occasional subjective effects.

Impressionist films also feature camera movements which convey subjectivity and enhance *photogénie.* Moving shots could suggest the characters' optical POV (Fig. 4.23). The moving camera could also convey subjectivity without optical POV, as in the carnival scene in Epstein's *Coeur fidèle.* Here

Fig. 4.22 In *Napoléon*, three images joined horizontally create an epic vista of the hero surveying his troops.

Fig. 4.23 In *Napoléon*, Gance mounted the camera on a horse's back, putting us in the hero's position as he flees from pursuing soldiers.

Fig. 4.24 In *Coeur fidèle*, the camera is mounted on the swing along with the couple so that the background whirls past as the woman sits unmoving in the foreground.

the heroine sits miserably on a carnival ride with the fiancé her parents have forced upon her (Fig. 4.24).

Until 1923, camera devices for fostering *photogénie* and expressing subjectivity were the main distinguishing traits of Impressionism. In that year, however, two films appeared that experimented with quick editing to explore characters' mental states. Gance's *La Roue*, released in February, contains several scenes with very fast cutting. In one sequence, many short shots convey the overwrought emotions of the hero, Sisif. A railway engineer, he has fallen in love with Norma, a woman whom he has raised from a child and who thinks she is his daughter. He is driving the train upon which she is riding into the city to be married. In despair, he opens the throttle of the train, planning to crash it and kill himself and everyone aboard (Figs. 4.25–4.31). Figures 4.25 through 4.31 are respectively eleven, fourteen, fourteen, seven, six, five, and six frames long. Given that projection speeds were about twenty frames per second at this time, each shot would last less than a second, and the shortest would remain on the screen only for about a quarter of a second. Here excitement is conveyed less through acting than through a rhythmic rush of swift details.

Later in *La Roue*, Sisif's son Elie, who also loves Norma, has fallen over a cliff during a fight with her husband. As he dangles, he hears Norma calling and running to his rescue. Suddenly a close-up of his face introduces a radically abbreviated series of shots. Each is only one frame in length, showing Elie and Norma in situations from earlier scenes in the film. This barrage of instantaneous flashbacks is too brief to register on the eye (since twenty of them would pass in a single second!). The effect is a flicker, suggesting the confusion of Elie's emotions as he recognizes Norma's voice and then falls to his death. This scene is the first known use of single-frame shots in film history. Such segments of rhythmic montage made *La Roue* an enormously influential film during the 1920s.

A second film, Epstein's *Coeur fidèle*, which appeared in the autumn of 1923, also drew upon fast editing. We have already seen how the moving camera in the carnival scene helps suggest the heroine's unhappiness. The editing enhances this effect. As in *La Roue*'s train scene, details appear in a series of about sixty brief shots of the objects around the whirling-swings ride. Most of these shots are well under one second, and many are only two frames long. One brief segment, for example, shows the man the woman actually loves looking on from the ground (Fig. 4.32), a quick long shot of

Fig. 4.25

Fig. 4.26

Fig. 4.27

Fig. 4.28

Fig. 4.29

Fig. 4.30

Fig. 4.31

Fig. 4.32

Fig. 4.33

Fig. 4.34

Fig. 4.35

Figs. 4.25–4.31 In *La Roue*, a long series of shots, gradually decreasing in length, suggests the train's dangerous acceleration, Norma's growing anxiety, and Sisif's anguish.

Fig. 4.32 A shot lasting fifteen frames from *Coeur fidèle*.

Fig. 4.33 The next shot contains nineteen frames.

Figs. 4.34 and 4.35 Two two-frame shots follow.

the ride and crowd (Fig. 4.33), then quick flashes of two frames each of the heroine and her thuggish fiancé (Figs. 4.34, 4.35).

After the release of *La Roue* and *Coeur fidèle*, fast rhythmic editing became a staple of Impressionist filmmaking. It appears in the disorienting opening sequence of *Menilmontant*, where the violence of a double murder is conveyed through details caught in close, short shots. Gance pushed the technique he had innovated even further in the final scene of *Napoléon* by using swift editing in a triptych sequence, with rapid changes in three side-by-side frames, combined with multiple superimpositions. With fast cutting, the Impressionists achieved something of the "visual rhythm" they had called for in their writings.

Since the Impressionists were interested primarily in the effects of camerawork and editing on the subjects filmed, fewer distinctive traits of the movement lie in the area of mise-en-scene. Still, we can make some generalizations about this aspect of their style. Perhaps most importantly, the Impressionists were concerned about lighting objects so as to enhance their *photogénie* as much as possible (Fig. 4.36).

If filters placed over the lens could enhance a shot's photographic effect, then shooting through some translucent object placed in the setting of the scene could do the same. The Impressionists often shot through textured curtains (Fig. 4.37). In *Kean*, the hero's first meeting with the woman he will love has him holding a gauzy curtain up between them (Figs. 4.38, 4.39).

Finally, the Impressionists often tried to use striking settings. They did so in two opposing ways: first, by employing modernist decor and, second, by filming in real locations.

In French society in general, "modern" design of the type now labeled "Art Deco" was fashionable at the time. Some of the filmmakers used celebrated architects and artists as designers (Figs. 4.40, 4.41). As we saw earlier in this chapter, however, much French filmmaking of the 1920s depended in part on location shooting, and the Impressionists found *photogénie* in natural landscapes (Fig. 4.42). L'Herbier obtained unprecedented permission to shoot in the Alhambra in Spain for *El Dorado*, and part of *Feu Mathias Pascal* was done on location in Rome. The last portion of *La Roue* was filmed largely in the Swiss Alps, resulting in some arresting shots (Fig. 4.43).

The Impressionists' stylistic devices were startlingly innovative, yet most of their narratives were conventional. The plots place characters in extremely emotion-laden circumstances. A situation may trigger memories, which lead to flashbacks, or it may inspire visions of the characters' desires, or it may lead the character to get drunk, motivating distorted views of his or her surroundings. Impressionist characters faint, go blind, or fall into despair, and these states are vividly rendered through camera techniques.

As a result, Impressionist narratives depend to a considerable extent upon psychological motivation. As in classical narratives, cause and effect operate, but causes arise largely from characters' conflicting traits and obsessions. In L'Herbier's *Feu Mathias Pascal*, for example, a man living in a small French town marries, and his mother-in-law makes the couple miserable. In despair he seizes upon an accident that makes it appear that he has died. He takes up a new identity in Rome and falls in love—triggering visions and dreams of a new life. The entire film centers around his motivations and reactions.

Fig. 4.36 In Epstein's *L'Affiche*, the tools that the heroine uses in making artificial flowers are turned into a striking still life through arrangement and lighting.

Fig. 4.37 In Albert Dieudonné's *Catherine*, the heroine and her lover look through a curtained window.

Fig. 4.38

Fig. 4.39

Figs. 4.38 and 4.39 In *Kean,* we see a shot/reverse shot of the hero and heroine through a curtain that suggests their POVs.

Fig. 4.40

Fig. 4.41

Fig. 4.40 For *L'Inhumaine,* L'Herbier had the great French modern artist Fernand Léger design the laboratory of the scientist-hero.

Fig. 4.41 The exterior of the heroine's house was done by Rob. Mallet-Stevens—who was using similar designs for some of the most up-to-date buildings in Paris.

Fig. 4.42

Fig. 4.43

Fig. 4.42 In *L'Inondation,* Delluc films a character walking along a country road with the sun opposite the camera, transforming the landscape into one of the film's many lovely compositions.

Fig. 4.43 In *La Roue,* a fight leaves the heroine's husband lying atop a cliff high above a snowy landscape.

In Impressionist films, the devices of camerawork, editing, and mise-en-scène which we have described do not occur continuously throughout the narrative. Instead, the action usually progresses in a conventional fashion, punctuated by scenes in which we linger over characters' reactions and mental states. At the beginning of *El Dorado,* for example, there is a lengthy scene in which the heroine thinks of her sick son, with filters suggesting her lack of attention to the events around her (Figs. 4.9, 4.10). Yet much of the film is a conventionally melodramatic story of how she came to be in this situation and how she strives to escape from it.

Only a few Impressionist films attempted to create innovative narrative patterns which would make character subjectivity the basis for an entire film's form. Dulac achieves this in a relatively simple way with *The Smiling Madame Beudet;* this brief film contains only the simplest of plots, concentrating almost entirely on the heroine's fantasy life and hatred of her husband. In one of the Impressionist movement's most daring films, *La Glace à trois faces,* Epstein created a shifting, ambiguous plot. Three very different women describe their relations with the same man, and their tales create a contradictory idea of him. In the final scene, after writing to each woman with a different excuse for not meeting her, he has a fatal car accident. Nearly all the narrative information has been filtered through the three women's perceptions, and our direct views of the hero reveal little about him. The final, symbolic shot shows him reflected in a triple mirror, suggesting the impossibility of pinning down any "truth" about him. Few narrative films of the silent era departed so thoroughly from classical storytelling conventions. The innovations of *La Glace à trois faces* would resurface in the European art cinema of the 1950s and 1960s.

THE END OF FRENCH IMPRESSIONISM

Of the three European movements that overlapped during the 1920s, French Impressionism lasted the longest, from 1918 to early 1929. Late in the decade, several factors contributed to its decline. As the movement became better established, the interests of its filmmakers became more diverse. In addition, significant changes within the French film industry made it more difficult for some of them to retain control over their own work.

In the late 1910s and the first half of the 1920s, the Impressionists formed a tightly knit group, supporting each other in their mission to establish an alternative, artistic cinema. By mid-decade, they had succeeded to a considerable extent. While many of their films did not attract large audiences, they often received favorable reviews and were appreciated by the audiences of the ciné-clubs and art theaters. In 1925, Léon Moussinac, a leftist critic sympathetic to the Impressionists, published *Naissance du cinéma* ("The Birth of the Cinema"); there he summed up the movement's stylistic traits and the theoretical views of its filmmakers. Largely based on Delluc's writings, Moussinac's account stressed expressive techniques like slow motion and superimpositions, and it singled out the Impressionist group as the most interesting French filmmakers. His summary came at an appropriate time, since no significant concepts were developed in Impressionist theory after this point.

There was also a growing sense that the very success of Impressionism had led to a diffusion of its techniques and hence to a lessening of their impact. In 1927, Epstein remarked: "Original devices such as rapid montage or the tracking or panning camera are now vulgarized. They are old hat, and it is necessary to eliminate visibly obvious style in order to create a simple film."[3] Indeed, Epstein increasingly presented simple stories in a quasi-documentary style, using nonactors and eliminating flashy Impressionist camerawork and editing. His last Impressionist film, *Finis Terrae,* portrays two young lighthouse keepers on a rugged island; subjective camera techniques appear mainly when one youth falls ill. Epstein's early sound film, *Mor-Vran* (1931) eschews Impressionist style altogether in a restrained, poetic narrative of villagers on a desolate island.

Perhaps because the style's techniques were becoming somewhat commonplace, other Impressionist filmmakers began to experiment in different directions. If the era 1918–1922 can be said to have been characterized primarily by pictorialism, and the period 1923–1925 by the addition of rhythmic cutting, then the later years 1926–1929 saw a greater diffusion in the movement. By 1926 some Impressionist directors had achieved considerable independence by forming their own small producing companies. Moreover, the support provided by the ciné-clubs and small cinemas now allowed the production of low-budget experimental films. As a result of both these factors, the late Impressionist period saw a proliferation of short films, such as Kirsanoff's *Menilmontant* and the four films produced by Les Films Jean Epstein.

Another factor diversifying the Impressionist movement was the impact of experimental films. As we shall see in Chapter 8, Surrealist, Dadaist, and abstract films often shared the programs of the ciné-clubs and art cinemas with Impressionist films in the mid- to late 1920s. These tendencies were summed up under the term *cinéma pur* ("pure cinema"). Dulac wrote and lectured extensively in favor of *cinéma pur,* and in 1928 she abandoned commercial filmmaking to direct a Surrealist film, *The Seashell and the Clergyman.* Thereafter she concentrated on abstract short films.

Such stylistic diffusion might eventually have destroyed any unity among the Impressionists' work and ended the movement. In any event, the late 1920s saw a swift decline in these directors' independence. For one thing, their situation as small producers had always been shaky. They did not own their own studios but had to rent facilities for shooting. Each film had to be financed separately, and a filmmaker's credit was typically based on the success of the previous film.

Moreover, by the late 1920s, the large distribution firms were less interested in financing Impressionist films. In the first years of the movement, as we have seen, there had been some hope that these distinctive films might be competitive in the United States and Germany. Only a few Impressionist films, however, were exported to these markets, and even fewer met with success. The experiments of the late 1920s were hardly calculated to make these films more competitive, either at home or abroad.

Ironically, by 1926 the French economy as a whole was doing better than at any earlier point since the war's end. Inflation was finally curbed in that year. From 1926 to the end of the decade, France experienced the same boom period that most other countries were enjoying. By the late 1920s the film industry was showing some signs of strength. Several of the larger production firms merged during 1929 to form two major companies: Pathé, Natan, and Cinéromans merged into Pathé-Natan, and a separate combination of three firms created Gaumont-Franco-Film-Aubert. (As we shall see in Chapter 13, the strength of the French film industry was largely illusory and definitely transitory.)

The Impressionists fared badly during the late 1920s, with most losing their independent companies. In 1928 Cinéromans absorbed L'Herbier's Cinégraphic, reediting his expensive production, *L'Argent.* L'Herbier quit, but he was forced into more commercial projects in the sound era. That same year, Les Films Jean Epstein went out of business, though Epstein obtained independent backing for his modest non-Impressionist films. The tangled production history and huge budget of *Napoléon* made it impossible for Gance to remain independent; thereafter he was strictly supervised by his backers, and his subsequent films contain, at best, a shadow of his earlier experimentation.

The introduction of sound in 1929 made it virtually impossible for the Impressionists to regain their independence. Sound production cost far more, and it became more difficult to scrape together financing for even a short, low-budget avant-garde feature. In 1968, L'Herbier recalled the situation:

> When sound arrived, the working conditions in the profession became very difficult for a director like me. It was out of the question, for economic reasons, to envision films in the talking era like those which we had made in the silent era, perhaps even at the author's [i.e., the director's] expense. One had to censor oneself considerably and even, in my case, to adopt forms of cinema which I had always held in contempt. All at once, we were constrained, on account of talk, to do canned theater pieces, pure and simple.[4]

Although the French cinema of the 1930s created several distinctive trends, none of the major Impressionist filmmakers played a prominent role in those developments.

◆ NOTES AND QUERIES

FRENCH IMPRESSIONIST THEORY AND CRITICISM

The Impressionists' theoretical writings are still less well known, especially to English-language readers, than are those of the Soviet Montage group and more recent writers. There are some helpful basic sources in English, however. For brief introductions to Impressionist theory, see David Bordwell, *French Impressionist Cinema: Film Culture, Film Theory, and Film Style* (New York: Arno, 1980), chap. 3, and Stuart Liebman, "French Film Theory, 1910–1921," *Quarterly Review of Film Studies* **8,** 1 (Winter 1983): 1–23.

An extensive sampling of writings by Impressionists and by critics supportive of avant-garde cinema has been translated in Richard Abel's *French Film Theory and Criticism 1907–1939*, vol. 1 (Princeton, N.J.: Princeton University Press, 1988): Abel introduces each section of this book, providing a historical context for the writings. Collections of the writings of two major Impressionist theorists have made their work more accessible: Louis

Delluc, *Écrits cinématographiques*, I, "Le Cinéma et les Cinéastes" (Paris: Cinémathèque Française, 1985), II (in two volumes) "Cinéma et Cie" (same, 1986 and 1990), and III, "Drames de Cinéma" (same, 1990); and Jean Epstein, *Écrits sur le cinéma*, 2 vols. (Paris: Éditions Seghers, 1974 and 1975). The complete run of an important film journal to which several of the Impressionists contributed essays has been reprinted: *L'Art Cinématographique No. 1–8* (New York: Arno, 1970).

RESTORATION WORK ON *NAPOLÉON*

Like many other types of silent cinema, French Impressionist films are seldom seen by modern audiences. Few prints are in distribution, and some films have disappeared or survive only in truncated versions. For instance, Kirsanoff's first film, *L'Ironie du destin* (1924), is apparently lost forever, and there is probably no print of *La Roue* as long as the original version. Restoration efforts continue, however. In 1987 the Cinémathèque Française completed work on a pristine new print of Dulac's *Gossette*, of which only fragments had previously been viewable.

Undoubtedly the most famous restoration project has been Gance's *Napoléon*. It is not clear that this epic was ever shown exactly as Gance intended it. The longest version ran about six hours, but showings of it did not include the two side screens for the triptych sequences. Subsequent versions cut the film by more than half, and the triptychs were often eliminated. As the film was edited and reedited, scenes vanished.

Its reconstruction was initiated in 1969 and largely carried out by historian Kevin Brownlow. Jacques Ledoux, curator of the Royal Film Archive of Belgium, coordinated the search for footage preserved in other archives around the world. By 1979, a lengthy version premiered at the Telluride Film Festival. Over the next few years, other gala screenings were held in theaters and museums—but because more footage kept turning up, some of these versions were even longer. To complicate matters, Francis Ford Coppola arranged for a much-publicized run, with live orchestral accompaniment, at Radio City Music Hall in New York. The event was a huge success financially, but the Coppola release version *removed* about twenty minutes of footage to fit into a four-hour time slot. (This shortened version was released on videotape.) Later, even more footage turned up, and a second triptych sequence was recovered; even so, the film is incomplete. For an account of the reconstruction work to 1982 (as well as a history of the film's production and exhibition in the 1920s), see Brownlow's *Napoléon: Abel Gance's Classic Film* (New York: Knopf, 1983). The first chapter of Norman King's *Abel Gance: A Politics of Spectacle* (London: British Film Institute, 1984) discusses the ideological implications of the revival of Gance's work.

Napoléon is an unusual case, but it indicates that we should view with caution claims about "restored" or "reconstructed" versions. Sometimes these are simply new prints of the film, not versions which duplicate it as it was originally seen. Many preserved films lack all their intertitles, and new ones may be added that are derived from a source other than the original film (a script, a censorship document) and hence may not be exact replicas. Some restoration work adds colors or edits together surviving fragments largely on the basis of educated guesswork. Finally, some footage often remains lost. For example, the so-called restored version of the 1927 German Expressionist film *Metropolis,* released with a pop-music score in 1984, was actually missing well over an hour of footage—since those portions of the film are not known to survive anywhere. The history of the cinema includes the history of the preservation of films.

◆ REFERENCES

1. Henri Diamant-Berger, "Pour sauver le film français," *Le Film* **153** (16 Feb. 1918): 9.
2. Dimitri Kirsanoff, "Problèmes de la photogénie," *Cinéa-Ciné pour tous* **62** (1 June 1926): 10.
3. Rémy Duval, "M. Jean Epstein," *Comoedia* **5374** (23 Sept. 1927): 3.
4. Jean-André Fieschi, "Autour du Cinématographie: Entretien avec Marcel L'Herbier," *Cahiers du cinéma* **202** (June–July 1968): 41.

5

GERMANY
IN THE 1920s

THE GERMAN SITUATION AFTER
WORLD WAR I

Although Germany lost World War I and suffered severe economic and political problems as a result, it emerged from the war with a strong film industry. From 1918 to the Nazi rise to power in 1933, the German film industry ranked second only to Hollywood in size, technical sophistication, and world influence. Within a few years of the armistice, German films were seen widely abroad, and a major stylistic movement, Expressionism, arose in 1920 and continued until 1926. The victorious France could not rejuvenate its film industry, so how did Germany's become so powerful?

The German industry's expansion during World War I was due largely to the isolation created by the government's 1916 ban on most foreign films. The demand by German theaters led the number of producing companies to rise from 25 (1914) to 130 (1918). By the end of the war, however, the formation of the Universum Film Aktiengesellschaft (Ufa) started a trend toward mergers and larger companies.

Even with this growth, if the government had lifted the 1916 import ban at the end of the war, foreign films might have poured in again—chiefly from the United States. Unlike the situation in France, however, the German government supported filmmaking throughout this period. The ban on imports continued until December 31, 1920, giving producers nearly five years of minimal competition in their domestic market. The expansion of the war years continued, with about 300 film production companies in existence by 1921. Moreover, by 1922 most anti-German sentiment in enemy countries had been broken down, and German cinema became famous internationally.

Ironically, much of the film industry's success came as Germany underwent enormous difficulties stemming from the war. By late 1918, the war had pushed the country deep into debt, and there was widespread hardship. During the last month of the war, open revolt broke out, demanding the end of the monarchy and the war. On November 9, just two days before the armistice, the German Republic was declared, abolishing the monarchy. For a few months radical and liberal parties struggled for control, and it seemed as if a revolution similar to the one in Russia would occur. By mid-January 1919, however, the extreme left wing was defeated, and an election led to a coalition government of more moderate liberal parties. In general, the German political climate drifted gradually toward the right during the 1920s, culminating in the ascension of the Nazi party in 1933.

Internal strife was intensified by the harsh measures the Allies took in their treatment of Germany. The war officially ended with the signing of the infamous Treaty of Versailles on June 28, 1919. Rather than attempting to heal the rift with Germany, Great Britain and France insisted on punishing their enemy. A "war guilt" clause in the treaty blamed Germany as the sole instigator of the conflict. Various territories were ceded to Poland and France (with Germany losing 13 percent of its prewar land). Germany was forbidden to have more than 100,000 soldiers in its army, and they were not to carry weapons. Most crucially, the Allies expected Germany to pay for all wartime damage to civilian property, in the form of reparations payments of money and goods. (Only the United States demurred, signing its own peace treaty with Germany in 1921.) Resentments over these measures eventually helped right-wing parties come to power.

In the short run, these reparations gradually pushed the German financial system into chaos. The reparations arrangement required that Germany regularly send high payments in gold and ship food, coal, steel, heavy equipment, and other basic goods to the Allies. Although Germany was never able to fulfill the amounts demanded, domestic shortages soon developed and prices rose. The result was inflation, beginning at the war's end and becoming "hyperinflation" by 1923. The government printed nearly worthless paper money in great quantities, and food and consumer goods became scarce and outrageously costly. In early 1923, the mark, which had been worth approximately 4 to the dollar before the war, had sunk to about 50,000 to the dollar. By the end of 1923, the mark had fallen to around 6 billion to the dollar. People carried baskets of paper money simply to purchase a loaf of bread.

It might seem at first glance that such severe economic problems could not benefit anyone. Many people suffered: retirees on pensions, investors with money in fixed-rate accounts, workers whose earnings lost value by the day, renters who saw housing costs spiral upward. Big industry, however, benefited from high inflation. For one thing, people had little reason to save, since money lost its value sitting in a bank account or a mattress. Wage earners tended to spend their money while it was still worth something, and movies were among the products that were readily available. Film attendance was high during the inflationary period, and many new theaters were built.

Moreover, inflation encouraged export and discouraged import, giving German companies an international advantage. As the exchange rate of the mark fell, consumers were less likely to purchase foreign goods. Conversely, exporters could sell goods cheaply abroad, compared with manufacturers in other countries. Film producers benefited from this competitive boost. Importers could bring in relatively few foreign films, while countries in South America and eastern Europe could buy German films more cheaply than they could the Hollywood product. German film producers also got help from an extension of the import ban of 1916. Thus, for about two years after the war, the German film market was isolated from competition, and even after imports were permitted in 1921, unfavorable exchange rates protected the domestic cinema.

The favorable export situation fostered by high inflation fit in with the film industry's plans. Even during the war, the growth of the industry led to hopes for export. But what sorts of films would succeed abroad? More than any other country in postwar Europe, Germany found answers to that question.

GENRES AND STYLES OF GERMAN POSTWAR CINEMA

Partly because the German film industry operated in near isolation between 1916 and 1921, there were few radical changes in the types of films being made. The fantasy genre continued to be prominent, typified in films starring Paul Wegener, like *The Golem* (1920, Wegener and Henrik Galeen) and *Der verlorene Schatten* ("The Lost Shadow," 1921, Rochus Gliese). Directly after the war, the leftist political climate led to a brief abolition of censorship, and that in turn fostered a vogue for films on prostitution, venereal disease, drugs, and other social problems. The widespread belief that such films were pornographic led to the reinstitution of censorship. The same sorts of comedies and dramas that had dominated production in Germany and most other countries during the mid-teens continued to be made. We can, however, single out a few major trends of genre and style that gained prominence in the postwar era: the spectacle genre, the German Expressionist movement, and the *Kammerspiel* film.

SPECTACLES

Before the war, the Italians had gained worldwide success with historical epics, such as *Quo Vadis?* and *Cabiria.* After the war, the Germans tried a similar tactic, emphasizing lavish spectacles. Some of these films attained a success similar to that of the Italian epics and, incidentally, revealed the first major German director of the postwar era, Ernst Lubitsch.

Spectacular costume films appeared in a number of countries, but only companies able to afford large budgets could use them to compete interna-

Fig. 5.1 In *Madame Dubarry*, large sets and hundreds of extras re-create Revolutionary Paris.

tionally. Hollywood, with its high budgets and skilled art directors, could make *Intolerance* or *The Last of the Mohicans*, but productions on this scale were rare in Great Britain and France. During the inflationary period, however, the larger German companies found it relatively easy to finance historical epics. Some firms could afford extensive backlots, and they expanded studio facilities. The labor to construct sets and costumes was affordable, and crowds of extras could be hired at low wages. The resulting films were spectacular enough to compete abroad and could earn stable foreign currency. When Lubitsch made *Madame Dubarry* in 1919, for example, the film reportedly cost the equivalent of about $40,000. Yet when it was released in the United States in 1921, experts there estimated that such a film would cost perhaps $500,000 to make in Hollywood—at that time, a high price tag for a feature film.

Lubitsch, who became the most prominent director of historical epics, had begun his film career in the early 1910s as a comedian and director. His first big hit came in 1916 with *Schuhpalast Pinkas* ("Shoe-Palace Pinkas"), in which he played a brash young Jewish entrepreneur. It was his second film for the Union company, one of the smaller firms that merged to form Ufa, where he directed a series of more prestigious projects. Ossi Oswalda, an accomplished comedienne, starred in several comedies directed by Lubitsch in the late teens, including *Die Austernprinzessin* ("The Oyster Princess," 1919) and *Die Puppe* ("The Doll," 1919). But it was with Polish star Pola Negri that Lubitsch achieved international recognition.

Negri and Lubitsch first worked together in 1918 on *Die Augen der Mumie Ma* ("The Eyes of the Mummy Ma"). This melodramatic fantasy took place in an exotic Egyptian locale, and it was typical of German productions of the late 1910s. Negri's costar was the rising German actor Emil Jannings, and with these two Lubitsch went on in 1919 to make *Madame Dubarry*, based loosely on the career of Louis XV's mistress (Fig. 5.1). It was enormously successful, both in Germany and abroad. Lubitsch went on to make similar films, most notably *Anna Boleyn* (1920). In 1923 he became the first major German director hired to work in Hollywood. (Negri had preceded him under a long-term contract with Paramount.) Lubitsch quickly became one of the most skillful practitioners of the classical Hollywood style of the 1920s.

Historical spectacles remained in vogue as long as severe inflation enabled the Germans to sell them abroad at prices that no other country's film industry could match. But in the mid-1920s, the end of inflation dictated more modest budgets, and the spectacle genre became considerably less important.

THE GERMAN EXPRESSIONIST MOVEMENT

In late February 1920, a film premiered in Berlin that was instantly recognized as something new in cinema: *The Cabinet of Dr. Caligari*. Its novelty captured the public imagination, and it was a considerable success. The film uses stylized sets, with strange, distorted buildings painted on canvas backdrops and flats in a theatrical manner (Fig. 5.2). The actors make no attempt at realistic performance; instead, they exhibit jerky or dancelike movements.

Fig. 5.2 The heroine of *The Cabinet of Dr. Caligari* wanders through the Expressionist carnival set. It almost seems that she is made of the same material as is the fairground setting.

Critics announced that the Expressionist style, by then well established in most other arts, had made its way into the cinema, and they debated the benefits of this new development for film art.

Expressionism had begun around 1908 as a style in painting and the theater—appearing in other European countries, but finding its most intense manifestations in Germany. Many tendencies of nineteenth-century art had stressed realism and an orientation toward outward appearances; for example, French Impressionist painters sought to capture fleeting qualities of light. Expressionism was one of several trends around the turn of the century that reacted against realism and turned toward extreme distortion to express an inner emotional reality rather than surface appearances.

In painting, Expressionism was fostered primarily by two groups. *Die Brücke* ("The Bridge") was formed in 1906; its members included Ernst Ludwig Kirchner and Erich Heckel. Later, in 1911, *Der Blaue Reiter* ("The Blue Rider"), was founded; among its supporters were Franz Marc and Wassili Kandinsky. Although these and other Expressionist artists like Oskar Kokoschka and Lyonel Feininger had distinctive individual styles, they shared some traits. Expressionist painting avoided the subtle shadings and colors that gave realistic paintings their sense of volume and depth. Instead, the Expressionist often used large shapes of bright, unrealistic colors with dark, cartoonlike outlines (Color Plate 5.1). Faces would frequently be livid green; Marc's most common motif was groups of blue horses. Figures might be elongated; faces wore grotesque, anguished expressions. Buildings might sag or lean, with the ground tilted up steeply in defiance of traditional perspective (Color Plate 5.2). Such distortions were difficult for films shot on location, but *Caligari* showed how studio-built sets could approximate the stylization of Expressionist painting.

A more direct model for stylization in setting and acting was the Expressionist theater. As early as 1908, Oskar Kokoschka's play *Murderer, Hope of Women* was staged in an Expressionist manner. The style caught on during the teens, sometimes as a means of staging leftist plays protesting the war or capitalist exploitation. Sets often resembled Expressionist paintings, with large shapes of unshaded color in the backdrops (Fig. 5.3). The performances were comparably distorted. Actors shouted, screamed, gestured broadly, and moved in choreographed patterns through the stylized sets (Fig. 5.4). The goal was to express feelings in the most direct and extreme fashion possible. Similar goals led to extreme stylization in literature, and narrative techniques such as frame stories and open endings were adopted by scriptwriters for Expressionist films.

By the end of the 1910s, Expressionism had gone from being a radical experiment to being a widely accepted, even fashionable, style. Thus when *The Cabinet of Dr. Caligari* premiered, it hardly came as a shock to critics and audiences. Other Expressionist films quickly followed. The resulting stylistic trend lasted until the beginning of 1927.

What traits characterize Expressionism in the cinema? Historians have defined this movement in widely differing ways. (See Notes and Queries.) Some claim that there are only a few true Expressionist films: those that resemble *The Cabinet of Dr. Caligari* in using a distorted, graphic style of mise-en-scene derived from theatrical Expressionism. Of such films only

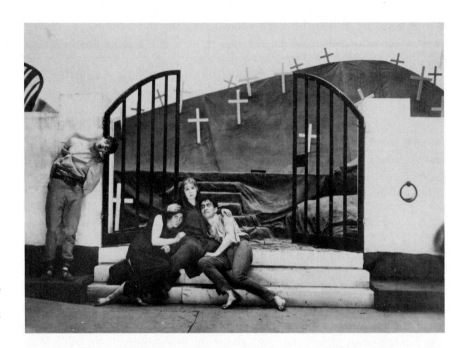

Fig. 5.3 A dark shape indicates a hill, and actors stare wide-eyed or assume grotesque postures in Fritz von Unruh's play, *Ein Geschlecht* (1918).

Fig. 5.4 Actors costumed as skeletons writhe within an abstract landscape of barbed wire in Ernst Toller's *Die Wandlung* (1919).

perhaps half a dozen were made. Other historians classify a larger number of films as Expressionist because the films all contain some types of stylistic distortion that *function* in the same ways that the graphic stylization in *Caligari* does. By this broader definition (which we will adopt here), there are close to two dozen Expressionist films, released in the period 1920–1927. Like French Impressionism, German Expressionism uses the various techniques of the medium—mise-en-scene, editing, and camerawork—in distinctive ways. We shall look first at these techniques, then go on to examine the narrative patterns that typically helped motivate the extreme stylization of Expressionism.

A CHRONOLOGY OF GERMAN EXPRESSIONIST CINEMA

1920 February: Decla company releases *Das Cabinet des Dr. Caligari (The Cabinet of Dr. Caligari)*, directed by Robert Wiene; it starts the Expressionist movement.

Spring: Decla and Deutsche Bioscop merge to form Decla-Bioscop; under Erich Pommer's supervision, Decla-Bioscop produced many of the major Expressionist films.

Algol, Hans Werckmeister

Der Golem (The Golem), Paul Wegener and Carl Boese

Genuine, Robert Wiene

Von Morgens bis Mitternacht (From Morn to Midnight), Karl Heinz Martin

Torgus, Hans Kobe

1921 November: Ufa absorbs Decla-Bioscop, which remains a separate production unit under Pommer's supervision.

Der müde Tod ("The Weary Death," aka *Destiny*), Fritz Lang

Das Haus zum Mond ("The House on the Moon"), Karl Heinz Martin

1922 *Dr. Mabuse, der Spieler (Dr. Mabuse, the Gambler)*, Fritz Lang

Nosferatu, F. W. Murnau

1923 *Schatten (Warning Shadows)*, Artur Robison

Der Schatz ("The Treasure"), G. W. Pabst

Raskolnikow, Robert Wiene

Erdgeist ("Earth Spirit"), Leopold Jessner

Der steinere Reiter ("The Stone Rider"), Fritz Wendhausen

1924 Autumn: Hyperinflation ends.

Wachsfigurenkabinett (Waxworks), Paul Leni

Die Nibelungen, in two parts: *Siegfried* and *Kriemhilds Rache (Siegfried* and *Kriemhild's Revenge)*, Fritz Lang

Orlacs Hände (The Hands of Orlac), Robert Wiene

1925 December: Ufa is rescued from bankruptcy by loans from Paramount and MGM.

Tartüff (Tartuffe), F. W. Murnau

Die Chronik von Grieshuus (The Chronicle of the Grey House), Arthur von Gerlach

1926 February: Erich Pommer is forced to resign as head of Ufa.

September: *Faust*, F. W. Murnau

1927 January: *Metropolis*, Fritz Lang

While the main defining traits of French Impressionism lay in the area of camerawork, German Expressionism is distinctive primarily for its use of mise-en-scene. In 1926, set designer Hermann Warm (who worked on *Caligari* and other Expressionist films) was quoted as believing that "the film image must become graphic art."[1] Indeed, German Expressionist films emphasize the composition of individual shots to an exceptional degree. Any shot in a film creates a visual composition, of course, but most films draw our attention to specific elements rather than to the overall design of the shot. In classical films, the human figure is the most expressive element, and the sets, costume, and lighting are usually secondary to the actors. The three-dimensional space in which the action occurs is more important than are the two-dimensional graphic qualities on the screen.

In Expressionist films, the expressivity associated with the human figure extends into every aspect of the mise-en-scene. During the 1920s, descriptions of Expressionist films often referred to the sets as "acting" or as blending in with the actors' movements. In 1924, Conrad Veidt, who played Cesare in *Caligari* and acted in several other Expressionist films, explained: "If the decor has been conceived as having the same spiritual state as that which governs the character's mentality, the actor will find in that decor a valuable

Fig. 5.5 In the Burgundian court in *Siegfried*, ranks of soldiers and decor alike form geometric shapes that combine into an overall composition.

Fig. 5.6 In *The Golem*, an animated clay statue emerges onto a rooftop, looking as if he is made of the same material as his surroundings.

Fig. 5.7 A symmetrical shot in *Algol* shows a corridor made up of repeated abstract black and white shapes and lines.

aid in composing and living his part. He will blend himself into the represented milieu, and both of them will *move* in the same rhythm."[2] Thus not only did the setting function as almost a living element, but the actor's body became a visual element.

In practice, this blend of set, figure behavior, costumes, and lighting fuses into a perfect composition only at intervals. A narrative film is not like the traditional graphic arts of painting or engraving. The plot must advance, and the composition breaks up as the actors move. Thus in Expressionist films the action often proceeds in fits and starts, and the narrative pauses or slows briefly for moments when mise-en-scene elements align into eye-catching compositions. (Such compositions need not be wholly static. An actor's dancelike movement may combine with a stylized shape in the set to create a visual pattern.)

Expressionist films had many tactics for blending the settings, costumes, figures, and lighting. These include the use of stylized surfaces, symmetry, distortion, and exaggeration and the juxtaposition of similar shapes.

Stylized surfaces might make disparate elements within the mise-en-scene seem similar. For example, Jane's costumes in *Caligari* are painted with the same jagged lines as are the sets (Fig. 5.2). In *Siegfried*, many shots are filled with a riot of decorative patterns (Fig. 5.5). In *The Golem*, texture links the Golem to the distorted ghetto sets, since both look as if they are made of soft clay (Fig. 5.6).

Symmetry offers a way to combine actors, costumes, and sets so as to emphasize overall compositions. Figure 5.5, the Burgundian court in *Siegfried*, uses symmetry, as do scenes in most of Lang's films of this period. Another striking instance occurs in *Algol* (Fig. 5.7).

Perhaps the most obvious and pervasive trait of Expressionism is the use of distortion and exaggeration. In Expressionist films, houses are often pointed and twisted, chairs are tall, staircases are crooked and uneven (compare Figs. 5.8–5.10).

To modern viewers, performances in Expressionist films may look simply like extreme versions of "silent-film acting." Yet Expressionist acting was deliberately heightened and exaggerated to match the style of the entire mise-en-scene. In long shot, gestures could be dancelike as the actors moved in patterns dictated by the sets. Conrad Veidt "blends into the represented milieu" in *Caligari* when he glides on tiptoe along a wall, his extended hand skimming its surface (Fig. 5.11). This is a case where a tableau involves movement rather than a static composition.

This principle of exaggeration governed close-ups of the actors as well (Fig. 5.12). In general, Expressionist actors work against an effect of natural behavior, often moving jerkily, pausing, and then making sudden gestures. Such performances should be judged not by standards of realism but by how the actors' behavior fits into the mise-en-scene as a whole.

A final, crucial trait of Expressionist mise-en-scene is the juxtaposition of similar shapes within a composition. Along with Wiene and Lang, F. W. Murnau was one of the major figures of German Expressionism, yet his films contain relatively few of the obviously artificial, exaggerated sets that we find in other films of this movement. He does create, however, numerous stylized compositions in which the figures blend in with their surroundings (Figs.

Fig. 5.8

Fig. 5.9

Fig. 5.10

Fig. 5.11

Fig. 5.12

Fig. 5.13

Fig. 5.14

Fig. 5.8 The old, sagging house in G. W. Pabst's *Der Schatz.*

Fig. 5.9 The leaning buildings and lamppost in Wiene's *Raskolnikow,* an adaptation of *Crime and Punishment.*

Fig. 5.10 A stairway in *Torgus* seems to lean dizzily, with a slender black triangle painted on each tread.

Fig. 5.11 In this famous shot from *The Cabinet of Dr. Caligari,* the diagonal composition of the wall dictates the movement of the actor, with his tight black clothes contributing to the compositional effect.

Fig. 5.12 In *Kriemhild's Revenge,* Marguerithe Schön's wide-eyed stare, together with her heavy make-up, the abstract shapes in her costume, and the blank background, create a stylized composition completely in keeping with the rest of the film.

Fig. 5.13 Count Orlak and his guest are placed within a nested set of four archways, with the hunched back of the vampire and the rounded arms of Hutter echoing the innermost arch. (Arches become an important motif in *Nosferatu,* associated closely with the vampire and his coffin.)

Fig. 5.14 In Murnau's *Tartuffe,* the title character's pompous walk is set off against the legs of a huge cast-iron lamp.

5.13, 5.14). A common ploy in Expressionist films is to pose human figures beside distorted trees to create similar shapes (Fig. 5.15).

For the most part, Expressionist films use simple lighting from the front and sides, illuminating the scene flatly and evenly to stress the links between the figures and the decor. In some notable cases, shadows are used to create additional distortion (Fig. 5.16).

Although the main traits of Expressionist style come in the area of mise-en-scene, we can make a few generalizations about its typical use of other film techniques. Such techniques usually function unobtrusively to display the mise-en-scene to best advantage. Most editing is simple, drawing upon continuity devices like shot/reverse shot and crosscutting. In addition, German films are noted for having a somewhat slower pace than other films of this period. Certainly in the early twenties they have nothing comparable to the quick rhythmic editing of French Impressionism. This slower pace gives

Fig. 5.15

Fig. 5.16

Fig. 5.15 A woman's stance in *The Stone Rider* echoes the shape of the stylized tree behind her.

Fig. 5.16 In *Nosferatu*, the vampire creeps up the stairway toward the heroine, but we see only his shadow, huge and grotesque.

us time to scan the distinctive compositions created by the Expressionist visual style.

Similarly, the camerawork is typically functional rather than spectacular. Many Expressionist sets used false perspective to form an ideal composition when seen from a specific vantage point. Thus camera movement and high or low angles are relatively rare, and the camera tends to remain at a straight-on angle and an approximately eye-level or chest-level height. In a few cases, however, a camera angle could create a striking composition by juxtaposing actor and decor in an unusual way (Fig. 5.17).

Like the French Impressionists, Expressionist filmmakers gravitated to certain types of narratives that suited the traits of the style. The movement's first film, *The Cabinet of Dr. Caligari*, used the story of a madman to motivate the unfamiliar Expressionist distortions for movie audiences. Because *Caligari* has remained the most famous Expressionist film, there is a lingering impression that the style was used mainly for conveying character subjectivity.

This was not the case in most films of the movement, however. Instead, Expressionism was often used for narratives that were set in the past or in exotic locales or that involved elements of fantasy or horror—genres which remained popular in Germany in the 1920s. *Der Schatz* takes place at an unspecified point in the past and concerns a search for a legendary treasure. The two feature-length parts of *Die Nibelungen, Siegfried* and *Kriemhild's Revenge,* are based on the national German epic and include a dragon and other magical elements in a medieval setting. *Nosferatu* is a vampire story set in the mid-nineteenth century, and in *The Golem*, the rabbi of the medieval ghetto in Prague animates a superhuman clay statue to defend the Jewish population against persecution. In a variant of this emphasis upon the past, the last major Expressionist film, *Metropolis*, is set in a futuristic city where the workers labor in huge underground factories and live in apartment blocks, all done in Expressionist style.

In keeping with this emphasis on remote ages and fantastic events, many Expressionist films have frame stories or self-contained stories embedded within the larger narrative structure. *Nosferatu* is supposedly told by the town historian of Bremen, where much of the action takes place. Within the narrative, the characters read books: the *Book of the Vampires* explains the basic premises of vampire behavior (exposition that would have been necessary, since this was the first of many vampire films), and entries in the log

Fig. 5.17 In *Tartuffe*, a high angle places an actor against a swirl of abstract lines created by a stairway.

Plate 1.1 *Faust aux Enfers* (*The Damnation of Faust*, 1903)

Plate 2.1 An unidentified Pathé film, c. 1905

Plate 2.2 *La Fille du Margrave* ("Margrave's Daughter," 1912)

Plate 2.3 An unidentified Urban-Eclipse film, c. 1907

Plate 2.4 *Jephtah's Daughter* (1909)

Plate 2.5 *The Will* (1912, Eclair)

Plate 5.1 "Dodo with a Feather Hat" (1911, Ernst Ludwig Kirchner)

Plate 5.2 "In a Village near Paris" (or "Street in Paris, Pink Sky," 1909, Lyonel Feininger)

Plate 6.1 El Lissitsky's Constructivist composition, "Beat the Whites with the Red Wedge."

Plate 8.1 *Cirano di Bergerac*

Plate 10.1 *Under a Texas Moon* (1930)

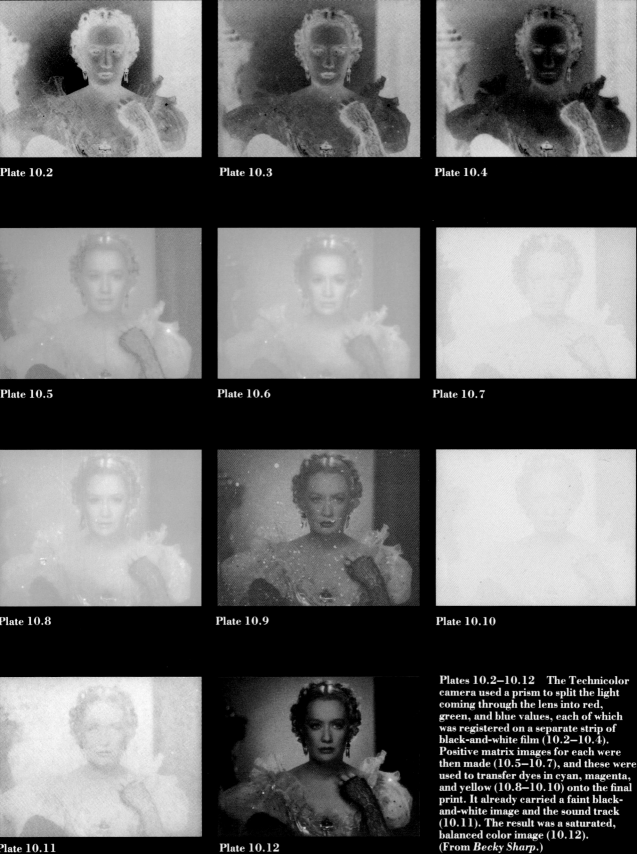

Plate 10.2

Plate 10.3

Plate 10.4

Plate 10.5

Plate 10.6

Plate 10.7

Plate 10.8

Plate 10.9

Plate 10.10

Plate 10.11

Plate 10.12

Plates 10.2–10.12 The Technicolor camera used a prism to split the light coming through the lens into red, green, and blue values, each of which was registered on a separate strip of black-and-white film (10.2–10.4). Positive matrix images for each were then made (10.5–10.7), and these were used to transfer dyes in cyan, magenta, and yellow (10.8–10.10) onto the final print. It already carried a faint black-and-white image and the sound track (10.11). The result was a saturated, balanced color image (10.12). (From *Becky Sharp*.)

Plate 10.13 *La Cucaracha*

Plate 10.14 *The Three Little Pigs*

Plate 10.15 *Bambi*

Plate 10.16 *Thugs with Dirty Mugs*

of the ship that carries Count Orlak to Bremen recount additional action. The central story of *Warning Shadows* (1923) consists of a shadow play that a showman puts on during a dinner party, with the shadow figures coming to life and acting out the guests' secret passions. *Tartuffe* begins and ends with a frame story in which a young man tries to warn his aging father that the housekeeper is out to marry him for his money; his warning takes the form of a film of Molière's play *Tartuffe,* which constitutes the inner story.

Some Expressionist films do take place in the present. Lang's *Dr. Mabuse, the Gambler* uses Expressionist style to satirize the decadence of modern German society: the characters patronize drug and gambling dens in night-clubs with Expressionist decor, and one couple lives in a lavish house decorated in the same style. In *Algol,* a greedy industrialist receives supernatural aid from the mysterious star Algol and builds up an empire; the sets representing his factories and the star are Expressionist in style. Thus in the cinema Expressionism had the same potential for social comment that it did on the stage. In most cases, however, filmmakers used the style to create exotic and fantastic settings that were remote from contemporary reality.

KAMMERSPIEL

Another German trend of the early 1920s had less international impact but led to the creation of a number of major films. This was the *Kammerspiel,* or "chamber-drama" film. The name derives from a theater, the *Kammerspiele,* opened in 1906 by the major stage director Max Reinhardt in order to stage intimate dramas for small audiences. Few *Kammerspiel* films were made, but nearly all are classics: Lupu Pick's *Shattered* (1921) and *Sylvester* (aka *New Year's Eve* or *St. Sylvester's Eve,* 1923), Leopold Jessner's *Backstairs* (1921), Murnau's *The Last Laugh* (1924), and Carl Dreyer's *Michael* (1924). Remarkably, all these films except *Michael* were scripted by the important scenarist Carl Mayer, who also co-scripted *The Cabinet of Dr. Caligari* and wrote other films, both Expressionist and non-Expressionist. [Another Mayer-scripted *Kammerspiel* directed by Leopold Jessner, *Erdgeist* (1923), is lost except for an excerpt that suggests it was made in Expressionist style.] Mayer can be considered the main force behind the *Kammerspiel* genre.

In many ways these films were opposed to the Expressionist drama. A *Kammerspiel* film concentrated on a few characters and explored a crisis in their lives in detail. The emphasis was on slow, evocative acting and telling details, rather than extreme expressions of emotion. The chamber-drama atmosphere came from the use of a small number of settings and a concentration on character psychology rather than spectacle. Some Expressionist-style distortion might appear in the sets, but it typically suggested dreary surroundings rather than the fantasy or subjectivity of Expressionist films. Indeed, the *Kammerspiel* avoided the fantasy and legendary elements so common in Expressionism; these were films set in everyday, contemporary surroundings, and they often covered a short span of time.

Sylvester, for example, takes place during a single evening in the life of a café owner. His mother visits his family for a New Year's Eve celebration. Jealousies and conflicts between the mother and the wife intensify until, as

Fig. 5.18 In *Sylvester*, a motif of shots using a mirror on the wall emphasizes the relationships among the characters within the family's drab home.

Fig. 5.19 Much of the action in *Backstairs* consists of the mailman's trips back and forth across the courtyard as he visits the heroine.

midnight strikes, the man commits suicide. Brief scenes of people celebrating in hotels and in the streets create an ironic contrast with the tensions of these three characters, but most of the action occurs in the small apartment (Fig. 5.18). As with most major *Kammerspiel* films, *Sylvester* uses no intertitles, depending on simple situations, details of acting and setting, and symbolism to convey the narrative events.

Similarly, *Backstairs* balances two settings. The boardinghouse kitchen in which the housekeeper works and the apartment of her secret admirer, the mailman, stand opposite each other in a grubby courtyard. The film's action never moves outside this area. When the heroine's departed fiancé mysteriously fails to write to her, the mailman tries to console her by forging letters from him (Fig. 5.19). Finally she visits the mailman in his little apartment— at which point the fiancé returns and is killed in a struggle with the mailman. The heroine then commits suicide by throwing herself into the courtyard from the top of the building.

As these examples suggest, the narratives of the *Kammerspiel* films concentrated on intensely psychological situations and concluded unhappily. Indeed, *Shattered, Backstairs,* and *Sylvester* all end with at least one violent death, and *Michael* closes with the death of its protagonist from illness. Because of the unhappy endings and claustrophobic atmospheres, these films intrigued mostly critics and highbrow audiences. Erich Pommer recognized this fact when he produced *The Last Laugh,* insisting that Mayer add a happy ending. This story of a hotel doorman who is demoted from his lofty post to that of lavatory attendant was to have concluded with the hero sitting in the rest room in despair, possibly dying. Mayer, upset at having to change what he saw as the logical outcome of his script's situation, added a blatantly implausible final scene in which a sudden inheritance turns the doorman into a millionaire to whom all the hotel staff cater. Whether this ludicrously upbeat ending was the cause, *The Last Laugh* became the most successful and famous of the *Kammerspiel* films. By late 1924, however, the trend ceased to be a prominent genre in German filmmaking.

GERMAN FILMS ABROAD

The exploration of distinctive types of films such as the spectacle, the Expressionist film, and the *Kammerspiel* drama helped the German industry break down prejudices abroad and gain a place on world film markets. Lubitsch's *Madame Dubarry* was one of the first postwar German films to succeed abroad. It showed in major cities in Italy, Scandinavia, and other European countries in 1920, becoming famous even in countries like England and France, where exhibitors had pledged not to show German films for a lengthy period after the war. In December 1920 *Madame Dubarry,* retitled *Passion,* broke box-office records in a major New York theater and was released throughout the United States by one of the largest distributors, First National. Suddenly American film companies were clamoring to buy German films, though few found the success of *Passion.*

More surprisingly, German Expressionism also proved an export commodity. There was particularly strong anti-German sentiment in France. Yet

The Cabinet of Dr. Caligari had an international reputation by late 1921 (having already had a mildly successful release in America after its triumph in Germany). In September the French critic and filmmaker Louis Delluc arranged for *Caligari* to be shown as part of a program to benefit the Red Cross. So great was the film's impact that it opened in a regular Parisian cinema in April 1922. A fashion for German film followed. Works by Lubitsch, as well as virtually all the Expressionist and *Kammerspiel* films, played in France over the next five years. A similar fad for Expressionism hit Japan in the early twenties, and in many countries, these distinctive films had at least limited release to art-house audiences.

Major Changes
in the Mid- to Late 1920s

Despite these early successes, however, the German industry could not continue making films in the same way. Many factors led to major changes. Foreign technological and stylistic influences had considerable impact. Moreover, the protection afforded the industry by the high postwar inflation ended as the German currency was stabilized in 1924. Success also created new problems, as prominent filmmakers were lured away to work in Hollywood. A continued stress on export led some studios to imitate Hollywood's product rather than seek alternatives to it. In the middle of the decade, a major trend called *Neue Sachlichkeit* displaced Expressionism. By 1929, the German cinema had changed greatly from its postwar situation.

THE TECHNOLOGICAL UPDATING
OF THE GERMAN STUDIOS

Technological resources for filmmaking developed rapidly in the course of the 1920s. Because inflation encouraged film companies to invest their capital in facilities and land, many studios were built or expanded. Ufa, for example, enlarged its two main complexes at Tempelhof and Neubabelsberg and soon owned the best-equipped studios in Europe, with an extensive backlot at Neubabelsberg that could accommodate several enormous sets. Here were made such large-scale productions as Lang's *The Nibelungen* and Murnau's *Faust.* Foreign producers, primarily from England and France, rented Ufa's facilities for shooting large-scale scenes.

Additional large facilities also became available. In 1922, an investment group converted a zeppelin hangar into the world's largest indoor production facility, the Staaken studio. The studio was rented to producing firms for sequences requiring large sets. Scenes from such films as Lang's epic *Metropolis* were shot in Staaken.

Other innovations during the 1920s responded to German producers' desire to give their films impressive production values. Designers pioneered the use of false perspectives and models to make sets look bigger. A marginal Expressionist film, *The Street* (1923), uses an elaborate model to represent a

Fig. 5.20 An elaborate use of false perspective in *The Last Laugh.*

Fig. 5.21 Hollywood-style backlighting in *The Loves of Pharaoh.*

Fig. 5.22 One portion of an elaborate tracking shot through a street in *Sylvester.*

cityscape in the background of one scene, with a real car and actors in the foreground. Tiny cars and dolls moving on tracks in the distance in *The Last Laugh* make the street in front of the hotel set seem bigger than it really is (Fig. 5.20). This was one case where the Germans were ahead of the Americans, and Hollywood cinematographers and designers picked up tips on models and false perspective by watching German films and visiting the German studios.

Aside from making more spectacular scenes, German producers wanted to light and photograph their films using techniques innovated by Hollywood during the 1910s. Since the Germans were eager to export films to the United States, a widespread assumption arose that filmmakers should adopt the new elements of American style, such as backlighting and the use of artificial illumination for exterior shots. Articles in the trade press urged companies to build better facilities: dark studios in place of the old glass-walled ones, endowed with the latest in lighting equipment.

The installation of American-style lighting equipment began in 1921, when Paramount made a short-lived attempt at producing in Berlin. It outfitted a Berlin studio with the latest technology, painting over the glass roof to permit artificial lighting. There Lubitsch made one of his last German films, *Das Weib des Pharoa* ("The Pharaoh's Wife," released in the United States as *The Loves of Pharaoh*, 1921), which was shot with extensive backlighting and effects lighting (Fig. 5.21). By mid-decade, most major German firms had the option of filming entirely with artificial light.

One German technological innovation of the 1920s became internationally influential: the *entfesselte camera* (literally, the "unfastened camera," or the camera moving freely through space). During the early 1920s, some German filmmakers began experimenting with elaborate camera movements. In the script for the *Kammerspiel* film *Sylvester*, Carl Mayer specified that the camera should be mounted on a dolly to take it smoothly through the revelry of a city street (Fig. 5.22). The film that popularized the moving camera, though, was Murnau's *The Last Laugh*. There the camera descends in an elevator in the opening shot; later it seems to fly through space to follow the blare of a trumpet to the protagonist, who is listening in a window high above. When he gets drunk at a party, the camera spins with him on a turntable (Figs. 5.23, 5.24). The film was widely seen in the United States and earned Murnau a contract with Fox. Another film made in the following year, *Variety* (1925, E. A. Dupont) took the idea of the moving camera even further (Fig. 5.25). Many other German films of the mid- to late 1920s contain spectacular camera movements.

As we saw in the previous chapter, the French Impressionist filmmakers were already experimenting with the moving subjective camera in the early 1920s. Their films, however, were not widely influential abroad. German filmmakers received worldwide credit for the new technique. Just as *Cabiria* had created a vogue for the tracking camera in the mid-teens, now *The Last Laugh* and *Variety* inspired cinematographers to seek ways of moving the camera more fluidly. During the late 1920s, a wide range of techniques like elevators, swings, cranes, and turntables "unfastened" the camera from its tripod. As a result, many late silent films from various countries contain impressive mobile framings.

Fig. 5.23

Fig. 5.24

Fig. 5.25

Once inflationary pressures ended in 1924, the German film industry could not continue the rapid expansion of its facilities. Most firms cut back between 1924 and 1926. Big-budget films became less common, and the large studios were less busy. Still, the new lighting equipment and expanded studios were in place, ready for use in the more modest productions that dominated the second half of the decade. The end of hyperinflation, however, had other, more serious effects on the film industry.

Figs. 5.23 and 5.24 In *The Last Laugh*, the background whirls past behind the protagonist, conveying his dizziness.

Fig. 5.25 *Variety* placed the camera on trapezes to convey the subjective impressions of acrobats.

THE END OF INFLATION

Although the high inflation of the postwar years benefited the film industry in the short run, it was impossible for Germany to continue functioning under the circumstances. By 1923, hyperinflation brought the country near chaos, and the film industry began to reflect this. At a time when a potato or a postage stamp could cost hundreds of millions of marks, budgeting a feature film months in advance became nearly impossible.

In November 1923, the government tried to halt hyperinflation by introducing a new form of currency, the Rentenmark. Its value was set at 1 million million of the worthless paper marks. (The Rentenmark was equal in value to the old German mark at the beginning of World War I. In other words, prices in 1923 were 1 million million times what they had been in 1914!) The new currency was not completely effective, and in 1924 foreign governments, primarily the United States, stepped in with loans to stabilize the German economy further. The sudden return to a stable currency caused new problems for businesses. Many firms which had been built up quickly on credit during the inflationary period either collapsed or had to cut back. The number of movie theaters in Germany declined for the first time, and some of the small production companies formed to cash in on inflationary profits also went under.

Unfortunately for film producers, stable currency made it cheaper in many cases for distributors to buy a film from abroad than to finance one in Germany. Moreover, in 1925 the government's quota regulations changed. From 1921 to 1924, the amount of foreign footage imported had been fixed at 15 percent of the total German footage produced in the previous year. Under the new quota, however, for every domestic film distributed in Germany, the company responsible received a certificate permitting the distribution of an imported film. Thus, theoretically, 50 percent of the films shown could be imported.

As a result of stabilization and the new quota policy, foreign, and particularly American, films made considerable inroads during the crisis years. This chart shows the percentage of types of films distributed in the years 1923–1929:

YEAR	TOTAL NUMBER OF FEATURES	GERMAN, %	AMERICAN, %	OTHER, %
1923	417	60.6	24.5	14.9
1924	560	39.3	33.2	24.5
1925	518	40.9	41.7	17.4
1926	515	35.9	44.5	16.3
1927	521	46.3	36.9	16.7
1928	520	42.5	39.4	18.1
1929	426	45.1	33.3	21.6

Although the import quota was not completely enforced, in 1925 the U.S. share of the German market edged past Germany's own for the first time since 1915, and Hollywood dominated the market in 1926 to a significant extent.

Perhaps the most spectacular event of the German film industry's post-stabilization crisis came in late 1925, when Ufa nearly went bankrupt. Apparently its head, Erich Pommer, failed to adjust to the end of hyperinflation. Rather than cutting back production budgets and reducing the company's debt, Pommer continued to spend freely on his biggest projects, borrowing to finance them. The two biggest films announced for the 1925–1926 season (German seasons ran from September to May) were Murnau's *Faust* and Lang's *Metropolis*. Both directors, however, far exceeded their original budgets and shooting schedules. Indeed, the films were not released until the 1926–1927 season.

As a result, in 1925 Ufa was deep in debt, with no prospects of its two blockbuster films appearing anytime soon. A crisis developed when a substantial portion of Ufa's debts were abruptly called in. Then, in late December, Paramount and MGM agreed to loan Ufa $4 million. Among other terms of the deal, Ufa was to reserve one-third of the play dates in its large theater chain for films from the two Hollywood firms.

The arrangements also set up a new German distribution company, Parufamet. Ufa owned half of it, while Paramount and MGM each held one-quarter. Parufamet would distribute at least twenty films a year for each participating firm. Paramount and MGM benefited, since a substantial number of their films would get through the German quota and be guaranteed wide distribution. After the deal was made, Pommer was pressured into resigning, and more cautious budgeting policies were initiated at Ufa.

It might seem that the Parufamet deal signaled a growing American control over the German market. Yet the deal had mostly short-term significance. By 1927, Ufa was again having debt problems. In March, it sold its main office building to pay off the American loan, and the following month the right-wing publishing magnate Alfred Hugenberg purchased controlling interest in Ufa, reduced its debts, and restored the firm to relative health. As we shall see in Chapter 12, Ufa eventually formed the core of the Nazi-controlled film industry.

The chart of films released in Germany from 1923 to 1929 reflects the basic strength that the industry had built up between 1916 and 1923. In 1927, the German percentages swung upward once more, and domestic films again outnumbered the Hollywood product.

THE END OF THE EXPRESSIONIST MOVEMENT

The production of Expressionist films was most intense in the period 1920–1924. The final years of the trend saw only two, both made by Ufa: Murnau's *Faust* and Lang's *Metropolis*. The latter's release in January 1927 marked the end of the movement. Two major factors in Expressionism's decline were the excessive budgets of the later films and the departure of Expressionist filmmakers to Hollywood.

Pommer, who had produced many of the Expressionist films at Decla, Decla-Bioscop, and Ufa, allowed Murnau and Lang to exceed their budgets on these two films. The resulting restructuring of Ufa and departure of Pommer meant that Expressionist filmmakers would no longer enjoy such indulgence. This aspect of late Expressionist films parallels what happened to some of the French Impressionists; two ambitious projects, *Napoléon* and *L'Argent*, curtailed Gance and L'Herbier's power within the film industry.

It might have been possible to make inexpensive Expressionist films, especially given that some of the early Expressionist successes had had low budgets. But by 1927, there were few filmmakers left who seemed interested in working in the style.

Robert Wiene, who had initiated the style with *Caligari*, went on to direct three more Expressionist films. The last of these, *The Hands of Orlac*, was made in Austria, where Wiene went on working, making non-Expressionist films. After the appearance of *Waxworks*, Paul Leni was hired by Universal in 1926; he made a series of successful films there before his death in 1929. Fox hired Murnau on the basis of the critical plaudits for *The Last Laugh*, and he departed for America upon finishing *Faust*.

Other personnel closely associated with the Expressionist movement also went to Hollywood. Both Conrad Veidt and Emil Jannings, who were among the most prominent Expressionist stars, left Germany in 1926, and each acted in several U.S. films before returning to Germany in 1929. Set designers were also snapped up. Rochus Gliese, Murnau's set designer, went with the director to Fox to do *Sunrise* and stayed on briefly to work for Cecil B. De Mille. Walter Reimann, who had worked on *Caligari* and other Expressionist films, left Germany to design the sets and costumes for Lubitsch's last silent film, *Eternal Love* (1929). Perhaps most crucially, after Pommer's resignation as head of Ufa in early 1926, he went to America. His most important project there was Swedish émigré director Maurice Stiller's *Hotel Imperial* (1926). By late 1927, after frustrating stints at Paramount and at MGM, Pommer returned to Ufa, no longer as head of the studio but merely one producer among many. His brief absence coincided with the depletion of Expressionist film personnel and with a move toward more cautious policies in the German film industry.

In 1927 Lang was the only major Expressionist director left in Germany. After publicity suggested that *Metropolis*'s high cost had caused Ufa's difficulties, Lang started his own production company. His next film, *Spione* (*Spies*, 1928) did not use Expressionist style. Its sets were closer to the clean lines of Art Deco than to the distortions of Expressionism. Although Lang and other German directors used Expressionist touches in their later films, the movement was over.

NEW OBJECTIVITY

A further reason for the decline of Expressionism lies in the changing cultural climate of Germany. Most art historians date the end of the movement in painting around 1924. The style had been current for about a decade and a half and had gradually filtered into the popular arts and design. It had become too familiar to retain impact as an avant-garde style, and artists turned in more vital directions.

Many artists moved away from the contorted emotionalism of Expressionism toward realism and cool-headed social criticism. Such traits were not specific enough to constitute a unified movement, but the trends were summed up as *Neue Sachlichkeit,* or "New Objectivity." For example, the savage political caricatures of George Grosz and Otto Dix are considered central to New Objectivity. Their paintings and drawings are as stylized as those of the Expressionists, but Grosz's and Dix's attention to the social realities of contemporary Germany set them apart from that movement (Fig. 5.26). Similarly, photography became increasingly important as an art form in Germany, particularly in the period 1927–1933. Such images ranged from Karl Blossfeldt's beautiful, abstract close-ups of plants to John Heartfield's bitingly satirical photomontages attacking the Nazis.

The avant-garde theater, too, became less concerned with the extreme emotions of the characters and more with the ironies of the social situation. Bertolt Brecht first came to prominence in the late 1920s and 1930s. His concept of the *Verfremdungseffekt* (commonly translated as the "alienation effect") was the opposite of Expressionist technique; Brecht wanted spectators to avoid total emotional involvement with the characters and action so that they could think through the ideological implications of the subject matter. The New Objectivity reached into literature as well, as exemplified by Alfred Döblin's novel, *Berlin Alexanderplatz* (1929), filmed by leftist director Piel Jutzi in 1931.

In the cinema, New Objectivity took various forms. One trend usually linked to New Objectivity was the "street film." In such films, characters from sheltered middle-class backgrounds are suddenly exposed to the environment of city streets, where they encounter representatives of various social ills, such as prostitutes, gamblers, black marketeers, and con men.

Fig. 5.26 George Grosz, "Street Scene" (1925).

Fig. 5.27 The hero follows a prostitute and encounters an ominous sign in *The Street.*

"Street films" came to prominence in 1923 with the success of Karl Grune's *The Street*. It tells the simple story of a middle-aged man's psychological crisis. From the safety of his apartment he sees visions of the excitement and romance that may be awaiting him in the street. Slipping away from his wife, he explores the city, only to be lured by a prostitute into a den of cardsharps and falsely suspected of a murder (Fig. 5.27). Eventually he returns home, but the ending leaves the sense that the denizens of the street lurk threateningly nearby.

The most celebrated German director of the second half of the decade, G. W. Pabst, rose to fame when he made the second major street film, *The Joyless Street*. (See Box.) Another major example was Bruno Rahn's *Dirnentragödie* ("Whores' Tragedy," aka *Tragedy of the Street*, 1928). In it the enduring Danish star Asta Nielsen plays an aging prostitute who takes in a rebellious young man who has run away from his middle-class home; she dreams of making a new life with him. He returns to his parents in the end, and she is arrested for murdering her pimp. The film used dark studio sets, a moving camera, and close framings to create the oppressive atmosphere of back streets and dingy apartments (Fig. 5.28).

Rahn's premature death and Pabst's move into other subject matter contributed to the decline of the mainstream street film in the late 1920s. In general these films have been criticized for their failure to suggest solutions

Fig. 5.28 *Tragedy of the Street* uses lengthy low-height tracking shots through the murky street set as prostitutes solicit clients.

G. W. PABST AND NEW OBJECTIVITY

G. W. Pabst's first feature was in the Expressionist style: *Der Schatz* ("The Treasure," 1923). His next, *The Joyless Street* (1925), remains the most widely seen of the street films. Set in Vienna during the period of hyperinflation, the film

Fig. 5.29 An Expressionist cityscape in *Secrets of a Soul*.

follows the fates of two women: Greta, the middle-class daughter of a civil servant, and Maria, a woman from a poverty-ridden home. When Greta's father loses his money, she is nearly prostituted, while Maria becomes the mistress of a rich man. *The Joyless Street* portrays the era's financial chaos, perhaps most vividly in the scenes of women lining up to buy meat from a callous butcher who extorts sexual favors in exchange for food. (Due to the film's controversial subject matter, it was often censored abroad, and truncated versions still circulate.)

Pabst's subsequent career was uneven. He turned out some ordinary films, such as the conventional triangle melodrama *Crisis* (1928). On the other hand, his *Secrets of a Soul* (1926) was the first serious attempt to apply the tenets of the new Freudian school of psychoanalysis in a film narrative. This desire for a scientific approach to psychological problems marks *Secrets of a Soul* as another variant of the New Objectivity. It is virtually a case study, following a seemingly ordinary man who develops a knife phobia and seeks treatment from a psychoanalyst. Though the depiction of psychoanalysis is oversimplified, the Expressionist style of some of the dream sequences (Fig. 5.29) adds considerable interest to the film.

Pabst also made another major New Objectivity film,

Fig. 5.30

Fig. 5.31

Fig. 5.32

Figs. 5.30–5.32 The first shot of *The Loves of Jeanne Ney*, moving from the villain's worn shoes propped carelessly against the woodwork to his hand searching the litter on a table for a cigarette butt to him lighting up, with a liquor bottle prominent in the foreground.

The Loves of Jeanne Ney, in 1928. The film's famous opening exemplifies what critics admired in his work. Rather than showing the villain immediately, the sequence begins with a tightly framed panning shot that builds a quick sense of his character through realistically observed details (Figs. 5.30–5.32).

Pabst's two late silent films starring the luminous American actress Louise Brooks, *Pandora's Box* (aka *Lulu*, 1929) and *Das Tagebuch einer Verlornenen* (*Diary of a Lost Girl*, 1929), enhanced his reputation and recently have received renewed attention. By the late 1920s he was a favorite with critics and intellectual audiences in Europe and the United States. Pabst also made some of the most notable early German sound films.

to the social ills that they depict. Their gloomy images of the streets suggest that the middle class could find safety only by retreating from social reality.

A number of factors led to the decline of New Objectivity in the cinema. For one thing, the increasing domination of German politics by extreme right-wing forces in the late 1920s and early 1930s led to a wider split between conservative and liberal factions. Socialist and Communist groups made films during this era, and to some extent these provided an outlet for strong social criticism (Chapter 14). Moreover, the coming of sound combined with greater control over the film industry by conservative forces to create an emphasis on light entertainment. The operetta genre became one of the most prominent types of sound filmmaking, and social realism became rare.

EXPORT AND CLASSICAL STYLE

Despite the appearance of some distinctive films in the mid- to late 1920s, the stress on export led big German companies to make films designed for international audiences. German subject matter was de-emphasized, with many films set in France and England, both major markets for German pictures. Moreover, German firms could easily film on location in London or Paris or the resort towns of southern France. Stories set in Germany frequently included foreign characters. In a 1927 Ufa film called *Die geheime Macht* ("The Secret Force"), a group of Russian nobles who flee the Soviet Revolution end up running a café in Paris; there the heroine is courted by a rich young Englishman.

Stylistically, many German films are virtually indistinguishable from the Hollywood product. German filmmakers had been exposed to American films from 1921 on, and many admired what they saw. Moreover, the heavy investment in new equipment and facilities during the inflationary period left a few German studios nearly on a par technically with the major Hollywood firms. The Germans' skill with the moving camera enhanced their grasp of American lighting techniques and continuity editing. During the late 1920s, German filmmakers often employed the 180° rule and over-the-shoulder shot/reverse shot (Figs. 5.33, 5.34).

This attempt to create a standardized quality film that did not seem distinctively German worked well for the industry in the late silent era. Exports rose, and Ufa released a significant number of its films in the American market (though these usually played only in city theaters that specialized in imported films). The political swing toward the radical right in the early 1930s, however, would eventually cut the German film industry off from the rest of the world once more.

◆ NOTES AND QUERIES

GERMAN CINEMA AND GERMAN SOCIETY

The German cinema of the 1920s, with its morbid subject matter and extreme stylization, has encouraged film researchers to treat the films as reflecting larger social trends. In a controversial study, Siegfried Kracauer has argued

Fig. 5.33

Fig. 5.34

Figs. 5.33 and 5.34 The style of many ordinary German films was virtually indistinguishable from that of Hollywood movies, as in this over-the-shoulder shot/reverse-shot scene in *Vom Täter fehlt jede Spur* ("No Trace of the Culprit," 1928, Constantin J. David).

that the films of the era after World War I reflect the German people's collective psychological desire to submit themselves to a tyrannical leader. Using this argument, he interprets many German films as prefiguring Hitler's rise to power in the early 1930s. See his *From Caligari to Hitler: A Psychological History of the German Film* (Princeton, N.J.: Princeton University Press, 1947). In his study, however, Kracauer ignores all the imported films German audiences were seeing in the 1920s. Moreover, he gives equal interpretive emphasis to popular films and to films which few people saw.

Noël Carroll criticizes Kracauer and offers an alternative view of German Expressionism in his "The Cabinet of Dr. Kracauer," *Millennium Film Journal* **1/2** (Spring/Summer 1978): 77–85. Paul Monaco attempts to improve on Kracauer by employing the criterion of popularity; see his *Cinema and Society: France and Germany during the Twenties* (New York: Elsevier, 1976). Tom Levin provides material for a further study of Kracauer's work in "Siegfried Kracauer in English: A Bibliography," *New German Critique* **41** (Spring–Summer 1987): 140–150.

WHICH FILMS ARE EXPRESSIONIST?

As with any stylistic movement in the cinema, historians have never agreed on which German films are "really" Expressionistic. Some establish limited guidelines and include only a few films; others assume that any film that possesses some traits of the style can be counted as Expressionist. In our account, we have included several films that other historians might deny are Expressionist; yet we have also termed some films "marginally" Expressionist that previous writers have placed within the movement. In reading such accounts and seeing the films, you should judge which descriptions of the movement are the most useful by comparing formal similarities among groups of films.

Barry Salt argues for a stringent view in "From Caligari to Who?" *Sight & Sound* **48,** 2 (Spring 1979): 119–123. Salt contends that only those German films which use flat, theatrical sets in the style of *The Cabinet of Dr. Caligari* can be counted as Expressionist. John D. Barlow provides a much broader analysis in *German Expressionist Film* (Boston: Twayne, 1982), even including *Kammerspiel* and street films within the Expressionist movement. A classic study of Expressionism remains Lotte Eisner's *The Haunted Screen: Expressionism in the German Cinema and the Influence of Max Reinhardt,* tr. Roger Greaves (Berkeley: University of California Press, 1969); Eisner, however, examines several styles and does not make clear distinctions between them and Expressionism.

EXPRESSIONISM, NEW OBJECTIVITY, AND THE OTHER ARTS

German culture of this era has received an enormous amount of attention. John Willett has written several overviews. His *Art and Politics in the Weimar Period, 1917–33* (New York: Pantheon, 1978) relates German culture to the international scene. Willett offers an excellent introduction in *Expressionism* (New York: World University Library, 1970). His *The Theatre of the Weimar Republic* (New York: Holmes & Meier, 1988) deals with late Expressionism, political theater, and the rise of Naziism.

Other overviews of the arts of this period are Peter Gay's *Weimar Culture: The Outsider as Insider* (New York: Harper & Row, 1968) and an anthology edited by Paul Raabe, *The Era of German Expressionism* (London: Calder & Boyars, 1974). Calder & Boyars has also published a series of translations of German Expressionist plays. For an introduction to both Expressionist and New Objectivity theater, see H. F. Garten, *Modern German Drama* (New York: Grove Press, 1959). Several representative German Expressionist plays are available in *An Anthology of German Expressionist Drama: A Prelude to the Absurd,* ed. Walter H. Sokel (New York: Doubleday, 1963).

For an English-language introduction to New Objectivity, see *Neue Sachlichkeit and German Realism of the Twenties* (London: Arts Council of Great Britain, 1979).

◆ REFERENCES

1. Quoted in Rudolf Kurtz, *Expressionismus und Film* (1926; rep., Zurich: Hans Rohr, 1965), p. 66.
2. "Faut-il supprimer les sous-titres?" *Comoedia* **4297** (27 Sept. 1924): 3.

6

SOVIET CINEMA IN THE 1920s

In France and Germany, avant-garde film movements began after World War I, whereas in the USSR, the Soviet Montage movement emerged during the 1920s. As in Europe, this avant-garde arose within a commercial film industry.

Although the new government controlled the industry in the USSR after the Bolshevik Revolution of 1917, it was not immediately able to finance filmmaking. Except for some educational and propaganda projects, films were expected to turn a profit. The Soviet Montage movement, which began in 1925, was initially successful partly because several of its films made money abroad—income that helped build up the Soviet film industry.

The post-Revolutionary era of the Soviet cinema can be divided into three periods. During War Communism (1918–1920), the Soviet Union was in a state of civil war and experienced great hardships, with the film industry struggling to survive. The New Economic Policy (1921–1924) was designed to bring the country out of its crisis, and the film industry slowly recovered. Finally, the period 1925–1933 saw growth and export as production, distribution, and exhibition expanded. This period also saw the experimentation of the Montage movement. Beginning in 1928, however, the First Five-Year Plan imposed strict state controls that were to hasten the movement's end.

THE HARDSHIPS OF WAR COMMUNISM, 1918–1920

Russia underwent two revolutions during 1917. The first, in February, eliminated the Tsar's aristocratic rule. In its place, a reformist Provisional Government was set up. This compromise did not satisfy the radical Bolshevik party, which favored a Marxist revolution to bring the worker and peasant classes to power. The Bolshevik cause gained support, especially from the military, when the Provisional Government failed to halt Russia's hopeless and unpopular struggle against Germany in World War I. In October, Vladimir Lenin led a second Revolution that created the Union of Soviet Socialist Republics.

The February Revolution had relatively little impact on the Russian film industry, which had expanded during the war. Films made just prior to the Revolution appeared, and a few films with political subject matter were rushed through production. Evgenii Bauer, a leading pre-Revolutionary director, made *The Revolutionary*, released in April; it supported Russia's continued participation in World War I. Yakov Protazanov's *Father Sergius*, produced between the two revolutions, was released in 1918. This film carried on the tradition of the mid-1910s Russian cinema, with its emphasis on psychological melodrama (pp. 59–60).

The major Russian production companies, however, quickly ceased operations. The Yermoliev troupe fled to the Crimea and eventually, in 1919, to Paris; there they established a successful company, Albatros (p. 91). Bauer's death in the spring of 1917, as well as the illness of his producer, Alexander Khanzhonkov, ended that company's existence. The third major pre-Revolutionary production company, Drankov, departed in the summer of 1918. The result was a production void which the new Soviet government would find difficult to fill.

After the October Revolution, the logical step under Marxist doctrine would have been the nationalization of the film industry—that is, acquisition of the industry by the government. The Bolshevik regime, however, was not yet powerful enough for this step. Instead, a new regulatory body, the People's Commissariat of Education (generally known as Narkompros), was assigned to oversee the cinema. The Commissar, or head, of Narkompros was Anatoli Lunacharsky. He was interested in film and occasionally wrote scripts. Lunacharsky's sympathetic attitude later helped create favorable conditions for the Montage directors.

During the first half of 1918, Narkompros struggled to gain control over film production, distribution, and exhibition. A few Soviets, or local workers' governing bodies, set up their own production units, making propaganda films promoting the new society. For example, the Petrograd Cinema Committee produced *Cohabitation*, released in 1918, made by a collective of directors and scripted by Lunacharsky. Under Soviet rule, large houses that had previously belonged to rich families were divided to provide dwellings for poorer families. In *Cohabitation*, a well-to-do professor and a poor janitor work at the same school; when the janitor and his daughter are assigned to live in

Fig. 6.1 *Cohabitation* ends with documentary shots of cheerful Revolutionary soldiers, giving this rather crudely made early Soviet film an air of historical immediacy.

Fig. 6.2 A scene in *Engineer Prite's Project* uses continuity editing, as a woman seated at a window drops something to attract the attention of two men passing below.

Fig. 6.3 A long shot shows them noticing the object and looking up.

Fig. 6.4 In a cut-in, the hero picks it up.

Fig. 6.5 In another shot, he looks up and right.

Fig. 6.6 In the reverse shot, the woman looks back at him. The rest of the scene proceeds in perfect continuity fashion.

the professor's large home, the latter's wife objects. Eventually all learn to live together in harmony (Fig. 6.1).

The year 1918 also saw the first directorial efforts of two young men who were to become major directors in the 1920s. In June, Dziga Vertov took charge of Narkompros's first newsreel; later he would be an important documentarist working in the Montage movement. Before the October Revolution, Lev Kuleshov made *Engineer Prite's Project* (released 1918) for the Khanzhonkov firm, where he had previously worked as a set designer. Only a few scenes from the film survive, but they indicate that, unlike his contemporaries in Russia, Kuleshov employed Hollywood-style continuity guidelines (Figs. 6.2–6.6). Kuleshov's later teachings and writings explored the implications of Hollywood continuity style in detail.

Despite these tentative signs of progress, however, Soviet production received two serious blows during 1918. Because the companies that had fled after the Revolution had taken whatever they could with them, the USSR badly needed production equipment and raw stock. (Neither was manufactured there.) In May, the government entrusted $1 million in credit to a film distributor who had operated in Russia during World War I, Jacques Cibrario. On a buying mission to the United States, Cibrario purchased worthless used material and absconded with most of the money. Russia had little foreign currency, and the loss was serious. It is little wonder that the government was reluctant to give the film industry further large sums. A second problem arose in June 1918, when a decree required that all raw stock held by private firms be registered with the government. Producers and dealers promptly hid raw film, and a severe shortage developed.

Fig. 6.2

Fig. 6.3

Fig. 6.4

Fig. 6.5

Fig. 6.6

Fig. 6.7 A decorated agit-train called the "V. I. Lenin." The sign at the top reads "Soviet Cinematograph," indicating that the train carried a projection setup.

For such reasons, few films were made in the USSR during 1919–1920. Most of these were newsreels and *agitki*, brief propaganda films with simple pro-Soviet messages. When one of the few private companies still producing, Russ, set out in 1919 to make a feature based on Tolstoy's *Polikushka*, the hardships of hunger and cold created incredible difficulties for the filmmakers, and the lack of positive film for release prints meant that *Polikushka* did not reach theaters until late 1922.

These were the years of the Civil War in the USSR, as the Reds, or Bolshevik forces, fought the Whites, Russians opposed to the Revolutionary government and supported by Britain, the United States, and other countries. In 1920, the Bolsheviks won, but at a terrible cost.

During the Civil War, a major concern was to get films out to troops and villagers in the countryside. Many of the far-flung areas had no movie theaters, and the Soviet government innovated the use of *agit-vehicles*. Trains, trucks, even steamboats (Fig. 6.7) visited the countryside. Painted with slogans and caricatures, they carried propaganda leaflets, printing presses, even small filmmaking setups. They put on theatrical skits or showed movies on an outdoor screen for local crowds.

Production, however, continued at a low level. In August 1919, Lenin finally nationalized the film industry. The main effect of this move was the discovery of many old films—both Russian and foreign—which had been stored away. These films provided most of what Soviet citizens saw in theaters until 1922.

The departure of the Yermoliev and Drankov companies, along with the dissolution of Khanzhonkov, meant that a generation of Russian filmmakers had largely disappeared. Who would replace them? Despite the hardships of War Communism, Narkompros established the State Film School in 1919. In 1920, the young director of *Engineer Prite's Project*, Lev Kuleshov, joined the faculty and formed a small workshop which was to train some of the era's important directors and actors.

Over the next few years, working in conditions of great deprivation and often without film stock for their experiments, Kuleshov's group explored the new art. They practiced acting and put on plays and skits staged as much like films as possible. Some of the skits used small frames with curtains, within which the actors stood to create "close-ups." Later they experimented with film scenes, either shooting their own footage or reediting older films. In doing so, they explored an editing technique which has come to be known as the *Kuleshov effect*.

The Kuleshov effect is based on leaving out a scene's establishing shot and leading the spectator to infer spatial or temporal continuity from the shots of separate elements. Often Kuleshov's experiments relied on the eyeline match. The workshop's most famous experiment involved recutting old footage with the actor Ivan Mozhukhin. (Since the experimental footage does not survive, we know about this and other experiments primarily from Kuleshov's recollections.) A close view of Mozhukhin with a neutral expression was selected. This same shot was repeatedly edited together with shots of other subject matter, variously reported as a bowl of soup, a dead body, a baby, and the like. Supposedly, ordinary viewers praised Mozhukhin's performance, believing that his face had registered the appropriate hunger, sorrow, or delight—even though his face was the same each time they had seen it. In another experiment, Kuleshov claims to have filmed close views of several women—one's eye, another's nose, yet another's ear—and edited them together into a sequence that viewers assumed showed one woman. In all these cases, the filmmaker built up a space or time that did not exist.

The major implication of Kuleshov's experiments was that in cinema the viewer's response depended less on the individual shot than on the editing—the *montage*, or "mounting" of the shots. This idea was to be central to the Montage filmmakers' theory and style. The move from classroom experimentation to film production would be difficult for Kuleshov's group, however, for the Soviet film industry's construction took several years.

RECOVERY UNDER THE NEW ECONOMIC POLICY, 1921–1924

By 1920, the hardships caused by the Civil War and the disorganization of the new government had created a severe famine in parts of the USSR. Faced with this crisis, in 1921 Lenin formulated the New Economic Policy (NEP), which allowed for a limited reintroduction of private ownership and capitalist-style dealings. As a result, hoarded raw stock reappeared, and film production by private firms and governmental groups increased.

In early 1922, Lenin made two statements that helped determine the course of Soviet filmmaking. First, he issued the so-called Lenin proportion, stating that film programs should balance entertainment and education—though not specifying how much of each type of film should be shown. He also declared (according to Lunacharsky), "Of all the arts, for us the cinema is the most important." Lenin probably meant that the cinema was the most powerful tool for propaganda and education among a largely illiterate population. In any event, his statement focused attention on the cinema and has been quoted innumerable times as an indication of the Bolshevik government's reliance on the new medium for propaganda.

In late 1922, the government attempted to organize the feeble film industry by creating a central distribution monopoly called Goskino. All private and government production firms were to release their films through Goskino, which would also control the import and export of films. The attempt failed, since several companies were powerful enough to compete with Goskino. In some cases private importers bid against Goskino for the same films, driving prices higher.

This was no small matter. During the NEP, the Soviet film industry became reliant on imports. In the early years after the October Revolution, the USSR had been cut off from the rest of the world, partly by the Civil War and partly by the refusal of most countries to deal with a Communist government. In 1922, the Treaty of Rapallo opened the way for trade between Russia and Germany. The treaty was a breakthrough for the USSR in its relations with the West, and Berlin became the main conduit for films going into and out of the USSR during the 1920s. Eager to beat their competitors into the vast new Soviet market, German film firms sold on credit, and lighting equipment, raw stock, and new films flowed into the USSR. A 1923 investigation found that 99 percent of all films in Soviet distribution were foreign. Since most of the film industry's revenues came from distributing imported pictures, foreign trade played a crucial role in its recovery.

Although the industry faced an uphill struggle, the NEP period saw a slow growth. Production centers were gradually set up in the non-Russian republics of the USSR so that ethnic populations could see films reflecting their own cultures. With the acquisition of raw stock, production of fiction features increased. In 1923, there appeared a Civil War drama which was as popular with Soviet audiences as were imported films: *Red Imps,* directed by Ivan Perestiani for the Georgian branch of Narkompros. The film concerns two teenagers, a brother obsessed with Fenimore Cooper's adventure books and a sister devoted to a novel about anarchism. When their father is killed by the Whites, the pair team up with a black street acrobat and set out to join the Red Army. As scouts, they live out the sorts of adventures they had previously read about (Fig. 6.8).

The year 1924 saw a further increase in production. Yuri Zhelyabuzhsky, who had gotten his start directing *agitki,* made *Cigarette-Girl of Mosselprom,* a contemporary comedy in which a street cigarette seller becomes a movie star by accident. Several scenes reflect the Soviet film situation of the day (Figs. 6.9, 6.10). Another popular film, *Palace and Fortress,* was

Fig. 6.8 In scenes like this, when the children leap from a bridge onto a train during the defense of their town, *Red Imps* captured something of the fast pace of American adventure films of the 1910s.

Fig. 6.9

Fig. 6.10

Fig. 6.9 In a sequence from *Cigarette-Girl of Mosselprom* set in a movie studio, a director reading a script sits in front of a German film poster.

Fig. 6.10 At the end, the heroine's film premieres in what may have been a typical movie theater of the day.

Fig. 6.11 As this shot of the hero and his mother indicates, *Palace and Fortress* used an old-fashioned style, with the camera facing the back wall straight on, the characters framed from a distance, and flat lighting coming from the front.

Fig. 6.12

Fig. 6.13

Figs. 6.12 and 6.13 In one shot from *The Extraordinary Adventures of Mr. West in the Land of the Bolsheviks*, a Soviet official gives a speech, and in the next Mr. West seems to be watching through binoculars—though the shots were clearly made in different spaces and times.

made by the veteran pre-Revolutionary director, Alexander Ivanovsky. It centered on a revolutionary of the era of Tsar Alexander II who is imprisoned and eventually goes mad (Fig. 6.11). *Palace and Fortress* became a favorite target of the Montage directors over the next few years as they advocated a new approach to filmmaking.

Members of the Kuleshov workshop of the State Film School also made their first feature in 1924. *The Extraordinary Adventures of Mr. West in the Land of the Bolsheviks* is a hilarious comedy about western misconceptions of the USSR. Mr. West, a naive American representative of the YMCA, reluctantly travels to Moscow, where thieves exploit his prejudices, pretending to defend him against "barbarous" Bolshevik thugs. Eventually he is rescued by real (and kindly) Bolsheviks. At the end, the film exploits the Kuleshov effect by combining newsreel and staged footage (Figs. 6.12, 6.13). With its playful use of acting and editing, *Mr. West* can be counted as a marginal Montage film. It brought the Soviet cinema to the verge of a truly avant-garde movement, as a new generation of directors interested in more radical stylistic exploration began working.

GROWTH AND EXPORT, INCREASING STATE CONTROL, 1925–1933

CHANGES IN THE FILM INDUSTRY

Because the centralized distribution firm Goskino had proved unable to organize the film industry, the government created a new company, Sovkino, on January 1, 1925. The few production firms that were allowed to keep operating were given a strong incentive to help Sovkino survive: they had to invest in stock in the new firm. Goskino continued in existence for a time, producing on a small scale; its main contribution was *Potemkin,* the most famous film of the Montage movement and the first Soviet film to have a major success abroad. A more extensive and long-lived company was Mezhrabpom-Russ (based on the old Russ collective that had made *Polikushka*). This private firm was owned and financed by a German Communist group, and it made a surprisingly large proportion of the most significant Soviet films—including Pudovkin's silent ones—before its dissolution in 1936. Specialist companies also held stock in Sovkino: Gosvoyenfilm made military propaganda until the late 1920s, and Kultkino produced educational films—including some by the major Montage-style documentarist, Dziga Vertov. Sevzapkino was based in Leningrad, and it later became simply the Leningrad studio of Sovkino. Working at Sevzapkino were a number of young and talented Montage directors, most notably the team of Grigori Kozintsev and Leonid Trauberg.

Sovkino faced a complex set of governmental demands. One policy dictated that the firm expand access to films throughout the USSR. Since 1917, the number of theaters had shrunk, due to the lack of films, the breakdown of projectors, the inability to heat the auditoriums, and similar factors. Lenin died in 1924, but his belief that the cinema should serve an

A CHRONOLOGY OF THE SOVIET MONTAGE MOVEMENT

1917   February: Tsar Nicholas II is overthrown; Provisional Government is established.
October: The Bolshevik Revolution

1918   Narkompros (the People's Commissariat of Education) takes charge of regulating the film industry.

1919   August: Nationalization of the film industry
Foundation of the State Film School

1920   Lev Kuleshov joins the State Film School and forms his workshop.

1921   The New Economic Policy is instituted.

1922   Formation of Goskino, the state film distribution monopoly

1923   Publication of Sergei Eisenstein's essay, "Montage of Attractions"

1924   *Kino-Eye*, Dziga Vertov
The Extraordinary Adventures of Mr. West in the Land of the Bolsheviks, Lev Kuleshov

1925   January: Formation of Sovkino, the new governmental distribution monopoly and production company
Strike, Sergei Eisenstein
Potemkin, Sergei Eisenstein

1926   *Mother*, Vsevolod Pudovkin
The Devil's Wheel, Grigori Kozintsev and Leonid Trauberg
The Cloak, Grigori Kozintsev and Leonid Trauberg

1927   *Zvenigora*, Alexander Dovzhenko

The House on Trubnoya, Boris Barnet

The End of St. Petersburg, Vsevolod Pudovkin

Moscow in October, Boris Barnet

SVD, Grigori Kozintsev and Leonid Trauberg

1928   March: The First Communist Party Conference on Film Questions is held.
October (aka *Ten Days That Shook the World*), Sergei Eisenstein
The Heir of Ghenghis-Khan (aka *Storm Over Asia*), Vsevolod Pudovkin
Lace, Sergei Yutkevich

1929   Sergei Eisenstein begins travels that will keep him abroad until 1932.
The New Babylon, Grigori Kozintsev and Leonid Trauberg
My Grandmother, Kote Mikaberidze
China Express (aka *Blue Express*), Ilya Trauberg
Man with a Movie Camera, Dziga Vertov
Arsenal, Alexander Dovzhenko
Old and New, Sergei Eisenstein

1930   Formation of Soyuzkino, a centralized company to control all production, distribution, and exhibition

1931   *Alone*, Grigori Kozintsev and Leonid Trauberg
Golden Mountains, Sergei Yutkevich

1932   *A Simple Case*, Vsevolod Pudovkin

1933   *Deserter*, Vsevolod Pudovkin

educational role continued to influence policy. The government insisted on getting films to workers and peasants in remote regions. Sovkino faced the formidable tasks of opening urban theaters and of sending over one thousand portable projection outfits to the countryside. Moreover, most workers and peasants could afford only tiny entrance fees, so the portable theaters operated at a loss.

How was Sovkino to pay for these portable projection outfits? Not through government subsidies, but through its profits on other enterprises. Many such profits would come from foreign films, which Sovkino imported and distributed in the USSR. During the second half of the decade, however, the company was pressured to reduce the number of imported films. Even reedited, as most such films were, they were considered ideologically harmful. A more desirable source of income was domestic production. Soviet films might make money within the USSR. Moreover, if they were sold abroad, they might earn much more. Sovkino thus had a strong incentive to export films. Partly by supporting the young Montage directors, Sovkino produced films that found an audience in the West, and the income that these exports generated bought new equipment and supported the expansion of the industry.

The first triumph abroad was Eisenstein's *Potemkin,* which proved enormously popular in Germany in 1926 and went on to show in many other countries. Other Soviet films, such as Pudovkin's *Mother,* soon followed and were exported very successfully. The foreign currency earned, especially by Montage-style films, facilitated the Soviet industry's purchase of foreign equipment.

Another goal for Sovkino was to make films that embodied the ideology of the Communist government so that its new ideals could be conveyed to the country's population. The early Montage films, with their dynamic depictions of Tsarist-period oppression and historical rebellions, were praised for their subject matter. Because these films were successful financially and critically, for a few years a new generation of filmmakers was able to continue experimenting in the avant-garde Montage style.

A NEW GENERATION OF DIRECTORS

The years after the Revolution saw widespread, enthusiastic experimentation by artists in every medium. They tried to approach artistic creation in a way appropriate to a completely new kind of society. One result was a trend in the visual arts called Constructivism, to which the Montage movement in the cinema was closely linked.

Despite its radical aims, Constructivism had precedents in pre-Revolutionary tendencies. Influences from French Cubism and Italian Futurism combined in Russia in a movement called Cubo-Futurism which led to a flamboyant attack on all traditional art forms. Artists affiliated with a second tendency, Suprematism, took a more spiritual, abstract turn. Simple geometrical shapes were combined into compositions. Kasimir Malevich's "Black Square" (1913) was a black square against a white background; in 1917 he created "White on White," a white background surrounding an off-center square of a slightly different shade.

In this pre-Revolutionary period, few of the Cubo-Futurist or Suprematist artists had political alliances. While they criticized traditional artistic styles, they did not see the artist as having a political role. After the Bolshevik Revolution, however, most artists supported the new government, and there were many debates as to how art and politics could be fused. Some of these avant-garde artists were given teaching posts or put in positions where they influenced official cultural policy, and Lunacharsky, while not entirely sympathetic to the modernist styles of the day, allowed them a relatively free hand.

The search for a socially useful art resulted in the rise of Constructivism around 1920. Manifestos and articles declared that artists who had been exploring abstract styles need not abandon their ways of working—they simply needed to apply them to useful ends. For the Constructivist, art inevitably fulfills a social function. It is not an object of rapt contemplation or a source of some enduring higher truth, as many nineteenth-century views of art had held. The artist is not an inspired visionary; he or she is a skilled artisan using the materials of the medium to create an artwork. Artists were often compared to engineers, using tools and a rational, even scientific approach.

The Constructivists also often compared the artwork to a machine. While earlier views of art frequently saw the work as analogous to a plant, with an organic unity and growth, the Constructivists stressed that it was put together from parts. This process of assemblage was sometimes referred to as *montage*, from the French word for the putting together of parts into a machine. (As we have seen, filmmakers applied the term "montage" to the editing of shots into a film.) This analogy between artwork and machine was seen positively. Because Soviet society focused on enhancing the USSR's industrial output, and also because communism stressed the dignity of human labor, the factory and the machine became symbols of the new society. Artists' studios were often seen as factories where laborers built useful products.

Because all human response was seen as based on scientifically determinable processes, the Constructivists considered that an artwork could be calculated to elicit a particular reaction. Thus artworks could be used for propagandistic and educational purposes promoting the new Communist society—if only the right ways of making them could be discovered. Many artists therefore jettisoned the notion that elite art forms (like opera and painting) were superior to popular art forms (like circus and poster). Art should be understandable to all, particularly to the workers and peasants so central to the Bolshevik cause.

Constructivism resulted in an extraordinary fusion of abstract graphic design and utilitarian function. For example, El Lissitsky used a geometrical composition straight out of Suprematism for a 1920 propaganda poster supporting the Bolshevik side in the Civil War (Color Plate 6.1). Constructivist artists designed textiles, book covers, workers' uniforms, street kiosks, even such mundane household items as ceramic cups and saucers—many using modernist abstract shapes.

In the early 1920s, Constructivism also affected the theater. The most important Constructivist theatrical director was Vsevolod Meyerhold, an established figure who offered his services to the Bolshevik government immediately after the Revolution. Meyerhold's bold methods of staging were to influence Soviet film directors. Set and costume designs in several major Meyerhold productions incorporated Constructivist design principles. In his 1922 production of *The Magnanimous Cuckold,* for example, the set somewhat resembled a large factory machine; it consisted of a series of bare platforms, with their supporting legs visible and a large propeller turning during the play. The actors performed in ordinary work clothes (Fig. 6.14). Meyerhold also pioneered the principle of *biomechanical* acting. The actor's body was assumed to be like a machine, and thus a performance consisted of carefully controlled physical movements rather than of the expression of inner emotions. Meyerhold's actors trained by doing exercises to gain mastery over their bodies, and their performances had an acrobatic quality.

Fig. 6.14 "Biomechanical" acting, work clothes, and a machine-like set in *The Magnanimous Cuckold.*

During the first half of the 1920s, when all these sweeping changes were revolutionizing the arts, a new generation of filmmakers was moving into the cinema. For them, the Revolution was a crucial formative event—partly because they were extraordinarily young. Indeed, Sergei Eisenstein was nicknamed "the old man" by his younger friends because he was all of twenty-six when he began his first feature film. Eisenstein came from a middle-class family in Riga, in the Baltics. His education gave him fluency in Russian, English, German, and French. He recalled that while on a visit to Paris at age eight, he saw a Méliès film and became interested in the cinema. Two years later he visited the circus and became similarly obsessed with this popular spectacle. Following his father's wishes, he began studying engineering in 1915. Eisenstein participated in the Revolution and during the Civil War put his engineering skills to work building bridges. He was drawn to the arts, however, and during this same period he also decorated agit-trains and helped design many theatrical skits for the Red Army. The combination of engineering and artistic work seemed anything but contradictory in the era of Constructivism, and throughout his life Eisenstein likened the production of his films to the building of those bridges.

In 1920, at the end of the Civil War, Eisenstein went to Moscow and joined the Proletkult Theater (short for Proletarian, or Workers', Cultural Theater). There he designed and co-directed many plays. In 1921, Eisenstein (along with his friend, Sergei Yutkevich, another future Montage film director) enrolled in a theater workshop under the supervision of Meyerhold, whom he would always consider his mentor. In 1923, Eisenstein directed his first theatrical production, *Enough Simplicity in Every Wise Man.* Although the play was a nineteenth-century farce, Eisenstein staged it as a circus. The actors dressed in clown costumes and performed in the acrobatic biomechanical style, walking on a tightrope above the audience or doing handstands as they spoke their lines. Eisenstein also produced *Glumov's Diary*, a short film to be shown on a screen on the stage (Fig. 6.15). At the same time that this play was performed, Eisenstein gained some early experience as a film editor: along with Esfir Shub (soon to become an important maker of compilation documentaries), he reedited a German Expressionist film, Fritz Lang's *Dr. Mabuse, the Gambler*, for Soviet release.

Eisenstein always maintained that his move from the theater to film came in 1924, when he directed a production of playwright S. M. Tretyakov's *Gas Masks*, not in a theater but in a real gas factory. According to Eisenstein, the contrast between the reality of the setting and the artifice of the drama was too great. A few months later, he began work on *Strike* (released in early 1925)—a film set and shot in a factory. It was the first major film of the Montage movement, and Eisenstein went on to make three more important works in that style: *Potemkin, October* (also known in an abridged version as *Ten Days That Shook the World*), and *Old and New* (also known as *The General Line*).

Fig. 6.15 Eisenstein takes a bow at the end of *Glumov's Diary*.

Eisenstein may have been young, but the oldest Montage director in terms of experience was Kuleshov (only eight years older actually), who had designed and directed films before the Revolution and then taught at the State Film School. Kuleshov's own Soviet films were only mildly experimental in style, but his workshop produced two important Montage directors.

Vsevolod Pudovkin had intended to train as a chemist until he saw Griffith's *Intolerance* in 1919. Convinced of the cinema's importance, he soon joined Kuleshov's workshop and trained as both an actor and a director. His first feature film typified the Constructivist interest in the physical bases of psychological response; he made *Mechanics of the Brain*, a documentary about Ivan Pavlov's famous experiments on stimulus-response physiology. In 1926 Pudovkin (born in 1893) helped found the Montage movement with his first fiction feature, *Mother*. Another Kuleshov workshop member, Boris Barnet (born 1902) had studied painting and sculpture, and he trained as a boxer after the Revolution. He acted in *The Extraordinary Adventures of Mr. West in the Land of the Bolsheviks* and other mid-1920s films, and he also directed *The House on Trubnoya* and other Montage-style films.

The other important filmmaker who, along with Kuleshov, had started directing about the time of the Revolution was Dziga Vertov (born 1896). During the mid-1910s, he wrote poetry and science fiction, composed what we now call *musique concrète*, and was influenced by the Cubo-Futurists. During 1916–1917, however, he studied medicine until becoming the supervisor of Narkompros's newsreel series in 1917. He went on in 1924 to make feature-length documentaries, some employing the Montage style.

The youngest Montage directors came out of the Leningrad theater milieu of the early 1920s. In 1921, while still in their teens, Grigori Kozintsev (born 1905), Leonid Trauberg (born 1902), and Sergei Yutkevich (born 1904) formed the Factory of the Eccentric Actor (FEKS). This theatrical troupe enthusiastically embraced the circus, the popular American cinema, the cabaret, and other entertainments. They issued provocative manifestos in the manner of the Cubo-Futurists' "Slap in the Face of Public Taste" (1912). In 1922 the FEKS group defined how their approach to acting departed from that of the traditional theater: "from emotion to the machine, from anguish to the trick. The technique—circus. The psychology—head over heels."[1] They staged theatrical events that adopted the techniques of popular entertainments, and by 1924, they moved into the cinema with a comic short, *The Adventures of Oktyabrina* (now lost). Yutkevich went on to make Montage films on his own; Kozintsev and Trauberg co-directed several important films of the movement.

Eisenstein, Kuleshov, Pudovkin, Vertov, and the FEKS group were the principal early exponents of Soviet Montage. Other directors picked up their influences and developed the style. In particular, filmmakers working in the non-Russian republics enriched the Montage movement. Foremost among these was Alexander Dovzhenko, the principal Ukrainian director. Dovzhenko had been in the Red Army during the Civil War, and served as a diplomatic administrator in Berlin in the early 1920s. There he studied art, returning to the Ukraine as a painter and cartoonist. In 1926 he suddenly switched to filmmaking and made a comedy and a spy thriller before directing his first Montage film, *Zvenigora*, in 1927. Based on obscure Ukrainian folk legends, *Zvenigora* baffled audiences but demonstrated an original style that emphasizes lyrical imagery above narrative. Dovzhenko went on to make two more important Montage films, *Arsenal* and *Earth*, also set in the Ukraine.

THE THEORETICAL WRITINGS OF MONTAGE FILMMAKERS

The mid-1920s saw a burgeoning in Soviet film theory, as critics and filmmakers sought to understand cinema scientifically. Like the French Impressionists, several Montage directors considered theory and filmmaking to be closely linked, and they wrote about their conceptions of cinema. They were united in an opposition to traditional films. All saw in montage the basis of revolutionary films that would inspire audiences. But the writings of the Montage directors differed in important ways.

In many respects, Kuleshov was the most conservative theorist of the group. He admired the succinct storytelling of American films, and he discussed montage chiefly as techniques of editing for clarity and emotional impact. This conception of montage influenced Pudovkin, whose two 1926 pamphlets on filmmaking were soon translated into western languages (in English as *Film Language*, 1929). Through Pudovkin, "montage" came generally to refer to dynamic, often discontinuous, narrative editing.

Vertov was far more radical. A committed Constructivist, he emphasized the social utility of documentary film. Vertov saw the fiction films of his contemporaries as "cine-nicotine," a drug that dulled the viewer's awareness of social and political reality. For him, "life caught unawares" would be the basis of a cinema of fact. Montage was less a single technique than the entire production process: choosing a subject, shooting footage, and assembling the film all involved selection and combination of "cine-facts." As for editing, Vertov emphasized that the filmmaker should calculate the differences between shots—light versus dark, slow motion versus fast motion, and so on. These differences, or "intervals," would be the basis of the film's effect on the audience.

Eisenstein developed the most complicated conception of montage. He insisted that montage was not limited solely to editing or even to Constructivist art in general. Montage was a universal formal principle that could also be found in traditional drama, poetry, and painting. In a bold essay of 1929, he suggested that the montage principle should be conceived as a *collision* of elements. He asserted that shots should not be seen as linked, as Pudovkin and Kuleshov believed, but rather as conflicting sharply with one another. For Eisenstein, this conflict imitated the Marxist concept of the dialectic, in which antithetical elements clash and produce a synthesis that goes beyond both. Montage could compel the spectator to sense the conflict between elements and create a new concept in his or her mind.

In "collision" montage, Eisenstein foresaw the possibility of an "intellectual" cinema. It would attempt not to tell a story but to convey abstract ideas, as an essay or political tract might. He dreamed of filming Marx's *Capital,* creating concepts through images and editing rather than through verbal language. Certain of his films took first steps toward intellectual filmmaking.

The filmmakers' theories did not always accord with their practice. Kuleshov and Pudovkin in particular proved more daring as filmmakers than their essays might suggest. All the core Montage directors, however, wrote about film technique as a vivid way to shape the new Soviet society by arousing and educating their audiences.

SOVIET MONTAGE FORM AND STYLE

Most non-Montage Soviet films tended to be topical comedies or conventional literary adaptations. In part because Montage directors emphasized physical conflict, in part because they sought to inculcate Bolshevik doctrine, they often chose uprisings, strikes, and other clashes in the history of the revolutionary movement. When two films were produced to mark the twentieth anniversary of the failed 1905 Revolution, for example, both were in the Montage style: *Potemkin* and *Mother.* Similarly, principal films celebrating the tenth anniversary of the Bolshevik Revolution—*October, The End of St. Petersburg,* and *Moscow in October*—used Montage style.

Other historical Montage films portrayed earlier revolutionary movements. Kozintsev and Trauberg's *New Babylon* dealt with the doomed 1871 Paris Commune; the same pair's *SVD,* with the Decembrist plot of 1825. Some presented Tsarist-period strikes (e.g., *Strike*) or the Civil War (e.g., *Arsenal*). Several Montage films, however, were dramas or comedies on contemporary social problems. For example, as the new government gave rise to a cumbersome bureaucracy, it became common to satirize the amount of red tape people had to go through to get anything done, as in the absurdist *My Grandmother,* made in the Republic of Georgia.

What about the narrative structure of Montage films? We have seen that French Impressionist films usually center around personal actions and psychology, while German Expressionism typically uses supernatural or legendary elements to motivate distorted style. The narrative patterns of Soviet Montage films differ considerably from both these other movements. On the

Fig. 6.16

Fig. 6.17

Fig. 6.18

Figs. 6.16–6.18 No action occurs during these three successive shots of an officer in *Storm Over Asia.*

one hand, there are almost no supernatural events (the one exception being Dovzhenko's *Zvenigora,* which uses elements from Ukrainian folklore). Moreover, many Montage films downplay individual characters as central causal agents. Instead, drawing on a Marxist view of history, Montage films often make social forces the source of causes and effects. Characters do act and react, but they do so less as psychologically distinct individuals than as members of different social classes.

Thus a single protagonist might represent a general type or class. Pudovkin was noted for using this approach, with the young heroes of *Mother* and *The End of St. Petersburg* symbolizing different types of supporters of the revolutionary cause. Some films went so far as to eliminate major characters and to use the masses as the protagonist. Eisenstein's early films—*Strike, Potemkin,* and *October*—all take this approach; in *October* even Lenin becomes one figure in the sweep of revolutionary events.

The Montage directors believed that such narratives would affect viewers most strongly if the stylistic devices created a maximum of dynamic tension. Thus their techniques were often diametrically opposed to the smooth, seamless continuity style of Hollywood-type films. In particular, these directors juxtaposed shots in vivid, energetic ways, and the main traits that distinguish the Montage style lie in the area of editing.

The search for dynamism through editing resulted in one of the most pervasive characteristics of Montage films: on average, they have a greater number of shots than does any other type of filmmaking of their era. While Hollywood practice was (and is) to use one shot per action, Montage filmmakers frequently broke individual actions down into two or more shots. Indeed, an unmoving character or object might be seen from different angles for several shots in a row (Figs. 6.16–6.18). Such editing reflects the directors' belief that cuts, in and of themselves, stimulate the spectator.

Beyond this greater quantity of shots, we can discern more specific strategies of editing, involving temporal, spatial, and graphic tensions.

While the goal of continuity editing is to create the illusion of a smooth flow of time within a scene, Montage cutting often created either overlapping or elliptical temporal relations. In *overlapping editing,* the second shot repeats part or all of the action from the previous shot. When several shots contain such repetitions, the time an action takes on the screen expands noticeably. Eisenstein's films contain some of the most famous examples of this tactic. *Potemkin* deals with a mutiny by sailors oppressed by their Tsarist officers; in one scene a sailor washing dishes gets upset and smashes a plate. This gesture, which would take only an instant, is spread across ten shots (Figs. 6.19–6.28). Such overlapping helps emphasize the first rebellious action of the mutiny. In *October,* scenes such as the raising of the bridges and Kerensky ascending the stairs in the Winter Palace take more time than they would in reality.

Elliptical cutting creates the opposite effect. A portion of an event is left out, so the event takes less time than it would in reality. One common type of elliptical editing in Montage films is the *jump cut,* whereby the same space is shown from the same camera position in two shots, yet the mise-en-

Fig. 6.19

Fig. 6.20

Fig. 6.21

Fig. 6.22

Fig. 6.23

Fig. 6.24

Figs. 6.19–6.28 Ten shots in the plate-smashing scene from *Potemkin*, showing the repeated action of the sailor raising his arm in contradictory directions.

Fig. 6.25

Fig. 6.26

Fig. 6.27

Fig. 6.28

Fig. 6.29

Fig. 6.29 A jump cut in *The House on Trubnoya:* Two successive close-ups show a woman's terrified face as she sees a streetcar bearing down on her; in the first her eyes are tightly closed, but a cut reveals them suddenly open.

Fig. 6.30 In *October,* a rapid burst of two-frame shots suggests the rat-tat of a machine gun.

Fig. 6.31 Near the end of *Storm Over Asia,* the Mongolian hero rebels against the British colonialists who have exploited him; single-frame shots alternate between him swinging his sword and the sword itself flashing against a dark background.

Fig. 6.30

Fig. 6.31

scene has been changed (Fig. 6.29). The contradictory temporal relations created by overlapping and elliptical editing compel the spectator to make sense of the scene's action.

Despite the use of ten shots to show the plate-smashing in *Potemkin,* the action occurs rapidly, because the individual shots are all short. In general, rapid, rhythmic editing is common in Montage films, whether or not the shots contain overlapping action. In early Montage films, the editing would sometimes accelerate until the shots were only a few frames long. Then, after *La Roue* and other fast-cut French Impressionist films were shown in the USSR in 1926, Montage filmmakers began to use strings of two- and one-frame shots. In most cases, however, rapid editing does not function to convey characters' subjective perceptions, as it would in French films. Instead, fast cutting may convey rhythmic sound (Fig. 6.30) or enhance the effect of explosive, often violent, action (Fig. 6.31).

As these examples of temporal relationships among shots suggest, Montage editing can also create conflict through spatial relationships. Again, the filmmakers do not guide the spectator through a clear, straightforward locale, as in a Hollywood film. Rather, the viewer must actively piece together what is going on—just as the spectators of Kuleshov's experiments were obliged to construct a coherent space and time. In the plate-smashing scene from *Potemkin,* for example, Eisenstein creates a contradictory space by mismatching the sailor's position from shot to shot. The sailor swings the plate down from behind his left shoulder (Fig. 6.22) and then is seen in the next shot with the plate already lifted above his right shoulder (Fig. 6.23).

The Soviet filmmakers also used intercutting to create unusual spatial relationships. As we have seen, intercutting was common in the cinema from the early teens, and it most often presented simultaneous actions in different spaces (as in Griffith's *The Birth of a Nation,* p. 74). In the USSR, it also served more abstract purposes, linking two actions for the sake of a thematic point. Near the end of *Strike,* for example, Eisenstein cuts from a police officer bringing his fists down violently as he orders a massacre of the strikers (Fig. 6.32) to a butcher's hands bringing a knife down to kill a bull (Fig. 6.33). The scene continues to cut between the death of the animal and the attack on the workers—not to suggest that these two events are happening simultaneously, but to get us to see the massacre as being like a slaughter. In *Mother,* Pudovkin uses intercutting more lyrically, moving between the hero in jail and the ice thawing on a river, suggesting the hero's hope as he learns of a plan to rescue him. There is no indication, as there might be in a French Impressionist film, that the hero is thinking of the ice; Pudovkin eventually gives the imagery a social meaning, as a political demonstration is intercut with the surging river.

The "slaughter" scene in *Strike* makes use of another common Montage device: the *nondiegetic insert.* The term "diegesis" refers to the space and time of the film's story; anything that is part of the story world is diegetic. A nondiegetic element exists outside the story world. In a sound film, for example, the voice of a narrator who is not a character in the film is nondiegetic sound. A nondiegetic insert consists of one or more shots depicting space and time unrelated to those of the story events in the film. The bull being slaughtered in *Strike* has no causal, spatial, or temporal relation to the workers. Its nondiegetic image is inserted to make a metaphorical point: the workers are being slaughtered like animals. The use of such nondiegetic shots to make a conceptual point was central to Eisenstein's theory of "intellectual montage."

October makes extensive use of intellectual montage. At one point Kerensky, the leader of the Provisional Government, is compared to Napoleon (Figs. 6.34, 6.35). The film's most complex use of intellectual montage comes when a leader calls upon soldiers to fight "For God and Country." There follows a lengthy series of nondiegetic shots of statues of gods and churches

Fig. 6.32 Intercutting in *Strike* compares a police officer . . .

Fig. 6.33 . . . to a butcher.

Figs. 6.34 and 6.35 *October* makes a conceptual point when a diegetic shot of Kerensky is followed by a nondiegetic insert of a statue of Napoleon.

Fig. 6.34

Fig. 6.35

Figs. 6.36 and 6.37 In *October*, nondiegetic shots point up the contradictory religious beliefs and simplistic ideas of patriotism used to convince soldiers to risk their lives.

Fig. 6.36

Fig. 6.37

Fig. 6.38 In one shot from the Odessa steps sequence in *Potemkin*, the steps create a set of strong diagonal lines from lower left to upper right, while the running figures move quickly down and rightward.

Fig. 6.39 In the next shot, the composition switches this orientation, with the row of unmoving rifles extending diagonally from upper left to lower right.

Fig. 6.38

Fig. 6.39

from widely differing cultures and then shots of military medals (Figs. 6.36, 6.37). Intellectual montage creates its effects through conflict; by juxtaposing shots that have no apparent causal connection, the filmmaker leads the audience to create a general concept that links them.

Montage directors carried conflictual editing further by creating striking *graphic contrasts* from shot to shot. A cut might bring a distinct directional change in the composition. The Odessa steps sequence in *Potemkin*, perhaps the single most famous scene in any Montage film, gains much of its effectiveness through graphic conflict (Figs. 6.38, 6.39). The cumulative effect of such cuts in this scene is to help heighten the tension. In other films, graphic conflict contributes to comedy (Figs. 6.40, 6.41).

One of the most striking graphic conflicts involves cutting from one image to the same image, but the latter is flipped right to left or even turned

Fig. 6.40

Fig. 6.41

Figs. 6.40 and 6.41 *My Grandmother*'s satirical treatment of bureaucracy uses a pair of shots in which canted framings juxtapose two typists.

Fig. 6.42

Fig. 6.43

Figs. 6.42 and 6.43 In Ilya Trauberg's *China Express*, a medium close-up of a soldier aiming a rifle rightward is followed by the same image, but with the soldier now facing left.

Fig. 6.44

Fig. 6.45

Figs. 6.44 and 6.45 Two quick shots from the demonstration scene in *Mother*.

upside down (Figs. 6.42, 6.43). Near the end of Pudovkin's *Mother*, mounted soldiers attack a workers' demonstration; the pace of the editing picks up, climaxing in a flurry of brief shots of soldiers riding past the camera, first to the right, then left (Fig. 6.44), then upside down (Fig. 6.45). Such cuts can be jarring, especially when they enhance the impression of violent action.

Although the Soviet directors considered cinema's artistic qualities to depend primarily on editing, they also realized that editing juxtapositions would be enhanced if the individual shots were as striking as possible. Thus they used camerawork in distinctive ways as well. Many shots in Montage films avoid the conventional chest-height, straight-on framing and utilize more dynamic angles. Low-angle framings place buildings or people against a blank sky, making characters look threatening (as in Fig. 6.46) or heroic

Fig. 6.46 A dynamic angle in *China Express*.

Fig. 6.47

Fig. 6.48

Fig. 6.49

Fig. 6.47 The heroine of *Mother* in the demonstration scene.

Fig. 6.48 In *Arsenal,* a train carrying Ukrainian soldiers seems to rush up at a steep angle, emphasizing its dynamic thrust.

Fig. 6.49 In *The End of St. Petersburg,* Pudovkin satirizes profiteers who want to carry on with Russia's participation in World War I by showing them only from the neck down.

Fig. 6.50 In *Earth,* Dovzhenko repeatedly emphasizes the vast farmlands of the Ukraine through framings that show almost nothing but sky.

Fig. 6.51 Pudovkin uses a similar device in *Deserter* to suggest the vulnerability of a workers' demonstration about to be attacked by police.

Fig. 6.50

Fig. 6.51

(Fig. 6.47). Canted or decentered framings dynamize the image (Figs. 6.48, 6.49). The Montage directors were also fond of placing the horizon line extremely low in the frame (Figs. 6.50, 6.51).

Montage directors also exploited special-effects cinematography. Vertov's playful documentary *Man with a Movie Camera* shows off the power of the cinema through split-screen framing and superimpositions (Fig. 6.52). Eisenstein's film about collective farming, *Old and New,* uses a superimposition of a bull towering above a field full of cows to suggest how important this one animal has been to the building of a successful farm (Fig. 6.53). While such camera tricks would be likely to be used for subjective effects in French Impressionism, Soviet directors often employed them to make symbolic points. (The building that "splits" in *Man with a Movie Camera* is the Bolshoi Theater in Moscow, home of traditional pre-Revolutionary opera and ballet.)

Because many Soviet films dealt with historical and social situations, some elements of their mise-en-scene tended to be realistic. Scenes might be shot on location in a real factory, as in *Strike* and *Mother.* Costumes often served primarily to indicate class position. Yet the Montage filmmakers also realized that dynamic tension between elements was not solely a matter of joining shots. Juxtapositions could be made within the shot as well, using mise-en-scene elements to heighten the impact on the viewer. Contrasting textures, shapes, volumes, colors, and the like, could be placed within a single frame (Fig. 6.54). Textures can work in a similar way (Fig. 6.55).

Fig. 6.52

Fig. 6.53

Fig. 6.54

Fig. 6.55

Fig. 6.56

Fig. 6.57

Fig. 6.58

Fig. 6.52 In *Man with a Movie Camera,* Vertov makes a huge building split like a broken egg by exposing each side of the frame separately and rolling the camera in opposite directions for each.

Fig. 6.53 A conceptual use of special effects in *Old and New.*

Fig. 6.54 In *Potemkin,* an officer glances suspiciously at some sailors. The composition splits into two distinct halves, dark and bright, with the lighting on the figures' faces matching the color of their costumes.

Fig. 6.55 In *New Babylon,* the heroine stands atop a barricade built by the Paris communards; her plain dress contrasts with the lacy frills on a department-store mannequin.

Fig. 6.56 In *Potemkin,* a high-angle shot down the side of the battleship shows men on the upper level, moving left to right, while the group on the deck below move right to left.

Fig. 6.57 A contrast in volumes in *Old and New,* as a bull looms hugely in the foreground while farmers and a cow appear as tiny figures below it.

Fig. 6.58 Similarly, *A Simple Case* arranges rows of mounted soldiers in depth, so that some appear large and some small.

We have seen how shots containing opposed directions of movement might be edited together. A single shot can use this principle by setting up more than one direction of figure movement (Fig. 6.56). Patterns might also create oppositions within the shot; in the plate-smashing scene from *Potemkin* (Figs. 6.19–6.28), the horizontal stripes of the sailor's shirt clash with the vertical stripes of the wall behind him. Although the precise effect of the juxtaposition is difficult to define, we can imagine that our impression of the scene would be very different if the wall were simply blank. Finally, mise-en-scene elements arranged in different planes in the depth of the shot could create juxtapositions of volume (Figs. 6.57, 6.58). When such shots, with their visual juxtapositions, are edited together with other shots, the multiple conflicting relationships can be complex indeed.

Fig. 6.59 A typical use of an unlit background in *Mother*.

Fig. 6.60 For the unglamorous role of the peasant heroine of *Old and New*, Eisenstein cast a real peasant.

Fig. 6.61 In *The Extraordinary Adventures of Mr. West in the Land of the Bolsheviks*, Khokhlova uses eccentric acting in playing a crook who vamps Mr. West.

Lighting also gives Montage films a distinctive look. Soviet films frequently use no fill light on the sets, so characters appear against black backgrounds (Fig. 6.59). Note also how the front of the officer's face is relatively dark, while the sides are strongly lit; this approach to lighting actors is common in Montage films.

Montage films used a variety of types of acting, ranging from the realistic to the highly stylized—often within the same film. Because so many characters in Soviet films were representatives of certain social classes or professions, directors used *typage*, casting nonactors whose physical appearances would instantly suggest what sort of people they were playing (Fig. 6.60). There was no need for the person to have the same job in real life as on the screen; for *Potemkin*, Eisenstein chose the small, fastidious man who plays the doctor because he "looked" like a doctor—though he actually made his living shoveling coal.

Typage was a gesture toward realism, but many performers in Montage films borrowed stylized techniques from Constructivist theater and from the circus: *biomechanics* and *eccentricity*. As in the theater, biomechanical film acting stressed physical control rather than subtle emotion. The Montage filmmakers delighted in having their actors punch one another or scramble about over factory equipment. Eccentricity emphasized the grotesque; performers behaved almost like clowns or slapstick comics. Alexandra Khokhlova, Kuleshov's wife and a member of his workshop, offered vivid instances of eccentric acting. Tall and gangly, she avoided the glamorous image of the female star; instead, she grimaced and used angular gestures (Fig. 6.61). Eisenstein's *Strike* and Kozintsev and Trauberg's silent films all contain eccentric performances.

Of the three avant-garde movements we have examined in Chapters 4 through 6, only the Soviet Montage style lasted into the early sound era. In Chapter 9 we shall discuss how the Montage filmmakers applied their approach to sound.

OTHER SOVIET FILMS

During the Montage movement's existence, perhaps fewer than thirty films were made in the style. Nevertheless, as in France and Germany, these avant-garde films were prestigious and influential. Many more conventional films contain a few Montage techniques, usually employed in a milder fashion. For example, Protazanov's *The White Eagle* (1928) begins with several dynamic views of statues against the sky (Fig. 6.62), a device which had become a cliché. Although *The White Eagle* has a story similar to those of some Montage films—the brutal repression of a strike by a provincial Tsarist governor—the rest of the film is done in the modified continuity style typical of European filmmaking in the 1920s.

Non-Montage films covered a wide range of genres. Although Soviet silent comedies are seldom seen today, there were plenty of them. Slapstick comedian Igor Ilinsky, a sort of Russian Jerry Lewis, was the decade's most popular star. In *The Tailor from Torzhok* (make by Protazanov in 1925 to

Fig. 6.62

Fig. 6.63

Fig. 6.64

Fig. 6.65

Fig. 6.66

Fig. 6.62 A Montage-style framing in a non-Montage film, *The White Eagle.*

Figs. 6.63 and 6.64 In *The Tailor from Torzhok*, the star mugs broadly, at one point glancing at the camera and crossing his eyes.

Fig. 6.65 In 1926, Leonid Leonidov appeared as Ivan the Terrible in Yuri Tarich's *Wings of a Serf;* his performance aided the film's widespread success abroad.

Fig. 6.66 Lavish production values in a conventional Soviet film, *Decembrists.*

publicize the government lottery), Ilinsky plays a tailor frantically seeking a winning lottery ticket he has lost (Figs. 6.63, 6.64). A light tone also prevails in the crime serial *Miss Mend* (co-directed by Kuleshov-workshop alumni Fyodor Ozep and Barnet in 1925). In this fantasy, three American workers from the "Rocfeller" company hear of a plot to poison the Soviet Union's water supply and, in a spirit of class solidarity, foil the villain.

Despite the Montage directors' downplaying of major stars, other films exploited the fame of established stage actors by casting them in dramas. In a few cases, top stars of the famous Moscow Art Theater, established by Stanislavsky in 1898 (and considered by many young filmmakers to be a bastion of conservative style) agreed to act in films (Fig. 6.65). Other Moscow Art Theater actors such as Ivan Moskvin and Mikhail Chekhov starred in films, and the only surviving film performance by the great Constructivist stage director Meyerhold is in *The White Eagle.*

A similar attempt at prestige came with historical epics and literary adaptations. Two popular films of this type were Viktor Gardin's *Poet and Tsar* (1927), a biography of the poet Pushkin, and *Decembrists* (1927, Alexander Ivanovsky). In a 1927 meeting to discuss the problems of Sovkino, Cubo-Futurist poet Vladimir Mayakovsky dismissed the former film contemptuously: "Take 'Poet and Tsar' for example. The picture is liked—but when you stop to think about it, what bosh, what a monstrosity."[2] Similarly, *Decembrists*, with its large ballroom sets (Fig. 6.66) looked like a tired version of Russian historical dramas of the pre-Revolutionary era. The Montage directors thought such films conservative and thus diametrically opposed to their own approaches to filmmaking.

THE FIVE-YEAR PLAN AND THE END
OF THE MONTAGE MOVEMENT

As we have seen, several of the early Montage films were successfully exported and were praised at home for their political content. As a result, during the period 1927–1930, the movement's activities intensified. At the same time, however, criticisms were increasingly being leveled at the Montage filmmakers by governmental and film-industry officials. The main charge was "formalism," a vague term implying that a film was too complex for mass audiences and that its makers were more interested in film style than in correct ideology.

Ironically, the very recovery of the film industry, which the export of Montage films helped create, led to criticisms of the movement. In 1927, for the first time the industry made more money from its own films than from imported ones. Official policy encouraged the industry to cut back its foreign trade. Sovkino and Lunacharsky came under attack for making films—including those of the Montage movement—that were more appropriate for sophisticated foreigners than for the uneducated peasant population at home. And as Montage filmmakers experimented with increasingly complex techniques, accusations of formalism intensified.

Criticized by the press, the major filmmakers had difficulties getting scripts approved and projects funded. Kuleshov came under fire first. Then Vertov had to move from his base in Moscow to make *Man with a Movie Camera* for the Ukrainian national company, Vufku. Critics also charged that Kozintsev and Trauberg's eccentric stylization was frivolous and obscure. Eisenstein's early prestige, gained through *Potemkin,* protected him at first, but as he explored the possibility of creating abstract ideas through intellectual montage in the late 1920s, he too faced growing criticisms. For a time Pudovkin was spared such attacks, and he managed to keep making Montage-style films until 1933, when his *Deserter* brought the movement to a close.

A turning point for the Soviet film industry came in March 1928, when the First Communist Party Conference on Film Questions was held. Until now, the government had left film matters largely to the control of Narkompros and other, smaller film organizations scattered through the republics. Now the Soviet Union was instituting the First Five-Year Plan, a major push toward expanding industrial output. As part of the Plan, the cinema was to be centralized. The goal was to increase the number of films made and to build equipment factories to supply all the industry's needs. Eventually, it was hoped, all film-related imports would be eliminated. Similarly, exportation would not be necessary, and all films could be tailored strictly to the needs of the workers and peasants.

The implementation of the Five-Year Plan in the cinema came slowly. Over the next two years, the government still put little money into the industry. This delay probably helped prolong the Montage movement. Soon, however, circumstances changed. In 1929, Eisenstein left the country to study sound filmmaking abroad. Spending most of his time working on abortive projects, first in Hollywood and then in Mexico, he did not return until 1932. Also in 1929, control over the cinema was taken away from Narkompros and turned over to the Movie Committee of the Soviet Union. Now Lunacharsky had little input, being only one of many members of the new body. In 1930, the film industry was further centralized by the formation of Soyuzkino, a company which was to supervise all production by the studios in the different republics and to handle all distribution and exhibition of films. The head of Soyuzkino was Boris Shumyatsky, a Communist party bureaucrat without film experience. Unlike Lunacharsky, Shumyatsky had no sympathy for the Montage filmmakers.

Soon the attacks on those filmmakers intensified. In 1931, for example, while Eisenstein was still in North America, an article criticized his films for their supposed "petty bourgeois" tendencies. If Eisenstein could strengthen his ties to the proletariat, the author concluded, he might "create real revolutionary cinema productions. But we must on no account minimize the difficulties confronting him. The way out of this crisis is possible only through a stubborn campaign for re-education, through merciless exposure and criticism of his first films."[3] All the major Montage filmmakers, and, indeed, modernist artists in every medium, eventually adopted more accessible styles.

During the early 1930s, the Soviet film industry moved toward an official policy that required all films to follow an approach called "Socialist Realism." We shall examine the era of intensified governmental control and Socialist Realism, from 1933 to 1945, in Chapter 12.

◆ NOTES AND QUERIES

FILM INDUSTRY AND GOVERNMENTAL POLICY: A TANGLED HISTORY

The film industry of any major producing country has a complex history, of course, but the Soviet situation in the fifteen years after the Revolution was particularly volatile. Many organizations disappeared soon after being formed. Governmental regulations attempted to make the industry both profitable and ideologically acceptable.

Several books offer detailed overviews. Jay Leyda's *Kino: A History of the Russian and Soviet Film* (3rd ed., Princeton, N.J.: Princeton University Press, 1983) provides an anecdotal account which gives a vivid sense of the events of the period. In his *The Politics of the Soviet Cinema 1917–1929* (Cambridge: Cambridge University Press, 1979), Richard Taylor explores the workings of the industry and governmental policy. Denise Youngblood's *Soviet Cinema in the Silent Era, 1918–1935* (Ann Arbor: UMI Research Press, 1985) provides a helpful indication of the kinds of criticism leveled at the Montage filmmakers, and she takes the history up to the institution of Socialist Realism as the film industry's official style. An older, but still interesting, source is Paul Babitsky and John Rimberg's *The Soviet Film Industry* (New York: Praeger, 1955). Many contemporary decrees and essays are translated in an anthology covering all aspects of Soviet cinema, *The Film Factory: Russian and Soviet Cinema in Documents 1896–1939,* ed. Richard Taylor and Ian Christie (Cambridge, Mass.: Harvard University Press, 1988).

THE KULESHOV EFFECT

Lev Kuleshov was an important theorist and teacher as well as a filmmaker. Modern historians have investigated the "Kuleshov experiments," none of which survives, and the "films without film," which the Kuleshov workshop staged in the early 1920s. Kuleshov's own accounts are available in English, in *Kuleshov on Film: Writings of Lev Kuleshov,* tr. and ed. Ronald Levaco (Berkeley: University of California Press, 1974), and *Lev Kuleshov: Fifty Years in Films,* tr. Dmitri Agrachev and Nina Belenkaya (Moscow: Raduga, 1987). Vance Kepley, Jr., discusses "The Kuleshov Workshop" in *Iris* **4,** 1 (1986), an issue devoted to Kuleshov (with most of the articles in French). A lengthy essay by Stephen P. Hill, "Kuleshov—Prophet without Honor?" appears in *Film Culture* 44 (Spring 1967).

THE RUSSIAN FORMALISTS AND THE CINEMA

During the period from 1914 to around 1930, a group of literary critics with close ties to the Cubo-Futurist and Constructivist movements created an important theoretical school called Russian Formalism. The Russian Formalists believed that artworks obeyed different principles than did other kinds of objects and that the theorist's task was to study how artworks were constructed to create certain effects. Working in Leningrad and Moscow, which were also the two centers of Russian film production, these critics wrote film reviews, essays on film theory, and even some scenarios for both Montage and non-Montage films. (For instance, Osip Brik scripted *Storm over Asia* and Viktor Shklovsky co-wrote Kuleshov's 1926 *By the Law.*) Several Soviet filmmakers, including Eisenstein, the FEKS group, and Kuleshov, had close links to Russian Formalism, which influenced their theoretical writings. Like the Montage directors, the Russian Formalists were attacked and forced after 1930 into more conventional approaches.

One volume of the Russian Formalists' film theory, *The Poetics of Cinema,* was published in 1927; it has been translated by Herbert Eagle as *Russian Formalist Film Theory* (Ann Arbor: Michigan Slavic Publications, 1981) and by Richard Taylor as *The Poetics of Cinema* in *Russian Poetics in Translation,* no. 9 (1982). Essays by both Montage directors and Russian Formalist critics have been published in *Screen* **12,** 4 (Winter 1971/1972) and *Screen* **15,** 3 (Autumn 1974). Material on FEKS, Russian Formalism, and eccentrism is available in *Futurism, Formalism, FEKS: 'Eccentrism' and Soviet Cinema 1918–36,* ed. Ian Christie and John Gillett (London: British Film Institute, n.d.). Several essays by Viktor Shklovsky appear in Taylor and Christie's *The Film Factory* (cited above).

◆ REFERENCES

1. Grigori Kozintsev, Leonid Trauberg, Sergei Yutkevich, and Georgi Kryzhitsky, *Eccentrism*, tr. Richard Taylor, in *The Film Factory: Russian and Soviet Cinema in Documents 1896–1939*, ed. Taylor and Ian Christie (Cambridge, Mass.: Harvard University Press, 1988), p. 58.

2. Quoted in Jay Leyda, *Kino: A History of the Russian and Soviet Film* (3rd ed., Princeton, N.J.: Princeton University Press, 1983), p. 229.

3. Ivan Anisimov, "The Films of Eisenstein," *International Literature* **3** (1931): 114.

7

THE LATE SILENT ERA IN HOLLYWOOD, 1920–1928

During World War I, the United States had become a global economic leader. The center of world finance shifted from London to New York, and American shipping carried goods all over the world. Despite a brief, intense recession in 1921 resulting primarily from the shift back to a peacetime economy, the 1920s were a period of prosperity for many sectors of society. Republican administrations were in power, and a conservative, pro-business approach dominated the country. American consumer goods, including movies, continued to make inroads in many foreign countries.

In contrast to this fiscal conservatism, society seemed to lose much of its restraint during the "roaring twenties." The passage of the Volstead Act (1919), outlawing all forms of alcoholic beverages, led to the excesses of the age of Prohibition. Bootleg liquor was readily available, and flouting the law by visiting speakeasies or attending wild drinking parties became common even among the upper classes. Before the war, women had grown their hair long, worn floor-length dresses, and danced sedately. Now they created scandals by bobbing their hair, wearing short skirts, doing the Charleston, and smoking in public.

Many sectors of society were shut off from the general prosperity and sophistication of the 1920s. Racism was rampant, with the Ku Klux Klan growing after its revival in 1915 and the stiffening of immigration quotas to keep certain groups out of the United States. Workers in agriculture and mining fared poorly. The film industry, however, benefited from the high level of capital available during this period, and its films reflected the fast pace of life in the "Jazz Age."

THEATER CHAINS AND THE STRUCTURE OF THE INDUSTRY

The American film industry, expanding hugely during World War I, continued to grow during the postwar decade. Despite a brief but severe depression in 1921, the era was one of general prosperity and intensive business investment. Between 1922 and 1930, total investment in the film industry leaped from $78 to $850 million. The average weekly attendance at American movie theaters doubled in the period between 1922 (40 million) to 1928 (80 million). Hollywood's exports continued to grow nearly unchecked until the mid-1920s and slowed only because virtually all foreign markets were sated.

Central to the industry's expansion was a strategy of buying and building movie theaters. By owning theater chains, the big producers had an ensured outlet for their films. Producers could then confidently raise budgets. Studios began competing in offering lavish production values. A new generation of directors came to prominence, and Hollywood also attracted more foreign filmmakers, who brought stylistic innovations. If the 1910s had seen the basic formation of the film industry, the next decade witnessed its expansion into a sophisticated set of institutions.

The most obvious indication of the growth of the film industry was its increasing vertical integration. The biggest firms jockeyed for power by combining production and distribution with expanding chains of theaters.

At first the main theater chains were regional. In 1917, in an attempt to challenge the power of the big Hollywood firms, a group of local theater chains formed its own production company, First National Exhibitors' Circuit. Its main member was the Stanley Company of America, a Philadelphia-based regional chain. Thus Hollywood firms like Famous Players–Lasky, Universal, and Fox were suddenly faced with a competitor that combined production, distribution, and exhibition.

This three-tiered vertical integration guaranteed that a company's films would find distribution and exhibition. The bigger the theater chain owned by the firm, the wider its films' exposure would be.

Although First National's production wing never became really profitable, it goaded other firms to integrate vertically. Adolf Zukor, head of Famous Players–Lasky and its distribution wing, Paramount, began buying theaters in 1920. In 1925, Famous Players–Lasky merged with Balaban & Katz, a Chicago-based theater chain controlling many of the biggest auditoriums in the Midwest. The result was the first production-distribution-exhibition firm with a truly national theater chain. Zukor marked the change by naming the theater circuit Publix Theaters. The firm as a whole became Paramount-Publix. By the early 1930s, it owned 1210 North American theaters, as well as some theaters abroad. Paramount-Publix's extensive holdings made it the subject of repeated governmental antitrust investigation and litigation that would lead to major changes in the film industry after World War II.

Another important firm that achieved vertical integration during this era was Loew's, Inc. Marcus Loew had begun as a nickelodeon owner, expanded into vaudeville, and built up a large chain of movie theaters by the late 1910s. In 1919, he moved into production by acquiring a medium-size firm, Metro, run by Louis B. Mayer. With the purchase of Goldwyn Pictures in

1924, Loew combined his production wing into Metro-Goldwyn-Mayer (MGM). After Paramount, MGM became the second largest of the Hollywood companies.

The chains owned by the vertically integrated firms contained few of the nation's 15,000 theaters. In the mid-1920s, the Publix chain had roughly 500 houses, while MGM had a mere 200. Yet the three main chains included many of the big first-run theaters, with seating capacities in the thousands and higher admission prices. By late in the decade, about three-quarters of box-office receipts came from these large theaters. Smaller urban theaters and those in rural areas had to wait to get a film on a subsequent run and often received well-worn prints.

As the big Hollywood companies expanded, they developed a system of distribution that would maximize their profits and keep other firms at the margins of the market. With the theaters they did not own, they employed *block booking*, which meant that any exhibitor who wanted certain films with high box-office potential had to rent other, less desirable films from the same company. Some exhibitors might be forced to book an entire year's program in advance. Since most theaters changed programs at least twice a week and each big firm usually made only around fifty films a year, a theater could deal with more than one firm. Similarly, the big companies needed films from other firms to keep their theater programs full. Thus the biggest firms cooperated among themselves. The movie business developed into a mature oligopoly during the 1920s.

Because the big theaters were so important, the major companies made them opulent to attract patrons, not simply through the films being shown but through the promise of an exciting movie-going experience. The 1920s were the age of the picture palace, seating thousands of patrons and offering fancy lobbies, uniformed ushers, and orchestral accompaniment to the films. The Balaban & Katz chain pioneered the use of air-conditioning in 1917; this was a major draw in a period when home air-conditioning was unknown and theater business ordinarily dropped off sharply in the summer months. Balaban & Katz houses and other big theaters also offered a lengthy program in addition to the main feature, including newsreels, comic shorts, orchestral interludes, and even live-action playlets and musical numbers.

The architecture of the picture palaces gave working and middle-class patrons an unaccustomed taste of luxury. There were two types of design: conventional and atmospheric. Conventional palaces were imitations of legitimate theaters, often incorporating elaborate ornamentation based on Italian baroque and rococo styles. Huge chandeliers, domes, and balconies were covered with stucco and gilt. The "atmospheric" palace gave the spectator the impression of sitting in an auditorium that opened onto a night sky. The dark-blue dome would have light-bulb stars, and moving clouds were cast onto the ceiling by projectors. The decor might imitate exotic places, such as a Spanish villa or an Egyptian temple. As the 1920s progressed, theaters got more and more flamboyant (Fig. 7.1). The Depression would soon put an end to such extravagant theater building.

The vertically integrated firms that controlled big theater chains—Paramount-Publix, Loew's (MGM), and First National—constituted the "Big

Fig. 7.1 Part of the interior of the Brooklyn Paramount (built in 1928). This theater combined the conventional and atmospheric approaches to picture-palace design, incorporating trees and false sky glimpsed through the alcoves but topping it all with an elaborately decorated ceiling.

Three," at the top of the American film industry. Trailing behind them, but still important, were the "Little Five," firms which owned few or no theaters: Universal, Fox, the Producers Distributing Corporation, the Film Booking Office, and Warner Bros.

Under founder Carl Laemmle, Universal continued into the 1920s concentrating on relatively low-budget films aimed at smaller theaters. Despite a strong distribution wing, the firm had few theaters. Universal attempted to build a chain in the mid-1920s but found the venture unprofitable and soon sold the theaters off. Several major directors (John Ford, Erich von Stroheim) and stars (Lon Chaney) worked there early in the decade, but they soon left, drawn away by higher salaries. For a time Universal employed the successful young producer Irving Thalberg, who helped the firm move into higher-quality, big-budget films; soon Thalberg also left, becoming a major force in shaping MGM's policies. Later in the decade, German-born Laemmle was in the forefront in hiring émigré directors, who brought a brooding, distinctive style to the studio's output.

Fox also continued to concentrate on lower-budget popular fare, including its Westerns with William Farnum and Tom Mix. Fox began to create a modest theater chain in 1925, making it one of the most important of the Little Five. The company had a small stable of prestige directors: John Ford, Raoul Walsh, F. W. Murnau, and Frank Borzage. It also continued to make many ordinary, low-budget films.

Warner Bros. was smaller, possessing neither theaters nor a distribution wing. It scored a considerable success, however, with a series of films starring a German shepherd dog, Rin-Tin-Tin. More surprisingly, Warners hired German director Ernst Lubitsch, and he produced several important films there. In 1924, Warners drew upon the new willingness of Wall Street investors to put money into the film industry. It began a major expansion, acquiring theaters and other assets. The firm's investment in new sound technology would thrust it into the forefront of the industry within a few years.

The two other members of the Little Five were relatively small firms. The short-lived Producers Distributing Corp. (1924–1928) was notable mainly for producing a series of Cecil B. De Mille's films after he left Famous Players–Lasky in 1925. The Film Booking Office was formed in 1922 and turned out popular action films for several years. In 1929, it became the basis for the production portion of a much more important new firm, RKO.

Standing apart from both the Big Three and the Little Five was United Artists (UA), formed by Mary Pickford, Charles Chaplin, Douglas Fairbanks, and D. W. Griffith in 1919. UA, which was an umbrella distribution firm, owned neither production facilities nor theaters. It existed to distribute films produced independently by its four owners, plus those of other major filmmakers it signed up over the years. Prior contractual commitments by the four founders delayed the firm's initial releases for a year, and Chaplin's first UA film, *A Woman of Paris*, was not a hit. In 1924, producer Joseph Schenck took over management of the firm. By adding stars Rudolph Valentino, Norma Talmadge, Buster Keaton, and Gloria Swanson, as well as prestigious producer Samuel Goldwyn, Schenck stepped up the rate of release of UA films. In general, however, UA failed to make a profit in most years.

THE MOTION PICTURE PRODUCERS AND DISTRIBUTORS ASSOCIATION

As the American film industry expanded, so too did efforts on the part of various social groups to increase censorship. By the late 1910s and early 1920s, there was increasing pressure for a national censorship law, and more local boards were being formed. Many postwar films used the sort of subject matter associated with the "roaring twenties": bootleg liquor, jazz music, flappers, and wild parties. Cecil B. De Mille's sex comedies presented adultery as a frivolous, even glamorous, pastime. Erich von Stroheim's *Blind Husbands* (1919) similarly treated a married woman's flirtation as a fascinating violation of social norms.

During this same period, a series of scandals focused attention on the less palatable aspects of the lifestyles of famous filmmakers, including sex scandals and flagrant violations of the new Prohibition law. Mary Pickford's image as "America's sweetheart" received a blow in 1920 when she divorced her first husband to marry Douglas Fairbanks. In 1921, comedian Roscoe "Fatty" Arbuckle was charged with rape and murder when a young actress died during a drunken party; although he was ultimately acquitted, the charges wrecked his career. The following year, director William Desmond Taylor was mysteriously murdered in circumstances that revealed his affairs with several well-known actresses. In 1923, the handsome, athletic star Wallace Reid died of a morphine addiction. The public suddenly viewed Hollywood as promoting excess and decadence.

Partly in an effort to avoid censorship and clean up Hollywood's image, the main studios banded together to form a trade organization, the Motion Picture Producers and Distributors of America (MPPDA). To head it, in early 1922 they hired Will Hays, then postmaster general under Warren Harding. Hays had already proved his flair for publicity by chairing the Republican National Committee when Harding was elected President. That flair, combined with Hays's access to powerful figures in Washington and his Presbyterian background, made him useful to the film industry.

Hays's strategy was to pressure the producers to eliminate the offensive content of their films and to include morals clauses in studio contracts. Despite Arbuckle's acquittal on the rape and murder charges, Hays banned his films. By 1924, the MPPDA had formulated a set of guidelines on subject matter that would render censorship laws unnecessary. These guidelines proved ineffectual, and Hays stiffened them in 1927 and 1930, finally cracking down with a strict Production Code in 1934.

Although the Hays Office, as the MPPDA came to be known, is usually thought of as a strategy to block domestic censorship, the organization also performed other services for the industry. The MPPDA gathered information on film markets at home and abroad, keeping up, for example, with censorship regulations in various countries. Hays established a foreign department which battled several European quotas that stifled American exports. In 1926, Hays's group successfully lobbied Congress to form the Motion Picture Division of the Department of Commerce. That division then helped promote the sale of American films abroad by gathering information and bringing more pressure against harmful regulations. Indeed, the formation of the MPPDA provided a clear signal that motion pictures had become a major American industry.

STUDIO FILMMAKING: DIRECTORS, STARS, GENRES

The expansion and consolidation of the Hollywood film industry was paralleled by a polishing of the classical continuity style that had developed in the 1910s.

By the 1920s, the big production firms had "dark" studios that kept out all sunlight and allowed entire scenes to be illuminated by artificial lights. Scenes' backgrounds were kept inconspicuous with a low *fill* light, while the main figures stood out by being outlined with a glow of *backlight*, usually cast from the rear top of the set (Fig. 7.2). The *key*, or brightest light, came from one side of the camera, while a dimmer secondary light from the other side created "fill" that softened shadows. This *three-point illumination system* (key, fill, backlighting) became the basis of Hollywood lighting. It created glamorous, consistent compositions from shot to shot.

By the 1920s, the continuity editing system had become sophisticated indeed. Eyeline matches, cut-ins, and small variations of framing could successively reveal the most important portions of a scene's space. In John Ford's 1920 Western, *Just Pals*, for example, a mother waits in anguish as her son supposedly drowns a litter of unwanted kittens. In fact he spares them and pretends that he has killed them. This complex action is gradually revealed through a series of carefully framed details observed by the heroine (Figs. 7.3–7.11).

With such techniques of lighting and editing, the Hollywood style had become highly flexible. During the 1920s, a generation of filmmakers came to the fore who would dominate American filmmaking for the next three decades and more. Some of them, like Ford and King Vidor, had started directing on a modest scale in the 1910s, but they were now famous. Similarly, although some of the stars of earlier years retained their popularity, others now came forward. Older genres developed, as when slapstick comedies and Westerns, typically relegated to short subjects, became more prestigious. New genres also appeared, such as the antiwar film. Perhaps most importantly, budgets grew as Hollywood consolidated its international control, and major directors found themselves able to make expensive films.

BIG-BUDGET FILMS OF THE EARLY 1920s

A film that typified several trends of the new decade was *The Four Horsemen of the Apocalypse*, directed by Rex Ingram and released in 1921. It was made by Metro, the production firm recently purchased by Loew's in its expansion. Ingram, who had directed several minor films, gained considerable control over this project, based on a best-selling novel. The film dealt with a South American family's changing fortunes during World War I, and it presented

Fig. 7.2 Light coming from the upper rear of the set outlines the characters in *The Marriage Circle*.

Fig. 7.3 Walking near town, the heroine of *Just Pals* pauses and looks off left.

Fig. 7.4 An eyeline match reveals what she sees, a little boy with a bag by a fence, looking off right.

Fig. 7.5 Another cut takes us to a medium shot of a woman, also by the fence, weeping.

Fig. 7.6 A second shot of the boy shows him looking through the fence apprehensively and beginning to empty the bag onto the ground.

Fig. 7.7 A cut to the ground shows a litter of kittens falling out of the bag.

Fig. 7.8 Finally a long shot shows the space: The woman and boy are by a river, and he throws the empty bag into the water.

Fig. 7.9 We see the bag hit the water in a closer view.

Fig. 7.10 The long-shot framing shows the pair moving away, the boy comforting the woman, who has not turned around to watch any of his actions.

Fig. 7.11 After seven shots of their actions, we return to a closer view of the heroine, reacting in horror.

a new view of the war. Although it still showed the Germans as evil "Huns," it presented the conflict as destructive rather than glorious (Fig. 7.12). The film's triumph was probably mainly due, however, to the fact that its doomed lovers were played by Rudolph Valentino and Alice Terry, who rose to immediate stardom (Fig. 7.13).

Valentino was soon hired by Paramount and became one of the matinee idols of the era, popularizing the "Latin lover" image in such films as *The Sheik* (1921, George Melford). He was willing to play in extremely melodramatic roles but also to mock his own image. His early death in 1926 provoked frenzied grief among his many fans. Alice Terry, who was married to Ingram, went on to act primarily in his later films. Ingram was ill suited to the restrictions of Hollywood, especially when Metro became part of the MGM merger in 1924. Unable to work under the strict regime of Louis B. Mayer and Irving Thalberg, Ingram made several films in France for the firm, including *Mare Nostrum* (1926). As with several nonconformist directors who worked for MGM, however, his career declined by the end of the 1920s.

Cecil B. De Mille had been extraordinarily prolific from 1914 on. During the 1920s, he moved into more sumptuous films at Paramount. One of his primary genres was the sex comedy, often starring Gloria Swanson, one of the top stars. De Mille's sophisticated comedies helped earn Hollywood a reputation for being inordinately risqué. He exploited expensive women's fashions, rich decors, and sexually provocative situations, as in *Why Change Your Wife?* (Figs. 7.14, 7.15).

When his films came under fire from censorship groups, De Mille responded with films that mixed equally steamy melodrama with religious subject matter. *The Ten Commandments* (1923) had a frame story depicting a young man who scoffs at morality and vows to break all the commandments; the central part of the film was a historical epic showing Moses leading the Jews out of Egypt (Fig. 7.16). De Mille's biggest religious production of this era was *The King of Kings* (1927), controversial because of its onscreen depiction of Christ. In the sound era, De Mille would become identified with historical epics.

Similarly, after D. W. Griffith's move to United Artists, he made several large-scale historical films. Just as he had been inspired by Italian epics like *Cabiria* to make *The Birth of a Nation* and *Intolerance*, now he was influenced by Lubitsch's postwar German films. Griffith's greatest success of the era

Fig. 7.12 The final scene of *The Four Horsemen of the Apocalypse* showed a military cemetery with innumerable crosses, suggesting the horrors of war.

Fig. 7.13 Glamorous photography in *The Four Horsemen of the Apocalypse* helped make Rudolph Valentino and Alice Terry stars.

Fig. 7.14

Fig. 7.15

Figs. 7.14 and 7.15 In *Why Change Your Wife?* Gloria Swanson plays a mousy wife who saves her marriage to Thomas Meighan by adopting a daring wardrobe.

Fig. 7.16

Fig. 7.17

Fig. 7.16 The Egyptian forces set out in pursuit of the fleeing Jews in front of a massive set in *The Ten Commandments*.

Fig. 7.17 A poignant moment in *Orphans of the Storm*, as the two separated sisters briefly encounter and then lose each other again in the streets of Paris.

was *Orphans of the Storm* (1922), set during the French Revolution. It starred the Gish sisters, Lillian and Dorothy, both affiliated with Griffith since the early 1910s (Fig. 7.17). Lillian's career in particular flourished during this decade, as she worked with such major directors as King Vidor (*La Bohème*, 1926) and Victor Sjöström. Griffith made another historical epic, *America* (1924), concerning the American Revolutionary War. His next film, however, was quite different: a naturalistic tale of difficulties in postwar Germany called *Isn't Life Wonderful* (1924). Griffith's mid-1920s films were increasingly unprofitable, and he soon abandoned independent production to make a few films for Paramount. He made two films in the early sound era, including the ambitious *Abraham Lincoln* (1930), but he then was forced into retirement until his death in 1948.

Not all filmmakers who commanded large budgets in Hollywood during the 1920s fit comfortably into its efficient system. Erich von Stroheim had begun in the mid-1910s as an assistant to Griffith. He also acted, typically playing the "evil Hun" figure in World War I films. Universal elevated him to director in 1919 with *Blind Husbands*, the story of a couple on a mountaineering holiday; the wife is nearly seduced away from her complacent husband by a scoundrel, played by von Stroheim (Fig. 7.18). The success of this film led Universal to give von Stroheim a larger budget for his second film, *Foolish Wives* (1922), in which he played another predatory role. Von Stroheim exceeded the budget considerably, partly by building a large set reproducing part of Monte Carlo on the studio backlot. Universal turned this to its advantage by advertising *Foolish Wives* as the first film to cost a million dollars. More problematically, von Stroheim's first version ran over six hours. The studio pared it down to roughly two and a half hours. (Abridged versions circulated until the 1970s, when an approximation of the 1922 version was restored.)

Von Stroheim's Hollywood career involved several such problems with excessive length and budgets. Producer Irving Thalberg replaced him when cost overruns threatened his next project, *The Merry-Go-Round* (1923). Von Stroheim then moved to the independent production firm Goldwyn (which

Fig. 7.18 Erich von Stroheim as the villainous seducer (termed by publicists "the man you love to hate") in *Blind Husbands*.

Samuel Goldwyn had by this point sold) to make *Greed*, an adaptation of Frank Norris's naturalistic novel, *McTeague*. The result was a nine-hour film, which von Stroheim cut by about half. By this point Goldwyn had become part of MGM, and von Stroheim again encountered constraints imposed by Thalberg. The final release print, taken out of von Stroheim's control, ran about two hours, shorn of one major plot line and many other scenes. This story of an uneducated dentist and his miserly wife was filled with naturalistic touches and was perceived as grim, even sordid, by most critics and audiences (Fig. 7.19). The excised footage was apparently destroyed, and *Greed* remains one of the great mutilated films.

Von Stroheim achieved a brief success at MGM with *The Merry Widow* (1925), a film that gained popularity mainly as a result of its sexual subject matter. He then moved to Paramount to make *The Wedding March* (1928), yet another film in which he starred as a seducer, this time nearly redeemed by love. Again von Stroheim contemplated a lengthy film which he hoped to release as two features; the studio reduced it to one, which did poor business. Von Stroheim's last major Hollywood project, an independent production for Gloria Swanson, was *Queen Kelly* (1928–1929), which was unfinished and only much later restored and shown. Von Stroheim ceased to direct in the sound era, but he acted in many important films, including Jean Renoir's *Grand Illusion* (1937).

Fig. 7.19 The ending of *Greed*, with the hero trapped in Death Valley and killing his old enemy, manifests the bleak tone that made *Greed* unpopular with its initial audiences.

MINOR GENRES GAIN RESPECTABILITY

After United Artists was started in 1919, Douglas Fairbanks was the first of its founders to release a film through the new company. *His Majesty, the American* (1919, Joseph Henabery) was one of the unpretentious, clever comedies that made Fairbanks a star. Soon, however, he moved from comedy to a more ambitious costume picture, *The Mark of Zorro* (1920, Fred Niblo). This film retained the star's comic flair but was longer and placed more emphasis on historical atmosphere, a conventional romance, dueling, and other dangerous stunts (Fig. 7.20). *The Mark of Zorro* was so successful that Fairbanks soon gave up comedy and concentrated on swashbucklers, often based on literature, such as *The Three Musketeers* (1921, Fred Niblo), *The Thief of Bagdad* (1924, Raoul Walsh), and *The Black Pirate* (1926, Albert Parker). Fairbanks remained one of the most consistently popular stars of the 1920s, though his success dissipated in the early sound era.

Fairbanks had been unusual as a silent comedian who worked exclusively in features from the beginning of his film career in 1915. In the 1920s, however, several of the great slapstick stars of the earlier period also aspired to work in longer films. (See Box.)

Another genre that gained in prestige during the 1920s was the Western. Previously Westerns had been cheap, short features shown primarily in small-town theaters. Then, in 1923, Paramount released *The Covered Wagon* (James Cruze), an epic of the westward trip of a wagon train. With a large cast, including major stars, and a thrilling scene of the wagons crossing a river, the film was a hit. The low-budget Western continued to be a staple of Hollywood production, but for decades the lavish Western would also command respect.

Fig. 7.20 Douglas Fairbanks, as Zorro, soars over a host of pursuers in *The Mark of Zorro*.

SILENT COMEDY IN THE 1920s

During the 1910s, most comedies that were based on physical action, or "slapstick," were shorts that accompanied more prestigious features (though the popular comic stars often proved bigger draws than those of the "main attraction"). During the 1920s, feature-length slapstick comedies became more common. Stars like Chaplin, Keaton, and Harold Lloyd concentrated on creating stronger stories that would support their elaborate physical gags. With their mastery of purely visual action, these comedians created one of the most prominent and enduring genres of the decade.

Harry Langdon came to the cinema somewhat later than the other major comics of this era. From 1924 to 1927, he made short comedies for Mack Sennett. In these he developed his typical persona, one quite different from the personas of his rivals. Langdon cultivated a baby-faced image, playing naive characters who react slowly to whatever happens to them (Fig. 7.21). By the mid-1920s, he also began making features: *Tramp, Tramp, Tramp* (1926, Harry Edwards), *The Strong Man* (1926, Frank Capra), and *Long Pants* (1927, Frank Capra). Langdon continued to appear in small roles into the 1940s, but, as with many other comics of this era, his appeal came primarily through visual humor.

Charles Chaplin continued to make hugely successful films in the early 1920s, when his contract with First National kept him from releasing through United Artists. In 1914, Chaplin had appeared in the first slapstick feature, *Tillie's Punctured Romance*, but subsequently he concentrated on shorts. In 1921, he returned to features with extraordinary success in *The Kid*. Here Chaplin played the familiar Little

Fig. 7.22 In *The Kid*, the Tramp coaches the foundling on tactics of street fighting, unaware that the rival's muscular father is looking on.

Tramp but shared the spotlight with the expressive child actor Jackie Coogan, who appeared as a foundling whom the Tramp raises (Fig. 7.22).

Chaplin soon became even more ambitious, making a drama, *A Woman of Paris*, in which he played only a walk-

Fig. 7.21 In a long take in *The Luck of the Foolish* (1924, Harry Edwards), Harry Langdon slowly eats a sandwich, registering his dawning realization that a shingle has accidentally fallen into it.

Fig. 7.23 The heroine's rich lover fetches one of his own handkerchiefs from a drawer in her apartment, a touch that establishes their intimate relationship visually, in *A Woman of Paris*.

Fig. 7.24 In *Safety Last*, Harold Lloyd created one of the most memorable comic images of the cinema when he dangled from a clock high up the side of a building.

Fig. 7.25 Trapped on a horse-drawn moving van in a passing police parade, the hero calmly lights his cigarette with a bomb tossed by an anarchist in *Cops* (1922, co-directed by Keaton and Eddie Cline).

on role. This bitterly ironic romance satirized high society. Its droll, even risqué, humor (Fig. 7.23) influenced other directors of sophisticated comedies. The public, however, stayed away from a Chaplin film without the Little Tramp. Chaplin brought back that beloved character in two very popular features, *The Gold Rush* (1925) and *The Circus* (1927).

Harold Lloyd quickly joined the vogue for slapstick features. Using the "glasses" character he had developed in the late teens, he made *A Sailor-Made Man* (1921, Fred Newmeyer), the story of a brash young man who wins his love through a series of adventures. Although Lloyd starred in a variety of types of comedies, he is best remembered for his "thrill" comedies. In *Safety Last* (1923, Newmeyer and Sam Taylor), he played an ambitious young man who has to climb the side of a skyscraper as a publicity stunt for the store where he works (Fig. 7.24). Some of Lloyd's films of this era featured him as the bumbling small-town boy who becomes a hero when confronted with a great challenge, as in *Girl Shy* (1924, Newmeyer and Taylor), *The Freshman* (1925, Newmeyer and Taylor), and *The Kid Brother* (1927, Ted Wilde). Lloyd's career lasted into the early sound era, but eventually the aging actor did not fit his youthful image, and he retired.

Buster Keaton had gotten his start in vaudeville when he was young and then moved into films as an actor in Fatty Arbuckle's short films of the late 1910s. When Arbuckle shifted to features in the early 1920s, Keaton took over his film production unit and directed and starred in a series of popular two-reelers. His trademark was his refusal to smile, and he became known as "the Great Stone Face." Keaton's early films revealed a taste for bizarre humor that bordered at times on surrealism (Fig. 7.25).

Fig. 7.26 The hero of *Sherlock Junior*, a projectionist, dreams, while his superimposed dream image goes out to enter the film being shown in the theater.

Keaton soon moved into features, though his offbeat humor and complex plots made him less popular than his main rivals, Chaplin and Lloyd. His first feature-length hit was *The Navigator* (1924, co-directed with Donald Crisp), a story of a couple cast adrift alone on a huge ocean liner. Keaton was fond of stories that exploited the cinematic medium, as in *Sherlock Junior* (1924), which contained an elaborate film-within-a-film dream sequence (Fig. 7.26). Keaton's finest film may be *The General* (1927, co-directed with Clyde Bruckman), a story of a daring rescue during the Civil War. Keaton and Bruckman created an almost perfectly balanced narrative structure, evoked period detail, and staged elaborate gags within single shots. Nonetheless, *The General* failed to win popularity.

In 1928, Keaton moved to MGM, where he made one film that was up to his old standard—*The Cameraman* (1928, Edward Sedgwick, Jr.). After the coming of sound, however, he was not allowed his customary freedom in improvising gags on the set. Keaton's career gradually declined in the early 1930s, when MGM began co-starring him with more aggressive comics like Jimmy Durante. From the mid-1930s, Keaton played in many minor films and took small roles during the sound era, but his career never revived before his death in 1966.

Although these major actors entered features, the comic short remained a popular part of theater programs. The most important producers of shorts remained Hal Roach, who had discovered Harold Lloyd, and Mack Sennett, formerly of Key-stone. Under their guidance, a new generation of stars emerged. The most famous of these were Stan Laurel and Oliver Hardy, who had worked separately in minor comedies for years before being teamed by Roach in *Putting Pants on Philip* (1927). This short film about an American (Hardy) trying to deal with the turmoil caused by his aggressively flirtatious, kilt-wearing Scottish cousin (Laurel) remains one of their most hilarious. Unlike some other silent comedians, Laurel and Hardy made an effortless transition to sound, and Roach graduated them to feature films in 1931. Another star of this period was Charlie Chase, who worked for Sennett. Chase was a thin, ordinary-looking man with a small moustache who depended not so much on his comic appearance as on his talents for staging elaborate indoor chases. Comics from the teens who had played supporting roles in Chaplin's and other stars' films, such as Chester Conklin and Mack Swain, now acquired series of their own under Sennett.

Fig. 7.27 The odd heroes of *Just Pals* awake after a night spent in a hayloft.

John Ford had made his start directing stylish, modest Westerns (p. 76). *Just Pals* (1920) was an unconventional film, the story of a loafer in a small western town who befriends a hobo boy and eventually becomes a hero by exposing a local embezzler (Fig. 7.27). In 1921 he moved from Universal to the Fox Film Corp. His first major success there was *The Iron Horse* (1924), a high-budget Western made in the wake of *The Covered Wagon*. This story of the building of the first transcontinental railroad exploited Ford's feeling for landscape. He soon became Fox's top director, working in a variety of genres. He made only one more Western during the decade: *3 Bad Men* (1926), with an impressive land-rush sequence. Surprisingly, he did not return to that genre until *Stagecoach* (1939), but he was identified with Westerns throughout his long career.

Frank Borzage had also directed a number of low-budget Westerns during the 1910s. These include *The Gun Woman* (1918), an intense story of a rugged dance-hall owner, the Tigress, who shoots the man she loves when he turns out to be a stagecoach bandit. Like Ford, Borzage moved into more prestigious filmmaking at the larger studios during the 1920s, though he quickly abandoned Westerns. Today he is often thought of in connection with melodramas, such as *Humoresque* (1920), a highly sentimental account of a Jewish violinist wounded in World War I. Some of Borzage's best films of the decade, however, were in other genres. *The Circle* (1925, MGM) was a sophisticated romantic comedy. In 1924 Borzage moved to Fox, where he joined Ford as a leading director. His first film there, *Lazybones* (1925), was a rambling, low-key comedy about a lazy young man who—unlike most Hollywood protagonists—has no goals but sacrifices his already shaky reputation to raise a child for the sister of the woman he loves.

After *The Cabinet of Dr. Caligari* was shown in the United States in 1921, horror films gradually became a minor American genre. Universal pioneered this type of film, primarily because one of its main stars was Lon Chaney. Chaney was a master of make-up—"the Man of a Thousand Faces"—and had a flair for macabre roles. He played Quasimodo in the original adaptation of *The Hunchback of Notre Dame* (1923, Wallace Worsley), for which Universal built extravagant sets re-creating medieval Paris, and the Phantom in the 1925 version of *The Phantom of the Opera* (Rupert Julian). Chaney's most consistently disturbing films, however, were made at MGM with director Tod Browning, whose taste for stories with perverse twists matched his own. In *The Unknown* (1927), for example, Chaney played a circus knife thrower, Alonzo, who pretends to be armless as part of his act. His beautiful partner (played by the young Joan Crawford) has a pathological fear of being touched by men and trusts only Alonzo. To gain her lasting love, he actually has his arms amputated, only to discover that she has now fallen in love with another man (Fig. 7.28). Chaney died prematurely in 1930, but Browning went on in the 1930s to make some notable horror films, such as *Dracula* (1931) and *Freaks* (1932). The horror film also received a boost in the late 1920s, when German directors began moving to Hollywood.

The gangster genre had not been particularly important in American filmmaking before the mid-1920s. There had been some films about petty gang crime, such as Griffith's *The Musketeers of Pig Alley* (1912) and Walsh's *The Regeneration* (1915). It was the rise of organized criminal activity associated with Prohibition, however, that helped make the flashily dressed, heavily armed gangster a prominent image in Hollywood films. One film did a great deal to establish the genre: Josef von Sternberg's *Underworld* (1927), made for Paramount.

Von Sternberg had started by independently producing and directing a gloomy naturalistic drama, *The Salvation Hunters* (1925), on a shoestring budget. It was championed by Charles Chaplin, and although the film failed at the box office, von Sternberg was hired by MGM for a brief and unfruitful period. *Underworld* was a big hit, however, in part due to its offbeat stars. Its odd hero is a homely, lumbering jewel thief, played by George Bancroft. He picks up a drunken Britisher (Clive Brook) and makes him into a refined assistant. The hero's world-weary mistress (Evelyn Brent) falls in love with the Britisher, and the hero, after plotting to kill the pair, magnanimously holds off a police raid to allow them to escape together. Von Sternberg filmed this story with the dense, dazzling cinematography that was to become his hallmark (Fig. 7.29). Von Sternberg went on to make another quirky gangster film starring Bancroft, an early talkie called *Thunderbolt* (1929). He also worked in other genres during the 1920s. *The Docks of New York* (1928) was a sordid story of a ship's stoker (Bancroft again) and a prostitute redeemed by each other's love; again the crowded scenery and textured, atmospheric lighting set von Sternberg's work apart. *The Docks of New York* prefigured the romantic melodramas that were to be the director's specialty in the 1930s.

Fig. 7.28 Lon Chaney frequently underwent lengthy make-up work and training for his roles, as when he learned to use his feet instead of hands to play the protagonist of *The Unknown*.

Fig. 7.29 Josef von Sternberg used backlight and smoke to create this atmospheric moment as the protagonist of *Underworld* guns down a rival. The film's style anticipated the later brooding *films noirs* ("dark films") of the 1940s.

NEW INVESTMENT AND BLOCKBUSTERS

During the mid-1920s, Wall Street investment increased the ability of the Hollywood studios to produce big-budget films. Epic films followed the trend initiated by *The Ten Commandments*, with colossal sets and lavish costume design. The newly formed MGM was particularly committed to prestige pictures. It undertook one of the decade's most ambitious projects, an adaptation

Fig. 7.30 Large sets and trick photography re-created Rome's Circus Maximus for the chariot race in *Ben-Hur*.

Fig. 7.31 The hero and heroine's romantic interlude ends as they are wrenched apart when he must depart for the front in *The Big Parade*.

Fig. 7.32 The "big parade" of men and equipment moving up to the front.

of General Lew Wallace's novel *Ben-Hur* (the second best-selling book, after the Bible, and an enormous stage hit as well). The production had originated in 1922 at the Goldwyn company, and the planners tried to give the film greater authenticity by filming on location in Italy—where, incidentally, labor costs were lower. Shooting in Italy, however, lacked the efficiency of studio work, and one accident during the filming of a naval battle may have resulted in some deaths of extras. In 1924, MGM inherited the project when it absorbed Goldwyn, and the process of completing the film was long and troubled. *Ben-Hur* finally appeared in 1926. Its chariot race was filmed in huge sets; a battery of cameras covered the action from many angles, permitting a breakneck pace in the editing (Fig. 7.30).

MGM also made an important pacifist war film, *The Big Parade* (1925). Its director, King Vidor, had learned his craft by studying the newly emerging classical Hollywood style in his hometown theater in Texas. He began his career by acting in and directing minor films in the 1910s. Moving to MGM when it formed in 1924, he worked in several genres. His *Wine of Youth* (1924) was a subtle story of three generations of women: a wise grandmother looking on helplessly as her daughter nearly divorces and her granddaughter takes this as a cue that she can settle for love outside marriage. *The Big Parade* was a much more ambitious project. It starred John Gilbert, the main romantic idol of the period after Valentino's death, as a rich young man who volunteers during World War I. The early portion of the story depicts his time behind the lines, as he falls in love with a French farm woman (Fig. 7.31). An abrupt switch moves the film into epic scenes of the war (Fig. 7.32). But, even more than *The Four Horsemen of the Apocalypse*, *The Big Parade* depicts the horrors of war. Now German soldiers are seen simply as other human victims of the combat. Alone in a foxhole with a dying German boy, the hero finds himself unable to kill the lad and instead lights him a cigarette. Other war films of the late 1920s and the 1930s followed this pattern, portraying war as grim and unglorious. *The Big Parade* became the first film to run more than a year on Broadway, and its success abroad was enormous.

Vidor made a very different sort of film with *The Crowd* (1928). A working-class woman marries a clerk, but they nearly break up when one of their children dies in a traffic accident. MGM, which was particularly prone to interfere with its directors' work, imposed a happy ending in which the family is reunited. Nevertheless, *The Crowd* stood apart from most Hollywood films in its nonglamorous depiction of everyday life.

Other studios than MGM carried on the trend toward big-budget films. In 1927, Paramount released *Wings* (William Wellman), another bittersweet tale of World War I, this time centering on two friends, Jack and David, who love the same girl and become pilots together. Jack fails to realize that his neighbor, Mary, is in love with him, and she follows him to France as a Red Cross driver. Mary was played by Clara Bow, who enjoyed a brief but intense period of stardom from the mid-1920s to early 1930s. She epitomized the jazz-age flapper, with an uninhibited natural sexuality; her most famous film, *It* (1927, Clarence Badger), earned her the name the "It" girl (with "It" being a euphemism for sex appeal).

Fig. 7.37

Fig. 7.38

Fig. 7.39

Fig. 7.40

Figs. 7.37–7.40 Four shots from the racetrack scene of *Lady Windermere's Fan* (1925), during which the views of various characters through binoculars reveal their attitudes toward a woman of shady reputation.

Pickford was not pleased with the result, and Lubitsch did not work again for the United Artists group. Instead, surprisingly, Warner Bros. hired him, and he became the minor studio's most prestigious director. Under the influence of Chaplin's *A Woman of Paris*, he made a series of sophisticated society comedies. These ingeniously suggested sexual appetites and rivalries bubbling beneath the surface of polite manners, a tactic that came to be known as "the Lubitsch touch." He mastered continuity editing and was able to indicate characters' attitudes simply by the ways in which they shifted position in the frame or through the directions of their glances from shot to shot (Figs. 7.37–7.40). Lubitsch's principal films for Warner Bros. were *The Marriage Circle* (1924; see Fig. 7.2), *Lady Windermere's Fan* (1925), and *So This Is Paris* (1926). He also returned to his old genre, the historical film, with *The Student Prince in Old Heidelberg* (1927) at MGM and *The Patriot* at Paramount (1928). He later proved to be one of the most imaginative directors during the early sound era.

THE SCANDINAVIANS COME TO AMERICA

Hollywood, and specifically MGM, also picked up on the important Scandinavian directors of the 1910s and early 1920s (pp. 63–69). The studio imported Benjamin Christensen, whose first American film, appropriately enough, was *The Devil's Circus* (1926); it harked back to the circus genre that had been so common in Scandinavian films of the 1910s (Fig. 7.41).

Fig. 7.41 This trapeze scene in *The Devil's Circus* exemplifies the kinds of "European" special effects and daring camera angles the Hollywood cinema was beginning to adopt in the mid-1920s.

Christensen went on to make several gothic thrillers, most notably *Seven Footprints to Satan* (1929). During the 1930s he returned to Denmark.

Mauritz Stiller was hired by MGM after the success of *The Story of Gösta Berling* in Berlin. With him went Greta Garbo, whom Stiller had discovered. MGM set the pair to work on *The Torrent*, but Stiller's eccentricities and inability to conform to strict accounting methods soon led to his replacement as director. German producer Erich Pommer, then working in a brief stint at Paramount, hired him to make *Hotel Imperial*, starring Pola Negri. This was Stiller's most notable Hollywood production, including some "Germanic" camera movements that involved placing the camera on an elaborate elevator system. It did not recapture the wit or intensity of his Swedish films, however, and after a few more aborted projects, Stiller returned to Sweden, where he died in 1928.

In 1923, Victor Sjöström also received an offer from MGM. Facing a waning Swedish film industry, he accepted and was renamed Victor Seastrom. His first American film, *Name the Man*, was a bit stiff but contained several landscape shots that recalled his earlier feeling for natural environments. His next project, *He Who Gets Slapped* (1924), was a vehicle for Lon Chaney; another Scandinavian-influenced circus film, it proved highly popular. Seastrom then made two films starring Lillian Gish, who had recently come to MGM after her long association with Griffith. She wanted to do an adaptation of *The Scarlet Letter* (1926), directed by Seastrom, who seemed perfectly suited to Hawthorne's tale of love and retribution. His sense of landscape emerged even more strongly here (Fig. 7.42). Similarly, the performances of Gish and Swedish actor Lars Hansen were strong, but MGM insisted on a comic subplot that vitiated the austere drama.

Gish and Hansen starred again in Seastrom's final American film, *The Wind* (1928). The story involves a woman who moves to the desolate, windswept western frontier to marry a naive rancher. She kills and buries a would-be rapist but then is driven to the brink of madness by visions of the wind uncovering his body. Despite a hopeful ending imposed by the studio, *The Wind* was a powerful film. Its grimness and its release as a silent film as sound was coming in doomed it to failure, however, and Seastrom returned to Sweden, to his original name, and to a long career acting in sound films.

EUROPEAN DIRECTORS AT UNIVERSAL

Universal, one of the larger studios among the Little Five, lent prestige to its production output by hiring several European directors. Among these was Paul Fejos, a Hungarian who had made his mark in Hollywood by directing an experimental independent feature, *The Last Moment* (1927), which depicted the last vision of a drowning man in a rapidly edited sequence using no intertitles. *Lonesome* (1928) was a simple story of a working-class couple's romance, portrayed with a naturalism that was unusual for Hollywood. His next film, the elaborate early musical *Broadway* (1929, which survives only in its silent version) used a huge expressionist-style nightclub set through which the camera swooped on a giant crane built expressly for this production (Fig. 7.43). After a few more minor Hollywood projects, including the foreign-

Fig. 7.42 The Reverend Arthur Dimmesdale walks through a forest of stumps in *The Scarlet Letter.*

Fig. 7.43 In *Broadway*, the camera pulls far back from the hero during a musical number in the expressionistic nightclub.

language versions of some early talkies, Fejos returned to work in various European countries in the 1930s.

Universal also hired Paul Leni, director of one of the main German Expressionist films, *Waxworks*. Leni's dark, vaguely expressionist adaptation of the hit Broadway gothic thriller *The Cat and the Canary* (1927) became an enormous success. He then directed a big-budget historical epic with overtones of the horror genre, *The Man Who Laughs* (1928), starring German actor Conrad Veidt in an expressionist performance as a man whose mouth has been cut into a permanent grotesque grin. These two films reinforced Universal's orientation toward horror films—a tendency that had begun with *The Hunchback of Notre Dame* and *The Phantom of the Opera* and which was to intensify in the sound era with such films as *Dracula* and *Frankenstein*. Leni's premature death in 1929, however, meant that others would take over the exploration of the genre.

MURNAU AND HIS INFLUENCE AT FOX

Undoubtedly the most prestigious acquisition of a European director occurred when Fox Film Corp. hired F. W. Murnau in 1925, in the wake of the universal acclaim for *The Last Laugh*. Murnau lingered at Ufa to make *Faust* (also a big hit in the United States) and then came to Hollywood. Fox allowed him an enormous budget to make its biggest picture of 1927, *Sunrise*. Scripted by Carl Mayer, who had done so many German Expressionist films, and designed by Rochus Gliese, who had worked with Murnau in Germany, the film was virtually a German film made in America. It was a simple but intense psychological drama of a farmer who attempts to murder his wife in order to run away with his lover from the city. When he cannot bring himself to commit the deed, he must regain his horrified wife's trust. The film was full of Germanic mise-en-scene with expressionist touches (Fig. 7.44). Even the American stars, Janet Gaynor and George O'Brien, were induced to give expressionist-style performances.

Fig. 7.44 Deep space and skewed false perspectives create an expressionist composition in *Sunrise*.

Sunrise was perhaps too sophisticated to be really popular, and its huge city sets (Fig. 7.45) made it so expensive that it did only moderately well for Fox. As a result, Murnau's fortunes declined. He went on to more and more modest projects: *Four Devils* (1929), yet another circus film, now lost; and *City Girl* (1930), a part-talkie that was taken out of Murnau's control and altered considerably. His last film began as a collaboration with documentarist Robert Flaherty (pp. 202–203). The two worked on a fiction film about Tahiti, *Tabu* (1931). After Flaherty abandoned the project, Murnau completed a flawed but beautiful love story made on location in the South Seas. He died in a car accident shortly before the film's release.

Despite Murnau's lack of popular success during his Hollywood career, *Sunrise* had an enormous impact on American filmmakers, especially at Fox. Both John Ford and Frank Borzage were encouraged to imitate it. Ford's sentimental World War I drama *Four Sons* (1928) looks very much like a German film, and the influence of Ufa's studio-bound style was to crop up in his sound films, such as *The Informer* (1935) and *The Fugitive* (1947).

Borzage's late-1920s films show even more directly the effects of his

Fig. 7.45 The huge city square constructed for *Sunrise* (with help from German false-perspective techniques that made it seem even larger).

Fig. 7.46 Diane and her sister in their garret apartment in *7th Heaven*. The upwardly slanting floor shows the influence of German set design.

Fig. 7.47 This elevator allowed the camera to move spectacularly with Diane and Chico seven flights up as they approached his apartment, which their love transforms into "heaven."

familiarity with Murnau's work. *7th Heaven* is an affecting melodrama about a forlorn Parisian prostitute, Diane, and a woman-hating sewer cleaner, Chico, who gradually gain each other's love and trust only to be separated by World War I. None of the film crew was European, but the set designs by Harry Oliver incorporated the sorts of false-perspective backgrounds that Murnau had used in *Sunrise* and some of his German films (Fig. 7.46). German-style virtuosic camera movements were imitated, most spectacularly in an elaborate vertical shot made from an elevator (Fig. 7.47). Borzage followed up the tremendous success of *7th Heaven* with a similar film, *Street Angel* (1928), starring the same actors, Janet Gaynor and Charles Farrell. They became the ideal romantic couple of the late 1920s. She won the first Best Actress award from the Academy of Motion Picture Arts and Sciences for these two films and *Sunrise* (at a time when the rules allowed an actor's entire year's output to be nominated). They starred together again in Borzage's late silent film, *Lucky Star* (1929), a dark, romantic love story which again displayed German influence and remained one of the rare Hollywood films with a wheelchair-bound hero.

European films, and especially those from Germany, also influenced Hollywood filmmaking more generally. *Flesh and the Devil* (1926), directed by the established filmmaker Clarence Brown, was fully of fancy camera movement, subjective camera effects, and other techniques derived from European avant-garde cinema (Fig. 7.48). It also starred the single most successful of the imported European stars, Greta Garbo. Here she was teamed with matinee idol John Gilbert, with whom she was linked romantically in real life (Fig. 7.49). Although Gilbert's career faded in the early sound era, Garbo remained one of MGM's top stars for more than a decade.

Many other Hollywood films of the late 1920s and the 1930s also reflected influences from European films, particularly those of the French Impressionist, German Expressionist, and Soviet Montage movements. Some stylistic changes, however, resulted from specifically American developments.

STYLISTIC AND TECHNOLOGICAL CHANGES

By the late 1910s, most of the major technological innovations in American filmmaking had already been made. Similarly, stylistic techniques of classical filmmaking were essentially in place. Only a few significant changes occurred during the 1920s.

One distinct change was a new approach to cinematography. Before about 1919, most films were shot with a hard-edged, sharp-focus look. Some filmmakers began to place gauzy fabrics or filters in front of their lenses to create soft, blurry images. Special lenses could keep the foreground action in focus while making the background less distinct. This technique enhanced the classical narrative style by concentrating the spectator's attention on the main action while deemphasizing less important elements. The result of such techniques was the *soft style* of cinematography. This style derived from still photography, and especially the Pictorialist school pioneered by such photographers as Alfred Stieglitz and Edward Steichen early in the century.

Fig. 7.48

Fig. 7.49

Fig. 7.48 The duel scene in *Flesh and the Devil*, handled with a rapid tracking movement back from a silhouetted scene; the opponents end offscreen at either side, with puffs of smoke coming into the frame, briefly leaving the result uncertain.

Fig. 7.49 A tiny spotlight created a romantic moment as John Gilbert lights a cigarette for Greta Garbo; the pair were cast as lovers in several more films.

D. W. Griffith was one of the early proponents of this style. He worked with cinematographer Hendrick Sartov, who had begun as a still photographer, to photograph soft-focus shots of Lillian Gish and some landscapes in *Broken Blossoms* (1919). They further explored the approach in *Way Down East* (1920; Figs. 7.50, 7.51). Other filmmakers pushed such techniques further. Erich von Stroheim sometimes placed coarse filters in front of the lens so that the scene was viewed through a textured screen (Fig. 7.52). During the 1920s, the soft style became more common in cinematography. It became dominant by the early sound era and remained prominent until a new hard-edged style became fashionable in the 1940s.

Another major innovation of this era came with the gradual adoption of a new *panchromatic* type of film stock. The film stock used previously had been *orthochromatic*; that is, it was sensitive only to the purple, blue, and green portions of the visible spectrum. Yellow and red light barely registered on it, so objects of these colors appeared nearly black in the finished film. For example, the lips of actors wearing ordinary red lipstick appear very dark in many silent films. Colors like purple and blue registered on the film stock as nearly white, so it was difficult to photograph cloudy skies: a blue sky with clouds simply washed out to a uniform white.

Panchromatic film stock, available by the early 1910s, registered the whole range of the visible spectrum, from purple to red, with nearly equal sensitivity. Thus it was capable of recording a sky with the clouds visible against the blue background, or red lips as shades of gray. But panchromatic stock had problems as well: it was expensive, it deteriorated quickly if not

Fig. 7.50 A shimmering soft-focus landscape shot in *Way Down East* that resembles high-art still photographs of the period.

Fig. 7.51 Soft-focus cinematography also considerably enhanced glamorous shots, as in this medium close-up of Lillian Gish.

Fig. 7.52 The entire wedding scene in *Greed* was filmed through a textured scrim placed in front of the lens.

Fig. 7.50

Fig. 7.51

Fig. 7.52

used right away, and it demanded much greater illumination to expose a satisfactory image. During the 1910s and early 1920s, it was primarily used outdoors in bright sunlight for landscape shots (to capture cloud scenes) or indoors for studio close-ups that could be brightly lit. By 1925, Eastman Kodak had made its panchromatic motion-picture stock cheaper and more stable; soon the stock was also made more sensitive, requiring less light for proper exposure. By 1927, the Hollywood studios were quickly switching over to panchromatic stock. The result was not a radical change in the look of films, but panchromatic did permit filmmakers to make shots of actors who were not wearing make-up and to shoot a greater variety of subjects without having to worry about using filters, special paint, make-up, and the like, to correct for the color deficiencies of orthochromatic. Panchromatic soon became the standard in other countries as well.

ANIMATION BECOMES MORE EFFICIENT AND POPULAR

The basic techniques of animated films had been invented during the 1910s (pp. 78–79), and the post–World War I period saw a boom in animation. New independent animation studios appeared, creating greater output and applying a division of labor that made the process of animation more efficient. Typically head animators laid out the basic poses for the scene, "in-betweeners" filled in the movements with additional drawings, other workers traced the drawings onto cels, still others filled in with paint, and a cinematographer photographed the results frame by frame. The result could be a series of cartoons released monthly or even biweekly. A whole new generation of animators set up shop as technical information about cels and the slash system was disseminated.

Typically animation companies produced series with continuing characters or themes. These films would be released through an independent distributor, but that distributor might sign a contract with one of the big firms to put the cartoons on its own program. The most successful independent distributor of this era was Margaret J. Winkler Mintz. By the early 1920s, she was financing and releasing the decade's three most popular series: the Fleischer brothers' "Out of the Inkwell" films, the cartoons based on Bud Fisher's beloved "Mutt and Jeff" comics, and some of Walt Disney's earliest efforts.

The Fleischer brothers, Max and Dave, had experimented with a new film technique called *rotoscoping* in the mid-1910s. The rotoscope allowed a filmmaker to take live-action films, project them onto a piece of paper, and trace the outlines frame by frame. Originally the brothers seem to have intended that the device be used for military purposes. Although the rotoscope was patented in 1915, World War I delayed further work on it. After the war, Max and Dave returned to work, this time tracing the live-action images as cartoon figures. They used a live-action prologue for each film in their series, featuring Max Fleischer as a cartoonist who creates Koko, a clown who pops "out of the inkwell." The first cartoon was released in late 1919, and several others followed sporadically through 1920.

Rotoscoping was not a technique to achieve efficiency, as earlier inventions in cartooning had been. Instead, by tracing the action one image at a time, the cartoonist could easily produce on cels characters that moved *as whole figures,* rather than stiffly, with only one or a few parts of their bodies, as in the slash and simpler cel systems. The Fleischer's new character, Koko the Clown, swung his limbs through space freely, and his loose outfit swirled about him as he went (Fig. 7.53). A reviewer of the period commented on this ease:

> [Koko's] motions, for one thing, are smooth and graceful. He walks, dances and leaps as a human being, as a particularly easy-limbed human being might. He does not jerk himself from one position to another, nor does he move an arm or a leg while the remainder of his body remains as unnaturally stiff as—as if it were fixed in ink lines on paper.[2]

The Fleischers also employed the standard techniques of cels, slashing, and retracing, but rotoscoping gave these devices new freedom. The "Out of the Inkwell" series prospered during the 1920s. In the early sound era, however, the Fleischers replaced Koko with the equally popular Betty Boop and Popeye.

The "Mutt and Jeff" series had begun as a popular comic strip in 1911. Its hapless stars were two moustached fellows, one tall, one short. The strip's artist, Bud Fisher, agreed in 1916 to allow the strip to be animated. His name was invariably given as the creator of the cartoon series, even though over the years Raoul Barré, Charles Bowers, and various other animation veterans actually drew the cartoons. Distributor Mintz contracted the series for release through Fox, and it remained popular through the 1920s (Fig. 7.54).

The young Walt Disney and his friend Ub Iwerks started their own commercial-arts firm in Kansas City in 1919. Failing to make money, they then worked for an ad agency, making simple animated films. There they started "Newman's Laugh-o-grams," a series of short animated films for local distribution. After this venture also failed, Disney moved to Hollywood. In 1923, he received backing from Mintz to create a series of "Alice Comedies," which proved to be his first success. With his brother Roy, he formed the Disney Brothers Studios, which would eventually grow into one of the biggest entertainment conglomerates of the twentieth century.

During the 1920s, the staff of the firm included several of the major animators who would create series for Warner Bros. and MGM in the 1930s: Hugh Harman, Rudolf Ising, and Friz Freleng. They all worked on the Alice series, which combined live action and cartoon images—a technique that was not new to cartooning (Fig. 7.55). In 1927, the Disney studio switched to full animation with the Oswald the Rabbit series. In a legal battle, however, Charles Mintz, husband of Disney's distributor, seized control of the character. Walt's solution was to invent a new character called Mickey Mouse. The first two Mickey cartoons failed to find a distributor. A third, *Steamboat Willie,* incorporated the new sound technology and proved a huge hit. It helped catapult Disney to the head of the animation business in the 1930s.

Other series of this period proved highly popular. Paul Terry, who had worked at various animation studios during the 1910s, started his own firm, Fables Pictures Inc., in 1921, launching a series called "Aesop's Fables."

Fig. 7.53 In *The Clown's Little Brother* (1919 or 1920), Koko struts across the frame in a rotoscoped motion that seemed effortless and lively in the context of 1910s animation.

Fig. 7.54 Mutt's attempts to help Jeff get out of the pot attached to his head will soon lead to dizzy escapades on a half-built skyscraper in *Where Am I?* (1925).

Fig. 7.55 In *Alice in the Wooly West* (1926), animated exclamation points express the live-action heroine's astonishment as she confronts the world of cartoon characters.

Fig. 7.56 The nightclub in which the protagonist fritters away his paycheck in *The Spendthrift* (1922), with the moral "A spendthrift blames everybody but himself for his misfortune."

Fig. 7.57 Felix politely tips his ears in *Felix the Cat in Futuritzy* (1928).

These were modern retellings of the classic fables. Terry used a virtual assembly-line division of labor to turn out one film per week; the results were amusing but usually conventional (Fig. 7.56). Terry left the company in 1928 to create Terrytoons, a firm he ran until 1955, when he sold it to television producers.

The single most popular series of the 1920s was based on Felix the Cat. Its nominal creator, Pat Sullivan, had opened his own studio in 1915, making ads and animated films. He began making Felix cartoons for Paramount around 1918. Although Sullivan signed all the films, the head of animation was actually Otto Messmer, who originated the character of Felix and directed the animation process. Mintz signed to distribute the series in 1922. The films achieved a huge success, partly through the appeal of the feline hero and partly through the flexible animation style. In these films, Felix's tail could fly off his body and become a question mark or a cane for him to lean on (Fig. 7.57). By the mid-1920s, the films had achieved a huge audience. Sullivan was also a pioneer in the use of tie-in products like dolls to further exploit the success of his cartoon character. Like most of the major animated series of the 1920s, Felix did not carry over well into the sound era, though there have been many later imitations of this character.

FILMS FOR AFRICAN-AMERICAN AUDIENCES

In 1915, the release of Griffith's *The Birth of a Nation* had led to many protests and boycotts on the part of African-Americans. Some envisioned the creation of black-controlled production firms that could provide an alternative perspective on race relations. A few sporadic attempts at production were initiated during the latter half of the 1910s, but the results were usually short films that were relegated to a minor role on programs. They either showed positive images of black heroism during World War I or perpetuated traditional black comic stereotypes.

During the 1920s, black roles in mainstream Hollywood films were small and rare. African-Americans appeared as servants, wastrels, comic children, and the like. Black actors seldom found regular work and had to fill in with other jobs, usually menial, to survive.

As moviegoers, African-Americans had little choice but to attend theaters that showed films designed for white audiences. Most theaters in the United States were segregated. In the South, laws required that exhibitors separate their white and black patrons. In the North, despite civil rights statutes in many localities, the practice was for the races to sit in separate parts of auditoriums. Some theaters, usually owned by whites, were in black neighborhoods and catered to local viewers. In such theaters, films with any black-oriented subject matter proved popular.

There were even a small number of films produced specifically for African-American audiences. Some of these used all-black casts, even though the directors and other filmmakers were white. The most prominent company of this kind in the 1920s was the Colored Players, who made several films, including two particularly significant ones. *Scar of Shame* (1926, Frank

Peregini) dealt with the impact of environment and upbringing on black people's aspirations. The hero, a struggling composer, strives to live a respectable middle-class existence; he is "a credit to his race," despite the attempts of sordid characters to corrupt him (Fig. 7.58).

That same year, the Colored Players also made a less preachy film, *Ten Nights in a Barroom* (1926, Charles S. Gilpin), an adaptation of a classic stage melodrama that had traditionally been played by white casts. Its complex flashback structure tells the story of a drunkard who reforms when he accidentally contributes to the death of his daughter in a barroom brawl (Fig. 7.59). Despite its low budget, *Ten Nights in a Barroom* was skillfully lit and edited in the classical style.

In a few cases, black filmmakers were able to work behind the camera. Oscar Micheaux was for several decades the most successful African-American producer-director. He began as a homesteader in South Dakota, where he wrote novels and sold them door to door among his white neighbors. He used the same method to sell stock to adapt his writings into films, creating the Micheaux Book and Film Company in 1918. Over the next decade he made thirty films, concentrating on such black-related topics as lynching, the Ku Klux Klan, and interracial marriage.

The energetic and determined Micheaux worked quickly under low budgets, and his films have a rough, disjunctive style. More than any other filmmaker, he depicted black concerns on the screen. *Body and Soul* (1924) explores the issue of the religious exploitation of poor blacks. Paul Robeson, one of the most successful black actors and singers of the century, played a false preacher who extorts money and seduces women (Fig. 7.60). Micheaux went bankrupt in the late 1920s and had to resort to white financing in the sound era. Nevertheless, he continued to average a film a year up to 1940 and made one more in 1948. Although much of his work is lost, Micheaux demonstrated that a black director could make films for black audiences.

The opportunities for African-Americans would improve somewhat during the sound era. Talented black entertainers were in greater demand in musicals, and major studios experimented with all-black casts. As we shall see in Chapter 9, one of the most important early sound films, King Vidor's *Hallelujah!*, attempted to explore African-American culture (p. 220).

The U.S. film industry's push into foreign markets during World War I had given it an enormous economic base for its expansion and consolidation during the 1920s. Most national film industries were too small to offer any significant resistance to American domination. Yet the cinema continued to be an international phenomenon, and many countries managed to make at least a few films of their own. Some countries in Europe were strong enough to support national industries and even to consider banding together to challenge American power. Moreover, for the first time, filmmakers in several countries were creating short experimental films that challenged the classical narrative approach of Hollywood cinema. We shall examine these trends in the next chapter.

Fig. 7.58 The conservatively dressed hero of *Scar of Shame* confronts the villainous gambler, marked by his sporty checked suit.

Fig. 7.59 The hero of *Ten Nights in a Barroom* holds his fatally wounded daughter.

Fig. 7.60 Paul Robeson as the villain in *Body and Soul*.

◆ NOTES AND QUERIES

THE REDISCOVERY OF BUSTER KEATON

After the great age of silent comedy ended, Charles Chaplin remained the most revered of the era's clowns. Although he controlled the rights to most of his features and refused to circulate them, most of his dozens of short comedies were commonly available. By contrast, few of the films of Buster Keaton circulated. As a result, a great deal was written about Chaplin, and he was generally ranked as much better than Keaton or Harold Lloyd.

The balance shifted dramatically in the mid-1960s, when Keaton films began to surface. Distributor Raymond Rohauer made new prints of most of Keaton's silent work. These were shown at the Venice Film Festival in 1965, where Keaton appeared to tremendous applause. That same year the British Film Institute presented him with a special award. Interviews and retrospectives followed. Keaton lived just long enough to enjoy this acclaim. He died in 1966, shortly before the publication of Rudi Blesh's biography, *Keaton* (New York: Macmillan, 1966). Blesh documented the decline in Keaton's career during the 1930s and helped revive interest in his early work.

Critics and historians recognized that Keaton had been a major director as well as a brilliant performer. His ability to arrange complex gags all within a single long-shot framing, his compositions in depth, his careful use of motifs, and the balanced structure of his scenarios all received attention.

For a description of Keaton's appearance at Venice and an interview with him, see John Gillett and James Blue, "Keaton at Venice," *Sight & Sound* **35,** 1 (Winter 1965–1966): 26–30. Studies of Keaton done in the wake of this revival include J.-P. Lebel's *Buster Keaton* (New York: Barnes, 1967) and David Robinson's *Buster Keaton* (Bloomington: Indiana University Press, 1969).

◆ REFERENCES

1. Advertisement, Paramount Pictures, *Photoplay* **19,** 4 (March 1921): 4.
2. From the *New York Times*, quoted in Donald Crafton, *Before Mickey: The Animated Film 1898–1928* (Cambridge, Mass.: MIT Press, 1982), p. 174.

8

INTERNATIONAL TRENDS
OF THE 1920s

W hile the Hollywood industry was consolidating its methods of narrative continuity, alternative and innovative movements arose within other film industries in France, Germany, and the USSR. These events took place within a more general reaction against the domination of international markets by Hollywood films. Some European companies united to resist American encroachment. At the same time, artists in other media and dedicated filmmakers worked outside the commercial establishment to create alternative types of cinema, both experimental and documentary. Less dramatically, several countries tried to compete with the United States by producing films more regularly.

"FILM EUROPE"

After World War I, many countries struggled against American films' continued domination of their markets. At first, nations competed against each other as well as against Hollywood, hoping to prosper in the international film market. The German government fostered the growth of a film industry by continuing the wartime ban on imported films. In France, despite many efforts, adverse conditions kept production low. For a few years, Italy continued to produce many films but could not regain its strong pre-1914 position. Other countries sought to establish even a small amount of steady production.

Exclusivite
Cosmograph
7 faubourg Montmartre

plus fort que
CALIGARI

NOSFERATU

LE VAMPIRE

LE FILM LE PLUS IMPRESSIONNANT

sera projeté exclusivement au

CINÉ OPÉRA, BOULEVARD DES CAPUCINES

DÈS LE 27 OCTOBRE

Fig. 8.1 A 1922 French advertisement for F. W. Murnau's *Nosferatu* called it "more powerful than *Caligari*."

This competition was exacerbated by lingering animosities. Great Britain and France were determined not to let German production thrive. Theater owners in both countries agreed not to show German films after the war, for a period of five years in Britain and for fifteen in France. Unofficial boycotts existed in Belgium and other countries that had suffered during the war.

Yet by 1921 glowing reviews of German films like Lubitsch's *Madame Dubarry* and Wiene's *The Cabinet of Dr. Caligari* made French and British audiences feel that they were missing important developments. In November, Louis Delluc held a Paris screening of *The Cabinet of Dr. Caligari* (at a charity benefit so that few could object). The film created a sensation, and a distributor quickly bought the French rights. *Caligari* opened in March 1922 and became an enormous hit. The exhibitors' ban was forgotten, and a vogue for German Expressionist films developed (Fig. 8.1). In late 1922, *Madame Dubarry* premiered in London, breaking that country's boycott. Postwar hostility was waning.

Moreover, by the early 1920s, European producers realized that American competition was too great for any one country to counter. The United States, with around 15,000 theaters, was the world's largest film market. Thus American producers garnered a huge, predictable income from domestic rentals alone. They could afford to sell films cheaply abroad because most foreign income was pure profit. Commentators also noted, however, that if the movie theaters of all European countries were gathered into a single continental market, it would be comparable in size to that of the United States. What if European film industries could cooperate by guaranteeing to import each other's films? European films might make as much money as Hollywood films did. Then their budgets could be raised, their production values would be better, and they might even be able to compete with American films in other world markets. This idea was gradually formulated as the "pan-European" cinema, or "Film Europe."

By 1922–1923, European film trade papers were calling for such cooperation, and in 1924, the first steps were taken to create a practical cooperation among European producing nations. Erich Pommer, head of the powerful German company Ufa, concluded a pact with Louis Aubert, a major Parisian distributor. Ufa agreed to release in Germany French films provided by the Aubert company, in exchange for Aubert's distribution of Ufa films in France. Previously, French-German deals had meant the sale of a film or two, but now mutual distribution became regular.

The Ufa-Aubert deal attracted wide notice. Pommer declared: "I think that European producers must at last think of establishing a certain cooperation among themselves. It is imperative to create a system of regular trade which will enable the producers to amortise their films rapidly. It is necessary to create 'European films,' which will no longer be French, English, Italian, or German films, but entirely 'continental' films."[1] The Ufa-Aubert agreement provided the model for later transactions. Exchange of films among France, Germany, Britain, and other countries increased during the second half of the 1920s.

Pommer's statement that producers should make "European films" reflects other tactics used to increase the international circulation of films.

Firms imported stars, directors, and other personnel to give an international flavor to their output. Similarly, a coproduction, in which a film would be financed and made by companies in two countries, guaranteed release in at least those two markets. A combination of these tactics might increase a film's breadth of circulation even further.

For example, British producer-director Graham Wilcox made *Decameron Nights* (1924), with Ufa providing its studio facilities and half the financing (Fig. 8.2). Actors from several countries participated, including American star Lionel Barrymore, English actress Ivy Close, and Werner Krauss (famous as Dr. Caligari). The result was highly popular in several countries, including the United States. Producers and filmmakers from abroad often worked in Germany, since the production facilities there were the best in Europe. In 1924, the young Alfred Hitchcock began working as a designer on British films made at Ufa, where he watched Murnau working on *The Last Laugh* (p. 118). His first two films as a director, *The Pleasure Garden* (1925) and *The Mountain Eagle* (1926), were British-German coproductions shot in Germany.

By mid-decade, Germany's film industry was the leader in an increasingly cooperative pan-European effort. To be sure, many big coproductions failed to gain the anticipated international success, since cautious producers tended to use standard formulas. "International appeal" also too often meant imitations of Hollywood-style films, with a loss of the distinctive national qualities that attracted viewers to movies like *Caligari* and *Potemkin*. Tactics like coproductions and international casts worked well enough, however, for stars to move freely among countries. Cross-border arrangements created Spanish-French, German-Swedish, and other multinational films. The wider circulation of films allowed production budgets to rise.

The Film Europe effort also led to import quotas in some countries. After Germany lifted its import ban in 1921, it had strictly limited the number of films admitted to the country. In 1925, it changed to a system whereby a distributor could import one film for every German film it had circulated the previous year. France attempted to imitate this plan in 1928 by introducing a modest limit of seven imported films for each French one distributed.

In 1927, Great Britain instituted a cautious quota calling for a small percentage of Brtish footage to be distributed and exhibited in the United Kingdom. Over the years, this percentage was to increase gradually, allowing the production sector to grow to meet the demand. Even countries with more limited production created quotas. In Portugal, for example, one-tenth of screen time had to be reserved for domestic films—usually newsreels or travelogues preceding an imported feature. Although these quotas were purportedly directed against all imported films, it was common knowledge that their main target was Hollywood films. Such quotas contributed to the Film Europe drive.

Between 1924 and 1927, the Europeans, led by Germany, Britain, and France, built the base for a continental market. Slowly their efforts reduced the number of American films and replaced them with European ones. This table shows the percentage of feature films released in Germany, France, and Britain in 1926 and 1929, by the main countries of origin:

Fig. 8.2 Ufa's large, technically sophisticated studios permitted the construction of epic-style sets of Renaissance Venice for the British-German coproduction, *Decameron Nights*.

COUNTRY OF ORIGIN	PERCENTAGE OF FILMS RELEASED IN:					
	GERMANY		FRANCE		BRITAIN	
	1926	1929	1926	1929	1926	1929
United States	45	33	79	48	84	75
Germany	39	45	6	30	6	9
France	4	4	10	12	3	2
Britain	0.4	4	0.4	6	5	13

Fig. 8.3 Expressionist mise-en-scene in L'Herbier's *Don Juan et Faust.*

Fig. 8.4 A corner in a room of Usher's mansion in Epstein's *The Fall of the House of Usher* displays the influence of German Expressionism.

Fig. 8.5 In *The Street,* Impressionist-style superimpositions depict the hero's visions of delights that await him in the city.

Germany, already the strongest, benefited most from cooperative efforts. France, struggling in a production crisis, gained least; the decline in American films there was largely offset by other imports. Still, Film Europe might gradually have improved Europe's situation had the effort continued.

Abrupt changes cut it short. In 1929, the introduction of sound began affecting Europe. Dialogue created language barriers, and each country's producers began to hope that they could succeed because English-language imports would decline. Several countries did benefit from audiences' desire for sound films in their own languages, and some national industries became major forces as a result of sound. Competitiveness among European nations reappeared.

In addition, the Depression began to hit Europe in 1929. Faced by hard times, many businesses and governments became more nationalistic and less interested in international cooperation. The rise of extreme left-wing and right-wing dictatorships in Europe and Asia increased divisiveness and territorial rivalries, in a trend that would eventually lead to another global war. Film Europe was moribund by the early 1930s, but some of its effects lingered on. Some films still circulated, and firms collaborated on coproductions.

THE "INTERNATIONAL STYLE"

Stylistic influences also circulated among countries. French Impressionism, German Expressionism, and Soviet Montage began as strictly national trends, but soon the filmmakers exploring these styles became aware of each other's work. By the mid-1920s, an international avant-garde style blended traits of all three movements.

Caligari's success in France in 1922 led French directors to add expressionist touches to their work. Impressionist director Marcel L'Herbier told two parallel stories of famous characters in *Don Juan et Faust* (1923), using expressionist-style sets and costumes in the Faust scenes (Fig. 8.3). In 1928, Jean Epstein combined Impressionist camera techniques with expressionist set design to create an eerie, portentous tone in *The Fall of the House of Usher*, based on Poe's story (Fig. 8.4).

At almost exactly the same time, French Impressionist traits of subjective camera devices were cropping up in German films. Karl Grune's *The Street*, an early example of the street film (p. 123), used multiple superimpositions to show the protagonist's visions (Fig. 8.5). *The Last Laugh* and *Variety* popularized subjective cinematographic effects that had actually orig-

Fig. 8.6

Fig. 8.7

Fig. 8.6 *The Cloak* contains grotesque elements that recall German Expressionism, such as this giant steaming teapot that heralds the beginning of a strange dream sequence.

Fig. 8.7 A low angle isolates the major characters against the sky in Soviet fashion as they march in protest (*Mutter Krausens Fahrt ins Gluck*).

inated in France (see Figs. 5.23–5.25). By the mid-1920s, the boundaries between the Impressionist and Expressionist movements were blurred.

The Montage movement started somewhat later, but imported films soon allowed directors to pick up on European stylistic trends. The very rapid rhythmic editing pioneered by Epstein and Abel Gance in 1923 was pushed further by Soviet filmmakers after 1926 (p. 144). Grigori Kozintsev and Leonid Trauberg's 1926 adaptation of Gogol, *The Cloak*, contained exaggerations in the acting and mise-en-scene that were reminiscent of major German Expressionist films (Fig. 8.6). In turn, from 1926 onward, Soviet Montage films wielded an influence abroad. Leftist filmmakers in Germany embraced the Soviet style as a means of making politically charged cinema. A shot from the final demonstration scene in *Mutter Krausens Fahrt ins Gluck* ("Mother Krausen's Journey to Happiness," 1929, Piel Jutzi; Fig. 8.7) echoes the climactic march in Pudovkin's *Mother* (Fig. 6.47). Soviet influence would intensify in the 1930s, when leftist filmmaking responded to the rise of fascism.

French, German, and Soviet techniques had an impact in many countries. Two of the most notable English directors of the 1920s reflected the impact of French Impressionism. Anthony Asquith's second feature, *Underground* (1928), used a freely moving camera and several subjective superimpositions to tell a story of love and jealousy in an ordinary working-class milieu (Fig. 8.8). Alfred Hitchcock's boxing picture, *The Ring* (1927), demonstrated his absorption of impressionist techniques in its many subjective passages (Fig. 8.9). Hitchcock also acknowledged his debts to German Expressionism, an influence evident in *The Lodger* (1926). For decades, he would draw upon avant-garde techniques he learned in the 1920s.

The international influence of the commercial avant-garde reached as far as Japan. By the 1920s, Japan was absorbing western modernism in various arts, primarily literature and painting. Futurism, Expressionism, Dada, and Surrealism were all welcomed. One young filmmaker, Teinosuke Kinugasa, was already well established in commercial production, having made over thirty low-budget pictures. He was also associated with modernist writers in Tokyo, however, and with their help, in 1926 he independently produced a bizarre film, *A Page of Madness*, that carried expressionist and impressionist techniques to new extremes. Taking a cue from *Caligari*, Kinugasa set the action in a madhouse, with distorting camera devices and

Fig. 8.8 As the heroine of *Underground* looks up at a building, a superimposition reminiscent of French Impressionism conveys her vision of the villain.

Fig. 8.9 Hitchcock used distorting mirrors in this shot of dancers to suggest the hero's mental turmoil during a party (*The Ring*).

Fig. 8.10 An enigmatic scene in *A Page of Madness*, in which an inmate obsessed with dancing appears in an elaborate costume, performing in an expressionist set containing a whirling, striped ball.

Fig. 8.11 In *The President* and other early films, Dreyer often calls as much attention to the set and incidental props as to the main action. [Compare this frame with Fig. 3.14 (*Atlantis*).]

expressionist mise-en-scene frequently reflecting the deranged visions of the inmates (Fig. 8.10; compare this with shots from *Caligari* and other Expressionist films in Chapter 5). The plot that motivates these strange scenes is full of flashbacks and fantasy passages. Kinugasa's next film, *Crossroads* (1928), was less difficult but still reflected influences from European avant-garde films. It was the first Japanese feature to receive a significant release in Europe.

The epitome of the international director of the late silent era was Carl Dreyer. He began in Denmark as a journalist and then worked as a script-writer at Nordisk from 1913 on, when the company was still a powerful force. Dreyer's first film as a director, *The President* (1919), used traditional Scandinavian elements, including stripped-down sets (Fig. 8.11), a relatively austere style, and dramatic lighting. His second film, *Leaves from Satan's Book* (1920), was also made for Nordisk; influenced by Griffith's *Intolerance*, it told a series of stories of suffering and faith.

At this point, one of the pioneers of Nordisk, Lau Lauritzen, departed, and the company declined. Both Dreyer and Benjamin Christensen left to work in Sweden for Svenska, Christensen making *Witchcraft through the Ages* while Dreyer did a bittersweet comedy, *The Parson's Widow* (1920). Over the next few years, Dreyer moved between Denmark and Germany, making *Michael* (1924) at the Ufa studio. Back in Denmark, he moved to the rising Palladium firm and made *Thou Shalt Honor Thy Wife* (aka *The Master of the House*, 1925). This chamber comedy shows a family deceiving an autocratic husband in order to make him realize how he has bullied his wife. This film established Dreyer's reputation internationally and gained particular popularity in France. After a brief sojourn in Norway making a Norse-Swedish co-production, Dreyer was hired by the prestigious Société Générale de Films (which was also producing Gance's *Napoléon*) to make a film in France.

The result was perhaps the greatest of all international-style silent films, *The Passion of Joan of Arc* (1928). The cast and crew represented a mixture of nationalities. The Danish director supervised designer Hermann Warm, who had worked on *Caligari* and other Expressionist films, and Hungarian cinematographer Rudolph Maté. The star, Renée Falconetti, was an Italian stage comedienne, and most of the cast was French.

Joan of Arc blended influences from the French, German, and Soviet avant-garde movements into a fresh, daring style. Concentrating his story on Joan's trial and execution, Dreyer used a great number of close-ups, often decentered and filmed against blank white backgrounds. The dizzying spatial relations serve to concentrate attention intensely on the actors' faces. Dreyer used the newly available panchromatic film stock, which made it possible for the actors to do without make-up. In combination with the close framings, this lack of make-up emphasized every facial detail. Falconetti gave an astonishingly sincere, intense performance as Joan (Fig. 8.12). The sparse settings contain touches of muted expressionist design (Fig. 8.13) and the dynamic low framings and the accelerated subjective editing in the torture-chamber scene suggest the influence of Soviet Montage and French Impressionism.

Despite criticisms that *Joan of Arc* depended too much on lengthy conversations for a silent film, it was widely hailed as a masterpiece. The

Fig. 8.12

Fig. 8.13

Fig. 8.14

Fig. 8.15

Fig. 8.12 A decentered close-up against a blank background in *The Passion of Joan of Arc* both disconcerts and allows us to watch Falconetti's moving performance in the title role.

Fig. 8.13 Warped windows in the courtroom set of *The Passion of Joan of Arc* recall Hermann Warm's earlier career in German Expressionist filmmaking.

Fig. 8.14 In *Vampyr*, the hero trails the disembodied shadow of a wooden-legged man and sees it rejoin its owner.

Fig. 8.15 The "dead" protagonist's point of view up through a window in his coffin as the vampiric old woman he has been investigating peers down at him.

producer, however, was in financial difficulties after *Napoléon*'s extravagances and was unable to support another Dreyer project. Since Danish production was deteriorating, Dreyer turned to a strategy common among experimental filmmakers: he found a patron. A rich nobleman underwrote *Vampyr* (1932) in exchange for being allowed to play its protagonist.

As the name suggests, *Vampyr* is a horror film, but it bears little resemblance to such Hollywood examples of that genre as *Dracula* (which Universal had produced the previous year). Instead of presenting bats, wolves, and clear-cut rules about vampires' behavior, this film evokes unexplained, barely-glimpsed terrors. A tourist who stays at a country inn in a foggy landscape encounters a series of supernatural events as he wanders around the neighborhood (Fig. 8.14). He finds that the illness of a local landowner's daughter seems to be connected with her mysterious doctor and a sinister old lady who appears at intervals. The protagonist's investigation brings on a dream in which he imagines himself dead (Fig. 8.15). Many scenes in *Vampyr* give a sense of dreadful events occurring just offscreen, with the camera tracking and panning just too late to catch them. Many visually degraded, cut prints of *Vampyr* circulate, but good 35mm copies reveal Dreyer's use of lighting, misty landscapes, and camera movement to enhance the macabre atmosphere.

Vampyr was so different from other films of the period that it was greeted with incomprehension. It marked the end of Dreyer's international wanderings. He returned to Denmark and, unable to find backing for another project, to his original career as a journalist. During World War II, he recommenced feature filmmaking.

THE SPREAD OF "ART CINEMA" INSTITUTIONS

During the years after World War I, the appearance of French Impressionist and German Expressionist films led many observers to distinguish between the mainstream commercial cinema and a separate "art cinema." Valid or not, this distinction has been widely used ever since.

Art films, with their more limited appeal, gave rise to a new set of institutions during the 1920s—what one historian has termed "the alternative cinema network."[2] Intellectually oriented journals, ciné-clubs, small art cinemas, exhibitions, and lectures all aimed at promoting the cinema as an art form. Filmmakers often supported these endeavors, writing essays, appearing at clubs and art houses, and even making films aimed solely at these small, elite venues.

The origins of this network can be traced to Delluc, who wrote theoretical essays and criticism for a serious fan magazine called *Le Film*, which he edited from 1917 to 1918. In it he championed early Impressionist films by Gance and L'Herbier and published the latter's first theoretical writings on the cinema. In 1919, Delluc called for the formation of a ciné-club devoted to artistic films, and in 1920 he started *Le Journal du Ciné-Club*. After three sporadic meetings of the first ciné-club, Delluc started another journal, *Cinéa*, which he later sold to finance his shoestring filmmaking. It became *Cinéa-Ciné pour tous* and published many essays by the Impressionists and by critics sympathetic to the movement.

In 1921, the author Ricciotto Canudo organized the Club des Amis du Septième Art ("Club of Friends of the Seventh Art"), known as CASA. The membership included artists and critics from Paris's artistic elite, and the meetings mixed discussions of films with programs of music, poetry readings, and dance. Suddenly film had gained a high-art cachet.

Canudo tirelessly promoted the cinema, and through his connections in the Paris art world, he persuaded the prestigious annual arts exhibition, the Salon d'Automne, to devote two evenings to the cinema annually from 1921 to 1923. These evenings included lectures and clips from important films—often from the French Impressionist and German Expressionist movements. Despite Canudo's premature death in late 1923, and the subsequent decline of CASA, his colleagues continued his work. In 1924 the cinema moved up another step in respectability, when a Paris art gallery, the Musée Galliera, held an exhibition on the art of the French cinema. Besides offering lectures and screenings, the exhibit displayed designs, posters, photographs, costumes, and other artifacts from recent French films—again, many of them Impressionist in style.

The climax of cinema's participation in exhibitions came in 1925, when one of this century's major art events, the Exposition International des Arts Décoratifs et Industriels Modernes, was held in Paris. This exposition was like a world's fair of decorative arts, and it popularized the modernist "Art Deco" style throughout the world. The cinema had its own gallery space, and a new film society was formed to show major recent films. Again, the Impressionists' work featured prominently.

Alternative cinema networks appeared in other countries as well. In 1924, a prestigious German art show, the Grossen Berliner Kunstausstellung, included a cinema section consisting of original set designs and models. Many Expressionist films, like *Caligari* and *Destiny*, were represented. The following year, a large exposition devoted entirely to the cinema was held in Berlin. The Kino und Photo Ausstellung (or "Kipho"), mixed commerce and art. The big companies publicized forthcoming films, and visitors saw displays of German Expressionist film design, including the full-sized dragon from *The Nibelungen*.

In keeping with the Film Europe effort, exhibitions in the later 1920s were more international. A major event in the Hague in 1928, the Internationale Tentoonstelling op Filmgebied, helped introduce the young Soviet Montage movement more fully to the Europeans. In 1929, the Deutsche Werkbund organized a big exposition in Stuttgart, Film und Foto. Here several programs of features and shorts surveyed the history of the avant-garde cinema, from *Caligari* on. By the end of the silent era, the important art films were already gaining the status of classics.

Another major component of the alternative cinema network appeared in 1924, when Jean Tedesco opened the first of Paris's *salles spécialisées* ("specialized theaters," known today as "art theaters"). Tedesco, a critic, had bought Delluc's *Cinéa* and transformed it into *Cinéa-Ciné pour tous*. He had long campaigned for a theater that would revive classics and show new offbeat films. His Théâtre du Vieux-Colombier created a repertory of classics which were shown in rotation; a few films that could find no commercial distributor premiered there. In 1928, that theater even produced Renoir's Impressionist film *The Little Match Girl*. By the second half of the 1920s, there were several specialized cinemas like the Théâtre du Vieux-Colombier, as well as a growing number of ciné-clubs in Paris and provincial towns.

Soon ciné-clubs and small specialized cinemas could be found abroad. In 1925, a group of London intellectuals, including Iris Barry, who later headed the Museum of Modern Art's film archive, and filmmaker Ivor Montagu, started the Film Society. It showed old films, imports without distributors, and, especially, in view of England's strict censorship laws, films that were not approved for public screening. The Film Society and other clubs became vital in showing Soviet films in Britain. The group lasted until 1938, but by the early 1930s, some art cinemas, including the long-lived Academy, had made it easier to see special-interest films, and film clubs existed in many parts of Britain.

The little-cinema trend reached the United States in 1925, when Symon Gould began the Film Arts Guild, renting a small New York theater for Sunday matinees of imported films. Within the next three years, the guild was able to move to full-time screenings, and additional art cinemas opened in New York and other cities. In 1928, the Filmarte opened in Hollywood, giving filmmakers there increased access to European avant-garde cinema. These theaters initially relied heavily on Expressionist and other German films, both new and old. Late in the decade, Soviet films became a staple of art-house programs. Émigré moviegoers helped support these theaters, and by the early 1930s, there was a healthy alternative cinema market in the United States.

Ciné-clubs and art theaters spread to Belgium, Japan, Spain, and many other countries. A filmmaker who failed to find a distributor could deal directly with these groups, shipping prints around the globe. As long as films remained fairly cheap to make, this limited circulation could generate a modest profit.

A growing number of journals promoted art films. Tedesco's *Cinéa-Ciné pour tous* continued to offer a forum for discussion of Impressionism and other artistic tendencies. It was supplemented by other French journals, including *L'Art Ciné-matographique*, which published only eight issues but served as an important outlet for Impressionist theory. The main international periodical of the era, *Close Up*, ran from 1927 to 1933. Its driving forces were editor Kenneth Macpherson and his wife Bryher, wealthy Britishers living in Switzerland. Frequent contributors included their friends, notably the American poet H. D. (Hilda Doolittle), who wrote passionate, personal accounts of European art films. *Close Up* championed noncommercial cinema of all types, including G. W. Pabst and the Soviet cinema, on which Bryher wrote the first book in English. Many small journals came and went during this period.

Art theaters, clubs, expositions, and publications helped support alternative types of films. Moreover, they affected decisions about which films would be saved as classics. During the 1930s, several major archives were formed, including the National Film Archive in London, the Museum of Modern Art in New York, and the Cinémathèque Française in Paris. Most people working in these archives had gained their knowledge during the 1920s and were sympathetic to alternative movements. Thus many films of this era were preserved, revived, and circulated in later decades.

FILM EXPERIMENTS OUTSIDE THE MAINSTREAM INDUSTRY

As specialized art films separated from the popular entertainment cinema during the 1920s, an even more radical type of filmmaking appeared. This was *experimental*, or independent avant-garde, cinema. Experimental films were usually short, and they were produced outside the film industry. Indeed, they were often deliberate attempts to undercut the conventions of commercial narrative filmmaking.

To support their work, filmmakers might use their own money, find a rich patron, or work part-time within the mainstream industry. Moreover, a new set of institutions had arisen to promote and exhibit art cinema. (See Box.) These ciné-clubs and specialized cinemas also provided venues for more radically experimental cinema. As with other types of filmmaking, experimental trends emerged soon after World War I as isolated phenomena in different countries before becoming more international.

During the early decades of the century, artists innovated a wide variety of modernist styles, including Cubism, abstract art, Futurism, Dadaism, and Surrealism. In many cases, painters or writers already established in these movements made one or two films. In other cases, young filmmakers became enchanted with the idea of creating an alternative, noncommercial cinema.

During the 1910s, a few experimental films resulted from these stylistic movements, but unfortunately none of these is known to survive. Even before 1910, Italian artists Bruno Corra and Arnaldo Ginna reportedly made short films using hand-colored abstract shapes. In 1914, a group of Russian Futurist painters made a parodic film called *Drama in the Futurists' Cabaret No. 13*, but little is known about this intriguing work.

A few Futurist films were made in Italy. One was *Vita futurista* ("Futurist Life"), made by a group of Futurist artists in 1916–1917. The movement was concerned with celebrating the new "machine age." Artists avoided conventional logic and were fascinated with capturing rapid actions, even portraying successive events as happening simultaneously. *Vita futurista* consisted of several unconnected, absurd segments, including the painter Giacomo Balla's courting and marrying a chair. Surviving illustrations show that the film used distorting mirrors and superimpositions in ways that may have anticipated the French Impressionists and later avant-garde filmmakers. A commercial producer made two films directed by Anton Bragaglia, a Futurist photographer: *Il Perfido canto* and *Thais* (both 1916). The first, which Bragaglia claimed contained innovative techniques, is lost. *Thais* survives, but it is less radical than the others, using a continuing narrative and sets, blurred focus, and costume designs that lend it a mildly Futuristic look.

Lacking sufficient evidence about these early experimental films, we must start our account of the independent avant-garde cinema with the 1920s. There were six major trends in experimental filmmaking: abstract animation, Dada-related production, Surrealism, *cinéma pur* ("pure cinema"), lyrical documentaries, and experimental narrative.

Abstract Animation. During the late nineteenth and early twentieth centuries, artists had moved toward works with increasingly nonobjective styles. Sometimes only the title enabled the viewer to tell what the shapes in a painting represented. In 1910, Wassily Kandinsky's "Abstract Watercolor" made the final break: the painting contained shapes and colors, but it depicted nothing. Other artists quickly followed suit, and pictorial abstraction became one of the major trends of modern art.

The nonrepresentational style took some time to make its way into film. In the late 1910s in Germany, a few artists believed that since film was a visual art like painting, its purest form would be abstract. One of them, Hans Richter, had studied art and worked with an Expressionist group. During World War I, Richter encountered a group of Dadaists in Switzerland, including a Swedish artist, Viking Eggeling, who had also lived in Germany. Eggeling was fascinated with the idea of using art as a universal means of spiritual communication. Richter and Eggeling returned to Germany and each worked on "scrolls": long strips of paper containing series of slightly different drawings. Both sought ways of transforming these into moving images that would be a sort of "visual music." The pair was allowed to use Ufa's facilities, and during 1920–1921, they experimented with animating short strips of frames photographed from the scrolls. Richter claims to have made the first abstract animated film, *Rhythmus 21*, in 1921, but it was not shown publicly until years later.

The earliest abstract animated film was apparently made in Germany by Walter Ruttmann. Ruttmann had also studied as a painter, working in abstract and Expressionist styles. From an early date, however, he was also interested in film. In 1913, he condemned the *Autorenfilm* (p. 38) as an attempt to inject quality into the cinema by drawing on literature:

You can't turn a film into a work of art by augmenting and exalting it with "quality." You can gather together the best mimes in the world, you can let them perform in the most exquisite paradise, you can adorn the programs of your film dramas with the names of the most eminent poets—art will never result *that way*. A work of art will result only if it is born of the possibilities and demands of its material.[3]

Ruttmann's attitude would be shared by many experimental filmmakers in the 1920s. In 1918, he too became intrigued with the idea of moving "paintings" and began to cast about for a means of creating them through film.

Apparently knowing little of commercial animation techniques, Ruttmann painted with oil on glass, wiping off portions of the wet paint and replacing them. He photographed each change from above with illumination from beneath the glass. His *Lichtspiel Opus I* was previewed in Frankfurt in early April 1921 and given a gala premiere in Berlin later that month. Ruttmann went on to make three similar short films, *Lichtspiel Opus 2* (1921), *Ruttmann Opus 3* (1924), and *Ruttmann Opus 4* (1925). (These are now known as *Opus I, Opus II,* and so on.) In each, abstract forms grow, shrink, and transmute in a lively fashion (Fig. 8.16). Ruttmann intended that his films be shown with original musical scores and with hand-coloring. These delightful short films earned him commissions to make theatrical commercials and special sequences in feature films, such as Kriemhild's "Dream of the Falcon" in Lang's *Siegfried*.

In the meantime, Richter had managed to make three similar short animated films, the *Rhythmus* series (tentatively dated 1921, 1923, and 1925). His partner, Eggeling, met an experienced animator, Erna Niemeyer; she traced his scroll drawings and photographed them to make *Diagonalsymphonie* (*Diagonal Symphony*). Eggeling saw his moving abstract images as the equivalent of music, dictating that the short film be shown without any sound accompaniment. It creates a series of variations on parallel white diagonal lines moving in complex patterns against a black background (Fig. 8.17). *Diagonal Symphony* was first shown in late 1924, and Eggeling died the following year.

The technique of abstract animation influenced commerical filmmaking, most notably in the work of a distinctive filmmaker, Lotte Reiniger. Trained as an actress during the 1910s, she was also skilled at cutting out elaborate and delicate silhouettes. During the early 1920s, she created special-effects sequences and advertisements. From 1923 to 1926, she worked on her most important film, *The Adventures of Prince Achmed*, assisted by Ruttmann and others. *Prince Achmed* was the first major animated feature (preceding Disney's *Snow White and the Seven Dwarfs*). *Prince Achmed* told an Arabian Nights fairy tale by means of silhouette figures photographed against subtly shaded backgrounds (Fig. 8.18). Reiniger created such silhouette fantasy films for decades in several countries.

On May 3, 1925, an important matinee of abstract films was held at an Ufa theater in Berlin. It included *Diagonal Symphony*, three of Ruttmann's *Opus* shorts, and Richter's *Rythmus* series. Also on the program, however, were two French Dada films, René Clair's *Entr'acte* and Dudley Murphy and Fernand Léger's *Ballet mécanique*. German filmmakers recognized a fresh experimental impulse. Richter and Ruttmann abandoned abstract animation

Fig. 8.16 In *Opus II*, Ruttmann creates subtle gradations of texture as abstract shapes slide across each other, blending and separating rhythmically.

Fig. 8.17 In *Diagonal Symphony*, complicated curved shapes swirl around the basic diagonal motif, which organizes the abstract patterns throughout the film.

Fig. 8.18 Shades of gray suggest the depth in a setting; the moving figures consist of jointed silhouette puppets in *The Adventures of Prince Achmed*.

Fig. 8.19 Len Lye based the abstract figures in *Tusalava* on Australian Aboriginal art.

to make films using real objects, and the tradition nearly disappeared at this point.

It resurfaced unexpectedly in 1929. The London Film Society provided a young New Zealander, the abstract painter and scriptwriter Len Lye, with the funds for a short film. The drawings occupied Lye from 1927 to 1929, while he supported himself as a curtain drawer in a theater. *Tusalava*, which premiered at the Film Society in 1929, baffled most spectators with its esoteric imagery (Fig. 8.19). Despite this initial reception, Lye went on to become one of the most important abstract animators of the sound era. During the 1920s, Oskar Fischinger was also trying out different animation techniques, including drawn abstract images, but his work, too, flourished primarily after the introduction of sound.

Dada Filmmaking. Dada was a movement that attracted artists in all media. It began around 1915, as a result of artists' sense of the vast, meaningless loss of life in World War I. Artists in New York, Zurich, France, and Germany proposed to sweep aside traditional values and to elevate an absurdist view of the world. They would base artistic creativity on randomness and imagination. Max Ernst displayed an artwork and provided a hatchet so that spectators could demolish it. Marcel Duchamp invented the "readymade" artwork, in which a found object is placed in a museum and labeled; in 1917, he created a scandal by signing a urinal "R. Mutt" and trying to enter it in a prestigious show. Dadaists were fascinated by *collage*, the technique of assembling disparate elements in bizarre juxtapositions. Ernst, for example, made collages by pasting together scraps of illustrations from advertisements and technical manuals.

Under the leadership of poet Tristan Tzara, Dadaist publications, exhibitions, and performances flourished during the late 1910s and early 1920s. The performance "soirées" included such events as poetry readings in which several passages were performed simultaneously. On July 7, 1923, the last major Dada event, the "Soirée du 'Coeur à Barbe' " ("Soirée of the 'Bearded Heart' "), included three short films: a study of New York by American artists Charles Sheeler and Paul Strand, one of Richter's *Rhythmus* abstract animated works, and the important American Dada artist Man Ray's first film, the ironically titled *Retour à la raison* ("Return to Reason"). The element of chance certainly entered into the creation of *Retour à la raison*, since Tzara gave Ray only twenty-four hours' notice that he was to make a film for the program. Ray combined some hastily shot live footage with stretches of "Rayograms" (Fig. 8.20). The soirée proved a mixed success, since Tzara's rivals, led by poet André Breton, provoked a riot in the audience.

This riot was symptomatic of the disagreements that were already bringing Dada to an end. By 1922, it was in serious decline, but key Dada films were still to come. In late 1924, Dada artist Francis Picabia staged his ballet, *Relâche* (meaning "performance called off"). Signs in the auditorium bore such statements as "If you are not satisfied, go to hell." During the intermission (or *entr'acte*), René Clair's *Entr'acte* was shown, with music by the composer who had done the music for the ballet as well—Erik Satie. The evening began with a brief film prologue (seen as the opening segment of

Fig. 8.20 Man Ray created "Rayogram" images without a camera by scattering objects like pins and tacks directly on the film strip, exposing it briefly to light, and developing the result.

Fig. 8.21   Fig. 8.22

Fig. 8.21 Clair's Dadaist fantasy *Entr'acte* concludes with an irreverent funeral scene in which the hearse is pulled, often at dizzying speed and over roller-coaster tracks, by a camel.

Fig. 8.22 Murphy and Léger's *Ballet mécanique* pays tribute to Chaplin with a moving puppet designed by Léger.

modern prints of *Entr'acte*) in which Satie and Picabia leap in slow motion into a scene and fire a cannon directly at the audience. Appearing in the intermission, the rest of the film consisted of unconnected, wildly irrational scenes (Fig. 8.21). Picabia summed up the Dada view when he characterized Clair's film: "*Entr'acte* does not believe in very much, in the pleasure of life, perhaps; it believes in the pleasure of inventing, it respects nothing except the desire to *burst out laughing*."[4]

Also in 1924, the casual collaboration of artists resulted in another major Dada film. American set designer Dudley Murphy had decided to mount a series of "visual symphonies," the first of which was a rather literal-minded ballet film, *Danse macabre* (1922). In Paris, he encountered Man Ray and modernist poet Ezra Pound, who inspired him to do a more abstract work. Ray actually shot some footage, but the French painter Fernand Léger completed the filming of *Ballet mécanique*. Murphy did the cinematography, and Léger directed a complex film juxtaposing shots of objects like pot lids and machine parts with images of his own paintings. There were prismatic shots of women's faces, as well as an innovative shot of a washerwoman climbing a flight of steps, repeated identically many times. Léger had hoped to make a film about Charlie Chaplin, and he opened and closed *Ballet mécanique* with an animated figure of the comedian rendered in an abstract style (Fig. 8.22).

Like Léger, Dada artist Marcel Duchamp made one foray into cinema during this era. By 1913, Duchamp had moved away from abstract painting to experiment with such forms as ready-mades and kinetic sculptures. The latter included a series of motor-driven spinning discs. With the help of Man Ray, Duchamp filmed some of these discs to create *Anémic cinéma* in 1926. This brief film undercuts traditional notions of cinema as a visual, narrative art. All its shots show either turning abstract discs (Fig. 8.23) or similar discs with sentences containing elaborate French puns. By emphasizing simple shapes and writing, Duchamp created an "anemic" style. (*Anémic* is also an anagram for *cinéma*.) In keeping with his playful attitude, he signed the film "Rrose Sélavy," a pun on the phrase *Eros, c'est la vie* ("Eros is life").

Both *Entr'acte* and *Ballet mécanique* were on the 1925 Berlin program, and they convinced German filmmakers like Ruttmann and Richter that modernist style could be created in films without completely abstract, painted images. Richter, who had been linked with virtually every major modern art

Fig. 8.23 One of the spinning discs that create the "anemic" form of *Anémic cinéma*.

Fig. 8.24 In *Ghosts before Breakfast*, a man's head flies off his body as a target is superimposed over him.

Fig. 8.25 Man Ray's *L'Étoile de mer* uses split-screen cinematography to create Surrealist juxtapositions of starfish in jars, roulette wheels, and other objects.

Fig. 8.26 Split-screen technique creates a bizarre effect in *The Seashell and the Clergyman*: The officer, dressed in baby clothes, seems to split in two.

movement, dabbled in Dada. In his *Ghosts before Breakfast* (1928) special effects show objects rebelling against their normal uses. In reverse motion, cups shatter and reassemble. Bowler hats take on a life of their own and fly through the air, and the ordinary laws of nature seem to be suspended (Fig. 8.24).

Riven by internal dissension, the European Dada movement was largely over by 1922. Many of its members formed another group, the Surrealists.

Surrealism. Surrealism resembled Dada in many ways, particularly in its disdain for orthodox aesthetic traditions. Like Dada, Surrealism sought out startling juxtapositions. André Breton, who led the break with the Dadaists and the creation of Surrealism, cited an image from a work by the Comte de Lautréamont: "Beautiful as the unexpected meeting, on a dissection table, of a sewing machine and an umbrella."[5] The movement was heavily influenced, however, by the emerging theories of psychoanalysis. Rather than depending on pure chance for the creation of artworks, Surrealists sought to tap the unconscious mind. In particular, they wanted to render the incoherent narratives of dreams directly in language or images, without the interference of conscious thought processes. Max Ernst, Salvador Dalí, Joan Miró, and Paul Klee were important Surrealist artists.

The ideal Surrealist film differed from Dada works in that it would not be a humorous, chaotic assemblage of events. Instead, it would trace a disturbing, often sexually charged story that followed the inexplicable logic of a dream. With a patron's backing, Dadaist Man Ray moved into Surrealism with *Emak Bakia* (1927), which used many film tricks to suggest a woman's mental state. At the end she is seen in a famous image, her eyes closed, with eyeballs painted on them; she opens her eyes and smiles at the camera. Many Surrealists denounced the film as containing too little narrative. Ray's next film, *L'Étoile de mer* ("The Starfish," 1927), hinted at a story, based on a script by Surrealist poet Robert Desnos. It shows a couple in love, interspersed with random shots of starfish, trains, and other objects (Fig. 8.25). At the end the woman leaves with another man, and her cast-off lover consoles himself with a beautiful starfish.

Germaine Dulac, who had already worked extensively in regular feature filmmaking and French Impressionism, turned briefly to Surrealism, directing a screenplay by poet Antonin Artaud. The result was *The Seashell and the Clergyman* (1928), which combines Impressionist techniques of cinematography with the disjointed narrative logic of Surrealism. A clergyman carrying a large seashell smashes laboratory beakers; an officer intrudes and breaks the shell, to the clergyman's horror. The rest of the film consists of the priest's pursuing a beautiful woman through an incongruous series of settings. His love seems to be perpetually thwarted by the intervention of the officer (Fig. 8.26). Even after the priest marries the woman, he is left alone drinking from the shell. The initial screening of the film provoked a riot at the small Studio des Ursulines theater, though it is still not clear whether the instigators were Artaud's enemies or his friends, protesting Dulac's softening of the Surrealist tone of the scenario.

Perhaps the quintessential Surrealist film was created in 1928 by novice director Luis Buñuel. A Spanish film enthusiast and modernist poet, Buñuel had come to France and been hired as an assistant by Jean Epstein. Working in collaboration with Salvador Dalí, he made *Un Chien andalou* (*An Andalusian Dog*). Its basic story concerned a quarrel between two lovers, but the time scheme and logic are impossible. The film begins with a sequence in which a man inexplicably slices the heroine's eye with a razor—yet she appears, unharmed, in the next scene. As the quarrel goes on, ants crawl from a hole in a man's hand, the hero hauls a piano stuffed with rotting mules' carcasses across a room, and a pair of hands protrudes through the wall to shake a cocktail (Fig. 8.27). Throughout, intertitles announce meaningless intervals of time passing, as when "sixteen years earlier" interrupts an action that then continues without pause.

Dalí and Buñuel followed this film with a longer, even more provocative one, *L'Age d'or* ("The Age of Gold," 1930). The tenuous plot concerns two lovers kept apart by the woman's wealthy parents and a disapproving society. An early scene shows a pompous ceremony at the seaside in which presiding bishops wither to skeletons. Later, a man who is shot falls up to the ceiling, and the heroine sucks on the toes of a statue to express her sexual frustration. The film teems with erotic imagery (Fig. 8.28), and the ending portrays a figure clearly intended to represent Christ emerging from a sadistic orgy. *L'Age d'or* provoked riots during its initial screenings, and it was banned. It remained almost impossible to see for over four decades.

During the early 1930s, Surrealism as a unified movement was breaking up. Some artists became involved in leftist or anarchist politics, and Dalí earned their wrath through his fascination with Hitler. By 1933, the European phase of the movement was over, but, as with Dada, Surrealism's influence was felt strongly in the era after World War II.

Cinéma Pur. In the wake of works like *Ballet mécanique*, some filmmakers realized that they could organize nonnarrative films around abstract visual qualities of the physical world. Since commercial cinema, especially that of Hollywood, was strongly associated with narrative, such abstract films seemed untainted, owing nothing to literary or theatrical influences. These filmmakers were not unified by membership in any modernist movement, like Dada or Surrealism. Indeed, they largely avoided the irreverence of Dada and the psychic explorations of Surrealism. These diverse, widely scattered filmmakers wanted to reduce film to its most basic elements in order to create lyricism and pure form.

Indeed, the early French proponents of this approach termed it *cinéma pur*, or "pure cinema." One of these was Henri Chomette, who had worked as an assistant director for commercial filmmakers like Jacques de Baroncelli and Jacques Feyder. In 1925, a commission from a rich count for an experimental short led to the earliest "pure" film, *Jeux des reflets et de la vitesse* ("The Play of Reflections and Speed," 1925). For the "speed" portion Chomette mounted his camera at various angles on a moving subway car, often filming in fast motion. He juxtaposed these shots with views of a series of shiny objects. His next film, *Cinq minutes de cinéma pur* ("Five Minutes of Pure Cinema," 1926), was made for the growing circuit of specialized cinemas (Fig. 8.29). After these two films, Chomette became a commercial director.

Fig. 8.27 In *Un Chien andalou*, a doorbell is inexplicably represented by hands shaking a cocktail.

Fig. 8.28 During an elegant party, the heroine of *L'Age d'or* finds an ox in her bed.

Fig. 8.29 *Cinq minutes de cinéma pur* begins by dissolving among shots of shiny crystals in changing patterns against a black background.

Figs. 8.30 and 8.31 *Thème et variations* alternates machine parts and plants with a ballerina's dance, suggesting an abstract graphic similarity between different kinds of movements and shapes.

Fig. 8.30

Fig. 8.31

Fig. 8.32 Filming one of his own kinetic sculptures, the "Light-Space Modulator," Moholy-Nagy created shifting patterns of shadows and reflected light, produced by its moving metallic parts, for *Lichtspiel, schwarz-weiss-grau.*

Fig. 8.33 In this shot from Ralph Steiner's *H₂O*, the reflections on the surface of the water create an image so abstract that we can barely recognize its subject.

Following her venture into Surrealism, Germaine Dulac embraced *cinéma pur* in *Disque 927* (1928), *Thème et variations* (1928), and *Arabesque* (1929). As the titles suggest, Dulac tried to make her short, lyrical studies equivalent to musical pieces (Figs. 8.30, 8.31). With the coming of sound, Dulac could not finance her films independently, and, unwilling to return to mainstream filmmaking, she worked primarily in newsreels after 1929.

The concept of pure cinema surfaced in other countries, though not always under that name. Some photographers experimented briefly with cinema. Laszló Moholy-Nagy, a Hungarian photographer and sculptor, created several films in the late 1920s and early 1930s. Among these was *Lichtspiel, schwarz-weiss-grau* ("Play of Light, Black-White-Gray," 1930), made while he was teaching at the Bauhaus. The title is a pun on *Lichtspiel*, which means both "movie" and "play of light" (Fig. 8.32). Similarly, American photographer Ralph Steiner's H_2O (1929) consisted of increasingly abstract images of water (Fig. 8.33). Steiner made two similar films and then went on to photograph some of the most important documentaries of the next decade. The "pure cinema" impulse has had a strong influence on experimental filmmakers since the 1920s.

Lyrical Documentaries: The City Symphony. Some filmmakers experimented by taking their cameras outdoors and capturing poetic aspects of urban landscapes. Their films formed another new genre, the "city symphony." These works were part documentary, part experimental film.

The earliest known city symphony, and, indeed, perhaps the first experimental film made in the United States, was made by modern artist Charles Sheeler and photographer Paul Strand in 1920. It was shown as a scenic short in a commercial theater in New York the following year under the title *New York the Magnificent*, but the filmmakers later dubbed it *Manhatta*, and that is the title by which it has come to be known. The pair filmed scenes near the Battery Park area of southern Manhattan, creating evocative, often nearly abstract views of the city (Fig. 8.34). Although the film had little distribution initially, it was revived in art theaters during the second half of the decade and probably inspired later filmmaking.

By that era, the city symphony had become more common. In 1925, Brazilian director Alberto Cavalcanti, working in France, made *Rien que les heures* ("Nothing but the Hours," 1926). It juxtaposes two different types of material: candid documentary shots and staged scenes. Shopkeepers open

Fig. 8.34

Fig. 8.35

Fig. 8.34 A dramatic view of the street far below through a balustrade in *Manhatta*.

Fig. 8.35 A drunken, perhaps dying old woman wandering the streets forms one motif in *Rien que les heures*.

Fig. 8.36

Fig. 8.37

Figs. 8.36 and 8.37 In *Berlin*, Ruttmann cuts from an abstract moving image of bars forming an "X" to a similar composition created by a railroad crossing gate.

their shutters, patrons eat at cafés, a pimp kills a woman, an old lady staggers through the streets (Fig. 8.35). Cavalcanti refuses to develop any of these situations into a coherent narrative, instead weaving together motifs to suggest the passage of time all over Paris.

Cavalcanti's film was followed by Walter Ruttmann's feature, *Berlin: die Symphonie der Grossstadt* (*Berlin, Symphony of a Great City*, 1927). It also provided a cross-section of life in a single city across one day. Coming from the tradition of abstract animation, Ruttmann begins the film with some geometrical shapes, matching them graphically with documentary images (Figs. 8.36, 8.37). Subsequent shots explore the abstract qualities of machines, building façades, store-window displays, and the like. Ruttmann also includes social commentary, as when, during the noontime segment, he cuts from a homeless woman with her children to plates of food in a fancy restaurant. *Berlin* circulated widely in commercial theaters and was one of the silent era's most influential documentaries.

The poetic city symphony proved fertile ground for young filmmakers working for the art-cinema and ciné-club circuit. For example, the Dutch documentarist Joris Ivens began as cofounder of a major club, the Filmliga, in Amsterdam in 1927. His first completed film was a lyrical, abstract study of a drawbridge, *The Bridge* (1928). Its success in art-film circles led to other films, including *Rain* (1929). *Rain* is a short exploration of the changing look of Amsterdam before, during, and after a shower: the sheen of water on tile roofs and windows and the spatter of raindrops in the canals and in puddles (Fig. 8.38). Again, *Rain* was well received among art-cinema audiences across Europe and inspired many imitations.

Fig. 8.38 Ivens captures the effects of the last few drops of a shower in a puddle on a brick pavement (*Rain*).

The city-symphony genre was diverse. The film could be lyrical, displaying the effects of wind and water. Henri Storck, who had formed the ciné-club for the Belgian seaside town of Ostende, recorded the town's summertime sights in his *Images d'Ostende* (1929). In contrast, the young Jean Vigo, who was to direct two quasi-Surrealist features in the early sound era, began with *À propos de Nice* ("Concerning Nice," 1929), a harsh satire of wealthy vacationers in a French resort town. Similarly, Dziga Vertov's *Man with a Movie Camera* commented on Soviet society by weaving together several cities in a single "day-in-the-life-of" documentary. Vertov demonstrated the power of the cinema by showing the filmmaking process within his film and by using extensive special effects (Fig. 6.52). The city symphony has proved an enduring genre among documentarists and experimental filmmakers.

Experimental Narrative. By the late 1920s, filmmakers in several countries were using the new techniques and styles of the independent experimental cinema to question narrative conventions. In the United States, some experimental directors adapted techniques from German Expressionism and French Impressionism into cinematic forms suited to low-budget, independent production. During the late 1920s, noncommercial European filmmakers pushed both narrative and abstract techniques still further.

In the United States, some filmmakers outside the commercial industry wanted to treat film as a modern art. Few of the more radical experimental films made in Europe during this era were shown in America, however. Experimental filmmakers were inspired mainly by German Expressionist and French Impressionist films.

Like Dreyer, Robert Florey was an international director, though on a more modest scale. Born in France, he was thoroughly familiar with both the Impressionist and the Expressionist movements. He came to Hollywood in 1921, serving as United Artists' technical adviser on French subjects and eventually directing minor features. In 1927, he turned to experimental filmmaking, directing the short *The Life and Death of 9413—a Hollywood Extra* (aka *Life and Death of a Hollywood Extra*). This ingenious film, made for a reported $100, combined close shots of actors against black backgrounds with stylized miniature scenes, made of simple paper cut-outs and erector-set objects shot with an ordinary light on a kitchen table (Fig. 8.39). The film was a witty satire on Hollywood's uncaring treatment of aspiring talent. Florey's cinematographer, Gregg Toland, went on to photograph many major films, including *Citizen Kane*. The special effects were devised by Slavko Vorkapich, another émigré fascinated with avant-garde technique; during the 1930s, he created elaborate montage sequences for several Hollywood movies. *Hollywood Extra* was given a commercial release, through the intervention of Charles Chaplin, and Florey went on to make three more experimental shorts. The only one that survives, *The Love of Zero* (1928), contains many innovative camera techniques, but it is not as appealing as the earlier film. Florey soon moved back into commercial production, directing many stylish middle- and low-budget features, ranging from the Marx Brothers' first film, *The Coconuts* (1929), to the horror film *Murders in the Rue Morgue* (1932). Some of these show the impact of German Expressionism.

Fig. 8.39 A split-screen effect in *The Life and Death of 9413—a Hollywood Extra* juxtaposes the hero's naive face with his abstract vision of Hollywood.

Fig. 8.40

Fig. 8.41

Fig. 8.40 The hero of *The Tell-Tale Heart* sits on the floor of his apartment, the design of which is modeled on that of *The Cabinet of Dr. Caligari*.

Fig. 8.41 An expressionist set, apparently depicting a crypt (*The Fall of the House of Usher*).

Almost simultaneously, some filmmakers drew upon the idea of using German Expressionism to bring stories by Edgar Allan Poe to the screen. Amateur director Charles Klein's *The Tell-Tale Heart* (1928) imitated *Caligari* by explicitly presenting its story as the vision of an insane man (Fig. 8.40). Klein's film circulated among the newly formed art cinemas. In Rochester, New York, two film and photography enthusiasts, James Sibley Watson and Melville Webber, co-directed *The Fall of the House of Usher* (1928). This film's oblique narrative technique depends on the spectator's foreknowledge of Poe's story. Impressionist-style subjective camera techniques and expressionist decor are combined in an attempt to capture the eerie atmosphere of the original (Fig. 8.41). Watson and Webber went on to make an even more impenetrable narrative, *Lot in Sodom* (1933), replete with superimpositions and black backgrounds.

A few European works pushed even further in exploring narrative conventions during the late 1920s. One such film was the short feature *Borderline*, created by the group around the international intellectual journal *Close Up* (p. 191). Its editor, Kenneth Macpherson, directed, and the poet H. D. was one of the actors. *Borderline* centers on two couples, one black, one white, living in a small Swiss town. When the white man begins an affair with the black woman, sexual and racial tensions escalate. The film mixes objective and subjective scenes without clear-cut transitions. The African-American stage actor and singer Paul Robeson played the black husband, and H. D. gave an intense performance as the jealous white woman. Dynamic compositions reflected the influence of the Soviet cinema (Fig. 8.42), but the film was unique in its elliptical style. It remained the *Close Up* group's only completed experiment.

The Belgian Charles Dekeukeleire discovered the cinema through the work of the French Impressionists. After working as a critic, he turned to filmmaking in 1927, just as the ciné-club movement was spreading. Planning, shooting, and even processing his own footage, he made four silent experimental films over the next few years. Outstanding among these were *Impatience* (1929) and *Histoire de détéctive* ("Detective Story," 1930), bold films which had little precedent in any artistic tradition. *Impatience* lasts for nearly forty-five minutes but consists only of relentless repetitions of four elements: a woman (alternatively naked and dressed in a motorcyclist's outfit), a motorcycle, mountain scenery, and a set of three swinging abstract blocks. No

Fig. 8.42 Paul Robeson in *Borderline*.

Fig. 8.43 *Impatience* seems to suggest a narrative situation, yet its insistent repetition of shots like this one of the woman against a blank background also forces us to see it as abstract.

two of these elements is ever seen in the same shot. Although the film seems to hint at a minimal narrative situation (perhaps the woman is riding the motorcycle through the mountains?), it simply shows us the same sorts of shots over and over (Fig. 8.43).

Histoire de détéctive is even more complex. Purportedly the film made by a detective investigating why a man has lost all interest in life, it consists mainly of lengthy written passages, punctuated by banal images of the lives of the man and his wife which add little to the intertitles. In a period when cinematic stories were supposed to be told visually, Dekeukeleire's film was widely condemned. He made one more silent film, *Flamme blanche* ("White Flame," 1931), a semidocumentary story of police brutality during a Communist party rally. Faced with an uncomprehending reaction to his work, Dekeukeleire turned to documentary filmmaking during the sound era. His two silent masterpieces, however, were indications of how far experimental films could go in defying the norms of narrative cinema.

Independent avant-garde cinema depended on the fact that silent filmmaking was relatively inexpensive. The advent of sound increased costs considerably, and even ciné-clubs and art cinemas usually preferred to show sound films. The rise of fascism led several experimental directors to move toward political documentaries. Still, the tradition of experimentation outside commercial institutions continued in changed form in the 1930s and beyond.

DOCUMENTARY FEATURES GAIN PROMINENCE

Before the 1920s, documentary filmmaking had largely been confined to newsreels and scenic shorts. Occasional feature-length documentaries had been made, but these had not established the genre as significant. During the 1920s, however, the documentary achieved new stature as it increasingly became identified with artistic cinema. We can distinguish three main tendencies in the documentaries of this era: the exotic film, the attempt at direct recording of reality, and the compilation documentary.

The exotic documentary was particularly important in the United States. It came dramatically to public attention in 1922 with the release of Robert Flaherty's *Nanook of the North*. An explorer and prospector in Alaska and Canada, Flaherty had shot some amateur footage of Eskimo culture. He determined to make a feature film following the life of an Eskimo family. Eventually, in 1920, a fur company agreed to finance the venture. Flaherty spent sixteen months in the region of Hudson Bay, filming Nanook and his wife and son. Every scene was planned in advance, with Nanook making many suggestions about what sorts of action to include (Fig. 8.44). Flaherty balanced authenticity with arranged scenes, as when the Eskimos built an oversize igloo with one side open so that the family could be filmed going to bed.

Fig. 8.44 Carefully staged action in *Nanook of the North* as the hero prepares to launch his kayak and join his friends in the hunt.

The major Hollywood film firms refused to distribute *Nanook*, but the independent Pathé Exchange released it. It met with great success, undoubtedly in part because of the engaging personality of its hero. As a result,

Paramount supported Flaherty in an expedition to Samoa to direct a similar film, *Moana*. He set out in 1923, only to find the natives had adopted western-style customs. Flaherty persuaded his "actors" to return to traditional clothing and, in order to inject drama into the film, to reenact a painful, obsolete tattoo ritual. Flaherty had now fallen into his lifelong habit of running far beyond schedule and shooting immense amounts of footage. *Moana* was not ready for release until 1926 and did not duplicate the success of *Nanook*. Flaherty would not complete another film for eight years.

Fig. 8.45 A documentary spectacle as thousands of nomads brave frigid mountains in a search for pastureland in *Grass*.

Nanook's triumph also enabled the producer-director-photographer team of Ernest B. Schoedsack and Merian Cooper to create their first feature, *Grass: A Nation's Battle for Life* (1925). Also financed and distributed by Paramount, it recorded a dangerous migration of Iranian nomads seeking pastures for their flocks (Fig. 8.45). *Grass* was popular enough to permit Schoedsack and Cooper to make *Chang* (1928), a staged account, shot on location, of a peasant family battling dangers in their native Siamese jungle. *Chang* reflected a move toward fiction-based filmmaking, and Schoedsack and Cooper were to combine their interest in exoticism and their impulse toward fiction in producing the immensely successful *King Kong* in 1933.

The documentary form was particularly important in the Soviet Union. There all three types of documentary—recording of reality, compilation, and exoticism—found expression.

Dziga Vertov had taken charge of Soviet newsreel filmmaking during the Revolution. By the early 1920s he had formulated his theory of the "kino eye," claiming that the camera lens, due to its recording abilities, was superior to the human eye. He put this claim to the test in 1922, establishing a new newsreel series, *Kino-Pravda*. [The name was derived from the national Bolshevik newspaper, *Pravda* ("Truth"), started by Lenin in 1912.] Each installment of the newsreel focused on two or three episodes of current events or ordinary life. Vertov also, however, believed that special effects were part of the camera's superior ability to report the truth. Thus he often used split-screen effects or superimpositions to comment on his subjects (Fig. 8.46). Vertov also made feature-length documentaries, mixing footage photographed directly from life with special effects that conveyed ideological points (Fig. 6.52). When sound was introduced in the Soviet Union, Vertov insisted upon having a mobile recording machine that could be taken on location in factories and mines for use in making *Enthusiasm* (1931), a documentary on the First Five-Year Plan in steel production.

Fig. 8.46 In *Kino-Pravda* (number 21, 1925), Lenin's face is superimposed in the sky above his tomb.

During this era, Soviet filmmaker Esfir Shub virtually single-handedly invented the compilation film. She had reedited foreign films for Soviet release during the early 1920s. Her real interest, however, was in documentary. She aspired to assemble scenes from old newsreels into new films. The Soviet authorities refused to give her access to such footage until 1926. Among the old reels, she found the home movies of Tsar Nicholas II, around which she based *The Fall of the Romanov Dynasty* (1927; Fig. 8.47). The favorable reception of this film allowed her to make two additional features: *The Great Road* (1927), on the Soviet Revolution, and *The Russia of Nicholas II and Leo Tolstoy* (1928), on the pre-Revolutionary era. Having used much of the footage she had discovered, Shub continued her career as an editor in the sound era.

Fig. 8.47 In *The Fall of the Romanov Dynasty*, Esfir Shub includes newsreel footage of the destruction of the statue of Tsar Alexander III in Moscow in 1921.

Fig. 8.48 The new railroad is used to tether a camel in *Turksib*.

The many ethnic groups included in the new Soviet Union led directors of documentaries to foster an exoticism not unlike that of Flaherty's *Nanook*. In 1929, Viktor Turin made *Turksib*, chronicling the epic construction of the Turkestan-Siberian railway. Although the film emphasized the achievements of the Soviet state, it also recorded the reactions of the indigenous peoples living along the railway's route (Fig. 8.48). This exotic appeal made *Turksib* popular on the art-cinema circuit in the West. Similarly, in *Salt for Svanetia* (1930) Mikhail Kalatozov recorded in sparse but beautiful detail the efforts to bring salt to a remote mountain village near the Black and Caspian Seas.

The work of Flaherty, Schoedsack and Cooper, Vertov, Shub, and other documentarists was to have a considerable impact during the 1930s, when the actuality film became more prominent.

COMMERCIAL FILMMAKING INTERNATIONALLY

Throughout this period, hundreds of films aimed at a popular market continued to be made annually worldwide. Some countries' industries imitated Hollywood cinema fairly directly, while a few devised recognizable (though not avant-garde) styles. Several countries which previously had only sporadic production began making films more regularly, while production in some declined.

JAPAN

One of the most powerful studio systems grew up in Japan, where filmmakers forged a distinctive style. The first studios were built during the Russo-Japanese War (1904–1905). Japan's victory in the conflict established it as a world power. Soon industrial growth intensified. Japan supplied the warring nations of Europe with matériel and began dominating Asia with consumer goods. As Japan modernized, U.S. films entered the market. Japanese audiences, though fond of American films, preferred the domestic product and sustained local production.

The two most powerful companies were Nikkatsu and Shochiku. Nikkatsu (short for Nippon Katsudo Shashin) was organized in 1912 out of several smaller firms. Shochiku was founded in 1920 by two brothers who ran a conglomerate of kabuki theaters and vaudeville houses. Both Nikkatsu and Shochiku were vertically integrated, owning distribution companies and theaters. The industry gained a professional identity by forming a trade association and by creating a film magazine, *Kinema Jumpo* ("Movie Times").

In September 1923 an earthquake devastated Tokyo, but the movie business emerged stronger than before. In rebuilding theaters, exhibitors expanded and modernized them. Vertical integration allowed Japanese firms to control and profit from American imports.

Shooting a feature in two weeks or less, Shochiku, Nikkatsu, and dozens of smaller studios pumped out 600 to 800 films per year. By 1928, Japan was producing more films than any other country, a position it would hold for a decade and reassume after World War II. Production was sustained through tight vertical integration, the big firms' investments in other entertainment businesses, and an avid urban audience.

As in other countries, the earliest Japanese features drew upon indigenous theater. The two major genres were the *jidai-geki*, or historical film, and the *gendai-geki*, the film of contemporary life. *Jidai-geki* borrowed heavily from the kabuki theater, particularly in the swordfight films (*chambara*) featuring acrobatic martial arts and bold samurai. *Gendai-geki* films were typically melodramas of romance or family life, influenced by the *shimpa* theater, which had been modeled on nineteenth-century western drama. All genres also adhered to the kabuki convention of having women's roles played by men.

Film exhibition also bore the marks of traditional theater. Exhibitors had to compete with kabuki performances, which consumed half a day or more, so shows in the largest cities tended to be very long, sometimes running over five hours. In addition, all films were accompanied by a commentator called the *katsuben* or *benshi*. Standing near the screen, the *benshi* (usually a man) would explain the action, imitate the dialogue of all the characters, and comment on their behavior. Carrying on the tradition of onstage narrators in kabuki and puppet theater, the *benshi* added the excitement of live performance to the film show. Some *benshi* became stars, attracting audiences regardless of what film was playing.

After World War I, companies cast off theatrical traditions and started to modernize their films. In the early 1920s, women began playing female parts. The fast-paced U.S. imports encouraged directors to break with the predominant long-shot style. Directors adopted Hollywood continuity principles, and close-ups and shot/reverse-shot editing became widespread. The *jidai-geki* directors, notably Masahiro Makino, intensified action sequences by adding American-style rapid editing. Some directors, such as Kaoru Osanai and Minoru Murata in their *Souls on the Road* (1921), blended theatrical performance with more American-style cutting and flashback construction.

Fig. 8.49 Dyamic swordfighting in *Komatsu Riyuzo* (1930).

New genres sprang up as well. The modern comedy centering on young people was initiated by *Amateur Club* (1920). Its director, Thomas Kurihara, had worked in Hollywood as an assistant to Thomas Ince. With the modern reconstruction of Tokyo after the 1923 earthquake, the urban comedy of manners became an important genre. American imports also accelerated modernization, as when Yutaka Abe modeled *Woman Who Touched the Legs* (1926) on Lubitsch's *The Marriage Circle* (1924). A genre of "salaryman" (*sarariman*) comedies portrayed the tribulations of the downtrodden company employee trying to succeed. One master of the salaryman film was Yasujiro Shimazu (*Sunday*, 1924).

The very few films that survive from this period indicate that despite low budgets, Japan's studios created one of the world's most innovative cinemas. Kinugasa's *Page of Madness* (p. 187) represents an experimental extreme, but ordinary films also displayed great pictorial dynamism. *Chambara* fight scenes relied on fast-motion, abrupt cutting, hand-held camera movements, and carefully choreographed swordplay (Fig. 8.49). Many films flaunted deep-space compositions and striking angles and lighting (Fig. 8.50). The imaginative storytelling and style pioneered in the 1920s would be elaborated in the outstanding accomplishments of Japanese cinema in the following decade.

Fig. 8.50 The blind factory owner in *Town of Love* (1928) is given hard crosslighting.

Fig. 8.51 The rye field Hepworth planted for *Comin' Thro' the Rye*. Its cycle, from plowing to harvesting, creates a bucolic background for key scenes of the central love story.

GREAT BRITAIN

In the postwar years, the British film industry also optimistically set out to compete directly with Hollywood, largely by imitating its methods. Pioneer producer-director Cecil Hepworth expanded his company in 1919, and a few other important firms, such as Stoll and Ideal, both formed during the war, made ambitious films that they hoped would be released in the United States. Among these, Hepworth was the main figure to try and make distinctively British films. As he put it, "It was always in the back of my mind from the very beginning that *I was to make English pictures, with all the English countryside for background and with English atmosphere and English idiom throughout.*"[6] His own favorite was *Comin' Thro' the Rye* (1924), which exploited the beauties of the English countryside to tell an old-fashioned love story (Fig. 8.51). Despite its location photography, however, the film proved unable to compete with the more lively Hollywood films that still occupied around 90 percent of British screen time. Shortly after its completion, Hepworth's firm was bankrupt, and he turned to running a film laboratory.

Other British filmmakers, imitating Hollywood films but unable to command the high budgets of American productions, also found it difficult to compete. By the mid-1920s production slumped. Finally, in 1927, the government passed a quota to support British production. Investment picked up slowly in the last years of the decade, though the expenses connected with the introduction of sound in 1929 set the recovery back somewhat. The growth of the British industry into a mature studio system would occur during the 1930s.

ITALY

A somewhat similar situation existed in Italy after the war. Initially producers tried to revive the palmy days of Italian prewar production, mostly by relying on the formulas of that period. Expensive costume pictures remained a staple. In 1923, the Unione Cinematografica Italiana (UCI), a large new firm started four years earlier, produced a lavish remake of the 1913 hit, *Quo Vadis?*. Drawing upon tactics associated wih the budding Film Europe movement, UCI brought in a German, Georg Jacoby, to co-direct with Gabriellino D'Annunzio. A German cinematographer was also imported, and the cast was international (Fig. 8.52). The film's lukewarm reception suggested that epics would not regain Italy its former glory. Further attempts were made, however. In 1924, one of the most important Italian directors, Augusto Genina, made *Cirano di Bergerac*, from Rostand's play *Cyrano de Bergerac*. The producers took the unusual step of adding hand-stenciled color to the entire lengthy feature (Color Plate 8.1). Another genre prominent in this period was the strongman film, including *Maciste all'inferno* ("Maciste in Hell," 1926).

The competition from American and other imported films was too great, however. During the early 1920s, Italian films made up only 6 percent of those screened. In 1926, output sank to a mere twenty features.

Fig. 8.52 German Emil Jannings—one of the foreign actors imported for *Quo Vadis?*—as Nero.

In 1922, the government was taken over by the Fascist party, whose leader, Benito Mussolini, considered the cinema "the strongest weapon" of the state. In 1923, the government formed L'Unione Cinematografica Educativa (LUCE) to make documentaries. Fiction films responded little to the Fascist regime, however, until the 1930s.

One notable event occurred at the end of the silent era. Alessandro Blasetti, the leader of a group of young critics and theorists who opposed the continued reliance on old formulas, made his first film, *Sole (Sun)* in 1929. For this tale of the reclamation of marshes for farmland, Blasetti drew heavily upon influences from Soviet Montage films and other European avant-garde cinema. The brief surviving portion displays rapid editing for maximum conflict, subjective techniques, and unusual camera angles, all combined with dazzling photography of the marshland settings. Blasetti's film received considerable praise as the first major Fascist fiction film. During the next few years, he was to become one of Italy's most important directors, when the introduction of sound and increasing government support revived Italian filmmaking.

Fig. 8.53 The bumbling hero of *The Good Soldier Schweik* stands to attention after squatting in an open-air latrine. A passing officer awards him a medal, prompting him to comment, "This shows that, no matter where, luck can smile on a soldier."

SOME SMALLER PRODUCING COUNTRIES

A number of countries began producing on a more stable basis. Often their films were inexpensively made and designed primarily for the domestic market. Such industries continued to draw heavily upon national literature and to exploit local scenery and customs to set their films apart from the dominant Hollywood product.

For example, although films had regularly been made in Czechoslovakia since 1908, the first well-equipped filmmaking studio was not built until 1921. In 1924, actor-director Karel Lamač constructed a second, the Kavalírka studios. Here Lamač made *The Good Soldier Schweik* (1926), which helped create a national film tradition. It was based upon Jaroslav Hašek's popular satire on militarism. Lamač chose a few episodes from the sprawling tale and found an actor who resembled the Schweik of the original illustrations (Fig. 8.53).

Similarly, Spanish cinema expanded slightly during this period. During the 1910s, Spanish films were usually adaptations of plays. Small firms came and went, as investors dabbled in producing a film or two. During the 1920s, more stable filmmaking companies formed, notably Film Española. Among its most prolific and popular directors was José Buchs. His *Curro Vargas* (1923), a costume picture set in the nineteenth century, typifies small national film production. It mixes picturesque exterior locales with interiors filmed in sets built on open-air stages (Figs. 8.54, 8.55). Spanish audiences enjoyed seeing locally made films, and production rose to fifty-nine features in 1928. The coming of sound, however, temporarily brought the industry to a virtual standstill.

Production was even more sporadic in Belgium, but a few small companies made occasional features. In 1919, André Jacquemin formed a firm,

Fig. 8.54

Fig. 8.55

Figs. 8.54 and 8.55 In *Curro Vargas*, the hero's entry into a building shows him moving from an old street to a sunlit interior setting built on an open-air stage.

Fig. 8.56 Location shooting in Brussels in *Le Portrait de l'amiral*.

Fig. 8.57 An Egyptian crowd scene in *Die Sklavenkönigen*.

Le Film Cinématographique Belge, which produced a feature, *Le Portrait de l'amiral* (1922, directed by François Le Forestier). Adapted from a Belgian novel, the film used local settings to enhance its appeal (Fig. 8.56). Although this film was aimed mainly at the domestic audience, it also did well in other French-speaking markets.

Occasionally a firm in a smaller producing country would make a big-budget costume picture in order to break into the world market. The Austrian producer Alexander Joseph "Sascha" Kolowrat-Krakowsky took this tack. He had begun as a producer in the early 1910s, forming the Sascha firm in 1914. In 1918, Kolowrat visited the United States to study production methods. He decided that making spectacles was the way to succeed in the Austrian and even the U.S. markets. He produced two big-budget pictures, *Sodom und Gomorrah* (1922) and *Die Sklavenkönigen* ("The Slave Queen," 1924), both directed by Hungarian Mihály Kertész. (By the end of the decade, he would go to work in Hollywood under the name Michael Curtiz, directing many films, including *Casablanca*.) *Die Sklavenkönigen* was a typical epic designed for international appeal. Based on an adventure novel by H. Rider Haggard, it highlighted crowds of extras and large sets (Fig. 8.57), as well as impressive special effects depicting Moses parting the Red Sea. Such films occasionally succeeded on world markets, but they were not enough to form the basis for regular production in a minor industry.

During the 1920s, the strength of America's hold on world markets became apparent. Many countries, however, resisted that hold. Moreover, a new set of institutions assumed that artistic cinema was distinct from the commercial product. Challenging alternatives to Hollywood filmmaking arose. The introduction of sound at the end of the decade massively altered many countries' filmmaking, sometimes adversely, sometimes positively.

◆ NOTES AND QUERIES

DIFFERENT VERSIONS OF SILENT CLASSICS

Dudley Murphy and Fernand Léger's *Ballet mécanique* is commonly seen in museum and classroom screenings in the United States today—yet almost invariably we see it in a shortened version. The film premiered at the Internationale Ausstellung für Theatertechnik ("International Exhibition of Theater Technology") in Vienna in 1924. A copy of this full version was preserved by Frederick Kiesler, a modernist architect (who designed a small art theater for the Film Guild in New York in 1929). His widow donated it to the Anthology Film Archives (New York) in 1976. This version contained additional footage not seen in most prints, including several shots of Léger's paintings.

In the meantime, however, Léger had reedited a shorter version, which he donated to the Museum of Modern Art in 1935. This abridgment is the basis for most current prints. Other versions of *Ballet mécanique* also exist. For an account of the film's production and subsequent career, see Judi Freeman, "Léger's *Ballet mécanique*," in Rudolf E. Kuenzli, ed., *Dada and Surrealist Film* (New York: Willis Locker & Owens, 1987), pp. 28–45.

The distribution history of *The Passion of Joan of Arc* has been even more confusing. Dreyer himself claimed that he was unable to edit the final version of the film released in France, Denmark, and elsewhere, yet there is evidence that he did in fact edit it. The film's negative was apparently burned in a laboratory fire. A shortened sound rerelease of the film was made in the United States in 1933, and another sonorized version was made in France in 1952. The Cinémathèque Française in Paris preserved a lengthy print which was copied and widely circulated. On the assumption that this print was still missing significant portions, the Dansk Filmmuseum in Copenhagen undertook a painstaking reconstruction. Then, in the early 1980s, a print made in 1928 from the original negative was discovered in Norway. Surprisingly, this print turned out to be only slightly different from the standard Cinémathèque version that had been circulating for decades. A few shots were longer, and the visual quality was clearer, but in this case the familiar version of a silent classic was apparently quite close to the original. See Tony Pipolo, "The Spectre of *Joan of Arc:* Textual Variations in the Key Prints of Carl Dreyer's Film," *Film History* **2,** 4 (November–December 1988): 301–324.

◆ REFERENCES

1. C. de Danilowicz, "Chez Erich Pommer," *Cinémagazine* **4,** 27 (4 July 1924): 11.
2. Richard Abel, *French Film: The First Wave, 1915–1929* (Princeton, N.J.: Princeton University Press, 1985), pp. 239 ff.
3. Quoted in Walter Schobert, *The German Avant-Garde Film of the 1920's* (Munich: Goethe-Institut, 1989), p. 10.
4. Quoted in Rudolf E. Kuenzli, *Dada and Surrealist Film* (New York: Willis Locker & Owens, 1987), p. 5.
5. Quoted in Patrick Waldberg, *Surrealism* (New York: McGraw-Hill, n.d.), pp. 24–25.
6. Cecil Hepworth, *Came the Dawn: Memories of a Film Pioneer* (London: Phoenix House, 1951), p. 144. Emphasis in original.

PART THREE

THE DEVELOPMENT OF SOUND CINEMA, 1926–1945

Two major social upheavals dominated the period 1930–1945: the Great Depression and World War II.

On October 29, 1929—"Black Tuesday"—a Wall Street crash signaled the beginning of the Depression in America. The slump quickly spread to other countries and lasted through most of the decade. Huge numbers of workers lost their jobs, banks failed in record numbers, farms were foreclosed, manufacturing declined, and currency plunged in value. Fierce competition on international markets shattered the cooperative spirit that had been developing among European countries during the 1920s.

These economic disturbances took place in a threatening political climate. Italy had had a fascist government since 1922. In 1933, Adolf Hitler became Chancellor of Germany, instituting the Nazi regime. The Japanese government was also moving to the right and asserted its imperialist goals by invading Manchuria in 1931. In many countries, socialist parties' resistance to the spread of fascism led to political polarization.

The United States and its western European allies tried to appease Hitler, but Germany's invasion of Poland on September 3, 1939, precipitated World War II. Until 1945, the German-Italian-Japanese Axis powers battled the United States, western European countries, and other Allies. Although it caused massive destruction in some parts of the world, the war boosted the U.S. economy, as the country recovered from the Depression partly by expanding its armaments industry.

The spread of sound in the cinema coincided with the early years of the Great Depression. Warner Bros. had successfully added music and sound effects to some of its films in 1926–1927. By 1929, sound had been adopted throughout the American studios, and theaters were quickly being converted. During that same year, early American sound films were enjoying long runs in European capitals.

Inventors in several countries had been working simultaneously on sound systems, and sound was introduced in various ways around the world. Crude sound equipment initially rendered many films static and talky. From the beginning, however, resourceful filmmakers injected visual and auditory interest into their sound pictures (Chapter 9).

During the 1930s, most of the big Hollywood companies encountered financial difficulties; some went bankrupt. Nevertheless, they continued to make hundreds of films a year and to develop new technology and genres (Chapter 10).

Sound boosted some national film industries. Britain

built up a studio system that imitated Hollywood's. Japan found its own successful variant upon the Hollywood system and managed to control its domestic market. India's small production sector grew during the 1930s by offering the population films in their own languages and exploiting the popular musical genre (Chapter 11).

The politically extreme regimes of the period, both right- and left-wing, led governments to take control of entire film industries. The Soviet Union completed its consolidation of its nationalized industry, instituting strict policies for subject matter and style. The Nazis moved more circumspectly but also gradually absorbed the German film business and installed strict censorship. The Italian government adopted a different approach, offering financial incentives to film companies and encouraging them to provide the public with light entertainment (Chapter 12).

The French cinema was still in its ongoing crisis. Its myriad of small production companies did not comprise a coherent studio system. Individual filmmakers created a lyrical style known as "Poetic Realism." During the middle of the decade, leftists made optimistic films in support of the short-lived Popular Front government. Once the war began, however, Germany quickly overran much of France, and French filmmakers who did not go into exile found themselves working under the tight control of the Nazi occupiers (Chapter 13).

The growing power of fascist regimes resulted in a move toward political documentary in western countries. At the same time, some governments sponsored factual films. In a few cases, experimental filmmakers were able to continue working independently, creating works that remained far outside the mainstream cinema (Chapter 14).

9

THE INTRODUCTION
OF SOUND

Most silent films were accompanied by live music, ranging from a piano or an organ to a full orchestra. Sound effects were roughly matched to the screen action. In addition, from the cinema's beginning, inventors attempted to join the image to mechanically reproduced sound, usually on phonograph records. These systems had little success before the mid-1920s, primarily because sound and image proved difficult to synchronize and because amplifiers and loudspeakers were inadequate for theater auditoriums.

The introduction of synchronized sound is usually dated from 1927, when Warner Bros. released the enormously successful *The Jazz Singer*. But the process of inventing and disseminating sound technology occurred at different rates in different countries and involved many competing systems and patents.

Sound had economic and technological implications, but it also affected style. Some critics and directors feared that extensive dialogue scenes in adapted plays would eliminate the flexible camera movements and editing of the silent era. (See Notes and Queries.) Most filmmakers soon realized that if sound could be used imaginatively, it offered a valuable new stylistic resource. In 1933, Alfred Hitchcock commented on the difference between musical accompaniment for silent films and musical scores in sound films: "I was greatly interested in music and films in the silent days, and I have always believed that the coming of sound opened up a great new opportunity. The accompanying music came at last entirely under the control of the people who made the picture."[1] Now sound and image could be combined in predictable ways during production.

SOUND IN THE UNITED STATES

Of the three countries that dominated the world's conversion to sound—the United States, Germany, and the USSR—the U.S. film industry was the first to move successfully into sound production. Executives had long anticipated the introduction of sound. The only question was, which system would be technically viable and profitable? Several alternatives were put on the market.

Lee DeForest first demonstrated his **Phonofilm** in 1923. This *sound-on-film* process converted sound into light waves reproduced on a photographic stripe running alongside the images on a regular 35mm film strip. This system offered synchronization advantages. If the film broke and had to be repaired, the same number of frames of image and sound would be eliminated. Since DeForest was determined to be independent, his company remained small, though the sale of Phonofilm patent rights abroad promoted the spread of sound in some countries.

During the 1910s and early 1920s, Western Electric, a subsidiary of one of the world's largest companies, American Telephone & Telegraph, was developing recording systems, amplifiers, and loudspeakers. Heavily funded researchers combined these components so that sound on phonograph records could be kept in satisfactory synchronization with the image. In 1925, Western Electric marketed its *sound-on-disc* system, but most Hollywood studios were too cautious to adopt it.

The Western Electric system was offered at a moment when the small firm of Warner Bros. was expanding. Using Wall Street financing, Warner Bros. was investing in distribution facilities and theaters, trying to become vertically integrated. It also created a radio station in Los Angeles to promote its films. The equipment came from Western Electric, which also managed to interest Sam Warner in its film recording system.

Initially the brothers Warner considered sound a substitute for live entertainment on film programs. By recording vaudeville acts and using orchestral accompaniment for features, they could save on costs in their own theaters and offer similar savings to other exhibitors. They signed major singers, comics, and other performers to exclusive contracts. Warner Bros. tested the **Vitaphone** process in a series of short films. The first public screening, on August 6, 1926, began with eight shorts, including a speech by Will Hays and an aria from *I Pagliacci* by Giovanni Martinelli. The feature, *Don Juan* (Alan Crosland), starring John Barrymore, had recorded music but no dialogue. The showing was successful, and Warners made more shorts and features with music.

On October 6, 1927, *The Jazz Singer* (Alan Crosland) premiered. Most sequences had only orchestral accompaniment, but in four scenes the vaudeville star Al Jolson sang and even spoke briefly ("You ain't heard nothin' yet"). The film's phenomenal success suggested that sound might provide more than a cheap way of reproducing stage acts and music. Warners made more "part-talkies," and in 1928 the first "100% all-talkie," *The Lights of New York* (Bryan Foy), became another hit.

Warner Bros. was first into the field of sound, but another firm was a close second. As Western Electric was developing its disc system, two engineers, Theodore Case and Earl Sponable, created a sound-on-film system, partly based on DeForest's. Fox Film Corporation invested in the Case-Sponable system. Like Warners, Fox was a small but expanding company which hoped that sound would give it a competitive advantage. Fox renamed the Case-Sponable system **Movietone** and demonstrated it in 1927 with short films of vaudeville acts and musical numbers. The showing was a success, but Fox soon found that most big-name theatrical talent had signed contracts with Warner Bros. Fox then concentrated on sound newsreels, including highly popular coverage of Charles Lindbergh's solo flight to Paris. Other uses for Movietone included a musical score for F. W. Murnau's 1927 feature *Sunrise* and some part-talkies in 1928.

The fourth major system was another sound-on-film technology developed by RCA (Radio Corporation of America, a subsidiary of General Electric and Westinghouse). Dubbed **Photophone**, it was demonstrated in early 1927 and for a short time promised to rival the most successful system to date, Warner's Vitaphone, in becoming the industry standard.

The five largest producing companies in Hollywood—MGM, Universal, First National, Paramount, and Producers Distributing Corporation—had proceeded cautiously in relation to sound. If firms acted individually, they might choose incompatible equipment. Since each firm's theaters had to show other companies' films, the lack of a common standard would hurt business. In February 1927 they signed the "Big Five Agreement," pledging to act together in adopting whichever sound system proved most advantageous. The two available choices were the Western Electric and the RCA systems. By 1928, Western Electric had a sound-on-film technology available, and it also offered more favorable contracts. The Big Five opted for Western Electric's system.

Because many theaters had already installed phonograph-style projectors, the Hollywood firms continued for a few years to release two different kinds of prints of most films: some with phonograph discs, some with sound-on-film (Fig. 9.1). Only Warners continued to use discs. In 1931, however, it joined the rest of the industry by switching to sound-on-film.

The rejected RCA system, Photophone, did not disappear. David Sarnoff, RCA's general manager, created a new vertically integrated motion-picture company. He bought the Film Booking Office, thus acquiring a distribution outlet and a studio, and he purchased the Keith-Albee-Orpheum circuit of vaudeville houses to provide a theater chain. In October 1928 Sarnoff formed Radio-Keith-Orpheum, known as RKO. Since Photophone was compatible with the Western Electric system, many theaters in the United States bought Photophone equipment, and the system enjoyed considerable success abroad.

Once the Hollywood studios decided what systems to adopt, they quickly began installing equipment in theaters. Independent theaters often used one of the cheaper sound systems. Smaller theaters often could not afford to buy any sound equipment at all, especially since the spread of sound coincided with the onset of the Depression. As a result, many American films were released in both sound and silent versions. Still, by about mid-1932, the conversion to sound was virtually complete in the United States.

Filmmakers and technical workers struggled to cope with the unfamiliar, often clumsy, new technology. Microphones were insensitive and hard to move; it was difficult to mix sound tracks; and scenes frequently had to be shot by multiple cameras in soundproof booths. (See Box.)

Fig. 9.1 In the early years of sound, many theaters had projectors, like this Western Electric model, that could play both sound-on-disc and sound-on-film.

EARLY SOUND TECHNOLOGY AND THE CLASSICAL STYLE

Early sound technology posed stylistic problems for the film industry. The first microphones were omnidirectional and thus picked up any noise on the set. Cameras, which whirred as they filmed, had to be placed in soundproof booths. Moreover, initially all the sounds for a single scene had to be recorded at once; there was no "mixing" of sound tracks recorded separately. If music were to be heard, the instruments had to play near the set as the scene was filmed. The microphone's placement limited the action. It was often suspended over the set on heavy rigging; a technician moved it about within a limited range, trying to point it at the actors (Fig. 9.2).

Fig. 9.3 The crew and equipment, including four camera booths, at Warner Bros.'s Vitaphone sound studio in Brooklyn, c. 1926. The man in the dark suit, second from left, has his hand on a single microphone hanging from the ceiling. The empty set for a musical short involving a piano is visible at the rear.

Fig. 9.2 In a Warner Bros. sound studio, an exterior dialogue scene for an early talkie is shot. The orchestra plays at the side, and three cameras in booths face the couple on the bench. Note the man on top of the booth, center, moving the microphone slightly to catch the pair's voices. Two additional microphones are suspended above the orchestra. Wires carry the sound from all three microphones to a sound recording booth not visible here.

Figure 9.2 shows three cameras filming a simple scene of two people on a bench. This technique, *multiple-camera shooting*, was widely adopted because each scene had to be filmed straight through in its entirety. Although it would have been technically possible to shoot all the action in a lengthy take with one camera, filmmakers were reluctant to surrender the flexibility and emphasis that the continuity editing system had given them in the silent era. In order to be able to use devices like establishing shots, cut-ins, and shot/reverse shots and still match sound and lip movement smoothly from shot to shot, directors filmed the scene from a variety of vantage points. One camera might have a normal lens and make the long shot, while another in the next booth made medium shots with a telephoto lens and a third filmed the action from a slightly different angle. At times more than three cameras were used.

Even Warner Bros.'s Vitaphone shorts, which primarily displayed classical music and vaudeville acts, used multiple cameras in order to permit shot changes (Fig. 9.3). For example, *Behind the Lines*, from the second Vitaphone program (shot August 1926), shows popular wartime entertainer Elsie Janis leading a group of soldiers in a series of songs; the seven-minute film's action was shot straight through, using two camera positions. The finished film cuts back and forth between these two positions (Figs. 9.4, 9.5). Note the stage-type backdrop in Warners' sound studio.

In feature films, multiple-camera shooting did not exactly duplicate silent-film style. The presence of the bulky booths made it difficult to get precise framings; in a conversation scene, for example, one shot might be taken at an angle to the characters, while the reverse shot is in profile (Figs. 9.6–9.8). Also, since the cameras tended to be lined up in front of the scene, portions of the space often overlapped between shots (Figs. 9.9–9.11). Incidentally, during the early years of sound, the track occupied part of the left of the rectangular frame used just for the image in the silent era. Thus many early sound films had square images (as in Fig. 9.9). The Academy of Motion Picture Arts and Sciences soon recom-

Fig. 9.4

Fig. 9.5

Figs. 9.4 and 9.5 A perfect match on action as the view shifts from one camera to a second covering the scene: a soldier climbing onto a truck bed being used as a stage.

mended putting black strips at the top and bottom of the image to re-create a rectangular frame; this "Academy ratio" (or "Academy aperture") remained standard until the advent of widescreen ratios in the 1950s.

Other aspects of early sound technology limited filmmakers' choices. The camera booths had wheels, but these usually served to move the camera between setups. Generally they

Fig. 9.6

Fig. 9.8

Fig. 9.7

Figs. 9.6–9.8 In a scene from *The Lights of New York*, made with multiple-camera shooting, one camera shows the Hawk and his two thugs, a second uses a telephoto lens to take a closer view of the thugs from an angle, and a third, also with a telephoto lens, frames Hawk in profile.

Fig. 9.9

Fig. 9.10

Fig. 9.11

Figs. 9.9–9.11 In *Hallelujah!* (1929, King Vidor), three shots show the action from similar standpoints; note how the central character is seen at one side of the frame in the second shot and then at the other side in the third.

it became increasingly possible to record more than one track of sound for a scene and to mix them into a single final track. This new technology facilitated recording the nondiegetic atmospheric music for a film after its images had been shot and edited; sound effects could be added to a scene, or prerecorded songs could be played back for singers to lip-sync

were too noisy and awkward for tracking shots. Instead, camera operators could make short panning movements through the booth windows to keep the action centered. As a result, short reframing pans became a more common stylistic feature than they had been in the silent era. The microphones initially were insensitive, and hence studios often insisted that actors take diction lessons and speak slowly and distinctly. Many early talkies move at a slow pace, and the performances seem stilted to modern ears.

Technicians worked quickly to solve such problems. Studios soon built padded metal "blimps" that silenced the camera but were far less awkward to use than booths. Microphone booms came into use: poles that moved the microphone overhead to follow moving sources or swing from actor to actor (Fig. 9.12). Perhaps most important, by 1931

Fig. 9.12 William Wellman directing *The Star Witness* (1931); the camera is muffled in a studio-built blimp, and the microphone hangs on a boom above the actors.

during the shooting. Combining and recombining sounds became as easy as selecting and arranging shots, and multiple-camera shooting ceased. As we shall see in the next chapter, during the 1930s Hollywood moved further toward overcoming the stylistic limitations that sound had created.

Significantly, some filmmakers, primarily those working in other countries, avoided the constrictive multiple-camera system or employed it sparingly. Sacrificing the polished lip synchronization and matches on action that the Hollywood technology provided, these filmmakers shot much of their footage silent and dubbed in sound later, however loosely it fit the images. This allowed the use of a moving camera, fast cutting from a wide range of angles, and other techniques seldom used in early Hollywood sound films.

While many early sound films were static and full of dialogue, some filmmakers responded to the new technical limitations imaginatively. The musical, a genre made possible by the new invention, offered opportunities for resourceful uses of sound. Even a pedestrian backstage musical like the immensely successful *The Broadway Melody* (1929, Edmund Goulding) had clever moments. The opening, set in a block of music rehearsal rooms, creates a cacophony of different pieces being played simultaneously, as well as abrupt cuts from one sound to another as the editing moves in and out of the soundproof rooms. Another show-business musical, Rouben Mamoulian's first feature, *Applause* (1929), helped restore extensive camera movements to the sound film.

Ernst Lubitsch brought the wit of his silent films to *The Love Parade* (1929), a costume musical set in a mythical eastern European country. In a comedy of sexual role reversals, Count Albert marries Queen Louise, only to discover that he has no authority, either in his marriage or in state affairs. Although the film was shot primarily in the studio, Lubitsch avoids multiple-camera shooting in most scenes. He simply has the character complete a line a few seconds before the cut and resume speaking a few seconds into the next shot. With no dialogue carrying over the cut, sound could be more easily edited. During some of the musical numbers, where the singing continues over the cut, Lubitsch does resort to multiple cameras (Figs. 9.13, 9.14).

Yet other musical numbers avoid multiple cameras by using the suggestive "Lubitsch touch." As the Count stands in his window singing "Paris, Please Stay the Same," Lubitsch cuts to reverse shots showing attractive women watching him from other windows—presumably some of his many romantic partners. Then the scene switches to another window, where the

Fig. 9.13

Fig. 9.14

Figs. 9.13 and 9.14 In the "My Love Parade" number in *The Love Parade*, multiple-camera shooting causes an awkward cut with only a slight change of angle on the characters.

Fig. 9.15 A tracking shot through a cotton field as the family sings and carries in their crop in *Hallelujah!*.

Count's valet sings another verse, and we see reverse shots of maids watching him, with similar risqué overtones. Finally, in yet another window, the Count's dog barks a bit of the same tune, with female dogs emerging from nearby bushes to listen.

Hallelujah! (1929, King Vidor) circumvents stylistic obstacles in other ways. Vidor persuaded MGM to make a musical featuring only African-Americans. No portable sound equipment was available, yet roughly half the footage was filmed silent on location. Unhampered by booths, Vidor could move the camera freely outdoors (Fig. 9.15). *Hallelujah!* did employ multiple-camera shooting in some scenes (Figs. 9.9–9.11). Even these studio scenes, however, have a distinctive quality, since much of the dialogue, whether postsynchronized or shot direct, was partially improvised by the actors. They often speak quickly, even interrupting each other, creating a more lively pace than that of most early talkies.

Although the studio insisted on including two Irving Berlin songs, the film's sound track emphasizes African-American folk music and spirituals. The performers play authentic banjos, kazoos, and a church harmonium. Despite *Hallelujah!*'s somewhat melodramatic treatment of southern black religious and sexual mores, its attempt to deal with a milieu largely neglected by Hollywood, as well as its creative use of sound, made it significant.

Germany challenges Hollywood

In 1918, three inventors came up with a German sound-on-film system, **Tri-Ergon**. During the years 1922–1926, the inventors tried to innovate the process, and the giant firm Ufa took an option on it. Probably because of Ufa's mid-1920s financial woes, however, the firm did not move into sound production.

In August 1928, various international companies pooled their sound patents, including those for Tri-Ergon, and formed the Tonbild-Syndikat ("Sound Film Syndicate"), usually referred to as Tobis. A few months later, major electronics and recording firms formed a second company, Klangfilm, to exploit another sound-on-film system. After a brief court battle, in March 1929 the two companies merged into Tobis-Klangfilm, soon to be the most powerful sound firm outside the United States. In April, spurred by news of Vitaphone's successes, Ufa signed a contract with Tobis-Klangfilm and began building sound studios.

The interests controlling Tobis-Klangfilm, which included powerful Swiss and Dutch financial groups, were determined to compete with the American firms. When Warners opened its immensely successful *The Singing Fool* (1928, Lloyd Bacon) in Berlin in the following year, Tobis-Klangfilm obtained a court injunction to stop the film's run. The firm claimed that the Vitaphone equipment Warners had installed in the theater infringed its patents. When it became apparent that Tobis-Klangfilm's officials were bent on keeping American sound systems out of Germany, the Motion Picture Producers and Distributors Association (MPPDA) declared that all American firms would stop sending films to German theaters and stop importing German films to the United States.

This period of uncertainty slowed the German transition to sound. Producers were reluctant to make sound films, for lack of wired theaters and for fear of being unable to export to the United States. Reciprocally, exhibitors hesitated to buy expensive projection systems when there were few sound films available. The first German talkie, *The Land without Women* (Carmine Gallone) was finished in 1928, but it was not until early 1930 that sound production and exhibition accelerated. By 1935 virtually all of Germany's theaters were wired.

In the meantime, the American firms discovered that their boycotts were not working. Both Warner Bros. and RKO started paying licensing fees to Tobis-Klangfilm in order to bring their films and equipment into Germany. Tobis-Klangfilm also set up foreign subsidiaries and made patent-sharing agreements with sound firms in several countries. By obtaining further court orders to block American equipment shipped from Switzerland, Czechoslovakia, and elsewhere, Tobis-Klangfilm threatened to gain control over large portions of the world market.

Soon the MPPDA and firms linked to the Western Electric system reached a settlement with Tobis-Klangfilm. On July 22, 1930, all parties agreed to an international cartel that would divide up the world market. Tobis-Klangfilm received exclusive rights to sell sound equipment in Germany, Scandinavia, most of eastern and central Europe, and a few other countries. American manufacturers gained control of Canada, Australia, India, the USSR, and other regions. Some countries, such as France, remained open to free competition. Anyone distributing sound films in any territory had to pay a fee to the appropriate member of the cartel. Although there were countless patent cases and battles over high licensing fees internationally, the global sound-film cartel operated until 1939, when World War II put an end to it.

In the meantime, several musical films made in Germany competed successfully on the international market. Erik Charell's *The Congress Dances* (1931) combined lavish historical costumes and sets with lengthy and elaborate camera movements. Less elaborate, but no less infectiously cheerful, is *Three from the Filling Station* (1930, Wilhelm Thiele). Early on, three friends return home to discover bailiffs repossessing all their furniture. The three dance about, singing a nonsense song, "Cuckoo," and smilingly bidding farewell to each item as it is carried out; the scene is shot from a variety of vantage points. Finally the trio decide to move to the country, and they jump out the window into their car.

Like many important early sound films, *Three from the Filling Station* avoids multiple-camera shooting and moves the action out of the studio whenever possible. The filmmakers even built the set of the Kuckuck ("cuckoo") gas station twice (Figs. 9.16, 9.17). Scenes that could be postsynchronized or that use only music were shot in the outdoor set, while those that needed synchronized sound were shot in the studio.

A very different sort of musical became one of the most widely seen of German sound films. Hollywood director Josef von Sternberg directed Emil Jannings (who had worked with Sternberg in Hollywood before the arrival of talkies forced him to return to Germany) in *The Blue Angel* (1930). The film also brought world fame to Marlene Dietrich, until then a minor actress.

Fig. 9.16

Fig. 9.17

Figs. 9.16 and 9.17 In Figure 9.16, the three heroes dance about to a prerecorded song in the outdoor gas-station set in *Three from the Filling Station*. Figure 9.17 shows a second set for the station, built in the studio and used for recording direct sound.

Fig. 9.18

Fig. 9.19

Figs. 9.18 and 9.19 A cut-in in *The Blue Angel* maintains lip synchronization, though the scene was shot with one camera. Note that Lola's head is in a slightly different position after the cut, and Rath is holding her powder case higher. Their poses would have remained identical across the cut with multiple-camera shooting.

Jannings plays Professor Rath, a repressed, unpopular high-school teacher. In the first scene, street sounds establish Rath's dreary neighborhood and his morning routine. The first break in his routine is in fact a moment of silence, when he whistles to his beloved canary and receives no response. The bird has died. Rath is plunged into a completely different world when he tries to catch some of his students at the Blue Angel, a sordid bar where they have gone to hear the sexy singer, Lola-Lola. He falls in love with Lola himself, gives up his job to marry her, and becomes a clown in order to help earn money. Eventually he dies in despair after Lola is unfaithful to him.

Sternberg avoided multiple-camera shooting almost entirely, yet he still managed to create dialogue scenes with excellent lip synchronization (Figs. 9.18, 9.19). *The Blue Angel* is also famous for its realistically motivated offscreen sound. An offscreen bell becomes a motif associated with Rath's routinized life. When he assigns his students a punitive essay, there is silence as they write; he opens a window, and we hear a boys' choir singing nearby. Aside from its ingenious use of sound, *The Blue Angel*'s international success was based in part on Dietrich's sultry performance as Lola. It led her to a Hollywood career, and there she made several more important films with Josef von Sternberg in the 1930s.

THE USSR PURSUES ITS OWN PATH TO SOUND

While western countries struggled with incompatible systems and patent disputes, the Soviet filmmaking establishment remained relatively isolated. In 1926, two inventors, P. T. Tager and A. Shorin, independently began working on sound-on-film systems. In the same year, a demonstration of the German Tri-Ergon equipment was given in Moscow, but it did not lead to links with Soviet companies. In 1929, just as the Soviet industry was arranging to obtain sound equipment from western companies, Tager and Shorin declared their systems ready. Vsevolod Pudovkin tried to use **Tagefon** for *A Simple Case*, but technical problems forced him to release the film silent. Dziga Vertov managed to use **Shorinfon** on location in his documentary feature *Enthusiasm*, but there were many difficulties, and the film, begun in 1929, was not released until April 1931.

The first Soviet sound films were released in March 1930: Abram Room's *Plan for Great Works* (a compilation documentary with postdubbed sound only) and some vaudeville and musical shorts. At that point only two theaters were wired for sound. By 1931, however, enough theaters were equipped that sound films came out more frequently. Aside from *Enthusiasm* in April, the next month Yuri Raizman's silent Montage-style film *The Earth Thirsts* (originally 1930) was rereleased with a track of music, songs, and sound effects. Other silent films soon received the same treatment. More new sound films also appeared: in the fall of 1931, Grigori Kozintsev and Leonid Trauberg's *Alone* appeared, soon followed by Sergei Yutkevich's *Golden Mountains*.

The transition to sound began during the First Five-Year Plan, when the Soviet film industry was trying to expand and become self-sufficient in all areas. Moreover, the Depression hit the Soviet Union hard; prices and demand for its principal exports, grain and other raw materials, fell sharply. Consequently, as late as 1935, some theaters could show only silent versions of sound films; a few films were shot only in silent versions that year. By 1936, however, the USSR had completed the transition to sound with virtually no help from abroad.

Many western observers resisted sound film, fearing that static, dialogue-ridden scripts would ruin the artistic qualities achieved by the silent cinema. A more flexible view emerged from the famous 1928 "Statement on Sound," signed by Sergei Eisenstein, his associate Grigori Alexandrov, and V. I. Pudovkin. They warned against sound's "unimaginative use for 'dramas of high culture' and other photographed presentations of a theatrical order." Simply filming characters talking would destroy the concept of montage, which depended upon abrupt juxtapositions: *"Only the contrapuntal use* of sound vis-à-vis the visual fragment of montage will open up new possibilities for the development and perfection of montage."[2] That is, sound should not simply duplicate the image but should add to the image in some way: off-screen sound could add narrative information, incongruous sound effects or music could change the tone of a scene, nondiegetic sounds could comment ironically on the action.

The filmmakers of the Montage movement welcomed sound as a way of creating juxtapositions to affect audiences more powerfully. For example, Kozintsev and Trauberg's *Alone* had been almost completed as a silent film before they added a sound track. Rather than using simple postsynchronized dialogue and effects, they took advantage of the new technology by employing startling and contradictory sound. In one scene, the heroine makes a phone call (Figs. 9.20, 9.21). As cuts move us inside and outside the phone booth, we hear an inconsistent succession of sounds: outside, a babble of voices and typewriters clacking in a nearby office; inside, the voices continue at the same volume level, but the typewriters are not heard. After the heroine hangs up—viewed from outside the booth—there is a sudden and unmotivated silence. At no point do we hear her voice.

Pudovkin's first sound film, *Deserter* (1933), proved to be the last film of the Montage movement. It uses sound in vivid ways. In one scene the sound track is edited very rapidly. The heroine is selling a workers' news-paper on the street; during this, a cheery nondiegetic waltz alternates with diegetic women's voices. These sounds are heard in quicker succession, until only a single note of the music and a single word are heard, passing back

Fig. 9.20

Fig. 9.21

Figs. 9.20 and 9.21 A scene in *Alone* that creates "counterpoint" by using contradictory sound sources.

Fig. 9.22 Sound counterpoint in Pudovkin's *Deserter*.

and forth. Another scene uses sound ironically. At an outdoor café, a desperate man on strike tries to steal food from a rich man's table (Fig. 9.22). The shot of the rich man lasts for about half a minute with virtually no movement, yet loud, cheerful music plays. As the food arrives, the music switches to a conga rhythm for the attempted theft and the worker's expulsion. This inappropriate music creates a bitter conceptual irony comparable to Eisenstein's visual treatment of Kerensky in *October* (pp. 145–146).

Such experimentation with sound, however, ran counter to the official policy of Socialist Realism instituted in 1934, and in later years sound was put to far more straightforward uses.

THE INTERNATIONAL ADOPTION OF SOUND

Synchronized sound movies were invented in a few countries, but they soon became an international phenomenon. Three other countries produced important films in the early years. At the same time, language barriers were surmounted so that dialogue films could circulate around the world.

FRANCE

During the silent era, Léon Gaumont had persistently tried to devise a French sound system. In October 1928, Gaumont presented a program of sound shorts and a feature with postdubbed songs. Like the Warner brothers, he wanted to replace live musicians and other entertainment. The early sound market in France, however, was dominated by American and German systems. In October, Paramount wired its first-run Paris theater and showed a short film starring the French music-hall star Maurice Chevalier. Other successful screenings, such as *The Jazz Singer* in January 1929, led to a race by French producers to make sound features. Since French studios were still being wired, the earliest, largely undistinguished, films were produced in London (including the first French sound feature, *Les Trois masques*, "The Three Masks," 1929) and Berlin (e.g., *L'Amour chante*, "Singing Love," 1930).

Since France was an important market, German interests sought to capture part of the production sector. In early 1929, Tobis-Klangfilm set up a subsidiary, the Société Française des Films Sonores Tobis, in Paris. Tobis produced many major French films, including the first three sound features of René Clair, which influenced filmmakers in many countries.

Uncertainty concerning sound led to a dip in French production. By 1930, however, most of the main studio buildings were wired, using either American or German systems or one of several minor French brands. Wiring went on until 1934, since many theaters were small and independently owned.

Despite the weakness of the French film industry during this period, several filmmakers experimented with the new technique. *La Petite Lise* ("Little Lise," 1930, Jean Grémillon) tells a simple, melodramatic story of Berthier, a long-term prisoner released from a South American prison, who returns to Paris to find his fragile daughter Lise, who has secretly become a prostitute. Grémillon shot some scenes in the studio with synchronized dialogue, but he achieved variety by filming others silent, adding sound later. For example, in the opening scene at the prison in Cayenne, he cuts freely among several striking exterior compositions of officers calling the roll (Fig. 9.23). The film also makes powerful use of offscreen sound (Fig. 9.24). Much of the dreary atmosphere of Lise's hotel is conveyed by a sonic motif of trains passing.

Other scenes avoid simple synchronization of sound and image. In a transition from Lise's room to a factory where Berthier seeks work, the sound of a buzz saw in the factory begins before the cut to the new location, creating an early example of a *sound bridge* (a technique whereby the sound of one scene bleeds over the transition to the scene that precedes or follows it). Later in the film, sound creates a flashback. As Berthier contemplates confessing to the killing, there is a cut from him to the prison in Cayenne and then back to him. Only then, as we see his thoughtful face again, do we hear his memory: the warden's telling him he is to be freed, a line spoken in the film's first scene.

René Clair became the most widely known of early French sound directors, as *Sous les toits de Paris* (*Under the Roofs of Paris,* 1930), *Le Million* (1930), and *À nous, la liberté!* ("For Us, Liberty," 1931) found an international audience. His imaginative use of camera movements, stretches of silence, and sonic puns helped quiet the fears of critics who believed that sound would result in static dialogue pictures. We shall see his influence cropping up in far-flung national cinemas, from Hollywood to China.

À nous, la liberté! involves two escapees from prison. Emile becomes a rich but miserable gramophone manufacturer, while Louis remains a happy, Chaplinesque hobo. The opening uses several lengthy tracking shots to show the prisoners working on an assembly line making toy horses (Fig. 9.25). These shots establish camera movements and industrial tedium as important motifs. Later, the workers in Emile's factory are shown in similar shots of boring assembly lines (Fig. 9.26).

Although *À nous, la liberté!* uses dialogue, it also employs music extensively—something many filmmakers favored in the early sound period. Clair also liked to surprise his audience by using the "wrong" sound for an object. In one scene, Louis lounges in a field overlooking the factory. We hear music and singing—the sounds of nature itself, which Louis "conducts." A close

Fig. 9.23 In *La Petite Lise*, distant framings eliminate the problem of lip synchronization; voices could be postdubbed in an exterior scene shot silent.

Fig. 9.24 Berthier's intense longing to return to Lise is conveyed simply in a lengthy shot of him staring at her picture, accompanied by the offscreen sounds of other prisoners.

Fig. 9.25

Fig. 9.26

Figs. 9.25 and 9.26 René Clair uses tracking shots to compare work in a prison and in a factory in *À nous, la liberté!*

Fig. 9.27 In *À nous, la liberté!* a "singing" flower's shape recalls the horns of the gramophones manufactured in Emile's factory.

shot of a flower trembling in the wind is accompanied by a soprano voice so that it seems to be singing (Fig. 9.27).

Ironically, Clair's success led him to leave France and work in England and the United States from 1934 to 1946. Grémillon and other early sound directors like Jean Renoir, however, participated in the creation of important French trends during the 1930s.

GREAT BRITAIN

In the mid-1920s, British film theaters began imitating American practice by adding vaudeville acts and prologues to their programs. The 1928 premiere of Vitaphone shorts aroused some interest, but there was no rush to convert to sound. Even *The Jazz Singer,* in September, failed to create a stir. Jolson's next film, *The Singing Fool,* however, opened to enormous acclaim in early 1929, and the push to wire theaters and studios began.

Western Electric's and RCA's systems were the principal ones on the market. Under the terms of the 1930 Paris agreement, 25 percent of the British market was reserved for Tobis-Klangfilm equipment, while 75 percent belonged to the American firms. But Tobis encountered technical difficulties as a result of having allied itself with the small British Phototone, and it could not exploit its share of the market. Several British companies offered cheaper sound outfits, but these provided poor reproduction. British Thomson-Houston (a subsidiary of General Electric) introduced reliable equipment in 1930, but it ran third behind the two American firms in the number of theaters wired. By 1933, all but the smallest British cinemas could reproduce sound.

The production companies, the weakest segment of the industry, had more trouble coping with the expense of converting to sound. The flow of investments into the British film industry after the 1927 Quota Act had slowed. By 1929, most of the new "quota" companies were in trouble, and their problems were compounded by the fact that their recent silent films were of little value in the big first-run cinemas. The main exception to this pattern was British International Pictures (BIP), which had been founded in 1927 by John Maxwell. Maxwell quickly wired his Elstree studio facility with RCA equipment. Rather than aiming for the largely closed American market, as other companies did, he concentrated on Europe and the British Commonwealth countries. His first production, Alfred Hitchcock's first talkie, *Blackmail,* was a big hit in 1929. BIP went on to make inexpensive sound films aimed at the British market, and the company remained profitable.

Blackmail was one of the most imaginative early sound films. Refusing to surrender the camera movement and rapid editing of the silent era, Hitchcock avoided multiple-camera shooting, finding a variety of other ways to work sound into his scenes. The opening sequence is a fast-cut episode in which the heroine's policeman boyfriend helps apprehend a criminal; the many shots of the police van speeding through the streets and the criminal trying to trick his pursuers were all shot silent, with only music added. Later, in the jail, the camera tracks forward behind the two police officers in another scene shot silent and postdubbed (Fig. 9.28).

Fig. 9.28 By filming the policemen from the back in this tracking shot in *Blackmail,* Hitchcock could add their dialogue to silent footage without having to synchronize the sound with their lip movements.

as well as occasional open-air shows in bullrings and similar venues; even for these casual screenings, portable sound equipment was brought in.

Interestingly, silent screenings lingered on longer in some middle-size markets with small production sectors. In 1937, about 800 of Belgium's nearly 1000 theaters had been equipped for sound. Only 100 were still considered real possibilities for wiring. Belgium managed to produce a small number of sound films, six in 1937. In Portugal, 185 of the country's 210 theaters were wired; it had one sound studio, and made four features and about a hundred shorts in the first nine months of 1937. Brazil had 1246 theaters, 1084 of which had sound capability; in 1937 it produced four sound features.

Ultimately many of those theaters which had not bought sound systems by the mid-1930s went out of business. They had survived primarily by showing old silent films or silent versions of sound films, but these became increasingly hard to get. By the mid-1930s sound had come to dominate international exhibition, as well as production in those countries that could afford it.

CROSSING THE LANGUAGE BARRIER

Sound filming created a problem for all producing countries: the language barrier threatened to limit export possibilities. Silent films could be translated through the simple substitution of intertitles, but talkies were another matter.

The earliest screenings of sound films explored several solutions to the problem. Sometimes films were shown abroad with no translation at all. Since sound was still a novelty, this occasionally worked, as when the German version of *The Blue Angel* went over well in Paris. During the early sound era Hollywood made several big "revue" musicals, such as *King of Jazz* (1929), that consisted of strings of musical numbers that could be enjoyed without a knowledge of English.

Because the mixing of sound was impossible in the early years, dubbing a new sound track in a foreign language was clumsy and expensive. It involved, for example, rerecording all the music at the same time that the dialogue was put in, making lip synchronization difficult. Some dubbed films were successful in 1929, but others failed because the voices matched badly with the lip movements. Firms also added subtitles to some films, but these were often rejected as distracting. Other solutions, like eliminating the dialogue and substituting intertitles or even editing in narrators explaining the action in a different language, proved wholly unacceptable.

By 1929, many producers decided that the only way to preserve foreign markets was to reshoot additional versions of each film, with the actors speaking different languages in each. Advertised as the world's first "multilingual" film, the British production *Atlantic* was released in German and English (1929, E. A. Dupont). Similarly, the first German talkie, *Das Land ohne Frauen,* also appeared in an English version, *The Land without Women.* In 1929 MGM set up an elaborate program of multilingual production, importing actors and directors to make French, German, and Spanish versions of its pictures. Paramount attempted to economize by producing its multilinguals in France, purchasing its Joinville studio, near Paris, in 1929. The

Joinville facilities were equipped like a big Hollywood studio, and there Paramount turned out dozens of films in as many as fourteen languages. Germany's Tobis-Klangfilm also made many multilinguals.

The assumption was that multilinguals would be relatively cheap to make, since the same scripts, sets, and lighting plans could be used. As one version was finished, a new group would move in and begin shooting the same film again. The cast and crew were usually changed for each version, though in some cases directors and stars who could speak two or more languages would work on more than one version. In some cases stars might even learn their lines phonetically, as when Laurel and Hardy were called upon to make Spanish versions of their films.

After about two years, it became apparent that multilinguals would not solve the language problem. The market for each version was too small to warrant the additional expense, and audiences did not welcome minor actors in roles made famous by stars like Gary Cooper or Norma Shearer.

By 1931, the technique of mixing separate sound tracks had been refined. The original music and sound effects could be combined with new voices, and methods of synchronizing voice and lip movements had improved. Moreover, subtitles were accepted more widely. By 1932, dubbing and subtitles enabled talkies to cross the language barrier, and they have remained in use ever since.

Still, the introduction of sound boosted film production in several countries, since audiences wanted to hear native performers speaking their own languages. France, for example, gained a bigger share of its own exhibition market than it had enjoyed during the 1920s. Many small countries in eastern Europe and Latin America began producing more films. Most spectacularly, Indian production, which had been very limited in the silent era, developed during the 1930s into one of the world's major studio systems. We shall examine some of these results of the coming of sound in Chapter 11.

◆ NOTES AND QUERIES

FILMMAKERS ON THE COMING OF SOUND

During 1928–1933, sound seemed to many filmmakers both promising and threatening. Most realized that it offered new aesthetic possibilities, but many feared that static versions of plays might dominate production. Some directors offered views of how sound could be used creatively.

Predictably, the Soviet Montage filmmakers, who had written extensively on film theory in the silent era, discussed sound. *The Film Factory: Russian and Soviet Cinema in Documents 1896–1939*, ed. Richard Taylor and Ian Christie (Cambridge, Mass.: Harvard University Press, 1988), contains essays by several filmmakers, including Vsevolod Pudovkin ("On the Principle of Sound in Film," pp. 264–267), Esfir Shub ("The Advent of Sound in Cinema," p. 271), and Dziga Vertov ("Speech to the First All-Union Conference on Sound Cinema," pp. 301–305).

Writings on sound by several major French filmmakers of the 1920s and 1930s, such as Jacques Feyder (pp. 38–39), René Clair (pp. 39–40), Abel Gance (pp. 41–42), and Marcel Pagnol (pp. 55–57) are available in English in Richard Abel's *French Film Theory and Criticism 1907–1939: A History/Anthology*, vol. 2 (Princeton, N.J.: Princeton University Press, 1988). The most successful and influential of French directors in the early sound era, Clair blended his writings from the period with commentary added years later, reflecting on his own initial reactions to sound; see his *Cinema Yesterday and Today,* ed. R. C. Dale and trans. Stanley Appelbaum (New York: Dover, 1972), pp. 126–158.

Hollywood directors wrote relatively little on the subject, but two significant articles appear in Richard Koszarski, ed., *Hollywood Directors 1914–1940* (London: Oxford University Press, 1976): Edmund Goulding's "The Talkers in Close-Up" (pp. 206–213) and Frank Borzage's "Directing a Talking Picture" (pp. 235–237). Writing from a very different perspective, Carl Dreyer offered thoughts on how filmmakers could adapt plays as sound films and still avoid static dialogue scenes in his "The Real Talking Film," in Donald Skoller, ed., *Dreyer in Double Reflection* (New York: Dutton, 1973), pp. 51–56.

SOUND AND THE REVISION OF FILM HISTORY

The topic of the introduction of sound provides examples of how historians can overturn widely accepted accounts by discovering new data or devising new arguments to account for existing evidence.

For instance, one historical puzzle was how a small firm like Warner Bros., whose financial records show heavy losses in the mid-1920s, managed to innovate sound and grow quickly into a major company. In 1939, Lewis Jacobs suggested that Vitaphone was "a desperate effort to ward off bankruptcy." [See his *The Rise of the American Film* (rep., New York: Teachers College Press, 1968), p. 297.] Other historians repeated and embroidered this account; in *The Movies* (New York: Bonanza Books, 1957), Richard Griffith and Arthur Mayer even attributed Sam Warner's 1927 death to the strain of the "grim race with time" to save his debt-ridden company (pp. 240–241). In the mid-1970s, however, economic historian Douglas Gomery argued that Warners' debts were a sign of the firm's healthy expansion and that the introduction of sound was far from a frantic bid to avoid ruin. [Gomery's numerous articles on this topic include "The Coming of Sound: Technological Change in the American Film Industry," in Tino Balio, ed., *The American Film Industry,* 2nd ed. (Madison: University of Wisconsin Press, 1985), pp. 229–251.]

The widespread resistance to the coming of sound on the part of filmmakers and critics has led some historians to treat its introduction as a major break in the cinema's stylistic history. By this account, early talkies virtually eliminated editing and camera movement. In the 1950s, however, André

Bazin took a novel approach by asking "if the technical revolution created by the sound track was in any sense an aesthetic revolution" ["The Evolution of the Language of Cinema," in Hugh Gray, ed. and trans., *What Is Cinema?* (Berkeley: University of California Press, 1967), p. 23]. More recently, David Bordwell, Janet Staiger, and Kristin Thompson offer evidence to support Bazin's view, showing that many stylistic traits of the classical Hollywood cinema changed surprisingly little with the introduction of sound. [See their *The Classical Hollywood Cinema: Film Style and Mode of Production to 1960* (New York: Columbia University Press, 1985).]

◆ REFERENCES

1. Stephen Watts, "Alfred Hitchcock on Music in Films," *Cinema Quarterly* **2**, 2 (Winter 1933–1934): 81.
2. Sergei Eisenstein, Vsevolod Pudovkin, and Grigori Alexandrov, "Statement on Sound," in Richard Taylor and Ian Christie, eds., *The Film Factory: Russian and Soviet Cinema in Documents 1896–1939* (Cambridge, Mass.: Harvard University Press, 1988), p. 234.

10

THE HOLLYWOOD STUDIO SYSTEM, 1930–1945

Between 1930 and 1945, the United States suffered a severe Depression and then an equally spectacular recovery during World War II. In 1932, as the Depression was entering its depths, unemployment reached 23.6 percent. In 1933, nearly 14 million people were out of work. The dollar's buying power was high—admission at some local movie theaters might be only a dime—but most people had little to spend on anything but necessities.

The stock market hit its lowest level in mid-1932, just before the presidential election, and Franklin Roosevelt swept to the first of four victories by blaming the disaster on Herbert Hoover. Roosevelt's administration moved to bolster the economy. The National Recovery Administration, established in 1933, cast a lenient eye on big-business practices such as trusts and oligopolies, while also displaying a new tolerance of labor unions. Both policies had a major impact on Hollywood. The government also fostered economic growth by spending on roads, buildings, the arts, and other areas under the Works Progress Administration (established in 1935). The WPA put 8.5 million people back to work, thus building up buying power and aiding industries to recuperate.

Recovery was uneven, and a recession in 1937–1938, though not as severe as the original crisis, caused similar problems. By 1938, however, increased government intervention was pulling the country out of the Depression. The outbreak of war in parts of Europe accelerated that process. Although the United States remained neutral until the Japanese attack on Pearl

Harbor on December 7, 1941, armaments companies were allowed to sell abroad from November 1939. America declared itself "the arsenal of democracy," selling arms to its allies around the world and then building up its own combat capability. This increased manufacturing gradually absorbed the available labor force. Although there were still 3 million unemployed when the United States entered the war in 1941, by late in the war some jobs were unfilled.

The war expanded the American economy. Between 1940 and 1944, for example, the output of manufactured goods quadrupled. Fully 40 percent of the nation's gross national product supported the war effort, but the newly employed workers at home (including many who had previously been housewives or servants) gained purchasing power and a higher standard of living. Despite shortages of some products, most American industries increased their sales, often by 50 percent or more. The film industry shared in this wartime boom, as attendance rose dramatically.

THE NEW STRUCTURE OF THE FILM INDUSTRY

During the silent era the Hollywood film industry had developed into an oligopoly in which a small number of companies cooperated to close the market to competition. While the structure of this oligopoly remained relatively stable into the 1930s, the coming of sound and the onset of the Depression caused some changes.

Only one large new company was formed as a result of the coming of sound: RKO (short for Radio-Keith-Orpheum), created to exploit RCA's sound system, Phonofilm. Fox's successful innovation of sound-on-film led it to expand considerably during the late 1920s, but the beginning of the Depression forced Fox to cut back on its investments. Most notably, it sold its newly acquired controlling interest in First National to Warner Bros. Thus Warners, which had been a small company, grew into one of the largest firms of the 1930s.

By 1930, the Hollywood oligopoly had settled into a structure that would change little for nearly twenty years. Eight large companies dominated the industry. First were the "Majors," also called the Big Five. In order of size, they were Paramount (formerly Famous Players–Lasky), Loew's (generally known by the name of its production subsidiary, MGM), Fox (which became 20th Century-Fox in 1935), Warner Bros., and RKO. To be a Major, a company had to be vertically integrated, owning a theater chain and having an international distribution operation. Smaller companies with few or no theaters formed the "Minors," or Little Three: Universal, Columbia, and United Artists. There were also several independent firms. Some of these made expensive, or "A," pictures comparable to those of the Majors (for example, Samuel Goldwyn and David O. Selznick). Those firms (such as Republic and Monogram) making only cheaper, or "B," pictures were collectively known as "Poverty Row." We shall survey each of the Majors and Minors briefly and then look at the phenomenon of independent production.

Paramount.   Paramount began as a distribution firm and expanded by buying up large numbers of theaters (pp. 69–70 and 157–158). This strategy succeeded in the 1920s, but once the Depression hit, the company earned far less money and owed sizable amounts on the mortgages of its theaters. As a result, Paramount declared bankruptcy in 1933 and underwent court-ordered reorganization until 1935. During that time it produced films but did not make money. In 1936, Paramount theater executive Barney Balaban became president of the entire company and made it profitable again (so successfully that he retained his post until 1964).

In the early 1930s Paramount was known partly for its "European"-style productions. Josef von Sternberg made his exotic Marlene Dietrich films there, Ernst Lubitsch continued to add a sophisticated touch with his comedies, and French import Maurice Chevalier was one of the major stars. The studio also depended heavily on radio and vaudeville comedians. The Marx Brothers made their earliest, most bizarre films there (most notably *Duck Soup,* directed by Leo McCarey in 1933), and Mae West's suggestive dialogue attracted both audiences and controversy.

In the second half of the decade, Balaban turned Paramount in a more thoroughly American direction. Bob Hope and Bing Crosby, consistently among the top box-office attractions of the World War II period, helped sustain the studio, as did tough guy Alan Ladd and comedian Betty Hutton. One of the studio's popular wartime directors, Preston Sturges, made several satirical comedies. Throughout the 1930s and 1940s, Cecil B. De Mille continued as a mainstay of the studio he had helped start, with a series of big-budget historical films.

Loew's/MGM.   Unlike Paramount, MGM did well all the way through the 1930–1945 period. With a smaller theater chain, it had fewer debts and was the most profitable American film firm. This was partly due to the quiet guidance of Nicholas Schenck, who managed Loew's from New York. The more visible producers, such as Louis B. Mayer and Irving Thalberg, ran the West Coast studio on a policy of high-profile, big-budget films (though MGM made many ordinary and B pictures as well).

MGM's films often looked more lavish than those of other studios. Budgets for features averaged $500,000 (higher, for example, than the $400,000 Paramount and 20th Century-Fox were spending). Cedric Gibbons, head of the art department, helped create an MGM "look," with large, white, brightly lit sets. MGM boasted that it had under contract "more stars than there are in Heaven." Important directors who worked consistently for MGM included George Cukor and Vincente Minnelli.

In the early 1930s, MGM's biggest star was the unglamorous, middle-aged Marie Dressler, remembered today mainly for her Oscar-winning performance in *Min and Bill* (1930) and her sardonic role in *Dinner at Eight* (1933). Later in the decade Clark Gable, Spencer Tracy, Mickey Rooney, and Judy Garland all became major drawing cards. It is some measure of MGM's emphasis on quality that Rooney, who was acting in A musicals like Busby Berkeley's *Strike Up the Band* (1940), could simultaneously be delegated to the relatively low-budget, but popular, "Andy Hardy" series. Greta

Garbo was more a prestige star than a box-office draw in the United States, but her films did well in Europe; once the war broke out and European markets were closed to American films, MGM let her go. During the war, major new stars emerged for the studio, including Greer Garson, Gene Kelly, and Katharine Hepburn—the latter teaming up with Spencer Tracy.

20th Century-Fox.   Partly as a result of its expansion after the innovation of sound, Fox entered the Depression in the worst shape of any of the Majors. The company remained in trouble until 1933, when Sidney Kent, former head of distribution for Paramount, took over and helped turn the firm around. One crucial step was a merger with a smaller company, Twentieth Century, in 1935. This deal brought in Darryl F. Zanuck as head of the West Coast studio, which he ran with an iron hand.

20th Century-Fox had relatively few long-term stars. Folk humorist Will Rogers was immensely popular up to his death in 1935, while skating star Sonja Henie and singer Alice Faye both gained fame for a few years. But the studio's biggest draw was child star Shirley Temple, who topped national box-office polls from 1935 to 1938. Her popularity waned as she grew up, and 20th Century-Fox's biggest wartime profits came instead from Betty Grable musicals. (A photograph of Grable in a bathing suit was supposedly the favorite pin-up among the troops.) Major directors who worked steadily at Fox during this period included Henry King, Allan Dwan, and John Ford.

Warner Bros.   Like Fox, Warner Bros. had been borrowing and expanding just before the Depression began. It coped with its debts not by declaring bankruptcy but by selling off some holdings and cutting costs. Harry Warner ran the company from New York, insisting on making modest but predictable profits on a relatively large number of low-budget projects.

The effects on the films were apparent. Although in total assets Warners was as big as MGM, its sets were much smaller, and its stable of popular actors—James Cagney, Bette Davis, Humphrey Bogart, Errol Flynn, and others—worked in more films. Plots were recycled frequently (the screen-writing department came to be known as the "echo chamber"), and the studio concentrated on creating popular genres and then mining them: the Busby Berkeley musical, the gangster film, the problem film based on current head-lines, the "bio-pic." Once the war began, Warners launched a series of successful combat films. The fact that many Warners films of the era have become classics attests to the ability of the studio's filmmakers to succeed with limited resources.

RKO.   This was the shortest-lived of any of the Majors. In 1928, the Radio Corporation of America (RCA) could not convince any studio to adopt its sound system, so it went into the movie-making business itself (p. 215). Yet RKO always lagged behind the other Majors. By 1933 it was in bankruptcy, and the firm was not reorganized until 1940. At that point, the general wartime prosperity helped RKO achieve profitability—though its problems would return shortly after the war's end.

RKO had no stable policy during this period, and it lacked big stars. Katharine Hepburn, for example, was popular during the early 1930s, but a series of indifferent or eccentric films labeled her "box-office poison." There were isolated hits, such as the 1933 fantasy *King Kong,* but the studio's only consistent money-makers during the 1930s were Fred Astaire and Ginger Rogers, whose series of musicals ran from 1934 to 1938. To a considerable extent, RKO's slim profits depended on its distribution of animated films made by an independent firm, Walt Disney.

During the early 1940s RKO turned to producing prestigious Broadway plays, including *Abe Lincoln in Illinois* (1940). One controversial young theatrical producer hired at this time was Orson Welles. His *Citizen Kane* (1941) would later be remembered as the single most important RKO film, though it was considered financially disappointing at the time. During these years RKO's B unit, supervised by Val Lewton, produced some of the most creative low-budget films of Hollywood's studio era.

Universal. Although it had an extensive distribution system and was the largest of the Little Three, Universal had constant money problems during the era 1930–1945 (and beyond). It held few major stars, and its successful filmmakers tended to move to bigger studios. Universal's early strategy was to promote new stars in visually striking horror films. The firm made stars of Bela Lugosi (*Dracula,* 1931), Boris Karloff (*Frankenstein,* 1931), and Claude Rains (*The Invisible Man,* 1933). After 1935, Universal increasingly targeted small-town audiences, building up another new star, the cheerful teenage singer Deanna Durbin. B series were important to the studio, as with the Sherlock Holmes films of the 1940s, starring Basil Rathbone, and the slapstick Abbott and Costello series.

Columbia. Under the consistent leadership of studio head Harry Cohn, Columbia weathered the Depression and remained profitable. Despite low budgets, it turned out popular films, often by borrowing stars or directors from bigger studios (thus avoiding the costs of keeping stars under contract). The studio's most important director, Frank Capra, remained there throughout the 1930s. His 1934 film *It Happened One Night* starred Claudette Colbert (loaned out from Paramount) and Clark Gable (from MGM); film, director, and stars all won Oscars, and the picture was one of Columbia's biggest hits.

Although several major directors worked briefly at Columbia—most notably, John Ford for *The Whole Town's Talking* (1935), George Cukor for *Holiday* (1938), and Howard Hawks for *Only Angels Have Wings* (1939) and *His Girl Friday* (1940)–they did not stay. The studio was largely dependent on its B Westerns and other cheaper fare (including 3 Stooges films) during this era.

United Artists. The sound era saw the beginning of a slow decline for UA. D. W. Griffith, Mary Pickford, and Douglas Fairbanks all retired in the early to mid-1930s, and Charles Chaplin released a feature only about once every five years. UA distributed films for other prominent independent producers, such as Alexander Korda, David O. Selznick, Walter Wanger, and Samuel Goldwyn, but all moved to other firms by the end of World War II. As a result, UA was the only company whose profits fell during most of the wartime boom years.

UA's releases during this period reflect their diverse origins in a batch of independent producers. Prestigious British imports like *The Private Life of Henry VIII*, slapstick musicals with popular Broadway star Eddie Cantor, a few of Alfred Hitchcock's American films (including *Rebecca* and *Spellbound*), and some of William Wyler's finest works (*Dodsworth, Wuthering Heights*) helped provide a varied output. Unlike in the silent period, however, UA now had to fill out its feature schedule with low-budget, even B, pictures.

The Independents.   There was little real competition among the Majors, the Minors, and the independents. Each group had a different function within the industry. The Majors provided the bulk of the A pictures for big theaters. The Minors supplied the extra films needed and catered to smaller theaters that did not belong to the Majors. A few independent firms made prestige films, while others, like Monogram and Republic, filled in the second halves of double features with B pictures, most of them falling into the action genres, like Westerns, crime thrillers, and serials.

Some small independent producers were even further removed from the Hollywood mainstream, producing low-budget films for specific ethnic groups. Oscar Micheaux (p. 181) continued making films with black casts. The introduction of sound led to production in a variety of languages. In cities where there were large enclaves of Jewish immigrants, for example, there was a demand for films in Yiddish. While there had been silent films distributed with Yiddish intertitles, the talkies fostered a brief flowering of Jewish-oriented production in the 1930s. Films such as *Uncle Moses* (produced by Yiddish Talking Pictures in 1932) were shown in theaters which also exhibited movies imported from the two other centers of Yiddish filmmaking, the USSR and Poland. Edgar G. Ulmer, who had worked briefly in Hollywood, made one of the most internationally successful Yiddish films, *Green Fields* (1937). Other directors adapted works from the popular theater. Many Yiddish films centered on family crises and the clash between traditional values and modern urban life. The films featured frequent musical interludes. The outbreak of World War II crushed Yiddish filmmaking in Poland in 1939, and by 1942, Yiddish-language production had ceased in the United States as well.

Despite the limited successes of various types of independent production, it would have been virtually impossible for a new company—large or small—to gain a significant share of the film market. The existing Hollywood firms had created a secure, stable situation in which they loaned each other stars, played each other's films in their theaters, and cooperated in other ways. In one of their most prominent joint actions, they worked to fight outside pressure for censorship of movies through the Motion Picture Producers and Distributors Association. (See Box.)

EXHIBITION PRACTICE IN THE 1930s

Sound and the Depression significantly changed the way theaters presented movies. Warner Bros. initially viewed sound as a way of eliminating live orchestral accompaniment of features and stage acts in the theater. Its effort

"THE HAYS CODE": SELF-CENSORSHIP IN HOLLYWOOD

The popular image of Will Hays and other officials of the Motion Picture Producers and Distributors Association (MPPDA) casts them as sour puritans imposing censorship on the film industry. The reality is more complex. The MPPDA was a corporation owned jointly by the film companies themselves. One of the MPPDA's tasks was to help *avoid* censorship from the outside.

The MPPDA was formed in 1922 to improve public relations after a series of Hollywood scandals, to provide a lobbying link to the era's sympathetic Republican administrations, and to handle foreign problems like quotas. Similar functions continued into the 1930s, but the MPPDA became more famous for its policy of industry self-censorship: the Production Code (often called the Hays Code).

The early 1930s were an age of conservatism. Many believed that lax morality during the 1920s "jazz age" had been one cause of the Depression. State and municipal film censorship boards, formed in the silent era, tightened standards. Pressure groups promoting religious beliefs, children's welfare, and the like protested against sex, violence, and other types of subject matter. In 1932–1933, a series of studies by the Payne Fund investigated the effects of filmgoing on audiences—particularly children. More voices demanded regulation of filmmaking.

By early 1930, outside pressure for censorship forced the MPPDA to adopt the Production Code as industry policy. The Code was an outline of moral standards governing the depiction of crime, sex, violence, and other controversial subjects. Provisions of the Code demanded, for example, that "methods of crime should not be explicitly presented" and that "sexual perversion or any inference to it is forbidden." (In this period, "sexual perversion" referred primarily to homosexuality.) All Hollywood films were expected to obey the Code or risk local censorship. In enforcing the Code, MPPDA censors often went to absurd lengths. Even respectably married couples had to be shown sleeping in twin beds (to suit British censors), and the mildest profanity was forbidden. When *Gone With the Wind* was filmed in 1939, there was lengthy controversy before the MPPDA finally permitted Clark Gable to speak the famous line "Frankly, my dear, I don't give a damn."

The MPPDA's efforts were initially resisted by the film companies. Most of the firms were in financial trouble, some moving into or near bankruptcy as theater attendance fell. Sex and violence could boost theater patronage. Gangster films and sex pictures, however, drew the wrath of censors and pressure groups. Films like *The Public Enemy* (1931), *Little Caesar* (1930), and *Scarface* (1932) were seen as glorifying criminals. Although the protagonists were killed in the end, it was feared that youngsters would copy the tough-guy images of James Cagney and Edward G. Robinson. More notoriously, several films centered on women who trade sexual favors for material gain. *Baby Face* (1933) and *Red-Headed Woman* (1932) showed women attaining elegant apartments, clothes, and cars through a series of affairs. Even *Back Street* (1932, John M. Stahl), in which the heroine lives modestly and truly loves the man who keeps her, was found offensive. According to the Code's author, the film approved "of extra-marital relationship, thereby reflecting adversely on the institution of marriage and belittling its obligations."[1]

Mae West presented a formidable challenge to the MPPDA. She was a successful Broadway performer and playwright whose fame rested on sensational plays like *Sex* (1926). Although the MPPDA fought to keep her out of films, Paramount, facing bankruptcy, hired her; for a few years she was the company's top money-maker. Her first star vehicle, *She Done Him Wrong* (1933, Lowell Sherman), took in many times its costs. A typical bit of dialogue occurs as the virtuous young hero chides the heroine, Lou, by asking her, "Haven't you ever met a man that could make you happy?" Lou replies, "Sure . . . lots of times." West's drawling delivery could make any line seem salacious.

The timing of the premiere of *She Done Him Wrong* could not have been worse. The first Payne Fund studies had just appeared. Moreover, in early 1933, the Roosevelt administration took over, severing Hays's ties to Republican officials in Washington. With growing ferment against the film industry, a national censorship law seemed to be in the offing. As a result, in March 1933, Hays pushed the film industry to enforce the Code.

Still, studios hungry for patrons tested the Code's limits. Mae West's films continued to cause problems. *Belle of the*

Fig. 10.1 The seal of approval as it appeared in the 1930s at the beginning of films passed by the MPPDA.

Nineties (1934) was recut at the insistence of the New York State Censorship Board. The negotiations concerning this film coincided with mounting pressure from religious groups, especially the Catholic Legion of Decency. (The legion had a rating system that could condemn films either for young people or for all Catholics. This stigma could cause the industry considerable lost revenues.)

The danger of increased official censorship was too great to be ignored, and in June 1934, the MPPDA established a new set of rules. Member studios releasing films without MPPDA seals of approval (Fig. 10.1) now had to pay a $25,000 fine. More importantly, a film without a seal was barred from any MPPDA member's theaters—which included most first-run houses. This rule forced most producers to comply with the Code. Of course, "objectionable" material was still used, but it became more indirect. A strategic fade-out might hint that a couple was about to make love; extreme violence could occur just offscreen; sophisticated dialogue could suggest much without violating the Code.

The MPPDA may have been repressive, but it blocked potentially more extreme national censorship. In practical terms, the Code was not a tool of the prudish minds of MPPDA officials but a summary of the types of subject matter that could get movies cut by local censors or banned for Catholic viewers. The Code saved Hollywood money by pressuring filmmakers to avoid shooting scenes that would be snipped out. The MPPDA did not seek to eliminate every risqué line or violent moment. Instead, it allowed the studios to go just far enough to titillate the public without crossing the lines defined by local censorship authorities.

was successful, and by 1930 most theaters showed only filmed entertainment. In effect, creative control of programming had at last been taken entirely out of the hands of local theater managers, who received their entire shows in the form of films.

The Depression cut short the age of the movie palace. Many theaters no longer could afford ushers to show patrons to their seats. Managers also needed to bring in extra income, and so they offered candy, popcorn, and beverages in the lobbies. Since many moviegoers had little to spend on entertainment, exhibitors resorted to playing double and even triple features, in addition to the usual short films. The second film was often a cheap B picture, but it gave the moviegoer the impression of getting twice as much. Just as importantly, the double feature had an intermission during which the spectator could buy refreshments.

Managers also lured patrons with giveaways. There might be a drawing for a door prize, or a souvenir pillow might come with every ticket. Most effective were "dish nights," when each ticket came with a piece of chinaware (purchased in bulk by the theater). Families were thus encouraged to attend weekly to collect a whole set of crockery.

As attendance expanded during World War II, some of these incentives declined. B-film production was less important, but the double feature remained, as did the concession stand. Many big movie houses deteriorated during the Depression, but they were still ready to accommodate the renewed crowds of moviegoers.

CONTINUED INNOVATION IN HOLLYWOOD

During the 1920s, the expansion of the industry had included the formation of many technical companies and studio departments. The innovation of sound, which created such an upheaval in the business, had been one result of this growth in the technological-support side of the industry. During the 1930s and 1940s, these companies and departments continued to innovate.

Through the efforts of the studios, key manufacturers, and coordinating institutions like the Academy of Motion Picture Arts and Sciences, film technology became more versatile and sophisticated.

SOUND RECORDING

Methods of sound recording improved steadily. Early microphones were omnidirectional, picking up unwanted noise from crew and equipment. Gradually unidirectional microphones, which could be aimed in the direction of the desired sound source, were developed. While early booms to hang and move the microphone above the set had been large and clumsy, lighter booms soon made recording more flexible (Fig. 10.2). Through innovations in multiple-track recording, by late 1932, music, voices, and sound effects could be registered separately and later mixed onto one track. (Musical numbers were generally recorded first, with the singers moving their lips to a playback.) Also in 1932, identical edge numbers began to be printed on both the image and sound negatives, permitting close synchronization even of short shots.

By 1932, the results of such improvements were apparent in many films. Actors no longer had to move gingerly or to enunciate their dialogue slowly, and thus the lugubrious pace of many early talkies gave way to a livelier rhythm. The new flexibility is apparent in such disparate films of 1932 as *Trouble in Paradise* (Ernst Lubitsch), *I Am a Fugitive from a Chain Gang* (Mervyn LeRoy), and *Dr. Jekyll and Mr. Hyde* (Rouben Mamoulian).

While early sound films had often avoided using much nondiegetic atmospheric music, multiple-track recording fostered the introduction of what came to be called the *symphonic score,* in which lengthy musical passages played under the action and dialogue. Several composers who were trained in the tradition of post-Romantic European classical music, including Max

Fig. 10.2 A lightweight boom aims a small microphone directly at the actors during the production of Lloyd Bacon's *San Quentin* (1937).

Steiner, Erich Wolfgang Korngold, Miklós Rózsa, David Raksin, and Bernard Herrmann, wrote scores to heighten moods of romance or suspense.

Steiner in particular helped establish the norms for studio music. His emphatic score for *King Kong* (1933) was an influential early use of the symphonic approach. Steiner also commonly quoted easily recognizable tunes to emphasize a scene's meaning, as in *Sergeant York* (1940), where "Give Me That Old Time Religion" forms a motif associated with the hero's religious faith. Like many musical techniques in the sound cinema, this quotation practice derived from live accompaniment of silent films. Composers usually claimed that they tried to make the music unobtrusive. Like continuity editing, set design, and other techniques, most music was supposed to serve the narrative without drawing attention to itself.

CAMERA MOVEMENT

Many early sound films contained camera movements, but in executing them, filmmakers often had to shoot silent and add sound later or create elaborate means to move the bulky camera booth. Moving shots tended to stand out from the rest of the film, which might well be made with multiple cameras. Such disparities were not good for continuity. Once blimps came into use, a new problem surfaced: the cameras were too heavy for traditional tripods, and they were difficult to move between shots. The solution was a camera support that was both strong and mobile, and individual cinematographers and service firms created new versions of the sorts of dollies and cranes used at the end of the silent era.

Again 1932 was a breakthrough year, with the introduction of the Bell & Howell Rotambulator. This was a 700-pound dolly that could raise the camera vertically from 18 inches to 7 feet, and the operator could pan, tilt, or track with ease. The Fearless Company's Panoram Dolly (1936) could pass through a 36-inch doorway. The spectacular tracking shots of some late 1930s and 1940s films, where the camera traverses two or more rooms, depended on such equipment.

Craning movements also became more common. Universal's *All Quiet on the Western Front* (1931) used the giant 50-foot crane that had been built in 1929 for *Broadway*. The famous movement of pulling back above a huge railway platform full of wounded Confederate soldiers in *Gone With the Wind* employed a building crane. Large cranes could also be used in the studio, usually to create spectacular shots in historical epics, musicals, or fantasies (Fig. 10.3). In MGM's 1939 musical fantasy *The Wizard of Oz*, the camera swooped over the Munchkin City and the Yellow Brick Road. Most cranes, however, were small models suitable for unobtrusive vertical and diagonal movements.

TECHNICOLOR

Undoubtedly the most striking innovation of this era was color filmmaking. We have seen how silent films employed various nonphotographic processes

Fig. 10.3 The crane Busby Berkeley used at Warner Bros. to film elaborate musical numbers, seen here between takes of *Wonder Bar* (1934).

that colored the film after it had been shot. There were also several attempts to introduce photographic color processes in the silent period. The Technicolor firm's two-strip system had been used occasionally in Hollywood films during the 1920s, and it survived into the early sound era. It was costly to use, however, and it rendered colors mainly as pinkish orange and greenish blue (Color Plate 10.1).

In the early 1930s, Technicolor introduced a new system involving a camera that used prisms to split the light coming through the lens onto three strips of black-and-white film, one each for the primary colors (Color Plates 10.2–10.12). This technique was introduced publicly in a 1932 Disney short cartoon, *Flowers and Trees*. Pioneer Pictures, a small independent production firm owned by a major stockholder in Technicolor, produced a live-action musical short, *La Cucaracha*, in 1935 (Color Plate 10.13). It demonstrated that Technicolor could render vivid colors with live actors in the studio. That same year, the feature *Becky Sharp* (Color Plate 10.12) showed that color could add to the appeal of a historical drama. Technicolor's ability to produce bright, saturated colors suggested that for some films, the extra cost (nearly 30 percent higher than that of black-and-white films) was justified. (Color Plates 11.1, 15.1, and 15.10 show other examples of three-strip Technicolor.) The Majors began using color, but the Technicolor company monopolized the process, supplying all cameras, providing supervisors for each production, and processing and printing the film.

Today we regard color as a realistic element in films, but in the 1930s and 1940s, it was often associated with fantasy and spectacle. It could be used for exotic adventures like *The Garden of Allah* (1936), swashbucklers like *The Adventures of Robin Hood* (1939), or musicals like *Meet Me in St. Louis* (1944).

Fig. 10.4 The actors in *The Woman in Red* (1935) sit in front of a back-projection screen, at the upper left, upon which an ocean background will be projected during filming.

SPECIAL EFFECTS

The term "special effects," used in connection with the 1930s, usually conjures up thoughts of films like *King Kong* and *The Wizard of Oz*. Yet, as the president of the American Society of Cinematographers pointed out in 1943, "Ninety per cent of the trick and special effects shots in Hollywood movies are made with no thought of fooling or mystifying the audience. The great majority of camera trickery is used simply because filming the same action by conventional means would be too difficult, too expensive, or too dangerous."[2] Because special effects promoted ease, efficiency, and safety, they were used frequently and had a considerable impact on films of this period.

Most trick photography in the silent era was done by the cinematographer during shooting. Multiple-camera filming and other complications associated with sound led to trick work's becoming the responsibility of specialists. Studios added special-effects departments that often invented and built equipment to meet the demands of specific scenes.

Special-effects work usually involved combining separately shot images in one of two ways: through *rear projection* (also called back projection) or *optical printing*. In rear projection, the actors perform in a studio set as an image filmed earlier is cast onto a screen behind them by a projector (Fig. 10.4). In most scenes in which characters ride in cars, for example, the vehicle is filmed in a studio while the background landscape passes on a screen (Fig. 10.5). Rear projection saved money, since actors and crew did not have to go on location. (A small crew, or "second unit," would travel to make the rear-projection shots.) For example, much of the 1938 MGM film *Captains Courageous* took place on the deck of a fishing schooner, yet the actors worked entirely in the studio, with a tank of water below them and rear projection providing seascapes.

Fig. 10.5 This scene from Fritz Lang's 1936 film *Fury* uses the rear-projection technique.

Fig. 10.6 Only the lower left portion of this shot from *Queen Christina* (1932) was built in the studio; the ships, water, rooftops, and sky have been added with a matte painting.

The optical printer offered more options for rephotographing and combining images. Essentially an optical printer consisted of a projector aimed into the lens of a camera. Both could be moved forward and backward, different lenses could be substituted, and portions of the image could be masked off and the film reexposed. Images could be superimposed, or portions could be joined like pieces of a jigsaw puzzle; a single image could be enlarged or its speed altered.

Typically the optical printer was used to save money by filling in portions of studio sets. By blocking off a part of a frame with a *matte,* the cinematographer could leave an unexposed portion into which the special-effects expert could later insert a *matte painting* (Fig. 10.6).

Far more complex were *traveling mattes.* Here the effects cinematographer would make two or more masks for each separate frame of the trick passage and expose the film twice, frame by frame, using the complementary masks in turn to cover one portion of the film. Traveling mattes were commonly used to make *wipes,* where a line passes across the screen, removing one shot gradually as the next appears. In 1933, wipes became fashionable as a way of replacing fades or dissolves when RKO optical-printer expert Linwood Dunn created elaborate transitions, moving in fan, sawtooth, and other shapes, in *Melody Cruise* and *Flying Down to Rio* (Fig. 10.7).

The optical printer was often used to create *montage sequences.* These brief flurries of shots used superimpositions, calendar pages, newspaper headlines, and similar images to suggest the passage of time or the course of a lengthy action (Fig. 10.8).

There were many other types of special effects. Entire scenes could be played by miniatures, as in the plane takeoffs and landings in Hawks's *Only Angels Have Wings.* Frame-by-frame three-dimensional animation was used occasionally, most notably to turn small puppets into the giant ape in *King Kong.* Other tricks involved simple mechanical devices, like the trapdoor elevator and dry-ice fumes that make the Wicked Witch seem to melt in *The Wizard of Oz.*

Fig. 10.7 A wipe with a zigzag edge provides a transition from one shot to another in *Flying Down to Rio.*

Fig. 10.8 In *Mr. Deeds Goes to Town,* superimposed newspaper headlines create montage sequences summarizing the public's changing perception of the protagonist.

Fig. 10.9 In *A Farewell to Arms* (1932, Frank Borzage), the romantic scene in which the main characters fall in love consists of soft, glittering images.

Fig. 10.10 *Shanghai Express* (1932) employs an extensive range of soft grays to create glamorous images of Marlene Dietrich.

Fig. 10.11 A depth composition in *Twentieth Century* (1934).

Figs. 10.12 and 10.13 Deep-space compositions that keep all planes in focus, from *The Public Enemy* (1931) and *Jezebel* (1938).

CINEMATOGRAPHY STYLES

During the early 1930s, most cinematographers aimed for a "soft" image, based on the important stylistic trend of the 1920s (pp. 176–177). Now, however, the soft look became less extreme and more pervasive. Camera experts did not use as many obvious filters or smeared, distorting glass masks. Instead, studio laboratories typically processed film to make it look grayer and softer. Moreover, in 1931 Eastman Kodak introduced a Super Sensitive Panchromatic stock suitable for use with the more diffused incandescent lighting that the innovation of sound had necessitated. Some films might use a sparkling, low-contrast image to convey a sense of glamor or romance (Fig. 10.9). Others went for a less blurry look while still avoiding sharp blacks and whites (Fig. 10.10).

Most Hollywood filmmakers of the 1930s clustered actors together in a relatively shallow area and then cut among them using shot/reverse shot. Others created compositions in greater depth, sometimes with the foreground plane slightly out of focus (Fig. 10.11) but sometimes also using deep focus (Figs. 10.12, 10.13).

Director Orson Welles and cinematographer Gregg Toland took such deep-focus shots further and used them more extensively in *Citizen Kane* (1941). Many of *Kane*'s depth shots used optical printing to combine sharply focused planes that had been filmed separately. Some shots, however, placed foreground elements very near the lens and background elements at a considerable distance, keeping everything in sharp focus; this occurs most spectacularly in the long take of the contract-signing scene (Fig. 10.14). Welles went further along the same path in his second film, *The Magnificent Ambersons* (1942), for which cinematographer Stanley Cortez achieved many crisply focused depth shots without using trick photography (Fig. 10.15). The influence of these visually innovative films soon spread throughout the industry. Staging in widely separated planes with deep focus became common practice (Fig. 10.16).

Overall, technological innovations of the 1930–1945 era did not fundamentally change the classical Hollywood approach to filmmaking. Narrative action and character psychology still remained central, and continuity rules still promoted spatial orientation. Sound, color, deep focus, and other techniques enhanced the style.

Fig. 10.12

Fig. 10.13

Fig. 10.14

Fig. 10.15

MAJOR DIRECTORS

In addition to the established directors working in Hollywood, the introduction of sound and the troubled political situation in Europe brought an influx of stage directors and émigrés into the film studios.

THE OLDER GENERATION

Charles Chaplin was one of the greatest opponents of talking pictures. As his own producer and a phenomenally popular star, he was able to go on making "silent" films, with only music and sound effects, longer than anyone else in Hollywood. His output, however, slowed considerably. He made two features without dialogue, *City Lights* (1931) and *Modern Times* (1936). The latter reflected the left-wing views that would get him into trouble with the government and the public after the war. In it, the Little Tramp loses a dreary assembly-line job, gets thrown in jail after being mistaken for the leader of a demonstration, and joins forces with a poor young woman as they seek work. Despite its concentration on Depression-era problems, it was a very funny film (Fig. 10.17). Oddly enough, so was Chaplin's first talkie, *The Great*

Fig. 10.14 Deep focus with one character close to the camera, a second in the middle ground, and a third in extreme depth, in *Citizen Kane*.

Fig. 10.15 The ballroom scene of *The Magnificent Ambersons* presents a vast set in clear focus behind the foreground couple.

Fig. 10.16

Fig. 10.17

Fig. 10.16 A simple shot/reverse-shot situation in *Casablanca* (1943) places Rick close to the camera in front of a sharply focused deep playing space.

Fig. 10.17 In *Modern Times*, factory worker Charlie tests a new machine that feeds the workers automatically while they stay on the job.

Fig. 10.18 Chaplin expresses Hynkel's lust for power when he dances with an inflatable globe, tossing it about until it bursts.

Fig. 10.19 Thief and potential victim in one of the gleaming Art Deco sets of *Trouble in Paradise*.

Dictator (1940), a comedy on the unlikely subject of Nazi Germany. The resemblance between Hitler's moustache and Chaplin's had often drawn comment, and Chaplin took advantage of their physical similarities to play Hynkel, dictator of Tomania (Fig. 10.18).

Josef von Sternberg had directed his second sound film, *The Blue Angel*, in Germany (p. 221). He returned to Hollywood with the film's star, Marlene Dietrich, and they made six more films together, including *Morocco* (1930) and *Blonde Venus* (1932). While the stories were conventional melodramas, their style placed them among the era's most beautiful films. Sternberg's fascination with textures and dense compositions intensified. In particular, costume, lighting, and cinematography glamorize Dietrich to an extent that has seldom been equalled (see Fig. 10.10). Von Sternberg also made films without Dietrich during this period, including two somber literary adaptations, *An American Tragedy* (1931) and *Crime and Punishment* (1935).

Ernst Lubitsch adjusted quickly to sound with *The Love Parade* (p. 219). He went on to make many popular musicals and comedies. Foremost among these was *Trouble in Paradise* (1932). It begins with a witty scene in which an elegant couple dine together in a Venetian hotel and then discover that each is a thief out to rob the other. They fall in love and continue to ply their trade until a scheme to rob a rich woman almost leads to the man's falling in love with the victim (Fig. 10.19). Lubitsch also directed Greta Garbo's penultimate film, *Ninotchka* (1939). Along with *The Great Dictator*, Lubitsch's *To Be or Not to Be* (1942) was one of the rare comedies about the Nazis.

John Ford continued to be remarkably prolific during the 1930s, signing twenty-six films during the decade, plus several more in the early 1940s before he went into the Navy. Working principally at 20th Century-Fox, he directed some of the studio's most popular stars, making a trio of films with Will Rogers [*Dr. Bull* (1933), *Judge Priest* (1934), and *Steamboat Round the Bend* (1935)] and a costume picture, *Wee Willie Winkie* (1937), starring Shirley Temple. Despite his early concentration on Westerns, he made only one during this era, but it was one of the genre's classics, *Stagecoach* (1939). It traced the trip of a motley group of people through dangerous Indian territory. Ford here first used the unearthly cliff formations of Monument Valley, a setting that would become his trademark in later Westerns.

That same year Ford directed *Young Mr. Lincoln*, in which a murder case solved by Lincoln suggests the combination of simplicity and shrewdness that will eventually make him President. *How Green Was My Valley* (1941) was the richly nostalgic story of a close-knit Welsh coal-mining family's gradual disintegration. Ford creates deeply emotional situations while using great stylistic restraint. Although he uses conventional shot/reverse shots and cut-ins in some cases, Ford downplays the most important or sentimental moments by staying in long shot or holding quietly on a silent scene as the characters ponder what has happened (Figs. 10.20, 10.21). Ford also used considerable depth in his staging and cinematography, stylistic traits that were to influence Orson Welles, who studied *Stagecoach* before making *Citizen Kane*.

Howard Hawks, who had begun directing in the mid-1920s, became much more prominent during this era. Like Ford, he worked in a wide variety of genres, concentrating on succinct handling of plot and performance and

Fig. 10.20

Fig. 10.21

displaying a mastery of rapid pacing and continuity editing. Hawks has explained his approach in a typically down-to-earth fashion: "I try to tell my story as simply as possible, with the camera at eye level. I just imagine the way the story should be told and I do it. If it's a scene that I don't want anybody to monkey with or cut, I don't give them any way to cut it."[3]

If Ford's *Stagecoach* is the quintessential Western, then Hawks's *His Girl Friday* (1940) is a model sound comedy. The hilarious script (from Ben Hecht and Charles MacArthur's play *The Front Page*) involves a newspaper editor who tries to prevent his ex-wife from giving up reporting to remarry. He lures her into trying to expose some crooked politicians who plan to execute a mentally incompetent killer in order to swing their election. Cary Grant, Rosalind Russell, and a bevy of character actors deliver the wise-cracking dialogue at breakneck speed, while Hawks records the action primarily with "invisible" shot/reverse shots and reframing movements.

Hawks's aviation adventure film *Only Angels Have Wings* (1939) is set in a small South American port where a flying service tries to get mail through a narrow mountain pass. Using simple resources, Hawks creates an intense atmosphere of danger and romance. Much of the action takes place in and around a single building, at night or in a fog, as the characters wait for each returning flight (Fig. 10.22). As often happens in Hawks films, the characters, male and female alike, have to prove themselves tough and stoic enough to deal with their problems.

William Wyler had begun directing in the late silent era, making mostly inexpensive Westerns. His breakthrough came in 1936, when he began working for independent producer Samuel Goldwyn. He made *These Three* (1936), an adaptation of Lillian Hellman's play *The Children's Hour,* and several other distinguished films over the next few years. These included *Jezebel* (1938; Fig. 10.13), *Wuthering Heights* (1939), and another Hellman adaptation, *The Little Foxes* (1941). On the last two, Gregg Toland was Wyler's cinematographer, and both films display deep-focus imagery similar to that of Ford's and Welles's films.

Veteran director Frank Borzage continued to specialize in sentimental

Fig. 10.20 In *Young Mr. Lincoln*, the climactic courtroom revelation is played out in a carefully arranged framing in depth, with no closer shots to emphasize the characters' emotions.

Fig. 10.21 Similarly, in *How Green Was My Valley*, a composition reminiscent of D. W. Griffith's films lingers over the family's silent reaction to bad news. (Compare with Fig. 3.42.)

Fig. 10.22 The hero talks down a plane in trouble in *Only Angels Have Wings*.

Fig. 10.23 In the famous final scene of *Stella Dallas*, Stella stands outside in the rain, weeping as she watches her daughter's wedding, and then turns to leave forever.

melodramas. *A Farewell to Arms* (1932) adapted Hemingway's novel of an American soldier and a British nurse who fall in love during World War I. Borzage and cinematographer Charles B. Lang filmed the characters in a glimmering soft-focus style that enhances the intense romanticism (see Fig. 10.9). By contrast, King Vidor continued to work in a variety of genres, from Westerns to melodramas. His 1937 remake of *Stella Dallas* is a classic instance of the latter, telling the story of a working-class woman who marries a factory owner's son. Her inability to overcome her vulgar upbringing eventually threatens her daughter's marriage to a society man, so she selflessly divorces her husband and gives up her daughter for adoption by the new, and refined, wife (Fig. 10.23).

Raoul Walsh also worked in various genres, making several major action films in the late 1930s and early 1940s. *The Roaring Twenties* (1939), a gangster film, contrasts the lives of three World War I veterans. The film is notable partly for several spectacular montage sequences, including a representation of the stock-market crash as a ticker-tape machine that swells to huge size and shatters. *High Sierra* (1940) is the sympathetic story of a killer fleeing through the mountains to escape the police; he meets a crippled girl whom he befriends. The film was a turning point in the career of Humphrey Bogart, who had previously played mostly villainous supporting roles; the next year he would play tough detective Sam Spade in *The Maltese Falcon*.

NEW DIRECTORS

The introduction of sound brought several stage directors from New York to Hollywood. Among these was George Cukor, who specialized in prestigious literary adaptations, such as *Camille* (1936), with Greta Garbo, and *David Copperfield* (1935), with W. C. Fields. Cukor worked mostly at MGM during this period. Rouben Mamoulian also came from Broadway; his *Applause* (1929) drew attention for its fluid camera movements. Similarly, his adaptation of *Dr. Jekyll and Mr. Hyde* (1932) begins with an unusually extended subjective tracking shot as we watch through his eyes as he enters a lecture hall. Another director who came from Broadway was Vincente Minnelli, who specialized in musicals. He joined MGM's musicals unit in 1940. This unit, under producer Arthur Freed, was soon to gather some of the finest musical talent in Hollywood, including Judy Garland, Gene Kelly, and Fred Astaire. Minnelli did choreography for Busby Berkeley films, including *Strike Up the Band* (1940), and then graduated to directing with *Cabin in the Sky* (1943), a musical with an all-star black cast. His most celebrated film of the war era was *Meet Me in St. Louis* (1944), with Garland.

Other new directors of this era appeared from the ranks of screenwriters. Preston Sturges wrote scenarios during the 1930s, working on *The Power and the Glory* (1933, William K. Howard), a film with a complex flashback structure that was a precursor to *Citizen Kane*. Sturges began directing with *The Great McGinty* (1940), a political satire, and went on to make a string of popular comedies throughout the war years. In *The Miracle of Morgan's Creek* (1944), for example, he poked fun at American prudishness. A young woman winds up pregnant after a wild party and claims that she married the father (whose name she remembers only as being something like "Ignatz Ratsky-watsky"). When he proves hard to locate, her mild-mannered boyfriend helps her avoid disgrace by marrying her; she then bears sextuplets, and the family becomes the focus of a media furor. Despite toning down by the MPPDA, the film remains audacious. For a while, Sturges was one of Paramount's most popular directors.

Another scriptwriter-turned-director was John Huston, who had worked on the screenplays of *Jezebel* and *High Sierra*. We shall discuss his directorial debut, *The Maltese Falcon*, as an early instance of the *film noir*. He was in the military for much of the war, making some major war documentaries, and returned to Hollywood after 1945.

Orson Welles, the most influential director to emerge in the years 1930–1945, had already achieved success in a number of other fields. (See Box.)

CITIZEN KANE AND THE MAGNIFICENT AMBERSONS

While still a young man (he was born in 1915), Orson Welles was directing unusual productions of theatrical and radio plays. For example, in 1936 he staged *Macbeth* with an all-black cast and set it in a Haitian jungle. In 1938, he gained nationwide notoriety with a radio adaptation of H. G. Wells's *The War of the Worlds*, treating it as a news bulletin and panicking thousands of listeners who believed that a Martian invasion was in progress.

In 1939, Welles was put under contract by RKO. His first completed project was *Citizen Kane*, one of the most admired of all films. Welles received an extraordinary degree of control over his work, including the right to choose his cast and to edit the final film. Not surprisingly, the resulting film was controversial. It was a veiled portrait of publishing magnate William Randolph Hearst and his long-term affair with film star Marion Davies. Hearst tried to have *Kane* suppressed, but it was released in 1941, with many audiences being aware of its subtext.

Both the narrative structure and the style of *Kane* were dazzlingly complex. Beginning with the death of Charles Foster Kane, the film switches to a newsreel that sketches out his life. A reporter is assigned to discover the meaning of Kane's mysterious last word, "Rosebud." He interviews people who had known Kane, and a series of flashbacks reveals a contradictory, elusive personality. Ultimately the reporter's quest fails, and the ending retains an ambiguity rare in classical Hollywood films.

Stylistically, *Kane* was flamboyant, drawing extensively on RKO's resources. For some scenes, Welles used quiet, lengthy takes. Other passages, notably the newsreel and several montage sequences, used quick cutting and abrupt changes in sound volume. To emphasize the vast spaces of some of the sets, Welles and cinematographer Gregg Toland worked at achieving deep-focus shots, placing some elements close to the camera, others at a distance (Fig. 10.14). Recent research has revealed that many of these very deep shots were made using several types of special effects (Fig. 10.24). Optical-printer work combined several tracking shots imperceptibly into one (as in the crane shot through a nightclub skylight, where a flash of lightning hides the joint between the two shots) and made the sets more impressive by combining miniatures and matte paintings with real-size sets. It has been claimed that over half of *Citizen Kane*'s shots contain special effects. The sound track was also altered substantially after filming. All these stylistic aspects of *Citizen Kane* proved

Fig. 10.24 In this shot from *Citizen Kane*, the large objects in the foreground were filmed separately and combined with the set and actors beyond.

highly influential to filmmakers during the 1940s.

Welles's second RKO feature was *The Magnificent Ambersons*. The plot does not use flashbacks, but it covers a lengthy period, the decline of a wealthy family as industrialization encroaches on a midwestern town. Welles establishes a nostalgic atmosphere in a prologue, narrated by him, which is a montage sequence depicting turn-of-the-century life. The film gradually adopts a grimmer tone as this genteel lifestyle disappears.

Stylistically, *Ambersons* takes *Kane's* techniques in less extravagant directions. Still, there are elaborate camera movements, as when Aunt Fannie has hysterics and the camera tracks through several rooms as Georgie tries to calm her. The deep-focus effects were more often done in a single exposure (Fig. 10.15), and a larger budget allowed Welles to build entire sets and downplay optical-printer work.

After adverse audience reactions at previews, RKO took *Ambersons* out of Welles's control and cut it drastically, adding scenes made by the assistant director and editor. This truncated version was given a minor release. No complete version of the film survives, but even so it remains a flawed masterpiece. (See Notes and Queries.)

ÉMIGRÉ DIRECTORS

Foreign filmmakers continued to come to Hollywood. Some were lured by higher salaries or the chance to work in the world's best-equipped studios. Increasingly, however, the spread of fascism in Europe and the onset of World War II drove filmmakers to seek refuge in the United States.

Dissatisfied with his lack of authority in England and fascinated by the technical possibilities offered in Hollywood, Alfred Hitchcock signed a contract with David O. Selznick. His first American film, *Rebecca* (1940), was a prestigious literary adaptation and won a best-picture Academy Award, but it was not typical of the suspense films he is more famous for. Among his several wartime films was *Shadow of a Doubt* (1943). A man driven to seduce and kill rich widows visits his sister's family in a small California town. He charms everyone, but his young niece is shattered when she ferrets out the truth about him. Through location shooting, Hitchcock created a sense of small-town normalcy with which to contrast the villain's secret crimes.

The German exodus to Hollywood which had begun in the silent era accelerated after the Nazis gained power in 1933. Fritz Lang arrived in 1934. Although he was able to work fairly steadily (about a film a year up to 1956), Lang seldom had much control over his projects and never gained the prestige he had had in Germany. He worked in many genres, making Westerns, spy pictures, melodramas, and suspense films. *You Only Live Once* (1937) is the affecting story of a young ex-convict who tries to go straight but is falsely accused of a murder; he escapes from jail the night before his execution, but he and his wife are hunted down and shot.

Two other new arrivals were Billy Wilder and Otto Preminger. Wilder had been a scriptwriter in Germany and resumed this career in Hollywood, teaming up with Charles Brackett for many screenplays, including those for *Ninotchka* and *Ball of Fire*. His first solo directorial effort was a comedy, *The Major and the Minor* (1942), and his grim study of alcoholism, *The Lost Weekend* (1945) was voted an Oscar as best picture. Although Preminger was Jewish, he was brought to Hollywood to play Nazi villains. He managed, however, to slip into directing in the early 1940s. Wilder and Preminger made two of the period's classic *films noirs*.

GENRE INNOVATIONS AND TRANSFORMATIONS

Many genres from the silent era continued uninterrupted into the sound period. Technical changes within the industry and social ones in the larger sphere, however, caused some new genres to arise and some new variants to be introduced into old ones.

THE MUSICAL

The introduction of sound promoted the musical as a major genre. Some early "revue" musicals simply strung numbers together. Others, like *The Broadway Melody*, were backstage stories, motivating their numbers as performances by their characters. There were also operetta musicals, exemplified by *The Love Parade*, which played out their stories and numbers in fantasy locales. Finally, there were "integrated" musicals, where the singing and dancing occurred in ordinary settings. (Backstage musicals often mixed a few integrated numbers in with those performed on stage.) The revue musical soon died out, but the other types all remained prominent.

A delightful example of the operetta subgenre was Rouben Mamoulian's *Love Me Tonight* (1932). The film begins with a sequence influenced by René Clair's early sound films: a Parisian street gradually comes to life in the early morning, with each rhythmic noise contributing to a beat that leads into a musical number. In a celebrated sequence, a song passes from person to person, with the scenes being linked by dissolves. The protagonist, a tailor, sings a song, "Isn't It Romantic?" (Fig. 10.25), which is picked up by a composer, who in turn sings it to soldiers on a train; when they sing it around their campfire, a gypsy hears it and plays it for his friends, and it makes its way to the heroine, a princess who sings the song on the balcony of her provincial castle.

Fig. 10.25 Maurice Chevalier sings into three mirrors in *Love Me Tonight*.

The backstage musical was typified by a series of films made by Warner Bros. and choreographed by Busby Berkeley. The film that established many conventions of the genre was *42nd Street* (1933, Lloyd Bacon). A naive chorus girl rises to sudden stardom when the lead player is injured just before the opening of a big Broadway show. The director encourages her: "You *can't* fall down, you *can't,* because *your* future's in it, *my* future, and everything all of us have is staked on you. All right now, I'm through, but you keep your feet on the ground, and your head on those shoulders of yours, and Sawyer, you're going out a youngster, but you've *got* to come back a star!" Of course she does become a star, and the stage show includes some of Berkeley's elaborate dance numbers, made using a crane and overhead camera platform (Fig. 10.26).

Among the most popular musicals were those starring Fred Astaire and Ginger Rogers, choreographed by Hermes Pan. In *Swing Time* (1936, George Stevens), for example, Astaire plays a vaudeville hoofer who courts Rogers, a dance instructor. Whether having a backstage plot or an integrated plot,

Fig. 10.26 Busby Berkeley creates an abstract pattern by shooting a dance number from directly overhead in *42nd Street*.

Fig. 10.27 The "Let's Face the Music" number in *Follow the Fleet* (1936, Mark Sandrich).

Fig. 10.28 The protagonists compete at throwing theatrical fits in *Twentieth Century*.

Fig. 10.29 The heiress relaxes as the reporter attempts to demonstrate his skill at hitchhiking in *It Happened One Night*.

Astaire-Rogers musicals were romances, and many of the dance numbers become part of the couple's courtship. Despite initial misunderstandings and antagonisms, the elegant meshing of their movements shows that they are made for each other (Fig. 10.27).

MGM also made many musicals during this era. Mickey Rooney and Judy Garland were paired in several films about teenagers putting on shows, such as *Strike Up the Band* (1940, Busby Berkeley). Garland became a star in the lavish Technicolor fantasy, *The Wizard of Oz* (1939, Victor Fleming). One of her finest films was Minnelli's *Meet Me in St. Louis.* Another MGM star whose career began during this period was Gene Kelly, whose dance style was often boisterous and athletic, as in the "Make Way for Tomorrow" number in *Cover Girl* (for which Kelly was loaned to Columbia; 1944, Charles Vidor).

THE SCREWBALL COMEDY

In screwball comedy, the romantic couple at the center of the story are eccentrics, often portrayed through slapstick. The films are usually set among wealthy people who can, despite the hardships of the Depression, afford to behave oddly. The romantic couple may initially be antagonistic, as in George Cukor's *The Philadelphia Story* (1940). Or the couple's love may cross class lines; then the wealthy parents must be converted (as in Capra's *You Can't Take It with You,* 1938) or thwarted (as in Cukor's *Holiday,* 1938).

Screwball comedy began in 1934 with two very different films. Hawks's *Twentieth Century* is utterly cynical in its treatment of its lead actors, Carole Lombard and John Barrymore. A hammy theatrical entrepreneur makes a star of a beautiful store clerk and then seduces her. She soon behaves as theatrically in everyday life as he does; during the film's second half, set on a train, they quarrel and throw tantrums (Fig. 10.28). The other major screwball comedy of 1934, Capra's *It Happened One Night,* is more sentimental. With its spoiled heroine fleeing her father in order to marry a superficial playboy, it popularized the "madcap heiress" character. A down-to-earth reporter aids the heroine in order to gain a scoop, and the two fall in love (Fig. 10.29). The image of a rich spoiled woman would be pushed to its limits in Hawks's *Bringing Up Baby* (1938).

The genre developed quickly, and Capra remained one of its main exponents. In his *Mr. Deeds Goes to Town* (1936), a small-town man becomes a national idol when he uses his unexpected inheritance to help dispossessed farmers. Venal lawyers try to have him declared insane, although he is only eccentric, as Capra demonstrates from the start (Fig. 10.30).

Early films in the genre dealt with the Depression. In *It Happened One Night,* the reporter strives to regain his job by writing a story about the fugitive heiress. In *My Man Godfrey,* a homeless man hires on as a butler to an eccentric wealthy family; the characters frequently mention "forgotten men"—a Depression-era term for the unemployed, many of whom were veterans of World War I. Later in the decade, however, many screwball comedies' plots ignored contemporary social problems, especially those of unemployment. In *Holiday,* the hero longs to quit his lucrative job and find

Fig. 10.30

Fig. 10.31

Fig. 10.32

his purpose in life; all the film's positive characters value individualism while despising snobbishness and wealth (Fig. 10.31). *You Can't Take It with You,* a paean to idiosyncracies, concerns a large family who take into their home people who quit dull jobs in order to pursue personal interests.

The comedy of sexual antagonism also continued unabated. In Sturges's *The Lady Eve* (1941), a female cardsharp sets out to fleece the heir to a brewing fortune; instead, they fall in love, and when he discovers her background and rejects her, she vows revenge (Fig. 10.32). Similarly, in *Ball of Fire* (1941, Hawks), a nightclub singer fleeing the law bamboozles a coven of naive professors and then falls in love with one of them.

The screwball genre flourished between 1934 and 1945. Sturges contributed a bitter late example with *Unfaithfully Yours* (1948), in which an orchestra conductor believes his wife has a lover and during a concert fantasizes murdering her in three ways, each to an appropriate musical piece. Hawks also made two postwar screwball comedies. In *I Was a Male War Bride* (1948), a French officer suffers a series of humiliations when he must dress as a woman in order to accompany his fiancée to the United States after World War II; *Monkey Business* (1952) portrays the delirious effects of a youth serum on seemingly respectable people.

Fig. 10.30 In *Mr. Deeds Goes to Town,* the hero is more concerned with playing his tuba than with a lawyer's news of his large inheritance.

Fig. 10.31 The independent, positive characters in *Holiday* celebrate eccentricity by jokingly awarding the hero a toy giraffe.

Fig. 10.32 In *The Lady Eve,* brewing heir Charles Pike suffers the comic humiliation typical of the screwball comedy.

THE HORROR FILM

During the early sound era, the horror film became a major genre. Some horror films had been made during the 1920s, mainly by Universal and usually starring Lon Chaney (pp. 168–169). The pattern for many future films was set in 1927 with Paul Leni's popular *The Cat and the Canary,* in which a group of people meet in an isolated mansion to hear a will read.

Universal repeated such successes in its horror cycle, beginning with the vampire film *Dracula* (1931, Tod Browning). Although it betrayed its origins as a stage version of Bram Stoker's original 1897 novel and suffered from some of the slowness of early sound films, *Dracula* became a hit largely due to Bela Lugosi's performance in the title role. Shortly thereafter, James Whale's *Frankenstein* (1931) made a star of Boris Karloff, who played the monster with the help of heavy make-up. The Universal horror cycle hit its stride from 1932 to 1935. Whale made *The Old Dark House* (1932), which balanced suspense and comedy by trapping a cast of eccentrics in an isolated

Fig. 10.33 *The Mummy* uses make-up, lighting (including a tiny "pin" light reflected in the eyes), and Boris Karloff's menacing performance to create an eerie atmosphere on a low budget.

Fig. 10.34 The opening scene of *Cat People*, in which the heroine sketches a leopard, typifies the simple, but disturbing, juxtapositions of the Val Lewton horror films.

country home on the proverbial dark and stormy night. He also directed *The Invisible Man* (1933) and *The Bride of Frankenstein* (1935).

One of the most stylish and effective of these films was *The Mummy*, directed in 1932 by Karl Freund, the German cinematographer who had shot *The Last Laugh* and many other important films during the silent era. The mummy of an ancient Egyptian priest returns to life in modern times and attempts to kill a woman he believes to be a reincarnation of his dead love (Fig. 10.33). In later years the Universal horror cycle was dissipated by formulaic repetition.

A second significant cycle of horror films was made in RKO's B unit during the early 1940s. Producer Val Lewton took charge of production there in 1942. A small number of directors worked under Lewton—Jacques Tourneur, Mark Robson, and Robert Wise—but the producer created a consistent tone and style for the films. Making a virtue of budget necessities, the Lewton films avoided graphic depictions of monsters or violence, concentrating instead on characters threatened by unseen terrors. In Tourneur's *Cat People* (1942), the heroine is obsessed with a black leopard in the zoo and seems to have inherited a supernatural ability to transform into a killer cat (Fig. 10.34). Tourneur also directed another of the Lewton unit's most effective films, *I Walked with a Zombie* (1943). These titles were chosen by the studio and assigned to Lewton, and he and his collaborators came up with extraordinarily poetic and frightening films to fit them.

THE SOCIAL PROBLEM FILM

The Depression created a new focus on social problems, and many 1930s films dealt with them, frequently adopting a realistic style that was far from the escapism often associated with this era. In 1934, for example, King Vidor made *Our Daily Bread*, which portrayed a group of unemployed people who start a cooperative farm. Despite various challenges, including a drought, they eventually succeed. The scene of the group digging a long channel and irrigating their land uses editing and framing to create an exhilarating image of collective triumph somewhat reminiscent of Soviet films of the era.

Warner Bros. was particularly committed to social problem films. In *I Am a Fugitive from a Chain Gang* (1932, Mervyn LeRoy), a World War I veteran is falsely accused of a theft. While a fugitive, he attempts to pawn his war medal, only to be shown dozens of such medals that unemployed veterans had pawned. In the end he disappears into the night, explaining how he now lives: "I steal," an ironic suggestion that the legal system has pushed him into the underworld. *Wild Boys of the Road* (1933, William Wellman) depicted the plight of homeless orphaned or abandoned children.

Fritz Lang made one of the finest social problem films, *Fury* (1936, MGM), on the subject of lynching. While traveling to meet his fiancée, the hero is arrested in a small town and falsely accused of murder. The citizens burn down the jail, and he is apparently killed. In fact he survives but is so embittered that he nearly allows his attackers to be convicted of his murder before the heroine persuades him to step forward. The film depicts newsreel cinematographers filming the attempted lynching. At the trial, this footage is

Fig. 10.35

Fig. 10.36

Figs. 10.35 and 10.36 A newsreel image of a woman during the lynching scene in *Fury*, and the woman's reaction to the footage in court.

used as evidence, and the defendants are forced to confront their own actions (Figs. 10.35, 10.36).

John Ford contributed an important social problem film with *The Grapes of Wrath* (1940), an adaptation of John Steinbeck's novel about displaced Oklahoma farmers during the Depression. The Joad family is driven off their land by the great drought that created the "dust bowl" in the Plains states. Traveling to California for work, they are exploited as migrant workers. They temporarily find a haven in a government-run camp that suggests the benefits of the Roosevelt administration. Near the end, however, the hero leaves to join the struggle for workers' rights, telling his mother, "Wherever there's a fight so hungry people can eat, I'll be there."

After the United States entered the war, increased employment and prosperity led to fewer social problem films. The genre revived in the postwar era with such films as *Gentlemen's Agreement* (1947, Elia Kazan) and *Crossfire* (1947, Edward Dmytryk).

THE GANGSTER FILM

Somewhat related to the social problem film was the gangster genre. Although there had been occasional films about small-time street gangs in the silent era, the first major movie with a gangster protagonist was von Sternberg's *Underworld* (1927; p. 169). The genre became more prominent in the early 1930s with *Little Caesar* (1930, Mervyn LeRoy), *Public Enemy* (1931, William Wellman), and *Scarface* (1932, Howard Hawks). Gangster films were topical, deriving material from the organized crime that grew up during Prohibition (1920–1933).

Gangster films centered on a ruthless criminal's rise to power. Like many films in the genre, *Public Enemy* hinges on the contrast between two men (friends or brothers), one of whom gets an honest job while the other turns to crime. Typically, the growing status of the gangsters in these films is signaled by their increasingly expensive clothing and flashy cars (Fig. 10.37).

Like other gangster films, *Public Enemy* was widely criticized for glamorizing violence. The Hays Code forbade the sympathetic depiction of criminals. Producers defended the genre by claiming that they were simply examining a social problem. *Public Enemy* begins with a title saying it wants

Fig. 10.37 After his first big payoff, the protagonist of *Public Enemy* is measured for a new suit.

Fig. 10.38 Tom mutters "I ain't so tough" after being shot, a scene designed to deglamorize his criminal career.

"to honestly depict an environment that exists today in a certain strata [sic] of American life, rather than glorify the hoodlum or the criminal." The protagonists of these films all die violently in the end, so the studios argued that the plots showed that crime does not pay. Tom, in *Public Enemy*, is gunned down by a rival gang (Fig. 10.38) and his body is dumped ignominiously at his home. Similarly, the main character in *Scarface* is killed during a violent shoot-out with police. Still, pressure groups insisted that such endings did not wipe out the impression that crime was lively and exciting. For such reasons, the release of *Scarface* was delayed, and the producers were forced to add scenes—not filmed by Hawks—of officials and reformers decrying the gangs' power and violence.

The studios tried to avoid censorship pressures while retaining the excitement associated with the gangster genre. Actors closely identified with criminal roles, such as James Cagney and Edward G. Robinson, might instead play tough, violent cops, as Cagney does in *G-Men* (1935, William Keighley). Or the gangster might become less central, with the story focusing on other characters tempted toward a life of crime, as in *Dead End* (1938, William Wyler) and *Angels with Dirty Faces* (1938, Michael Curtiz). In the latter, two friends grow up, one becoming a gangster, the other a priest; a group of children idolize the gangster. Finally the priest persuades the gangster to pretend to be terrified just before his execution so that children will be disillusioned and not take him as a role model.

FILM NOIR

To some extent the cynical, violent narratives of the gangster films were taken over by the *film noir*. This was a term applied by French critics in 1946 to a group of U.S. films made during the war and released abroad in quick succession after 1945. *Noir* means "black" or "dark" but can also imply "gloomy." Less a genre than a stylistic and narrative tendency, *film noir* is often considered to have started in 1941 with Huston's *The Maltese Falcon* or even earlier with the B film *Stranger on the Third Floor* (1940, Boris Ingster). Most *films noirs* involve crime, but the tendency crosses genres. It includes social problem films like Wilder's *The Lost Weekend* and spy films like Lang's *Ministry of Fear* (1944).

The *film noir* tendency derives from the American hard-boiled detective novel, which originated in the 1920s. In such harsh, tawdry works as *Red Harvest* (1929), Dashiell Hammett reacted against traditional British detective fiction, which often involved staid country-house settings and upper-class characters. Other major authors of hard-boiled fiction included Raymond Chandler, James M. Cain, and Cornell Woolrich. Many of their novels and stories were adapted as films, starting with Hammett's *The Maltese Falcon*. Filmic influences came from German Expressionism, French Poetic Realism (Chapter 13), and the stylistic innovations of *Citizen Kane*.

Like their literary models, *films noirs* were mainly aimed at male audiences. Their protagonists are almost invariably men, usually detectives or criminals characterized by pessimism, self-doubt, or a cold, detached view of the world. Women are usually sexually alluring but treacherous, leading the protagonists into danger or using them for selfish ends. A common setting for a *film noir* would be a big city, especially at night; shiny, rain-slicked pavements, dark alleyways, and sleazy bars are common milieux. Many of the films use distinctive high and low angles, low-key lighting, extreme wide-angle lenses, and location shooting, though some *films noirs* contain few of these traits.

The Maltese Falcon established many of the conventions of the *film noir.* Humphrey Bogart became a major star in the role of Sam Spade, a private detective who must decide whether to turn in the treacherous femme fatale who has hired him and whom he (perhaps) loves. In a long take he bitterly explains why he must send her to prison and promises to wait for her during the many years of her sentence. Brigid is taken away in an elevator by the police, marked as the archetypal *film noir* heroine by the shadow on her face (Fig. 10.39).

Fig. 10.39 Our last view of the femme fatale of *The Maltese Falcon.*

Film noir's debt to German film of the 1920s may be reflected in the fact that four important émigrés worked extensively in this tendency. Lang's *Dr. Mabuse der Spieler* and other German works anticipated *film noir,* and his Hollywood career developed this tendency. In *Ministry of Fear,* for example, the hero is released from an insane asylum after the mercy killing of his wife. Whiling away time before his train, he wanders into a grim charity fête and accidentally becomes enmeshed in a battle against Nazi spies. Lang's association with independent producer Walter Wanger led to two other notable wartime *films noirs: Woman in the Window* (1944) and *Scarlet Street* (1945). Robert Siodmak began making B films in Hollywood in 1941, achieving a reputation in *film noir* in 1944 with *Phantom Lady* and *The Suspect* (1945); after the war he would lead this tendency with such films as *The Killers* (1946).

Another German émigré, Otto Preminger, rose to fame with a major *film noir. Laura* (1944) concerns an embittered working-class detective who investigates the murder of a sophisticated advertising executive and falls in love with her through her diary and portrait. *Laura*'s flashbacks, apparent dream sequence, and plot twists were an extreme case of *film noir* narration.

Perhaps the definitive wartime example of the *film noir* came from yet another émigré. The script for Billy Wilder's *Double Indemnity* (1944) originated in a unique combination of hard-boiled authors, with Raymond Chandler adapting a James M. Cain novel. A woman seduces an insurance salesman into helping her murder her husband; gradually the scheme unravels in mutual suspicions and betrayals. The film unfolds in a series of flashbacks as the dying salesman speaks into a dictaphone, confessing to his friend, an insurance investigator who is hot on his trail. Many typical traits of the *film noir* are present: the venality of both the main characters, the voice-over narration by the insurance salesman, the somber urban setting, and the doomed romance. (*Film noir* was the one type of Hollywood film that permitted an unhappy ending, though abrupt—and often unconvincing—happy endings were sometimes added.) *Double Indemnity* also used a conventional lighting motif: venetian blinds and other parts of the sets cast shadows across the scene (Fig. 10.40).

Fig. 10.40 *Film noir* shadows fall across the set as Walter Neff sneaks up the back stairs to his apartment in *Double Indemnity.*

Fig. 10.41 The hero of *Objective Burma* gives a journalist a captured Japanese flag as a souvenir.

THE WAR FILM

During the period 1930–1945, films about war passed through remarkable changes. The disillusionment of World War I had resulted in a pacifism that dominated films of the 1930s. (Until Pearl Harbor, most citizens opposed American entry into the hostilities.) Lewis Milestone's *All Quiet on the Western Front* (1930) was one of the most uncompromisingly pacifist films, showing a sympathetic young German hero and ending unhappily with his death. Throughout the decade, war was depicted as tragic and senseless. Warner Bros. made two versions of *Dawn Patrol* (1930, Howard Hawks; 1938, Edmund Goulding), about a commander who agonizes over sending pilots out to be killed. Even the musical *Golddiggers of 1933* contains a number—"Remember My Forgotten Man"—about World War I veterans impoverished by the Depression.

After Pearl Harbor, however, the film industry supported the cause wholeheartedly. Combat films were upbeat and often showed Americans from various ethnic backgrounds united in battling the Axis. In Hawks's *Air Force* (1943), men named Winocki, Quincannon, and Weinberg form part of a bomber crew.

Most war films featuring the Nazis treated them simply as cold-hearted killers. Propaganda directed against the Japanese, however, was often more racist in tone, drawing upon stereotypical images. In *Objective Burma* (1945, Raoul Walsh), for example, the hero leads a division of paratroopers to recapture part of Burma from the Japanese (Fig. 10.41), who are referred to at one point as "monkeys" (a common racial epithet used during World War II). In one scene they discover the bodies of American soldiers tortured and killed by the Japanese forces. A reporter with the group comments on the horrors he has seen in his career: "But this, this is different. This was done in cold blood by a people who, who claim to be civilized. Civilized and degenerate moral idiots! . . . Wipe 'em out! Wipe 'em off the face of the earth!"

One of the few combat films that presented a less gung-ho image was Ford's *They Were Expendable* (1945), a story of PT-boat sailors who fight valiantly but go down to defeat in the Philippines. Some are evacuated, but others, including one of the protagonists, must stay behind to face capture or death. Ford, who had been in the Navy and been injured filming combat footage for his documentary *The Battle of Midway* (1942), made several realistic scenes of PT boats in combat for *They Were Expendable*. Ford later remarked of this film: "I *despise* these happy endings—with a kiss at the finish—I've never done that. Of course, they *were* glorious in defeat in the Philippines—they kept on fighting."[4] As Ford suggests, *They Were Expendable* presented a remarkably unvarnished picture of heroism.

ANIMATION AND THE STUDIO SYSTEM

Before 1910, animated films had been novelties. By the 1930s, however, labor-saving devices had made them a part of nearly every film program. The Majors and Minors all regularly released a cartoon series, either under contract with an independent firm or in their own animation units.

Some of these series were highly standardized, turned out with efficient, assembly-line systems. For nearly forty years after 1930, Paul Terry provided his Terrytoons biweekly for Fox/20th Century-Fox. Universal released films by Walter Lantz from 1929 through 1972; Lantz's most famous character, Woody Woodpecker, debuted in 1941. Columbia had its own short-film division, Screen Gems, which made cartoons starring Krazy Kat, Scrappy, and others until 1949.

At the opposite end of the scale from these series were those produced by the Walt Disney Studio, an independent company devoted solely to making cartoons. Disney's enormous success in 1928 with the Mickey Mouse short *Steamboat Willie* had brought animation into the sound age and given it respectability. The studio went on centering cartoons around Mickey but also established a series of "Silly Symphonies," based on musical pieces and containing no continuing characters. *Skeleton Dance* (1928) featured a macabre celebration in a graveyard.

By 1932, Disney could move from Columbia to distribute through the prestigious United Artists. Critics all over the world suddenly hailed these shorts, with their fluid movements and minimal dialogue, as the answer to the problems of the all-talkie sound film. The studio also was among the first to pick up on three-strip Technicolor, beginning with *Flowers and Trees* in 1932. Disney dominated the cartoon category of the Oscars with such films as *The Three Little Pigs* (1933), whose song "Who's Afraid of the Big Bad Wolf?" became an anthem of Depression-period America. The firm spent a great deal of money on such films, and its huge staff of artists had the leisure to create detailed, shaded backgrounds, lots of figure movement, and bright color schemes (Color Plate 10.14).

In 1937, Disney switched to RKO as a distributor—a move that bolstered that shaky firm when it released the first American feature-length cartoon, *Snow White and the Seven Dwarfs* (1937). Despite being terrified by the Witch, children were enchanted by the dwarfs, and the film was a huge hit. The studio continued its series of popular short cartoons, starring Mickey Mouse, Donald Duck, Goofy, and Pluto. It also planned several additional features. *Bambi* (1942) took the studio's propensity for realistic backgrounds further, with soft pastel paintings for the natural settings (Color Plate 10.15). The film also extensively employed the new multiplane camera, an elaborate animation stand introduced in *The Old Mill* (1937). The multiplane permitted the settings and figures to be divided up onto several cels in layers. These could be moved frame by frame at varying rates toward or away from the camera, giving a powerful illusion of gliding through a three-dimensional space.

The Disney studio was working at its peak during the early 1940s, making *Pinocchio* (1940) and *Dumbo* (1941) as well as *Bambi*. Part of the staff was diverted to war propaganda and informational films, but full-time work on both features and shorts resumed after 1945.

Other studios found animators who, with more limited means, could imaginatively exploit the cartoon's potential for absurdist illogic and rapid, distorted movements. In 1927, Paramount began releasing films by Max and Dave Fleischer, inventors of the "Out of the Inkwell" series. In 1931, they

Fig. 10.42 In *A Dream Walking* (1934), Olive Oyl, Bluto, and Popeye all end up sleepwalking on an unfinished skyscraper.

introduced Betty Boop, and Koko the Clown became a supporting character. Betty was a sexy innocent wandering through a variety of adventures, sometimes encountering ghosts and monsters. The Fleischers utilized popular songs; in *Minnie the Moocher* (1932), Cab Calloway's band provides the sound track as Betty explores a scary cave.

Betty had to be toned down considerably after the Hays Code was enforced in 1934. A supporting player who had first appeared in *Popeye the Sailor,* a Betty cartoon of 1933, now became the studio's main star. The gravel-voiced Popeye, with his simple credo ("I yam what I yam and that's all what I yam") and his strengthening cans of spinach, rescued girl friend Olive Oyl and adopted child Swee' Pea from the villainous Bluto and other menaces (Fig. 10.42).

After Disney's success with *Snow White and the Seven Dwarfs,* the Fleischers released the feature-length *Gulliver's Travels* (1939), which employed realistic rotoscoped movements for the title character while using more caricatural portrayals for the Lilliputians. The other Fleischer feature, *Mr. Bug Goes to Town* (aka *Hoppity Goes to Town,* 1941), achieved a more consistent stylized look. By that point, however, the brothers had overextended themselves. In 1942, Paramount maneuvered them out of their own animation firm and took over the Popeye series, as well as the new Superman series (1941 on). The Fleischers were never able to regain their prominence as animators.

In 1930, Warner Bros. started its own cartoon unit, on its regular Hollywood lot, hiring as its heads former Disney animation team Hugh Harman, Rudolf Ising, and Isadore "Friz" Freleng. Like many early sound cartoons, the Warner Bros. shorts were built around popular songs from the studio's feature musicals. The series was labeled "Looney Tunes," and most of the early entries starred a little black boy named Bosko.

In 1934, Harman and Ising moved to MGM, taking Bosko with them. Over the next few years Warners hired a new generation of animators who were to put it at the top of the short-cartoon business: Frank Tashlin, Bob Clampett, Tex Avery, and Chuck Jones, who, along with Freleng, each headed a unit within the animation section. The Warners system was more casual than the usual cartoon factory, and this group swapped ideas with a team of writers in informal "jam sessions." They developed superstars Porky Pig, Daffy Duck, Bugs Bunny, and Elmer Fudd.

The Warners group did not have the resources to create detailed backgrounds or elaborate groups of moving figures to match the Disney product. Instead, the animators depended on speed, topicality, and a silly humor that contrasted with the sentimentality and cuteness of most contemporary cartoons. Clampett specialized in dazzlingly fast motion; in trying to avoid his induction notice in *Draftee Daffy* (1943), Daffy whizzes about his house as a lightning bolt or shower of sparks. Avery's taste ran to wild visual puns.

Many Warners cartoons refer self-consciously to the fact that they are cartoons. In *You Ought to Be in Pictures* (1940, Freleng), Porky decides to become a star in regular features and quits his job with the Warners animation unit (in a scene with the unit's producer, Leon Schlesinger). In several Warners cartoons, a black silhouette rises up from the audience and interrupts the action; in *Thugs with Dirty Mugs,* a spectator who says he has seen the cartoon before calls the police and informs on the gangsters (Color Plate 10.16; note also the caricature of Warners star Edward G. Robinson). Warners shorts appealed as much to adults as to children and became immensely popular.

The same adult appeal was injected into MGM's cartoon series when Tex Avery moved there from Warner Bros. in 1942. Avery created a new repertoire of stars, including wisecracking Screwy Squirrel, unlikely super-hero Droopy Dog, and an unnamed Wolf, perpetually expressing extravagant (and frustrated) lust for curvaceous heroines. Avery continued his penchant for literalizing dreadful puns, as when the wolf in *The Shooting of Dan McGoo* (1945) has one foot in the grave (a little grave complete with tombstone encloses his boot like a slipper). Avery would continue pushing cartoons to manic limits for a decade after the war.

Hollywood enjoyed great prosperity during the war. That prosperity was to continue briefly after 1945, but later in the decade new challenges would change the film industry profoundly.

◆ NOTES AND QUERIES

THE CONTROVERSY OVER ORSON WELLES

Orson Welles's career, especially during the making of *Citizen Kane* and *The Magnificent Ambersons,* has remained the subject of controversy. During the 1950s and 1960s, when auteurist criticism began hailing directors as the central creators in the filmmaking process (see Chapter 19), Welles was often singled out as a major example. Critics analyzed the thematic unities of his works. For some samples, see André Bazin, *Orson Welles: A Critical View,* trans. Jonathan Rosenbaum (1972; New York: Harper & Row, 1978); Ronald Gottesman, ed., *Focus on Orson Welles* (Englewood Cliffs, N.J.: Prentice-Hall, 1976); and Joseph McBride, *Orson Welles* (New York: Viking, 1972).

In 1971, Pauline Kael attempted to counter this approach in a long essay, "Raising Kane," which ascribed certain aspects of *Citizen Kane* to other people who had worked on it, especially script collaborator Herman Mankiewicz. See *The Citizen Kane Book* (Boston: Little, Brown, 1971), which also contains the original shooting script. Kael's essay prompted several indignant responses, including Peter Bogdanovich's "The Kane Mutiny" in 1972 (reprinted in *Focus on Orson Welles,* cited above).

This controversy, plus the stylistic daring of Welles's two early films, has led historians to examine the films' production circumstances closely. Two detailed accounts of the making of *Citizen Kane* have revealed much about the respective roles of Welles and his collaborators. See Robert L. Carringer, *The Making of **Citizen Kane*** (Berkeley: University of California Press, 1985) and Harlan Lebo, ***Citizen Kane:*** *The Fiftieth-Anniversary Album* (New York: Doubleday, 1990). See also Carringer, ***The Magnificent Ambersons:*** *A Reconstruction* (Berkeley: University of California Press, 1993). The laserdisc editions of both films (from the Criterion Collection) contain production documents, also assembled by Carringer.

◆ REFERENCES

1. Martin Quigley, *Decency in Motion Pictures* (New York: Macmillan, 1937), p. 33.
2. William Stull, "Process Cinematography," in Willard D. Morgan, ed., *The Complete Photographer: A Complete Guide to Amateur and Professional Photography*, vol. 8 (New York: National Educational Alliance, 1943), p. 2994.
3. Joseph McBride, *Hawks on Hawks* (Berkeley: University of California Press, 1982), p. 82.
4. Peter Bogdanovich, *John Ford* (Berkeley: University of California Press, 1968), pp. 83–84.

11

OTHER STUDIO SYSTEMS

During the 1930s and early 1940s, Hollywood's studio system was the basis for the most successful film industry in the world. Industries elsewhere took other forms. In some countries, such as the USSR and Germany, state-run monopolies developed during this period. In others, like France and Mexico, small producers renting studio space put out films, often haphazardly, hoping for quick profits. Still others had well-developed studio systems that were either imitations of or variants on the Hollywood models. This chapter examines four countries' studio systems: Britain, Japan, India, and China.

QUOTA QUICKIES AND WARTIME PRESSURES: THE BRITISH STUDIOS

In 1936, a British trade paper commented, "When one recalls the wretched, bleak sheds, barns and huts, the mud and general discomfort of many British studios of 15 years ago, it is possible to realise the strides and opportunities of today, when physical hardships are reduced to a minimum thanks to bold and considerate planning."[1] The occasion was the opening of the Pinewood Studios, part of a construction boom in English production centers during the mid-1930s. Two decades after Hollywood cinema began to consolidate its studio system, British film companies finally expanded into a comparable, if smaller, system.

What enabled the British film industry to expand at this relatively late date? Midway through the 1920s, fewer than 5 percent of the features released in Great Britain originated domestically. Responding to this situation, in 1927 the government passed the Quota Act. It required that distributors make at least a certain percentage of British films available and that theaters devote a minimum portion of screen time to such films. The percentages were to rise over ten years, to 20 percent by 1937.

The result was a sharp rise in the demand for British films. American companies distributing their output in the United Kingdom needed to buy or make films there to meet the quota, and English importers also needed to have a certain amount of domestic footage on offer.

The quota was largely responsible for the British cinema's expansion during the early 1930s. In fact, production increased so much that the quota was consistently exceeded. A considerable portion of production, however, was devoted to making "quota quickies"—cheap, short films that barely met the legal requirements for a feature. Many quota quickies sat on distributors' shelves, virtually unseen, or made up the second half of double features; spectators often walked out after seeing the American film. One estimate in 1937 suggested that half again as many features were released in the UK as in America, even though the British market was not even a third the size of the American market.

The British studio system came to resemble a less stable version of Hollywood's. There were a few large, vertically integrated companies, several midsize firms without theaters, and many small independent producers. Some firms, particularly the smaller ones, concentrated on quota quickies. Other British firms opted to produce films with moderate budgets, aimed at generating a modest profit solely in Britain. A few tried the strategy of making expensive films, hoping to break into the American market. Although all these companies competed with each other to some extent, they formed a

Fig. 11.1 An aerial view of British International Pictures' studio complex, built in 1926 and expanded after the coming of sound.

Fig. 11.2 Alfred Hitchcock, leaning on the railing in the foreground, directs *Sabotage* (1936) in one of the large street sets built for the film at Gaumont-British's Lime Grove Studios, Shepherd's Bush.

loose oligopoly. Bigger firms commonly rented studio space to each other and to small independents. The quota requirements made room for all.

The two main firms, Gaumont-British and British International Pictures (BIP) had been formed during the silent era but now expanded significantly. BIP's new studio (Fig. 11.1) was the biggest of several in the London suburb of Elstree, which came to be called "the British Hollywood." (As in Los Angeles, the other British studios were scattered about the outskirts of London.) Both firms practiced a division of labor similar to that used in the Hollywood system, though BIP was particularly noted for its rigid adherence to production roles and lack of emphasis on creativity by individual employees. Both had extensive backlots where large sets could be built (Figs. 11.1, 11.2). Gaumont-British and BIP were roughly comparable to the Hollywood Majors in that both were vertically integrated, distributing films and owning theater chains.

There was also a group of smaller firms, somewhat similar to Hollywood's Minors: British and Dominion (headed by Herbert Wilcox), London Film Productions (Alexander Korda), Associated Talking Pictures (Basil Dean). All produced, some distributed, but none owned theaters. Wilcox's policy was to make modest films in his studio at Elstree, targeting the British market. Dean called Associated Talking Pictures' Ealing facility "the studio with the team spirit," encouraging filmmakers to make high-quality pictures, often from stage plays.

Korda was the most prominent and influential of these producers in the early 1930s. A Hungarian émigré who had already produced and directed in Hungary, Austria, Germany, Hollywood, and France, he formed London Film in 1932 to make quota quickies for Paramount. Soon, however, he switched

Fig. 11.3 Lavish sets and crowd scenes re-created the French Revolution in Korda's production *The Scarlet Pimpernel.*

to a big-budget approach, hoping to crack the American market. He leased a studio and in 1933 contracted to make two films for United Artists. The first, *The Private Life of Henry VIII* (1933, Korda) provided a breakthrough for Korda and the British film industry. Enormously successful at home, its profits in the United States topped those of any previous British release. Charles Laughton won a best-actor Academy Award and became an international star. United Artists signed to distribute sixteen more Korda films.

Korda continued making expensive costume pictures, and some other producers imitated him. Korda's fourth film for UA, *The Scarlet Pimpernel* (1935, Harold Young), was a hit second only to *Henry VIII*. Leslie Howard became known abroad for his portrayal of the seemingly foppish Sir Percy Blakeley, who secretly rescues aristocrats from the guillotine in Revolutionary France (Fig. 11.3). At Denham, Korda built Britain's largest studio complex in 1936. Only a few of his epics were spectacularly profitable, however. *Things to Come* (1936, William Cameron Menzies) was set in the space-age future, after a disastrous war. The high budget required for the fanciful sets and costumes prevented the film from returning its costs.

The Private Life of Henry VIII started a brief boom in British production. Financiers eagerly provided backing, hoping for more American profits. The most significant figure to take advantage of the new prosperity was J. Arthur Rank, one of the entrepreneurs who started British National Films in 1934. He quickly moved toward vertical integration in 1935 by forming General Film Distributors and building the huge Pinewood Studios. (Pinewood remains one of the world's major production centers; several of the James Bond and Superman films were shot there more recently.) Within a decade, Rank's empire would become the most important force in the British film industry.

The production boom made higher-quality filmmaking possible. In 1931, Gaumont-British gained control of a smaller firm, Gainsborough. With it came the talented producer, Michael Balcon, who supervised filmmaking for both companies. Despite pressure from the owners to make films with "international" appeal, Balcon favored fostering distinctive stars and directors who could make specifically British films. These often did better than some of the more expensive, but lifeless, costume films. For example, Gaumont-British made musicals starring the popular Jessie Matthews. Her biggest international hit was *Evergreen* (1934, Victor Saville), in which she plays both the Edwardian music-hall star Harriet Green and her daughter. Years after the mother's retirement and death, the daughter masquerades as the mother, gaining enormous publicity by playing the apparently unaging star (who is "ever green"; Fig. 11.4).

Balcon also signed Alfred Hitchcock to a contract with Gaumont-British. Since his success with the early talkie *Blackmail* (p. 226), Hitchcock had moved from company to company, trying several genres, including comedies and even a musical. At Gaumont-British (and its subsidiary Gainsborough), he returned to his element, making six thrillers, from the *The Man Who Knew Too Much* (1934) to *The Lady Vanishes* (1938). Hitchcock would become identified with this genre throughout his long career.

One of Hitchcock's strengths was his ability to frame and edit shots in such a way as to allow spectators to grasp characters' thoughts. In *Sabotage* (1935), for example, there is a virtuosic scene in which a woman has just learned that her husband is a foreign agent and has accidently caused the death of her brother. A lengthy series of shots shows her serving dinner, while anguishing over her brother's death (Figs. 11.5–11.10).[2] Hitchcock's use of characters' points of view would remain a defining stylistic trait throughout his career.

Hitchcock's thrillers were also notable for their humor. In *The 39 Steps* (1935), the innocent hero is accused of a murder and flees handcuffed to a woman who believes him guilty. This situation leads to amusing complications

Fig. 11.4 *Evergreen* began diminutive song-and-dance star Jessie Matthews's reign as queen of the British musical.

Figs. 11.5–11.10 Part of a series of shots in Hitchcock's *Sabotage* that uses subtle variations in framing and eyeline direction. The heroine glances at her brother's chair and is tempted to stab her husband, who caused the boy's death.

Fig. 11.5

Fig. 11.6

Fig. 11.7

Fig. 11.8

Fig. 11.9

Fig. 11.10

and, inevitably, to romance. *The Lady Vanishes* contains similar lighthearted sparring between the hero and heroine, as well as a subplot concerning a pair of obsessive cricket fans who ignore all dangers while trying to learn the outcome of the latest match.

Delightful though Hitchcock's English thrillers are, they betrayed their low budgets and technical limitations. Hitchcock wanted access to better studio facilities and to more dependable financing. In 1939, he signed a contract with David O. Selznick to make films in Hollywood. Beginning with *Rebecca* (1940), which won an Oscar as best picture, Hitchcock did well and stayed there throughout his long career.

The British production boom suffered a severe setback in 1937. Several producers had received extensive investments and loans but had few profitable films. As a result, many sources of funding dried up, and responsible production firms suffered along with opportunists. Alexander Korda's policy of big-budget films had been only partially justified. Despite a few notable successes, the American market remained largely closed to British imports. Moreover, the Quota Act of 1927 was due for renewal. There had been much criticism of the original quota for encouraging quickies. Uncertain over what the new quota would require, producers delayed projects. Feature output sank during the 1937–1938 crisis.

This crisis triggered changes in the industry. Partly as a result of his extravagance, in late 1938 Korda lost his financial backing. London Film's main asset, the huge Denham studio, passed into the control of Rank's growing empire. Korda continued producing films, now having to rent space in Denham. During World War II he spent three years in Hollywood as an independent producer; his films there included Ernst Lubitsch's satire on Naziism, *To Be or Not to Be* (1942). After the war, Korda returned to reorganize London Film Productions. He produced a number of important films up to his death in 1955, but none so influential as some of those he had made in the 1930s.

The crisis also drove Basil Dean out of film production in 1938. Michael Balcon, after spending an unsatisfying year supervising quota films for MGM, took over Associated Talking Pictures and renamed it Ealing Studios. He continued producing quality films on a small scale, a policy that would gain prominence after the war with successful comedies.

Britain's crisis diminished after Parliament passed the Quota Act of 1938. It specified that higher-budget films would count double or in some cases triple toward satisfying quota requirements. The output of quota quickies declined as both British and American producers attempted to make or purchase films of higher quality to qualify for extra quota credit.

Film magnate J. Arthur Rank had come through the crisis relatively unscathed, and he rapidly added to his holdings. In 1939, he moved further into vertical integration by purchasing part interest in Odeon Theatres, one of the largest cinema circuits in the UK. Over the next few years Rank acquired or built studios until his companies owned over half of Britain's production space. In 1941, he gained controlling interest in Odeon Theatres and Gaumont-British. Rank also formed Independent Producers, an umbrella company to fund the films of several small firms. From 1941 to 1947, companies in Rank's conglomerate financed about half the films made in Britain.

Due to the high level of production in Britain during the 1930s, many negligible films were inevitably made. The quota quickies were not entirely pointless, however. For one thing, they kept employment in the film industry high, despite the Depression. For another, they provided a training ground for important directors—just as films made in Hollywood's B units and Poverty Row studios did. Michael Powell, one of the most important directors of the 1940s and 1950s, worked extensively in cheap quota films. In *The Night of the Party* (1934, Gaumont-British), using a script which he later called a "piece of junk,"[3] Powell scraped together a cast from the stars under contract to the studio and created a bizarre and amusing film running a mere sixty-one minutes.

Fig. 11.11 Michael Redgrave as the hero of Carol Reed's *The Stars Look Down*, in a scene shot in a Cumberland mining village.

Beyond the quota quickies, many solid, middle-budget films were made. These often starred music-hall performers, such as George Formby and Jack Hulbert. They had a huge following in Britain, but their brand of humor could not be understood elsewhere. These unpretentious pictures also gave rise to significant filmmakers. For example, future director David Lean was working during the 1930s as an editor. Carol Reed got his start making films for Basil Dean's Associated Talking Pictures. His breakthrough came with the more ambitious *The Stars Look Down*, made in 1939 for a small independent firm. It drew upon important traditions of British documentary and leftist filmmaking (Chapter 14) to depict the plight of oppressed coal miners and to advocate the nationalization of the industry. At the beginning, a narrator's voice says, "This is a story of simple working people." Location filming in Cumberland lent the film authenticity (Fig. 11.11), and the climactic coal-mine disaster was convincing, despite being shot in studio sets.

By the end of the 1930s, Britain's industry had passed through its crisis, and the industry's situation looked promising. World War II was to give it a further boost.

THE EFFECTS OF THE WAR

For the United Kingdom, the war began on September 3, 1939. Anticipating immediate German bombing, the government closed down all film showings and production. Soon it became clear that such measures were unnecessary, and theaters reopened. Military officials did, however, requisition many of the country's film studios for such wartime uses as supply warehouses. Some of the industry's personnel also went into military service.

Such problems were balanced, however, by a sharp rise in attendance, as people sought to escape the privations of wartime. Theaters stayed open even during the worst nights of the Battle of Britain in August and September 1940, when many London citizens slept on the Underground's platforms to avoid the bombing. Despite such hardships, weekly attendance rose from 19 million in 1939 to 30 million in 1945.

The Ministry of Information encouraged wartime filmmaking. It required that all film scripts be checked to make sure that they in some way supported the war effort, and producers patriotically cooperated in creating a positive image of Britain. There was little stifling of creativity. The Ministry of Infor-

Fig. 11.12

Fig. 11.13

Figs. 11.12 and 11.13 The contrast of an idyllic family picnic and a distant aerial combat in *In Which We Serve.*

Fig. 11.14 A scene during the bombing of London in the same film.

mation even put money into some commercial films. Wartime austerity also made it undesirable to spend money on imported films. Moreover, the new quota was still in effect, and British films were in demand. Due to the lack of studio space and personnel, however, far fewer films were made during the war. From between 150 and 200 annually during the mid-1930s, production sank to just under 70 films a year.

Due to cutbacks on quota quickies, the average budget and quality rose. Some of these films were polished studio productions comparable to Hollywood's. For example, Thorold Dickinson made *Gaslight* (1940) for Rank's main production firm, British National. A melodrama concerning a wife's well-founded fears that her husband is trying to drive her mad, the film used a tight script, three-point lighting, large sets, and other Hollywood-style techniques. Indeed, a version of the same story was made in 1944 at MGM by George Cukor.

Several independent production companies came to prominence during the war. In 1942, an Italian émigré, Filippo del Guidice, formed Two Cities and persuaded the renowned actor and playwright Noel Coward to script, direct, and star in a film. *In Which We Serve* centers on the crew of a British ship sunk by the Germans. While the survivors cling to a life raft, flashbacks tell their stories, focusing on the upper-class captain, a middle-class officer, and a working-class sailor.

In Which We Serve (co-directed by David Lean) emphasizes the parallels among these characters. In one scene, as the captain and his wife and children picnic in the south of England, he watches a dogfight between British and German planes in the sky high above (Figs. 11.12, 11.13). The wife wistfully remarks that she tries to think of the fights as games so that they won't bother her. Shortly thereafter, in a scene set in the London home of the middle-class officer, his wife and mother-in-law hear bombers approaching. The wife remarks in an annoyed tone, "Oh, there they are again," but soon a low angle shows the two women listening worriedly to the whine of the bomb that will soon kill them (Fig. 11.14). Such scenes contribute to the film's treatment of the war as a daily problem for all classes, sometimes remote and sometimes suddenly dangerous.

The popular and profitable *In Which We Serve* attracted Rank, who gained control of Two Cities in exchange for an agreement to finance its subsequent films. These included Lean's *This Happy Breed* (1944), an adaptation of Coward's play *Blithe Spirit* (1945, Lean), and Laurence Olivier's first directorial effort, a patriotic Technicolor adaptation of Shakespeare's *Henry V* (1945). Olivier began the film with a "flying" shot over an elaborate model of Renaissance London, moving down into the Globe Theatre. The opening scenes take place on a reconstruction of the Globe's stage (Color Plate 11.1). Then, as in the play, the narrator's voice urges us to imagine the wider settings of the historical action, and the bulk of the film occurs in stylized studio sets based on medieval illuminated manuscripts. The rousing Battle of Agincourt was the only portion shot entirely on location. *Henry V* celebrated England's ability to triumph against superior forces.

One small but important production firm was The Archers, formed by the team of Michael Powell and Emeric Pressburger. After directing quota quickies, Powell made his first major film *The Edge of the World* (1937). Shot on a remote island off the western coast of Scotland, it showed how young people's migration into urban areas was depopulating the region. Hungarian-born Pressburger had scripted five Powell-directed films prior to the formation of The Archers. The most prominent of these was *49th Parallel,* a war film financed by the Ministry of Information and J. Arthur Rank. It traces the episodic progress of a band of Nazi infiltrators traveling across Canada. The group's members are gradually killed or captured as they meet resistance from a disparate series of Canadian citizens, including a French-Canadian trapper, a British esthete (Fig. 11.15), and a Canadian hitchhiker. *49th Parallel* was unusual for wartime propaganda, characterizing the German soldiers as fallible individuals rather than inhuman beasts and even making one of them a positive figure.

Fig. 11.15 In *49th Parallel,* Leslie Howard plays a British intellectual escaping by camping in the Canadian wilderness. Nazis who invade his camp and burn his Picasso painting and copy of Thomas Mann's *The Magic Mountain* goad him to defend democracy.

In 1943, Powell and Pressburger formed The Archers, financed initially by Rank's new Independent Producers Ltd. Rank offered them considerable freedom. Their first Archers film, *The Life and Death of Colonel Blimp,* followed a model British soldier through three wars. The film was somewhat critical of the current government, positing that traditional English values of fair play that had served in earlier combats were inadequate for the threat posed by the barbaric Nazis. Like *49th Parallel,* it contained a German character who appears in a largely sympathetic light, maintaining his friendship with the hero despite their being on opposite sides.

Colonel Blimp was the first of fourteen films that were to carry the credit "Written, produced and directed by Michael Powell and Emeric Pressburger." Although Powell was the director, the phrase indicated that the two were equal partners. Their films were often extremely romantic and even melodramatic, yet outlandish twists of narrative and style set them apart from conventional studio films. *A Canterbury Tale* (1944), for example, a patriotic story set in the traditional center of the Anglican church, has three narrative strains, one of which focuses on a local magistrate who creeps about pouring glue into the hair of young girls to keep them from distracting soldiers. The collaboration of Powell and Pressburger would remain fruitful until 1956. Indeed, in general the strength that the British film industry gained in the 1930s and during World War II carried over briefly, until the early 1950s.

INNOVATION WITHIN AN INDUSTRY: THE STUDIO SYSTEM OF JAPAN

Britain's studios failed to achieve the stability of Hollywood's, but Japan succeeded. The industry's growth after the 1923 earthquake and the advent of talking pictures strengthened a studio system much like America's.

Two large, vertically integrated companies, Nikkatsu and Shochiku, dominated several smaller firms. Despite the Depression and the increased expense of sound-film production, feature output remained high (400 to 500 per year in the early 1930s), and new theaters were constantly built. Most important, Japan was virtually the only country in which U.S. films did not overshadow the domestic product. Nikkatsu and Shochiku could profit from showing Hollywood films in their theaters while limiting American penetration of the market.

A third major player entered the game in 1934. Ichiro Kobayashi was a show-business entrepreneur who mounted extravagant stage revues. He formed Toho ("Tokyo Takarazuka Theater Company") by buying and merging two small companies specializing in talkies. Along with creating Toho as a production firm, Kobayashi erected movie theaters in Japan's major cities.

While bringing Toho's production up to speed, Kobayashi used imported films to build up attendance at his theaters. He also hired many major directors, such as Teinosuke Kinugasa and the swordfight specialist Masahiro Makino. Toho became Shochiku's chief competitor. Nonetheless, the two vertically integrated companies cooperated to keep Hollywood at bay. Shochiku began to buy up smaller firms to keep pace with Toho, and the expenses of sound filming forced marginal production houses out of business. The industry consequently became more centralized in the course of the 1930s, with three majors and six to ten lesser firms.

The audience's appetite for films remained keen. The Depression was easing by the mid-1930s, and movies had become a central part of urban life. After the 1923 earthquake, the rebuilding of Tokyo had created a westernized popular culture, and the passion for western clothes, jazz, whiskey, and fads continued throughout the 1930s. Japanese moviegoers were as familiar with Harold Lloyd and Greta Garbo as they were with their own stars.

In the same period, Japan embarked on ambitious military plans. The nation was Asia's dominant power, having defeated China and Russia in war and having annexed Korea. As political parties proved ineffectual, military factions gained influence in government. Some officers argued that modern Japan had to expand its markets and its sources of labor and materials. In 1932 Japan announced its imperialist aims by invading Manchuria.

The search for "national autonomy" led to government regulation of the economy under a declared "emergency"—one that was to last for thirteen years. At first, however, filmmaking and other aspects of popular culture were comparatively unaffected. Censorship was tightened somewhat, but on the whole the genres that had flourished in the 1920s continued to be exploited.

POPULAR CINEMA OF THE 1930s

The historical film *(jidai-geki)* was still the realm of swordfights, chases, and heroic deaths. The directors Daisuke Ito and Masahiro Makino continued to contribute to the genre, encouraging filmmakers to use rapid cutting and imaginatively staged fight scenes. Among the many satires of the *chambara* was Toho's *Enoken as Kondo Isamu* (Fig. 11.16).

More psychologically oriented *jidai-geki* began to come from younger directors such as Hiroshi Inagaki and Mansaku Itami (*Kakita Akanishi*, 1936). The most prominent member of this group was Sadao Yamanaka. His *A Pot Worth a Million Ryo* (1935) is a warm comedy in which a gruff samurai befriends an orphan. *Humanity and Paper Balloons* (1937), Yamanaka's most famous film, shows a masterless samurai *(ronin)* unable to find work and eventually driven to suicide. Yamanaka filmed this quietly ironic tale in a distinctive manner, with low camera positions, deep perspectival framings,

Fig. 11.16 The popular vaudeville comedian Enoken plays a reluctant swordsman.

Fig. 11.17 The atmospheric tenement setting of the opening discovery of the suicide in *Humanity and Paper Balloons.*

and somber lighting (Fig. 11.17). This was Yamanaka's last film; drafted and sent to the Chinese front, he died there in 1938.

The *gendai-geki,* or contemporary-life film, included many genres: student and salaryman comedies, the *haha-mono* ("mother film"), and the *shomin-geki,* the film about lower-class life. From the early 1930s through the war, these and kindred genres were the bulwark of the major studios. Shochiku's stars Kinuyo Tanaka and Shin Saburi and Toho's Hideko Takamine and Setsuko Hara made their reputations in these unpretentious films portraying work, romance, and family life in Japan's cities and towns.

Yasujiro Shimazu had helped create Shochiku's "*Kamata* flavor," an atmosphere of poignant cheerfulness associated with the *gendai-geki* made in the firm's suburban Tokyo studio, and he continued it in such lighthearted talkies as *Our Neighbor Miss Yae* (1934). Heinosuke Gosho, formerly Shimazu's assistant, carried on the Shochiku tradition in the early sound comedies *Madam and Wife* (1931; see p. 228) and *The Bride Talks in Her Sleep* (1933), as well as in the melodramas *The Dancing Girl of Izu* (1933) and *Woman of the Mist* (1936; Fig. 11.18). In such films Gosho won fame as a master of the *shomin-geki.*

Also working in the *gendai-geki* was Mikio Naruse. He started at Shochiku with salaryman films and contemporary comedies before discovering his more astringent, pessimistic tone. *Apart from You* (1933), *Nightly Dreams* (1933), and *Street without End* (1934) won critical praise despite their bleak look at prostitutes, sailors, and struggling single mothers. These melodramas established Naruse as an outstanding director of actresses and, in their lengthy dissolves and brooding close-ups, revealed his ability to build up a sense of society's suffocating pressures on women (Fig. 11.19).

Moving to Toho, Naruse quickly established himself with a series of feminine dramas. The most famous was *Wife, Be Like a Rose!* (1935), an urban comedy which modulates into harsh melodrama. Kimiko has picked out a young man to marry, but she must locate her runaway father. She talks him into returning for her wedding. The confrontation of the father and the

Fig. 11.18 A young woman in love with a student discovers that he is not interested in her *(Woman of the Mist).*

Fig. 11.19 *Street without End:* The young wife, spurned by her husband's family, goes to his sickbed.

Fig. 11.20 A high-angle shot of the daughter's grief in *Wife, Be Like a Rose!*

Fig. 11.21 A characteristic Shimizu track-back from marching students drilling during a country outing *(Star Athlete).*

high-strung mother who secretly wants him back shows Naruse's skill in handling complex emotional situations (Fig. 11.20). The film's last shots, tracking in and out on Kimiko and her mother, abandoned by the father once more, intensify our awareness that Kimiko's marriage will be devoted to taking care of her mother. *Wife, Be Like a Rose!*—one of the few Japanese films of the 1930s to be seen in the west—won critical accolades and established Naruse as a major director.

The successes of Yamanaka, Gosho, and Naruse confirmed studios in their policy of encouraging directors to specialize in certain genres and to cultivate personal styles. This practice differentiated the company's product and fed fans' interest. In addition, many of the *gendai-geki* directors had started in the 1920s, when genre innovations and stylistic originality were prized. As a result, Japanese films of the 1930s experimented with storytelling and technique to a degree not common in most western sound cinema. For example, Tomu Uchida's *Police* (1933) presents a plot straight out of Warner Bros. (two old friends from the neighborhood, one a cop, the other a gangster) but enlivens it with bold compositions, bursts of hand-held camerawork, and rapid intercutting between past and present.

Hiroshi Shimizu, another exponent of humanistic comedy, also displayed a distinctive style. His films centering on children (e.g., *Four Seasons of Children,* 1939) won him most fame, but he also excelled at adult subjects, as seen in *Arigato-San (Mr. Thank You,* 1936) and *Star Athlete* (1937). Shimizu's stylistic signature is the shot in which the action moves straight at or away from the viewer, while the camera tracks backward or forward to keep up with the figure (Fig. 11.21). Shochiku's flexible policy allowed Shimizu to travel across Japan in search of ideas, shooting films on location from sketchy notes rather than scripts. The arrangement proved productive: between 1924 and 1945 Shimizu directed an astonishing 130 films.

By common consent, the two most influential Japanese directors of the 1930s were Yasujiro Ozu and Kenji Mizoguchi. They contrasted in almost every way. Ozu worked only for Shochiku, while Mizoguchi began with Nikkatsu and became a free-lance. Ozu started in comedies and *shomin-geki,* and he maintained an everyday humor in virtually all of his films. Mizoguchi, whose first films were melodramas, probed every situation for grim psychological and social implications. Ozu was a master of editing and the static, closely framed shot, while Mizoguchi cultivated a style of long-shot framings, long takes, and camera movements. On the set Ozu was quietly insistent, while Mizoguchi exploded into demonic tantrums. Ozu and Mizoguchi illustrate how the Japanese studio system permitted directors an enormous range of originality. (See Box.)

Avoiding the strict division of labor practiced in Hollywood, Shochiku and Nikkatsu had cultivated a "cadre" system in which the director and scriptwriter had considerable control over their projects. Oversight tended to be even less stringent at smaller firms. Toho favored a "producer" system, which, like that of Hollywood in the 1930s, made a producer supervise several directors at the same time. While Toho films did have a somewhat more glossy mass-manufactured look, directors could still work in idiosyncratic ways at most studios before 1938. After that, they had to face the demands of a nation engaged in total war.

YASUJIRO OZU AND KENJI MIZOGUCHI

At age twenty-four Ozu began directing with a *jidai-geki*, but he quickly turned to the film of contemporary life. Between 1928 and 1937 he made thirty-five features, running the gamut from student slapstick (*Days of Youth*, 1929) and urban comedy of manners (*An Introduction to Marriage*, 1930) to gangster movie (*Walk Cheerfully*, 1930). He made his fame with two salaryman films (*Tokyo Chorus*, 1931; *I Was Born, But . . .*, 1932) and consolidated it with three masterpieces of 1933 (*Woman of Tokyo, Dragnet Girl*, and *Passing Fancy*). His first sound feature was *The Only Son* (1936), a *shomin-geki* about a mother following her son to Tokyo to discover that he has not succeeded despite the education she has drudged for years to provide. Ozu characteristically followed this quietly despairing film with a lighthearted satire on the wealthy classes, *What Did the Lady Forget?* (1937).

Ozu was deeply influenced by the Hollywood cinema, particularly the social comedies of Chaplin and Lubitsch and the gag comedies of Harold Lloyd. Like many Shochiku directors, he adopted the 1920s American comedy style—brief shots of actors and details of setting, edited together crisply and concisely. But Ozu extended this style in several ways. At unexpected moments he inserted shots of unobtrusive objects or adjacent landscapes (Fig. 11.22). In dialogue scenes, he systematically filmed from within a 360-degree circle surrounding the characters, changing the view by multiples of 45 degrees (usually 180 degrees). This strategy consistently violates Hollywood's traditional 180-degree continuity editing. He edited as much for visual pattern as for dramatic emphasis; his 360-degree cutting produces close "graphic matches" between two shapes. Figures 11.23 and 11.24 are a graphically continuous version of shot/reverse shot.

Fig. 11.23 In *Passing Fancy*, the man grabs the woman's arm as he faces her.

Fig. 11.24 Ozu cuts to a position 180 degrees opposite, showing the man on the other side.

Most strikingly, Ozu refused certain resources of film technique. He was the last major director to convert to sound. He also limited his use of camera movements. Above all, he restricted his camera position by filming only from a low height, regardless of subject. This tactic again allowed him to draw attention to the composition of the shot, balancing the dramatic value of the actor and the milieu with the purely visual design of the frame (Fig. 11.25).

Ozu's style amplified his intimate dramas. His comedies, like those of Lubitsch and Lloyd, are based on embarrassment and psychological revelation, qualities which could be sig-

Fig. 11.22 A boiling teakettle punctuates the drama in Ozu's *Woman of Tokyo*.

Fig. 11.25 Like the previous illustrations, this frame from *The Only Son* illustrates Ozu's low-height camera.

Fig. 11.27 Shirts on a clothesline are echoed by the salaryman as he exercises in the morning *(I Was Born, But . . .).*

Fig. 11.26 A cutaway to an industrial wasteland in *Inn in Tokyo* (1935).

Fig. 11.28 *Sisters of Gion:* Umikichi learns that her sister has been taken to the hospital.

naled by a judiciously placed close-up of an expression or a gesture. His social dramas, lingering on the cycle of life within an indifferent city, were intensified by enigmatic urban landscapes (Fig. 11.26).

Several of Ozu's films mix comedy and drama so thoroughly that the style alternates between humorous commentary and poetic abstraction. *I Was Born, But . . .*, for instance, is at once a satire on the bootlicking salaryman, a comedy about brattish children, and a sober study of lost illusions. At any moment, Ozu may create a low-key pictorial joke (Fig. 11.27). His films' poignant evocation of missed opportunities, regrets, and foreknowledge of separation is reinforced by a measured style that finds even the most mundane object an occasion for contemplation. Ozu's distinctive handling of narrative and technique influenced Yamanaka, Shimizu, and Naruse.

Mizoguchi began directing five years before Ozu. In the high-output 1920s, his forty-two films established him as an eclectic director with artistic pretensions. He made melodramas, crime dramas, even imitations of German Expressionism, but he did not become recognized as a major director until the 1930s.

Across a variety of genres, Mizoguchi concentrated on the social dilemmas facing the Japanese woman. In *White*

Fig. 11.29 Ashamed, Ayako shrinks away from her lover, and from the viewer *(Naniwa Elegy)*.

Fig. 11.31 . . . before she backs into the distant wall . . .

Fig. 11.30 In *The Downfall of Osen,* Osen's gangster lover goes in to her with a sword and the shot stands vacant for a moment . . .

Fig. 11.32 . . . and he confronts her.

Threads of the Waterfall (1933), a circus entertainer works to send a poor student to school; the lovers end by committing suicide. In *The Downfall of Osen* (1935) a gangster's girlfriend sends a young man to medical school; after he has become successful, he finds his benefactor in a railroad station, old and demented. In *Oyuki the Madonna,* modeled on Maupassant's "Boule de Suif," a prostitute gives her life to save a rebel leader. Mizoguchi's two outstanding melodramas of the mid-1930s, *Naniwa Elegy* (1936) and *Sisters of Gion* (1936), show women swapping sexual favors for power only to find that men will not honor their bargains. He later saw these two bitter films as marking the beginning of his

maturity: "It is only since I made *Naniwa Elegy* and *Sisters of Gion* that I have been able to portray humanity lucidly."[4]

Mizoguchi was drawn to situations of high emotion—men's sadistic abuse of women and children, women's distraught response to the threat of poverty or solitude, scenes of harsh bargaining and quarrels. But in filming he adopted what would, after World War II, be called a "dedramatizing" approach. His staging and framing put scenes of emotional intensity at a distance, inviting the spectator to react less viscerally to the material.

Mizoguchi thus tends to stage highly charged scenes in long shot (Fig. 11.28). Often the characters turn away from the viewer (Fig. 11.29), or they are hidden by a wall or a shadow (Figs. 11.30–11.32). Only at the end of *Naniwa*

Elegy and *Sisters of Gion* does Mizoguchi give us abrupt, intense close-ups of his protagonists, each woman challenging the audience to reflect on why she must suffer (Fig. 11.33).

Moreover, the camera records the action steadily, refusing to cut in to a character's reaction. To an unprecedented extent Mizoguchi exploits the long take. There are only 270 shots in *Oyuki*, fewer than 200 in *Naniwa Elegy*, and fewer than 125 in *Sisters of Gion*. Further, these long takes are seldom designed to follow the movements of the actors, as in the work of Ophüls and Welles. Mizoguchi's long takes force us to watch painful acts of self-sacrifice unfold at a relentless pace.

Ozu and Mizoguchi were among the most honored directors of their day, one representing the heights of the *shomin-geki*, the other exemplifying a prestigious cinema of social polemic. Their work suggests the richness of what came to be recognized as the first "golden age" of Japanese cinema.

Fig. 11.33 For the first time in the film, as Ayako is turned out into the streets by her family, we have a clear frontal view of her: the curt final shot of *Naniwa Elegy*.

THE PACIFIC WAR

Japan's all-out attack on China in 1937 marked the beginning of the war in the Pacific. The government banned existing political parties, tightened its alliance with Nazi Germany and Fascist Italy, and mobilized the home front around a war-based economy.

The film industry was slowly brought into line with the new policies. In this jingoistic atmosphere, western culture became suspect. Studios were ordered not to include jazz, American dancing, or scenes which might undermine respect for authority, duty to emperor, and love of family. In April 1939, Japan's Diet passed a law modeled on Goebbels's edicts to the Nazi industry. It called for nationalistic films portraying patriotic conduct. The Home Ministry established the Censorship Office, which would review scripts before production and order revisions where necessary.

American films were still playing in Japan, and some Japanese directors could dodge the terms of the 1939 Motion Picture Law. Still, political constraints were now much stronger than ever before. For instance, the Censorship Office rejected Ozu's script for *The Flavor of Green Tea over Rice* because the married couple's last meal was not the "red rice" traditionally reserved for seeing off a warbound husband.

As the Chinese war intensified, the government forced the film companies to consolidate. In 1941 authorities agreed to a three-part reorganization. One group was dominated by Shochiku, another by Toho, and a third, unexpectedly, by the small firm of Shinko. Shinko's key executive was Masaichi Nagata (who had produced Mizoguchi's *Naniwa Elegy* and *Sisters of Gion* for his independent firm Dai-Ichi Eiga). Nagata used the consolidation scheme to gain control over Nikkatsu, whose production facilities were absorbed into his group.

Nagata's group was renamed Daiei (for Dai-Nihon Eiga, or "Greater Japan Motion Picture Company"). Nikkatsu was allowed to keep its theater holdings separate, so Daiei initially had difficulties in exhibiting its product. After the war, Daiei would become Japan's major force on the international scene.

All companies participated in the war effort. The government supported the production of newsreels, documentary shorts, and films celebrating the uniqueness of Japanese art. The most elaborate example of the last category is Mizoguchi's *Story of the Last Chrysanthemum* (1939), an adaptation of a popular play. Kikugoro Onoe is expected to become a kabuki actor like his father and uncle, but he is a lackluster performer. When he takes up with the maid Otoku, his family disowns him. Her faith enables him to keep trying to perfect his art. At the climax, he gives a devastating performance and is hailed by the audience, while Otoku dies alone. The film won a prize from the Education Ministry.

Mizoguchi's sympathy for women, along with his interest in theatrical performance and stylization, makes *Last Chrysanthemum* one of his most important works. He continues to employ long takes, wide-angle lenses, dramatic chiaroscuro lighting, and slow rhythm. The camera, poised at a distance, often forces the viewer to scan the frame to pick out the significant action (Fig. 11.34).

Alongside tributes to the purity of Japanese culture were patriotic films supporting the war effort. Tomotaka Tasaka's *Five Scouts* (1939) set the pattern for subsequent efforts, stressing the unity of the fighting group and the quiet heroism of its members. As in many Japanese battle films, the enemy is not seen; war is not a sordid struggle among men but a test of the purity of the Japanese spirit. Tasaka's *Mud and Soldiers* (1939) and Kimisaburo Yoshimura's *Story of Tank Commander Nishizumi* (1940) continued to promote the image of the modest, humane Japanese soldier.

Fig. 11.34 Kikugoro's mother scolds him for associating with the maid Otoku, who watches apprehensively in the background.

Fig. 11.35 A stupendous gathering of the samurai in *The Abe Clan* (1938).

The *jidai-geki* adjusted to the war period by becoming more stately and grandiose. In *The Abe Clan* (1938) family honor vies with friendship in a setting that downplays violence and emphasizes the spectacular beauty and power of the martial code (Fig. 11.35). Contemporary-life films celebrated national ideals in a more prosaic way. Because of Kobayashi's ties to governmental agencies, Toho led the charge with stridently patriotic vehicles. Shochiku offered such films as Shimazu's *A Brother and His Younger Sister* (1939), in which a young man abandons petty office politics and carries his sister and mother off to a fresh start in China; a clod of earth clings to their plane wheel, bringing a bit of Japan to the world they are building.

In attacking American forces at Pearl Harbor in December 1941, Japan declared war on the United States and Britain. Japanese forces seized western colonies throughout the Pacific and soon dominated East and Southeast Asia. By mid-1942, Japan seemed a new imperial power, holding major islands as well as Siam, Burma, Singapore, Vietnam, Hong Kong, Taiwan, and major portions of China. Japan promised to lead the "Greater East Asia Co-Prosperity Sphere," but usually the Japanese occupation was at least as harsh as its colonial predecessors.

Full-scale war reduced resources on the home front. The government cut screenings to two and a half hours, rationed film stock, and limited studios to releasing two features per month. Production dwindled to about a hundred features in 1942, seventy in both 1943 and 1944, and fewer than two dozen in 1945. With most men drafted and most women working in factories or community groups, film attendance fell drastically.

Patriotic efforts became more shrill. Toho produced the extravaganza *The War at Sea from Hawaii to Malaya* (1942), directed by Kajiro Yamamoto and released on the first anniversary of the Pearl Harbor attack. The film's historical sweep and excellent miniatures and special effects made it an outstanding propaganda piece. Yamamoto exploits the unseen-enemy convention in a chilling scene: on the night before the Pearl Harbor attack Japanese sailors on a battleship listen quietly to a radio broadcast from an American nightclub. Other films celebrated kamikaze raids and the struggle against partisans in China.

Home-front films continued to emphasize patience, humility, and cheerful stoicism. In Naruse's *Hideko the Bus Conductor* (1941) the gracious heroine (played by the beloved Hideko Takamine) brightens her rural community. *A Diary of Our Love* (1941) shows a husband returning wounded from the war and being nursed back to health by his devoted wife. Shiro Toyoda's direction uses Mizoguchi's oblique, long-shot aesthetic to mute the sentimental story (Fig. 11.36).

In such films as *A Diary of Our Love* and Naruse's *Oh, Wonderful Life* (1944), a comic musical which occasionally reverses the sound track, directors continued to explore novel techniques. On the whole, however, most films of the 1939–1945 period are virtually indistinguishable from Hollywood or high-budget European films of the era. The seriousness of the war effort demanded noble, solemn technique, and the daring experimentation of the 1930s was felt to be frivolous. Even Ozu and Mizoguchi toned down their styles for their Pacific War efforts.

Ozu's output slackened in the war period, when he was repeatedly drafted. His only films were *Brothers and Sisters of the Toda Family* (1941) and *There Was a Father* (1942). The first, quite close in plot to Shimazu's *Brother and His Younger Sister*, shows an upper-class family recalled to its duty by the youngest members. While carrying a serious message, the film contains Ozu's characteristically quirky comedy. *There Was a Father* proved more severe; not a trace of humor enlivens this tale of a teacher who sacrifices himself to the greater national need.

Toda Family and *There Was a Father* contain much lengthier shots than Ozu had used before; the camera dwells on the actors' moments of deliberation and resignation. Ozu continues to exploit 360-degree shooting space, a quiet handling of dramatic moments (Fig. 11.37), and transitions composed of landscapes and objects (Fig. 11.38). After *There Was a Father*, Ozu went to Singapore to plan a battlefront film, but he was captured and spent the remainder of the hostilities as a prisoner of war.

Mizoguchi fared better. He was entrusted with one of the most prestigious projects of the war, a new version of a classic tale of self-sacrifice. *Genroku Chushingura* (aka *The Loyal Forty-Seven Ronin*) was shot in 1941,

Fig. 11.36 The husband in *A Diary of Our Love* watches his wife prepare his food, framed in a distant window.

Fig. 11.37 The decentered deathbed scene from *There Was a Father*, determined by Ozu's low camera height.

Fig. 11.38 Throughout *Brothers and Sisters of the Toda Family*, the changing of households by the mother and daughter is signaled by shots of their plants and bird.

Fig. 11.37

Fig. 11.38

Fig. 11.39

Fig. 11.40

Fig. 11.39 A retainer weeps while his lord goes into a garden to be executed (*Genroku Chushingura*).

Fig. 11.40 In a distant framing reminiscent of Mizoguchi's 1930s work, a woman struggles to keep her brother from assassinating Lord Kira (*Genroku Chushingura*).

with one part released in December and the second part two months later. It tells how a lord's retainers patiently suffer indignity before avenging his death.

Earlier film versions told the story with vigorous swordplay and overblown emotions. Predictably, Mizoguchi dedramatized the tale. For three hours he dwells on the ronin's slow preparation for the deed, their calm acceptance of their mission, and their resignation to their ultimate punishment. The long take is carried to extremes, with the entire film comprising only 144 shots (making each shot, on average, over ninety seconds long). The climactic battle takes place offscreen, recounted through a letter read by the lord's widow. Mizoguchi's long takes, monumental compositions, and majestic crane shots ennoble a drama of fidelity to duty (Figs. 11.39, 11.40).

After spending some months in China scouting a film, Mizoguchi returned to direct several films, including the *jidai-geki Musashi Miyamoto* (1944) and *The Famous Sword Bijomaru* (1945). Both betray the industry's paucity of means in the last phase of the war, and except for some very long takes, they are far more orthodox in style than *Genroku Chushingura*.

Of the several directors who made their debuts during the war, the most promising was Akira Kurosawa. A scriptwriter and assistant director at Toho, he worked for Yamamoto before being entrusted with directing *Sanshiro Sugata* (1943), a tale of martial arts set in the late nineteenth century. *Sanshiro* brings hurly-burly action back to the period film, which had become static and solemn under the influence of wartime ideology. The plot centers on a classic martial-arts conflict: Sanshiro, a hot-headed young judo fighter, must learn restraint under the guidance of a harsh but wise master. The combat sequences are handled with a kinetic bravura, using elliptical editing, slow motion, and sudden changes of angle (Figs. 11.41, 11.42). *Sanshiro Sugata* was a major influence on postwar *jidai-geki* films, and it was the ancestor of Hong Kong martial-arts films and the "spaghetti Westerns" of Sergio Leone.

The film's success led Kurosawa to make a sequel (*Sanshiro Sugata II*,

Fig. 11.41

Fig. 11.42

Fig. 11.41 One of Sanshiro's opponents is hurled endlessly through the air . . .

Fig. 11.42 . . . before crashing against a wall, causing a window frame to float down in slow motion *(Sanshiro Sugata).*

1945). More significant, however, was his second film, the home-front drama *The Most Beautiful* (1944). Several women are working at a plant which manufactures precision lenses for airplanes' gunsights. The plot shows in episodic fashion a string of personal dramas, some comic, some intensely serious. Lacking the physical exuberance of the judo films, *The Most Beautiful* reveals Kurosawa's interest in the psychology of stubborn, almost compulsive dedication to a social ideal. Both *Sanshiro* and *The Most Beautiful* fitted wartime ideology, but they also showed Kurosawa to be a virtuosic, emotionally intense director.

Gradually, three years of Allied "island hopping" pushed Japan's forces back. In August 1945, after months of firebombing Tokyo and other cities, U.S. planes dropped atomic bombs on Hiroshima and Nagasaki. Japan surrendered soon afterward.

Like most of the nation's institutions, the film studios were hard-hit, but even the devastation of the war and the reforms of American occupation could not loosen the major companies' control. The Japanese studio system would retain control for three more decades.

INDIA: MYTHOLOGICALS, DEVOTIONALS, SOCIALS

In India, with its twelve major languages and twenty secondary ones, the silent cinema was a widely accessible entertainment. The images carried the burden of the story, and the films took their plots from well-known tales in the epics *Ramayana* and *Mahabarata.* Although intertitles were in as many as four languages, and sometimes an explainer akin to the Japanese *benshi* accompanied screenings, the Indian silent film found a national audience. Following the work of D. G. Phalke in the 1910s (p. 48), several production companies sprang up in Bombay and Calcutta. By the mid-1920s, India was producing over a hundred feature films annually, more than England, France, or the USSR.

Indian producers sought to imitate Hollywood's studio system, but they could not achieve oligopolistic vertical integration. An attempt was made by Madan Theatres, the most powerful exhibition chain at the end of the 1920s. The firm bought American sound equipment and built a studio in the Calcutta suburb of Tollygunge (giving birth to the nickname "Tollywood"). Madan

Theatres released the first Indian talking films in 1931, but problems of cash flow forced Madan to sell its studio and most of its theaters. Thereafter, the Indian market would be a free-for-all in which production firms, distributors, and exhibitors vied for power.

The fragmentation of the market was increased by the coming of sound, which broke the national audience into language-based groups. Calcutta firms monopolized Bengali-language production, Bombay controlled production in Marathi, and both cities made films in Hindi, the principal language. Slowly some production emerged in Madras, specializing in southern languages.

At first, producers controlled the market. The earliest talking feature, the Imperial Film Company's *Alam Ara* ("Beauty of the World," 1931; Hindi language) proved a huge success, and other producers quickly converted to sound. The major firms were Prabhat, founded in 1929 and operating in a suburb of Bombay; New Theatres, founded in 1930 in Calcutta; and Bombay Talkies, founded in 1934. All were modeled on Hollywood studio complexes, with sound stages, laboratories, and commissaries. Although the producers sought to imitate Hollywood's efficient planning and scheduling, they prided themselves on running friendly, "one-big-family" operations.

By the mid-1930s, film companies were turning out a total of about 200 films a year, most of them in Hindi. Although the number of theaters increased throughout the 1930s and 1940s, it did not keep pace with the expansion of production or the growing urban population. Exhibitors competed frantically to show the most popular movies. Production companies manipulated the theater owners through block booking.

The success of the Indian talking picture owed much to its musical sequences. Folk performance and Sanskrit theater were based on music, and these traditions found their way into the cinema. For decades nearly all films, regardless of genre, contained song and dance interludes. An early and influential example is *Chandidas* (1932; Bengali language; Fig. 11.43). It featured both songs and a continuous musical background in the manner of Hollywood underscoring. Initially, most stars sang their own parts, but during the 1940s firms began to use "playback singers" who prerecorded the songs for the actors.

The genres of the 1930s had been established in the silent era. The "mythological" film, using a plot derived from legend and the literary epics, had been a mainstay since Phalke's day. More westernized were the stunt films, adventure stories modeled on Douglas Fairbanks and Pearl White. Most of these were cheap productions akin to Hollywood's B pictures; those featuring the masked outlaw woman Nadia were especially popular.

The "social" film, a romantic melodrama set in contemporary times, was introduced in the mid-1920s and became an important genre in the sound era. One of the most famous socials was New Theatres' *Devdas* (1935; Hindi), which used naturalistic dialogue to show the suffering of lovers torn apart by an arranged marriage. Other socials addressed contemporary problems of labor, the caste system, and sexual equality.

Another major genre was the "devotional," a biographical tale of a religious figure. The most popular example is *Saint Tukaram* (1937; Marathi), made by Prabhat. A poor villager who spends his days singing holy songs is persecuted by the corrupt Brahmin priest. Tukaram's faith creates several

Fig. 11.43

Fig. 11.44

miracles, and he is eventually taken to Nirvana in a heavenly chariot (Fig. 11.44). The hero's gentle personality, the understated performances, and the lyrical beauty of the songs, nearly all composed by the historical saint, led many critics to judge *Saint Tukaram* the masterpiece of 1930s Indian film-making.

By 1939, the nation's film industry was apparently robust. Although the market was still dominated by foreign films, the rise of the talkie had greatly increased audiences for Indian cinema. India had become the third-largest film producer in the world, and *Saint Tukaram* won a prize at the Venice Film Festival. The mobilization for World War II improved the national economy.

The wartime boom also revealed, however, that the film industry was fundamentally unstable. In search of quick profits, entrepreneurs began to form independent production companies, and black-marketeers used film projects to launder cash. The independents lured stars, directors, and song-writers away from the studios, often paying bonuses in under-the-table deals. Now the older firms had to compete for personnel, and a star might consume half a film's budget. The studios' one-big-family ideology collapsed when stars and creative personnel realized their market value. Moreover, the independents did not have to maintain the massive overhead which encumbered the studios; a producer would simply rent studio space and hire personnel as needed. Now that many more companies were offering films, distributors and theater owners could make the studios compete for screens.

The industry's failure to achieve vertical integration proved fatal to the big companies. Prabhat, New Theatres, and Bombay Talkies continued to make films throughout the war, but their power ebbed. Only the government's wartime restrictions on investment and raw film stock kept the "mushroom producers" from overrunning the market. Once the war was over, black-market profiteering ran unchecked. Although film production expanded and became even more significant internationally, India's studio system was at an end.

Fig. 11.43 *Chandidas:* The low-caste woman sings with the holy man before his altar.

Fig. 11.44 The bird-chariot that carries the hero to heaven at the climax of *Saint Tukaram.*

CHINA: FILMMAKING CAUGHT BETWEEN LEFT AND RIGHT

For a brief period during the 1930s, Chinese film entrepreneurs struggled to create a small studio system in the face of serious difficulties. During the 1920s, Chinese production had mostly been spread among many small companies which made a few films before going out of business. The market was largely supplied by imports, principally U.S. films. In 1929, only 10 percent of the 500 films released were made in China. The introduction of sound, however, gave a little boost to domestic filmmaking. While educated urban audiences were used to western culture, many workers and peasants wanted more familiar fare and could not read subtitles.

There were two relatively large Chinese firms, though neither was vertically integrated. The Mingxing Film Company had been founded in 1922 in Shanghai, the center of Chinese film production. By the 1930s, it was the largest producer. In 1930, a former cinema owner started the Lianhua Film Company, Mingxing's primary competitor. There were also three small producers: Yihua (founded in 1932), Diantong (1934), and Xinhua (1935). For the most part these companies turned out melodramas patterned after popular literature.

The political temper of the times, however, injected controversy into this system. Jiang Jie-shi (Chiang Kai-shek) had seized power in a bloody coup d'état in 1927, establishing the right-wing Guomindong government. The government's forces were engaged in an armed conflict with Mao Ze-dong's Communist insurgents, who controlled portions of the country outside the largest cities. In 1931, when the Japanese invaded Manchuria and overran other portions of the country, Jiang Jie-shi mistakenly decided that it was more important to fight the Communists than the Japanese. In this atmosphere, a split developed between right-wing nationalists on the side of the Guomindong and leftists who, while not Communists, sympathized with the oppressed working and peasant classes.

These two groups struggled to control the output of the budding studios. In 1932, a Communist cultural group, the League of Left-Wing Writers, formed the Film Group to guide and encourage leftists in the film industry. Although most of the members were scenarists, many important actors and directors also belonged. They were not necessarily Communists but typically came from urban, middle-class backgrounds. They were thoroughly familiar with western filmmaking. Although they never came to dominate the film industry or have any real power, they were to create some of the decade's most significant films.

The right-wing nationalist government of Jiang Jie-shi set up strict censorship to control the cinema. As a result, leftists in the studios had to craft their films subtly to convey their ideas. The leader of the Film Group, scenarist Xia Yan, became head of the script team at the Mingxing company. His adaptation of a novel, *Spring Silkworms* (1933, Cheng Bugao), was the first major left-wing film of the decade. It follows the life of a peasant family during the yearlong cycle of raising worms and harvesting silk. Documentary-style scenes explaining the process are interspersed with scenes of family life; at the end, the family suffers through an unfair drop in the prices paid for silk. The emphasis on the dignity of labor and on the plight of peasants made this a controversial film. Although left-wing films were popular, they also created censorship problems. Xia Yan was fired from the Mingxing company the following year and moved to Lianhua.

The owner of the second-largest company, Lianhua, was loyal to the nationalist cause, and the Film Group found it harder to infiltrate the firm. Nevertheless, one of the three production units was dominated by leftists in the early 1930s. Lianhua produced two important liberal films in 1934. The first was *The Goddess,* written and directed by Wu Yonggang. In Chinese, "goddess" was the term for a prostitute, and the story treats the heroine in a straightforward fashion rather than creating a melodrama. She struggles against an unjust society, saving money to send her son through school; when her money is stolen, she kills the thief and her pimp. The second film, *The Highway* (aka *The Big Road,* directed by Sun Yu), follows a group of unemployed men as they get jobs constructing a road that will serve as a defense against the Japanese invaders. The film emphasizes their friendship and the joys of physical labor.

The three small companies reflected the struggle between right-wing and left-wing tendencies in more extreme ways. Yihua was dominated by members of the Film Group from its founding in 1932. The following year, right-wing extremists destroyed its filmmaking facilities, but the company rebuilt, producing more innocuous fare from 1934 on. The Diantong firm was even more overtly leftist in its orientation; after it had produced only four films, the government shut it down. Xinhua, founded in 1935 by right-wing extremists, met no opposition.

In 1937, the left-wing elements of the Chinese cinema seemed to be in resurgence. Xia Yan was rehired by the Mingxing company, which produced two extremely popular, controversial films. *Street Angels* (Yuan Muzhi) combined influences from Frank Borzage melodramas and René Clair musicals to portray the lives of an itinerant trumpet player and his friends, living opposite a prostitute and her sister. The cheerful treatment of the characters' lives is belied by the ending, in which the prostitute is killed by the gang that controls her, and the other characters are left with little hope of a better life.

Crossroads (Shen Xiling) follows the lives of four graduates who cannot find jobs (Fig. 11.45). The protagonist feuds with the unseen woman in the flat next to his, unaware that she is the worker he has been interviewing to write an exposé on factory conditions (and with whom he has fallen in love). The ending implies that the couple will go off to join the Communists in fighting the Japanese.

Such films suggest that the Chinese film industry might have expanded in the late 1930s. In 1937, however, the Japanese overran Shanghai. All the producers except Xinhua ceased production (Xinhua closed in 1942). China's filmmakers dispersed, some going to the few areas of the country under Communist control, others fleeing to Guomindong territory. Many of those who had worked at the Mingxing Film Company would become important filmmakers in the era just after the Communist Revolution of 1949.

Fig. 11.45 An ironic juxtaposition of a doll in a college graduate's gown with a Mickey Mouse figurine in the hero's apartment *(Crossroads).*

Our four examples—Britain, Japan, India, and China—indicate that studio systems of filmmaking could take many forms. A group of filmmaking firms could form a solid oligopoly, with some companies being vertically integrated. In Britain and Japan, the larger firms distributed their own films and owned theater chains. The scale of production and the power of domestically made films in the local market helped determine how stable such a system would be. India's studio system was more artisanal, with many producers competing against each other. Finally, the Chinese industry struggled to develop in a way that imitated western models, only to be overwhelmed by political circumstances. In the next chapter, we shall examine how other film industries functioned under political dictatorships.

◆ NOTES AND QUERIES

Japanese Cinema Rediscovered

Most of the Japanese films discussed in this chapter were unknown in the West before the 1970s. This was partly because the industry's output was almost completely destroyed—junked by the studios, obliterated in wartime bombardment, burned during the American occupation. We must judge Yamanaka on only two films, while only one of Mizoguchi's 1920s films survives intact. Several major Ozu, Kinugasa, and Mizoguchi titles are missing.

The meager access we have to the prewar Japanese cinema is a product of fairly recent interest. After World War II, critics in Europe and the United States knew Japanese cinema principally through Kurosawa's and Mizoguchi's 1950s work. These films quickly became examples of international "art cinema." (See Chapters 18 and 19.) French critics revered Mizoguchi as a director who exemplified the power of mise-en-scene, a quasi-mystical ability to stage a shot with evocative force. "He has," wrote Philippe Demonsablon, "one single aim: to render a note so pure and sustained that the smallest variation will be expressive."[5] In the late 1960s a few of Ozu's postwar works, notably *Tokyo Story* (1953), joined this select company.

In the early 1970s, more of the 1930s films returned to circulation, along with Kinugasa's *Page of Madness* (1926; p. 187). Retrospectives were held in London, New York, and Paris, while the Japan Film Library Council (later the Kawakita Memorial Film Institute) made prints available to universities and museums. It became evident that Ozu's and Mizoguchi's films of the 1930s and early 1940s were at least the equal of their postwar work and looked startlingly ahead to the "modern" cinema of 1960s Europe.

The reevaluation of the period was crystallized in Noël Burch's book *To the Distant Observer* (Berkeley: University of California Press, 1979). Burch treated the Japanese cinema of the 1920s and 1930s as a critique of western filmmaking, indeed of western conceptions of representation and meaning. His focus on style called attention to the non-Hollywood aspects of the films, which Burch traced to long-standing Japanese traditions in literature and the visual arts.

The 1980s saw retrospectives of Gosho, Naruse, and Shimizu and revived interest in the monumental *jidai-geki* of the late 1930s. Kurosawa's memoirs of the era were published in *Something Like an Autobiography*, tr. Audie E. Bock (New York: Knopf, 1982). An approach similar to Burch's was developed in David Bordwell's *Ozu and the Poetics of Cinema* (Princeton, N.J.: Princeton University Press, 1988) and Donald Kirihara's *Patterns of Time: Mizoguchi and the 1930s* (Madison: University of Wisconsin Press, 1992), though these authors emphasized the films' ties to contemporary popular culture and social change.

Film history remains a provisional discipline, highly dependent on what production companies and archives preserve. Despite gaps in our knowledge, however, Japanese cinema of the interwar era is clearly as important as that of the United States or Europe.

◆ REFERENCES

1. Quoted in Robert Murphy, "A Rival to Hollywood? The British Film Industry in the Thirties," *Screen* **24,** 4–5 (July–October 1983): 100.
2. Sequences of frames from this scene have been reproduced in prominent critical and analytical studies but in scrambled order and missing several shots. See François Truffaut, *Hitchcock* (New York: Simon and Schuster, 1966), pp. 77–79. (The photograph on p. 77 is a production still rather than a frame enlargement.) David A. Cook reproduces Truffaut's layout of illustrations, adding the claim that the production still is a frame, in his *A History of Narrative Film*, 2nd ed. (New York: Norton, 1990), pp. 343–344.
3. Michael Powell, *A Life in Movies: An Autobiography* (London: Heinemann, 1986), p. 231.
4. Quoted in Peter Morris, *Mizoguchi Kenji* (Ottawa: Canadian Film Archive, 1967), p. 10.
5. Quoted in *ibid.*, n.p.

12

CINEMA AND THE STATE: THE USSR, GERMANY, AND ITALY, 1930–1945

D uring the 1930s, left- and right-wing dictatorships controlled a few national film industries, most notably in the USSR, Germany, and Italy. The governments treated cinema as a medium of propaganda and entertainment, and both these functions continued under wartime conditions.

Governmental control took different forms. The film industries of the various countries that made up the USSR were nationalized when the Soviet government seized their property in 1919. That centralized control increased during the 1930s. State control could take other forms, however. The Nazi regime that came to power in Germany in 1933 supported capitalism, so it did not seize the privately owned film industry. Instead, the Nazis nationalized the industry by quietly buying companies. In Italy, the situation was quite different. There the government supported the industry and censored films, but it did not nationalize production.

THE SOVIET UNION: SOCIALIST REALISM AND WORLD WAR II

The First Five-Year Plan centralized the Soviet film industry under one company, Soyuzkino, in 1930 (pp. 152–153). The purpose was to make the industry more efficient and to free the USSR from having to import equipment and films. In order to dominate the home market, the film industry had to

Fig. 12.1 A heroic image of Soviet labor in *Men and Jobs.*

boost the number of films being made. By 1932, new factories were supplying the necessary raw stock, and the conversion to sound had been accomplished with little help from abroad (pp. 222–224). Low production and inefficiency, however, remained problems.

The period 1930–1945 also saw a tightening of controls on the types of films being made. Boris Shumyatsky became head of Soyuzkino at its formation. He was directly responsible to Josef Stalin, who took a great interest in the cinema. Shumyatsky favored entertaining and easily comprehensible films, and under his regime the avant-garde Montage movement died out. In 1935, he oversaw the introduction of the doctrine of Socialist Realism into the cinema.

FILMS OF THE EARLY 1930s

Before the introduction of Socialist Realism several significant films appeared. *Men and Jobs* (1932, Alexander Macheret) combined the Montage style with an emphasis on production reflecting the First Five-Year Plan. An American expert arrives to help build a dam. His initial condescension breaks down, and he decides to stay on and help the new Soviet state (Fig. 12.1). A stranger film was made by Alexander Medvedkin, who spent the early 1930s traveling in a train, shooting and showing films in villages throughout the Soviet Union. His early shorts made in this fashion do not survive, but his only feature, *Happiness* (1934), does. A peasant, Kymyr, resists the reforms of the Revolution and seeks happiness through personal wealth, while his oppressed wife, Anna, eventually enters a collective farm and persuades Kymyr to join her. Medvedkin uses comic exaggeration to portray the initial poverty of the couple and the stupidity of soldiers and priests (Fig. 12.2). Largely ignored in 1934, *Happiness* was revived in the 1960s, and critics recognized it as an important film.

Fig. 12.2 Stylization in *Happiness:* The hero and heroine's poverty leads their horse to graze on their thatched roof.

SOCIALIST REALISM AND *CHAPAYEV*

The central tenet of Socialist Realism was *partiinost'*—roughly, "party-mindedness." That is, artists had to propagate the Communist party's policies and ideology. The models for this were the European realist novelists of the nineteenth century. Authors like Balzac and Stendhal had criticized bourgeois society. Of course, Soviet authors were not supposed to be critical of socialist society. Unlike critical realism, Soviet realism was based on a second tenet: *narodnost'*. This untranslatable term ("people-centeredness") means that artists should depict the life of ordinary people in a sympathetic way.

Socialist Realist artworks were supposed to be free from "formalism," stylistic experiments or complexities that would make them hard to understand. Thus Socialist Realism ruled out the Montage style of filmmaking. In order to serve the party and the people, art was supposed to educate and provide role models, particularly in portraying a "positive hero."

The "realism" in Socialist Realism was based in part on Frederick Engels's equation of truth with the "reproduction of typical characters in typical circumstances." For Stalinists, "typical" designated traits associated with Communist ideals, not with the way things actually are. This means that many Socialist Realist artworks give an optimistic, idealized image of Soviet society, far removed from actual life under Stalin. As party goals changed over the years, so did Socialist Realism, and proper artistic methods were endlessly debated.

Although some traits associated with Socialist Realism had already appeared in cinema, the first film to provide a complete model of the new doctrine was *Chapayev* (1934, Sergei and Georgy Vasiliev). Based on a fictionalized account of an actual officer in the Civil War, *Chapayev* furnished a hero for audiences to admire. Moreover, Chapayev's cheerful, handsome assistant, Petja, is a "typical" (i.e., idealized) working-class figure with whom people could identify (Fig. 12.3). He provides a romantic subplot as well, flirting with Anna, a female soldier. In an association of romance and work that was common in Soviet films, the two fall in love as Petja teaches her to fire a machine gun. *Chapayev* told its story in simple terms. When Chapayev explains a point of military strategy to another officer, he lays out small potatoes to represent the soldiers, with a large potato for the commander (Fig. 12.4).

Chapayev was an enormous success, both with audiences and with film officials promoting Socialist Realism. Shumyatsky praised its concentration on individual characters, contrasting it with the mass heroes in Montage films of the 1920s. He also pointed out that the film does not hide the hero's faults. At first, Chapayev is shown as unschooled in military history, and he follows his own impulses rather than obeying orders calculated to benefit the Bolshevik cause. Shumyatsky declared that Chapayev "presents himself at the beginning of the film as a typical 'innate' Bolshevik."[2] Indeed,

Fig. 12.3 This framing of Chapayev and Petja against the sky became the single most famous image of the Soviet Socialist Realist cinema.

Fig. 12.4 Chapayev's use of potatoes to explain military technique showed how a film could employ familiar means of storytelling that peasants and workers could grasp.

Chapayev follows one of the most common patterns of Socialist Realist narratives, that of a protagonist who learns to subordinate his or her desires to the people's good. *Chapayev* became one of the most influential films in the history of the Soviet cinema.

THE DOCTRINE OF SOCIALIST REALISM

Socialist Realism was an aesthetic approach introduced at the 1934 Soviet Writers' Congress. A. A. Zhdanov, a cultural official, explained:

> Comrade Stalin has called our writers engineers of human souls. What does this mean? What duties does the title confer upon you?
>
> In the first place, it means knowing life so as to be able to depict it truthfully in works of art, not to depict it in a dead, scholastic way, not simply as "objective reality," but to depict reality in its revolutionary development.[1]

Writers and artists in all media were required to serve the Communist party's goals in their work and to follow a set of vague official tenets. This policy would remain more or less strictly in force until the mid-1950s. Film soon took up the new doctrine. (See Box.)

Artists were obligated to adhere to the policy of Socialist Realism. Stalin ruled as an absolute dictator, and harsh repression enforced government policy. The secret police ferreted out dissent in all walks of life. From the 1920s on there was a policy of "purges," whereby party members who were considered not to support Stalin wholeheartedly were expelled, imprisoned, exiled, or executed. This reign of terror peaked during 1936–1938, with "show trials" in which party leaders made scripted confessions that they had participated in "counter-revolutionary" activities.

Artists were not immune from such persecution. Eisenstein's early mentor, the foremost theatrical director of the 1910s and 1920s, Vsevolod Meyerhold, disappeared during the 1936–1938 purges. Major writers like Sergei Tretyakov and Isaac Babel were secretly executed. Artists such as composer Dmitri Shostakovich chafed under the Socialist Realist doctrine but had to obey it.

Socialist Realism became official policy in the cinema in January 1935, at the All-Union Creative Conference of Workers in Soviet Cinema. *Chapayev*, which had premiered only two months earlier, was referred to throughout the conference. By contrast, Eisenstein was singled out for attack, in an obvious effort to discredit the Montage movement. Other "formalist" directors were forced to admit past "mistakes"; Lev Kuleshov declared: "Like my other colleagues whose names are linked with a whole series of failed productions, I want, whatever the cost, to be, and I shall be, an outstanding revolutionary artist but I shall only be one when my flesh and blood, my whole organism and being are merged with the cause of the Revolution and the Party."[3] Despite this self-abasement, Kuleshov also offered an eloquent defense of the beleaguered Eisenstein.

Filmmakers could not hope to keep a low profile. Stalin was extremely interested in the cinema, viewing many films in his private quarters. Shumyatsky, as Stalin's direct representative, ruled the industry. There was an elaborate censorship apparatus, whereby film scripts had to be reviewed repeatedly before being accepted. After shooting began, films could also be revised or shelved at any stage. This cumbersome bureaucratic system, and the fact that most scripts were rejected, slowed output: throughout the 1930s, the number of finished films remained far below the total planned. A film might take years to make, undergoing minute ideological scrutiny. The most spectacular case of such interference came with Eisenstein's first Soviet sound project, *Bezhin Meadow,* which Shumyatsky shelved in 1937.

Relatively few filmmakers suffered the most extreme penalties of the purges. There were several victims, however. Critic and scenarist Adrian Piotrovsky, who had scripted Kozintsev and Trauberg's 1926 Montage film *The Devil's Wheel,* was arrested in 1938 and died in a prison camp. Cinematographer Vladimir Nilsen, a student of Eisenstein's, also disappeared. Konstantin Eggert, a traditional director, was prevented from making any films after 1935. Several other filmmakers suffered penalties.

Hoping to boost production and create a popular cinema, Shumyatsky decided to build a "Soviet Hollywood." He spent two months touring the American studios in 1935 and determined to replicate their technical sophistication and efficiency. His grand expansion project progressed during 1937, though it was never completed. Indeed, Shumyatsky never raised production to the level called for in the Five-Year Plans. While over a hundred films were scheduled in most years, actual release figures remained modest. After ninety-four films came out in 1930, the total steadily declined to a low of thirty-three in 1936 and averaged about forty-five for the next few years.

Ironically, the final result of Shumyatsky's policies was his own arrest in January 1938. One of the reasons cited for his removal from power was the waste of money and talent in the abandonment of *Bezhin Meadow.* He became the film world's most prominent victim of the purges later in 1938, when he was executed. From that point on, Stalin played an even more central role in making decisions about the ideological acceptability of films.

THE MAIN GENRES OF SOCIALIST REALISM

Chapayev's huge success made the Civil War film an important genre of Socialist Realist cinema. Although the Civil War had caused great hardships, many veterans looked back on it as a pre-Stalinist era when Communist goals were clear-cut and rapid changes were possible. *We from Kronstadt* (1936, Yefim Dzigan) is virtually a loose remake of *Chapayev,* except that it has a typical hero rather than one based on a historical figure. It is set in 1919, during heavy fighting around Kronstadt. The sailor Balachov is initially undisciplined, accosting a woman on the street and only reluctantly sharing his rations with the workers and children of nearby Petrograd. Gradually, after escaping execution by the White troops and enduring hardships in battle, he learns to fit selflessly into the Revolutionary cause (Fig. 12.5).

Chapayev also helped make the biographical film a major genre. Famous figures of the Revolution and Civil War eras were often the focus, but films dealt increasingly with great people of the pre-Revolutionary era, even tsars. Despite the fact that the USSR was supposedly becoming a classless society, this period saw the development of a "cult of personality." Stalin was hailed as the embodiment of Communist ideals, and his role in the Revolution was exaggerated by historians. Because Stalin saw parallels between himself and

Fig. 12.5

Fig. 12.6

great leaders of Russia's past, these men became suitable subject matter for laudatory films.

Important intellectuals who supported the Revolution could furnish the basis for biographical films. *Baltic Deputy* (1937, Alexander Zarkhi) is set directly after the October Revolution and gives a fictionalized account of an actual scientist who welcomed the Bolshevik regime, braving the scorn of his colleagues. In fact, many intellectuals had resisted the Revolution, and *Baltic Deputy* was designed to show that all classes could unite under communism. The elderly professor makes friends with a group of sailors (Fig. 12.6). In the end the professor's book is published, and Lenin sends him a congratulatory letter.

The writer Maxim Gorky was promoted as the greatest Socialist Realist author, with his 1906 novel *Mother* (the basis for Pudovkin's 1926 film) considered the model of the doctrine. After his death, three films based on Gorky's memoirs of his early life were made by Mark Donskoi (*Childhood of Gorky*, 1938; *Among People*, 1939; *My Universities*, 1940). The Gorky Trilogy stresses the hero's lack of formal education. Coming from a deprived background, he moves from job to job, encountering oppressive aspects of tsarist society but also occasionally finding people who resist—a kindly local chemist arrested for revolutionary activities, a crippled child who treasures the slightest pleasant moment. Near the end Gorky helps a peasant woman in labor in a field (Fig. 12.7). The Trilogy implies that Gorky's greatness as a writer arose from his close ties with the people.

Stalinist historians singled out two tsars, Ivan the Terrible and Peter I (known as "the Great"), as "progressive" rulers who carried out reforms that constituted important steps away from feudal society and toward capitalism. Their actions thus helped prepare the way for communism.

Vladimir Petrov's two-part epic, *Peter the First* (1937–1938) was the first tsarist film and established some important conventions. Although a

Fig. 12.5 Soviet films of the 1930s continued to use the dynamic low-angle framings that had originated in the silent era. This shot from *We from Kronstadt* suggests the protagonist's innate heroism.

Fig. 12.6 An idealistic image of solidarity across social classes, as the scientist-hero of *Baltic Deputy* lectures on botany to attentive Revolutionary sailors.

Fig. 12.7

Fig. 12.8

Fig. 12.7 The young Gorky walks along the shore triumphantly holding up a newborn baby. Despite the hardships that he has experienced, the ending implies that this child will grow up in the freedom created by the Revolution.

Fig. 12.8 Grotesque helmets dehumanize the Teutonic invaders in *Alexander Nevsky*.

monarch, Peter is also a man of the people. He leads armies in battle and makes shrewd diplomatic moves but is not above carousing in taverns with his men or hammering vigorously in a blacksmith shop. He teaches a class in navigation, dismissing a nobleman's lazy son and promoting a talented servant.

Such conventions appear again in the film that returned Eisenstein to the forefront of the Soviet cinema, *Alexander Nevsky* (1938). Nevsky was a medieval prince who had led a defense of Russia against European invaders. The similarities to the contemporary situation, with war threatening from Nazi Germany, made *Alexander Nevsky* a major patriotic project. The film's anti-German tone was clear (Fig. 12.8). At the end, Nevsky speaks directly into the camera: "Those who come to us with sword in hand will perish by the sword."

Eisenstein's first completed sound film fit into the doctrine of Socialist Realism: its narrative was simple and it glorified the accomplishments of the Russian people. Nevsky, like the young Gorky and Tsar Peter, mingles with the peasants and bases his final strategy on a joke he hears by a campfire. Eisenstein also managed, however, to preserve something of the fruits of Montage experimentation in the 1920s. There are frequently several shots of the same action with different framings, and many cuts yield discontinuities. The renowned sequence of the battle on an ice-covered lake is a virtuosic piece of extended rhythmic editing. The music by Sergei Prokofiev helped smooth over the eccentric editing style and enhanced the legendary, larger-than-life qualities of the film.

In early 1935, Stalin remarked to Dovzhenko, "Now you must give us a Ukrainian *Chapayev*."[4] The subject was to be the Ukrainian Civil War hero, Nikolai Shchors. Of course Dovzhenko took this suggestion as a mandate. Over the next few years he worked on the project, constantly scrutinized by Stalin and lesser officials. *Shchors* (1939) displays Dovzhenko's typical lyricism, especially in the startling opening scene of a battle erupting in a vast field of sunflowers (Fig. 12.9). His humor is also evident in the scene in which one of Shchors's officers solicits donations in a theater (Fig. 12.10).

Fig. 12.9

Fig. 12.10

Fig. 12.11

Fig. 12.12

Fig. 12.13

Fig. 12.9 Dovzhenko balances a tall sunflower against an explosion in the opening shot of *Shchors*.

Fig. 12.10 In *Shchors*, a Red officer politely asks for money from a bourgeois theater audience, a machine gun at his side.

Fig. 12.11 In *Suvorov*, the hero is framed against the sky, towering over his victorious troops.

Fig. 12.12 Shimmering cinematography and a diagonal composition in *Lone White Sail*, as middle-class passengers try to capture a fugitive sailor from the rebellious "Potemkin" battleship.

Fig. 12.13 The death of the hero in *Bezhin Meadow* uses a wide-angle lens to achieve an arresting deep-focus composition.

Pudovkin contributed to this genre with *Suvorov* (1941), which deals with the late years of a famous general in the wars against Napoleon. The opening scene is typical of such films (Fig. 12.11). Again, although Suvorov is of noble origins, he fraternizes with the common people. He wins his battles despite the opposition of the stupid tsar, Paul I. In the scene where Suvorov comes to visit the tsar, he slips repeatedly on the polished floor, clearly out of his element at the elegant court. Down-to-earth portrayals of historical figures would continue during the wartime period.

Stories of "typical," heroic ordinary people also were common. *Lone White Sail* (1937, Vladimir Legoshin) portrays the adventurous participation by children in the 1905 attempted revolution. (The film is set in Odessa and contains references to *Potemkin*.) It is also an excellent example of Shumyatsky's attempts to make Hollywood films, being shot in a polished continuity style that blends well with Socialist Realism (Fig. 12.12).

Eisenstein's aborted project, *Bezhin Meadow*, would have been the story of a boy who places loyalty to his collective farm above his relationship with his abusive father. Unfortunately, the negative of *Bezhin Meadow* was destroyed during a bombardment in World War II, and all that survives today is a reconstruction made from printing frames from each shot as still photographs. Even this slight record of the film indicates that it would have been one of the era's masterpieces. Eisenstein experimented with an extreme depth of field that looked forward to the films of Toland and Welles (Fig. 12.13).

A Member of the Government (1940, Alexander Zarkhi and Josif Heifits) deals with an idealized peasant woman. Alexandra is beaten by her drunken

Fig. 12.14

Fig. 12.15

Fig. 12.14 A composition in depth as Alexandra and a friend wait for a boat to pick up the collective farm's milk in *A Member of the Government.*

Fig. 12.15 *Jolly Fellows* blends slapstick humor and American jazz.

husband, who resents her devotion to their collective farm. The local party official, however, assures her that "you have your role in history." She persists, becoming the presiding officer of the farm (Fig. 12.14). Eventually she is elected her region's deputy to the Supreme Soviet in Moscow and addresses a huge crowd there.

Some of the era's most popular films were musical comedies. Grigori Alexandrov, who had been Eisenstein's assistant, became the main exponent of musicals with *Jolly Fellows* (aka *Jazz Comedy*, 1934). It concerns a cheerful singing farmer who is mistaken for a famous jazz conductor. When a party is held in his honor, his flute lures his animals into the house, and they create havoc (Fig. 12.15). There was criticism of the film's frivolity, but Alexandrov had the ultimate protection: Stalin loved it. Alexandrov's *Volga-Volga* (1938), the story of a woman mail carrier who writes a wildly popular song, became Stalin's favorite movie.

The other important director in this genre was Ivan Pyriev, who specialized in "tractor musicals" that glorified life on collective farms. Both *The Rich Bride* (1938) and *Tractor Drivers* (1939) show cheerful competitions among peasants to exceed work quotas. In 1935, miner Alexei Stakhanov had purportedly set a record for cutting coal, and the government promoted similar accomplishments by workers in all areas. "Stakhanovite" record breakers were glorified in the press, got special privileges, and even received fan mail.

In *The Rich Bride,* a collective's accountant conspires to marry the best female tractor driver in order to share her privileges. He breaks up her romance with the best male driver by falsifying her lover's work record, but the deception is discovered and the couple is reunited. The notion that the best Stakhanovite female peasant should marry the best male peasant reappears in *Tractor Drivers.* The heroine, Marianne, is so famous for exceeding her plowing quotas that suitors constantly pester her. She pretends to be engaged to Nazar, one of the farm's less productive tractor drivers. The farm's supervisor is appalled at this mismatch and asks Klim, another Stakhanovite, to teach Nazar how to work better. Klim agrees, though he secretly loves

Marianne himself. Eventually, despite Nazar's improvement, Marianne discovers Klim's love for her, and the two best workers marry. Throughout the film, the tone is energetic. Although most peasants on real collective farms spent as much time as possible working in their private gardens, in *Tractor Drivers* several songs are performed in the fields as the characters work cheerfully (Fig. 12.16).

Fig. 12.16 The collective farm's mail carrier sings animatedly about the joys of doing his job well as he rides through the broad fields of the Ukraine in *Tractor Drivers*.

THE SOVIET CINEMA IN WARTIME

Tractor Drivers was made during a period of nervousness about the threat of Nazi Germany. Klim, an ex-soldier, undertakes to give the other drivers military training, and the farm supervisor declares, "A tractor is a tank!" Two years after the film's release, the war began.

Before World War II, the United States, England, and other countries usually avoided making anti-Nazi films, since they still exported films to Germany. The USSR was under no such constraints and made several films on the Nazis during the late 1930s. *Professor Mamlock* (1938, Adolf Minkin and Herbert Rappoport), for example, was set in Germany shortly after the Nazi government came to power. It concerns a great Jewish doctor who tries to stay out of politics and disowns his son when the youth joins a Communist group. When the doctor is forced out of his job, he denounces the Nazis and is shot. The Communists vow to fight on.

Despite the fact that the Communists and Nazis were at extreme opposite ends of the political spectrum, on August 23, 1939, a startled world learned that the USSR and Germany were signing a nonaggression pact. Having received no assurances of support from Britain and France, Stalin decided to avoid invasion by negotiating with the Germans. As part of the agreement, Hitler allowed the USSR to seize the Baltic republics and to invade Finland. During the nearly two years that the pact was respected, anti-German films of the 1930s, including *Alexander Nevsky* and *Professor Mamlock,* were withdrawn from circulation.

The first fiction film to deal with the Finnish invasion was *Front-Line Girl Friends* (1941, released abroad as *The Girl from Leningrad*). It focuses on a unit of Red Cross nurses. As in many American war films, the central group is made up of such character types as a frivolous party girl who fears the sight of blood and an underage volunteer who insists on being allowed to go to the front (Fig. 12.17). With its spectacular battle scenes and depiction of the nurses' courage, the film was a huge hit in the USSR and was popular abroad as well.

Despite the nonaggression pact, Germany abruptly invaded the USSR on June 22, 1941. By early the next year, it occupied most Soviet territory west of Moscow. In the course of the war, German soldiers pillaged much of this area and committed numerous atrocities. They bombarded Moscow heavily but never managed to capture it. Beginning in October, however, most filmmaking activities were swiftly moved to studios in the unoccupied republics. Mosfilm and Lenfilm, for example, withdrew to Alma-Ata, the capital of Kazakhstan. Such an enormous effort caused considerable confusion, and the small studios had to be expanded in order to accommodate this huge increase in activity. Women workers had to be trained to take the place of male

Fig. 12.17 Nurses volunteering for duty in *Front-Line Girl Friends.* The towering white statue of Stalin is typical of the many images of party heroes that appear in Soviet films of this era.

filmmakers who had gone into the military.

These problems interrupted feature filmmaking. Early wartime releases included features made before the invasion, shorts, and newsreels. Newsreel production was centered in the vacated Mosfilm studios. The need for quickly produced films about the war was also met in part by a series of "Fighting Film Albums." These were cheaply made compilations of short segments, combining reports, documentary sketches, satirical scenes, musical numbers, or fictional episodes. Pudovkin made "Feast at Zhirmunka" for *Fighting Film Album 6* (1941). It shows Nazis committing atrocities against women and children in an occupied village where the men have gone off to be guerrilla fighters. One woman lays out a feast for the soldiers, eating some of it first herself when they suspect the food has been poisoned. Reassured, they eat and drink, realizing too late that the woman has poisoned the food, killing herself in order to kill them. This brief, bitter story ends with the woman's husband declaring, "All right, Germany. We're not going to forget." *Fighting Film Album 6* also contained a group of war songs and a documentary on women in the Soviet air force. N. Sadkovich directed another brief fiction segment, "Three in a Tank," for *Fighting Film Album 8* (1942). In it, two Soviet soldiers and their German hostage face being burned alive inside a tank. The German is terrified, but the two Soviet men calmly plan to use dynamite to blow up themselves and the Germans surrounding the tank. Soviet troops arrive in the nick of time (Fig. 12.18).

Although some segments of the Film Albums were effective, they were made far from the actual fighting and the occupied areas. Hence they often were naive and unrealistic. Eisenstein commented that they were "more passionate than well planned."[5]

Fiction features about the war began appearing in 1942. In order to stress the hatefulness of the German enemy, these often focused on women and children as victims of battles or atrocities. Based on a true incident, *Zoya* (1944, Leo Arnstam) concerns a young guerrilla captured, tortured, and hanged by the Nazis. Most of the film consists of flashbacks to her school days, when an old librarian tells her of Nazi book burnings. Victor Eisimont's *Once There Was a Girl* (1945) uses a small girl's viewpoint to give a poignant

Fig. 12.18 The triumphant end of "Three in a Tank," as a dead German soldier falls into the foreground and victorious Soviet troops rush over him.

portrayal of the hardships suffered by the citizens during the long siege of Leningrad.

Mark Donskoi's *The Rainbow* (1944) is set in a Ukrainian village paralyzed by both a heavy snow cover and the occupying German troops. The Nazis continue to commit atrocities among the villagers and to hang captured Soviet partisans, but the occupation has drifted into routine. The German commander has settled comfortably in and taken a mercenary village woman as his mistress. Aside from this woman, the other Ukrainians quietly resist their oppressors. In one powerful scene, a woman partisan who has returned to give birth is questioned under torture (Fig. 12.19). Finally Soviet troops, camouflaged in white, swoop down on the village and liberate it as a rainbow appears in the sky. Despite its broad character types, *The Rainbow* was considered an unusually realistic war film, and it influenced some filmmakers of the Italian Neorealist movement.

Fig. 12.19 The heroic partisan in *The Rainbow* refuses to speak, even when the Nazis kill her baby. Carrying its body, she herself is then shot.

The sufferings of the wartime period did not encourage the production of comedies, but a few appeared, especially after the 1943 Battle of Stalingrad brought more hope to the USSR. For example, *Wedding* (1944, Isidor Annensky) was a satire on pre-Revolutionary provincial pretensions, adapted from a Chekhov vaudeville. It lampooned the middle-class guests at a wedding party; the heavy make-up and broad acting were reminiscent of the "eccentric" style of Soviet comedies of the Montage movement (Fig. 12.20).

Biographical films continued to be an important genre during the war. Petrov followed *Peter the Great* with *Kutuzov* (1944), depicting the famous general's defense of Moscow against Napoleon in 1812. Shortly after this film was made, Petrov described the contemporary relevance of Socialist Realist biographical films:

Fig. 12.20 Two of the caricatural middle-class guests in *Wedding*.

> I am not inclined to view *Peter the Great* from a single historical perspective. I think that in some ways it is a contemporary film. The life and activities of the great Reformer of Russia seem to me very close to the life and actions of the Soviet people, who have also from day to day established the basis for a new life. It is the same for *Kutuzov*. The film was made and shown during the war. After the conquest of each village rooted out the enemy, after each new victory, the spectator saw those events as an echo of the old ones.[6]

Since Stalin was the supreme military leader of the USSR during World War II, he could be seen as a parallel both to the progressive tsars and the triumphant generals.

Stalin identified in particular with Ivan the Terrible, and during the war Eisenstein worked on a three-part film on that subject. Two parts were completed. They are elaborate, full of exaggerated acting, labyrinthine sets, and richly embroidered costumes (Fig. 12.21). Again Prokofiev wrote a musical track that emphasizes the heroic nature of the plot's events. The first film creates a grandiose image of Ivan, conquering invaders and resisting efforts by the nobility to undercut his unification of Russia. It was given the Stalin Prize in early 1946.

The second part of *Ivan the Terrible* fared badly. Eisenstein emphasized Ivan's doubts about his ruthless eradication of the noble class in Russia (Fig. 12.22). Stalin and his officials deplored this depiction of Ivan as hesitating in his "progressive" actions, and the second part of the film was suppressed in 1946. Eisenstein, suffering from heart disease, concentrated on writing

Fig. 12.21

Fig. 12.22

Fig. 12.21 Eisenstein uses lighting to create a looming image of the tsar in *Ivan the Terrible*, Part 1.

Fig. 12.22 Ivan kneels and begs forgiveness from the head of the church in *Ivan the Terrible*, Part 2.

film theory until his death in 1948. The second part of *Ivan the Terrible* was not released until 1958.

During 1943–1944, Soviet troops pushed westward, regaining territory and occupying eastern Europe. In early 1945, the Red Army advanced on Berlin, and the German government surrendered on May 8. The war had brought enormous losses to the USSR. The film industry was faced with reestablishing production in the regular studios and rebuilding the Lenfilm facilities, virtually ruined during the Siege of Leningrad. Nevertheless, as one of the victorious powers, the Soviet government retained control of its nationalized film industry. Such would not be the case for Nazi Germany.

THE GERMAN CINEMA UNDER THE NAZIS

Despite the departure of many German filmmakers for Hollywood during the 1920s, several major films were made between 1930 and the Nazi takeover in 1933. Some of these came from veteran silent directors, others from important newcomers.

The first sound film of Fritz Lang, who had been central to the German Expressionist movement of the 1920s (pp. 111–115), was one of his finest.

Figs. 12.23 and 12.24 In *M*, Fritz Lang creates an apparent "match on action" by cutting from a shot of the criminal boss gesturing during a conference concerning the child murderer to a police commissioner making a similar gesture at a parallel meeting of the police.

Fig. 12.23

Fig. 12.24

M (1931) tells the story of the search for a serial killer of children. The police dragnet so inconveniences the underworld of Berlin that the criminals capture the killer and try him in a kangaroo court. In portraying the two manhunts, Lang uses sound and image to create parallels between the police and the highly organized criminal world (Figs. 12.23, 12.24). He also exploits off-screen space for shock value (Fig. 12.25). Such stylistic inventiveness demonstrated Lang's immediate grasp of sound cinema. He also made a sequel to his 1922 *Dr. Mabuse, the Gambler*. In *Das Testament des Dr. Mabuse* ("The Last Will of Dr. Mabuse," 1933), the arch-criminal Dr. Mabuse continues to run his gang from an insane asylum and even from beyond the grave.

Veteran silent director G. W. Pabst made three notable films in this early sound era: *Westfront 1918* (1930), *The Threepenny Opera* (1931), and *Kamaradschaft* ("Comradeship," 1931). Both *Westfront 1918* and *Kamaradschaft* were pacifist films, pleas for international understanding in an era when nationalism and militarism were growing in Germany. The first portrays the senselessness of World War I; the second shows German miners risking their lives to save fellow French workers after a mine disaster.

Westfront 1918 creates an antiwar stance through bitter symbolism and a realistic depiction of battlefront conditions (Fig. 12.26). One scene shows the protagonist, Karl, coming home on leave and finding his wife in bed with the butcher's delivery boy. This scene uses many subtly varied framings to trace Karl's reactions, changing from rage to bitter resignation. Only in the wrenching final scene in a field hospital full of maimed and dying soldiers does Karl, himself near death, forgive his wife (Fig. 12.27). The film closes with a title, "The End?!" accompanied by the sound of explosions. Pabst made films in France during much of the Nazi regime, but he returned to Germany to work during World War II.

Max Ophüls, a stage director, began his film career in the early sound period. His first important work was *The Bartered Bride* (1932). An adaptation of the Smetana operetta, *The Bartered Bride* used several stylistic devices

Fig. 12.25 The balloon we have seen the murderer buy for a little girl escapes and bounces in telephone wires, suggesting her murder taking place offscreen.

Fig. 12.26 An exhausted student, sent back from the trenches for help, walks past a group of soldiers preparing coffins while a shell explodes in the background in *Westfront 1918*.

Fig. 12.27 The penultimate shot of *Westfront 1918* shows the dying Karl declaring he will go back to his unfaithful wife, for "we are all guilty."

Fig. 12.26

Fig. 12.27

Fig. 12.28 A group photograph at the end of *The Bartered Bride* becomes a freeze-frame and then a framed photograph (labeled "In memory of the year 1859").

that would typify Ophüls's style, including deep staging, elaborate camera movements, and direct address to the audience (Fig. 12.28). Ophüls hit upon his characteristic tone in *Liebelei* (1933), in which the innocent daughter of a violinist and a dashing lieutenant fall in love. Ophüls came to be known for creating an intense romanticism. In one scene of *Liebelei*, the camera begins by simply following the couple as they dance (Fig. 12.29). Then they whirl vertiginously around the camera as the background swirls by (Fig. 12.30). Finally, the camera pauses on the music box to which they have been dancing as they move away from our view (Fig. 12.31) and the scene fades out.

One of the most acclaimed directorial debuts of the period was Leontine Sagan's *Mädchen in Uniform* ("Girls in Uniform," 1931). It deals with a sensitive girl, Manuela, sent to a private school run by a tyrannical headmistress (Fig. 12.32). Manuela develops a crush on her only sympathetic teacher, and after blurting out her love at a party, she attempts suicide. *Mädchen in Uniform* was a rare early attempt to deal sympathetically with lesbianism. Sagan made a second film in England (*Men of Tomorrow*, 1932) before returning to her main career in the theater.

By 1933 all of these directors—Lang, Pabst, Ophüls, and Sagan—were working outside Germany, in part because a new political regime had gained power.

THE NAZI REGIME AND THE FILM INDUSTRY

Although Germany emerged from World War I with a relatively liberal government, the political climate moved rightward during the 1920s. In 1933, the fascistic Nationalsozialistische Deutsche Arbeiterpartei ("National Socialist German Workers' Party," known as the Nazis) gained parliamentary control and Adolf Hitler became chancellor. The Nazis became the only legal political party, and Hitler ruled as a dictator.

Nazi ideology was based on extreme nationalism: a belief that Germany was naturally superior to the rest of the world. This notion in turn stemmed from a view that Germans belonged to a pure "Aryan" race, and that other ethnic groups, especially Jews, were inferior and dangerous. Nazis also held that women were innately subordinate to men and that citizens owed unquestioning obedience to government leaders. Thus the new German regime

Figs. 12.29–12.31 In *Liebelei*, the camera dances with the characters and then discreetly loses them.

Fig. 12.29

Fig. 12.30

Fig. 12.31

opposed not only the Communist ideology of the USSR but also the democratic principles of other nations.

Hitler led his party to power in part by appealing to feelings of humiliation stemming from Germany's defeat in World War I. The country had been forced to disarm its military forces; soldiers could not even carry rifles. The Nazis managed to convince many people that the defeat had been caused by Jews. Similarly, the economic problems caused by the Depression were blamed on Jews and Communists. Hitler promised to restore both the economy and national pride.

The Nazi regime had a profound effect on the film industry. Like Stalin, Hitler was a movie fan; he cultivated friendships with actors and filmmakers and often screened films as after-dinner entertainment. Even more fascinated with the cinema was his powerful Minister of Propaganda, Dr. Josef Goebbels, who controlled the arts during the Nazi era. Goebbels watched films every day and socialized with filmmakers. In 1934 he gained control of censorship, and until the end of the war he personally examined every feature film, short, and newsreel that was released. Despite his hatred of communism, Goebbels admired Eisenstein's *Potemkin* for its powerful propaganda, and he hoped to create an equally vivid cinema expressing Nazi ideas.

Fig. 12.32 The headmistress inspects the schoolgirls in *Mädchen in Uniform*.

Goebbels moved to control other aspects of the film industry. The virulently anti-Semitic attitudes of the Nazi party led to an effort in April 1933 to remove all Jews from the film industry. Jews were forbidden to work for any film establishment—even in foreign companies' distribution offices. This precipitated an exodus of filmmaking talent. Many Jews fled, including Max Ophüls, Billy Wilder, and Robert Siodmak. Anyone holding left or liberal views was also in danger, and many non-Jews who could not stomach Nazi policies departed. Fritz Lang was offered a high position in the film industry but went into exile, first in France and then in the United States. Actor Conrad Veidt, though of Aryan origin, reportedly wrote "Jew" on the racial form required of each film worker and left the country. Ironically, in Hollywood he went on to play Nazi villains (most famously, Major Strasser in *Casablanca*).

In April 1935, the Nazis' anti-Semitic campaign continued with a ban on screenings of all pre-1933 films produced with the involvement of Jews. This move coincided with increasingly harsh measures being enacted by the government; the "Nuremberg laws" in September, among other things, stripped Jews of their citizenship and forbade marriages between Jews and non-Jews. Goebbels later ordered the production of anti-Semitic films.

Goebbels's main effort to control the German cinema came with the gradual nationalization of the film industry. When the Nazis came to power, there was no pressing need for the government to take control. Most shares in the largest company, Ufa, belonged to the powerful right-wing media mogul Alfred Hugenberg (who was briefly Minister of Economics in the new regime). Although many Ufa officials opposed the Nazis, the company made some of the earliest Fascist films. Moreover, in June 1933, the government set up the *Filmkreditbank*. The Credit Bank supported production in the wake of the Depression, but it also allowed the Nazis to oversee filmmaking, since projects had to meet ideological requirements in order to receive loans.

Nationalization was not tried immediately for another reason: Goebbels did not want to alienate other countries. Germany's film industry depended on exports. It also needed imports, primarily from the United States and France, to satisfy German theaters' needs. Some nations, however, resisted dealing with Nazi Germany. Both imports and exports fell sharply during the mid-1930s. At the same time, production costs in Germany were ballooning. The government had two options: to subsidize production (as Fascist Italy did) or to nationalize the industry.

The Nazis chose nationalization because it offered them greater control over the films. The process of nationalization, however, proceeded differently from that in the USSR. Instead of openly seizing private firms, as the Soviet government had done, during 1937–1938 the Nazi regime secretly bought controlling interests in the three main film-producing companies—Ufa, Tobis, and Bavaria—and two important smaller firms, Terra and Froelich. By 1939, eighteen independent production firms existed, but they made fewer than one-third of that year's features.

The nationalization of the film industry was completed in 1942. All German film companies were assembled under a giant holding firm, called Ufa-Film (but abbreviated as Ufi, to distinguish it from the old Ufa). Ufi was vertically integrated, controlling 138 firms in all sectors of the industry. By now, Hitler had seized Austria and Czechoslovakia, and Ufi absorbed their national film industries.

Despite this effort, the number of films produced in Germany did not meet the demand, and production declined after the war began in 1939. The Nazis were more successful, however, in controlling the types of films made.

FILMS OF THE NAZI ERA

Because of the repellent nature of Nazi ideology, modern audiences have seen few films from this era. The exceptions tend to be the more heavily propagandistic films like *Triumph of the Will* and *Jud Süss,* which are studied primarily as historical documents. Nevertheless, most films made during the period were intended as entertainment and have little or no overt political content. Of the 1097 features made from 1933 to 1945, only about one-sixth were banned by postwar Allied censors for containing Nazi propaganda. Since all films had to receive Goebbels's approval, they certainly could not attack Nazi ideology. Many are, however, ordinary studio films not very different from those made in Hollywood or England during the same period.

Some of the earliest strongly propagandistic films appeared in 1933: *SA-Mann Brand* ("SA-Man Brand," Franz Seitz), *Hans Westmar* (Franz Wenzler), and *Hitlerjunge Quex* ("The Quicksilver Hitler Youth," Hans Steinhoff). These were intended to win adherents to the party by glorifying Nazi heroes. The films take place shortly before the Nazis seized power, and they depict the era as a struggle between vicious Communists and stalwart young Hitler supporters.

Hans Westmar is based loosely on the life of Horst Wessel, one of the first to die for the Nazi cause and author of the party's fighting song. The film portrays late 1920s Berlin as sinking under Jewish, Communist, and decadent foreign influences. Young Westmar disgustedly visits a café that serves only

Fig. 12.33 The hero's zeal for the Nazi cause in *Hans Westmar* sometimes verges on fanaticism. Later propaganda films toned down such extreme behavior.

English beer and features a black jazz band. A Jewish play is on at the Piscator-Bühne (a real leftist theater of the day), and a cinema is showing Boris Barnet's 1927 Soviet comedy, *The Girl with the Hat Box.* Villainous Communists plot to take over Germany by exploiting working-class poverty. Westmar proves so adept at winning converts to the Nazi cause that the Communists assassinate him (Fig. 12.33).

Hitlerjunge Quex was, like many Nazi films, designed to appeal to adolescents. The protagonist, Heini, is attracted to a Hitler Youth group, despite his drunken Communist father's opposition (Fig. 12.34). The most effective scene shows him visiting a Communist youth camp where the leaders press wine and beer on the young visitors; he then wanders off and encounters a Hitler Youth camp where the children participate in healthy sport. Again, after Heini joins the Hitler Youth, his valiant service leads the Communists to murder him. Although the Communist organizations in both *Hans Westmar* and *Hitlerjunge Quex* contain stereotyped Jewish members, anti-Semitism is a minor part of these propaganda films, which mainly attack the German Communist party.

For modern audiences, the most famous filmmaker of the Nazi era is Leni Riefenstahl. She had started as an actress in the silent era and had directed herself in one sound feature, *The Blue Light* (1932), starring as a mountain sprite. Her two main films, *Triumph of the Will* (1935) and *Olympia* (1938), are virtually the only Nazi propaganda films which are studied today for their artistic qualities.

Triumph of the Will is a documentary feature made on the occasion of the Nazi party congress in Nuremberg in 1934. Hitler intended the event to demonstrate, both in Germany and abroad, his control of a powerful and unified group of followers. He asked Riefenstahl to direct the film, and he put enormous resources at her disposal. She oversaw sixteen camera crews, and the huge buildings erected for the event were designed to look impressive in the film (Figs. 12.35, 12.36). Using skillful cinematography, editing, and

Fig. 12.34 The young hero of *Hitlerjunge Quex* expresses delight as he receives his Hitler Youth uniform.

Figs. 12.35 and 12.36 Facilities for filming *Triumph of the Will* included a camera elevator, visible in Figure 12.35 on the supports of the banners in the giant open-air auditorium. It permitted moving shots of the vast crowds, carefully arranged for the camera, as in Figure 12.36.

Fig. 12.35

Fig. 12.36

Fig. 12.37 Since 1919, German soldiers had been forbidden to bear arms. In *Triumph of the Will* they parade carrying shovels in place of rifles—but the threat posed by Hitler's troops is still clear.

Fig. 12.38 Riefenstahl juxtaposes a series of shots of bodies soaring against the sky in the diving sequence in the second part of *Olympia*.

Fig. 12.39 Fears of Jewish corruption are exploited in *Jud Süss* when Süss rapes the heroine. She is played by Kristina Söderbaum, who portrayed idealized blonde Aryan heroines in several of Veit Harlan's films.

music, Riefenstahl created an impressive two-hour pageant of Nazi ideology and fervor. She also displayed to a nervous world Germany's military strength (Fig. 12.37).

Made as a record of the 1936 Olympic Games, held in Berlin, *Olympia* contains far less overt Nazi propaganda than *Triumph of the Will* had. Nevertheless, it was financed by the government, again on a lavish scale. The intention was that the film would show Germany as a cooperative member of the world community and thus quell fears about Nazi aggression. It was also hoped that the games would result in a series of prizes for Aryan participants, demonstrating the racial inferiority of their competitors.

Riefenstahl deployed even more camera crews to film the events and to catch crowd reactions. The huge amount of footage generated required two years to edit, and the final film was released in two feature-length parts. There were glimpses of Hitler and other Nazi officials viewing the games, but Riefenstahl concentrated on creating a sense of friendly competition among the athletes and on the beauty and suspense of the events. At times that sense of beauty became almost abstract, as in the famous diving sequence (Fig. 12.38). The medals won by several non-Aryan athletes, most prominently the black American track star Jesse Owens, also helped undercut the original propaganda purposes of the film.

During the Nazi era, films attacking the enemies of the Third Reich continued to appear. Some were anti-British, since Great Britain epitomized the kind of parliamentary democracy that the Nazis opposed. In *Carl Peters* (1941, Herbert Selpin), for example, British secret agents use underhanded means to battle the hero in colonizing parts of Africa. The USSR continued to be a favorite target, since the Nazis aimed to enslave and exterminate Slavic populations. *GPU* (1942, Karl Ritter) associates Soviet communism with women's equality, peace, and disarmament; the GPU (Soviet secret police) acts as a band of assassins furthering the USSR's plans for world domination. (In fact the GPU had been used primarily to persecute Soviet citizens.) After the German defeat at Stalingrad in 1943, one of the turning points of the war, the Nazis were not anxious to call attention to the USSR, and anti-Soviet features disappeared.

The most notorious of the "enemies" films were a few anti-Semitic features. These were ordered by Goebbels in 1939, shortly after Hitler first publicly discussed total annihilation as the "final solution" to the "Jewish problem." Five such films appeared, during 1939–1940. Among the most insidious of them was *Jud Süss* ("Jew Süss," 1940, Veit Harlan). A historical epic set in the eighteenth century, *Jud Süss* was based on the stereotype of the grasping Jewish moneylender. Süss loans money to an impoverished duke and gains enough power to try and turn the duchy into a Jewish state. He commits hideous crimes, including raping the heroine and torturing her lover (Fig. 12.39). *Jud Süss* was widely seen and incited violence against Jews.

Der ewige Jude ("The Eternal Jew," 1940, Fritz Hippler) was a documentary film exploiting similar myths, depicting Jews as a homeless race, spreading corruption by wandering through Christian lands. Footage of poverty-stricken inhabitants of the Warsaw ghetto is accompanied by a narrator's voice saying that Jews spread disease. A scene from Warner Bros.'s 1934 film, *House of Rothschild*, a positive depiction of the Jewish banking family, is taken out of context to "prove" a supposed Jewish conspiracy to control international finance. *Der ewige Jude* was so viciously anti-Semitic that it proved unpopular. After 1940, hatred of Jews appeared only in isolated scenes, not as the basis for entire films—partly because the Nazis wanted to divert attention from the exterminations then occurring in concentration camps.

Propaganda also drummed up enthusiasm for the war effort. Some militarist films showed life in uniform to be full of comradely cheer. In *Drei Unteroffiziere* ("Three Petty Officers," 1939, Werner Hochbaum), the heroes spend their time finding romance while on leave, singing as they march along, and occasionally participating in bloodless battles. The Nazis also, however, promoted a fanatical belief in "blood and soil," glorifying death in battle for the fatherland. Goebbels's pet project of the war period, *Kolberg* (1945, Veit Harlan), fostered this notion. In 1943, *Kolberg* was envisioned as a vast historical epic, the German *Gone With the Wind*. Because of the growing shortages caused by the war, the film was not actually finished until 1945. So obsessed was Goebbels with his project that he drew nearly 200,000 troops away from the fighting to act as extras. The result was a lavish film, shot on the new Afgacolor film stock introduced early in the war.

Kolberg dramatizes an actual incident in the Napoleonic wars, as the citizens of a small Prussian town take up arms to defend themselves when the local military authorities want to surrender. The people are eventually defeated, but the film highlights their courageous resistance to the French. Apparently Goebbels hoped that ordinary citizens would rise up and save Germany from its impending defeat. That did not happen. By the time *Kolberg* premiered on January 30, 1945, Allied bombing had closed most Berlin cinemas. The film remained virtually unseen as the city fell to Soviet troops.

Although most features were intended primarily as entertainment, political content often underlay the drama. For example, *Der Herrscher* ("The Ruler," 1937, Veit Harlan) portrays a powerful, aging industrialist who decides to marry his young secretary. His family attempts to have him declared insane, but he triumphs and disinherits them, leaving his factory to the German people. His children and their spouses are selfish: one checks a watch during the mother's funeral; others speculate on who will inherit her jewelry. The protagonist wins out, and his last line is "A born leader needs no teacher to guide his genius." The parallel with Hitler, who expected German citizens to follow him unquestioningly, was clear.

Goebbels also believed that the cinema was valuable as pure entertainment and did not demand even implicit Nazi ideology in every film. The tradition of German musicals that had begun in the early sound era continued during the Third Reich. The biggest hit of 1935, for example, was *Amphitryon* (Reinhold Schüntzel), a comedy set in large, abstract white sets representing ancient Rome, with anachronistic touches like Mercury delivering his messages on roller skates. Danish director Detlef Sierck (known after World War II in the United States as Douglas Sirk) made several films in Germany in the late 1930s, including the popular musical melodrama *Zu neuen Ufern* ("Toward New Shores," 1937). It is the story of a famous English music-hall singer who, taking the blame for a check her lover has forged, is sent to prison in Australia (Fig. 12.40). After a series of misfortunes there she eventually finds a happy marriage.

Fig. 12.40 The heroine of *Zu neuen Ufern* at the height of her success, before her unjust conviction sends her to prison in Australia.

Fig. 12.41 Rugged Luis Trenker, star and director of *Der Kaiser von Kalifornien*, embodied the ideal hero in many popular adventure films of the Nazi era.

One of the most unusual films of the Nazi era was *Der Kaiser von Kalifornien* ("The Kaiser of California," 1936, Luis Trenker). It starred Trenker in the story of Johann August Sutter, who accidentally discovered gold in California and set off the gold rush of 1849 (Fig. 12.41). Much of the film was shot on location in the United States, and it suggested none of the hostilities that were to lead to war between America and Germany several years later.

The prolific Veit Harlan made a number of nonpropaganda films, such as *Jugend* ("Youth," 1938), made by Tobis shortly after it was taken over by the government. *Jugend* involves an illegitimate young woman who has been taken in by her conservative uncle, a pastor. She is in turn seduced and abandoned by her cynical cousin and drowns herself. The film's style and even its strict morality are not much different from what one would expect in a contemporary Hollywood film (Fig. 12.42).

One little-known director working during this period was Helmut Käutner. In *Auf Wiedersehen, Franziska* ("Till We Meet Again, Franziska," 1941) he employs Ophülsian camera movement to portray romance, though with greater realism and a more subdued tone than Ophüls displayed. A traveling reporter has an affair with and later marries Franziska, a sensitive young woman. Despite their genuine love, Franziska grows withdrawn and morose as a result of his lengthy absences, which each begin with his saying, "Auf wiedersehen, Franziska," as he departs on a train. This bittersweet psychological study is marred only by the ending, aimed at satisfying the Nazi authorities. The husband returns after Germany's invasion of Poland and goes into the military, with Franziska, implausibly recovered from her malaise, seeing him off at the train with an optimistic, "Wiedersehen, Michael." Still, such films indicate that there is more variety to Nazi-period cinema than is sometimes believed.

THE AFTERMATH OF THE NAZI CINEMA

After the Allies captured Germany, they faced the problem of what to do with the people who had participated in the making of Nazi films. Goebbels was beyond punishment, having committed suicide during the fall of Berlin. Some filmmakers fled the country. Karl Ritter, director of *GPU* and one of the Nazi era's most popular directors, went into exile in Argentina. Others tried to maintain a low profile. Riefenstahl returned to her home in Austria, but her notoriety ensured that she would be investigated. Her interrogators concluded that she could not be charged with any crime, but she was not permitted to work on films again until 1952, when she completed her long-planned *Tiefland*. Many other filmmakers were also blacklisted while their Nazi-period activities were probed.

Veit Harlan was the only filmmaker charged and tried. There was considerable evidence that *Jud Süss* had been used to incite SS troops to arrest Jews and had been shown to audiences to weaken opposition to sending Jews to concentration camps. Harlan, however, claimed that he and the other filmmakers involved had been forced to make the film and had not intended it as propaganda. Two trials failed to produce enough evidence to convict him.

Fig. 12.42 The large, brightly lit sets in *Jugend* resemble those used in big Hollywood studio productions of the same era.

It is virtually impossible to assess how willingly such filmmakers co-operated with the Nazi regime. Some of them undoubtedly distorted the truth to protect themselves. Riefenstahl, for example, claimed that *Triumph of the Will* simply documented an unstaged event and that she financed *Olympia* herself, though ample evidence exists to prove these claims false.

ITALY: PROPAGANDA VERSUS ENTERTAINMENT

"Why," complained an Italian writer in 1930, "has there been no birth of a cinema inspired by the great fascist revolution to stand beside that inspired by the communist revolution?"[7] The question seems reasonable, since Mussolini ascended to power in 1922, only five years after the Bolshevik Revolution and a decade before the Nazi regime in Germany. Yet during the 1920s, Italian fascism made few attempts to commandeer the media. The agency LUCE, which controlled documentary and newsreel films, was the government's only major effort to centralize propaganda.

There were several reasons for this relaxed policy. Fascist ideology, based almost completely on nationalism, was more vague than communism or Naziism. Mussolini's regime was also more unstable, relying upon a loose coalition of provincial landowners, disaffected intellectuals, superpatriots, and a passive middle class. Although the Fascist government sought to regiment public life, it tended to leave private interests alone. It assisted industries, but it did not nationalize them. Italy thus offers a third example of how cinema fared under authoritarian rule in the 1930s and 1940s.

INDUSTRY TENDENCIES

At the end of the 1920s, the entrepreneur Stefano Pittaluga sought to revive Italy's film industry by creating a vertically integrated company. Pittaluga took over several small production companies, distribution firms, and theater chains. He bought the old Cines studio and reopened it with great fanfare in 1930. For a few years, the new Cines dominated Italian production, chiefly because it had the only sound recording facilities. Still, Cines could not heal the ailing industry. Exhibition prospered, but foreign films, chiefly American, ruled. The coming of sound accelerated the decline in production. In 1930, only twelve Italian features were made; in 1931, only thirteen.

As the Depression hit the Italian economy, the government began to aid several industries. A series of laws in 1931–1933 set up measures to protect the cinema. The government guaranteed subsidies according to box-office receipts; theaters were obliged to program a certain number of Italian films; foreign films were taxed; and a fund was established to award prizes to high-quality films. In 1932 Mussolini's regime also established the Venice Film Festival as an international showcase for the Italian product.

Such efforts encouraged producers to enter the market. After 1932, as Cines's power faded, Lux, Manenti, Titanus, ERA, and other production companies formed. By the late 1930s national production had risen to around forty-five features per year.

On the whole, however, the legislation did not improve conditions. Most films were commercially unsuccessful. Soon the government acknowledged that the film industry was an important ideological force that should not deteriorate. In 1934, the Undersecretariat of State for Press and Propaganda established the Direzione Generale della Cinematografica ("General Direction of Cinema"), to be headed by Luigi Freddi.

Although Freddi had supervised the Fascist party's propaganda office, he brought to his new position a surprisingly laissez-faire attitude toward governmental intervention. He suggested that the state should encourage and reward the industry but not dictate to it. Convinced that Italian audiences would reject heavily propagandistic films, he supported producers' desire for a cinema of "distraction" along Hollywood lines. A trip to Berlin confirmed Freddi's convictions. The Nazis had damaged German cinema, he claimed, by "blind and authoritarian coercion."[8] An entertained public, Freddi believed, was a quiescent public.

Freddi's views led the government to a series of new policies. In 1935 it established the Ente Nazionale Industrie Cinematografiche ("National Office for the Cinema Industry," or ENIC), which was given authority to intervene in all domains of film. ENIC took over Pittaluga's company, producing some films and coproducing others. It also absorbed some theater chains and began distributing films.

After Cines's studio burned in 1935, Freddi oversaw the building of a modern government-owned studio complex, Cinecittà ("Cinema-city"), on the outskirts of Rome. The facility soon housed twelve sound stages. From Cinecittà's opening in 1937 to 1943, more than half of all Italian films were shot there. In 1935, Freddi also established a film school, the Centro Sperimentale ("Experimental Center") in 1935. Two years later, the Centro launched its journal, *Bianco e nero* ("White and Black"), which made important contributions to film theory and has continued to this day. The Centro turned out many of the major Italian directors, performers, and technicians.

The government's investment in film culture yielded international prestige. The Venice Biennale arts festival, as well as the Film Festival, promoted

Italy as a modern, cosmopolitan country. Foreign directors such as Max Ophüls, Gustav Machaty, Jean Epstein, and Abel Gance arrived to make films.

Strong legislation also came forward. One law guaranteed government backing for most large-budget films, which in turn encouraged banks to invest in production. The "Alfieri law" of 1938 gave producers direct aid based on a percentage of ticket sales, thus favoring popular films and high-output firms. Just as dramatic was the "Monopoly law" of the same year, which gave ENIC control over all imported films and led four of the major Hollywood firms to withdraw their product from Italy. As a result, 1941 production nearly doubled to a record eighty-three features.

The Italian cinema never became a state-based political cinema like that of Germany or the USSR. ENIC controlled only a small fraction of the market and made only a few films. Mussolini, like Stalin, previewed virtually every feature made in his country, but he almost never banned a film. At the same time, despite government assistance, the Italian industry did not become self-supporting. Throughout the 1930s the average Italian production lost money. In general, the regime subsidized a fragile business while leaving it largely in private hands.

A CINEMA OF DISTRACTION

The comparative autonomy of the industry did not make the Italian cinema free of propaganda. LUCE's documentaries and newsreels extolled Mussolini's regime, and some explicitly Fascist features were made. The tenth anniversary of the party's founding led to two commemorative films, *Camicia nera* ("Black Shirt," 1932) and *Vecchia Guardia* ("The Old Guard," 1933), somewhat similar in thrust to Germany's *Hans Westmar*. The invasion of Ethiopia in 1935 inspired several propagandistic works, such as *Lo Squadrone bianco* ("The White Squadron," 1936), as did the support of Franco in the Spanish Civil War. Fascist policies were more indirectly glorified in patriotic historical spectacles like *1860* (1934) and *Scipione l'Africano* (1937).

Figs. 12.43 and 12.44 Fascist spectacle in *Scipione l'Africano* and *Lo Squadrone bianco*.

Fig. 12.43

Fig. 12.44

Although most Fascist intellectuals hated communism, many shared Goebbels's admiration for Soviet films. They hoped that Italian films could move toward a nationalistic, propagandistic cinema. These so-called Fascists of the left particularly welcomed epic spectacle. The masses, they hoped, would burst with pride at the sight of camels crossing Ethiopia, of tumultuous battles in Spain, and of Rome's elephants charging into heathen hordes (Figs. 12.43, 12.44). The regime, however, often disapproved of the spectacles' portrayal of the party. In addition, many of the films were financial disappointments. Not until World War II did a strongly propagandistic streak emerge in Italian cinema, as it did in most countries. Before then, a cinema of distraction was the norm.

Several popular genres flourished. Italian studios turned out romantic melodramas, typically set among the rich. When presented in a glossy modern decor, these were known as "white-telephone" films. A prototype was Gennaro Righelli's *La Canzone dell'amore* ("The Song of Love," 1930), with later examples being Mario Camerini's *T'amero sempre* ("I Will Love You Always," 1933) and Goffredo Alessandrini's *Noi vivi* (*We the Living*, 1942). An outstanding entry is Max Ophüls's *La Signora di tutti* ("Everybody's Lady," 1934), a mordant critique of the star-making machinery of the publicity industry. In flashback, the plot shows an innocent girl seduced by the father of the man she loves. When their romance sours, she becomes a film star. Eventually she commits suicide (Fig. 12.45). Virtually every scene of *La Signora di tutti* is full of emotional turmoil, which Ophüls films with great intensity. At climactic moments his camera sweeps across the action, losing and then finding characters with a giddy abandon that recalls *Liebelei*.

The other major genre of the era was comedy. As in other countries, sound film quickly brought forth romantic comedies built around infectious tunes. Sound also encouraged dialect humor, and many successful comedians—Ettore Petrolini, Vittorio De Sica, Totò—came to cinema from music halls and regional theater. De Sica moved into mainstream romantic comedy in such Cines products as *Gli uomini, che mascalzoni* ("What Scoundrels Men Are," 1932). *Il Signor Max* ("Mr. Max," 1937), in which De Sica portrays a poor man pretending to be rich, proved him to be a top box-office attraction (Fig. 12.46). Later Aldo Fabrizi's Roman dialect comedy yielded him a comparable success. The postwar Neorealist movement owed a large debt to popular comedy: De Sica became a major Neorealist director, and Fabrizi's teaming with Anna Magnani in *Campo de' fiori* ("Field of Flowers," 1943; Fig. 12.47) looked ahead to *Open City*.

The range of Italian production of the period is neatly exemplified by the work of Alessandro Blasetti. After the critical success of *Sole* (1929; p. 207) he made *Resurrectio* (1930), a romantic melodrama that combined the rapid cutting and elaborate camera movements of the silent "international style" with experimental sound techniques. Both *Nerone* (1930) and *La Tavola dei poveri* (1932) joined the current of dialect comedies. Blasetti argued unfashionably that artists should creatively interpret Fascist ideology. This he sought to do in *Vecchia Guardia*, a history of the early days of the party that resembled *Hitlerjunge Quex* and embarrassed officials. Blasetti's massive *1860* not only brought regional dialects to the historical film but borrowed from the heroic imagery of the Soviet cinema (Fig. 12.48). Blasetti also made white-telephone films, a historical swashbuckler, psychological dramas, and

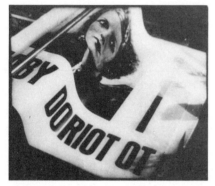

Fig. 12.45 At the star's death, her publicity machine halts *(La Signora di tutti)*.

Fig. 12.46 De Sica as Signor Max, emphasized by Hollywood-style edge lighting.

Fig. 12.47 Fish peddler Aldo Fabrizi encounters Anna Magnani in *Campo de' fiori*.

Fig. 12.48

Fig. 12.49

Fig. 12.48 A martial angle from Blasetti's epic *1860*.

Fig. 12.49 Fairy-tale atmosphere for peplum musclemen: the call to battle in *The Iron Crown*.

the important comedy *Four Steps in the Clouds* (1942). His fantasy pageant, *The Iron Crown* (1941), pushes the peplum formulas of the Italian silent cinema to an eccentric extreme (Fig. 12.49), adding a hint of a pacifist message. When Goebbels saw *The Iron Crown*, he is said to have remarked: "If a Nazi director had made it, he would have been put up against a wall and shot."[9]

A NEW REALISM?

Between 1940 and 1942, Italy's battlefield successes boosted the film business. The 1938 legislation had streamlined the industry, creating over a dozen production-distribution combines. The adroit Luigi Freddi, who was by 1941 president of ENIC and supervisor of Cinecittà, revived Cines as a semigovernmental company. Though never as all-embracing as Ufi in Germany, during 1942–1943 Freddi's Cines produced more films than any other firm. Overall, film attendance increased and output rose to unprecedented levels: 89 features in 1941, 119 in 1942. This surge in production allowed young directors to start careers, and many of these men would achieve fame in the postwar era.

Even in wartime conditions, however, the regime did not commandeer the industry. The General Direction, under Freddi's successor Eitel Monaco, actually liberalized censorship. More generally, during the late 1930s anti-Fascist attitudes grew strong among younger intellectuals, who were dismayed by the regime's military adventures and doctrinaire educational system. This atmosphere fostered a broadening of artistic options.

One trend looked back to nineteenth-century theatrical traditions. This trend was called *calligraphism* for its decorative impulses and its retreat from social reality. Typical examples are Renato Castellani's *Un Colpo di pistola* ("A Pistol Shot," 1942) and *Via della cinque lune* ("Five Moon Street," 1942), by Luigi Chiarini, the first head of Centro Sperimentale.

A younger generation, however, was debating the merits of realistic art. Influenced by Hemingway, Faulkner, and other American authors, writers argued for a return to an Italian tradition of regional naturalism (epitomized in the *verismo* of Giovanni Verga, a turn-of-the-century novelist). Similarly, in the pages of *Bianco e nero*, *Cinema*, and other journals, critics called for the director to film the problems of ordinary people in actual surroundings.

Fig. 12.50 *The White Ship:* In a scene reminiscent of *Potemkin*, Rossellini shows sailors at one with their machines.

Aspiring filmmakers were impressed by the Soviet Montage films shown at Centro, by French Poetic Realism, and by Hollywood populist directors like Capra and Vidor. In 1939 Michelangelo Antonioni envisioned a film about the Po River that would tell a story while recording life along the river. A 1941 essay by Giuseppe De Santis praised American Westerns, Soviet landscape shots, Renoir's 1930s films, and some works of Blasetti as forerunners of an aesthetic that would blend fiction and documentary into "a true and genuine Italian cinema."[10]

Such debates gained support from films that were released during the war years. Several of these manifest a new reliance upon regional dialects, location shooting, and nonprofessional actors. In Roberto Rossellini's *La Nave bianca* ("The White Ship," 1941), for instance, a naval war drama is filmed in semidocumentary fashion (Fig. 12.50). Forerunners of this trend can be found, notably Walter Ruttmann's *Acciaio* (1933) and Amleto Palermi's *Porto* (1935), but three films of the early 1940s seemed to move sharply toward a "new realism."

Blasetti's *Four Steps in the Clouds* (1942) centers on a traveling salesman frustrated by his boring life. On a trip to the countryside, he reluctantly pretends to be the husband of a pregnant girl whose family has cast her out. At first he is embarrassed by her family's mistreatment of him, but he comes to see the rural interlude as a break from his routine. In building a populist comedy on such topics as out-of-wedlock pregnancy and the sterility of married life, *Four Steps* gave the genre a quietly ironic melancholy.

The second breakthrough film was De Sica's fifth effort as director, *The Children Are Watching Us* (1943). If Blasetti turns the sentimental comedy somber, De Sica makes melodrama border on tragedy. A woman is tempted to leave her husband and little boy for her lover. De Sica and his scriptwriter Cesare Zavattini complicate this familiar situation by telling the story largely from the son's point of view. In a startling finale, after the mother drives the father to suicide, the little boy rejects her. The family is well-to-do, but *The Children Are Watching Us* avoids the elegance of the white-telephone films and offers a strong social critique (Fig. 12.51).

Fig. 12.51 *The Children Are Watching Us:* De Sica frames the troubled family against a vista of apartment windows, suggesting that other urban tragedies surround them.

Fig. 12.52

Fig. 12.53

Fig. 12.52 A crane shot in *Ossessione:* As the seedy store owner pumps gas for a lorry . . .

Fig. 12.53 . . . the camera rises to reveal the café where his wife waits.

The boldest manifestation of the realistic trend was Luchino Visconti's *Ossessione* ("Obsession"), released in 1943. Adapted from James M. Cain's novel *The Postman Always Rings Twice,* the film traces how a drifter's passion for a café owner's wife leads them to murder her husband. Visconti's camerawork is as elaborate as that in any studio product (Figs. 12.52, 12.53), but his mise-en-scene has an unexpected grittiness. By setting the drama in the sun-drenched, impoverished Po valley, he refuses the glamour of mainstream Italian production. The steamy heat soaks people's clothes; a coil of flypaper sways over the couple's dinner table. Staggering home from a tavern, the husband crawls into a ditch and vomits. Apart from broaching the forbidden subject of adultery, Visconti's version adds a homosexual theme to Cain's original.

After controversial first showings, *Ossessione* was withdrawn from distribution. Still, it remained a point of reference. A 1943 article by Umberto Barbaro called for a *neo-realismo* comparable to that seen in French films like *Quai des brumes,* and he suggested that *Ossessione* could point the way.

Today these films by Blasetti, De Sica, and Visconti seem close to mainstream traditions. *Four Steps* developed out of popular comedy, while the others owe a good deal to melodrama. *Ossessione* is closer to American *film noir* than to postwar Neorealism. All three films exploit the star system and display studio lighting techniques (Fig. 12.54). Even their location shooting is offset by Hollywood-style studio sets and rear projections (Fig. 12.55). At the time, however, what attracted attention was their "realistic" depiction of social problems long concealed by Freddi's cinema of distraction.

In 1943, the Allies invaded southern Italy, and Mussolini's government fled north to establish the Republic of Salò. Fascist loyalists and German troops occupied the northern and central regions, where they were fought by an armed resistance movement. Italian film production dropped precipitously and did not revive until 1945. Then the memories of the resistance and visions of a cinema that recorded everyday life would provide major sources for the Neorealist movement.

Fig. 12.54 Rich chiaroscuro lighting intensifies the meeting between the drifting hero and the boss's sultry wife *(Ossessione).*

Fig. 12.55 The traveling salesman's bus trip, shot in a studio bus, complete with careful lighting and rear projection *(Four Steps in the Clouds).*

The Soviet, German, and Italian industries of this period exemplify three ways in which a government may control its film industry. In the USSR, nationalization had occurred early on, in an open fashion. The Nazis covertly acquired film companies and forced them to produce films supporting the regime. The Italian government used more indirect means to ensure the film industry's cooperation. After the war, the Soviet system lasted until the late 1980s. The defeat of the Nazis left the German industry in a shambles. In Italy, where the industry had not been nationalized, the transition to peacetime filmmaking went more smoothly.

◆ NOTES AND QUERIES

THE CASE OF LENI RIEFENSTAHL

Leni Riefenstahl has been the most enduringly controversial of the Third Reich's filmmakers. *Triumph of the Will* and *Olympia* can be said to have an aesthetic quality that surpasses their propagandistic purposes. Indeed, along with Carl Orff's oratorio *Carmina Burana,* they are among the most admired of all Nazi-era artworks. Riefenstahl was neglected for decades after the war, but the rise of feminism caused traditional film history to be reexamined, and she was rediscovered and acclaimed as one of the most important female directors. The beauty of her films was often stressed more than their historical role, and she was welcomed at feminist film festivals. Susan Sontag has discussed this trend, arguing that the beauty and the Fascist ideology of Riefenstahl's films were inextricably linked, in her "Fascinating Fascism" (1975), reprinted in Bill Nichols, ed., *Movies and Methods* (Berkeley: University of California Press, 1976), pp. 31–43.

The issue of Riefenstahl's attitude toward the Nazis has also been much debated. She claimed that she was interested only in art when she made the films and that she knew nothing of oppressive Nazi policies. David Stewart Hull presents a description of her filmmaking based largely on Riefenstahl's own claims in *Film in the Third Reich* (Berkeley: University of California Press, 1969), especially pp. 73–76 and 132–137. More recently, Glenn B. Infield's research has used government records and other archival material to show that at least some of Riefenstahl's claims are untrue. See his *Leni Riefenstahl: The Fallen Film Goddess* (New York: Crowell, 1976). Richard Meran Barsam analyzes the film in detail in *Filmguide to **Triumph of the Will*** (Bloomington: Indiana University Press, 1975). For Riefenstahl's most recent version of her activities, see her *The Sieve of Time: The Memoirs of Leni Riefenstahl* (London: Quartet Books, 1992).

◆ REFERENCES

1. A. A. Zhdanov, "Soviet Literature—the Richest in Ideas, the Most Advanced Literature," in *Soviet Writers' Congress 1934: The Debate on Socialist Realism and Modernism* (1935; rep. London: Lawrence and Wishart, 1977), p. 21.
2. Boris Shumyatsky, *A Cinema For the Millions* (Extracts), tr. Richard Taylor, in Taylor and Ian Christie, eds., *The Film Factory: Russian and Soviet Documents 1896–1939* (Cambridge, Mass.: Harvard University Press, 1988), p. 359.
3. "For a Great Cinema Art: Speeches to the All-Union Creative Conference of Workers in Soviet Cinema (Extracts)," in *ibid.,* p. 355.

4. Quoted in Jay Leyda, *Kino: A History of the Russian and Soviet Film,* 3rd ed. (Princeton, N.J.: Princeton University Press, 1983), p. 353.
5. Quoted in Neya Zorkaya, *The Illustrated History of the Soviet Cinema* (New York: Hippocrene Books, 1989), p. 175.
6. Quoted in Sagalovitch, "Vladimir Petrov: Maître du film historique," in *Les Maîtres du cinéma soviétique au travail* (Service cinématographique de l'U.R.S.S. en France, 1946), pp. 75–76.
7. Quoted in Gian Piero Brunetta, "The Conversion of the Italian Cinema to Fascism in the 1920's," *Journal of Italian history* **1** (1978): 452.
8. Quoted in David Forgacs, *Italian Culture in the Industrial Era 1880–1980* (Manchester: Manchester University Press, 1990), p. 72.
9. Quoted in Elaine Mancini, *Struggles of the Italian Film Industry during Fascism* (Ann Arbor: UMI Research Press, 1985), pp. 170–171.
10. Giuseppe De Santis, "Towards an Italian Landscape," in David Overbey, ed., *Springtime in Italy: A Reader on Neo-Realism* (London: Talisman, 1978), p. 127.

13

FRANCE, 1930–1945: POETIC REALISM, THE POPULAR FRONT, AND THE OCCUPATION

France felt the effects of the worldwide Depression comparatively late. Bank failures began in late 1930, and economic production declined from the second half of 1931 on. The government failed to counter these problems, and the slump lingered throughout the 1930s. The film industry was hit hard by the Depression, and its already unstable production sector became even more fragmented. Other studio systems we have examined, such as those of Britain, Japan, and Italy, were more organized and prolific. Still, French cinema of this era was more significant than its industrial conditions would suggest. A surprising proportion of the films produced were notable. Filmmakers like René Clair and Jean Renoir did their most important work during the 1930s, and French films had an influence around the world second only to that of Hollywood films. A weak studio system offered filmmakers flexibility and freedom.

Throughout Europe, economic problems created political turmoil. Italy, Germany, Spain, and smaller countries near France were establishing Fascist governments. Right-wing parties were pushing France in the same direction, and during the mid-1930s a coalition of leftist groups, the Popular Front, opposed them and briefly came to power. This movement had a short-lived but significant impact on filmmaking.

France's involvement in World War II, beginning in September 1939, cut off most filmmaking activity. When German forces captured Paris in June 1940, a right-wing French government was established in Vichy, in the south.

The German Occupation lasted until August 1944. During these four years, the conditions of film production and exhibition changed radically, and many filmmakers had to flee or go into hiding. Those who remained, however, managed to keep the French industry alive. Some of the resulting films are distinctive for their tone of fantasy, isolation, and escapism. Although World War II altered many countries' films, there can be few places where the break between the 1930s and the early 1940s was so dramatic as in France.

THE INDUSTRY AND FILMMAKING DURING THE 1930s

France's film production had declined precipitously from its glory days before World War I, when it dominated world screens. The coming of sound gave it a boost, since audiences were eager to hear dialogue spoken in French, and prosperity early in the decade slightly bolstered production. The following figures for numbers of features made during the 1930s, however, show that the French industry was eventually hit by the Depression:

1929:	52	1933:	158	1937:	111
1930:	94	1934:	126	1938:	122
1931:	139	1935:	115	1939:	91
1932:	157	1936:	116		

By way of contrast, the United States, Germany, and Japan were each producing hundreds of films each year.

Even more than in the 1920s, much of the French production sector consisted of small firms. These were privately owned and often made only one film, borrowing heavily to do so and going out of business quickly. Some dishonest entrepreneurs formed small firms in order to get loans to make films. In some cases filmmakers found themselves working for nothing after their employers absconded with the money. Other projects had to be halted for lack of funds. During the 1930s, 285 small firms made only one film apiece, and dozens more managed to produce only a few. Even the largest producer, Pathé-Natan, made only sixty-four films in the decade—about as many as Paramount was producing annually.

Size was no guarantee against corruption and mismanagement. Two of the largest firms, formed through mergers during the healthier period of the late 1920s, ran into trouble in the mid-1930s. Rather than cooperating to form an oligopoly, as the big firms in more stable studio systems did, the French firms tried to drive each other out of business. In 1934, Gaumont-Franco-Film-Aubert nearly went bankrupt, and only a government-sponsored loan saved it. Pathé-Natan ran into similar problems by 1936, complicated by the fact that one of its heads, Bernard Natan, was discovered to have been embezzling funds. He went to jail, and the company had to be broken into smaller firms.

The situation was not altogether gloomy, however. Government regulation and the coming of sound both helped loosen the American hold on the

Fig. 13.1 Surrealist style in *L'Affaire est dans le sac*, as a mysterious stranger helps the hero into a car for a bizarre hat-stealing mission.

Fig. 13.2 In *Zero for Conduct*, the kindly teacher Huguet imitates Charlie Chaplin during recess, to the delight of the schoolboys.

Fig. 13.3 The pillow-fight scene ends with a triumphant slow-motion procession by the schoolboys, with a musical accompaniment played partially backward.

French market. In 1935, for the first time since World War I, French films made up over half of the domestic market. Moreover, film attendance, which had dropped during the Depression, began to rise, and theater income increased.

The decentralized structure of French film production helps explain why so many enduring films were made during this decade. Small companies lacked the elaborate production bureaucracy that characterized filmmaking in the United States, Germany, and the USSR. Instead, as in Japan, directors were often able to work on their own, supervising many phases of production. This situation, combined with a large number of talented actors, screenwriters, designers, cinematographers, composers, and other creative personnel, contributed to the creation of several distinctive trends.

During the early 1930s, the silent period's tendency toward fantasy and surrealism continued. René Clair's innovative early musicals, *Sous les toits de Paris* (1930) and *À nous, la liberté!* (1931), made him the most prominent French filmmaker. *Le Million* (1931) was another imaginative musical, centering on a lengthy comic chase for a lost lottery ticket. Clair substituted music for diegetic sound effects and used extensive camera movement. After two minor efforts, Clair departed for England, where he made one notable comedy, *The Ghost Goes West* (1935). Interrupted by the war in an attempt to return to France, he spent the war period in Hollywood.

The Surrealist tradition was also continued in a few works, though these were not as violent and chaotic as Luis Buñuel's *Un Chien andalou* and *L'Age d'or* (pp. 196–197). In 1932, Pierre Prévert directed *L'Affaire est dans le sac* ("It's in the Bag") from a script by his brother Jacques, a major playwright and poet. Shot on a tiny budget and using sets from other movies, *L'Affaire est dans le sac* is an anarchic comedy concerning, among other things, people who sell, steal, and wear inappropriate hats (including a man who searches in vain for a Fascist-style beret) and a rich industrialist's daughter who is courted by men of various social classes. The film uses an exaggerated style (Fig. 13.1) to reinforce the oddities of the plot. After the failure of this film, the Prévert brothers were unable to make another film together until a decade later, but Jacques scripted several of the most important French films of the era.

The most promising young filmmaker of the early 1930s, Jean Vigo, also worked in a Surrealist vein. After two shorts, his main work consists of a brief feature, *Zero for Conduct* (1933; banned and not shown publicly in France until 1945) and *L'Atalante* (1934; restored version released 1990).

Zero for Conduct is the more overtly Surrealist of the two, presenting boarding-school life from the viewpoint of the children. Most of the teachers are seen as grotesques, with the one exception of Huguet (Fig. 13.2), who encourages the boys to rebel. One night they defy their teachers and start a pillow fight in their dormitory (Fig. 13.3). The final scene shows four of the boys staging a rebellion during a commemoration day at the school.

In *L'Atalante*, Vigo presents an intensely romantic story of a barge captain who marries a woman from a village along his route. After a short honeymoon period, she longs for something beyond the barge's routine. Intrigued by the exotic souvenirs of the first mate, Père Jules, and tempted by a passing peddler, she runs away to Paris, and her husband refuses to admit his longing for her (Fig. 13.4). Eventually Père Jules tracks the wife down, and the couple are reunited.

Vigo died in 1934, at the age of twenty-nine. His death and the inability of the Prévert brothers to make further films cut short the Surrealist impulse in French film. Clair's departure similarly made the fantasy genre less prominent in France.

Many important French films of the 1930s were high-quality studio productions. Some were literary adaptations, such as *Crime and Punishment*, from the Dostoyevsky novel (1935, Pierre Chenal). Two distinguished stage actors, Pierre Blanchar and Harry Baur, give impressive performances as Raskolnikov and Porphyre, and the elaborate interior sets display a slight influence from German Expressionism (Fig. 13.5).

Jacques Feyder, who had worked briefly in the Impressionist style during the 1920s, returned to France in 1932 after a short stay in Hollywood. His most famous film of this decade is *La Kermesse héroïque* (*Carnival in Flanders*, 1935), a comedy set in a Flemish town in the early seventeenth century. When news arrives that the Duke of Alba is marching on the town, the men panic and hide, but the women welcome the invading army into their homes (and beds) for a festival. The delighted duke leads his troops away the next day, sparing the town. Of Belgian origin himself, Feyder insisted on a meticulously correct duplication of the architecture and costumes of the period (Fig. 13.6).

Carnival in Flanders has been interpreted as favoring collaboration with the enemy at a time when the Fascist threat was growing. In fact, Feyder and Charles Spaak had written the script in the mid-1920s, when pacifist films were becoming common. They were unable to find a producer then, and the timing of the film's eventual appearance proved unfortunate. It was not well received in France or Belgium but was immensely popular in Germany and England, and it won a director's prize at the Venice Film Festival and an Oscar as best foreign film in the United States.

Less prestigious and more typical of quality French filmmaking in the 1930s is Marc Allégret's 1934 *Lac aux dames* ("Women's Lake"). Its slim

Fig. 13.4 After his wife's departure, the tortured barge captain of *L'Atalante* plays checkers with first mate Père Jules, surrounded by the latter's strange collection of souvenirs. These odd objects provide the main Surrealist motif in the film.

Fig. 13.5 The hallway outside Raskolnikov's room in *Crime and Punishment* shows a hint of Expressionist style.

Fig. 13.6 Lazare Meerson, the greatest French set designer of the interwar period, created an authentic Renaissance Flemish town for *Carnival in Flanders*.

Fig. 13.7 A picturesque location shot in *Lac aux dames.*

Fig. 13.8 The frame story in *Le Roman d'un tricheur* takes place in an unabashedly theatrical set representing a sidewalk café, but the narrator's voice takes us into a series of flashbacks.

Fig. 13.9 In *Le Drame de Shanghai,* Pabst creates a sense of the sleazy underworld of Shanghai.

plot involves a young man who works as a swimming teacher at a Tyrolean lake and is besieged by female admirers. He has been separated from the woman he really loves, and an innocent rich girl who develops a crush on him finally helps him reunite with her. As in many French films of this era, this conventional story gains interest through beautiful cinematography (Fig. 13.7) and its stars. *Lac aux dames* introduced both Jean-Pierre Aumont and Simone Simon, and the character actor Michel Simon plays a small role. Although the French industry was relatively small, it had many popular stars and character actors during the 1930s. Raimu, Michèle Morgan, and Jean Gabin often proved to be drawing cards abroad as well—something that had seldom been the case in the 1920s.

A unique filmmaker in this studio tradition was Sacha Guitry, a successful author of sophisticated comic plays and fiction. He turned to the cinema, starring in, adapting, and directing several of his own works. Critics and filmmakers deplored Guitry's unabashed defense of his "filmed theater," yet many of them shared the audience's delight in these witty, well-constructed comedies. Outstanding among them is *Le Roman d'un tricheur* (*The Story of a Cheat*, 1936), based on a Guitry novel about a confidence man and cardsharp. Guitry innovates by having the trickster's voice narrate the tale, filling in for all the characters' dialogue—women as well as men (Fig. 13.8).

Julien Duvivier, who participated in all the main trends of French filmmaking in the 1930s, made *Poil de carotte* in 1932. (In 1925 he had directed an earlier version in the Impressionist style.) The protagonist is a boy whose cheerful personality is worn down by a tyrannical mother and an indifferent father. He nearly commits suicide before the father belatedly reveals that he loves him. *Poil de carotte*'s sophisticated style and rural location shooting create a touching story seen largely from the boy's viewpoint.

Quite a few of the high-quality French films of this period were created by foreign, especially German, directors. Many German and French filmmakers moved between Berlin and Paris, and even after most multilingual production had been abandoned in favor of dubbing or subtitles, many French films were still reshot in German versions, and vice-versa.

G. W. Pabst had two lengthy sojourns in France. During the first, he directed a multilingual version of *Don Quixote* (1933), starring the legendary opera star Fédor Chaliapin. After a disappointing visit to Hollywood that resulted in a single film, Pabst returned to France to direct three more features, all melodramas. In *Le Drame de Shanghai* ("Shanghai Drama," 1938), the heroine, Kay, is a nightclub singer who has for years been working for an underworld gang in Shanghai; when her innocent daughter, who has been away at school for years, comes to visit, Kay tries to go straight but is forced to kill one of the gang members so that her daughter can escape from China just as the Japanese invade. Pabst used the exotic setting to create an effective *film noir* (Fig. 13.9). Surprisingly, once the war began, Pabst decided to return to Germany, where he worked under the Nazi regime.

Max Ophüls also worked regularly in Paris during the 1930s, making seven intensely romantic features in the vein of *Liebelei.* In *Le Roman de Werther* ("The Romance of Werther," 1938), Ophüls adapted Goethe's novel of doomed love. The hero comes to serve as an official in a small town, falls in love with his superior's fiancée, Charlotte, and eventually commits suicide (Fig. 13.10). Ophüls fled to the United States once World War II began.

Other émigrés found France a way station to Hollywood. Anatole Litvak, a Russian Jew who had worked for a while in Germany, fled the Nazis and worked briefly in France. *Mayerling* (1936), the story of a prince's doomed love for a commoner, was shot in a style virtually indistinguishable from that of polished Hollywood productions, and it was extremeley popular abroad. Actors Charles Boyer and Danielle Darrieux became international stars; they and Litvak all went to work in Hollywood. Fritz Lang also paused briefly in France, having left Germany to avoid working under the Nazis. He made a fatalistic romantic drama, *Liliom* (1934), before moving on for a long-term stay in the United States. Similarly, Billy Wilder, Robert Siodmak, Curtis Bernhardt, and others worked briefly in France but soon went on to careers in Hollywood.

Fig. 13.10 Ophüls comments on the action using his characteristic camera movement in *Le Roman de Werther*, tilting up to a crucifix as the clergyman tells Charlotte to reject Werther's love.

While these prestigious studio productions relied on polished technique, romantic stories, and stars, there were several films made that stressed everyday realism. Prominent among these is a film that, like *Zero for Conduct* and *Poil de carotte*, deals sympathetically with children: *La Maternelle* (1933), by Jean Benoît-Lévy and Marie Epstein. Benoît-Lévy, who was primarily a documentarist, and Epstein, who had scripted three films for her brother Jean in the 1920s, had previously collaborated on some silent features on social issues involving children. Their most important film, *La Maternelle*, focuses on neglected and abused children attending a kindergarten. An educated, but impoverished, young woman, Rose, takes a menial job there and becomes the object of the children's repressed longings for love—especially those of Marie, abandoned by her prostitute mother (Fig. 13.11). Avoiding studio glamour and stars, Benoît-Lévy and Epstein filmed in an actual working-class kindergarten and used children with no acting experience (Fig. 13.12). This simple story was well received by French and foreign audiences. As a result, Benoît-Lévy and Epstein collaborated again, on *Itto* (1934), one of the few films about France's North African colonies that treats the native population sensitively.

Fig. 13.11 In *La Maternelle*, Marie sees Rose as her mother figure. Resenting her romance with the school-board director, she tries to commit suicide and finally is adopted by the couple.

Another filmmaker emerged in the 1930s whose work was highly individualistic and centered in everyday reality. Like Sacha Guitry, Marcel Pagnol was already a highly successful playwright, but unlike Guitry's, his plays were leisurely character studies. Upon seeing *The Broadway Melody*, Pagnol decided that sound films were an ideal way of recording plays. He supervised the film adaptation of his hit play, *Marius* [1931, directed by Alexander Korda, who was soon to revolutionize the British cinema by directing *The Private Life of Henry VIII* (p. 268)]. When the producer, Paramount, declined a sequel despite the film's huge success, Pagnol went on to produce *Fanny* (1932, Marc Allégret) himself. With the profits, he set up his own production firm, producing one popular film after another. He directed the third entry in the trilogy, *César* (1936).

The "Marius" trilogy covers about twenty years in the lives of its three central characters, yet many of its scenes contain little action. Instead, the inhabitants of a waterside district of Marseille bicker and carry on lengthy discussions. Although the slow pace derived in part from the stage origins of the films, Pagnol was also striving to capture the meanderings and shifts in tone that characterize everyday conversation.

By 1936, Pagnol's success permitted him to equip his own studio facilities in Marseille. His actors and crew remained fairly constant from film to

Fig. 13.12 Realism in *La Maternelle*: Rose with Fondant, a child from an abusive home who never smiles. Although she draws him out of his shell, he dies at home of unexplained causes.

Fig. 13.13 Pagnol's celebration of fertility: As the couple sow their field in the final scene of *Harvest*, the heroine reveals to her husband that she is pregnant.

film, forming the "Pagnol family." They lived and worked together wherever the location scenes for the films were being shot. Pagnol's oft-quoted formula was "The Universal is attained by staying at home,"[1] and his most successful films of the late 1930s and early 1940s were made in the Provence region around his hometown, Marseille. They were less stagy than the trilogy and told simple stories of village life. In *La Femme du boulanger* (*The Baker's Wife*, 1938), the departure of the baker's wife with another man causes the baker to stop making bread, and the villagers band together to fetch her back. *Regain* (*Harvest*, 1937) celebrates the fertility of the earth, as a lonely peasant and an outcast woman join forces and struggle to raise a family and build a farm in a deserted village (Fig. 13.13).

POETIC REALISM

Many of the best-remembered French films of the 1930s belong to a tendency that has been termed "Poetic Realism." This was not a unified movement, like French Impressionism or Soviet Montage; it is rather a general tendency. Poetic Realist films often center on characters living on the margins of society, either as unemployed members of the working class or as criminals. After a life of disappointment, these shabby figures find a last chance at intense, ideal love. After a brief period they are disappointed again, and the films end with the disillusionment or deaths of the central characters. The overall tone is one of nostalgia and bitterness.

There were some forerunners of Poetic Realism in the early 1930s. We have already examined Jean Grémillon's 1930 film *La Petite Lise* (pp. 224–225), which provides a mature early example of this tendency. A convict returns from his prison to find that his daughter has been forced into prostitution. When she accidentally helps kill a pawnbroker, he protects her by taking the blame for the crime. Another early example of the tendency is Feyder's *Pension Mimosas* (1934). Its story centers on a woman who runs a boardinghouse and falls in love with her adopted son. Her elaborate attempts to thwart his falling in love with anyone else lead to his suicide. Aside from this tragic plot, the film depends on the precise establishment of atmosphere through the settings—the Pension Mimosas boardinghouse of the title, a local casino, and other sets, all designed by Lazare Meerson (who did the sets for *Carnival in Flanders* and other important films of the decade).

The Poetic Realist trend began in earnest in the mid-1930s, and its main filmmakers were Julien Duvivier, Marcel Carné, and Jean Renoir.

Duvivier's main contribution to the tendency was *Pépé le Moko* (1936), a film that typifies Poetic Realism. Pépé is a gangster hiding out in the notorious Casbah section of Algiers, where the police dare not arrest him. Although he has a mistress already, he falls in love with a sophisticated Parisian, Gaby, who visits the district for a casual adventure. Their love is doomed, since if he leaves the Casbah he will be caught. Duvivier captures a sense of Pépé's confinement in the Casbah district, despite the fact that most of the shots were made either in the studio or in the south of France (Fig. 13.14). At the end of the film, Pépé ventures out in order to leave Algiers with Gaby. He is arrested at the dock and asks permission to watch

Fig. 13.14

Fig. 13.15

her ship depart; as it pulls out to sea, he kills himself. Such a fatalistic ending is typical of Poetic Realist films.

Pépé was played by Jean Gabin, one of the most popular actors of the period and the ideal doomed Poetic Realist hero. Handsome enough to play leads in light comedies and dramas, heavy-featured Gabin was also a plausible working-class protagonist. He starred in Carné's two major Poetic Realist films: *Quai des brumes* (*Port of Shadows*, 1938) and *Le Jour se lève* (*Daybreak*, 1939).

In *Quai des brumes*, Gabin plays Jean, a deserter from the French Foreign Legion who encounters a beautiful woman, Nelly (played by Michèle Morgan, who formed, with Gabin, the "ideal couple" of the period). They fall in love, but she is protected by a powerful gangster. Although Jean kills the gangster, he is himself gunned down by a member of the gang at the end and dies in Nelly's arms. The dark, foggy cinematography of German cameraman Eugen Schüfftan and the atmospheric sets, with their rain-dampened brick streets, by Alexandre Trauner, created a look that typified Poetic Realism.

Le Jour se lève is another major example of Poetic Realism. Again Gabin plays the protagonist, François, a worker who commits a murder in the first scene and is trapped in his apartment by police. Throughout the night he recalls the circumstances leading up to his present pass, and we see them in three flashbacks showing how the villainous Valentin (the murder victim) had seduced the innocent young woman with whom François was in love. The simple story was not as important as the brooding atmosphere, created in part by Alexandre Trauner's set (Fig. 13.15). This studio-built version of a working-class district illustrates the mixture of stylization and realism in Poetic Realism. Maurice Jaubert's music supplies a simple drumbeat for the opening and closing scenes. Above all, Gabin's portrayal of François pensively waiting for his doom created the ultimate hero of Poetic Realism (Fig. 13.16). *Le Jour se lève* was released just three months before the German invasion of Poland. During the war, Carné would emphasize doomed romance and downplay realism in two of the most popular films of the era.

Fig. 13.14 *Pépé le Moko* uses setting to create a sense of the hero's entrapment in the Casbah of Algiers.

Fig. 13.15 The tall, thin set in *Le Jour se lève* emphasizes the isolation of the hero, trapped in his apartment on the top floor.

Fig. 13.16 One of the most famous images of Poetic Realism, with the trapped François looking out his window, surrounded by bullet holes created by the police outside.

Fig. 13.17 A typical Renoirian use of deep staging as Toni bends over Marie after she has tried to drown herself and his friend rushes in from the background.

The most significant director of 1930s French cinema was Jean Renoir. Although his filmmaking career stretched from the 1920s to the 1960s, his output during this one decade was a remarkable case of concentrated creativity. He made a wide variety of films, some in the Poetic Realist strain. His first sound film, *On purge Bébé* (roughly, "Baby's Laxative," 1931) was a farce that Renoir made in order to get backing for other projects. His next film was completely different, and can be seen as another forerunner of Poetic Realism. *La Chienne* ("The Bitch," 1931) concerns a mild accountant and amateur painter who is unhappily married; he stumbles into an affair with a prostitute whose pimp exploits the hero by selling his paintings. The hero ends up murdering the prostitute and escaping to become a cheerful panhandler. *La Chienne* introduced many elements that would characterize Renoir's work. There are virtuosic camera movements, scenes staged in depth, and abrupt switches of tone. The hero's murder of his mistress seems to make the film the sort of tragedy that would characterize Poetic Realism, yet he wanders off into contented poverty. Similarly, though the film is realistic in style, Renoir begins and ends it with the curtain of a puppet stage, thus suggesting that it is a stylized performance.

Renoir's other most notable films of the early 1930s include *Boudu sauvé des eaux* (*Boudu Saved from Drowning*, 1932) and *Toni* (1935). *Boudu* is the comic story of a tramp saved from suicide by a bourgeois bookseller who tries unsuccessfully to reform him. *Toni* is a more somber film dealing with the Italian and eastern European immigrant workers who came to France during the 1920s. It was produced by Marcel Pagnol and was shot entirely on location in the south of France. Its actors were largely unknown and spoke the dialect of the region. Toni is an Italian drifter who comes to France to work in a quarry; he marries his landlady Marie but falls in love with Josefa, who marries another man. When she learns the truth, Marie attempts suicide and then rejects him (Fig. 13.17). Toni takes the blame when Josefa kills her brutal husband. A posse shoots him as a new group of foreign workers arrives. *Toni* was a crucial forerunner of the Italian Neorealist movement.

Fig. 13.18 Again Renoir uses deep staging as one of the young men opens a window and watches the wife and daughter swinging in the inn yard in *A Day in the Country*.

In the mid-1930s, Renoir made a few films influenced by the leftist Popular Front political group, and we shall examine these shortly. He also made a nonpolitical short feature, *Une Partie de campagne* (*A Day in the Country*, 1936). This film creates a delicate balance of the humorous and tragic. A Parisian family picnicking at a country inn encounter two young men who seduce the wife and young daughter—to the delight of the wife and the regret of both the daughter and her seducer, who fall in love and must part. Throughout the film, Renoir conveys both the pleasure of the outing and the sense of loss that would follow it (Fig. 13.18). Due to bad weather, the film was never actually finished, and it was released only in 1946, with two titles summarizing the missing portions.

Fig. 13.19 In *Grand Illusion,* Commander von Rauffenstein picks the last flower in his prison camp in tribute to the French officer's death.

Renoir's *Grand Illusion* (1937) took a pacifist stance at a time when war with Germany was increasingly probable. This drama of French prisoners in World War I suggests that class ties are more important than national allegiances. The upper-class German camp commander and the French officer understand each other better than do the officer and his French subordinates. When the French officer sacrifices his life so that some of his men may escape, the German commander plucks the only flower in the prison, suggesting that their class is dying out (Fig. 13.19). In contrast, it is the working-class Maréchal and his Jewish friend Rosenthal who gain hope by escaping at the end.

This contrast between the declining aristocratic class and the working class reappeared in a more sardonic form in Renoir's last film of the decade, *Rules of the Game* (1939). Here a famous aviator causes confusion by falling in love with the wife of a French aristocrat who is in turn trying to break off with his mistress. These characters form part of a large gathering at the aristocrat's château. The servants' intrigues parallel the romantic confusion among the upper class, as a local poacher gets a job as a servant and immediately tries to seduce the gamekeeper's wife. The many romantic entanglements come to a head in a lengthy and virtuosic party scene at the château, as characters dodge in and out of rooms and forge and break relationships. Despite the characters' foolish actions, no one becomes a villain. As one of them remarks, "In this world, the scary thing is that everyone has his reasons." This line has often been taken as emblematic of Renoir's cinema, where there are seldom villains—only fallible people reacting to each other. In *Rules of the Game,* Renoir employed large, intricate sets and extensive camera movement to convey a sense of the characters' constant interactions (Fig. 13.20). In the end, a death is caused through the confusion, and it is covered up by the host. The film implies that the outworn aristocratic class is fading.

Rules of the Game was a failure at the time of its release. Audiences did not understand its mixture of tones, and it was perceived as attacking the ruling classes. The film was released just before France entered World War II, and it was soon banned.

Despite the weakness of the production sector, the French cinema of the 1930s created a high proportion of important films, thanks partly to the large number of talented people working in the industry. Lazare Meerson designed the sets for Clair's films *Sous les toits de Paris* and *À nous, la liberté!*

Fig. 13.20 The long hallway set in the château of *Rules of the Game,* where characters enter and exit unpredictably, conveying a sense of bustling activity in all the rooms.

and for Feyder's *Carnival in Flanders.* He also trained Alexandre Trauner, who worked consistently with Carné. Major French composers worked in the cinema as well: Georges Auric provided the music for *À nous, la liberté!;* Arthur Honegger scored *Crime and Punishment;* Josef Kosma contributed the haunting music for *A Day in the Country.* Most importantly, Maurice Jaubert composed music for *Zero for Conduct, L'Atalante, L'Affaire est dans le sac, Quai des brumes, Le Jour se lève,* and other films before his death in 1940 during the German invasion. Similarly, a surprisingly small number of script-writers contributed to many of the significant films of the decade, with the two most important being Charles Spaak (several Feyder and Renoir films) and Jacques Prévert (Carné and Renoir films).

Brief interlude: the popular front

During the 1930s, a gap widened between extreme right-wing and left-wing political parties. Leftists struggled against the rise of Fascist elements in France. Before 1934, these leftist parties did not cooperate: the Parti Communiste Français ("Communist party of France," or PCF) worked against the more moderate Socialists, and both disdained the middle-class Radical Socialists. In various countries, the Communists tried independently to defeat the Fascists. By 1933, however, the German wing of the party had failed to prevent Hitler's ascension to power.

In early 1934, the French political scene changed rapidly. Financier Serge Stavisky was revealed as a swindler who had the blessing of high government officials. In February, rightists protested with the violent "Stavisky riots," which brought down the Radical-Socialist government. The PCF responded with further riots, and several people were killed. The PCF decided to join forces with the rival Socialists, and in July a coalition party called the "Popular Front" was formed. In the autumn of 1935, even the moderate Radical Socialists were admitted into the Front.

By now the Depression was hitting the working class particularly hard: unemployment reached a record 460,000 by late 1935, and wages had fallen substantially. Economic problems and a fear of fascism led to a Popular Front victory in the elections in the spring of 1936. Socialist Léon Blum became head of the government. In May and June, a massive series of strikes broke out—including some of the film-producing companies. Blum's government passed important legislation benefiting the working class, including a forty-hour week and paid vacations.

There were soon divisions within the Popular Front, however. When the Spanish Civil War broke out in July 1936, Blum wanted to support the Republican cause against Franco's Fascist troops. Both right-wing groups and elements of the Popular Front opposed this move. Controversial economic decisions, such as proposals to nationalize certain industries, led to further dissension, and in 1937 Blum's government toppled.

Brief as it was, the Popular Front had a noticeable impact on the cinema. Although the PCF and the Socialists had each produced a few short propaganda films in the early 1930s, their first joint effort came in 1936. In January, the Popular Front formed a group called Ciné-Liberté to make films and issue a magazine. Members of the group included Renoir, Marc Allégret (who had directed *Fanny* and *Lac aux dames*), Feyder, and Germaine Dulac. Ciné-Liberté produced a feature film to be used as propaganda in the upcoming spring elections: *La Vie est à nous* ("Life Belongs to Us"). Both the PCF and the Socialists continued to make a few short propaganda and documentary films during the 1930s. The last major left-wing feature was *La Marseillaise* (1938). As Renoir was the most prominent director in Ciné-Liberté, he was a logical choice to supervise the collectively made *La Vie est à nous* and to direct the epic production of *La Marseillaise*. (See Box.)

Aside from its direct participation in the production of a few films, the Popular Front inspired several commercial films. Foremost among these were two about workers' cooperatives. Renoir's *The Crime of Monsieur Lange* (1935) concerns life in a building that includes apartments, a laundry, and a publishing firm. The publisher, Batala, exploits his workers, mismanages the business, and seduces an innocent laundress. When he is forced to flee his creditors and is thought to have been killed in a train wreck, Monsieur Lange, one of his writers, leads the workers in reorganizing the publishing firm into a cooperative. Everyone in the building cheerfully takes part in the publication of Lange's successful Western series, "Arizona Jim," and the firm gets back on its feet. When Batala unexpectedly returns, Lange kills him in order to protect the cooperative and flees with his lover, Valentine, the owner of the laundry.

Although Renoir's previous film, *Toni,* had been concerned with the working class, *Monsieur Lange* was his most overtly left-wing film to date. (It was largely as a result of *Monsieur Lange* that Renoir was asked to supervise *La Vie est à nous*.) It is one of the rare cases where Renoir includes a truly villainous character, the monstrous Batala. Renoir uses his distinctive technique to suggest the unity among the people of the entire building by organizing the setting around a central courtyard across which the characters can

POPULAR FRONT FILMMAKING: *LA VIE EST À NOUS* AND *LA MARSEILLAISE*

These two productions were created outside normal channels. *La Vie est à nous* was made in early 1936, to be used in the Popular Front's election campaign. It was largely financed through collections taken up at PCF meetings, and both the cast and crew donated their labor. It was shot quickly, in about two weeks. Although often referred to as a Renoir film, those who worked on it stressed that *La Vie est à nous* was a collaborative project. Renoir supervised the production and directed only a few sequences, while other scenes were directed by Jacques Brunius, Jean-Paul Le Chanois, and Jacques Becker. Completed a few weeks before the May elections, the film was shown in private Popular Front meetings and rallies.

La Vie est à nous was innovative in its form as well as in its production circumstances. Taking further the mixture of staged and documentary footage Brecht and Dudow had used in *Kuhle Wampe* (p. 347), Renoir's team mixed scenes and documents in a collage style. What begins as a documentary about France is revealed to be a lecture staged in a classroom; we follow some of the children out into the street as they discuss their poverty, and then a woman directly addresses the camera, giving a straightforward message. Other elements include still photographs, occasional intertitles, newsreel footage, and signs. Several Popular Front officials appear as themselves, yet well-known actors play the workers and peasants who support them. In one scene, a movie screen behind an industrialist illustrates what he is saying (Fig. 13.21). Later a "family photo album" mocks the "200 fami-

Fig. 13.22 The "200 families" were the richest in France and were commonly blamed by leftists for the country's financial woes. Here a "family album" lampoons real-life targets like Eugène Schneider, "cannon merchant."

Fig. 13.23 In *La Marseillaise*, a group of French aristocrats in exile listen nostalgically to a song about France.

lies" of France (Fig. 13.22). At one point, the filmmakers show newsreel footage of Hitler speaking but substitute a dog's barking on the sound track.

La Vie est à nous disappeared after the May elections, and a print resurfaced only in 1969. It was then hailed for its inventive approach and became highly influential.

La Marseillaise is a historical epic depicting the events of the French Revolution surrounding the fall of the monarchy in 1792. Made in support of the Popular Front, the film was

Fig. 13.21 In *La Vie est à nous*, an industrialist complains of how workers have destroyed equipment and burned farm produce to protest low wages and prices; on the screen behind him, a film shows scenes of the destruction.

Fig. 13.24 A tracking shot begins on some children playing leapfrog . . .

Fig. 13.26 . . . pauses on boys playing marbles . . .

Fig. 13.25 . . . moves to the right past a large crowd looking off right . . .

Fig. 13.27 . . . and ends on a group of men battering down the gates of the Tuileries Palace—an event which will lead to the abolition of the French monarchy.

to be financed through a subscription system: members of the large labor union, the Confédération Générale du Travail, would buy coupons good toward the cost of tickets when the film eventually appeared. Not enough tickets were purchased, however, and Renoir had to set up a special company to produce the film. This firm was not much different from the many little one-film production companies in France during this period. *La Marseillaise* had a regular commercial release in early 1938, but by that point the Popular Front's mass support had dissipated.

The film was praised by the leftist press but proved unpopular, perhaps partly because Renoir refused to make Louis XVI and the aristocrats of his court into stock villains. Instead, he treats them sympathetically, as dignified members of a dying class, rather like the upper-class figures in *Rules of the Game* (Fig. 13.23). Moreover, Renoir shows only a few of the important events of the Revolution; he concentrates on everyday occurrences, focusing primarily on a group of soldiers from Marseille who march to Paris to join the fighting, bringing with them the new song that will become the national anthem. Renoir also uses few stars, giving the main roles to minor actors with real accents from the south of France.

The film is full of the spectacular tracking shots typical of Renoir's work. One of these exemplifies his "bottom-up" approach to history in this film, encompassing both trivial and momentous events (Figs. 13.24–13.27). This mixture may have made *La Marseillaise* too undramatic for contemporary audiences.

Fig. 13.28 Deep staging in *The Crime of Monsieur Lange* simultaneously shows characters in the concierge's apartment in the foreground, the courtyard in the middle ground, and the laundry in the background.

Fig. 13.29 Jean and Mario, two of the unemployed heroes of *La Belle équipe*, stand in front of a poster advertising skiing holidays ("Why shiver in Paris? Stockpile healthiness among the eternal snows").

Fig. 13.30 Charles and Jean, the remaining protagonists, introduce the triumphal final dance that signals the success of their café.

Fig. 13.31 The pessimistic final shot of the original ending of *La Belle équipe*. As Jean is arrested for the murder of his partner, he declares, "It's all over. It was a wonderful idea."

interact. Deep staging juxtaposes events in different parts of the building (Fig. 13.28).

Julien Duvivier's *La Belle équipe* ("The Glorious Team," aka *They Were Five*, 1937) begins with five unemployed workers. An ironic juxtaposition places two of them before a vacation poster (Fig. 13.29) at a time when many working-class people had never been able to afford to leave their grim urban neighborhoods. When the five men win a lottery, they determine to start a cooperative riverside café near Paris. Many little touches indicate the egalitarian quality of the project: each of the five has a sign over his bed with the word "President," and the café's name is Chez Nous ("Our Place"). Yet various problems gradually lead two of the protagonists to drop out of the project, and one dies in an accident during a party at the unfinished café. By the end, the remaining two have resolved their jealous feud over a woman and preside over the Chez Nous's grand opening (Fig. 13.30). In fact, Duvivier had wanted an unhappy ending in which Jean kills Charles over the woman they both love and is arrested while sitting in the empty café (Fig. 13.31). The producer, however, insisted on a happy ending.

Duvivier's original intention for *La Belle équipe*'s ending suggests that the main films inspired by the Popular Front were not very far removed from

Fig. 13.29

Fig. 13.30

Fig. 13.31

Poetic Realism. While the villainous Batala may be killed in *The Crime of Monsieur Lange*, Lange and Valentine must pay the price by fleeing from France. *La Belle équipe* would have ended with the cooperative project in a shambles. The aspirations of the Popular Front are evident in a less obvious way in other Poetic Realist films that deal sympathetically, if pessimistically, with working-class heroes.

FILMMAKING IN OCCUPIED AND VICHY FRANCE

THE SITUATION IN THE FILM INDUSTRY

When Germany unleashed World War II by invading Poland on September 1, 1939, France and Great Britain honored their diplomatic commitments and declared war on Germany. Many French filmmakers were mobilized, and production of twenty films was suspended.

Poland collapsed swiftly, however, and the British and French did little to prevent it. The period to April 9, 1940, was the *drôle de guerre*, or "phony war." During this time, 2 million French troops remained in the field, but virtually no fighting occurred. It was widely assumed that an Allied blockade would eventually defeat Germany. By October 1939, film production resumed, and it continued throughout the phony war.

In the spring of 1940, Germany attacked again, occupying Denmark on April 9 and moving in quick succession into Norway, the Netherlands, and Belgium. On June 5, Germany invaded France; meeting weak resistance, it occupied Paris on June 14. Two days later a right-wing French government was set up in Vichy, a resort town. The southern portion of France remained an "unoccupied" zone for over two years, with the Vichy government holding power at the pleasure of the Germans.

The film industry was enormously disrupted by these events. Jews, leftists, and others fled into the unoccupied zone or went abroad. Feyder, for example, made one film in the south and then went to Switzerland in 1942; he was unable to direct again until after the war. Renoir worked in the United States during the 1940s. Some refugees returned to the occupied zone after production resumed there in June 1941. Two separate film industries developed.

Vichy Cinema. During late 1940, the Vichy government created the Comité d'Organisation de l'Industrie Cinématographique (COIC) to support and control the industry. Producers had to go through an elaborate application process to get permission to make a film, and censorship under the Vichy regime was even harsher than that in the German-controlled zone. In addition, the rightist government strove to eliminate Jews from the film industry.

The southern zone had only a few small studios, including Pagnol's in Marseille. Equipment and raw stock were scarce and sometimes had to be obtained on the black market. Producers also faced a lack of funding. Until May 1942, films made in the unoccupied zone were banned from the German zone; thus they showed only in the limited market of southern France and French North Africa. Moreover, there were few French investors in the area.

Some financing came clandestinely from Jewish and American sources or openly from Italian investors. For example, the French firm Discina was closely linked with the Scalera company of Rome. The two firms co-produced some important films, including Jean Delannoy's *L'Eternel retour* ("The Eternal Return," 1943), Carné's *Les Visiteurs du soir* ("Visitors of the Evening," 1942), and Carné's *Les Enfants du paradis* (*Children of Paradise*, 1945, completed by Pathé after Italy's defeat). Italian firms also invested in other film enterprises in southern France and provided a market for some French films. Abel Gance's *Le Captaine Fracasse* (1943) was another Italian-French coproduction.

The COIC helped alleviate financial problems by arranging for low-interest government loans for production. Films made with such loans include Grémillon's *Lumière d'été* ("Summer Light," 1943) and *Le Ciel est à vous* ("The Sky Is Yours," 1944) and Robert Bresson's *Les Anges du péché* ("Angels of Sin," 1943). Later the COIC attempted to foster quality production with an annual prize of 100,000 francs for the best films of the year. *Les Visiteurs du soir* won in 1942 and *Les Anges du péché* in 1943. (This prize may have been modeled on those given in Italy.) Finally, once southern films were allowed into the German zone, they shared in the generally high profits of the war period.

Occupied France.   The situation in the occupied zone was quite different. Initially there was no French production, and a ban on imports of American, British, and French films from the Vichy area gave the Germans a monopoly on screenings. Some German films, especially the infamous *Jud Süss*, were successful. Audiences preferred French films, however, and attendance dropped in 1941. In May of that year, German officials allowed French production to resume. Many filmmakers who had fled returned to the better-equipped studios of Paris. Once new French films began appearing in the cinemas, attendance rose again. With no competition from American films, French production actually became more profitable during the war.

Why did the German authorities permit French production? For one thing, it was widely assumed at that point, by the Germans and many French, that Germany would win the war. Its leaders planned to create a "New Europe," under German control. France would contribute to that new order. Moreover, strong European production could help Germany break the American domination of world markets, thus fulfilling—though in a less cooperative spirit—the old "Film Europe" goal of the 1920s. A healthy French film industry could also demonstrate to other occupied countries the benefits of cooperating with the Germans.

In addition, there was considerable German investment in France's film industry. That investment came mainly through the formation in 1940 of a German company, Continental, in Paris. Continental was a subsidiary of the giant firm Ufa, which, as we saw in the previous chapter, was becoming the single centralized film company in Germany. Of the approximately 220 features made in both parts of France during the Occupation, 30, or nearly one-seventh, were produced by Continental. By way of contrast, the largest French producer, Pathé-Cinéma, made fourteen films during the same period. Most production companies were still small firms, making from one to eight films during the war. Continental was vertically integrated, owning its own studios, laboratories, and the biggest French theater chain; it released its films through Ufa's Paris distribution subsidiary. Continental signed up several major French stars and directors and produced some of the most popular—and controversial—films of the Occupation.

German censorship of French films was surprisingly lenient, concentrating on eliminating references to the United States and Great Britain. One area of official control was strict, however. Several regulations were passed to prevent Jews from participating in the film industry, and prewar films with Jewish actors were banned. During the war, about 75,000 French Jews were sent to concentration camps in Germany, and few of them survived. Most Jewish filmmakers, however, managed to flee or hide, and some kept working clandestinely.

France was divided until November 1942, when Germany occupied its southern portion, keeping the Vichy regime as a figurehead government. From then on the southern production facilities functioned mainly as places for Parisian firms to go for location shooting.

It is sometimes assumed that all French filmmakers who worked in France during the Occupation were collaborating with the enemy. Many, however, felt they were keeping the French film industry alive during an extremely difficult period. While a few films reflected Fascist ideals, others were pro-French. Quite a few filmmakers also served secretly in the French Resistance movement. There was a resistance group for cinema, the Comité de Libération du Cinéma Français; members included Grémillon, director Jacques Becker, and actors Pierre Blanchar and Pierre Renoir.

The Allied military push that eventually defeated the Germans began in late 1942. From this point on, the French Resistance expanded. Allied bombing within France damaged some film facilities, with five studios destroyed and 322 theaters damaged or leveled. A shortage of materials hampered production late in the war, and by July 1944, all production ceased. Filmmakers in the Resistance movement fought in the general uprising during August, while secretly filming the liberation of Paris.

Some filmmakers suspected of collaborating were punished. A few, such as Sacha Guitry and Maurice Chevalier, were briefly imprisoned but then exonerated. Director Henri-Georges Clouzot was briefly barred from filmmaking for having made a supposedly anti-French film, *Le Corbeau* ("The Crow," 1943). In order to see why such punishment was meted out, we need to look at the kinds of films made during the Occupation.

FILMS OF THE OCCUPATION PERIOD

Most films made during the Occupation were comedies and melodramas of the sort that had appeared before the war. Censorship in the German and Vichy zones forced filmmakers to avoid subject matter relating to the war and other social problems.

The most notable films of this period fit into the "prestige" category, close to what would later be called the "Cinema of Quality" (Chapter 17). Belying their straitened circumstances, these films were expert productions, with impressive sets and major stars. Cut off from contemporary reality, they conveyed a mood of romantic resignation. Some films, however, also could

Fig. 13.32 In *L'Assassinat du Père Noël*, Cornusse plays Santa Claus for the villagers while mysterious events are occurring.

be interpreted as suggesting resistance to oppression—vague allegories of French indomitability.

Perhaps the first such film was Christian-Jacque's *L'Assassinat du Père Noël* ("The Murder of Santa Claus," 1941). Set in a snow-covered mountain village, it tells the story of a mapmaker, Cornusse, who plays Santa Claus for the local children every year (Fig. 13.32). On Christmas Eve, odd events occur: a sinister figure steals a saint's relics from the church, and the village's baron, returned from an enigmatic absence, courts Cornusse's ethereal daughter. All ends well, with Cornusse's visit miraculously curing a crippled boy. Cornusse tells him that a French sleeping beauty will someday be awakened by a Prince Charming. Although *L'Assassinat du Père Noël* was the first production by Continental, the German firm, its symbolic message was presumably apparent to many French filmgoers.

Marcel L'Herbier, who had been a major figure in the French Impressionist movement of the 1920s, made his most personal film since that time with *La Nuit fantastique* ("The Fantastic Night," 1942). In it, a poor student works in a Parisian produce market and dreams nightly of an angelic woman in white. One day the woman wanders through the market, taking him on a strange journey through a nightclub, a magic shop, and an insane asylum. When he wakes again, the woman reappears, and they go off together into a permanent dreamlike realm. L'Herbier revived Impressionist subjective techniques for *La Nuit fantastique*, using reversed sound, slow motion, and split-screen effects to convey the hero's dreaming visions. Similarly, Pierre Prévert managed to rekindle something of the anarchic spirit of *L'Affaire est dans le sac* in his 1943 feature, *Adieu . . . Leonard!* Leonard, a thief, undergoes a series of comic adventures and then ends up abandoning society and going off with his friends in a gypsy caravan.

Escapist fantasy of a more romantic and morbid kind is apparent in two major films of the midwar period. Marcel Carné's *Les Visiteurs du soir* (1942), a romance set in medieval times, employs elaborate costumes and settings (Fig. 13.33). Yet because of shortages, many period costumes had to be made of cheap cloth. The crew injected poison into the scarce fruit in the banquet scenes to prevent hungry extras from eating it. In *Les Visiteurs*, a man and a woman are sent by the Devil to corrupt the inhabitants of a castle. The man falls in love with the princess he is supposed to seduce, and ultimately the Devil turns them both to statues (Fig. 13.34). This ending has been widely interpreted as another allegory of France's resistance to German Occupation. Two prominent Jewish film artists, set designer Alexandre Trauner and composer Joseph Kosma, collaborated anonymously on the film.

A similar story of doomed love appeared in Jean Delannoy's *L'Eternel retour* (1943), from a Jean Cocteau script based on the Tristan and Isolde legend. Cocteau set the story in contemporary times but on an isolated island. The hero, Patrice, goes to fetch a young wife, Natalie, for his elderly uncle. Falling in love with her, he lives out a doomed existence in which his evil cousin Achille (a dwarf) plots against him. Eventually Patrice and Natalie, both coldly beautiful, idealized characters, accept death as the only way that they can stay together. This sort of fatalism, with little hope of resistance, typified much French filmmaking of the Occupation period.

The era was also notable for two films by Jean Grémillon, whose *La Petite Lise* had been a major early sound film and an early entry in the Poetic

Fig. 13.33

Fig. 13.34

Fig. 13.35

Fig. 13.36

Realist tendency. In *Lumière d'été* (1943), a love triangle among older peo-ple—Cri-Cri, a dancer who now runs a mountain hotel, Patrice, a local nobleman, and Roland, an alcoholic artist—is played off against a more innocent romance between a young engineer, Julien, and a young woman, Michèle. Patrice tries to seduce Michèle, but after a masked ball and a car crash, the relationships sort themselves out, and Julien and Michèle end up together. The film's settings (Fig. 13.35) and acting made it stand out in the period. Because of its sordid depiction of its characters, the film was nearly banned by the Vichy authorities, who demanded strong, upright French figures.

La Ciel est à vous (1944) is more upbeat. Here Grémillon shows the family of a garage owner sacrificing everything so that the wife, Thérèse, can establish a long-distance solo flying record. The story uses conventional Hollywood-style suspense, showing the family struggling to finance the trip and waiting as Thérèse loses radio contact on her record-breaking flight. With its patriotic motifs (Fig. 13.36), the film lauded French heroism and even revived a bit of the spirit of the Popular Front.

Fig. 13.33 The Devil's emissaries approach the immense castle set in the opening scene of *Les Visiteurs du soir*.

Fig. 13.34 The Devil hears the heartbeats of his victims and realizes he has failed to completely subjugate them.

Fig. 13.35 An effective use of a location setting in the mountains in Grémillon's *Lumière d'été*.

Fig. 13.36 At the opening of a small airport in *La Ciel est à vous*, French flags are draped conspicuously in the background.

Fig. 13.37

Fig. 13.38

Fig. 13.37 Robert Bresson used the black and white costumes of the nuns, in combination with careful lighting and composition, to create an arresting visual style in *Les Anges du péché.*

Fig. 13.38 Jewish designer Alexandre Trauner worked clandestinely on *Children of Paradise* to create enormous sets reconstructing the theater district of mid-nineteenth-century Paris.

Fig. 13.39 The bittersweet pantomime involving Pierrot, Columbine, and Harlequin in *Children of Paradise* suggests the sense of lost love that pervades the film's offstage romances.

The most important filmmaker to begin a career during the Occupation period was Robert Bresson, whose first feature, *Les Anges du péché,* appeared in 1943. An audacious *film noir* set in a convent, it deals with nuns who try to reform female criminals. Bresson's characteristic narrative of spiritual redemption emerged in mature form, with a rebellious nun and a murderess unpredictably helping each other find peace. The austere visual style also looked forward to Bresson's later films (Fig. 13.37). Bresson's next film, *Les Dames de Bois de Bologne* ("The Ladies of the Bois de Bologne") began production late in the Occupation period but was not released until a year after the liberation of France. It shares some traits of the Occupation films, since its narrative is cut off from contemporary society, dealing with a high-society woman who tries to take revenge on her ex-lover by tricking him into marrying a woman who has been a prostitute.

Perhaps the two most famous films of the Occupation period are *Children of Paradise* and *Le Corbeau.* Carné's three-hour feature was, again, made under difficult circumstances, in the lean late war period. A vast tapestry of the theater world in nineteenth-century Paris (Fig. 13.38), the story traces the romantic entanglements of several characters, centering around the famous mime Baptiste Debureau and Garance, an actress, whose thwarted love echoes their onstage roles (Fig. 13.39).

Nothing could be further from the mood of romantic melancholy that pervades *Children of Paradise* than the cynicism of Clouzot's *Le Corbeau.* The film is set in a small French town where a series of poison-pen letters signed "Le Corbeau" reveal various secrets about several of the most respected members of the community. The panicky townspeople react with unreasoning suspicions. The protagonist, Dr. Germain, receives a letter falsely accusing him of having an affair with a married woman and of being an abortionist. He is seduced by Denise, a young woman whom the community is quick to condemn for her loose morals—despite the fact that she is one of the few to refuse to enter into the hysterical suspicions and accusations prompted by Le Corbeau's letters (Fig. 13.40).

At the time of *Le Corbeau*'s release in 1943, its unpleasant subject matter led to its being widely condemned as anti-French—especially since it had been produced by the German-backed Continental company. Clouzot was banned from filmmaking after the Liberation in 1944, and the film has remained controversial. Yet some have argued that *Le Corbeau* was a specific attack on the sorts of right-wing values that undergirded the Vichy government.

The end of the Occupation brought many changes for French filmmaking, including the renewed competition with imported American films. Yet most of the filmmakers of the wartime period kept working, and the decentralized industrial structures survived into the postwar era.

Fig. 13.40 At the funeral of one of the "Crow's" victims in *Le Corbeau*, the villagers pass around another poison-pen letter.

◆ NOTES AND QUERIES

RENEWED INTEREST IN THE POPULAR FRONT

Most surveys of film history written before the 1970s cover René Clair's work, Poetic Realism, and the Occupation—but not the Popular Front. This brief, but important, movement drew attention mainly in the late 1960s and after, when there was a renewed interest in critical political cinema. (See Chapter 23.) In particular, *La Vie est à nous* and *La Marseillaise*, which had been treated simply as examples of Renoir's work, have been examined in their specific political contexts.

An early study (1966) of the Popular Front cinema is Geffredo Fofi's "The Cinema of the Popular Front in France (1934–1938)," translated in *Screen* **13**, 3 (Winter 1972–1973): 5–57. A collective text on *La Vie est à nous* appeared in *Cahiers du cinéma* in 1970 and has been translated as Pascal Bonitzer et al., "*La Vie est à nous:* A Militant Film" in Nick Browne, ed., *Cahiers du Cinéma: 1969–1971: The Politics of Representation* (Cambridge, Mass.: Harvard University Press, 1990), pp. 68–88. See also Elizabeth Grottle Strebel's "Renoir and the Popular Front," *Sight and Sound* **49**, 1 (Winter 1979–1980): 36–41, and Ginette Vincendeau and Keith Reader, eds., *La Vie est à nous!: French Cinema of the Popular Front 1935–1938* (London: British Film Institute, 1986).

The most extensive study in English, Jonathan Buchsbaum's *Cinema Engagé: Film in the Popular Front* (Urbana: University of Illinois Press, 1988), takes issue with these earlier studies and deals only with those films actually produced by left-wing French political parties during the 1930s. For a broader overview that treats many films of the 1930s in relation to the Popular Front, see Geneviève Guillaume-Grimaud's *Le Cinéma du Front Populaire* (Paris: Lherminier, 1986).

◆ REFERENCE

1. Quoted in Pierre Lagnan, *Les Années Pagnol* (Renens: 5 Continents, 1989), p. 111.

14

LEFTIST, DOCUMENTARY, AND EXPERIMENTAL CINEMAS, 1930–1945

The era from the early Depression to the end of World War II brought about particularly dramatic changes for filmmakers who worked outside the mainstream commercial industry. Economic hardship and sound technology made it prohibitively expensive for many individual experimenters and documentarists to work independently. To a considerable extent, the 1920s generation of experimental filmmakers turned in other directions. A new group then took their places, sometimes by depending on cheaper, recently developed amateur equipment.

The rise of fascism, civil wars in China and Spain, and the move toward global conflict pushed many filmmakers, who were often leftist in their sympathies, to politicize their work. Some who had begun by making lyrical films turned to documentary work, recording epochal events. At first, political films tended to be pacifist, equating militarism with imperialist aggression. Later, when the Axis powers began invading their neighbors, leftists came to support the war effort to resist them.

THE SPREAD OF POLITICAL CINEMA

During the 1920s and early 1930s, Soviet films, particularly those of the Montage movement, galvanized viewers around the world. Some audiences were interested primarily in these films' stylistic innovations, but others also saw them as models for strongly leftist cinema. Politicized filmmakers displayed the influence of the Soviets. Thus this era's leftist films, though made in different countries, often resemble each other.

THE UNITED STATES

Politically active filmmakers in the United States started by confronting the issues of poverty and racism. Communist groups had produced a few documentaries during the 1920s, but the first regular association was formed in 1930. Several film enthusiasts in New York joined with a Communist still-photographers' organization to create the Workers' Film and Photo League. (The word "Workers" was soon dropped.) Soon a national network of Film and Photo Leagues grew up, cooperating to shoot footage for newsreels that could be shown at socialist gatherings. The filmmakers received no payment, and costs were made up by donations, benefits, and screenings of classic films. The leagues used silent cameras purchased cheaply after the advent of sound. Their early films mainly recorded demonstrations, strikes, and hunger marches that took place around the country (Fig. 14.1).

Fig. 14.1 *Workers Newsreel Unemployment Special* (1931, edited by Leo Seltzer) documented widespread hunger and protests against government policy, as with this longshoremen's march.

Members of the Film and Photo League in New York included Paul Strand and Ralph Steiner, who had made lyrical documentaries (Strand's *Manhatta*) and abstract films (Steiner's H_2O) in the 1920s. Photographer Margaret Bourke-White joined the group, as did Thomas Brandon, who after the war would become an important 16mm distributor for film societies and classes. The leagues' other activities included providing lecturers to leftist gatherings, writing criticism that denounced Hollywood films and upheld alternative cinema, and protesting screenings of Nazi films.

During 1935, the New York branch published a short-lived newsletter, *Filmfront*, that contained translations of essays by leftist theorists and critics, including Dziga Vertov. A report issued by the leagues in 1934 made explicit the links with his "kino-eye" theory (p. 203):

> "The Film and Photo Leagues" were rooted in the intellectual and social basis of the Soviet film . . . in the same way as the Soviet cinema began with the kino-eye and grew organically from there on . . . the Leagues started also with the simple newsreel documents, photographing events as they appeared to the lens, true to the nature of the revolutionary medium, they exploited in a revolutionary cinematic way.[1]

By the mid-1930s, however, some members were moving on to more ambitious projects, and the leagues were moribund by 1937.

In 1935, several filmmakers left to form a loose collective, Nykino, whose name (roughly, "cinema now") again suggests a conscious imitation of Soviet cinema. Nykino made only a few films, including documentaries, and one notable satire on the sanctimonious promises made to the poor during the Depression. *Pie in the Sky* (1934) was set principally in a dump, where actors improvised gags on church and government institutions (Fig. 14.2). By early 1937, Nykino was transformed into a nonprofit filmmaking firm, Frontier. Frontier was quite successful for a few years in making longer documentaries with impressive photography by, among others, Ralph Steiner and Paul Strand. The former was cinematographer on *People of the Cumberland* (1938, directed by Sidney Meyers and Jay Leyda), which dealt with unionization in the Cumberland Mountain region.

Frontier's last and longest film was *Native Land*, shot in the late 1930s, though not released until 1942. It was directed by Paul Strand and Leo

Fig. 14.2 Two homeless men satirize the welfare system in *Pie in the Sky*.

Fig. 14.3 A staged shot in depth from *Native Land*, showing police looming ominously in the foreground as they break up a peaceful demonstration among strikers.

Hurwitz and photographed by Strand. *Native Land* is a quasidocumentary, restaging actual incidents in which working-class people struggle against oppressive forces of capitalism. In one episode, sharecroppers who try to organize and obtain higher prices for cotton are chased by police; a black farmer and a white one flee together, but they are both shot down. The incident stresses that workers of different races must cooperate to defend themselves. Other episodes show peaceful union activities broken up by police or company goons (Fig. 14.3).

Leftist cinema declined during the 1940s, due in part to increasing anti-Communist pressures and radical sympathizers' disillusionment after Stalin's purges and show trials. Fearing the spread of fascism, the Communists also decided to support the American government during the war. Some former members of the Film and Photo Leagues worked on government- and corporate-sponsored documentaries.

GERMANY

Leftist filmmaking began relatively early in Germany, since that country had been the first to import the Soviet films of the 1920s. Moreover, the Communist party and other left-wing groups in Germany became more active as the influence of right-wing political parties like the Nazis grew in the late 1920s and early 1930s.

In 1926, the International Workers' Relief, a Communist organization concerned with fostering the growth of the USSR, formed Prometheus, a film firm that would distribute Soviet films. It scored a big success in 1926 with *Potemkin* (p. 136) and subsequently released many more imported pictures. During the late 1920s, Prometheus also produced German films, including Piel Jutzi's *Mother Krausen's Journey to Happiness* (1929). By this time, Germany was suffering sharply rising unemployment as a result of the Depression. Jutzi's film reveals in grim detail the life of a family trapped in a tiny apartment; when the son is arrested as a thief after losing his job, his mother commits suicide. Only his sister, who ends by joining in a Communist demonstration with her fiancé (see Fig. 8.7), represents a sense of hope for German society. The film's title was an ironic commentary on the plight of the poor, for whom suicide seems one path to "happiness."

Prometheus also produced the most prominent German Communist film of this era, *Kuhle Wampe* (1932, Slatan Dudow), named for the workers' camp in which it is set. The script was written by Bertolt Brecht, the leftist playwright who invented the "epic" theater and whose *The Threepenny Opera* had recently been an enormous hit. Brecht believed that theater spectators should be distanced from the actions they witnessed so that they could think through the implications of the events rather than remaining emotionally involved with the story. He applied this idea in *Kuhle Wampe*, which explores unemployment, abortion, the situation of women, and other issues in a series of episodes from the life of a single family. The son commits suicide after failing for months to find a job: "One fewer unemployed" a title ironically comments at the beginning of this scene (Fig. 14.4). Ultimately the daughter of the family, nearly abandoned by her fiancé after she becomes pregnant, finds help through Communist youth activities, and the family gains a semblance of normal life at the tent city of the unemployed, Kuhle Wampe. Intertitles, songs by Kurt Weill (composer of *The Threepenny Opera*), and a lengthy sequence at a Communist youth sports festival all help give *Kuhle Wampe* the feel of a political tract.

Prometheus went out of business in 1932, and another producer finished the film. By that point, however, the Communist cinema was fighting a lost battle. The Nazis came to power in 1933, and Brecht and Weill soon were both working in the Hollywood cinema—where their approach fit in uneasily.

BELGIUM AND THE NETHERLANDS

In Belgium, which had suffered a lengthy occupation by the Germans during World War I, documentarists and experimentalists were quick to respond to the growth of fascism. Charles Dekeukeleire, who had manipulated narratives in frustrating ways in his silent films (pp. 201–202), turned to political film with *Flamme blanche* ("White Flame," 1931). He combined documentary footage of a Communist rally with staged scenes of police hunting down a young demonstrator hiding in a barn (Fig. 14.5).

Dekeukeleire's friend Henri Storck had started a ciné-club in his hometown, the Belgian seaside resort of Ostende, in the 1920s. He also had made several poetic documentaries and city symphonies, including *Images d'Ostende* (1929). During the early 1930s, however, his career took a political turn. In 1932 he made an anti-fascist, pacifist compilation documentary, *Histoire d'un soldat inconnu* ("History of an Unknown Soldier"). Storck's approach to editing was novel, juxtaposing stock footage of governmental and religious leaders supporting the military with bizarre imagery that created a bitterly ironic comment on warmongering (Figs. 14.6, 14.7).

Dutch filmmaker Joris Ivens, who had also been involved in a ciné-club and made films in abstract and city-symphony genres during the 1920s (p. 199), became more politically oriented. After the success of *The Bridge* and

Fig. 14.4 Brecht's technique of distancing the audience from the action appears after the suicide in *Kuhle Wampe*, when a neighbor woman turns to the camera and repeats the phrase used earlier in an intertitle: "One fewer unemployed."

Fig. 14.5 A Soviet-influenced composition in *Flamme blanche*, with a dynamic low-angle framing isolating a threatening police officer's head against a blank sky.

Fig. 14.6

Fig. 14.7

Figs. 14.6 and 14.7 Utilizing Soviet-style intellectual montage, Storck compares a yapping lapdog to a pompous politician.

Rain, he was invited to make a documentary on the steel industry, *Song of Heroes* (1932), in the Soviet Union. At that point, Henri Storck was invited by a left-wing ciné-club in Brussels to make a film exposing the oppressive treatment of coal miners in the Borinage region of Belgium, and he asked Ivens to collaborate with him.

The result was *Misère au Borinage* ("Misery in Borinage," generally known as *Borinage,* 1933). Storck and Ivens made the film clandestinely, dodging authorities to film workers reenacting scenes of clashes with police, evictions, and marches (Fig. 14.8). *Borinage*'s powerful treatment of its subject led to its banning in Belgium and the Netherlands, though it was widely seen in ciné-clubs. Ivens returned to the Netherlands to make another film on the exploitation of workers, *New Earth* (1934), in which he showed how thousands of workers who helped create dikes and new land suddenly ended up unemployed. Thereafter Ivens's remarkable career took him around the world, as he recorded left-wing activities over the next several decades.

Fig. 14.8 Workers carry a homemade picture of Karl Marx during a reenacted demonstration scene in *Borinage.*

GREAT BRITAIN

Socialist ciné-clubs and filmmaking groups were particularly active in Britain, in part as a reaction to strict censorship that forbade public screenings of Soviet and other leftist films.

In October 1929, a group of Communist trade unions created the Federation of Workers' Film Societies to encourage the formation of such clubs. In November, the London Workers' Film Society was established, and during the 1930s, the movement spread to other British cities. The federation distributed 35mm prints of leftist German and Soviet films to such groups, and it also issued a newsreel, the *Workers' Topical News.*

It soon became apparent, however, that the key to both production and distribution would be 16mm equipment. In 1932, several Communists filmed a May Day demonstration against Japanese aggression in Manchuria (Fig. 14.9). At that point, however, there was no regular distribution mechanism for 16mm films. In 1933, Rudolph Messel formed the Socialist Film Council, the first leftist group in the United Kingdom that systematically used 16mm. Messel asked local groups to submit footage of the oppression of labor. He edited this material into several films, including *What the News Reel Does Not Show* (1933), which juxtaposed footage of the Soviet Five-Year Plan with scenes in London slums.

In 1934, another socialist group, the Workers' Theatre Movement, formed Kino, a production-distribution firm that concentrated on 16mm films. Kino (the Russian word for "cinema") also distributed Soviet films. Also in 1934, the Workers' Film and Photo League was established to coordinate the activities of leftist film groups. (Following its American prototype, the league soon eliminated the word "Workers" from its name.) Finally, leftist Ivor Montagu, one of the main founders of the Film Society in 1925, established the Progressive Film Institute to make documentaries and distribute more Soviet films.

Most films produced by these groups during the 1930s were made by leftist sympathizers who were not themselves members of the working class. One exception was Alf Garrard, a carpenter and amateur filmmaker. After a successful strike by his union, he received support from the Film and Photo League to make secretly a film of actual construction work and combine it with restaged scenes of the strike made with the help of his fellow workers (Fig. 14.10). The film was intended to promote unionism. Dozens of other films of this era documented unemployment, marches, strikes, and other aspects of labor's struggle.

The middle of the decade saw a shift in British political filmmaking. In 1935, the Communist International changed its policy. Rather than concentrating on class struggle, it encouraged leftists around the world to oppose the spread of fascism. Partly as a result, during the second half of the 1930s, European groups reacted to two civil wars, in Spain and China. British leftists were to play an important role in documenting the plight of the former. The beginning of World War II caused a severe decline in socialist filmmaking activity in Britain.

Fig. 14.9 *Against Imperialist War— May Day 1932* is an early example of the many films of protests and marches made by British leftists. The filmmakers commonly juxtaposed peaceful marchers and a police presence.

Fig. 14.10 Shots taken with a hidden camera made *Construction* (1935) a convincing view of working-class conditions.

Fig. 14.11 Ivor Montagu's *The Defense of Spain* used a common convention of newsreels, an animated map. In this case it shows the flow of "propaganda money" among countries that supported Franco's Fascist attacks against the Republican government.

Fig. 14.12 A shot in *Spanish Earth* juxtaposes defensive barbed wire with more traditional sights of Madrid.

INTERNATIONAL LEFTIST FILMMAKING IN THE LATE 1930s

The Spanish Civil War began in 1936, when Fascist leader Francisco Franco instigated an insurrection against the elected Republican government. While Hitler and Mussolini both backed Franco, the United States, Britain, and France withheld aid. Only the USSR helped those loyal to the Spanish government. This uneven conflict led thousands of volunteers to rally to the Spanish Republican cause and go to fight or succor victims of the war.

Filmmakers supported the cause. Russian cinematographer Roman Karmen shot newsreel footage which Esfir Shub later edited into a compilation feature, *Spain* (1939). The American leftist production firm Frontier made *Heart of Spain* (1937), shot on the spot and edited in New York by Paul Strand and Leo Hurwitz. Ivor Montagu's Progressive Film Institute made a 16mm Civil War film, *The Defense of Madrid* (1936; Fig. 14.11), which Montagu shot in the Spanish capital while it was under attack. Kino distributed *The Defense of Madrid* and raised £6000 for Spanish relief.

After *Borinage* and other films in the early 1930s, Joris Ivens was prominent enough that important leftist writers and artists brought him to the United States. His first assignment was *Spanish Earth* (1937), on the Civil War, written and narrated by Ernest Hemingway. Ivens emphasized the juxtaposition of ordinary events—women sweeping a street, men planting a vineyard—with the destruction of war (Fig. 14.12). American composers Virgil Thomson and Marc Blitzstein arranged a score from Spanish folk songs. The Roosevelts viewed and approved the film, but its circulation was limited mainly to film clubs.

The Chinese civil war received less attention, primarily because little was known in the outside world about Mao Zedong's attempt to overthrow Jiang Jie-shi's (Chiang Kai-shek's) government—a struggle that had been going on since the 1920s. In 1937, American Harry Dunham managed to reach Mao's forces in their stronghold in Yenan and record events there. The resulting footage was edited in the United States at Frontier Films, by Jay Leyda and Sidney Meyers, and released as *China Strikes Back* (1937). This film had a major impact, introducing Mao to much of the world. One of its results was that Stalin for the first time took Mao seriously as a Communist revolutionary leader. Consequently, cinematographer Roman Karmen, who had filmed the Spanish Civil War, went to China and made a Russian feature documentary, *In China* (1941). Ever interested in leftist struggles, Joris Ivens also went to China, but the official government prevented him from journeying to Mao's stronghold. With American backing, Ivens made *The Four Hundred Million* (1938)—named for China's population at that time. Unable to show the civil war, Ivens concentrated on the country's struggle against the Japanese invasion and on its vast landscapes (Fig. 14.13). The Maoist revolution would continue to fascinate Ivens, and five decades later he would make his final film in China.

Aside from these major conflicts, oppressed groups around the world attracted the attention of leftist filmmakers. In 1934, for example, the radical administration of Mexican President Lázar Cárdenas financed *The Wave*. Scripted and photographed by Paul Strand and directed by the young Austrian

Fig. 14.13

Fig. 14.14

Fred Zinneman, *The Wave* dealt with Indian fishermen who try to resist unfair exploitation by local buyers. Although it was a fiction film, it used nonactors and documentary-style filming to emphasize the reality of the social injustice portrayed (Fig. 14.14). Such films also became less common during the 1940s, as World War II claimed filmmakers' attention.

Fig. 14.13 In *The Four Hundred Million,* Ivens suggests the vast, bleak beauty of China.

Fig. 14.14 The fishermen work on their nets while discussing their plight in *The Wave.*

GOVERNMENT- AND CORPORATE-SPONSORED DOCUMENTARIES

THE UNITED STATES

After Franklin Roosevelt's inauguration as President in early 1933, the American government turned more toward solving the problems relating to the Depression. As a result, some filmmakers who had started in the early 1930s as members of the leftist Film and Photo Leagues moved into government-sponsored documentary filmmaking.

In the mid-1930s, the Resettlement Administration wanted to disseminate information on the Dust Bowl, the huge area of southern Plains states whose drought conditions contributed to the Depression. Pare Lorentz, a young intellectual interested in politics, had never made a film, but he was given a minuscule $6000 budget to make *The Plow That Broke the Plains* (1936). Convinced of the socially beneficial uses of cinema, he wanted to show *The Plow* as a short on commercial-film programs. He hired Ralph Steiner, Paul Strand, and Leo Hurwitz, all members of the New York Film and Photo League, as cinematographers. The group found themselves up against the Hollywood establishment, which regarded their work as government-supported competition. Just finding a firm willing to sell them raw film stock was difficult. No distributor would release *The Plow That Broke the Plains*. A major selling point was achieved when Virgil Thomson agreed to write a score for the film, drawing upon folk songs as motifs.

Fig. 14.15 *The River* shows a cabin threatened by severe soil erosion to suggest the need for government action.

Despite running over budget, the film proved a success. The manager of New York's Rialto Theater booked it and publicized it widely. The result was bookings into thousands of theaters nationwide. This triumph and White House approval led to a higher budget for Lorentz's next film, *The River* (1937), photographed by Willard Van Dyke and again provided with a rousing score by Thomson. The filmmakers demonstrated how logging had led to massive erosion in the Mississippi valley (Fig. 14.15). A huge flood forced them to extend the shooting schedule but provided dramatic footage for use in arguing for the benefits of the government's Tennessee Valley Authority dam program. After Lorentz's previous triumph, Paramount distributed *The River,* and it also proved widely popular.

Roosevelt admired *The River* and had the U.S. Film Service formed to make films for various government agencies. Lorentz, as head of this service, began to assemble a group of filmmakers to work on several projects. Joris Ivens, for example, was brought in to make *The Power and the Land* for the Rural Electrification Agency. Lorentz, however, proved to have little administrative ability, and the service was dissolved in 1940. Its projects were turned over to individual government bodies, so *The Power and the Land* (1941) finally was completed by the Rural Electrification Agency. Soon, with the beginning of the war, the military would make some documentaries, while others were commissioned from Hollywood firms.

Some of the filmmakers who worked in the Film and Photo Leagues and for the U.S. government were able to find institutional sponsorship to make significant documentaries. For example, the American Institute of Planners commissioned *The City* for the 1939 New York World's Fair. This film was directed by Ralph Steiner and Willard Van Dyke, from an outline by Pare Lorentz. Again music played a key role, with Aaron Copland composing the score.

The City resembled government documentaries, and particularly *The River,* in its presentation of a problem—overcrowded cities—followed by a solution—rebuilding through city planning. Humorous vignettes caught by concealed cameras, combined with fast pace, created entertainment value as well as informational content. In one celebrated scene, an automated café serves food to lunch-hour customers as if they were on an assembly line. Other scenes emphasize traffic and congestion (Fig. 14.16). Sponsorship of documentaries by institutions and corporations would become increasingly important in succeeding decades.

GREAT BRITAIN

While the American government's sponsorship of documentaries was short-lived, in the United Kingdom a major national filmmaking body was built up during the early 1930s. It produced so many classic documentaries that for years historians focused a great deal of attention on this "realist" streak of British cinema, often to the exclusion of other, more entertainment-oriented filmmaking there.

This burgeoning of the documentary mode resulted largely from the efforts of Scottish-born John Grierson. Educated in the United States during

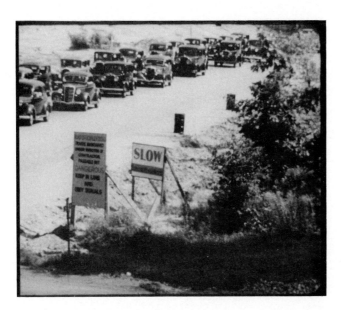

Fig. 14.16 *The City* emphasizes urban congestion in a sequence of outbound weekenders inching along a road, ironically accompanied by jaunty Aaron Copland music.

the 1920s, Grierson was impressed by how effective American popular culture, particularly in the forms of advertising and the cinema, was in affecting mass audiences. He deplored, however, the way Hollywood cinema missed its opportunity to combine entertainment with education. Grierson also admired the Soviet cinema, not simply for its artistic innovations but also because the films were designed to affect viewers intellectually and were government-sponsored. He helped prepare the version of *Potemkin* released in the United States. Finally, he strongly approved Robert Flaherty's tactic of locating corporate funding outside the commercial-film industry for *Nanook of the North* (sponsored by a fur company). At the same time, he thought Flaherty was too fascinated by primitive cultures and not concerned with influencing modern society.

Grierson returned to Britain in 1927 and encountered a sympathetic supporter in Sir Stephen Tallents, head of the Empire Marketing Board, a government institution charged with promoting British products around the world. Tallents arranged financing to allow Grierson to make a documentary on herring fisheries (supposedly because a key official in the Treasury was an expert on the herring industry). The result was a short feature, *Drifters*, released in 1929. Grierson's interest in Soviet Montage cinema was apparent: he cuts quickly among parts of the fishing boats, and his images present ordinary work as heroic (Fig. 14.17).

British exhibitors were not keen on showing documentaries, so *Drifters* premiered at the Film Society, on a program with *Potemkin.* Its favorable press converage led to bookings in many commercial theaters. Still, throughout the 1930s, Grierson and his colleagues faced resistance to commercial screenings of their films, and Grierson increasingly stressed distribution of 16mm prints to schools and educational groups.

In 1930, the Empire Marketing Board hired Grierson to form a permanent film unit. He recruited a number of young, mostly liberal filmmakers, including Paul Rotha, one of the founding members of the Film Society and

Fig. 14.17 *Drifters* deemphasizes the scientific and economic side of British fisheries, stressing the dynamism and dignity of the workers' labor.

Fig. 14.18 The train in *Night Mail*, with accompanying narration: "This is the night mail crossing the border / Bringing the check and the postal order / Letters for the rich, letters for the poor / The shop at the corner and the girl next door."

the author of an influential early book on the subject, *Documentary Film* (1935). This group tried to foster a positive image of the working class. Most were, however, inexperienced and learned cinematic technique on the job. They shot short, silent films that usually received limited distribution. Many were simply advertisements shown in railway stations.

In 1933, before the Empire Marketing Board could turn to more ambitious films, it was dissolved. Tallents moved over to handle public relations for the General Post Office (GPO), a large government institution that oversaw many areas of communications, including radio and early television. Tallents took Grierson and his circle with him, and they became the GPO Film Unit. This unit came to include several people who would remain among the country's most important documentarists: Basil Wright, Arthur Elton, Edgar Anstey, Harry Watt, Alberto Cavalcanti, and Stuart Legg.

The GPO Film Unit was prolific. Many of its films were simple didactic works distributed mainly to schools. In some cases, where a more poetic or dramatic approach was taken, the films had wider theatrical circulation. One of the most popular was *Night Mail* (1935, Basil Wright and Harry Watt). Its subject was simple: a typical journey of the daily overnight train from London to Glasgow. Its form, however, was complex and lyrical. A promising young composer, Benjamin Britten, contributed the score, while W. H. Auden wrote a poetic voice-over commentary. A wide variety of shots moved from such mundane details as a farmer receiving his newspaper to distant views situating the train in the grandeur of the British countryside (Fig. 14.18).

Grierson also sought backing from industry, and the GPO Film Unit's staff made several important documentaries on diverse subjects. Production of tea in British colonies in India and Ceylon was an important industry, and in 1935, Basil Wright directed *Song of Ceylon* for the Ceylon Tea Propaganda Board. This film deals only briefly with the tea trade, concentrating instead on the beauties of Ceylonese culture, both past and present. Indeed, the impressive images and dense sound track hint that modern commerce is an intrusion on this society.

In that same year, 1935, Arthur Elton and Edgar Anstey directed a very different kind of sponsored film. The Gas, Light and Coke Company commissioned *Housing Problems* in hopes of promoting the use of gas heat and light in modernized housing. Elton and Anstey responded by experimenting with direct recording of sound on location to interview working-class people in their own grim apartments. This interview approach has since become pervasive in both documentary films and television. Though the subjects apparently were previously interviewed and are repeating their memorized statements for the camera, the effect of real people describing their problems remains poignant (Fig. 14.19). At the end, interviews with satisfied people who have natural gas in their homes suggest that public utilities can improve living standards. Nevertheless, the effect of the earlier interviews with the slum dwellers lingers and creates a pervasive tone of social criticism.

Fig. 14.19 Crude location lighting and a direct interview approach emphasize the stark reality of a working-class woman's situation in *Housing Problems*.

This emphasis on outside sponsorship led to a major shift in the GPO Film Unit. Arthur Elton left to form the country's most important corporate film unit for Shell Oil. Stuart Legg and Basil Wright each set up an independent production firm to make films for commercial sponsors. Grierson himself quit the unit in 1937, creating a firm to match sponsors with filmmakers; in 1939 he went to Canada, where he was instrumental in founding the National Film Board.

Grierson was replaced as head of the GPO Film Unit by Alberto Cavalcanti, the Brazilian-born filmmaker who had helped establish the city-symphony genre in the 1920s with *Rien que les heures* (p. 198). His main film for the GPO was *Coal Face* (1936), a documentary on the coal industry that again made use of a complex sound track with a rhythmic commentary and music by Britten. Cavalcanti and the other remaining staff moved away from Grierson's fierce independence and concentration on an educational approach. Under Cavalcanti, the unit produced films that drew more upon the narrative techniques of commercial cinema, as did *North Sea* (1938, Harry Watt). Influenced by Flaherty, the group employed reenactments of events.

In 1940, the GPO Film Unit was absorbed by the Ministry of Information. World War II was in its early stages, and soon the unit became central to wartime documentary filmmaking.

AN ISOLATED CASE: ROBERT FLAHERTY IN BRITAIN

After the commercial failure of *Moana* in the mid-1920s, Robert Flaherty had briefly collaborated with F. W. Murnau on *Tabu* (p. 175). After withdrawing from that project, he was at loose ends. In 1931, Grierson, still trying to vitalize the Empire Marketing Board's film production, hired Flaherty.

Flaherty embarked upon a film on British industries, shooting in factories and mines. He proved too undisciplined for government filmmaking, but some of his voluminous footage formed the basis for *Industrial Britain* (1933), one of the few successes enjoyed by Grierson's Empire Marketing Board unit.

By 1931, Flaherty had conceived a project on the bleak, remote Aran Islands off the west coast of Ireland. Michael Balcon, head of Gaumont-British, Britain's largest film company, agreed to fund a feature. Flaherty and

Figs. 14.20 and 14.21 Flaherty uses the traditional continuity editing technique of shot/reverse shot to create an unexpected encounter between a young boy and a giant shark in *Man of Aran*.

Fig. 14.20

Fig. 14.21

his crew spent years on one of the islands, hunting out local people to play roles. Flaherty emphasized the tireless efforts of the Arans' inhabitants to compost seaweed and grow crops on rocky land and to fish among gigantic waves; this drama was embodied in the story of a couple and their young son.

Flaherty also added a scene of the islanders harpooning huge basking sharks from open boats, even though such hunts had ceased long before the inhabitants had been born. (He had similarly resurrected an obsolete tattoo ritual in *Moana*.) He had harpoons constructed, based on antiques, and the islanders learned how to execute the dangerous shark hunt. Flaherty's insistence on such suspense yielded some dramatic scenes. In particular, there is a haunting moment when the young boy Mikeleen climbs down the cliffs to the water's edge and finds himself looking down into the maw of a huge shark (Figs. 14.20, 14.21).

Man of Aran finally premiered in 1934 and did well, both with critics and audiences. It was picked as best film at the Venice Film Festival. Yet it also stirred up considerable controversy. Many documentarists thought it was escapist fiction. Leftists, including some connected with the Film and Photo League, attacked it for failing to deal with the social situation of the islanders, including their exploitative absentee landlords. Despite his reservations about Flaherty, Grierson defended the film:

> It is of course reasonable for later generations of film-makers to want a documentary tougher, more complex, colder and more classical, than the romantic documentary of Flaherty. It is fitting that it should want a documentary in which both material and theme are found in our own social organization and not in literary idyll. But there are considerations one must watch carefully. The first one is that Flaherty was born an explorer, and that is where his talent is. . . .
>
> Not half-a-dozen commercial films in the year can compare with *Man of Aran* in simple feeling and splendid movement. I am all for congratulating Flaherty on pushing the commercial film brilliantly to its limit. I am all for commending his fortitude in yet another sickening encounter with commercialism.[2]

Nevertheless, *Man of Aran* led to a break between Grierson and Flaherty. The latter, unable to find work, returned to the United States, where he would make *The Land* (1942) and *Louisiana Story* (1948).

WARTIME DOCUMENTARIES

The beginning of World War II abruptly changed the status of documentary filmmaking. Leftist filmmakers who had criticized capitalist governments recognized the necessity for switching to a position supporting the battle against fascism. The military establishments within the warring countries called upon professional filmmakers, and major directors previously associated primarily with fiction films switched to documentary. Documentaries became far more popular. In those days before television news, families who had members in the military or who were directly endangered could witness wartime events at their local theaters, in newsreels and documentaries.

HOLLYWOOD DIRECTORS AND THE WAR

The United States stayed out of the escalating European conflict until December 7, 1941. Then the Japanese launched an unprovoked, devastating attack on the American naval base at Pearl Harbor, Hawaii. Germany declared war on the United States a few days later, and global conflict became inevitable.

The U.S. government called directly upon the Hollywood establishment to make films supporting the war effort. Immediately after Pearl Harbor and the German declaration, the Pentagon asked the prominent Columbia director Frank Capra to make a series of propaganda films. These were to explain to American soldiers and sailors why their country was in the war and especially why they were obliged to help foreign countries in the fight against Germany, Italy, Japan, and other members of the Axis. This was especially necessary in the case of the USSR, which had previously been portrayed as a Communist threat to the American public.

Capra himself entered the military as a major. He has recalled watching Leni Riefenstahl's *Triumph of the Will* and deciding that the best way to motivate soldiers to fight was by drawing upon existing films that portrayed the enemy's power. He created a series called "Why We Fight," based primarily on footage captured from German and other enemy sources, combined with material from the Allies. The directors he supervised compiled this footage, explaining military strategies through animated maps (supplied by the Disney studio). A forceful narrator told the audience exactly what to think about the images (Fig. 14.22). The series consisted of seven films: *Prelude to War* (1942), *The Nazis Strike* (1942), *Divide and Conquer* (1943), *The Battle of Britain* (1943), *The Battle of Russia* (1943), *The Battle of China* (1944), and *War Comes to America* (1945). Major Hollywood figures like actor Walter Huston (as narrator) and composer Alfred Newman worked anonymously on some of the films. The series was required viewing for military recruits, but some of the films were also shown publicly.

Other Hollywood directors soon entered the service, recording aspects of the war in powerful documentary films. John Ford joined the Navy as the Chief of the Field Photographic Branch. Since military intelligence anticipated the Japanese attack on Midway Island, Ford and his cameraman were

Fig. 14.22 In *The Battle of Britain,* animation turns the map of Europe into a Nazi whale about to devour the United Kingdom.

Fig. 14.23 Lightweight 16mm cameras carried during bombing runs created spectacular aerial footage for *Memphis Belle*, including this shot of a plane's tail against the squadron's vapor trails.

Fig. 14.24 In *Let There Be Light*, the camera lingers on the jubilant face of a traumatized soldier who has regained his voice under treatment; his therapist is glimpsed in the left foreground.

there to record this turning point in the war. Using 16mm cameras, they captured the attack and American response, including a memorable shot of the American flag being hoisted amid the turmoil of battle. Ford edited this footage with shots of actors speaking the sentiments of archetypal American people; he also used traditional folk music on the sound track. The result was a paean to American strength, *The Battle of Midway* (1942, co-produced by 20th Century-Fox and the Navy). Ford was later decorated for wounds received during the attack, and *The Battle of Midway* garnered an Oscar as best documentary.

William Wyler served in the Air Force, where he supervised *Memphis Belle* (1944), a film on bombing runs over Germany (Fig. 14.23). John Huston had established his reputation as a director of fiction films early in the war with *The Maltese Falcon*. He made two exceptionally candid films during the war. In *San Pietro* (generally known as *The Battle of San Pietro*, 1944), he was assigned to show why the Allied advance through Italy was taking so long. He used footage taken by frontline camera operators as the troops moved through Italian villages. The film came close to being banned when Huston juxtaposed actual soldiers' voices with shots of their body bags. After some revision, the film was released.

Huston ran up against further censorship problems with his next project, *Let There Be Light*. The military initially delegated him to make a film about the rehabilitation of victims of shell shock. Employing direct sound, Huston shot extensive candid records of interviews with traumatized soldiers undergoing therapy. This film was virtually unprecedented in using unrehearsed, direct recording of people's responses to offscreen questions (Fig. 14.24). *Let There Be Light* captured the soldiers' illnesses so effectively that it was banned by the U.S. government and thus had no influence on the subsequent development of documentary filmmaking. It did not become available to the public until the 1970s. Nevertheless, it anticipated the documentaries of the Direct Cinema era, and especially the "unbiased" approach of Frederick Wiseman.

GREAT BRITAIN

As a result of Germany's invasion of Britain's allies in eastern Europe, primarily Poland and Czechoslovakia, Britain declared war on Germany on September 3, 1939. Just under a year later, on August 13, 1940, the Germans launched a bombing campaign against Britain, known as the "Battle of Britain" or "the Blitz." Bombers targeted civilian areas as well as military sites, and thousands of Londoners regularly slept on the platforms of Underground stations. Many citizens were killed, and there was massive destruction in the southern and eastern areas of England. Within months the Britishers' determined resistance led Nazi Germany to turn more of its attention to the USSR.

The British documentary cinema contributed to the united front against the Nazi attack. Some films were made by units within the military services. The Army and the Royal Air Force co-produced *Desert Victory* (1943, Roy Boulting), a feature-length account of one of the turning points of the war, the North African campaign and defeat of the Germans at El Alamein. Dozens

Fig. 14.25

Fig. 14.26

of camera operators exposed huge amounts of film in the desert, often in the thick of battle (Fig. 14.25). Stock footage, maps, and staged footage were also used, yielding a clear, dramatic account of the campaign. Rapid editing enhanced the excitement of the battle scenes. *Desert Victory* was very popular in many countries, winning an Oscar as best documentary in the United States.

Fig. 14.25 Prime Minister and Minister of Defence Winston Churchill flashes his familiar "V for Victory" sign while visiting the troops in *Desert Victory*.

Fig. 14.26 An American soldier and a Scot, both members of the bombing team in *Target for Tonight*.

As soon as the war began, the General Post Office Film Unit became the Crown Film Unit, dedicated to making war-related films. Some members of the unit were documentarists who had worked under Grierson. Harry Watt, for example, directed *Target for Tonight* (1941), showing a typical bombing raid over Germany. Virtually all the action, from the establishment of the home base and personnel to the return of the planes, is staged; the opening emphasizes, however, that "each part is played by the actual man or woman who does the job." The action goes beyond simple exposition of information, drawing upon conventions of fictional war films. Little touches lend human interest, as when a pilot misplaces his helmet. Similarly, *Target for Tonight* makes its bombing unit a mixture of nationalities (Fig. 14.26). Perhaps in part because of these "fictional" aspects, the film was enormously popular.

One crucial documentarist came to the fore during this period. Humphrey Jennings, an artist and a poet, had been acting, editing, and scripting for the GPO since 1934. He had directed one significant film, *Spare Time* (1939), on Britain's leisure activities. Along with his close collaborator, editor Stewart McAllister, Jennings devised a style that lyrically evokes the lives of ordinary British citizens. The pair frequently edited together shots taken in different locales, but with the sound from one locale continuing uninterrupted. The counterpoint invites the viewer to see the connections among events.

Jennings's approach proved suited to depicting the home front once war broke out. Rather than celebrating the more dramatic glories of combat, he concentrated on the quiet resilience of the British public. With Watt and Pat Jackson, Jennings made *The First Days* (1939), on London's preparations for the inevitable bombing. The title of *London Can Take It!* (1940, also co-

Fig. 14.27

Fig. 14.28

Fig. 14.27 Staged action in *Fires Were Started* allowed Jennings to cut among details of the fire-fighting, such as this close shot of two men on a roof.

Fig. 14.28 Children walk though the rubble of war as the narrator addresses Timothy: "When you joined us we'd been fighting for exactly five years. We've hated it, but we've kept on at it to save our skins. And also we had a feeling, deep down inside us, that we were fighting for you. For you and all the other babies."

directed with Watt), on the Blitz, suggests the determined mood that Jennings captured in his wartime films.

Similarly, *Listen to Britain* (1942, co-directed with Stewart McAllister) reflects the pair's fascination with sound. Using only music and sound effects, they move freely among everyday routines continuing incongruously during the reminders of war. A scene inside the National Gallery, for example, shows a concert against a backdrop of empty frames whose paintings have been removed for safekeeping. The concert music continues over views outside the hall, including a girl sitting reading while a barrage balloon floats overhead. As the music ends, the scene shifts to a factory, with the music giving way to loud clanging as a tank is assembled. In other cases, popular songs span a range of shots in different places.

In 1943, Jennings made a feature documentary, *Fires Were Started,* on the role of the National Fire Service in putting out blazes started by German incendiary bombs during the Blitz. The film was completely staged, using a small group of characters to lend human interest to the story. Jennings portrays them off-duty, playing pool, drinking beer, listening to music. For the fire scenes, several bombed-out buildings were set ablaze so that Jennings could set up careful compositions and get enough footage to edit scenes in the style of a fiction film (Fig. 14.27). Despite all this manipulation of events, actual fire fighters who participated considered the film highly authentic.

Just as Jennings had captured the home front during the war, he meditated on the approaching postwar era in *A Diary for Timothy* (1945). The narration, written by E. M. Forster, addresses a baby born on the fifth anniversary of Britain's entry into the war, attempting to tell him not simply what went on but why the war was fought (Fig. 14.28). The film juxtaposes scenes of Timothy's first six months with other everyday and war-related events, as when a scene of John Gielgud rehearsing *Hamlet* is intercut with police coping with a bombing. *A Diary for Timothy* attempted to convey the experiences of wartime to the young generation who had to build a new society.

Jennings made a few films after the war's end, but they failed to recapture the poignancy and optimism that had made him the foremost documentarist of the war. He died in an accident while scouting locations in 1950.

The Crown Film Unit itself was abolished in 1952, though its alumni continued to work prominently in sponsored documentaries after the war.

GERMANY AND THE USSR

Overtly propagandistic films comprised a relatively small proportion of German production during the Nazi era. Most programs included newsreels and documentary short films, however, and these consistently contained Nazi propaganda. As in other countries, established filmmakers sometimes worked on these. For example, Walter Ruttmann, who had created experimental and documentary films in the 1920s, made a few shorts (Fig. 14.29). In 1940, the four newsreel series were merged into one series, the *Deutsche Wochenschau,* under Goebbels's control.

During the early years of the war, theater attendance rose because viewers wanted news from the front. Initially newsreels portrayed the obstacles German soldiers encountered and overcame abroad (Fig. 14.30); death and suffering were never shown. After the disastrous German defeat at Stalingrad in 1943, however, many spectators avoided newsreels as mere window dressing. The *Deutsche Wochenschau* became pure agitation in favor of total war, stressing the fearsomeness of the enemy.

Soviet documentaries took a different approach, stressing the suffering and destruction caused by the German invaders. As the war progressed, filmmakers could also inspire the public with genuinely heroic victories. The counterattack against the Fascist forces was shown vividly in *Defeat of the German Armies Near Moscow* (1942, Leonid Varlamov and Ilya Kopalin; seen in the United States as *Moscow Strikes Back,* it won an Academy Award). *Stalingrad* (1943, Varlamov) depicted the yearlong siege that proved to be the turning point in the war. Dovzhenko spent the war supervising documentary production, including the heartfelt *The Fight For Our Soviet Ukraine* (1943, Yulia Solntseva and Y. Avdeyenko; Fig. 14.31).

After the end of World War II, documentary films were less frequently seen in theaters. Techniques that had been invented for military cinematography, however, were to affect fiction filmmaking. Similarly, documentaries had accustomed audiences to seeing real events depicted in film programs, and in some cases a greater realism emerged in entertainment films.

THE INTERNATIONAL EXPERIMENTAL CINEMA

After the heyday of avant-garde cinema in the 1920s, the 1930s was a period of decline. The greater expense of sound production discouraged some filmmakers from experimentation. Others moved toward documentary, often of a political nature. Official policy under the Nazi regime forbade modernist styles in the arts as "decadent," and most filmmakers either went into exile (as when Hans Richter moved to the United States) or cooperated with the new regime (as we have just seen with Walter Ruttmann).

Fig. 14.29 Walter Ruttman put his flair for abstract images to work for the Nazis in *Deutsche Waffenschmieden* ("German Armaments," 1940), as in this shot of a factory worker inspecting the interior of a new gun barrel.

Fig. 14.30 The *Deutsche Wochenschau* depicted the hardships of German troops operating during the winter on the Russian-Ukrainian front, as in this shot of an airplane taking off amid heaps of snow and ice.

Fig. 14.31 Dovzhenko's familiar flower motif was used in *The Fight for Our Soviet Ukraine,* here juxtaposed with real destruction wrought by the Germans. (Compare with Fig. 12.9.)

Fig. 14.32 *A Bronx Morning* celebrates the charm of ordinary city life.

Fig. 14.33 *Douro, Faina Fluvial* returns repeatedly to shots of this dramatic bridge from many angles.

Fig. 14.34 Many shots in *Autumn Fire* show cityscapes and the countryside without the characters.

Nevertheless, experiment did not disappear entirely. Avant-garde narratives and lyrical films, such as the city symphony, remained popular, especially for beginners. The influence of Surrealism lingered, and independent animation saw a resurgence. During the war, the United States and Canada became centers of alternative cinema, both for émigrés and for a new generation of filmmakers.

EXPERIMENTAL NARRATIVES AND LYRICAL FILMS

During the late 1920s and early 1930s, a small support system for amateur experimental filmmaking developed in the United States. Amateur filmmaking clubs proliferated, and the availability of 16mm film stock made production cheaper. Small cinemas and ciné-clubs rented and showed such films. The Film and Photo Leagues distributed some experimental films along with their leftist ones, and the Amateur Cinema League provided another outlet. Some filmmakers rented out their own work through the mail.

Experimental narrative films took many directions. In 1931, Austrian émigré Charles Vidor made *The Spy*, an adaptation of Ambrose Bierce's short story, "An Occurrence at Owl Creek Bridge." A man condemned to death seems to escape, and the long chase culminates in the discovery that the escape was only a vision in his mind just before his hanging. Vidor went into the Hollywood industry, where he directed many feature films.

The city symphony was a favorite genre for those working on slim budgets. Aspiring New York photographer and filmmaker Jay Leyda created *A Bronx Morning* (1931). This poetic documentary weaves together simple motifs of actions caught in the streets as shops open and people come outdoors to socialize (Fig. 14.32). The film's photography and editing won Leyda a place at the National Film School in the USSR, where he studied with Eisenstein and assisted him in the abortive *Bezhin Meadow* project (p. 299). In Portugal, Manoel de Oliveira filmed *Douro, Faina Fluvial* ("Douro, River Work," 1931) at the mouth of the Douro River. Oliveira used the subject as a pretext to experiment with editing together dynamic compositions (Fig. 14.33). Although he made only a few films over the next decades, much later Oliveira became a prolific director of features.

Herman Weinberg was a movie enthusiast who worked at an early art theater and wrote reviews. He made experimental short films, the only surviving example of which is *Autumn Fire* (1931). It combines lyrical documentary with a slim narrative thread, cutting between estranged lovers: a woman in rural settings and a man in the city (Fig. 14.34). Weinberg went on to a career as a film critic and historian.

SURREALISM

In 1930, the French poet and artist Jean Cocteau shot his first film, *Blood of a Poet* (released in 1932). His financing came from a rich nobleman, the Vicomte de Noailles (who had also backed Luis Buñuel and Salvador Dali's *L'Age d'or* in 1930). *Blood of a Poet* established the dream and psychodrama genres as central to the experimental cinema. Cocteau's film was intensely personal, drawing upon motifs, like the lyre and a muse figure, that appeared in his poetry and drawings. Developing upon the dreamlike narrative of *Un Chien andalou* (p. 197), Cocteau made his hero an artist whose statue comes to life and sends him through a mirror into a mysterious corridor. Behind its doors he sees bizarre scenes symbolically connected to his art (Fig. 14.35).

After *Un Chien andalou* and *L'Age d'or*, Luis Buñuel spent part of 1930 in Hollywood, hired as an "observer" to learn filmmaking method at MGM. (With dubbing not yet practical, studios needed Spanish-language directors.) His intractable attitude lost him the job, and he spent the next few years in France, helping dub Hollywood films into Spanish. He also became interested in making a documentary on Las Hurdes, an isolated, extremely primitive area in Spain. With a tiny budget provided by an interested teacher, Buñuel made *Las Hurdes* (aka *Land without Bread*, 1932), emphasizing the region's stultifying poverty and disease. The catalogue of misery, presented in the dispassionate manner of a travelogue, created an eerie echo of the Surrealism of Buñuel's earlier work (Fig. 14.36). Two decades later, he remarked, "I made *Las Hurdes* because I had a Surrealist vision and because I was interested in the problem of man. I saw reality in a different manner from the way I'd seen it before Surrealism."[3] The film was shot silent and shown in that form privately in 1933. The Spanish government banned it, however, on the grounds that it presented the country in a negative light. In 1937, it was finally released in France, with the music and narrator heard in modern prints.

After this point, Buñuel worked as an editor and co-director on several Spanish films and then went to the United States early in the 1940s, where he did odd filmmaking jobs. His career as a director of feature films did not blossom until after the war.

Another, very different Surrealist completed one film during this era. Self-taught American artist Joseph Cornell had begun painting in the early 1930s, but he quickly became known chiefly for his assemblages of found objects inside glass-sided display boxes. Mixing antique toys, maps, movie-magazine clippings, and other emphemeral items mostly scavenged from New York secondhand shops, these inexplicable but suggestive assemblages created an air of mystery and nostalgia. Although Cornell led an isolated life in Queens, he was fascinated by ballet, music, and cinema. He loved all types of films, from Dreyer's *The Passion of Joan of Arc* to B movies, and he amassed a collection of 16mm prints.

In 1936, he completed *Rose Hobart*, a compilation film that combines clips from scientific documentaries with reedited footage from an exotic Universal thriller, *East of Borneo* (1931). The fiction footage centers around *East of Borneo*'s lead actress, Rose Hobart. Cornell avoids giving more than a hint as to what the original plot, with its cheap jungle settings and sinister turbaned villain, might have involved. Instead, he concentrates on repetitions of gestures by the actress, edited together from different scenes; on abrupt mismatches; and especially on Hobart's reactions to items cut in from other films, which she seems to "see" through false eyeline matches. In one pair of shots, for example, she stares fascinatedly at a slow-motion view of a falling drop creating ripples in a pool (Color Plates 14.1, 14.2). Cornell specified

Fig. 14.35 In *Blood of a Poet*, the artist sees a painting with a living head and arm.

Fig. 14.36 *Las Hurdes* shows victims of genetic defects resulting from inbreeding, one of the chronic problems in the remote Spanish region.

that his film be shown at silent speed (sixteen frames per second instead of the usual twenty-four) and through a purple filter; it was to be accompanied by Brazilian popular music. (Modern prints are tinted purple and have the proper music.)

Rose Hobart seems to have had a single screening in 1936, in a New York gallery program of old films treated as "Goofy Newsreels." Its poor reception led Cornell not to show it again for over twenty years. He continued to edit together films—mostly instructional shorts and home movies—in rough form. In the 1960s, he gave these to experimental filmmaker Larry Jordan, who completed some of them as *Cotillion, The Children's Party,* and *The Midnight Party* (1940s? to 1968). Many other scraps of films remain unfinished, though Cornell continued his work in painting and assemblage pieces until his death in 1972.

Although relatively few Surrealist films were made during this era, this approach has intermittently continued to influence the cinema ever since.

ANIMATION

Some of the most significant experimental films of the 1930s employed animation techniques. This was partly because animated films required relatively little expenditure for sets, actors, and other necessities of live-action fiction filmmaking. Instead, with a camera, a few simple materials, and a great deal of patience, a single filmmaker or a small group could create richly imaginative works. Moreover, the stylization of animation made it suitable for advertising films, so some artists could support themselves by making both ads and more personal projects.

Most European animators continued to avoid traditional cel animation, probably because they associated it with Hollywood commercialism. Instead, they devised ingenious alternative means of creating motion frame by frame.

One of the most dedicated individualists of this period was Berthold Bartosch, a Czech artist who had made animated educational films in Vienna and Berlin during the years just after World War I. He had also assisted Lotte Reiniger on *The Adventures of Prince Achmed,* which gave him skill in shooting layers of translucent material to create land, sky, and sea effects (see Fig. 8.18, p. 193). In 1930, the publishing house of Kurt Wolff (which had discovered Franz Kafka in the 1920s) commissioned Bartosch to make a film based on a book of socialist woodcuts by Frans Masereel. Bartosch set up an animation stand in the Parisian art cinema Théâtre du Vieux-Colombier. Using black-tinted glass, smears of soap, and other materials, over the next two years he created *The Idea* (1932). The film is an allegory of a single worker's conception, personified as a nude woman, which he presents to his fellow workers but which is suppressed by corporate and social tyranny. Although the human figures were simple, stiff-jointed cut-outs, they moved about in evocative, subtly shaded cityscapes (Fig. 14.37). Although Bartosch made a few ads over the next few decades, he never completed another major film.

Bartosch's film inspired two important animators to move into filmmaking. Russian-born Alexandre Alexieff had become a stage designer and book

Fig. 14.37 The hero of *The Idea* speaks to factory workers of his idea. The film was shot on a transparent table with light from below.

Fig. 14.38

Fig. 14.39

Figs. 14.38 and 14.39 Faces swirling in a void transmute into each other quickly and frighteningly in *A Night on Bald Mountain.*

illustrator in Paris. After seeing *The Idea,* he decided to try and create the effect of engravings in motion pictures. Around 1934, he and his American partner Claire Parker (whom he married in 1941) invented an animation technique they called the "pinboard." It consisted of a frame around a stretched fabric in which were embedded half a million double-pointed pins. By pushing pins in different areas of the board to various heights and lighting them from the side, Alexieff and Parker could create images in shades of gray. Moving some of the pins between each frame generated images textured in ways that no other type of animation could duplicate.

They quickly achieved a masterpiece, *Night on Bald Mountain* (1934), set to Mussorgsky's tone poem of that name. In keeping with the *Walpurgisnacht* subject matter of this musical piece, Alexieff and Parker animated a series of weird images that mutate (Figs. 14.38, 14.39) and fly toward and away from the camera with dizzying speed. The film was well received by critics and film-society audiences, but the pair had to turn to advertising films to make a living. These short films, made by animating objects one frame at a time, are today considered classics. Alexieff and Parker were able to make one other pinboard film during this period, a charming two-minute piece called *En passant* ("In Passing," 1943), to illustrate a French-Canadian folk song. It was produced by the National Film Board of Canada, after the two had fled the war and were living in the United States.

Abstract animation also survived during the 1930s. In Germany, Oskar Fischinger pursued his attempts to link moving shapes to music. Supporting his small company primarily by doing advertising, Fischinger explored the possibilities of color in abstract animation. For example, *Circles* (1933) was made for an ad agency. The first color film made in Europe, the three-minute short delivered the brief message "Toliras reaches all [social] circles." The bulk of the film consisted of complex patterns of circles rotating and pulsating to music (Color Plate 14.3). By 1935, Fischinger was making cigarette and toothpaste commercials while completing *Composition in Blue,* in which three-dimensional objects cavort in an abstract blue space.

Fischinger realized he could not remain in Nazi Germany and moved to Los Angeles. There he was able to make a few animated films, including one short produced by MGM as *An Optical Poem* (1937). It was fairly well received as a novelty, but the animation unit of MGM was not sympathetic to Fischinger's approach. He worked briefly at the Disney studio, and a few

Fig. 14.40 The animated skeletons of a bird and a fish try to take the hero's hard-won orange in *The Mascot.*

touches in the design of *Fantasia* and *Pinocchio* have been attributed to him. Still, most of his work in America was carried on with little support. His most important film after his move to America, however, was *Motion Painting No. 1* (1947), funded by the Guggenheim Foundation. It consists of a single lengthy "shot," lasting roughly ten minutes, of the frame-by-frame brush strokes of a painting gone mad, building up to a whole composition, then another composition on top of the first, and so on. Six layers of transparent Plexiglas were laid on top of the first to achieve the effect—which Fischinger created in the camera for months on end without developing it to see if his technique was working! The result, timed to one of Bach's *Brandenburg Concertos,* is a dazzling exercise in continuous extension of lines of color. After the late 1940s, Fischinger could find no financial support, and he turned to abstract painting.

The other major experimenter in abstract animation who had begun work during the silent era was Len Lye. After *Tusalava* in 1929 (p. 194), he tried to make similar films but found no backing. He began painting directly on film. Eventually Grierson's GPO Film Unit assisted Lye by financing his projects or finding backers for him. Like Fischinger, he explored the possibilities of the new color processes that were becoming available in the mid-1930s. *Colour Box* (1935) animated jittery shapes to dance music. It was very popular and influenced the Disney animators who worked on *Fantasia.* In *Rainbow Dance* (1936), Lye took live-action images originally shot on black-and-white stock and manipulated the layers of the color film-stock emulsion to produce extraordinarily vibrant solid hues (Color Plate 14.4). The film's only reference to the Post Office came at the end with a slogan, "A Post Office Savings Bank puts a pot of gold at the end of the rainbow for you." Beginning in the late 1930s, when sponsorship declined, Lye directed imaginative documentaries for the GPO, such as *When the Pie Was Opened* (1941), a modest short film about making rationed food palatable.

In the United States, painter Mary Ellen Bute began making abstract animated films in the 1930s. Like Fischinger, she used familiar pieces of music and created moving shapes that synchronized to the changes in the sound. Her first films, like *Synchrony No. 2* (1935) and *Parabola* (1937) were in black and white, but with *Escape* (1937), she introduced color (Color Plate 14.5). An astute businesswoman, Bute managed to distribute her films herself directly to ordinary commercial cinemas that ran them as cartoons before the feature. She was to continue to make occasional shorts until the 1960s.

While Bartosch, Alexieff and Parker, Fischinger, Lye, Bute, and others were exploring the resources of pictorial animation, the world's foremost puppet animator, Ladislav Starevicz, who had begun in Russia (p. 51) and emigrated to Paris after the Revolution, continued working. One of his longest works, *The Mascot* (1934), mixes live action and puppets in a story of a poor seamstress who crafts stuffed toys to support her sick daughter. Some of these come to life and the protagonist, a toy dog, sets off in search of an orange for the child. Among his many adventures, the dog encounters various grotesque figures at an inn (Fig. 14.40). This scene displays Starevicz's expertise at moving many characters at once and in giving them mobile, expressive faces. Starevicz continued making occasional animated films in Paris until his death in 1965.

DEVELOPMENTS IN THE UNITED STATES DURING WORLD WAR II

The early 1940s proved transitional for experimental cinema in the United States. Hans Richter came to New York and started the City College Institute of Film Techniques in 1943, where he supervised training in various genres of film. Buñuel, Duchamp, and other European artists fled Naziism, and although most were not involved with film projects, their presence helped spur America to become the leading force in postwar modern painting.

Several West Coast filmmakers worked in abstract animation. John and James Whitney's *Five Film Exercises* (completed 1944) employed sound tracks consisting of synthesized music (well before the advent of electronic music). The painter Harry Smith explored the *batik* technique, which applied layers of paint to 35mm film strips and controlled the pattern by means of tape or wax. In some of Smith's early abstractions, textured patches sketchily fill in the constantly changing shapes, while speckles of color overlay the design (Color Plate 14.6).

One of the most daring abstract films of the war period was the 16mm *Geography of the Body* (1943) by Willard Maas and Marie Menken. Through extreme close-ups, a man's body becomes a sensuous landscape of hills and crevices (Fig. 14.41).

Experimental narrative also continued, most significantly in the work of Maya Deren. Deren initially studied literary criticism and then became interested in dance, working as secretary to the choreographer Katherine Dunham. From Dunham Deren acquired an enduring interest in Caribbean cultures, particularly the dance and religion of Haiti.

Fig. 14.41 Abstraction through framing in *Geography of the Body*.

Fig. 14.42 Air and space as gauzy barriers in *Meshes of the Afternoon.*

Fig. 14.43 *Meshes of the Afternoon:* The abject figure of the early sequences . . .

Fig. 14.44 . . . becomes a cool assassin.

In 1943, Deren and her husband Alexander Hammid collaborated on what would become the most famous American avant-garde film, *Meshes of the Afternoon.* A woman (played by Deren) has a series of mysterious encounters with a hooded figure whose face is a mirror. She passes through chambers (Fig. 14.42), splits into several personalities, and eventually dies.

The drifting protagonist and the dream structure were conventions of what came to be called the *trance film.* Strong cues that the images are projections of the heroine's anxieties also initiated a long line of "psychodramas" in American experimental film. Stylistically *Meshes* creates a nonrealistic spatial and temporal continuity through false eyeline matches of the sort already exploited in the avant-garde tradition.

Hammid (whose original name was Hackenschmied) had made some experimental narratives himself in his native Prague, and *Meshes* has strong resemblances to *Un Chien andalou, Blood of a Poet,* and *Vampyr.* But Deren disavowed any connection with the European tradition of experiment, rejecting the continental version of Surrealism for relying too much on the unconscious. "Creativity," she noted, "consists in a logical, imaginative extension of a known reality."[4] Moreover, making a woman the protagonist alters the implications of the role changes (Figs. 14.43, 14.44).

Deren went on to make another psychodrama, *At Land* (1944), in which she plays a woman emerging from the sea and crawling across a variety of landscapes. This film was almost completely Deren's own creation, with Hammid serving occasionally as a technical adviser. In the following year, she began a series of dance films and pursued her interest in the relation between artistic form and communal ritual. She also became America's most charismatic advocate for experimental cinema.

The economic and political turmoil of the years 1930–1945 helped foster the documentary cinema, especially that made by left-leaning filmmakers. After World War II ended, the Cold War would create a less receptive atmosphere for such films, and leftists often faced an uphill struggle or outright censorship.

During the 1930s and early 1940s, experimental filmmakers had often worked in near isolation and with little financial support. Their situation improved somewhat, however, after 1945, with the spread of specialized art cinemas, the growth of international film festivals, and new grant support for filmmaking. We shall examine these trends in Part Four.

◆ REFERENCES

1. Quoted in Vlada Petric, "Soviet Revolutionary Films in America (1926–1935)" (unpublished dissertation, New York University, 1973), p. 443.

2. Quoted in Paul Rotha, *Robert J. Flaherty: A Biography,* ed. Jay Ruby (Philadelphia: University of Pennsylvania Press, 1983), p. 153.

3. Quoted in Francisco Aranda, *Luis Buñuel: A Critical Biography,* tr. and ed. David Robinson (New York: Da Capo Press, 1976), pp. 90–91.

4. Quoted in VèVè A. Clark, Millicent Hodson, and Catrina Neiman, *The Legend of Maya Deren: A Documentary Biography and Collected Works,* vol. 1, Part 2: *Chambers (1942–1947)* (New York: Anthology Film Archives/Film Culture, 1988), p. 566.

PART FOUR

THE POSTWAR ERA:
1946–1960s

The end of World War II created enormous changes in the film industries of most countries. Europe, Japan, the USSR, and the Far East suffered immense damage during the war, and rebuilding required will and money. The United States, buoyed by a new prosperity with the end of the Depression, was able to assist many of these countries and to consolidate its position as leader of the west in the Cold War with the Soviet Union.

In many of the major film-producing countries, the years after the war saw attendance reach an all-time high. But eventually—soon in the United States, by the end of the 1950s in most European countries—patronage slackened disastrously. The United States pioneered new means of wooing audiences back, with color, widescreen, and "bigger," more distinctive pictures, but the "golden age" of the vertically integrated studio system came to an end (Chapter 15).

The United States was not alone in postwar prosperity. Most European economies recovered quickly, and this helped national cinemas come to world prominence. Governments stepped up protection of domestic cinemas, arguing that film was a key representative of national culture. From Europe came a vastly influential film movement—Italian Neorealism—and a self-consciously artistic cinema that borrowed extensively from trends in modernism in the other arts (Chapters 16 and 17). Japanese cinema won international fame in the same period (Chapter 18).

The USSR and its eastern European satellites continued to sustain state-controlled production, although countries experimented with degrees of centralization. Filmmakers from Poland, Czechoslovakia, and Hungary achieved fame in the postwar era. Intermittent thaws in official Soviet policy allowed directors greater latitude, a rhythm of freedom and constraint found as well in Mao's China (Chapter 18).

Elsewhere, Third World film industries were increasing in power. India led the way in output, while Argentina, Brazil, and Mexico were also major producers. All of these industries also produced significant genres and directors (Chapter 18).

The new films of Europe, the Soviet bloc, Latin America, and Asia were made more visible through international film trade and accompanying institutions such as coproduction arrangements and festivals. The circulation of these films, along with their roots in artistic traditions, encouraged critics and filmgoers to treat cinema as the art of the director. The new frame of reference, which took the filmmaker as *auteur* ("author"), had profound effects on how films were made and consumed in the postwar era (Chapter 19).

Near the end of the 1950s, a new generation of filmmakers surged to prominence all over the world. Energized by the *auteur* idea of personal expression, they created "new waves" and "young cinemas" which were formally experimental and thematically challenging (Chapter 20).

The art cinema and new waves operated within the commercial film industry, but more marginal filmmaking practices continued to offer alternatives. Both documentary and experimental filmmakers sought to express their personal visions in their works, and they pioneered technologies and artistic strategies which influenced mainstream fictional cinema (Chapter 21).

15

AMERICAN CINEMA IN THE POSTWAR ERA, 1946–1967

The United States came out of World War II a prosperous country. Workers had earned good money in military industries but had had little chance to spend it. Returning troops rejoined their spouses or married, ready to set up households and buy consumer goods. The birthrate, increasing during the war, skyrocketed, and the new generation was tagged the "baby boom."

European countries, whether on the winning or losing side, faced vast rebuilding, and Japan's infrastructure was in ruins. The United States took on the role of a world superpower, helping its allies and former enemies. At the same time, the USSR struggled to assert its authority. In 1946, when Stalin began taking steps to keep control of the eastern European countries captured during the war, Winston Churchill declared that an "iron curtain" divided the East from the West. In 1949, Mao Zedong's revolution succeeded in China, and the Soviets conducted their first nuclear-weapon test. It seemed as if a new era of Russian imperialism was beginning.

President Truman adopted a policy of "containment," trying to counter Soviet influence throughout the world. From 1950 to 1952, the United States fought alongside South Korean troops against the Communist North in an indecisive civil war. The United States and the USSR jockeyed for sway over nonaligned nations. The Cold War between the United States and the USSR would last for almost fifty years.

The sense of Communist encroachment around the world led to an era of political suspicion in the United States. During the late 1940s, intelligence agencies investigated individuals suspected of being spies or subversives. A congressional committee delved into Communist infiltration of government and business, and under President Dwight Eisenhower (1953–1961) a Cold War policy held sway.

Yet even as the U.S. government sought to make a united front against communism, American society seemed to fracture into distinct demographic segments. One powerful group was composed of teenagers, who had money to buy cars, records, clothes, and movie tickets. As teenage crime rose, the image of the "juvenile delinquent" emerged as well. Other social groups also gained prominence. The civil rights movement accelerated, primarily under the guidance of pacifist Martin Luther King, Jr. In 1954, the Supreme Court decision in the case of *Brown v. Board of Education* took a step toward ending legal discrimination by mandating school desegregation.

The legacy of this struggle emerged in the 1960s, during the presidencies of John F. Kennedy and Lyndon Johnson. They promoted more liberal domestic policies (which Johnson termed the "Great Society"), including the introduction of Medicare and Medicaid, and the passage of the Civil Rights Act of 1964. Johnson's "War on Poverty" instituted work-study programs in colleges and created the Job Corps. At the same time, however, these administrations carried on the policy of containing communism. The United States had begun to support the French fight against Ho Chi Minh's Communist forces in Vietnam in the 1950s. In 1963, America entered the hostilities. Over the next nine years, the United States would send hundreds of thousands of soldiers into a war that became increasingly unpopular at home.

THE COLD WAR'S POLITICAL IMPACT ON HOLLYWOOD

During the 1930s, many Hollywood intellectuals had been sympathetic to Soviet communism; some had even joined the American Communist party. Their left-wing leanings had been reinforced during World War II, when the Soviet Union was one of America's allies in the battle against the Axis. America's move toward a staunch anti-Communist policy after the war placed many of these leftists in a compromised position. For years the FBI had compiled information on Communists or sympathizers in the Hollywood community. By 1947, Congress was investigating Communist activities in the United States as part of the nationwide search by the House Un-American Activities Committee (HUAC) for purportedly subversive elements in government and private life.

In May 1947 a number of individuals—among them the actor Adolphe Menjou and the director Leo McCarey—declared in secret interviews with congressional representatives that they were willing to name Hollywood people with Communist ties. In September, Republican J. Parnell Thomas chaired a HUAC hearing that set out to prove that the Screen Writers' Guild was dominated by Communists. Forty-three witnesses were subpoenaed.

The "friendly" witnesses, led off by Jack Warner of Warner Bros., labeled several screenwriters "Communists." Gary Cooper, Ronald Reagan, Robert Taylor, and other stars expressed concern over leftist content in scripts. The "unfriendly" witnesses, most of them screenwriters, were seldom allowed to state their views. Most avoided denying that they had been Communists, stressing instead that the First Amendment guaranteed them freedom of expression in their work. Ten who testified were cited for "contempt of Congress" and briefly jailed. German leftist Bertolt Brecht, who had been working in Hollywood during the war and who had never belonged to any Communist party, gave a neutral response and immediately left for East Germany.

Vociferous public protest led Congress to suspend the hearings for four years. The ten unfriendly witnesses who had testified, however, found their careers collapsing as producers blacklisted them. Most of the "Hollywood Ten"—scriptwriters John Howard Lawson, Dalton Trumbo, Albert Maltz, Alvah Bessie, Samuel Ornitz, Herbert Biberman, Ring Lardner, Jr., and Lester Cole; director Edward Dmytryk; and producer Adrian Scott—were unable to work openly in the film industry. Dmytryk later cooperated with HUAC and returned to the Hollywood fold.

The 1947 HUAC hearings concentrated on showing that the subject matter of Hollywood films had been tainted by Communist ideas—hence the emphasis on screenwriters. In 1951, the committee resumed its hearings, this time aiming to expose all allegedly Communist personnel. Many former Communists or sympathizers saved themselves by naming others. Actors Sterling Hayden and Edward G. Robinson and directors Edward Dmytryk and Elia Kazan were among this group. People who were named but who refused to cooperate, such as actress Gale Sondergaard, found themselves on a new blacklist.

Some of the blacklisted filmmakers saved their careers by going abroad. Director Joseph Losey moved to England, Jules Dassin to France. Others worked under pseudonyms. Dalton Trumbo wrote the script for *The Brave One*, which won him an Oscar—under a false name—in 1956. In 1960, Otto Preminger declared that he would give Trumbo screen credit for the script of *Exodus,* and producer Kirk Douglas did the same for Trumbo's contribution to *Spartacus* (1960). From that point, the blacklist slowly crumbled. Only about one-tenth of its victims, however, were able to resume their film careers. The HUAC hearings had left a legacy of distrust and wasted talent.

THE DECLINE OF THE HOLLYWOOD STUDIO SYSTEM

The film industry also faced economic problems. Directly after the war's end, prospects seemed excellent. As consumer goods flowed off assembly lines once more, returning troops and well-heeled workers began to spend money at an unprecedented rate. At first they flocked to the movies. The box-office earnings for 1946 were the highest in U.S. film history; adjusted for inflation, they probably remain the highest of all time.

Hollywood's international market was also expanding. Late in the war, the studios turned the Foreign Department of the MPPDA into a new trade organization, the Motion Picture Export Association of America (MPEAA). The MPEAA was responsible for coordinating American exports, negotiating prices, and making sure that Hollywood firms presented a united front abroad. The government, seeing cinema as propaganda for American democracy, assisted film export through Commerce Department initiatives and diplomatic pressures.

Many countries passed protectionist laws, establishing quotas, production subsidies, and restrictions on exporting currency. The benefits were ambivalent at best. In 1947, Britain imposed an extra tax on imported films, and the MPEAA responded by announcing that the Majors would no longer offer new films to the country. The boycott won the day after eight months, and the British government repealed the duty and permitted more film revenues to be remitted to the United States. Elsewhere, protectionist action often strengthened American domination. U.S. firms could export currency indirectly by investing in foreign films and importing them to the United States. Alternatively, Hollywood could spend "frozen funds" in shooting films abroad. These "runaway" productions also avoided the high cost of U.S. labor.

While some countries struggled to rebuild their industries domestically, Hollywood came to rely more on exporting its product. Before the war about one-third of U.S. box-office income had come from abroad, but by the mid-1960s the figure had risen to around half—a proportion that has been constant ever since.

After 1946, however, Hollywood's domestic fortunes began to sag. Attendance steadily shrank, from about 98 million viewers per week in 1946 to about 47 million in 1957. About 4000 theaters closed in the same decade. Output and profits fell. One of the Big Five, RKO, passed through several owners, including Howard Hughes, before ceasing production in 1957. What ended the "golden age" of the studios, begun so auspiciously during the 1910s?

After the war, the film industry faced two challenges that fundamentally transformed its structure. First, a crucial court case altered the way Hollywood did business. Second, Americans' moviegoing habits changed profoundly.

THE PARAMOUNT DECISION

Since the 1910s, the Hollywood studios had expanded cooperatively to create an oligopoly, controlling the American film industry. Almost from the beginning, the U.S. government had investigated this situation. In 1938, the Justice Department initiated a suit, the *United States v. Paramount Pictures, Inc. et al.*, usually called the "Paramount case." The government accused the Big Five [Paramount, Warner Bros., Loew's (MGM), 20th Century-Fox, and RKO], plus the Little Three (Universal, Columbia, and United Artists), of violating antitrust laws by colluding to monopolize the film business. The Big Five owned theater chains, block-booked films, and used other unfair means to keep independent films out of the big first-run houses. Although the Little Three did not own theaters, they were accused of cooperating to exclude other firms from the market.

After a complex series of decisions, appeals, and legal maneuvers, the U.S. Supreme Court handed down a decision in 1948. It declared that the eight companies had been guilty of monopolistic practices. The Court ordered the Majors to divest themselves of their theater chains. It also directed the eight Hollywood firms to end block booking and other practices which hampered independent exhibitors. To avoid further litigation, the Hollywood companies filed a series of consent decrees, agreements that set up compromises with the Court. Over the next decade, all eight moved to comply with the Court's orders. The Big Five remained production-distribution companies but sold off their theater chains.

Some obvious benefits resulted from the industry's new policy. Independent theaters, which had previously depended on cheap films from small firms, had access to a wider range of films (though competition from television soon drove many out of business). With access to bigger theaters, lesser studios could make bigger-budget films. Among these were Universal's Technicolor bio-pic *The Glenn Miller Story* (1954, Anthony Mann) and Columbia's all-star *From Here to Eternity* (1953, Fred Zinnemann). Finally, the divorcement decrees encouraged independent production. Stars and directors broke away to start their own companies. Between 1946 and 1956, the annual number of independent films more than doubled, to about 150. United Artists, which existed solely to distribute independent films, alone released fifty films a year.

Overall, however, the structure of the industry changed little. Independent producers could not afford to start large distribution circuits, which would require many local offices and high overhead. Virtually all independent firms had to distribute their films through the established companies. By the mid-1950s, all the big Hollywood firms scheduled independent productions as part of their annual release schedules. The Majors and Minors continued to dominate distribution and to reap the bulk of box-office receipts.

CHANGING LIFESTYLES AND COMPETING ENTERTAINMENT

A second cause of the decline of the studio system involved social and cultural changes. During the 1910s and 1920s, theaters had been built near mass-transportation lines in downtown neighborhoods, where they were easily accessible. After the war, many Americans had enough money saved up to purchase homes and cars. Suburban housing sprang up, and many people now commuted by car to the city center. With small children, they had little inclination to make the long trip into town for a film. Thus changing demographics contributed to the late 1940s slump in moviegoing.

Initially, families were inclined to settle in and listen to the radio. Within a few years they were watching television. Americans owned 32 million sets in 1954, and by the end of the decade, 90 percent of homes had television. The suburban lifestyle and broadcast entertainment, along with growth in other leisure activities (such as sports and recorded music), made the film industry's profits plunge by 74 percent in the 1947–1957 decade.

When suburban couples did decide to go out to the movies, they tended to be more selective than moviegoers in the past. Rather than attending a local theater regularly, they would choose an "important" film—one based on a famous literary work, or distinguished by its stars, or displaying lavish production values. Catering to this audience, the big producers cut back on the number of films they released, concentrating on ways to provide big attractions.

WIDER AND MORE COLORFUL SCREENS

The television image of the early 1950s was small, indistinct, and black-and-white. Film producers attempted to draw spectators out of their living rooms and back into theaters by changing the look and sound of their movies.

Color filmmaking was an obvious way to differentiate movies from television, and during the early 1950s, the proportion of Hollywood color films jumped from 20 to 50 percent. Many employed Technicolor, the elaborate three-strip, dye-transfer process perfected in the 1930s (p. 242). Technicolor's monopoly, however, led independent producers to complain that the studios got preferential access. A court agreed, and in 1950 Technicolor was obliged to offer its services more widely. In this same year, however, Eastman introduced a single-strip ("monopack") color film. Eastman Color could be exposed in any camera and was simple to develop. Technicolor ceased to be a camera stock in 1955, but the firm continued to prepare release prints in its imbibition process until 1975.

The simplicity of Eastman's monopack emulsion helped increase the number of films shot in color. By 1967, with color television becoming common, Hollywood had committed itself to virtually 100 percent color production. In addition, the studios were now dependent on selling TV rights, and the networks demanded color films for broadcast.

Eastman Color lacked Technicolor's rich saturation, transparent shadows, and detailed textures. (An example of late 1940s Technicolor is Color Plate 15.1.) Still, many cinematographers believed that the monopack stock looked better in the widescreen dimensions of the day. Unfortunately, Eastman Color images tended to fade—especially if the footage was hastily processed. By the early 1970s many prints and negatives had turned a puttyish pink or a sickly crimson (Color Plate 15.2).

At the time, however, color films provided an appeal that television could not match. So did bigger images. Between 1952 and 1955, many widescreen processes were introduced—or rather, revived, since all had been tinkered with in the early sound era.

Cinerama, a three-projector system that created a multipaneled image, premiered in 1952. *This Is Cinerama* was a travelogue in which the audience was treated to a roller-coaster ride, a plane flight through the Grand Canyon, and other thrills. The film played at a single New York theater for over two years at unusually high admission prices, grossing nearly $5 million.

Less elaborate was CinemaScope, introduced by 20th Century-Fox and first displayed in *The Robe* (1953). 'Scope became one of the most popular widescreen systems because it utilized conventional 35mm film and fairly simple optics. Virtually all studios adopted 'Scope; only Paramount clung to its own system, VistaVision, introduced in *White Christmas* (1954). Later there came processes involving 70mm film. (For more details on these processes, see Box.)

WIDESCREEN CINEMA IN HOLLYWOOD

Before 1954, American films were almost always shot and shown in a trim rectangle at the proportions of 1.37:1. (The arrival of sound had led studios to modify the common silent ratio of 1.33:1.) The early 1950s technical innovations drastically widened the image, creating new aesthetic problems and opportunities for filmmakers.

Several incompatible formats competed. Some utilized wider film gauges. Todd-AO, for example, replaced the usual 35mm width with 65mm; the finished film would measure 70mm in width, allowing the extra 5 mm for stereophonic sound tracks. Todd-AO was framed at a 2:1 aspect ratio. Such Todd-AO features as *Oklahoma!* (1955) were released on 70mm prints (Fig. 15.1). Alternatively, Paramount's VistaVision process utilized 35mm film but ran it horizontally through the camera so that a greater negative area was exposed.

Cinerama achieved a wider picture by combining sep-

Fig. 15.2 The Cinerama process (in publicity material).

arate images. Three adjacent camera lenses exposed three strips of film simultaneously. Theaters showed the film on three mechanically interlocked projectors, yielded a sprawling 2.85:1 image on a curved 146-degree screen (Fig. 15.2). Projectionists faced the constant risk of a reel's breaking and falling out of synchronization with the others. In addition, odd images resulted from the "blend lines" separating the three panels (Fig. 15.3).

Fig. 15.1 Two "fish-eye" Todd-AO lenses, one center left and one on the boom above, shooting *Oklahoma!;* a CinemaScope version was shot simultaneously. (The 'Scope camera is center right.)

Fig. 15.3 The curved Cinerama screen and its three panels made horizontal action bulge in perverse ways (*How the West Was Won*, 1963).

Fig. 15.4 A publicity photograph displays not only Marilyn Monroe but also the "squeezing" and "unsqueezing" of the CinemaScope process.

The most popular widescreen system was CinemaScope, introduced by 20th Century-Fox in *The Robe* (1953). The CinemaScope camera was equipped with an anamorphic lens that took in a wide angle of view but squeezed it onto a strip of 35mm film. The film could be shown by attaching a comparable lens to the projector: the picture would be "unsqueezed" to create normal-looking images (Fig. 15.4). CinemaScope was initially standardized at 2.55:1 (for magnetic sound) or 2.35:1 (for optical sound). Compared with most other widescreen systems, CinemaScope was inexpensive, technically simple, and fairly easy to use in shooting.

Some widescreen systems mixed these options. One process, displayed most famously in the highly praised *Ben-Hur* (1959), combined anamorphic lenses with 65mm film to create images in a 2.76:1 ratio. The process eventually came to be known as Ultra Panavision 70. The Panavision company's improvements in anamorphic optics, its lightening of 70mm cameras, and its sophisticated laboratory techniques for reducing and blowing up different formats established it as the industry's leader in widescreen technology.

At first, Hollywood's creative personnel feared that the wide screen would immobilize the camera and lead to long takes. Some editors were afraid to cut quickly, worrying that viewers would not know where to look in a rapid series of wide compositions. A few early widescreen films, such as *The Robe, Oklahoma!,* and *How to Marry a Millionaire* (1953), were rather theatrical, employing long shot framings, frontal staging, and simple cutting.

Almost immediately, however, directors applied classical stylistic principles to widescreen composition. They exploited lighting and focus to emphasize the main figures, and they used depth to guide the spectator's eye gracefully across the frame (Fig. 15.5). Orthodox editing returned, complete with shot/reverse shots and analytical cuts (Figs. 15.6, 15.7). Alternatively, directors who had already exploited long takes and depth compositions packed the wide frame with significant detail.

By the mid-1960s, three sorts of widescreen systems dominated U.S. production. Anamorphic 35mm was established at a ratio of 2.35:1, while nonanamorphic 35mm was typically shown at 1.85:1. In the 70mm gauge, virtually all films were nonanamorphic and shown at a ratio of 2.2:1. Wider 70mm movies were usually blow-ups from anamorphic 35mm. These widescreen systems would remain the principal options available for Hollywood filmmaking during the decades that followed.

Fig. 15.5 Soon directors learned to leave areas of the widescreen image open in order to direct the audience to the salient information (*Carmen Jones*, 1954).

Figs. 15.6 and 15.7 Shot/reverse shot in CinemaScope (*Heaven Knows, Mr. Allison*, 1957).

After 1954 virtually all Hollywood films were designed to be shown in some format wider than 1.37:1. Hollywood continued to shoot many films in the Academy sound ratio, but the projectionist had to mask the projector aperture to create a wide image in the theater. In order to compete with America, major foreign industries developed their own anamorphic widescreen systems, including Sovscope (the USSR), Dyaliscope (France), Techniscope (Italian Technicolor), Shawscope (Hong Kong), and TohoScope (Japan).

Wider images required bigger screens, brighter projection, and modifications in theater design. Producers also demanded magnetically reproduced stereophonic sound. During the early 1950s, Hollywood studios gradually converted from the optical sound recording introduced in the late 1920s to magnetic sound recording, using ¼-inch audiotape or magnetically coated 35mm film. These innovations permitted engineers to enhance widescreen presentations with multiple-channel sound. Cinerama used six channels, while CinemaScope used four. But the extra expense, and a conviction that audiences paid more attention to the image than to the sound, kept most exhibitors from installing magnetic projector heads and multichannel sound systems. Although films' music, dialogue, and sound effects were recorded magnetically during production, most release prints encoded the sound information on optical tracks.

Other innovations of the period were transitory fads. Stereoscopic, or "3-D," films had been toyed with since the beginning of cinema, but the process made a reappearance during the postwar recession years. *Bwana Devil* (1952) employed Natural Vision, a system which required two strips of film to be shown one atop the other. The viewer wore polarized glasses that merged the two images into a sensation of depth. *Bwana Devil* attracted large audiences, and all the major studios undertook 3-D projects, the most noteworthy being *House of Wax, Kiss Me Kate* (both 1953), and *Dial M for Murder* (1954). By 1954, however, the craze was over. Even more short-lived was the effort to add odors to films. In 1958, "AromoRama" and "Smell-O-Vision" appeared, to largely negative response. Both stereoscopic and olfactory processes have been revived, always as an occasional novelty.

THE RISE OF THE INDEPENDENTS

As the big Hollywood studios cut back on the number of films they created, independent production became more prominent. Independent producers hired the personnel needed to make a film on a one-time-only basis, creating a "package" in order to get financing. Once the film was made, it would often be released through one of the Big Five or Little Three distributors. These big firms discovered they could reduce overhead costs by cutting back on the number of actors and filmmakers they had under long-term contract. They increasingly filled out their regular release schedules by buying up more independently made films. By 1954, only MGM was making all its own pictures. In early 1959, about 70 percent of the features in production were being made by independent companies. During the 1960s, virtually all Hollywood films were independent packages, while the studios produced TV series.

The independents were a highly diverse lot. United Artists, one of the largest independent firms, was essentially a corporate entity, holding no studio facilities and providing financial assistance to the producer. By contrast, Universal made its studio resources available to such independent producer-directors as Hitchcock, who utilized studio staff and equipment as part of his contractual arrangement with the company.

Some of the packages put together by independent producers were for big-budget films, comparable to what the major studios would supply the biggest first-run theaters. These were often historical spectacles or adaptations of best-selling novels. For example, Kirk Douglas produced the epic *Spartacus* in 1960, in Technicolor and Super Technirama 70; its all-star cast included Douglas, Laurence Olivier, Tony Curtis, and Jean Simmons, and the film was released through Universal. 20th Century-Fox director Otto Preminger began producing on his own, releasing through Columbia and United Artists such adaptations of best-sellers as *Anatomy of a Murder* (1959), *Exodus* (1960), and *Advise and Consent* (1962).

Less powerful independent producers were left to fill the gap that occurred when the major producers drastically cut back their output of cheaper films. As of 1954, 70 percent of American theaters still showed double features, and they needed inexpensive, attention-getting fare. The demand was met by independent companies that produced cheap "exploitation" pictures. Having no major stars or creative personnel, these films cashed in on topical or sensational subjects which could be "exploited." Exploitation films had existed since World War I, but in the 1950s they gained new prominence. Exhibitors, now free to rent from any source, found that the low-priced product could often yield a nicer profit than could the big studio releases, which obliged the exhibitor to turn back high percentages of box-office revenues.

Exploitation companies cranked out cheap horror, science-fiction, and erotic films. Among the most bizarre were those written and directed by Edward D. Wood. *Glen or Glenda* (aka *I Changed My Sex*, 1953) was a "documentary" about transvestism narrated by Bela Lugosi and starring Wood as a young man confused about his wardrobe preferences. *Plan 9 from Outer Space* (1959), a science-fiction invasion story, was filmed in an apartment, with the kitchen serving as an airplane cockpit. Lugosi died during the filming and was doubled by a chiropractor who scarcely resembled him. Wood's films, ignored or mocked on their release, became cult classics in later decades. (See Notes and Queries.)

More upscale were the exploitation items made by American International Pictures (AIP). AIP films were targeted at what company head Sam Arkoff called "the gum-chewing, hamburger-munching adolescent dying to get out of the house on a Friday or Saturday night."[1] Shot in a week or two with a young cast and crew, the AIP film exploited high-schoolers' taste for horror (*I Was a Teenage Frankenstein*, 1957), juvenile crime (*Hot Rod Girl*, 1956), science fiction (*It Conquered the World*, 1956), and music (*Shake, Rattle and Rock*, 1956). As AIP grew, it invested in bigger productions, such as beach musicals (*Muscle Beach Party*, 1964) and an Edgar Allan Poe horror cycle beginning with *House of Usher* (1960).

Roger Corman produced his first exploitation film (*The Monster from the Ocean Floor*, 1954) at a cost of $12,000. Soon Corman was directing five to eight films a year, most for AIP. They had a rapid pace, tongue-in-cheek humor, and dime-store special effects, including monsters apparently assembled out of plumbers' scrap and refrigerator leftovers (Fig. 15.8). According to Corman, he shot three black comedies, *A Bucket of Blood, Little Shop of*

Fig. 15.8 A publicity still from Corman's *Attack of the Crab Monsters* (1956).

Horrors, and *Creature from the Haunted Sea* (all 1960) over a two-week period for less than $100,000, at a time when one ordinary studio picture cost $1 million. Corman's Poe cycle won him some critical praise for its imaginative lighting and color, but the films still appealed to teenagers through the scenery-chewing performances of Vincent Price.

Obliged to work on shoestring budgets, AIP and other exploitation companies pioneered efficient marketing techniques. AIP would often conceive a film's title, poster design, and advertising campaign, test it on audiences and exhibitors, and only then begin writing a script. Whereas the major distributors adhered to the system of releasing films selectively for their first run, independent companies often practiced "saturation booking" (that is, opening a film simultaneously in many theaters). The independents advertised on television, released films in the summer (previously thought to be a slow season), and turned drive-ins into first-run venues. All these innovations were eventually taken up by the Majors.

The exploitation market embraced many genres. William Castle followed the AIP formula for teen horror, but he added extra gimmicks, such as skeletons which shot out of the theater walls and danced above the audience (*The House on Haunted Hill,* 1958), as well as electrically wired seats which jolted the viewers (*The Tingler,* 1959). With the slackening of censorship controls, the 1960s saw growth in erotic exploitation. "Nudies" surfaced from the 16mm "stag film" world and could be seen in decaying picture palaces in America's downtown neighborhoods. Eroticism became mixed with gore in Herschell Gordon Lewis's *Blood Feast* (1963) and *2000 Maniacs* (1964). Russ Meyer began in nudies before discovering his idiosyncratic blend of parodically overblown sex scenes and gruesome violence (*Motorpsycho,* 1965; *Faster Pussycat, Kill! Kill!,* 1966).

Occasionally independent production took a political stance. Herbert Biberman's *Salt of the Earth* (1954) followed the tradition of 1930s left-wing cinema in its depiction of a miners' strike in New Mexico. Several blacklisted film workers, including some of the Hollywood Ten, participated. Most of the parts were played by miners and unionists. The hostile atmosphere of the "anti-Red" years hampered the production, and the projectionists' union blocked its theatrical exhibition.

Less politically radical was the "New York School" of independent directors. Morris Engel shot *The Little Fugitive* (1953), an anecdote about a boy's wandering through Coney Island, with a hand-held camera and post-dubbed sound. Engel's later independent features, *Lovers and Lollipops* (1955) and *Weddings and Babies* (1958), used a lightweight 35mm camera and on-the-spot sound recording in a manner anticipating Direct Cinema documentary (p. 566). Lionel Rogosin blended drama and documentary realism in *On the Bowery* (1956) and *Come Back, Africa* (1958). Shirley Clarke, known for her dance and experimental shorts, adapted the play *The Connection* (1962) and made the semidocumentary *The Cool World* (1963; Fig. 15.9). Jonas and Adolfas Mekas modeled *Guns of the Trees* (1961) and *Hallelujah the Hills* (1963) on the experiments of the French New Wave.

The most famous member of this "off-Hollywood" group was John Cassavetes. A New York actor committed to the "Method" approach, Cassavetes made a career on the stage and in television. He scraped up donations to direct *Shadows* (1961). "The film you have just seen was an improvisation":

Fig. 15.9 Shirley Clarke directing *The Cool World*.

this curt closing title announced Cassavetes's key aesthetic decision. The story, about two black brothers and their sister in the New York jazz and party scene, was unscripted; the actors shared creative choices about dialogue and delivery with the director. Although shooting in a semidocumentary style, with a grimy, grainy look (Fig. 15.10), Cassavetes also relied upon deep-focus compositions and poetic interludes familiar from contemporary Hollywood cinema. *Shadows* won festival prizes and led Cassavetes to undertake

Fig. 15.10 The roughly shot beating of Ben (*Shadows*).

a pair of ill-fated Hollywood projects. He returned to independent cinema, financing his films by acting in mainstream pictures.

ART CINEMAS AND DRIVE-INS

The burst of independent production typified a larger strategy. Many producers responded to the decline in theater attendance by targeting specific segments of the population. Before the 1950s, most studio productions were intended for a family audience. Now films designed only for adults, children, or teenagers appeared more frequently.

Aiming at children and adolescents, Disney moved into live-action features with adventure classics (*Treasure Island,* 1950), adaptations of juvenile literature (*Old Yeller,* 1957), and fantasy-comedies (*The Absent-Minded Professor,* 1961). These low-cost films were routinely among each year's top grossers.

In the mid-1950s, the "teenpics" market opened in earnest, as viewers born during World War II began making their consumer strength felt at the box office. Rock and roll musicals, juvenile delinquency films, and science-fiction and horror items attracted the teenage market, with exploitation companies like AIP leading the way. The major studios reacted with "clean-teen" comedies and romances featuring Pat Boone and a succession of Tammys and Gidgets. America's burgeoning youth culture, centered on dating, pop music, souped-up cars, and fast food, began to be exported around the world and shaped cinema in other countries. From the 1960s on, the teenage market became the target for most Hollywood motion pictures, and few films became hits without appealing to it.

The demographic-target tactic also created new kinds of exhibition. Although a few little theaters had specialized in showing foreign films since the 1920s, the art-house audience became a more significant force after World War II. With thousands of veterans going to college through the GI Bill, an older, educated audience, many of whose members had traveled in Europe during the war, emerged, and "art films" held some appeal for it.

The film industry had economic reasons for importing more films. American films were flooding into countries whose production was debilitated, but many governments restricted the amount of funds that could be taken out. American companies had to invest their profits in the country or buy goods there for export. Importing foreign films proved one way of transferring profits legally.

Moreover, with U.S. production in decline, importing art films provided smaller theaters with low-cost product. Some independent exhibitors, faced with sagging attendance, found that they could fill their houses by booking foreign films and appealing to the local elite. Imported films were not broadcast on television, so these exhibitors suffered no competition.

As of 1950, there were fewer than 100 art theaters in the entire country, but by the mid-1960s, there were over 600, most in cities or college towns. They were usually small, independent houses decorated in a modernist style calculated to appeal to an educated clientele. The lobbies often displayed art exhibits, and the refreshment counters were more likely to offer coffee and cake than soda and popcorn.

Shadows, The Cool World, and similar U.S. independent fare got some circulation in art theaters, but the staple programming came from Europe. The flow of imports began directly after the war ended, with Roberto Rossellini's *Open City,* released in 1946, earning high grosses and helping to create an interest in films made abroad. Carl Dreyer's *Day of Wrath,* Marcel Carné's *Children of Paradise,* and Vittorio De Sica's *The Bicycle Thief* were among many that accustomed American audiences to reading subtitles. English films consistently dominated the import market. Michael Powell and Emeric Pressburger's *The Red Shoes* broke out of the art-cinema circuit to become one of the top-grossing films of 1948. During the 1950s, some imports, from countries with looser censorship controls, turned sex into an attraction for art cinemas. French director Roger Vadim's *And God Created Woman* (1957) made Brigitte Bardot a star in the United States. Quite often the "sophistication" of imported films owed more to daring subject matter than to complex form or profound themes.

Drive-in theaters presented another attractive alternative for exhibitors during a period of falling box-office receipts. The owner did not need an expensive building—only a screen, a cheap speaker for each parking space, a concession stand, and a ticket booth. Farmland was relatively cheap, and the drive-in's typical location, just outside town, made it handy for the new suburban population. Now people who seldom frequented the big downtown theaters could easily go to the movies. Admission was also affordable, as films playing in drive-ins were often far past their first runs.

The first drive-in dated from 1933, but there were still only two dozen in the whole country in 1945. By 1956, more than 4000 "ozoners" were operating. This figure was approximately equal to the number of "hardtop" theaters that closed during the postwar era. During the early 1950s, about one-quarter of total box-office income came from drive-ins.

Drive-ins were not ideal venues for viewing. The tinny speakers yielded atrocious sound, rain would blur the picture, and cold weather required exhibitors to close down for the season or provide (feeble) heaters. But drive-ins proved successful with their target audiences. Despite their cheap tickets, most showed two or even three features. Parents could bring their children and avoid the cost of a baby-sitter. Since people could circulate during the film without clambering over their neighbors, concession stands did better business in drive-ins than in other theaters. Some drive-ins specialized in teenpics, and the prospect of sharing a darkened front seat for several hours brought many adolescent couples to the local "passion pit."

CHALLENGES TO CENSORSHIP

Exploitation movies, imported films, and independent producers' "adult" themes and subjects inevitably posed problems. Films were failing to win approval from local censorship boards. A turning point in regulation came when an Italian film, Roberto Rossellini's *The Miracle* (1948), was denied an exhibition permit by the New York State Board of Censors on the grounds that it was blasphemous. It told the story of a retarded peasant woman who is convinced that her unborn child is the son of God. In 1952, the Supreme Court declared that films were covered by the First Amendment's guarantee of free speech. Later court decisions made it clear that films could be censored only on grounds of obscenity, and even that was narrowly and vaguely defined. Many local censorship boards were dissolved, and few films were banned.

The industry's own self-censorship mechanism, the Motion Picture Association of America (MPAA, formerly the Motion Picture Producers and Distributors Association), also faced problems enforcing its Production Code (pp. 239–240). The MPAA's main weapon for obliging distributors to submit their films for its approval was its rule that no theater belonging to the association would show a movie without a certificate of approval. Once the five Majors had to divest themselves of their theater chains, however, exhibitors were free to show unapproved films.

And producers began to supply them. One way of competing with television, which had extremely strict censorship, was to make films with more daring subject matter. As a result, producers and distributors pushed the Code further and further. When the MPAA refused to approve the mildly risqué *The Moon Is Blue* (1953, Otto Preminger), United Artists released it nevertheless. Preminger was persistent in flaunting the Code, and UA distributed his film about drug addiction, *The Man with the Golden Arm* (1955), without an MPAA certificate. Other films that failed to obtain certificates included *The Pawnbroker* (1965), *Who's Afraid of Virginia Woolf?* (1966), and *Alfie* (1966). It became apparent that the Code not only was ineffectual but was creating lucrative publicity for the films it rejected.

In 1966, the MPAA stopped issuing certificates. Instead, films that failed to conform to its guidelines were labeled "Suggested for Mature Audiences." This procedure also proved ineffectual, and it soon gave way to a more systematic rating system.

HOLLYWOOD ADJUSTS TO TELEVISION

Television posed a threat to certain staple products of theaters' programs. Newsreels, for instance, were largely abandoned after television news proved more efficient and immediate. Animated films were edged out more slowly; for two decades after the war, film programs still included short cartoons, and the major animators continued to create works of comic imagination and technical finesse. At MGM, Tex Avery's manic frenzy worked at full heat in *King-Sized Canary* (1947; Color Plate 15.3) and *The Magical Maestro* (1952), while William Hanna and Joseph Barbera made the Tom and Jerry series perhaps the most bloodthirsty films coming out of Hollywood.

The Warner Bros. cartoon unit became, if anything, even more bizarrely inventive than it had been during the war. Bob Clampett's *The Great Piggy Bank Robbery* (1946) takes Daffy Duck at a breakneck pace through a surrealistic parody of *film noir.* Chuck Jones, who had begun as a head animator at Warners in the late 1930s, reached the top of his form, combining Wagnerian opera and Bugs Bunny illogic in *What's Opera, Doc?* (1957). He invented the Road Runner series with *Fast and Furry-ous* (1949; Color Plate 15.4) and continued to direct its unpredictable variations on violence until his departure from the studio in 1961. During the 1950s, Jones also created several distinctive cartoons without the studio's stars. In *One Froggy Evening* (1955) a construction worker discovers a miraculous singing frog—which he attempts to exploit for money, until discovering that it sings only when alone with him (Color Plate 15.5).

Newer and smaller than the units at MGM and Warners was United Productions of America (UPA), formed in 1948 and releasing through Columbia. UPA cartoons placed their recurring characters, Mr. Magoo and Gerald McBoing Boing, in distinctive modernistic backgrounds. One of the founders of UPA, John Hubley, left to form his own company in 1952. Hubley and his wife, Faith, made such films as *Moonbird* (1960; Fig. 15.11) in a decorative style that elaborated on the more spare UPA approach. UPA succumbed to the small screen in 1959, when it was sold and began making cartoons for television.

Fig. 15.11 Sketchy, distorted figures against a semiabstract background in *Moonbird.*

Walt Disney continued to distribute his cartoons through RKO until 1953, when he formed his own distribution firm, Buena Vista. Although Disney continued to turn out short films, his most profitable works were his feature-length cartoons, introduced every few years and perpetually rereleased. As usual, these were often sanitized adaptations of children's classics, although *Alice in Wonderland* (1951; Color Plate 15.6) displayed a slapstick verve that was missing from more solemn undertakings such as *Cinderella* (1950) and *Sleeping Beauty* (1959). The studio returned to its tradition of combining live action and animation in the enormously successful *Mary Poppins* (1964).

By the mid-1960s, however, broadcast animation had captured the audience. The major studios virtually stopped producing animated shorts; MGM's last Tom and Jerry films (directed by Jones) were released in 1967, and Warner Bros. shut down its animation unit in 1969. Now Bugs, Daffy, Popeye, and their peers could be found on Saturday morning television, not in the local theater.

Yet in other ways Hollywood accommodated itself to television. The industry moved rapidly to take advantage of its new competitor.

For one thing, the networks needed enormous quantities of programs to show. In the early 1950s, about one-third of broadcast material consisted of old films, mostly B pictures from Monogram, Republic, and other Poverty Row studios. In 1955, the bigger studios started selling the TV rights to their own libraries. In 1961, NBC launched the first weekly prime-time film series, "Saturday Night at the Movies," and by 1968, there was a comparable film showcase on every weeknight. Rising fees for this programming made television sales a significant, predictable part of a film's income.

Moreover, the Hollywood studios started creating television shows. In 1949, Columbia converted its short-subject division, Screen Gems, to TV production. Among its products was the hit series, "Father Knows Best" (1954–1962). When the networks moved from live broadcasting to showing filmed series in 1953, the demand for material intensified. Independent producers fulfilled the need, as with "I Love Lucy," created by the Desilu company (which took over the RKO studio when that firm ceased production in 1957). As film production declined at the big studios, they generated income by renting out their production facilities for independent filmmaking, both for theatrical release and television broadcast.

Perhaps the shrewdest use of the new medium was made by Walt Disney. Disney adamantly refused to sell his cartoons to television, since their carefully paced theatrical rereleases would yield profits for the indefinite future.

In 1954, Disney contracted with ABC to produce an hour-long weekly show, "Disneyland." The series became a hit, running for decades under several names. The show permitted Disney to publicize his theatrical films and his new theme park (opened in 1955). Disney filled his program with shorts and excerpts from the studio library. And when his TV series struck a chord, as it did with its saga of Davy Crockett, a reedited version of the programs could be released as a profitable theatrical feature.

After the first few years, the Hollywood firms as corporate entities did not suffer from the competition with television. They simply adjusted by expanding their activities to encompass both entertainment media. The film-based component of the industry, however, did decline. In the 1930s, the Majors released close to 500 features annually, but by the early 1960s the average was under 150. Box-office receipts continued to fall until 1963, when television had effectively saturated the American market. After that point, attendance rose a bit and leveled off at around a billion admissions per year. Still, it has never come close to the levels of the pre-TV era.

STORIES, STYLES, AND GENRES

Even as the industrial base of Hollywood filmmaking began to crack, the classical style remained a powerful model for storytelling. In addition, it underwent some important modifications during the postwar decades.

Citizen Kane's plot had a complexity seldom seen in Hollywood sound cinema, and it created a vogue for subjective narrative techniques (p. 251). This trend intensified in the postwar decade. The first several scenes of *Dark Passage* (1947) are entirely presented through the eyes of the protagonist. In *Hangover Square* (1945), distorted music suggests the demented imagination of a composer who compulsively strangles women, while *Possessed* (1947) conveys a woman's growing madness through exaggerated noises. In *Lady in the Lake* (1946) the image presents detective Philip Marlowe's optical viewpoint for virtually the entire film. Characters punch or kiss the camera, and during his inquiry Marlowe is visible to us only when we glimpse him in a mirror (Fig. 15.12). Such films rely on techniques of camerawork and mise-en-scene pioneered by French Impressionism and German Expressionism.

Similarly, narrative construction became more intricate. *Kane*'s investigation plot, interrupted by flashbacks of people recounting the past, became a model. Some films experimented with flashbacks: *Crossfire* (1947) and *Stage Fright* (1950), for example, incorporate flashbacks which the audience later learns are lies. The melodrama *The Locket* (1946), in which a husband tries to find out about his wife's past, contains a flashback-within-a-flashback-within-a-flashback. None of these innovations threatened the premises of classical narrative filmmaking—a protagonist-centered chain of cause and effect, a "linear" drive toward coherence and closure. Indeed, the fact that most of the experiments with plot time involve a crime to be solved or a mystery to be unveiled suggests that the new complexity of structure was partly motivated by genre conventions. During the 1960s, films influenced by the European art cinema took time-juggling to extremes, as in *The Pawnbroker* (1965).

While some directors were exploring complex storytelling tactics, others

Fig. 15.12 *The Lady in the Lake:* "Our" mirror image and a subjective point of view.

were embracing an unprecedented realism of setting, lighting, and narration. The trend toward location shooting, initiated during the war years when the government imposed a limit on budgets for set construction, continued. The semidocumentary film, usually a police investigation or crime tale, staged a fictional narrative in existing locales and was often filmed with the aid of lightweight equipment developed in wartime. *13 Rue Madeleine* (1947) and *The Naked City* (1948) used portable photofloods to light rooms for filming. *The Thief* (1952) was filmed in Washington, D.C., and New York City, often concealing its camera; one shot, with the camera on a cart, tracked for five blocks. Such films, based on actual incidents, frequently featured a thunderous voice-over narration that evoked wartime documentaries and radio broadcasts.

A complex flashback narrative and a semidocumentary feel might be found in the same film. *Sunset Blvd.* (1950), a memory narrated by a dead man, exploits actual Hollywood locations. One of the most intricate examples of artifice in the semidocumentary is Stanley Kubrick's *The Killing* (1956). Several men carry out a precisely timed robbery of a racetrack. Kubrick gives us virtually newsreel images of the track and the races, and the film uses a dry "voice of God" commentator to specify the day and time of many scenes. Yet *The Killing* also manipulates time in a complex way. We see a bit of the robbery, and then the film skips back to show events leading up to that phase. As the film traces different lines of action, events are presented several times.

Kane had reinvigorated the use of long takes and deep-space imagery (p. 246), and these techniques, taken up during the war, became even more prominent during the late 1940s and early 1950s. Scenes might now be filmed in a single shot (the so-called *plan-séquence*, or "sequence shot"). (See Figs. 15.13–15.18.) Often the long take featured very fluid camera movement.

Fig. 15.13 In *The Asphalt Jungle* (1950), a three-minute sequence shot with movement in depth replaces traditional cutting. Within a deep-focus composition, the truck driver quarrels with Gus, the owner of the diner.

Fig. 15.14 Gus shoves him out the door . . .

Fig. 15.15 . . . and continues to berate him . . .

Fig. 15.16 . . . before coming to the foreground to advise Dix to lie low.

Fig. 15.17 Dix leaves . . .

Fig. 15.18 . . . and Gus goes to the rear to make a phone call.

Fig. 15.13

Fig. 15.14

Fig. 15.15

Fig. 15.16

Fig. 15.17

Fig. 15.18

Fig. 15.19

Fig. 15.20

Fig. 15.21

Fig. 15.19 Deep focus for the gun-obsessed boy in *Gun Crazy* (1949).

Fig. 15.20 Deep focus for claustrophobic atmosphere (*The Whip Hand*, 1951).

Fig. 15.21 Cinematographer John Alton's low-key lighting typified *film noir* (*T-Men*, 1948).

facilitated by new "crab" dollies that allowed the camera to move freely in any direction. In addition, the vivid deep focus that had been a Welles-Toland trademark was widely imitated (Figs. 15.19, 15.20).

Many of these innovations were associated with *film noir*, the "dark" style which continued to be important until the end of the 1950s. Adventurous cinematographers pushed chiaroscuro lighting to exaggerated extremes (Fig. 15.21). *Noir* films became more outrageously baroque, with canted compositions and layers of visual clutter (Fig. 15.22). These stylistic developments attracted enough notice to make them the target of satire. *Susan Slept Here* (1954) mocks the flashback narrative by having an Oscar statuette narrate the film. The "Girl Hunt" ballet in the musical *The Band Wagon* (1953) and Frank Tashlin's *It's Only Money* (1962) parody the excesses of *film noir*.

In black-and-white dramas, low-key lighting schemes continued well into the 1960s, but films in other genres exploited a brighter, high-key look (Fig. 15.23). Most melodramas, musicals, and comedies of the 1950s avoided chiaroscuro. Deep-focus cinematography continued well into the 1960s for black-and-white films, but color films usually cultivated shallow-focus imagery. And for some time, aggressive deep focus of the Wellesian sort proved impossible to achieve with CinemaScope's anamorphic lenses.

In the mid-1960s, under the influence of Direct Cinema and New Wave movements, cameramen began using long-focal-length lenses to flatten the shot's space and produce soft, blurry contours. The telephoto lens became

Fig. 15.22 *Kiss Me Deadly* (1955): A densely cluttered shot with violence at its center.

Fig. 15.23

Fig. 15.24

Fig. 15.25

more common than the wide-angle one. In 1962, Arthur Penn's black-and-white *The Miracle Worker* showcased sharp-edged focus and crisp lighting (Fig. 15.24), but five years later the much flatter imagery in his color *Bonnie and Clyde* (Fig. 15.25) derived from long lenses.

During the same period, in contrast with the long-take tendency of the immediate postwar years, directors began to use flashier and more rapid editing. Richard Lester's *A Hard Day's Night* (1964) and *Help!* (1965) fractured the Beatles' musical numbers into dozens of discontinuous shots (Figs. 15.26, 15.27). Lester's zany technique derived less from Soviet Montage or French New Wave than from television commercials and British eccentric comedy. Rapid editing was further popularized in *A Funny Thing Happened on the Way to the Forum* (1966, Lester), *The Graduate* (1967, Mike Nichols), and *Bonnie and Clyde*.

Lester's films created a vogue for wordless scenes, often montage sequences, backed by pop songs. The most famous example is probably *The Graduate*'s Simon and Garfunkel vocals commenting on the hero's anomie. The integration of full-length songs into action scenes in virtually all genres became a staple of American cinema in the 1960s. Film studios became affiliated with music companies, saw the benefits of "cross-plugging" movies and recordings, and made the sound-track album a source of profit. This trend continued into the 1990s, when virtually every film was obliged to include rock music, if only in the credits.

UPSCALING GENRES

With greater competition for the entertainment dollar, the major firms gave nearly all genres a higher gloss. And as studios cut back on the number of films produced, each movie had to be more distinctive. Executives enhanced production values with bigger stars, opulent sets and costumes, and the resources of color and widescreen technology. Even minor genres benefited from efforts to turn B scripts into A pictures.

The postwar Western was set on the "big-picture" trail by David O. Selznick with *Duel in the Sun* (1945). Several directors were fired from this passion-drenched Technicolor saga before King Vidor completed it. It earned large grosses and set the pattern for *Red River* (1948), *Shane* (1953), *The Big Country* (1958), and other monumental Westerns.

Fig. 15.23 High-key lighting in *The Bad and the Beautiful* (1952).

Fig. 15.24 *The Miracle Worker:* Deep focus and the wide-angle lens.

Fig. 15.25 *Bonnie and Clyde:* During the final shoot-out, Clyde Barrow's dying descent is filmed with a long lens, which softens focus and flattens space.

Fig. 15.26 Discontinuity in *A Hard Day's Night:* As "Can't Buy Me Love" plays on the sound track, the Beatles romp in a soccer field . . .

Fig. 15.27 . . . and immediately are seen relaxing.

More modest Westerns also benefited from lavish production values, the maturity and range of the directors and stars, and a new narrative and thematic complexity. The genre helped John Wayne and James Stewart consolidate their postwar reputations, with Stewart becoming wealthy from his profit participation in a cycle directed by Anthony Mann (beginning with *Winchester 73*, 1950). Color cinematography enhanced the majestic scenery of *The Naked Spur* (1953, Mann) and the rich costume design of Hawks's *Rio Bravo* (1959; Color Plate 15.7). At the same time, social and psychological tensions were incorporated. A Western might be liberal (*Broken Arrow*, 1950), patriarchal (*Red River; The Gunfighter*, 1950), youth-oriented (*The Left-Handed Gun*, 1958), or psychopathic (the Ranown cycle directed by Budd Boetticher; Sam Peckinpah's *Ride the High Country*, 1962).

Enhanced production values also drove the melodrama to new heights. At Universal, producer Ross Hunter specialized in "women's pictures," and central to his revamping of the genre was Douglas Sirk. Sirk was an émigré (p. 311) who had made anti-Nazi pictures and *films noirs* during the 1940s. Working with cinematographer Russell Metty, Sirk lit Universal's plush sets in a melancholy, sinister low key. Psychologically impotent men and gallantly suffering women (*Magnificent Obsession*, 1954; *All That Heaven Allows*, 1955; *Written on the Wind*, 1956; *Imitation of Life*, 1959) play out their dramas in expressionistic pools of color and before harshly revealing mirrors (Color Plates 15.8, 15.9). Critics in later decades believed that Sirk's direction undercut the scripts' pop-psychology traumas and pat happy endings. An eerily boisterous counterpart to Sirk's melodramas was supplied by Hunter's other specialty: Doris Day romantic comedies, from *Pillow Talk* (1959) on.

No genre benefited more from the new upgrading than the musical, believed to be Hollywood's most durable product. Every studio made musicals, but the postwar decade was ruled by MGM. The studio's three production units mounted everything from operatic bio-pics to Esther Williams aquatic extravaganzas. "Backstage" musicals like *The Barkleys of Broadway* (1949) were balanced by "folk" musicals like *Show Boat* (1951). Adaptations of Broadway hits (e.g., *Kiss Me Kate*, 1953) were matched by original scripts (e.g., *Seven Brides for Seven Brothers*, 1954). A film might be built around a set of career hits from a single lyricist-composer team. *The Band Wagon* (1953), for example, was based on the songs of Howard Dietz and Arthur Schwartz.

The most lauded musical unit at MGM was overseen by Arthur Freed, a top producer since *The Wizard of Oz*. The Freed unit showcased the best talents—Garland, Astaire, Vera-Ellen, Ann Miller, and, above all, Gene Kelly, the wiry, wide-grinning dancer who added athletic modern choreography to the MGM product. *On the Town* (1949, co-directed by Kelly and Stanley Donen), a frenetic tale of three sailors on a day pass in Manhattan, was not the first film to stage its numbers on location, but the choreography and the cutting gave the film a hectic urban energy (Color Plate 15.10). In *Brigadoon* (1954, Vincente Minnelli) and *It's Always Fair Weather* (1955, Kelly and Donen) Kelly made the musical a sour comment on masculine frustations in postwar America.

More lighthearted was *Singin' in the Rain* (1951, Kelly and Donen), widely considered the finest musical of the period. Set during the transition to talkies, the film pokes fun at Hollywood pretension while satirizing the style of early musicals and creating gags with out-of-sync sound. The numbers include Donald O'Connor's calisthenic "Make 'Em Laugh"; Kelly's title number, blending swooping crane shots with agile choreography that exploits puddles and umbrellas; and the "Broadway Melody" number, an ebullient homage to MGM's early sound musicals.

Although MGM continued to turn out striking musicals after the mid-1950s, it was no longer the leader. Goldwyn's *Guys and Dolls* (1955), Paramount's *Funny Face* (1956), United Artists' *West Side Story* (1961), Columbia's *Bye Bye Birdie* (1963), and Disney's animated ventures all made the "big musical" a box-office stalwart. Twentieth Century-Fox based several musicals on Broadway hits—*The King and I* (1956), *Carousel* (1956), and *South Pacific* (1958), followed a few years later by the biggest blockbuster of all, *The Sound of Music* (1965). Warners contributed to the genre with George Cukor's *A Star Is Born* (1954) and Doris Day vehicles such as *The Pajama Game* (1957) before dominating the 1960s with *The Music Man* (1962), *My Fair Lady* (1964), and *Camelot* (1967).

Rock and roll brought new dynamism to the postwar musical. *Rock around the Clock* (1956) paved the way, and soon both Majors and independents went after teenage record buyers. After crooning rather than jittering in his debut, *Love Me Tender* (1956), Elvis Presley went on to present a fairly sanitized version of rock and roll in thirty musicals over the next dozen years. The genre was mocked in Frank Tashlin's *The Girl Can't Help It* (1956), which nonetheless managed to include "straight" numbers by popular bands.

Westerns, melodramas, and musicals had been major genres for several decades, but the inflation of production values and the betting on big pictures brought another genre to prominence. The biblical spectacle had proved lucrative in the hands of Cecil B. DeMille in the 1920s and 1930s, but it had lain untouched until DeMille revived it in *Samson and Delilah*, the top-grossing film of 1949. When *Quo Vadis?* and *David and Bathsheba* (both 1951) also garnered huge profits, a cycle of historical pageants was launched. The genre's need for crowds, colossal battles, and grandiose sets made it natural for widescreen processes, and so *The Robe, Ben-Hur, Spartacus,* and *The Fall of the Roman Empire* (1964) all showcased new image technologies.

"Those who see this motion picture produced and directed by CECIL B. DEMILLE will make a pilgrimage over the very ground that Moses trod more than 3,000 years ago." Thus opens *The Ten Commandments* (1956), the most enduringly successful of the biblical epics. (Some observers noted that the credit gives Moses only second billing.) The film used 25,000 extras and cost over $13 million, a stupendous amount for the time. Despite ambitious special effects like the parting of the Red Sea, DeMille's staging often harked back to the horizontal blocking of his 1930s films (Fig. 15.28).

Soon historical epics were treating virtually every period. There were Egyptian pageants (*Land of the Pharaohs*, 1955; *Cleopatra*, 1963), chivalric adventures (*Ivanhoe*, 1952; *El Cid*, 1961; Color Plate 15.11), and sagas of twentieth-century war and revolution (*Lawrence of Arabia*, 1962; *Doctor Zhivago*, 1965). Most of these attracted audiences, but because of budget overruns in production, some proved unprofitable in the long run.

Another genre was revived by the new commitment to big pictures. As

Fig. 15.28 *The Ten Commandments:* Pharaoh and his counselors, staged in a classic linear medium shot.

Fig. 15.29 A production still from *The Incredible Shrinking Man.*

the market in science-fiction writing expanded after the war, producer George Pal proved that the atomic age offered a market for science-fiction movies. The success of his *Destination Moon* (1950) gave him access to Paramount budgets for *When Worlds Collide* (1951) and two prestigious productions based on works by H. G. Wells, *The War of the Worlds* (1953) and *The Time Machine* (1960). Using color and sophisticated special effects, Pal's films helped lift science-fiction to a new respectability. *Forbidden Planet* (1956), with electronic music, an "Id-beast," and a plot based on *The Tempest,* was a somewhat more forced effort to dignify the genre. Disney's *20,000 Leagues under the Sea* (1954) and the precise stop-motion work of Ray Harryhausen (e.g., *The Seventh Voyage of Sinbad,* 1959) aided the rebirth of the fantasy film.

Less expensive science-fiction and horror films portrayed technology in a struggle with unknown nature. In *The Thing* (1951), scientists and military men discover an all-devouring monster in the Arctic wastes. In *Invasion of the Body Snatchers* (1955), an average town is overrun by pods who clone the citizens and replace the humans with unfeeling replicas. Opposed to these paranoid fantasies were "pacifist" ones, exemplified in *The Day the Earth Stood Still,* in which an alien urges earthlings to give up war. Special effects dominated films which portrayed eccentric science and misbegotten experiments, such as *The Fly* (1958) and *The Incredible Shrinking Man* (1957; Fig. 15.29). Such films were interpreted in immediate historical terms, often as commentaries on Cold War politics or the nightmarish effect of nuclear radiation.

The effect of amplifying B-film material was perhaps most visible in the rise of the big-budget espionage film. Hitchcock's elegant *North by Northwest* (1959) featured an innocent bystander caught up in a spy ring, but the catalyst for genre upscaling was Ian Fleming's fictional British agent James Bond. After two screen adaptations of the novels, 007 became a proven commodity with the phenomenally profitable *Goldfinger* (1964). The Bond films had erotically laced intrigues, semicomic chases and fight scenes, outlandish weaponry, wry humor, and dazzling production design (Fig. 15.30). Over

Fig. 15.30 The fight in the Fort Knox set of *Goldfinger*, designed by Ken Adam.

three decades, producers Harry Salzman and Albert Broccoli ran through several directors and main actors. The Bond films, probably the most profitable series in the history of cinema, spawned imitations and parodies throughout the 1960s and 1970s.

Lower-budget movies, in order to compete with the new scale of expenditures, had to find their own selling points. The crime film, for instance, became more violent. Menacing *films noirs* like *Out of the Past* (1947) seemed subdued in comparison to the souped-up sadism of *Kiss Me Deadly* (1955), the brutality of a thug running down a little girl in *Underworld USA* (1961), and the opening of Don Siegel's *The Killers* (1964), in which gunmen terrorize a school for the blind.

By the early 1960s, a genre film might be either a lavish blockbuster or a stark, seedy exercise. When the distinguished Hitchcock made a black-and-white thriller called *Psycho* (1960) without major stars and on a B-picture budget, he launched a cycle of grand guignol (e.g., *What Ever Happened to Baby Jane?*, 1962), that continued for decades. The prestigious *In Cold Blood* (1967), shot in anachronistic black and white, cultivated a low-budget *noir* look in adapting a best-seller, chiefly because the style enhanced the brutal amorality of young murderers determined to "put hair on them walls." After fifteen years of dressing up genre formulas, leading filmmakers began to dirty them up.

MAJOR DIRECTORS: SEVERAL GENERATIONS

A few major directors ceased working or lost impetus fairly soon after the war. Lubitsch died in 1947. Josef von Sternberg, who had left Paramount in the mid-1930s and worked sporadically through the 1940s, ended his career with two films for Howard Hughes and *The Saga of Anatahan* (1953), a Japan-U.S. coproduction exuding the misty atmosphere of his prewar work. Frank Capra made the perennially popular *It's a Wonderful Life* (1946), a mixture of homespun comedy and astonishingly cruel melodrama, but his few subsequent features had little influence.

The Great Dictator had been the last bow of Charles Chaplin's Tramp, and his experiments with other personae, coupled with controversies about his politics and personal life, made his popularity sink. *Monsieur Verdoux* (1947) centered on a quiet gentlemen who murders his wives; *Limelight* (1952) was a testament to comic theater. Threatened with political persecution in the United States, Chaplin settled in Switzerland. *A King in New York* (1957) satirized American politics, while *A Countess from Hong Kong* (1967) bade farewell to the urbane comedy of *A Woman of Paris*.

Overall, however, a number of veteran directors continued to be central players in the postwar period. DeMille, Frank Borzage, Henry King, George Marshall, and others who started directing during World War I remained surprisingly active into the 1950s and even the 1960s. Raoul Walsh, for example, turned out masculine action films, and *Colorado Territory* (1949) and *White Heat* (1949) remain models of the trim, understated efficiency of Hollywood classicism.

John Ford, producing films through his Argosy company, was still the most visible director of the eldest generation. His Irish comedy-drama *The Quiet Man* (1952) gave its backer, the B-studio Republic, immediate credibility. The sparkling location photography, the interplay of spirited romance and brawling comedy, and a buoyant epilogue in which the performers gravely salute the audience have made *The Quiet Man* one of Ford's most enduring pictures, a utopian fulfillment of the nostalgic longing for home that permeates *How Green Was My Valley*.

The bulk of Ford's postwar work was in the Western genre. *My Darling Clementine* (1946) is an ode to frontier life, shot in the rich depth and chiaroscuro which Ford had pioneered a decade earlier. His "Cavalry trilogy" (*Fort Apache*, 1948; *She Wore a Yellow Ribbon*, 1949; *Rio Grande*, 1950) pays homage to the close-knit military unit. *Sergeant Rutledge* (1960) and *Two Rode Together* (1961) raise issues of rape and miscegenation in the manner of "liberal Westerns," and each experiments a bit: the former with flashback narrative, the latter with an unmoving long take. *The Man Who Shot Liberty Valance* (1962), widely taken as Ford's elegy for the frontier myth, has the simplicity of a fable. The heroic side of the West dies in the corruption brought by the railroad and Washington politics.

The Searchers (1956), arguably Ford's most complex Western, centers on Ethan Edwards, who pursues the Comanche who have killed his brother's family and carried off his niece Debbie. His saddle partner Martin Pawley gradually realizes that Ethan intends not to rescue Debbie but to kill her for becoming an Indian wife. Seldom had the Western shown such a complex protagonist, in which devotion and pride struggle against violent racism and sexual jealousy. At the film's climax, as Ethan is about to kill Debbie, their shared memory of her childhood links them again in a new bond and he is purged of his murderous impulse.

The continuity of Ford's style is evident in *The Searchers*. The film's color scheme reflects the changing seasons across Monument Valley (Color Plate 15.12). Fordian depth of space emerges in an evocative motif of doorway framings (Figs. 15.31–15.33). Even John Wayne's final gesture of clasping his forearm is modeled on a gesture Harry Carey had used in *Straight Shooting* (1917). For film critics and young filmmakers of the 1970s, *The Searchers* typified the emotional richness of the Hollywood tradition.

Other veteran directors continued to practice their craft despite the studios' decline. William Wyler directed prestigious dramas and studio pic-

Fig. 15.31 *The Searchers:* The motif is established in the first shot when the mother opens the door onto the desert.

Fig. 15.32 Later, Ford ironically reminds us of the destroyed home by shooting through the opening of the smokehouse in which the mother's body lies.

Fig. 15.33 The end of a search: After bringing Debbie back to the settlement, Ethan cannot reenter civilization.

Fig. 15.34

Fig. 15.35

Fig. 15.34 Moderated deep focus in *The Best Years of Our Lives.*

Fig. 15.35 *Adam's Rib* (1949): A long take records the wry byplay between an attorney (Katharine Hepburn) and her district attorney husband (Spencer Tracy).

Fig. 15.36 *The Cobweb* (1955): In a sanitarium, characters confront each other before the controversial drapes.

tures into the 1960s, winning large box-office revenues with *The Best Years of Our Lives* (1946) and *Ben-Hur* (1959). The deep-focus, wide-angle look was already muted in *Best Years* (Fig. 15.34); Wyler seemed content to leave it to directors working in genres more oriented to suspense or action. Howard Hawks made comedies and action-adventure films until 1970. King Vidor turned to spectacles (*War and Peace,* 1956) after directing overblown, delirious melodramas such as *The Fountainhead* (1949). George Stevens created several of the era's biggest hits, notably *Shane* (1953) and *Giant* (1956).

Of the directors specializing in melodramas, comedies, and musicals, Vincente Minnelli and George Cukor stand out for their shrewd use of long takes. Cukor's quietly watching camera permits the players full sway in their performances (Fig. 15.35). Minnelli's more distant framing emphasizes the characters' interactions with the setting. Cukor's *A Star Is Born* (1954) daringly activates the edges of the 'Scope frame, while Minnelli's melodramas juxtapose characters with symbolic decor (Fig. 15.36).

Some émigré directors, such as Renoir and Ophüls, returned to Europe fairly soon after the Armistice, but others flourished in postwar Hollywood. The most successful was Alfred Hitchcock. (See Box.) Fritz Lang continued to make sober, somber genre pictures that radiated paranoid unease, such as *Rancho Notorious* (1952) and *The Big Heat* (1953; Fig. 15.37). Billy Wilder became a top director noted for irony-laden dramas (*Sunset Blvd.*, 1950; *Ace in the Hole,* 1951; *Witness for the Prosecution,* 1958) and cynical erotic comedies (*The Seven-Year Itch,* 1955; *The Apartment,* 1961; *Irma La Douce,* 1963). *Some Like It Hot* (1959), less mordant than Wilder's usual work, delighted audiences with its cross-dressing gags (Fig. 15.38).

Fig. 15.37 The rogue cop finds his way blocked in Lang's *The Big Heat* (1953).

Fig. 15.38 *Some Like It Hot:* Jack Lemmon, as "Daphne," dancing a passionate tango with Joe E. Brown.

ALFRED HITCHCOCK

Apart from the filmmakers who were also performers (Chaplin, Jerry Lewis), Hitchcock was probably the most publicly recognizable director of the postwar years. The press delightedly reported his remarks: "Actors are cattle"; "A film is not a slice of life but a slice of cake"; "Ingrid, it's only a movie" (after Bergman had sought to understand her role's motivation). His walk-on appearances, quizzically observing the crises his plots set in motion, guaranteed a moment of laughter. His image as the "Master of Suspense" was marketed through shrewd spin-offs: chatty trailers, a mystery magazine, and a television show, with Hitchcock introducing each episode in phlegmatically ghoulish tones.

Above all, the films themselves carried the stamp of his fussy, childish delight in discomfiting the audience. Like his mentors the Soviet Montage directors, he aimed at a pure, almost physical response. His goal was not mystery or horror but suspense. His plots, whether drawn from novels or his own imagination, hinged on recurring figures and situations: the innocent man plunged into a vortex of guilt and suspicion, the mentally disturbed woman, the charming and amoral killer, the humdrum locale with tensions seething underneath. The consistency of his stories and themes furnished evidence for the European critics who proposed that an American studio director could be the creator—the "author"—of his work (p. 493).

Hitchcock flaunted his stylistic ingenuity, embedding into each script a set piece that aroused suspense in the teeth of outrageous implausibility. An assassination is attempted during an orchestra concert (*The Man Who Knew Too Much*, 1956). A crop-dusting airplane tries to shoot down the protagonist (*North by Northwest*, 1959). Sometimes Hitchcock set himself a technical challenge. *Rope* (1948) consists of eight long takes. In *Rear Window* (1951), by contrast, hundreds of shots are assembled to induce the viewer to share the hero's belief that a man living across the courtyard has committed murder (Color Plates 15.13, 15.14).

Many critics found Hitchcock's postwar work to be his finest. *Strangers on a Train* (1951) employs taut crosscutting to divide our sympathies between hero and villain (Figs. 15.39, 15.40). The semidocumentary *The Wrong Man* (1956) invests a drab news story with a harsh anguish. *Vertigo* (1958) uses location shooting and Bernard Herrmann's haunting score to pull the spectator into a hallucinatory tale of a man obsessed with a woman whom he believes he has killed (Color Plate 15.15). Hitchcock's films gave Cary Grant, James Stewart, and Henry Fonda dark, brooding roles suited to their maturing star images.

Hitchcock's calculations of public taste were farsighted. *Psycho* (1960) triggered several cycles of homicidal films, up to the "slasher" movies of the 1980s; *The Birds* (1963) anticipated the "vengeful nature" horror film. Like most veteran directors, he floundered in the mid-1960s, but *Frenzy* (1972) proved that he could still craft a plot which outfoxed the audience and that his technical virtuosity could leave viewers at once anxious and amused.

Fig. 15.39 *Strangers on a Train:* While the hero desperately tries to finish a tennis match in time . . .

Fig. 15.40 . . . the villain scrabbles for the lighter he needs in order to frame the hero for a murder; Hitchcock makes the audience root for both.

Fig. 15.41 In the U.S. Senate Preminger's 'Scope frame registers different reactions to a blustering speech (*Advise and Consent*, 1962).

Another émigré, Otto Preminger, cultivated a distinctive personality both as an actor (in Wilder's *Stalag 17*, 1953) and as a director. His despotic temper was sometimes compared to von Stroheim's, but Preminger was no spendthrift; as his own producer, he counted every penny. Partly to trim shooting time, he pushed the long-take technique even further than Cukor and Minnelli. The average shot in *Fallen Angel* (1945) lasts about half a minute, the same as in the 'Scope *Carmen Jones* (1954).

Although Preminger ingeniously composed his CinemaScope frame (Fig. 15.41), most of his long takes refuse expressive effects. There are seldom elaborate camera maneuvers or virtuoso performances; the camera simply observes poker-faced people, most of whom are lying to one another (Fig. 15.42). This impassivity makes Preminger's *films noirs* and adaptations of middlebrow best-sellers intriguingly opaque.

Just the opposite aesthetic strategy was pursued by Orson Welles. Discharged from RKO after *The Magnificent Ambersons* (1942), Welles became a vagabond director. He turned in pictures for Columbia, Republic, and Universal, but he produced most of his films on a shoestring, with funds scraped together from European backers and his film performances (e.g., in Reed's rather Wellesian *The Third Man*, 1949).

Fig. 15.42 A neutral long take in *Anatomy of a Murder* (1959): A defense attorney tries to convince his client's wife to play the role of loyal spouse.

Welles directed and starred in versions of *Macbeth* (1948), *Othello* (1952), and *The Trial* (1962), but he also made espionage films (*Mr. Arkadin*, 1955) and crime thrillers (*The Lady from Shanghai*, 1948; *Touch of Evil*, 1958). To all he brought the flamboyant technique he had pioneered in *Kane*—Gothic chiaroscuro, deep-focus imagery, sound tracks of shattering dynamic range, brooding dissolves, abrupt cuts, overlapping and interruptive dialogue, and intricate camera movement. The climax of *The Lady from Shanghai*, a shoot-out in a funhouse hall of mirrors, is less a plausible resolution of the drama than a virtuoso display of disorienting imagery (Fig. 15.43). *Touch of Evil*, beginning with one of the most baroque camera movements in Hollywood history, brought the *film noir* to new heights. In *Chimes at Midnight* (1967), an adaptation of Shakespeare's *Henry IV* plays, Welles presented the most kinetic, harrowing battle sequence of the era (Fig. 15.44). Welles haunted the studio system of the 1970s and 1980s, hoping to complete his long-running projects (*Don Quixote*, *The Other Side of the Wind*).

Fig. 15.43 *The Lady from Shanghai:* The final shoot-out in a mirror maze.

Fig. 15.44 *Chimes at Midnight:* A deep-space view of a chaotic battle, with the camera flanked by the warriors' furiously scuffling legs.

Fig. 15.45 In a long take, Terry toys with Edie's glove, keeping her with him while he expresses his reluctant interest in her (*On the Waterfront*).

Welles had come to Hollywood from New York left-wing theater, and several other directors followed him. Jules Dassin started in this vein before turning out harsh crime films (e.g., *Brute Force,* 1947; *The Naked City,* 1948). Joseph Losey worked in the Federal Theatre project and directed Brecht's play *Galileo* (1947) before entering filmmaking with *The Boy with Green Hair* (1948). HUAC hearings drove Dassin and Losey into exile.

During the 1930s the Group Theatre transplanted to America the naturalistic acting "Method" taught by Stanislavsky's Moscow Art Theater. The most influential Group alumnus was Elia Kazan, who established himself in Hollywood while continuing to direct the Broadway premieres of *Death of a Salesman, A Streetcar Named Desire,* and *Cat on a Hot Tin Roof.* After specializing in liberal social-problem films, Kazan moved rapidly to prestigious adaptations of works by Tennessee Williams, *A Streetcar Named Desire* (1951) and *Baby Doll* (1956), as well as to socially critical films such as *A Face in the Crowd* (1957), which warns of the political abuses of television.

After the war Kazan and two New York colleagues founded the Actors Studio. They believed that Stanislavsky's "Method" required the actor to ground the performance in personal experiences. Improvisation was one path to a natural, if sometimes painful and risky, portrayal. Kazan's conception of Method acting found its most famous exponent in Marlon Brando. A prototypical Method exercise occurs in Kazan's *On the Waterfront* (1954), in which Terry picks up and toys with Edie's casually dropped glove. Keeping her glove becomes a pretext for making her linger with him, but as he straightens the fingers, plucks lint from it, even tries it on, it also expresses his awkward attraction to her and provides an echo of the childhood teasing he recalls (Fig. 15.45). Method acting was to have an enormous influence on Hollywood through Kazan, Brando, James Dean, Karl Malden, and other Actors Studio participants.

Nicholas Ray worked with the Group Theatre before serving as assistant director to Kazan on *A Tree Grows in Brooklyn* (1945). He began directing with a painful tale of a runaway couple drawn into the outlaw life, *They Live*

Fig. 15.46 Judy, Plato, and Jim are brought together unbeknownst to each other in the first scene of *Rebel without a Cause.* The CinemaScope framing tucks them into discrete pockets of the police-station set.

Fig. 15.47 Deep focus in the wide image: Ray's *King of Kings.*

by Night (1948). Always a fringe figure, Ray specialized in films about men whose toughness masks a self-destructive compulsion. *In a Lonely Place* (1950) implicates a Hollywood scriptwriter in a murder, revealing his narcissistic exploitation of others. In the offbeat Western *Johnny Guitar* (1954), the weary gunfighter is dominated by the hard-as-nails saloon lady; the film climaxes with a showdown between two gun-toting women. *Rebel without a Cause* (1954) showcases James Dean as another tormented hero, childishly passive and uncertain; it also demonstrates Ray's forceful use of the CinemaScope frame (Fig. 15.46). After several other "male melodramas," Ray ended his Hollywood career with two historical epics, *King of Kings* (1961; Fig. 15.47) and *55 Days at Peking* (1963).

Another group of postwar directors emerged from scriptwriting: Richard Brooks (*The Blackboard Jungle*, 1955; *Elmer Gantry*, 1960), Joseph Mankiewicz (*All about Eve*, 1950; *The Barefoot Contessa*, 1954), and Robert Rossen (*Johnny O'Clock*, 1947; *The Hustler*, 1961). The most idiosyncratic talent was Samuel Fuller, who had been a scenarist for a decade before he directed his first film, *I Shot Jesse James* (1948). A former reporter for New York tabloids, Fuller brought a B-film sensibility to every project. He relied on intense close-ups, off-center framings, and shock editing to underscore his tales of underworld treachery or men facing death in combat.

Fuller goes straight for the viscera. During a fistfight in *Pickup on South Street* (1953), a man is dragged down a flight of stairs, his chin thonking on

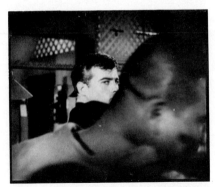

Fig. 15.48 Using karate on a villain, and the viewer, in *The Crimson Kimono.*

Fig. 15.49 Thrusting the violence in the audience's face: A fight from Mann's *The Tall Target* (1951).

each step. At the showdown of *Forty Guns* (1957) a cowboy punk uses his sister as a shield. The lawman coolly shoots her. As she falls, he proceeds to fire several rounds into the astonished youth. In *China Gate* (1957) a soldier hiding from an enemy patrol steps on a spike trap, and Fuller cuts from shots of his sweating face to extreme close-ups of the spikes protruding from his boot. Fuller enjoys staging fight scenes that assault the viewer (Fig. 15.48). The opening of *The Naked Kiss* (1963) turns its fury on the audience, with a woman striking directly into the camera.

Other directors had a comparable, if less raw, aggressiveness. Robert Aldrich built *Kiss Me Deadly* (1955) and *Attack!* (1956) out of the hollow dialogue and outrageous sadism of pulp fiction. Don Siegel's police films, along with *Invasion of the Body Snatchers*, show a rapid pace learned during his days as an editor at Warners. Anthony Mann, like Fuller and Aldrich strongly influenced by Welles, staged fight scenes in great depth, hurling his combatants at the audience. (Fig. 15.49). "In the films of these hard-edged directors," wrote critic Manny Farber, "can be found the unheralded ripple of physical experience."[2]

Some new directors specialized in grotesque comedy. Frank Tashlin, former animator and children's book illustrator, made several imaginative satires on 1950s culture (*The Girl Can't Help It*, 1956; *Will Success Spoil Rock Hunter?*, 1957), as well as directing Jerry Lewis when Lewis split with his comedic partner, Dean Martin.

Martin and Lewis had been hugely successful in several Paramount program pictures (Fig. 15.50). After working with Tashlin, Lewis negotiated a contract with Paramount to direct his own films. Before changing tastes ended Lewis's directing career, he made nine uniquely peculiar comedies. Some were simply anthologies of skits in a single locale; *The Bellboy* (1960), for instance, offers cartoonish gags set in a Miami hotel. In other films, Lewis gave his idiot-child character a spastic, demonic frenzy. His schizophrenic persona was further split when, in *The Nutty Professor* (1963), he portrayed both "himself" and a suave lady-killer modeled on Dean Martin. Lewis also

Fig. 15.50 Martin, Lewis, and their fiancées stare at the comedy act that will replace them (*The Caddy*, 1953).

displayed a visual flair. *The Ladies' Man* (1961) presents a women's boarding-house as a colossal cutaway set (Color Plate 15.16).

The oldest practitioners in the years 1945–1965 learned their craft in the silent cinema or the talkies; the postwar newcomers typically started in theater or in the studio system. The youngest generation, who began making films in the mid-1950s, often started in television. John Frankenheimer, Sidney Lumet, Martin Ritt, and Arthur Penn directed live broadcast drama in New York before turning to feature films. They brought to cinema a "television aesthetic" of big close-ups, constricted sets, deep-focus cinematography, and dialogue-laden scripts. *The Young Stranger* (1956, Frankenheimer), *Twelve Angry Men* (1957, Lumet), *Edge of the City* (1957, Ritt), and *The Miracle Worker* (1962, Penn) exemplified this trend. These directors became significant Hollywood figures in the early 1960s, and they were among the first to borrow from European art cinema and New Waves in *Mickey One* (1965, Penn), *The Pawnbroker* (1965, Lumet), and *Seconds* (1966, Frankenheimer).

Despite the unheavals in the industry, directors from several generations and backgrounds made postwar Hollywood films a central force in world cinema. The system had lost economic stability, but the genres and styles of classical filmmaking supplied a framework within which directors could create idiosyncratic, powerful films. The ambitious young filmmakers who came to prominence in Europe in the early 1960s usually turned to postwar Hollywood for inspiration.

As the size of Hollywood's domestic audience leveled off in the mid-1960s, studios proved slow to understand that the big picture was no longer a sure thing. The enormous cost overruns on *Cleopatra* (1963) guaranteed that it would lose money, but blockbuster successes like *The Sound of Music* (1965) suggested to some that wholesome fare could still command the market. The failures of *Doctor Dolittle* (1967), *Thoroughly Modern Millie* (1967), and *Star!* (1968) shattered this hope. Top-grossing films like *Virginia Woolf, Bonnie and Clyde,* and *The Graduate* were aimed largely at young adults who were not shocked by profanity, adultery, and mayhem. "Hollywood now is run by Wall St. and Madison Ave., who demand 'Sex and Violence,' " wrote Ford after completing his last feature, *Seven Women* (1965). "This is against my conscience and religion."[3] Hollywood was changing once more, and it would encounter recession and retrenchment before it recovered.

◆ NOTES AND QUERIES

Widescreen Formats in Subsequent History

Widescreen formats established in the early 1950s have continued to govern theatrical filmmaking, but other technological changes have affected films' presentation.

Since only "road-show" theaters had 70mm equipment, wide-gauge films were also released in 35mm copies for neighborhood and suburban theaters.

With the decline in U.S. 70mm production (*Ryan's Daughter,* 1970, was the last such film for many years), 35mm returned to dominance. Today, however, some big-budget features are filmed in 35mm but released in 70mm, which can produce excellent blow-ups and better sound. This means that a 35mm film might be shot in one aspect ratio but shown in others. If a film is shot in anamorphic 35mm, 35mm prints will usually be exhibited in the 2.35:1 ratio, while 70mm prints of the film will be shown at the standard of 2.2:1.

When films are shown in nontheatrical situations, they often appear in ratios drastically different from those originally intended. A 16mm print of a CinemaScope film may be anamorphic, or it may be "matted" to a widescreen ratio less than the correct 2.35:1, or it may be a "flat" version that fills the 1.37 frame fully. The latter two versions can be projected without a special lens, but they exclude much of the original image.

Broadcast television, which was designed to accord with the Academy film ratio of 1.37:1, routinely shows widescreen films in flat versions. To cover the action in a widescreen original, television engineers devised the *pan-and-scan* process, which introduces camera movements or cuts that were not in the original. To avoid such problems, some cinematographers shoot widescreen films with eventual television presentation in mind. This is easiest when filming "full-frame" (i.e., at the 1.37:1 ratio). This squarer image is more appropriate for versions that will appear on television and videocassette. In filming wider ratios, the cinematographer may take the television frame into account by leaving blank areas in the composition. Currently, many films are released on laserdisc video in a "letterbox" format which approximates the wider theatrical image, and even cable channels are starting to program such versions of classic widescreen films.

For a discussion of widescreen ratios of the 1950s and their continuation into the present, see John Belton, *Widescreen Cinema* (Cambridge, Mass.: Harvard University Press, 1992).

EXPLOITATION FILMS AND CONNOISSEURS OF "WEIRD MOVIES"

Since the 1970s, exploitation movies have become cult items. Some fans find hilarity in the overblown dialogue, stiff performances, and awkward technique. This so-bad-it's-good attitude was popularized in Harry and Michael Medved, *The Golden Turkey Awards* (New York: Putnam, 1980). Other aficionados consider the exploitation films a direct challenge to the idea of normality presented by the Hollywood mainstream. Arising at the time of Punk and No Wave music, this notion of the subversive potential of rough technique and bad taste is exemplified in the "fanzines" *Film Threat* and *That's Exploitation!* With the new availability of exploitation items on video, a "psychotronic" subculture has grown up around violent films, both old and more recent.

"Incredibly Strange Films," *Re/Search* no. 10 (1986) gathers information on exploitation items of the 1960s. The magazine *Video Watchdog* specializes in comparing versions of exploitation horror films. Rudolph Grey's *Nightmare of Ecstasy: The Life and Art of Edward D. Wood, Jr.* (Los Angeles: Feral, 1992) compiles attractively odd interviews. Autobiographies of more successful exploitation filmmakers are William Castle, *Step Right Up! I'm Gonna Scare the Pants Off America: Memoirs of a B-Movie Mogul* [New York: Pharos, 1992 (orig. 1976)]; Roger Corman (with Jim Jerome), *How I Made a Hundred Movies in Hollywood and Never Lost a Dime* (New York: Random House, 1990); and Sam Arkoff (with Richard Trubo), *Flying through Hollywood by the Seat of My Pants* (New York: Birch Lane, 1992).

◆ REFERENCES

1. Sam Arkoff and Richard Trubo, *Flying through Hollywood by the Seat of My Pants* (New York: Birch Lane, 1992), p. 4.
2. Manny Farber, "Underground Films [1957]," in *Negative Space* (London: Studio Vista, 1971), p. 17.
3. Quoted in Tag Gallagher, *John Ford: The Man and His Films* (Berkeley: University of California Press, 1986), p. 437.

16

POSTWAR EUROPEAN CINEMA: NEOREALISM AND OTHER TRENDS

n 1945 much of Europe lay in ruins. Thirty-five million people were dead, over half of them civilians. Millions of survivors had lost their homes. Factories were obliterated, damaged, or obsolete. Great cities—Rotterdam, Cologne, Dresden—were rubble. All European countries were massively in debt; Britain had lost one-quarter of its prewar wealth, while Denmark's economy had regressed to its 1930 level. In all, this conflagration was the most devastating the world had yet seen.

THE POSTWAR CONTEXT

Europe would have to start again. But according to what principles? Socialists and Communists believed that social revolution could start from scratch in this "year zero," and in some countries left-wing parties won substantial popular support. By 1952, however, the left's power had waned, and Europe's most industrially advanced countries were dominated by conservative and middle-of-the-road parties. World War II had demonstrated that a modern government could oversee a nation's economy. Consequently, most European countries introduced centralized economic planning. This mildly "socialistic" reform, along with emerging welfare-state policies pioneered in Scandinavia, blunted some left-wing demands for radical change.

The victory of moderate reconstruction took place in a changed international context. The Allies' victory demonstrated that Europe would no longer enjoy central power in world affairs. The postwar world was bipolar, dominated by the United States and the USSR. The Cold War between these two superpowers would now affect every nation's internal politics.

The United States helped consolidate the new Europe. In 1947, the European Recovery Plan, popularly known as the Marshall Plan, offered billions of dollars in aid. By the time the plan ended in 1952, industrial and agricultural production in Europe had surpassed prewar levels. Europe's "great boom" in employment, standard of living, and productivity was under way.

In exchange for helping Europe rebuild, however, the United States expected political allegiance. In 1949 the United States presided over the formation of the North Atlantic Treaty Organization (NATO), a military alliance which committed members to oppose the USSR and national Communist parties.

Postwar reconstruction proceeded along a course which resisted radical change and absorbed Europe into the American sphere of influence. But there were still many local conflicts with U.S. policy. Many governments resisted the imposition of American will, sometimes by means of legislation that tried to constrain the power of American capital. Another area of conflict was the reemergence of the "European idea."

The growth of American power after World War I had convinced many Europeans that only a "United States of Europe" could compete in the new arena (p. 184). This idea was revived in the 1940s, when it became evident that countries would need to cooperate in order to rebuild. Moreover, the United States supported the pan-European idea because continental prosperity would resist communism and offer markets for American goods.

The United Nations (founded in 1945), the Organization for European Economic Cooperation, and, in 1957, the European Economic Community (known as the Common Market) certainly constituted steps toward the goal of European unity. Yet the dream of a Europe without national boundaries was not realized. Nations insisted on their distinct cultural identities. Many Europeans argued that in the wake of American economic and political domination had come a cultural imperialism—that in advertising, fashion, and mass media Europe was already becoming a colony of the United States. In the postwar era, then, we find a complex, often tense interplay among national identity, European unity, resistance to America, and allegiance to it.

FILM INDUSTRIES AND FILM CULTURE

The war had drastically cut the flow of American films to most countries. This cleared space for the domestic industry and nurtured indigenous talent. After the war, however, the American companies strove to reintroduce their product into the lucrative European market.

U.S. foreign aid paved the way for American movies' reentry into European markets. Hollywood's overseas negotiations were conducted by the

Motion Picture Export Association of America (p. 373), and the agency used its power forcefully. In France, the U.S. government backed up film export agreements. The MPEAA also argued that Hollywood films were excellent propaganda against Communist and Fascist tendencies. This argument carried most weight in Germany. The American firms could also resort to boycotts, as proved necessary in Denmark in 1955–1958.

Hollywood's strategy was to make each country's domestic industry strong enough to support the large-scale distribution and exhibition of American films. Penetration was quick. By 1953, in virtually every country American films occupied at least half of all screening time. Europe would remain Hollywood's major source of foreign revenue.

WEST GERMANY: "PAPAS KINO"

West Germany offers a case study in how thoroughly the United States could dominate a major market. Between 1945 and 1949, Germany was occupied by the four Allied powers. In 1949, the merged western zones became the German Federal Republic (commonly known as West Germany), and the Russian zone became the German Democratic Republic (East Germany). West Germany received millions of dollars in aid under the Marshall Plan and other programs, a policy justified by American strategists' belief that the country would become a bulwark against communism. By 1952, the German "economic miracle" produced a standard of living almost 50 percent above that of the prewar period.

Superficially, the film industry seemed healthy as well. Production climbed from 5 films in 1946 to 103 in 1953 and did not fall below 100 during the 1950s. Attendance surged and coproductions flourished. Hildegard Neff, Curt Jurgens, and other German stars gained wide recognition.

Yet the industry failed to foster an internationally competitive cinema. Soon after 1945, American movie companies had convinced the U.S. government to cooperate in making the German market an outpost of Hollywood. The old Ufi monopoly was dismantled and replaced by hundreds of production and distribution companies. Since the German empire was lost, these firms could count only on the domestic market, and this was dominated by American firms. The latter controlled a large part of distribution and were permitted to use blind- and block-booking tactics already outlawed in the United States. With no quota restrictions, up to two-thirds of German theaters' screening time was occupied by American films.

As in other countries, the bulk of production leaned toward popular entertainment, literary adaptations, and remakes of classics. The most popular genre was the *Heimat* ("homeland") film, the tale of village romance, which represented 20 percent of the domestic output. Much quality production of the era consisted of war films or biographies of statesmen and professionals.

Some postwar cinema seriously scrutinized the war and its effects. Peter Lorre's *Der Verlorene* (*The Lost One*, 1951) uses flashbacks to present a doctor haunted by the wartime murders he has committed. The film, like many of its era, makes macabre play with mirrors and shadows, but Lorre also adorns his performance with mildly expressionist touches (Fig. 16.1). In addition, the early postwar years saw the emergence of the *Trümmerfilm* ("rubble film"), which dealt with the problems of reconstructing Germany (p. 473).

Not until the end of the 1950s did filmmakers suggest that traces of Naziism lingered on. Wolfgang Staudte's *Roses for the State Prosecutor* (1959) and *Fairground* (1960) show ex-SS men prospering under Germany's economic miracle. More oblique in its treatment of the past is Lang's thriller *The Thousand Eyes of Dr. Mabuse* (1960). Here a criminal doctor uses hidden television cameras to spy upon the guests at the Hotel Luxor. By invoking the figure of Mabuse (in the postwar years considered a parallel to Hitler), by suggesting that many characters share his voyeurism (Fig. 16.2), and by stipulating that the Luxor was built by the Nazis for espionage purposes, *Thousand Eyes* hints that the Fascist era survives into the present.

The charge could well have been addressed to the industry at large. Although some Nazi filmmakers (such as Leni Riefenstahl) were forbidden to work, most were rehabilitated under Allied policy. Some Nazi supporters were given prestigious posts; Veit Harlan directed eight films in the postwar decades. This continuity with the Fascist era, and the dully complacent film culture that it spawned, would be attacked by young directors of the 1960s, who called for an end to *Papas Kino,* "Papa's cinema."

RESISTANCE TO U.S. ENCROACHMENT

For U.S. firms, Germany was the model of a quiescent European market, just active enough to permit profitable domination. But most European film industries retained greater independence. This was largely due to a wave of protectionist legislation. By 1948, American films were dominating European exhibition, and many national industries, still rebuilding after the war, were in a slump. Producers' organizations pleaded for help, and most governments responded.

One strategy, already exercised in the interwar years, was that of setting quotas on American films or on screen time allotted to the domestic product. In 1948, France limited American imports and required that at least twenty weeks per year be devoted to the French product. In the same year, Britain's New Films Act required that at least 45 percent of screen time be reserved for British feature films. Italy's "Andreotti law" of 1949 required that eighty days per year be set aside for Italian films, and numerical quotas on imports soon followed.

Another strategy was to restrict American firms' income. This might be done before the fact by levying charges on each film's expected earnings. Alternatively, a flat rate might be charged. The Andreotti law required that for each imported film, the distributor had in effect to give Italian film production an interest-free loan of 2.5 million lire. Or a country's legislation might provide for "freezing" American earnings, requiring that they be kept and invested in the country. In France, for instance, a 1948 agreement provided for a freezing of $10 million in earnings per year.

Besides defensive protectionist legislation, most European countries took steps to make their industries competitive. Governments began to finance

Fig. 16.1 Echoes of *M:* Peter Lorre's hand dawdling as he is about to kill his wife in *The Lost One.*

Fig. 16.2 "Innocent" voyeurism in *The Thousand Eyes of Dr. Mabuse:* A false mirror allows the millionaire to spy on the woman he wishes to seduce.

production. Sometimes, as in Denmark, a tax on movie tickets created a fund which could advance monies to producers judged worthy. In several countries, the national government established an agency through which banks could loan money to film projects; the most famous instance is Britain's National Film Finance Corporation, established in 1949. A government might also offer cash prizes for scripts or films judged artistically or culturally significant. Sometimes the government subsidized a project outright, through a mechanism that would return to producers a percentage of ticket income or tax. European producing companies soon became dependent on government aid.

Protectionist legislation and government support were somewhat successful. Film output rose significantly in France, Italy, and the United Kingdom after 1950. But the new interventionism aided American firms as well. Most governments encouraged companies to invest their frozen funds in domestic production, which yielded further profits for Hollywood. The Majors might also earn money from exporting films to U.S. "art theaters." Frozen-funds policies encouraged U.S. companies to undertake "runaway" productions. American firms also established foreign subsidiaries. These were eligible for local government assistance and could lobby for Hollywood's interests within each country. In some countries, the Hollywood Majors were able to buy distribution outlets, thus controlling the access which domestic films had to their own market. At the same time, quotas became rather insignificant because they coincided with the 1950s downturn in American production: the major companies did not have a great many films to export.

One tactic for challenging Hollywood's domination moved toward the 1920s goal of "Film Europe" by creating *coproductions*. In a coproduction, producers drew the cast and crew from two or more countries under the auspices of bilateral agreements allowing the production to qualify for subsidies from each nation. Typically, each coproduction had a majority and a minority partner, and the responsibilities of each were stipulated by the international accords. Thus, in a French-Italian coproduction, if the French company was the primary participant, the director had to be French, but an assistant director, a scriptwriter, one major actor, and one secondary performer had to be Italian. Coproductions spread out financial risks, allowed producers to mount bigger-budget fare that might compete with Hollywood, and gave access to international markets. The coproduction quickly became central to western European filmmaking.

Similarly, while Hollywood set the international standard in most film technology, a few European innovations competed on the Continent. At the end of the 1940s Eclair and Debrie introduced lightweight cameras with relatively large magazines and reflex viewing, which allowed the cameraperson to see, during filming, exactly what the lens was recording. These cameras were taken up throughout Europe, as was the German Arriflex (dating back to 1936 but improved in 1956). The Arriflex would become the standard nonstudio 35mm camera of the postwar era. In 1953, a French inventor devised the Pancinor, a zoom lens that did not appreciably damage image quality.

Another international initiative of the postwar era was the film festival. It was, most evidently, a competition among quality productions for prizes awarded by panels of experts. Thus films shown "in competition" would be prestigious representatives of a nation's film culture. The prototype was the Venice festival, run under Mussolini's patronage between 1932 and 1940. In the postwar era, film festivals helped define the public's conception of advanced European cinema. Festivals also showcased films which might attract foreign distributors. Winning a prize gave a film an economic advantage: the director, producer, and stars gained fame (and perhaps investment for their next ventures). At the same time, many films would be shown "out of competition"—screened for the press and interested producers, distributors, and exhibitors.

The Venice Film Festival was revived in 1946. Festivals in Cannes, Locarno, and Karlovy Vary began in the same year. The postwar years saw a steady increase: Edinburgh (beginning in 1947), Berlin (1951), Melbourne (1952), San Sebastian and Sydney (1954), San Francisco and London (1957), Moscow and Barcelona (1959). There were festivals of short films, animation, horror films, science fiction, and experimental films. There also appeared an enormous number of "festivals of festivals," usually noncompetitive events which showcased outstanding works from the major festivals. In North America, festivals began in New York, Los Angeles (known as Filmex), Denver, Telluride, and Montreal. By the early 1960s, a film devotee could attend festivals year-round.

It would be too simple to treat coproductions, technological innovations, and festivals as straightforward European counterattacks on American domination. Just as U.S. companies invested in European cinema, so they also participated in coproductions through their continental subsidiaries. Hollywood filmmakers had access to Arriflexes and used them on occasion, and they had their own zoom lens, the Cooke Zoomar. American films often won both prizes and distribution contracts at European festivals. Hollywood could even pay tribute to its peers by creating (in 1947) a special category of the Academy Awards. A winner of the award for Best Foreign Film stood a good chance of success in the United States, where American firms and theaters would reap a share of the benefits.

Some pan-European initiatives created genuine worldwide cooperation. In 1947 the International Federation of Ciné-Clubs was founded in order to join independent film societies in twenty countries. By 1955, there was a European confederation of Cinemas d'Art et d'Essai—theaters that programmed more innovative and experimental films, often aided by tax rebates. An older organization was the International Federation of Film Archives (FIAF), founded in 1938 but suspended during the war years. FIAF contacts were renewed at a 1945 conference, and in the next decade membership jumped from four to thirty-three archives. The growth in international film consciousness spurred governments to fund archives that would take up the burden of systematically documenting and preserving the world's film culture. Major American archives like the Museum of Modern Art, the International Museum of Photography in Rochester, and the Library of Congress Motion Picture Division joined the international effort.

Most European film industries enjoyed moderate health during the 1950s. Production increased within a modest range, sometimes exceeding prewar levels. Television and other competitive leisure activities had not yet emerged on a large scale, and the new generation of postwar youth swelled the theaters. As a result, in the most populous countries, the period 1955–1958 represented a peak in postwar attendance. Hollywood and its European counterparts had reached a mutually profitable stability.

THE RETURN OF MODERNISM

Most European films continued popular traditions from earlier decades: comedies, musicals, melodramas, and other genres, sometimes imitative of Hollywood. But now European films competed more successfully internationally and won prestige at film festivals. A growing population of young people was interested in less standardized fare. There was also a new generation of filmmakers trained during the war. More broadly, European social and intellectual life began to revive. Artists envisaged the possibility of continuing the modernist tradition founded in the early decades of the century. In a rebuilding Europe, modernism, always promising "the shock of the new," became revitalized.

These circumstances fostered the emergence of an international "art cinema." This cinema largely turned its back on popular traditions and identified itself with experimentation and innovation in the "high arts" of literature, painting, music, and theater. In certain respects, the postwar art film marks a resurgence of the modernist impulses of the 1920s, explored in French Impressionism, German Expressionism, and Soviet Montage. Sometimes there were specific debts to these earlier movements: the Italian Neorealists followed the Soviet filmmakers in using nonactors in central roles, while some Scandinavian directors had distinct expressionist leanings. In other ways, though, postwar filmmakers forged a revised modernism suitable to the sound cinema.

Postwar modernism can be described by three stylistic and formal features. First, filmmakers sought to be more true to life than they considered most classical filmmakers had been. The modernist filmmaker might seek to reveal the unpleasant realities of class antagonism or to bring home the horrors of fascism, war, and occupation. The Italian Neorealists, filming in the streets and emphasizing current social problems, offer the most evident example.

This *objective* realism led filmmakers toward episodic, slice-of-life narratives which avoided Hollywood's tight plots. The camera might linger on a scene after the action concluded or refuse to eliminate those moments in which "nothing happens." Similarly, postwar European modernist films favored open-ended narratives, in which central plot lines were left unresolved. This was often justified as the most realistic approach to storytelling, since in life, few events neatly tie up everything that went before.

Stylistically, many modernist filmmakers came to rely on the long take—the abnormally lengthy shot, typically sustained by camera movements. The long take could be justified as presenting the event in continuous "real time," without the manipulations of editing. Similarly, new acting styles—halting delivery, fragmentary and elliptical speeches, and refusal to meet other players' eyes—were often seen as running counter to the rapid, smoothly crafted

Fig. 16.3

Fig. 16.4

performances of American cinema. Faithfulness to objective reality could also imply a minute reproduction of the acoustic environment. In many postwar French films, for example, silence calls attention to small noises.

Fig. 16.3 The bleached-out nightmare in Bergman's *Wild Strawberries* (1957).

Fig. 16.4 Authorial commentary on the characters' lack of feeling in *Il Grido*.

Modernist filmmakers' drive to record objective reality was balanced by a second tendency. They also sought to represent *subjective* reality—the psychological forces that make the individual act in particular ways. The whole of mental life now lay open to exploration. As in the United States, flashback construction became very common, particularly for exploring recent history in a personal way. Filmmakers plunged still further into characters' minds, revealing dreams, hallucinations, and fantasies. Here the influence of German Expressionism was often evident (Fig. 16.3). The emphasis on subjectivity increased throughout the 1950s and the 1960s.

A third factor in the European art film of the postwar era is what we might call *authorial commentary*—the sense that an intelligence outside the film's world is pointing out something about the events we see. Here film style seems to be suggesting more about the characters than they know or are aware of. In a shot from *Il Grido* (1957), Antonioni evokes the bleakness of the characters' relationship by framing them, backs to the camera, against a barren landscape (Fig. 16.4). In *Le Plaisir* (1952), Ophüls's camera pans and tracks down from cherubs in the church to prostitutes in the pews, suggesting that the women are blessed by their attendance at a young girl's confirmation. At the limit, such narrational commentary can become *reflexive*, pointing up the film's own artifice and reminding the audience that the world we see is a fictional construct.

Such narrational commentary is usually far from clear-cut in its implications; one can imagine alternative interpretations of the shots just mentioned. In fact, ambiguity is a central effect of all three forces in the postwar modernist European film. The film will typically encourage the spectator to speculate on what might otherwise have happened, to fill in gaps, and to try out different interpretations.

In Michael Cacoyannis's *Stella* (Greece, 1955), for example, the two lovers, Milto and Stella, have quarreled and separated. Each one has picked

Figs. 16.5 and 16.6 Crosscutting to suggest that the separated lovers are dancing with each other.

Fig. 16.5

Fig. 16.6

another partner, and each couple has gone to a different nightspot. But Cacoyannis crosscuts the two lovers: Milto dancing to Greek music, Stella dancing to bebop (Figs. 16.5, 16.6). The editing makes them appear to be dancing with each other. This might be taken as representing mental subjectivity: perhaps each one would prefer to be with the other. Alternatively, the viewer could interpret the crosscutting as making an external comment, perhaps suggesting that the couple belong together even if they are not aware of it. In a stylistic choice typical of postwar modernism, the film invites the spectator to consider multiple meanings.

Such ambiguities had surfaced in the works of avant-gardists such as Buñuel, Cocteau, and Maya Deren, but now they were absorbed by directors working in commercial feature production. These directors also owed a debt to classical traditions, such as the post-*Kane* tendency toward deep-space staging and deep-focus shooting (Figs. 16.7, 16.8). Sometimes, however, the modernist film reworked classical devices for the sake of greater realism, subjective depth, narrational commentary, or ambiguity. Our example from *Stella* uses standard crosscutting in this way. Fantasies and dream sequences were common currency of mainstream cinema; the modernist filmmaker made them more prominent and even sometimes untrustworthy. Films like *Le Jour se lève* and *Citizen Kane* had popularized flashback construction in the 1940s, so the modernist filmmaker could count on audiences being prepared for more complicated manipulations of time. Europeans' reliance on continuity editing remained constant, although directors like Jacques Tati and Bresson reworked the technique. The long take was already common in Hollywood, but few Americans used it as systematically and disorientingly as Antonioni or Ophüls.

In all, the modernist cinema located itself between the intelligible, accessible popular cinema and the more radical experimentation of the avant-garde. Often coproduced for a pan-European audience, films of this trend were seen in North America, Asia, and Latin America as well.

Several countries participated in the trend toward cinematic modernism. Italy was the most significant, so we devote most of what follows to it; we close the chapter by examining Spain as an example of Italian Neorealist influence. In the following chapter we consider other countries which contributed to the European art cinema of the postwar period.

Fig. 16.7 Deep space and deep focus in *The Devil's General* (West Germany, 1955, Helmut Käutner).

Fig. 16.8 Hollywood-style depth in *Justice est faite* (France, 1954, André Cayatte).

ITALY: NEOREALISM AND AFTER

The most important filmmaking trend of the era appeared in Italy during the years 1945–1951. Neorealism was not as original or as unified a movement as once was thought, but it did create a distinct approach to fictional film-making. Moreover, this approach had an enormous impact on cinema in other countries.

ITALIAN SPRING

With the fall of Mussolini, the Italian film industry lost its organizational center. As in Germany, Allied military forces in Italy cooperated with the American companies in trying to secure U.S. domination of the market. Most production firms became small-scale affairs. While domestic companies struggled, Neorealist cinema emerged as a force for cultural renewal and social change.

During the waning years of the Fascist regime a realist impulse arose in literature and film (pp. 317–319). *Four Steps in the Clouds, The Children Are Watching Us, Ossessione* and other films led some filmmakers to envision a new cinema. "We are convinced," wrote Giuseppe De Santis and Mario Alicata in 1941, "that one day we will create our most beautiful film following the slow and tired step of the worker who returns home."[1] Once Italy was liberated in the spring of 1945, people in all walks of life were eager to break with old ways. Parties formed a coalition government, aiming to make left-liberal ideas the basis of a reborn Italy. Filmmakers were ready to bear witness to what was called "the Italian Spring." The "new realism" imagined during the war years arrived. (See Box.)

What made these films seem so realistic? Partly the contrast with many of the films that preceded them. Italian films had become known across Europe for their magnificent studio settings. But the government's Cinecittà studios were heavily damaged in the war and could not support opulent productions. Filmmakers moved into the streets and the countryside. Since Italy had long mastered postsynchronization for dubbing foreign movies, crews could shoot on location and dub in dialogue later.

Another novelty was a critical examination of recent history. Neorealist films presented contemporary stories from a "popular front" perspective. For example, Roberto Rossellini's *Open City* derived its plot from events of the winter of 1943–1944. The principal characters are caught up in the struggle against the German troops occupying Rome. Trust and self-sacrifice bind together the sabotage agent Manfredi, his friend Francesco, Francesco's fiancée Pina, and the priest Don Pietro. The film portrays the Resistance as uniting Communists and Catholics with the populace.

Similarly, Rossellini's *Paisà* (known in English as *Paisan*) presents a kaleidoscopic vision of the Allied invasion of Italy. The film's six episodes follow the movement of the American forces from Sicily north to the Po valley. More fragmentary and documentary-like than *Open City, Paisan* focuses not

NEOREALISM AND AFTER
A CHRONOLOGY OF EVENTS AND SELECTED WORKS

1945   Spring: Mussolini is executed; Italy is liberated.
Open City, Roberto Rossellini

1946   June: Popular referendum carries liberal and left-wing parties to government power.
Paisan, Roberto Rossellini
Il Sole sorge ancora ("The Sun Always Rises"), Aldo Vergano
Vivere in pace ("To Live in Peace"), Luigi Zampa
Il Bandito ("The Bandit"), Alberto Lattuada
Shoeshine, Vittorio De Sica

1947   *Germany Year Zero*, Roberto Rossellini
Caccia tragica (*Fugitive*), Giuseppe De Santis
Senza pietà (*Without Pity*), Luigi Zampa

1948   April: Moderate Christian Democratic party wins election.
La Terra trema ("The Earth Trembles"), Luchino Visconti
The Bicycle Thief, Vittorio De Sica
Bitter Rice, Giuseppe De Santis
Il Mulino del Po (*The Mill on the Po River*), Alberto Lattuada
La Machina ammazzacattivi (*The Machine to Kill Bad People*), Roberto Rossellini
L'Amore (*Love*) [episode-film consisting of *Una Voce umana* (*The Human Voice*) and *Il Miracolo* (*The Miracle*)], Roberto Rossellini

1949   December: Andreotti law establishes quotas and subsidies.
Stromboli, Roberto Rossellini

1950   *Miracle in Milan*, Vittorio De Sica
Francesco, guillare di Dio (*The Little Flowers of Saint Francis*), Roberto Rossellini
Cronaca di un amore (*Story of a Love Affair*), Michelangelo Antonioni
Luci del varietà (*Variety Lights*), Alberto Lattuada and Federico Fellini

1951   *Umberto D.*, Vittorio De Sica
Roma ore 11 (*Rome 11 O'Clock*), Giuseppe De Santis
Bellissima ("The Most Beautiful"), Luchino Visconti
Europa 51, Roberto Rossellini

1952   *The White Shiek*, Federico Fellini
I Vinti (*The Vanquished*), Michelangelo Antonioni

1953   December: Conference on Neorealism is held in Parma.
Amore in città (*Love in the City*), collective work overseen by Cesare Zavattini
I Vitelloni ("The Young Calves"), Federico Fellini
Stazione termini ("Final Station"), Vittorio De Sica
Signora senza camilie (*The Lady without the Camellias*), Michelangelo Antonioni
Pane, amore e fantasia (*Bread, Love, and Fantasy*), Luigi Comencini

1954   *Senso*, Luchino Visconti
La Strada ("The Road"), Federico Fellini
Voyage to Italy, Roberto Rossellini

Fig. 16.9 *The Bicycle Thief:* Ricci and his wife prepare to pawn their sheets in order to reclaim his bicycle.

only on the struggles between the Italian partisans and the occupying forces but also on the frictions, misunderstandings, and occasional affinities that arise between the populace and the Yankee troops. Thematically, *Paisan* is as much about differences of language and culture as it is about the historical events it portrays.

Soon filmmakers turned from partisan heroics to contemporary social problems, such as party factionalism, inflation, and widespread unemployment. Few Neorealist films represent postwar suffering more vividly than Vittorio De Sica's *Ladri di biciclette* ("The Bicycle Thieves," aka *The Bicycle Thief*). This story of a worker whose livelihood depends upon his bicycle shows the brutal rapacity of postwar life (Fig. 16.9). Ricci turns to every institution—police, Church, labor union—but none can recover his stolen bicycle, and most are indifferent to his plight. He and his son Bruno must wander the city in a futile search.

To this social criticism *The Bicycle Thief* counterpoints the disintegration of trust between Ricci and Bruno. The film's climax comes when, in despair, Ricci tries to steal a bicycle himself. Bruno watches in shock. Their search has stripped away his illusions about his father. Ricci is spared arrest, and Bruno, now sorrowfully accepting his father's frailties, acknowledges his love by slipping his hand into Ricci's. The film's scriptwriter, Cesare Zavattini, often expressed the desire to make a film that simply followed a man through ninety minutes in his life. *The Bicycle Thief* is not that film, but at the time it was seen as a step toward Alicata and De Santis's ideal of following the worker's "slow and tired tread."

Some films charted the problems of the countryside. *Bitter Rice* depicts, somewhat sensationalistically, the exploitation of young women driven to low-wage farm work and herded into prisonlike dormitories. The most well known of these regional works is Visconti's *La Terra trema* ("The Earth Trembles"). The film portrays the ill-fated rebellion of Sicilian fishermen against the marketers who exploit them. Like other films of the period, it expresses fading hopes for deep social change.

In 1948, the Italian Spring ended. Liberal and left-wing parties were defeated at the polls. At the same time, the country was rebuilding. National income was starting to exceed prewar levels, and Italy was moving gradually into a modernizing European economy. The film industry discovered that it could export films, even to the United States.

Back in 1942, when Vittorio Mussolini, the head of the film industry, saw Visconti's *Ossessione,* he stormed out of the theater shouting, "This is not Italy!" Most Neorealist films elicited a similar reaction from postwar officials. The portrait of a desolate, poverty-stricken country outraged politicians anxious to prove that Italy was on the road to democracy and prosperity. The Catholic Church condemned many films for their anticlericalism and their portrayal of sex and working-class life. Leftists attacked the films for their pessimism and lack of explicit political commitment.

Few Neorealist works were popular with the public. Audiences were more drawn to the American films which came flooding into Italy. The state under-secretary in charge of entertainment, Giulio Andreotti, found a way of slowing the advance of American films while also curbing the embarrassing excesses of Neorealism. The so-called Andreotti law, which went into effect in 1949, not only established import limits and screen quotas but also provided for loans to production firms. To grant a loan, however, a government committee had to approve the script, and films with an apolitical slant were rewarded with larger sums. Worse, a film could be denied an export license if it "slandered Italy."[2] The Andreotti law created preproduction censorship.

This move coincided with a general drift away from the "purer" Neorealism of the 1944–1948 period. Soon after the war, some filmmakers sought to acquire a Neorealist look by shooting traditional romances and melodramas in regions that would supply picturesque local color. Other directors explored a vein of allegorical fantasy (such as in De Sica's *Miracle in Milan* and Rossellini's *The Machine to Kill Bad People*) or historical spectacle (Visconti's *Senso*). There also emerged "rosy Neorealism," films which melded working-class characters with 1930s-style populist comedy. Against this background, De Sica and Zavattini's *Umberto D.*, which depicted the lonely life of a retired man, could only strike officials as a dangerous throwback. The film begins with a scene of police breaking up a demonstration of old pensioners, and it ends with Umberto's aborted suicide attempt. In a public letter to De Sica, Andreotti castigated him for his "wretched service to his fatherland, which is also the fatherland of . . . progressive social legislation."[3]

NARRATIVE INNOVATIONS

By the early 1950s, the Neorealist impulse had spent its force. At the 1953 Parma Congress on Neorealism, journalists and filmmakers began to discuss what the movement had been. There had been no Neorealist manifesto or program, only an appeal for greater realism and an emphasis on contemporary subjects and the life of the working class. Soon, however, several critical positions emerged.

One view treated Neorealism as committed reportage, calling for reform in the name of the political unity that had been briefly achieved during the Resistance and the Italian Spring. Another position emphasized the moral dimension of the films, suggesting that the movement's importance lay in its ability to make characters' personal problems gain universal significance.

A more abstractly theoretical position, held by the French critics André Bazin and Amédée Ayfre, fastened on the ways in which Neorealism's documentary approach made the viewer aware of the beauty of ordinary life. In this respect, Bazin and Ayfre echoed the ideas of Cesare Zavattini, De Sica's scriptwriter and the most tireless advocate of a distinctive Neorealist aesthetic. Zavattini sought a cinema which presented the drama hidden in everyday events, like buying shoes or looking for an apartment. He insisted on presenting events in all their repetitive ordinariness. An American producer told Zavattini that a Hollywood film would show a plane passing overhead, then machine-gun fire, then the plane falling out of the sky but a Neorealist film would show the plane passing once, then again, then again. But, Zavattini replied, "It is not enough to have the plane pass by three times; it must pass by twenty times."[4] This ideal was seldom realized in Neorealist practice, but Zavattini's formulation allowed filmmakers and film theorists to imagine a radically "dedramatized" cinema that would be approached in the 1960s.

Most historians of cinema find Neorealism influential not only for its political attitudes and its world view but also for its innovations in film form. Many of these had precedents, but the international prestige of the Neorealist movement brought them to attention as never before.

The prototypical Neorealist film is often thought to be shot on location, using nonactors filmed in rough, offhand compositions. Actually, however, few Neorealist films display all these features. Most interior scenes are filmed in studio sets, and these are carefully lit (Fig. 16.9). Sound is almost invariably postdubbed, which allows control after filming; the voice of the protagonist in *Bicycle Thief* was supplied by another actor. While some performers are typically nonprofessionals, more common is what Bazin called the "amalgam" technique, whereby nonactors are mixed with such stars as Anna

Fig. 16.10

Fig. 16.11

Magnani and Aldo Fabrizi. In sum, Neorealism relies no less on artifice than do other film styles.

Moreover, the films are edited according to the norms of classical Hollywood style. While few Neorealist images are as self-consciously composed as those in *La Terra trema*, shots virtually always balance elements within the frame. (See Figs. 16.10, 16.11.) Even when filmed on location, scenes contain smooth camera movements, crisp focus, and choreographed staging in several planes (Figs. 16.12, 16.13). The Neorealist film typically includes a sweeping musical score which recalls opera in its underlining of a scene's emotional development.

In its conception of storytelling, the Neorealist movement broke fresher ground. Sometimes the films rely extensively upon coincidences, as when in *Bicycle Thief* Ricci and Bruno happen to spot the thief near the house of the psychic they have visited. Such plot developments, in rejecting the carefully motivated chain of events in classical cinema, seem more objectively realistic, reflecting the chance encounters of daily life. Among with this tendency goes an unprecedented use of ellipsis. Neorealist films often skip over important causes for the events we see. As Bazin pointed out, in *Paisan* the Germans' massacre of a farm family is revealed with startling suddenness: in one scene, the partisan guerrillas are in the field awaiting a plane, and in the next scene, the guerrillas discover a baby crying beside the bodies of his parents.

This loosening of plot linearity is perhaps most apparent in the films' unresolved endings. Halfway through *Open City*, Francesco escapes from the Fascists, but the plot does not return to him again. In *Bicycle Thief*, Ricci and Bruno walk off into the crowd without a bicycle. How will the family keep going? The film does not tell us.

Neorealist films employ Hollywoodian deadlines, appointments, and "dialogue hooks" to connect scenes, but the result is likely to seem merely a string of events. Scene B is apt to follow scene A simply because B happened later, not because scene A made it happen. The bulk of *Bicycle Thief* is organized around the search for the bicycle, and this traces the chronology of the day, from the morning through lunch to late afternoon.

Fig. 16.10 *La Terra trema:* Visconti's rich compositional use of seascape.

Fig. 16.11 Neorealism as historical spectacle (*Il Mulino del Po*).

Fig. 16.12 In *Bitter Rice*, the camera starts from a close-up of women's striding legs . . .

Fig. 16.13 . . . and slowly cranes up to reveal the entire rice paddy.

Fig. 16.14 Edmund pauses in his wanderings when a bombed-out church emits organ music (*Germany Year Zero*).

Similarly episodic are the final sequences of Rossellini's third postwar film, *Germany Year Zero*. Edmund, the boy who exemplifies the moral confusions of defeated Germany, flees his family and wanders the streets of Berlin. The film's final fourteen minutes follow him through a single night and the following morning, concentrating on random events. Edmund watches a prostitute leave her client, plays hopscotch on the empty streets, scuffs through the rubble of buildings, tries to join other boys in a soccer game, and drifts around the city (Fig. 16.14). From high in a shattered building, after he watches his grandfather's coffin carried out, he jumps to his death. While a suicide is a traditional conclusion to a story, Rossellini leads up to it by a string of everyday, accidentally glimpsed, events.

Presented with a plot consisting of events that may not be causally connected, the viewer no longer knows which are the "big scenes" and which are simply filler material. Neorealist storytelling tends to "flatten" all events to the same level, playing down climaxes and dwelling on mundane locales or behaviors. Bazin wrote eloquently about how *Bicycle Thief*'s walk through Rome lets the viewer notice the difference between Ricci's and Bruno's gaits.[5] In *Umberto D.*, one scene is devoted to the maid waking up and starting her day's kitchen work; Bazin praised this for dwelling on trivial "microactions" that traditional cinema never shows us.[6] (See Box.) This unorthodox approach to narrative construction enabled Neorealist filmmakers to draw the viewer's attention to the "irrelevant" details that constitute daily life.

Neorealism sought to embrace ordinary life in all its varying moods. In *Paisan*, mildly comic or pathetic scenes alternate with ones full of violence. Probably the most famous example of mixed tone in films of the period is the scene depicting the death of Pina in *Open City*. It reveals how a fairly orthodox film style can convey severe wrenches of emotional timbre.

Rossellini starts the scene at a pitch of suspense when German soldiers cordon off a block of apartments and begin searching for underground par-

UMBERTO D.: THE MAID WAKES UP

The sequence begins with the maid in bed, watching a cat walking across the roof. She rises and goes into the kitchen, where, after several tries, she lights the fire (Fig. 16.15). (The wall bears the marks of many matches scratched there.) She looks out the window again and sees the cat walking on the roof; she looks out another window and then walks back to the kitchen. She goes to the cupboard, then to the table, and finally to the sink, where she sprays ants off the wall (Fig. 16.16). She fills the coffeepot, walks around a bit more, and then returns to the stove, where she checks herself for signs of her pregnancy.

Going to the table, she sits and starts to weep as she grinds the morning coffee (Fig. 16.17). As she grinds, she stretches out her foot to shut the door (Fig. 16.18). Then she sits up, wipes her eyes, and rises to take the coffee to her mistress.

As is often the case with Neorealist films, the realistic details play a narrative role. Bazin rightly praises the sequence for presenting the maid's life in all its "dailiness," but we should also note that a degree of drama is inserted as well. The maid has just discovered that she is pregnant. The force of the scene derives from the tension between her drab routine and her numb anxiety about her future.

Fig. 16.15

Fig. 16.17

Fig. 16.16

Fig. 16.18

Fig. 16.19

Fig. 16.20

Fig. 16.21

Fig. 16.22

Fig. 16.23

Fig. 16.24

Fig. 16.19 *Open City:* To make the old man seem to be dying, Don Pietro has had to knock him unconscious with a frying pan.

Fig. 16.20 Pina breaks free from the guards . . .

Fig. 16.21 . . . and runs after Francesco; she is seen from his viewpoint on the truck.

Fig. 16.22 In a reverse shot, Francesco calls out . . .

Fig. 16.23 . . . just before Pina is shot.

Fig. 16.24 Don Pietro and Marcello grieve over Pina's body.

tisans. Don Pietro and Marcello pretend to be visiting a dying man. They hide the partisans' munitions in an old man's bed, a ploy which triggers farcical comedy when he refuses to pretend to be dying (Fig. 16.19).

The tone shifts again when Pina sees that the Germans have captured her fiancé, Francesco, and are marching him toward their trucks. She breaks free from the guards and runs after his departing truck (Figs. 16.20, 16.21). Don Pietro, watching in horror, presses Marcello's face into his cassock. Francesco shouts, "Hold her back!" (Fig. 16.22). Suddenly there is a burst of machine-gun fire. In the next shot, from Francesco's viewpoint, Pina is hit and falls (Fig. 16.23). Grim music starts. The last four shots of the scene, all taken in newsreel fashion with long lenses, show Marcello and Don Pietro running to the dead woman and kneeling by her (Fig. 16.24).

The clarity of Rossellini's style allows him to drive home some unsettling narrative qualities. In a more classical film, Francesco would see who killed Pina and would spend the rest of the film seeking revenge. But here Pina is cut down by an anonymous burst of fire, and the killer's identity is never revealed. In addition, the emotional tone switches abruptly, from suspense to comedy to suspense and finally to shock and sorrow. Even more disturbing, Pina has been established as the film's heroine, and her sudden death constitutes a shock for which few viewers in 1945 would have been prepared. Like the death of André Jurieu in Renoir's *Rules of the Game*, Pina's murder suggests that in real life—as opposed to the movies—good people may die pointlessly.

Neorealism's stylistic and narrative devices influenced the emergence of an international modernist cinema. Location shooting with postdubbing; the amalgam of actors and nonactors; plots based on chance encounters, ellipses, open endings, and microactions; and extreme mixtures of tone—all these strategies would be developed by filmmakers around the world over the next four decades.

BEYOND NEOREALISM

Apart from works like *Umberto D.*, rosy Neorealism was the dominant form the movement took in the early 1950s. The huge success of Luigi Comencini's *Pane, amore e fantasia* (*Bread, Love, and Fantasy*) led to a string of imitations that continued well into the 1960s. Rosy Neorealism retained some use of locations and nonprofessional actors, and it occasionally took on social problems, but it absorbed Neorealism into the robust tradition of Italian comedy. As economic recovery continued to move Italy toward greater prosperity, Neorealism's focus on poverty and suffering came to seem less welcome to most audiences.

During the same period of time, the domestic film industry was becoming more oriented to an international market. Although hundreds of American films were successfully released in Italy in the late 1940s, the Italian government froze the profits within the country. This encouraged Hollywood studios to reinvest the money in Italian film production, distribution, and exhibition. Italy also sustained American runaway productions, supplying casts and crews.

Many traditional genres proved exportable. Blasetti's hugely lucrative *Fabiola* (1948) revived the lavish costume picture. Audiences in Europe and America developed a taste for "peplum," musclemen sagas such as *Ulysses* (1954) and *Revolt of the Gladiators* (1958). Also successful was the *commedia all'italiana* featuring veteran comic stars like Vittorio De Sica and Totò along with such postwar arrivals as Sophia Loren, Vittorio Gassman, Alberto Sordi, and Marcello Mastroianni. Among the most successful films were *I Soliti ignoti* ("Suspicious Persons," aka *Big Deal on Madonna Street*, 1956) and *Divorce Italian Style* (1962). Carlo Ponti and Dino de Laurentiis led a new generation of producers who set their sights beyond the Italian border and turned the rebuilt Cinecittà studios into a film factory.

Other filmmakers moved toward more intimate psychological portrayal. The focus fell upon how social circumstances affected the personal relations among individuals. Michelangelo Antonioni, one of the major directors of the period, noted:

> It no longer seems to me important to make a film about a man who has had his bicycle stolen. . . . Now that we have eliminated the problem of the bicycle (I am speaking metaphorically), it is important to see what there is in the mind and in the heart of this man who has had his bicycle stolen, how he has adapted himself, what remains in him of his past experience, of the war, of the period after the war, of everything which has happened to him in our country.[7]

An interest in the effects of war and recovery marks the early 1950s work of both Rossellini and Antonioni. Each director reveals how individuals' lives are altered by a milieu of postwar confusion.

After Rossellini's "war trilogy" of *Open City, Paisan,* and *Germany Year Zero,* his filmmaking attempted to revivify humanism in what he perceived as a decaying society. "We live," he once asserted, "in a world that is scarcely human—in fear and anguish. Humankind drinks whiskey to arouse itself, then takes tranquilizers to calm down."[8] He saw himself as continuing the Neorealist project by bringing people to an awareness of the demands of spiritual truth, self-knowledge, and obligation to others. Rossellini's films became highly didactic, showing how the practical world mistakes sensitive individuals for simpletons, heretics, or lunatics. In *The Miracle,* he presents the story of a bewildered goatherd, who believes she is pregnant with a holy child. She is cast out by the villagers and must go into the mountains to bear the child alone. In *Francesco, giullare di Dio* ("Francesco, God's Juggler," aka *The Little Flowers of St. Francis*), Saint Francis of Assisi and his scampering, childlike disciples become models of gentleness and charity in a corrupt world.

In the films starring Ingrid Bergman, Rossellini presents a woman's gradual discovery of moral awareness. A selfish and calculating war refugee comes to quiet acceptance of her husband's love after a mystical experience on the edge of a volcano (*Stromboli*). A mother shattered by her son's suicide devotes her life to relieving the suffering of others; her charity can only seem mad, and she winds up imprisoned in an asylum (*Europa 51*). And an emotionally numb Englishwoman finds Italy frighteningly alive, even in its catacombs. Only after the accidental passing of a religious procession does she—perhaps—begin to love her husband once more (*Voyage to Italy*). (See Box.)

Rossellini concentrates on the extraordinary person who can rediscover time-honored values in the postwar world. By contrast, Antonioni's films focus on how ambition and class mobility make individuals lose their moral sensitivity. In *Story of a Love Affair,* for example, the heroine and hero accidentally caused the death of a friend years ago. Now she has become the wife of a wealthy industrialist, while he is an itinerant car salesman. Her husband's curiosity about her past leads him to hire a detective, and eventually his investigation reunites the lovers. As their passion takes hold once more, they begin to plot to murder the husband.

Narratively, many Italian art films of the early 1950s draw on such Neorealist conventions as ellipses and open endings. In particular, the focus on individuals' psychological states led Rossellini and Antonioni toward a dedramatized approach derived from Neorealism's concentration on mundane events. Now a film's plot might mix scenes of banal conversation with scenes showing the characters reacting to their environment or simply walking or driving through a landscape.

LUCHINO VISCONTI AND ROBERTO ROSSELLINI

The two major directors to emerge from Neorealism were almost exact contemporaries. Both grew up in wealthy households, took up film as an amateur pastime, and launched their professional filmmaking under the auspices of Mussolini's fascism. Both men led unorthodox personal lives, Visconti acknowledging his homosexuality and Rossellini getting involved with a number of women (most notably Ingrid Bergman, who bore him a daughter, Isabella, outside marriage).

The aristocrat Visconti became interested in film through assisting Jean Renoir in filming *A Day in the Country* (1936). Visconti took up left-wing causes, and during the war he was drawn into partisan work. His first film, *Ossessione*, played a key part in the realist revival during the last years of Fascist cinema. "The term 'neo-realism,' " he declared, "was born with *Ossessione*."[9] *La Terra trema* started out as a vehicle for the Communist party, but Visconti financed it from his personal fortune.

Visconti was a major theater director, and his films flaunted sumptuous costumes and settings, florid acting, and overpowering music. *Senso* opens at a performance of *Il Trovatore* and uses Verdi's music throughout. *The Damned* (1969) was originally to be called *Götterdammerung*, in order to compare the moral decay of Germany under Naziism with Wagner's opera *Twilight of the Gods*. Throughout, the use of color exaggerates the slide from tradition to decadence (Color Plate 16.1). Visconti's film version of Mann's *Death in Venice* (1971) models its hero on Mahler, and *Ludwig* (1973) makes Wagner a protagonist. Visconti aimed for intense emotion: "I love melodrama because it is situated right on the border between life and the theater."[10]

La Terra trema, Senso, Rocco and His Brothers (1960), *The Leopard* (1963), *The Damned, Ludwig,* and *Conversation Piece* (1974) all trace the decline of a family in a period of drastic historical upheaval. Visconti evokes the lifestyles of the rich, but he also usually reveals the class conflict that those lifestyles conceal. Foreign powers conspire with the ruling class to oppress the populace (*Senso*); the aristocrats must give way to democracy (*The Leopard*); a bourgeoisie collapses through its own corruption (*The Damned*).

More and more Visconti relied upon a languid, pan-and-zoom shooting style, as if history were a vast stage production and the director were guiding the spectator's opera glasses slowly over its details. As the Essenbach family in *The Damned* listen to a Bach sonata, the camera drifts slowly from one face

Fig. 16.25 Von Essenbach, with his discreet Nazi badge, lost in contemplation of classical music (*The Damned*).

to another, studying the bourgeois self-absorption which the Nazis will exploit (Fig. 16.25). In *Death in Venice*, the camera scans for the boy Tadzio among the pillars, ferns, and silver tea trays of the luxurious hotel.

Rossellini, by contrast, was resolutely antispectacle. "If I mistakenly make a beautiful shot," he once remarked, "I cut it out."[11] His direct approach matched his straightforward faith in rudimentary values. *Open City* turns the partisans into Christ-like martyrs, and *The Little Flowers of St. Francis* shows the childlike joy of Christian charity. At the film's end, Francesco instructs his followers to whirl around until they fall to the ground (Fig. 16.26). Rossellini sometimes advocates a more secular humanism that praises fantasy and imagination (*The Machine to Kill Bad People*), devotion to good works (*Europa 51*), and acceptance of imperfect love (*Voyage to Italy*). Later he celebrates the great artists, inventors, and philosophers of the western world (*Socrates*, 1970; *Blaise Pascal*, 1972; *The Age of the Medici*, 1972; *Descartes*, 1974).

However forthright Rossellini's message may have been, his manner of treatment repeatedly led him into modernist ambiguities. His penchant for mixed tone, episodic narratives, ellipses, and open endings often makes the films more evocative than their straightforward themes might suggest. By comparison with Visconti's elegance, Rossellini's style seems

Fig. 16.26 Once they fall to the ground, Francesco's spinning followers are to spread the gospel in whatever directions their heads point.

awkward. But often his simplest effects, in context, yield complex results, as in his use of *temps morts*, "dead time." Rossellini punctuates his stories with empty intervals of characters simply sitting or walking or thinking. The spectator must infer the characters' attitudes. In *Voyage to Italy*, Katherine pretends to be asleep when her husband returns from Capri, and Rossellini suggests a welter of emotions merely by intercutting shots of each partner.

Like Visconti, Rossellini also came to rely on a pan-and-zoom style after the early 1960s. But Visconti's scanning frame unrolls an endless spectacle, while Rossellini uses the pan-and-zoom for its simplicity and cheapness and for its ability to present the action neutrally, freeing us from any character's consciousness (Color Plate 16.2).

In the last fifteen years of his life, Rossellini launched a series of television films that would introduce the great figures and forces in history. This vast enterprise brought forth *La Prise du pouvoir par Louis XIV* (*The Rise to Power of Louis XIV*, 1966), the Pascal and Medici films, *The Messiah* (1975), and other works. As costume dramas, these films are remarkably unspectacular. Full of talk, dominated by static long takes, they dwell on daily life in each era. Whereas Visconti imagines history as a vast opera, Rossellini dedramatizes it.

Visconti became a model for other Italian directors of an operatic turn, such as Franco Zeffirelli, Francesco Rosi, and Liliana Cavani. Rossellini's version of cinematic modernism, in the name of realism, humanism, and education, centrally influenced the new generation of the 1960s. "Here is our cinema," wrote Jacques Rivette, "those of us who are in our turn preparing to make films (did I tell you, it may be soon)."[12]

Fig. 16.27 The celebrated museum scene of *Voyage to Italy:* Katherine comes face to face with the ardent physicality of ancient statuary.

The canonical example of the dedramatized tale is Rossellini's *Voyage to Italy*, in which the bickerings between Katherine and her husband alternate with scenes of her excursions to tourist sights around their villa. The excursion episodes suggest her romantic yearnings, her uncertainty about the role of physical pleasure, and her wish for a child (Fig. 16.27), and she gradually recognizes the sterility of her marriage. *Voyage to Italy* pointed toward a filmmaking that would build scenes not around an intricate plot but around episodes in which casual, "undramatic" incidents would reveal characters' passing moods and barely articulated problems.

The museum scene in *Voyage to Italy* is notable for its lengthy camera movements, and in this respect it is characteristic of a stylistic development in Italian films of the early 1950s. More and more, directors used slowly paced tracking shots to explore characters' relations within a concrete environment. Antonioni's early 1950s films pushed this tendency to an extreme by relying upon very lengthy takes. A scene might consist of only two or three shots, each one running abnormally long. (The average shot in *Story of a Love Affair* lasts thirty-four seconds; in *The Lady without the Camellias*, it lasts almost a minute.) A scene might even be handled in a single shot, as in *Story of a Love Affair*'s *plan-séquence* ("sequence shot"). (See Box.)

THE BRIDGE SCENE FROM *STORY OF A LOVE AFFAIR*

The two lovers, Paola and Guido, meet to rehearse their murder of her husband. But Paola, who initiated the plot, is now fearful, and Guido, intent on carrying out the crime, must force her to go along. Antonioni stages the action so that once Guido confronts her with the plan, she moves evasively away from him. (The stages of the shot are depicted in the accompanying photos.)

In the course of the scene, the camera situates itself within the center of the couple's circular movement. It establishes a simple but powerful pattern of panning and tracking. At first, it follows Paola (Figs. 16.29–16.33); then it stays on Guido after she has left (Figs. 16.34–16.35). When she pulls away, the camera again lingers on him (Figs. 16.36–16.37). Then the camera pans with her as she backs away shouting about Giovanna's murder; concentrating on her makes his sudden entrance into the frame more violent (Figs. 16.38–16.40). The shot ends as it began, looking down the sidewalk along the bridge. (Compare Figs. 16.30 and 16.42.) In all, Antonioni compresses a great deal of tension and surprise into a single shot in a relatively simple locale.

Fig. 16.29 . . . but then pans right to reveal Paola in the foreground. The car is merely tracing out the route that her husband's car will follow on the night of the murder.

Fig. 16.28 *Story of a Love Affair:* Antonioni disorients us from the start with a long shot that seems to make the distant car significant . . .

Fig. 16.30 Guido comes to join her.

Fig. 16.31 He tells her that their scheme can't fail.

Fig. 16.32 Nervous, Paola turns away to avoid him . . .

Fig. 16.33 . . . and walks to the other side of the bridge.

Fig. 16.34 He follows her and turns away as she looks vacantly out at the murder route.

Fig. 16.35 She leaves him and walks out frame right.

Fig. 16.36 He joins her again . . .

Fig. 16.37 . . . only to have her once more abruptly leave the frame.

Fig. 16.40 Furiously Guido bursts into the frame and slaps her face.

Fig. 16.38 More quickly now, Guido follows her again and confronts her. He reminds her that he killed for her once before, and she helped him.

Fig. 16.41 He turns and walks back along the bridge in the direction he had come.

Fig. 16.39 She backs away. "You killed her!"

Fig. 16.42 Paola reluctantly follows. The shot fades out.

Fig. 16.43 *La Strada:* As Gelsomina sits by the roadside, a carnival band strolls out of nowhere.

After the early 1950s, much of Italian "quality" cinema would center on individual problems. Instead of documenting a historical moment by depicting group struggles, filmmakers probed middle-class and upper-class characters for the psychological effects of contemporary life.

Alternatively, the filmmaker might treat the middle and lower classes in a more poetic way, as Federico Fellini did in a series of films beginning with *Variety Lights* (1950, co-directed with Lattuada). In Fellini's works of the 1950s, Neorealistic subject matter is given a lyrical, almost mystical treatment. In *La Strada* ("The Road," 1954), for instance, Fellini's tale of victimized innocence has the simplicity of a parable. The itinerant entertainers Zampano and Gelsomina live in the grim countryside, but occasionally this realm overlaps with a more mysterious one (Fig. 16.43). Marxist critics attacked Fellini for deviating from Neorealism, but he claimed that he remained true to its spirit of "sincerity."[13] In any event, Fellini's work, no less than that of Rossellini and Antonioni, turned Italian filmmaking from the verisimilitude of Neorealism toward a cinema of imagination and ambiguity.

A SPANISH NEOREALISM?

Spain offers an illuminating case study in the powerful influence of Italian Neorealism. At first glance, no country could have seemed more inhospitable to the Neorealist impulse. Once Franco's forces won the civil war in 1939, he established a Fascist dictatorship. After World War II Spain gradually reentered the world community, but it remained an authoritarian country until the mid-1970s.

The film industry was controlled by a government ministry that censored scripts before filming, required dubbing of all films into the "official" Castilian dialect, and created a state monopoly on newsreels and documentaries. The regime demanded pious, chauvinistic films. The result was a procession of Civil War dramas (*cine cruzada*), historical epics, religious films, and literary adaptations (including a *Don Quixote de la Mancha*, 1947, that compared the idealistic hero with Franco). At a less prestigious level, the industry turned out popular musicals, comedies, and bullfight films. The domestic industry also furnished locales for coproductions and runaway projects.

In the early 1950s, however, countercurrents became visible. CIFESA, the biggest production company of the 1940s, overinvested in high-budget productions and collapsed. As a reaction to the superproduction approach, several low-budget films, most notably *Furrows* (1951), began to treat social problems, and some used location filming and nonprofessional actors in the Neorealist manner. At the film school IIEC (founded in 1947), students were able to see foreign films that were banned from public exhibition. In 1951 during an Italian film week, IIEC students viewed *The Bicycle Thief, Miracle in Milan, Open City, Paisan,* and *Story of a Love Affair.* Soon afterward, several IIEC graduates founded a journal, *Objetivo,* which discussed Neorealist ideas.

The immediate impact of Neorealism is most evident in the work of the two best-known Spanish directors to emerge in the 1950s, Luis Garcia Berlanga and Juan Antonio Bardem. "B & B," as they came to be known, had been in the first graduating class of IIEC, and in the early 1950s they collaborated on several projects. *Welcome, Mr. Marshall* (1951), scripted by Bardem and directed by Berlanga, is a comic fable reminiscent of De Sica's *Miracle in Milan*. A small town transforms itself into a picturesque stereotype in order to benefit from the Marshall Plan (Fig. 16.44).

Fig. 16.44 The schoolteacher holds classes on how to dress and act like the clichéd Spaniard in *Welcome, Mr. Marshall.*

Enormously popular in Spain, *Welcome, Mr. Marshall* satirized America's expanding power, took jabs at Hollywood movies and Spanish folk genres, and made a quiet appeal for popular unity. It set the tone for later Berlanga films such as *Calabuch* (1956), which mocked the arms race, and it promulgated what came to be called *la estética franquista* ("the Franco aesthetic"), a sardonic or an ironic treatment of apparently safe subjects.

Welcome, Mr. Marshall was selected as Spain's official entry to the Cannes festival, and despite controversy about its "anti-American" outlook, it won a special mention. The film also launched Bardem's career. Soon his stature was reaffirmed internationally with *Death of a Cyclist* (1955), which won the best-film prize at Cannes, and *Calle Mayor* (*Main Street*, 1956), which won the Critics' Prize at Venice.

Berlanga blended Neorealist impulses toward regional realism with a penchant for sardonic comedy. Bardem, by contrast, favored a more somber scrutiny of psychological states that owed a good deal to 1950s Italian developments. *Calle Mayor*, a fierce indictment of small-town narrowness and masculine egotism, recalls *I Vitelloni*, but without Fellini's indulgent humor (Fig. 16.45). Similarly, *Death of a Cyclist* derives to some extent from *Story of a Love Affair*; it even stars Lucia Bose, the heroine of Antonioni's film. Bardem's plot shows how an affair between a rich man's wife and a university professor is shattered when their car kills a passing bicyclist. In trying to conceal their crime, the couple break up. The film ends with the wife, perhaps deliberately, running over her lover on the site of the accident. Bardem's

Fig. 16.45 Young wastrels in a small town (*Calle Mayor*).

Fig. 16.46 Antonioniesque alienation and anomie in *Death of a Cyclist*.

editing creates narrational commentary on the affair, and the deep-focus landscape shots isolate his protagonists in compositions that recall Antonioni (Fig. 16.46).

As the work of Berlanga, Bardem, and others gained international attention, an alternative Spanish film culture began fitfully to surface. The growth of ciné-clubs in various universities led to a conference at Salamanca in 1955. This event assembled filmmakers, critics, and scholars to discuss the future of the nation's cinema. Bardem denounced Spanish film as "politically, useless; socially, false; intellectually, inferior; aesthetically, nonexistent; and industrially, sick."[14] After Bardem's denunciation, he was arrested while filming *Calle Mayor* and was released only after international protests.

The Salamanca talks did not sway the industry but did encourage filmmakers to test the limits of government policy. Such resistance was helped by the production company UNINCI, founded in 1951 and responsible for *Welcome, Mr. Marshall*. In 1957, Bardem joined UNINCI's board of directors and soon persuaded Luis Buñuel to return to Spain to make a film. The government welcomed Buñuel's return, and his script was accepted with only one change (which Buñuel claimed was an improvement). *Viridiana* (1961) won the highest award at the Cannes festival, but when Church officials declared it blasphemous, the government banned the most famous Spanish postwar film. UNINCI dissolved. The rebellion of young filmmakers and critics had gone too far, and the experiment in Spanish Neorealism was over.

◆ NOTES AND QUERIES

CONTROVERSIES AROUND NEOREALISM

As with most film movements, historians differ about how unified and uniform Italian Neorealism was. At a 1953 conference on Neorealism, Zavattini, Visconti, and other participants could not agree on what characterized the movement. A 1974 conference of scholars saw even less coherence; many believed that Neorealism was a loose ethic, not an aesthetic or a political position. A good survey of the range of opinions can be found in Chapter 4 of Mira Liehm's *Passion and Defiance: Film in Italy from 1942 to the Present* (Berkeley: University of California Press, 1984).

Historically, Neorealism can be studied from several perspectives. For one thing, the film movement had parallels with a postwar "neorealist" literature, as exemplified in the novels of Elio Vittorini, Pratolini, and Cesare Pavese. These writers' works are discussed in Sergio Pacifici, *A Guide to Contemporary Italian Literature: From Futurism to Neorealism* (Cleveland: Meridian, 1962).

There is also the tricky question of the ties of Neorealism to the political left. In the immediate postwar period, an aesthetic of realism arose within the Communist party. Its proponents sought to create a "national-popular" strategy that would show a progressive, critical realism to be part of Italian cultural history. See David Forgacs, "The Making and Unmaking of Neorealism in Postwar Italy," in Nicholas Hewitt, ed., *The Culture of Reconstruc-*

tion: European Literature, Thought and Film 1945–1950 (New York: St. Martins, 1989), pp. 51–66. Communist critics at first favored the Neorealist films, and the directors, while not Marxists, often had leftist sympathies. Very soon, however, relations cooled. As early as 1948, *Bitter Rice* was attacked for its sex and its lack of "typical" characters. In 1950–1954, when many directors shifted toward psychological analysis, Marxist attacks intensified.

Since the mid-1950s, the debate about the political underpinnings of Neorealism has continued, and not only in Italy. For a sample, see Liehm, *Passion and Defiance* (cited above), as well as Pierre Sorlin, "Tradition and Social Change in the French and Italian Cinemas of the Reconstruction," in Hewitt, ed., *The Culture of Reconstruction* (cited above), pp. 88–102.

◆ REFERENCES

1. Quoted in Millicent Marcus, *Italian Film in the Light of Neorealism* (Princeton, N.J.: Princeton University Press, 1986), p. 16.
2. Quoted in Mira Liehm, *Passion and Defiance: Film in Italy from 1942 to the Present* (Berkeley: University of California Press, 1984), p. 91.
3. Quoted in Marcus, *Italian Film in the Light of Neorealism*, p. 26.
4. Ibid., p. 70.
5. André Bazin, *What Is Cinema?* vol. 2, ed. and trans. Hugh Gray (Berkeley: University of California Press, 1971), pp. 54–55.
6. Ibid., pp. 81–82.
7. Quoted in Pierre Leprohon, *Michelangelo Antonioni: An Introduction* (New York: Simon and Schuster, 1963), pp. 89–90.
8. Quoted in Mario Verdone, *Roberto Rossellini* (Paris: Éditions Seghers, 1963), p. 89.
9. Quoted in Gaia Servadio, *Luchino Visconti: A Biography* (New York: Franklin Watts, 1983), p. 78.
10. Quoted in Marcus, *Italian Film in the Light of Neorealism*, p. 183.
11. Quoted in Peter Brunette, *Roberto Rossellini* (New York: Oxford University Press, 1987), p. 14.
12. Jacques Rivette, "Letter on Rossellini," in Jim Hillier, ed., **Cahiers du Cinéma: The 1950s: Neo-Realism, Hollywood, New Wave** (Cambridge, Mass.: Harvard University Press, 1985), p. 203.
13. Federico Fellini, "My Experiences as a Director," in Peter Bondanella, ed., *Federico Fellini: Essays in Criticism* (New York: Oxford University Press, 1978), p. 4.
14. Quoted in Virginia Higginbotham, *Spanish Film under Franco* (Austin: University of Texas Press, 1988), p. 28.

17

POSTWAR EUROPEAN CINEMA: FRANCE, SCANDINAVIA, AND BRITAIN

Italian Neorealism provided an influential model of social realism and psychological ambiguity, but it was not the only trend in Europe during the postwar era. France achieved recognition for its prestigious "Tradition of Quality," the return of several important prewar directors, and the emergence of modernist experimenters. Scandinavian filmmaking attracted attention with offshoots of theatrical tradition that shaped emerging art-cinema conventions. British filmmaking, on the whole less inclined to experiment, found a new fame in English-speaking countries. Coproductions, export, and festivals helped films find international audiences.

FRENCH CINEMA OF THE POSTWAR DECADE

THE INDUSTRY RECOVERS

Before the Nazi Occupation, France's production sector consisted of many small firms, often created solely for the purpose of making one film. Pathé and Gaumont, the major vertically integrated companies, produced few films themselves. They rented studio facilities to other firms and served as distributors and exhibitors.

After the Liberation in 1944, free-for-all competition reemerged. Pathé and Gaumont, while occasionally producing big-budget films, could not supply the market. Filmmakers were forced back to the "artisanal" system of finding smaller production companies or individual producers. In 1947, there were over 200 registered firms, but nearly all had little capital, and banks were reluctant to finance projects.

The problems were intensified by governmental indifference. In May 1946, Prime Minister Léon Blum and U.S. Secretary of State James Byrnes signed an agreement which eliminated prewar quotas on American films. The pact guaranteed that exhibitors would reserve only sixteen weeks per year for French films; the rest of the year would be given over to "free competition." Although the Blum-Byrnes accord was defended as a way to encourage production, film workers protested that it actually made France an open market for American films. Immediate results bore out the charge: a year after the accord, the number of imported American films increased tenfold, and French output dropped from ninety-one features to seventy-eight. With double bills outlawed and with Hollywood companies making deep inroads in countries which had previously relied upon French films, there were fewer outlets for the domestic product.

Two governmental measures responded to the outrage in the industry. In late 1946, the French government established the Centre National de la Cinématographie (CNC, "National Cinema Center"). This agency began to regulate the industry by establishing standards for financial solvency, providing subsidies for filmmaking, and encouraging documentary and artistic efforts. In effect CNC was a revision of the centralized organization of production under the Vichy regime. By 1949, the agency was regularly subsidizing production, and in the same year, it founded Unifrance Film, a publicity agency aiming to promote French film abroad and coordinate the nation's festival entries. The CNC was part of a broader effort toward centralized economic planning, which included nationalization of banks, utilities, and transportation industries.

The government took a second step by enacting protectionist legislation. A 1948 law set a new import quota of 121 American films per year, a figure that remained roughly constant over the next decade. The same law provided for major bank loans to stable companies. The legislation also created an admission tax earmarked for financing future productions. If a film proved successful, ticket surcharges would build up a large fund that would assist the producer in financing his next project. This policy encouraged firms to aim at making popular films with presold stars and stories. A 1953 revision in the law created a development fund for new projects and included a provision for the encouragement of short films.

Government assistance helped feature output rise to about 120 films per year. While the industry never regained the international power it had enjoyed early in the century, it was fairly healthy. Television had not yet penetrated France, and moviegoing remained popular. Although the three major companies—Pathé, Gaumont, and Union Générale Cinématographique—owned or had contractual arrangements with the best first-run theaters, their production output dwindled; Pathé gave up film production altogether and made an arrangement for Gaumont to supply its theaters. The larger production houses—Discina, Cinédis, Cocinor, and Paris Film Pro-

POSTWAR FRENCH FILM CULTURE

Since World War I, French intellectuals took a keen interest in cinema. (See Chapter 5.) After 1945, their enthusiasm, constrained by the war, burst out anew. The German occupation had denied them American movies for five years, but now in a single month they might see *Citizen Kane, Double Indemnity, The Little Foxes,* and *The Maltese Falcon.* The Cinémathèque Française, which had gone underground during the war, began regularly showing older films from around the world. As students gathered in Parisian cafés and lecture halls to argue about Marxism, Existentialism, and phenomenology, so too did they flock to movie theaters and spend hours talking and writing about films.

The atmosphere of *cinéphilie* ("love of cinema") must have been heady. The ciné-club movement was revived, and by 1954 there were 200 clubs with approximately 100,000 members. The Catholic Church's lay group on public education formed an agency that arranged screenings for millions of viewers. University courses began to teach cinema, and an academic discipline called "Filmology" was elaborated. Several film journals were launched, most notably *L'Écran français* (published secretly during the Occupation, openly beginning in 1945), *La Revue du cinéma* (founded 1946), *Cahiers du cinéma* (1951), and *Positif* (1952). Soon after the war's end, publishers had brought out film histories by Georges Sadoul and theoretical works by André Bazin (Fig. 17.1), Jean Epstein, André Malraux, and Claude-Edmonde Magny.

Certain issues came to the fore. One, central to all thinking about film since the early years, was the question of cinema as an art. Some critics argued that film was analogous to theater; others suggested that it had more in common with the novel. At the same time, many critics proposed fresh ways to think about film style and technique; Bazin, for instance, responded to the revelation of wartime Hollywood films by closely examining the aesthetic potential of deep focus and

Fig. 17.1 André Bazin, the preeminent French film theorist.

long takes. Such discussions led to more abstract speculation too. Film theory, as an inquiry into the nature and functions of cinema, was revived in this philosophical milieu. (See Notes and Queries.)

Postwar French film culture has long served as the paradigm case of intellectual ferment around cinema. The ideas explored by several brilliant thinkers have permanently shaped the direction of film studies and filmmaking. Out of the debates in ciné-clubs, the screenings of esoteric classics and recent Hollywood products, and the articles in *Cahiers du cinéma* and *Positif,* the New Wave of the 1950s would be born.

duction—were able to fill exhibitors' demands, in the process becoming strong distributors. The national film school, Institut des Hautes Etudes Cinématographiques (IDHEC), founded in 1943, trained technicians for industry positions. Coproductions, especially with Italian companies, flourished under the coordination of the CNC.

Throughout the 1950s, as today, international audiences enjoyed French police thrillers, comedies, costume dramas, and star vehicles. The major stars—Gérard Philipe, Jean Gabin, Yves Montand, Fernandel, Simone Signoret, Martine Carol, and Michèle Morgan—were known around the world. And France, along with Italy, would become a vanguard for the emerging "modernist" currents of the 1950s and 1960s. The audience's interest in cinema as a part of artistic culture (see Box), along with the relatively artisanal condition of smaller production companies, enabled some writers and directors to experiment with film form and style.

THE TRADITION OF QUALITY

The first decade of the postwar French cinema was dominated by what a 1953 critic dubbed the "Tradition of Quality." Originally the term was quite broad, but it was soon identified with particular directors and screenwriters.

The Tradition of Quality aimed to be a "prestige" cinema. It relied heavily upon adaptations of literary classics. Often the scriptwriter was considered the creative equal or even the superior of the director. Performers were drawn from the ranks of top-flight stars or from leading theaters. The films were often steeped in romanticism, particularly of the sort made famous by Poetic Realism before the war (p. 328). Again and again in these films lovers find themselves in an unfeeling or threatening social environment; most often, their affair ends tragically. The woman is persistently idealized, treated as mysterious and unattainable (Figs. 17.2, 17.3). Stylistically, much of the Tradition of Quality resembles the A-picture romantic dramas of Hollywood and British cinema, such as *Arch of Triumph* (1948) and *Brief Encounter* (1945). All the resources of studio filmmaking—lavish sets, special effects, elaborate lighting, extravagant costumes—are used to amplify these refined tales of passion and melancholy (Fig. 17.4).

In certain ways the Cinema of Quality prolonged traditions developed under the Occupation. The French had perfected a literary, studio-bound romanticism that culminated in the Marcel Carné-Jacques Prévert collaboration *Children of Paradise* (p. 342). It is no surprise that among the most famous films in the canon of Quality is the first postwar Carné-Prévert project *Les Portes de la nuit* ("Gates of the Night," 1946). In this allegory of postwar life, a young couple flee the black-marketeer who has kept the woman as his mistress. In the course of the night they encounter the figure of Destiny, a tramp who continually warns them of their fate. A hugely expensive film, featuring colossal street sets (Fig. 17.5) and a fabricated waterfront, *Les Portes*

Fig. 17.2 Many films in the Tradition of Quality dwell on the moment when the male protagonist is captivated by a woman's distant image (*Symphonie pastorale*).

Fig. 17.3 *Le Diable au corps:* At night a woman waits for her lover at dockside, and the camera glides toward her while waves of reflections play across her body.

Fig. 17.4 Lovers pause to study the graffiti on a statue while strolling through a murky yard littered with tomb carvings (*Les Portes de la nuit*).

Fig. 17.5 A studio set for *Les Portes de la nuit;* like *Children of Paradise,* the film was designed by Alexander Trauner.

Fig. 17.6 Morbid rituals in *Forbidden Games*.

de la nuit was a financial failure. Carné and Prévert did not collaborate on any projects again, but the director persisted in his efforts to create a symbolic cinema, notably in *Juliette ou la clef des songes* ("Juliette, or the Key of Dreams," 1951).

More successful was the scriptwriting team of Jean Aurenche and Pierre Bost. After working under the Occupation, they rose quickly in the postwar period, turning out adaptations of classics by Feydeau, Colette, Stendhal, and Zola. Aurenche and Bost became the prototypical scenarists of the Tradition of Quality. Their *Symphonie pastorale* ("Pastoral Symphony," 1946), an adaptation of André Gide's novel, plays up the fateful attraction of a father and son for the same blind girl. In *Le Diable au corps* ("Devil in the Flesh," 1947), Aurenche and Bost use flashbacks to tell another story of lost adolescent love. While crowds joyously celebrate the end of World War I, the teenager François recalls his affair with Marthe, a soldier's fiancée. Just as the soldier returns from the war, Marthe dies giving birth to François' child. *Le Diable au corps* solidified the reputation of its star, Gérard Philipe, and gave director Claude Autant-Lara his first postwar success. Aurenche and Bost were to collaborate frequently with Autant-Lara.

Most English-language audiences encountered Aurenche and Bost through *Jeux interdits* (*Forbidden Games*, 1952), directed by René Clément. Here children form the romantic couple. An orphaned refugee girl is taken in by a farm family. She and the family's youngest son begin to collect dead animals in order to bury them in elaborate graves (Fig. 17.6). The film has a touch of Buñuel in the way that the children's morbid rituals unwittingly satirize the Church's own death obsession. On the whole, however, Aurenche and Bost lyricize their subject, contrasting broadly comic rivalries among peasant families with the children's devotion to each other and to the beauty of death.

The Tradition of Quality encompassed other scriptwriter-director teams. One of the most notable was that of Charles Spaak, who had written many of the most famous films of the 1930s, and André Cayatte, a lawyer who began making social-problem films in the 1950s. Like other products of the Quality tradition, the Cayatte-Spaak films, such as *Justice est faite* ("Justice Is Done," 1950) and *Nous sommes tous des assassins* ("We Are All Killers," 1952), are polished studio-bound projects; but in harshly criticizing the French judicial system, they avoid the usual romanticism and take a didactic, even preachy, attitude.

Most of the Tradition of Quality directors were young men who had launched their careers after the coming of sound, usually during the Occupation. Somewhat detached from this group was their contemporary Henri-Georges Clouzot, who had achieved notoriety with *Le Corbeau* ("The Raven," 1943; p. 342). Clouzot became internationally famous by specializing in mordant suspense films like *Quai des orfèvres* (1957), *The Wages of Fear* (1953), and *Les Diaboliques* (*Diabolique*, 1955). Clouzot, like the director-writer teams, continued the tradition of tightly scripted, fatalistic romances and thrillers associated with the French cinema of the 1930s and 1940s.

THE RETURN OF OLDER DIRECTORS

While young directors were achieving prominence, much older men like Marcel L'Herbier, Abel Gance, and Jean Epstein continued to work. With the possible exception of Epstein's *Le Tempestaire* ("Master of the Winds," 1947), no films by these directors had much influence on the course of French cinema. More significant was a middle generation of directors who had begun their careers in the late 1920s and early 1930s. Julien Duvivier, René Clair, Max Ophüls, Jean Renoir, and others had fled to Hollywood. After the war ended, they returned to their homeland.

Repatriation failed to revive Duvivier's career, but other exiled directors reestablished their reputations. They came to embody a postwar alternative to the Tradition of Quality—that of the veteran director not beholden to screenwriters but to a trusted cadre of assistants and technicians who could enable him to express his own personality.

Clair, for example, returned from a mildly successful stay in England and Hollywood to direct seven features. For nearly all of these, he relied on Léon Barsacq for set design (much as he had frequently turned to Lazare Meerson in the 1930s). Upon his return, Clair established continuity with his native tradition with *Le Silence est d'or* ("Silence Is Golden," 1947). Maurice Chevalier plays a turn-of-the-century film producer-director who oversees a love affair (Fig. 17.7). Later films continued Clair's work in light comedy, but several were dramas in keeping with prevailing Cinema of Quality tastes. Throughout, Clair retained some of the playful exuberance of his early works, often paying homage to silent cinema (Fig. 17.8).

Max Ophüls directed four films in Hollywood before returning to Paris, where he had worked a decade earlier. He renewed his career with four films: *La Ronde* (1950), *Le Plaisir* (1952), *Madame de . . .* (*The Earrings of Madame de . . .*, 1953), and *Lola Montès* (1955). For each film Ophüls called upon virtually the same collaborators: scriptwriter Jacques Natanson, cinematographer Christian Matras, costume designer Georges Annenkov, and set designer Jean d'Eaubonne. All four films were literary adaptations set in picturesque locales and periods; they were full of international stars, gorgeous sets, ingratiating music, and extravagant costumes.

Yet these were not ordinary prestige pictures. *La Ronde* aroused controversy for its casual treatment of promiscuity, and *Lola Montès* provoked such a storm of attacks that several prominent directors signed a public letter defending it. Refusing to moralize or preach, Ophüls detachedly observes courting rituals at all levels of society. Sexual conquest usually brings no lasting pleasure, especially for the predatory and foolish males who fill Ophüls's films. Instead, Ophüls emphasizes the subterfuges through which women satisfy their desires. The romantic tales of deceived love that he presented in his American films give way to a more explicit treatment of feminine sexual identity. In *Lola Montès*, the title character is a courtesan who rises through society and ends up as a performer in a circus, an object of fantasy but lifeless, withdrawn, and wholly artificial.

Fig. 17.7 Chevalier directs in *Silence est d'or*, Clair's tribute to silent film.

Fig. 17.8 A ballroom scene in *Les Grands manoeuvres* (1955), with a dancing couple seen in a white iris created by the view through a rolled-up newspaper.

Fig. 17.9 The *meneur de jeu* in *La Ronde*.

The films center on casual liaisons, extramarital affairs, and seduced innocence—all topics betraying Ophüls's roots in theater and operetta of the 1920s. Yet he makes stock situations more complex by means of episodic plot construction, presenting the film as a set of sketches (three in *Le Plaisir*), offering sharply separated flashbacks (*Lola Montès*), recycling characters across distinct episodes (as in *La Ronde*), or following an object passed among characters (the earrings in *Madame de . . .*). This construction echoes the rhythm of arousal, brief fulfillment, and long-term dissatisfaction that is central to the theme of unconsummated love. Each little story restarts the whirligig of desire.

Ophüls distances us from his characters by several means—through irony, through a sense of a predetermined plot pattern that the characters do not realize, and especially through a narrator who addresses us directly. In *Lola Montès*, the ringmaster becomes a master of ceremonies who leads the circus audience, and us, into episodes from Lola's past. In *La Ronde*, the narrator strolls through what seems to be a street, mounts a theater stage to address us, and then is revealed to be in a film studio, turning the carousel that is the film's symbol of the endless dance of love (Fig. 17.9). Ophüls's narrators conjure up the fictional world we will see, setting the plots in motion for our pleasure. This reflexivity made Ophüls's works seem highly modernist to many young French critics.

A comparable self-consciousness pervades the films' style. In a period when other directors were following the Neorealist impulse to move toward a simpler approach to staging and shooting, Ophüls required all the artifice of the French studio cinema to create his rococo world of restaurants, parlors, ballrooms, artists' lofts, and cobblestone streets. The lines of his compositions are sweeping arabesques which recall the frilly curves of the writing in the credit sequences. His camera sweeps as well, following characters as they stroll, dance, flirt, or race to their destinies. Even more than his Hollywood films, his French efforts return to the tradition of the *enfesselte camera*, the "unfastened camera," of the German studio cinema of his youth (p. 306).

These tendencies of Ophüls's work are evident in a single shot from *La Ronde* (Figs. 17.10–17.14). At one level, the play of hiding and revealing the action repeats the rhythm of frustration and satisfaction of desire in the narrative's episodes; but the sheer zest in the graceful dance of the camera with the characters is itself a source of the audience's—and director's—pleasure. James Mason wrote in a poem about Ophüls: "A shot that does not call for tracks / is agony for poor dear Max. . . . / Once, when they took away his crane / I thought he'd never smile again."[1]

Jean Renoir was the last of the exiled prewar directors to return to French filming. (He continued to live in Beverly Hills for decades after the war, occasionally teaching at Los Angeles universities.) After one postwar film for RKO, he undertook two international projects, *The River* (1951) and *The Golden Coach* (1953), before directing *French Cancan* (1955) in Paris. It became his first popular success of the postwar era and was followed by the less well-received *Eléna et les hommes* (1956), *The Testament of Dr. Cordelier* (1959), *Picnic on the Grass* (1959), and *The Elusive Corporal* (1962). His last film, made for French and Italian television, was *The Little Theatre of Jean Renoir* (1970). When not filming, Renoir (like Visconti and Ingmar Bergman) was active in the theater, writing and directing plays.

Fig. 17.10

Fig. 17.11

Fig. 17.12

Fig. 17.13

Fig. 17.14

Fig. 17.10 *La Ronde:* When the guilty wife comes to call on the young poet, he rushes to greet her.

Fig. 17.11 In a reflexive gesture that announces the sheer artificiality of the set, the camera passes through the wall to show her entering.

Fig. 17.12 As the couple move toward the parlor, Ophüls "loses" and then "finds" them through a play of props that momentarily block our view.

Fig. 17.13 She sits on the divan, and the camera is drawn a bit closer each time the poet tremblingly lifts a layer of veiling from her face.

Fig. 17.14 As he removes the hat, her face is finally revealed to us.

Right after the war, Renoir's reputation was in eclipse. French ciné-clubs began a Renoir revival in the late 1940s, and the January 1952 *Cahiers du cinéma* used the release of *The River* to reevaluate his work. In that issue, André Bazin published a major essay on the director, "The French Renoir," which argued that he had made unique contributions to the nation's cinema. The 1950s saw a steady rise in Renoir's critical stock. A critics' forum at the 1958 Brussels World's Fair voted *Grand Illusion* one of the twelve best films of all time, and in 1965, the reconstructed version of *Rules of the Game* was released to international acclaim. Ever since, *Rules* has been routinely cited as the greatest film of all time, and many critics have declared Renoir cinema's supreme artist.

Yet few critics would have rested that evaluation on Renoir's postwar work. While many directors exploited the sort of deep-space staging and complex camera movements that Renoir had favored in the 1930s, he largely abandoned such techniques and developed a simple, direct style centered on the performer. Stressing lengthy rehearsals and slow nurturing of roles, Renoir began staging action in a flatter and more frontal way, especially in *The Golden Coach*, which pays homage to Italian classical theater (Color Plate 17.1). With *The Testament of Dr. Cordelier*, he explored the television technique of shooting with multiple cameras, so as to preserve the continuity of the actor's performance. Although Renoir did not exploit the long take as Rossellini did in his historical films, *Picnic on the Grass* made extensive use of zooms and telephoto framings, giving the actors considerable freedom of movement while the cameraman panned to follow them. Renoir's later career concludes with a shot in which the entire cast of the film bows to the camera (Fig. 17.15).

Fig. 17.15 The last shot of Renoir's last film, *The Little Theatre of Jean Renoir.*

Fig. 17.16 *The River:* Three girls reflect on new life . . .

Fig. 17.17 . . . and Renoir's camera moves serenely to the enduring river.

This theatrical directness went along with a more serene vision of life. Renoir claimed to have learned a new acceptance while filming *The River*: "The only thing that I can bring to this illogical, irresponsible, and cruel universe is my love."[2] His work was balanced between a worship of the sensuality of nature and a meditation on art as the repository of human values. *Picnic on the Grass* mocks artificial insemination and celebrates the joy of unbridled passion, while *Dr. Cordelier* shows the grotesque results of tampering, Dr. Jekyll-like, with nature. Correspondingly, *The Golden Coach* treats the theater as a supreme achievement: a sharing of experience through sensuous artifice. Renoir's Technicolor contrasts the pale pastels of the viceroy's court with the bright, saturated hues of the *commedia dell'arte* players (Color Plate 17.2).

The themes of art and nature intermingle in *The River*. Three teenage girls are growing up in a Bengali river town. Harriet, who narrates the film from the vantage point of adulthood, writes poetry and dreams up stories. Valerie, the oldest girl, becomes infatuated with a wounded American veteran, while Melanie, daughter of a British father and an Indian mother, quietly accedes to her role in Indian society and urges the tormented soldier to "accept everything." Renoir delicately balances two cultures, western and Indian, counterposing the girls' fantastic intrigues with the Indian community's seasonal rituals. The girls are initiated into adulthood through the cycle of life: the death of a little brother, the birth of a sister. In the last shot, the camera rises past the three girls reacting apprehensively to the baby's first squalls (Fig. 17.16). The ceaselessly flowing river becomes the center of the image (Fig. 17.17), as the rhythms of nature frame the ongoing passions of everyday life. Yet westerners can learn this acceptance only through art, as embodied in Harriet's poem:

> The river runs, the round world spins;
> Dawn and lamplight; midnight, noon.
> Sun follows day, night, stars, and moon;
> The day ends, the end begins.

If Renoir sees art as an entryway to nature, Jean Cocteau treats it as a path to myth and the supernatural. Cocteau considered himself above all a poet, even though his creative output included novels, plays, essays, drawings, stage designs, and films. He was centrally involved with many of the most important avant-garde developments in France after World War I: Diaghilev's ballets, Picasso's paintings, the music of Satie, Stravinsky, and *Les Six*, and the experimental cinema of the early sound era (p. 362). After a decade of stage work, Cocteau began writing scripts during the Occupation (for Delannoy's *L'Eternal retour*, 1943, and Bresson's *Dames du bois du Boulogne*, 1945).

After the war, Cocteau returned to filmmaking in earnest. Working frequently with the composer Georges Auric and the actor Jean Marais, Cocteau directed *Beauty and the Beast* (1945), *L'Aigle à deux têtes* (*The Eagle with Two Heads*, 1947), *Les Parents terribles* (1948; from his own play), *Orphée* (*Orpheus*, 1950), and *Le Testament d'Orphée* (*Testament of Orpheus*, 1960). Most are self-consciously "poetic" works, seeking to create a marvelous world sealed off from ordinary reality and to convey imaginative truths through evocative symbols.

While *Beauty and the Beast* remains an exemplary case of rendering a fairy tale on film, *Orphée* has proved the most influential of Cocteau's work of this period. The film freely updates the myth of Orpheus, the poet who tries to rescue his wife Eurydice from death. Cocteau's Orphée lives in contemporary Paris, with a cozy bourgeois home and a loving wife. But he becomes fascinated with the Princess, who roars through the city in a black limousine and who seems to have captured Cégeste, a dead poet whose cryptic verses are broadcast on the car radio. The Princess, an emissary of death, falls in love with Orphée and captures Eurydice. In Cocteau's personal mythology, the Poet becomes a charmed being, courting death in the attempt to discover enigmatic beauty.

Fig. 17.18 *Orphée:* The mirror as threshold and curtain.

In *Orphée* Cocteau creates a fantasy world through striking cinematic means. The afterlife, *la Zone*, is a maze of factory ruins raked by searchlights—at once a bombed-out city and a prison camp. The dead return to life in reverse motion, while slow motion renders the trip to death's world as a floating, somnambulistic journey. Mirrors become the passageways between death and life. When Orphée dons the magic gloves, he penetrates the quivering liquid curtain of the mirror (Fig. 17.18).

Cocteau conceived rich images that could be translated into many media, confirming his belief that the poet is not merely a writer but rather someone who creates magic through any imaginative means. His career typifies the intense interest which creative writers like Jean-Paul Sartre, Claude Mauriac, Françoise Sagan, and Raymond Queneau took in the cinema. In addition, Cocteau's commitment to a cinema of private vision, even obsession, influenced New Wave directors and the American avant-garde.

Fig. 17.19 *Antoine et Antoinette* (1947): Location shooting in the Paris Métro.

Although Clair, Ophüls, Renoir, and Cocteau reasserted their distinctive identities in the postwar period, none represented a radical challenge to the prestige cinema. Two other directors struck a compromise with the Tradition of Quality while also reviving aspects of the 1930s realist tradition. Roger Leenhardt's first feature, *Les Dernières vacances* ("The Last Vacation," 1947) resembles the contemporary Aurenche-Bost output in its treatment of a young man's lost love, but the plot also puts economic factors to the fore in a way atypical of the Cinema of Quality. Jacques Becker gave the neighborhood film of the 1930s a new realism of setting (Fig. 17.19). His *Casque d'or* ("Golden Cask," 1952) is a turn-of-the-century drama of life among petty thieves and criminals. The doomed romance of Marie and the carpenter Jo, heightened by a radiant romanticization of the enigmatic woman (Fig. 17.20), creates an ambience not far from the Cinema of Quality. *Le Trou* ("The Hole," 1960), the story of a prison break, concentrates both on the mechanics of escape and on the need for trust among the prisoners as they cooperate in their flight. Many critics saw Becker's film as a humanistic call for collective unity reminiscent of 1930s Popular Front cinema.

Fig. 17.20 Simone Signoret as Marie, seen through her lover's eyes in *Casque d'or.*

NEW INDEPENDENT DIRECTORS

One provision of the 1953 aid law encouraged the production of short films of artistic quality, and several filmmakers benefited from this. The veteran

Jean Grémillon and the older Roger Leenhardt and Jean Mitry made several shorts in this period, but the most notable talents to emerge belonged to a younger generation. Alain Resnais, Georges Franju, and Chris Marker got their start making short poetic documentaries (Chapter 21). Alexandre Astruc launched his career with *Le Rideau cramoisi* ("The Crimson Curtain," 1952), a symbolic Poe-like short containing no dialogue. Agnès Varda's short feature *La Pointe courte* (1954) has a regional realism recalling *La Terra trema*, but it also presents abstract compositions and a stylized, discontinuous editing of conversations (p. 528). In the work of Astruc and Varda we find the first stirrings of the New Wave.

More central to mainstream cinema at the time was the eccentric, Stetson-wearing Jean-Pierre Melville. An ardent lover of American culture, he changed his name in honor of Herman Melville. In 1946, he became a producer in order to direct. He worked as an independent, eventually owning his own studio. He produced, directed, wrote, edited, and occasionally starred in his films, once claiming that he never had enough employees to make up a decently long credits list.

Melville's first film, *Le Silence de la mer* ("The Silence of the Sea," 1949), now seems one of the most experimental works of its day. During the German Occupation, an officer is assigned to live with an old man and his niece. The officer tries, in halting French, to engage them in conversation; but they ignore him and never speak in his presence. A tense silence envelops almost every scene. The most minute sounds, particularly the ticking of a clock, become vivid. The voice-over narration often daringly reiterates what the images show, and even introduces dialogue with such lines as "And he said . . ." As the German becomes more worn down by the pair, he too lapses into silence and is unable to talk freely with his friends outside the household. At last he leaves. The niece, looking at him blankly, finally speaks: "Adieu."

A similar freedom of treatment dominates *Les Enfants terribles* ("The Terrible Children," 1950), Melville's adaptation of Cocteau's novel. Again there is a voice-over commentary (spoken by Cocteau), which slips in and out between characters' lines and almost becomes a participant in the dialogue. Melville respects Cocteau's personal mythology—the film opens with a snowball fight reminiscent of that in *Blood of a Poet* (1932)—while giving the piece a self-consciously theatrical quality. Characters look at or speak to the camera, and Melville occasionally treats the action as if it occurred on a stage (Figs. 17.21–17.23). *Les Enfants terribles* exemplifies the rethinking of

Fig. 17.21 *Les Enfants terribles:* A scene begins with a shot facing an auditorium . . .

Fig. 17.22 . . . the camera pulls back to reveal a curtain as seen through a window . . .

Fig. 17.23 . . . then the camera pans left to show us the children's bedroom.

Fig. 17.21

Fig. 17.22

Fig. 17.23

the relation between film and other arts that was taking place in postwar modernism.

Melville gained most fame for such dry, laconic gangster films as *Bob le flambeur* (1955), *Le Doulos* (1962), *Le Deuxième souffle* ("Second Breath," 1966), and *Le Samourai* ("The Samurai," 1967). Expressionless men in trenchcoats and snap-brim hats stalk through gray streets to meet in piano bars. Almost completely impassive, they behave as if they have watched too many Hollywood *films noirs*—driving American sedans, pledging loyalty to their pals, dividing duties for a caper they intend to pull. Melville dwells on long silences as gunmen size each other up, stare at their reflections, or stoically realize that a deal has failed.

The films teem with bravura techniques—hand-held camerawork, long takes, and available-light shooting (Fig. 17.24). Melville also experiments with narration. The plot of *Le Doulos* leaves out crucial scenes, leading us to misjudge the hero's motives as severely as do the gang members he seems to have betrayed. *Bob le flambeur* has a "hypothetical" sequence, introduced by the voice-over narrator: "Here's how Bob planned it to happen." We then see the robbery of the casino, played silently (Fig. 17.25). This is very different from the way the heist turns out (Fig. 17.26).

Melville loved to watch movies. ("Being a spectator is the finest profession in the world."[3]) Many of his films are tributes to American cinema (Fig. 17.27), and he brought to French film some of the audacious energy of Hollywood B pictures. If Renoir fathered the New Wave, Melville was its godfather.

Experiments in narrative structure and sound were contributed by two other major directors of the period: Robert Bresson and Jacques Tati. In the decade after Bresson's Occupation work (p. 342), he made only two films, *Diary of a Country Priest* (1951) and *A Man Escaped* (1956). At first glance, Bresson's reliance upon literary sources and his tendency to collaborate with famous authors on dialogue link him to the Tradition of Quality, and his interest in religious subjects struck a strong chord during the revival of Catholicism in postwar France. In fact, however, his approach to filmmaking was decidedly idiosyncratic.

Fig. 17.24 An off-the-cuff shot from *Two Men in Manhattan* (1958), where Melville acted as his own cinematographer.

Fig. 17.25

Fig. 17.26

Figs. 17.25 and 17.26 Alternative versions of the robbery in *Bob le flambeur.*

Fig. 17.27 In *Le Silence de la mer*, Melville pays homage to the deep focus of *Citizen Kane* (p. 251, Fig. 10.24).

Fig. 17.28

Fig. 17.29

Fig. 17.30

Fig. 17.31

Fig. 17.32

Fig. 17.33

Fig. 17.28 *Diary of a Country Priest:* As the priest walks into the church, he picks up a fallen prayerbook and discovers that the inscription is in the same handwriting as a cruel anonymous letter he has received. We make the discovery with him, and share his curiosity to learn who has been persecuting him. But then we hear a door opening. He quickly puts the book in front of a pew and walks out of the frame.

Fig. 17.29 Bresson holds on the book for eleven seconds, tracking in as the offscreen steps approach.

Fig. 17.30 The suspense is resolved when the governess from the manor house comes into medium shot, kneels, and opens the book.

Fig. 17.31 She looks up.

Fig. 17.32 Bresson cuts to a medium-close shot of the priest walking into the chapel and looking briefly at her . . .

Fig. 17.33 . . . before he makes his way to the altar, eyes lowered. As he kneels, the scene fades out. Her motivations, and his reactions, have been suppressed.

Bresson's films show little but suggest much. Often the most important actions take place outside the frame or in sequences which are skipped over. His insistent close-ups of feet, hands, and objects lead him to omit traditional establishing shots. Characters avoid looking at one another; when gazes meet in a Bresson film, it is often a climax. Bresson's abrupt cutting, short scenes, brief track-ins or track-outs, and laconic sound tracks demand the viewer's utmost concentration. The reward is a remarkable balance between a penetration of the characters' experiences and a sense that their inner states remain elusive and mysterious. (See the passage discussed in Figs. 17.28–17.33.) Bresson's intense concentration on physical details often "fills in" for psychological analysis. The mystery and ambiguity of Bresson's style proved suited to his treatment of solitary individuals who struggle to survive a spiritual or physical ordeal.

No such Christian subjects can be found in the films of Jacques Tati. Born a year later than Bresson, Tati became a vaudeville mime and acrobat in the early 1930s. He made comedy shorts and, during the Occupation, starred in other directors' films. Like Bresson, he worked slowly: in the first decade after the war he directed only two features, *Jour de fête* ("Holiday," 1949) and *Les Vacances de M. Hulot* (*Mr. Hulot's Holiday*, 1953). Both were outstanding successes and quickly earned him a reputation as a master of film comedy.

At one level, Tati's films are satiric commentaries on the rituals of modern life—vacations, work, housing, travel. Declaring himself an anarchist, he believed in freedom, eccentricity, and playfulness. *Jour de fête* centers on the day a carnival comes to a rural town. Tati plays François, the postman who tries to do his duty while all about him are at leisure. In *Mr.*

Fig. 17.34

Fig. 17.35

Fig. 17.36

Fig. 17.34 *Jour de fête:* On the road in the distance, François pauses to drive away a buzzing bee . . .

Fig. 17.35 . . . which then plagues a farmer on a hilltop in the foreground . . .

Fig. 17.36 . . . before returning to François.

Hulot's Holiday, Tati is Hulot, whose insistence on a fun-filled week disrupts the tidy routines of other vacationers.

A stiff-legged beanpole capable of outrageously mechanical gestures, Tati was one of the cinema's great clowns. Like Keaton, he was also one of its most innovative directors. His films lack firm plots; things simply happen, one after the other, and nothing much is ever at stake. The film accumulates tiny, even trivial events—like the microactions of Neorealism (p. 420), only treated as gags. These gags are accentuated by Tati's unique style. He tends to film the scene from a distance and let the viewer scan the frame for the details that make up a gag. Sometimes, like Keaton, he stages gags in carefully composed long shot (Figs. 17.34–17.36). Tati guides the viewer's attention in such shots by sound effects as precise as those of Melville or Bresson. *Mr. Hulot's Holiday* is dominated by the percussive chuggings of Hulot's car, the low thump of the hotel restaurant's swinging door, and the hollow ricochet of a ping-pong ball as it invades the hotel parlor.

The Tradition of Quality yielded a cinema that was artistic but hardly modernist in the strong sense. The adaptations of literary masterworks remained within the conventions of mainstream filmmaking. Ophüls, Renoir, and Cocteau, however, saw themselves as expressing their personal visions, and they reinforced the idea that a strong directorial personality might break away from tradition. These directors, along with Melville, Bresson, and Tati, moved the French cinema into the vanguard of postwar modernism.

SCANDINAVIAN REVIVAL

Denmark and Sweden proved to have the two most influential Scandinavian national cinemas. As with Italian Neorealism and French postwar cinema, their first contributions to 1940s art cinema were made during the war.

Denmark had a strong film industry in the 1910s, but it lost its international standing during World War I. Late in the 1930s Danish cinema regained some ground, thanks partly to generous government policies that taxed ticket prices to create a fund for artistic and cultural filmmaking.

The Germans invaded Denmark in 1940. As elsewhere, the Nazis' ban on film imports from the Allied countries spurred domestic production. Documentary and educational films continued to be made under the Occupation, but the most important film, made for the country's major firm, Palladium, was Carl Theodor Dreyer's *Day of Wrath* (1943). This somber study of witchcraft and religious dogma in a seventeenth-century village marked Dreyer's return to Danish feature filmmaking after almost two decades. The film caused a sensation and was widely interpreted as an anti-Nazi allegory. When it was shown abroad after the war, it proved no less controversial, but more for its solemn tempo, its restrained technique (Fig. 17.37), and its teasing ambiguities. *Day of Wrath* reestablished Dreyer on the international film scene. (See Box.)

Swedish cinema had also been in eclipse since Victor Sjöström and Mauritz Stiller were lured to Hollywood. Sweden was not invaded by the Nazis, but its policy of neutrality shut out any foreign films considered propagandistic. The lack of competition stimulated the local industry. In 1942, the major studio Svensk Filmindustri hired Carl-Anders Dymling as head. He brought in Sjöström as artistic supervisor of production, a gesture that was considered to symbolize a return to the great Swedish filmmaking tradition.

Once the war ended, Danish and Swedish filmmaking benefited from Scandinavia's rapid recovery. Annual film outputs averaged 15 to 20 features in Denmark and twice that in Sweden—lower figures than the wartime peaks, but remarkably high for small countries. Here quality filmmaking was comparatively cheap. Production was dominated by large companies which insisted on small budgets and short shooting schedules. Denmark levied an entertainment tax to subsidize "artistic" films, and in 1951, under pressure from filmmakers, Sweden initiated a comparable policy.

Apart from Dreyer, the most famous Scandinavian filmmakers of the postwar decade were Swedish. Like Sjöström and Stiller, most of these men had ties to a rich theatrical tradition. During the second half of the nineteenth century, the Norwegian Henrik Ibsen and the Swede August Strindberg had made Scandinavian drama world famous. Both playwrights had a penchant

Fig. 17.37 Chiaroscuro lighting and slow performance in *Day of Wrath*.

CARL THEODOR DREYER

etween the generation of Sjöström and Stiller, who made their first films in 1912, and the generation who began work in the 1930s, only one Scandinavian director came to worldwide prominence. Dreyer's career prefigured that of the traveling "international" director of the postwar period, with films made in Denmark, Sweden, Norway, Germany, and France, notably *The Passion of Joan of Arc* and *Vampyr* (p. 188). There followed a decade of inactivity, broken by some documentary shorts and *Day of Wrath*. After the Swedish *Two People* (1945), Dreyer made *Ordet* (*The Word*, 1954) and *Gertrud* (1964), both in Denmark. He died while planning a film on the life of Jesus.

Dreyer's earliest films revealed his fondness for static, highly pictorial compositions which alternate with intense close-ups of actors' facial expressions. In *Jeanne d'Arc* and *Vampyr* he also explored unusual camera movements—gymnastic rotations in the former, subtly misleading tracking movements in the latter. After *Vampyr*, Dreyer became convinced that the sound cinema required a more "theatrical" technique. His last four films, all adaptations of plays, are largely confined to interior settings and elaborate their action through lengthy dialogue exchanges. Using very long takes, Dreyer records dialogue in rigid, harmonious compositions (Fig. 17.38). The camera arcs gracefully across parlors as characters slowly move from a sofa to a table, from a doorway to a bedside. "Camera movement," he wrote, "gives a fine soft rhythm."[4] Dreyer's version of modernism acknowledges the film's source in a literary text and creates a "minimal" cinema of minutely varied pace, much more subdued than the aggressive theatricality of Visconti or Bergman.

Through this ascetic style Dreyer presents the ineffable mystery of faith and love. In *Day of Wrath* Anne goes to the

Fig. 17.38 A conversation in *Gertrud*.

stake acknowledging she is a witch; but we wonder whether the community has merely convinced her that she is guilty. *Ordet* ends with one of the most daring scenes in film history: a miracle created by a child's faith. In *Gertrud* the woman who demands absolute devotion retreats into isolation, worshipping an ideal of pure love.

Dreyer's films were not popular successes, but his singleminded tenacity within the commerical film industry and his rigorous exploration of powerful themes won him critical regard. His contributions to modernist technique influenced Jean-Luc Godard, Jean-Marie Straub, and other young directors.

for fantasy and expressionism, and their plays often used complex symbols to suggest characters' emotional states. Strindberg had also developed an intimate psychological drama called the *Kammerspiel*, or "chamber play." Typically, the *Kammerspiel* was set in a single room and staged in a small theater that would bring the audience very close to the actors. (See pp. 115–118 for a discussion of the influence of *Kammerspiel* on silent German cinema.) Of the filmmakers marked by these modernist trends, the two most influential were Alf Sjöberg and Ingmar Bergman.

After making one film in 1929, Sjöberg became the major director at Stockholm's Royal Dramatic Theatre. He returned to filmmaking in 1939 and completed several films during the war. One of the most original was *The Heavenly Play* (1942), which fused the silent-film traditions of naturalistic landscape and symbolic drama (Fig. 17.39) to create an allegorical fantasy of Protestant redemption.

More influential outside Sweden was Sjöberg's *Torment* (1943), scripted by Bergman. A high-school student tortured by his Latin teacher, nicknamed

Fig. 17.39 Chiaroscuro and expressionist setting in Sjöberg's *The Heavenly Play*.

Fig. 17.40 *Torment:* The school's sinister, endless flights of stairs recur in the city streets.

Fig. 17.41 Caligula as Nosferatu (*Torment*); compare Fig. 5.16.

Fig. 17.42 Two time periods in one shot: Julie, sitting in the foreground, tells of an episode from her childhood; in the background her mother talks with her as a child.

Caligula, discovers that the man is a lecher, a Nazi sympathizer, and a murderer. *Torment*'s sympathy with teenage rebellion emerges not only from its rather schematic story but also from a visual style derived from German Expressionism. Looming architecture and long, sharp shadows turn the entire city into a prison (Fig. 17.40). The pudgy Caligula, with his round spectacles and fussy manner, becomes a wartime Caligari, and his shadow threatens the lovers in a gesture that echoes Murnau's vampire in *Nosferatu* (Fig. 17.41).

After the war, Sjöberg continued to move between theater and cinema. After staging Strindberg's 1888 naturalist play *Miss Julie*, he adapted it to the screen in 1950. The film concentrates upon the performances, especially Anita Björk's skittery Julie, but it also expands the original *Kammerspiel*. In Strindberg's play, characters recount their memories in monologues. Sjöberg dramatizes the scenes as flashbacks which combine past and present in the same shot (Fig. 17.42). Conventions of what would become art cinema can be found in Strindberg's original *Kammerspiel*, but Sjöberg adds a modernist ambiguity derived from film's power over space and time.

Like Sjöberg, Ingmar Bergman came from the theater. After a stint as a scriptwriter this prodigiously energetic man began directing in 1945. Before he turned forty, he had completed nineteen films and directed over sixty plays.

Bergman's postwar films gained him a reputation as a serious artist commanding many genres. His earliest films were domestic dramas, often centering on alienated young couples in search of happiness through art or nature (*Summer Interlude*, 1950; *Monika*, 1952). Soon, with a repertory of skillful performers at his call, he focused on the failures of married love—sometimes treated comically, as in *A Lesson in Love* (1954), but other times presented in probing, agonizing psychodramas such as *Sawdust and Tinsel* (aka *The Naked Night*, 1953). He moved to more self-consciously artistic works: the Mozartian *Smiles of a Summer Night* (1955); the parablelike *The Seventh Seal* (1956); a blend of expressionist dream imagery, natural locales, and elaborate flashbacks in *Wild Strawberries* (1957). For many viewers and critics, Bergman's career climaxed with a trilogy of three portentous *Kammerspiel* films—*Through a Glass Darkly* (1961), *Winter Light* (1962), and *The Silence* (1963).

Brink of Life (1957) illustrates Bergman's adoption of theatrical technique. The plot centers on three women in a maternity ward during a critical period of forty-eight hours. The sense of a *Kammerspiel* world is reinforced by the first shot, which shows the ward's door opening to admit Cecilia, who is in labor. The film will end with the youngest woman, Hjördis, resolutely going out the door, departing for an uncertain future. The women's pasts are revealed through dialogue. In addition, each actress is given one hyperdramatic scene. The first, and perhaps most impressive, presents Cecilia's reaction to the death of her baby. Characteristically, Bergman dwells on this display of shame, anguish, and physical pain. In a drugged haze, cradled by a maternal nurse, Cecilia recalls her worries about the delivery, accuses herself of failing as a wife and mother, and alternates among sobs, cries of agony, and bitter laughter. The monologue runs for over four minutes, filmed in very long takes and stark frontal close-ups (Figs. 17.43, 17.44). Here Bergman employs the cinematic device of the close-up for theatrical purposes, intensifying the viewer's focus on Ingrid Thulin's performance.

Fig. 17.43 **Fig. 17.44**

Fig. 17.43 At the climax of Cecilia's speech, in a shot lasting almost two minutes, she claws forward into extreme close-up, her face starkly lit . . .

Fig. 17.44 . . . before falling back exhausted into the nurse's arms.

By the late 1950s, Bergman was enjoying an international success. *Smiles of a Summer Night, The Seventh Seal, Wild Strawberries, Brink of Life,* and *The Virgin Spring* (1959) won major festival prizes; *The Virgin Spring* and *Through a Glass Darkly* won Academy Awards. Bergman became the most widely known European filmmaker of the postwar era.

ENGLAND: QUALITY AND COMEDY

British film output declined during the war, when personnel were conscripted and studio facilities were turned to military use. Yet high wartime attendance boosted the industry. The main companies, the Rank Organization, headed by J. Arthur Rank, and the Associated British Picture Corporation, expanded their domains. Associated British owned a major theater chain, while Rank controlled two others and owned the largest distribution firm, several studios, and two producing companies.

In 1944 a report entitled "Tendencies to Monopoly in the Cinematograph Film Industry" had recommended that the major companies' power be reduced. The "Palache report," as it came to be known, remained the center of debate for years, but it was not acted on soon, partly because the industry seemed robust. High attendance continued, with 1946 the biggest year ever. More British films were being made, and many were of high enough quality to be popular at home and competitive abroad. Moreover, because Rank needed many films for his theater chains, he supported several small independent producers. Rank also had ties with some of the American Majors, and English films began to enter the United States regularly, often becoming successful there. For a few years it seemed as though the intense competition between the British and American firms might diminish.

Yet trouble soon appeared. Production costs were rising, few films made profits, and Hollywood films commanded 80 percent of screen time. The left-wing Labour government, committed to fighting monopolies and protecting British industry from American competition, tackled these problems.

In 1947 the government imposed a 75 percent tariff on all imported American films. When the U.S. industry immediately threatened a boycott, the government compromised. In 1948 the government established a quota reminiscent of the prewar era: 45 percent of all screenings in Britain had to consist of British films. Many exhibitors and distributors, dependent on American films, opposed the quota, and it was soon reduced to 30 percent.

The Rank Organization was vertically integrated, and only a few firms controlled the industry, so the government could have forced companies to sell part of their holdings, as the American government did in the Paramount decision of 1948 (pp. 374–375). Those trying to cure the industry's woes, however, realized that "divorcement" decrees would be suicidal in Great Britain. If firms were forced to sell their theaters, American companies would simply buy them.

The government attempted another solution in 1949. The National Film Finance Corporation (NFFC) was founded with the purpose of loaning money to independent producers. Unfortunately, £3 million, over half the total amount loaned out, went to one of the largest independents, British Lion, which producer Alexander Korda had acquired in 1946. Soon British Lion went bankrupt, and its heavy losses weakened the NFFC's ability to support other firms.

In 1950, after a year of financial crisis, the government tried once more to bolster production. It reduced the entertainment tax charged on theater tickets but added a levy against ticket sales, part of which was given to producers. The "Eady levy," named after its planner, thus provided a production subsidy comparable to those which appeared at about the same time in Sweden, France, and Italy.

The Eady levy worked reasonably well and remained in force for several decades. Nevertheless, the film industry continued its decline during the 1950s, as competition with television increased. The problem of monopoly in the industry intensified. Rank and the Associated British Picture Corporation bought up more theaters, and smaller, independent exhibitors were forced out of business by declining attendance. Despite industry problems, however, the decade after the war saw a number of important films and trends.

British producers continued to debate whether to produce high-budget prestige films for export or more modest films aimed at home audiences. As always, many films were literary adaptations featuring famous actors. Laurence Olivier followed up his wartime success *Henry V* (1945) by directing and starring in *Hamlet* (1948) and *Richard III* (1953). Gabriel Pascal contin-

Fig. 17.45 *Oliver Twist:* An elaborate set re-creates Victorian London.

ued his association with the plays of George Bernard Shaw by making a lavish version of *Caesar and Cleopatra* (1946), with Vivien Leigh and Claude Rains. This approach to filmmaking is comparable to the French Cinema of Quality. In addition, two major British directors achieved international reputations during this period.

David Lean had his start during the war co-directing *In Which We Serve* (1942) with Noel Coward. His postwar career began with the release of *Brief Encounter* (1945), a story of a middle-aged man and woman, both trapped in unexciting marriages, who fall in love. They meet repeatedly but resist having a sexual affair. Lean's restrained romanticism centers around Celia Johnson's portrayal of the heroine.

Fig. 17.46 Location shooting in *Odd Man Out.*

Lean went on to make two popular adaptations of Dickens novels, *Great Expectations* (1946) and *Oliver Twist* (1948). Both featured Alec Guinness, who within a few years became the most popular actor in exported British films. *Oliver Twist* is typical of Lean's postwar films, containing large, dark sets, deep-focus compositions, and *film noir* lighting (Fig. 17.45). Lean also made comedies, such as *Hobson's Choice* (1953), in which a strong-willed heroine defeats her tyrannical father. Lean later gained wider fame with costume epics such as *Lawrence of Arabia* (1962) and *Doctor Zhivago* (1965).

The other prominent director of the postwar years was Carol Reed. Reed had begun directing in the late 1930s, but his international reputation was built upon *Odd Man Out* (1947), *The Fallen Idol* (1948), *The Third Man* (1949), *An Outcast of the Islands* (1951), and *The Man Between* (1953). Like Lean, Reed favored dramatic lighting, often intensified by flashy camera techniques. Thus *The Third Man* (possibly influenced by Orson Welles, who plays the villain) is full of canted framings and uses an unusual instrument, the zither, for its famous musical accompaniment.

Fig. 17.47 The wounded hero stares down at the table . . .

Reed's awareness of emerging art-cinema norms is evident in one of his most important films, *Odd Man Out*. An Irish Republican Army unit steals payroll money to fund its terrorist activities. During the robbery the hero (James Mason) is wounded. As he flees, he encounters a series of people who try to save him or to exploit him. While Reed shot some scenes in Irish slums (Fig. 17.46), several passages stress a more subjective realism (Figs. 17.47, 17.48).

Less famous than Lean and Reed, Michael Powell and Emeric Pressburger were undoubtedly the most unusual British filmmakers of the era. They had created their production company, The Archers, in 1943, and supported it with Rank's help. Writing, producing, and directing in collaboration, the pair made modest dramas in black and white and elaborate Technicolor productions.

Fig. 17.48 . . . and we see his point of view of a pool of beer, with various characters from earlier scenes of the film superimposed in the bubbles.

Typical of their offbeat approach is *I Know Where I'm Going!* (1945). A strong-willed young woman engaged to a rich industrialist attempts to join him on a Scottish island. As she waits for the weather to clear, she struggles against falling in love with a pleasant, but impoverished, Scottish landowner. Powell and Pressburger display their characteristic feeling for the British countryside, as well as their sympathy for eccentric characters. They even make the headstrong, greedy heroine sympathetic. Another intimate drama, *A Small Back Room* (1948), deals with the intriguing subject of an alcoholic whose job is to defuse unexploded bombs left in England after the war.

Powell and Pressburger also directed some of the most opulent color films ever made. Their most popular film, *The Red Shoes* (1948), and its successor, *The Tales of Hoffmann* (1951), use ballet to motivate deliriously stylized decors and cinematography. *A Matter of Life and Death* (aka *Stairway to Heaven*, 1946) centers on a British pilot who impossibly survives a fatal crash and argues in a heavenly courtroom (in his dream?) that he should be sent back to earth to join the woman he loves. Color film stock for the sequences on earth contrasts with a black-and-white rendition of Heaven.

One of Powell and Pressburger's color masterpieces is *Black Narcissus* (1947), a story of nuns trying to run a dispensary and school in a Tibetan palace formerly used as a harem. Sexual frustrations, a lack of understanding of local customs, and the general ambience of the setting drive some of the nuns to dereliction of duty, nostalgic fantasies, madness, and even attempted murder before the convent is finally abandoned. The directors create a vivid sense of the Himalayas, even though they shot the film wholly in the studio (Color Plate 17.3). The range of bright hues in the lush settings contrasts with the stark white of the nuns' habits (Color Plate 17.4).

Powell and Pressburger's most extravagant works contrast strongly with the modest product of Michael Balcon's Ealing Studios. Balcon, a veteran of the industry since the early 1920s, became head of Ealing in 1938. In the postwar period Ealing prospered because the Rank Organization helped finance production and released the studio's films through its large distribution network. Balcon achieved a consistency of tone across the studio by making decisions democratically (allowing the studio staff to vote at round-table meetings) and by giving filmmakers an unusual degree of independence.

Today Ealing Studios is usually associated with comedies starring Alec Guinness, Stanley Holloway, and other major British actors, but only about one-third of the company's output was in this genre. Indeed, one of the most successful Ealing films is a realistic drama about police life, *The Blue Lamp* (1950). Scenes in which a veteran cop explains the job to a new recruit give a systematic account of police procedure, in the tradition of the 1930s and wartime British documentaries. As in other Ealing films, many scenes were shot on location in poor or bombed-out areas of London (Fig. 17.49).

Fig. 17.49 The Ealing Studios, nestled in a suburban neighborhood, had no backlot on which to build sets. Directors filmed scenes on location, as in *The Blue Lamp*.

Ealing's reputation for comedies was established with three 1949 releases, *Passport to Pimlico* (directed by Henry Cornelius), *Whisky Galore!* (aka *Tight Little Island*, directed by Alexander Mackendrick), and *Kind Hearts and Coronets* (directed by Robert Hamer). *Kind Hearts*, in which Guinness plays eight different characters, swept him to international stardom. While many Hollywood-style comedies depended on slapstick or on sophisticated screwball situations, Ealing's humor was built on injecting a single fantastic premise into an ordinary situation. *Passport to Pimlico*, for example, takes place in the drab working-class London district of Pimlico, and much of the film was shot on location in realistic style. Yet the plot depends on a zany premise: researchers discover that the suburb is actually not part of England at all but belongs to the French district of Burgundy. As a result, following a maddeningly linear logic, Britishers must have a passport to enter Pimlico, and the residents are no longer subject to London's rationing restrictions. Like other Ealing comedies, *Passport to Pimlico* presents an imaginary escape from postwar austerity.

Fig. 17.50 A landscape of bombed-out London in *The Lavender Hill Mob*.

Another typical Ealing comedy is Charles Crichton's *The Lavender Hill Mob* (1951). The hero, played by Guinness, works guarding gold shipped to London banks. With a gang of mild-mannered crooks, he plans and executes a massive heist. The Ealing fantasy emerges when the gang disguises the bullion as souvenir Eiffel Towers. Yet the film mixes realism with stylization. The near-documentary opening sequence depicts the hero's daily routine. Scenes shot on location (Fig. 17.50) contrast with scenes which parody *film noir* and even Ealing's own *Blue Lamp* (Fig. 17.51). Crichton returned to prominence decades later with *A Fish Called Wanda* (1989), which many critics considered an updating of the Ealing tradition.

Fig. 17.51 When the Lavender Hill Mob plot their crime, the low-key lighting and deep-focus composition suggest Hollywood gangster films of the 1940s. (Compare p. 390, Figs. 15.20–15.22.)

The Ealing comedies depend on a notion of English eccentricity. In *The Lavender Hill Mob*, the hero entertains a sweet elderly woman by reading lurid crime thrillers to her. The last major film from the studio, *The Ladykillers* (1955), revolves around a dotty old lady who discovers that the string quintet players renting her spare room are actually a gang of robbers.

Distinctive though the Ealing and Archers films were, they fall into recognizable commercial genres and employ classical storytelling techniques. Yet the success of these films abroad depended largely on the same art theaters that showed Italian Neorealist or Scandinavian films. Although the films were not themselves modernist, they reinforced the trend toward international film circulation that fostered art-cinema trends elsewhere. In particular, they showed that the U.S. market could support European filmmaking to an unprecedented extent.

The pattern was set quietly by *I Know Where I'm Going!*, which became an unexpected hit in a New York art house. Soon afterward Olivier's *Henry V* (U.S. release 1946), ran for thirty-four weeks in a small Manhattan theater at high admission prices. In 1948, his *Hamlet* became such a hit in small theaters that it moved into wide release and won several Oscars. *Brief Encounter*, *Blithe Spirit*, and other British films prospered in the art-house circuit, with *The Red Shoes*, astonishingly, becoming the top U.S. box-office attraction of 1948. An Ealing comedy could make more money in art houses than in limited release to larger theaters.

In the mid-1950s, most of the older creative figures in the postwar era lost momentum. Powell and Pressburger broke up The Archers in 1956;

Powell's career was nearly curtailed by the scandal aroused by *Peeping Tom* (1960). Heavy losses forced Balcon to sell Ealing's studio facilities in 1955, though he made a few more films before losing the company. Some of the most successful directors of this era, such as David Lean and Carol Reed, went on to big-budget, American-financed projects. These developments cleared the way for a generation of filmmakers who would turn against the polished cinema of the postwar decade.

◆ NOTES AND QUERIES

POSTWAR FRENCH FILM THEORY

Postwar Paris saw a revival of theoretical writings about film as art. Some writers suggested that film aesthetics owed less to the theater than to the novel. In her book *The Age of the American Novel*, trans. Eleanor Hochman (New York: Ungar, 1972; originally published 1948), Claude-Edmonde Magny argued that the work of Hemingway and Faulkner showed strong affinities with the style of American cinema. She also suggested that the camera lens was like the organizing consciousness of the narrator in literary works. Alexandre Astruc spoke of the "camera-pen," *la caméra-stylo*, and predicted that filmmakers would treat their works as vehicles of self-expression in the way writers did (Alexandre Astruc, "The Birth of a New Avant-Garde: *La Caméra-Stylo*," in Peter Graham, ed., *The New Wave* (New York: Doubleday, 1968), pp. 17–24.

André Bazin also pointed out that a "novelistic" cinema seemed to be emerging in France and Italy. In his opinion, films by Bresson, Clément, Leenhardt, and other directors went beyond the theater's depiction of character behavior. These directors either plunged into the depths of psychology or moved beyond the individual to portray, in a realistic fashion, the world in which the characters lived. Many of Bazin's essays are collected in Hugh Gray, ed. and trans., *What Is Cinema? I* (Berkeley: University of California Press, 1967), and *What Is Cinema? II* (Berkeley: University of California Press, 1971); see also Bazin's *Jean Renoir*, trans. W. W. Halsey II and William H. Simon (New York: Simon and Schuster, 1973).

The comparison of film to literature also called a new attention to style and narrative construction. Theorists began to reevaluate the traditional analogy between film style and language by developing a notion of *écriture cinématographique*, or "filmic writing." Bazin revolutionized film criticism by his detailed discussions of how editing, camerawork, and deep-space staging offered expressive possibilities to the filmmaker. He and his peers were also sensitive to how filmic storytelling could create ellipses and could shift point of view. And by assuming the filmmaker to be a novelist-on-film, the critic could examine even a popular film as the vehicle of a personal vision. There arose debates about whether the filmmaker could be considered an *auteur*, or author, of his works (Chapter 19).

At the same time, Bazin and others began to ponder the possibility that cinema might be radically unlike all traditional arts. They argued that the film medium has as its basic purpose to record and reveal the concrete world in which we find ourselves. This line of thought treated cinema as a "phenomenological" art, one suited to capture the reality of everyday perception. For thinkers like Bazin and Amédée Ayfre (p. 436), the Italian Neorealist films exemplify cinema's power to reveal the ties of humans to their surroundings. A related development, the academic discipline of Filmology, emerged at the same period. For a discussion, see Edward Lowry, *The Filmology Movement and Film Study in France* (Ann Arbor: UMI, 1985).

Discussions of the theoretical trends of this era can be found in Dudley Andrew, *André Bazin* (New York: Oxford University Press, 1978), and Jim Hillier, ed., **Cahiers du Cinéma:** *The 1950s: Neo-Realism, Hollywood, New Wave* (Cambridge, Mass.: Harvard University Press, 1985), especially pp. 1–17.

THE POWELL-PRESSBURGER REVIVAL

For several years, Michael Powell and Emeric Pressburger remained marginal figures, but their reputations have risen substantially since the late 1970s.

The team made some films that were widely popular, but much of their work was so eccentric that it earned unfavorable reviews. Their baroque melodramas and fantasies lay outside the documentary tradition long considered the strength of British cinema. After the breakup of their production company in 1956 and the scandal surrounding Powell's *Peeping Tom* in 1960, most historians treated them as minor filmmakers. British auteurism tended to focus on Hollywood directors and treat English filmmaking as pallid and stodgy. Raymond Durgnat (writing as O. O. Green) presented an intelligent defense in "Michael Powell," *Movie* **14** (Autumn 1965): 17–20 [also, in revised form, in his *A Mirror for England* (New York: Praeger, 1971)]. This was, however, largely ignored.

By the mid-1960s *Peeping Tom* had acquired cult status. The National Film Theatre in London presented a Powell retrospective in 1970, and the National Film Archive and BBC restored a few important films. In 1977 Powell received an award at the Telluride Film Festival in Colorado. American director Martin Scorsese helped fund a re-release of *Peeping Tom*, and the film showed at the 1979 New York Film Festival, with Powell in attendance, to a sell-out crowd. See John Russell Taylor, "Michael Powell: Myths and Supermen," *Sight and Sound* **47**, 4 (Autumn 1978): 226–229; and David Thomson, "Mark of the Red Death," *Sight and Sound* **49**, 4 (Autumn 1980): 258–262. British historian Ian Christie has helped both in the restoration of Powell and Pressburger's films and in the dissemination of information on the pair. See his *Powell, Pressburger and Others* (London: British Film Institute, 1978) and *Arrows of Desire: The Films of Michael Powell and Emeric Pressburger* (London: Waterstone, 1985). See also Christie's "Powell and Pressburger: Putting Back the Pieces," *Monthly Film Bulletin* **611** (December 1984): back cover, for an account of how their films have been cut and, in some cases, restored.

Powell and Pressburger have influenced Martin Scorsese, Francis Coppola, Brian De Palma, George Lucas, and Derek Jarman. *Scorsese on Scorsese*, ed. David Thompson and Ian Christie (Boston: Faber and Faber, 1990) contains numerous references to Powell. Powell tells his own story in *Michael Powell: A Life in Movies* (London: Heinemann, 1986).

◆ REFERENCES

1. Quoted in Andrew Sarris, ed., *Interviews with Film Directors* (Indianapolis: Bobbs-Merrill, 1967), p. 295.
2. Quoted in Christopher Faulkner, *The Social Cinema of Jean Renoir* (Princeton, N.J.: Princeton University Press, 1986), p. 170.
3. Quoted in Rui Nogueira, ed., *Melville on Melville* (New York: Viking, 1971), p. 64.
4. Quoted in Sarris, *Interviews with Film Directors*, p. 111.

18

POSTWAR CINEMA BEYOND THE WEST

I n the mid-1950s, the world was producing around 2800 feature films per
year. About 35 percent of these came from the United States and western
Europe. Another 5 percent were made in the USSR and the eastern European
countries under its control. Although quantitatively small, the output of this
"Second World" dominated the Soviet bloc (where few films were imported
from the West) and had some impact in other regions.

Sixty percent of all feature films were made outside the western world
and the Soviet bloc. Japan accounted for about 20 percent of the world total.
The rest came from India, Hong Kong, Mexico, and other less industrialized
nations. Such a stunning growth in film production in the developing countries
is one of the major events in film history.

This chapter examines postwar filmmaking in selected nonwestern regions: Japan, the USSR and its satellites, and areas of what was coming to
be called the Third World.

GENERAL TENDENCIES

After World War II, international affairs were dominated by two "superpowers," the United States and the USSR. In the postwar settlements, the United
States brought Japan into the western alliance while the USSR took control
of portions of eastern Europe. For the next several decades, the bipolar power
split created competing spheres of influence.

Over the same period, colonies began to break away from the western European empires. Through negotiation or insurrection, Indonesia, the Philippines, India, Pakistan, Burma, Egypt, Cuba, and other countries gained independence in the 1940s and 1950s. Western policymakers feared that resources and markets would be lost if these new nations aligned themselves with the USSR. The 1949 Chinese revolution, which installed a government allied with Moscow, demonstrated that communism could take power in an underdeveloped nation.

Most decolonized nations joined the western camp, since local leaders had been trained there and conditions for investment and trade were firmly established. Under this "neocolonialism," such countries were politically sovereign but economically dependent on the western powers. Many countries in Latin America were prime examples of neocolonialism.

The Third World, where television had hardly penetrated and urban populations were growing rapidly, presented a huge market for films. The USSR and its satellite countries virtually banned American films, but in almost every other market Hollywood cinema ruled. As in Europe, U.S. firms established powerful regional distribution companies throughout the Third World, and exhibitors often favored the popular and cheap Hollywood product. The Motion Picture Export Association of American (MPEAA) negotiated favorable quotas and fiscal policies with local governments (p. 373). Soon, prewar conditions returned, with Hollywood movies occupying between 50 and 90 percent of screen time in most countries.

Yet as Hollywood cut back its output in the 1950s, it could not fill the appetites of Third World city populations who might go to the movies once a month or even once a week—a far higher average than that in the United States or most of Europe. And in most countries, indigenous stars, locales, and music remained powerful attractions.

Despite the U.S. companies' dominance of world markets, then, film production grew in the developing countries. Burma, Pakistan, South Korea, and the Philippines had had virtually no film production before the war, but in the 1950s each produced more films annually than almost any European country. In postwar Egypt, the growth of cities and an economic upturn created a filmmaking boom which made Egyptian films the most widely circulated Middle Eastern product. The most spectacular rise occurred in Hong Kong; film output grew from about 70 features in 1950 to over 250 in 1962—more than that of the United States and Britain combined.

Nonwestern film enterprises organized production in various ways. In the Soviet sphere of influence, the centralized vertical monopoly system established in the USSR was put in place. Directors, writers, and technicians were kept on salary whether working or not. At every step a film was subjected to financial and ideological scrutiny. The system was at its most inflexible in the Soviet Union and China; in the USSR, it drastically lowered output immediately after the war. The major eastern bloc nations, however, managed to increase production during the 1950s, thanks to more decentralized creative policies, a weakening of ideological controls, increased export possibilities, and overall growth in the economies.

Outside the eastern bloc, the most common option was artisanal, small-company production on the postwar European model. In India and South

Korea, where the government refused to support the industry, independent production created chaos, with speculators using cinema to turn a quick profit. In Mexico, where the state protected the industry, independent production proceeded in a somewhat more orderly fashion.

Some countries sought to imitate Hollywood's vertically integrated studio system. This strategy failed in Argentina and succeeded only partially in Brazil, but it proved successful in East Asia. Japan sustained its strong vertical oligopoly throughout the postwar era. A similar structure appeared in Hong Kong, when the major companies formed the "Big Eight" combine. By 1961 the prosperous Shaw Brothers company surpassed even Hollywood's "factory system" by building Movieland, a 46-acre complex of studios, sets, laboratory facilities, and dormitories. There 1500 performers and 2000 staff worked around the clock.

New countries earned some international notice. The Asian Film Festival (established in Tokyo in 1954) and the Moscow International Film Festival (1959) brought nonwestern cinemas to world attention. By and large, however, the rich film traditions of the Middle East, the Far East, Latin America, and the Indian subcontinent remained almost completely unknown in the West. Even today, archives and distribution companies do not hold many such films, and many nations have been unable to preserve representative examples of their own output. Thus any generalizations about tendencies in theme, structure, and style must remain tentative.

As in the West, most production was in popular genres: action and adventure films, romances, comedies, musicals, melodramas, and adaptations of literary classics. More "serious" works often concentrated on episodes of national history or depicted contemporary social problems. Some filmmakers sought to create a cinema that would be more realistic than mainstream production. Many directors were strongly influenced by documentary practices and Italian Neorealism. In addition, some countries brought forth a sector of filmmaking inspired by western art cinema.

Filmmakers in Japan, the "Second World," and the Third World were also influenced by formal trends of the West. Scriptwriters made flashback construction common. Directors began using wide-angle lenses to create deep-space staging and deep-focus cinematography (Figs. 18.1, 18.2). The zoom lens, revived in late-1940s Hollywood, gained wider international currency through its extensive use in Hungarian and Polish films of the late 1950s. In all, the postwar decades saw a return to the cross-national stylistic influences and the circulation of technology which World War II had momentarily halted.

Fig. 18.1 The distorting effect of the wide-angle lens in *The Cranes Are Flying* (USSR, 1957).

Fig. 18.2 Deep-focus staging puts the tolling bell in the foreground of this image from the Mexican film *María Candelaria* (1943).

JAPAN

World War II devastated Japan. American firebombing laid waste to the largest cities, and the dropping of atomic bombs on Hiroshima and Nagasaki left casualties and long-term suffering on an unprecedented scale. By the time Japan surrendered on August 15, 1945, it had lost almost 8 million soldiers and over 600,000 civilians. U.S. forces moved to occupy Japan, directing it toward allegiance with the "First World."

The Occupation was administered by General Douglas MacArthur; both he and his official bureaucracy were known as Supreme Commander of the Allied Powers (SCAP). SCAP's goal was to remake Japanese society. The large, family-run conglomerates, known as *zaibatsu*, were dissolved. Rural landlords' estates were given to tenant farmers. Universities were created, and the country had a new constitution. Women were granted the vote, and divorce and inheritance laws were liberalized.

The 1949 Chinese revolution made the American government fear the spread of communism throughout Asia. Japan was designated Asia's bulwark of western capitalism and democracy. In this Cold War atmosphere, some SCAP reforms, such as the encouragement of labor unions, were rapidly scaled back. With American economic assistance the economy was rebuilt. When the Korean War (1950–1953) gave Japan a crucial strategic role and a source of war-related business, the country began a period of unprecedented economic growth.

SCAP officials took a keen interest in the film industry. They reviewed wartime productions for "feudalistic" and "nationalistic" content. Hundreds of films were banned, many of them burned. SCAP encouraged films on democratic themes, such as women's rights and the struggle against militarism, and even insisted that modernization should include kissing scenes (long forbidden by Japanese tradition). But not wishing to strengthen left-wing sentiments, SCAP also discouraged films criticizing Japanese militarism or the wartime suppression of civil rights.

During the war, the film industry had consolidated its forces under three companies: Shochiku, Toho, and Daiei. (See p. 280.) Under Occupation auspices, independent production grew considerably, but the three vertically integrated firms controlled distribution and exhibition. The companies worked with SCAP authorities to plan films that obeyed the new policies. In turn, SCAP restrained labor activities which threatened to disrupt the studios.

With relative stability in the production sector, other companies could enter the market. During a 1946 strike at Toho, one union faction went off to form an alternative company, Shintoho ("New Toho"). At first, Shintoho shared distribution and theaters with the parent company, but in 1950, the units formally split into two vertically integrated firms. In 1951, Toei ("Eastern Film Company") also entered the field. By building theaters in the center of urban traffic and by winning control of the cheaper double-feature market, Toei became in 1956 the most profitable studio in the industry. And in 1954, the moribund Nikkatsu was reborn. It refurbished its studios and lured disaffected employees away from other firms. Soon it was, like its competitors, turning out a film a week.

The postwar era saw a rapid recovery and expansion of the industry. SCAP had admitted hundreds of American films to Japan, but despite their popularity, the domestic industry kept firm control of the market. By the mid-1950s, Japanese companies could count on 19 million viewers per week—twice the attendance in the United States and five times that in France. Overall, the decade brought unprecedented prosperity, with production increasing to almost 500 films a year by 1960. Thanks to this success, the industry was able to invest in the Fujicolor process (first seen in *Carmen Comes Home*, 1951) and in widescreen technology, which quickly became standard in Japanese studios.

Japanese cinema also burst onto the international scene. Masaichi Nagata, head of Daiei, began to concentrate on foreign markets. His breakthrough was *Rashomon*, which won the Golden Lion at the Venice Film Festival of 1951 and the Academy Award for the best foreign film. Though hardly a typical Japanese film, it immediately drew worldwide attention. Nagata began producing high-quality costume pictures suitable for export. "America was making action pictures," he explained. "France had love stories, and Italy realism. So I chose to approach the world market with the appeal of Japanese historical subjects. Old Japan is more exotic than Westernized Japan is to Westerners."[1] Such Daiei films as *Ugetsu Monogatari* (1953), *Sansho the Bailiff* (1954), and *Gate of Hell* (1954) won festival awards and increased western audiences' appetite for Japanese cinema.

Banned during the Occupation, historical films (*jidai-geki*) reappeared soon after the Americans had departed in 1952. The swordfight movie (*chambara*) remained the staple product, while more dignified *jidai-geki*, principally Teinosuke Kinugasa's *Gate of Hell* and Akira Kurosawa's *Seven Samurai* (1954), renewed the genre.

Still, Japanese production concentrated on the broad category of *gendai-geki*, the film set in the contemporary period. This type included extreme leftist films, pacifist and antinuclear films, "salaryman" comedies, musicals, films about delinquent youths, and monster movies (e.g., *Godzilla*, 1954). Most popular were the *shomin-geki*, or films of ordinary daily life. These melodramas of family crises or young romance sustained entire studios and often became sensational hits. Such films were seldom exported because they were regarded as too mundane and slowly paced for the international audience.

Directors who had made their initial successes in the 1920s and 1930s continued to play central roles in the postwar era. For example, Kinugasa continued to be known for his quality *jidai-geki*. His postwar production of *Actress* (1947), based on the life of a pioneer of modern Japanese theater, is less typical of his output than the florid *Gate of Hell* (1954). Shot on Eastman Color stock, the film self-consciously borrowed techniques of Japanese scroll painting, not only in its color schemes but also in its high-angle views (Fig. 18.3). Less famous than Kinugasa's films was the work of Hiroshi Shimizu,

Fig. 18.3 A high-angle shot in *Gate of Hell* recalling the "floating perspective" of Japanese prints.

who continued to produce excellent films about children. His *Children of the Beehive* (1948) used nonprofessional actors and real locations to portray the plight of war orphans. Shimizu founded an orphanage and used many of the children as players in subsequent films.

Mikio Naruse, who had worked for various studios in the 1930s, made several outstanding *shomin-geki* films for Toho, Shintoho, and Daiei. *Repast* (1951), *Lightning* (1952), *Mother* (1952), *Floating Clouds* (1955), and *Flowing* (1956) center on relations between mother and daughter, aunt and niece, sister and sister. In these dark melodramas, set in working-class neighborhoods, characters are plagued by sickness, debt, and jealousy. Hideko Takamine, one of the most accomplished actresses of the postwar period, often takes the role of the suffering heroine.

Less bleak is the postwar work of Heinosuke Gosho, who tempers the *shomin-geki* with muted lyricism. *Where Chimneys Are Seen* (1953), for example, tells a tale of marital mistrust, but Gosho lightens it with a wry motif: from different vantage points in the neighborhood, the same group of chimneys seems to be two, or three, or four. This hint that one's situation may seem different from different standpoints makes the married couple's tribulations seem less tragic than they believe.

The two most distinguished old masters of the postwar period were Kenji Mizoguchi and Yasujiro Ozu. As in the 1930s, Mizoguchi was drawn to social-problem films centering on women's suffering, and SCAP authorities were highly encouraging. *Victory of Women* (1946) presents a female attorney defending a woman who in a burst of mad despair has killed her child. *Women of the Night* (1948) portrays the life of prostitutes, a subject Mizoguchi was to take up again in his last work, *Street of Shame* (1956). In the same period, Mizoguchi launched a string of unique historical films with *The Life of Oharu* (1952), a somber adaptation of a literary classic. Mizoguchi's old associate Nagata saw the export possibilities in such prestigious fare, so under the auspices of the Daiei company Mizoguchi went on to make *Ugetsu Monogatari* ("A Tale of Ugetsu," 1953), *Sansho the Bailiff* (1954), *Chikamatsu Monogatari* (*The Crucified Lovers*, 1954), and *New Tales of the Taira Clan* (1955).

In his earliest postwar films, Mizoguchi continues to place figures at a considerable distance from the camera; the ultimate use of this technique comes in the distant and decentered framings of *The Loves of Sumako the Actress* (1947; Fig. 18.4). In more intimate scenes, Mizoguchi tends to film from a slightly high angle and uses wide-angle lenses to set the characters in depth, often framed by doorways and walls (Fig. 18.5).

Mizoguchi's early postwar films persist in using abnormally long takes. The average shot runs between forty and fifty seconds, and some takes last minutes. Unlike Ophüls or Antonioni, however, Mizoguchi often uses little or no camera movement. This has the effect of creating enormous dramatic pressure. For example, in *Victory of Women*, when the mother confesses to murdering her child, Mizoguchi stages the action as a frontal scene in which the gradual, frequently halted movement of the mother and her attorney toward the camera provides an accumulated dramatic impact (Figs. 18.6, 18.7).

After 1950, Mizoguchi's staging and shooting method became somewhat more conventional, using more close-ups and shot/reverse-shot cutting than previously. At the same time, he began to make more explicit use of Japanese

Fig. 18.4

Fig. 18.5

aesthetic traditions. Still working with his long-time screenwriter Yoshikata Yoda, Mizoguchi adapted famous works of literature, both classic and modern. He also began to present landscapes and vistas in ways that echoed Japanese pictorial styles (Fig. 18.8). The picturesque elegance of Mizoguchi's 1950s historical films made them the prototype of "Japaneseness" for western audiences.

In later decades, Yasujiro Ozu's postwar films would take on the same aura. After some *shomin-geki* in a realist vein (such as *Record of a Tenement Gentleman*, 1947), Ozu began a collaboration with screenwriter Kogo Noda that was to result in a string of major works. These films usually center upon family crises: marriage, separation, and death. In *Late Spring* (1949) a dutiful daughter faces the necessity of leaving her widowed father alone. In *Early Summer* (1951), several generations of a family are shaken by a daughter's impulsive decision to marry. *Tokyo Story* (1953) chronicles an elderly couple's visit to their grown, unfeeling children. In *Equinox Flower* (1958) and *An Autumn Afternoon* (1962), a father must accept his daughter's wish to leave the household. Ozu and Noda explore a few dramatic issues from various angles. Usually the film is suffused with a contemplative resignation to life's painful changes—an attitude embodied in the gentle smile and sigh of Chishu Ryu, Ozu's perennial actor of this period.

Fig. 18.4 The stage framed from a nearly illegible distance in *The Loves of Sumako the Actress*.

Fig. 18.5 A characteristic Mizoguchi interior, with doorways and windows framing characters in depth (*Street of Shame*).

Fig. 18.6 Two stages of a single shot: A mother confesses . . .

Fig. 18.7 . . . to killing her child (*Victory of Women*).

Fig. 18.8 The frightening kidnapping scene in *Sansho the Bailiff* relies on atmospheric effects of water and mist.

Fig. 18.6

Fig. 18.7

Fig. 18.8

Figs. 18.9 and 18.10 Ozu's version of shot/reverse shot in *Late Autumn* (1960).

Fig. 18.9   Fig. 18.10

A comparable calm pervades the director's style. The films adhere to the "rules" he set for himself in the 1930s: low camera position, 360-degree shooting space, cutting for graphic effects, transitional sequences that obey a logic of similarity and difference rather than strict spatial continuity. Avoiding the comparative flamboyance of his 1930s experiments, the late films rely on the more muted technique he had developed in the wartime films *Brothers and Sisters of the Toda Family* (1941) and *There Was a Father* (1942, p. 283). Now Ozu forswears dissolves and fades entirely. He stages conversations with the characters facing the camera head-on and looking over the lens (Figs. 18.9, 18.10). His color design turns mundane settings into abstract patterns (Color Plate 18.1). As ever, his camera is attracted by humble objects in the corner of a room, down a hallway, or on a thoroughfare (Fig. 18.11). The peaceful contemplation at the heart of the drama finds its correlative in a style that allows us time to look closely at the characters and their world. This quietude, sometimes broken by sly humor, makes Ozu's films seem undramatic. But he came to be recognized as one of the cinema's most sensitive explorers of everyday life.

As in other countries, many of Japan's most notable directors of the postwar decade began their career during the war. Keisuke Kinoshita's wartime efforts, notably *The Blossoming Port* (1943) and *Army* (1944), were home-front dramas lacking the strident nationalism sometimes seen in the genre. *Army*'s ending, in fact, is ambiguous enough to suggest a critique of militarist ideology. During the Occupation, Kinoshita made one of the first SCAP-approved pictures, *Morning for the Osone Family* (1946). Here 1930s militarism brings on a family's suffering, but the war's end promises them a bright future. Over the next four decades, Kinoshita directed many *gendai-geki*. His most widely seen film in the West is *Twenty-Four Eyes* (1954), a story of a dedicated teacher in a rural school during the war.

Kon Ichikawa's first film, a puppet adaptation of a kabuki play, was made near the end of the war but banned by SCAP. Trained as a cartoonist, Ichikawa acquired a reputation as an efficient craftsman, turning out several films for every major company. Ichikawa never specialized in a genre, but his postwar reputation rested largely upon his satirical and grotesque comedies like *Odd Obsession* (1959) and upon several intense dramas. *The Burmese Harp* (1956) shows a soldier forced to disguise himself as a monk and eventually won over to a humanistic pacifism. *Fires on the Plain* (1958) presents the Philippine front in the grim last days of the war, when starving

Fig. 18.11 Ozu reveals in an urban landscape the mysterious beauty of a still life (*Early Summer*).

Plate 16.1 *The Damned*

Plate 16.2 *The Rise to Power of Louis XIV*

Plate 17.1 *The Golden Coach*

Plate 17.2 *The Golden Coach*

Plate 17.3 *Black Narcissus*

Plate 17.4 *Black Narcissus*

Plate 18.1 *An Autumn Afternoon*

Plate 18.2 *The Fall of Berlin*

Plate 15.9   *Imitation of Life*

Plate 15.10   *On the Town*

Plate 15.11   *El Cid*

Plate 15.12   *The Searchers*

Plate 15.13   *Rear Window*

Plate 15.14   *Rear Window*

Plate 15.15   *Vertigo*

Plate 15.16   *The Ladies' Man*

Plate 15.1 *Sinbad the Sailor* (1947)

Plate 15.2 *The Adventures of Robinson Crusoe* (1952)

Plate 15.3 *King-Sized Canary*

Plate 15.4 *Fast And Furry-ous*

Plate 15.5 *One Froggy Evening*

Plate 15.6 *Alice in Wonderland*

Plate 15.7 *Rio Bravo*

Plate 15.8 *Written on the Wind*

Plate 11.1   *Henry V*

Plate 14.1   *Rose Hobart*

Plate 14.2   *Rose Hobart*

Plate 14.3   *Circles*

Plate 14.4   *Rainbow Dance*

Plate 14.5   *Escape*

Plate 14.6   *Abstraction #3 (1939–46)*

Plate 18.3   *Liliomfi*

Plate 18.4   *Two Stage Sisters*

Plate 19.1   *Kagemusha*

Plate 19.2   *Amarcord*

Plate 19.3   *Red Desert*

Plate 19.4   *Red Desert*

Plate 19.5   *Lancelot du Lac*

Plate 19.6   *L'Argent*

Plate 20.1   *Contempt*

Plate 20.2   *For a Few Dollars More*

Plate 20.3   *Innocence Unprotected*

Plate 20.4   *Dracula* (aka *The Horror of Dracula*, 1958)

Plate 21.1   *No. 5* (1950, Harry Smith)

Plate 21.2   *The Long Bodies*

Plate 21.4   *Blinkety Blank*

Plate 21.5   *Lapis* (1966, James Whitney)

Plate 21.6   *Allures* (1961, Jordan Belson)

Plate 21.7   *Bridges Go Round*

Plate 21.10   *The Hand*

Plate 21.11   *The Wonder Ring*

Plate 21.3   *Copycat*

Plate 21.8   *REcreation*

Plate 21.9   *Fist Fight*

Plate 21.12   *Anticipation of the Night*

Plate 21.13   *The Riddle of Lumen*

Plate 21.14   *La Peau de chagrin*
(1960, Vladimir Kristl)

Plate 21.15   *Castro Street*

Plate 21.16   *Hold Me while I'm Naked*

Plate 21.17   *La Verifica incerta*

soldiers resort to cannibalism. Immensely prolific and commercially successful, Ichikawa adroitly varied his style. Many of his films indulge in flamboyant technical tricks (direct address to the audience in *Odd Obsession*, decentered widescreen compositions in *Conflagration*, 1958, and *An Actor's Revenge*, 1963), while others, such as *The Burmese Harp*, are far more subdued.

The most widely acclaimed talent to come to prominence in the postwar period was Akira Kurosawa. Like most Japanese directors, Kurosawa began his career as a scriptwriter and an assistant director. He made several features during the war (see p. 284), one of which, a satiric *jidai-geki* called *The Men Who Tread on the Tiger's Tail* (1945), was banned by SCAP. Kurosawa quickly adapted to Occupation policy with *No Regrets for My Youth* (1946), a political melodrama about militarist Japan's suppression of political change. Kurosawa followed this with a string of social-problem films: crime (*Stray Dog*, 1949), government bureaucracy (*Ikiru*, "To Live," 1952), nuclear war (*Record of a Living Being*, 1955), and corporate corruption (*The Bad Sleep Well*, 1960). He also directed several successful *jidai-geki*, starting with *Seven Samurai* (1954), and including *The Hidden Fortress* (1958) and *Yojimbo* (1961). In addition, he tackled literary adaptations; *Throne of Blood* (1957) was a version of *Macbeth*. Virtually all of Kurosawa's works star the fierce, glowering Toshiro Mifune.

Western film culture greeted Kurosawa's *Rashomon* (1950) as both an exotic film and a modernist one. Drawn from two stories by the 1920s Japanese writer Ryunosuke Akutagawa, the film utilized flashback construction in a more daring way than any European film of the period. In twelfth-century Kyoto, a priest, a woodcutter, and a commoner take shelter from the rain in a ruined temple by the Rashomon gate. There they discuss a current scandal: a bandit has stabbed a samurai to death and raped his wife. In a series of flashbacks, the participants are shown testifying as to what happened after the rape. (Through a medium, even the dead samurai presents his testimony.) The problem is that each person's version, shown in flashback, differs drastically from the others. When we return to the present, and the three men waiting out the rain at the Rashomon gate, the priest despairs that humans will never tell the truth. The woodcutter abruptly offers his eyewitness testimony, producing another contradictory version.

Kurosawa's staging and shooting sharply demarcate the film's three major "time zones" (Figs. 18.12–18.14). These stylistic differences make for

Fig. 18.12 *Rashomon*'s "three styles": The present-day scenes in the temple during the cloudburst rely on compressed wide-angle and deep-focus compositions.

Fig. 18.13 The scenes of testimony in the hot, dusty courtyard employ frontal compositions. Witnesses address the camera as if the audience were the magistrate.

Fig. 18.14 The sensuous forest flashbacks emphasize close-ups, dappled sunlight, and mazelike tangled brush.

Fig. 18.12

Fig. 18.13

Fig. 18.14

great clarity of exposition, but they do not help the viewer determine exactly what happened in the grove. As with *Paisan* and other Neorealist works, the film does not attempt to tell us everything; indeed, it shows us inconsistent events. Like *The Bicycle Thief*, *Voyage to Italy*, and some of Bergman's works, Kurosawa's film leaves key questions unanswered at the end. *Rashomon*'s unreliable flashbacks were a logical step beyond 1940s Hollywood experiments in flashback technique (see p. 388), while its relativistic attitude toward truth made it significant within the emerging modernist tradition of art cinema.

For such reasons, Kurosawa has sometimes been considered the most "western" Japanese filmmaker, but this judgment ignores the extent to which his nation's cinema was westernized when he was learning his craft. His work is indebted to the flamboyant swordfight films and the humanistic social dramas of the 1930s. His commitment to social criticism, his penchant for sentiment and symbolism (e.g., *Rashomon*'s last-minute discovery of a baby in the temple ruins), his knack for picking prestigious projects, his technical virtuosity, and the timing of his international emergence all made him the most famous of many gifted Japanese directors. With the industry booming at home and Kurosawa and his peers representing exportable artistic quality, the postwar decade firmly established Japanese cinema on the international film scene.

POSTWAR CINEMA IN THE SOVIET SPHERE OF INFLUENCE

After the Allied victory in Europe, the United States and the USSR began to establish spheres of influence. The Soviet Union had acquired the Baltic republics in the 1939 pact with Hitler. In 1945 at Yalta, Stalin was granted preliminary control over territories held by Soviet troops, which included eastern Germany, most of eastern Europe, and Mongolia. China's 1949 revolution brought Communists to power and initially aligned the country with the USSR. By 1950 several countries had become Soviet satellites.

Most of those nations had worse economic and social problems than western Europe. Over 25 million Soviet citizens had been killed, and as many were now homeless. Hitler had resettled or massacred millions of Germans and eastern Europeans. Towns, bridges, waterways, and rail lines were destroyed. A 1947 famine took almost a million lives in Russia alone. Because Stalin distrusted American aid, no Marshall Plan funds helped rebuild eastern Europe. Eastern bloc leaders followed Moscow's example in developing heavy industry and collectivizing farms.

A pattern of cultural activity also emerged in the Soviet bloc countries. First there would be a period of tight political control. Writers and artists would be faced with strict demands for doctrinaire Communist art. This repression would be lifted by a moment of liberalization. But then this liberality would be perceived as threatening stability, and the government would enforce new restraints. This cycle of "freeze" and "thaw" would recur throughout the postwar era, and it emerged first in the Soviet Union.

THE USSR: FROM HIGH STALINISM TO THE THAW

The Soviet people lived in wartime stringency well into the 1950s. Leaders exhorted the workers to sterner sacrifices, insisting that the new enemy was the western alliance. Political repression returned in full force. Into prison camps poured captured soldiers, refugees, religious believers, and political prisoners.

The Communist party quickly reasserted its domination of the arts. In 1946 Minister of Culture Alexander Zhdanov, who had led the cultural purges of the late 1930s, launched a new campaign. The policy of Socialist Realism became, if anything, even more constraining than it had been in the 1930s. The writer or dramatist had to affirm Communist heroism and patriotism; there could be no ambiguity about characters' motives or purposes. The party harassed artists, charging them with disloyalty and neglect of political duty. Admitting to western influences, as Grigori Alexandrov did in acknowledging his debts to American comedy, brought accusations of "kowtowing to bourgeois culture." Just as Socialist Realism had stifled Soviet modernism in the early 1930s, Zhdanov's new policies assured that western European trends, particularly Neorealism, would have no influence on postwar Soviet film.

Film production was already a cumbersome bureaucratic process, and Zhdanov's campaign for ideological purity brought the studios to a virtual standstill. All the Soviet "film factories" produced seventeen features in 1948, fifteen in 1949, thirteen in 1950, and a mere nine in 1951. Now a script might wend its way through the bureaucracy for two years before getting approval. Dovzhenko's *Michurin* (1948) and Sergei Gerasimov's *Young Guard* (1948) were "corrected" during scripting and after filming. Other films, notably the second part of Eisenstein's *Ivan the Terrible* (1946), were banned outright.

Films that survived this system operated within narrow genre constraints. Fairy tales showed off the exotic cultures of the republics, and political dramas attacked American foreign policy. Biographies of artists and scientists continued the 1930s trend of Russian nationalism, with Stalin's image playing a central role (Fig. 18.15). "Artistic documentaries" about the war mixed newsreel footage with restaged scenes, portraying a larger-than-life Stalin deciding the fate of civilization. In all genres, the emphasis was on exceptional protagonists. Although such characters were said to derive their strength from the people, the ordinary person usually served only to inspire or assist the hero.

Most of the pioneering 1920s filmmakers became inactive. Kuleshov continued teaching but made no films. Poor health kept Eisenstein from revising *Ivan the Terrible*, and he died in 1948 without making another film. Pudovkin made two films after the war, and Dovzhenko, just one. Only Alexandrov, Yutkevich, Fridrikh Ermler, and Kozintsev worked steadily. A younger generation, consisting of Gerasimov, Mark Donskoi, Mikhail Romm, and Josef Heifits, became the central figures of postwar filmmaking. All had launched their careers in the early 1930s and had produced major Socialist Realist works. Particularly adept in adapting to policy was the Georgian

Fig. 18.15 The scientist receives his reward under the benevolent gaze of the leaders (*In the Name of Life*, 1947, Alexander Zharki and Josef Heifits).

Fig. 18.16 Static, friezelike mise-en-scene in *The Young Guard*.

Fig. 18.17 In Yutkevich's *Tales of Lenin* (1957), old-fashioned technique sanctifies the leader.

Fig. 18.18 *The House I Live In:* A subdued presentation of wartime homecoming: while the populace celebrates with fireworks, a soldier's greatcoat is draped over a chair and a reunited couple embrace offscreen.

Mikhail Chiaurelli, whose *The Vow* (1946) and *The Unforgettable Year 1919* (1951) took Stalin worship to dizzy heights.

All directors were vulnerable to criticism, however, and so they retreated into a uniformity of style. The inflated tendencies of the wartime cinema (see p. 303) were carried to extremes. The "artistic documentaries" showed the nation's leaders brooding in huge offices or striding down colossal corridors. In Chiaurelli's *The Fall of Berlin* (1949), the reunion of the couple takes place before a huge crowd, with Stalin towering above all (Color Plate 18.2). Even the more intimate *Young Guard* uses lengthy takes and long shots to present its heroes as a monumental ensemble (Fig. 18.16). Postwar Socialist Realist cinema was even more rigid and academic than the 1930s version.

The ponderousness of this approach soon became evident. In 1952, party spokesmen complained that most films lacked conflict: the fear of censorship had created blandness. At the party congress of the same year, the leadership demanded an increase in film output. The production process smoothed out. Now scripts about ordinary persons could be accepted, as long as the Communist party still played a positive role in the story. There emerged the short-lived genre of the "three-person film," centering on a husband-wife-lover conflict that is ultimately resolved by the intervention of a sympathetic party representative. Pudovkin's last film, *The Return of Vasily Bortnikov* (1954), exemplifies this trend.

Stalin's death in March 1953 triggered a power struggle that five years later would carry Nikita Khrushchev to leadership. In the course of the years 1953–1958, known broadly as the "Thaw," the party undertook some reforms. Taxes were lowered, thousands of political prisoners were freed from the camps, and the government invested in education and research. Most improvements were aimed at securing popular support, but in comparison with Stalin's reign, the Thaw proved liberating.

Reform crept into the film industry. New screenwriters were recruited; censorship was lightened. The biographical pictures and the artistic documentary went into decline. With "peaceful coexistence" now the official policy, Cold War subjects were played down. Comedies and musicals returned to favor. The republics' studios revived. By 1957 production had risen to ninety-two films.

Many directors of the older generation continued to turn out didactic, doctrinaire works (Fig. 18.17). But as "Make room for youth!" became a rallying cry, a number of recent graduates of the film school VGIK launched their careers. For example, Lev Kulidzhanov and Jakov Segel's muted *The House I Live In* (1957) traces the intertwined destinies of families in a housing complex before and during the war (Fig. 18.18).

In 1956, Khrushchev boldly attacked Stalin's dictatorial policies. He singled out the cinema as a prime vehicle of the "cult of personality," denouncing those films which praised Stalin's military genius. As a result, some of the most revisionist films of the Thaw treated the war genre in a new light. Grigori Chukhrai's first feature, *The Forty-First* (1956), portrays the developing sexual relation between a female soldier and her prisoner. The actor Sergei Bondarchuk made his directorial debut with *Destiny of a Man* (1959), which questions a Russian soldier's conduct in a Nazi concentration camp.

Fig. 18.19

Fig. 18.20

Near the end of the decade, two other war films represented a trend toward a new "humanism." *The Cranes Are Flying* (1957), directed by the veteran Mikhail Kalatozov, treats the home front unheroically. The protagonist is far from the "positive heroine" of Socialist Realism. While her fiancé is at the front, she has an affair with his brother, a weak black-marketeer, and suffers guilt over her infidelity. In the late 1940s, psychological conflicts had usually been considered "bourgeois," but *The Cranes Are Flying* shows that they had gained official sanction. Kalatozov relies upon the conventional deep-focus style (see Fig. 18.1), but he also experiments with hand-held camerawork and slow-motion shots, techniques that would become common in the 1960s. The film's optical subjectivity and imaginary sequences link it to trends in the European art cinema. Its modern look helped *The Cranes Are Flying* win the Grand Prize at the 1958 Cannes Film Festival.

The sense of renewal was strengthened by Chukhrai's World War II drama *Ballad of a Soldier* (1958). The teenage infantryman Alexei is granted a brief furlough to visit his mother. In the course of his trip, he encounters people coping with the problems of the war. He falls in love with a refugee girl. He reaches home so late that he must leave immediately. Since Chukhrai has opened the film by telling us that Alexei eventually died on the front, his final embrace of his mother (Fig. 18.19) becomes particularly poignant. The effect is strengthened by the shot's visual parallel to the nightmarish tank attack in the film's opening (Fig. 18.20). Alexei's fear of the war, his awkward kindness, and his sexual urges distinguish him from the stiff Bolshevik familiar from high Stalinism.

The Cranes Are Flying and *Ballad of a Soldier* display a conventional patriotism, a trust in paternal leaders, and mammoth battle scenes. Yet these and other films moved beyond the stern puritanism of earlier party dogma, offering "Socialist Realism with a human face." The postwar generation welcomed the sight of youthful sensitivity and passion on the screen, if only in the context of official doctrine and formulaic genres. Such films parallel the teenpics cultivated by Hollywood during the same period (Chapter 15).

By the end of the decade, films from the USSR had regained worldwide

Fig. 18.19 The ending of *Ballad of a Soldier.*

Fig. 18.20 The opening of *Ballad of a Soldier.*

prestige. In 1958 Part II of Eisenstein's *Ivan the Terrible* was released to great acclaim, and an international critics' poll voted *Potemkin* the best film of all time. The works of Vertov and Dovzhenko were being revived. New films were winning renown. Although the Thaw soon ended, Soviet cinema was rehabilitated in the eyes of the international film community.

POSTWAR CINEMA IN EASTERN EUROPE

At the close of the war the Soviet army occupied Czechoslovakia, Poland, Hungary, Albania, Bulgaria, Romania, Yugoslavia, and the eastern sector of Germany (to become the Deutsche Demokratische Republik, or DDR). Between 1945 and 1948, Communist governments arose in all these countries—first by forming coalitions with other parties, then by purging the coalitions of non-Communists and dissidents. By 1950, virtually all of eastern Europe had come under Soviet sway. Stalin saw these countries serving as "buffer states" against western invasion. They would also supply the USSR with materials and purchase Soviet goods.

In these "people's democracies," as in the USSR, one party ruled. The state collectivized agriculture, expanded heavy industry, and controlled wages and prices. During 1945–1948, all the countries' film industries were nationalized, often on the basis of film units within the army, resistance forces, or partisan groups. Many filmmakers who had in the prewar period supported left-wing causes received posts in the new structure.

Some production facilities needed little rebuilding. Czechoslovakian studios had served as the basis for Nazi productions and were able to resume filmmaking easily. In East Germany, the Soviets established the state monopoly Deutsche Film Aktiengesellschaft (DEFA) in the Tobis studios and the Ufa administration quarters. By contrast, Bulgaria, Romania, and Yugoslavia had virtually no prewar film tradition. There the governments, with Soviet aid, had to build film production from scratch.

Initially, eastern European industries copied the Soviet structure. Production was centralized, with scripts approved by a single hierarchical agency under the control of the party. Administrators assigned workers to projects. Bureaucrats demanded revisions at stages in the production process. Since distribution and exhibition were also under centralized control, the party might order the banning of a finished film.

One country deviated from this policy when it broke with the Soviet Union. In 1948 Marshal Tito, Communist ruler of Yugoslavia, launched a more market-oriented brand of socialism. As a result the film industry became decentralized. After 1950, Yugoslavian production was organized around independent enterprises consisting of artistic and technical workers. State subsidy of filmmaking was supplemented by a tax on admissions. While the party censored finished films, personnel were allowed to initiate projects and move among enterprises. Yugoslavia's industry became the most "commercial" in eastern Europe, entering into coproductions with the West and hosting runaway productions.

Again following Soviet precedent, the eastern European countries emphasized specialized film education. Advanced schools were started in Warsaw (in 1945; moved to Łódź in 1948), Budapest (1945), Belgrade (1946),

Prague (1947), Bucharest (1950), and Potsdam (1954). Technicians also studied at the Soviet film school VGIK. Such standardized training was believed to guarantee both professional competence and obedience to ideology.

Before the Communist parties achieved full power, left-wing directors worked in a variety of directions. Aleksandr Ford's *Border Street* (Poland, 1948), for example, shows how ordinary people are drawn into becoming Nazi sympathizers. In the DDR, Wolfgang Staudte's *The Murderers Are Among Us* (1946), a major *Trümmerfilm* ("rubble film"), makes almost neorealistic use of the ruins of Berlin (Fig. 18.21) in telling its story of a Nazi sympathizer who remains a powerful businessman. At the same time, however, Staudte draws upon the indigenous Expressionist tradition (Fig. 18.22).

Fig. 18.21 The "rubble film": *The Murderers Are Among Us.*

Left-wing humanism of this sort soon fell into disfavor. Eastern European countries embraced Zhdanov's narrow version of Soviet Socialist Realism. The Soviet Union's Russian chauvinism found its eastern equivalents in patriotic historical epics, revised to suit politically correct policy. Each nation developed its own variant on the war film, the collective-farm film, the factory-sabotage film, and the biography of the great national artist. To help its satellites adhere to the new policy, the USSR sent leading directors to shoot or supervise local productions and to suggest improvements in the domestic product.

Nevertheless, almost every country boasted some films which stretched or evaded the rules of Socialist Realism. In Poland, Ford's *Five Boys from Barska Street* (1954) and Jerzy Kawalerowicz's early work became noted for injecting humanist themes into the formulas. In Hungary, Zoltán Fábri's *Fourteen Lives in Danger* (1954) displayed a Neorealist tendency in its account of trapped miners. Some filmmakers found cartoon films to be a haven from Zhdanovism, and in Czechoslovkia and Yugoslavia outstanding animation studios developed (Chapter 21). Often the nationalistic emphasis of eastern European films of the period offered a degree of distance from Soviet policy: any patriotic film could be taken as asserting local pride in the face of Russian dominance.

Fig. 18.22 The return of Expressionism: *The Murderers Are Among Us.*

Stalin's death and Khrushchev's policy of "de-Stalinization" created a "thaw" within many eastern European governments. But citizens of these countries displayed a stronger spirit of independence and renewal than was common in the USSR. Eloquent intellectuals criticized the Soviet system. Most dramatically, people began to rebel. Strikes and riots broke out in East Germany and Poland; in 1956, Hungary teetered on the edge of revolution. Soviet tanks rolled in to quell the disturbances, but the upheavals revealed popular resentment of Communist rule.

The Thaw brought a cultural renaissance to many eastern European countries. Magazines, art groups, and experimental styles came forth to challenge official policies. Young people fresh from film schools could take advantage of the more liberal atmosphere. Intellectuals looked to the cinema to articulate new impulses. Although eastern European film did not pursue western-style modernism until the 1960s, the cinemas of the Thaw went further than their Soviet counterpart in loosening traditional narrative structure and in pursuing psychological and symbolic effects. During this period the most innovative and influential work emerged from Czechoslovakia, Hungary, and Poland.

Czechoslovakia's thaw was relatively brief, since many of the liberals who would have pressed for reform had already fallen victim to the Stalinist coup of 1948. In 1956–1958 new trends emerged in the work of two older filmmakers. Ladislav Helge, a committed but critical Communist, made *School for Fathers* (1957), while Ján Kadár's *House at Terminus* (1957) presented a study of social apathy under communism. A younger film school graduate, Vojtech Jasný, presented a poetic treatment of the cycle of seasons in *Desire* (1958), while Václav Krška's *Here Are Lions* (1958) offered a modernist use of flashbacks told from the viewpoint of a man on an operating table.

Hungary responded more radically to de-Stalinization, but in the cinema its thaw lasted only a little longer than that in Czechoslovakia. Between 1954 and 1957 three significant directors received international attention. Karoly Makk's first film, the period comedy *Liliomfi* (1954), not only proved a popular success but displayed technically sophisticated color design (Color Plate 18.3). Makk would prove to be one of Hungary's most important directors. Félix Máriássy's *Spring in Budapest* and *A Glass of Beer* (both 1955) introduced strongly neorealistic elements.

Particularly important were two films of Zoltán Fábri, a stage director who had moved into filmmaking after the war. His *Merry-Go-Round* (1955), a tale of reluctant peasants learning the joys of collective farming, displayed an energetic lyricism. Its zoom shots, brief flashbacks (both visual and auditory), quick editing, whirling camera movements, and slow-motion final images put it closer to western modernism than to Socialist Realism. In *Professor Hannibal* (1956), Fábri offered a satirical study of Hungary under right-wing rule in 1921.

Of the countries under Soviet sway, Poland proved to be the most hostile to communism. Many Poles remembered that during the war Stalin had refused to back the Polish government in exile, creating instead a puppet regime and using Soviet troops to help the Nazis wipe out the underground Home Army. The Poles resisted agricultural collectivization, and sporadic outbursts of demonstrations and strikes became a regular part of urban life. The moderate leader Wladyslaw Gomulka proposed a series of reforms. Polish filmmakers took advantage of de-Stalinization to reorganize film production and reexamine the nation's history.

In May 1955, the Polish industry established the Creative Film Unit system, a shift away from the Soviet-style centralized bureaucracy. As in Yugoslavia, filmmakers could join a regional production unit, which would rent studio facilities from the government. Each unit would consist of an artistic director (usually a film director), a literary director to develop scripts, and a production manager to oversee filmmaking. The Creative Film Units, bearing such names as Kadr ("Frame"), Start, Kamera, and Studio, proved efficient; they also allowed film-school graduates to gain strong positions in the industry.

During the 1950s, the "Polish School" became the most prominent cinema in eastern Europe. Aleksandr Ford's *Five Boys from Barska Street* (1954) won a major prize at Cannes. A series of documentaries, called the "black series," undertook unprecedented social criticism. Jerzy Kawalerowicz, who had begun his career under Socialist Realism, offered the complexly constructed *Shadow* (1955), which raises the question of a man's death and then only partially explains it through a series of oblique flashbacks. More famous outside Poland was Kawalerowicz's *Night Train* (1959); another exercise in narrative ambiguity, it has some affinities with the 1960s work of Bergman. Many other directors, most of them young, came to form part of the Polish School, but two proved particularly influential.

Andrzej Munk, a Lódź Film Academy graduate, gained fame with *The Man on the Tracks* (1956). An elderly mechanic is run down by a train; a nearby signal lamp is broken; was he a saboteur? The film's plot interweaves the investigation with a series of flashbacks. As a result, events are presented out of chronological order and some actions are shown several times. Common as this plot construction was in Hollywood and European cinema after *Citizen Kane*, it flouted official Socialist Realist aesthetics. Thematically, the revelation of the mechanic's good intentions makes *The Man on the Tracks* a critique of the Stalinist search for "wreckers."

Munk's *Eroica* (1957), a "Heroic Symphony in Two Parts," offers a similarly demystifying view of the war. The first part, a bitter comedy about a small-time con man during the Warsaw uprising, stands in sharp contrast to the more tragic story of Polish prisoners of war who comfort themselves with illusions about heroism (Fig. 18.23). Munk later undertook a major film about the Nazi concentration camps. He died in an automobile accident early in production, but what remains of *The Passenger* suggests that it might have resembled Resnais's *Hiroshima mon amour*. Apparently the finished film would have moved unpredictably from a woman's memories of serving as an officer at Auschwitz to her attempts to explain her life to her husband.

Andrzej Wajda, the most famous Polish director, was also a graduate of the Lódź film school. After Wajda worked as assistant director to Ford on *Five Boys from Barska Street*, Ford served as artistic supervisor for Wajda's first film, *A Generation* (1954). Roman Polanski, who played a minor role, remarked: "The whole Polish cinema began from it."[2] Wajda's next film, *Kanal* ("Sewers," 1957), created far more controversy, winning a special prize at the Cannes Film Festival. *Ashes and Diamonds* (1959) won a major prize at Venice and became known as the most important film made in eastern Europe.

As a teenager Wajda had served in the non-Communist underground Home Army. In the course of the trilogy, his representation of the underground evolves from ideologically correct criticism of the army (*A Generation*) through a grim celebration of its stubborn heroism (*Kanal*) to an ambiguous affirmation of the non-Communist Resistance (*Ashes and Diamonds*).

In the first film, Jacek, who dies in a crazy flourish standing atop a staircase (Fig. 18.24), is condemned, but he remains attractive in his reckless romanticism. *Kanal*, made at the height of the post-Stalin Thaw, is far more sympathetic to its young partisans. After the Warsaw uprising, they take to the sewers. The film's second half intercuts three groups' attempts to escape through the swampy labyrinths. Each band dies heroically. In *Ashes and Diamonds*, an overtly anti-Communist partisan becomes a positive, even seductive figure. Maciek, a young man grown cold-blooded in the Resistance, assassinates the Communist representative arriving in town and dies in a garbage heap, accidentally shot by a policeman. Although he is a political

Fig. 18.23 *Eroica:* Comic action in the foreground while a fleeing refugee is shot in the distance.

Fig. 18.24 The Home Army partisan Jacek in *A Generation.*

Fig. 18.25 *Kanal:* The alternation of pitch darkness and explosions of light.

Fig. 18.26 The studio-built sewers enable Wajda to squeeze the characters close to one another or thrust them into the camera lens (*Kanal*).

Fig. 18.25

Fig. 18.26

enemy, Maciek, with his machine gun, tight jacket, and dark glasses, became a charismatic figure for young audiences. The role made Zbigniew Cybulski known as "the Polish James Dean."

In the last two films, Wajda found a stylistic flamboyance to match his protagonists' bravado. *Kanal* won notoriety for its suspense, its violence, and its virtuosic style (Figs. 18.25, 18.26). In *Ashes and Diamonds* Wajda's startling visual effects become symbolic motifs. Maciek's first victim, blasted

Fig. 18.27 *Ashes and Diamonds:* Christianity in wartime.

Fig. 18.28 Resistance fighters remember their dead.

Fig. 18.29 The climax of *Ashes and Diamonds*, with the fireworks echoing the fiery wound and the flaming drinks.

Fig. 18.27

Fig. 18.28

Fig. 18.29

so fiercely that his back catches fire, collapses against a church door, revealing the bombed altar behind (Fig. 18.27). At the hotel bar, Maciek and his friend honor their fallen comrades by lighting glasses of alcohol, a secular equivalent of votive candles (Fig. 18.28). At the end, killer and victim embrace in a grisly dance while fireworks ironically signal the end of the war (Fig. 18.29).

Critics have contrasted Wajda's romantic celebration of doomed heroes with Munk's more ironic, demystifying attitude. Both directors used the war film to question the official historical record and to address controversial topics—the nature of resistance, the Polish tradition of gallantry. But Wajda's baroque visual effects, his taste for suspenseful plots, and his ambivalent use of religious imagery made his films startlingly different from most of the eastern European products.

As in the Soviet Union, the eastern European thaws lasted only a few years. After Hungary's aborted 1956 revolution, its Union of Film Workers was disbanded, ending hopes for a new production system. In 1957, a Prague filmmakers' conference condemned recent Polish films and demanded that a single ideological line be followed. Polish filmmakers found their works scrutinized and sometimes suppressed. A 1959 conference of Czech filmmakers reorganized production policy and called for major films to be banned. Most governments tightened control of their film industries. Soon, however, even more nonconformist filmmakers would appear.

PEOPLE'S REPUBLIC OF CHINA

During World War II, the Chinese civil war had moderated as both the governmental forces and the Communist revolutionaries battled the occupying Japanese army. After Japan's 1945 surrender, however, the civil war broke out anew. Despite U.S. backing, Jiang Jie-shi's forces had to flee to Taiwan in 1949. Under Mao Zedong the Communists established the People's Republic of China (PRC) on the mainland. While America considered Jiang's Guomindong the legitimate government, the USSR recognized the PRC in 1949, providing it with aid and military assistance.

During the civil war, film production remained centered in Shanghai. Many scriptwriters and directors were sympathetic to the revolutionary cause, and they frequently ran afoul of strict wartime censorship. Still, some films provided models for the postrevolutionary cinema. Most important of these was the two-part *The Spring River Flows East* (1947–1948, Cai Chusheng and Zheng Junli). The film proved immensely popular, partly because it encapsulated the experiences of many Chinese citizens under the oppressive Japanese occupation.

Three hours long, *The Spring River Flows East* covers the years 1931–1945 as it traces the fortunes of a husband and wife separated by war. Like many Chinese films, *The Spring River Flows East* resembles Hollywood films in its use of a lush symphonic score, skillful editing, and careful script construction. Scenes contrasting the husband's and wife's situations are carefully timed, as when a housewarming party for his new mansion is intercut with a scene of his family being evicted from their shack.

Fig. 18.30 Two of the positive characters in *Crows and Sparrows*, a leftist clerk and a maid, lead a group of children in a song.

Fig. 18.31 Fashionable clothes, liquor, and cigarettes mark the right-wing couple of *Crows and Sparrows* as corrupt.

Two other important films of this era spanned the transition between the civil war period and the postrevolutionary era. Zheng Junli's *Crows and Sparrows* (1949) offers a cross-section of prerevolutionary Chinese society by portraying the various inhabitants of an apartment block. The story contrasts the "sparrows," honest working-class people (Fig. 18.30), with the "crows," the decadent right-wing party boss and his wife who exploit them (Fig. 18.31). Like *Crows and Sparrows*, *San Mao, the Little Vagabond* (1949, Zhao Ming and Yang Gong) encountered censorship barriers under the Guomindong government and was finished after the revolution. Based on a comic strip, it centers on a suffering street urchin who gains hope when the revolution occurs. *San Mao* uses location shooting reminiscent of Italian Neorealism, and the boy's presence in actual celebrations of revolutionary victory lends the film a documentary power.

The Communist party quickly nationalized the Chinese film industry. Many filmmakers welcomed the victory of the Communists in 1949 and provided a continuity of personnel. The Beijing Film Studio was established in April 1949; its head was Yung Muzhi, who in 1937 had made the important left-wing film *Street Angels* (p. 289) and had studied filmmaking in Moscow for six years. The new Ministry of Culture also formed the Film Bureau. During 1949–1950, plans were made to centralize production, censorship, distribution, and exhibition. The popular films from western countries were gradually phased out. Since Chinese production could not meet the demand, films were brought in from the USSR and other Communist countries.

Despite the propaganda value of film, officials in charge of the industry faced a problem. China was mainly agricultural, with 80 percent of the population living in rural districts. In 1949, the nation had only about 650 theaters, concentrated in the port cities and catering to a middle-class, educated audience. Millions of Chinese had never seen a movie and could not assimilate the ideas depicted in Soviet films.

Like the Bolsheviks after the 1917 Revolution, the Chinese government worked to expand the exhibition network and to make films that peasants, workers, and soldiers could enjoy. Directly after the revolution, the government created mobile projection units that could tour films throughout distant regions. By 1960 there were about 15,000 such units. As inexperienced filmgoers gained access to films, the number of annual admissions to screenings also grew enormously, from 47 million in 1949 to 4.15 billion in 1959.

The USSR and eastern Europe were largely untouched by western-style modernism, and China remained even more distant from such influences. On the whole, Communist Chinese cinema reworked popular genres into political message films. Due to changes in governmental policy, periods of control alternated with periods of relaxation, a cycle reminiscent of the freeze-and-thaw rhythm of culture in the USSR.

Right after the revolution, officials obliged filmmakers to take Soviet Socialist Realism as their model. Soviet specialists lent their expertise as they did in eastern European countries, and Chinese filmmakers traveled to Moscow to study the industry there. New personnel were trained, initially at a school attached to the Beijing Film Studio (opened 1952) and later at the

Beijing Film Academy (1956). One noteworthy film of the era is *My Life* (1950, Shi Hui), structured as a series of flashbacks as an old beggar recalls his career as a policeman loyally serving various regimes since 1911. This panorama of his life provides the opportunity for many scenes of prerevolutionary oppression (Fig. 18.32). As the hero dies, his son participates in the revolution.

Strict control was relaxed somewhat in 1956–1957. Citing the ancient Chinese saying, "Let a hundred flowers bloom, let a hundred schools of thought contend," Mao Zedong invited constructive criticism of the government. This period of relative openness was comparable to the mid-50s Thaw in the USSR and eastern European countries.

Production had been slow to revive in the immediate postwar period, but it expanded under the "Hundred Flowers" movement. Filmmakers adapted literary works by leftist authors of the prerevolutionary "May Fourth" school (named for a major series of 1919 protests). One such film, Sang Hu's *The New Year's Sacrifice* (1956), centers on a woman forced to work as a rich family's servant. Despite its unrelentingly grim story, *The New Year's Sacrifice*, like most Chinese films of the 1950s and 1960s, displays polished production values of a type usually associated with Hollywood, including elaborate studio-built exteriors and rich color cinematography. *Girl Basketball Player No. 5* (1957, Xie Jin) creates a more optimistic mood by focusing on young people learning to work together. Again, however, the unhappy prerevolutionary heritage is stressed, since the team's coach had been fired during the 1930s for refusing to rig the outcome of a game. Such films hinted at a new range of subjects for filmmaking, but as criticisms of the government led to a general crackdown, the Hundred Flowers movement ended.

Official policy now declared the need for rapid growth in the Chinese economy, a policy known as the "Great Leap Forward." Among the results of this disastrous campaign was a huge famine, as peasants were forced onto collective farms and agricultural output plummeted. In the film industry, the Great Leap Forward led to unrealistically high goals for the number of movies to be produced, often on impossibly low budgets. More positively, new emphasis on ethnic diversity led to the establishment of regional film production centers, an action that would have long-range effects on Chinese filmmaking. While Beijing and Shanghai remained the main centers of production, during the years from 1957 to 1960, major regional studios were built: the Pearl River Studio in Guangzhou, the Xi'an Film Studio, and the Emei Film Studio in Chengdu. In addition, some significant films were made during the period. One was *The Lin Family Shop* (1959, Shui Hua), which presents a shopkeeper caught between corrupt Guomindong officials and the invading Japanese. Another polished studio production, *The Lin Family Shop* integrates the family's drama with its examination of 1930s politics.

The end of the Great Leap Forward led to another period of openness during the first half of the 1960s. Film production expanded and attendance increased. Prerevolutionary films were revived, and the national film archive (established in 1956) began to preserve them. As the PRC was becoming less dependent on Soviet aid, directors stressed indigenous Chinese traditions.

Fig. 18.32 A Chinese officer who serves the Japanese occupation government is seen surrounded by his instruments of torture in *My Life*.

Fig. 18.33 The climactic scene in *Serfs*, as the Tibetan hero honors the Chinese soldier who has saved him.

Fig. 18.34 Chunhua, right, is shocked when Yuehong shows up backstage late and tipsy in *Two Stage Sisters*.

As a result of this new interest in Chinese life, more films began dealing with the nation's fifty-five distinct minorities. Some films featured these minorities simply in order to display picturesque cultures. *Ashma* (1964, Liu Qiong), for example, is a pretty widescreen musical based on a legend of the Bai minority. Other films aimed to show a minority becoming united with the general population. In Li Jun's *Serfs* (1963) Tibetan peasants are oppressed by feudal landowners and religious leaders. The Chinese army liberates the serfs, with one soldier giving his life to save the hero. The hero pays tribute to him by spreading a traditional Tibetan friendship scarf across his corpse (Fig. 18.33). Like many Chinese films, *Serfs* introduces an elaborate metaphor of revolutionary struggle; the protagonist is struck dumb by a Buddhist priest's curse. Only in the final scene, when the victorious crowd cheers Chairman Mao outside the hero's hospital room, does he regain his voice, declaring, "I have so much to say."

There was also a renewal of the historical film. *Naval Battle of 1894* (1962, Lin Nong) is set during the Opium Wars and deals with an admiral trying to lead his men in a patriotic fashion in the face of governmental corruption. Skillful filming of elaborate miniature ships gives the film an epic quality. In the final scene the hero defiantly steers his ship into the enemy fleet; this is intercut with waves crashing on a coast, metaphorically suggesting the rebellion soon to begin.

Many films continued to glorify the ordinary individual who escapes from oppression by discovering the revolutionary movement. The most important director of this era, Xie Jin, proved adept at combining melodramatic narratives with political concerns. His *The Red Detachment of Women* (1961) tells of a poor serf who escapes from her tyrannical master and joins a revolutionary brigade made up of women. At first driven by revenge, she gradually learns to fight for the good of society. *Red Detachment* is enthusiastically propagandistic, using stirring music and energetic action sequences to create larger-than-life heroes.

Xie's most well-known film in the West is *Two Stage Sisters* (1965). When the protagonists become theater stars, Chunhua remains true to her art, while Yuehong succumbs to luxury and drink (Fig. 18.34). After the revolution the sisters bring plays to the peasants. Theater becomes another metaphor for revolution; Chunhua has yearned to have her own stage, but at the end she realizes that "we now have the biggest one"—all of China.

Xie's narrative unfolds in a manner worthy of the glossiest American productions. "*Two Stage Sisters* has a Hollywood quality to it, I think, especially in its structure, the way I shot it, the way I put it together."[3] As in many Chinese films of the period, elaborate camera movements combine with vibrant color design. When Chunhua is pilloried for defending Yuehong from a landowner's lustful advances, a track-back reveals a crowd and a vast set (Color Plate 18.4).

Such attempts to combine entertainment, high-level production values, diverse subject matter, and ideological education came to an abrupt end in 1966. In that year, huge political changes brought about by the Cultural Revolution drove many filmmakers into prolonged inactivity.

INDIA

Of the world's film output in the postwar years, a large share was contributed by India. During this period Indian films also began to win international renown.

The national independence movement achieved victory when the British government divided its colonial territory into the predominantly Hindu nation of India and the predominantly Moslem one of Pakistan. Although the partition was far from peaceful, India became independent in August 1947. Prime Minister Jawaharlal Nehru undertook many reforms, notably the abolition of the caste system and the promotion of civil rights for women. Nehru also pursued a policy of "nonalignment" that sought to steer a course between the western and Soviet powers.

Even after partition, India remained very diverse. As a republic, it was a union of states, each with its own culture, languages, and traditions. Most people were illiterate and lived in abject poverty. Population was increasing, reaching 440 million in 1961. Although most people lived in the countryside, the wartime boom brought many to the cities.

For both farmers and urban workers, cinema quickly became the principal entertainment. But Bombay Talkies, Prabhat, New Theatres, and other established studios owned no theaters and could not take advantage of the market (p. 287). After the studios collapsed as production firms, they rented their facilities to the hundreds of independent producers.

Banks avoided investing in motion pictures, so producers often financed projects with advances from distributors and exhibitors. But this arrangement gave distributors and exhibitors enormous control over scripts, casts, and budgets. The result was a cutthroat market in which many films remained unfinished, hits produced dozens of copies and sequels, and bankable stars worked in six to ten films at any one moment. Nevertheless, annual outputs soared, hovering between 250 and 325 films well into the early 1960s.

The government largely ignored this chaotic situation. Increasing taxes on filmgoing only intensified producers' frenzied bids for hits. A 1951 Film Enquiry Committee report recommended several reforms, including formation of a film training school, a national archive, and the Film Finance Corporation to help fund quality films. It took a decade before these agencies were established. Another initiative of the early 1950s, the creation of the Central Board of Film Censors, had more immediate impact. Coordinating the censorship agencies in the major film-producing regions, the board forbade sexual scenes (including kissing and "indecorous dancing"), as well as politically controversial material.

The exhibition-controlled market, the absence of government regulation, and the strict censorship encouraged standardized filmmaking. Most of the genres established in the 1930s continued, but the "historical," the "mythological" (stories drawn from Hindu religious epics), and the "devotional" (tales of gods and saints) became less popular than the "social," which took place in the present and might be a comedy, thriller, or melodrama.

More grandiose was the historical superproduction, initiated by *Chan-*

Fig. 18.35 The drum dance in *Chandralekha*, from Vasan, the self-proclaimed Cecil B. De Mille of India.

dralekha (1948), the biggest box-office hit of the decade. *Chandralekha* was produced and directed by S. S. Vasan, who set his tale of adventure and romance in huge sets and amidst massive crowds. Scenes like the spectacular drum dance (Fig. 18.35) sent producers scrambling for even bigger budgets. A decade later, a vogue for *dacoit* (rural outlaw) films appeared in the wake of *Gunga Jumna* (1961), another milestone in big production values.

While regional production grew during the two decades after the war, the national market was dominated by films in Hindi, the principal language. After the war Bombay was still the center of this "all-India" filmmaking. The India-Pakistan partition had cut the market for Bengali-language films by over half, so Calcutta companies scaled back or began making films in Hindi. After *Chandralekha*, Madras, in southern India, became a production center, and by the end of the 1950s its output surpassed Bombay's; but it too turned out many Hindi-language products.

The postwar Hindi film became highly standardized. Like many Hollywood films, it centers on a romantic or sentimental main plot, adds a comic subplot, and finishes with a happy ending. Since the coming of sound, virtually all Indian films had interlarded their plots with song and dance sequences. The Hindi film of the postwar era froze this tendency into a formula: an average of six songs and three dances. Even melodramas and grim crime thrillers would have the obligatory musical stretches. The idea was to create a "complete spectacle," an entertainment package that could dazzle an impoverished, illiterate audience. The actor Dilip Kumar and the actress Nargis became huge stars, while the music used in the films became a major drawing factor. (See Box.)

Virtually all filmmakers worked in this popular tradition. Mehboob Khan specialized in socials before making the biggest Indian box-office success, *Mother India* (1957), a melodrama of a rural woman's struggle to raise her family. V. Shantaram continued the populist tradition of the 1930s with films which criticized social inequities. His most famous film of the 1940s was *Dr. Kotnis* (1946), the story of an Indian physician in China; a typical later work is *Two Eyes, Twelve Hands* (1957) about a humane prison warden. Bimal Roy, the cameraman for the classic *Devdas*, moved to Bombay after the

MUSIC AND POSTWAR INDIAN FILM

It is often difficult to separate the history of cinema from the history of other media. In the United States, film was intricately bound up with theater, literature, radio, and television. Nonwestern cultures displayed the same complex relations between cinema and other media. Indian cinema offers an intriguing example.

Out of the approximately 2500 Indian sound films made before 1945 only one did not include song sequences. After World War II, music became even more important. Radio disseminated movie songs, advertising forthcoming releases. With the breakup of the studios, independent producers clamored for successful songwriters and lyricists, who were often as well paid as the biggest stars. A composer might write for several dozen films in a single year.

Early on, Indian film scores borrowed western symphonic motifs and orchestration, but it took the Hindi formula film to create the "hybrid score." A song or dance might draw on any musical tradition, from Greece and the Caribbean to Broadway or Latin America. The polyrhythms of Indian dance might blend with American jazz, an Italianate vocal line, and Spanish guitars.

In films of the 1930s and early 1940s, the actor had typically sung her or his own part. After the war, the task was almost always taken up by playback singers, professional performers who recorded the songs, which would then be played back during shooting and lip-synched by the actors.

Playback singers became as famous as the stars to whom they loaned their voices. Mukesh (whom Raj Kapoor called "my soul") was preeminent among male playback singers, while the outstanding female singer was Lata Mangeshkar (Fig. 18.36), who recorded 25,000 songs (a world record) over a period of forty years. Her chirrupy voice made her

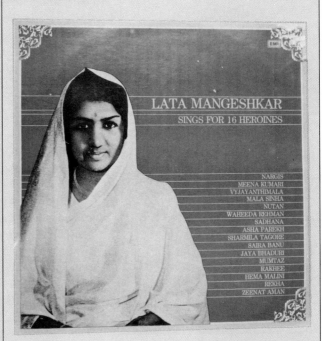

Fig. 18.36 Lata Mangeshkar, queen of Indian film music.

powerful enough to dictate terms to producers, directors, and composers.

Comic songs, love songs, songs of friendship or seduction, religious songs—each type had its place in the film and a use for the public. Eight out of ten Indian cassettes and discs sold today are movie music, and film songs are played on religious holidays and at weddings and funerals.

decline of the Calcutta film studios. His Neorealist-influenced *Two Acres of Land* (1953) celebrates the endurance of a rural family, while *Sujata* (1959) tentatively explores the issue of the "untouchable" caste.

Throughout the postwar era, European and Anglo-American film culture took the Bengali director Satyajit Ray as the preeminent Indian filmmaker. His first film, *Pather Panchali* ("Song of the Little Road," 1955), won a prize at the Cannes Film Festival, and its sequel, *Aparajito* ("The Undefeated," 1956), captured the Grand Prize at Venice. Most of Ray's work runs counter to the commercial Indian cinema and lies closer to the European art film. Yet he and his work do typify important aspects of Indian culture—chiefly the Bengali renaissance of the nineteenth century. The most famous Tagore, Rabindranath, turned the young Ray toward the liberal humanism that is the hallmark of his work.

After youthful training in drawing at Tagore's cultural center, Ray worked as an artist in a British advertising agency. He founded the Calcutta

Fig. 18.37 Durga dances in the rain in *Pather Panchali.*

Fig. 18.38 The beginning of the girl's song in *Three Daughters.*

Film Society in 1947, which brought European and American films to India. His cinematic influences crystallized in the late 1940s: Ford and Wyler; Renoir, whom he met during the filming of *The River*; and Italian Neorealism, especially *The Bicycle Thief*. He criticized the contemporary Indian cinema for its exaggerated spectacle and ignoring of reality. His film work would render Indian life through the subtle drama of naturalistic European cinema.

Pather Panchali, which took two years to make, was a turning point in postwar Indian film. A sober adaptation of a literary classic, it was shot extensively on location and used restrained acting. The story depicts a boy's life in a rural area, culminating in the death of his aunt and his sister. Ray continued Apu's story with *Aparajito*, which depicts his teenage years and the death of his parents. The trilogy concludes with *The World of Apu* (1960), in which Apu marries, confronts the death of his wife in childbirth, and comes to accept his son.

The trilogy's leisurely, "undramatic" action is based more on chronology than causality. Ray avoids dwelling on sentimental moments. In *Aparajito*, for instance, Apu hurries home to his dying mother. In most 1950s Indian cinema, this would provide the occasion for a touching deathbed scene, but here he simply arrives too late. In *The World of Apu*, the death of Apu's wife is kept offscreen. Ray's subdued approach to dramatic moments adhered to western standards of subtle, realistic filmmaking. "At last," declared De Sica's scriptwriter Cesare Zavattini, "the neorealist cinema that the Italians did not know how to do."[4]

Ray's films slowly accumulate moments that reveal characters' feelings. In *Pather Panchali*, Apu and his sister Durga are caught in a monsoon. He takes shelter under a tree, but she spins excitedly, washing herself in the pounding rain (Fig. 18.37). Most Indian films would have made this the excuse for a song sequence, but here, without dialogue, Ray conveys both Durga's childish exuberance and her awakening sensuality. The moment has a dramatic consequence too: Durga will die from the cold she catches. Similarly, in the episode film *Three Daughters* (1961), tradition would have dictated an elaborate number when the little girl Ratan sings to her employer, the haughty young postmaster consigned to her remote village. Instead, Ray stages the scene with subdued simplicity. The postmaster has just finished reading a letter from his sister, and as Ratan starts to sing, the camera tracks slowly in on him (Fig. 18.38). Ray quietly suggests that through Ratan's song, the young man recalls his sister.

Ray's international preeminence doubtless distorted western conceptions of Indian filmmaking. Still, he was not completely cut off from the popular tradition. His films were often successful with Bengali audiences, he made several popular comedies and children's films, and he even attempted a historical epic in Hindi (*The Chess Players*, 1977). His early works also had considerable influence on Indian cinema, turning filmmakers toward location shooting and a more understated acting style.

Ray's opposite number in almost every respect was Raj Kapoor. In 1954, the same year that *Pather Panchali* gained acclaim in the West, Kapoor's third feature, *Awaara* ("The Vagabond," 1951) became a stupendous success throughout the East, from the Middle East to the USSR. Over the next three decades, Kapoor was the master showman of the Hindi film. Kapoor directed and starred in much of his studio's output, becoming in the process probably the most internationally known Indian star of his generation. (It is said that in the Soviet Union parents named their sons after him.) Raj was the most prominent member of a star dynasty including his brothers Shashi and Shammi and his sons Rishi and Bhupendra.

Kapoor gave new formulas to the Hindi film. His scripts, often written by the veteran social critic K. A. Abbas, praise the virtuous poor and satirize the undeserving rich. Kapoor contributes ingratiating comedy as an idealistic, Chaplinesque common man (Fig. 18.39). Heart-wrenching melodrama centering on lovers or orphaned children alternates with farcical humor and erotic scenes. Kapoor portrayed himself as a populist entertainer: "My fans are the street urchins, the lame, the blind, the maimed, the have-nots, and the underdog."[5]

Such show-business hyperbole should not distract from the skill of Kapoor's direction, which displays a mastery of the classical narrative style. He was quick to keep up with western trends: chiaroscuro lighting and low-angle deep focus in the earlier works; a glossier, higher-key look in the late 1950s; vibrant color location shooting in Europe for *Sangam* (1964). *Awaara* has a complicated flashback structure and includes a flamboyant musical fantasy sequence. Kapoor's ingenuity and craftsmanship, no less than his shrewd judgment of public taste, set new standards for the all-India film.

Another major producer-director, Guru Dutt, struggled self-consciously against the conventions of Hindi cinema. After leaving Calcutta's Prabhat company for Bombay, Dutt began as a director of urban romantic drama and comedy and eventually founded his own production company. Like Kapoor, he was in demand as an actor.

Dutt established himself as a major director with *Thirst* (1957). This romantic drama about a sensitive poet (played by Dutt himself) became an unexpected hit (Fig. 18.40). Encouraged, he made *Paper Flowers* (1959), the first Indian CinemaScope film, but this melancholy tale of a film director's

Fig. 18.39 *Awaara:* The ne'er-do-well Raj Kapoor sings to the rich woman, played by Nargis, another major Hindi star.

Fig. 18.40 A production still from *Thirst*, with the poet and the prostitute who loves him.

decline was a commercial failure. After producing another unpopular film, *Master's Wife and Slave* (1962), he died from an overdose of sleeping pills, either by accident or suicide.

Dutt's dramas are dominated by a brooding romantic fatalism. The filmmaker in *Paper Flowers* fails in marriage, in his love affair with an actress, and finally in his vocation, becoming a drunkard whom his old studio will not even hire as an extra. Dutt's sorrowful depiction of the losing battle of the individual with social forces proved ill-suited to the Hindi formula. Unable to break away as completely as did Ray's, his "serious" films are poised between popular genres and "higher" drama.

This somber intensity informs Dutt's song numbers. Long tracking shots pick up the rhythm of the music and move in to and out from his characters' sorrowful faces. In *Thirst*, the hero Vijay sings as he stumbles drunkenly through seedy streets, commenting cynically on the exploitation around him: streetwalkers entice him, a mother sells her daughter to a passerby, a teenage prostitute is racked by a cough. Vijay's soliloquy becomes a wail of protest against urban misery. In such sequences, Dutt pushes the Hindi film away from musical comedy toward the pathos of western-style opera.

Like Dutt and Ray, Ritwik Ghatak was Bengali, but this background marked him in a different way. Ghatak was shattered to see his homeland become part of Pakistan in 1947, and the experience of exile was at the base of several of his films. He became a member of the Indian People's Theatre Association, a left-wing cultural movement that called for a return to indigenous arts and protest on behalf of the masses. In the early 1950s, Ghatak's interests shifted to cinema, a development intensified by his study of Soviet Montage directors and his viewing of Neorealist films at the Indian Film Festival of 1952.

Out of these impulses came his first film, *The City Dweller* (1953), which failed to get released. Returning to Calcutta after some scriptwriting in Bombay, Ghatak was able to make several films, including *Ajantrik* (*Pathetic Fallacy*, 1958), his children's film *The Runaway* (1959), and a trilogy on the Partition.

Ghatak pushed genre conventions to extremes. His only comedy, *Pathetic Fallacy*, is based on the premise that a cabdriver treats his ancient Chevrolet as more human than the people around him (Fig. 18.41). Ghatak's melodramas turned the Indian social film toward stark tragedy. He relished plot contrivances and lurid action from which Ray would have recoiled. The climax of *Subarnarekha* (1965) comes when a prostitute learns that her next customer is her drunken brother; she slits her throat with a scythe. Ghatak saw his harsh melodrama as harking back to Indian theater traditions and to mythical archetypes.

Whereas Ray sought to mute melodramatic conventions, Ghatak exaggerated them. Famous for making his sound tracks "thick," he used music symbolically. In the famous final scene of *The City Dweller*, the "Internationale" is heard playing at a political rally offscreen. Ghatak's later melodramas underscore scenes of suffering with startling whip cracks. In *The Cloud-Capped Star* (1960), the credits sequence establishes a complex matrix of musical associations which are abruptly cut off by the homely sound of rice boiling.

Fig. 18.41 The grotesque cabdriver in *Pathetic Fallacy* and his beloved car (production still).

In the mid-1960s Ghatak gave up directing for a time and took a teaching post at the Film Institute of India. "I barged into them," he said of his students. "I tried to win them over in favor of a different cinema."[6] The results would emerge in the 1970s under the rubric "Parallel Cinema."

LATIN AMERICA

Although Latin American nations had long been politically autonomous, they still depended on the industrialized world, which bought the raw materials and food they produced and sold them manufactured goods. Most of the continent was ruled by dictatorships and military regimes, and there were frictions among intellectuals, businessmen, traditional landowners, urban workers, and indigenous peasants. Populations usually consisted of a mix of native Indian, African, and European elements.

World War II forced many countries in the region to align themselves with the West. Governments formed alliances with the United States while accepting aid under the "Good Neighbor" policy. After the war, the major Latin American countries encouraged cooperation between local entrepreneurs and foreign investors. The state helped by funding or managing companies, and most countries moved back to import-export economies.

In the 1930s, Argentine films had been the most successful Spanish-language product in Latin America. During the World War II, the government took a position of neutrality. As a result, the United States refused to ship film materials to Argentina but sent raw stock, equipment, technical advisers, and loans to Mexican firms instead. U.S. policy, along with tactical errors by Argentine producers, enabled Mexico to become the production center of Latin America.

In the immediate postwar period, Central America and South America were dominated by films from the United States, a few European countries,

Fig. 18.42 *Throw Me a Dime:* Child beggars risk their lives running alongside trains.

Fig. 18.43 *House of the Angel:* Gauzy imagery, *film noir* lighting, and fluid tracking shots of body parts present the hazy present in which the heroine lives.

Fig. 18.44 The woman's past, filmed in canted angles and steep perspectives.

Mexico, and Argentina. Only Brazil offered any significant competition. Two studios—Atlântida of Rio de Janeiro, and Vera Cruz Studios of São Paulo—dominated postwar production. The vertically integrated Atlântida prospered through exploiting the popular *chanchada*, or musical comedy. Vera Cruz, despite its modern studio complex, went bankrupt in 1954.

Brazil, Mexico, and Argentina relied on genres that were counterparts to Hollywood cinema: musicals, family melodramas, action pictures, and comedies. Each genre, however, was adapted to each nation's culture. The cowboy became the Argentine gaucho, singers and dancers became performers in Rio's Carnival.

Conceptions of an alternative cinema emerged, however haltingly. As in Europe, ciné-clubs sprang up. There was also some influence from Italian Neorealism. Fernando Birrí, after studying at Italy's Centro Sperimentale, founded the Documentary Film School of Santa Fé, Argentina. There he and his students made the documentary short *Throw Me a Dime* (1958; Fig. 18.42). In Brazil, Nelson Pereira dos Santos made *Rio 40 Degrees* (1955), a semidocumentary about boys selling peanuts in the slums, and *Rio Northern Zone* (1957), a biography of a famous samba composer. Pereira dos Santos has stressed that

> Neorealism taught us, in sum, that it was possible to make films on the streets; that we did not need studios; that we could film using average people rather than known actors; that the technique could be imperfect, as long as the film was truly linked to its national culture and expressed that culture.[7]

Both Birrí and dos Santos would be central figures in Latin American left-wing cinema of the 1960s (Chapter 22).

A European-style art cinema emerged most visibly in Argentina, where Buenos Aires was a center of cosmopolitan culture. Leopoldo Torre Nilsson, the son of a veteran director, made several features before *House of the Angel* (1957) earned acclaim at the Cannes festival. Told as an ambiguous series of flashbacks, *House of the Angel* reveals a girl's personality stifled by political, sexual, and religious repression. She eventually succumbs to aristocratic decadence, living in a haze of memories and fantasies. Her suffocating life in the present is shot in a misty, mysterious style (Fig. 18.43). Scenes in the past are filmed more crisply, but with an expressionist flavor (Fig. 18.44)—not unexpected in a filmmaker who listed Lang, Murnau, and Bergman among his favorite directors.

After the success of *House of the Angel*, Torre Nilsson formed his own company. Most of his films were scripted by his wife, Beatriz Guido, a prominent novelist. His most renowned later work was *Hand in the Trap* (1961), which won a prize at Cannes. Of strongly European tastes, Torre Nilsson exemplified the international modernism characteristic of many Argentine artists.

Torre Nilsson's success occurred within the narrow confines of Argentine production. In the late 1940s Juan Perón's government established protectionist measures, but in 1950, the government struck a bargain with the Motion Picture Export Association of America that was similar to the pacts negotiated in Europe. U.S. companies and local distributors and exhibitors benefited, but local production was hurt. After a coup overthrew Perón, the military government lifted all controls on imports. A 1957 law gave the industry substantial subsidies, which encouraged independent production. Although output dropped to fewer than thirty films per year, conditions encouraged Torre Nilsson's prestige cinema, which attracted elite audiences and foreign prizes.

By contrast, the Mexican government vigorously supported a popular cinema. Thanks to U.S. assistance, the industry came out of the war strong. The government exempted the industry from income taxes and created the National Film Bank to help finance production. In 1954, it created nationalized companies to market films at home and abroad. In 1959, the government bought the country's leading studio facility; in the following year, the major theater chain was nationalized.

For almost twenty years after World War II, the Mexican cinema was second only to that of the United States as a presence in the Spanish-speaking Americas. Working-class audiences in the growing cities were drawn to Mexico's genres: the *comedia ranchera*, featuring the virile singing *charro*, or cowboy; the melodrama; the *pachuco* musical, centering on zoot-suited hustlers; and the *cabaretera*, or brothel film. Cantinflas, "Tin Tan" Germán Valdez, and Dolores del Rio were the best-known Spanish-speaking stars in the world. Mexican feature output ranged from 50 to 100 films per year. By the end of the 1950s, the industry was adapting to competition from television by exploiting the wide screen, color, nudity, and new genre formulas, such as horror films and Westerns.

Mexican films were often cheap, quickly shot formula pictures; the Film Bank would support only those projects deemed likely to turn a big profit; and the directors' union permitted few young people to enter the profession. Nevertheless, some directors stood out, especially during the "golden age" of 1946–1952. Most notable was Emilio "El Indio" Fernández. His wartime successes (e.g., *María Candelaria*, 1943; Fig. 18.2) were followed by *Enamorada* ("In Love," 1946), an adaptation of *The Taming of the Shrew*, and *Río Escondido* ("Hidden River," 1947), a didactic film about a teacher sent to reform a backward village. Fernández's melodramatic plots showcased the cinematography of Gabriel Figueroa, who cultivated picturesque, deep-focus landscape shots similar to those in Eisenstein's *Qué viva Mexico!* Other filmmakers of importance include Mathilde Landeta, the only woman director working in Mexico at the time, and Alejandro Galindo, who made somewhat left-wing social-problem films.

Audiences outside the Spanish-speaking countries knew the postwar Mexican cinema chiefly through the work of Luis Buñuel. After nearly a decade of working in the United States at odd film jobs, Buñuel moved to Mexico. The twenty films he made there between 1946 and 1965 revived his career.

Buñuel quietly accepted the conventions of mainstream cinema. His first Mexican film was a star-filled musical; his second was a comedy. His filming schedules were seldom more than four weeks long, his budgets ludicrously small. He developed a straightforward technique that was the antithesis of Fernández's showiness. Buñuel's very poverty of means gave him considerable control: he wrote his own scripts, and he could even slip in bits from his memories or dreams.

Fig. 18.45 The dead Julian chortling under the bed: Pedro's dream in *Los Olvidados.*

His third Mexican film, *Los Olvidados* ("The Young and Lost," 1950), depicts juvenile delinquents in a poor neighborhood of Mexico City. Shot largely on location, it opens with an introduction announcing that it is based strictly on facts. These elements encouraged many European critics to see the film as a Mexican version of Neorealism. Yet Buñuel offers no warm-hearted liberal optimism. Instead of the virtuous poor of *The Bicycle Thief,* he presents vicious youth gangs, unfeeling mothers, bitter vagrants.

By winning a prize at the 1951 Cannes Film Festival, *Los Olvidados* returned Buñuel to international prominence. Several of his Mexican films were distributed abroad, and in the late 1950s he participated in coproductions with France and Italy. After the scandal of his Spanish production *Viridiana* (1961; see p. 432), he made two prestigious films in Mexico, *The Exterminating Angel* (1962) and *Simon of the Desert* (1965). Both were more modernist than anything he had done since *L'Age d'or,* but even his entertainment films preserved his Surrealist impulses.

Buñuel charged Italian Neorealism with lacking authentic "poetry." In *Los Olvidados* the poetry is often provided by disturbingly erotic images. Neorealism never generated as unsettling and enigmatic a scene as Pedro's dream, featuring floating chickens, images of his mother bringing him a slab of meat, and a shot of a murdered boy grinning and bleeding under the bed (Fig. 18.45). In other films Buñuel draws his Surrealistic poetry from more conventional plots. The black comedy *The Criminal Life of Archibaldo de La Cruz* (1955) centers on a murderous obsession which is endlessly rehearsed. *Nazarin* (1958), based on a classic novel, comments on the ineffectiveness of naive religious faith.

Surrealism had flourished in Latin America, and like artists in painting and literature Buñuel showed that it was compatible with indigenous traditions. Unlike Torre Nilsson, he created modernist films within mass-entertainment genres. He sought, as he put it, to make films "which, apart from entertaining the audience, would convey to them the absolute certainty that they do not live in the best of all possible worlds."[8] The unpretentious, high-output Mexican industry enabled him to achieve this goal several times in the postwar decades.

As postwar film culture expanded the international market for movies, many of the directors we have discussed in this chapter won fame outside their regions. A handful, such as Kurosawa, Ray, and Buñuel, gained international recognition as innovative and unique artists. The forces that shaped this trend, the search for film "authors," are examined in the next chapter.

◆ NOTES AND QUERIES

De-stalinization and the disappearing act

After Khrushchev's "secret speech" denouncing Stalin in 1956, the leader's image was gradually removed from its place of honor in offices, public squares, and hearthsides. It was also removed from films made during the height of his reign.

Fig. 18.46

Fig. 18.47

Fig. 18.46 *Lenin in October*, with Stalin standing on the left.

Fig. 18.47 *Lenin in October*, minus Stalin but with a Wellesian foreground supplied by special effects.

During the early 1960s, Soviet archivists produced "revised" versions of 1930s classics which expunged all views of the leader. It was relatively easy to cut out shots in which Stalin appeared and redub sound tracks to eliminate references to him. But sometimes shots could not be cut without losing story information. Therefore, optical tricks were used to cover portraits of Stalin and his henchmen with large vases of flowers or pictures of Marx and Lenin. When Stalin himself was in the shot, matte work eliminated him, sometimes in bizarre ways. Mikhail Romm revised his *Lenin in October* (1937) by blocking Stalin out with huge foreground elements, such as a head or an elbow (Figs. 18.46, 18.47). The resulting shots resemble nothing so much as the exaggerated deep focus pioneered by Eisenstein and pursued by Orson Welles. See Alexander Sesonske, "Re-editing History: *Lenin in October*," *Sight and Sound* **53,** 1 (Winter 1983–1984): 56–58.

◆ REFERENCES

1. Quoted in "Industry: Beauty from Osaka," *Newsweek* (11 October 1955): 116.
2. Quoted in Boleslaw Michalek, *The Cinema of Andrzej Wajda*, trans. Edward Rothert (London: Tantivy, 1973), p. 18.
3. George S. Semsel, "Interviews," in Semsel, ed., *Chinese Film: The State of the Art in the People's Republic* (New York: Praeger, 1987), p. 112.
4. Quoted in Chidinanda Das Gupta, ed., *Satyajit Ray* (New Delhi: Directorate of Film Festivals, 1981), p. 61.
5. Quoted in Bunny Reuben, *Raj Kapoor: The Fabulous Showman* (Bombay: National Film Development Corporation, 1988), p. 380.
6. Quoted in Haimanti Banerjee, *Ritwik Kumar Ghatak: A Monograph* (Pune: National Film Archive of India, 1985), p. 22.
7. Quoted in Robert Stam and Randal Johnson, "The Cinema of Hunger: Nelson Pereira dos Santos' *Vidas Secas*," in Stam and Johnson, eds., *Brazilian Cinema* (Austin: University of Texas Press, 1982), p. 122.
8. Quoted in Francisco Aranda, *Luis Buñuel: A Critical Biography*, ed. and trans. David Robinson (London: Secker and Warburg, 1975), p. 185.

19

ART CINEMA
AND THE IDEA
OF AUTHORSHIP

I ndividuals and institutions affect history, but so do ideas. One of the most influential ideas in cinema history is the belief that a director is most centrally responsible for a film's form, style, and meanings. Most historians have made this assumption since at least the 1920s, but it was examined and articulated with particular force in postwar European film culture. The debates of that period, along with the films that were drawn into them, shaped filmmaking all over the world.

THE DIRECTOR AS AUTHOR

Since the mid-1940s, French directors and screenwriters quarreled over who could properly be considered the *auteur*, or author, of a film. The Occupation period had popularized the notion that the mature sound cinema would be the "age of the scriptwriter," but Roger Leenhardt and André Bazin claimed that the director was the main source of a film's value. These two critics wrote for the journal *Revue du cinéma* (1946–1949), which championed Welles, Wyler, and other American directors.

An important statement of this line of thought was Alexandre Astruc's 1948 essay on "the camera-pen" (*la caméra-stylo*). According to Astruc, the cinema had achieved maturity and would attract serious artists who would use film to express their ideas and feelings. "The filmmaker-author writes with his camera as a writer writes with his pen."[1] The modern cinema would be a personal one, and technology, crew, and cast would be no more than instruments in the artist's creative process.

In 1951, Jacques Doniol-Valcroze founded the monthly magazine *Cahiers du cinéma* ("Cinema Notebooks"). Bazin quickly became its central critic. The first issue reviewed *Sunset Boulevard* as a Wilder film, *Diary of a Country Priest* as a Bresson film, *The Little Flowers of Saint Francis* as a Rossellini film, and so on. Soon younger *Cahiers* critics such as Eric Rohmer, Claude Chabrol, Jean-Luc Godard, and François Truffaut began pushing the *auteur* approach to the point of provocation. The first scandal came in 1954, with Truffaut's essay, "A Certain Tendency in the French Cinema." He attacked the Cinema of Quality (p. 437) as "scenarists' films," works that revealed a lack of originality and a reliance upon literary classics. According to Truffaut, in this tradition the screenwriter hands in the script, and the director simply adds the performers and pictures, thereby becoming only a *metteur en scène,* a "stager." Truffaut named a few genuine *auteurs:* Renoir, Bresson, Cocteau, Tati, Ophüls, and others who wrote their own stories and dialogue. Fulfilling Astruc's dream of the *caméra-stylo,* these directors were true "men of the cinema."

In making the issue of screenwriting central, Truffaut was providing a rationale for *Cahiers*'s tastes. The journal had praised those European and American directors who composed or controlled their scripts. Truffaut's initial conception of authorship was also held by *Cahiers*'s rival magazine *Positif* (founded 1952). Marxist and Surrealist in its inclinations, *Positif* shared few of the *Cahiers* writers' tastes, but like them it concentrated primarily on directors who had a great deal of control over the scriptwriting process.

Some of the younger *Cahiers* critics went further, claiming that great directors in Hollywood had managed to express their vision of life without having any say in the screenplay. This hard-core version of auteurism proved most controversial throughout the 1950s and 1960s. Bazin could not accept the extreme views of his young colleagues, but critics elsewhere were quick to take up what came to be called the *politique des auteurs*—the policy of favoring certain directors through thick and thin. In the early 1960s American critic Andrew Sarris began promulgating what he called the "auteur theory" as a method of film criticism and history. The British journal *Movie* (founded 1962) was auteurist from the start. While Sarris and the *Movie* critics were sympathetic to the *Cahiers* European canon, they concentrated chiefly on Hollywood directors. (See Notes and Queries.)

Once we have declared, for example, Bergman to be an auteur because he writes his own scripts, how does this help us understand a Bergman film? Auteur critics argued that we can examine the film as if it were a piece of "pure" creation, like a novel. The film can be understood as expressing Bergman's view of life.

Moreover, considering Bergman an auteur allows us to look for common elements across his films. One motto of auteur criticism was Renoir's remark that a director really makes only one film and keeps remaking it. Recurrent subjects, themes, images, stylistic choices, and plot situations give the director's films a rich unity. Knowledge of the auteur's other films may thus help the viewer understand the one at hand. In particular, the auteur critic was sensitive to ways in which a director's work developed over time, taking unexpected turns or returning to ideas broached earlier.

Finally, auteur criticism tended to promote a study of film style. If a filmmaker was an artist like a writer or painter, that artistry was revealed not only in *what* was said but in *how* it was said. Like any creator, the filmmaker ought to be a master of the medium, exploiting it in striking and innovative ways. Auteur critics distinguished directors by uses of camerawork, lighting, and other techniques. Some critics drew a distinction between filmmakers who emphasized staging and camera placement (the so-called mise-en-scene directors like Ophüls and Renoir) and filmmakers who relied on editing ("montage" directors like Hitchcock and Eisenstein).

Such ideas of authorship meshed smoothly with the growing art cinema of the 1950s and 1960s. Most of the prestigious directors of the period wrote their own scripts; all pursued distinctive themes and stylistic choices in film after film. Film festivals tended to honor the director as the central creator. In a commercial context, Tati, Antonioni, and others became "brand names," differentiating their products from the mass of "ordinary" cinema. Such name recognition could carry a film into foreign markets.

The idea of authorship has become a commonplace in film criticism. Journalistic reviewers now commonly credit a film to its director. Many ordinary moviegoers use a rough auteurism as a criterion of taste, applying it not only to art-cinema directors but also to Hollywood filmmakers like Steven Spielberg and Brian De Palma (directors who themselves held auteur assumptions). Auteur criticism also helped create film studies as an academic discipline. (See Notes and Queries.)

During the 1950s and 1960s, auteurist critics tended to focus on filmmakers who developed the cinematic modernism discussed in the last three chapters. Auteurism sensitized viewers to narrative experiments that expressed a director's vision of life. It also prepared viewers to interpret stylistic patterns as the filmmaker's personal comment on the action. Auteur critics were especially alert for ambiguities that could be interpreted as the director's reflection upon a subject or a theme.

This chapter examines the careers of Luis Buñuel, Ingmar Bergman, Akira Kurosawa, Federico Fellini, Michelangelo Antonioni, Robert Bresson, Jacques Tati, and Satyajit Ray. They are not the only auteurs in the history of cinema, of course, and we are not arguing that they are the best directors. Each was significant in his country's film history, but there are good reasons to examine them in an international context as well.

For one thing, these eight directors typify broader tendencies in world film production. All made breakthrough films in the 1950s. All triumphed at film festivals and won international distribution, even gaining some foothold in the inhospitable American market. The institutions of film culture helped them to fame, and these directors' successes in turn strengthened the authority of coproductions, national subsidy programs, festivals, and film journals. Some, such as Antonioni and Bergman, made films outside their own country, and several more enjoyed the benefits of international funding. Their careers thereby highlight important trends in the postwar cinema.

In addition, these eight directors became the most celebrated exponents of 1950s and 1960s modernist filmmaking. Critics considered that each director had enriched film technique while also expressing an idiosyncratic vision of life. The directors' work exercised wide influence on other filmmakers. Since these directors all considered themselves serious artists, they shared auteurist assumptions with audiences and critics. Fellini inadvertently echoed Astruc: "One could make a film with the same personal, direct intimacy with which a writer writes."[2]

During the late 1960s and the 1970s, not all of these directors sustained their reputations. Most suffered critical and commercial setbacks (often as a result of an incompatibility with post-1968 political cinema). To a surprising extent, however, these directors regained critical acclaim after the mid-1970s, and throughout the following decades their work continued to command attention.

LUIS BUÑUEL (1900–1983)

Un Chien andalou (1928), *L'Age d'or* (1930), and *Las Hurdes* (1932) established Buñuel's distinctive personal vision, and most critics believed that he continued to express it in Mexico, Spain, and France. Bazin found Buñuel's films deeply moralistic; for Truffaut, they exemplified rigorous scripting and a concern for entertainment; for Sarris, they embodied the mystery of a style without style; and for the critics of *Positif,* Buñuel remained the great cinematic Surrealist, attacking bourgeois values with images of savage beauty.

His Mexican films of the postwar decade showed that he could insert his personal obsessions into accessible comedies and melodramas. *Viridiana* (Spain, 1961) may be regarded as the culmination of this trend. The novitiate Viridiana attempts to establish her uncle's farm as a Christian community, but her plans fall prey to the practical cynicism of her uncle's son Jorge and to the rapacity of the beggars who swarm over the farm. Her ideals chastened, Viridiana joins Jorge and his mistress in a game of cards while a child tosses Viridiana's crown of thorns onto a fire (Fig. 19.1). The protagonist's loss of innocence recalls that of the hero of *Nazarin* (1958), trying vainly to bring grace to a fallen world. As *Los Olvidados* (1950) had put Buñuel back on the map (p. 490), *Viridiana,* which won a major prize at Cannes, revived his fame during the 1960s—especially since he had made this blasphemous film under Franco's very nose.

In the 1960s, Buñuel moved toward more distinctly modernist experiments that had been partially sketched in *L'Age d'or. The Exterminating Angel* (1962) entraps partygoers in a house for days, their polite manners decaying under pressure. With *Diary of a Chambermaid* (1964) Buñuel began his "French phase," in which major stars and the scriptwriter Jean-Claude Carrière became central to his work. As he had used the Mexican commercial cinema for his ends, so he began to exploit the conventions of the European art film: the mixture of fantasy and reality in *Belle de jour* (1967), the episodic narratives in *The Milky Way* (1969), the ambiguous interwoven dreams of *The Discreet Charm of the Bourgeoisie* (1972), and the device of using two actresses to portray the same character in *That Obscure Object of Desire*

Fig. 19.1 The nun's crown of thorns becomes kindling (*Viridiana*).

Fig. 19.2 *Mort en ce jardin* (1956): In the jungle heat, ants invade the Bible.

(1977). Some of the films became substantial successes on the art-house circuit, and *Discreet Charm* won an Academy Award. At the end of his life, the elderly anarchist became that rarity, a modernist filmmaker whom audiences found entertaining.

In both mass-market films and art films, Buñuel's accessibility was partly due to the sobriety of his technique. Of major auteurs, he has the least distinctive style. In the Mexican films, he adheres to the conventions of classical Hollywood cinema, including moderate deep focus and restrained camera movements. His more self-consciously modernist films rely on simple staging, long takes, and panning movements to follow the actors.

Buñuel's straightforward style serves to heighten haunting images that disturb received notions of religion and sexuality. In *Un Chien andalou* Buñuel shows ants crawling out of a man's hand; thirty years later, they are gnawing their way through a Bible (Fig. 19.2). In *Susana* (1950), a spider scuttles across a cross-shaped shadow on the floor of a prison cell. The frigid housewife who becomes a prostitute in *Belle de jour* is visited by a Japanese client who shows her a box, from which there issue buzzing sounds; the audience never learns what the box contains.

Buñuel gives obsessions to his characters and then insidiously invites the audience to share them. In *The Criminal Life of Archibaldo de La Cruz* (1955), the hero is shown as a young boy, staring at a music box (Fig. 19.3); he comes to associate this with the death of his governess, shot by a stray bullet at the window (Fig. 19.4). As a grown man, he rediscovers the music box (Fig. 19.5). This stirs in him the desire to kill sexually alluring women. He never succeeds, but after he has practiced strangling a mannequin and drags it away, Buñuel calmly shows us the dummy's fallen leg (Fig. 19.6).

Fig. 19.3

Fig. 19.4

Figs. 19.3–19.6 Four shots from *Archibaldo de La Cruz.*

Fig. 19.5

Fig. 19.6

We, not Archibaldo, make the association with the slain governess, and find ourselves firmly within his morbid fantasy.

Buñuel's modernism emerges as well in his experiments with narrative construction. The films are full of repetitions, digressions, and movements between reality and fantasy. ("Don't worry if the movie's too short," he once told a producer. "I'll just put in a dream."[3]) His plots depend particularly on outrageous delays. *The Discreet Charm of the Bourgeoisie* is virtually nothing but a series of interrupted dinners. The ostensible action, something about corrupt businessmen smuggling cocaine, is buried in a series of bourgeois rituals gone awry: encountering a restaurant's staff gathered around the corpse of the manager, finding an entire army troop invading one's parlor. The film's surface consists of maddeningly banal conversations about tastes in food, drink, and decor. Whenever the story seems to have reached a climax, a character wakes up, and we realize that previous scenes—how many?—have been imaginary.

Most modernists attack narrative in order to turn the viewer's attention to other matters, but Buñuel treats narrative frustration as itself the basis of pleasure. The very title of *That Obscure Object of Desire* alludes to the impossibility of satisfying one's deepest wishes. Traveling on a train to Paris, the wealthy Fabert tells other passengers of his obsessive pursuit of the virginal Conchita. He gives her money, clothes, even a house of her own, and yet each time he tries to seduce her she eludes him. When he pulls away, she returns to lure him on and humiliate him more brutally. Whenever Fabert pauses in his tale, the passengers urge him to continue; their avid curiosity makes them stand-ins for us. At the end of Fabert's story, Conchita appears on the train, and the cycle of frustrated desire starts again. *Obscure Object* can be seen as a reflexive parable which makes cinematic narrative akin to sexual flirtation.

If the fun is in the waiting, not the ending, the Buñuel film will often stop arbitrarily. In *Belle de jour,* the supposedly crippled husband miraculously rises from his chair. In *Discreet Charm,* the Mirandan ambassador finally gets to eat a piece of leftover lamb from his refrigerator. And in the final scene of Buñuel's last film, a terrorist bomb destroys the chic shopping arcade through which Fabert still pursues Conchita. Buñuel's films at once criticize social conventions and play cunningly upon those narrative conventions that maintain our fascination with storytelling.

INGMAR BERGMAN (1918–)

Between 1945 and 1988, Bergman directed almost forty-five feature films. With *Smiles of a Summer Night* (1955), *The Seventh Seal* (1957), and *The Virgin Spring* (1960) he was recognized as a major director. He confirmed his success with two sets of chamber dramas (*Through a Glass Darkly,* 1961, *Winter Light,* 1962, and *The Silence,* 1963; then *Persona,* 1966, *Hour of the Wolf,* 1968, and *Shame,* 1968). Bergman was now at the height of his fame. Critics wrote articles and books on his work; his screenplays were translated; his films won festival awards and Oscars. He became an exemplar of the film director as artist.

Fig. 19.7 Art as a mysteriously powerful spell (*The Magician*).

Fig. 19.8 The ringmaster badgered by his performers in a deep-focus long take (*Sunset of a Clown*).

Fig. 19.9 Expressionistic dissolves open *Sunset of a Clown.*

Fig. 19.10 The Knight questions the "witch" in *The Seventh Seal.*

Soon, however, after some ill-judged projects and financial setbacks, Bergman could not get funding for his films. *Cries and Whispers* (1972) was paid for with his savings, some actors' investments, and money from the Swedish Film Institute. It had worldwide success, as did *Scenes from a Marriage* (1973) and *The Magic Flute* (1975). Pursued by tax authorities, Bergman abruptly began a period of exile and poorly received coproductions. He returned to Sweden to make *Fanny and Alexander* (1983), which was an international box-office triumph and winner of four Academy Awards. After the television film *After the Rehearsal* (1984) he retired from filmmaking.

Into his films Bergman poured his dreams, memories, guilts, and fantasies. Events from his childhood recur, from his earliest works to *Fanny and Alexander.* His loss of a lover shaped *Summer Interlude* (1951), while his domestic life was the basis of *Scenes from a Marriage.* Thus Bergman's private world became public property. In it dwell the nurturing woman, the severe father figure, the cynical man of the world, and the tormented visionary artist. They enact parables of infidelity, sadism, disillusionment, loss of faith, creative paralysis, and anguished suffering. The setting is a bleak island landscape, a stifling drawing room, a harshly lit theater stage.

Despite the obsessive unity of Bergman's concerns, there are several stages in his career. The early films portray adolescent crises and the instability of first love (e.g., *Summer with Monika,* 1953). The major films of the 1950s tend to explore spiritual malaise and to reflect upon the relation between theater and life. The bright spot is often a faith in art—symbolized in *The Magician* (1958) as a conjurer's illusion (Fig. 19.7).

The two trilogies of the 1960s solemnly undercut the religious and humanistic premises of the early work. God becomes distant and silent, while humans are shown to be confused and narcissistic. Even art, *Persona* and *Shame* suggest, cannot redeem human dignity in an age of political oppression. In the deeply pessimistic films of the 1970s, almost every human contact—that between parents and children, husband and wife, friend and friend—is revealed to be based on illusion and deceit. All that is left, again and again, is the memory of infantile innocence. This becomes the basis of

Fig. 19.9

Fig. 19.10

Fanny and Alexander, a film set in a world that has yet to know the catastrophes of the twentieth century.

"I am much more a man of the theatre than a man of the film."[4] Bergman was able to turn out films quickly partly because he cultivated a troupe of performers—Eva Dahlbeck, Gunnar Bjornstrand, Harriet Andersson, Bibi Andersson, Liv Ullmann, and Max von Sydow. His staging and shooting techniques have usually been at the service of the dramatic values of his scripts. His 1950s work applied deep-focus and long-take tactics to scenes of intense psychological reflection (Fig. 19.8). After *Cries and Whispers* he relied more on zoom shots. Throughout his career he drew on the expressionist tradition (Figs. 19.9, 19.10).

Perhaps more distinctive is a technique that owes a good deal to the *Kammerspiel* tradition of Strindberg and German cinema. Bergman pushed his performers close to the viewer, sometimes letting them challengingly address the camera (Fig. 19.11). In the chamber dramas, Bergman began to shoot entire scenes in frontal close-up, with abstract backgrounds concentrating on nuances of glance and expression (Fig. 19.12).

Persona is perhaps the furthest development of this intimate style. In a little more than sixty minutes, Bergman presents a psychodrama that challenges the audience to distinguish artifice from reality. An actress, Elisabeth Vogler, refuses to speak. Her nurse Alma takes her to an island. Having gained Alma's trust, Elisabeth then torments her; Alma retaliates with violence (Fig. 19.13). Several techniques suggest that the two women's personalities have begun to split. A hallucinatory image of a boy groping for an indistinct face further suggests a dissolution of identity (Fig. 19.14).

Fig. 19.11

Fig. 19.12

Fig. 19.13

Fig. 19.14

Fig. 19.11 *Summer with Monika:* "Have we forgotten," wrote Godard, ". . . that sudden conspiracy between actor and spectator . . . when Harriet Andersson, laughing eyes clouded with confusion and riveted on the camera, calls on us to witness her disgust in choosing hell instead of heaven?"

Fig. 19.12 The degradation of the artist (*Hour of the Wolf*).

Fig. 19.13 *Persona:* Elisabeth and Alma struggle.

Fig. 19.14 The mysterious child gropes for an image that is a composite of the film's two protagonists.

Bergman frames the story within images of a film being projected, suggesting the illusory nature of a world that can so deeply engross the spectator. At a moment of particular intensity, the film image burns, yanking the audience out of its involvement with the drama. *Persona*'s ambiguity and reflexivity made it one of the key works of modernist cinema.

Bergman's roots in modern theater and his treatment of moral and religious issues helped convince western intellectuals that cinema was a serious art. His films, and his personal image of the sensitive and uncompromising filmmaker, have played a central role in defining the postwar art cinema.

AKIRA KUROSAWA (1910–   )

In the years after *Rashomon* burst upon European audiences in 1950 (see p. 467), Akira Kurosawa became the most influential Asian director in film history. His use of slow-motion cinematography to portray violence eventually became a cliché. Several of his films were remade by Hollywood, and *Yojimbo* ("Bodyguard," 1961) spawned the Italian Western. George Lucas's *Stars Wars* (1977) derived part of its plot from *Hidden Fortress* (1958). At the beginning of the 1990s, many critics still regarded Kurosawa as the greatest living filmmaker.

Throughout his career, he had been considered the most "western" of Japanese directors, and although this is not completely accurate, his films proved highly accessible abroad. He drew many of his stories from western literature. *Throne of Blood* (1957) and *Ran* ("Chaos," 1985) are based on Shakespeare; *High and Low* (1963), on a detective novel by Ed McBain. Kurosawa's films have strong narrative lines and a good deal of physical action, qualities often believed to be untypical of Japanese films. Kurosawa admits that Ford, Gance, Capra, Wyler, and Hawks influenced him.

Critics looking for an authorial vision of the world found in Kurosawa's work a heroic humanism close to western values. Most of his films concentrate on men who curb selfish desires and work for the good of others. This moral vision informs such films as *Drunken Angel* (1948), *Stray Dog* (1950), and *Ikiru* ("To Live," 1952). It is central to *Seven Samurai* (1954), in which a band of masterless swordfighters sacrifice themselves to defend a village from bandits. Often Kurosawa's hero is an egotistical young man who must learn discipline and self-sacrifice from an older, wiser teacher. This theme finds perhaps its most vivid embodiment in *Red Beard* (1965), in which a gruff, dedicated doctor teaches his intern devotion to poor patients.

After *Red Beard,* however, Kurosawa's films slide into pessimism. *Dodes'kaden* (1970), made after he attempted suicide, presents the world as a bleak tenement community holding no hope of escape. *Kagemusha* and *Ran* depict social order as torn by vain struggles for power. Only *Dersu Uzala* (1975) reaffirms the possibility of friendship and charitable commitment to others.

The first few years of Kurosawa's postwar career established him in three genres: the literary adaptation, the social-problem film, and the *jidai-*

Fig. 19.15 The bureaucrat Watanabe waiting for death in *Ikiru.*

Fig. 19.16 In *Red Beard*, the young intern and a cook (both in the foreground) watch a disturbed girl try to make friends with a little boy amid a forest of quilts hung out to dry. The long lens flattens the space and creates an abstract pattern of slots and undulations.

geki, or historical film. To all these he brought that pluralistic approach to cinematic technique typical of Japanese filmmakers. His first film, *Sanshiro Sugata* (1943), displays immense daring in editing, framing, and slow-motion cinematography (p. 284). Soon after the war, perhaps as a result of exposure to a variety of American films, Kurosawa adopted a Wellesian shot design, with strong deep focus (Fig. 19.15). He later explored ways in which telephoto lenses could create nearly abstract compositions in the widescreen format (Fig. 19.16).

He also experimented with violent action. In *Seven Samurai*, the combat scenes were filmed with several cameras. The cameramen used very long telephoto lenses and panned to follow the action, as if covering a sporting event. Kurosawa began to apply the multiple-camera technique to dialogue, as in *Record of a Living Being* (aka *I Live in Fear*, 1955; Figs. 19.17–19.19). His revival of multiple-camera shooting (a commonplace of the early sound era; see p. 217) allowed the actors to play the entire scene without interruption and to forget that they were being filmed. Both telephoto filming and the multiple-camera technique have become far more common since Kurosawa began using them.

Throughout his career Kurosawa has been noted for his frantically energetic editing. In *Sanshiro Sugata* he boldly cuts into details without changing the angle, yielding a sudden "enlargement" effect. (See Figs. 19.20–

Fig. 19.17 *Record of a Living Being:* In the opening sequence, the supposedly mad Kiichi is brought in for his court hearing. A camera from one side of the set shows him in medium shot arguing with his sons.

Fig. 19.18 A second shot, taken by a camera with a less long lens, establishes them in a more frontal view.

Fig. 19.19 A third camera, from the right side of the set, uses a very long lens to supply a close-up of the old man's rage.

Fig. 19.17

Fig. 19.18

Fig. 19.19

Fig. 19.20

Fig. 19.21

Fig. 19.22

Figs. 19.20–19.22 Axial cutting enlarges an image abruptly (*Sanshiro Sugata*).

19.22.) When using the multiple-camera, telephoto-lens strategy, however, he has a penchant for disjunctive changes of angle. These editing strategies can dynamize tense or violent confrontations.

There is a more static side to Kurosawa's style as well. His 1940s films exploit extremely long takes, and his later works often utilize rigidly posed compositions, as in the startling opening of *Kagemusha*, which holds for several minutes on three identical men. (See Color Plate 19.1.) This tendency toward abstract composition can be seen in his settings and costumes. Early in his career, Kurosawa depicted environments in extremely naturalistic ways: no film was complete without at least one scene in a downpour and another in a gale. But this tendency has steadily yielded to a much more stylized mise-en-scene. After *Dodes'kaden*, the orchestration of color in the image has become Kurosawa's primary concern. Originally trained as a painter, he has lavished attention upon vibrant costumes and stark set design. In *Kagemusha* and *Ran*, the precise compositions of the early works give way to sumptuous pageantry captured by incessantly panning cameras.

Kurosawa's technical brilliance, along with his kinetic treatment of spectacular action, won the reverence of Hollywood's "movie brat" generation. (George Lucas and Francis Coppola helped finance *Kagemusha* and *Ran*.) In addition, his preoccupation with human values comprehensible to audiences around the world have made him a prominent director for almost fifty years.

Fig. 19.23 The holy fool worships the stolen statue in *I Vitelloni*.

FEDERICO FELLINI (1920–1993)

In 1957, after Fellini had made five feature films, André Bazin could already reveal a web of recurring imagery. He pointed out that the angel statue of *I Vitelloni* ("The Young Calves," 1953) reappears as the angelic wire-walking Fool in *La Strada* ("The Road," 1954; Figs. 19.23, 19.24). In other films, the angel's wings are associated with bundles of sticks carried on people's backs. Bazin's conclusion—"There is no end to Fellini's symbolism"[5]—is amply proved by the director's whole career. The films return compulsively to the circus, the music hall, the desolate road, deserted squares at night, and the seashore. *La Strada* begins by the seashore and ends there as well, with Zampano, who has left Gelsomina for dead, sobbing alone. In *La Dolce Vita*

Fig. 19.24 *La Strada:* Gelsomina and the acrobatic angel.

("The Sweet Life," 1960), Marcello is in almost exactly the same posture as dawn breaks over the sea and he cannot reply to the little girl who is calling him.

There are recurring characters as well, such as the holy fool, the narcissistic male, the nurturing mother figure, the sensual whore. There are invariably parades, parties, shows—all usually followed by bleak dawns and dashed illusions. And there are the odd, privileged moments that offer a glimpse of mystery (Figs. 19.25, 19.26). Echoing Renoir, Fellini admits: "I seem to have always turned out the same film."[6]

Fig. 19.25 *La Strada:* Gelsomina mimes a tree.

Fellini's ability to create a personal world on film was central to his fame during the 1950s and 1960s. *I Vitelloni* brought him to international attention, and *La Strada* became a huge success, winning the Academy Award in 1956. *La Dolce Vita* received the grand prize at Cannes, and its depiction of the orgiastic lifestyles of the idle rich shocked and tantalized audiences around the world. It quickly became one of the most profitable films Italy ever exported. With *8½* (1963), another Oscar winner, Fellini created perhaps the most vivacious modernist film of the era, a reflexive study of a film director unable to make the film he has planned. After *Juliet of the Spirits* (1965), a counterpart to *8½* told from a woman's viewpoint, Fellini adapted Petronius's *Satyricon* (1969). This loose, episodic spectacle established the new Fellini mode: teeming, grotesque spectacle reminiscent of *commedia dell'arte,* often lacking a linear narrative. He continued to work steadily throughout the 1970s and 1980s, always to a chorus of controversy. With Bergman, he became the most widely seen and intensively interpreted of European filmmakers.

Fig. 19.26 Teenagers scamper out of the forest to console the heroine of *Nights of Cabiria* (1956).

The films are frankly autobiographical. Fellini's school days inform the flashback scenes in *8½;* his adolescence in Rimini shapes *I Vitelloni,* the story of a band of young loafers, and *Amarcord* (1974), a lyrical treatment of a small town. His childhood fascination with Chaplin, Keaton, Laurel and Hardy, and the Marx Brothers emerges again and again, notably in the mimed comedy of Giuletta Masina's performances. Yet like Guido, the hero of *8½,* Fellini claimed not to know where memory leaves off and fantasy begins. He offers not literal autobiography but personal mythology: a life mixed with fantasy. This expressive side of Fellini, seen most clearly in *8½,* influenced other directors, such as Paul Mazursky (*Alex in Wonderland,* 1970), Bob Fosse (*All That Jazz,* 1979), and Woody Allen (*Stardust Memories,* 1980; *Radio Days,* 1986).

Up to *La Dolce Vita,* the films were firmly rooted in the real world, albeit one that harbored mysteries. With *8½* and *Juliet,* the realm of dream and hallucination opened up. In an important sense, the protagonist of each Fellini film became Fellini himself—or, rather, his imagination. *Satyricon* is a series of fragments unified by a phantasmagoric vision. He launched extravagant spectacles—*The Clowns* (1970), *Roma* (1972), *Casanova* (1976), *City of Women* (1980), *The Ship Sails On* (1983), each announcing itself as revealing more of the director's obsessions, fears, aspirations. For some critics, the films became increasingly narcissistic exercises; for others, they carried the consistent theme that only through the creative imagination could people find freedom and happiness.

There is also a less personal side to Fellini's work. Several of the films

Fig. 19.27 Cabiria shares a look of hope with the viewer.

Fig. 19.28 One of *Amarcord*'s many storytellers.

since the late 1950s fused autobiography and fantasy with an examination of social history. *La Dolce Vita* juxtaposes ancient Rome, Christian Rome, and modern Rome, and it judges contemporary life decadent. *Satyricon* draws the same analogy, comparing the emotionally empty protagonists to hippies. For Fellini, *Amarcord* is not simply a placid look back at his boyhood but also an attempt to show how Mussolini's regime fulfilled Italians' immature needs. *Casanova*'s obsessed, mechanical sexuality can be seen as portraying the protagonist as a proto-Fascist. *City of Women* reacts to the feminist movement, while *Orchestra Rehearsal* (1980) presents contemporary life collapsing under oppressive authority and random terrorism. As with Bergman, Kurosawa, and Ray, Fellini offers social criticism in the name of artistic sensitivity and human values. This attitude emerges clearly in *Ginger and Fred* (1986), which attacks the superficiality of television and celebrates the more intimate performance associated with a dancing team from the 1930s (consisting of Fellini's definitive couple, Giulietta Masina and Marcello Mastroianni).

Fellini's images depend on intricately staged action, and he proved a master of flamboyant costume, decor, and crowd movement (Color Plate 19.2). He happily continued the Italian tradition of total postsynchronization, preferring to control all dialogue and sound effects after filming. The canonical Fellini scene—a vast procession accompanied by lilting Nino Rota music—does not permit the direct sound recording favored by Bresson.

Like many of the auteurs who came to prominence in the 1950s, Fellini steadily turned away from interesting the audience in a story to interesting them in the very act of storytelling. At the end of *Nights of Cabiria*, the heroine, rescued by the dancing youths, smiles shyly at the camera (Fig. 19.27) and then glances away, as if uncertain of our existence. By *Amarcord*, Fellini structures the film around characters openly and casually chatting with us (Fig. 19.28). "It seems to me that I have invented almost everything: childhood, characters, nostalgias, dreams, memories for the pleasure of being able to recount them."[7]

MICHELANGELO ANTONIONI (1912–   )

Antonioni's fame emerged somewhat later than Fellini's, and his pessimistic, cerebral films stood out in sharp contrast to Fellini's life-affirming extravagance. Nonetheless, throughout the 1960s, he helped define European cinema's "high modernism."

Antonioni served his apprenticeship in Neorealism with several short films and five features running from *Story of a Love Affair* (1950) to *Il Grido* ("The Outcry," 1959). His most famous film was *L'Avventura* ("The Adventure," 1960); though booed at the Cannes Film Festival, it became an international success. *L'Avventura* was followed by *La Notte* ("The Night," 1961), *L'Eclisse* (*Eclipse*, 1962), and *Red Desert* (1964), the entire tetralogy constituting an exploration of contemporary life. Now one of the half-dozen most prominent directors in the world, Antonioni accepted a contract with MGM to make three films in English. The first, *Blow-Up* (1966), amply justified Hollywood's faith, earning praise and profits around the world. But *Zabriskie Point* (1969), Antonioni's rendition of student activism, was a financial di-

Fig. 19.29 The modern city becomes a labyrinth that dominates human beings (*L'Avventura*).

saster. After *The Passenger* (1975), Antonioni returned to Italy, breaking several years of silence with *The Mystery of Oberwald* (1981) and *Identification of a Woman* (1982).

Antonioni's historical significance rests principally on his early and middle-period films. During the first decade, he helped turn Italian Neorealism toward intimate psychological analysis and a severe, antimelodramatic style (p. 424). The films depicted an anomie at the center of Europe's booming economy, an "indifference" also portrayed in postwar Italian fiction. Antonioni's early portrayals of the rich could be seen as extending the social criticism inherent in the idea of Neorealism. But Antonioni found numb, aimless people in the working class as well. The sluggish, inarticulate drifter of *Il Grido* is far from the struggling hero of *The Bicycle Thief*, who at least has his wife and son to sustain him.

With the tetralogy of the early 1960s, what Andrew Sarris called "Antoniennui" deepens. *L'Avventura* undertakes a panoramic survey of the upper classes' alienation from the world they have made (Fig. 19.29). Vacations, parties, and artistic pursuits are vain efforts to conceal the characters' lack of purpose and emotion. Sexuality is reduced to casual seduction, enterprise to the pursuit of wealth at any cost. Technology has taken on a life of its own; an electric fan or a toy robot has a more vivid presence than the people who use it. ("It is things, objects, and materials that have weight today."[8]). One cliché of Antonioni criticism—the "lack of communication"—takes on its significance within his broader critique of how all personal relations have shriveled in the contemporary world.

Fig. 19.30 A reminder of the fatal elevator looms over the couple in *Story of a Love Affair*.

These thematic preoccupations are expressed in innovative narrative forms and stylistic patterns. After an increasingly episodic treatment of narrative in *I Vinti* (1952) and *Il Grido*, *L'Avventura* moved sharply toward pure modernist storytelling. Wealthy vacationers descend on a Mediterranean island, and Anna wanders off. Her friends cannot find her. Her lover Sandro and her friend Claudia return to the mainland to continue the search. Gradually, as they become attracted to one another, Anna is forgotten. What starts as a detective story becomes the tale of an ambivalent love affair haunted by guilt and uncertainty.

Other films in the tetralogy take different narrative paths. *La Notte* covers a twenty-four-hour period, tracing the ways in which a couple's random encounters illuminate their disintegrating marriage. *Red Desert* presents an industrial landscape pervaded by ambiguity, in which the washed-out color schemes may be attributed either to the disturbed psyche of the heroine Giuliana or to Antonioni's vision of the blighted modern world. All the films utilize a slow rhythm, with many *temps morts* (intervals of "dead time") between events. Scenes begin a bit before the action starts and linger after the action has ended. And all four films conclude with "open endings"— perhaps most notably *L'Eclisse*'s series of empty urban spaces where the two lovers might yet meet.

Fig. 19.31 The itinerant worker confronts his wife in *Il Grido*.

From the start of his career Antonioni demonstrated a mastery of deep focus (Fig. 19.30) and the long take with camera movement (pp. 427–429). The early works also pioneered the possibility of concealing the characters' reactions from the audience, often by means of setting (Fig. 19.31). *L'Avventura* systematically extends this strategy (Fig. 19.32). The film's last image

Fig. 19.32 *L'Avventura* often presents characters turned from the camera, rendering emotional states uncertain.

Fig. 19.33

Fig. 19.34

Fig. 19.33 *L'Avventura:* The ending.

Fig. 19.34 *L'Avventura:* Two strong diagonals divide the frame and isolate Claudia.

is an extreme long shot of the couple dwarfed by a building, staring out at Mount Etna, their backs resolutely to the viewer (Fig. 19.33). The viewer can hardly feel close to characters presented so dispassionately.

A similar detachment results from Antonioni's increasingly abstract compositions. He reduces human beings to masses and textures, figures on a ground (Fig. 19.34). With *Red Desert,* Antonioni's first color film, he pushed his abstraction further. He painted fruit gray (Color Plate 19.3); objects became blobs or slabs of color. In some scenes, space is flattened by long lenses; in others it becomes cubistic, as blocks and wedges of color fracture the shot (Color Plate 19.4).

In *Blow-Up,* the distancing effects of the previous films cooperate with a full-scale reflexivity. Thomas accidentally photographs a couple in the park; has he also filmed a murder? The more he enlarges his pictures, the more granular and abstract they become. Within a detective-story framework, the film probes the illusory basis of photography and suggests that its ability to tell the unvarnished truth is limited. Like *8½* and *Persona, Blow-Up* became a central example of modern cinema's interrogation of its own medium.

Antonioni's muted dramatization of shallow or paralyzed characters found a sympathetic response in an era that also welcomed Existentialism. Perhaps more than any other director, he encouraged filmmakers to explore elliptical and open-ended narrative. Juan Bardem, Miklós Jancsó, and Theo Angelopoulos learned from his distinctive style. Francis Ford Coppola's *The Conversation* (1974) and Brian De Palma's *Blow-Out* (1981) derive directly from *Blow-Up.* An entire generation identified film artistry with the silences and vacancies of Antonioni's world, and many viewers saw their own lives enacted there.

ROBERT BRESSON (1901–)

Bresson's reputation rests upon a comparatively small body of work. After his first two significant films, *Les Anges du péché* (1943) and *Les Dames du Bois du Boulogne* (1945; p. 342), he made only eleven films in forty years, most notably *Diary of a Country Priest* (1951), *A Man Escaped* (1956), *Pick-*

pocket (1959), *Au Hasard Balthasar* ("At Random Balthasar," 1966), *Mouchette* (1967), *Four Nights of a Dreamer* (1972), *Lancelot du Lac* (*Lancelot of the Lake*, 1974), and *L'Argent* ("Money," 1983). Yet since the early 1950s Bresson has been one of the most respected directors in the world. Championed by the *Cahiers* critics, praised by Sarris and the *Movie* group, his rigorous, demanding films display an internal consistency and a stubbornly individualistic vision of the world.

Bresson's reliance on literary texts gave him some credibility in the period when the Cinema of Quality reigned. His films are often structured around letters, diaries, historical records, and voice-over retellings of the action. Yet there is nothing particularly literary about the finished product. His work perfectly exemplifies Astruc's *caméra-stylo* aesthetic: he takes literary works as pretexts, but he composes by purely filmic means. Bresson is fond of contrasting what he calls "cinematography"—"writing through cinema"—with "cinema," or the ordinary filmmaking that is, he insists, merely photographed theater.[9]

Bresson concentrates on sensitive people struggling to survive in a hostile world. His two 1940s features weave vengeful intrigues around innocent victims. With *Diary of a Country Priest* and on through the early 1960s, a long second phase emerged in his work. Now the films presented austere images and very subdued acting. In most of these works, suffering is redeemed to one degree or another. The country priest dies with the realization "All is grace"; in *A Man Escaped,* Fontaine breaks out of a Nazi prison by trusting in his cellmate; after a fascination with crime, the pickpocket learns to accept a woman's love. During this phase Bresson gained his international reputation as the great religious director of postwar cinema.

After the mid-1960s, the films became far more pessimistic. Viewers who had identified Bresson as a "Catholic" director were puzzled by his turn to the secular, even sexual, problems of young people in modern society. Now his protagonists are led to despair and even suicide. In *Balthasar,* Marie dies after a juvenile gang has stripped and beaten her. Mouchette and the protagonists of *Une Femme douce* ("A Gentle Woman," 1969) and *The Devil Probably* (1977) kill themselves. In *L'Argent,* an unjust accident hurls a young man in and out of prison and toward unreasoning murder. Now Christian values offer no solace: the quest for the Grail in *Lancelot du Lac* fails; chivalry becomes a heap of bloodied armor.

However bleak they may be, Bresson's films radiate mystery. It is difficult to understand his characters because they are typically examined from the outside. The performers—Bresson calls them his "models"—are often nonactors or amateurs. They are preternaturally still and quiet, breaking their silence with a clipped word or a brief gesture. In this cinema, a sudden raising of the eyes becomes a significant event; a shared look, a climax. The models will often be filmed from behind, or in close-ups that fragment their bodies (Fig. 19.35).

The characters' world is rendered in the same spare strokes. After *Diary of a Country Priest,* Bresson began to avoid long shots. He typically creates a scene's space by showing small portions of it and linking shots through characters' eyelines (Figs. 19.36, 19.37). At other times his tightly framed camera movements suggest action by concentrating on details. In one scene

Fig. 19.35 *Pickpocket:* Michel's hand seems almost cut free from his arm as it moves freely into purses and pockets.

Fig. 19.36

Fig. 19.37

Figs. 19.36 and 19.37 Oblique eyeline matches in *Four Nights of a Dreamer:* "To set up a film is to bind persons to each other and to objects by looks."

Fig. 19.38 Most directors would show Mouchette going to school by establishing the locale with a long shot and then cutting in to a direct view of her walking along the street and joining her schoolmates. Instead, Bresson starts with a downward angle on the children's feet . . .

Fig. 19.39 . . . lets Mouchette come in, her back to us . . .

Fig. 19.40 . . . tracks a short way to follow her . . .

Fig. 19.41 . . . and then stops before the school gate. The effect is to cut characters free of locale for a brief moment, suspending our knowledge of where they are in order to concentrate on their physical behavior.

Fig. 19.38

Fig. 19.39

Fig. 19.40

Fig. 19.41

of *Mouchette,* for instance, by showing no faces, Bresson calls attention to Mouchette's discouraged gait and her shabby clothes (Figs. 19.38–19.41).

Bresson also needs no long shot of Mouchette's school because he has evoked the setting through the sounds of the school bell and the students' chatter. "Every time that I can replace an image by a sound I do so."[10] Against a background of pervasive silence, every object in a Bresson film takes on a distinct acoustic flavor: the scrape of the bedstead in Fontaine's cell, the clank of the knights' armor in *Lancelot du Lac,* the rusty bray of the donkey Balthasar. Offscreen sound will establish a locale or will provide a motif that recalls other scenes.

These enigmatic gestures, textures, and details are presented in a highly sensuous way. Bresson's images may be severe, but they are never drab. In *Les Anges du péché* the nuns' habits create an angular geometry and lustrous range of tonalities (see Fig. 13.37). His color films achieve vivid effects by minute means: a knight's armor stands out slightly by its sheen; a mail basket in a prison office becomes a vibrant blue (Color Plates 19.5, 19.6).

Bresson moved toward abbreviated, elliptical storytelling. From *Pickpocket* on, and especially in *Au Hasard Balthasar,* so much is left to the spectator's imagination that the very story events—"what happens"—become almost opaque. ("I never explain anything, as it is done in the theatre."[11]) What gives the Bresson film a sense of ongoing structure are the subtly varied, almost ceremonial, repetitions—daily routines, replayed confrontations, returns to the same locales. The spectator suspects, as the individuals involved do not, that the apparently random action is part of a vast cycle of events governed by God, fate, or some other unknown force.

Bresson never sought the commercial success enjoyed by Antonioni, Bergman, and Fellini. Yet he influenced filmmakers as varied as Jean-Marie Straub (who saw political implications in ascetic images and direct sound) and Paul Schrader (whose *American Gigolo* of 1980 reworks *Pickpocket*). Although Bresson never made his long-cherished version of the biblical book of Genesis, he remains one of the most distinctive auteurs of the last fifty years.

JACQUES TATI (1908–1982)

With true auteurist fervor Truffaut once declared that "a film by Bresson or Tati is necessarily a work of genius *a priori*, simply because a single, absolute authority has been imposed from the opening to 'The End.'"[12] The similarities between the directors are enlightening. Both began their film careers during the 1930s, worked on films during the war, and became prominent in the early 1950s. Both spent years on each film; Tati's output, with only six features between 1949 and 1973, was even slimmer than Bresson's. Both directors experimented with fragmented, elliptical narratives and unusual uses of sound.

Unlike Bresson, however, Tati made some very popular films. Since he was a performer as well as a director, he also became an international celebrity. From this perspective, Tati resembles Buñuel in making modernist films within an accessible, mainstream tradition.

Jour de fête ("Holiday," 1949) set the pattern for most of Tati's subsequent works. A small carnival comes to a village, the townsfolk enjoy a day off, and the carnival leaves the next day. In the midst of the celebration, the local postman François, played by Tati, continues to deliver the mail and decides to adopt American methods of efficiency. The circumscribed time and place, the contrast between humdrum routine and bursts of zany amusement, the bumbling character who disrupts everyone else's life, and the recognition that only children and eccentrics know the secret of fun—all these elements would reappear throughout Tati's later work. The loose plot, built out of elaborately staged gags and motifs rather than a strong cause-and-effect chain, would become a Tati trademark.

Jour de fête also inaugurated Tati's characteristic style. The comedy is not verbal (very little is said, and that often in a mutter or mumble) but visual and acoustic. Like Keaton, Tati relies on long shots that spread elements across the frame or in depth. Changes in sound source or level will shift our attention from one aspect of the shot to another, as when the pesky bee plagues a farmer and François (see Figs. 17.34–17.36).

An even bigger success was *Mr. Hulot's Holiday* (*Les Vacances de M. Hulot*, 1953). The scene is a seaside resort to which various middle-class city people repair; the action consumes the one week of their stay; the disruptive force is Mr. Hulot, who insists on making the most of his vacation. He shatters the routine meals, arranged outings, and quiet evenings playing cards. His splenetic car disturbs the guests, his outrageously unprofessional tennis game defeats all comers, and his antics on the beach bring woe to bystanders. Tati's performance captivated audiences around the world and was credited with single-handedly reviving the pantomime tradition of Chaplin and Keaton. Just as important, Tati the director had composed a film with a firm structure that owes little to traditional plotting. By alternating very

Fig. 19.42

Fig. 19.43

Fig. 19.42 A non-gag in *Mr. Hulot's Holiday:* The painter suspects Hulot of accidentally releasing his boat into the sea; both stand awkwardly for several moments.

Fig. 19.43 Two women greet one another in *Mon Oncle:* The winding pathway keeps them from walking straight toward each other. (Note the fish fountain, turned on only when a guest arrives.)

strong gags with empty moments that invite the spectator to see ordinary life as comic, *Mr. Hulot's Holiday* points forward to the more extreme experiments of *Play Time* (Fig. 19.42).

Back in Paris, Hulot launches a hilarious attack on modern work and leisure in *Mon Oncle* (*My Uncle*, 1958). The windows of a modernistic house seem to spy on passersby; plastic tubing extruded from a plant becomes a giant serpent. Again, Tati's long shots show individuals at the mercy of the environment they have created (Fig. 19.43). The result is a comic version of Antonioni's portrayal of urban alienation.

The international success of *Mon Oncle,* which won the Academy Award for best foreign film, enabled Tati to undertake his most ambitious project. On the outskirts of Paris he built a false city, complete with paved roads, water and electricity, and traffic (Fig. 19.44). He shot the film in 70mm, with five-track stereophonic sound.

Fig. 19.44 A production still showing a portion of Tativille.

Fig. 19.45

Fig. 19.46

The result was *Play Time* (1967), one of the most audacious films of the postwar era. Aware that audiences would watch for Hulot, Tati plays down his presence. Knowing that viewers rely upon close-ups and centered framings to guide their attention, Tati builds the film almost completely out of long shots and scatters his gags to all corners of the frame (Fig. 19.45). Sometimes, as in the lengthy sequence of the destruction of the Royal Garden restaurant, he packs several gags into the frame at once, challenging the spectator to spot them all (Fig. 19.46). At other moments, he simply dwells on a bit of trivial action and invites the spectator to consider it potentially funny (Fig. 19.47). Tati's satire of tourism and urban routine encourages us to see all of life as play time.

Since Tati initially insisted that *Play Time* be shown in 70mm, it did not get wide distribution and quickly failed. Tati went into bankruptcy, and his career never recovered. To the end of his life, he hoped to establish one theater somewhere in the world that would show *Play Time* every day, forever.

He made two more films. In *Traffic* (1971), Hulot helps a young woman deliver a recreational vehicle to an Amsterdam auto show. Simpler than *Play Time* or *Mr. Hulot's Holiday*, *Traffic* satirizes car culture. *Parade* (1973), shot for Swedish television, is a pseudo-documentary celebration of the circus and its audience. As usual, Tati blurs the boundary between performance and the comedy of everyday life (Fig. 19.48).

Before his death, Tati was planning another Hulot film, *Confusion*, in which his hero would work in television and be killed on camera. But the debts of *Play Time* haunted him, and in 1974 his films were auctioned off at

Fig. 19.45 The principal joke is on the left side of the frame, where M. Giffard has collided with the glass door. On the far right, the businessman is frozen mannequinlike in midstride; he will start to walk only at the end of the shot (*Play Time*).

Fig. 19.46 While the millionaire orders his meal from the splotches on the waiter's jacket, the restaurant owner (foreground left) prepares to calm his nerves with an antacid; this sets up a later joke, when Hulot accidentally drinks the fizzy potion, thinking it is champagne.

Fig. 19.47

Fig. 19.48

Fig. 19.47 A doorman aligned with door handles seems suddenly to sprout horns (*Play Time*).

Fig. 19.48 The audience in *Parade:* Only the three women in the foreground row are not photographic cut-outs.

an absurdly low price. Over the next two decades, however, rereleases of all the films demonstrated to new audiences that Tati had left behind a rich body of work that invites the spectator to see ordinary life as an endless comedy.

SATYAJIT RAY (1921–1992)

Ray triumphed in many media. After *Pather Panchali* ("Song of the Little Road," 1955) he made almost thirty feature films. As a commercial graphic artist, he revolutionized Indian book design. He wrote children's books, science-fiction novels, and detective stories. He also became an acclaimed musician, scoring his own films and those of other filmmakers.

Ray's artistic roots lie in the Bengali renaissance associated with the Tagore family. His own family boasted distinguished inventors, teachers, writers, and musicians. Ray brought this westernized humanistic culture of his youth to all his activities. He saw the central purpose of filmmaking as "the revelation of the truth of human behavior."[13] His films' refusal to single out villains links him to Renoir, and his reluctance to endorse collective political solutions testifies to an individualistic approach to life.

Ray's earliest period, running from *Pather Panchali* to *Charulata* (1964), centers on rudimentary human problems. In the Apu trilogy (*Pather Panchali*; *Aparajito*, "The Undefeated," 1956; *The World of Apu*, 1960), the problems are those of growing up and accepting responsibility in a world filled with frustration and death. In his works on the landowning aristocracy (most notably *The Music Room*, 1958), he portrays individuals who cling unreasonably to dying traditions. His "awakening woman" trilogy (most famously *Mahanagar*, or "The Big City," 1963, and *Charulata*) present women confined by Indian tradition and struggling to create their own identities. Whether the setting is a rural area or a city, Ray concentrates on the domestic life of families, courtship, and daily work.

As in a novel by Henry James, Ray's characters are judged by their eagerness to learn and their sensitivity to their surroundings. Apu observes the life around him before plunging into reading and, eventually, writing. At the beginning of *Charulata*, the wife, virtually imprisoned in the household, rushes from window to window, watching the world through binoculars.

The films of this first period reveal a craftsman's approach. Ray gained a sense of firm structure from his study of western cinema and of western music, with its "dramatic" sonata form so different from the open forms of Indian ragas. Ray also developed his style along European and Hollywood lines. Often his shot compositions draw parallels between situations in a before-and-after fashion (Figs. 19.49, 19.50).

The entire Apu trilogy is bound together by motifs of setting and camera placement (Figs. 19.51, 19.52). The most famous motif in the films is the train: glimpsed by the children in *Pather Panchali*, running in the background as the mother weakens in *Aparajito*, chugging through the neighborhood of Apu's apartment in *The World of Apu*. Sometimes the train symbolizes the great world that Apu craves to explore. When he wins a globe as a school prize, he thrusts it at his mother, loftily demanding: "Do you know what this is?" and offscreen the distant train is heard (Fig. 19.53). At other times the

Fig. 19.49 *Three Daughters* (1961): As Amulya walks home through the mud, the tomboy Puglee mocks him from behind a tree.

Fig. 19.50 Much later, Amulya marries Puglee, somewhat against her will. Unhappy, Puglee flees him, and when he goes out searching for her, Ray repeats the earlier camera setup, emphasizing Amulya's realization of his loss.

Fig. 19.51

Fig. 19.52

train is an impersonal force shuttling the family from the countryside to Benares, from a village to Calcutta. By the end, when Apu has reconciled with his son, the train is no more than a toy that can be left behind.

After the political upheavals of the late 1960s, Ray's work began to confront social issues more directly. A trilogy of "city" films portrays weak men trying to survive in a corrupt business world. In *The Middleman* (1975), for instance, Somnath is expected to provide a client with a woman. He is shocked when he learns that she is a friend's sister. Ray's conception of the cost of success is conveyed by cutting from Somnath's playing the pimp to a shot of his father at home, listening to a Tagore song on the radio: "Darkness is gathering over the forest."

Ray became more deliberately "modern." He adapted contemporary fiction by young writers and utilized flashbacks, negative footage, and freeze-frames. Yet he was uncomfortable with self-conscious technique: "As if being modern for a film-maker consisted solely in how he juggles with his visuals and not in his attitude to life that he expressed through the film."[14]

Many of the films of this period reflect the growing inability of Ray's humanism to comprehend the political uncertainties of modern India. His cinema was identified with the liberal politics of Prime Minister Nehru, and as Nehru's legacy faded, so did Ray's belief in India's moral progress. His optimism is more evident in the fantasy films he made for children, such as the lively *Goopi Gyne Bagha Byne* (1969).

At the end of this career, Ray seems to have synthesized individual concerns with contemporary political problems. *The Home and the World* (1984), a Tagore adaptation, presents the 1907 anticolonialist struggle by centering on a wife who breaks with her reclusive domestic life. *Public Enemy* (1989) is an updating of Ibsen's *Enemy of the People* and depicts the youth of a community rallying to the defense of a doctor who finds cholera-infested water in a temple. The film was relevant to an India still suffering from the disaster at the Bhopal chemical plant. Ray's 1980s work persists in asserting that any significant action, political or otherwise, can spring only from the consciousness and conscience of the sensitive individual.

Fig. 19.51 Alive, the old aunt dominates a composition of the porch (*Pather Panchali*).

Fig. 19.52 After she has died, the composition seems hollow.

Fig. 19.53 Apu offers his mother the globe (*Aparajito*).

◆ NOTES AND QUERIES

THE IMPACT OF AUTEURISM

To a great extent, the academic study of film in English-speaking countries arose from auteurism. The premise of individual artistic expression proved congenial to scholars trained in art, literature, and theater. Moreover, auteurism's emphasis on the interpretation of a film called on skills already cultivated by literary education.

During the 1960s, auteur-based courses began to appear in the American college curriculum. Trade publishers launched book series which translated French monographs and gave a forum to the *Movie* critics and their American counterparts. University presses started publishing academic studies such as Donald Richie's *The Films of Akira Kurosawa* (Berkeley: University of California Press, 1965) and Charles Higham's *The Films of Orson Welles* (Berkeley: University of California Press, 1970). In the mid- to late 1960s colleges and universities started film study programs, often emphasizing individual directors. The process by which auteurism helped lay the groundwork for contemporary film study is discussed in David Bordwell, *Making Meaning: Inference and Rhetoric in the Interpretation of Cinema* (Cambridge, Mass.: Harvard University Press, 1989).

AUTEURISM AND THE AMERICAN CINEMA

Only certain versions of auteurism proved controversial. Critics had been ascribing films to their directors since at least World War I. In the 1950s, no one doubted that the films of our eight auteurs could be treated as "personal expression" in some sense. But the young critics of the British journal *Sequence* and of the French magazines *Cahiers* and *Positif,* and later writers like Sarris and the *Movie* group, urged that Hollywood filmmakers who might have no input into their scripts could also be treated as expressive artists. Look at the body of their work, the critics urged, and you will see recurrent themes, stylistic patterns, and narrative strategies. In this light, not only Howard Hawks and John Ford but Otto Preminger and Vincente Minnelli could be revealed as sophisticated filmmakers with distinctive artistic visions. The "French revolution" in critical thought revealed artists in what most English-speaking intellectuals disdained as uniform, mass-produced entertainment.

By the early 1960s, French publishers were devoting entire volumes to Minnelli, Anthony Mann, and other American filmmakers. The breakthrough in English-language criticism came with Sarris's special 1963 issue of *Film Culture* on American cinema. Here he constructed a vast reference text on Hollywood directors, modeled on *Cahiers*'s encyclopedic special issues on American cinema. Sarris grouped filmmakers, ranking them as "Pantheon Directors" (Ford, Hitchcock, Griffith, von Sternberg, et al.), "Second Line" (Cukor, Ray, Sirk, et al.), "Fallen Idols" (Elia Kazan, Fred Zinnemann, et al.), and so on. Each entry was accompanied by a brief discussion of the director's career.

The *Film Culture* issue was expanded into Sarris's book *The American Cinema: Directors and Directions* (New York: Dutton, 1968), one of the most influential volumes on film ever published. Sarris's career surveys became the point of departure for many in-depth analyses, and auteurism became the overwhelmingly dominant approach to studying the history of the Hollywood cinema—a status it has never lost. The most diversified revision of the Sarris approach is Jean-Pierre Coursodon and Pierre Sauvage's two-volume collection *American Directors* (New York: McGraw-Hill, 1983).

Auteurism changed in the late 1960s. A group of writers associated with the British Film Institute sought to make the approach more rigorous by incorporating insights from structuralist linguistics and anthropology. Now an auteur's themes could be seen as organized around oppositions (e.g., desert versus garden). The oppositions might then be reconciled by mediating images or narrative actions. An early example of "auteur structuralism" is Geoffrey Nowell-Smith's *Visconti* (London: Secker and Warburg, 1967); the theory was most fully systematized in Chapter 2 of Peter Wollen's *Signs and Meaning in the Cinema* (London: Secker and Warburg, 1969; rev. ed., 1972).

Auteur structuralism was soon surpassed by a revision in *Cahiers*'s policy during the late 1960s (Chapter 23). The new generation of *Cahiers* critics adopted a Marxist position which treated auteur films as unwitting expressions of social ideology. The most influential formulation of this view was a 1970 essay by the *Cahiers* editors on John Ford's *Young Mr. Lincoln*. Here John Ford's direction was said to "rewrite" a script that could have simplistically celebrated the Lincoln myth. The conflict between the script and Ford's personal themes and motifs resulted in a film full of discordances; these in turn expressed contradictions within dominant ideology. For a general account of the *Cahiers* position, see Jean Narboni and Jean-Louis Comolli, "Cinema/Ideology/Criticism," a 1969 essay reprinted in Bill Nichols, ed., *Movies and Methods* (Berkeley: University of California Press, 1976), pp. 22–30. The *Young Mr. Lincoln* study has been widely reprinted. (See Nichols, *Movies and Methods*, pp. 493–529.)

Cahiers's new approach to authorship was extended during the 1970s by writers in the British journal *Screen* and other publications of the British Film Institute. Examples are several essays in Laura Mulvey and Jon Halliday, eds., *Douglas Sirk* (Edinburgh Film Festival, 1972); Phil Hardy, ed., *Raoul Walsh* (Edinburgh Film Festival, 1974); and Claire Johnston, ed., *The Work of Dorothy Arzner* (London: British Film Institute, 1975).

Some historians have accused the auteur approach of concentrating on individual innovation rather than institutional processes. Nonetheless, some notion of directorial authorship has remained central to most film scholarship. The development of auteur debates is traced in John Caughie's anthology *Theories of Authorship* (London: Routledge and Kegan Paul, 1981).

1950s AND 1960s MODERNIST CINEMA

As we have seen, non-American auteurs were often identified with a modernist trend in postwar cinema. During this period, several English-language critics examined this trend. Their discussions document art cinema's rise to authority in western film culture.

Penelope Houston's *The Contemporary Cinema* (Harmondsworth, England: Penguin, 1963) and John Russell Taylor's *Cinema Eye, Cinema Ear: Some Key Filmmakers of the Sixties* (New York: Hill and Wang, 1964) typify the response of mainstream British criticism to European and Asian auteurs. David Thomson's more offbeat *Movie Man* (New York: Stein and Day, 1967) incorporates both American and European auteurs within a tradition of inquiry into the nature of the "visual society." More explicitly than many of his contemporaries, Thomson made the issue of reflexivity central to modernist cinema. In addition, Parker Tyler recast modernist arguments for an American readership; see his essay *"Rashomon* as Modern Art" in *The Three Faces of the Film* (Cranbury, N.J.: Barnes, 1967) and his influential popularization *Classics of the Foreign Film* (New York: Bonanza, 1962).

More recent and historically framed surveys of modernist cinema are Roy Armes's *The Ambiguous Image: Narrative Style in Modern European Cinema* (London: Secker and Warburg, 1976) and Robert Phillip Kolker's *The Altering Eye: Contemporary International Cinema* (New York: Oxford University Press, 1983). Armes's discussion stops around 1968, while Kolker's moves into the late 1970s. Both retain an auteurist approach in tracing distinct strands within the modernist cinematic tradition.

◆ REFERENCES

1. Alexandre Astruc, "The Birth of a New Avant-Garde: *La Caméra-Stylo,*" in Peter Graham, ed., *The New Wave* (Garden City: Doubleday, 1967), p. 23.
2. Federico Fellini, *Comments on Film,* ed. Giovanni Grazzini and trans. Joseph Henry (Fresno: California State University Press, 1988), p. 64.
3. Luis Buñuel, *My Last Sigh,* trans. Abigail Israel (New York: Knopf, 1983), p. 92.
4. Quoted in Lise-Lone Marker and Frederick J. Marker, *Ingmar Bergman: Four Decades in the Theatre* (Cambridge: Cambridge University Press, 1982), p. 6.
5. André Bazin, *What Is Cinema? II,* ed. and trans. Hugh Gray (Berkeley: University of California Press, 1971), p. 89.
6. Fellini, *Comments on Film,* p. 77.
7. Quoted in Peter Bondanella, *Italian Cinema: From Neorealism to the Present* (New York: Ungar, 1983), p. 230.
8. Quoted in Andrew Sarris, ed., *Interviews with Film Directors* (Indianapolis: Bobbs-Merrill, 1967), p. 9.
9. See Robert Bresson, *Notes on Cinematography,* trans. Jonathan Griffin (New York: Urizen, 1977).
10. Quoted in "The Question," *Cahiers du Cinéma in English* no. 8 (February 1967): 8.
11. Quoted in Sarris, *Interviews with Film Directors,* p. 26.
12. François Truffaut, *The Films of My Life,* trans. Leonard Mayhew (New York: Simon and Schuster, 1975), p. 235.
13. Quoted in Chidananda Das Gupta, ed., *Satyajit Ray: An Anthology of Statements on Ray and by Ray* (New Delhi: Directorate of Film Festivals, 1981), p. 136.
14. Quoted in Marie Seton, *Portrait of a Director: Satyajit Ray* (Bloomington: Indiana University Press, 1971), p. 283.

20

NEW WAVES AND YOUNG CINEMAS, 1958–1967

The decade after 1958 saw extraordinary ferment in the international art cinema. Not only were major innovations introduced by older auteurs, but a host of "Young Cinemas," "New Cinemas," and "New Waves" criticized and rejuvenated the modernist tradition. Many of the younger filmmakers became the major figures of later decades.

THE INDUSTRIES' NEW NEEDS

Industrial conditions favored the arrival of fresh talent. Whereas American film attendance had declined after 1947, elsewhere audiences did not significantly dwindle until the late 1950s, when television began to provide cheap entertainment. In response, producers aimed at new audiences—sometimes through coproductions, sometimes by making erotic films. They also aimed films at the "youth culture" that emerged in most western countries in the late 1950s. In western Europe, sexual liberation, rock music, new fashions, the growth of soccer and other sports, and new forms of tourism such as Club Med became hallmarks of the generation coming to maturity around 1960. Trends toward an urban, leisure-class lifestyle were strengthened by an economic boom after 1958 that raised European living standards. Similar patterns emerged in Japan and eastern Europe.

Who could better attract this affluent audience than young filmmakers? Film companies began to open up production to beginning directors. These opportunities coincided with the expansion of professional film training. After the late 1950s, existing film academies in the USSR, eastern Europe, France, and Italy were joined by national film schools founded in the Netherlands, Sweden, West Germany, and Denmark. Throughout Europe, directors around thirty years old made their first features in the years 1958–1967.

Youth culture accelerated the internationalizing of film culture. Art theaters and ciné-clubs multiplied. The list of international film festivals now included San Francisco and London (both begun in 1957), Moscow (1959), Adelaide and New York (1963), Chicago and Panama (1965), Brisbane (1966), and San Antonio and Shiraz, Iran (1967). Festivals in Hyères, France, and Pesaro, Italy (both begun in 1965) were created as gathering points for young filmmakers.

FORMAL AND STYLISTIC TRENDS

Fig. 20.1 *The Age of Daydreaming* (1964): Shooting on the street, using a long lens that flattens perspective.

Each nation's New Cinema was a loose assortment of quite different filmmakers. Typically their work does not display the degree of unity that we find in the stylistic movements of the silent era. Still, some broad trends link the Young Cinemas.

The new generation was the first to have a clear awareness of the overall history of cinema. The Cinémathèque Française in Paris, the National Film Theatre in London, and the Museum of Modern Art in New York became shrines for young audiences eager to discover films from around the world. Film schools screened foreign classics for study. Older directors were venerated as spiritual "fathers": Renoir, for Truffaut; Lang, for Alexander Kluge; Dovzhenko, for the Soviet Andrei Tarkovsky. In particular, young directors absorbed the Neorealist aesthetic and the art cinema of the 1950s. Thus the New Cinemas extended several postwar trends.

Fig. 20.2 Shallow depth in a closer view, yielded by the telephoto lens (*Walkover*, 1965).

Most apparent were innovations in technique. In part, Young Cinema identified itself with a more immediate approach to filming. During the late 1950s and throughout the 1960s manufacturers perfected cameras that did not require tripods, reflex viewfinders that showed exactly what the lens saw, and film stocks that needed less light to create acceptable exposures. Although much of this equipment was designed to aid documentary filmmakers (see p. 567), fiction filmmakers immediately took advantage of it. Now a director could film with direct sound, recording the ambient noise of the world outside the sealed studio. Now the camera could take to the streets, searching out fictional characters in the midst of a crowd (Figs. 20.1, 20.2). This portable equipment also let the filmmaker shoot quickly and cheaply, an advantage for producers anxious to economize in a declining industry.

The 1960s fictional cinema gained a looseness that put it closer to Direct Cinema documentary (Chapter 21). Directors often filmed from a distance, using panning shots to cover the action and zoom lenses to enlarge details, as if the filmmaker were a journalist snooping on the characters (Fig. 20.3). It was during this period that close-ups and shot/reverse-shot exchanges began to be shot almost entirely with long lenses—a trend that would dominate the 1970s (Figs. 20.4, 20.5).

Fig. 20.3 A moment in the pan-and-zoom shot covering a conversation (*Es*, West Germany, 1965, Ulrich Schamoni).

Fig. 20.4

Fig. 20.5

Figs. 20.4 and 20.5 Shot/reverse shot employing a long lens in Milos Forman's *Black Peter* (1963).

Yet this rough documentary look did not commit the directors to recording the world passively. To an extent not seen since the silent era, young filmmakers tapped the power of fragmentary, discontinuous editing. In *Breathless* (France, 1960) Jean-Luc Godard violated basic rules of continuity editing, notably by tossing out frames from the middle of shots in order to create jarring "jump cuts" (Fig. 20.6). A film by the Japanese Nagisa Oshima might contain over a thousand shots. Older directors favored smooth editing, considering Soviet Montage unrealistic and manipulative, but now montage became a point of reference. At the limit, 1960s directors pushed toward a *collage* form. Here the director builds the film out of staged footage, "found" footage (newsreels, old movies), and images of all sorts (advertisements, snapshots, posters, and so on).

Yet young filmmakers also extended the use of long takes, one of the major stylistic trends of the postwar era (pp. 389–390). A scene might be handled in a single shot, a device which quickly became known by its French name, the *plan-séquence* ("sequence shot"; see pp. 427–429). The lightweight cameras proved ideal for making long takes. Some directors alternated lengthy shots and abrupt editing; French New Wave directors were fond of chopping off a graceful long take with sudden close-ups. Other directors, such as the Hungarian Miklós Jancsó, continued the Ophüls-Antonioni tradition by building the film out of lengthy, intricate traveling shots. Across the 1960s, telephoto filming, discontinuous editing, and complex camera movements all came to replace the dense staging in depth that had been common after World War II.

The narrative form of the postwar European art film relied upon an objective realism of chance events that often could not be fitted into a linear cause-and-effect story line. The objective realism of the Neorealist approach was enhanced by the use of nonactors, real locations, and improvised performance. The new techniques of Direct Cinema allowed young directors to go even further on this path. Accordingly, young filmmakers staged their stories in their own apartments and neighborhoods, filming them in a way that traditional directors considered rough and unprofessional. For instance, in *Los Golfos* ("The Drifters," Spain, 1960), Carlos Saura uses nonactors and improvisation to tell his story of young men's lives of petty crime. Saura incorporates hand-held shots and abrupt zooms (Fig. 20.7) to give the film a documentary immediacy.

The art cinema's subjective realism also developed further during this period. Flashbacks had become common in the postwar decade, but now

Fig. 20.6 In *Breathless*, Godard's jump cuts create a skittery, nervous style.

Fig. 20.7 The end point of a zoom-in from *Los Golfos*.

Fig. 20.8 *Daisies*: The long lens flattens women and man.

Fig. 20.9 *Everything for Sale* joins the New Cinemas in its self-conscious references to film history—a history which includes Wajda's early work. In a direct echo of *Ashes and Diamonds*, the mysterious young actor lights drinks while remarking that the partisans were symbols for his generation (compare Fig. 18.28).

filmmakers used them to intensify the sense of characters' mental states. *Hiroshima mon amour* (1959) led many filmmakers to "subjectivize" flashbacks. In addition, scenes of fantasy and dreams proliferated. All this mental imagery became far more fragmentary and disordered than it had been in earlier cinema. The filmmaker might interrupt the narrative with glimpses of another realm which only gradually becomes identifiable as memory, dream, or fantasy. At the limit, this realm might remain tantalizingly obscure to the very end of the film, suggesting how reality and imagination can fuse in human experience.

The art-cinema tendency toward authorial commentary likewise continued. François Truffaut's lilting camera movements around his characters suggested that their lives were a lyrical dance. In *Daisies* (Czechoslovakia, 1966), Vera Chytilová uses camera tricks to comment on her heroines' mocking view of men (Fig. 20.8).

Directors combined objective realism, subjective realism, and authorial commentary in ways that generated narrative ambiguity. Now the spectator could not always tell which of these three factors was the basis for the film's presentation of events. In *8½* (1963), some scenes indiscernibly blend memory with fantasy images. Younger directors also explored ambiguous uses of narrative form. In Jaromil Jireš's *The Cry* (Czechoslovakia, 1963), events may be taken as either objective or subjective, and the question is left open as to whose subjective point of view might be represented. Open-ended narratives also lent themselves to ambiguity, as when we are left to wonder at the end of *Breathless* about the heroine's attitude toward the hero.

As films' stories became indeterminate, they seemed to back away from documenting the social world. Now the film itself came to seem the only "reality" which the director could claim. Combined with young directors' awareness of the history of their medium, this retreat from objective realism made film form and style *self-referential*. Many films no longer sought to reflect a reality outside themselves. Like modern painting and literature, film became reflexive, pointing to its own materials, structures, and history.

Reflexivity was perhaps least disturbing when the film built its plot around the making of a film, as in *8½*, Godard's *Contempt* (1963), and Andrzej Wajda's *Everything for Sale* (1968), a memorial to Zbigniew Cybulski, the deceased star of *Ashes and Diamonds* (Fig. 20.9). Even when filmmaking is not an overt subject, reflexivity remains a key trait of New Cinemas and of 1960s art cinema generally. Erik Løken's *The Hunt* (Norway, 1959) starts with a voice-over commentary remarking, "Let's begin," and ends with the narrator asserting: "We can't let it end like this." In *Breathless*, the hero talks to the audience, while *Shoot the Piano Player* (Fig. 20.10) affectionately echoes silent cinema.

The collage films, which juxtapose footage from different sources or periods, contribute to a similar awareness of the artifice of film. And New Cinemas could even cite each other, as when Gilles Groulx's *Le Chat est dans le sac* ("The Cat Is in the Bag," Canada, 1964) deliberately echoes a French New Wave film (Figs. 20.11, 20.12). In all, the films acknowledge the mechanisms of illusion-making and an indebtedness to the history of the medium. This made the New Cinemas major contributors to postwar cinematic modernism.

Fig. 20.10 Irises in *Shoot the Piano Player* pay homage to silent film.

Fig. 20.11

Fig. 20.12

Figs. 20.11 and 20.12 *Le Chat est dans le sac* cites Godard's *Vivre sa vie*.

Many countries sustained New Waves and New Cinemas, but this chapter concentrates on the most influential and original developments in western and eastern Europe, Great Britain, and the USSR.

FRANCE: NEW WAVE AND NEW CINEMA

In France during the late 1950s, the idealism and political movements of the immediate postwar years gave way to a more apolitical culture of consumption and leisure. The rising generation was dubbed the *nouvelle vague*, the "new wave" that would soon govern France. Many of these young people read film journals and attended screenings at ciné-clubs and *art et essai* ("art and experiment") cinemas. They were ready for more offbeat films than those of the Cinema of Quality.

The film industry had not fully tapped these new consumers. In 1958 film attendance started to decline sharply, and several big-budget films failed. At the same time, government aid fostered risk taking. In 1953, the Centre National du Cinéma established the *prime de la qualité* ("subsidy for quality"), which allowed new directors to make short films. A 1959 law created the *avance sur recettes* ("advance on receipts") system, which financed first features on the basis of a script. Between 1958 and 1961, dozens of directors made their first full-length films.

FRENCH NEW CINEMA AND THE NOUVELLE VAGUE
A CHRONOLOGY OF MAJOR RELEASES

1959   *Le Beau Serge* ("The Good Serge"), Claude Chabrol
       Les Cousins (*The Cousins*), Claude Chabrol
       Les Quatre cents coups (*The 400 Blows*), François Truffaut
       Hiroshima mon amour ("Hiroshima My Love"), Alain Resnais
       Les Yeux sans visage (*Eyes without a Face*), Georges Franju

1960   *À bout de souffle* (*Breathless*), Jean-Luc Godard
       Les Bonnes femmes ("The Good Girls"), Claude Chabrol
       Tirez sur le pianiste (*Shoot the Piano Player*) François Truffaut
       Zazie dans le métro ("Zazie in the Subway"), Louis Malle

1961   *Lola*, Jacques Demy
       Une Femme est une femme (*A Woman Is a Woman*), Jean-Luc Godard
       L'Année dernière à Marienbad (*Last Year at Marienbad*), Alain Resnais
       Paris nous appartient (*Paris Belongs to Us*), Jacques Rivette

1962   *Jules et Jim* (*Jules and Jim*), François Truffaut
       Le Signe du lion ("The Sign of the Lion"), Eric Rohmer
       Vivre sa vie (*My Life to Live*), Jean-Luc Godard
       Cléo de 5 à 7 (*Cléo from 5 to 7*), Agnès Varda
       L'Immortelle ("The Immortal One"), Alain Robbe-Grillet

1963   *Le Petit soldat* ("The Little Soldier"), Jean-Luc Godard
       Ophélia, Claude Chabrol
       Les Carabiniers ("The Riflemen"), Jean-Luc Godard
       Le Mépris (*Contempt*), Jean-Luc Godard

       Muriel, Alain Resnais
       Judex, Georges Franju
       Adieu Philippine, Jacques Rozier

1964   *La Peau douce* (*The Soft Skin*), François Truffaut
       Bande à part (*Band of Outsiders*), Jean-Luc Godard
       Une Femme mariée (*A Married Woman*), Jean-Luc Godard
       Les Parapluies de Cherbourg (*The Umbrellas of Cherbourg*), Jacques Demy

1965   *Alphaville*, Jean-Luc Godard
       Pierrot le fou ("Crazy Pierrot"), Jean-Luc Godard
       Le Bonheur ("Happiness"), Agnès Varda

1966   *Masculin-Feminine*, Jean-Luc Godard
       Fahrenheit 451, François Truffaut
       La Guerre est finie ("The War Is Over"), Alain Resnais
       Suzanne Simonin, la Réligieuse de Denis Diderot ("Suzanne Simonin, the Nun by Denis Diderot"), Jacques Rivette
       Les Créatures ("The Creatures"), Agnès Varda
       La Collectionneuse ("The Collector"), Eric Rohmer

1967   *Made in USA*, Jean-Luc Godard
       Deux ou trois choses que je sais d'elle (*Two or Three Things I Know about Her*), Jean-Luc Godard
       La Chinoise ("The Chinese Woman"), Jean-Luc Godard
       Weekend, Jean-Luc Godard
       Les Demoiselles de Rochefort (*The Young Girls of Rochefort*), Jacques Demy
       Trans-Europe Express, Alain Robbe-Grillet
       Ma nuit chez Maud (*My Night at Maud's*), Eric Rohmer

Such a broad development naturally included quite different trends, but two major ones are crucial. One centers on the *Nouvelle Vague*, or "New Wave," group. The other trend, often identified with the "Left Bank" group, involves a slightly older generation who now moved into feature production. Both groups are represented in the accompanying chronology. (See Box.)

THE NEW WAVE

The French New Wave (Nouvelle Vague) is largely responsible for the romantic image of the young director fighting to make personal films that defy the conventional industry. Ironically, most directors associated with the New Wave quickly became mainstream, even ordinary filmmakers. But certain members of the group not only popularized a new conception of personal cinema but also provided innovations in film form and style.

The principal Nouvelle Vague directors had been film critics for the magazine *Cahiers du cinéma*. (See p. 436.) Strong adherents of the auteur policy, these men believed that the director should express a personal vision of the world. This vision would appear not only in the film's script but also in its style. Most of the *Cahiers* group started by directing short films, but by the end of the decade, most turned to features. They helped each other by financing projects and sharing the services of two outstanding cinematographers, Henri Decae and Raoul Coutard.

The New Wave's initial impact came from four films of 1959–1960. Claude Chabrol's *Le Beau Serge* and *Les Cousins* explored the disparity between rural and urban life in the new France. The first film almost became the French entry at Cannes; the second won a major prize at the Berlin festival. François Truffaut's *The 400 Blows*, a sensitive tale of a boy becoming a thief and a runaway, won the best-direction prize at Cannes and gave the New Wave great international prestige. The most innovative early New Wave film was Jean-Luc Godard's *Breathless*, a portrait of a petty criminal's last days. As Chabrol, Truffaut, and Godard followed up their debuts, other young directors launched first features.

Many New Wave films satisfied producers' financial demands. Shot on location, using portable equipment, little-known actors, and small crews, they could be made quickly and for less than half the usual cost. Often a film would be shot silent and postdubbed. And for three years several New Wave films made high profits. The trend brought fame to Jean-Paul Belmondo, Jean-Claude Brialy, Anna Karina, Jeanne Moreau, and other stars who would dominate the French cinema for decades. Moreover, Nouvelle Vague films proved more exportable than many bigger productions.

As the very name "New Wave" indicates, much of the group's success can be attributed to the filmmakers' rapport with their youthful audience. Most of the directors were born around 1930 and were based in Paris. By concentrating on urban professional life with its chic fashions and sports cars, its bars, all-night parties, and jazz clubs, this cinema suggested that the café scene was being captured with the immediacy of Direct Cinema. The films also have thematic affinities. Authority is to be distrusted; political and romantic commitment is suspect. The characters' gratuitous actions bear traces of pop Existentialism. And in an echo of Poetic Realism, the Tradition of Quality, and American crime movies, the films often center on a *femme fatale*.

The New Wave directors also share some basic narrative assumptions. Like Antonioni and Fellini, these filmmakers often build their plots around chance events and digressive episodes. They also intensify the art-cinema convention of the open-ended narrative; the famous ending of *The 400 Blows* made the freeze-frame technique a favored device for expressing an unre-

Fig. 20.13 Antoine Doinel, at the edge of the sea, turns to the audience in world cinema's most famous freeze-frame (*The 400 Blows*).

solved situation (Fig. 20.13). At the same time, the mixture of tone characteristic of Italian Neorealism gets pushed to the limit. In Truffaut, Godard, and Chabrol, farcical comedy is often only an instant away from anxiety, pain, and death.

Finally, the Nouvelle Vague was the first group of directors to refer systematically to prior film traditions. For these former critics, film history was a living presence. In *Breathless,* the hero imitates Humphrey Bogart, while the heroine comes from Preminger's *Bonjour Tristesse* (1958). Partygoers in *Paris Belongs to Us* screen *Metropolis,* while in *The 400 Blows* the boy steals a production still from Bergman's *Summer with Monika.* Celebrating their own notoriety, the directors cited each other or their friends at *Cahiers du cinéma* (Fig. 20.14). Such awareness of a film's debt to history helped usher in the reflexive filmmaking of the 1960s.

Since the *Cahiers* critics favored a cinema of personal vision, it is not surprising that the New Wave did not coalesce into a unified stylistic movement like German Expressionism or Soviet Montage. The development of the directors' careers during the 1960s suggests that the New Wave was only a brief alliance of varied temperaments. The two most exemplary and influential directors were Truffaut and Godard (see Box), but several of their colleagues also made careers in the film industry.

"You become a director," Claude Chabrol wrote, "when you find the money to make your first film."[3] His wife's inheritance financed *Le Beau Serge,* which won a *prime de la qualité* that nearly covered its costs before it was released. The success of *Les Cousins* allowed Chabrol to make several films quickly. His admiration for Hitchcock turned him toward moody psychodramas, often with touches of grotesque humor (*Les Bonnes femmes, Ophélia*). Chabrol churned out lurid espionage pictures before embarking on a series of psychological thrillers: *La Femme infidèle* ("The Unfaithful Wife," 1969), *Que la bête meure* (*This Man Must Die,* 1969), *Le Boucher* ("The Butcher," 1970), and others. Like Hitchcock, Chabrol traces how the tensions of middle-class life explode into madness and violence. By the early 1990s Chabrol had made over forty features and several television episodes, remaining the most commercially flexible and pragmatic of the directors to emerge from *Cahiers.*

Fig. 20.14 In Claude Chabrol's *Les Cousins*, a browser finds a book on Hitchcock, written by Eric Rohmer and . . . Claude Chabrol.

FRANÇOIS TRUFFAUT AND JEAN-LUC GODARD

Friends, *Cahiers* critics, co-directors (on a 1958 short), and eventual adversaries, Truffaut and Godard usefully define the poles of the New Wave. One proved that the young cinema could rejuvenate mainstream filmmaking; the other, that the new generation could be hostile to the comfort and pleasure of ordinary cinema.

A passionate cinéphile, François Truffaut grew up as a ward of the critic André Bazin. After a notable short film, *Les Mistons* ("The Brats," 1958), Truffaut managed to finance a feature, *The 400 Blows*. This film about a young runaway established an autobiographical strain in Truffaut's work. His next features revealed two more tendencies that would recur over his career: the offhand, affectionately parodic treatment of a crime plot (*Shoot the Piano Player*) and the somber but lyrical handling of an unhappy love affair (*Jules and Jim*). For many worldwide audiences, these three films defined the New Wave.

Stylistically, Truffaut's early films flaunt zoom shots, choppy editing, casual compositions, and bursts of quirky humor or sudden violence. Sometimes such devices capture the characters' vitality, as in Antoine Doinel's frantic rush around Paris in *The 400 Blows* or in the waltzlike camera movements that surround Jules, Jim, and Catherine during their country outings. The extreme shifts of mood in *Shoot the Piano Player* are accented by abrupt cutaways; when a gangster swears, "May my mother die if I'm not telling the truth," Truffaut cuts to a shot of an old lady keeling over. But Truffaut's technique increasingly injected a subdued romanticism, as when he dwells on Charlie's numb face at the end of *Shoot the Piano Player* or turns Catherine's image into a freeze-frame (Fig. 20.15).

Truffaut remained true to the *Cahiers* legacy by inserting into each film references to his favorite periods of film history and his admired directors (Lubitsch, Hitchcock, Renoir). *Jules and Jim*, set in the early days of cinema, provided an occasion to incorporate silent footage and to employ old-fashioned irises.

Truffaut sought not to destroy traditional cinema but to renew it. In the *Cahiers* spirit he aimed to enrich commercial filmmaking by balancing personal expression with a concern for his audience: "I have to feel I am producing a piece of entertainment."[1] Over two decades he made eighteen more films. As if seeking more direct contact with the viewer, he took up acting, performing in his own works and in Spielberg's *Close Encounters of the Third Kind* (1977). His output includes light entertainments [*Vivement dimanche!* ("Finally Sunday!"), 1983], bittersweet studies of youth (*Stolen Kisses*, 1968), and more meditative films (*The Wild Child*, 1970). Late in his life, he created intense studies of psychological

Fig. 20.15 A snapshot image, thanks to the freeze-frame (*Jules and Jim*).

obsession (*The Story of Adele H.*, 1975; *The Green Room*, 1978; Color Plate 26.9). Of Truffaut's last films only *The Last Metro* (1980) achieved international success, but he remained the most popular New Wave director.

Far more abrasive was the work of Jean-Luc Godard. Like Truffaut, he was a stormy and demanding critic. He soon became the most provocative New Wave filmmaker. Of his early works only *Breathless* had notable financial success—due in part to Belmondo's insolent performance and Truffaut's script. The film was also recognizably New Wave in its hand-held camerawork, jerky editing, and homages to Melville and Monogram B pictures. Over the next decade, Godard made at least two features per year, and it became clear that he, more than any other *Cahiers* director, was redefining film structure and style.

Godard's work poses fundamental questions about narrative. While his first films, such as *Breathless* and *A Woman Is a Woman*, have fairly straightforward plots, he gradually moved toward a more fragmentary, collage structure. A story is still apparent, but it is deflected into unpredictable paths. Godard juxtaposes staged scenes with documentary material (advertisements, comic strips, crowds passing in the street), often with little connection to the narrative. Far more than his New Wave contemporaries, Godard mixes conventions drawn from popular culture, such as detective novels or Hollywood movies, with references to philosophy or avant-garde art. (Many of his stylistic asides are reminiscent of Lettrist and Situationist works; see p. 575.) The inconsistencies, digressions, and disunities of Godard's work make most New Wave films seem quite traditional by comparison.

Breathless identified Godard with the hand-held camera and the jump cut (see Fig. 20.6). His subsequent films explore film style more widely, interrogating conventional film techniques. Compositions are decentered; the camera moves on its own to explore a milieu; one of Godard's most influential

Fig. 20.16 The painterly flatness of the Godard frame (*Vivre sa vie*).

innovations was to design shots which seem astonishingly flat (Fig. 20.16).

Nothing could be further from Truffaut's accommodating attitude to his audience than Godard's assault on sense and the senses. In Truffaut's *La Nuit américaine* (*Day for Night*, 1973) filmmaking becomes a merry party, after which everyone can be forgiven. Godard's *Contempt*, by contrast, treats filmmaking as an exercise in sadomasochism. To secure his job, a scriptwriter leaves his wife alone with a venal producer and then taunts her with his suspicions of infidelity. His games and her contempt for him lead to her death. Fritz Lang, playing himself as the director, is seen to be a slave in exile. Ironically, Godard's critique of the film world uses the resources of the big-budget film to create ravishing color compositions (Color Plate 20.1).

Such works aroused passionate debate. After the mid-1960s Godard continued to develop, always in ways that aroused attention. Even his detractors grant that he is the most widely imitated director of the French New Wave, perhaps the most influential director of the entire postwar era. With characteristic generosity Truffaut remarked: "There is the cinema *before* Godard and the cinema *after* Godard."[2]

Fig. 20.17 Parisian landscapes and a weary man's gait in *Le Signe du lion*.

Although Eric Rohmer was nearly ten years older than most of his *Cahiers* friends, his renown came somewhat later. A reflective aesthete, Rohmer adhered closely to André Bazin's teachings. *Le Signe du lion* is akin to *The Bicycle Thief*, consisting largely of a homeless man's meanderings through the hot Parisian summer (Fig. 20.17).

After this work, Rohmer embarked on his "Six Moral Tales," wry studies of men and women struggling to balance intelligence with emotional and erotic impulses. In the first feature-length tale, *La Collectionneuse*, the nymphlike Haydée tempts the overintellectual Adrien but remains just out of his reach (Fig. 20.18). After the success of this film, Rohmer was able to complete his first series with *My Night at Maud's* (1967), *Claire's Knee* (1970), and *Love in the Afternoon* (1972). In the 1980s he completed a second series, "Comedies and Proverbs," and launched another, "Tales of Four Seasons." Deflating his characters' pretensions while still sympathizing with their efforts to find happiness, Rohmer's cinema has the flavor of the novel of manners or of Renoir's films.

Whereas Rohmer favors the concise, neatly ironic tale, the films of Jacques Rivette, another *Cahiers* critic, struggle to capture the endlessness of life itself. *L'Amour fou* (1968) runs over four hours, *Out 1* (1971) twelve. Such abnormal lengths allow Rivette gradually to unfold a daily rhythm behind which intricate, half-concealed conspiracies are felt to lurk.

Paris Belongs to Us initiated this paranoid plot structure. A young woman is told that the unseen rulers of the world have driven one man to suicide and will soon kill the man she loves. The film owes much to Lang, whose parables of fate and foreboding Rivette admired. *Paris Belongs to Us* also introduces Rivette's fascination with the theater. In one plot strand, an aspiring director tries to stage *Pericles* in makeshift circumstances (Fig. 20.19). *L'Amour fou* develops the motif more elaborately by following a 16mm film crew documenting a theater troupe's production (Fig. 20.20). Considered marginal in the prime Nouvelle Vague period, Rivette's work became influential on the French cinema of the 1970s.

More stylized in technique are the films of Jacques Demy, whose career was launched with *Lola* (dedicated to Max Ophüls in memory of *Lola Montès*). This and *Baie des anges* ("Bay of Angels," 1963) introduced the artificial decor and costumes that became Demy's trademark. With *The Umbrellas of Cherbourg* Demy broke even more sharply with realism by having all the dialogue sung. Michel Legrand's pop score and Demy's vibrant color schemes helped the film achieve a huge commercial success. In *Les Demoiselles de Rochefort*, an homage to MGM musicals, Demy created the sense that an entire city's population was dancing to the changing moods of his protagonists (Fig. 20.21). Most of Demy's films disturbingly contrast sumptuous visual design with banal, even sordid plot lines.

The "New Wave" label was often applied to directors who had little in common with the *Cahiers* group. Niko Papatakis's savage *Les Abysses* (1963), for instance, seems chiefly indebted to the Theater of the Absurd in its

Fig. 20.18 Flirtation among the intelligentsia: Rohmer's characteristic world already formulated in *La Collectionneuse*.

Fig. 20.19 A theater rehearsal with sinister overtones (*Paris Belongs to Us*).

Fig. 20.20 Filming the theater rehearsal in *L'Amour fou*.

Fig. 20.21 The rapture of a city dancing: *Les Demoiselles de Rochefort*.

Fig. 20.22 *Les Abysses*: An adaptation of the story of the murderous Papin sisters; here they savagely peel away wallpaper.

Fig. 20.23 Joviality echoing the Marx Brothers (*Zazie dans le métro*).

Fig. 20.24 In *La Pointe courte*, the couple declaim philosophically while in the background fishermen go about their work.

depiction of two housemaids' frenzied psychodrama (Fig. 20.22). By contrast, the mainstream Louis Malle could appropriate a New Wave style for his *Zazie dans le métro* (Fig. 20.23). In general, the "New Wave" rubric allowed a variety of young filmmakers to emerge.

FRENCH NEW CINEMA: THE LEFT BANK

The late 1950s brought to prominence another loosely affiliated group of filmmakers—since known as the *rive gauche*, or "Left Bank," group. Mostly older and less movie-mad than the *Cahiers* crew, they tended to see cinema as akin to other arts, particularly literature. Some of these directors—Resnais, Varda, and Franju—were already known for their unusual short documentaries (see pp. 563–564). Like the New Wave, however, they practiced cinematic modernism, and their emergence in the late 1950s benefited from the youthful public's interest in experimentation.

Two works of the mid-1950s were significant precursors. Alexandre Astruc, whose *caméra-stylo* manifesto had been an important spur to the auteur theory (see p. 492), made *Les Mauvaises rencontres* ("Bad Meetings," 1955), which uses flashbacks and a voice-over narration to explain the past of a woman brought to a police station in connection with an abortionist. More important is Agnès Varda's short feature *La Pointe courte* (1955). Much of the film consists of a couple's random walks. But the nonactors and real locales conflict with the couple's archly stylized voice-over dialogue (Fig. 20.24). The film's elliptical editing was without parallel in the cinema of its day.

The prototypical Left Bank film was *Hiroshima mon amour*, directed by Alain Resnais from a script by Marguerite Duras. Appearing in 1959, it shared the limelight with *Les Cousins* and *The 400 Blows*, offering more evidence that the French cinema was renewing itself. But *Hiroshima* differs greatly from the works of Chabrol and Truffaut. At once highly intellectual and viscerally shocking, it juxtaposes the present and the past in disturbing ways.

A French actress comes to Hiroshima to perform in an antiwar film. She is attracted to a Japanese man. Over two nights and days they make love, talk, quarrel, and gain an obscure understanding. At the same time, memories of the German soldier she loved during the Occupation well up unexpectedly. She struggles to connect her own torment during World War II with the ghastly suffering inflicted in the 1945 atomic destruction of Hiroshima. The film closes with the couple's apparent reconciliation, suggesting that the difficulty of fully knowing any historical truth resembles that of understanding another human being.

Duras builds her script as a duet, with male and female voices intertwining over the images. Often the viewer does not know if the sound track carries real conversations, imaginary dialogues, or commentary spoken by the characters. The film leaps from current story action to documentary footage, usually of Hiroshima, or to shots of the actress's youth in France (Figs. 20.25–20.27). While audiences had seen flashback constructions

Fig. 20.25

Fig. 20.26

Fig. 20.27

throughout the 1940s and 1950s, Resnais made such temporal switches sudden and fragmentary. In many cases they remain ambiguously poised between memory and fantasy.

In *Hiroshima*'s second part, the Japanese man pursues the French woman through the city over a single night. Now her inner voice takes the place of flashbacks, commenting on what is happening in the present. If the film's first half is so rapidly paced as to disorient the spectator, the second part daringly slows to the tempo of their walking, her nervous avoidance, his patient waiting. The rhythm, which forces us to observe nuances of their behavior, anticipates that of Antonioni's *L'Avventura*.

Hiroshima mon amour was shown out of competition at Cannes in 1959 and awarded an International Critics' Prize. It caused a sensation, both for its scenes of sexual intimacy and for its storytelling techniques. Its ambiguous mixture of documentary realism, subjective evocation, and authorial commentary represented a landmark in the development of the international art cinema.

Hiroshima lifted Resnais to international renown. His next work, *Last Year at Marienbad*, pushed modernist ambiguity to new extremes. In this tale of three people encountering each other in a luxurious hotel, fantasy, dream, and reality—if there is any to be discovered—mix (Fig. 20.28). Resnais's next film *Muriel*, uses no flashbacks, but the past remains visible in a young man's amateur movies of his traumatic tour of duty in Algeria. Even more explicitly than *Hiroshima*, the film takes up political questions; the Muriel of the title, never seen, is an Algerian tortured by French occupiers. Resnais emphasizes the anxiety of the present through a jolting editing far more precise than the rough jump cuts of the New Wave (Figs. 20.29, 20.30).

Figs. 20.25 and 20.26 *Hiroshima mon amour*: As the couple lie in bed, Resnais cuts abruptly to a shot of the woman's German lover. The grayer tonality of the film stock helps mark the distant past.

Fig. 20.27 Later in the sequence, a long shot of the woman meeting her German lover in wartime dissolves slowly to the present, creating a lingering "body landscape" that compares the two men.

Fig. 20.28 *Last Year at Marienbad*: People cast shadows but trees don't.

Fig. 20.29

Fig. 20.30

Figs. 20.29 and 20.30 *Muriel*: When Alphonse rises from a table Resnais cuts to him in a different locale but in the same part of the frame.

Fig. 20.31 A dead-white mask echoing silent film make-up in Franju's *Eyes without a Face*.

Fig. 20.32

Fig. 20.33

Figs. 20.32 and 20.33 The protagonist of *L'Immortelle* peers out through a blind, and the phantom woman he pursues, in still photograph, peers back.

Fig. 20.34 Cléo sings to the camera.

The success of *Hiroshima mon amour* helped launch features by other Left Bank filmmakers. Georges Franju's *Eyes without a Face* (Fig. 20.31) and *Judex* offered cerebral, slightly Surrealist reworkings of classic genres and paid homage to directors like Lang and Feuillade. Resnais's editor Henri Colpi was able to make *Une Aussi longue absence*, a tale of a café keeper who believes that a tramp is her returning husband. With its fragmentary scenes and unexpected cuts, it anticipates *Muriel*. Marguerite Duras, who wrote Colpi's film as well as Resnais's, was eventually drawn to filmmaking (Chapter 26).

The fame of Resnais's work enabled another literary figure to move into directing. After scripting *Last Year at Marienbad*, the novelist Alain Robbe-Grillet embarked as a director with *L'Immortelle*. It continues *Marienbad*'s rendition of "impossible" times and spaces (Figs. 20.32, 20.33). Robbe-Grillet's second film, *Trans-Europe Express*, is self-consciously about story-telling, as three writers settle down in a train to write about international drug smuggling. The films shows us their plot enacted, with all the variants and revisions that emerge from the discussion.

The *Hiroshima* breakthrough also helped Agnès Varda make a full-length feature, *Cléo from 5 to 7*. Despite its title, the film covers ninety-five minutes in the life of an actress awaiting the results of a critical medical test. Varda distances us from this tense situation by breaking the film into thirteen "chapters" and by including various digressions (Fig. 20.34). The film's exuberance, in surprising contrast to its morbid subject, puts it close to the New Wave tone, but its experiment in manipulating story duration has an intellectual flavor typical of the Left Bank group.

Varda's films after *Cléo* include the controversial *Le Bonheur*, which disturbed viewers by suggesting that one woman can easily take the place of another. In a typically modernist attack on traditional morality, Varda quotes Renoir's *Picnic on the Grass*, in which a character remarks: "Happiness may consist in submitting to the order of Nature."

Both the New Wave and the Left Bank groups had only a few years of success. French film attendance continued to decline. Some works by novice directors, notably Jacques Rozier's *Adieu Philippine*, ran up huge production costs. By 1963, the New Cinema was no longer selling, and it was as difficult for a young director to get started as it would have been ten years earlier. Tenacious producers such as Georges de Beauregard, Anatole Dauman, Mag Bodard, and Pierre Braunberger assisted the major filmmakers, but far more bankable were directors like Claude Lelouch, whose *A Man and a Woman* (1966) used New Cinema techniques to dress up a traditional romantic plot.

Nevertheless, the French cinema of the 1960s was one of the most widely admired and imitated in the world. The Tradition of Quality had been supplanted by a vigorous cinematic modernism.

ITALY: YOUNG CINEMA AND SPAGHETTI WESTERNS

During the late 1950s and early 1960s, the Italian film industry fared much better than the French. Higher ticket prices offset the decline in attendance, American imports were decreasing, and Italian films were gaining a large share of domestic revenues. The international market proved accessible to horror films, comedies like *Divorce Italian Style* (1961), and revived "mythological" epics like *Hercules Unchained* (1959). U.S. and European firms continued to seek Italian coproductions. Cinecittà churned out films, and in 1962 Dino De Laurentiis built a huge studio outside Rome. By the early 1960s, Italy had become western Europe's most powerful production center.

The most visible directors were Fellini and Antonioni, whose early 1960s films consolidated their reputations as auteurs (Chapter 19). Expansion in the industry also enabled dozens of new directors to embark on careers. Most went immediately into the popular genres, but a few became more celebrated and influential. As we might expect, they were often characterized in relation to the Neorealist tradition.

The most straightforward updating of Neorealism occurred in the work of Ermanno Olmi. From the first scene, which shows a young man waking up while his parents prepare breakfast, *Il Posto* ("The Job," aka *The Sound of Trumpets,* 1961) seems to continue the patient observation of daily life conducted in *Umberto D.* (p. 421). *Il Posto* is also characteristic of international Young Cinema in the way it loosens its narrative beyond the Neorealist norm. The young man's application for a civil service job, the petty office routines, and the melancholy lives of the clerks are presented in an anecdotal, digressive fashion. The romance plot line remains unfulfilled. Olmi's alternation of satiric touches with quiet sympathy resembles the attitude of young Czech filmmakers like Jiří Menzel.

Neorealism's socially critical impulse was intensified by new filmmakers identified with the left. Perhaps closest to the Neorealist source was the work of the Taviani brothers, Vittorio and Paolo, who would gain international prominence in the 1970s. Francesco Rosi, who had assisted Visconti on *La Terra trema,* merged a semidocumentary inquiry into a Sicilian bandit's death with nonchronological flashbacks in *Salvatore Giuliano* (1961). Marco Bellocchio brought a New Left critique of orthodox communism to the screen with *Fists in the Pockets* (1966) and *China Is Near* (1967). Gillo Pontecorvo, older than these filmmakers, made one of the most important contributions to the trend in *Battle of Algiers* (1966). This restaged semidocumentary drew upon the conventions of *cinéma vérité* to render the immediacy of the Algerian war for independence; but in using a complex flashback construction, Pontecorvo, like Rosi, showed the influence of Resnais and other experimenters.

The Neorealist impulse also encountered a radical modernism in the work of Pier Paolo Pasolini. An unorthodox Marxist, a homosexual, and a nonbeliever steeped in Catholicism, Pasolini generated a furor in Italian culture. He was already famous as a poet and novelist when he entered filmmaking. He worked on several scripts, notably for Fellini's *Nights of Cabiria,* and he cast his own films on a principle that De Sica could have accepted: "I choose actors for what they are and not for what they pretend to be."[4] Yet Pasolini claimed to take from Chaplin, Dreyer, and Mizoguchi the idea that the filmmaker could reveal the epic and mythic dimensions of the world.

The bleak examination of urban poverty in *Accatone* (1961) and *Mama Roma* (1962) was hailed as a return to Neorealism. Yet Pasolini's treatment of the milieu seems to owe more to Buñuel's *Los Olvidados,* not only in the scenes of savage violence but in the disturbing dream imagery (Fig. 20.35). Pasolini criticized Neorealism as being too tied to Resistance politics and too attached to a surface veracity. "In neorealism things are described with a certain detachment, with human warmth mixed with irony—characteristics which I do not have."[5]

Pasolini's first films also display what he called *pasticchio,* the "jumbling together" of a wide range of aural and visual materials. In compositions reminiscent of Renaissance paintings, characters spew forth vulgar language. *Cinéma-vérité* street scenes are accompanied by Bach or Mozart. Pasolini explained these disparities of technique by claiming that the peasantry and the lowest reaches of the urban working class retained a tie to preindustrial mythology, which his citation of great artworks of the past was meant to evoke.

The tactic of stylistic "contamination," as Pasolini called it, was perhaps least disturbing to audiences in *The Gospel According to St. Matthew* (1964) which—unlike his previous writings and films—won praise from the Church. The biblical tale was presented with greater realism than would be found in Hollywood or Cinecittà epics. Pasolini made Jesus a fierce, often impatient preacher, and he dwelt on the characters' gnarled features, wrinkled skin, and broken teeth. *The Gospel,* however, is not simply a Neorealist scripture. Techniques are jumbled together. Bach and Prokofiev vie with the African *Missa Luba* on the sound track. Faces out of Renaissance paintings are filmed

Fig. 20.35 Accatone dreams that his friends lie dead around him.

Fig. 20.36 A thief steals the prostitute's purse in a distant, abstract composition from Bertolucci's *La Commare secca.*

Fig. 20.35

Fig. 20.36

Fig. 20.37

Fig. 20.38

Fig. 20.39

Fig. 20.40

Fig. 20.41

Fig. 20.37 Disorienting time juggling in *Before the Revolution*: The aunt sorts photographs from her life on her bed.

Fig. 20.38 After a close-up of some of the pictures . . .

Fig. 20.39 . . . Bertolucci cuts to the bed, empty, and tracks in; she comes into the room in the background.

Fig. 20.40 Then Bertolucci resumes showing pictures, again spread on the bed . . .

Fig. 20.41 . . . before the aunt slowly turns the pictures over one by one. The shot of the empty bed presents an ambiguity of time: Is the shot out of order, or does it mark a new occasion on which the aunt returned to the bed and laid out the photos once again?

in abrupt zoom shots. Jesus' trial before Pilate is viewed by a hand-held camera within a crowd of onlookers, as if a news reporter could not get closer.

Pasolini, the experimental writer turned filmmaker, somewhat resembles Robbe-Grillet, while Bernardo Bertolucci represents an Italian parallel to the directors of the Nouvelle Vague. At age nineteen he was assistant director on *Accatone,* and Pasolini supplied the script for his first film, *La Commare secca* ("The Grim Reaper," 1962). A devoted cinéphile, he spent his teenage vacations watching movies at the Cinémathèque Française. Although Bertolucci identified strongly with the New Wave filmmakers, the careful construction and technical elegance of his films put them closer to the work of older modernists like Resnais. In *La Commare secca,* offscreen detectives interrogate murder suspects, and flashbacks supply each suspect's version of events. This familiar modernist device, exploited in *Citizen Kane* and *Rashomon,* is here applied to a classic Neorealist situation—a purse theft that recalls both *The Bicycle Thief* and *Nights of Cabiria.* Pasolini's script creates variants on the device by interrupting one flashback with another and by flashing still further back to show the victim preparing to go out on the morning of the crime. Bertolucci's visual style is far smoother than Pasolini's, using slow tracking shots and studied compositions (Fig. 20.36).

Bertolucci's most celebrated film of the era was the autobiographical *Before the Revolution* (1964). A tale of a young man who falls in love with his aunt, it parades references to *Cahiers du cinéma* and Hollywood directors and displays the director's mastery of art-cinema procedures of disorientation (Figs. 20.37–20.41). Avoiding the radical disjunctions of Godard, Bertolucci made mildly modernist films of great technical polish, a quality that he would exploit in his successes of the 1970s and 1980s.

The industry's prosperity allowed Olmi, Pasolini, Bertolucci, and many other directors to enter filmmaking. As in France, however, the period of opportunity was rather brief. A crisis emerged in 1963–1964, when the costume epic fell out of favor and major companies suffered from expensive failures, principally Visconti's *The Leopard* (1963) and Aldrich's *Sodom and*

Gomorrah (1963). In 1965 the government intervened and offered an aid policy resembling that of France: prizes for quality efforts, guaranteed bank loans, credits from special funds.

While this policy led to a new filmmaking boom, producers turned to low-budget production in new genres, such as sex films and James Bond imitations. Mario Bava introduced new eroticism, baroque set designs, and bizarre camera movements into fantasy-based thrillers (*Black Sabbath*, 1963; *Blood and Black Lace,* 1964). The most internationally successful Italian genre was the "spaghetti Western," as it came to be known in English, and its most successful practitioner was Sergio Leone.

A fan of American comic strips and *films noirs,* Leone was as dedicated a film fan as were the New Wave directors. He worked as assistant director for his father, Roberto Roberti, for De Sica (on *The Bicycle Thief*), and for American directors on runaway productions. After directing two costume epics, Leone moved to the genre which producers hoped would restabilize the industry.

A Fistful of Dollars (1964), *For a Few Dollars More* (1965), and *The Good, the Bad, and the Ugly* (1966) became the prototypical spaghetti Westerns. Laconic, stubble-jawed Clint Eastwood saunters through a world of grotesque absurdity modeled on Kurosawa's samurai films. Leone's Westerns have a harsh realism—seedy towns, grubby ponchos, and violence more gruesome than most audiences had ever seen. But they also display an almost operatic splendor. Vast landscapes (filmed cheaply in Spain) are juxtaposed with widescreen close-ups of eyes or hands. Wide-angle lenses distort depth (Color Plate 20.2). Leone's flamboyant visual style pushes the Western conventions to the level of sheer ceremony, so a face-off in a bar becomes as prolonged and stylized as a confrontation in Eisenstein's *Ivan the Terrible.* Yet Leone often deflates his supercharged scenes with grimly ironic humor.

In each film, Ennio Morricone's musical score heroicizes the action with soaring strings or mocks it with an abrupt whistle or a twang. Leone called Morricone his "scriptwriter" because the composer could replace a line of dialogue with a sudden expressive chord.[6] Morricone also helped Leone magnify the thematic implications of a film, as when, at the end of *For a Few Dollars More,* the parallel between a gunfight and a bullfight emerges not only from the *corrida*-shaped arena but also from throbbing Mexican brass on the sound track.

The huge success of the *Dollars* trilogy spurred the production of spaghetti Westerns and made Leone, Morricone, and Eastwood world famous. Although Leone worked in a popular genre, his florid, highly personal reinterpretation of its conventions proved as significant as the efforts of those art-cinema directors who revised and challenged the Neorealist tradition.

YOUNG GERMAN FILM

In February 1962, at the Oberhausen Film Festival, a new impulse in West German cinema was articulated. Twenty-six young filmmakers signed a manifesto declaring the old film dead. In the face of a decaying industry and a dwindling audience, the signatories promised to help German cinema regain international renown. After three years of lobbying and public debate, the central government established the Kuratorium Junger Deutsch Film ("Commission for Young German Film") in early 1965. This agency provided interest-free loans on the basis of scripts by directors who had proved themselves with notable short films.

During its brief existence, the Kuratorium financed nearly two dozen feature films. All were low-budget projects, in which the filmmaker paid the actors little and filmed almost completely on location. But many of these *Rücksackfilme* ("backpack films") had the shock of novelty. They depicted contemporary Germany as a land of broken marriages, soured affairs, rebellious youth, and casual sex. They suggested that the legacy of Naziism lingered into the present. And after nearly two decades of respectful adaptations of classics, the Young German Film forged alliances with experimental writing. This was a cinema of *Autoren*. Unlike the French auteur critic-filmmakers, the young Germans sought a cinema of literary quality.

Later the Oberhauseners would admit that the manifesto was largely a bluff, but several signatories, such as Edgar Reitz and Volker Schlöndorff, managed to sustain careers. From a long-range international perspective, the two most noteworthy debuts of the period were those of Alexander Kluge and Jean-Marie Straub.

Trained as a lawyer, Kluge moved into experimental writing and—after seeing *Breathless*—filmmaking. He became the most tireless advocate of the Young German Film. A signer of the Oberhausen manifesto, Kluge played a central role in lobbying for the Kuratorium. He also helped establish West Germany's first film production school, at Ulm. During the same period, he made a series of shorts. In 1965 he was given Kuratorium funding for what became *Abscheid von Gestern* ("Departure from Yesterday," aka *Yesterday Girl*, 1966). Kluge's stylistic flourishes—jump cuts, fast motion, interruptive titles, hand-held tracking shots—and his fragmented, elliptical storytelling firmly locate *Yesterday Girl* in the 1960s Young Cinema. Anita G. might be a French New Wave heroine: she drifts through cities, tries to hold a job, indulges in petty theft, has love affairs, and winds up pregnant and in prison.

Unlike his French contemporaries, though, Kluge sought to give Anita a historical significance. Her story is intermingled with a host of documents: a children's story from the 1920s, direct-cinema interviews, old photographs and songs. Anita's plight illustrates the continuity between the old Germany and the new; the film's epigraph is "We are separated from yesterday not by an abyss but by the changed situation." Although Kluge's narrative technique does not encourage the audience to identify wholly with Anita, there are moments of subdued pathos (Fig. 20.42). After the international recognition granted *Yesterday Girl*, Kluge became the Young German Film's most articulate theorist, championing films that would free the audience's imagination in new ways.

Far less public a figure was the French-born Jean-Marie Straub. As a youth he was deeply impressed by Bresson's *Les Dames du Bois du Boulogne* and the films of Lang and Dreyer. With his wife, Danièle Huillet, Straub adopted two works of Heinrich Böll as *Machorka-Muff* (1963) and *Nicht versöhnt* (*Not Reconciled*, 1965).

Like Kluge, Straub juxtaposed fictional and documentary materials.

Fig. 20.42 *Yesterday Girl*: On the run, Anita must change her clothes at the roadside.

Fig. 20.43 Depth and decentering in *Not Reconciled.*

Machorka-Muff, which points up the rise of militarism in postwar Germany, is presented in snippets of dialogue, action, and internal monologue, all intercut with landscapes and newspaper headlines. The film squeezes Böll's novelette *Berlin Diary* into eighteen minutes.

Not Reconciled is even more daringly compressed. In only fifty minutes Straub and Huillet trace a continuity between World War I, World War II, and the present through the story of three generations of a family. The deliberately inexpressive, even stilted acting, the great number of characters, the unsignaled switches between present and past, and the staccato fragmentation of the scenes make *Not Reconciled* almost incomprehensible on a first viewing. The plot complexities are accompanied by a self-conscious visual beauty (Fig. 20.43) and direct sound—a rarity among young filmmakers, who typically kept costs low by using postdubbing. Although German distributors refused to handle *Not Reconciled,* it enabled Straub and Huillet to win Kuratorium funding for a feature on the life of Bach. This film and subsequent efforts would have considerable international influence.

By the end of 1967, the Young German Film could point to many successes. *Yesterday Girl* and Volker Schlöndorff's *Young Törless* (1966) each won eight festival prizes, and other films did well on the international market. But directors, differing on principles and forced to compete for scarce resources, became more divided. The mainstream industry successfully lobbied for a new form of subsidy, and in January 1968, the Film Promotion Law went into effect. It shut out first-time directors and favored producers who turned out quick, low-budget commercial series. In addition, the new law also controlled content with a provision that refused sponsorship to films that were "contrary to the constitution or to moral or religious sentiments."[7]

Some beginning filmmakers used Kuratorium money and producers' interest in the young audience to make espionage thrillers and bedroom comedies. Eckhardt Schmidt, director of *Jet-Generation* (1967), remarked: "I prefer filming a naked girl rather than chattering about problems."[8] But many young filmmakers critical of the German "economic miracle" would make their voices heard throughout the decade.

NEW CINEMA IN THE USSR AND EASTERN EUROPE

YOUNG CINEMA IN THE SOVIET UNION

The "thaw" after Stalin's death in 1953 ended quickly: in the political sphere, with the 1956 crushing of the Hungarian Revolution; in the artistic domain, with the 1958 attacks on Boris Pasternak's novel *Dr. Zhivago.* But in 1961, Khrushchev launched a new "de-Stalinization" campaign, calling for openness and greater democracy. Intellectuals and artists responded eagerly, and a Soviet youth culture began to emerge.

In the cinema, most older directors continued to work in traditional ways. Heifits's *Lady with the Little Dog* (1960), for example, continued the stolid 1950s deep-focus technique in telling its story of a love affair in a declining class (Fig. 20.44). Still exploiting the monumental style, Mikhail

Fig. 20.44 The continuation of deep-focus shooting in the prestigious literary adaptation *The Lady with the Little Dog.*

Romm displayed a more liberal stance in *Nine Days of One Year* (1962), a social-problem film about nuclear radiation. Although Romm had been a major Stalinist filmmaker, he proved a progressive force after the thaw, training and encouraging several of the important directors of the postwar decades.

A new emphasis on youth could be seen in several films about children. Other filmmakers, like their counterparts abroad, concentrated on young adults in the contemporary world. Vasily Shukshin, a fiction writer, directed *There Was a Lad* (1964), in which a good-natured trucker encounters teenage life in the USSR (Fig. 20.45).

The most celebrated young director was Andrei Tarkovsky. The son of a major poet, he studied under Romm at VGIK. Like many of his contemporaries, Tarkovsky became interested in European art cinema, particularly Bergman, Bresson, and Fellini. His first feature was *Ivan's Childhood* (1962). After winning the Grand Prize at Venice, it became one of the most widely admired Soviet films of the 1960s.

The plot of *Ivan's Childhood* adheres to many conventions of the Soviet World War II film. A boy vows to avenge his parents' deaths and becomes a scout for a band of partisans. But Tarkovsky treats this material with an unusual lyricism (Figs. 20.46, 20.47). The wordless opening sequence, a dream in which Ivan floats through the trees to greet his mother and take a drink of water, establishes a cluster of visual motifs. After Ivan has died at the hands of the Nazis, the film concludes with a glowing sequence of fantasy images. The ambiguity is characteristic of 1960s art cinema: the sequence could be Ivan's final reverie, or it could be the filmmaker's free elaboration and comment. The authorities resented Tarkovsky's effort "to replace narrative causality with poetic articulations."[9]

The new liberalization soon ended. After Khrushchev denounced *I'm 20* (1963, Marlen Khutsiev) for insulting the older generation, the new cinema encountered greater resistance. In 1964 Khrushchev was forced to resign, and the conservative Leonid Brezhnev took over as Party Secretary. Under the rubric "harmonious development," Brezhnev halted reforms and tightened

Fig. 20.45 Youth culture in "socialist humanism": In *There Was a Lad*, a disdainful Muscovite confronts locals at a club dance.

Figs. 20.46 and 20.47 Tarkovsky's battle-scarred landscapes in *Ivan's Childhood* have a Bergmanesque starkness and stand in contrast to the lush tranquility of nature in Ivan's imagination.

Fig. 20.46

Fig. 20.47

Fig. 20.48 *Andrei Rublev*: The mystical tactility of Tarkovsky: A bloody hand slumping into a stream produces a milky stain.

Fig. 20.49 As Tartars pillage a town, geese float down from the sky (*Andrei Rublev*).

control of culture. Nonconformist films were reshot or banned. Andrei Konchalovsky's *Asya's Happiness,* finished in 1966, was withdrawn for its supposed insults to the peasantry. Alexander Askoldov's *Commissar* (1967) was suppressed for its positive portrayal of Jewish characters. After Grigori Chukhrai's *Beginning of an Unknown Era* (1967) was shelved, he closed his experimental studio.

The fate of Tarkovsky's second feature exemplifies the difficulties filmmakers faced. *Andrei Rublev* (1965), a long, somber drama of the life of a fifteenth-century icon painter, followed the strategy Tarkovsky had pursued in *Ivan's Childhood.* Once more he took a formulaic genre—here, the biography of the great artist—and infused it with mysteriously poetic imagery (Figs. 20.48, 20.49). *Andrei Rublev* also had disturbing contemporary overtones. Surrounded by viciousness and cruelty, Rublev gives up speaking, stops painting, and abandons religious faith. Some viewers saw Tarkovsky's film as an allegory of art crushed by social oppression. Goskino administrators denied it a release.

Despite political pressures, several films of the Brezhnev era broached issues of importance to youth and intellectuals. Two significant women directors emerged: Larissa Shepitko, who centered *Wings* (1966) on a female pilot learning to become a school supervisor, and Kira Muratova, whose *Brief Encounters* (1968) shows a man from the viewpoints of the two women who love him.

The studios of the Soviet republics, closer to folk traditions and less vulnerable to official reprimands, produced some oblique, poetic films. Older than the "new" directors, Serge Paradzhanov grew up in Georgia, graduated from VGIK in 1951, and during the 1950s made several films in the Ukraine. His *Shadows of Forgotten Ancestors* (1965) tells of a man haunted by the death of the woman he loved. The folklike story, however, is rendered in a flurry of hysterically modernist techniques. Jerkily hand-held, the camera races through landscapes. Paradzhanov gives us shots taken from treetops, ceremonially still compositions, and abrupt subjective images (Fig. 20.50). Paradzhanov's aggressive style made authorities limit the film's distribution in the USSR but also helped it garner over a dozen international prizes.

Fig. 20.50 A man is struck by an axe, and blood dribbles down the camera lens (*Shadows of Forgotten Ancestors*).

Once Brezhnev's regime was firmly in place, Paradzhanov, Tarkovsky, and other innovative directors found it difficult to launch projects. Instead, the industry and the Party made Sergei Bondarchuk's massive *War and Peace* (1967) the official emblem of Soviet film. The film was trumpeted as the most costly production in history and won a huge success in the export market. Bondarchuk cautiously inserted a few self-consciously contemporary techniques (slow motion, hand-held camera), but on the whole he revived the monumental tradition. A new period of "stabilization"—later to be known as "stagnation"—set in, and not until the early 1970s would Soviet cinema and other arts have the chance to explore new avenues.

NEW WAVES IN EASTERN EUROPE

The USSR's resistance to cinematic experimentation had its parallels in some eastern European countries. Still, in the early 1960s "New Waves" sprang up in Poland, Czechoslovakia, Yugoslavia, and Hungary.

During the late 1950s, eastern Europe's economy strengthened, and countries sought to enter western markets. Films proved to be valuable export items. In addition, economic reforms led many governments to increase artistic freedom. Each New Wave typically participated in a broader cultural renaissance including literature, drama, painting, and music.

Several eastern European countries simultaneously developed production structures that were more decentralized than the rigidly controlled Soviet hierarchy. In 1955 Poland had pioneered the system of "creative film units"; in each one directors and scriptwriters worked under the supervision of a senior filmmaker. In 1963, both Czechoslovakia and Hungary adopted variants of the film-unit system. Yugoslavia's decentralized system, in place since 1950, was revised in 1962 to allow filmmakers to form independent companies to make a single film. Since nearly all these countries were threatened by the advance of television, the reorganization offered possibilities of competition.

Consequently, filmmakers in these countries were freer to try fresh subjects, themes, forms, and styles than were their Soviet counterparts. The films that emerged linked eastern European cinema to the art cinema that had been flourishing in western Europe since the war. Because eastern Europe had always imported more foreign films than had the Soviet Union, directors and audiences were more aware of other New Cinemas. And as eastern European films entered festivals and international distribution circuits, western viewers encountered innovative examples of cinematic modernism.

Young Cinema in Poland.   In the early 1960s it might have seemed that Polish filmmaking had lost none of its force. Andrzej Wajda's *Innocent Sorcerors* (1960) adapted his style to a more intimate subject, a couple's night together. *Mother Joan of the Angels* (1961), by Jerzy Kawalerowicz, offered a daring tale of possession in a convent. By 1960 the Polish system of producing films by independent units was working smoothly, and strict Socialist Realism was firmly in the past.

Yet political pressures were intensifying. Films were seldom banned, but they might be denounced by critics and politicians, and this slowed the progress of older directors. After *Innocent Sorcerors,* Wajda made no film in Poland for several years, opting instead for international coproductions. His Polish historical epic *Ashes* (1965) did not find much favor. Similarly, Kawalerowicz made the long, brooding *Pharaoh* (1966) after six years of preparation. On the whole the older directors of the Polish School seemed to have run out of energy.

In the early 1960s, there was the possibility that Poland's younger directors would cultivate a modest, realistic approach in contrast to the "baroque" tendencies of Wajda and Kawalerowicz. A few intimate films based on sociological observation did appear, but the two most celebrated young directors avoided such realism and moved toward a strongly dramatic, technically flamboyant approach to youthful subjects.

Roman Polanski was an actor before going to film school and attracting international attention with a short, *Two Men and a Wardrobe* (1958). After spending a few years in Paris, he returned to Poland to make *Knife in the Water* (1962). At one level the film is an intimate suspense drama. An unhappily married couple take a young hitchhiker along on a sailing trip, and the tension builds as the husband taunts the young man mercilessly. *Knife in the Water* could be defended as politically accurate in attacking the new "red bourgeoisie" who lived in western luxury. But the young man can hardly be a positive hero, since he is at best naively confused and at worst somewhat cynical.

Polanski avoids most of the technical innovations of the European New Cinemas, relying on orthodox cutting and vivid deep-focus shots that keep the characters in tense confrontation (Fig. 20.51). Yet in other ways *Knife in the Water* relies on art-cinema conventions. The opening derives from *Voyage to Italy,* although by 1962 Polanski needed none of the expository dialogue that Rossellini required: we can infer that the couple are quarreling when the wife gets out of the car to let her husband drive. The film's finale, with the couple reunited in their car and the husband wondering if the young man is really dead, became an emblem of the lack of closure in 1960s cinema.

Jerzy Skolimowski, scriptwriter for *Innocent Sorcerors* and *Knife in the Water,* became the Polish director closest in style and theme to the Parisian Nouvelle Vague. *Identification Marks: None* (1964), assembled out of student

Fig. 20.51 Harsh, Wellesian depth in *Knife in the Water.*

footage, shows a draft-dodger moving through Polish youth culture. *Walkover* (1965) centers on a prizefighter who eventually wins a factory boxing match. *Barrier* (1966) draws upon Felliniesque fantasy to portray contemporary Polish youth rebelling against cynicism and bureaucracy. In each film, Skolimowski's hero (usually played by the director) is a sensitive drifter disillusioned by society but still hoping to find happiness in a woman's love.

Skolimowski's films exhibit the casual improvisation we find in early Truffaut or Godard. They also have a flashy, almost exhibitionistic style. There are long takes, with complex camera movements and zooms; abstract, often perplexing compositions (Fig. 20.52); and surreal images of the contemporary city (Fig. 20.53). In *Identification Marks: None*, after a traffic accident a hand covers the lens; only then do we realize that the shot represents the protagonist's optical point of view.

The late 1960s marked an end to the Polish School. After *Knife in the Water*, Polanski went into exile. In Belgium Skolimowski made *Le Départ* (1967), a Nouvelle Vague echo; the banning of his next Polish production, *Hands Up!* (1968), led him to work in England and western Europe.

The Czech New Wave.   Czechoslovakia offered more favorable conditions for a New Cinema. The years 1962–1966 saw steps toward "market socialism" and a mood of reform. The cinema took an active part in cultural renewal. A decentralized production system placed a director-scriptwriter team at the head of each unit. As television became the main source of popular entertainment, the cinema became subsidized by the state. By 1968, production units had become independent and censorship had diminished.

The Czech New Wave crested in the period 1963–1967, winning international prizes and even Academy Awards. Although some nations in the Soviet sphere disapproved of the new Czech films, elsewhere they were almost as influential as the Nouvelle Vague.

The younger directors, most of them graduates of the film school FAMU, made their entry with short films in the early 1960s. All the filmmakers knew Italian Neorealism, the Polish School, and the French New Wave, and all to some degree felt the effects of Direct Cinema. But like most New Waves, the Czech phenomenon can only loosely be considered a stylistic movement. For the most part filmmakers shared only conditions of work, thematic concerns, and an urge to move beyond Socialist Realist formulas.

One tendency was toward an art-cinema realism. Jaromil Jireš's *The Cry* (1963), often considered the first manifestation of the Czech New Wave, used nonactors and Direct Cinema technique to explore the life of a couple expecting a baby. Ewald Schorm's *Courage for Every Day* (1964) and *Return of the Prodigal Son* (1966) owed more to Antonioni in their probing of the problems of the middle-class professional.

Jiří Menzel, who found international success with *Closely Watched Trains* (1966) and *Capricious Summer* (1967), took to an extreme that shifting of tone which Neorealism made a major principle of postwar cinema. In *Closely Watched Trains*, Menzel mixes solemn issues with erotic jokes, satire on authority, and moments of sheer absurdity. The film shifts instantly from

Fig. 20.52 Dazzling reflections in *Identification Marks: None*.

Fig. 20.53 False depth and flatness (*Walkover*).

Fig. 20.54 After a hospital is bombed, Menzel's flat, Keatonesque shot shows Milos, miraculously unscathed, lifting his coat off the rack.

Fig. 20.55 The final shot of *Intimate Lighting*: obstinate eggnog.

Fig. 20.56 The long lens picks out details in documentary fashion (*The Firemen's Ball*).

mocking the young hero's petty ambitions to appreciating his courage, however inadvertent, in participating in partisan sabotage. Individual images display reflexive wit (Fig. 20.54).

The single Czech feature made by Ivan Passer presents a gentler blend of comedy and social criticism. A sketch of the reunion of two musicians, *Intimate Lighting* (1965) contrasts city and country manners, amateur and professional music making, and traditional and modern conceptions of women's roles. The fragmentary incidents have a muted pathos and humor: a hen hoping to hatch a car, hosts and guests patiently trying to drink eggnog that will not leave their glasses (Fig. 20.55).

Milos Forman was also influenced by Neorealism and Direct Cinema, but his films present more caustic social criticism than do those of Menzel and Passer. His first feature, *Black Peter* (1963), centers on a teenager similar to Menzel's Milos. Barely holding down a job, constantly at odds with his father, clumsily seeking romance, Peter becomes a comic emblem of confused Czech youth. In the first half of *Loves of a Blonde* (1965), Forman focuses with cruel hilarity on the effects of an army unit assigned to a factory town where women vastly outnumber men. In the second half, the heroine pursues a traveling piano player to Prague, where she learns that neither he nor his parents care for her. The film's grim undertones blend with Forman's satire of meaningless work and official morality.

At the center of *Black Peter* and *Loves of a Blonde* are long seriocomic scenes of couples flirting at a dance. In *The Firemen's Ball* (1967), Forman builds an entire plot around such a situation. Concentrating on the single evening of a party honoring a retiring fire chief, Forman does not develop characters in depth. Instead, he fills his film with incisive running gags and revelations of human vanities. As the ball goes on, prizes are stolen, an impromptu beauty contest creates a scandal, couples make love, and an old man's home burns down. Stylistically, *The Firemen's Ball* exemplifies the emerging worldwide tendency to use long lenses and documentary techniques to film staged material (Fig. 20.56). Forman's portrait of socialist society, with its frustrated sexuality, incompetent bureaucracy, and petty pilfering, drew torrents of criticism.

Besides impulses toward satiric realism there were efforts to find a more formally complex approach on the model of Resnais, Fellini, or Robbe-Grillet. Jan Nemeć's first feature, *Diamonds of the Night* (1964), takes as its situation two young men's escape from a train carrying them to a concentration camp. This incident, a likely basis for a Socialist Realist war film, triggers an exercise in 1960s modernism. The physical frenzy of the boys' flight is rendered via documentary techniques: hand-held camera, high-contrast cinematography (Fig. 20.57), and a sound track dominated by gasping and thrashing noises. Nemeć goes on to interrupt the action with fragmentary, jumbled flashbacks which mix indiscernibly with fantasy scenes (Fig. 20.58).

If *Diamonds of the Night* owes something to *Hiroshima mon amour*, Nemeć's next film, *Report on the Party and the Guests* (1968), echoes *Last Year at Marienbad*. As if to compensate for the virtual absence of dialogue in *Diamonds of the Night*, Nemeć fills this film with talk—the empty absurdities of bourgeois life. These become only the prelude to a symbolic critique of a Stalinist police state. Banned upon completion and released two years later, *Party and the Guests* proved to be the most controversial film of Czech New Cinema.

The New Wave pushed toward even purer fantasy. In Vojtech Jasný's *Cassandra Cat* (1963), a magical cat wreaks havoc when its special eyeglasses turn people different colors. Jan Schmidt's *End of August in the Hotel Ozone* (1966), about survivors of an atomic war, also became an abstract political allegory. Nemeć's third feature, *Martyrs of Love* (1966), consists of a trio of three Surrealistic tales on the border between fantasy and reality. In a remark that would have provoked the wrath of Communist officials a few years before, Nemeć summed up the attitude of many Czech filmmakers: "The director must create his own world, a world independent of reality."[10]

The work of Vera Chytilová partakes of several of these trends. Her *Something Different* (1963) intercuts the lives of Eva, a gymnast who trains arduously, and Vera, a bored housewife. Since Eva and Vera never meet, the viewer is obliged to compare their situations. Chytilová also links the stories through film style. The piano music accompanying Eva's training is heard over scenes of Vera's life, while shots in one story graphically resemble those in another (Figs. 20.59, 20.60). Eva's story is filmed in a modified Direct Cinema style, while Vera's is presented as a more conventional fiction, setting up an interplay between two trends in the Czech New Wave itself.

With *Daisies* (1966) Chytilová moves into symbolic fantasy, satirizing a

Fig. 20.57 Harsh, Direct Cinema techniques rendering the boys' escape in *Diamonds of the Night*.

Fig. 20.58 The central fantasy of the empty tramcar in Nemeć's *Diamonds of the Night*.

Fig. 20.59

Fig. 20.60

Figs. 20.59 and 20.60 In *Something Different*, Vera's meeting with the bike boy cuts to another vertical and centered shot in Eva's practice session.

Fig. 20.61 *Daisies*: The interchangeable heroines as disassembled parts.

society of consumption and waste. Like *Something Different*, the film concentrates on two women, but now their personalities are robotically identical. Taking them through a string of sight gags and escalating bouts of eating and mayhem, Chytilová mocks female stereotypes when special effects reduce the heroines to cut-outs and pin-ups (Fig. 20.61).

Menzel, Passer, Forman, Nemeć, and Chytilová were the most widely known filmmakers of the New Wave, but many others played a role in reviving Czech production. In 1966–1967, the government attempted to retighten cultural policy. Authorities attacked liberal writers and banned several films, including *Daisies* and *Report on the Party and the Guests*. The year 1968, an important benchmark in cinemas around the world, would put the Czech New Wave to a crucial test.

Yugoslavian New Film. Since 1948, Yugoslavia had evolved its own nationalistic, market-based version of socialism. In 1960–1961 and in 1966–1967, workers' councils gained more power over industrial production, and this tendency benefited cinema workers. A revised film law (1962) gave regional republics greater autonomy in filmmaking and allowed filmmakers to create independent enterprises. Such companies could compete for generous state subsidies. Soon the number of production units tripled.

These conditions encouraged Yugoslavia's "New Film" (*Novi film*). Influenced by Neorealism, the Nouvelle Vague, and recent eastern European cinemas, young directors advocated experimenting with film form in the name of socialist humanism. As in other countries, filmmakers and critics wrote for periodicals and translated articles from foreign journals.

The peak period of New Film, 1963–1968, revealed active groups in Belgrade, Zagreb, and Ljubljana. Two directors had particularly strong impact outside Yugoslavia.

Aleksandar Petrović, whose *Two* (1961) helped launch New Film, represented an "intimate cinema" that examined personal problems in contemporary society. His *Days* (1963) portrays the empty life of a young urban couple. *Three* (1966) is a triptych of World War II stories. Petrović called for "personal films" that "claimed the right to subjective interpretations of the lives of individuals and society, the right to 'open metaphors,' leaving room for viewers to think and feel for themselves."[11]

Petrović's most widely known film, *I Even Met Happy Gypsies* (1967), is an open-ended study of a tough gypsy merchant of goose feathers whose romantic involvement with two women leads him to murder. Petrović relies on long lenses and hand-held shots, and he uses nonactors speaking their various native languages. The overall effect is of pseudo-documentary realism in the portrayal of an oppressed minority.

Far more freewheeling, close to the flamboyant experimentation of the Czech fantasists, are the works of Dušan Makavejev. Makavejev's first feature, *Man Is Not a Bird* (1965), announced his penchant for deflating the pretentions of politics with earthy humor: in one scene, lovers copulate to Beethoven's Ninth Symphony, played for the edification of workers. In *Love Affair, or the Tragedy of a Switchboard Operator* (1967) Makavejev utilizes a collage form which owes something to Resnais and Godard but which is treated with his bawdy humor. While Chytilová's *Something Different* crosscuts two simultaneous lines of action, Makavejev alternates the progress of a love affair with flashforwards that show the affair's grisly outcome. The film also includes newsreel footage and lectures on criminal behavior. The viewer learns quickly that the affair ends in the death of Isabella, but which of her two lovers killed her? The film mixes gruesome scenes (an autopsy, a search for rats) with racy comedy and satire on socialist ideals.

At one level, Makavejev's next film, *Innocence Unprotected* (1968), is a Direct Cinema inquiry into the life of Aleksic Dragoljub, a professional acrobat who also made the first Serbo-Croatian sound movie. Interviews with Aleksic and his surviving collaborators are interrupted by intertitles, newsreels, and extracts from the original film (also called *Innocence Unprotected*). Makavejev further "decorates" the found footage with tinting, toning, handcoloring (Color Plate 20.3), and ironic musical accompaniment. The collage strategy allows Makavejev to mock Nazi and Communist politics, satirize show business, celebrate naive filmmaking, and pay tribute to the national pride expressed in Aleksic's "very good old film." Through their collage form, *Love Affair* and *Innocence Unprotected* create the sort of "open metaphors" Petrović had called for in New Film.

New Cinema in Hungary. The French New Wave made a very strong impact in Hungary. As one filmmaker put it, "Everybody went to Paris to see Truffaut's and Godard's films. . . . At the time, people imitated them, but that was liberating."[12] Such influences would not have had much consequence, however, without favorable production circumstances.

As the political scene liberalized and television became more popular, production became decentralized. In 1958, the Béla Balázs studio (named after the pioneer film theorist and scriptwriter) was created to give graduates of the film academy a chance to make shorts and first features. In 1963, the industry adopted the Polish "creative film unit" system, which assigned each director a place in a unit but also allowed him or her to propose a project to another unit. The units were coordinated by MAFILM, which also allocated studio facilities. The industry's reorganization yielded an output of twenty or more films per year, twice the 1950s average.

Like other New Cinemas, Hungary's included two generations. In the

MIKLÓS JANCSÓ

Miklós Jancsó graduated from the Hungarian Film Academy in 1950, at the age of twenty-nine, and after making some short films he directed a fairly orthodox feature in 1958. His second feature, *Cantata* (1962), a story of a young doctor seeking to rekindle his relation with his peasant father, was filmed in the manner of Antonioni, a key influence on Jancsó. Not until the mid-1960s did he emerge as a distinct auteur.

Jancsó's major films concentrated on upheavals in Hungary's tumultuous history: World War II, military coups, and popular rebellions. He follows Soviet Montage cinema in creating drama out of collective action and historical movements. In Jancsó films, individuals have little psychological identity. Instead, they become emblematic of social classes or political factions. The drama emerges out of the ways in which they are caught in a historical process.

Distancing us from the characters, the films avoid subjective devices like fantasy and refuse flashbacks and flashforwards. What comes to the fore are naked displays of power. In *The Red and the White* (1967), after a peasant woman has numbly obeyed a Cossack officer's order to strip, a superior appears and curtly orders the troops to execute the officer. In *The Round-Up* (1965) the occupying Austrians promise a peasant that he can escape execution if he can find a partisan who has killed more men than he has. Before suffering torture or execution, victims must march in file, form circles, strip or lie down or swim a river—that is, undergo absurd ceremonies which merely display their subjection to the will of authority. Coming from a generation appalled by the revelation of wartime atrocities and the Nazi death camps, Jancsó suggests that power is exercised through public humiliation and minute control of the victim's body.

Jancsó's manner of treatment suits his dramas. After *My Way Home* (1965), he exploited abnormally long takes; the average shot in *Silence and Cry* (1968) runs two and a half minutes. Jancsó presents the moment-by-moment oscillations in power by means of a dynamic camera that renders every situation fluid and filled with tension. The intricacies of this camera-and-character choreography go beyond even the complex shot from *Story of a Love Affair* (pp. 427–429); to illustrate even a single Jancsó shot would require several pages. In *The Round-Up* the camera often emphasizes geometrical patterns in the Austrians' search for partisans (Fig. 20.62). *The Red and the White* uses both immense landscape views and medium shots, sometimes tracking, panning, and zooming all at once (Figs. 20.63–20.68).

In few auteurs' work do structure, style, and theme mesh so precisely as in Jancsó's. His narrative construction and cinematic technique present a spectacle of power that is at once abstractly symbolic and concretely historical. He became the principal example of the artistic originality and seriousness that could be achieved in an eastern European film industry.

Fig. 20.62 *The Round-Up*: Geometric figures of power fill the wide screen.

early 1960s older directors such as Karoly Makk, Zoltán Fábrí, and István Gaal seized new opportunities. Most widely seen was the work of Miklós Jancsó, who made his first feature in 1958 when he was thirty-seven but who achieved fame with the films he made after he turned forty. (See Box.)

The younger generation of directors consisted largely of those who had graduated from the Academy for Theatre and Cinematography during the late 1950s. Entranced not only by the Nouvelle Vague but also by the Young

Fig. 20.63 The floating fluidity of Jancsó's long takes in *The Red and the White*: The youth flees the White soldiers at the river . . .

Fig. 20.64 . . . comes up to the hospital cabin . . .

Fig. 20.65 . . . and hides among the wounded . . .

Fig. 20.66 . . . before a nurse comes out . . .

Fig. 20.67 . . . and the camera follows her to the edge of the cabin . .

Fig. 20.68 . . . where she and the other nurses discover the Whites' atrocities at the river's edge.

Polish Cinema and European auteurs like Bergman and Antonioni, Hungarian directors pursued the goals of most New Cinemas: to rethink their country's past and to present a portrait of contemporary youth.

For example, István Szabó presented his films as "the autobiography of a generation."[13] *The Age of Daydreaming* (1964) portrays a new socialist technocracy: confident young people wear western sports clothes, take beach vacations, and talk of their love affairs while watching footage of Nazi horrors. Szabó sometimes romanticizes their lives with Nouvelle Vague techniques, as in lyrical slow-motion shots or citations of Truffaut, but as the film goes on, it questions material success.

Szabó's next film, *Father* (1966), probes the main character's mind in a way typical of the European art cinema generally. As in the films of Kluge and Straub, a play with time serves to pose questions about politics and history. Tako believes his father to be a war hero, but upon investigating his life, the son finds that history is more complicated. An interplay of memory, dreams, fantasy, and history in the hero's experience creates the ambiguity so characteristic of 1960s modernism. Just as *Hiroshima mon amour* treats newsreels as both documents and symbolic commentary, Szabó inserts footage of the 1956 uprising into his story, generating both a mild collage effect and a plausible sense that the characters are involved in the historical event (Figs. 20.69, 20.70). In his attempt to fuse the concerns of contemporary youth with a critical study of his nation's past, Szabó typified the efforts of most directors in eastern Europe's New Waves.

Fig. 20.69

Fig. 20.70

Fig. 20.69 Szabó cuts from newsreel shots of the 1956 Hungarian rebellion . . .

Fig. 20.70 . . . to shots of his heroes marching with a crowd.

THE JAPANESE NEW WAVE

After a high-school girl is raped by a thuggish student, she agrees to seduce older men so that he can shake them down. When she becomes pregnant, the student gets money for her abortion by sleeping with an older woman. As the student is beaten to death by a gang, the young woman, riding with a man who has picked her up, tries to escape and is dragged to her death.

Aptly titled *Cruel Story of Youth* (1960), this film by the young Nagisa Oshima would scarcely have been recognizable as Japanese to western connoisseurs of Kurosawa, Mizoguchi, and Ozu. Yet it is a typical product of the Japanese New Wave. The movement is all the more remarkable in being one of the few New Cinemas deliberately created by a film industry.

The Japanese studios had jumped on the youth bandwagon early. During the mid-1950s, the newly revived swordfight movie catered to adolescent boys, while romantic melodramas were aimed at teenage girls. In 1956, *Season of the Sun,* adapted from a scandalous best-seller, brought forth a series of "sun-tribe" (*taiyozoku*) movies which depicted spoiled young people living an amoral, licentious lifestyle. Crime thrillers, rock-and-roll musicals, and swordplay films were ground out relentlessly, particularly at less prestigious studios like Nikkatsu and Toei. Thanks to the new strategy, 1958 movie attendance rose to just over a billion, a postwar high.

Shochiku, the most conservative Japanese studio, noted its rivals' triumphs with youth fare and observed the box-office success of French young cinema. The company decided to launch a Japanese New Wave. In 1959 the firm promoted a young assistant director, Nagisa Oshima, and allowed him to direct his own scripts. The success of his first films led Shochiku to promote other assistants. Nikkatsu followed suit, giving newly appointed directors substantial assignments.

At first, New Wave films attracted critical praise and proved somewhat popular with young audiences. But they could not halt a downturn in the box office. By 1963, the popularity of color television had pulled attendance to half its 1958 level. The studios tried desperately to win back the audience by lowering ticket prices, by making more violent swordplay films (e.g., the *Zatoichi* "blind swordsman" series), and by pioneering new genres—the *yakuza* (gambler-gangster) film and the "pink film" (soft-core pornography). Some of the New Wave directors contributed interestingly to these trends, but soon most of the filmmakers quit their studios.

Only a few years earlier this would have meant leaving filmmaking. Unlike European countries, Japan had a strong, vertically integrated studio system, and until the 1960s no one could easily work outside it. Moreover, the government did not encourage new talent through subsidies and prizes. But theaters' habits of showing double features created a larger appetite for releases than the studios could profitably satisfy. As a result, many New Wave directors were able to create independent production companies. While young directors' films were sometimes distributed by the big studios, a central role was played by the Art Theater Guild (ATG), a chain of specialized theaters. In 1964, the ATG began financing and distributing films, and it became the mainstay of the New Wave generation.

Like Young Cinemas elsewhere, the Japanese New Wave attacked mainstream cinematic traditions. Complex flashback structures, intrusions of fantasy and symbolism, and experiments with shot design, color, cutting, and camerawork became common. Directors splashed jarring compositions across the wide screen, and the hand-held camera and disjunctive editing came to the fore. But since mainstream Japanese films had explored such techniques before, they were perhaps less disruptive than the subjects, themes, and attitudes portrayed in the New Wave works.

No films had so savagely criticized Japanese society, revealing oppression and conflict behind the image of a tranquil, prosperous nation. Theft, murder, and rape were rendered casually. The directors flaunted the vulgarity of their heroes and heroines, and often the critique was framed in political terms. The Japanese directors went further than even their German contemporaries in showing that authoritarian forces continued to rule their country long after democracy had supposedly come.

All these qualities are evident in the work of Nagisa Oshima. Like his contemporary Truffaut, before getting into directing he wrote inflammatory film criticism. But as a former student activist, he gave his articles a political slant alien to the French auteur critics. Oshima complained that Japanese society stifled the individual in the name of superficial harmony. He called for a personal cinema of the "active subject," in which the director expressed his deepest passions, anxieties, and obsessions. This view, a cliché in the West and one basis of postwar art cinema, was a breakthrough in Oshima's group- and tradition-dominated nation. He and his New Wave peers created Japan's postwar modernist cinema.

Oshima saw flickers of "active subjectivity" in the wave of late 1950s student demonstrations against renewing the U.S.-Japan Security Treaty (known as "Ampo"). For the first time the Japanese abandoned their time-honored role of obedient sufferer and saw themselves as able to change their fate. But Oshima quickly came to believe that the Ampo demonstrations led only to disillusionment. He traces this process in *Night and Fog in Japan* (1960), a scathing critique of the Communist party and the student left. Oshima intercuts student political activities from the 1950s with Ampo treaty demonstrations during 1960, rearranging their order to bring out parallels. He frames the two time schemes within a wedding ceremony which symbolizes a cynical surrender of political ideals. Shochiku shelved *Night and Fog in Japan* almost immediately after release, claiming that it was failing, but Oshima charged that the studio bowed to political pressures after the recent

Fig. 20.71 Just before the ending of *Cruel Story of Youth*, with the heroine's face split by the wide frame.

Fig. 20.72 The quarreling leftists, framed in cramped, telephoto shots (*Night and Fog in Japan*).

assassination of a Socialist leader. In protest he quit Shochiku, though several of his later films were produced with the company.

Throughout these films and others, Oshima pursues the question of how individual desires of the active subject, however warped, reveal the rigidity of political authority. His two major representations of these desires—criminality and eroticism—produced films that remain disturbing today. Moreover, Oshima refused to cultivate an identifiable style. *Cruel Story of Youth* frames most scenes in medium shots and tight, decentered close-ups (Fig. 20.71). *Night and Fog in Japan*, comprising only forty-five shots, relies on disorienting camera movements that whip across theatrically poised tableaux (Fig. 20.72). *Violence at Noon* (1966), by contrast, uses naturalistic staging and around 1500 shots. Each film's style, Oshima maintained, sprang from his feelings and attitudes of the moment.

Other directors created more conventional methods of stylization while still expressing a degree of social criticism. Hiroshi Teshigahara, associated with a Surrealist group and the novelist Kobo Abe, found international success with *Woman in the Dunes* (1963). This tale of a man trapped in a gigantic sand pit with a mysterious woman was widely interpreted as an allegory of how an arid society could be overcome by a primal eroticism.

More central to the New Wave was Yoshishige Yoshida, whom Shochiku promoted to director when Oshima's earliest work became successful. Yoshida admired Resnais and Antonioni, whose emphasis on pictorially striking

Fig. 20.73 The poise of Mizoguchi displayed in the swordfight film (Shinoda's *Assassination*, 1965).

Fig. 20.74 *Pigs and Battleships*: The rage of youth against the world.

images shows up in his work. His sensuous camera movements in *Akitsu Springs* (1962) owe less to Oshima than to *Last Year at Marienbad*. The film's concerns, however, remain resolutely historical, suggesting that in the postwar era Japan lost its chance for true democracy. Another Shochiku alumnus was Masahiro Shinoda, an assistant to Ozu and an admirer of Mizoguchi. Shinoda's films have a fastidiousness of visual design that echoes 1930s Japanese classicism (Fig. 20.73).

Closer to Oshima's political perspective was the other major director to emerge from the New Wave, Shohei Imamura. Declaring his interest in "the lower part of the human body and the lower part of the social structure,"[14] Imamura sought to record Japan's forgotten regions, oppressed classes, and lustful impulses.

As a young director at Nikkatsu, Imamura became identified with the New Wave principally through his outrageously satiric *Pigs and Battleships* (1961). This story of a teenage thug whose gang raises pigs on black-market garbage is less stylized than Oshima's work of the period, but the political critique remains sharp. Presenting a society of petty racketeers, prostitutes, and mothers anxious to sell their daughters to GIs, Imamura equates the Japanese with the pigs feeding off refuse from U.S. warships. The hero dies in a moment of rebellion, cut down as he machine-guns a row of buildings (Fig. 20.74).

Like Oshima's men, Imamura's are typically driven by perverse anti-social desires, but he often regards his heroes more mockingly, as in *The Pornographers* (1966). The final scene of *Pigs and Battleships* establishes the central Imamura character as the tough woman who fights for herself in a world dominated by men. *The Insect Woman* (1963) celebrates the pragmatism of three generations of postwar women who use prostitution and theft to win a measure of independence. In *Intentions of Murder* (1964) a woman, made pregnant by her rapist, abandons him to death and lives for the sake of her son.

The Japanese New Wave brought recognition to many other filmmakers, both older directors like Kaneto Shindo (notable for *The Island,* 1960) and younger talents like Susumu Hani (*Bad Boys,* 1960; *She and He,* 1963). In addition, it created a climate of acceptance for experimentation. Seijun Suzuki's Nikkatsu films, with their eccentric black humor and comic-book exaggerations, made him a cult figure with young audiences. Similarly, Koji Wakamitsu exploited the "pink" genre in gruesome, stylized films like *Violated Women in White* (1967). Executives were distressed to find that the New Wave which they had created led young audiences to expect outrageous formal innovations and attacks on authority in even routine studio products.

GREAT BRITAIN: "KITCHEN SINK" CINEMA

As Italy had cultivated the spaghetti Westerns and as Japan had aimed at teenage movies, British filmmaking responded to the decline in filmgoing by creating new sorts of films. Hammer Films, a small independent production company, rose to prominence with a series of internationally popular horror films. Many were loose remakes of 1930s Universal films, including *Dracula* (aka *The Horror of Dracula,* 1958, Terence Fisher) and *The Mummy* (1959, Terence Fisher). Gorier than their predecessors, they also boasted polished production values, including elegant color cinematography (Color Plate 20.4).

The horror vogue paved the way for one of the most unusual films of this period, Michael Powell's *Peeping Tom* (1959). Although it was not produced by Hammer, its scriptwriter had worked there. It concerned a shy young assistant cinematographer who is also a psychotic killer, making 16mm films of his female victims in their death throes. Since Powell had co-directed some of the most prestigious films of the postwar era, such as *The Red Shoes* and *A Matter of Life and Death* (Chapter 17), critics could not fathom why he should take on this sordid tale. Yet *Peeping Tom* explores the roots of sexual violence with a complexity unusual for its time, presciently linking child abuse to the victim's later crimes. It also raises the question of how the film medium itself arouses erotic impulses (Fig. 20.75).

If horror films constituted one of the most distinctive portions of the mainstream cinema, the "Kitchen Sink" trend (so-called for its depiction of grubby, everyday life) was Britain's equivalent of the French New Wave. Its principal directors emerged out of the Free Cinema group (p. 562).

During the mid-1950s, plays and fiction centering on rebellious working-class protagonists created a class-conscious, "angry young man" trend. The most important of these works was John Osborne's play *Look Back in Anger,* directed on the stage by Tony Richardson in 1956. In 1959, Richardson and others formed a production company, Woodfall, in order to move from the documentary shorts of Free Cinema into feature filmmaking.

Fig. 20.75 The image of one of the terrified victims in *Peeping Tom* is partially projected on the protagonist as he stands before the cinema screen.

Fig. 20.76 Like many Kitchen Sink films, *Look Back in Anger* stresses the grim industrial landscapes that surround the characters.

One of the first Woodfall films was an adaptation of *Look Back in Anger* (1959) starring Richard Burton. The alienated hero runs a candy stall in an open-air market and rants to his mates about the injustices of the class system. His best friend is his elderly landlady, whom he accompanies on a visit to her husband's grave (Fig. 20.76). Like other films of this tendency, *Look Back in Anger*'s sober realism owes a good deal to location shooting.

Although *Look Back in Anger* was a commercial failure, another Woodfall film made at the same time, and released shortly before it, did well at the box office. *Room at the Top* (1959, Jack Clayton) was adapted from a novel about a cynical working-class hero who marries a factory owner's daughter in order to better his lot. Dwelling on the disillusionment of life in Britain's provincial cities, *Room at the Top* was unusual in its sexual frankness and its depiction of class resentment.

Perhaps the quintessential film of the Kitchen Sink trend is Karel Reisz's *Saturday Night and Sunday Morning* (1960). Arthur deeply resents his factory job and his passive parents (Fig. 20.77), yet at the end he and his fiancée stand staring at a suburban housing development, a shot suggesting that they face the same dreary life.

Saturday Night and Sunday Morning was based on an Alan Sillitoe novel, and he adapted his own short story for Richardson's *The Loneliness of the Long Distance Runner* (1962), the story of a sullen prisoner in a reform school who trains as a cross-country runner. Like other Angry Young Man films, *Loneliness* uses techniques borrowed from the French New Wave, including fast motion to suggest excitement during the hero's crimes and hand-held camerawork for scenes of his exhilarating open-air jogging. In an echo of Truffaut's *The 400 Blows*, *Loneliness* ends with a freeze-frame as the boys assemble gas masks.

Lindsay Anderson, like the *Cahiers du cinéma* directors, had been a film critic, and he lambasted the British cinema for its stodgy refusal to face contemporary life. His first feature, *This Sporting Life* (1963), takes as its protagonist a miner who tries to become a professional rugby player while carrying on a troubled affair with his landlady (Fig. 20.78). Anderson indicts capitalist society through the corrupt sports promoters whom the hero encounters.

Fig. 20.77 This shot from the opening scene of *Saturday Night and Sunday Morning* shows the protagonist at work, as we hear his voice speaking over: "Don't let the bastards grind you down, that's one thing I've learned."

Fig. 20.78 The hero of *This Sporting Life* in a rare cheerful interlude, playing with his lover's son as she looks on. Kitchen Sink films often contrast the peace of the countryside with the oppression of the industrialized city.

Kitchen Sink cinema was a short-lived trend. *This Sporting Life* failed, and the unexpected success of another, very different, Woodfall film swerved filmmakers in new directions. Turning away from harsh realism, Richardson adapted a classic British comic novel in *Tom Jones* (1963), tapping Osborne for the screenplay. Backed by United Artists, the big-budget color film borrowed heavily from the French New Wave (Fig. 20.79). It became a huge hit and won several Academy Awards.

Fig. 20.79 Tom Jones turns and asks the audience if they saw his landlady pick his pocket.

Turning from working-class life in the industrial cities, filmmakers began to attach themselves to the vogue for portraying the lifestyle of "swinging London." English clothes and British rock and roll were suddenly fashionable, and London came to be seen as the capital of trendiness, social mobility, and sexual liberation. A series of films probing the shallowness of the "mod" lifestyle found success in art theaters around the world.

For example, in *Darling* (1965, John Schlesinger) a thoughtless, trivial model rises in society through a string of love affairs and finally marries an Italian prince. *Darling* uses many techniques derived from the Nouvelle Vague, such as jump cuts and freeze-frames. *Alfie* (1966, Lewis Gilbert) offered a male reversal of *Darling*, in which a selfish charmer seduces a series of women, ducking all problems until confronted with the illegal abortion of one of his victims. *Alfie* follows *Tom Jones* in letting the hero share his thoughts with the viewer by means of asides to the camera.

Reisz's *Morgan, a Suitable Case for Treatment* (1966) joined the working-class hero of the Kitchen Sink period with a comic critique of swinging London. A man from a Marxist family tries desperately to prevent his wife from divorcing him and marrying a snobbish art-gallery owner. *Morgan* assimilates art-cinema conventions in its fantasy scenes, in which the hero compares people to gorillas and envisions his execution (Fig. 20.80).

Apart from the new prominence of the London lifestyle, creative talents left Kitchen Sink realism behind. The success of *Tom Jones* led Richardson to Hollywood, while Albert Finney, Tom Courtenay, Richard Harris, and Michael Caine became international stars. Hollywood's tactics in financing British films changed as well. The intimate, realistic film would often be associated with a more overtly political cinema, while many notable later British works were either expensive prestige films (often made with American backing) or inventive genre pictures.

Fig. 20.80 Morgan imagines his execution in a junkyard decorated with pictures of famous Marxists.

Cinematic modernism, revived in the decade after World War II, became even more prominent in the years 1958–1967. While established directors consolidated the trend, young auteurs experimented with novel techniques and applied them to new subjects. Now art-cinema films were likely to be fragmentary and nonlinear in their time and space, provocative and puzzling in their storytelling, ambiguous in their thematic implications.

Moreover, many Young Cinemas were explicitly, and critically, political. In this respect, the Nouvelle Vague, influential in so many ways, lagged behind. Outside France, many filmmakers assaulted myths about national history, cast a severe eye on contemporary social conditions, celebrated rebellions against authority, and dissected the mechanisms of repression. Older directors like Resnais and Jancsó and youthful talents like Godard, Pasolini, Straub, Kluge, Chytilová, Makavejev, and Oshima were laying the grounds of a "political modernism." This trend would become central to international cinema in the decade after 1968.

◆ NOTES AND QUERIES

CENSORSHIP AND THE FRENCH NEW WAVE

The Nouvelle Vague was not socially or politically critical in the fashion of most Young Cinemas, partly because French censorship remained strong throughout the period. Films treating France's colonial wars (in Indochina until 1954, in Algeria until 1962) were suppressed. After some mayors had banned Vadim's *Les Liaisons dangereuses* (1960), the Centre National de la Cinématographie strengthened its power over controversial scripts and films. According to a 1961 decree, no film could be shot unless the script was approved by the president of the CNC, and the Ministry of Information had final say over which films could be shown. Politically critical films circulated clandestinely, and police began raiding political meetings and ciné-clubs. As a result of the new policy, films by Resnais (*Muriel*, 1963) and Godard (*Le Petit soldat*, 1960) were delayed or banned because of their references to the Algerian war.

NEW FILM THEORY

The success of Fellini, Bergman, and the other postwar directors discussed in Chapter 19 encouraged the auteur theory developed in France, Britain, and America. Similarly, the young or first-time directors of the late 1950s and early 1960s triggered new ways of thinking about cinematic meaning in general and modernist filmmaking in particular.

The most influential trend in film theory of this period was that of *semiology*. Of ancient origins, "semiotics," or the study of signs in culture, was revived in this century by the linguist Ferdinand de Saussure and taken up on the Continent in the postwar era. One of the most influential codifications of semiological doctrine was Roland Barthes's book *Elements of Se-*

miology (1964). Soon this perspective was applied to film, most notably by Christian Metz. [See *Film Language: A Semiotics of the Cinema,* trans. Michael Taylor (Chicago: University of Chicago Press, 1990; originally published 1968).] Italian proponents of semiology include Umberto Eco [notably his *La Strutture assente* of 1968, revised as *A Theory of Semiotics* (Bloomington: Indiana University Press, 1976)] and Pier Paolo Pasolini, who proposed the controversial idea that cinema uses nonlinguistic signs to duplicate our perception of everyday reality and psychological states. Pasolini, like Metz and others, felt a special need to explain the innovativeness of the second phase of postwar film modernism. He proposed that the Young Cinema depended heavily on a "free indirect discourse" that combines the author's point of view with that of a character. [See Pasolini, "The Cinema of Poetry," in Louise K. Barnett, ed., *Heretical Empiricism* (Bloomington: Indiana University Press, 1988), pp. 167–186.] As this line of argument suggests, the new film theory did not immediately seek to overturn the auteur approach to criticism; rather, it often promised to put auteurism on a more rigorous, even "scientific" basis.

◆ REFERENCES

1. Quoted in Peter Graham, ed., *The New Wave* (Garden City, New York: Doubleday, 1968), p. 92.
2. Quoted in Jean-Luc Douin, *Godard* (Paris: Rivages, 1989), p. 26.
3. Claude Chabrol, *Et Pourtant je tourne . . .* (Paris: Laffont, 1976), p. 181.
4. Quoted in Oswald Stack, *Pasolini on Pasolini* (Bloomington: Indiana University Press, 1969), p. 49.
5. Quoted in ibid., p. 109.
6. Quoted in Noël Simsolo, *Conversations avec Sergio Leone* (Paris: Stock, 1987), p. 93.
7. Quoted in "Young German Film," *Film Comment* **6,** 1 (Spring 1970): 44.
8. Quoted in " . . . Preferably Naked Girls," in Eric Rentchsler, ed., *West German Filmmakers on Film: Visions and Voices* (New York: Holmes & Meier, 1988), p. 42.
9. Andrei Tarkovsky, *Sculpting in Time: Reflections on the Cinema,* trans. Kitty Hunter-Blair (London: Faber and Faber, 1989), p. 30.
10. Quoted in Peter Hames, *The Czechoslovak New Wave* (Berkeley: University of California Press, 1985), p. 187.
11. Quoted in Daniel J. Goulding, *Liberated Cinema: The Yugoslav Experience* (Bloomington: Indiana University Press, 1985), p. 72.
12. Quoted in Jean-Pierre Jeancolas, "Le Cinéma hongrois de 1963 à 1980," in Jean-Loup Passek, ed., *Le Cinéma hongrois* (Paris: Pompidou Center, 1979), p. 48.
13. Quoted in Graham Petrie, *History Must Answer to Man* (Budapest: Corvina, 1978), p. 107.
14. Quoted in Audie Bock, *Japanese Film Directors* (Tokyo: Kodansha, 1978), p. 293.

21

DOCUMENTARY AND EXPERIMENTAL CINEMA IN THE POSTWAR ERA, 1945–MID-1960s

In the two decades after World War II documentary and avant-garde film-making underwent enormous changes around the world. New technologies and institutions altered the basis of independent filmmaking. These developments were often connected to the rise of the commercial art cinema and the emergence of New Waves.

Both documentarists and avant-gardists renewed the idea of a personal cinema. In the 1930s, the Spanish Civil War, Stalin's rigged trials of his former associates in Moscow, and the rise of fascism and militarism had led to genocide and a world war. Now many artists turned from political commitment (Chapter 14) to a conception of individual expression. This impulse, most notable in the rise of Abstract Expressionist painting in the United States and Europe, was also visible in experimental film. Even the postwar documentary film became more of a vehicle for the filmmaker's beliefs and feelings than had been usual before.

A second prevailing idea was a new interest in capturing unpredictable events on film. Before 1950, most documentary cinema had sought to control chance to a great degree. The filmmaker might record a casual action, but that would be smoothly absorbed into a larger structure of meaning by virtue of editing and voice-over commentary. Most major documentarists, from Vertov and Flaherty to Lorentz and Jennings, had resorted to even more strongly controlling techniques, such as staging scenes for the camera. But Neorealism, particularly in Zavattini's pronouncements, had seen truth in the uncontrolled event. In the 1950s lightweight cameras and sound equipment allowed documentarists to eliminate the artifice of voice-over commentary and preplanned structure, creating a cinema centered on the spontaneous moment.

At the same time, avant-gardists revived Dada and Surrealist conceptions of the revelatory accident. John Cage, for example, composed musical pieces which incorporated chance and environmental sounds. His *Imaginary Landscape no. 4* (1951) consisted of twelve radios tuned to different stations according to chance. Postwar experimental filmmakers, as well as workers in other arts, often adapted Cagean ideas by incorporating accidents as part of self-expression. Lucky aberrations of light or color could become part of a larger form. By the late 1950s and early 1960s, the sort of objectivity courted by documentarists entered the avant-garde as well. In the work of the Fluxus group and of Andy Warhol, the artist no longer expressed personal feelings but rather invited the spectator to scrutinize a process or witness an improvised scene. This approach risked boring the audience, and several avant-gardists, like their documentary counterparts, asked audiences to accept a cinema which refused to arouse and fulfill the narrative appetites to which Hollywood catered.

TOWARD THE PERSONAL DOCUMENTARY

At the end of the war most documentary filmmaking remained in the hands of large institutions. Pathé, news organizations, and the Hollywood studios issued newsreels and informational films for theatrical exhibition. Government agencies in many countries supported documentary units, which produced informational and propaganda films for schools and civic organizations. Corporations sponsored films which promoted products, as when Shell Oil backed Flaherty's lyrical *Louisiana Story* (1948).

After the early 1950s, fewer documentaries appeared on theater programs. Television journalism displaced the weekly newsreels, and studios ceased to produce them. Yet television also provided a new market. For example, before the war the feature-length documentary had been rare, but by the early 1960s it became more common, aimed at television broadcast or occasional theatrical exhibition.

In the postwar era most of the older documentarists slackened their pace. Vertov supervised a newsreel series until his death in 1954. After *Louisiana Story* Flaherty was unable to complete a film, though before his death in 1951 he produced several shorts. John Grierson left the National Film Board of Canada in 1945 but then presided over several efforts to make documentary-style fiction films and documentary television series. Only Joris Ivens remained active as a director, teaching and making films in Poland, China, Cuba, and other nations aligned with the USSR.

A new generation of documentarists appeared during the first decade after the war. Although some had begun their careers during the war, the freer circulation of films in peacetime helped their work became known internationally. Most of these individuals worked within well-tried genres, but others innovated more significantly.

Fig. 21.1

Fig. 21.2

Fig. 21.3

Fig. 21.1 Flirtation on the stoop (*In the Street*, Helen Levitt, Sidney Loeb, and James Aree).

Figs. 21.2 and 21.3 *Farrebique*: During labor, Berthe clutches the sheet, and Rouquier dissolves to a flower opening as a shriek is heard and her baby is born.

In the film of nature and exploration, for example, the Swede Arne Sücksdorff used telephoto lenses and hidden cameras to bring the viewer into the midst of wildlife in *The Great Adventure* (1954). Oceanographer Jacques Cousteau perfected undersea photography in a series of films exploring marine life (*The Silent World*, 1956; *World without Sun*, 1964).

The film of social observation also attracted idiosyncratic talents. The tabloid photographer Weegee toured the seamy side of city life in *Weegee's New York* (1950). Less sensationalistic was *In the Street* (1952), an unpolished evocation of the world of the New York poor (Fig. 21.1). Perhaps the most important observational film of the period was Georges Rouquier's *Farrebique* (1946), a chronicle of the struggles of a French peasant family through 1944–1945. Much of the film was staged and drew on conventions of fictional cinema (Figs. 21.2, 21.3). Yet Rouquier minimizes voice-over commentary in order to savor the regional dialect, and he skillfully evokes the routines and travails of the Farrebique farm.

The film of reportage, though largely replaced by television coverage, still held a place, especially when it could present an event in fresh ways. Kon Ichikawa's *Tokyo Olympiad* (1965), for example, did not try to duplicate television coverage of the 1964 Olympics but instead used over 150 cameramen and a virtuosic barrage of techniques to capture the human toil of the

Fig. 21.4 Haanstra pokes fun at the gestures of salesmen in a Dutch auto show (*Alleman*).

Fig. 21.5

Fig. 21.6

Fig. 21.7

games. Similarly, the "city symphony" continued in such works as Frank Stauffacher's *Sausalito* (1948), Francis Thompson's *N. Y., N. Y.* (1957), and Bert Haanstra's *Alleman* (*Everyman*, 1960; Fig. 21.4).

The compilation documentary had become a staple of the wartime film diet, and it retained its importance in the years that followed. One of the most powerful was Henri Cartier-Bresson's *Le Retour* (1946), using U.S. military footage to show the liberation of the Nazi POW camps and the prisoners' return to their homes (Fig. 21.5). The feature-length compilation film flourished in the hands of a new generation of filmmakers. Frédéric Rossif's *To Die in Madrid* (1962; Fig. 21.6) marked the mainstream success of a politically critical use of the genre. With *Point of Order* (1964), a recapitulation of the Senate's 1954 investigation of charges against Senator Joseph McCarthy, Emile De Antonio established himself as one of the most skillful exponents of the compilation genre (Fig. 21.7).

Ethnographic cinema was rejuvenated as anthropologists began to give it more professional standards. Flaherty's approach to exotic societies—a search for drama, an emphasis on the clash of humans and nature, a willingness to restage events—gave way to an attempt to record remote cultures more neutrally and accurately. During the 1950s, the American John Marshall filmed customs of the Bushmen of the Kalihari desert, and anthropologist Robert Gardner helped him assemble the footage into *The Hunters* (1956). Following four men hunting a giraffe, the film adheres to the Flaherty tradition, but it marked an important stage in the more sober recording of folkways (Fig. 21.8). Gardner went on to make the most famous American anthropological film, *Dead Birds* (1963). Here he recorded, with a minimum of interference, the Dani people of Indonesia as they fought a war.

Most innovative documentarists of the postwar era worked on an artisanal basis or on a film-by-film arrangement with a funding group. The National Film Board of Canada (NFB) had been formed in 1939 by John Grierson, and it concentrated on short animated and documentary films. Despite its government funding, the board sought to institutionalize innovation—to give idiosyncratic talents a bureaucratic structure which could help them express individual viewpoints. A typical NFB documentary is *City of Gold* (1957, Colin Low and Wolf Koenig). Ostensibly a historical view of the gold rush in Dawson City, it was framed as a meditation on the contrasts between the town as it had been in the 1890s and the modern town, in which

Fig. 21.5 Labor-camp inmates are fed in *Le Retour.*

Fig. 21.6 The compilation film as an investigation of the past: The Spanish Civil War in *To Die in Madrid.*

Fig. 21.7 *Point of Order*: After accusing Senator Joseph Welch's associate of espousing communism, Senator Joseph McCarthy tries to shrug off Welch's rebuke ("Until this moment, Senator, I never truly gauged your cruelty or your recklessness").

Fig. 21.8 Boys of the Kalihari desert practice archery (*The Hunters*).

Fig. 21.9

Fig. 21.10

Fig. 21.9 In *City of Gold*, old-timers from gold-rush days gossiping, with a modern Coca-Cola ad in the background.

Fig. 21.10 Reisz's Lambeth boys drive back through Whitehall, the framing juxtaposing their youthful rowdiness with a postcard London cityscape.

the narrator had been raised (Fig. 21.9). Of those who stayed in the town despite finding no gold, he concludes, "These men found their El Dorado."

The trend toward individual innovation was most evident in several filmmakers who found ways to express their personal attitudes via the documentary. This trend arose simultaneously with *Cahiers du cinéma*'s auteur policy, which emphasized the director's personal vision in fictional and commercial film. Not surprisingly, many of the directors of "personal" documentaries moved into mainstream fiction production.

In Great Britain the personal documentary came to prominence in a short-lived movement called "Free Cinema." Karel Reisz, Lindsay Anderson, and other members of the group had been associated with the film magazines *Sequence* (1947–1952) and *Sight and Sound*. In these forums they had expressed hostility to both commercial filmmaking and the current state of British documentary. They called for a "free" cinema which would express the director's commitment to deep personal views. Thanks to the British Film Institute's Experimental Film Fund and to occasional corporate sponsorship, several of the Free Cinema filmmakers were able to make short documentaries before becoming the core filmmakers of the British Kitchen Sink cinema (Chapter 20).

Most of the films expressed the directors' attitudes toward contemporary, urbanizing Britain. Popular culture formed a central subject. Anderson's *O Dreamland* (1953) reflected on the public's need for a cheap night out, while Tony Richardson's *Momma Don't Allow* (1956) and Reisz's *We Are the Lambeth Boys* (1958) rendered teenagers' lifestyles with considerable affection (Fig. 21.10). More traditional subjects were treated with a new restraint. Anderson's film about Covent Garden's markets, *Every Day Except Christmas* (1957), emphasized work routines and earthy language, while his *Thursday's Children* (1954) offered an optimistic view of a school for deaf children by capturing the pupils' spontaneous cheerfulness (Fig. 21.11).

In France as well, personal expression emerged in the documentary. The government funded films about art and culture, both subjects which

Fig. 21.11 A deaf child learns about speaking by touching her teacher's jaw in *Thursday's Children*.

traditionally allowed filmmakers to inject their own viewpoints. By 1953, the government was actively encouraging short quasi-experimental films. In addition, *Cahiers du cinéma*, like *Sequence*, considered artistic cinema to depend upon directorial expression (under the auspices of the auteur idea; Chapter 19). Pierre Braunberger, Anatole Dauman, Paul Legros, and other producers gave directors a free hand in the making of poetic or essayistic documentaries.

Alain Resnais achieved his reputation as a documentarist with a series of films on art. *Van Gogh* (1948), which won a prize at Venice and an Academy Award, set forth a new method of portraying a painter's work. Instead of considering each painting as a whole and in chronological order, Resnais delineated Van Gogh's private world across his entire career. He panned over a canvas to show the rhythm of a line and intercut details from different paintings without supplying an orienting long shot. Resnais modified his tactic for *Guernica* (1951), intercutting Picasso's sketches and notes with photographs and headlines from the Spanish Civil War. More controversial was *Les Statues meurent aussi* ("Statues Also Die," 1953), which Resnais codirected with his friend Chris Marker. This study of African art in western museums implies that the colonizers destroyed the cultures of the lands they invaded. The film was banned.

Resnais's two most honored documentaries explore the nature of historical memory. *Nuit et brouillard* (*Night and Fog*, 1957) gives a clipped, unsensationalized image of the Nazi concentration camps akin to Resnais's treatment of the atomic bomb in *Hiroshima mon amour*. He cuts between a deserted prison seen today—in a bright countryside filmed in full color—and newsreel footage of the camps in operation. Instead of playing up the horror, *Night and Fog* dwells upon the impossibility of ever truly capturing the past. As the camera probes the ruins, the commentator asks: "How to discover what remains of the reality of these camps?" (Fig. 21.12). At the end, the commentary suggests that the impulses which created the holocaust are far from extinguished today.

More optimistic is *Toute la mémoire du monde* ("All the World's Memory," 1957), a study of the French national library. Resnais's camera glides through the gloomy storerooms and stacks, creating a series of metaphors: the library as labyrinth, as prison (Fig. 21.13), and as gigantic brain. The film's somber lyricism celebrates the desire to know the truth and to remember the past.

Resnais's work ran parallel to that of Georges Franju. Both men were born in 1912, made their first significant film in 1948, and moved to fiction features after the explosion of the New Wave in the late 1950s. Of Franju's numerous documentaries, the most influential were *Le Sang des bêtes* (*Blood of the Beasts*, 1948) and *Hôtel des invalides* (1951). In these films Franju set out to disturb his audiences in a way reminiscent of the Surrealists and of Buñuel's *Las Hurdes*.

Le Sang des bêtes records a day in a slaughterhouse. It emphasizes the casual professionalism of the butchers and the violence necessary to put meat on plates. But Franju also juxtaposes images of suffering animals with the homes and churches surrounding the slaughterhouse. Accidental details of

Fig. 21.12 "No description, no image can restore their true dimension: endless, uninterrupted fear": The barracks in *Night and Fog*.

Fig. 21.13 A book shut into its cell in *Toute la mémoire du monde*.

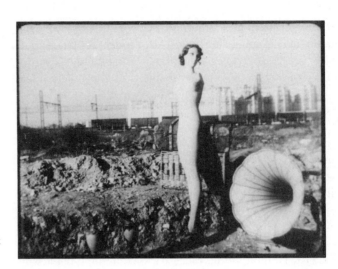

Fig. 21.14 A junkyard yields Surrealist icons in *Le Sang des bêtes.*

Fig. 21.15 The juxtaposition of the military past and its consequences in *Hôtel des invalides.*

Fig. 21.16 "But first, look at her—to the point where she becomes an enigma, as words endlessly repeated become unrecognizable": the closing of Marker's *Description of a Struggle.*

this quiet neighborhood take on bizarre aspects (Fig. 21.14). In this context, a shot of calves' heads stacked like cabbages exudes the disturbing poetry sought by Buñuel and Dalí.

Hôtel des invalides does much the same for a national war memorial. In this monument to war's glory, the film discloses images of suffering (Fig. 21.15). Franju dwells on the ominous overtones of military memorabilia, as when a general's bust resembles a shattered skull. Franju later brought this vision of the disquieting aspects of everyday life to feature films.

The films of Chris Marker, more cerebral and freely structured than those of Resnais and Franju, epitomize the use of documentary for personal expression. A professional photographer and a world traveler, Marker produced a series of essayistic documentaries expressing complex opinions and ironic wit.

Marker explores two documentary modes. One is the travelogue, which he treats as a pretext for a free-ranging reflection on western ideas of exotic cultures. *Dimanche à Pekin* (*Sunday in Peking,* 1956) and *Lettre de Sibérie* (*Letter from Siberia,* 1958) take banal, almost tourist-movie images and, through a dense poetic commentary, meditate on the storybook clichés representing non-European cultures. *Letter from Siberia* is both a parody of the travelogue and a highly formalized reflection on documentary film's inability to capture the truth of a culture. In the film's most famous sequence, Marker demonstrates the power of voice-over commentary by running the same series of shots three times, each time changing the narration to create different meanings.

Marker also made political documentaries. In *Cuba Sí!* (1961), he appraises Castro's revolution in the face of U.S. attacks. *Le Joli mai* (1963) brought a political critique to bear on the new trend of Direct Cinema. But Marker's highly personal stance often confounds orthodox leftist positions. His reflections on Israel (*Description of a Struggle,* 1961) mix praise, criticism, humor, and a tourist's fascination (Fig. 21.16).

While Resnais, Franju, and Marker were defining varieties of the personal documentary, another French filmmaker was bringing this attitude to the ethnographic film. In 1946, the young anthropologist Jean Rouch took a 16mm camera on his first field trip to Niger, and on a later visit he took along a portable tape recorder. The short ethnographic documentaries he made led to his being named head of the newly created International Commission of Sociological and Ethnographic Film.

Rouch's influence began to be felt with his controversial *Les Maîtres fous* ("The Mad Masters," 1957). While in Ghana in 1955, he was asked by priests of the Hauka cult to film their ceremonies of possession. Rouch recorded cult members in a trance, pacing frenziedly, foaming at the mouth, and eventually eating a dog. What differentiates this film from sensationalized portraits of "primitive" Africa is the fact that the participants adopt the identities of the colonialists who rule them. By day the cultists are dockers and cattle herders, but at the ritual, one becomes an army captain, another the governor, a third an elegant French lady (Fig. 21.17). Rouch's doctoral thesis argued that in parodying their rulers, the Hauka release their feelings of imperialist oppression. "This violent play," the film's commentary warns, "is only the reflection of our civilization."

Les Maîtres fous caused a scandal. Many African countries banned it, and both Europeans and Africans urged Rouch to destroy it. Nonetheless, it won a prize at the Venice Film Festival and reinforced Rouch's desire to document the effects of colonialism in the Third World. His next film, *Moi un noir (Treichville)* ["Me, a Black Man (Treichville)," 1959], shows people in the Ivory Coast consciously imitating western life. Surrounded by the trappings of European culture, menial laborers take new names: Edward G. Robinson, Tarzan, Dorothy Lamour. The hand-held camera follows them drinking, searching for jobs, and drifting through dance halls. Rouch also displays their aspirations, notably the dream of Edward G. Robinson to become a prizefighter. *Moi un noir* becomes an intriguing mixture of fiction and documentary (Fig. 21.18). Rouch showed the edited film to Robinson, whose comments during the screening were added to the sound track.

Ethnographic film, in Rouch's eyes, was of paramount importance for westerners because it showed the differences among societies, preventing Europeans from "trying to transform [other cultures] into images of ourselves."[1] Rouch was criticized for delineating the psychological effects of colonialism without presenting Africans who seek to change their lives through social action. But he saw his project in less political terms. He sought to give ethnographic film a human dimension, not only by showing westerners other cultures but also by using the filmmaking act to create a bond between the researcher and the subject. Having brought Edward G. Robinson into the movies, he made him his assistant. (Years later, under his given name Oumarou Ganda, Rouch's protagonist became one of Niger's most important filmmakers.) Rouch made films, he claimed, primarily for the people he filmed and for himself, to preserve his experiences in the culture. His involvement with his subjects, and his willingness to break technical rules if they interfered with human immediacy, also led him toward another documentary trend, Direct Cinema.

Fig. 21.17 *Les Maîtres fous*: The celebrants stalk up and down in a frenzy. At this point in his career, Rouch used a long lens which allowed him to stay at a distance from the action, an approach he would later abandon.

Fig. 21.18 In a dance hall, Edward G. Robinson is "in" the story action and so ignores Rouch's camera, while Eddie Constantine and the others frankly acknowledge it.

DIRECT CINEMA

Between 1958 and 1963, documentary filmmaking was transformed. Documentarists began to utilize lighter and more mobile equipment, to work in smaller crews, and to reject traditional conceptions of script and structure. The new documentary sought to study individuals, to reveal the moment-by-moment development of a situation, to search for instants of drama or psychological revelation. Instead of staged scenes dominated by a voice-over narration, the new documentary would let the action unfold naturally and permit people to speak for themselves.

Called "candid" cinema, "uncontrolled" cinema, "observational" cinema, and *cinéma vérité* ("cinema truth"), this trend was most generally known as Direct Cinema. The name suggests that the new technologies recorded events with an unprecedented immediacy and that the filmmaker avoided the more indirect documentation—restaging, narrational commentary—of earlier documentarists.

Several factors influenced the new approach. Most generally, Italian Neorealism had intensified documentarists' urge to capture everyday life. Technological innovations, such as the growth of 16mm production and the emergence of sound-on-tape, provided a new flexibility. (See Box.) Moreover, television needed motion pictures to fill airtime, and network news organizations sought a fresh approach to audio-visual journalism. In the United States, Canada, and France documentarists affected by these conditions forged distinct versions of Direct Cinema.

THE UNITED STATES: DREW AND ASSOCIATES

In the United States, Direct Cinema emerged under the auspices of the photojournalist Robert Drew. Drew wanted to bring to television reporting the dramatic realism he found in *Life* magazine's candid photography. In 1954, he met Richard Leacock, who had worked on *Native Land* (p. 345) and had been cinematographer for Flaherty's *Louisiana Story* (1948). With the backing of Time, Inc., Drew hired Leacock, Don Pennebaker, David and Albert Maysles, and several other filmmakers.

Drew produced a series of short films aimed at television broadcast. The ground-breaking one was *Primary* (1960), a report on the Wisconsin primary contest between John Kennedy and Hubert Humphrey. Leacock, Pennebaker, the Maysles, and Terence Macartney-Filgate all worked as cinematographers. Although the film contained some lip-sync sound, its visual authenticity attracted more attention. The camera followed the politicians working the streets, riding from town to town, and nervously relaxing in hotel rooms (Figs. 21.19–21.21). *Primary*'s drama was heightened by crosscutting between the two candidates and by voice-over news reports, which largely replaced explanatory commentary.

Shortly afterward, Drew and Leacock were commissioned to make several films for ABC television, notably *Yanki, No!* (1960), an examination of anti-U.S. feelings in Latin America, and *The Children Were Watching* (1960), a study of school integration. Between 1961 and 1963, Drew Associates made

Fig. 21.19 The most famous shot in *Primary*: Albert Maysles' camera, held above his head, follows Kennedy through a crowd of supporters . . .

Fig. 21.20 . . . into a corridor (note the distortions created by the wide-angle lens) . . .

Fig. 21.21 . . . and onto the stage, where another Drew cameraman can be glimpsed waiting to capture a reverse angle.

NEW TECHNOLOGY FOR THE NEW DOCUMENTARY

Eastman Kodak introduced the 16mm gauge in 1923, chiefly for home movies and educational films. During the 1930s, some American avant-gardists began using the gauge for experimental work (p. 367). During World War II, 16mm came into wider use. It was well suited for combat filming, and 16mm prints of educational and propaganda films circulated among military stations and on the home front. The U.S. government donated 16mm projectors to schools and civic organizations so that they could screen government releases. After the war, documentary and experimental filmmakers around the world eagerly took up the format.

Television arrived in Europe and North America in the early 1950s. In those pre-videotape days, the cheapness and flexibility of 16mm made it the standard gauge for reportage, commercials, and TV films. Manufacturers began to produce professional 16mm cameras. These usually had zoom lenses and reflex viewfinders which allowed the filmmaker to sight directly through the lens during filming. In 1952, the Arriflex 16 established a new standard for ease of operation and became the model for most professional 16mm. In addition, Eastman and other companies developed a range of 16mm film stocks, often very "fast" emulsions that permitted filming in relatively low light.

Two further developments led to Direct Cinema. Before the mid-1950s nearly all professional 16mm cameras were so heavy that steady shots could be obtained only if the camera was anchored to a tripod. Yet attaching a standard camera to a tripod was time-consuming; by the time the camera was set up, the action had usually passed. Using a tripod encouraged documentarists to restage events. In addition, the bulky camera made subjects aware of the act of filming. Only filmmakers using amateur equipment, such as Rouch in his ethnographic shorts and Stan Brakhage in his experimental *Desistfilm* (1953), could easily shoot hand-held.

Around 1958, several manufacturers introduced lighter 16mm professional cameras. The Auricon Cinevoice and the Eclair Cameflex each weighed around 60 pounds, light enough to be anchored on a shoulder brace. An improved model of the Arriflex 16 weighed just 22 pounds. The prototype KMT Coutant-Mathot Eclair, made available to Rouch for

Chronique d'un été (1961), weighed less than 20. Holding such a camera, the filmmaker could pan quickly, walk with the subject, ride in a car, follow the situation wherever it led.

Just as important were improvements in sound recording. Documentaries had relied on voice-over narration partly because filmmakers could not easily record lip-synchronized sound outside the studio. It was far less trouble to add music, background noise, and commentary to a string of images than to let the participants speak for themselves. Only in highly prepared circumstances—a politician giving a speech before a microphone, a person interviewed in a studio—was it possible to record lip-sync sound during filming. Even the relatively spontaneous Free Cinema films suffered from the limitations of sound recording.

During the early 1950s, both fiction and documentary filmmakers began to replace optical sound-on-film recording with magnetic sound, recorded on tape. Documentarists consequently tried to capture sound on-site with a portable tape recorder. The Swiss company Nagra introduced a tape recorder for filmmaking in 1953 and made an improved version available four years later.

The problem now was synchronizing the picture track with sound recorded on the spot. Around 1958, engineers devised the *Pilotone* system, by which an electric pulse is sent from the camera to the recorder and registered on one track of the tape. In playback, the pulse automatically adjusts the speed of the tape to correspond to the picture. Most early versions of the Pilotone system used a cable to connect the camera to the recorder. This umbilical cord hampered the freedom of movement which Direct Cinema sought, so engineers created radio-transmission systems. A quartz crystal or a tuning fork in the camera emitted a pulse that the recorder picked up and recorded as a guide for synchronization. The wireless system, first used extensively in the United States, became standard internationally by the mid-1960s.

Although synchronization and camera noise still posed problems, by 1958 portable 16mm cameras and recorders, along with smaller microphones and faster film stocks, had triggered a revolution in filmmaking practice.

twelve more films, including *Eddie* (1961), *Jane* (1962), and *The Chair* (1962). Ten of these films became known as the "Living Camera" series. By now they fully exploited direct sound.

Drew, who exercised editorial control over most of the films made by the company, saw documentary as a way of telling dramatic stories. "In each of the stories there is a time when man comes against moments of tension, and pressure, and revelation, and decision. It's these moments that interest us most."[2] For Drew, Direct Cinema gripped audiences through what came to be called its "crisis" structure. Most Drew-unit films center on a high-stakes situation to be resolved in a few days or hours. The film arouses the viewer's emotion by showing conflict, suspense, and a decisive outcome. *Primary* exploits the crisis structure, as does *The Chair*, which shows lawyers' struggles to save a rehabilitated convict from execution. The crisis puts the participants under stress and reveals their personalities. Often, as in *Eddie* or *Jane*, the protagonist fails to achieve the goal, and the film ends with a scrutiny of his or her emotional reaction.

Drew used multiple crews on most films, tracing out several lines of action and intercutting between different forces racing against the clock. He encouraged each cameraman to efface himself, to accustom the subjects to his presence, and to respond intuitively to the developing drama. The approach was that of feature journalism, where the reporter balances respect for the facts with subjective judgments about selection and emphasis.

Soon Drew's filmmakers left the unit to form their own companies. The Maysles brothers departed to make *Showman* (1962), a study of film producer Joseph E. Levine, and *What's Happening! The Beatles in New York* (1964). Far more episodic than the Drew films, the Maysles projects avoided the crisis structure and offered casual, sketchy portraits of show-business celebrities. *What's Happening!*, the first Direct Cinema film in the United States to omit voice-over narration entirely, was simply a diary of the Beatles' tour, rousing one professional television producer to complain: "As most documentary filmmakers understand the film, it was hardly a film at all."[3]

Don Pennebaker and Richard Leacock also left Drew Associates, forming their own firm. Pennebaker made a study of handicapped twins (*Elizabeth and Mary,* 1965) and specialized in films documenting American popular music (*Don't Look Back,* 1966; *Monterey Pop,* 1968; *Keep on Rockin',* 1970). Leacock went on to make *Happy Mother's Day* (1963), showing how the birth of quintuplets disrupts a small town; *A Stravinsky Portrait* (1964); and *Ku Klux Klan—The Invisible Empire* (1965).

Leacock, the most proselytizing of U.S. Direct Cinema filmmakers, advocated what he called "uncontrolled cinema." The filmmaker would not interfere with the event; the filmmaker simply observed, as discreetly and responsibly as possible. Leacock believed that a self-effacing crew could become so integrated into a situation that people would forget they were being filmed.

Less interested in drama and suspense than Drew, Leacock also believed that the filmmaker could bear witness to social processes that normally went unseen. Although we think we know what happens on a battlefield or in a courtroom, Leacock claimed, our preconceptions arise from the stereotypes we have absorbed—often from fictional films. But if we take a camera and tape recorder onto the scene, we will find that our preconceptions are usually wrong. The purpose of uncontrolled cinema, Leacock claimed, is "to find out some important aspect of our society by watching our society, by *watching how things really happen* as opposed to the social image that people hold about the way things are *supposed* to happen."[4] Leacock's concern for Direct Cinema's power to reveal social institutions through face-to-face interactions was to prove significant for a generation of filmmakers.

DIRECT CINEMA IN BILINGUAL CANADA

Television was also a major impetus for the emergence of Direct Cinema in Canada. The creation of national broadcasting in 1953 encouraged documentarists at the National Film Board (NFB) to shoot in 16mm and rapidly make topical works. Two movements emerged at almost exactly the same time, one among English-speaking Canadians, the other among Francophones in Québec.

The NFB's "B unit" made several films for "Candid Eye," an English-language series broadcast in fall 1958 and fall 1959. These films took a candid-camera approach, with hidden cameras and telephoto lenses. With a few exceptions—notably the first film in the series, *The Days before Christmas* (1958)—they did not employ lip-sync sound. Terence Macartney-Filgate encouraged use of the hand-held camera in this film, in his study of the Salvation Army (*Blood and Fire*, 1958), and in his examination of the plight of migrant tobacco pickers (*The Back-Breaking Leaf*, 1959).

Avoiding scripts and letting the structure emerge from editing, the Candid Eye directors shared Drew's belief in an objective, observational cinema. While Drew was influenced by *Life* photojournalism, however, the Canadian group looked instead to British Free Cinema and to photographer Henri Cartier-Bresson, who sought the exact moment of insight which illuminates everyday, unspectacular incidents. Thus the Candid Eye films lack the crisis structure of the Drew unit's work.

Fig. 21.22 *Les Raquetteurs*: A snowshoe winner breasts the tape . . .

The Candid Eye series ended by 1960, but filmmakers associated with it went on to other documentaries. The most distinctive was *Lonely Boy* (1962), a portrait of singer Paul Anka by Wolf Koenig and Roman Kreitner. This ironic exposé of how popular music exploits both its stars and its public showed how Direct Cinema techniques could be used to slant the viewer's attitudes. In one sequence, we hear Anka explain how he calculates a gesture while we see him onstage making the gesture, which might have seemed spontaneous without his voice-over. The filmmakers present Anka as confessing to manipulating his fans.

Fig. 21.23 . . . and is met by his supporters. The camera walks along with them . . .

The NFB's move to Montreal in 1956 had created more French involvement in the agency. In 1958, three French filmmakers shot *Les Raquetteurs* ("The Snowshoers"), a humorous and affectionate report on a convocation of snowshoe enthusiasts. Although shot in 35mm without direct sound, the film was a landmark for Direct Cinema in Canada. The cinematographer Michel Brault plunged into the action in a manner that looked forward to the Drew unit's wide angles and fluid camera (Figs. 21.22–21.24).

Praise for *Les Raquetteurs* encouraged the NFB to establish a French-language unit consisting of Brault, Gilles Groulx, Claude Jutra, Marcel Fournier, and others. *La Lutte* ("The Match," 1961), *Golden Gloves* (1961), and *Québec-USA* (1962) revealed the French team's proficiency with the new equipment and the members' dedication to a committed version of Direct Cinema. Unlike the Candid Eye group, which embraced an aesthetic of objectivity, the French team identified with the people and their urban popular culture.

The urge to explore the social identity of the Francophone community

Fig. 21.24 . . . to have their picture taken.

came to the fore in the feature-length *Pour la suite du monde* ("For the Rest of the World," aka *Moontrap,* 1963). Cameraman Michel Brault, the poet Pierre Perrault, and their sound recordist lived for a year in an isolated French Canadian village, where a variant of seventeenth-century French was still common speech. Consisting primarily of interviews with people recalling the community's history, *Pour la suite du monde* illustrates what Perrault called *cinéma vécu* ("lived cinema"). "Nothing is more real than an old man telling of an event he has lived through. Often the facts themselves may not have any value but the telling of them has."[5] Perrault brought to light the history and customs of the French Canadian population through several later films.

FRANCE: CINÉMA VÉRITÉ

In France, Direct Cinema emerged not out of television but out of Jean Rouch's ethnographic inquiries. The key film, and the single most influential work of Direct Cinema in any country, was *Chronique d'un été* (*Chronicle of a Summer,* 1961), which Rouch made in collaboration with the sociologist Edgar Morin. Out of their collaboration came yet another model of Direct Cinema—one in which the filmmakers did not simply observe or sympathize but rather prodded and provoked.

After a prologue in which Rouch and Morin interview Marcelline, a market researcher, *Chronique d'un été* shows her asking people on the street, "Are you happy?" (Fig. 21.25). In the clichéd and defensive responses of the passersby, the sequence reveals the superficiality of casual poll taking. The rest of the film scrutinizes the opinions and memories of a group of Parisians (Fig. 21.26). Students and working people discuss their lives with Morin, who presses them to explain themselves. Gradually the interviewees come to know one another, a process which the film documents.

In an extension of Rouch's technique in *Moi un noir,* the last portion of *Chronique d'un été* shows the subjects discussing the film which Rouch and Morin have made. Their comments—the footage is said to be boring, truthful,

Fig. 21.25 "Are you happy?" (*Chronique d'un été*).

Fig. 21.26 Marcelline's walk through Les Halles: As the camera tracks further back, she recites her memories of the war into a portable tape recorder in her handbag.

embarrassing, even indecent—become part of our film (Fig. 21.27). In an epilogue, Rouch and Morin appraise the success of their enterprise and anticipate the reaction of the public.

Chronique lacks the suspenseful drama of the Drew films. The film centers on ordinary people explaining their lives, while Morin's insistent questioning makes Direct Cinema a provocative force. Rouch and Morin did not accept Leacock's demand that the camera efface itself. Viewers of *Chronique* are given occasional shots of equipment or technicians. For Rouch, the camera was not a brake on the action but an accelerator: "You push these people to confess themselves. . . . It's a very strange kind of confession in front of the camera, where the camera is, let's say, a mirror, and also a window open to the outside."[6] An inquiry into personal history and psychology, *Chronique* encourages its subjects to define themselves through performances for the camera.

Chronique's prologue calls the film "a new experiment in cinema-truth [*cinéma vérité*]." The important word is "new," since Morin believed that the emerging technology and the willingness to explore everyday life permitted filmmakers to go beyond Vertov's *Kino-Pravda* ("film-truth"; p. 203). But the label got applied to far more than *Chronique*, and even American filmmakers began to call their work *cinéma vérité*. A 1963 conference of filmmakers found it too biased a term, but up to the present, *cinéma vérité* remains a synonym for Direct Cinema.

A more hybrid version of Direct Cinema was explored in two films by Mario Ruspoli, shot by Michel Brault (cameraman on several French Canadian films as well as *Chronique*). *Les Inconnus de la terre* ("The Unknown Ones of the Land," 1961) studies the poor peasants of the Lozère region, observing peasants discussing their problems. *Regard sur la folie* ("A Look at Madness," 1962) visits an asylum in the same area.

Ruspoli's films lie midway between the American "observational" method and the Rouch-Morin "provocational" one. At times, the camera style is discreet, even surreptitious (Fig. 21.28). Yet, even more than Rouch, Ruspoli flaunts the act of recording, showing his crew and ending *Regard sur la folie* with the camera turning from a conversation between doctors to advance toward us (Fig. 21.29). We are continually aware of the filmmaker's presence even if the subjects are not.

A direct criticism of Rouch and Morin's method is to be found in Chris Marker's *Le Joli mai* ("The Pretty May," 1963). Marker could not embrace

Fig. 21.27 Marcelline explains that despite the camera's presence she behaved sincerely in her scenes.

Fig. 21.28

Fig. 21.29

Fig. 21.28 The long lens films from a distance as a doctor, wearing a microphone, consoles an old woman in *Regard sur la folie.*

Fig. 21.29 Referring to the end of *Chronique d'un été*, Ruspoli's camera leaves a conversation behind and confronts the viewer.

Fig. 21.30 *Le Joli mai*: "The others don't count much for you, do they?" "The others? What others?"

Fig. 21.31 In the shooting-gallery scene that opens "The Return of Fantomas," *Le Joli mai* builds up the atmosphere of political menace pervading "happy" Paris.

Fig. 21.32 A "snapshot" made possible by the lightweight 16mm camera: Kazimierz Karabasz's *Musicians* (Poland, 1960).

the Direct Cinema trend, preferring always to retain the voice of a narrator who reflects on the images before us. *Le Joli mai* absorbs Direct Cinema techniques into a larger meditation on freedom and political awareness.

The first part of the film inquires into the state of happiness in Paris in May 1962, the moment when the Algerian war ended. Marker's aggressive questioning of smug or oblivious people pushes the camera-as-catalyst tactic to the point of rudeness. He also criticizes the limited, apolitical notion of happiness from which *Chronique* began. (Marker ironically dedicates his film "To the happy many.") A clothes salesman says that his goal in life is to make as much money as possible; a couple in love are indifferent to social issues (Fig. 21.30). Part Two, opening with mysterious evocations of terrorism and right-wing reprisals (Fig. 21.31), consists of interviews with people who seek political solutions to contemporary problems.

Harsh and acerbic, shot through with Marker's quirky humor and poetic digressions, *Le Joli mai* asks *cinéma vérité* to recognize the complexity of life and the political forces governing French society at a historical turning point. Yet Marker's meditation has its base in Direct Cinema: his evidence consists partly of his lip-sync interviews. "Truth is not the destination," he conceded, "but perhaps it is the path."[7]

The American, Canadian, and French exponents of Direct Cinema were keenly aware of each others' work. Many of them first met at a 1958 seminar. At a conference at Lyon in 1963, Direct Cinema documentarists debated their differences. Should the camera observe, empathize, or challenge? Is it more authentic to film with several cameras at once? Should the director be the camera operator? Above all, what is the responsibility of the director to the people, their lives, and the event recorded? Direct Cinema, apart from its technical and technological innovations, raised perennial issues of the ethics of documentary film.

By the mid-1960s, several sophisticated 16mm and 35mm cameras offered all filmmakers the flexibility of Direct Cinema. The trend revolutionized documentary; after the early 1960s, most documentarists utilized the hand-held camera to snatch bits of arresting action (Fig. 21.32). Direct Cinema also gave ethnographic filmmaking a new flexibility. It shaped the course of several national cinemas: the French Canadians Groulx and Jutra moved into features on the basis of their NFB work, while directors in Third World countries made Direct Cinema central to their style (Chapter 22).

The open-ended, episodic narratives of Direct Cinema also reinforced tendencies in the fiction films of the art cinema. Stylistically, most of the New Waves of 1958–1967 pledged themselves to the hand-held camera, available light, and apparently off-the-cuff shooting (Chapter 20). (Few directors, however, undertook the harder task of recording direct sound.) More mainstream films, such as *Dr. Strangelove; or, How I Learned to Stop Worrying and Love the Bomb* (1963), *Seven Days in May* (1964), and *A Hard Day's Night* (1964) invoked Direct Cinema techniques when a sense of spontaneous action was required. Even fiction films set in the distant past or the future could intensify their realism (Fig. 21.33). And Direct Cinema became a central tool of western militant cinema of the 1960s, which relied on unstaged interviews, footage shot on the fly, and the ease of taped sound. In both technology and technique, Direct Cinema exercised a powerful international influence throughout the 1960s and 1970s.

EXPERIMENTAL AND AVANT-GARDE CINEMA

The experimental film also renewed itself after World War II. The wider availability of 16mm equipment made experimental filmmaking more feasible for the nonprofessional. Most schools, universities, and museums in the United States had 16mm projectors and could show experimental films. Foreign classics had been available on 16mm from the Museum of Modern Art, but after the war new companies began to circulate experimental films in that gauge. In Europe, which largely lacked 16mm distribution, newly founded or reopened film archives screened classic experimental films.

A growing number of institutions nurtured experimental cinema. Hundreds of ciné-clubs sprang up in cities and universities throughout Europe; because of censorship laws, avant-garde works barred from general screenings could only be shown in such venues. An international federation of ciné-clubs was created in 1954. International festivals appeared as well, most significantly the Experimental Film Competition at Knokke-le-Zoute, Belgium, begun in 1949. Occasionally European governments offered funding for imaginative "cultural films." In France, theaters designated to show *art et essai* (artistic and experimental) films received some governmental subsidy.

The most dramatic growth of an experimental film culture occurred in the United States. Here 16mm film stock and equipment were available, universities and art schools began film production departments, and the wartime work of Deren, Maas, Menken, the Whitney brothers, and other experimentalists started to circulate. Moreover, Hans Richter, Oskar Fischinger, and other older avant-gardists had emigrated to America. Experimental film acquired a public identity with Richter's feature-length *Dreams that Money Can Buy* (1946), a batch of vaguely surrealist sketches by prominent avant-gardists.

Throughout the period most filmmakers funded their work in the time-honored ways: from their own pocketbooks or from a patron. Although the U.S. government and private foundations stepped up support for the fine arts generally, only a few filmmakers won grants. Still, in the postwar era, a number of new exhibition venues emerged. Frank Stauffacher's "Art in Cinema" series, presented at the San Francisco Museum of Art immediately after the war, crystallized interest on the West Coast. The New York City film society Cinema 16 was founded in 1949 and grew to a membership of 7000. In 1960, Canyon Cinema in San Francisco became a similar venue. Students at Dartmouth, Wisconsin, and other universities founded campus film societies, and many were eager for alternatives to commercial fare. A national association of film societies, the Film Council of America (later the American Federation of Film Societies), began in 1954.

Distribution, always a problem for independent American cinema, also expanded considerably. Amos Vogel started a Cinema 16 distribution library,

Fig. 21.33 In Peter Watkins's *The War Game* (1966), the staging of a nuclear attack on Britain gains intensity through use of Direct Cinema; here, a hand-held shot captures a fireman collapsing by a child.

Fig. 21.34 A low angle turns a dancer's leap into a sailing abstract shape (*A Study in Choreography for Camera*).

and other companies followed. The founding of the Film-Makers' Cooperative in New York in 1962 marked a milestone. The co-op accepted all work, making no judgment of quality, and received a flat percentage for rentals. A year later the Canyon Cinema Cooperative was established on the West Coast.

Fifteen years after Maya Deren rented the Provincetown Playhouse to screen her films, the United States had developed an infrastructure for supporting the avant-garde cinema. Tastemakers had emerged: Deren, Vogel, the critic Parker Tyler, and Jonas Mekas, editor of the key New York journal *Film Culture* (founded 1955), organizer of the Film-Makers' Cooperative, and film reviewer for *The Village Voice*. By 1962, anyone with access to 16mm or even 8mm equipment could make a film, and it had a chance of being distributed and discussed. While New York was displacing Paris as the capital of modern painting, the United States had become the leading force in avant-garde cinema.

As in earlier epochs, experimental filmmakers were more closely tied to the world of the fine arts than to the commercial film industry. Some filmmakers continued to animate abstract paintings or illustrate passages drawn from classical music (e.g., Jean Mitry's *Pacific 231*, 1949). One of the most common genres of the postwar era was the dance film, which carried further the camera and editing manipulations of Dulac's *Thème et variations* (p. 198). An early and famous instance was Deren's *A Study in Choreography for Camera* (1945; Fig. 21.34).

Stylistically, several postwar filmmakers were influenced by Surrealism and Dada. During the 1950s others found inspiration in contemporary trends which favored an intuitive, personal approach to creation. Abstract Expressionist painting had centered on the spontaneous creativity of the artist, who might splatter and drip paint as Jackson Pollock did. Critics compared this

Fig. 21.35 Poets Gregory Corso and Allen Ginsberg spar in *Pull My Daisy*.

"gestural painting" to the writings of Jack Kerouac and other "Beats," who advocated an impulsive, nonintellectual approach to experience.

Some avant-garde painters and poets moved into film. In Paris, the Lettrist movement of the late 1940s experimented with the pure sound of verse and the arrangement of letters on the printed page; it soon made filmmaking integral to its program. A breakaway Lettrist group eventually founded the "antiart" Situationist International, which also produced several films. In the early 1960s in the United States, experimental films were made by artists associated with Pop Art and the Fluxus group. Avant-garde composers, such as Steve Reich and Terry Riley, assisted their filmmaker friends by scoring films or performing live accompaniment.

At certain moments, experimental filmmaking spread beyond the fine-arts world and made contact with wider audiences. Typically, this occurred when the filmmakers addressed a distinct subculture of viewers. For example, *Pull My Daisy* (1959) attracted attention because of its ties to the Beat milieu: its narration was written and recited by Jack Kerouac, and its veneer of loose improvisation reflected the "hip" attitude to life (Fig. 21.35). Soon afterward, experimental films drew audiences in the worldwide "counterculture."

ABSTRACTION, COLLAGE, AND PERSONAL EXPRESSION

The new avenues of expression encouraged the continuation of many tendencies of the prewar period. Dada and Surrealist influences continued throughout the postwar era. For example, Dada's antiart impulses can be seen in the films made by the French Lettrists. Their leader, Isidore Isou, argued that linguistic signs were more important than images. In an updating of the strategy of Duchamp's *Anémic cinéma* (1926; p. 195), he argued for a *cinéma discrépant* ("cinema of discrepancy"), in which the soundtrack dominates the image. Guy Debord's Lettrist film *Hurlements en faveur de Sade* ("Howls for de Sade," 1952) carried out Isou's program by eliminating all images. A silent black screen alternates with a white screen that is accompanied by a voice-over harangue.

Surrealist imagery pervaded the work of the Polish animator Walerian Borowczyk. His *Les Jeux des anges* ("Games of Angels," 1964), made in France, presents a series of undefinable objects and nonsense syllables flying past the camera before what seem to be disembodied human organs start to fight. *Renaissance* (1963) uses stop-motion in reverse to make messy heaps of material on a floor assemble into a series of ordinary but disquieting objects: a table, a stuffed owl, an antique doll (Fig. 21.36). In the end, a grenade explodes the still life.

Besides Dada and Surrealist tendencies, four major trends dominated avant-garde filmmaking between the late 1940s and the early 1960s: abstract film, experimental narrative, the lyrical film, and the experimental compilation film.

Abstract Film. The abstract film had emerged in the 1920s with such works as Ruttmann's *Lichtspiel Opus 1* and Eggeling's *Diagonal Symphony*

Fig. 21.36 The reassembly process nears completion in *Renaissance*.

(pp. 192–194). Several Americans who made abstract films during the war (p. 367) continued their experiments in the postwar decades. Harry Smith, who created his early abstractions directly on the film strip, began to use a camera to shoot painted imagery (Color Plate 21.1). Douglass Crockwell employed cut-outs, frame-by-frame painting, and color-veined blocks of wax in *Glen Falls Sequence* (1946) and *The Long Bodies* (1947; Color Plate 21.2). Marie Menken painted designs on film that present one pattern onscreen and another when one examines the film strip (for example, *Copycat*, 1963; Color Plate 21.3).

The Canadian Norman McLaren practiced a great many forms of animation, including Cohl's technique of animating three-dimensional objects (dubbed by McLaren "pixillation"). It was, however, principally his abstract animation that garnered praise for his unit at the National Film Board. Soon after Len Lye, McLaren mastered painting and scratching directly on film, and his hand-painted *Begone Dull Care* (1949) and *Blinkety Blank* (1955; Color Plate 21.4) were shown and admired in art cinemas throughout North America.

Two other exponents of abstraction, John and James Whitney, won a prize for their *Variations* (1943) at Knokke in 1949. John went on to experiment with computer imagery, while James Whitney devised a dot-painting method that could generate mandala shapes and kinetic patterns reminiscent of Op Art (Color Plate 21.5). In a similar vein was the abstract animation of Jordan Belson, who sought to induce Zen-like states (Color Plate 21.6).

Smith, McLaren, the Whitneys, and Belson presented rich, elaborate works, but other filmmakers took a more reductive approach to abstraction. The Viennese filmmaker Dieter Rot created his "Dots" series (1956–1962) by punching different-size holes in black leader. When projected, the holes appeared as shifting or expanding white discs. Perhaps the height of such reduction was reached in *Arnulf Rainer* (1960). Here the Austrian Peter Kubelka created a film wholly out of clumps of pure white and black frames, which created a rhythmic flicker onscreen and produced spectral afterimages in the viewer's eye (Fig. 21.37).

All these experiments relied on filming purely abstract designs, often frame by frame. The filmmaker could also shoot objects in ways which brought out their abstract qualities. This approach, earlier identified with *cinéma pur* (p. 197), had been launched by Léger and Murphy's *Ballet mécanique* (1924), and it was taken up throughout the postwar era. Charles and Ray Eames's *Blacktop* (1950) recalls Ivens's *Rain* in its scrutiny of the patterns formed by foaming water. In Kubelka's *Adebar* (1957) printing processes turn footage of people dancing in a café into a flow of negative images, inverted or flipped end for end. Shirley Clarke's *Bridges Go Round* (1958) employs more complicated laboratory effects, including tinting and superimposition to bring out the bridges' soaring arcs (Color Plate 21.7).

Pure pictorial design and the abstract handling of familiar objects mix frantically in the witty films of the American Robert Breer. While in Paris in the early 1950s, he experimented with single-frame filming. The technique was established in animation, but instead of changing a single object or

Fig. 21.37 Peter Kubelka before his flicker film *Arnulf Rainer*.

drawing frame by frame, Breer hit on the idea of making each frame a completely different image. In *REcreation* (1956), abstract images swirl together with close-ups of tools, writing utensils, toys, photos, and drawings (Color Plate 21.8). Breer went on to incorporate animated footage, handwriting, and other material, as in *Fist Fight* (1964; Color Plate 21.9). His films establish a new threshold of minimal clarity: in the context of single-frame images, a shot of four or five frames becomes distinct and vivid. The avant-garde equivalent of cartoons, Breer's works exude the gentle humor and childlike wonder that we find in the paintings of Paul Klee.

Some European films were abstract in yet another sense. Their makers organized the images into rigorous patterns according to formulaic rules. Whether the shot displayed a pure design or a distinct object, the filmmaker could build the shots into an unfolding structure that owed nothing to narrative. The most evident precursor of this approach is Dekeukeleire's *Impatience* (1929; p. 201), with its few motifs inexorably reiterated. In postwar Austria, avant-garde artists were under the sway of formalistic painting and the serial music of Schoenberg and Webern, so it is not surprising that the two major proponents of structural abstraction were the Viennese Peter Kubelka and Kurt Kren.

Building on the discoveries of Breer, as well as on the rhythmic cutting of the French Impressionists and the Soviet Montage directors of the 1920s, Kubelka formulated a theory of "metrical" film: "Cinema is not movement. Cinema is a projection of stills—which means images which do not move—in a very quick rhythm."[8] Kubelka concluded that the basic units of cinema were not shots but the single frame and the interval between one frame and

Fig. 21.38 Metric editing in Kubelka's *Schwechater* (1958). Single-frame images of people in a tavern are combined by following arithmetical rules.

the next. The director could assemble frames into a fixed series and then build the film out of variations and manipulations of that series (Fig. 21.38).

For example, because the musical phrase to be used in *Adebar* (1957) lasted twenty-six frames, Kubelka decided that all his shots of dancing couples would be either thirteen, twenty-six, or fifty-two frames. These shots would combine to form "phrases." Kubelka then varied the phrases according to a set of self-imposed rules; for example, a cut could link only positive and negative images. *Adebar* ends when all the combinations of shots have been exhausted. The process consumes a mere ninety seconds.

Like Kubelka, Kurt Kren worked with shot units of only a few frames, but his exercises in structural abstraction paid more attention to the imagery. His frame-by-frame patterning is applied to material that evokes strong associations. For example, *2/60 48 Köpfe aus dem Szondi Test* ["2/60 48 Heads from the Szondi Test," 1960 (Kren numbers and dates his films)] atomizes a

Fig. 21.39

Fig. 21.40

Fig. 21.39 Kren's *2/60*: The effect onscreen is that of turning heads, blinking eyes, and transformed features.

Fig. 21.40 Early flash images from Kren's *5/62*: People watch from windows.

set of photo-cards from a psychological test (Fig. 21.39). His *5/62 Fenstergucker, Abfall, Etc.* ("5/62 Window Watchers, Garbage, Etc.," 1962) teases the viewer with repeated shots ordered according to strict rules. At the start, each shot of the window watchers lasts only a single frame (Fig. 21.40). As the film goes on, each image extends to two frames, then three, then five, and so on. Kren's formulas are less mathematically intricate than Kubelka's, but their patterning is more geared to the spectator's memory of specific images.

Experimental Narrative. In *Entr'acte, Un Chien andalou, Histoire de détective,* and other films the 1920s experimentalists had challenged the

Fig. 21.41

Fig. 21.42

Fig. 21.43

Fig. 21.44

Fig. 21.45

Fig. 21.41 *Mother's Day*: Mother's "lovely boys and girls" are frozen in childish postures recast by adult fantasy.

Fig. 21.42 A game of hopscotch in *The Lead Shoes*, with the lens enhancing the quality of heaviness evoked by the title.

Fig. 21.43 *Bells of Atlantis:* A superimposition reminiscent of French Impressionism. (Compare Fig. 4.8, p. 93.)

Fig. 21.44 In *Fireworks*, the protagonist, played by Anger himself, stares at himself in a shot that recalls the mirror imagery in Cocteau's films.

Fig. 21.45 Photos of pain/ecstasy burn in *Fireworks*.

storytelling conventions already developed by the world's film industries. After World War II filmmakers continued to create narratives that differed significantly from those produced by mainstream film industries.

Deren's *Meshes of the Afternoon* and *At Land* (p. 368) had crystallized the tendency toward "psychodrama" that emerged in the symbolic dramas of the Surrealists and French Impressionists of the 1920s. American filmmakers found the psychodrama a congenial form for expressing personal obsessions and erotic impulses. In its fluid mixture of subjective and objective events, the genre anticipated the exploration of narrative ambiguities that characterizes the postwar European art cinema.

Psychodramas commonly present fantasy tales through highly stylized techniques. James Broughton's *Mother's Day* (1948) offers an adult's fantasy projection of childhood. Adults play children's games, framed in striated, off-center tableaux (Fig. 21.41). By contrast, distorting lenses intensify the grotesque plot of Sidney Peterson's *The Lead Shoes* (1949; Fig. 21.42).

As in *Meshes* and Surrealist works, postwar psychodramas are often presented as dreams. Ian Hugo's *Bells of Atlantis* (1952) uses languorous superimpositions to create an underwater world (Fig. 21.43), but according to Anaïs Nin's voice-over commentary, "This Atlantis could only be found at night by the route of the dream." Similarly, Kenneth Anger's *Fireworks* (1947) elaborates a dream structure reminiscent of *Blood of a Poet* (p. 362; Fig. 21.44). The story of a young man drawn to a sailor and then beaten by a gang of sailors ends with the hero awakening alongside his lover as flames consume photographs of dream images (Fig. 21.45).

Fig. 21.46

Fig. 21.47

Fig. 21.46 *Un Chant d'amour*: Prisoners share smoke through a straw.

Fig. 21.47 Tensions between a couple in Brakhage's *Reflections on Black*.

Fig. 21.48

Fig. 21.49

Fig. 21.48 John takes his life in Maclaine's tense and brooding *The End*.

Fig. 21.49 A U.S. missile targets Khrushchev in *Science Friction*.

Gregory Markopoulos also used dreams and hallucinations to motivate erotic fantasy. Like Anger, he structured his films around protagonists who stood in for himself; like Cocteau, he filled his narratives with references to classical mythology. He made *Psyche* (1947) while a student at the University of Southern California and then completed several films (*Lysis*, 1948; *Charmides*, 1948) in his hometown of Toledo, Ohio. In *Swain* (1950), an inmate of a mental hospital fantasizes escape from his prison and from confining masculine roles.

Anger and Markopoulos brought male homosexual themes and imagery into films with an explicitness not previously seen in the avant-garde. So did Jean Genet in *Un Chant d'amour* ("Song of Love," 1950), which presents desire among prisoners and guards with Surrealist touches but without the alibi of dream or hallucination (Fig. 21.46). Psychodramatic narratives express heterosexual drives as well. Stan Brakhage's *Reflections on Black* (1955) presents a series of variations on male-female relationships through a mysterious blind man's visit to an apartment house (Fig. 21.47).

Apart from dramas of erotic longings and personal anxiety, postwar experimental films offered large-scale narratives. Some, like Christopher Maclaine's sepulchral *The End* (1953), warned against nuclear holocaust (Fig. 21.48). Several filmmakers offered satiric or mystical fables. Stan VanDerBeek's Pop-flavored *Science Friction* (1959) stages the Cold War through animated cut-outs taken from TV imagery and news-media caricature (Fig. 21.49). Harry Smith's cut-out animations, culminating in *Heaven and Earth Magic* (1958), present bizarre narratives dominated by occult symbolism (Fig. 21.50).

Fig. 21.50 Esoteric imagery in *Heaven and Earth Magic.*

Fig. 21.51 The improvised "hanging-out" narrative: Jack Smith as the Spirit of Listlessness in *Little Stabs at Happiness.*

Far more loosely organized are the anecdotal, almost home-movie narratives cultivated by filmmakers influenced by the Beat and hipster milieus. *Pull My Daisy* is one instance of this genre; another is Ken Jacobs's *Little Stabs at Happiness* (1959), featuring Jack Smith, founder of a vaudeville act called "The Human Wreckage Revue" (Fig. 21.51). Ron Rice's *Flower Thief* (1960) follows the misadventures of the roguishly goofy Taylor Mead, one of the "stars" of American experimental film.

European animators were particularly noteworthy for their experiments with narrative. After the war, several of the newly socialist eastern European countries formed small, state-supported animation units which often allowed filmmakers a considerable degree of creative freedom. In Czechoslovakia, for example, the puppet animator Jiří Trnka started working in 1945. As with many eastern European animators, his work made veiled comments on the contemporary political situation while celebrating national culture, especially folklore. The latter tendency is evident in *Old Czech Legends* (1953). Trnka's last film, *The Hand* (1965), is an allegory of artistic freedom. A little artisan who makes flowerpots is pressured by a huge, officious hand into making a sculpture of it; when he finally agrees, he must work in a giant cage (Color Plate 21.10). Ironically, Trnka was able to make this fable of state-controlled art in a Communist-supported studio.

Another major Czech animator, Karel Zeman, seemed to comment on the nuclear-arms race in his feature *The Invention of Destruction* (aka *The Fabulous World of Jules Verne*, 1957). It combines live action, special effects, and animation to create an elaborate science-fiction film about a menacing factory hidden inside a mysterious island (Fig. 21.52).

The most prominent of the eastern European animation units was in Yugoslavia. Founded in 1956, the Zagreb studio gained a reputation for highly stylized cartoons, most of them specifically aimed at an adult, art-cinema audience. The films, with simple or lyrical stories that needed little or no dialogue, had considerable international appeal. The comedies usually satirized modern life, as in *Ersatz* (1961, Dušan Vukotić), where a man's visit

Fig. 21.52

Fig. 21.53

to the beach ends when everything—including the hero and the scenery—turn out to be inflatable imitations.

Jan Lenica began work in Poland, moved to France, and also worked in Germany. His French-made *A* (1964) typifies much European narrative animation by combining the humorous and the threatening. A writer is tyrannized by an enormous letter "A" that invades his home (Fig. 21.53), and just as he thinks he has finally gotten rid of it, a giant "B" appears.

Alexandre Alexieff and Claire Parker, back in France after the war, continued to support themselves by doing advertisements. They also made more pinboard (p. 365) films. *The Nose* (1963), an adaptation of a Gogol tale, alludes evocatively to the original story rather than presenting it in linear fashion (Fig. 21.54).

The Lyrical Film. As continuations of prewar genres, abstract film and experimental narrative appealed to well-established avant-garde conventions. But new genres were created as well. The most influential is called the *poetic* or *lyric* film. Here the filmmaker seeks to capture a personal perception or emotion, much as a poet conveys a flash of insight in a brief lyric. The film lyric aims to convey a sensation or a mood directly, with little or no recourse to narrative structure.

It was Stan Brakhage who defined the genre of the lyric in *The Wonder Ring* (1955), *Flesh of Morning* (1956), *Nightcats* (1956), and *Loving* (1956). For Brakhage, the lyrical film records the act of seeing and the flow of imagination. In his "first-person" filmmaking a jerky pan becomes a glance; a flash frame, a glimpse; a flurry of cuts, sensory transport. Brakhage's films capture light as it radiates, reflects, refracts, dapples, and dazzles. *The Wonder Ring*, commissioned by Joseph Cornell when he heard that the New York City elevated train was about to be destroyed, gives us the city as a stream of layers, warped and fractured by the glass of the train windows (Color Plate 21.11). The abstract patterns suggest light hitting the eye and stirring associations.

Fig. 21.52 In *The Invention of Destruction*, real people are dwarfed by animated machines in a style that recalls nineteenth-century engravings.

Fig. 21.53 The protagonist confronts his nemesis in *A*.

Fig. 21.54 The discomfited hero tries to retrieve his nose, now grown into a government official.

Fig. 21.55 Motifs of light, fertility, and fluidity merge in *Window Water Baby Moving*.

The most elaborate of Brakhage's films of this period is *Anticipation of the Night* (1958). Here a sketchy psychodrama about a man hanging himself is recast by the lyric approach. The protagonist is not even a body, only a shadow. Most of the film is an exploration of surface, hue, and movement in the visible world. An aggressive hand-held camera makes light smear and blur across the frame. Brakhage links shots by texture or color, as when a light-streaked stretch of night footage is cut to a burst of light through treetops (Color Plate 21.12). *Anticipation of the Night* established the lyric film as one of America's central contributions to avant-garde cinema.

Brakhage pursued the genre with a series of films about his family. In *Window Water Baby Moving* (1959) Jane Brakhage's pregnancy and childbirth is rendered in flashbacks and a weave of pictorial motifs (Fig. 21.55). Other filmmakers utilized the lyric form—Charles Boultenhouse in *Hand Written* (1959), Bruce Baillie in *To Parsifal* (1963)—but it remains identified with Brakhage. (See Box.)

Brakhage's shots of his family, pets, and household showed that the lyric form could work with intimate, home-movie material. The lyric mode led filmmakers to explore the film journal or diary, in which the filmmaker records impressions of daily existence (e.g., Jonas Mekas's *Walden*, completed 1969). There was also the film "portrait": Markopoulos's *Galaxie* (1966) consists of thirty brief films depicting friends.

The experimental narrative and the lyric film incorporate abstract imagery and structure. Broughton's hard-edged compositions emphasize the design of the shot, while Anger's play with lighting and focus softens outlines and makes the image fairly abstract. Brakhage's films exploit reflections, spectral diffusion, and hand-painting on the film strip. Markopoulos interrupts his erotic quest tales by brief clusters of single-frame shots, "film phrases" which recall the abstract modules of Kren and Kubelka. And the animators who worked in narrative often used abstraction; Zagreb films display flat, painterly backgrounds (Color Plate 21.14). In most narrative and lyric works, however, abstraction carries symbolic overtones, enhances expressive qualities, or conveys that direct perception which Brakhage believed to be the mission of art.

MAYA DEREN AND STAN BRAKHAGE

The figure of Maya Deren dominated the first decade of postwar experimental film in the United States. She achieved recognition with two films made in wartime (p. 368), won a prize at the Cannes Film Festival, and became the emblematic figure of the American avant-garde. Renting a New York theater for her screenings, sending flyers to film societies to advertise her work, lecturing mesmerically, she inspired an intellectual public with a new respect for artistic film. Brakhage attracted notice in the mid-1950s, after Deren's principal contributions were made. A far more solitary and intransigent figure, he won fame through the originality and quantity of his work and its affinities with contemporary artistic developments.

Deren's postwar films marked a new phase in her creative development. After the psychodramas *Meshes of the Afternoon* and *At Land* she made the nonnarrative dance film *A Study in Choreography for Camera* (1945), an exploration of the unique ways in which framing and editing could create an "impossible" time and space (Figs. 21.56, 21.57). A similar examination of movement dominates *Meditation on Violence* (1948), a choreographic study of Chinese boxing.

Ritual in Transfigured Time (1946) combines techniques of the dance films with the trancelike narrative of the psychodrama. A woman whose identity shifts across two bodies drifts through three rituals—domestic work (Fig. 21.58), flirtatious socializing, and sexual pursuit. Slow motion, freeze-frames, and Deren's elliptical match cuts "transfigure" the time of these social rites. Deren saw deep affinities between artistic form and the rote gestures of social ceremonies. "Historically, all art derives from ritual. In ritual, the form is the meaning."[9]

Fig. 21.57 . . . and through a match-on-action cut the movement continues in a studio.

Fig. 21.58 *Ritual in Transfigured Time*: Winding yarn as an image of both unwinding time and women's domestic rituals.

Fig. 21.56 *Choreography for Camera*: The dancer lifts a leg in a forest . . .

Supported by a Guggenheim grant, Deren went to Haiti to make a film on Voudoun dance and ritual. Although she never completed the film, she did publish a book, *Divine Horsemen: The Voodoo Gods of Haiti* (1953). Before her death in 1961, she finished another dance film, *The Very Eye of Night* (1959).

In New York, Deren adopted the image of a Voudoun priestess, gifted with the power to bless her friends and curse her enemies. An extroverted, dynamic organizer, she formed a community of filmmakers in 1953, eventually named the

Independent Film Foundation, which held monthly meetings for screenings, lectures, and heated disputes.

In specialized journals and the general press, Deren promoted avant-garde cinema. She also elaborated a provocative theory of film form and expression. She distinguished between a "horizontal" cinema that emphasizes action and plot and a "vertical" cinema that "probes the ramifications of the moment," emphasizing not what is happening but "what it feels like or means."[10]

The possibility that cinema could dwell on the imaginative resonance of the instant, manifested in *Meshes* and in Markopoulos's psychodramas, was taken in nonnarrative directions by Brakhage. During his stay at the Institute of Fine Art in San Francisco and in his travels between Colorado, California, and Manhattan, Brakhage came to know experimentalists of the older generation—Broughton and Peterson on the West Coast; Deren, Menken, Maas, and Cornell in New York. He absorbed ideas from all of them but quickly forged his own personal style.

Brakhage's main contribution lay in his development of the film lyric. His "domestic" films, such as *Window Water Baby Moving* (1959) and *Thigh Line Lyre Triangular* (1961); his "cosmic" cycle *Dog Star Man* (completed 1964); his 8mm series *Songs* (1964–1969); and his cycle *Scenes from Under Childhood* (completed 1970) defined the genre. His output was prodigious—over fifty films in the 1960s, nearly a hundred in the 1970s.

Brakhage conceived of the artist as a visionary who perceives and feels more deeply than others. He sought to capture on film untutored vision, a sense of space and light unspoiled by knowledge and social training:

> Imagine an eye unruled by man-made laws of perspective, an eye unprejudiced by compositional logic, an eye which does not respond to the name of everything but which must know each object encountered in life through an adventure of perception. How many colors are there in a field of grass to the crawling baby unaware of "Green"? . . . Imagine a world alive with incomprehensible objects and shimmering with an endless variety of movement and innumerable gradations of color. Imagine a world before the "beginning was the word."[11]

Brakhage believed that even unpleasant sights—a rotting dog in *Sirius Remembered* (1959), autopsies in *The Act of*

Fig. 21.59 A corpse's flesh as lyric material in Brakhage's *The Act of Seeing with One's Own Eyes.*

Seeing with One's Own Eyes (1970; Fig. 21.59)—become revelatory visual experiences when seized by the artist's innocent eye.

This Romantic trust in the creative imagination went along with a modernist insistence on abstraction and intricate formal play. Brakhage's transformation of everyday objects into sheer patterns puts him in the tradition of *cinéma pur* (p. 197; Color Plate 21.13). His work bears traces of currents outside the cinema as well—the poetry of Kenneth Rexroth and Robert Duncan, the photography of his teacher Minor White, and the painting of Abstract Expressionism. Critics found in Brakhage's roaming camera the spontaneity of Pollock's "gestural painting."

Brakhage's work encouraged filmmakers to trust their immediate impressions and to make even editing and laboratory work serve direct emotional expressiveness. By "deprofessionalizing" film craft—refusing sharp focus and "correct" exposure, exploiting light-struck footage, showing the splices, filming everyday surroundings with an amateur camera obedient to the movements of the body—he exemplified the notion of the *caméra-stylo* in a way that would have surprised Astruc (p. 492). Making a film was now as personally expressive as writing a poem on a piece of paper.

The Experimental Compilation Film. This postwar trend also has few antecedents in earlier years, though Joseph Cornell's *Rose Hobart* (1939; p. 363) is an important one. In this genre the filmmaker either gathers footage from a variety of sources and cuts it together or trims and rearranges someone else's finished film. The result conveys an emotion or builds up metaphorical associations. Unlike the compilation documentary, the avant-garde assemblage film avoids an overt message and uses the original footage in satiric or shocking ways.

Perhaps the earliest postwar assemblage films came from the Lettrist movement in Paris. Isidore Isou's *Traité de bave et d'éternité* ("Treatise on Slime and Eternity," aka *Slime and Eternity*, 1951) incorporates casual footage, scratched film, black screen, and flicker. Isou's unflagging commentary in *Traité* is deliberately out of synchronization. Maurice Lemaître's *Le Film est déjà commencé?* ("Has the Film Already Started?" 1951) portrays a phantasmagoric visit to the movies. Anticipating many of the devices that avantgardists would exploit in coming years, Lemaître pulls together clips from *Intolerance*, coming attractions, and previous Lettrist films and then mixes these bits with negative and tinted footage, perforation strips, and flash frames—all accompanied by snatches of classical music and the sneering voice of a commentator reading the critical reviews that the film will receive.

Other European avant-gardists produced such assemblage films during the 1950s and early 1960s. Guy Debord's *Sur le passage de quelques personnes à travers une assez courte unité de temps* ("On the Passage of a Few People through a Rather Brief Moment in Time," 1959) combines news footage, advertising shots, and snatches of fiction films with scenes staged and shot by Debord himself, thus becoming a kind of avant-garde parallel to *Night and Fog* and preparing a path for the collage features of European modernism of the 1960s.

In the United States, the sculptor Bruce Conner brought the avant-garde compilation film to notice with *A Movie* (1958). Conner juxtaposes thrilling scenes from Westerns and jungle pictures with eerie newsreel shots of death-defying stunts and man-made disasters, interspersed with repetitions of the film's title. The four-minute *Cosmic Ray* (1961) is an orgiastic montage of reportage and stock footage, linking sexuality and violence and timed to Ray Charles's song, "What'd I Say."

Encouraged by the support for experimental filmmaking, avant-gardists in all these genres moved toward works of ambitious length and thematic breadth. Markopoulos's *Twice a Man* (1963) takes nearly an hour to unfold the interwoven points of view of four characters. Bruce Baillie's *Mass: For the Dakota Sioux* (1964) uses the Roman Catholic liturgy as a framework for

Fig. 21.60

Fig. 21.61

Fig. 21.60 Baillie's richly textured superimpositions in *Mass* evoke an America choked by technology and mournful routine.

Fig. 21.61 Cosmic superimpositions in *Prelude: Dog Star Man.*

a series of lyrics portraying the degradation of contemporary America (Fig. 21.60). Brakhage extended the lyric form in *Dog Star Man* (1965), a five-part cycle of films that seeks to fuse nature, everyday human life, the necessity of death, and the rhythms of the cosmos (Fig. 21.61). Brakhage also separated out all the footage in the film, peeling away the layers of superimposition, and called the four and a half hours that resulted another film, *The Art of Vision* (1965). The avant-garde film was laying claim to the monumentality of the Joycean novel, Picasso's "Guernica," and other modernist work in rival arts.

In a similar effort toward a broad statement, Bruce Conner made *Report* (1965), a complex meditation on the assassination of John Kennedy. By means of television news material, Academy "countdown" leader, and advertising footage Conner not only evokes the nation's horror and grief but also suggests that the assassination and funeral became media events. His sound track,

Fig. 21.62 "And here it comes—the gun-metal gray limousine . . .": Commentary as counterpoint in Conner's *Report.*

drawn from news broadcasts, creates unsettling echoes with the image (Fig. 21.62). Conner completed *Report* on a Ford Foundation grant; that he and eleven other experimental filmmakers received such funding attests to the status which experimental film had achieved within American culture.

Work was done on a more intimate scale too. As 16mm became a semiprofessional gauge, 8mm (introduced by Kodak in 1932) became the most popular home-movie format. Jacobs and Conner began shooting in 8mm in the early 1960s, and Brakhage made an 8mm series, *Songs* (1964–1969), notably the optically dense *23rd Psalm Branch* (1967). Throughout the decade the personal film lyric proved well suited for 8mm and its offspring super 8mm (introduced in 1965). Some filmmakers hoped to sell their films in 8mm editions, as fine artists sold prints; in the smaller gauge, the avant-garde film might become a respectable, and collectible, artistic commodity.

By the early 1960s, all the genres of experimental cinema were thriving. In the United States, a small, active infrastructure—magazines, distribution cooperatives, exhibition venues—supported and promoted avant-garde film-making. A canon of recognized masterworks and major directors was starting to form. At the same time, experimental trends were swept up within a broader social phenomenon. Avant-garde cinema became more strongly affiliated with the fine arts, with the mass culture of youth, and with a nonconformist counterculture. The result came to be called *underground* cinema.

UNDERGROUND AND EXPANDED CINEMA

While the experimental film culture was consolidating in the late 1950s and early 1960s, strange things were happening in the art world. William Burroughs created his novel *Naked Lunch* by cutting and pasting together his manuscript at random. Cellists performed suspended from wires. La Monte Young's musical piece *Composition 1960 no. 2* consisted of building a fire in the auditorium. In Paris sculptors constructed elaborate machines whose sole purpose was to self-destruct. A Japanese artist laid a clean canvas on the floor and called the result "Painting to be Stepped On" (1961, Yoko Ono). Choreographers were making entire dances out of natural movements, while painters reworked comic strips, advertisements, and magazine illustrations. "Happenings" offered theatergoers plotless, often random pieces of activity that might continue indefinitely. Under the influence of John Cage and others, avant-garde art was blurring the line between the order of art and the disorder of life (which might reveal an unpredictable order of its own).

Boundaries among the media were also dissolving. Painters staged theater pieces and turned musical scores into graphic designs. Composers collaborated with poets and dancers in what came to be called the "Theater of Mixed Means." Computers made it possible to compose music, generate sounds, create imagery, and merge the results. Multimedia shows coordinated painting, film, music, light, and performance. Intermedia events fell between existing media; George Brecht's "Drip Event" (1962), which consisted of letting water drip from any source into any empty vessel, could be regarded as music, theater, or even kinetic sculpture.

This nonconformist, vaguely threatening art intrigued the public outside the art world. American newspapers and magazines began discussing avant-garde art, and with the arrival of Pop Art in 1962, the new experiments came to public consciousness as never before. At the same time, the youth culture of the late 1950s was becoming the counterculture of the 1960s. Many young people rejected traditional values and embraced rock and roll, "mind-expanding" drugs, and Zen and Hindu religious doctrines. For a time, avant-garde artists were automatically taken as part of this social tendency, and experimental filmmakers found themselves in the "underground."

In the theater, underground experiments were associated with sexual explicitness, as in the bacchanals of the Living Theatre, or with political critique, as in the work of San Francisco's Bread and Puppet troupe. Within the film community, "underground" initially meant "independent" and "anti-Hollywood." Stan VanDerBeek popularized the term in a 1961 collage-essay which referred to a very diverse group of filmmakers (Brakhage, Clarke, Mekas, Hugo, Breer, Lye, and others). Soon, virtually all experimental films were called underground movies, since they offered glimpses of a world which Hollywood ignored.

Films intended for quite different purposes were absorbed into the underground aesthetic. Conner's compilations became successful shorts at midnight showings. Abstract films formed part of light shows or were screened as "head" movies. Harry Smith suggested that film societies play Beatles songs while showing his early abstractions. Avant-garde institutions encouraged this manner of appropriating the films. In 1961 Mekas began setting up midnight screenings at New York theaters, and some theaters started exhibiting the more notorious films. In 1964 Mekas opened the Film-makers' Cinematheque as a venue for experimental work. Independent film festivals became underground meeting points. A chain of West Coast theaters habitually showed midnight programs of avant-garde films.

Some experimental films fit the "underground" label reasonably well. A film lyric might evoke the mellow spirituality and cosmic consciousness promised by eastern religions and marijuana or LSD. Brakhage's "domestic" films, with their presentation of childbirth and lovemaking, achieved some underground currency, while Bruce Baillie's polished lyrics were taken to embody the serene affirmation popularly associated with California lifestyles. In *Castro Street* (1966) slow dissolves through switch engines and oil refineries reflect what Baillie called "the essential image of *consciousness*"[12] (Color Plate 21.15).

Most audiences expected that underground films would flaunt a raunchy eroticism. The expectation was met in the films of George and Mike Kuchar, twins who began collaborating on 8mm films when they were twelve. *A Tub Named Desire* (1960), *Born of the Wind* (1961), *A Town Called Tempest* (1961), *Lust for Ecstasy* (1963)—the very titles indicate the high trashiness of the brothers' ambitions. Their cast lists parody "Coming Attractions" taglines: "Steve Packard as Paul—who made love with his body, waste with his bowels." At age nineteen the Kuchars began to work separately, and throughout the 1960s both turned out lurid extravaganzas of frustrated male sexuality. The garish mise-en-scene of George Kuchar's *Hold Me while I'm Naked* (1966) becomes a travesty of the rich colors of Sirk and Minnelli (Color Plate 21.16).

Fig. 21.63

Fig. 21.64

Quite different from the Kuchars' neurotic parodies of Hollywood melodramas, and even more closely identified with the cinematic underground, is Kenneth Anger's *Scorpio Rising* (1963). Anger links motorcycle culture to homoeroticism, diabolism, the death wish, and the desires aroused by the mass media (Fig. 21.63). He creates an aggressive montage of staged scenes, off-the-cuff documentary shots, and imagery drawn from comic strips, movies, and mystical traditions. In addition, each episode is accompanied by a rock-and-roll song, anticipating the structure of music videos.

The most notorious underground movie was Jack Smith's *Flaming Creatures* (1963). In about forty minutes, transvestites, naked men and women, and other "flaming creatures" enact a rape and an orgy. Shot in a jerky, awkward style and harshly overexposed, *Flaming Creatures* created the underground's noisiest scandal. After the first screening, the theater management canceled all underground shows. *Flaming Creatures* could not pass New York City censorship requirements, so it was screened free at the Gramercy Arts Theater while donations were solicited. At the 1963 Knokke-le-Zoute festival, the film was denied a screening, but Mekas seized the projection booth and ran the film until authorities cut the power. In 1964, New York police shut down the Gramercy. When Mekas changed to another venue, detectives burst in and seized *Flaming Creatures*. Coinciding with this crackdown was the arrest of a Los Angeles exhibitor for showing *Scorpio Rising*. In court, both cases ended in a victory for the prosecution, with Mekas and Smith given suspended sentences. The underground cinema had lived up to its name.

Women filmmakers also helped establish the underground mode. Barbara Rubin's *Christmas on Earth* (1963) portrays a largish orgy, with characters in masks or painted faces. The film's two reels are projected simultaneously, with one image inserted inside the other. An equally controversial piece was Carolee Schneeman's *Fuses* (1967), which presents copulation through an ecstatic burst of film-lyric superimpositions, applied paint, and rephotographed imagery (Fig. 21.64).

Fig. 21.63 Scorpio in his lair, surrounded by mass-culture imagery of rebellion.

Fig. 21.64 Distortion and overpainting in Schneeman's *Fuses* (1967).

Fig. 21.65 Red Grooms's *Fat Feet* (1966) creates a circuslike atmosphere through slapstick comedy and exaggerated cut-outs recalling his 1959 Happening "The Burning Building."

Underground cinema drew upon new modes of visual arts and performance. Some experimentalists followed the cross-media pollination of the art world and postulated an "expanded cinema." The phrase included computer-generated films (e.g., VanDerBeek's *Collideoscope,* 1966, made at Bell Laboratories) as well as multimedia performances integrating dance, music, and theater. Expanded-cinema adherents began to revive Gance's idea of triptychs in multiscreen events. Stan VanDerBeek's *Movie-Movies* (1965) used hand-held projectors to present film images and slide projections. In Stony Point, New York, VanDerBeek built a "Movie-Drome" which projected films on a dome while spectators lay back to watch.

Avant-gardists were questioning the specific identity of their media, and filmmakers began to ask what counted as cinema. Nam June Paik's *Zen for Film* (1964) consisted of clear film which accumulated scratches and dirt as it was replayed; on some occasions Paik projected it on his own body. In presenting *March of the Garter Snakes* (1966) Standish Lawder began with slides which contained paint and wax; in the heat of the projection lamp, the colors ran, producing movement. Ken Jacobs performed shadow plays in which "close-ups" and "long shots" mimicked film technique. At this point, expanded cinema merged with light shows and even the behavior of light in the everyday world.

As filmmakers borrowed ideas from multimedia artists, so painters and performance artists moved into film. The Pop artists Claes Oldenburg, Rudy Burckhardt, and Red Grooms had staged Happenings, theater events jammed with shocking, puzzling, or frantic action. Some of these artists made films derived from their performance pieces (Fig. 21.65). Fluxus, a neo-Dada group, presented more minimal theatrical works, typified by George Brecht's "Drip Event."

The most significant underground filmmaker to come from the art world was Andy Warhol. A 1962 gallery exhibit brought to public notice a group of painters who took their material from mass culture and treated it in

Fig. 21.66 Sequential variations on an image in Warhol's *Marilyn Diptych* (1962) . . .

Fig. 21.67 . . . and in *Kiss*.

ambiguously straight-faced ways. Roy Lichtenstein presented blown-up, hand-painted comic-strip panels; James Rosenquist painted still lifes of housewares and detergents; Claes Oldenburg built oversize, inflated, sagging hamburgers. Warhol portrayed row upon row of Campbell's soup cans and portraits of Marilyn Monroe and Elvis Presley. All this Pop Art could be seen as ironically criticizing American life or as cheerfully celebrating the energy of the mass media.

As Warhol began to win fame as a Pop painter and printmaker, he took up cinema. He made a variety of films, but the ones which made him notorious were stunningly simple. A man sleeps (*Sleep,* 1963); a man eats a mushroom (*Eat,* 1963); couples kiss (*Kiss,* 1963). Some of the films were related to procedures Warhol used in his graphic art (Figs. 21.66, 21.67); but transposed to cinema, his artistic strategies caused a furor.

Warhol's first films were unnerving largely because of what they did not do. They lacked credit lists and titles. They were silent, even when they

Fig. 21.68 *Eat*: The punch marks at the beginning and the end of a raw roll of film deface Robert Indiana as he chews a mushroom.

Fig. 21.69 Good grooming and flirtation in *My Hustler*.

showed people talking. They told no stories. There was typically no cutting within the scene, and only occasionally would the camera pan or zoom. Usually Warhol or the cameraperson simply loaded the camera, turned it on, and let it record action until the film ran out. The only editing consisted in splicing the camera rolls together, so light flares and punched footage appeared in the finished film (Fig. 21.68). Astonishingly long (*Sleep* consisted of three hours of footage; *Empire*, 1964, was designed to be shown over eight), Warhol's films posed so many challenges that most viewers took them as put-ons—an attitude encouraged by his own comments. "They're experimental films; I call them that because I don't know what I'm doing."[13]

Warhol took up sound films in 1965 and turned toward performance and rudimentary narratives. For *The Life of Juanita Castro* (1965), *Vinyl* (1965), and *Kitchen* (1965) playwright Ronald Tavel provided the actors with semiscripted situations; Warhol had told him he wanted "not plot, but incident."[14] Narcissistic amateur performers chatter aimlessly and aggressively, each one vying to control the scene while parading what she or he perceives as "star quality." Most scenes are rendered in very long takes, with gaps sometimes signaled by "strobe cuts" (flashes of bright light) and disconcerting zaps on the sound track. In 1966, always alert for new opportunities, Warhol joined the expanded-cinema trend with *Up Tight*, two side-by-side films with music provided by a rock group, the Velvet Underground. This led to *The Chelsea Girls* (1966), a three-hour feature which presented a string of scenes on two screens.

During the next two years, Warhol moved toward more recognizable narrative form in *I, a Man* (1967), *Bike Boy* (1967), *Nude Restaurant* (1967), and *Lonesome Cowboys* (1967). After being seriously wounded when one of his circle shot him, Warhol gave up film directing, although he lent his name to films conceived and directed by Paul Morrissey and he signed some later video work.

Warhol's cinema was an extension of his celebrity lifestyle and the group-manufacture process behind his pictures. Just as many "Warhol" silkscreens were made by his staff and merely signed by him, he came up with ideas for his films but the staging and shooting were usually carried out by others. Hovering on the fringes of the Factory, his silver-foil-lined studio and social gathering point, Warhol presented himself as a bland, passive onlooker, naively enthusiastic about everything. "The world fascinates me. It's so nice, whatever it is."[15] His films had the impassive ambiguity of Pop paintings, but they also encapsulated several broader qualities of 1960s avant-garde art.

First, they manifested in a deadpan way the eroticism that had made a scandal of *Flaming Creatures* and *Scorpio Rising*. *Couch* (1964), for instance, consisted of seventy minutes of couples engaging in sexual activity in one corner of the Factory. Moreover, the films' nonchalant depiction of sadomasochism and male homosexuality marked a stage beyond the oblique and overwrought imagery of *Fireworks* and Markopoulos's works. The second half of *My Hustler* (1965) takes place entirely in a cramped bathroom, where gay prostitutes discuss their careers, indulge in casual caresses, and groom themselves painstakingly (Fig. 21.69).

Related to the films' eroticism was Warhol's investment in the "Camp" sensibility. "Camp," as defined in a famous essay by Susan Sontag, "is the love of the exaggerated, the 'off,' of things-being-what-they-are-not."[16] Associated with the gay subculture, Camp taste elevated the excessive and extravagant. Kenneth Anger and Jack Smith also manifested Camp, but Warhol celebrated it forthrightly in his parodies of Hollywood genres and in the performances of several of his "superstars," notably the transvestites Holly Woodlawn and Jackie Curtis.

Eroticism and campiness gave Warhol's work an underground cachet, but he also won attention with more radical qualities. For example, the idea of reflexivity, already important in European art cinema (p. 520), had been significant in American art criticism since the rise of Abstract Expressionist painting. Many experimental films of the period exploited reflexivity quite literally; Stanton Kaye's *Georg* (1964), for instance, presents its fictional story as a film diary, so we are constantly aware of the frame, the cuts, and the sound recording. Critics often took the amateurish techniques of Warhol's work to be reflexive, acknowledging the film as film and thus breaking the audience's illusory involvement with the action (or nonaction) on the screen.

The early films' offhand, plotless shapes also manifested the ideal of indeterminacy in art. Cage had pioneered this attitude in the 1940s, as had the Happenings and the Fluxus events a decade later. Warhol, an apt borrower, gave his films a random, unfinished quality. Often the camera reels could be cut together in any sequence. On initial release of *The Chelsea Girls* the order of the reels was determined by the projectionist.

Finally, in its passive rendering of objects and events, Warhol's work embodied an avant-garde aesthetic of boredom. Cage and other artists had insisted that repetition of even the most trivial action would eventually yield a deeper interest. But Warhol seemed to value boredom in itself. "The more you look at the same exact thing, the more the meaning goes away, and the better and emptier you feel."[17] By projecting the early silent films at sixteen frames per second (although they were shot at the normal twenty-four), Warhol guaranteed that his slight material would be stretched to the limit of endurance.

Warhol ascended into Manhattan's world of discothèques and celebrity parties at the moment when the avant-garde was becoming part of the "art business." Dealers, critics, museums, collectors, and news media turned the art world into a realm of rapid changes in fashion and a market which demanded stylistic innovation and fresh talent. Warhol's films participated in this cultural change and helped bring the underground above ground. By embracing more structured narrative situations, he bid for a broader audience. *The Chelsea Girls* achieved some commercial distribution and attracted unprecedented media attention. His "superstars"—the jittery and shrill Edie Sedgwick; the vacantly beautiful Nico and Joe Dalessandro; the amphetamine-driven Ondine; the perpetually spacy Viva, retelling anecdotes from her Catholic girlhood—had a screen presence that gave the late films entertainment value.

Warhol's rise in the art world certainly helped the films achieve fame, but their influence went beyond the shifts of fashion. His early work was praised for a refreshing simplicity that revived the tradition of Lumière. More generally, his work signaled a reaction against the expressive psychodramas

Fig. 21.70 A typically enigmatic image from Iimura's *Dance Party in the Kingdom of Lilliput* (1964).

and rich, dense imagery of the 1940s and 1950s. The films' awkwardness, superficiality, and self-mockery seemed an antidote to an avant-garde that was becoming too serious and pretentious. Finally, by attracting dealers, curators, and critics, Warhol raised hopes that avant-garde cinema might find a home in museums and galleries, gaining prestige and funding. In all, Warhol became as important to the world of avant-garde cinema as Godard was to the art cinema.

The work of Smith, Anger, and Warhol, as well as the continuing traditions typified by Brakhage, Conner, Jacobs, and others, played a central role in creating an international underground. American experimental films had won recognition at the Brussels Experimental Film Competition of 1958 and elsewhere. In 1963, after the Belgian scandal of *Flaming Creatures*, Mekas and the critic P. Adams Sitney toured Europe with the Exposition of the New American Cinema. Two years later the tour went to South America and Japan. Independent cooperatives sprang up in London and Toronto (both 1966), Holland, Montreal, Italy (1967), and Hamburg (1968), and many of these distributed canonical works of the American avant-garde.

Underground cinema outside the United States explored recognizable genres and styles. In Vienna, Kurt Kren filmed Otto Muehl's "Material-Actions," aggressive and shocking spectacles in which people were rolled in mud and apparently tortured and mutilated. Kren subjected the footage to the same rigorous organization he had applied in his earlier structure-based works. In *La Verifica incerta* ("Uncertain Verification," Italy, 1964), Gianfranco Baruchello and Alberto Grifi developed the avant-garde compilation film by scavenging worn, faded, scratched, and dubbed clips from American CinemaScope films. The filmmakers cut their snippets together in ways which expose Hollywood clichés and create purely formal disjunctions, as when, distorted by the anamorphic squeeze, Gregory Peck closes the door twice (Color Plate 21.17). An even greater expansion of European avant-garde cinema would take place in the late 1960s and throughout the 1970s.

In Japan, powerful and scandalous underground works appeared quite early, notably *Love* (1962) and *Onan* (1963) by Takahiko Iimura (Fig. 21.70). On the whole, though, the freedom of directors like Oshima and Suzuki in the commercial cinema delayed a broad underground movement. The arrival of U.S. work intensified interest. Soon many taboo-breaking films were shown in art galleries, cafés, and universities.

Between 1958 and 1968, international experimental filmmaking enjoyed a period of vitality and variety without parallel since the first avant-garde epoch of the 1920s. Through its alliance with a worldwide youth-based counterculture, experimental film also prepared the way for the politically active roles which mainstream filmmakers were soon to play.

◆ NOTES AND QUERIES

WRITING THE HISTORY OF THE POSTWAR AVANT-GARDE

The experimental film in America has benefited from strong polemicists and critics with a vivid sense of history. Parker Tyler proved one of the sharpest observers of emerging trends, identifying the "trance film" and dubbing the film of hipsters hanging out the "pad movie." Tyler produced an astute chronicle of the avant-garde in essays collected in *The Three Faces of the Film* (New York: Barnes, 1967) and *Sex Psyche Etcetera in the Film* (New York: Horizon, 1969). Later he accused underground filmmakers of infantile exhibitionism [*Underground Film: A Critical History* (New York: Grove, 1969)].

The assimilation of avant-garde cinema to the underground aesthetic is evident in Sheldon Renan's *An Introduction to the American Underground Film* (New York: Dutton, 1967). *The New American Cinema: A Critical Anthology*, ed. Gregory Battcock (New York: Dutton, 1967), collects important manifestos and critical essays. From the West Coast came Gene Youngblood's *Expanded Cinema* (New York: Dutton, 1970), a fund of technical information as well as a document of the 1960s merger of electronics, space exploration, parapsychology, Zen, and cosmic consciousness.

P. Adams Sitney, who became a devotee of experimental cinema before leaving high school, emerged as the most scholarly critic of the avant-garde. In *Film Culture* and his own periodical, *Filmwise*, he printed interviews with filmmakers and close critical discussions of the films. In the early 1970s he elaborated a comprehensive history of the postwar American avant-garde, plotting a shift from the trance film through the lyric to the "mythopoeic" form (*Dog Star Man, Scorpio Rising*). Sitney saw the filmmakers as part of a Romantic tradition, with each movement seeking to represent an essential aspect of the human mind: dream in the psychodramas, perception in the lyric, and the collective unconscious in the myth films. Sitney elaborated this argument in "The Idea of Morphology," *Film Culture* no. 53–55 (Spring 1972): 1–24, and developed it at full length in *Visionary Film: The American Avant-Garde 1943–1978*, 2nd ed. (New York: Oxford University Press, 1979; originally published 1974). Sitney's wide-ranging scheme, as well as his sensitive scrutiny of films, made his work the standard historical account. His framework is utilized in Marilyn Singer, ed., *A History of the American Avant-Garde Cinema* (New York: American Federation of the Arts, 1976).

Three other monographs offer different treatments. Steven Dwoskin's *Film Is: The International Free Cinema* (Woodstock, N.Y.: Overlook, 1975) supplies essays on the international avant-garde. Dominique Noguez offers an institution-based account in *Une Renaissance du cinéma: Le cinéma "underground" américain: Histoire, économique, esthétique* (Paris: Klincksieck, 1985). David James situates experimental filmmaking in relation to Hollywood cinema and militant film in *Allegories of Cinema: American Film in the Sixties* (Princeton, N.J.: Princeton University Press, 1989).

◆ REFERENCES

1. Quoted in Mick Eaton, ed., *Anthropology—Reality—Cinema: The Films of Jean Rouch* (London: British Film Institute, 1979), p. 63.

2. Quoted in Gideon Bachmann, "The Frontiers of Realist Cinema: The Work of Ricky Leacock," *Film Culture* no. 22–23 (Summer 1961): 18.

3. Quoted in Stephen Mamber, **Cinéma Vérité** in America: Studies in Uncontrolled *Documentary* (Cambridge, Mass.: MIT Press, 1974), p. 146.

4. Quoted in James Blue, "One Man's Truth: An Interview with Richard Leacock," *Film Comment* **3**, 2 (Spring 1965): 18.

5. Quoted in Louis Marcorelles, *Living Cinema* (New York: Praeger, 1973), p. 82.

6. Quoted in "Jean Rouch," *Movie* **8** (April 1963): 22.

7. Quoted in Mark Shivas, "New Approach," *Movie* **8** (April 1963): 13.

8. Peter Kubelka, "The Theory of Metrical Film," in P. Adams Sitney, ed., *The Avant-Garde Film: A Reader of Theory and Criticism* (New York: New York University Press, 1978), p. 140.

9. Maya Deren, "An Anagram of Ideas on Art, Form, and Film," in VèVè A. Clark, Millicent Hodson, and Catrina Neiman, *The Legend of Maya Deren: A Documentary Biography and Collected Works,* vol. 1, pt. 2: *Chambers (1942–1947)* (New York: Anthology Film Archives/Film Culture, 1988), p. 629.

10. Quoted in "Poetry and the Film: A Symposium," in P. Adams Sitney, ed., *The Film Culture Reader* (New York: Praeger, 1970), p. 174.

11. Stan Brakhage, *Metaphors on Vision,* ed. P. Adams Sitney (New York: Film Culture, 1963), n.p.

12. Quoted in *Film-Makers' Cooperative Catalogue* no. 4 (New York: Film-Makers' Cooperative, 1967), p. 13.

13. Quoted in "Nothing to Lose," *Cahiers du cinéma in English* no. 10 (May 1967): 42.

14. Quoted in Stephen Koch, *Star-Gazer: Andy Warhol's World and His Films* (New York: Praeger, 1973), p. 63.

15. Quoted in "Nothing to Lose": 42.

16. Susan Sontag, "Notes on Camp," in *Against Interpretation and Other Essays* (New York: Delta, 1966), p. 279.

17. Andy Warhol and Pat Hackett, *POPism: The Warhol '60s* (New York: Harcourt Brace Jovanovich, 1980), p. 50.

PART FIVE

THE CONTEMPORARY CINEMA: SINCE THE 1960s

By the mid-1960s, film was widely recognized as not only a mass entertainment medium but also a vehicle of "high culture." The achievements of postwar European modernism, the increasing influence of the *auteur* idea, and new developments in documentary and experimental film had established cinema as a vital contemporary art.

Very quickly, however, this art faced challenges from other directions. From the early 1960s to the mid-1970s, the world was shaken by a series of political crises.

The Third World, home to three-quarters of the world's population, had been the site of most political strife since 1945. The violence intensified during the 1960s and 1970s. African states were torn by ethnic conflict and civil wars. Right-wing juntas seized power in South America, and guerrilla movements arose to fight them. Egypt and Israel went to war in 1967 and again in 1974, while Palestinian resistance groups embarked on military actions throughout the Middle East.

Western leaders sought to contain Communist expansion in newly independent nations. The first notable failure was Cuba, which after Castro's 1959 revolution quickly aligned itself with the USSR. Some African states followed suit. Most dramatically, the war in Vietnam demonstrated the extent to which a western power would go to block the formation of another Communist state. The United States, which committed itself heavily to the Vietnam conflict in 1965, had to withdraw a decade later. As Mao's 1949 revolution in China had symbolized Asians' struggle against western colonialism, the 1975 victory of Ho Chi Minh's National Liberation Front, along with the ascent of Cambodia's Khmer Rouge in the same year, came to represent the power of guerrilla warfare in the name of socialist revolution.

In the United States, a more militant Black Power movement emerged alongside African-Americans' civil rights movement. Left-wing regimes, many identified with the Soviet Union, sprang up in Africa and Latin America. At the same period throughout the west, the postwar youth culture became a "counterculture," a realm in which young people could explore lifestyles outside the mainstream. With the intensification of political conflicts during the 1960s, college students participated in revolutionary politics as never before. The years 1968–1969 marked a high point in the radicalization of youth in Europe, Asia, and the Americas.

In the face of all this, cinema became politicized on a scale not seen since World War II. In the Third World and elsewhere, political documentaries and socially realistic fiction, often on the model of Italian Neorealism, became vital forces (Chapter 22). More startling, the innovations of postwar modernist filmmaking were melded with the new radical-left orientation to create a "political modernism" which made commercial cinema experimental to a degree comparable to the avant-garde movements of the 1920s (Chapter 23).

By the mid-1970s, many revolutions had failed, as in Latin America, or had revealed a repressive side, as in Vietnam, Cambodia, and China. Filmmakers began to imagine a "micropolitics" that would promote social change at a grass-roots level, within institutions. The extreme tendencies of political modernism waned in commercial 35mm production: filmmakers developed less challenging approaches to story-telling and style. Even the Third World, home of the most militant alternative cinemas, began to produce films for an international audience and to work in widely accessible forms (Chapters 23, 26, 27). Political modernism hung on somewhat longer in the avant-garde sector, but by the end of the 1980s 16mm and super-8mm filmmakers had largely returned to variants of "purer" modernism or had embraced "postmodern" modes of experimentation (Chapter 24).

The political culture of the 1960s and 1970s underwent crucial changes with the crises of the Communist world in the mid-1980s. By the end of the decade, Chinese communism had been shaken by internal rebellion and had moved toward capitalism, while the USSR and the whole of eastern Europe renounced Marxism-Leninism and eagerly sought to join the market economies of the west. The absence of clear-cut alternatives to the Soviet variant of communism left western versions of capitalism and democracy the most powerful players on the globe (Chapter 26).

The waning of stringent political modernism was also due to the decline of cinemagoing. Television and other leisure activities coaxed audiences away from movie theaters, and the boom in home video intensified this tendency. Between 1970 and 1988, attendance fell by a third in West Germany and France, by almost half in Japan, by almost two-thirds in Spain and the United Kingdom, and by almost three-quarters in Italy. Most developing countries saw a similar decline.

In the United States, the slump in attendance leveled off at around a billion annually. This provided the film industry with enough stability for a new consolidation and a further conquest of foreign markets (Chapter 25). For much of the 1970s and 1980s, a rejuvenated Hollywood was the central attraction for the world's filmgoing public. Filmmakers outside the U.S. tried to join Hollywood or devised ways to compete with it. Distributors and exhibitors sought to profit from its products or to block their entrance into domestic markets. In any event, Hollywood could not be ignored. At the same time, innovative alternatives to classical filmmaking continued to arise, from a revision of the strategies of European art cinema (Chapter 26) and from indigenous traditions in the developing world (Chapter 27).

22

THIRD WORLD CINEMA, 1960s–1970s: MASS PRODUCTION AND REVOLUTIONARY POLITICS

Tensions between the western powers and the Soviet bloc did not lessen during the 1960s, but there were signs that the bipolar-world model was fracturing. Growing rivalry between China and the Soviet Union led to an open break in 1960, and during the rest of the decade eastern European peoples strained to loosen Moscow's hold. At the same time, the Third World proclaimed in the mid-1950s appeared to be coming into its own. Colonies became sovereign states, and many of their leaders rejected both Soviet and western ways. "Third Worldism," as it came to be called, was the hope that the "peripheral" countries would not only find true liberation but use the experience of oppression to build more just societies.

Economic development was first on the agenda, but regions were moving at an uneven pace. Mexico, Hong Kong, Singapore, Taiwan, and South Korea were briskly becoming manufacturing centers. India and Africa, by contrast, were not developing fast enough to offset the rapid rise in their populations.

Political violence intensified the difficulties of development. Apart from the major confrontations between East and West—in Cuba, Vietnam, and the Middle East—the Third World suffered coups d'états, external aggression, civil wars, and ethnic strife. These struggles often gave rise to revolutionary hopes. By the late 1960s, radical observers suggested that sovereignty, nationalism, and economic reform were not enough to help the developing nations. Militants argued that the countries' class systems, holdovers from colonial days, would have to be restructured by means of socialist revolution.

"Fidelismo," the belief in patient guerrilla warfare of the sort that had succeeded in Cuba, fortified many resistance movements in Latin America, Africa, and Asia.

Film history was profoundly affected by these events in the Third World. As industrialization spread, so did filmgoing. The continued growth of Third World cities—at the rate of 10 to 11 million people per year in the 1960s—expanded the audience. Significantly, this occurred as filmgoing was declining in Europe and the United States. A larger proportion of the world film audience was made up of Indians, Africans, and Asians.

Just as important, a greater number of films were being produced in the Third World. In 1950, the world was releasing about 2000 feature films per year, but by 1980 Asia alone was producing that many. Unlike the clothes manufactured in Singapore or the watches made in Hong Kong, most of these eastern films would never be available in the West.

Of the 3500 or so features made worldwide in the mid-1970s, the 8 percent made in the United States and the 30 percent made in Europe had global reach. They might be seen in a comfortable theater in Algeria or Buenos Aires or on a canvas screen hung up in a village square in the Ivory Coast or Venezuela. Yet cheaper films from other countries were filling the cracks. Soon the most powerful Third World film industries—notably those of India and Hong Kong—penetrated the less developed nations.

A distinct trend grew out of the political upheavals of the decade. Filmmakers treated cinema as a tool of social change and a weapon of political liberation. The bulk of this chapter examines the explosion of revolutionary filmmaking in the Third World. In Latin America, this was initiated by Brazil's Cinema Nôvo and became more overt in Cuba, Argentina, and Chile. In Black Africa, politicized cinema arose as both an expression of indigenous culture and a criticism of neocolonialist regimes. In China, a strict form of revolutionary filmmaking was undertaken as an act of official policy.

Mass-Production Industries and the Growth of Hong Kong

Japan remained the world's most prolific film-producing country throughout the 1960s and early 1970s. But certain Third World countries also increased their output significantly, largely because they targeted their product at the rapidly increasing populations of Third World cities.

Egypt continued to produce between forty and sixty historical dramas, comedies, and cabaret musicals per year. Its principal film market was Africa and the Middle East. In Latin America, production expanded, particularly in Brazil, but Mexico continued to dominate South American markets. Thanks to government support, Mexico's annual output jumped to over a hundred features in the early 1970s.

Already geared to rapid production, India pushed its annual output to over 450 films by 1975, putting it ahead of Japan. Films in Hindustani predominated, but films in other languages gained a wider share of the market as well. The romantic, colorful Indian films, always adorned with exuberant music, won a huge audience across the Third World.

Several other Asian film industries expanded. South Korea and Pakistan increased output to over a hundred features a year, the Philippines to twice that. By 1975, Asian countries outside India and Japan yielded one-quarter of the world's entire output.

The most successful of the new competitors was located in the British Crown Colony of Hong Kong. The colony established a mass-production studio system in the 1950s. After 1970, when its output leveled off at around 120 features per year, the system became one of the most influential national cinemas of the sound era.

The Hong Kong industry had grown in the 1950s on the basis of family melodramas, Cantonese opera films, and swordfight movies. These genres continued throughout the next decade, principally under the aegis of the colony's biggest company, Shaw Brothers. The Shaws had established an entertainment empire in Singapore. Moving to Hong Kong in 1958, the indefatigable entrepreneur Run Run Shaw built a lavish studio, Movietown. The huge complex held ten shooting stages, numerous backlots (including an artificial lake), an actor's training school, and laboratory and sound facilities. In addition, Movietown housed dormitories and apartments for Shaw's thousands of performers and staff. The studio worked in round-the-clock shifts. Although Shaw films had an average budget of only U.S. $100,000, they dominated Hong Kong production. Shaw Brothers was vertically integrated, owning distribution agencies and theater chains throughout East Asia.

During the 1960s Run Run Shaw pioneered the revision of the martial-arts film (the *wuxia pian,* or film of "martial chivalry"). Earlier films of the genre had emphasized Confucian philosophy, but Shaw's directors stressed action and stunts. Borrowing from Peking-opera acrobatics, Japanese samurai films, spaghetti Westerns, and even James Bond films, the Hong Kong swordplay film became a dazzling spectacle. Zhang Che, the most successful practitioner of the genre, made top grossers like *The Assassin* (1967), *Golden Swallow* (1968), and *Wandering Swordsman* (1970). Che's assistant directors and instructors went on to become important directors in the 1970s.

More innovative and widely renowned was King Hu, whose *Come Drink with Me* (1965) marked the emergence of the new martial-arts trend. Set almost wholly within an inn, *Come Drink with Me* builds its action out of intrigues, masquerades, and flare-ups among the guests. Hu's rapid editing, sweeping widescreen compositions, and Chinese opera acrobatics shaped the martial-arts film for decades. "Working on that film," he recalled, "I began to realize that if the plots are simple, the stylistic delivery will be even richer."[1]

Hu left Hong Kong for Taiwan, where he established a studio for martial-arts filmmaking. There he made two more "inn films" and *A Touch of Zen* (1971). The latter project was on a scale unprecedented in the *wuxia pian.* Three years in the making and based upon intricacies of Buddhist philosophy, the original version ran three hours. *A Touch of Zen* pushes stylization to new extremes. While "flying swordsmen" were a convention of martial-arts

Fig. 22.1 Airborne combat in *A Touch of Zen*. The fighters are propelled by trampolines hidden in the setting.

Fig. 22.2 Hsu Feng preparing to fire an arrow, without a bow, in King Hu's *The Valiant Ones*.

fiction and film, Hu intensifies the urgency of the action. His warriors execute fantastic leaps, hovering to slash or punch before landing gracefully, already coiled for a new encounter (Fig. 22.1).

Hu's later films *The Fate of Lee Khan* (1973), *The Valiant Ones* (1975), and *Raining in the Mountain* (1979) amplify the balletic excitement of *A Touch of Zen*. Nimble performers (Fig. 22.2) hurl themselves over rocks, ricochet off walls and treetrunks, and swoop down from the sky. In Hu's work the martial-arts film achieved a new kinetic grace, and his Taiwanese productions had an enduring influence on Hong Kong directors.

The new martial-arts film developed under the auspices of Raymond Chow, who served as head of production for Run Run Shaw. In 1970 Chow broke away to found his own company, Golden Harvest. Chow aimed his product at a broad international market. He found immediate success in films starring the Asian-American martial artist Bruce Lee.

Lee had worked in minor roles in U.S. films and television before Golden Harvest's *The Big Boss* (aka *Fists of Fury*, 1971) burst onto screens. It propelled Lee to stardom and made kung fu, the art of punching and kickboxing, a worldwide fad. Chow built upon Lee's success with *Fist of Fury* (aka *The Chinese Connection*, 1972) and *The Way of the Dragon* (aka *The Return of the Dragon*, 1972), each of which broke Hong Kong box-office records. Lee was loaned out to appear with minor Hollywood actors in the

Fig. 22.3 In *Enter the Dragon*, Bruce Lee licks his own blood to fuel his rage.

Fig. 22.4 *The Chinese Connection*: In slow motion, Bruce Lee leaps into the air and kicks to pieces the sign reading: "No Dogs or Chinese Allowed."

bigger-budget U.S. production *Enter the Dragon* (1973). Lee's death under mysterious circumstances in 1973 made him a cult hero.

The most famous Chinese-American star in history, Lee played a key role in opening foreign markets to Hong Kong films. He also saw himself as an emblem of the excellence of Chinese martial arts, a point made explicit in *Fist of Fury*, which celebrates Shanghai's resistance to Japanese occupation during World War II. Lee's films, enjoyed throughout the Third World, were often taken as symbolizing the rebellious pride of insurgent Asia.

Although Lee directed only one film, *The Way of the Dragon,* he controlled his star image carefully. Typically he plays a superman, unquestionably the best fighter around but keeping his full force in reserve until the explosive climax (Fig. 22.3). Lee insisted on more realistic combat scenes than were the norm in Hong Kong films, displaying his skills in longish takes and long shots. Some moments of spectacle, however, are intensified by camera tricks and editing (Fig. 22.4).

After Lee's death, producers cast about for substitutes (often named Bruce Le, Leh, or Li), but the kung-fu film rapidly declined in quality. Nevertheless, foreign audiences had embraced the genre, and Raymond Chow's enterprise grew. By the mid-1970s, Golden Harvest and Shaw Brothers produced about one-third of all Hong Kong films. Chow controlled the largest theater circuit in the colony and 500 other theaters across Asia. The martial-arts film, as developed under Shaw and Chow, contributed conventions to action-based genres around the world and won Hong Kong films a high place in international markets.

BRAZIL: CINEMA NÔVO

In the late 1950s young cinéphiles in Rio de Janeiro began meeting at movie theaters and coffee houses. Intrigued by both Hollywood classics and contemporary European art films, the young men wrote articles calling for a change in filmmaking. Given opportunities in the commercial industry, they launched a movement: *Cinema Nôvo,* the Portuguese term for "New Cinema."

In outline, Cinema Nôvo's history conforms to that of many Young Cinemas, particularly the Parisian Nouvelle Vague. Yet the differences are also striking. Although Brazil was in many ways a westernized country, it remained firmly a part of the "underdeveloped" Third World. The cinéphiles, far more politically militant than their counterparts in France, wanted their films to speak for the disenfranchised people of their country—the ethnic minorities, the peasants and landless laborers. Influenced by Italian Neorealism as well as the New Wave, the directors sought to record their nation's dilemmas and aspirations.

Cinema Nôvo films combined history and myth, personal obsessions and social problems, documentary realism and Surrealism, modernism and folklore. In mixing populist nationalism, political criticism, and stylistic innovation, Cinema Nôvo recalled the Brazilian Modernist movement of the 1920s. It also chimed well with contemporary literary experiments and Augusto Boal's "theater of the oppressed." The young directors became a link between the western New Cinemas of the early 1960s and later Third World movements.

The most populous country in South America, Brazil had a topography stretching from drought-parched areas to tropical beaches. Its population included groups of African, Amerindian, European, and Far Eastern descent. Through a policy of "developmental nationalism" President João Goulart sought to unify and modernize the country. His plan for achieving industrial capitalism required that people recognize the country's backwardness. Although under fire from both right and left, Goulart supported many liberal cultural initiatives.

Cinema Nôvo was one such effort. Nelson Pereira dos Santos had already made his mark with the Neorealistic *Rio 40 Degrees* (1955) and was to serve as producer, editor, and inspiration to a group of younger men who came from film schools and film criticism. Like many New Wave directors before them, Brazil's filmmakers first tried their hands at short films. Ruy Guerra, Glauber Rocha, and Joaquim Pedro de Andrade made shorts while they were in their teens and early twenties. The anthology film *Slum Times Five* (1962) included episodes by Carlos Diegues, de Andrade, and others. Within a year, distinctive Cinema Nôvo features began to appear. Drawing on stylistic resources of other New Cinemas—hand-held camera, zoom shots, *plans-séquences,* underplayed dramatic moments, *temps morts,* ambiguous leaps between fantasy and reality—these directors turned out politically critical works.

Many films concentrated on life outside the cities. Glauber Rocha's *Barravento* ("The Turning Wind," 1962) is set in Bahia. Firmino returns from the city and tries to persuade the fishermen to free themselves from bondage to the owner of their nets. He also comes into conflict with Aruan, a local holy man (Fig. 22.5). Eventually Aruan becomes the new force of social consciousness.

Fig. 22.5 *Barravento* is filmed with a hand-held, zooming camera that dynamizes the *capoeira* fight/dance between Firmino and Aruan.

Rocha's next film, *Black God, White Devil* (1963), is more disjunctive. Set in the *sertão*, Brazil's harsh northwestern plain, it shows the oppression of the peasants by messianic religious leaders and vicious bandits. Between the two forces stand the credulous follower Manuel and the gunman Antonio das Mortes (Fig. 22.6). The story is modeled on folk ballads, and songs comment ironically on the action. When Antonio kills the bandit Corisco, a choir sings "The power of the people is the strongest power," followed immediately by a lengthy take of Manuel and his wife fleeing across the wastelands. "Sad, ugly films . . . screaming, desperate films where reason does not always prevail"[2]—Rocha's description of Cinema Nôvo's style of this period fits his own work perfectly.

Nelson Pereira dos Santos dealt with peasant life more austerely in *Vidas secas* ("Barren Lives," 1963). Adapted from a classic novel, the film traces the attempts of Fabiano to find work during the 1940s drought. The dedramatized, almost wordless opening sequences introduce his family's trek across the arid *sertão* (Fig. 22.7). In the course of the film, the family picks up scraps of work, but Fabiano is unjustly arrested and beaten. The film ends as it began, with quasi-documentary images of the family on the move.

Fig. 22.6 Hired by a landowner and a priest to kill the religious agitator Sebastião, Antonio das Mortes takes aim at his real target.

Ruy Guerra made one of the earliest Cinema Nôvo films, *Os Cafajestes* ("The Loafers," 1962), but his fame arrived with *Os Fuzis* ("The Guns," 1963). Soldiers arrive in a famine-ridden town to guard a landlord's warehouse. As the starving peasants pray for miracles, the soldiers idle away their time drinking, firing their rifles, and chatting with the truck driver Gaucho. At the film's climax, Gaucho leads an aborted rebellion. Guerra uses striking wide-angle close-ups as well as long shots which dramatize the alignment of political forces (Fig. 22.8).

These films' stylistic differences reveal the influence of the European auteur theory. Guerra's crisp deep-focus imagery, the bleached dedramati-

Fig. 22.7 The hand-held camera is used to follow the family's endless search for a home in *Vidas secas*.

Fig. 22.8 *Os Fuzis:* A truckload of onions in the right foreground is off-limits to the peasants, kept passive and frightened by the soldiers.

zation of Pereira dos Santos, and the flamboyant zooms and jerky cutting of Rocha mark each film as the product of a distinct sensibility. Most Cinema Nôvo directors followed Rocha in seeing the auteur theory as a vehicle of political critique. He considered cinematic authorship a reaction to the dominance of Hollywood; making idiosyncratic films was itself a revolutionary act.

The worldwide popularity of samba and bossa nova music and the building of the modernistic capital Brasília helped promote Cinema Nôvo as the expression of an energetic, modernizing country. More concretely, the films were oriented toward Goulart's ideology of consciousness raising. They show peasant Brazilians oppressed by illiteracy, subsistence living, and military and clerical rule. The *sertão* films exemplify what Rocha called an "aesthetics of hunger," the revelation of how centuries of suffering could burst into cathartic rebellion. "Cinema Nôvo shows that the normal behavior of the starving is violence."[3]

President Goulart's reforms aroused fears in conservative circles. In 1964, the military seized power. For more than two decades afterward, generals ruled. Guerra, who left the country soon after the coup, declared that Cinema Nôvo ended in 1964. Yet the movement was not yet interrupted. Despite the authoritarian regime, politically critical art flourished. Cinema Nôvo directors continued to work, and new filmmakers entered the industry.

Several Cinema Nôvo directors reflected on the failure of the Goulart government. Their films often focus on the tormented intellectual, cut off from both the bourgeoisie and the people. Gustavo Dahl's *The Brave Warrior* (1967) ends with an idealistic politician about to shoot himself in the mouth. Rocha gave this despair an extravagant treatment in *Terra em transe* ("Land in Anguish," 1967). In the country of Eldorado, a political myth is played out within the delirious consciousness of a revolutionary poet. *Terra em transe* is a Surrealistic interrogation of the artist's political role, culminating in an Eisensteinian sequence: while police fire at the poet, churchmen and businessmen hold a raucous celebration.

Despite the new regime, Brazilian film culture was advancing. Universities were starting film courses, an annual festival was begun in Rio, and new magazines appeared. The collapse of the Atlântida and Vera Cruz companies (p. 488) had seemed to end all prospects for a national film industry, but both Goulart and his military successors sponsored state initiatives aimed at rebuilding it. Legislation dictated tax exemptions, uniform ticket prices, and bigger screen quotas for the local product. The Grupo Executivo da Indústria Cinematográfica (GEICINE) was created in 1961 to coordinate film policy. In 1966, GEICINE was absorbed into the Instituto Nacional do Cinema (INC), which supported production through loans and prizes. Cinema Nôvo had a strong influence on the agency. The INC also assisted coproductions, which sharply increased national film output.

This expansion was aided by an abrupt turn of political events. As inflation increased in 1967–1968, so did strikes and protests. A second coup took place, installing hard-line generals. They pushed through legislation curtailing civil liberties and dissolving political parties. Leftist forces launched urban guerrilla war, and between 1969 and 1973 Brazil was a battleground between terrorists and the military regime.

As usual, Rocha was quick to comment on contemporary conditions. *O Dragão da maldade contra o santo guerreiro* ("The Evil Dragon versus the Holy Saint," aka *Antonio das Mortes*; 1969) revisits the subject of *Black God, White Devil,* but now the mystic and the bandit are seen as affirmative forces. No longer are the peasants benighted victims; revolution arises out of folk rituals, such as theater and festival. Accordingly, Rocha's technique is more stylized. The people become the audience as the antagonists play out their conflicts in a bare, semitheatrical arena (Fig. 22.9). In asking spectators to consider his films as part of an evolving personal vision, Rocha continued to take European auteur cinema as a model. Yet he also pushed toward political militancy. He saw *Antonio* as an instance of "guerrilla filmmaking" in which the cold-blooded killer had obvious analogies with the new regime.

Fig. 22.9 *Antonio das Mortes*: In the town square Antonio and Corisco reenact the battle which climaxed *Black God, White Devil.*

As part of the military government's plan to centralize cultural activities, film policy was recast. Censorship became much stiffer. In 1969, an agency was created to control filmmaking. Empresa Brasileira de Filmes (Embrafilme) was charged with organizing film export and financing production, much as France's CNC did. Through low-interest loans to successful firms, Embrafilme helped boost production to a postwar high of ninety-one films in 1971. The agency would eventually absorb the INC and fuel Brazil's export success in the 1980s.

Although production was flourishing, political repression drove many artists out of the country. Rocha and Diegues made films elsewhere, while Guerra returned to make a film in 1970 and then departed once more. The Cinema Nôvo directors who stayed altered their filmmaking in distinctive ways.

One trend, which encompassed music and theater as well, was called "tropicalism." This was a comic and grotesque celebration of indigenous popular culture. Instead of Cinema Nôvo's didactic insistence on the backwardness of rural life, tropicalism treated folk culture as brimming with vitality and wisdom. Joaquim Pedro de Andrade's *Macunaíma* (1970), for example, is an exuberant comic epic blending Brazilian myths with contemporary satire. Filmed in brilliant color, full of surreal gags and sudden switches of tone, *Macunaíma* became the first Cinema Nôvo film to win large audiences in Brazil.

Throughout *Macunaíma* the lazy, deluded hero is confronted with cannibalism as a way of avenging oneself on enemies. This motif, an echo of 1920s literary movements, became another element of Cinema Nôvo work of the period. The metaphor of cannibalism showed authentic Brazilian culture ravenously incorporating colonial influences. In *How Tasty Was My Little Frenchman* (1972), Pereira dos Santos's Direct Cinema technique and voiceover narration show a French colonialist captured by a tribe of Tupinamba. He is allowed to live among them before he is executed and eaten. The film dwells satirically on the cultural and economic dynamics of imperialism, as when the greedy colonist and the white trader open a grave in their search for treasure (Color Plate 22.1).

Both tropicalism and cannibalism were in the tradition of Brazil's "festive left," which traditionally paid homage to popular culture. Rocha saw in these qualities a way for filmmakers to connect with myth and to guide people toward "anarchic liberation."[4] These trends could win a wider audience than did the astringent realism or flamboyant experiments of earlier Cinema Nôvo efforts. The competition of television serials and erotic comedies (the *pornochanchada*) also pushed filmmakers toward more accessible, spectacle-centered works.

As Cinema Nôvo became a prestige cinema, winning financial support from INC and Embrafilme, a more extreme avant-garde arose to challenge it. Colleges, ciné-clubs, and archives began to screen specimens from the *udigrudi*, or "underground." Rogerio Sganzala's *Red Light Bandit* (1968), Andrea Tonacci's *Bla Bla Bla* (1968), and Julio Bresanne's *Killed the Family and Went to the Movies* (1969) were all-out assaults on good taste. Gruesome scenes of murder and vomiting were recorded in deliberately sloppy technique. This self-proclaimed "aesthetics of garbage" savagely mocked the aesthetics of hunger, and many scenes parodied films by Rocha, Guerra, and their peers. Cinema Nôvo, its edge blunted by exile or cooperation with the state-controlled film industry, was no longer a disruptive force.

Diegues and Guerra continued to make politically critical films in exile. Rocha became even more militant. He denounced Cinema Nôvo's formative influences, Neorealism and the Nouvelle Vague, declaring that Third World revolution would overturn both Hollywood and the tradition of European authorship represented by Godard, Rossellini, and Eisenstein. In this he echoed the manifestos of "imperfect cinema" and "Third Cinema" elsewhere in the hemisphere.

Years before, Rocha and his colleagues had been, as Diegues put it, "making political films when the [French] New Wave was still talking about unrequited love."[5] The young Rio cinéphiles had helped launch a tradition of political modernism that swept through the world during the next decade.

POLITICAL FILMMAKING IN THE THIRD WORLD

Although the film industries of Hong Kong and other Third World nations aimed their products at mass audiences in developing countries, they were hardly likely to present revolutionary ideas. And although Cinema Nôvo struck a compromise between auteur cinema and political critique, it was addressed to cultivated viewers who appreciated European art cinema. In the late 1960s, Third World directors began making politically critical films aimed at large audiences.

In some countries, politicized cinema arose from the same concerns for social criticism that had propelled filmmakers in the 1950s. Actors or directors who had found success in a well-organized industry were in a strong position to make critical films. The Egyptian Youssef Chahine, for instance, was able to exploit his commercial reputation to direct such populist films as *The Land* (1969; Fig. 22.10). In Turkey the actor Yilmaz Güney also benefited from a growing national industry. His popularity enabled him to direct *Umut* ("Hope," 1970), in which Güney stars as a taxi man hoping to strike it rich in the lottery. The film's emphasis on daily routine and its episodic structure put it in the lineage of Neorealism and the early 1960s art cinema, while its slow pace and use of "dead time" exemplify a resistance

Fig. 22.10 A smooth crane shot reflects the technical prowess of Egypt's well-established film industry (*The Land*).

to action-filled plotting (Fig. 22.11). *Umut* inspired a new, "engaged" film-making in Turkey.

Similarly, in India Mrinal Sen's *Bhuvan Shome* (1969) sprang largely from the individual filmmaker's urge to launch a social critique. Sen had participated in the left-wing Indian People's Theatre Movement and had made films since 1956, but *Bhuvan Shome*, a comic satire on neocolonialist bureaucrats (Fig. 22.12), led him to what he called "a taste for pamphleteering."[6] Along with Ritwik Ghatak, the leftist director who had gone into teaching (p. 487), Sen helped create the New Indian Cinema of the early 1970s.

Chahine, Güney, and Sen exemplify the general politicized tendency of Third World filmmaking in the late 1960s. But Third Worldism called for a more militant film practice. Many believed that Third World revolution was in the offing. In 1962 Algeria won a war of independence from France. African colonies, newly liberated, showed promise of indigenous rule. Some guerrilla wars in Latin America were initially successful. The Palestine Liberation Organization, founded in 1964, promised to win Palestinians a homeland. Fidel Castro had led a revolution in Cuba, and the U.S.-backed Bay of Pigs invasion had been easily repelled. China's split with Moscow in 1960 seemed to signal the emergence of a non-Soviet-style communism, and Mao Zedong's pronouncements carried enormous authority among radicals throughout the 1960s. In Vietnam, Ho Chi Minh's National Liberation Front had managed to resist U.S. intervention in the war with the corrupt regime in the South.

Such developments seemed to point toward a mass revolution of oppressed peoples. The writings of Algerian psychiatrist Frantz Fanon argued that all colonized people had to recognize that their minds had been restructured by western domination. "People of the world," Mao urged in 1964,

Fig. 22.11 *Umut*: As Djabbar (played by Güney) and his customer talk of finding buried treasure, they drive through a neighborhood whose wealth mocks their dreams.

Fig. 22.12 Bhuvan Shome, a cold bureaucrat on vacation in a village, learns about life outside the office from a warm-hearted rural woman (production still).

"unite and defeat the U.S. aggressors and all their running dogs!"[7] At the 1966 Conference of Solidarity in Havana, speakers advocated that Asia, Africa, and Latin America organize to fight western imperialism and neocolonialism.

The ideal of tricontinental revolution inspired many filmmakers. In the Middle East, for instance, there grew up a New Cinema movement dedicated to Third World revolution. Egyptian anticolonialist films such as Salah Abou Seif's *Cairo '30* (1966) and Tewfik Saleh's *The Rebels* (1968) inspired filmmakers in Lebanon, Tunisia, and Egypt to make more militant features. Palestinian and Algerian resistance organizations made short propaganda pieces. Moroccans established a journal, *Cinema 3* (the "3" standing for Third World). In December 1973, concurrent with a conference of nonaligned countries, Algiers hosted a meeting of Third World filmmakers. Similar activities took place in Asia, Africa, and Latin America.

The fundamental premise of revolutionary Third World film was that all art, even that which purports only to be entertainment, is deeply political. The stories that are told, the views with which the viewer is asked to sympathize, the values implicit in the action, and even the way in which the story is told—all were held to reflect political ideologies. The domination of Hollywood films in the Third World thus provided an obvious target. Revolutionary cinema would not only reject the politics that masqueraded as entertainment, not only attack the imperialist ideology carried by American movies, but also offer the viewer a politically liberating film experience.

To some extent this process could be carried on through traditional means, such as documentary or socially critical films set in the present day. But in Latin America and Africa, filmmakers forged new genres of fictional films.

One common type was the historical examination of mass struggles against imperialism. In almost every country, filmmakers found incidents of resistance or rebellion which could be made relevant to the contemporary scene. There was also the "exile" film, which portrayed the experiences of individuals cut off from their roots and reflecting on their native country from abroad. African filmmakers studying abroad in the 1960s often made films in this genre, while Latin American filmmakers used it to examine their political exile in the 1970s. Yet another genre was one which plumbed indigenous cultures, seeking to reveal a national identity untainted by colonialism. In this genre (known in African cinema as the "return to the sources") filmmakers drew upon folklore, myth, and ritual and then transformed such elements so as to reflect critically upon native traditions or contemporary politics.

Stylistically, militant Third World filmmakers refused the technical gloss identified with Hollywood spectacle. The lightweight cameras and informal lighting of Direct Cinema offered the opportunity of making films cheaply and quickly. Such techniques also created a sense of a more direct, intimate encounter with the event. The rawness of style was itself a political statement. Yet aesthetic subtleties were also open to the filmmakers. Cuban and Chilean directors followed the lead of Rocha in making the hand-held camera an aggressive, kinetic force. Moreover, since virtually no sound recording was done during filming, postsynchronization offered rich possibilities of manipulating the sound track in relation to the image. Cuban directors, Argentina's Cine Liberación, and the New Chilean directors also revived Soviet Montage techniques as part of their rejection of Hollywood continuity style.

Most militant Third World filmmakers came from the middle classes, and many had been trained in Europe. Most were intellectuals with deep knowledge of American and European film traditions. As a result, their films often blend formal innovation with direct emotional appeal. Many films of this tradition challenged western conceptions of cinematic art by showing that mass audiences were not as intolerant of experimentation as Hollywood and Europe had trained them to be. An aesthetically rich film could also address the audience's political concerns.

LATIN AMERICA

In 1963 the Mexican novelist Carlos Fuentes wrote: "South of your border, my North American friends, lies a continent in revolutionary ferment—a continent that possesses immense wealth and nevertheless lives in a misery that you have never known and barely imagine."[8] It was this revolutionary ferment, and the challenge it flung at Europe and the United States, which many Latin American filmmakers sought to advance.

Throughout most of the century Latin America had been economically dependent on the western-controlled world market. Most countries exported natural resources in order to develop their industrial infrastructures. But the 1960s saw a stagnation in trade throughout Latin America. This in turn encouraged the growth of authoritarian military regimes, which sought to attract northern investment and repress political dissent. Many activists went underground. During the early 1970s Brazil was only one of several South American countries to be assailed by guerrilla warfare and urban terrorism.

In addition, the United States sought to stifle left-wing activity that could disrupt business. President Kennedy sponsored the Cuban exiles who invaded at the Bay of Pigs in 1961, President Johnson quashed a 1964 uprising in the Dominican Republic, and the Central Intelligence Agency sought to subvert uncooperative regimes, notably that of Salvador Allende in Chile. Such actions only intensified the sense of Latin America as a battle-ground between economic imperialism and mass insurgence.

Outside Cuba, the only country to undergo a left-wing revolution, few artists took sides in this conflict. Latin American novelists of the 1960s were more famous for their evocative "magical realism" than for partisan positions. Some painters were more socially critical: the Argentine Antonio Berni made disturbing collages out of junked First World commodities, while the Colombian Fernando Botero mocked authority in his eerie paintings of inflated, vacantly staring priests and generals. Closer to cinema was the *nueva canción* ("new song") movement which began in Chile as a mix of indigenous sources with politically critical lyrics. The music spread throughout Latin America, becoming internationally popular via the Cuban singer Silvio Rodriguez. Film played an equally important role in presenting revolutionary ideology through popular art.

Fig. 22.13 In a nervous hand-held shot, the Indian Corachi confronts his landlord (*Tarahumara*).

Fig. 22.14 Intellectual montage in *Hour of the Furnaces*: The bull, evoking the slaughter of the workers in Eisenstein's *Strike*, represents the oppression of Argentines working in the beef-export industry.

In Cuba, filmmaking was sponsored by Fidel Castro's regime, but elsewhere militant filmmakers usually gathered in twos or threes, often working with political groups or labor unions. It might happen, as in Argentina and Chile, that a new government would support or at least tolerate their activities, but the resurgence of right-wing regimes drove filmmakers into exile. By the mid-1970s, many worked outside their native countries.

More than other Third World filmmakers, Latin American directors were haunted by Hollywood cinema. American films had dominated southern markets since the mid-1910s. Hollywood's flirtation with South American locales and music during the 1930s and 1940s, although presenting stereotyped images, intensified audience interest in U.S. genres and stars. The dreamlike glamour of the studio cinema profoundly influenced the countries' cultures. The Argentine novelist Manuel Puig has recalled that for him the American films shown on his small town's movie screen created a "parallel reality . . . which, I was convinced, existed somewhere beyond my town, and in all three dimensions."[9]

Politicized Latin American directors sometimes assimilated elements of the Hollywood product they knew so well, but they also turned to foreign models of socially critical cinema. As in the 1950s, Italian Neorealism was a pervasive influence, particularly in the handling of nonprofessional actors and location shooting. Direct Cinema documentary was also an important source, as it had been for the Cinema Nôvo group. In *Tarahumara* (1964), for instance, the Mexican Luis Alcoriza uses the hand-held camera much as Guerra had in *Os Fuzis* (Fig. 22.13). For both aesthetic and economic reasons, most Latin American directors shot on location with nonprofessional performers, using a lightweight camera and postsynchronizing dialogue.

In editing, filmmakers usually relied on the principles of Hollywood continuity. There were, however, some experiments that harked back to Soviet silent cinema, particularly Eisenstein's "intellectual montage." For example, the Argentine *La Hora de los hornos* (*Hour of the Furnaces*, 1968) crosscuts a soft-drink ad with the slaughter of a bull (Fig. 22.14). Similarly, the use of sound intensifies the thematically pointed editing. In the Cuban film *Memories of Underdevelopment* (1968) newsreel shots of victims of military torture are intercut with society women applauding. The discreet insensitivity of the ruling elite is underscored by the sound track, which simply presents the delicate pattering of the women's hands.

All these stylistic tendencies, along with elements drawn from European Young Cinemas, led Latin American film to blur the boundaries between documentary and fiction. The use of nonactors, the immediacy of the hand-held camera, the interpolation of newsreel footage, and the focus on topical issues gave the films the urgency of reportage, even if their action was set in the past. At the same time, by assimilating modernist techniques—fragmentary flashbacks, elliptical narration, to-camera address—directors avoided the stolidity of Soviet Socialist Realism.

Driven by a desire to capture the continent's political aspirations, new directors sought a more immediate contact with the public than was characteristic of most other Young Cinemas. In Cuba, directors merged experimental form with entertainment. Elsewhere, directors explored ways of incorporating the ordinary person into the process of production or projection.

Like the tropicalist Cinema Nôvo works, some films drew on folklore traditions, particularly oral storytelling. Other films were designed to provoke discussion after the screening. For a time, the Latin American cinema sustained the political modernism of Cinema Nôvo and other movements while addressing a wider public than the Brazilian directors reached.

Latin American filmmakers also resembled the Soviet Montagists and the Italian Neorealists in their eagerness to connect theory and practice. In the late 1960s, critical discussion of political cinema generated essays and manifestos, notably Fernando Solanas and Octavio Getino's "Towards a Third Cinema" (1969) and Julio Garcia Espinosa's "For an Imperfect Cinema" (1969). No theoretical "line" characterized all Third World cinema (see Notes and Queries), but such writings, accompanied by films of striking energy and force, crystallized issues faced by revolutionary filmmakers around the globe.

Cuba: Cinema of Revolution.　In 1956, a band of exiles landed on Cuba's shores, determined to overthrow President Fulgencio Batista. Less than three years later, Batista fled the country. On New Year's Day 1959 Fidel Castro led his guerrilla forces into Havana. Latin America had seen its first revolution since World War II.

Castro quickly expropriated land, executed officials of the hated Batista regime, and nationalized the economy. Cuba identified itself as a socialist state and swung its allegiance toward the USSR, a policy intensified by a U.S. embargo. After the fiasco of the U.S.-sponsored invasion at the Bay of Pigs in 1961 and the missile crisis of 1962, Cuba became a Soviet satellite.

While the USSR provided the country with exports and financial aid, Fidel's comrade-in-arms Che Guevara promoted the idea of assisting revolts throughout South America. For much of the Third World Cuba came to symbolize anti-imperialist revolution. In addition, the vibrancy of Cuban literature and music attracted worldwide attention and made the nation a central influence on other Latin American countries.

Motion pictures helped create Cuba's new way of life. The first act of Castro's government in the artistic sphere was the 1959 creation of the Instituto Cubano del Arte e Industria Cinematograficos (ICAIC, "Cuban Institute of Film Art and Industry"). Headed by Alfredo Guevara, Che's brother, ICAIC became a center of the new Cuban film culture. In 1960 it founded a film archive and a film journal, *Cine cubano.* By 1965 ICAIC ran all production, distribution, and exhibition in the country. It trained all personnel and oversaw import and export. By replacing commercial advertising with dynamic and engaging posters made by in-house artists (Color Plate 22.2), ICAIC influenced graphic design throughout the world. In a gesture reminiscent of Soviet and Chinese mobile projection units, ICAIC established *cine moviles,* trucks that visited remote areas to hold screenings.

ICAIC also produced a great many films. Under earlier governments, filmmaking had been a cheap, small-scale affair, consisting almost wholly of routine genre pictures and pornographic films. ICAIC had to create a production base. Thanks to government support, directors and crews who had made films before the revolution, and extensive support by foreign talent, large-scale filmmaking began in 1960. By the early 1970s, the new government had turned out 500 newsreels, 300 documentary shorts, and over 50

Fig. 22.15 In *Hanoi, Tuesday the 13th* the editing makes President Johnson's wife Lady Bird . . .

Fig. 22.16 . . . seem to be laughing at a suffering Vietnamese.

features. Since the relatively prosperous Cubans were devoted moviegoers, ICAIC could recoup production costs in the home market. In addition, many of the new Cuban films were ripe for export to Europe and the USSR.

Because Cuba had few trustworthy prerevolutionary directors, ICAIC had to assign films to untried talents. Former ciné-club members Julio Garcia Espinosa and Tomás Gutiérrez Alea had made only experimental shorts before the revolution. Humberto Solas directed his first feature, the large-scale *Lucia* (1968), when he was only twenty-six. The young directors of ICAIC became Cuba's equivalent of Europe's Young Cinemas or Brazil's Cinema Nôvo.

In the early 1960s, ICAIC concentrated on documentary shorts, which not only offered good training grounds for beginning talent but also answered the need for promulgating government policies. The outstanding exponent of the new Cuban documentary was Santiago Alvarez, creator of *Now!* (1965), *Hanoi, Tuesday the 13th* (1967), *79 Springtimes* (1969), and other short films. Alvarez combined stock footage, titles, animation, and wide-ranging sound sources to create partisan agit-films in the Soviet Montage vein (Figs. 22.15, 22.16).

Despite Cuba's alignment with Moscow, artists did not embrace Socialist Realism. ICAIC's members debated the nature of revolutionary art, and filmmakers were open to influences from many sources. The feature films of the early years often bore the stamp of Neorealism. Espinosa and Alea had studied at Italy's Centro Sperimentale, and Alea's *Stories of the Revolution* (1960) borrowed its episode structure from Rossellini's *Paisan*. The Neorealist scriptwriter Cesare Zavattini contributed to the script of Espinosa's *The Young Rebel* (1961).

The major works of Cuba's revolutionary cinema emerged in the crucial years 1966–1971. During these years the drive to build Cuba's economy led Castro to promote central planning and call on the populace for an enormous moral and physical sacrifice. As part of this campaign, Cubans celebrated 1968 as the culmination of the "Hundred Years of Struggle" that began with Cuba's first efforts to throw off Spanish colonization. After Havana's 1966 Tricontinental Solidarity Conference, Cuba also took the lead in fostering anticolonial revolution, with Che calling for "two, three, many Vietnams."

Filmmakers began to go beyond the Neorealist model and adopt strategies of cinematic modernism. The Cuban directors knew the works of Antonioni, Bergman, Resnais, and the Nouvelle Vague. They cited other films in an affectionate or critical spirit. They also drew on characteristic art-cinema techniques: abrupt flashbacks and flashforwards, fantasy sequences, hand-held camerawork, elliptical editing, and the mixing of staged footage, documentary, and animation into a cinematic collage.

Yet the Cuban directors did not simply mimic the European art cinema. As with the Cinema Nôvo directors, circumstances and commitments drove them to explore a politicized modernism. This ran parallel to efforts in capitalist countries (Chapter 23). In Cuba, however, the directors consistently modified modernist techniques in order to make them accessible to wide audiences. ICAIC welcomed experimentation which demystified the filmmaking process. Alfredo Guevara urged filmmakers "to reveal all the tricks, all the resources of language; to dismantle all the mechanisms of cinematic

Fig. 22.17

Fig. 22.18

hypnosis."[10] Because Cuban filmmakers tended to use familiar genres, they made film form less ambiguous or obscure than did the most experimental Brazilian and European directors.

Alea's *Death of a Bureaucrat* (1966), for instance, updates that perennial socialist genre, the satire on bureaucracy. Animation, newsreels, and still photos interrupt the action with bits of grotesque comedy that recall Makavejev (Fig. 22.17). The film rushes through affectionate homages to Fellini, Buñuel, and Hollywood comedians (Fig. 22.18). Even ICAIC art is mocked when a painter is seen using a live octopus as a model for a poster portraying American imperialism.

Similarly comic in tone is Espinosa's *Adventures of Juan Quinguin* (1967), a parody of Hollywood Westerns centering on a young revolutionary. Other films, notably *Memories of Underdevelopment* and *Lucia* (both 1968), offered more serious models of critically assimilating other traditions. (See Box.) Another important attempt to create an accessible political modernism was Manuel Octavio Gomez's *First Charge of the Machete* (1969). One of several historical films celebrating the Hundred Years of Struggle, *First Charge* re-creates an 1869 revolt, when the machete became a weapon of the oppressed sugar-cane cutters. Gomez made the film as if it were a 1969 news report, complete with to-camera interviews, direct sound, hand-held shooting, and high-contrast film stock (Fig. 22.19).

The intermingling of fiction and documentary, already seen in various New Cinemas, became a central strategy for Cubans who wished to make their experimentation accessible. The hand-held camera portrayed the ferocity of a battle, accentuated personal confrontations, or conveyed a character's confused perceptions. Documentary-style voice-over commentary helped the audience adjust to disorienting visual techniques. The most innovative Cuban filmmakers recognized the need for what Espinosa in 1969 called "imperfect" cinema—popular, addressed at problems, and helping to make spectators into "co-creators" of the work.

While winning large audiences, Cuban directors followed the Soviet filmmakers of the 1920s in adapting modernist techniques to the need of a propagandistic cinema. The debt to the Soviet tradition is explicitly noted in

Fig. 22.17 An animated arrow identifies the dead uncle as a loyal Cuban, faithfully listening to a Castro speech (*Death of a Bureaucrat*).

Fig. 22.18 A tit-for-tat fight between bureaucrats in a cemetery evokes Laurel and Hardy (*Death of a Bureaucrat*).

Fig. 22.19 Like many Cuban films, *First Charge of the Machete* uses Direct Cinema technique to present staged events with an aggressive immediacy.

TWO REVOLUTIONARY FILMS: *MEMORIES OF UNDERDEVELOPMENT* AND *LUCIA*

In the fall of 1968, there premiered two films which exemplified the diversity of the Cuban postrevolutionary cinema. Both became paradigms of political filmmaking within Latin America.

Memories of Underdevelopment, directed by Tomás Gutiérrez Alea, portrays an intellectual uncertain about his allegiance to the revolution. Sergio's contempt for those who leave Cuba for the United States is counterbalanced by his self-centered lifestyle and his unwillingness to build the new society.

Alea uses art-cinema techniques already associated with the "alienated bourgeois" in European cinema to characterize a man out of synchronization with the revolution. Abrupt flashbacks, fantasy scenes, and a continuous inner monologue expose Sergio's creative paralysis and unfulfilled sexual desires (Fig. 22.20). Somewhat in the manner of Antonioni, Alea follows Sergio on aimless walks through the city. There is even a reflexive scene in which Alea tells Sergio of his new film, "a collage that will have a bit of everything"—referring to *Memories of Underdevelopment* itself.

While utilizing the techniques of cinematic modernism, the film is far less obscure and ambiguous than its European counterparts. Momentary uncertainties are quickly resolved by the verbal commentary or the narrative situation. The inner monologue gives thematic significance to the long-held telephoto image in which Sergio's face disintegrates (Fig. 22.21).

Alea's collage of fiction and documentary enables him to exploit principles of Eisenstein's intellectual montage (p. 145). In context, the juxtapositions also reflect Sergio's bitter, paralyzed consciousness. At the film's climax, as the Cuban missile crisis unfolds, Alea cuts between Sergio in his penthouse and newsreels of Havana's mobilization (Fig. 22.22). The film's final images of crashing waves cites the beginning of *Potemkin*; over shots of the breakers we hear Cuban tanks rumbling into battle.

Lucia also confronts its main characters with political crises. The film celebrates the Hundred Years of Struggle through three episodes from Cuban history, each centering upon a woman named Lucia. "Lucia 1895" shows a woman wooed by a Spanish secret agent; he uses her love to gain knowledge of her brother's rebel band. In "Lucia 1933" a woman and her revolutionary lover watch his party descend into corruption. "Lucia 196–" is a comedy in which a vibrant woman learns to resist her tyrannical husband.

Humberto Solas was infatuated with Resnais and Antonioni during his youth, but each episode of *Lucia* explores different trends within cinematic modernism. "Lucia 1895" oscillates between dazzlingly overexposed images, associated with the comfortable bourgeois life, and scorched, high-contrast ones of the Spanish-American War and of Lucia's imagination (Fig. 22.23). In a pastiche of Visconti's *Senso*,

Fig. 22.20 Sergio, the emasculated intellectual, pulls his wife's stocking over his face and stares at his lipstick-smeared reflection (*Memories of Underdevelopment*).

Fig. 22.21 As Sergio walks to the camera, his features dissolve into a grainy blur; his voice intones: "You're alone . . . . You're nothing, you're dead."

Lucia's love for Rafael is rendered operatic by soaring romantic music and the couple's histrionic poses (Fig. 22.24).

"Lucia 1933" yields an understated lyricism reminiscent of Truffaut. Soft lighting, abbreviated scenes, and sudden shifts of mood evoke 1960s French cinema (Figs. 22.25, 22.26). "Lucia 196–" portrays contemporary Cuban society by means of a third stylistic approach. Now the staging is loose and naturalistic (Fig. 22.27). Direct Cinema observational tactics recall Forman and other Czech directors, as

Fig. 22.22 The sound of Sergio flicking his lighter eerily evokes his isolation when heard under the shots of tanks and a populace determined to resist invasion.

Fig. 22.23 A nun blesses the war's victims in a high-contrast subjective image from *Lucia*.

Fig. 22.24 *Lucia*: Operatic emotions of the bourgeoisie.

Fig. 22.25 *Lucia*: A more muted romantic scene, reminiscent of Antonioni.

Fig. 22.26 After Aldo has been killed, Lucia's gaze at the camera irresistibly recalls the finale of *The 400 Blows* (p. 524).

Fig. 22.27 Tomas confronts Lucia after she has disobeyed him and returned to work.

does the dry comedy when under Tomas's jealous, but sleepy, eye a teacher helps Lucia learn to read. The folkish pop tune "Guantanamera" becomes a recurring musical commentary. Such technical virtuosity enabled Alea and Solas to com-pare political processes across a variety of epochs, moods, and styles. *Memories of Underdevelopment* and *Lucia* convinced critics that cinema from the Third World could be aesthetically accomplished as well as politically engaged.

Fig. 22.28 *Days of Water* invokes and updates *Potemkin*: a hand-held camera records the people's massacre of the bourgeoisie on a flight of steps.

Gomez's *Days of Water* (1971). Insurgent peasants fire in the countryside and hit people in the city (an echo of the "impossible geography" of Montage films). In a climax which recasts *Potemkin*'s Odessa Steps massacre, stylized bourgeois figures are slain on a staircase (Fig. 22.28).

Between 1972 and 1975, however, Cuban directors retreated from experimentation. Problems with the nation's economy led to a cut in film production. Solas's *A Day in November* (1972) was never released. Acrimonious national debates about writers' loyalty made artists cautious. Instead, ICAIC intensified the emphasis on popular forms. Filmmakers began to borrow Hollywood genres—the police thriller in *The Strange Case of Rachel K* (1973), the Western in *The Man from Maisinicú* (1973). Several directors' first features broached fresh issues within accessible formats. Sergio Giral's *The Other Francisco* (1974) adapted a classic novel but interrogated the author's attitude toward slavery. In *De cierta manera* (*One Way or Another*, 1974) Sara Gomez's criticism of Cuban *machismo* sparked a national debate.

By the mid-1970s, Cuban cinema commanded respect around the world. While the Cinema Nôvo films succeeded chiefly with elite viewers, the Cubans demonstrated that Third World cinema could blend modernist conventions with narrative forms to which mass audiences had become accustomed.

Argentina: Third Cinema.   During the 1950s the Argentine documentarist Fernando Birrí had created a critical and realistic "cinema of discovery" that made him an inspirational figure among South American filmmakers (p. 488). Argentina had also pioneered a Latin American art cinema in the works of Leopoldo Torre Nilsson (p. 488). During the early 1960s, the country had its own mild New Wave, or *Nueva Ola*, consisting of filmmakers who presented the young Buenos Aires middle class much in the manner of Chabrol or Malle. And in the late 1960s, Argentina was the scene of one of the most influential movements within militant filmmaking.

After the fall of the nationalist President Juan Perón, a series of regimes tried to eliminate his support among the people. A 1966 military coup shut down the Argentine legislature, disbanded political parties, and suppressed the labor movement. The regime tried to impose a distribution quota on U.S. films, but gave in to pressure from the MPEAA. Most commercial filmmakers turned out sanctioned works, based on folklore or official versions of Argentine history.

At the same time, the left, the middle class, student groups, and Perónists worked to unseat the military government. A parallel political cinema was exemplified in Jorge Cedrón's *Operación masacre* ("Operation Massacre," 1969), which revealed the government's attempt to murder key Perónists. The most influential political films came from the Cine Liberación group. Founded by the left-wing Perónists Fernando Solanas and Octavio Getino,

Fig. 22.29

Fig. 22.30

Figs. 22.29 and 22.30 Through the similarity of the figures' outstretched arms, the other-worldliness of art is confronted by the reality of political violence (*Hour of the Furnaces*).

Cine Liberación played a central role in defining political cinema in Latin America.

Solanas and Getino's major film was *La Hora de los hornos* (*The Hour of the Furnaces*, 1968). This four-hour work blended Direct Cinema, staged scenes, and a dense sound track to create a film tract of a complexity akin to the work of Vertov and Chris Marker. The film's three parts were designed to provoke argument and action. "Neocolonialism and Violence," dedicated to Che Guevara, shows Argentina exploited by Europe, the United States, and ruling elites. Part II, "An Act for Liberation," dissects the failures of Perónism. The third part, "Violence and Liberation," centers on interviews with activists discussing prospects for change.

Hour of the Furnaces bombards the spectator with a collage of images and sounds. As in Cuban films and Soviet Montage cinema, the disjunctive techniques of modernism are turned to agitational ends. Opposites collide: founders of the country and contemporary middle-class golfers, a massacre of mountain people and a contemporary disco. The "myth of a universal culture" is mocked by cutting from an academic painting to a man dragged off by police (Figs. 22.29, 22.30). The sound track intensifies the disjunctions. When contemporary pop music is heard while the camera tracks through museums, the film suggests the co-opting of intellectuals by the mass media.

Hour of the Furnaces goes beyond purely internal complexity and reaches directly out to its audience. The film was circulated among workers' groups and shown in secret meetings. Although Solanas and Getino took a Perónist line, they wanted the film to be interrupted by discussions among the audience. At one point the film halts: "Now it is up to you to draw conclusions, to continue the film. You have the floor."

Out of the experience of making and screening *Hour of the Furnaces* came several Cine Liberación manifestos defining a "Third Cinema." Solanas and Getino equated First Cinema with the Hollywood movie, which overwhelmed its viewer with spectacle and made each viewer a consumer of bourgeois ideology. Second Cinema was auteur-centered art cinema. In fostering individual expression, this was a step forward, particularly in Cinema Nôvo works; but its time was now past. Third Cinema used film as a weapon for liberation, making every participant a "film-guerrilla." The director was part of a collective, not only a mass movement but a production cadre working on behalf of the oppressed.

In line with the formal innovations of *Hour of the Furnaces*, Solanas and Getino called for Third Cinema to break with individual protagonists and orthodox narrative. At the same time, the conditions of reception would have to be transformed. Solanas and Getino urged filmmakers to create secret distribution circuits among insurgent groups. When the screening is clandestine, the viewer takes a risk simply in coming, and this renders the viewer a "participant-comrade," ready to think and debate. Solanas and Getino had called *Hour of the Furnaces* a "film-act"; now they urged filmmakers to treat a movie as a concrete tactic within a larger struggle.

The Cine Liberación articles remained vague in ideology. They spoke the language of populist rebellion rather than of Cuban-style revolution. Still, "Towards a Third Cinema" became as important as Espinosa's "Imperfect Cinema" essay in formulating the aspirations of radical film in the underdeveloped countries.

During the early 1970s, Argentina was coming apart. Government repression was met by insurrections and terrorism. Solanas and Getino contributed by filming two documentary interviews with the exiled Perón. They also founded a magazine, *Cine y liberación*. Getino directed *El Familiar* (1972), an allegorical fiction feature on the destiny of Latin America. Other filmmakers continued to make Perónist films, and ultra-left groups such as Cine de Base emerged.

By 1973, the military authorities could not contain the upheaval or cure the nation's economic problems. Perón returned to serve as president. The Cine Liberación leaders began working for his regime. Solanas became head of an independent filmmaking association, while Getino took charge of the national censorship board. Getino readmitted all banned films, liberalized censorship, and offered financing to exhibitors and film unions. A new film law was drafted which would increase government support to the industry. Cine de Base and the FAS group remained underground, making films which denounced Perónism as fascism.

Perón soon confirmed such suspicions by cracking down on the left. He died in 1974, and his wife Isabel succeeded him. She could not check the country's inflation and the urban guerrilla war which blazed between left and right. In the chaos, all reform of the cinema was forgotten. The Cine Liberación directors fled, Getino to Peru, Solanas to Paris. Both continued to work in exile.

In 1976, the military seized power and launched a brutal assault on the opposition. Over the years as many as 20,000 people disappeared, most killed by death squads. Film production virtually halted. The Sono Film studio closed in 1977, and Torre Nilsson died in exile a year later. Not until the mid-1980s would Argentine cinema reemerge from the shadows of the generals.

New Chilean Cinema. Political cinema in Chile followed a pattern similar to that enacted in Brazil and Argentina. In the 1960s an energetic critical cinema emerged in a hostile political environment. It became aligned with a liberal government before being cast out by a coup and a repressive military regime in the 1970s.

Chilean film culture grew during the 1960s, when the University of Chile organized a national film archive and a department of experimental cinema. Joris Ivens visited to teach. A film festival was founded at Viña del Mar in 1962, and in 1967 this event hosted the first continental meeting of Latin American filmmakers. Artists in other media, spearheaded by the Communist poet Pablo Neruda, began to agitate for social change.

Chilean film production was minuscule until 1967, when the moderate government of Eduardo Frei began to offer some support to the industry. Young directors quickly came forward. Raul Ruiz's *Tres tristes tigres* (*Three Sad Tigers*, 1968) presents a casually bizarre view of middle-class intellectuals drifting through bars, indifferent to politics. Aldo Francia's *Valparaiso mi amor* ("Valparaiso My Love," 1969) traces the history of a teenage girl whom poverty drives to prostitution. In *Bloodstained Nitrate* (1969) Helvio Soto shows how an 1879 Andean war gave British firms access to nitrate deposits. Miguel Littín's *El Chacal de Nahueltoro* (*The Jackal of Nahueltoro*, 1969) investigates a murderer's life, disclosing the causes of his crime in his social milieu.

Fig. 22.31 A mysterious cutaway to a barroom full of bottles in Ruiz's *Tres tristes tigres.*

The Chileans' political situation was similar to that faced by the Argentine Cine Liberación, but their films are closer to Cuban work in their mixture of popular fiction and art-cinema techniques. *Bloodstained Nitrate* draws on the Hollywood Western, while the flashbacks of *The Jackal of Nahueltoro* recall European art cinema. *Valparaiso mi amor* relies on a straightforward realism, but *Tres tristes tigres* uses Surrealist images to undercut the conventions of kitsch melodrama (Fig. 22.31).

Most of these directors aligned themselves with the Marxist Salvador Allende and his Popular Unity party. As with *Hour of the Furnaces*, political groups projected *The Jackal of Nahueltoro* in political meetings and union halls (Fig. 22.32). In 1970, Allende won a narrow victory at the polls. He moved toward socializing the economy, nationalizing copper and other key industries. Immediately the United States led an effort to undermine his government, creating an "invisible blockade" against Chile. At the same time, Allende faced criticism from the radical wing of his party, who wanted reforms to move faster.

Fig. 22.32 The execution scene of *The Jackal of Nahueltoro*: Based on a real-life case, the film was used in campaigns against the president, who refused to pardon the killer.

After Allende's triumph, Miguel Littín, among the most militant of the young filmmakers, composed a manifesto recalling Espinosa's imperfect cinema and the Solanas-Getino idea of Third Cinema. "The people are the generators of action and finally the true creators; the filmmaker is their instrument of communication."[11] Littín became head of Chile Films, a government agency which produced several documentary films. He hoped to create an exhibition network which would add discussions to screenings in the manner urged by Cine Liberación.

Littín stayed with Chile Films less than a year. At the same time, the film industry faced growing economic problems. As part of the U.S. boycott of Allende, the MPEAA companies ceased shipping prints and demanded advance payment for rentals. Soon Chilean audiences, among the most movie-addicted on the continent, had only a choice among European and Soviet-bloc titles.

Under Allende the New Cinema directors offered more radical films. Soto's *Voto + Fusil* (*The Vote and the Gun*, 1970) presents three generations of the Chilean left reuniting at dinner and rethinking their positions. Francia's

Fig. 22.33 In *The Penal Colony*, an interview presumably free of police surveillance . . .

Fig. 22.34 . . . suddenly reveals an observing officer in the next shot.

It's No Longer Enough to Pray (1971) urges Latin American Catholics to engage in political activism. Ruiz made several films, many taking a wry attitude to official politics; his *The Penal Colony* (1971) conveys the invasiveness of a police state (Figs. 22.33, 22.34).

Despite a barrage of economic difficulties, CIA attempts to subvert the government, and growing violence between right and left, Allende was reelected in March 1973. But soon, in the most violent coup in twentieth-century Latin America, the military seized power. Thousands of Chileans perished. Allende died when the army bombarded the presidential palace.

General Augusto Pinochet Ugarte took command and proclaimed a state of siege. He dissolved the constitution, disbanded the congress, and outlawed political parties. The military destroyed film schools and production centers, burning film and smashing equipment. Workers at Chile Films were fired or arrested.

Most of the young Chilean filmmakers fled. Soto went to Spain. In Cuba Patricio Guzman completed *The Battle of Chile* (1973–1979), a documentary account of the Allende years. In Paris Littín finished *The Promised Land* (1973), a symbolic account of an earlier coup. Ruiz settled in Paris as well, rapidly turning out dry, quirky films such as *Dialogue of Exiles* (1974). Littín went on to work in Cuba and Mexico, producing historical epics celebrating the resistance of Latin American peoples. In all, Chilean filmmakers produced dozens of works outside their native land. But their exile proved a long one. Pinochet's reign lasted sixteen years.

Throughout South America, the revolutionary ferment of the 1960s waned during the next decade. In 1960, most governments had been moderately democratic, but by 1973, dictators ruled virtually every country. No nation followed Cuba's lead in creating a revolution. Indeed, Cuba was showing signs of the authoritarian rule characteristic of Soviet satellites.

As repressive regimes came to power, filmmakers emigrated to Europe, Mexico, and Cuba. Rocha shot *Der Leone Has Sept Cabecas* (*The Lion Has Seven Heads*, 1970) in the People's Republic of the Congo; he described the film as "a communiqué on the cinema of the 1960s," a dialogue with Eisenstein, Brecht, and Godard.[12] Guerra returned to his native Mozambique, assisting its Marxist government by building a film institute and shooting documentaries.

Other exiles worked in closer proximity to their targets, serving as guerrilla provocateurs in Solanas and Getino's sense. The most famous example was the Bolivian Jorge Sanjinés. In the early 1960s, Sanjinés created a film school and ciné-club while making some short agitational films. With friends he made several features, the outstanding one being *Blood of the Condor* (1969). The film attacked the American Peace Corps and its policies forcing birth control onto Indian communities. The premiere triggered a street demonstration, and the film played a large role in banning the Peace Corps from Bolivia.

A 1971 fascist coup forced Sanjinés into exile, during which he completed *The Courage of the People* (1971). Mixing documentary photographs, survivors' testimony, and staged sequences, the film exposes the 1967 massacre of striking miners by the Bolivian government. Now barred from returning to Bolivia, Sanjinés and his Ukamau Group set *The Principal Enemy* (1971) in Peru. The film depicts the problems of guerrilla warfare in the era of Che Guevara's mobilization of regional peasants. *Get Out of Here!* (1976) treats missionaries among Ecuador's tribal communities as carriers of U.S. imperialism.

While *Blood of the Condor* resembles other militant filmmaking of its period, Sanjinés's exile films created a more novel aesthetic. Encouraging nonactors to reenact their own experiences, he treated films as collective efforts—an idea in line with Third Cinema and imperfect-cinema manifestos. Refusing to structure the plot around individuals, the Ukamau Group created a mass hero reminiscent of 1920s Soviet filmmaking. But they employed long shots and long takes rather than montage, as Sanjinés explained:

Fig. 22.35 The long take of the people's tribunal in *The Principal Enemy*.

> Jumping right away to close-ups of the assassin—in *The Principal Enemy*—in the crowded plaza where the popular tribunal was held didn't serve our purposes, because the surprise that is always produced by directly cutting to a close-up was opposed to what we were trying to develop in the sequence shots, which was to engage the participation of the viewer by means of the internal power of the people's collective participation.[13]

The *plan-séquence* was utilized in the postwar European cinema to capture the moment-by-moment flow of psychological states (p. 426), but here it signifies an oppressed group's solidarity (Fig. 22.35). Guided by political commitment and formal exploration, the guerrilla cinema of exile practiced by Sanjinés and the Ukamau Group continued the traditions of Latin American revolutionary cinema into the 1970s.

BLACK AFRICAN CINEMA

During the mid-1970s, militant filmmaking waned in Latin America, but in Africa it began to come into its own. Black African colonies won independence in the early 1960s. A decade later most of the major countries had produced at least one feature-length film. In a region which suffered two protracted wars, forty coups and revolts, and several devastating droughts and famines, it is remarkable that even this many films appeared.

Still, most countries lacked the finances, equipment, and infrastructure to found a film industry. Regional film distribution was controlled by European and American interests, which dumped cheap films on the market. Pictures from Egypt, India, and Hong Kong dominated the theaters. Moreover, individual countries' audiences were usually too small to support a national industry of any consequence.

African filmmakers therefore began to seek cooperation. A biennial festival was established in Carthage, Tunisia, in 1966, and another (FES-PACO) in Burkina Faso. A continental association, the Fédération Pan-Africaine des Cinéastes (FEPACI) was established in 1970 to facilitate exchange of information and to help lobby governments to support production.

Senegal, Ivory Coast, and other French-speaking nations were the earliest and strongest sources of black African cinema. These were among the

Fig. 22.36 Assimilated Africans dance, apparently oblivious to their compatriots' living conditions, in *À nous deux, France*.

Fig. 22.37 In *Xala*, the briefcase-carrying businessman pleads with a *marabout*, or "magic healer," to restore his potency.

Fig. 22.38 *Sambizanga*: The protagonist's husband is seized by the police. Like many Third World filmmakers, Maldoror uses long lenses and a hand-held camera in order to suggest a documentary record.

most industrially developed nations, and film production benefited from contributions from the French Ministry of Cooperation. From 1963 to 1980, the ministry offered both financing and production facilities, eventually assisting more than a hundred films. The drawback was that the films circulated only to cultural centers, not commercial theaters, so most were not seen by the broad population.

The first generation of indigenous African filmmakers included Paulin Vieyra and the novelist Ousmane Sembene (both from Senegal), Med Hondo (Mauritania), Desiré Ecaré (Ivory Coast), and Oumarou Ganda (Niger). Their contemporary Sarah Maldoror (from Guadeloupe) worked in various African countries. Many were left-wing artists: Sembene was a Communist who learned filmmaking in Moscow; Maldoror, also trained in Moscow, was the wife of an Angolan revolutionary leader.

Several directors began with short films portraying exile life. Vieyra's *Afrique sur Seine* ("Africa on the Seine," 1955), made while he was at the French film school IDHEC, displays the influence of Italian Neorealism in its portrayal of the daily life of African students in Paris. Sembene's *La Noire de . . .* (*Black Girl*, 1966) shows the misery of a woman brought to France to serve as a kitchen maid. Desiré Ecaré's *Concerto pour un exil* ("Concerto for an Exile," 1967) and *À nous deux, France* ("Let's Go, France!" 1970) are satirical studies of assimilated Africans who mimic French ways (Fig. 22.36).

Directors also turned to neocolonialism as a subject. Sembene's *Borom Sarret* (1963), often considered the first indigenous black African film, is a poignant study of a day in the life of a cart driver in Dakar. In quasi-documentary fashion, using voice-over inner monologue, Sembene shows that independence has not lessened Africa's poverty and suffering. *Mandabi* (*The Money Order*, 1968) is a rough comedy about cultural transition, while *Xala* ("The Curse of Impotence," 1974) turns a Buñuelian ferocity on neocolonialist elites who exploit the masses whom they are supposed to represent (Fig. 22.37).

Critiques of colonial regimes also formed the basis of African films. Sembene's *Emitai* ("God of Thunder," 1972) portrays the clash of French soldiers with a native tribe in World War II. The anticolonial insurrection in Angola was dramatized in Sarah Maldoror's *Sambizanga* (1972), which depicts the imprisonment of a revolutionary leader and the struggle of his wife to free him (Fig. 22.38). Once Angola's Marxist faction won sovereignty in 1975, it produced films recalling the war and summoning people to support the new regime. Other African nations which adopted socialist governments, such as Mozambique and Ethiopia, made films denouncing their colonialist past.

In the 1970s African filmmakers also sought to return to the sources of their cultures. As elsewhere in the Third World, indigenous cultures had long been concealed or distorted by western images. Sebastien Kamba's *La Rançon d'une alliance* ("The Price of a Union," Congo, 1973) traces the effects of clan rivalry before the arrival of the Europeans. Haile Gerima's *Harvest: 3000 Years* (Ethiopia, 1975) portrays peasants' attempts to overturn a feudal land system.

The most famous film of the "return to the sources" tendency is Sembene's *Ceddo* ("Outsider," 1977). The film shows the clash among Islam,

Fig. 22.39 In *Ceddo*, a contemporary Catholic ceremony interrupts the seventeenth-century story and reveals the bishop's crosier to be a *sampa*, or tribal scepter.

Christianity, and indigenous tribal traditions. Stately in its unfolding of the kidnapping of a princess, the film occasionally cuts ahead to Senegal in the future (Fig. 22.39).

Ceddo is characteristic of African cinema in another way. Believing that oral storytelling is an important part of African culture, many directors have sought to transpose its subjects, plots, and techniques into cinematic terms. Sembene, for example, self-consciously adopts the role of a *griot*, the traditional storyteller.

> Often the worker and the peasant don't have the time to pause on the details of their lives: they live them and do not have the time to tie them down. The filmmaker, though, can link one detail to another to put a story together. There is no longer a traditional story-teller in our days, and I think the filmmaker can replace him.[14]

Fig. 22.40 *La Noire de . . .*: Colonial clichés challenged by the black servant's inner monologue.

Sembene's use of types (the pauper, the trickster) and certain subjects (magic, abrupt shifts of fortune) harks back to folktale conventions. In *Ceddo*, the legendary quality of the plot and the presence of a commenting *griot* further signal that the film is to be taken as a contemporary revision of oral tradition.

Related to Sembene's *griot* conception is the freedom of commentary in his sound track. His own voice dominates *Borom Sarret*, speaking to the audience directly of the character's hopes and disillusionment. *La Noire de . . .* has a remarkable scene in which the illiterate servant has received a letter from her mother. Her French employers, concerned about propriety, begin to write a responding letter for her. We see the husband write a banal letter and hear her protesting inner monologue (Fig. 22.40). Playing between French and the Wolof language, Sembene's films accentuate the clash of modernity and tradition.

Fig. 22.41 The sexual activities of the heroine of *Touki-Bouki* are juxtaposed to the throbbing movements of the ocean.

Sembene's style remained closer to mainstream realism than did that of other African filmmakers. Djibril Diop Mambéty's *Touki-Bouki* (Senegal, 1973), the most avant-garde film made upon the continent during the period, alludes to African folktales while drawing upon techniques of European modernist cinema (Fig. 22.41). Similarly experimental was Med Hondo, who made most of his films while in exile in Paris. He began in a surreal vein

Fig. 22.42 While gunfire and shrieks are heard, the protagonist of *Soleil O* tears banknotes off his body and burns them.

Fig. 22.43 In *Les Bicots-négres, vos voisins*, a narrator links the history of cinema to that of the colonization of Africa.

close to Rocha with *Soleil O* ("O Sun," 1970), which portrays an unemployed African possessed by a vision of a guerrilla revolution sweeping through Asia, Africa, and Latin America. *Les Bicots-négres, vos voisins* ("The Dirty Negroes, Your Neighbors," 1973) reveals the conditions of African workers in France. Both films use collage techniques parallel to those of political modernist films elsewhere, mixing documentary, realistic fiction, animation, photomontages, and direct address (Figs. 22.42, 22.43).

Hondo was one of the strongest advocates of an African version of Third Cinema. He demanded that film reflect popular political struggles and that it convey cultural differences. "The physical time of an Arab or African film is different from a Western film. . . . It's a matter of another mode of breathing, of another manner of telling a story. We Africans live with time, while the Westerners are always running along behind it."[15] Aware of European and American film traditions but determined to represent central aspects of their own cultures, Hondo and his contemporaries sustained a distinctively African approach to political filmmaking throughout the 1970s.

CHINA: CINEMA AND THE GREAT PROLETARIAN CULTURAL REVOLUTION

The "revolutionary cinema" of the People's Republic of China (PRC) differed sharply from that found elsewhere in the Third World. As in Cuba, a Communist government controlled filmmaking. But whereas ICAIC encouraged experimentation, China opted for a narrow, dogmatic conception of revolutionary cinema.

After the 1949 revolution, PRC filmmaking had, like postwar Soviet filmmaking, alternated between periods of strict government supervision and phases of liberalization (Chapter 18). During the early 1960s, filmmakers had considerable latitude, but in 1966, a bizarre shift in policy brought a period of repression without parallel in the postwar period.

Although Mao Zedong remained the venerated leader of the revolution and chairman of the Communist party, he had become marginal to policymaking. The chairman of the PRC, Liu Shaoqui, and the party's secretary-general, Deng Xiaoping, held the real power. They undertook reforms, allowing some private enterprise for farmers, giving bonuses to productive workers, and requiring examinations for university admission. Mao, who favored complete equality and no hint of capitalist enterprise, sought to regain control. He decided to exploit the "cult of Mao" in order to destroy the party hierarchy and rebuild it with loyal followers.

In 1966, Mao declared the "Great Proletarian Cultural Revolution," a sweeping program that was to dominate Chinese society for the next decade. With the help of the People's Liberation Army (PLA), he purged many of his enemies and seized the national newspaper. Soon he controlled Beijing, but strong resistance sprang up elsewhere. Mao then called upon high-school and university students to form a youth army, the Red Guard. Their task was to attack and humiliate intellectuals, artists, bureaucrats, and other proponents of "western" thinking.

The Red Guard's assaults on teachers soon closed schools and universities. Students rampaged through museums and burned libraries. Red Guards roamed the country, identifying "enemies" and forcing them to submit to "self-criticism" before a large crowd. Some victims were tortured or executed, while others committed suicide or died in prison.

Mao's thought dominated all debates. Bookstores now carried virtually nothing but his writings. A sampling was published as *Quotations from Chairman Mao*, the "little red book" that was printed in over a billion copies and flourished zealously by Red Guards as they carried out his policies.

Mao considered untutored peasants to be the ideal revolutionary citizens. Consequently, hundreds of thousands of city dwellers were sent to the farms to perform manual labor and live in primitive dormitories. After this process of "reeducation," citizens were supposed to return home, although many died in the countryside.

By the late 1960s, the party consisted almost entirely of Maoists. Liu had been arrested and later died in prison; Deng was exiled to the countryside. In gaining control, however, Mao had created chaos. Some regions were torn by armed conflict. To settle matters, Mao turned the PLA against the Red Guards, many of whom took their turn in long "rehabilitation" stays in the countryside.

During the Cultural Revolution, the arts were strictly controlled. Mao's wife, Jiang Qing, was part of a group of high officials, later termed the "Gang of Four," who took charge of cultural affairs. A minor film actress during the 1930s, Jiang Qing supervised the creation of a Maoist cinema. Her first step was to close down the film industry. For the only time in cinema history, a government simply withdrew feature films from audiences. All foreign films and pre-1966 Chinese films were banned, and no new Chinese features were released between 1966 and 1969. The public still went to the movies, but they saw only newsreels, mostly records of Mao reviewing troops or riding in parades.

Jiang Qing and her associates sought an ideologically acceptable approach to fiction filmmaking. They settled upon a genre called the "revolutionary model performance" film. Such films were versions of stage works that blended modernized Peking opera (one of Mao's favorite art forms), somewhat traditional ballet, and revolutionary military subjects. These were the only types of films made from 1970 to 1972, and only seven of them were released. The revolutionary model performance films were screened incessantly. Deprived of all other entertainment, audiences saw them over and over; to avoid attending rendered one's commitment to Maoism suspect.

The most famous of these performance films is *The Red Detachment of Women* (1971, Pan Wenzhan and Fu Jie). It is a record of a 1964 ballet, which was in turn an adaptation of Xie Jin's 1961 film (p. 480). The ballet, with a score by a collective of composers, told of an actual detachment of female soldiers in the Chinese Civil War of the 1930s. The lack of dialogue and the simple action made the story easy for peasant audiences to follow. The characters of *The Red Detachment of Women* represent types familiar from Soviet and Chinese Communist fiction: the sadistic landlord, the good Maoist leader, the vengeful heroine who must learn Communist discipline.

Fig. 22.44 A mixture of traditional ballet and Maoist militarism as the soldiers drill in *The Red Detachment of Women.*

Fig. 22.45 The heroine gestures triumphantly just before shooting the villainous landlord who had beaten her.

Eliminating psychological development, the plot concentrates on the detachment's training for the climactic battle. The dancers wear traditional ballet slippers and go up on point, yet they also flourish rifles and strike aggressive poses (Figs. 22.44, 22.45). Chinese filmmakers never embraced the Direct Cinema approach, preferring to use long-tried studio methods reminiscent of 1930s Hollywood. In *Red Detachment*, the performance is shot as if on a theater stage, using artificial trees and backdrops.

In 1973, other types of features began to be made. All emphasized political subjects, with stock characters enacting Maoist doctrine. *Breaking with Old Ideas* (Li Wenhua, 1975), a drama about an agricultural college, illustrates how schematically Mao's ideas were treated. He had written that young people were his "revolutionary successors," but he believed that they should not be well educated, since education gave students advantages over other people and made them elitist. He believed that universities should not use strict admission requirements, since these kept peasants and workers out.

In *Breaking with Old Ideas*, an enthusiastic Maoist, Principal Lung, takes charge of a college from which the administrators have barred untutored peasants and workers. Lung questions the young people, admitting one enthusiastic boy solely because he has worked as a blacksmith. Other peasants recommend a woman who had been abused by a landlord before the revolution and has since become an expert rice farmer. When Lung asks if she is literate, she writes, "Chairman Mao is our liberator." Triumphant music wells up, and she is immediately accepted. Lung goes on to impose his policies on the conservative administrators.

The Cultural Revolution lasted well into the 1970s. As Mao grew senile, the Gang of Four ruthlessly pursued his policies. After Mao's death in September 1976, Deng Xiaoping, who had been rehabilitated in 1973, took control. The Gang was arrested in October 1976 and convicted two years later.

The Cultural Revolution devastated China. As many as a million people may have died in its turmoil. A generation missed its chance to be educated, and industrial development halted. In the cinema as well, the Cultural Revolution created what Chinese call "the lost ten years." Not until the early 1980s did a recovery become visible.

Although politically activist films continued to be made after the mid-1970s, militant Third Worldism faded. In Latin America, insurgent groups were defeated. The masses were not mobilized, and military regimes proved ready to terrorize the population. Right-wing juntas drove some Cinema Nôvo directors, Sanjinés, and the Chilean and Argentine filmmakers into exile. In Africa, most countries lapsed into neocolonial states ruled by authoritarian parties and charismatic dictators. Third Worldism often helped establish a new capitalist class, as the films of Sembene and his African colleagues often point out.

Mao's Cultural Revolution was discredited with the downfall of the Gang of Four, and the revelation of Khmer Rouge atrocities eliminated Cambodia as a viable model of Asian socialism. The most visible Third World revolutionary activity became international terrorism, often pursued by Palestinian groups and sponsored by Middle Eastern nations.

The 1973 rise in oil prices by the petroleum-producing Arab states dealt most Third World economies a staggering blow. The underdeveloped countries began to accumulate the debts that would haunt them into the next century. After a decade of revolutionary rhetoric, most Third World countries remained impoverished agricultural nations ruled by business leaders and military figures cooperating with the western powers or the Soviet bloc.

Revolutionary filmmaking, however, had not been confined to the Third World. It had its counterpart in the developed countries as well. As we have already seen, many European and Asian New Waves, such as the Young German Film and the Japanese New Wave, were critical or left-wing in their orientation. Revolutionary agendas arose everywhere during the 1960s, and the cinema of the First and Second Worlds played a part in formulating them.

◆ NOTES AND QUERIES

DEFINING THIRD WORLD REVOLUTIONARY CINEMA

Three essays set the agenda for Third World political filmmaking: Rocha's "Aesthetics of Hunger" (1965), Espinosa's "For an Imperfect Cinema" (1969), and Solanas and Getino's "Third Cinema" manifesto (1969). The authors all subsequently reconsidered their ideas. Espinosa explained that he conceived "imperfection" not as clumsiness but as an acknowledgment of the filmmaker's political position.[16] Solanas explained that not all big productions were necessarily First Cinema, just as not all auteur-based films were necessarily Second Cinema. Third Cinema did, however, express anti-colonialism and social change.[17] Writing later in the 1970s, Getino noted ruefully that "the force and cohesion of the popular movements in these countries—and in Argentina—were not as strong as we had imagined."[18]

Most expansively, in a 1971 essay, "The Aesthetics of the Dream," Rocha defined three types of revolutionary art: that useful for immediate political action (e.g., *Hour of the Furnaces*), that which opens up political discussion (e.g., most of Cinema Nôvo), and a revolutionary art based on the people's dreams, as reflected in magic and myth.[19] This art of the dream had been ignored by the traditional left, Rocha claimed, although he glimpsed it in the 1968 youth revolutions. (See Chapter 23.)

As the force of Third World cinema was waning, film scholars began to study the phenomenon extensively. Some took the position that there was a tricontinental Third Cinema, characterized by recurrent political themes and formal conventions. The most extensive argument for this view is set forth in Teshome Gabriel, *Third Cinema in the Third World: The Aesthetics of Liberation* (Ann Arbor, Michigan: UMI Research Press, 1982). A condensed statement of his position is "Towards a Critical Theory of Third World Films," in Jim Pines and Paul Willemen, eds., *Questions of Third Cinema* (London: British Film Institute, 1989), pp. 30–52. The view is criticized by Julianne

Burton in "Marginal Cinemas and Mainstream Critical Theory," *Screen* **26,** 3–4 (May–August 1985): 2–21. Gabriel replies in "Colonialism and 'Law and Order' Criticism," *Screen* **27,** 3–4 (May–August 1986): 140–147.

◆ REFERENCES

1. Quoted in Stephen Teo, "The *Dao* of King Hu," in *A Study of Hong Kong Cinema in the Seventies* (Hong Kong: Urban Council, 1984), p. 34.
2. Quoted in Randal Johnson and Robert Stam, eds., *Brazilian Cinema* (Austin: University of Texas Press, 1982), p. 70.
3. Ibid.
4. Quoted in Sylvie Pierre, *Glauber Rocha* (Paris: Cahiers du Cinéma, 1987), p. 139.
5. Quoted in Johnson and Stam, *Brazilian Cinema*, p. 33.
6. Quoted in Aruna Vasudev, *The New Indian Cinema* (Delhi: Macmillan, 1986), p. 29.
7. *Quotations from Chairman Mao Tse-Tung* (Peking: Foreign Languages Press, 1967), p. 82.
8. Quoted in Jean Franco, "South of Your Border," in Sohnya Sayres et al., eds., *The 60s without Apology* (Minneapolis: University of Minnesota Press, 1984), p. 324.
9. Manuel Puig, "Cinema and the Novel," in John King, ed., *On Modern Latin American Fiction* (New York: Noonday, 1987), p. 283. See also Puig's novel *Betrayed by Rita Hayworth*, trans. Suzanne Jill Levine (New York: Vintage, 1981).
10. Quoted in Julianne Burton, "Revolutionary Cuban Cinema, First Part: Introduction," *Jump Cut* no. 19 (1978): 18.
11. "Film Makers and the Popular Government: Political Manifesto," in Michael Chanan, ed., *Chilean Cinema* (London: British Film Institute, 1974), p. 84.
12. Quoted in Pierre, *Glauber Rocha*, p. 180.
13. Jorge Sanjinés and the Ukamau Group, *Theory and Practice of a Cinema with the People*, trans. Richard Schaaf (Willimantic, Conn.: Curbstone, 1989), p. 43.
14. Quoted in Noureddine Ghali, "An Interview with Sembene Ousmane," in John D. H. Downing, ed., *Film and Politics in the Third World* (New York: Autonomedia, 1987), p. 46.
15. Abid Med Hondo, "The Cinema of Exile," in ibid., p. 71.
16. Julio Garcia Espinosa, "Meditations on Imperfect Cinema . . . Fifteen Years Later," *Screen* **26,** 3–4 (May–August 1985): 94.
17. Quoted in "L'Influence du 'Troisième Cinéma' dans le monde," *Revue tiers monde* **20,** no. 79 (July–September 1979): 622.
18. Octavio Getino, "Some Notes on the Concept of a 'Third Cinema,' " in Tim Barnard, ed., *Argentine Cinema* (Toronto: Nightwood, 1986), p. 107.
19. Quoted in Pierre, *Glauber Rocha*, pp. 129–130.

23

CRITICAL POLITICAL CINEMA OF THE 1960s AND 1970s

Third World revolutionary cinema foreshadowed trends which emerged in the developed countries. Here too people were pushing for social change—through protest, through resistance to authority, and sometimes through violent confrontation. Between the mid-1960s and the mid-1970s filmmaking and film viewing became political acts to a degree not seen since World War II.

In the Soviet bloc countries, many citizens strained to liberalize Communist societies, and the most politically provocative works of eastern European and Soviet cinema often asserted the individuality of the artist's imagination. In western Europe and North America, unorthodox left-wing groups criticized government policies, educational institutions, and economic conditions. Radical politics entered daily life. As was often said, the "personal" had become "political."

Many western radicals were suspicious of exactly that democratic humanism which Soviet bloc reformists craved. Capitalist society, many believed, maintained an "illusory democracy" and "repressive tolerance." Radicals often took Third World leaders like Mao, Che Guevara, and Castro as models of popular revolution. By the mid-1970s, however, militancy gave way to a "micropolitics" that focused pragmatically on particular issues. What one historian has called "the political culture of dissent" began to permeate everyday life in the western countries.[1]

EASTERN EUROPE AND THE USSR

THE PRAGUE SPRING AND ITS AFTERMATH

The major upheaval in the Soviet bloc took place in Czechoslovakia. After internal struggles, in January 1968 reformer Alexander Dubcek took control of the Czech Communist Party. Dubcek encouraged debates, even raising the possibility of a multiparty system. By late June, reform was in the air. Over sixty scientists, artists, and scholars signed the "Two Thousand Words" manifesto, calling for workers' self-management, criticism of party authority, and rejection of old-line communism.

The "Prague Spring" had enormous influence on culture. "In the last few weeks," the film director Jan Nemeć said, "I have been possessed by such a feeling of joy and liberation—maybe madness—nothing holds me any more."[2] The banned films of 1967 were made available, and New Wave directors felt at liberty to experiment.

But the euphoria was short-lived. On August 20, 1968, the USSR ordered half a million Warsaw Pact troops to invade Czechoslovakia. Government officials were flown to Moscow in handcuffs. With Soviet backing, conservatives halted reforms. In April 1969, Dubcek's successor Gustav Husák oversaw "normalization"—that is, elimination of the 1968 reforms and punishment of rebellious individuals. Thousands of intellectuals and artists were forbidden to write, perform, or teach. In two years, almost 200,000 Czechs emigrated.

Officials banned any films that exuded the Prague Spring spirit of social critique. A striking instance is Jiří Menzel's *Larks on a String*. Menzel had already made an international reputation with *Closely Watched Trains* (1966) and *Capricious Summer* (1967; p. 541). *Larks on a String* is set in 1948, when, as a title ironically informs us, the working class took power in Czechoslovakia. Professionals, intellectuals, and waiters now sort scrap in a junkyard. Menzel mixes comedy, romance, and satire in his characteristically poignant way. In the opening scene, the hero and heroine portray loyal socialist workers for a staged newsreel; ostentatious posters and banners conceal the junkyard behind them (Color Plate 23.1). Completed in 1969 but denied release, *Larks on a String* was charged with "contempt for the working class" and kept Menzel out of filmmaking for five years.

"Normalization" forced changes in the Czech film industry. The film-unit production system was abolished, and control was recentralized. One studio head went to prison. The new regime demanded that political subjects be treated in an affirmative, heroic way—a return to Socialist Realism. Expectably, officials complained of the New Wave's experimentation and "pessimism." In 1973, four New Wave films, including *The Firemen's Ball* and *Report on the Party and the Guests*, were banned.

The attacks destroyed the Czech New Wave. Many of the best directors emigrated. Milos Forman had already planned to leave, but the repressions drove out Nemeć, Ivan Passer, Ján Kadár, and others. Of the New Wave filmmakers who stayed, most were denied work until the mid-1970s. For example, Vera Chytilová, director of *Something Different* (1963) and *Daisies*

(1966), managed to make the modernist fantasy *The Fruit of the Garden* (1969) before the new freeze set in. For the next six years she submitted scripts and sought projects. She was put off, denied permission to attend foreign festivals, and finally judged "elitist" and "uncommitted."[3] Not until Chytilová wrote a letter to President Husák charging officials with illegality and sexism was she permitted, in 1976, to return to directing.

For a few months, it appeared that democratic reform could alter a Communist society, but the invasion put into action what would be known as the "Brezhnev doctrine," the policy that the USSR would intervene in any satellite permitting dissent. The Prague rebellion showed that free discussion could lead to dangerous political unrest, and most Communist regimes pulled back from the liberalizing of the mid-1960s. The Prague Spring of 1968 warned eastern European artists that another thaw had ended.

A parallel debacle took place in Yugoslavia. In Zagreb intellectuals centered around the journal *Praxis* had launched critiques of Soviet-style communism since the early 1960s. These humanistic Marxists, much like the leftists of the West, declared their opposition to any social institutions "which cripple human beings, arrest their development, and impose on them patterns of simple, easily predictable, dull, stereotyped behavior."[4] In the same period, the Central Committee of the Yugoslavian party demanded economic reform. During the events of spring 1968, students occupied Belgrade University. Tito intervened to break the strike, and government repression intensified. By 1972, the rising Croatian nationalist movement provoked the government to arrest, try, and purge political dissenters.

Yugoslavian film culture of the late 1960s strongly resembled that of western Europe. Politically and erotically outspoken, Yugoslavian New Film infuriated conservative factions. Zika Pavlović's *Ambush* (1969) and Krsto Papić's *Handcuffs* (1969) saw traces of the Stalinist past continuing into the present, while Aleksandar Petrović's *The Master and Margarita* (1972) compared Stalinism with current attacks on cinema. The Zagreb Film Festival of 1970 took as its theme "Sexuality as an Effort to Achieve a New Humanism." As pressures increased after 1968, official critics labeled the New Films "black films" because of their "defeatism" and "nihilism."

Fig. 23.1 The calculated effrontery of Makavejev's *WR*: In a cult-of-Stalin fiction feature, the leader declaims that the USSR will fulfill Lenin's legacy. This is followed by . . .

Dušan Makavejev offered the most scandalous black film of the era in *WR: Mysteries of the Organism* (1971). Like his earlier works, it juggles newsreel footage, extracts from older fiction films, and a story; it is also, centrally and explicitly, about sex. A biography of Wilhelm Reich, radical sex theorist, is mixed with Direct Cinema footage of current erotic practices in the United States, newsreels of the Chinese revolution, and a grotesque story about Milena, a Yugoslavian woman who believes that "communism without free love is a wake in a graveyard." *WR* epitomizes counterculture irreverence, not least in its outrageous juxtapositions (Figs. 23.1, 23.2). In suggesting that erotic freedom would revitalize Marxism, Makavejev was attacking Communist prudery head-on.

In the early 1970s, the *Praxis* group was forcibly disbanded. The government denied distribution to *WR*, *The Master and Margarita*, and other black films. Petrović, who had won worldwide fame with *I Even Met Happy Gypsies* (1967), was forced out of his post at the Film Academy. The party

Fig. 23.2 . . . a shot of a patient receiving electroshock therapy.

Fig. 23.3 *Iconostasis*: The icon painter and his creation.

expelled Makavejev and Pavlović, and the former joined the band of wandering directors exiled from eastern Europe.

Polish cinema felt a government crackdown like that in Czechoslovakia, but it recovered more easily. In the spring of 1968, the Polish government was debating the need for economic reform. In May, an uprising at Warsaw University was suppressed. Students and dissidents were arrested, and censorship tightened. The Creative Film Unit system, which had operated since the mid-1950s, was replaced by a centralized organization. Venerated figures like Aleksander Ford were removed from their supervisory positions.

After workers' strikes in the early 1970s, however, Wladyslaw Gomulka lost control and was replaced by a more concessive leadership. The freer atmosphere reanimated Polish cinema. The production units were reorganized in 1972, with filmmakers having even more control than they previously had. A literature-based cinema won favor with audiences and solidified the production units. Andrzej Wajda returned to the center of Polish cinema with *Landscape after Battle* (1970), *Wedding* (1972), and *Land of Promise* (1975). Several new talents appeared, most notably Krsysztof Zanussi, a former physics student who brought his scientific training to bear on contemporary dramas in *The Structure of Crystals* (1969), *Illumination* (1972), and *Balance* (1974).

Other eastern European cinemas flourished in the postinvasion era. In Romania, which had only loose ties to the USSR, the late 1960s saw a liberalization. More experimentation was permitted, and in the early 1970s decentralized production units were formed. The Bulgarian government created a production-unit system in 1968, and three years later it installed new management in the industry. The nation's most celebrated film was Todor Dinov and Hristo Hristov's *Iconostasis* (1969), somewhat similar to Tarkovsky's *Andrei Rublev* in its echoes of folk and religious art (Fig. 23.3). After 1971, Bulgarian cinema underwent a renaissance, with several films winning international recognition.

It was Hungary, however, that moved to the forefront of eastern European cinema in the aftermath of the Prague Spring. The economic reforms created in the late 1960s remained intact, and decentralized planning and a mixed economy continued well into the mid-1970s. A critical political cinema continued in Hungary, and the four production units were each making about five films per year. Because directors such as Miklós Jancsó, Marta Mészáros, and István Szabó were closely tied to western trends, they are considered later in this chapter.

DISSENT AND STAGNATION IN THE USSR

While there was no "Moscow Spring," the early 1960s spawned a USSR youth movement of sorts. Students scrutinized the history of communism and debated party conduct. Liberals and religious believers formed dissident and pro-democracy organizations. Writers circulated *samizdat* ("self-published") articles and books. When Soviet tanks rolled into Czechoslovakia, protesters crowded Red Square.

Facing a declining economy and a conflict with China, Party Secretary Leonid Brezhnev sought "détente" with the West while dealing harshly with dissent on the home front. Christians and intellectuals were imprisoned or sent to mental hospitals. Physicist Andrei Sakharov's Human Rights Committee was steadily undermined by the secret police. In 1970, Aleksandr Solzhenitsyn won the Nobel Prize for literature, but after his novel *The Gulag Archipelago* (1973) revealed the horrors of Stalin's prison camps, he was deported and forbidden to return.

In cinema, production averaged about 130 features annually. But the new freeze demanded a return to Socialist Realism, now called "pedagogical realism." Energetic factory workers and World War II heroes came back to the screen. Some of the more idiosyncratic directors of the New Wave, such as Vasily Shukshin, produced well-crafted literary adaptations. In the late 1960s Andrei Konchalovsky had proposed a film on Che Guevara, but he too turned to safe sources, such as Turgenev for *A Nest of Gentlefolk* (1969).

In the regional republics, however, intense anti-Russian nationalism created a "poetic cinema." Dovzhenko's peasant lyricism offered filmmakers a distant precedent, and Paradzhanov's *Shadows of Forgotten Ancestors* (1965) reopened the way toward a personal treatment of folk material. Georgy Shengelaya's *Pirosmani* (1969) used the artist-biography genre to treat a folk painter, a subject which carried nationalistic connotations but also justified experiments in abstract shot design (Color Plate 23.2). Similar efforts were the Ukrainian Yuri Ilienko's *White Bird with a Black Mark* (1972) and the Georgian Otar Ioseliani's *Pastorale* (1977).

Two other directors associated with the poetic tendency emerged as central to the new Soviet cinema. Andrei Tarkovsky's *Andrei Rublev*, suppressed in 1966, premiered in Paris in 1969. After widespread acclaim abroad it was released in the USSR. By then Tarkovsky had completed his third feature, *Solaris* (1972), widely touted as Russia's answer to *2001*. Its ambiguous depiction of the hero's delusions is motivated by its space-travel premise, but typically Tarkovskian are passages of mystical contemplation: weeds coiling under water, an endless freeway, and the awesome final images (Fig. 23.4). Tarkovsky wanted to avoid an ideological message: "The image is not a certain *meaning*, expressed by the director, but an entire world reflected as a drop of water."[5]

The reflection of the artist's world is carried to an extreme in *The Mirror* (1975), a poetic blend of childhood memories, documentary footage, and

Fig. 23.4 In *Solaris* the hero kneels before his father as the camera retreats to a God's-eye perspective.

Fig. 23.5 *The Mirror*: The enigma of memory and fantasy.

Fig. 23.6 In *The Color of Pomegranates*, the tableau shot recalls folk art.

fantastic imagery. As Tarkovsky's voice recites his father's poetry offscreen, the camera slides across a room, moving from a cat lapping a puddle of milk to the mother at the window, tearfully watching the rain. A barn burns in a downpour; a man is almost blown over in a windy landscape; a woman levitates (Fig. 23.5). While the mainstream *Slave of Love* (Nikita Mikhalkov, 1976) was enjoying worldwide success, Soviet authorities declared *The Mirror* incomprehensible and gave it a cramped, unprofitable release.

Sergei Paradzhanov remains the most vivid example of how the personal became political in the Soviet cinema. After his Ukrainian feature *Shadows of Forgotten Ancestors* (p. 539) won international success, Paradzhanov used his new fame to protest the treatment of dissidents. In 1968, he was arrested on charges of "Ukrainian nationalism"; upon his release he was transferred to the Armenian studio, where he made *The Color of Pomegranates* in 1969. Although the script is based on the life of the Armenian poet Sayat Nova, a prologue tells us that the film will not be a conventional biography. Long-take shots frame characters, animals, and objects in rigid frontal tableaux (Fig. 23.6). Editing serves merely to link these shots or to cut jarringly into the static portraits. The film's mise-en-scene presents Sayat Nova's poetic imagery: waterlogged books opened out to dry on rooftops, carpets bleeding as they are washed, chicken feathers scattering over the dying poet (Fig. 23.7). Although Paradzhanov's style differs drastically from Tarkovsky's, both directors contemplate the changing textures of objects through time.

The Color of Pomegranates was probably the most shockingly experimental film made in the USSR since the late 1920s. It was immediately shelved, although a shorter, revised version (the one currently available) achieved limited release in 1971. Forbidden to direct, Paradzhanov fought back. He wrote a pamphlet on his problems and those of Soviet cinema. In January 1974 he was accused of homosexuality, trafficking in stolen art objects, and "incitement to suicide." He was sentenced to several years at hard labor.

In the eastern bloc, Socialist Realist policy obliged the artist to serve society—or rather its representative, the Communist party. The major eastern

Fig. 23.7 Sayat Nova's death in *The Color of Pomegranates*.

European directors such as Chytilová, Jancsó, and Makavejev believed that their visions were in harmony with some socialist position, even if that position was not currently in favor. But the poetic cinema of Tarkovsky and Paradzhanov presented the artist's vision as independent of all needs of the collective. Their highly personal films thus boldly challenged the Soviet orthodoxy and echoed trends in the West that sought political liberation in the unconstrained imagination of the individual.

POLITICAL CINEMA IN THE WEST

The year of the Prague Spring, 1968, also marked a height of social protest in the western countries. As in the Third World and eastern Europe, young people played a key role.

By 1966, more students were questioning authority and rejecting traditional American values. Some were drawn to the "New Left," a diverse movement propounding a spontaneous, libertarian Marxism opposed to orthodox Soviet varieties. University students were central to the New Left in the United States, Britain, Japan, West Germany, and even Franco's Spain. Another element in youth politics was loosely known as the "counterculture." It spanned a range of alternative lifestyles, free-flowing eroticism, immersion in rock music, experiments in communal living, and drug use in the name of expanded consciousness. Although some countercultural bohemians considered themselves apolitical, many felt allied with the New Left.

The international politics of youth focused on several issues. A central one was America's role in the Vietnam War, which steadily intensified after American planes began bombing North Vietnam in 1965. U.S. organizations such as Students for a Democratic Society actively opposed the war. This opposition began as protest but hardened into resistance, as young men refused the draft and activists blocked induction centers. In 1967–1969, resistance turned to confrontation, with activists occupying buildings and fighting police in the streets.

By then, the issue of Vietnam had become part of a broader push for social change. Throughout the "First World" the student movement launched a critique of postwar capitalist society. The university was seen as a machine of social control, cranking out well-behaved managers and technicians. Around the world students protested crowded classes, poor facilities, impersonal teaching, and "irrelevant" programs. The Berkeley free-speech movement of 1965 became a prototype of campus rebellion around the world.

The Vietnam War, the weakness of traditional left parties, the specter of neocolonialism, and the consumption-based economies of the West led students to question their culture. Many charged that western society created an artificially "normal" life in order to restrain impulses toward freedom and self-management. Wilhelm Reich, who saw fascism as springing from sexual repression, and Herbert Marcuse, who attacked the irrationality of "one-dimensional society," introduced the generation of the 1960s to a wide-ranging social critique. Yippies and other countercultural groups attacked "Amerika" in less theoretical terms. "The left," declared Jerry Rubin, "demands full employment for all—we demand full unemployment for all."[6]

Other social movements shaped the radical politics of the period. In the United States the Black-Power movement emerged around 1965. While the civil rights movement stressed legal and nonviolent reform, Black Power called for a more aggressive stance—crystallized in the public mind by the militant Black Panther party, founded in 1966. African-American students protested segregation and demanded black studies programs. During the same period the Women's Liberation movement emerged in the United States and Britain, influenced by the civil rights movement and reacting against the sexism of New Left leadership. Gay and lesbian groups, which had become more outspoken in the early 1960s, often joined the New Left and the counterculture.

By the end of 1967, all these tendencies had converged. There began two years of political upheaval unparalleled in the West since World War II. The events of 1968 led many to believe that western society was on the brink of social revolution.

In that year, when students in Madrid closed the university, over a thousand were sent to military service. In Germany, student leader Rudi Dutschke was shot in the head. In the insurrection that followed, police killed two people and arrested a thousand. In London, a peace march sparked a battle between police and 20,000 demonstrators. At Japan's Nihon University, students locked administrators in their offices and shut down classes. Italian students' seizure of universities was supported by strikes among workers and high-school students.

Similar tremors shook 200 U.S. campuses, notably Columbia, San Francisco State, Wisconsin, and Michigan. In April Martin Luther King fell victim to a white assassin, and riots broke out in scores of ghettos. Two months later, Robert Kennedy, widely perceived as America's best hope for moderate social change, was shot by a Palestinian. At the Democratic Convention in Chicago, police assaulted thousands of demonstrators protesting President Johnson's prosecution of the Vietnam War. By the end of the year, armed black students were occupying Cornell University buildings, and 400,000 American students claimed to be revolutionaries.

For many historians, events in Paris during May 1968 typify the radical energies and frustrations of the period. The Stalin worship of the 1950s had turned many students against the Communist party. Trotskyite and Maoist factions quarreled. Other groups, such as the Situationist International, injected a freewheeling critique of the consumer society. Housing shortages, unemployment, the unions' collusion in keeping wages down, and vastly overcrowded universities led to an explosive situation.

The beginning of 1968 saw French film culture embroiled in politics. (See Box.) Soon after, at Nanterre and the Sorbonne, students confronted administrators and police, demanding university reforms and social change. Mass marches were met with tear gas and truncheons. On May 10, 20,000 demonstrators built cobblestone barricades and battled charging police. Three nights later, half a million students, workers, and professionals marched through Paris, forcing the government to reopen the Sorbonne and release arrested student leaders. Students occupied the universities anew, seeking to create models of a festive, nonexploitative society. In solidarity 10 million French citizens went out on strike.

FILM ACTIVITIES DURING THE MAY EVENTS IN PARIS

French film culture was deeply involved in the upheavals of 1968. Early in February, the government tried to remove Henri Langlois as curator of the Cinémathèque Française. Resnais, Truffaut, Godard, Bresson, Chabrol, and others coordinated demonstrations of hundreds of filmmakers. On February 14, 3000 people demonstrating in support of Langlois clashed with police. Thanks to press coverage and threats from film companies, Langlois was reinstated.

As the May uprising unfolded, Godard spearheaded an effort to halt the Cannes Film Festival, leading demonstrators to occupy the theaters. Truffaut called on all to support the events in Paris: "The colleges are occupied! The factories are occupied! The stations are occupied! It's political action on an unprecedented scale! And you want this activity to stop at the doors of the festival? . . . There must be solidarity!"[7] After Godard and Truffaut halted a screening by holding the curtains closed, the Cannes festival shut down.

In Paris, students at the state film school IDHEC quickly began making newsreels and "ciné-tracts." The issues broadened as cinéastes and cinéphiles launched a critique of film under capitalism. A large number of professional film workers established the États Générales du Cinéma (EGC). The EGC aimed to create an alternative French system of production, distribution, and exhibition. Members, many of them technicians and projectionists, went on strike "to denounce and destroy the reactionary structures of a cinema which has become a commodity."[8]

The EGC called for public ownership of the film industry, workers' control of production, abolition of censorship, and elimination of the government's Centre Nationale de Cinématographie (see p. 435). The EGC prepared several projects, involving Malle, Resnais, and other influential figures, and it laid plans for autonomous production units (akin to those in eastern Europe) which could undertake noncommercial projects. Members also stressed the need for educating viewers in new ways of watching film.

Throughout May and June, the EGC held sessions. It quickly became a filmmaking cooperative, turning out documentaries over the following two years. But without government support there was no way to implement the ambitious EGC proposals. As de Gaulle regained power, most film personnel resumed work as usual. In July, many of the filmmakers involved in the EGC formed the Société des Réalisateurs ("Society of Film Directors"), which took as its goal the defense of artistic freedom. Beyond this, the May movement created some long-term political commitment, a "parallel cinema" of militant engagement, and alternative production and distribution structures.

The May events led many to think that de Gaulle's government might fall in the June elections, but he won a landslide majority. Life gradually returned to routine as the government cracked down on extreme-left groups.

In April 1970, President Nixon's widening of the Vietnam War into Cambodia touched off a new wave of protest in the United States. Nearly 400 colleges went on strike, students on many campuses burned their ROTC buildings, and sixteen states called out the National Guard. Two students were shot at Mississippi's Jackson State University and four students were killed at Ohio's Kent State University.

Already, however, the radical movement was losing unity. By 1970, the student left in most countries had failed to ally itself with working-class issues. In the United States, the Black Panthers and the New Left fell out. Many feminists, gays, and lesbians saw the New Left as oppressive and formed their own organizations. In 1969–1970, some radicals, convinced that only violence could defeat "the system," formed terrorist cadres, such as the Weathermen in the United States, the Red Brigade in Italy, and the Red Army Faction (Baader-Meinhof) in Germany. Often modeling themselves on Third World guerrillas, these groups brought bombing, kidnapping, and political assassination to western capitals in the 1970s.

Radical political movements steadily lost their authority as New Left ideas were incorporated into more mainstream Socialist and Communist parties. The excesses of the Chinese Cultural Revolution (p. 628) and the revelations of Solzhenitsyn's *Gulag Archipelago* suggested that communism led to totalitarian rule. With the middle class governing the western democracies, there was a growing awareness that social change was more likely to come through issue-oriented, grass-roots activism.

The militancy of the late 1960s was thus replaced by a "micropolitics." Activists concentrated on small-scale issues—cooperatives, communes, squatters' movements, and the ecology movement. "Working within the system" became no longer a reproach. German leftists adapted a Maoist phrase, calling for social change by "the long march through the institutions."

The growth of gay and lesbian movements shows how radical energies could change concrete situations. In 1969 gay men in New York City fought off a police raid on the Stonewall bar. Throughout the period 1969–1973, gay and lesbian activism flourished in Britain, Canada, Australia, West Germany, and France. Groups changed laws and altered attitudes toward homosexuality.

Similarly, during the 1970s Women's Liberation broadened into the feminist movement. Some participants hoped for a radical restructuring of social consciousness, but others emphasized step-by-step progress toward equality and justice. Italian feminists helped liberalize divorce laws, while throughout Europe and North America similar groups altered abortion statutes. In country after country there arose women's shelters, clinics, legal services, child-care centers, and bookstores—an alternative "woman's culture."

Most broadly, both the militant radicalism of the late 1960s and the micropolitics of the 1970s changed fundamental attitudes. The goals of universities, the social and sexual inequality within western democracies, and matters of sexual orientation became part of public awareness as never before.

Filmmakers participated vigorously in the politicization of culture. We can identify three broad tendencies from the late 1960s to the mid-1970s. *Engaged cinema* uncompromisingly aligned itself with revolutionary social change. Its purpose was explicitly propagandistic, and its favored genre was the documentary. Alongside engaged cinema there emerged a *political modernism*. This tendency, an outgrowth of the postwar art cinema and Third World trends such as Cinema Nôvo (Chapter 22), created a radical aesthetic that fused left-wing politics with innovative forms and styles. Finally, even the commercial fictional film and the mainstream art cinema bore the traces of the emerging "political culture."

ENGAGED CINEMA: COLLECTIVE PRODUCTION AND MILITANT FILMS

"In our hands film is not an anaesthetic, a sterile, smooth-talking apparatus of control. It is a weapon to counter, to talk back to and to crack the facade of the lying media of capitalism."[9] This 1971 statement represents the standpoint of many leftist filmmakers throughout the West. During the 1960s and early 1970s a cinema of political engagement, addressing itself to concrete social problems and arguing for radical social change, emerged on a scale not seen since the 1930s.

In bypassing the mainstream media, engaged cinema was forced to adopt alternative production methods. A project might be financed by a political organization, as when the Vietnam Veterans Against the War supported *Winter Soldier* (United States, 1972). Sometimes an individual filmmaker or small group might scrape up funding from donors; this occurred with Noriaki Tsuchimoto's series of films on Japan's Minamata pollution tragedy (e.g., *Minamata: The Victims and Their World*, 1972). In rare cases, independent producers arranged funding for radical work. In France Marin Karmitz's MK Productions had supported militant cinema since 1964.

Particularly characteristic of the era was the attempt to create filmmaking collectives. Militant filmmakers would band together and work in subgroups on separate projects. Rental fees helped finance more films. Britain's Cinema Action and Berwick Street Collective, Italy's Militant Cinema Collective, Denmark's Workshop, Sweden's New Film, Belgium's Fugitive Cinema, Greece's Band of 6, the Chicago-based Kartemquin, and other groups utilized the collective mode of production. Often the group's collective structure itself embodied left-wing ideals of equality and shared responsibility.

The prototype of the engaged-cinema collective was the U.S. group Newsreel. In late 1967, students aligned with Students for a Democratic Society decided to make films that would counter the mainstream media's representation of protests against the Vietnam War. This group became New York Newsreel. Early in 1968 another group formed San Francisco Newsreel.

The Newsreel logo—the flickering word synchronized with machine-gun fire—announced the militant, confrontational quality of the films. The Newsreel groups specialized in coverage of individual events, such as the occupation of a campus, a strike, or a demonstration. Beginning as a "full democracy," the Newsreel collective soon adopted a steering-committee system whereby every film was screened for the entire membership and was released only if a majority supported it.

A parallel development took place in France. During May 1968, striking film workers created *ciné-tracts*, short 16mm films made simply and circulated for a few weeks. These sometimes led to the formation of collectives. For example, the spontaneously created Medvedkine group, including Godard and Chris Marker, made *Lutte de class* ("Class Struggles," 1969) in a provincial clock factory. Godard then teamed up with Jean-Pierre Gorin to form the Dziga-Vertov Group, while Marker and another collaborator formed the larger and more robust collective SLON (later ISKRA). Other production units sprang up, each with its own ideological alignments. Such collectives formed France's "oppositional," or "parallel," cinema.

Collectives usually depended upon alternative distribution and exhibition structures. Marin Karmitz created a distribution company and ran three Parisian theaters. In the United States, New Day Films and Women Make Movies circulated feminist works, while Newsreel distributed films from Third World countries along with its own projects. Holland's alternative distribution network, The Free Circuit, led to the creation of production collectives. Other independent distribution agencies included Belgium's Cinélibre, Holland's feminist Cinemien, Sweden's Cinema of the People, and Britain's The Other Cinema.

Like Solanas and Getino of Cine Liberación, engaged filmmakers in the West sought to change the context in which their work was shown. Some avoided traditional theaters and preferred that the films be screened in clubs, union meetings, and campus or community centers. Many filmmakers also hoped that the audience would discuss the film. In some countries, these alternative venues created a parallel outlet for films. In France, the festival of Hyères, created as a showcase for young directors, became an international meeting place for engaged cinema. In 1972, the first New York Women's Film Festival was held, quickly followed by similar events in Toronto and elsewhere.

New film journals—*Jump Cut* and *Women and Film* in the United States, *Champ libre* in Canada, *Filmkritik* and *frauen und film* in West Germany, and *Cinéthique* in France, among many others—also promoted radical film-making. Older magazines, such as the U.S. *Cineaste* and the Parisian *Cahiers du cinéma*, moved to a left political position. Most of these journals became central sources of information about new films.

Even though radical leftism declined in the mid-1970s, engaged film-making remained central to the micropolitics of the era. A June 1979 alter-native-cinema conference in New York assembled over 400 political activists working in film and video in the United States. In some countries, government liberalization led to funding for militant film. The new Labor government in Britain assisted Liberation Film and Cinema Action, while in France the regional Maisons de la Culture allotted budget money for local media groups. Some parallel distribution and exhibition circuits proved successful in pro-moting films about nuclear power, day care, ethnic rights, and similar issues.

In the United States and Great Britain, feminist filmmaking pioneered the turn to issue-centered, grass-roots problems. By 1977, 250 women's films had been produced in the United States alone. Although some feminist films were made under the auspices of New York Newsreel in 1968–1969, the first major Newsreel effort came from the San Francisco wing. *The Women's Film* (1970) was followed by New York Newsreel's *Janie's Janie* (1971). Other feminist engaged films of the period were Julia Reichert and Chuck Klein's *Growing Up Female* (1970) and Kate Millett's *Three Lives* (1970). British feminist cinema was initiated by the London Women's Film Group (founded 1972), and it often sought to link women's concerns with labor issues.

As the international women's movement grew, films on rape, self-de-fense, and housekeeping were paralleled by explorations of women's history, the latter most widely seen in the U.S. films *Union Maids* (1976) and *With Babies and Banners* (1978) by the Women's Labor History Project. Women's filmmaking groups emerged in other countries as well, with France's Musi-dora, Italy's Feminist Film Collective, and Australia's Sydney Women's Film Collective being among the most active.

In general, engaged filmmakers adopted the techniques and forms es-tablished by Direct Cinema documentary in the late 1950s. The new 16mm technology of lightweight cameras, portable tape recorders, and faster film stocks could be used for agitational moviemaking, often by people without formal training. But the engaged filmmakers typically avoided purely descrip-tive observation of the type advocated by Leacock (p. 568). Direct Cinema technique supplied evidence, but the film as a whole was likely to be defiantly rhetorical in confronting its audience.

The typical engaged film draws upon both spontaneously shot reportage and more or less staged interviews. Most Newsreel films, such as *Break and Enter* (1971), combine street footage of demonstrations and interviews with participants. A film might strongly emphasize reportage, as does *Some of Your Best Friends* (1972), which records gay activists' invasion of a psychiatric conference. The filmmaker's reliance on candid footage could go beyond the single event, the normal province of Direct Cinema, and suggest broader trends, as does Pierre Perrault in his survey of political agitation in Québec, *A Country without Good Sense!; or, Wake Up, My Good Friends!!!* (1970). As in any compilation film, reportage could be enhanced by the sound track (in Newsreel films, often rock and roll) or interpolated footage, as when Newsreel's *Oil Strike* (1969) includes a company promotional film to mock management's public-relations face.

During the 1970s engaged filmmakers also explored the interview technique. Now entire films were built around talking heads. In feminist filmmaking, this led to a genre of "film portraits," often in an effort to create positive role models of women. *The Women's Film* consists of intercut interviews with five women talking about work and married life, followed by footage of them meeting in consciousness-raising groups. *Three Lives, Growing Up Female,* and *Union Maids* all render the individual's report on her experience through lengthy close-ups. This tendency recalls Shirley Clarke's *Portrait of Jason* (p. 668) and probably owes something to the central role of the consciousness-raising group in the Women's Liberation Movement. A similar strategy is at work in the lesbian or gay "confessional" film, such as *Lavender* (1972). In *Word Is Out* (1977) the accumulation of several interviews seeks to provide a panoramic view of various aspects of gay and lesbian life.

Over the 1970s, some feature-length engaged documentaries played commercial theaters. In the United States, Peter Davis's *Hearts and Minds* (1974), Cinda Firestone's *Attica* (1974), Jill Godmilow's *Antonia* (1974), *Word Is Out, Union Maids,* and *With Babies and Banners* drew broad audiences.

The engaged filmmaker who consistently achieved this scale of commercial recognition was Emile De Antonio. His first film, *Point of Order* (1963), was devoted to the hearings investigating Senator Joseph McCarthy. *Point of Order* showed that mainstream news-footage shots could sustain a politically critical film with no nudging from an anonymous voice-over narrator. *Rush to Judgment* (1966), a brief for a multiple-assassin theory of the John Kennedy murder, brought interviews into the compilation mix.

"Radical scavenging" allowed De Antonio to include footage that was too controversial for its original users. *In the Year of the Pig* (1969), an analytical history of the Vietnam War, drew upon material shot for television that was too grisly or embarrassing to broadcast. ("Out-takes," De Antonio commented at the time, "are the confessions of the system."[10]) *In the Year of the Pig* makes its case through a variety of techniques. In the hallucinatory opening, brief, almost subliminal images of battle and peasants' suffering interrupt a black screen while the drone of airplanes and helicopters rises chillingly. The rest of the film puts the argument in more analytical terms, juxtaposing expert and eyewitness testimony with news footage of speeches, ceremonies, battles, and Vietnamese life. De Antonio's editing uses one

Fig. 23.8 On the sound track, Lyndon Johnson reviews his trip to Saigon: "We never heard a hostile voice, and we never shook a hostile hand"; on the image track, he presides over the crowd (*In the Year of the Pig*).

Fig. 23.9 Filming into a mirror, Lampson, Wexler, and De Antonio interview Weather Underground fugitives who went into hiding after their Greenwich Village bomb factory exploded.

interview to contradict another and undercuts official accounts by contrary evidence. Although the film has virtually no voice-of-God narration, interviewees' remarks become voice-over commentary for the images (Fig. 23.8).

In the Year of the Pig gained a wide audience on campuses and in some theatrical venues. So did *Millhouse: A White Comedy* (1971), in which De Antonio's compilation technique satirizes Richard Nixon. The more serious *Underground* (1976) provided an opportunity to reflect on developments since the 1960s. In 1975, while five Weather Organization members were sought by the FBI, De Antonio, Mary Lampson, and Haskell Wexler filmed lengthy interviews with them, interspersing their memories and reflections with biographical and newsreel footage (Fig. 23.9).

A comparable sense of stock taking informs *Milestones* (1975), by Robert Kramer and John Douglas. Kramer was a founder of New York Newsreel who also developed a semifictional approach to New Left politics in the independent features *In the Country* (1966), *The Edge* (1968), and *Ice* (1970). Like the earlier features, *Milestones* was shot in Direct Cinema fashion, using improvised performances. Featuring several protagonists and running for over three hours, the film aimed at a broad assessment of the successes and failures of the New Left.

POLITICAL MODERNISM

In seeking to rouse the viewer to political reflection or action, the engaged filmmaker drew upon Direct Cinema technology and the tradition of leftist documentary. Other militant filmmakers explored modernist traditions. These directors combined politically radical themes and subjects with aesthetically radical form, pushing further the impulses of Brazil's Cinema Nôvo and Cuba's postrevolutionary cinema.

The political modernists took inspiration from the Soviet Montage cinema of the 1920s. Eisenstein and Vertov became models of political consciousness and formal innovation. Even more pervasive was the influence of the Marxist playwright Bertolt Brecht. (See Box.) In addition, many radical filmmakers sought to surpass the postwar art cinema. Its techniques had become fairly familiar and its mildly critical liberalism seemed reformist, not revolutionary. The political modernist director would transform character subjectivity, reflexivity, and ambiguity in the name of radical critique. At the forefront of this political modernism stood Jean-Luc Godard and Nagisa Oshima.

Before the May events, Godard was already fusing political criticism with modernist aesthetics. His films mounted an almost sociological examination of French life, accompanied by harsh attacks on American foreign policy (for example, *Masculin-Feminine*, 1966, and *Two or Three Things I Know about Her*, 1967). In *La Chinoise* ("The Chinese Girl," 1967) a Maoist study group turns into a terrorist cadre. *Weekend* (1967) shows the bourgeoisie, preoccupied with greed, murder, and gruesome sexuality, overtaken by

BRECHT AND POLITICAL MODERNISM

Although Bertolt Brecht (Fig. 23.10) was closely identified with Soviet communism in his lifetime, his creative work contributed to a strong "unorthodox Marxist" tradition in the arts. For thirty years his plays explored many forms of theater, some explicitly political, others closer to musical, parable, and "problem drama": *The Threepenny Opera* (1928), *The Rise and Fall of the City of Mahagonny* (1929), *Mother Courage and Her Children* (1941), *The Good Woman of Szechuan* (1943), and others.

Brecht's film *Kuhle Wampe* (1932, directed by Slatan Dudow; see p. 347) was not as influential for western cinema as were his theatrical productions and his writings. The hugely successful 1950s tour of his East German troupe, the Berliner Ensemble, introduced European audiences to Brecht's theater. When he died in 1956, his influence was still growing.

In a pungent, often humorous style, Brecht attacked traditional, or "Aristotelian," theater, on the grounds that it tries to absorb the audience completely. The spectator is supposed to identify with individual characters, feel their emotions, and accept the premises of the play's world. A committed Marxist, Brecht saw art as inevitably political. Impressed by Eisenstein's *Potemkin,* he also believed that playwrights would cease to focus on individuals and would eventually represent mass movements.

Brecht contrasted the drama of hypnotic empathy with Asian theater and the boxing match, which encourage spectators to take a more detached attitude to what they see. Brecht proposed several techniques which might accomplish this: breaking the play into episodes, interspersing titles, separating text from music or performance, and letting the performers speak the lines as if quoting them. These and other devices created the *Verfremsdungeffekt,* often translated as "alienation effect" but better rendered as "estranging" or "distancing." Through this effect, the spectator would evaluate the action critically and see larger historical forces at work behind it. The spectator could then start to understand how to change the world that created the characters' problems.

Fig. 23.10 Brecht, in a photo from Godard's *La Chinoise* (1967).

Brecht's influence emerged in cinema in the early 1960s, notably in Godard's *Vivre sa vie* (1962). His ideas energized a generation of political modernist filmmakers who sought to break that "illusion of reality" which classical fiction films created for the spectator. Filmmakers used collage structures, disjunctive editing, stylized framing and acting, and interspersed titles to achieve "anti-illusionist" works that would provoke reflection.

Brecht's influence also extended to less avant-garde films, such as *How I Won the War* (1967), *Oh What a Lovely War!* (1969), and *O Lucky Man!* (1973). Some critics claimed that even Sirk, Hitchcock, and Ford were "Brechtian." In many cases, filmmakers and critics recast and distorted the dramatist's ideas. Nevertheless, the versions of Brechtian theory in circulation during the 1960s and 1970s remain central to understanding critical political cinema of the era.

an absurd guerrilla band while Third World emigrants stand by awaiting their chance for revolt. With the eruptions of 1968, Godard turned his energies to a more severe and cerebral political modernism.

During the May events, he produced several ciné-tracts, short films consisting of demonstration footage and still photographs, usually with a few

Fig. 23.11 In *Un Film comme les autres* Godard appropriates advertising imagery and then attacks it through his own graffitilike comments.

Fig. 23.12 Godardian flattening of space put at the service of political critique in *Luttes en Italie*.

words scribbled over each one (Fig. 23.11). His films of 1968 alternate such material with dialogues of characters exploring political positions: a young man and a woman in a black vacuum in *Le Gai savoir* ("Joyful Wisdom," 1968), a group of workers and students (all barely visible in tall grass) in *Un Film comme les autres* ("A Film Like the Others," 1968). After *One Plus One* (aka *Sympathy for the Devil,* 1968), which juxtaposes a Rolling Stones rehearsal with staged scenes depicting political repression and black revolution, Godard joined the young Communist Jean-Pierre Gorin in forming the Dziga-Vertov Group.

The collective marked itself as politically modernist, declaring that it would struggle not only against political repression but also against "the bourgeois concept of representation."[11] Renouncing his previous films, Godard converted to Maoism and support for Third World revolution. Because his name guaranteed funding, usually from European television, the Dziga-Vertov Group turned out several films quickly, notably *British Sounds* (1969), *Wind from the East* (1969), *Luttes en Italie* ("Struggles in Italy," 1969), and *Vladimir and Rosa* (1970). The group dissolved when Godard had a severe motorcycle accident, but after his recovery he and Gorin made *Tout va bien* ("Everything's Fine," 1972) and *Letter to Jane* (1972), which are linked with the earlier work.

Each Dziga-Vertov Group film is an assemblage of diverse material, juxtaposing Direct Cinema footage (street scenes, labor actions, conversations) with titles and highly stylized tableaux (Fig. 23.12), often with direct address to the camera. Unlike Godard's earlier works, where such material interrupts a more or less coherent narrative, the Dziga-Vertov Group films largely lack stories. Rapid montages of still photos and blank frames alternate with long takes, either completely static or slowly tracking right or left. On the sound track, voices read extracts from Marx or Mao or exhort the viewer to criticize the image. Noises, as in the lengthy tracking shot down an auto assembly line in *British Sounds,* also assault the audience. Impossible to consume as entertainment or as engaged documentary, the films carry the modernist project to an abrasive extreme.

Tout va bien withdraws from this forbidding extreme, subscribing instead to Brecht's notion of "culinary"—that is, pleasurable—political art. The film has, for one thing, a fairly clear story. A radio journalist (Jane Fonda) and

Fig. 23.13 *Tout va bien*: A factory on strike, rendered as a "dollhouse" set.

her lover (Yves Montand), a director of TV commercials, accidentally get locked into an occupied factory. The experience makes them rethink their relation to each other, to the aftermath of May 1968, and to French society in 1972. Yet this story is "estranged" by a host of Brechtian devices: male and female voice-overs that plan how the film is to be made, hands signing checks to the stars, to-camera interviews by the characters, a cutaway set (Fig. 23.13), virtuoso left-and-right tracking shots along supermarket check-out counters, and alternate versions of scenes. *Tout va bien* remains a prototypical Brechtian film; its reflexivity invites the audience to consider the political implications of film form and style.

Fig. 23.14 "Each time, one image comes to replace the other . . . keeping, of course, the memory": Images of Palestinian struggle presented in a personification of the process of montage (*Ici et ailleurs*).

After 1972, Godard created a media facility, Sonimage, in Grenoble, France, with the photographer Anne-Marie Miéville. The male-female dialogue of *Tout va bien* became central to their mid-1970s work. *Ici et ailleurs* ("Here and Elsewhere," 1976), for example, returns to the assemblage form of the Dziga-Vertov Group work, while Godard and Miéville in voice-over reflect on the Palestinian liberation movement and discuss visual and auditory representation (Fig. 23.14). Several Godard-Miéville films include video imagery, which allows for still more varied juxtapositions of image, sound, and written language.

For most critics of the decade 1967-1977, Godard personified the political modernist, creating a formally and ideologically exploratory cinema. The work of the Japanese director Nagisa Oshima was not as widely seen, but it was no less aggressive and disturbing.

The Japanese New Wave filmmakers had begun producing politically critical films in the late 1950s (p. 550). A decade later, Oshima and other directors recorded and supported current social activism against the Vietnam War, education policies, and renewal of the American-Japanese security treaty. Oshima made several films about student politics, notably *Diary of a Shinjuku Thief* (1968) and *He Died after the War (Story of a Young Man Who Left His Will on Film)* (1970). He also turned his attention to the social problems of Koreans (in *Death by Hanging* and *Three Resurrected Drunkards,* both 1968) and of Okinawans (in *Dear Summer Sister,* 1972), groups which were suffering discrimination at Japanese hands.

Oshima also continued to explore modernist techniques of disjunction and distancing. He became especially drawn to strategies of repetition, replaying actions or episodes from different perspectives and offering none as definitively true or accurate. Twenty minutes into *Three Resurrected Drunkards,* the film begins again, as if the projectionist has put on the wrong reel, and continues, repeating each shot before it slowly starts to change. The device makes the three Japanese students "become" Koreans. In *He Died after the War* (known in English-language distribution as *The Man Who Left His Will on Film*), the militant student Motoki tries to decipher the footage left behind by a friend. Visiting the sites his friend filmed, Motoki sees each one trigger violence.

Repetition is also central to *Death by Hanging,* based on an actual criminal case. R, a young Korean convicted of rape and murder, is about to be hanged. To convince him of his guilt, police and bureaucrats stage elaborate reenactments of his crime until they (perhaps) kill an innocent victim themselves. Only then does R accept his guilt, "for the sake of all Rs." The

Fig. 23.15 In an abstract, purified set, R is about to be executed (*Death by Hanging*).

film's stylized sets (Fig. 23.15) and grotesque comedy stress its central issues: Koreans as an oppressed minority, capital punishment as political control, and sexual murder as an inevitable outcome of social repression. Oshima urged that the original criminal's letters become high-school reading.[12]

Unlike Godard, Oshima alternated very experimental films like *Three Resurrected Drunkards* and *Death by Hanging* with more accessible works like *Boy* (1969), the story of parents who make a living by shoving their child into traffic and then collecting payment for his injuries. *Ceremonies* (aka *The Ceremony*, 1971) is likewise fairly traditional in its treatment of the familiar Oshima theme of how society frustrates young people's sexual drives. The story plots the political and erotic intrigues within a family ruled by a rapacious father. The relatives gather only at funerals and weddings. Oshima's insistence that exploitation, incest, and guilt pervade the Japanese extended family form a critique of the serene domestic life presented in Ozu's work.

The works of Godard and Oshima are central cases, but they do not exhaust all the tendencies within political modernism. There were at least four other trends: collage construction, fantasy and parable, a stylized presentation of myth and history, and minimalism.

Collage Construction. An exemplary modernist strategy, collage construction has origins in Cubist painting. Most broadly, the collage film assembles bits of footage that are not intrinsically connected. Instead of trying to make the linkage seem natural or even "invisible," as in Hollywood's use of stock footage, the modernist filmmaker emphasizes the disparities among the images or sounds, forcing the viewer to make an imaginative leap. We have already seen this strategy used for metaphorical or poetic effect in Joseph Cornell's *Rose Hobart* (ca. 1936), Chris Marker's *Letter from Siberia* (1957), and Bruce Conner's short films; but in the late 1960s many filmmakers exploited it for political critique.

Radical filmmakers working with fictional narrative typically employ the collage principle in a more linear fashion. Such films set up a story and then elaborate on it with footage drawn from other realms. Brecht and Dudow's *Kuhle Wampe* pioneered this approach in a mild way, and we have already seen it in Makavejev's films (p. 545). Very similar to *WR: Mysteries of the Organism* is Vilgot Sjöman's *I Am Curious (Yellow)* (1967) and *I Am Curious (Blue)* (1967). Sjöman's story of a young woman seeking sexual liberation is

Fig. 23.16

Fig. 23.17

Figs. 23.16 and 23.17 Through editing, Martin Luther King seems to be looking at Lena, heroine of *I Am Curious (Yellow)*.

treated in Direct Cinema terms (with a good deal of reflexivity), but it is interrupted by titles and cutaways (Figs. 23.16, 23.17).

Fantasy and Parable. Political modernism after 1967 also embraced more fantastic possibilities. The return of Buñuel to international fame rekindled interest in the Surrealist tradition, which had nursed revolutionary aspirations since the 1920s. Many viewers considered *The Discreet Charm of the Bourgeoisie* (1972) and *The Phantom of Liberty* (1974) to be sly comments on official repressions of the 1968 rebellions. Closer to the ferocity of Buñuel's first films is *Viva la muerte!* ("Long Live Death!" 1971), by the Spanish playwright Ferdinand Arrabal. A Spanish boy fantasizes his father's torture at the hands of the Church and the army. The boy is also obsessed with his mother, whom he imagines bathing in the blood of a slaughtered bull. Arrabal's cheerfully perverse fantasies put the film in the modernist tradition, and he savors gruesome imagery. A shot of the father being tortured is rendered peculiarly beautiful through tinting (Color Plate 23.3). Traces of the Surrealist impulse are also evident in Alexander Jodorovsky's grotesque *El Topo* ("The Mole," 1971) and his mystical *The Holy Mountain* (1973).

Less indebted to Surrealism in the use of fantasy was Pier Paolo Pasolini. *Hawks and Sparrows* (1965) initiated his interest in contemporary political parables, but his subsequent work in this vein was more scathing. *Teorema* (1968) shows a blankly handsome young man taken in by a bourgeois family; one by one, their lives are changed in ways at once sordid and miraculous. *Pigpen* (1969) sets side by side two stories about perverse appetites: a young mountain climber becomes a cannibal, and an industrialist is eaten by pigs. In these films, Pasolini's technique has a Buñuelian restraint, throwing into relief the absurd spectacle of a disintegrating society.

History and Myth. Instead of portraying a past event neutrally, or simply retelling a myth, the radical filmmaker might treat it through nonrealistic techniques and then draw analogies with contemporary political struggles. For example, Yoshishige Yoshida's trilogy *Eros plus Massacre* (1969), *Heroic Purgatory* (1970), and *Martial Law* (1973) uses decentered framing and stylized lighting to show how Japanese activism in different eras parallels that of the late 1960s.

Similarly, Pasolini consistently teased a political critique out of his adaptations of classical myths and contemporary history. In *Medea* (1969),

Fig. 23.18 *The Confrontation*: A struggle in the past restaged as if in the present.

among masked choristers and pink rocks the classical heroine embodies the conflict between colonization and the people it dominates. Pasolini's last film, *Salò, or the 120 Days of Sodom* (1975), stages the final days of Italian fascism as a spectacle out of the Marquis de Sade. Here Pasolini's technique of *pasticchio* ("mixing"; p. 532) frames mutilation and sexual assault in classical compositions and sets them to the music of Orff's *Carmina Burana*.

In the wake of 1968, Miklós Jancsó's treatment of history also became more defiantly unrealistic. *The Confrontation* (1969) centers on left-wing debates in Hungary during the immediate postwar period. As usual, Jancsó concentrates on group dynamics. Activists ransack a university library, bully other students, argue with their opponents, and purge a leader on orders from the party. Jancsó's sinuous camera movements and very long takes are now accompanied by a more stylized mise-en-scene. Characters sing and dance spontaneously, and although the events are set around 1948, the students wear the sport shirts and blue jeans of the sixties (Fig. 23.18).

Jancsó began to create political allegories fusing past, present, and future events. *Agnus Dei* (1970) shows the 1919 Hungarian Revolution in the countryside, concentrating on an epileptic priest and a mysterious White officer who may represent the fascism that will overtake Europe. Jancsó's subsequent films extend his examination of power to the entire history of the West. Attila's murder of his brother (*Technique and Rite*, 1971), the plot against Julius Caesar (*Rome Wants Another Caesar*, 1973), and Elektra's legendary struggle with Aegisthos (*For Elektra*, 1974) become ritualized dialogues and ceremonial encounters, rendered in elaborate choreography and long takes. (*For Elektra* is composed of only ten shots.)

Red Psalm (1971), for many critics Jancsó's masterpiece, balances these generalizing tendencies with national elements and more idiosyncratic symbolism. Although no actual event or period is designated, the story portrays a struggle of Hungarian peasants against landowners and soldiers. Followed by a zooming, panning, and tracking camera, victims and oppressors float through an abstract, expanding and contracting space (Figs. 23.19-23.24). Beginning with a peasant woman holding a dove and ending with the same woman brandishing a rifle, *Red Psalm* draws on revolutionary symbols. When someone is killed, the victim may return to life, now wearing a red flower. *Red Psalm* becomes a pageant that restages the revolutionary tradition in the light both of Brecht and of art-cinema modernism.

Fig. 23.19

Fig. 23.20

Fig. 23.21

Fig. 23.22

Fig. 23.23

Fig. 23.24

A stylized treatment of history and myth was also explored by the Greek director Theo Angelopoulos. Influenced by Mizoguchi, Antonioni, and Dreyer, Angelopoulos began his career under the dictatorship of the Greek generals in the late 1960s. His first feature, *Reconstruction* (1970), displayed a by-then conventional reshuffling of present and past, as flashbacks interrupt the investigation of a murder. But the cryptic dialogue, which supplies little information about character relations, and the camera's dwelling on still compositions and landscapes (Fig. 23.25) made the film seem dedramatized even by art-cinema standards.

Fig. 23.19 One phase of one shot in *Red Psalm*: From a woman with a dove . . .

Fig. 23.20 . . . the camera pans left to a soldier's pistol . . .

Fig. 23.21 . . . before glimpsing a balladeer drifting into the background.

Fig. 23.22 The camera follows him to a group of peasants . . .

Fig. 23.23 . . . who surround the soldier . . .

Fig. 23.24 . . . and entice him into a dance.

Fig. 23.25 The police investigation in *Reconstruction*.

Fig. 23.26 Moving through history and staging classic plays in small towns, the traveling players become the conscience of Greek culture.

Like the early Jancsó, Angelopoulos plumbed his nation's history for political lessons for the present. Despite censorship under the military regime, *Days of '36* (1972), a film about the murder of a militant union leader, showed how the government protected the assassin. The result, shot in long takes and 360-degree panning movements, became an allegory of political repression. Under the same regime Angelopoulos produced *The Traveling Players* (1975), a four-hour panorama of Greek political strife between 1939 and 1952. Over the years the theater troupe performs the same play, a mythical piece which comments upon the changing political situation. As in *Reconstruction,* Angelopoulos rearranges the time sequence, but now he blends historical periods within a single shot. The soliloquies and performances, along with Angelopoulos's long-shot framings, yield a dry anti-illusionism consistent with early-1970s interpretations of Brecht (Fig. 23.26).

Minimalism. The spareness of Angelopoulos's technique relates him to another trend of post-1968 political modernism. Some filmmakers pursued a strategy of minimalism—sparse narratives rendered in a rigorous, ascetic style.

Outstanding examples are found in the work of Chantal Akerman, one of the most influential women directors of the era. Akerman's minimalism derived less from European sources than from encounters with Warhol's work (p. 593) and North American "Structural" cinema (Chapter 24). *Je, tu, il, elle* (1974) was a spare narrative of sexual encounters rendered in long takes. Her most influential film was *Jeanne Dielman, 23, Quai du commerce, 1080 Bruxelles* (1975; the title gives the main character's name and address in Brussels).

Over 225 minutes, Akerman presents three days in the life of a housewife who works as a prostitute in her home. The film's first half presents Jeanne's life in a style as meticulous as her housekeeping. The low-height camera, centered down a corridor or across a kitchen table, records every bit

Fig. 23.27 *Jeanne Dielman*: Household routine made unfamiliar through use of long takes.

of business—dressing, washing dishes, greeting a customer, making a meat-loaf. After one client's visit, however, Jeanne's routine mysteriously breaks down and she starts to make errors. Finally, she stabs a client and goes to sit at the dining table—virtually the only time we have seen her relax.

Jeanne Dielman is a landmark in feminist modernism. By slowing plot action to a standstill, Akerman obliges the viewer to look at the empty intervals and domestic spaces that mainstream cinema skips over. In one sense, *Jeanne Dielman* moves toward fulfilling Neorealist Cesare Zavattini's dream of recording eight hours in a person's life; the film could even be considered an expansion of the sequence of the maid's awakening in *Umberto D.* (p. 421). But Akerman treats domestic space as harboring sexual repression and financial exploitation. Housekeeping is woman's work, as is prostitution (as Jeanne's address on "Commerce Pier" indicates).

Similarly, Akerman's minimalist style recalls Bresson, Ozu, Mizoguchi, and experimental cinema, but she uses spare technique for purposes of political critique. The static camera and the rectilinear, low-height compositions estrange the viewer from the action while dignifying household chores as aesthetically and socially significant (Fig. 23.27).

Despite the diversity within political modernism, the mid-1970s saw the trend drop off, at least in 35mm filmmaking. Although the exploration of myth and history continued, the collage form and Surrealist fantasy virtually vanished. Minimalism was adapted to less formally radical ends. As left-wing positions became assimilated into mainstream politics, radical production groups were difficult to sustain. Oshima disbanded his company Sozosha in 1973, a year after the end of Godard and Gorin's Dziga-Vertov Group. The scandals surrounding Makavejev's *Sweet Movie* (1974) and Oshima's *In the Realm of the Senses* (1975) were triggered by their sexual content, not modernist technique or political stance. Godard announced his return to more accessible narrative in *Sauve qui peut (la vie)* ["Let one who can save (one's life)," aka *Every Man for Himself,* 1979]. By the end of the 1970s, most political modernists were making less radical, and less radically experimental, works.

THE POLITICIZATION OF MAINSTREAM NARRATIVE AND THE ART FILM

During the 1960s and 1970s, mainstream European and Asian cinema became politicized to some degree. In Italy, directors were more willing to investigate the Fascist past; even spaghetti Westerns became more partisan (for example, Sergio Leone's *Duck, You Sucker!*, 1972). In Sweden Bo Widerberg made *Adalen 31* (1969), a study of labor strife. In Japan, the "pink films" of Koji Wakamitsu became frenzied studies of sexual repression and terrorism. The British *Sunday, Bloody Sunday* (1971) inserted male homosexuality into a domestic melodrama.

The most commercially successful integration of left-wing politics and classical narrative cinema took place in the genre of the "political thriller." Here a plot would be built around the investigation of an actual government scandal, mentioned by name or thinly disguised. The political thriller offered the excitement of a detective film and the shock of an exposé. The inclusion of major stars also assured wide circulation.

Fig. 23.28 Pseudo-documentary touches in *The Mattei Affair*.

The political thriller had been pioneered by Francesco Rosi in *Salvatore Giuliano* (1961), and he continued to exploit it in *The Mattei Affair* (1972), *Lucky Luciano* (1974), and *Exquisite Corpses* (1975). Rosi's films intercut the inquiry with key events in the past while drawing upon documentary techniques, such as newsreel footage, dates, and explanatory captions (Fig. 23.28). Although the genre was almost exclusively male territory, Nadine Trintignant's *Défense de savoir* ("Right to Know," 1973) was a comparable study of collusion between police and the extreme right. The most famous exponent of the political thriller was Costa-Gavras. A Greek who became a French citizen, Costa-Gavras started as a director of thrillers (*The Sleeping Car Murder,* 1965) before he made *Z* (1969), one of the most widely seen political films of the era.

Fig. 23.29 A hand-held shot follows the dissident to his assassination in *Z*.

"Any similarity to actual events, or persons living or dead, is not coincidental. It is intentional." Signed by Costa-Gavras and the scriptwriter Jorge Semprun, the opening title of *Z* announces a political agenda. The film retells the events surrounding the assassination of a popular opponent of the dictatorial Greek colonels. The investigating magistrate, a political moderate, exposes the right-wing conspiracy, but then he falls victim too. By 1969, many New Cinema techniques—glimpsed flashbacks, slow motion, freeze-frames, hand-held shots (Fig. 23.29)—had become easily understood, and Costa-Gavras used them to create suspense and rapid-fire action. The presence of the star Yves Montand helped *Z* gain international recognition.

Fig. 23.30 Spanish peasant life as a breeding ground for political rebellion (*Pascal Duarte*).

Costa-Gavras then made *The Confession* (1970), a re-creation of a political purge in postwar Czechoslovakia; *State of Siege* (1973), an attack on American attempts to oust the Tupamaro guerrillas of Uruguay; and *Special Section* (1975), an exposé of French collaboration with the Germans during World War II. The films rested upon a body of research, but critics from all political persuasions faulted the action-packed intrigue and the schematic hero/villain characterizations. Costa-Gavras replied that only by working within mainstream conventions could he bring information to a broad audience. He refused the slow pace and intellectual demands of political modernism:

The general public is not sufficiently trained to reflect upon a film while it is being projected. They have become accustomed to the rapid pace of American cinema, and I have to confess that I feel closer to this rhythm too. It's only after the film that the spectator can truly reflect upon it. Or reject it.[13]

For two decades Costa-Gavras remained the dean of the political thriller (*Missing*, 1982; *Betrayed*, 1988; and *Music Box*, 1989).

Other genres became political vehicles. Louis Malle's period drama *Lacombe Lucien* (France, 1974) shows a young peasant seduced by Fascist politics, while in the more elliptical *Pascal Duarte* (Spain, 1975) Ricardo Franco traces how an equally violent youth becomes a rebel during the Spanish Civil War (Fig. 23.30). Comedy also assimilated left-wing themes. In France, Diane Kurys made the highly popular *Diabolo Menthe* (1977), an affectionate portrait of post-1968 youth, following it two years later with *Cocktail Molotov*, set in the days of May. Political subjects were taken up in Italian comedies as well, most famously in Lina Wertmuller's *The Seduction of Mimi* (1972), *Love and Anarchy* (1973), and *Swept Away* (1974). *Seven Beauties* (1976) offers a critique of Italian male pride, showing how a cocky hustler must humble himself to survive in a Nazi prison camp (Fig. 23.31).

Marco Ferreri's grotesque comedies offer a more deadpan, enigmatic attitude. *Dillinger Is Dead* (1969) builds enormous suspense as it observes a businessman coming home late, preparing a meal, watching home movies, and murdering his wife. In this masculine version of Akerman's *Jeanne Dielman*, the minute depiction of the husband's habits reveals the pettiness of his business ethos (Fig. 23.32). In Ferreri's *La Grande bouffe* ("The Big Blowout," 1973) a batch of businessmen literally kill themselves through gorging and fornication.

Along with such mainstream filmmakers, directors working within the art cinema were equally affected by the climate of the era. Avoiding the extremes of Brechtian alienation and stylization, many established directors nevertheless continued the tradition of postwar modernism while incorporating political material. Carlos Saura, for instance, had already made *The Hunt* (1965), an attack on the machismo ethos in Spain. *The Garden of Delights* (1970) took a more Buñuelian slant, showing a perverse ruling class living between fantasy and reality (Fig. 23.33).

In *If . . .* (1968), Lindsay Anderson intensified the critique of British society that had driven the Kitchen Sink films (p. 553). An upper-middle-class boys' school becomes a microcosm of social revolution as four radical students rebel against repressive officials. *If . . .* adopts Godardian techniques by introducing major segments with intertitles; its alternation of color and black-and-white film stock (though used simply through economic necessity) becomes a mildly Brechtian distancing device. The final scene, in which the boys fire from a roof into a crowd, refers to the ending of Vigo's anarchistic *Zero for Conduct*. With its fantasy sequence and concluding freeze-frame, *If . . .* invoked conventions of the contemporary art cinema.

Postwar European films had used strongly demarcated flashbacks to compare past and present; *Hiroshima mon amour* had made the time shifts more rapid and ambiguous; directors of the 1960s had pushed the technique to fragmented extremes. In the 1970s, the flashback continued to be a tool

Fig. 23.31 *Seven Beauties*: The street hustler forced to bargain for his comforts in a prison camp.

Fig. 23.32 In *Dillinger Is Dead*, the husband takes a fantasy swim "inside" a movie.

Fig. 23.33 The imaginary life of the upper classes, attacked in *The Garden of Delights*.

Fig. 23.34 *The Spider's Stratagem*: Standing in the past, Draifa tells the young Athos in the present about his father (the man at the window in the background); the technique serves the thematic purpose of questioning the need for sanctified historical heroes.

for exploring political change across history. The Hungarian Istvan Szabó employed the device to chronicle the lives of people in an apartment building in *25 Firemen's Street* (1973). Through a rhythmic alternation of eras, André Téchiné's *Souvenirs d'en France* ("Memories of France," 1974) chronicles the effects of labor struggles on a family over several decades. Karoly Makk's *Love* (Hungary, 1970) uses swift montage and abrupt flashbacks to contrast the lives of two women waiting for the return of a political prisoner.

Bernardo Bertolucci, always in touch with contemporary trends, employed flashbacks in more innovative ways in *The Spider's Stratagem* (1970). Here characters look exactly the same "now" as they did thirty years before, and from the past they speak to someone in the present (Fig. 23.34). Bertolucci's *The Conformist* (1971) is perhaps the prototype of the politicized art film. It presents a precise play among memory, fantasy, and reality in its portrayal of a sexually repressed man driven to become a Fascist political assassin. A simpler flashback structure frames *1900* (1975), a sweeping fresco of the rise of fascism presented through the parallel lives of two friends, one a leftist peasant and the other a weak-willed son of the gentry.

Directors of the postwar generation reflected the new era in distinct ways. Fellini's *Satyricon* (1969) was widely interpreted as his sour commentary on current social decline, and in *Amarcord* (1973) he produced a half-nostalgic, half-mocking portrayal of Fascist spectacle. A colossal steamship holds the villagers spellbound, and a gigantic head of Mussolini looms frowning over a parade (Color Plate 19.2). Antonioni's *Zabriskie Point* (1970) made common cause with student revolution through a hallucinatory love-in at Death Valley and a series of shots detailing the slow-motion explosion of an American home. *The Passenger* (aka *Profession: Reporter,* 1975) shifted to the Third World, where Antonioni's characteristic questions about identity are played out in a political intrigue involving arms shipments.

The Swiss director Alain Tanner declared himself also stirred by the May events, and throughout the ensuing decade his films reflected upon the legacies of 1968. With Michel Soutter, Claude Goretta, and others Tanner founded the Groupe Cinq ("Group 5") in 1968 in order to make films for Swiss television. Tanner's early features, influenced by British Free Cinema and the Nouvelle Vague, lay firmly in the European art-cinema tradition, using reflexivity [*Charles mort ou vif* ("Charles Dead or Alive," 1969)] and

Fig. 23.35 In an epilogue set in the future, Jonah scribbles on the commune's mural (*For Jonah, Who Will Be 25 in the Year 2000*).

the investigation-via-flashbacks structure (*The Salamander*, 1971). Thereafter he specialized in wistful studies of how the absence of radical change blocked personal relationships. His most famous film was *For Jonah, Who Will Be 25 in the Year 2000* (1976). Here eight "children of May" (*M*ax, *M*arco, *M*arguerite, *M*adeleine, and so on) form a commune in the era of dashed hopes and political "normalization." Black-and-white images represent their utopian desires, and Tanner ends the film with an ambivalent image of the future (Fig. 23.35).

Fig. 23.36 *Padre padrone*: The stick is transferred.

If Tanner focuses on middle-class characters longing for change, the brothers Paolo and Vittorio Taviani concentrate on the revolutionary aspirations of the peasantry and the working class. The Tavianis undertook a populist retelling of Italian revolutionary history in *Subversives* (1967), *Under the Sign of Scorpio* (1968), *St. Michael Had a Cock* (1971), and *Allonsanfan* (1974). Their first international success was *Padre padrone* ("Father-Boss," 1977), the story of an illiterate shepherd boy who becomes a scholar of linguistics through an obstinate revolt against his father. The film begins with the author of the original autobiography whittling a branch as he introduces the tale. He then hands the stick to the actor playing the father (Fig. 23.36), who enters the schoolroom to fetch his son, and the fictional story begins. Apart from introducing a Brechtian distance, the scene suggests that the son, now grown, realizes that harsh authority is necessary if youth is to define itself.

Attention to women's concerns gave a new impetus to the careers of female art-cinema directors. The Hungarian Marta Mészáros had made several short films during the 1960s. Her first feature, *The Girl* (1968), was followed by several others, notably *Riddance* (1973), *Adoption* (1975; winner of a Grand Prize at the Berlin Film Festival), and *Nine Months* (1976). Mészáros's work balances a consideration of women's relation to social forces, particularly class structure, with a probing of intimate relationships. Taken together, her films dramatize a vast range of feminine experience, from school, dating, and marriage to work, childbirth, and family life. She particularly explores mother-daughter relationships. Her style emphasizes realism and authorial commentary, both inflected by close-ups of her heroines' bodies; in *Adoption* she builds an entire sequence out of women's hands at work in a factory.

Agnès Varda had been directing since the early 1950s, though her fame came only with the rise of the Nouvelle Vague (see p. 530). She was active in the cinematic left, making a short on the Black Panthers and contributing to the collective film *Far from Vietnam* (1967). After *Lions Love* (1969), a relaxed celebration of the American counterculture, Varda made several short films before her next feature, *One Sings, the Other Doesn't* (1976). Like many political films of the mid-1970s, it takes stock of the previous decade—here, by tracing the course of two women's friendship from 1962 to 1974. Wanting to focus attention on abortion and childbearing as seen from her liberal-feminist viewpoint, Varda deliberately aimed *One Sings* at a wide audience. "In France, our film has already been seen by 350,000 people. . . . If the meaning of the film and its feminist point of view is even half or two-thirds as strong as that of a more radical film, at least we've gotten a lot of people *thinking*, and not in the wrong direction."[14]

The late 1960s and early 1970s saw new women directors emerge within the art cinema. In France, Nelly Kaplan, who had been Abel Gance's assistant since 1954, made her first feature. *The Pirate's Fiancée* (aka *A Very Curious Girl,* 1969) shows a young village woman exploited by the local men until she begins blackmailing them with tape recordings of intimate secrets. Liliane de Kermadec's *Aloïse* (1974) launched the career of Isabelle Huppert as a woman imprisoned for opposing World War I. Several French actresses took up directing, notably Diane Kurys, Anna Karina, and Jeanne Moreau. In Canada, the experimental filmmaker Joyce Wieland made the reflexive melodrama *The Far Shore* (1976). Some filmmakers focused on particular feminist issues, while others dealt with subjects of broader political concern, including the "politics of everyday life."

On the whole, mainstream cinema and art cinema adapted to the political culture of the post-1968 era. Classical narrative conventions assimilated political themes and subject matter, especially in the political thriller and the comedy. Art-cinema directors who retreated from the extreme experimentation of political modernism nevertheless took micropolitics and the culture of dissent to be fruitful subjects. Tanner, calling himself "marginal" within commercial filmmaking, spoke for many: "My position is not to be as radical as Godard, but to try to force the commercial world to open their doors to outside experiences."[15] As radical political modernism left the realm of 35mm commercial filmmaking in the late 1970s, most politicized fictional filmmaking in the western world worked within the bounds of classical or art-cinema narrative. Political modernism survived longer in the experimental 16mm sector (Chapter 24).

NEW CINEMA IN WEST GERMANY: THE POLITICAL WING

The "New German Cinema," a phrase coined in the early 1970s, denotes an even more amorphous group than most New Cinemas of recent decades. The label covers filmmakers pursuing very different agendas. Several directors did not practice critical political cinema (Chapter 26). But those who took up left-wing filmmaking vividly illustrate the trends of the late 1960s and after.

The Oberhausen manifesto of 1962 (p. 534) stimulated some socially critical filmmaking, particularly for television, but not until 1968 did left-wing students at Berlin's Institute of Film and Television launch a series of engaged documentaries and fiction films aimed at working-class audiences. More ambitious were the films of the "Berlin School," which echoed the German proletarian films of the late 1920s (p. 346) in their focus on working-class life. Rejecting the idealized realism of the Berlin School, the feminist Helga Reidemeister concentrated on documenting the domestic life of the working class, notably in *The Purchased Dream* (1977), a compilation from four hours of super-8mm material which a family had shot.

Political modernism was also a strong force in the New German Cinema. The 1968 upheavals and their political culture strengthened the Brechtian documentary drama practiced by playwrights Peter Weiss and Rolf Hochhuth. In film, political modernists continued the social critique implicit in much Young German Film of the early 1960s, but they gave it a more radical edge in response to the rise of the counterculture and the New Left.

Alexander Kluge, a moving force in the Young German Film (pp. 534–535) exemplifies the collage trend in political modernism. By intercutting fiction, documentary, written titles, and other material, his films continued the strategies of *Yesterday Girl* (1966), confronting the spectator with gaps "in which fantasy can take root." "The film is composed in the head of the spectator; it is not a work of art that exists on the screen by itself."[16] Kluge hoped that this countercultural openness would permit the film to become less a preplanned message and more the basis of an ongoing dialogue between filmmaker and audience.

Fig. 23.37 *Artists at the Top of the Big Top: Perplexed*: A circus acrobat pirouettes on Leni's head, thanks to Kluge's framing.

Artists at the Top of the Big Top: Perplexed (1968) was a reaction to the radical students at the Berlin Film Festival who pelted Kluge with eggs and charged him with elitism. The story of Leni Peickert's attempt to create a new kind of circus is interrupted by news photos, newsreels, shots from Eisenstein's *October,* color footage, and references to current ideas that only through a "work of mourning" could Germany come to terms with its Nazi past. The circus of Leni's imagination (Fig. 23.37) never comes to pass, and she winds up working as a television producer. In its open-textured way, *Artists at the Top of the Big Top* presents the difficulty of utopian political change and suggests that only a "long march through the institutions"—here, existing media conditions—will lead to social change.

The alternation of documentary and fiction within Kluge's films takes place in a more theatrical fashion in the work of Hans-Jürgen Syberberg. Syberberg came to notice with a series of Direct Cinema documentaries in the late 1960s, but his most famous films are the trilogy *Ludwig: Requiem for a Virgin King* (1972), *Karl May* (1974), and the eight-hour *Hitler: A Film from Germany* (1977). The spirit of Brecht, whom Syberberg has called his "foster father," mingles with a Wagnerian giganticism in the first and last of these works. Swirling smoke, vast auras of colored light, and mournful music enfold monumental tableaux representing the twilight of German culture (Fig. 23.38). The *Hitler* film's reflexivity, with references running from Edison and

Fig. 23.38 The phantasmagoric blend of cinema, music, and German history (*Hitler: A Film from Germany*; production still).

Fig. 23.39 Impersonally rendered musical performance in *The Chronicle of Anna Magdalena Bach.*

Riefenstahl to *Citizen Kane,* makes it a history of the cinema in which Hitler, turning politics into mythical drama, becomes "the greatest filmmaker of all time."

Probably the most controversial practitioners of political modernism in the New German Cinema were Jean-Marie Straub and Danièle Huillet. After *Not Reconciled* (1965), they made the feature-length *The Chronicle of Anna Magdalena Bach* (1968). In one sense it employs the collage aesthetic, setting together shots of documents from Bach's day, brief staged narrative scenes, and lengthy performances. But for most of its length it is a remarkable effort in minimalism. Straub and Huillet present elliptical, fragmentary episodes from Bach's life and use static shots or a slightly moving camera to record lengthy stretches of performances, always without showing the audience (Fig. 23.39). As in *Not Reconciled* and later works, they counter most production practice in fictional film by using direct sound, thereby capturing the specific auditory character of each space. From one perspective, the film resembles *Artists at the Top of the Big Top* in being a "materialist" study of artistic labor, with Straub and Huillet suggesting that Bach's music arose in part from particular social and political conditions.

The combination of collage construction, direct sound, and ascetic treatment of narrative and style returns in *History Lessons* (1972), an adaptation of a Brecht novel, and *Sinai Dogs: Fortini Cani* (1977). Straub and Huillet also explore minimalist ways of adapting theater pieces: *Othon* (1969) uses the hand-held camera to present a classical French play in contemporary Rome, while the opera *Moses and Aaron* (1974) is played out in a desert arena with stylized arrangements of solo singers and chorus (Fig. 23.40). Opposed to all forms of entertainment cinema, Straub and Huillet's films interrogate artistic tradition, probing classic novels and plays for contemporary political implications. (*The Chronicle of Anna Magdalena Bach* is dedicated to the people of Vietnam; *Moses and Aaron,* to a terrorist.)

The more commercially successful New German films adapted political commentary to the conventions of mainstream cinema. The most prominent

Fig. 23.40 *Moses and Aaron*: The protagonists sing, backed by an invisible chorus.

new genres were the *Arbeiterfilm* ("worker film"), which used realistic story-telling technique to portray the life of the contemporary working class, and the *Heimatfilm* ("homeland film"), which focused on rural life.

Among the many directors working within the art cinema, Volker Schlöndorff stands out. His 1970 *Heimatfilm, The Sudden Wealth of the Poor People of Kombach,* draws on mildly Brechtian techniques to trace the capture and execution of a gang of peasant bandits. Schlöndorff attracted international attention by co-directing *The Lost Honor of Katherina Blum* (1975) with his wife, Margarethe von Trotta. The film shows a woman accused of aiding a terrorist and hounded by the police and the scandalmongering press. Throughout most of the film, the viewer is led to believe Katherina is an innocent victim (Color Plate 23.4). Once she has gained the viewer's sympathy, the plot reveals that love led her to help the young man. The narrational processes of classical filmmaking coax the audience to sympathize with a subversive act.

After another film with Schlöndorff, von Trotta began directing on her own. *The Second Awakening of Christa Klages* (1977) pursues the narrative strategy of *Katherina Blum* by aligning the audience with a feminist robber on the run. In a period when terrorism, plane hijackings, and assassinations created headlines, such a focus on a criminal woman had a vivid political impact.

Von Trotta's career exemplifies the extent to which West Germany's production subsidy system enabled women directors to work in numbers unparalleled in other nations. Many of them produced politically inflected art films. For example, Helga Sanders-Brahms's *Violence* (1971) is an "anti-road movie," alternating static road maps with a tale of how two assembly-line workers kill an immigrant. In an *Arbeiterfilm, The Employee* (1972), Sanders-Brahms traces a computer programmer's descent into madness, while her *Last Days of Gomorrah* (1974) shows a future society in which television gratifies all desires.

Rainer Werner Fassbinder was perhaps the best-known director of the New German Cinema, partly because of his aggressive personality and self-destructive lifestyle. Fassbinder was influenced by the French New Wave and the political modernism that intensified in the late 1960s. Beginning as an actor, playwright, and theater director, Fassbinder revealed a taste for grotesque comedy, splashy violence, and strong realism of characters' regional dialects. Yet he rejected the Brechtian theory that was important for Kluge, Straub, and others. He insisted that politically critical art had to engage the spectator's feelings. "With Brecht you see the emotions and you reflect upon them as you witness them but you never feel them. . . . I let the audience *feel and think.*"[17]

After his early, strongly Godardian short *The Little Chaos* (1966; Fig. 23.41), Fassbinder made eleven films with the Antiteater, a troupe of actors and technicians. Some of the films recast Hollywood genres, while others show the influence of the Nouvelle Vague and Straub and Huillet. Fassbinder then acquainted himself with Douglas Sirk's Hollywood melodramas (p. 392), which he took as a model of a socially critical cinema that was also emotionally engaging. He was struck by the arbitrarily upbeat endings (he called them "unhappy happy ends") and by the way that Sirk blocked full identification with the characters. With *The Merchant of Four Seasons* (1971)

Fig. 23.41 *The Little Chaos*: Fassbinder plays a robber in his first film.

Fig. 23.42

Fig. 23.43

Fig. 23.42 *Katzelmacher* (1969): Loafing couples, shot in a flat, frontal manner.

Fig. 23.43 *The Bitter Tears of Petra von Kant* takes place entirely in the luxurious apartment of a fashion designer; Fassbinder's filming of the richly decorated set recalls von Sternberg.

Fig. 23.44 *Far from Vietnam*: The director as laconic and detached commentator.

Fassbinder initiated a second phase in his work, that of domestic melodramas. Once more he proved highly prolific, using rapid shooting schedules and low budgets to turn out several features, notably *The Bitter Tears of Petra von Kant* (1972), *Fear Eats the Soul* (1973), *Effie Briest* (1974), and *Fox and His Friends* (1974).

Early in his career Fassbinder often framed figures in a sober, mug-shot fashion (Fig. 23.42). In his "Hollywood revisionist" phase, he accepted the conventions of continuity editing in order to keep the drama paramount, yet much of the fascination of these films derives from Fassbinder's dwelling on gazes or distant views or his using elements of decor to veil characters' emotional states (Fig. 23.43).

The early Antiteater films experiment with narrative, while the later political melodramas are gripping, emotion-laden stories aimed at a broader public. Most of Fassbinder's films are about power. He often focuses on victimization and conformity, showing how members of a group exploit and punish outsiders. Fassbinder insists that the victim often accepts the standards the group applies, so he or she comes to believe that the punishment is deserved. Ali in *Fear Eats the Soul* literally internalizes the racial prejudice he suffers, collapsing from an ulcer—a common illness of immigrant workers.

Coming after the failures of 1968, Fassbinder's work is often interpreted as acknowledging the impossibility of radical change. No Brechtian aesthetic could promise a social revolution. The movement of Fassbinder's career from anarchistic and severe political modernism to works that use the less disturbing conventions of Hollywood and the art cinema reflects a general trend within European critical political cinema during the 1970s.

The same change is conveniently summarized in two European films from the beginning and the end of the period. In 1967, thirteen left-wing directors, mostly French, collaborated on *Far from Vietnam*. The film sought to mobilize intellectuals against the war by a series of episodes—some fictional (e.g., Resnais's), some compiled from newsreel footage (e.g., Marker's), one essayistic (Godard's; Fig. 23.44). In 1978, fourteen German directors, coordinated by Kluge, made *Germany in Autumn*. Like *Far from Vietnam* it brings together disparate tendencies within current filmmaking. But now the hope is not to change international policy; the goal is to understand national life in a climate of terrorism and right-wing oppression. Certain episodes, particularly Fassbinder's drug-hazed confrontation with his lover, dramatize the extent to which the political had become personal (Fig. 23.45). *Germany in Autumn* exemplifies the turn from broad activism toward a micropolitics, while indicating that critical filmmaking remained central to the 1970s political culture of dissent.

Fig. 23.45 *Germany in Autumn*: The director as confused and dispirited participant.

◆ NOTES AND QUERIES

Film Studies and the New Film Theory

The era which this chapter surveys witnessed the enormous growth of academic film studies in Britain, Europe, and North America. The political movements of the late 1960s influenced many film courses; instructors and students often analyzed the ideological implications of mainstream Hollywood film and considered critical political films as "oppositional" cinema.

Along with these developments went major changes in film theory. Building on semiological ideas of the early 1960s (see Notes and Queries, Chapter 20, p. 556), film theorists in the wake of 1968 sought to explain how cinema functioned politically while providing pleasure. The newly radicalized editors of *Cahiers du cinéma* proposed a taxonomy that distinguished films wholly in the grip of dominant ideology from those which use political critique opportunistically (e.g., *Z*). The editors left a space for committed works, for modernist efforts, and for those mainstream films which could be read "symptomatically," as if they were "splitting under an internal tension."[18] Another early theoretical effort, drawing upon current psychoanalytic ideas, was Jean-Pierre Baudry's 1970 essay "Ideological Effects of the Basic Cinematographic Apparatus." Baudry suggested that the very technology of film—camera shutter, screen, light beam—manifested a bourgeois world view.

Feminists also posed theoretical questions about film's role in promoting patriarchal values. Journals like *Camera Obscura* and *frauen und film* took as part of their task the elaboration of a feminist film theory. The most influential essay in this direction was Laura Mulvey, "Visual Pleasure and Narrative Cinema" (1975), which generated a vast range of comment. By the end of the 1970s, not only had film study established itself as a discipline, but women's cinema found an audience among feminists.

These and other important essays can be found in Bill Nichols, ed., *Movies and Methods*, vol. 1 (Berkeley: University of California Press, 1976) and vol. 2 (Berkeley: University of California Press, 1985); Philip Rosen, ed., *Narrative, Apparatus, Ideology: A Film Theory Reader* (New York: Columbia University Press, 1986); Constance Penley, ed., *Feminism and Film Theory* (London: Routledge, 1988); and Nick Browne, ed., *Cahiers du cinéma 1969–1972: The Politics of Representation* (Cambridge: Harvard University

Press, 1990). Historical overviews can be found in introductions to the above volumes, as well as in Christine Gledhill, "Recent Developments in Feminist Film Theory," in Mary Ann Doane, Patricia Mellencamp, and Linda Williams, eds., *Re-Vision: Essays in Feminist Film Theory* (Frederick, Md.: University Publications of America, 1984), pp. 18–48; and David Bordwell, *Making Meaning: Inference and Rhetoric in the Interpretation of Cinema* (Cambridge, Mass.: Harvard University Press, 1989), pp. 43–104.

◆ REFERENCES

1. See H. Stuart Hughes, *Sophisticated Rebels: The Political Culture of European Dissent, 1968–1987* (Cambridge, Mass.: Harvard University Press, 1988), pp. 3–14.
2. Quoted in Tomáš Mottl, "Interview with Jan Nemeć," in *The Banned and the Beautiful: A Survey of Czech Filmmaking, 1963–1990* (New York: The Public Theatre, 15 June–5 July 1990), p. 46.
3. Vera Chytilová, "I Want to Work," *Index on Censorship* **5**, 2 (Summer 1976): 17–20.
4. Mihailo Marcović, quoted in Gale Stokes, ed., *From Stalinism to Pluralism: A Documentary History of Eastern Europe since 1945* (New York: Oxford University Press, 1991), p. 120.
5. Andrei Tarkovsky, *Sculpting in Time: Reflections on the Cinema,* trans. Kitty Hunter-Blair (London: Faber, 1989), p. 110.
6. Jerry Rubin, *Do It!* (New York: Simon and Schuster, 1970), p. 86.
7. Quoted in Alomée Planel, *40 Ans de festival: Cannes, le cinéma en fête* (Paris: Londreys, 1987), p. 142.
8. Quoted in Sylvia Harvey, *May '68 and Film Culture* (London: British Film Institute, 1978), p. 123.
9. Marilyn Buck and Katen Ross, "San Francisco Newsreel," in John Stuart Katz, ed., *Perspectives on the Study of Film* (New York: Little, Brown, 1971), p. 235.
10. Quoted in Colin J. Westerbeck, Jr., "Some Out-Takes from Radical Film-Making: Emile De Antonio," *Sight and Sound* **39**, 3 (Summer 1970): 143.
11. Quoted in Abraham Segal, "Godard et le groupe Dziga-Vertov," *L'Avant-scène du cinéma* nos. 171–172 (July–September 1976), p. 50.
12. See Nagisa Oshima, "À propos *La Pendaison*," in *Écrits 1956–1978* (Paris: Gallimard, 1980), p. 188.
13. Quoted in John J. Michalczyk, *Costa-Gavras: The Political Fiction Film* (Philadelphia: Art Alliance Press, 1984), p. 46.
14. Ruth McCormick, "*One Sings, the Other Doesn't:* An Interview with Agnès Varda," *Cineaste* **8**, 3 (1978): 28.
15. Quoted in Jim Leach, *A Possible Cinema: The Films of Alain Tanner* (Metuchen, N.J.: Scarecrow Press, 1989), pp. 30–31.
16. Quoted in Stuart Liebman, "Why Kluge?" *October* no. 46 (Fall 1988): 13–14.
17. Quoted in John Sandford, *The New German Cinema* (London: Eyre Methuen, 1980), p. 102.
18. Jean-Louis Comolli and Paul Narboni, "Cinema/Ideology/Criticism," in Bill Nichols, ed., *Movies and Methods*, vol. 1 (Berkeley: University of California Press, 1976), p. 27.

24

DOCUMENTARY AND EXPERIMENTAL FILM SINCE THE LATE 1960s

Many filmmakers became more politically committed during the late 1960s and early 1970s, and this had long-range effects on both documentary and avant-garde films. Left-wing documentarists, often trained in Newsreel or other collectives, continued to work independently. In the mid-1970s several experimental filmmakers tried to merge avant-garde formal strategies with the criticism of ideologies. By the 1980s, social and political critique—often from the standpoint of feminists, homosexuals, and ethnic minorities—had become a central feature of the world's documentary and experimental filmmaking.

This development took shape against the background of other trends. In documentary, the Direct Cinema impulse continued, but often in a subdued form which merged it with more traditional methods. A few documentarists began questioning the very possibility of adequately recording reality. The experimental cinema was dominated by a reflexive and form-centered movement known as Structural Film. Eventually, reactions set in and other avenues were explored. Both documentary and the avant-garde were profoundly affected by the growing presence of broadcast television and home video.

DOCUMENTARY CINEMA

DIRECT CINEMA AND ITS LEGACY

Direct Cinema, in one guise or another, continued to be the most powerful force in documentary. The veterans David and Albert Maysles made one of the most important American *cinéma-vérité* films, *Salesman* (1969), a dogged chronicle of an unsuccessful Bible salesman begging, cajoling, and bullying prospective customers. For Allan King's *A Married Couple* (Canada, 1969), the director and crew lived with a Toronto family and shot over seventy hours of film; observing a string of quarrels, the filmmakers watched the marriage disintegrate.

The most widespread use of Direct Cinema was in the emerging genre of "rockumentaries." With the success of D. A. Pennebaker's Bob Dylan film *Don't Look Back* (1966) and *Monterey Pop* (1968), filmmakers realized that lightweight cameras and direct sound recording made it possible to shoot appealing films quickly and comparatively cheaply. *Woodstock* (1970) and *Let It Be* (1970) were records of single, memorable performances, while others were structured around tours. Both tendencies met in the most provocative instance of the genre, the Maysles' *Gimme Shelter* (1970). The film intercuts a Rolling Stones tour with a single concert in which the camera records a Hell's Angel fatally stabbing a member of the audience. The whole action is framed by the Maysles brothers' reviewing of the footage at the editing machine while Mick Jagger looks on.

Mercilessly parodied in *This Is Spinal Tap* (1984), the rockumentary proved to be the most theatrically successful documentary genre. Aimed at young moviegoers, it offered performances and sound quality unavailable on broadcast television. By the time Jonathan Demme made *Stop Making Sense* (1984), the concert had become secondary to the filming; David Byrne storyboarded the Talking Heads' performance for the shooting.

The dominance of Direct Cinema techniques led filmmakers to extend and interrogate them. Norman Mailer's *Beyond the Law* (1968) and *Maidstone* (1970) were semi-improvised narratives in the tradition of John Cassavetes's *Shadows*, with Direct Cinema veteran Don Pennebaker supplying cinematography. Some rockumentaries also included staged fictional scenes, as in *200 Motels* (1971), *Renaldo and Clara* (1977), and *Pink Floyd—The Wall* (1982).

More critical was Jim McBride's *David Holtzman's Diary* (1967); by using Direct Cinema techniques to treat a fictional man's life, McBride suggests that they are purely conventional. Similarly, Shirley Clarke's *Portrait of Jason* (1967) at first seems a pure instance of Direct Cinema. Clarke records long monologues of a black homosexual prostitute, and in the manner of Rouch, she hovers offscreen asking Jason increasingly probing questions. But Clarke also criticizes Direct Cinema's selectivity and invisible editing by keeping to a single camera position, using long takes, and acknowledging shot changes by letting the screen lose focus and fade to black. Thus *Portrait of Jason* resembles the work of Warhol: an exhibitionistic performer is berated by others (here, his friends offscreen) and collapses in psychic pain (Fig. 24.1).

McBride and Clarke were exceptional in criticizing Direct Cinema. More standardized uses of the approach continued throughout the 1970s and 1980s. The technology and techniques proved well adapted to capturing the filmmaker's personal experiences. Kazuo Hara's *My Intimate Eros: Love Song 1974* (Japan, 1974) records the filmmaker's obsessive search for the woman who has left him. In *Best Boy* (1979) Ira Wohl traces how his cousin, a middle-aged man with a learning disability, leaves his family to enter a

Fig. 24.1 Assailed by his friends for "acting," Jason breaks down (*Portrait of Jason*).

hospital. Michael Moore's ironic *Roger & Me* (1989) chronicles his attempts to confront the chairman of General Motors with the reality of Michigan plant closings.

Direct Cinema attracted other directors because of its ability to capture the immediate texture of social and political processes. The most famous filmmaker to exploit this capacity was Frederick Wiseman, whose Direct Cinema documentaries since the late 1960s virtually defined the "pure" extreme of the style. (See Box.)

FREDERICK WISEMAN AND THE TRADITION OF DIRECT CINEMA

In the spring of 1966, a middle-aged lawyer produced and directed a film about conditions at a Massachusetts hospital for the mentally ill. He filmed everyday activities as well as a show put on by the patients. The result, titled *Titicut Follies* after the patients' name for their show, was released in 1967 and set off a storm of protest. Since that directorial debut, controversy has pursued Wiseman through almost twenty feature-length documentary films. In the process, his work has become emblematic of Direct Cinema.

The Drew unit concentrated upon situations of high drama, and the Rouch-Morin approach to *cinéma vérité* emphasized interpersonal relations (Chapter 21). Wiseman pursued another path, focusing on the mundane affairs of social institutions. The titles are indicative: *Hospital* (1970), *Juvenile Court* (1972), *Welfare* (1975), *Sinai Field Mission* (1977), *Racetrack* (1985). *Law and Order* (1969) records police routine, while *The Store* (1983) moves behind the scenes of a Dallas department store.

Wiseman typically does not follow individuals facing a crisis or solving a problem. He assembles a film out of slices of day-to-day life in a business or government agency. Each sequence is usually a short encounter that plays out a struggle or expresses the participants' emotional state. Then Wiseman moves to another situation and other participants. He has called this a "mosaic" structure, the result of assembling tiny pieces into a picture of an institution. Using no narrator, Wiseman creates implications by making shrewd juxtapositions between sequences and by repeating motifs across the film (Figs. 24.2, 24.3). The meaning, he insists, is in the whole.

His first films reflect a conception of institutions as machines for social control. He declared himself interested in "the relationship between ideology and practice and the way power is exercised and decisions rationalized."[1] Wiseman records the frustrations of ordinary people facing a bureaucracy, and he captures the insular complacency of those used to exercising power. In his most famous film, *High School* (1968), secondary education becomes a confrontation between bewildered students and oppressive or obtuse teachers: schooling as control and conformity.

Fig. 24.2

Fig. 24.3

Figs. 24.2 and 24.3 The controlling hand as a motif in *High School*.

In his later work, Wiseman claimed to take a more flexible and open-minded approach reminiscent of Leacock's "uncontrolled cinema" (p. 568):

> You start off with a little bromide or stereotype about how prison guards are supposed to behave or what cops are really like. You find that they don't match up to that image, that they're a lot more complicated. And the point of each film is to make that discovery.[2]

This concern for complexity may be one reason that Wiseman's "mosaics" have grown to vast proportions. *Canal Zone* (1977) runs almost three hours, while *Deaf and Blind* (1988) consists of four two-hour parts. It is as if his search for comprehensiveness and nuance has forced Wiseman to amass more and more evidence, searching for all sides of the story. Nevertheless, in his films of the late 1970s "personal" confrontations continue to encapsulate micropolitical struggles for survival.

Wiseman carries on the Leacock tradition of fly-on-the-wall observation. The cameraman and the recordist (Wiseman) efface themselves (Fig. 24.4). The filmmakers ask no questions and hope that the subjects never look into the lens. Wiseman creates classical continuity through eyeline matches, cutaways, and sound overlaps. We seem to be on the scene, invisible observers of social rituals of authority and humiliation. Yet Wiseman insisted that his documentaries were subjective creations, "reality fictions" expressing highly personal judgments. Many of his targets agreed.

Fig. 24.4 A trainee's family admires his rifle during a visit to boot camp (*Basic Training*). As in a fiction film, the participants seem oblivious to the presence of the filmmakers.

Wiseman showed that the apparently neutral methods of Direct Cinema could create strong reactions through selection and emphasis. Yet some filmmakers believed that his films hid their "fictional" side. The films exemplified a "transparency" that documentarists would react against in the name of "anti-illusionism" and skepticism about the truth claims of Direct Cinema.

Fig. 24.5 *The Emperor's Naked Army Marches On*: The vengeful veteran assaults another ex-soldier when he refuses to acknowledge his role in wartime atrocities.

While Wiseman adhered to the American tradition of Direct Cinema, effacing the presence of the filmmaker, other directors adopted the Rouch-Morin model of provocation (p. 571). *Field Diary* (1982), by the Israeli documentarist Amos Gitai, begins with a very long take as the filmmakers move through a town in the Gaza Strip and try to interview its Palestinian mayor. They continually confront Israeli soldiers, who cover the lens and demand identity papers from the sound recordist (Color Plate 24.1). Kazuo Hara's *The Emperor's Naked Army Marches On* (1987) follows a Japanese veteran who insists that the emperor take the blame for war crimes. Tracking down witnesses, the veteran invades their homes (Fig. 24.5).

Claude Lanzmann's *Shoah* (1985), a twelve-hour document of the Nazis' extermination of the Polish Jews, recalls Resnais's *Night and Fog* (p. 563) in studying bland contemporary landscapes that were the sites of unspeakable cruelty (Fig. 24.6). Here, however, no stock footage takes us into the past; Lanzmann presents only what he called "traces of traces," interviews with witnesses, Jewish survivors, and former Nazis (Fig. 24.7). In the provocateur tradition of Morin and Marker, Lanzmann is present throughout, guiding, goading, and challenging his interviewees.

Shoah, Wiseman's films, and most of the others mentioned above, are quite pure instances of Direct Cinema. Each is built principally out of the

Fig. 24.6

Fig. 24.7

Fig. 24.6 The extermination camp at Belzic, seen today (*Shoah*).

Fig. 24.7 Dr. Franz Grassler, former Nazi officer: "We at the Commission tried to maintain the ghetto for its labor force" (*Shoah*).

Fig. 24.8 *Harlan County USA*: In a moment worthy of the Drew unit, the cameraman and sound recordist follow a sheriff reluctantly serving a warrant on a strikebreaker.

filmmaker-recordist's immediate confrontation with a concrete situation. Usually no narrator or nondiegetic music guides the audience's attention. The standard documentary format of the 1970s, however, was less stringent. It blended Direct Cinema interviews (often including an offscreen questioner), scenes shot on the fly (often without direct sound), and compilation footage, the whole glued together by commentary and music. De Antonio's *In the Year of the Pig* (1969) pioneered this synthetic format, which dominated the next twenty-five years.

A highly visible example is Barbara Kopple's *Harlan County USA* (1976). Chronicling a thirteen-month strike of Kentucky coal miners, much of the film is in the Direct Cinema vein. The camera crew records the strikers' changing tactics, with particular attention given to the wives' forming a strong picket line and blocking the entry of scab workers. The film has as much drama as any crisis-structure film from the Drew unit (p. 568)—quarrels among the strikers, thugs firing at picketers, and a confrontation between the women and the strikebreakers (Fig. 24.8).

Kopple frames the immediate drama, however, with background history concerning struggles in the mining industry. She draws upon archival footage and interviews with older citizens. And Kopple, a former member of Newsreel (p. 643), suggests broader points in the manner of De Antonio. There is no voice-over commentator, but superimposed titles supply basic information;

Fig. 24.9 Archival footage used to create Soviet-style montage: A newsreel shot of soldiers moving in to break a strike in the 1930s . . .

Fig. 24.10 . . . gives way to a shot of present-day police arriving to clear the roads, matched in frame position and direction of movement (*Harlan County USA*).

Fig. 24.11 Advertising imagery tapping pornographic appeals (*Not a Love Story*).

regional folk music comments sympathetically on the action; and editing patterns make points in a manner that Leacock would find judgmental (Figs. 24.9, 24.10). The result has the immediacy of Direct Cinema but supplies historical context and leaves no doubt about the filmmaker's sympathies.

The synthesis of Direct Cinema material, archival footage, titles, and music proved especially apt for examining controversial figures of the recent past, as in *Lenny Bruce without Tears* (1972), *The Times of Harvey Milk* (1984), *What Happened to Kerouac?* (1985), *Let's Get Lost* (1988, Bruce Weber), and similar portrait documentaries. Other filmmakers began to use the synthetic format to record lengthy processes. The makers of *So That You Can Live* (UK, 1981) revisited a Welsh family over five years, and the film chronicles not only the maturing of the family members but also the growing sensitivity of the filmmakers. Michael Apted's *28 Up* (UK, 1985) interviews people at ages seven, fourteen, twenty-one, and twenty-eight. Over the years of its making, the filmmakers increasingly stress the ways in which social class shaped their subjects' lives.

The synthetic documentary format also dominated critical political cinema. By putting "talking heads" into context, filmmakers constructed oral histories of social movements in *Union Maids* (1976) and *With Babies and Banners* (1978). *The Wobblies* (1979) traces the history of a left-wing party, while *Before Stonewall* (1984) does the same for gay culture and activism in the United States. Other filmmakers used the synthetic format to report on contemporary political struggles—nuclear power accidents (*We Are the Guinea Pigs*, 1980), civil wars in Latin America (*When the Mountains Tremble*, 1983), and apartheid (*We Are the Elephant*, South Africa, 1987).

When mixing archival footage with interviews, filmmakers oriented toward social criticism and change followed Newsreel and De Antonio in using individual testimony to challenge accepted positions or images. In *The Life and Times of Rosie the Riveter* (1980, Connie Field), a study of women who worked in the defense industry during World War II, information films about plant safety are undercut by women's accounts of accidents on the job. *Common Threads: Stories from the Quilt* (1989, Robert Epstein and Jeffrey Friedman) juxtaposes media coverage of AIDS with the personal stories of five people afflicted with the disease. The interviews in Bonnie Sherr Klein's *Not a Love Story* (Canada, 1981), a study of pornography, move along a spectrum of opinions, ending with an attack upon erotic advertising (Fig. 24.11).

The synthetic format proved central to the work of Marcel Ophüls (son of Max Ophüls). His four-and-a-half-hour film about the Nazi Occupation, *The Sorrow and the Pity* (Switzerland, 1970), identified him with the investigative political documentary. Ophüls brought to light a history that many French preferred to hide behind heroic Resistance legends. Newsreels and interviews portray citizens acquiescing comfortably to their German masters and turning a blind eye to the holocaust.

Either in its pure form or in the more synthetic version, Direct Cinema, along with its goal of recording social and political processes "behind the scenes," sustained political filmmaking throughout the 1970s and 1980s. At the same time, however, another trend was gathering force, and this called into question the idea that cinema could directly record any reality.

THE QUESTIONING OF DOCUMENTARY ACTUALITY

Political modernism, as defined by Godard, Oshima, Straub and Huillet, and others, set many documentary filmmakers thinking about their work. Throughout film history, and particularly since the advent of Direct Cinema, documentarists claimed to offer immediate access to reality. If the Brechtians' critique of "transparent" and "illusionist" filmmaking (p. 647) was right, though, documentary could appear even more manipulative than the Hollywood fiction film. Perhaps documentary only seemed to capture reality.

The problem was not that of the filmmaker's bias. Many documentarists had acknowledged their own subjectivity, and directors like Franju and Marker had made it integral to their essayistic films (p. 564). What came to the fore now was the idea that perhaps the very forms and techniques of documentary were invisible conventions, no more inherently valid than the conventions of fictional narratives. Most documentaries presented themselves as descriptions or stories; yet these very forms carried a persuasive effect, asking the audience to accept a tacit social or political perspective. Most documentaries used voice-over commentary; but who was the speaker, and whence came the voice's authority? Documentaries showed archival footage or on-the-spot interviews; but what gave these images any power to penetrate reality, to present not only facts but truths?

This line of thought was most explicitly posed by film theorists and critics (see Notes and Queries), but it was not merely academic. Documentaries became more reflexive, turning a critical eye on documentary tradition itself. A rudimentary instance is *The Atomic Cafe* (1982, Kevin Rafferty, Jayne Loader, and Pierce Rafferty). This compilation film reviews the history of the testing and deployment of nuclear weapons by the United States, from Hiroshima to the mid-1960s. In the De Antonio vein, commentary is reduced simply to subtitles identifying place, time, and occasionally sources of the footage. But much of the footage does not function as a transparent record of events. Since the shots come from educational and propaganda films, *Atomic Cafe* dwells on the ways in which these documentary genres spread oversimplified ideas of nuclear war (Fig. 24.12). The film implies that the public's acceptance of Cold War policies was strengthened by the conventions of popular media.

The reflexive film might go further and scrutinize its own use of documentary conventions. Raul Ruiz's *Of Great Events and Ordinary People* (France, 1978) takes its title from John Grierson's remark: "We wait for the cinema to give us an event, a great event which can show us ordinary people." Yet in this film events and people are visible only through the distorting lenses of the media. "What I am calling the everyday," remarks Ruiz the narrator, "is a parody of TV documentary." Ruiz mocks news broadcasts, Marker's *Le Joli mai*, and the talking-heads convention. Titles announce what we will see, promising "stock footage" and "shots which block the view" (Fig. 24.13). The film's ostensible subject—political attitudes in a Paris neighborhood before an election—is all but lost in tangents and rambling anecdotes. *Of Great Events and Ordinary People* delights in a digressive reflexivity that shows how much of reality the traditional documentary must ignore.

Fig. 24.12 A Cold War film uses animation to cure a pessimistic citizen of "nuclear blindness" (*The Atomic Cafe*).

Fig. 24.13 In Ruiz's *Of Great Events and Ordinary People*, an unidentified looker reminds us of the convention of over-the-shoulder views.

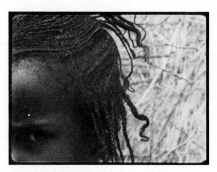

Fig. 24.14 Decentered framings and jerky editing accentuate the "invisible" conventions of the ethnographic film (*Reassemblage*).

Fig. 24.15 *Song of Ceylon*: As in Deren's *Ritual in Transfigured Time*, Jayamanne presents stylized images of social rituals. Unlike Deren, however, she criticizes ethnographic discourse by means of a dramatized sound track.

Chris Marker, an old hand at reflexivity and the essayistic form, contributed to the new "meta-documentary" with *Sans soleil* (aka *Soleil noir, Sun Less*, 1982), perhaps his most obscure and challenging film. A whimsical examination of the byways of Japanese city life is set against glimpses of other nations, while a woman's voice reads extracts from a man's letter about visiting a foreign country. In the vein of *Letter from Siberia, Sans soleil* questions current documentary clichés ("global culture," "the rise of Asia") while also interrogating assumptions of ethnographic cinema.

This interrogation paralleled work by others. Trinh T. Minh-Ha's *Reassemblage* (1982) films village life in Senegal in ways which refuse to transmit standard forms of anthropological knowledge (Fig. 24.14). Laleen Jayamanne's *Song of Ceylon* (1985) presents tableaux of western leisure activities and courting rituals, accompanied by an anthropological description of a Sri Lankan exorcism (Fig. 24.15). Invoking Basil Wright's *Song of Ceylon* (1935), made for Grierson's GPO Film Unit (p. 354), Jayamanne questions how western documentary traditions represent nonwestern cultures.

Another strategy of meta-documentary was that of making a film about the impossibility of making the film originally intended. One of the earliest instances was Marcel Hanoun's *Octobre à Madrid* ("October in Madrid," France, 1964); more recent ones are Michael Rubbo's *Waiting for Fidel* (Canada, 1974) and Jill Godmilow's *Far from Poland* (United States, 1984). Another reflexive documentary centered on an aborted project is Hellmuth Costard's *A Little Godard to the Production Board for Young German Cinema* (West Germany, 1978). The film begins with a director laboriously filling out an application for funding. Costard comments on the state of contemporary German cinema and the possibility of developing new equipment for super-8mm projects. The account of his (failed) application is intercut with a visit to Hamburg by Jean-Luc Godard, also failing to get backing for a film. Costard playfully accentuates his point—"Is it possible to make a work of unfettered imagination in Germany today?"—while revealing the processes behind the scenes of documentary filmmaking.

Some meta-documentaries of the 1970s and 1980s were even more skeptical, using reflexivity to explore the possibility that no documentary neutrally captures actuality. One implication of *Sans soleil, Reassemblage, Of Great Events and Ordinary People,* and kindred films is that any documentary carries a large freight of artifice—in its conventions, its appeal to ideology, and its reliance on the tricks of fictional filmmaking. Some documentarists began to doubt whether film could ever truthfully represent the world.

More commonly, as in *The Atomic Cafe* and *A Little Godard*, the film does not question the power of all documentary filmmaking; it seeks only to demystify certain forms or production processes. This moderate position has precedents in earlier documentary films, which used reflexivity in order to reveal a deeper truth that ordinary documentaries miss. In *Man with a Movie Camera*, for instance, Vertov shows people filming, editing, and watching the film we see; but this is in order to assert a new truth about reality, that of the harmonious integration of all labor into Soviet life (p. 148). Ruspoli's *Regard sur la folie* (p. 571) and Clarke's *Portrait of Jason* make us aware of the act of filming, but principally to assure us of the actuality of the events portrayed.

One of the most celebrated 1980s examples of this moderate position is Erroll Morris's *The Thin Blue Line* (1988). While revealing documentary artifice, Morris also tries to penetrate the truth of a murder case. As in the synthetic format of the 1970s, there is no voice-over commentary, and interviews with participants mingle with stock footage. Morris's reflexivity poses the problem of documentary reenactment by including highly artificial restagings of the crime and the investigation, including the police interrogation of their suspect (Color Plate 24.2). At first, the reenactments may seem merely dramatic license, but when they change to accommodate new or contradictory testimony, the film suggests that the original event can be known only through distant, and biased, retellings. Morris increases skepticism about his restagings when a judge tells of his father's seeing John Dillinger killed: the images consist of footage from an old gangster movie replaying the outlaw's death.

Yet out of the layers of lies, cover-ups, uncertainties, and conjectures a plausible case emerges—plausible enough that the film helped free a falsely convicted man. *The Thin Blue Line* grants that personal bias, cultural predispositions, and cinematic conventions often mislead us; but it also declares that the documentarist can find a persuasive approximation to truth. This is a more tentative position than that adopted by Vertov, Flaherty, or proponents of Direct Cinema, but it does secure a place for documentary as a legitimate way of discovering reality.

Whatever doubts western documentarists and theorists had about the truth of documentary, filmmakers in the disintegrating Soviet bloc seized upon the mode as a way of exposing decades of lies. The Polish Filmmakers Association sponsored *Workers 80* (1980), a record of the Solidarity movement. In Hungary, a strong documentary movement emerged, exemplified in such films as *Pretty Girls* (1986), an exposé of how the Miss Hungary pageant led women into prostitution. Most strikingly, under Mikhail Gorbachev's policy of *glasnost*, Soviet filmmakers began to make stinging documentaries about history and contemporary life. Films about the Chernobyl nuclear disaster, about the grip of Stalinism on everyday life, and about scandals in the military and the bureaucracy poured forth. Marina Goldovskaya's *Solovki Regime* (1988) shows how a monastery was used as a Stalinist prison camp. She follows *Night and Fog* in cutting between the camp in the past and its placid present, supplementing the juxtapositions with interviews, newsreels, and excerpts from a staged documentary about camp conditions. Juris Podnieks' *Is It Easy to Be Young?* (1987), mixes rough Direct Cinema techniques with provocative, Rouch-like interviews in tracing teenagers from their attendance at a 1985 rock concert to their participation in the Afghanistan war. As the Soviet Union and the eastern bloc countries began to shake free of communism, reflexivity was far from their filmmakers' concerns.

FROM STRUCTURALISM TO PLURALISM IN AVANT-GARDE CINEMA

During the late 1960s and early 1970s experimental filmmaking sustained its postwar renaissance. Established experimental genres and styles continued. Film portraits and diaries were still made—some, like Jonas Mekas's

Fig. 24.16 Marcel Broodthaers interviews the replica of Jeremy Bentham in *Figures of Wax* (1974).

autobiographical series, of mammoth length. The cut-out animation of Larry Jordan recalled the Surrealist collages of Max Ernst (Color Plate 24.3), and the Belgian artist Marcel Broodthaers used Dadaist strategies to question the instituton of the museum and art history (Fig. 24.16).

Perhaps the most innovative Surrealist work was done in Czechoslovakia by the animator Jan Švankmajer. Trained in the marionette section of the Academy of Fine Arts but influenced by Czech Surrealism of the 1930s, Švankmajer turned away from the mainstream animation developed by Jiří Trnka in the 1950s (p. 582). His first short film, *The Last Trick* (1964), combined puppets and frame-by-frame animation in a bizarre duel of two magicians trying to outdo each other with outlandish tricks.

In Švankmajer's films, images of fear, cruelty, and frustration exude black humor. Every object has a rich texture and tactile appeal, yet the events follow the illogic of dreams. Slabs of meat slither about; antique dolls are ground up and boiled into soup; faces in old prints stare enigmatically as enraged puppets smash each other with mallets. In Švankmajer's first feature, *Alice* (1988), loosely based on Carroll's *Alice in Wonderland*, the heroine dips her finger into a jar only to find marmalade laced with carpet tacks. *Dimensions of Dialogue* (1981) plays out a repulsive metaphor for communication: heads made of vegetables and tools devour each other and then vomit each other out (Color Plate 24.4).

The countercultural underground tendency also flourished after the late 1960s. Soon, however, the more commercially marketable elements of underground cinema obliterated its more experimental aspects. Andy Warhol lent his name as producer to self-consciously camp features directed by Paul Morrissey (e.g., *Trash*, 1970; *Andy Warhol's Frankenstein*, 1973). Amplifying the Kuchar brothers' parodies of Hollywood melodrama, John Waters produced *Pink Flamingos* (1972), *Female Trouble* (1974), and other low-budget films reveling in bad taste and shock effects. In a comparable vein were the early super-8mm films of the Spaniard Pedro Almodóvar and his first "above-ground" 16mm feature, *Pepi, Luci, Bom and Other Girls in the Neighborhood* (1980). By the mid-1970s, the underground film had become a marketable genre. It became the "midnight movie" or the cult film playing campus film societies, and it provided Morrissey, Waters, Almodóvar, and other directors an entry to commercial features.

STRUCTURAL FILM

As the underground film gained popularity in the late 1960s, a more intellectual approach to experimentation was taking shape. The American critic P. Adams Sitney called this tendency "Structural Film." Although Sitney later regretted using this term, it gained wide currency in experimental circles around the world.

If underground filmmakers emphasized shocking subject matter, Structural filmmakers stressed challenging form. They concentrated the spectator's attention on a nonnarrative shape or system that organized the film. Usually this form unfolded gradually, engaging the spectator in a process of noticing fine detail and speculating on the film's overall pattern.

A prime instance is Hollis Frampton's *(nostalgia)* (1971). It consists of twelve shots; in each one, a photograph resting on a hot plate slowly burns to ashes (Fig. 24.17). The single-take recording forces us to watch the images flame and crumble. The sound track also consists of twelve units, and in each module the narrator discusses his memories of each photo. But each chunk of narration describes not the photo onscreen but the photo that is to come next. The spectator imagines what the next photo will look like, but she or he can never directly check the description with the picture. By the time the photo appears, the verbal description is gone. The idea of nostalgia— a longing for a past that cannot be recaptured—is manifested in the very structure of the film.

Frampton's film is also about the process by which images are born and die, and this reflexivity is characteristic of Structural cinema. A Structural film might be "about" camera movement or photographic texture or the illusion of motion. In *Serene Velocity* (1970), Ernie Gehr creates pulsating views down a corridor by alternating shots in which only the focal length of the lens changes (Fig. 24.18). Structural films were often called "anti-illusionist" because they drew attention to the ways in which the medium transforms the object filmed. As in *(nostalgia)* the viewer becomes sharply aware of the act of viewing; one often "watches oneself watching."

Fig. 24.17 A photograph starts to burn on a heating coil in *(nostalgia)*.

Fig. 24.18 Alternating shots of a corridor, taken with a zoom lens set at different focal lengths, create a rhythmic push-pull effect in *Serene Velocity*.

Fig. 24.19 One of Yoko Ono's Fluxfilms consists exclusively of walking buttocks [*No. 4 (Bottoms)*, 1966].

Structural principles had been explored in earlier avant-garde works. *Eat* (1963) and other early Warhol films emphasized stasis and minimal change, while his use of entire camera rolls as the units of the film suggested a "modular" construction which was explored by Structural filmmakers. During the 1960s, Minimalist sculptors, painters, and composers also concentrated attention on bare-bones forms and slight changes in materials. Yvonne Rainer's dance piece "Trio A" (1966) focused attention on small movements and more ordinary, worklike gestures.

Particularly important sources for Structural Film were experiments by the loose group of American painters, composers, and performance artists known as Fluxus. Influenced by Duchamp's Dada work (p. 195) and Cage's theories of indeterminacy (p. 559), Fluxus artists sought to dissolve the bounds between art and life. They "framed" mundane events or actions—a dripping tap, a paintbox—as artworks. "Fluxfilms" pioneered the Structural approach, often by recording such banal gestures as eating and walking. Mieko Shiomi's *Disappearing Music for Face* (1966) records a fading smile at 2000 frames per second, creating onscreen movement so slow as to be imperceptible. Conceptual artist Yoko Ono made several Fluxfilms (Fig. 24.19) and with her husband, John Lennon, continued on a minimalist line. Their forty-five minute *Fly* (1970) follows a fly crawling over a woman's body.

Structural films vary in their organizing principles. Some center completely on a single process of gradual change, inviting the spectator to notice minute differences from moment to moment. For example, Larry Gottheim's *Fog Line* (1970) shows, from a fixed long shot and over an interval of eleven minutes, a field with fences and cattle gradually becoming visible as a fog lifts. This gradual-change approach usually relies on the static camera setup, the long take, or some form of rephotography. In David Rimmer's *Surfacing on the Thames* (Canada, 1970), an optical printer reduces riverboats to slightly changing granular patches reminiscent of Impressionist painting (Color Plate 24.5).

Other Structural films complicate their form through repetition. George Landow's *Film in Which There Appear Sprocket Holes, Edge Lettering, Dirt*

Fig. 24.20 *Film in Which There Appear Sprocket Holes, Edge Lettering, Dirt Particles, Etc.*: Loops of a laboratory test in which the woman on the right blinks but the woman on the left does not.

Particles, Etc. (1966) takes a strip of test footage featuring a woman's face, copies it so that four shots fill the frame, and then loops the result so that the strip accumulates scratches and dirt in successive printings (Fig. 24.20). Paul Sharits's films alternate solid-colored frames and tableaux of aggressive actions. The result bombards the viewer with flickering colors and subliminal imagery (Color Plate 24.6). Ken Jacobs's *Tom, Tom the Piper's Son* (1969) employs rephotography to dissolve a 1905 American Mutoscope & Biograph film into frozen gestures and patches of light and dark.

Several Structural filmmakers organized their work around a rigorous, almost mathematical set of rules. Kurt Kren's and Peter Kubelka's early 1960s work (p. 577) anticipated this tendency. In *Serene Velocity*, Gehr adjusted focal length according to a strict set of procedures, moving from the least distinct changes to the most radically different ones. J. J. Murphy's *Print Generation* (1974) is guided by a similar plan. After reprinting casual footage until it became blobs and smears of light, Murphy arranged the shots into arithmetical patterns that develop from dimly visible imagery to recognizable figures and then back into abstraction.

Structural filmmakers also explored the sort of "phase" patterns that fascinated minimalist composers like Steve Reich and Philip Glass. In Wojciech Bruszewski's *Matchbox* (Poland, 1975), a shot of a hand thwacking a matchbox against a tabletop is shown again and again, each time with the sound increasingly out of synchronization with the image. The spectator gradually notices the mismatch and then waits edgily for the return to perfect synchronization.

At its most elaborate, the Structural film combined several of these tendencies. George Landow's *Diploteratology or Bardo Folly* (1967) begins with looped footage of a woman waving and then moves to extreme close-up imagery that compares cellular structures to burning film. *Bleu Shut* (1970), a comic Structural film, contains an absurd system—a game in which contestants guess the names of boats—which is interrupted by looped imagery and concluded by people making grotesque faces at the camera (Fig. 24.21).

The most famous Structural film, *Wavelength* (1967) by the Canadian Michael Snow, offers a rich mixture of techniques. It begins as a descriptive study of a single loft apartment, with the camera fixed at a distance from the windows. People enter and leave, and a death seems to occur, but the camera refuses to budge, preferring to register the slight changes in illumination in the apartment. At the same time, the film flaunts a technique: the zoom, which abruptly and spasmodically enlarges the frame at intervals, indifferent to the action in the room. Over the forty-five minutes of the film, as the lens enlarges the back wall (Fig. 24.22), it reveals a photograph of waves on the ocean. (So the film traces a literal "wave length.") In addition, bursts of color periodically wash out the shot, serving as reflexive reminders of the flatness of the cinematic image.

Several of Snow's films reflexively display the resources of the moving frame. *Wavelength* exhibits the perceptual effects of the zoom; ⟷ (called *Back and Forth*, 1969) explores pan shots; *Breakfast* (1976) emphasizes how the tracking shot alters space (Fig. 24.23). For the majestic *La Région centrale* (*Central Region*, 1971), Snow filmed a rocky wasteland with a multiple-

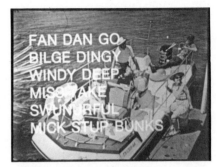

Fig. 24.21 Name the boat: One of the quiz shots in Robert Nelson's *Bleu Shut*.

Fig. 24.22 The camera zooms in on a distant wall, oblivious to the dead man in the foreground (*Wavelength*).

Fig. 24.23 The camera's movement across the table pushes the food against the wall, creating a cubistic flattening (*Breakfast*).

Fig. 24.24 Michael Snow adjusts his filming machine in the Canadian landscape; during shooting, the camera's gyrations were operated by remote control.

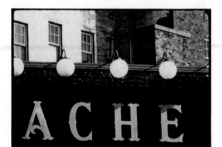

Fig. 24.25 *Zorns Lemma*: An "A" word.

Fig. 24.26 A 9.5mm home movie, with its central perforations, askew frame lines, and other "structural" essentials, whizzes through the frame in Le Grice's *Little Dog for Roger*.

jointed machine that executes pans, crane shots, and other movements (Fig. 24.24).

In the United States, perhaps the most versatile exponent of Structural Film was Hollis Frampton. Trained in science and mathematics but steeped in the history of painting and literature, Frampton declared his opposition to the romantic sensuousness of his predecessors. According to Frampton, to understand an artwork a viewer had to recover its "axiomatic substructure"[3]—a notion that made Brakhage shudder.

Frampton created important films in nearly every vein of Structural explorations. His *Lemon* (1969) epitomizes the film of gradual change. Reprinted loops create modules in *Palindrome* (1969), while *Artificial Light* (1969) presents wide-ranging variations on a central body of footage. Frampton based other films on mathematical procedures or elaborate private codes. *(nostalgia)* combines gradual-change techniques in the shot with out-of-phase combinations of sound and image.

Frampton's celebrated *Zorns Lemma* (1970) merges several strains within Structural cinema. The film's first section, over a blank screen, consists of a woman's voice reading an ABC rhyme taken from a colonial American primer. The second portion consists of one-second shots showing single words, usually found on signs (Fig. 24.25), arranged in alphabetical order. Gradually, as Frampton runs through the alphabet again and again, every time using a different set of words, each letter's slot is filled by an arbitrary image—fire, ocean waves, grinding hamburger. By the end of this section, the film has created a unique pictorial alphabet, each image correlated with one letter.

The film's final section consists of several long takes of a man, a woman, and a dog slowly crossing a snowy field as voices read a medieval text about light. While the middle section exemplifies the rigorously systematic side of Structural Film, the fixed camera and final long takes present a gradual change in the manner of *Fog Line* and other meditative works. The formal complexity of *Zorns Lemma* has invited a broad range of interpretations. Is it about the child's acquisition of language, the rivalry between sight and sound, or the superiority of nature and human relations to artificial systems like the alphabet?

Frampton's films, like other Structural works, often invite the spectator to watch himself or herself undergoing the very experience of the film. This "participatory" relation between the viewer and the film led Sitney to suggest that the Structural trend was fundamentally about human consciousness, the ways in which the mind builds patterns and draws conclusions on the basis of sensory information.

British filmmakers drawn to the Structural idea found this psychological approach disagreeable. At the London Co-op, "Structural/Materialist" filmmakers such as Peter Gidal and Malcolm Le Grice insisted that the most honest film was only about the medium itself. By drawing the spectator's attention to filmic qualities, the films produced knowledge about the "material" processes of cinema. Le Grice's *Little Dog for Roger* (1967), which subjects old home movies to a dizzying range of printing techniques (Fig. 24.26), exemplifies this stance. Structural/Materialist ideas influenced many British filmmakers, including Chris Welsby (*Seven Days*, 1974) and John Smith (Fig. 24.27), who turned landscapes into formal systems far more strict and elaborate than those visible in *Fog Line* and *Central Region*.

Outside the English-speaking countries, the Structural impulse had a less cerebral tint. Many filmmakers applied Structural techniques to erotic material. In Paul de Nooiyer's *Transformation by Holding Time* (Netherlands, 1977), a man photographs a nude woman in Polaroid snapshots and then mounts each one on a grid close to us (Fig. 24.28). The film's distinct shape is concluded when the photos fill the frame, reconstructing the woman's body from several vantage points. Other filmmakers used the static camera and rephotography of the Structural approach to evoke emotions recalling the film lyric (Color Plate 24.7). Through this hedonistic treatment of Structural premises, many avant-gardists kept the tendency alive through the 1980s.

Underground film reached a broad public through accessible humor and shock value, but most Structural films were aimed at a sophisticated audience interested in reflexivity and other rarefied aesthetic issues. The films' affinities with art-world movements carried them into museums and art galleries. The Museum of Modern Art and the Whitney Museum of American Art undertook regular screenings of experimental film, and the American Federation of the Arts began to distribute avant-garde works. A 1974 exhibition of Structural Film in Switzerland led several European museums to acquire prints.

Art schools and film departments also welcomed the intellectual rigor of Structural Film. In addition to its art-world affiliations, the trend offered excellent ways to introduce pupils to particular film techniques. As the discipline of film studies gained ground in the 1970s, Structural Film won academic support, and filmmakers moved into teaching positions.

Structural Film further benefited from an expansion of avant-garde institutions. In 1966, the Millennium Film Workshop of New York began as a production cooperative and screening venue. Jonas Mekas opened the An-

Fig. 24.27 Editing turns goalposts into purely material configurations in John Smith's *Hackney Marshes—November 4th 1977* (1977).

Fig. 24.28 *Transformation by Holding Time*: An underground image recast by a Structural sensibility.

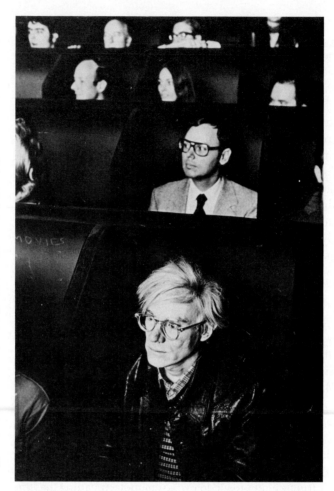

Fig. 24.29 Between 1970 and 1974, New York's Anthology Film Archives held screenings in the "Invisible Cinema," an auditorium designed to enhance each individual's absorption in the film experience. Here Andy Warhol sits in one of the auditorium's partitioned and shielded seats.

thology Film Archives (Fig. 24.29) in 1970 as a repository for a canon of masterpieces, including many in the postwar avant-garde. In response the Collective for Living Cinema (founded 1973) offered younger artists a venue. During the same period, filmmakers began to receive funding from the National Endowment for the Arts (established 1965), state arts councils, and the Jerome Foundation (established by railroad heir and experimental filmmaker Jerome Hill).

Cooperatives and collectives grew stronger. In Britain, Cinema Action and The Other Cinema were formed to distribute experimental work. Bruce Elder in Canada, Peter Gidal in England, Birgit Hein in Germany, and other Structural filmmakers wrote essays that attracted public attention and helped fund work in this vein. The British Film Institute expanded its aid to experimental production, as did the Canadian Arts Council. The Goethe Institute of West Germany and the Alliance Française offered touring packages of experimental films.

By the mid-1970s, formal experiment in the avant-garde film had gained support from cultural institutions throughout Europe and North America.

INDEPENDENT ANIMATION OF THE 1970s AND 1980s

With the decline of studio animation in the late 1960s, the cartoon became identified with children's entertainment, on television or in Disney's occasional theatrical features. But the sales of underground comics, the revival of interest in superheroes, the "graphic novels" produced in Europe and Japan, and the growing public for offbeat newspaper comics like Nicole Hollander's "Sylvia," Matt Groening's "Life in Hell," Lynda Barry's "Ernie Pook's Comeek," and Gary Larson's "The Far Side" showed that comic-strip art still attracted young adults and aging baby-boomers. In this atmosphere, new film animators came to the fore.

Some had clearly European sources. *Heavy Metal* (Canada, 1981, Gerald Potterton) derived from a French magazine of sword-and-sorcery fantasy. The twin brothers Steve and Tim Quay, Americans working in Britain, modeled their puppet animation on Jan Švankmajer's Surrealist fantasies. In the Quay's evocative *Street of Crocodiles* (1986), an emaciated figure explores a Victorian street whose buildings house decaying dolls, sawdust, writhing screws, and sinister machinery (Color Plate 24.8).

Other animators took their inspiration from the American tradition. Sally Cruikshank's cel-animation satires of American consumerism recall 1970s "headcomix" and *Yellow Submarine*, but the jazzy music and the incessantly pulsing backgrounds also evoke Fleischer's Betty Boop films (Color Plate 24.9). George Griffin's reflexive *Lineage* (1979) allows Mr. Blockhead to dial up any genre of animated film. Griffin's punning title refers not only to the history of the animated film but also to the "lines" with which he creates virtuosic parodies of early silent animation and the minimal abstract film (Color Plate 24.10).

More women began drawing comic strips in the 1970s, and more also took up animation. Often they expressed feminist concerns through evocative imagery or symbolic narratives. Susan Pitt's *Crocus* (1971) shows a couple's lovemaking interrupted by a baby's offscreen cries and by birds, a Christmas tree, and other phallic objects floating above them (Fig. 24.30). In Kathy Rose's *Pencil Bookings* (1978), the animator tries to discipline her errant characters (Fig. 24.31) and then joins them in their fantasy world.

In the West, most independent animators came from art schools and funded their work through grants and television commissions. The new animated shorts, no longer able to

Fig. 24.30 A cucumber hovers over the couple in *Crocus*.

Fig. 24.31 The realistically rotoscoped heroine confronts her cartoonish creation.

serve as theatrical fillers, were shown on alternative television and in film societies, museum programs, and touring programs such as the annual "Tournée" package of festival prize-winners.

Although avant-garde filmmakers never became central to "gallery culture," their work was considered worthy of academic analysis and public and private funding. Structural Film played a central role in making experimental film culturally respectable.

REACTIONS AND ALTERNATIVES
TO STRUCTURAL FILM

As institutional support expanded for the Structural project, North American filmmakers launched ambitious, even epic works. Michael Snow's *Rameau's Nephew by Diderot (Thanx to Dennis Young) by Wilma Schoen* (1974) runs four and a half hours. Its segments systematically explore paradoxes of language and sound effects in the cinema. Frampton conceived *Magellan*, a thirty-six-hour film to be shown in installments over 371 days. It remained unfinished at Frampton's death in 1984.

For many filmmakers, however, Structural Film was an overintellectual, apolitical dead end. Its acceptance as "high art" meant that the avant-garde had lost its critical edge. In addition, a younger generation who had not lived through the innovations of the 1960s had little sympathy with modernism, particularly in its purist guises. As a result, new experimental tendencies manifested themselves in the 1970s and 1980s. Some filmmakers revisited narrative. Others turned experimental techniques toward political criticism or theoretical debate. Still others embraced a harsh and passionate personal expression.

Structural Film, especially in North America, had been dominated by men, but the reactions to the Structural movement were led by women. This tendency paralleled the growth of feminist documentary and feature filmmaking during the 1970s. During the next decade, in the United States and Great Britain, minority women also played an increasing part in the changes in experimental cinema.

Perhaps the most direct development out of Structural Film was the "Deconstructive" film. The term (originally referring to a type of philosophical analysis) became applied to a certain kind of reflexive experimental work. Avant-garde films had for decades called attention to the cinema as a medium, from Vertov's *Man with a Movie Camera* (1928) through Conner's *A Movie* (1958) and the technique-centered Structural films. Deconstructive filmmakers went a step further. They targeted mainstream moviemaking, and they aimed to reveal its illusory artifice.

An early example is Hellmuth Costard's *Fussball wie noch nie* ("Football as Never Before," 1970). Here an entire soccer match is shown by concentrating on one player; we see the ball only when it comes near him. Inevitably, long stretches of empty time alternate with bursts of action. Costard's approach recalls that of Warhol and the gradual-process Structural film, but it primarily encourages the viewer to reflect upon the conventions of normal television coverage.

Deconstructive films often rework footage from an existing film, as does Ken Jacobs's *The Doctor's Dream* (1978), which reorders shots of a 1930s Hollywood fictional short according to an arbitrary numerical principle. The filmmaker may also create new scenes which display conventions of orthodox style. In Manuel De Landa's *The Itch Scratch Itch Cycle* (1976), a couple's argument is refilmed and recut so as to survey shot/reverse-shot options. A didactic example of the Deconstructive film is Noël Burch's *Correction Please; or, How We Got into Pictures* (Great Britain, 1979).

Deconstructive films such as these often targeted conventional narrative cinema. Yet in subverting storytelling, filmmakers had to invoke its conventions and appeals. This roundabout return to narrative was characteristic of a general interest in storytelling shared by many filmmakers seeking to avoid the impasse of Structural Film.

Women filmmakers were in the forefront of the return to narrative, with Jackie Raynal's *Deux fois* ("Two Times," 1970), Chantal Akerman's *Je, tu, il, elle* (France, 1974), Joyce Wieland's *The Far Shore* (1976), and the films of Yvonne Rainer. Rainer moved to film because of her wish to present emotion in a more direct way than she could in dance. Her *Lives of Performers* (1972), *Film about a Woman Who . . .* (1974), and *Kristina Talking Pictures* (1976) dominated the American "New Narrative" tendency.

Fig. 24.32 *Film about a Woman Who . . .*: Title questioning image.

Rainer's films take up subjects familiar from Hollywood melodrama—love affairs, relations among women, and definition of the self through memory. But the plots remain fragmentary, and character relations are vague or even inconsistent. The same character may be played by different actors; a voice cannot always be assigned to a figure. Dramatic events occur offscreen, presented on the sound track or in captions. Onscreen we see photographs and still lifes, performances and recitations. Occasionally a text interrogates the image (Fig. 24.32).

Journeys from Berlin/1971 (1980) exemplifies Rainer's approach. Several lines of material alternate. A rolling title chronicles West Germany's treatment of political criminals. There are long-held cityscapes, overhead views of Stonehenge and the Berlin Wall, and glimpses of a man and a woman on city streets. In a string of psychoanalytic sessions the doctor changes from a woman to a man to a child (Color Plate 24.11). We hear a young girl reading an adolescent's diary from the early 1950s and a kitchen dialogue between a man and a woman discussing revolutionary movements in the West. At intervals the camera tracks across a mantelpiece crowded with objects referred to elsewhere in the film, including a heap of spaghetti (Fig. 24.33).

Fig. 24.33 The mantelpiece as landscape and still life in *Journeys from Berlin/1971*.

Rainer's film is partly autobiographical, begun while she was living in Germany; but it also tries to find analogies between the political realm and everyday life, as when the patient's attempted suicide is paralleled to the death of terrorist Ulrike Meinhof. In a version of intellectual montage, *Journeys from Berlin/1971* confronts opposing facts and standpoints. Unlike Eisenstein's or Godard's dialectical editing of images, however, Rainer's montage juxtaposes pieces of language. For example, the kitchen dialogue of the couple constantly undercuts political ideals with the daily feelings of individuals confronted with ethical dilemmas. The dominance of speech in many New Narratives led to their being called the "New Talkies."

The New Narratives of the 1970s retained some of the rigor and playfulness of Structural cinema. Rainer's delayed hookups between image and sound (asking the spectator, for instance, to remember the spaghetti when the patient mentions it) recall the participatory processes of *(nostalgia)*. Structural impulses also returned in James Benning's films, in which sketchy narratives are played out in vast, gradually changing Midwest landscapes. His *One Way Boogie Woogie* (1977) carries color motifs and barely noticeable actions through sixty long shots lasting one minute each (Color Plate 24.12).

Fig. 24.34 In *Dallas Texas—After the Gold Rush* (West Germany, 1971), Wyborny creates mysterious dramas played in long shots reminiscent of early cinema.

Fig. 24.35 The home of Constance Fallaburr, adjacent to Zurich airport (*The Falls*).

Fig. 24.36 French psychoanalyst Jacques Lacan argued that the self first becomes constituted by an image at the "Mirror Stage" in childhood. This doctrine is represented when Mimi/Musetta meets another Mimi as herself in Sally Potter's *Thriller*.

The less studiously designed tableaux of Klaus Wyborny allow us equally brief glimpses of melodramatic situations (Fig. 24.34).

At another extreme, the Englishman Peter Greenaway gleefully disclosed obscure, exfoliating narratives lurking within nearly every structural principle—numbers, colors, alphabets. His films, though based on categorical structures, are far from minimal; they are jammed with whimsical anecdotes and arcane references. In *A Walk through H* (1978) an art exhibit turns into a fantastic journey through the paintings' mazelike landscapes (Color Plate 24.13). While *Zorns Lemma* employs the alphabet as a nonnarrative structure, in Greenaway's *The Falls* (1980) alphabetical order forms the basis of a three-hour survey of how a mysterious public health disaster affected ninety-two people whose surnames begin with "Fall" (Fig. 24.35). As the spectator struggles to assemble a larger story out of the Falls' dossiers, Greenaway parodies the clichés of experimental film through negative footage, tinted shots, looping, and rephotographed shots of rippling water.

During the 1970s, commitment to political modernism waned in the commercial art cinema, but it gained ground in the experimental realm. Influenced by Godard and Straub and Huillet (pp. 535–536), filmmakers used a minimal visual style and lengthy spoken commentary to criticize the political power of visual media and other sign systems.

One group of films, strongly influenced by contemporary film theory, combined storytelling with techniques drawn from Structural and Deconstructive filmmaking in order to criticize ideologies. For instance, Sally Potter's *Thriller* (Great Britain, 1979) cites classical storytelling in order to deconstruct it: Mimi, protagonist of Puccini's opera *La Bohème*, investigates her own death. This paradoxical plot line unrolls as an exploration of how women's identities are historically defined by language and conventional imagery. By means of ideas drawn from literary and psychoanalytic theory, *Thriller* plumbs the ideological underpinnings of myths and classic artworks (Fig. 24.36). Laura Mulvey and Peter Wollen's *Riddles of the Sphinx* (Great Britain, 1977) and Joanna Kiernan's *Dream-Work* (United States, 1980) also exemplify the trend toward "theory" films.

Fig. 24.37

Fig. 24.38

Fig. 24.37 The family portrait as stifling tableau in *Lawale* (West Germany, 1969, Dore O. Nekas).

Fig. 24.38 *Daughters of Chaos*: Girls together in a home movie.

Political filmmaking in the wake of 1968 posited that "the personal is political." By the mid-1970s many feminist filmmakers were finding political implications in the avant-garde's realm of "personal" filmmaking. Women filmmakers took up lyric and Structural techniques to reveal domestic space from the standpoint of women's memory and imagination. The way had been pointed by the Canadian Joyce Wieland (*Water Sark*, 1965; *Hand Tinting*, 1967) and the German Dore O. Nekas (Fig. 24.37). Younger filmmakers such as Michelle Citron (*Daughter Rite*, 1978) and Marjorie Keller (*Daughters of Chaos*, 1980) reworked their parents' home-movie footage in order to discover how female roles and attitudes take shape within family life (Fig. 24.38). Such films redefined the Brakhagean film lyric. Instead of yielding security and artistic inspiration, the home often creates anxiety, pain, and oppression, and the spontaneous self-expression of *Anticipation of the Night* is replaced by a suggestion that a sense of self is constructed through social processes.

Another social critique was driven by more belligerent emotions. In the late 1970s, Punk rock became a force in pop music, while Neo-Expressionism and graffiti art emerged in the world of painting. Jagged, visceral narrative films shot on super 8mm appeared in Manhattan music clubs, bars, and cabarets. Vivienne Dick's *She Had Her Gun All Ready* (1978) centers on the sadistic relationship between an aggressive woman and her passive partner. In Scott B and Beth B's *The Black Box* (1979), mysterious thugs kidnap and torture a young man (Fig. 24.39). The audience is assaulted in turn when the theater lights flash on and off in synchronization with the punishing rays of the "black box."

Rejecting virtually all avant-garde trends of the moment, Punk and "No Wave" filmmakers scavenged ideas from B movies, exploitation films, *film noir*, and pornography. Kodak's introduction of synchronized-sound super 8mm in 1974 enabled directors to shoot long dialogue scenes and enhance the films with a microphone buzz which would grate the nerves when magnified on rock-club sound systems. Punk filmmakers' assault on the audience expressed their rejection of contemporary society.

In the United States the hard-core Punk trend, tied to a volatile music scene and lifestyle, ended rapidly. Punk filmmakers moved to features and music videos, while the aesthetic was appropriated in the Punk-flavored features *Liquid Sky* (1983), *Alphabet City* (1984), and *Repo Man* (1984). In Lizzie Borden's dystopian *Born in Flames* (1983), aspects of feminist Punk

Fig. 24.39 A prototype of Punk and No Wave cinema: a production still from *The Black Box*.

Fig. 24.40 *Born in Flames*: Underground radio, with activist disc jockeys inciting revolt.

Fig. 24.41 From the bar scene of *The Deadman*: The "rough aesthetic," using Direct Cinema techniques and quasi-pornographic material in order to "defy the law to which fear subjects us."

meld with rap music in a portrayal of women guerrillas uniting to fight the government in a future society (Fig. 24.40).

Elsewhere, Punk and quasi-Punk movements took on longer-term significance. In Japan, college and high-school students created Punk-oriented super-8mm films with *noir* leanings, often inflected by ideas drawn from violent Japanese comic strips (*manga*). In Masashi Yamamoto's feature-length *Dark Carnival* (1981), a rock singer wanders through the Shinjuku area of Tokyo, discovering the ugly, horrific side of city nightlife. Shunichi Nagasaki's *Heart, Beating in the Dark* (1982) presents a tale of a young man and woman spending a night together copulating, the event interrupted by mysterious flashback and fantasy scenes; in some of these she portrays him and he plays another woman. An annual festival sponsored by a Tokyo magazine encouraged young filmmakers to create experimental small-gauge work, and festival winners found producers offering to back projects.

In the USSR, Punk 16mm filmmakers worked outside the official film culture in the early 1980s. With Gorbachev's new policies, this underground cinema surfaced. Many of its products, closely tied to Soviet rock and roll, were harsh, chaotic, and obscene in the American Punk vein. Evgeny Yufit founded what he called "necro-realism" in films of degeneracy, death, and absurdity shot in a frantic, rough-edged style.

The brutal intensity of Punk and No Wave was one more sign of a return to expression in the 1970s and 1980s avant-garde. Another indication was a defiant interest in pornography, criticized as a misrepresentation of women's sexuality but also celebrated as a subversive source of pleasure. Elfi Mikesch and Monika Treut's *Seduction: The Cruel Woman* (West Germany, 1983), with its sadomasochistic tableaux; Claudia Schillinger's *Between* (West Germany, 1989), with its fantasies of bondage and masturbation; Peggy Ahwesh and Keith Sanborn's *The Deadman* (United States, 1991; Fig. 24.41)—all aimed defiant gestures at mainstream viewers and fastidious avant-garde tastes. Warhol, who influenced undergound film, Structural Film, and Punk film, could also be discerned as one source of this aggressively erotic work.

Fig. 24.42 The masked and looped imagery of Structural Film, the New Talkies' use of intertitles to narrate the action, and handscratches reminiscent of Brakhage evoke dreams and a sexually charged anger in Su Friedrich's *Gently Down the Stream* (1981).

Some filmmakers aimed for a cooler, less emotional eclecticism. Film-makers joined artists in other media in ransacking both high and low culture, thereby creating what came to be called the "postmodern" avant-garde. (See Notes and Queries.) Barbara Hammer, Abigail Child, and Su Friedrich drew on Structural, New Narrative, and Punk techniques, as well as soap operas and *film noir* imagery, to present stories centering on childhood trauma and sexual desire (Fig. 24.42). The psychodramas of Cocteau, Deren, and Markopoulos had been set in mythical or exotic places, but in Leslie Thornton's *Peggy and Fred in Hell* series (1983–) the symbolic rooms and emblematic journeys are littered with bits of classic films, the Old Testament, citizens' band radio, and TV commercials (Fig. 24.43).

A tendency to ransack mass culture could also be seen in the assemblage mode pioneered by the Lettrists and Bruce Conner. Craig Baldwin's paranoid compilation *Tribulation 99: Alien Anomalies under America* (1992) linked conspiracy theories, science fiction, and Millennarian fantasies into a super-market-tabloid history of the world (Fig. 24.44). Even in the USSR a post-modern assemblage style emerged. The satiric compilation films of Igor and

Fig. 24.43 In the prologue to *Peggy and Fred in Hell* (1983), the little girl sings "Billy Jean" in a room cluttered with flotsam of the media age.

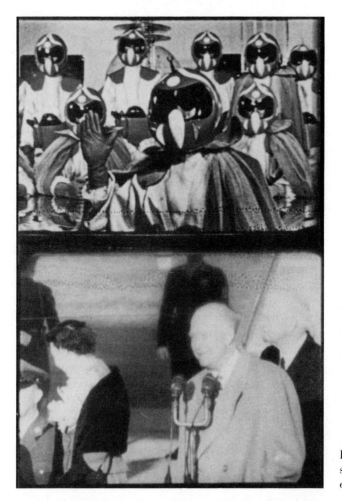

Fig. 24.44 *Tribulation 99*: In a tabloid-style juxtaposition, aliens from the earth's core greet President Eisenhower.

Gleb Aneinikov (*Tractors*, 1987) mock clichés of Socialist Realism in ways reminiscent of that unofficial Soviet version of Pop Art called "Sots Art."

At the end of the 1980s, observers of the international avant-garde cinema were split in their prognosis. For many critics, the fragmentary and diverse reactions to Structural Film, the soaring costs of 16mm, and the discontinuation of the super-8mm gauge all signaled the end of the postwar experimental film. Experimentalists, particularly in Europe where government subsidies supported more offbeat work, were seeking to reach mainstream or art-house audiences. In Britain, support for small-scale filmmaking was drastically cut in the late 1980s, while in the United States the National Endowment for the Arts began to refuse funding to work judged blasphemous or obscene. Museums' budget deficits forced them to orient exhibits toward broader tastes. In becoming an elite art, avant-garde film had become a province of universities, largely unsupported by the fine-arts market and prey to dwindling government funding.

There was a growing sense that in all media avant-garde activity had reached stasis. Many critics proposed that the idea of one stylistic movement succeeding another was no longer valid. In this sense, "postmodernism" was understood not as a particular style but rather as a steady state of pluralism. Artists would pursue a great variety of styles, none of which would dominate. If Structural Film was the last unified and widespread movement in experimental film, then the diverse, rapidly mutating responses to it suggested that the cinematic avant-garde had become "postmodern."

Yet in North America particularly, the avant-garde often reached beyond the art world to social minorities and subcultures. The 1950s filmmakers had drawn strength from the Beat generation; the 1960s underground films had won audiences in the counterculture; the Structural films and the New Talkies had taken root in universities, and the Punk films had arisen from the music-club milieu. Now the avant-garde won a following among groups defined by ethnic and sexual identity. These audiences did not care whether a film responded to the Structural trend; they were more concerned with films that articulated their interests and even entertained them while doing so.

The avant-garde had long nurtured gay and lesbian cinema. In the 1970s and 1980s, as gay activists openly challenged heterosexual society (Chapter 23), filmmakers made more frankly homosexual works. The West German Rosa von Praunheim undertook a string of militant quasi-underground films beginning with *It Is Not the Homosexual Who Is Perverse but the Society in Which He Lives* (1971), which surveys New York gay life through the experiences of a young man. More widely seen was the work of Derek Jarman, an English painter and set designer. Jarman's short super-8mm films are reminiscent of Brakhage in their jittery camerawork and of Warhol in their impassive treatment of male bodies. *Sebastiane* (1976), his first feature, sets its action in the era of the Roman Empire, and the film's dialogue is all spoken in (subtitled) Latin. Its loose plot follows the fortunes of a Christian soldier who is ultimately martyred as much for resisting an officer's sexual advances as for refusing to fight on pacifist grounds (Fig. 24.45). Jarman was a strong influence on the "New Queer Cinema" which emerged in several countries and which found an international venue at the New York Lesbian and Gay Experimental Film Festival founded in 1987.

Fig. 24.45 *Sebastiane* creates a homoerotic version of the saint's martyrdom.

Emerging African- and Asian-American filmmakers also worked in the experimental vein. In London, the Sankofa Film and Video Collective and other groups tackled British black issues while also absorbing avant-garde elements. For example, Martina Attile's *Dreaming Rivers* (1988), with its deathbed visions of a woman who has emigrated to London from the West Indies, has precedents in Deren's trance films.

The momentum and rhetoric of post-1968 political filmmaking continued in the "identity politics" of the avant-garde of the 1980s and 1990s. Marginality was celebrated, as it had been in the underground and Punk films. Gay, lesbian, and ethnic-minority films often sustained the viewers' sense of community. At the same time, several experimentalists sought to move toward mainstream or art-house audiences. By the early 1990s Derek Jarman, Lizzie Borden, and a few others had succeeded.

NEW MERGERS

Avant-garde and documentary cinema had mingled since the 1920s, and they continued to do so into the 1980s. Godfrey Reggio's *Koyanisqaatsi* (1983), an updated city symphony with a New Age aura, captured a wide audience. John Akomfrah's *Handsworth Songs* (Great Britain, 1986) merged the "race-riot" report and the experimental essay, while Isaac Julien's *Looking for Langston* (Great Britain, 1989) opened up the artist-biography film with imagery reminiscent of Cocteau. Some "alternative ethnographies" also straddled the two modes (Fig. 24.46).

The most far-reaching crossovers of the era, however, took place between film and the electronic media—television, cable, and videocassette. For documentary, the shift to the small screen was fairly smooth. Since the 1950s, television had been an important funding source and exhibition venue for documentaries; most of Wiseman's films, for instance, were initially made for broadcast. The introduction of *portapaks*—in 1965, cameras using 1-inch reel-to-reel tape, then in 1971 ones using ¾-inch tape in "U-matic" cartridges—gave video the flexibility of Direct Cinema. The U-matic system quickly replaced 16mm film for much broadcast reporting. Home video players, which went on the market in the late 1970s, increased viewer demand for compilation films (particularly combat footage) and how-to documentaries (sports training, exercise tapes, language lessons). The cassette format encouraged schools, libraries, and businesses to acquire documentaries.

The rise of video had a more complex effect on the experimental cinema. Throughout the 1970s, fairly strict lines separated avant-garde film from video art, which was largely confined to performance pieces and gallery installations. In the early 1980s, George Kuchar and Punk filmmakers embraced video when portable video cameras using ½-inch tape became available in Beta and VHS cassette formats. Some experimentalists clung to the vanishing super-8mm gauge, but by the end of the decade, avant-garde film and video art had grown much closer together. Festivals exhibited the two side by side; cooperatives distributed works in both formats; artists moved between them; and some works, such as Thornton's *Peggy and Fred in Hell*, employed both. Moreover, video distributors made avant-garde classics avail-

Fig. 24.46 Chick Strand's *Mujer de milfuegos* ("Woman of a Thousand Fires," 1976) presents a Latin American woman's housekeeping as a ritual that becomes ecstatically joyful.

Fig. 24.47 *Mongoloid*: Bruce Conner applies his associational compilation skills to a Devo tune.

able to the general public. Video fulfilled Brakhage's dream that average citizens could collect experimental films to watch at home.

At the level of form and style, the two media intertwined. Music videos borrowed from the avant-garde tradition, with many reworking conventions of the trance films. Some experimentalists' song-based films looked forward to the music-video format: *Scorpio Rising* furnished an early model, while Bruce Conner's *Mongoloid* (1978; Fig. 24.47) and Derek Jarman's *Broken English: Three Songs by Marianne Faithful* (1979) also pointed the way.

In the late 1980s, documentarists and avant-garde filmmakers freely incorporated television and video materials. The stylized reenactments in *The Thin Blue Line* refer as much to "true-crime" reportage as to Flaherty's restagings, while Todd Haynes's *Poison* (1991) cites not only Anger's *Fireworks*, Genet's *Chant d'amour*, and *film noir* but soap operas and "unsolved-mysteries" programs.

Structural Film continued the tradition of *cinéma pur* launched by Chomette and Dulac in the 1920s (p. 197). It aimed to expose "film as film"—its ultimate materials, its essential procedures. Yet Michael Snow remarked in 1989: " 'Film as film' is reaching its end. . . . Film will continue as a video representation/reproduction."[4] This prophecy is probably too absolute, but certainly experimental filmmakers, faced with the discontinuation of super 8mm and the great expense of 16mm, turned increasingly to the video format. By the end of the 1980s, Japan's New Cinema and the USSR's necro-realism had become largely video movements. Film-based works also found ways to cross over. *Tribulation 99* attracted "psychotronic" video fans, and Erica Beckman incorporated video games into *Cinderella* (1986; Color Plate 24.14). In various ways avant-garde filmmakers were appropriating the electronic media in order to expand their audience. The same strategy was pursued by Hollywood, on a scale appropriately more colossal.

◆ NOTES AND QUERIES

RETHINKING DOCUMENTARY

Direct Cinema, the documentaries of the 1960s and 1970s, and the more reflexive works of those and later years triggered a burst of interest in the history and practice of documentary cinema. Wiseman generated an enormous amount of attention, while certain films—*Salesman, A Married Couple, Gimme Shelter, Hearts and Minds* (1974)—became focal points of controversy. Alan Rosenthal's *The New Documentary in Action* (Berkeley: University of California Press, 1971) and *The Documentary Conscience* (Berkeley: University of California Press, 1980) present interviews with influential practitioners. His anthology, *New Challenges for Documentary* (Berkeley: University of California Press, 1988), gathers useful essays.

As documentary practice was changing from "pure" Direct Cinema to a more synthetic form derived from the work of De Antonio and others, film academics turned attention to matters of style and structure. Scholars built

THE IDEA OF STRUCTURE /693

taxonomies, distinguished trends, noted rejections of tradition, and explored questions of practice (reenactment, continuity editing) and ethics (the exploitative dimensions of Direct Cinema). For examples, see Bill Nichols, *Ideology and the Image* (Bloomington: Indiana University Press, 1981), and *Representing Reality: Issues and Concepts in Documentary* (Bloomington: Indiana University Press, 1992); Thomas Waugh, ed., *"Show Us Life": Toward a History and Aesthetics of the Committed Documentary* (Metuchen, N.J.: Scarecrow Press, 1984); Noël Carroll, "From Real to Reel: Entangled in Non-Fiction Film," *Philosophic Exchange* (1983): 5–45; and Willem De Greef and Willem Hesling, eds., *Image Reality Spectator: Essays on Documentary Film and Television* (Leuven: Acco, 1989).

THE IDEA OF STRUCTURE

Structural Film was one manifestation of a growing interest in film form during the 1960s and 1970s.

The wide-ranging intellectual movement known as "Structuralism" originated in France in the 1950s. Its proponents, such as the anthropologist Claude Lévi-Strauss and the linguist Émile Benveniste, argued that human thought was patterned somewhat as languages are. Consciousness and all its products—myth, ritual, and social institutions—were traceable not to individual minds but to collective "structures" manifested in language or other cultural systems. Although as a philosophical position Structuralism had largely collapsed by the late 1960s, its influence in the arts grew. Structuralist studies led film theorists to examine mythical patterns in Westerns and other genres. Examples of this approach are Jim Kitses, *Horizons West: Studies of Authorship within the Western* (Bloomington: Indiana University Press, 1970), and Rick Altman, *The American Film Musical* (Bloomington: Indiana University Press, 1987).

At about the same time, the issue of structure was broached by a competing tradition stemming from experimental music. Serial composition, as initiated by Arnold Schoenberg and Anton Webern, posited that the artist could control all "parameters"—melody, harmony, rhythm, and so on—by devising a single generative system. This serial conception of structure was elaborated more generally in Umberto Eco's *La Struttura assente* (1968) and was applied to film in Noël Burch's *Theory of Film Practice*, translated by Helen R. Lane (Princeton, N.J.: Princeton University Press, 1973; originally published 1969). Whereas the mythic approach emphasizes the organization of social meanings, the serial approach stresses the "purer" process of sheer pattern making.

Thus by 1969, when Sitney dubbed certain American films "Structural," the term had already taken on several meanings. He added yet another. In the Structural film, "the *shape* of the whole film is predetermined and simplified, and it is that shape that is the primal impression of the film."[5] Here "structure" means neither deep organization of meaning (the French Structuralist concept) nor serialist control of part-whole relations. Other critics found other terms ("minimalist film," "literal cinema") more apt, but Sitney's formulation crystallized the movement in the minds of viewers and filmmakers. Many subsequent films owe as much to his definition as to any films in the movement.

Important recastings of the idea of Structural Film can be found in a 1972 essay by Paul Sharits, "Words Per Page," in Richard Kostelanetz, ed., *Esthetics Contemporary* (Buffalo: Prometheus, 1978), pp. 320–332, and in two anthologies: Annette Michelson, ed., *New Forms in Film* (Montreux: 1974), and Peter Gidal, ed., *Structural Film Anthology* (London: British Film Institute, 1976). Malcolm Le Grice's *Abstract Film and Beyond* (Cambridge, Mass.: MIT Press, 1977) tells the history of experimental film from the standpoint of British Structural aspirations.

THE AVANT-GARDE AND POSTMODERNISM

Postwar experimental cinema, like the international art cinema, operated under the auspices of modernism in the arts (pp. 412–414). Frampton, for example, often invoked James Joyce's *Ulysses* as a model for his *Magellan* project. But the rise of Pop Art led many art historians toward a new tolerance of mass culture and a rejection of the grand ambitions of "high modernism." Artists in all media began to draw upon popular culture, to emphasize fragmentation, to acknowledge the power of the art market in the creation of trends, and to regard all styles of the past as equally available for parody and pastiche. These were some of the traits identified as "Postmodernism." The term itself, initially applied to a new style of architecture, spread quickly to the other arts and even became a name for the postwar era of "finance capitalism."

The most plausible candidates for Postmodernist experimental film came from the New Narrative, Punk cinema, and later developments, but historians of avant-garde film were reluctant to take up the concept. Film critics applied the term "Postmodern" more comfortably to commercial narrative films like *Blade Runner* or *True Stories* than to the works of Rainer or Greenaway.

Russell Ferguson et al., eds., *Discourses: Conversations in Postmodern Art and Culture* (New York: New Museum of Contemporary Art, 1990) includes interviews with many filmmakers, some of whom work under the "Postmodern" label. Noël Carroll argues that Postmodernism in film is better understood as "post-Structural-Film." (See his article, "Film," in Stanley Trachtenberg, ed., *The Postmodern Moment: A Handbook of Contemporary Innovation in the Arts* (Westport, Conn.: Greenwood Press, 1985), pp. 100–133.) For other views, see *Millennium Film Journal* nos. 16–18 (Fall–Winter 1986–1987) and J. Hoberman, *Vulgar Modernism: Writing on Movies and Other Media* (Philadelphia: Temple University Press, 1991). The literature on Postmodernism is voluminous, but one of the most accessible accounts is Robert Hughes, *The Shock of the New* (New York: Knopf, 1981), pp. 324–409. An important statement is Frederic Jameson, *Postmodernism; or, the Cultural Logic of Late Capitalism* (Durham, N.C.: Duke University Press, 1991).

◆ REFERENCES

1. Quoted in Ira Halberstadt, "An Interview with Fred Wiseman," *Filmmakers News-letter* **7**, 4 (February 1974): 25.
2. Quoted in Thomas W. Benson and Carolyn Anderson, *Reality Fictions: The Films of Frederick Wiseman* (Carbondale: Southern Illinois University Press, 1989), p. 149.
3. Hollis Frampton, "Notes on Composing in Film," in *Circles of Confusion: Film—Photography—Video: Texts 1968–1980* (Rochester, N.Y.: Visual Studies Workshop Press, 1983), p. 119.
4. Quoted in *International Experimental Film Congress* (Toronto: Art Gallery of Ontario, 1989), p. 42.
5. P. Adams Sitney, "Structural Film," in Sitney, ed., *The Film Culture Reader* (New York: Praeger, 1970), p. 327.

25

HOLLYWOOD'S FALL AND RISE: SINCE THE 1960s

In the United States, between the late 1960s and the early 1970s, social activists clashed with authority to an extent not seen since the Great Depression. The liberal stance of the civil rights movement had given way to the more radical position of Black Power. Opposition to U.S. involvement in the Vietman War had intensified. Martin Luther King and Robert F. Kennedy were assassinated; police attacked demonstrators during the 1968 Chicago Democratic party convention; and President Nixon widened the war. Campuses exploded; 400 closed or went on strike during 1970.

The withdrawal of U.S. forces from Vietnam in 1973 could not heal the deep divisions in American society which the war had created. The New Left collapsed, partly due to internal disputes, partly because the shooting of students at Kent State University in 1970 seemed to prove the futility of organized action. Nixon rose to power partly on middle-class voters' resentment of eastern liberals, the left, and the counterculture.

The international upheavals of this period led to a critical political cinema (Chapter 23). Emile De Antonio, the Newsreel group, and other American filmmakers practiced an "engaged" filmmaking of social protest. At the same time, the Hollywood industry tried to woo the younger generation with countercultural films, and the effort brought forth some experiments in creating an American art cinema.

Responding to the U.S. government's turn to the right in the early 1970s, left and liberal activists embraced a "micropolitics." They sought grass-roots social change by organizing around concrete issues (abortion, race- or gender-based discrimination, welfare or environmental policy). Many American documentary filmmakers participated in these movements (p. 643). At the same period, however, this activism was fiercely opposed by the rise of the "New Right," conservative organizations which proved able to organize local support for school prayer, the abolition of newly won abortion rights, and other issues. The struggle between reform movements and New Right forces was to become the central political drama after the mid-1970s, and many films (*Jaws, Nashville, 9 to 5, Tootsie*) bear the traces of it.

The drama was played against the backdrop of a waning U.S. economy, prey to oil embargoes and brisk competition from Japan and Germany. The 1970s ended the postwar era of prosperity. This period coincides with Hollywood's rediscovery of the blockbuster and the rise to power of the "movie brats," the most influential ones (George Lucas, Steven Spielberg, Francis Ford Coppola) becoming the new creative leaders of the industry.

The Reagan administration (1980–1988), largely a representation of New Right agendas, relaxed controls on business and rolled back 1960s social programs. During this period of increased financial speculation more conglomerates acquired Hollywood firms, and such enterprises found ways to tie films to music and publishing subsidiaries.

As a figurehead, Reagan provided an image of an America once more in possession of superior values and know-how. Although this image crumbled in the face of mounting federal deficits and the Iran-Contra scandal, Reagan could claim credit for occupying the White House when eastern European countries and the Soviet Union were beginning to break with Cold War policy. A movie-star president who used lines from Warner Bros. pictures in his speeches, whose high-technology Strategic Defense Initiative was nicknamed "Star Wars," and who was wounded in an assassination attempt by a young man obsessed with *Taxi Driver*—in all these ways, Reagan typified the extent to which Hollywood film pervaded the very consciousness of the country. But in the 1980s, American cinema was no longer trying to be countercultural. Addressing diverse audiences, becoming a major source of "infotainment" news and commentary, it was at the center of mass culture.

The Film Industry:
Recession and Rejuvenation

Ben-Hur, The Sound of Music, Doctor Zhivago, and other big productions of the early and middle 1960s won unprecedented profits. Producers eagerly sank huge sums into more blockbusters, hoping that they offered an answer to the threat of television. But costly flops like *Doctor Dolittle* (1967) and *Star!* (1968) proved that the strategy could lead to disaster. At the same time, the major companies faced new competition from "instant majors" like the TV networks ABC and CBS, which began producing theatrical films. Moreover, American movie attendance leveled out at about 1 billion each year.

The prosperity of the 1960s ended. Between 1969 and 1972 the major companies lost $500 million. As recession gripped the industry, banks forced companies to cut back production, cooperate with competitors, and avoid big-budget films. Exhibitors began building cheap shopping-mall theaters and dividing older houses into two or more auditoriums. The result was a generation of shoe-box theaters with poor sight lines and garbled sound.

Producers cast about for new attractions. One possibility was opened by changes in national censorship standards. Throughout the 1950s and 1960s, the power of the Hays Office to dictate film content had been eroding. By the mid-1960s, many major films were distributed without a Production Code seal, and others won a seal despite nudity or profanity. When *Who's Afraid of Virginia Woolf?* (1966) won huge profits despite requiring that under-eighteen patrons be accompanied by an adult, the way was paved for indus-trywide classifications.

In 1968, the MPAA companies created a rating system coded by letter: G (general; all ages admitted), M (mature; adults and mature young people), R (restricted; viewers under sixteen to be accompanied by parent or guard-ian), and X (no one under sixteen admitted). The new system presented the industry as being sensitive to public concern while still allowing filmmakers license to represent violence, sexuality, or unorthodox ideas. The new latitude helped make hits out of *Bob & Carol & Ted & Alice* (1969), *The Wild Bunch* (1969), and *Midnight Cowboy* (1969). Many later films succeeded by pushing the standards of acceptability further. Eventually the rating system was re-vised, raising the age for R and X films and replacing the "mature" category with "PG" (indicating films for which "parental guidance" was suggested).

Recession-driven producers also noted that *The Graduate* (1967) and *Bonnie and Clyde* (1967) had garnered huge ticket sales by appealing to young audiences. Nearly half of U.S. filmgoers were between sixteen and twenty-four years old. Studios launched a cycle of "youthpix," films which offered subject matter unavailable on television. The prototypical youth movie was *Easy Rider* (1969), a chronicle of two drug dealers' motorcycle trip across America. Made for less than half a million dollars, it became one of the most successful films of its year and triggered a host of imitators.

The youthpix cycle included films of campus rebellion (e.g., *The Straw-berry Statement*, 1970), countercultural dramas (*Alice's Restaurant,* 1969), nostalgia pieces (*The Last Picture Show*, 1971), and anarchic comedies (*M*A*S*H*, 1970; *Harold and Maude*, 1971). When *Yellow Submarine* (Great Britain, 1968, George Dunning) became a phenomenal hit by offering a string of "psychedelic" vignettes illustrating Beatles songs, producers realized that animation could also win college audiences. Ralph Bakshi aimed *Fritz the Cat* (1972), the first cartoon to receive an X rating, at an audience accustomed to the drugs-and-free-love ethos of underground comics (Color Plate 25.1). Bruno Bozzetti's Italian feature, *Allegro non troppo* (1976, Color Plate 25.2), a parody of *Fantasia*, also found success, partly because of the Disney film's reputation as a "head" movie.

The films of student rebellion proved unsuccessful, but countercultural attitudes, diluted to mockery of the establishment and celebration of sex and drugs, eventually proved marketable. Gross, youth-oriented slapstick come-dies starring Cheech Marin and Tommy Chong (*Up in Smoke*, 1978) and performers associated with the television show "Saturday Night Live" (Chevy Chase, Bill Murray, John Belushi, Dan Aykroyd, Steve Martin), as well as films directed by John Landis (*Animal House*, 1978) and Ivan Reitman (*Meatballs*, 1979), became staple program pictures and helped pull Hollywood out of its slump.

In the early and mid-1970s the industry also benefited from several box-office hits. Many of these traded on familiar genres (the war film *Patton*, 1970; the musical *Fiddler on the Roof*, 1971; the caper film *The Sting*, 1973), and some were throwbacks to the blockbuster strategy of the 1960s (e.g., a cycle of "disaster" pictures starting with *The Poseidon Adventure*, 1972). But more striking was a string of modestly budgeted but stupendously successful films by young or unknown directors: Francis Ford Coppola's *The Godfather* (1972), William Friedkin's *The French Connection* (1971) and *The Exorcist* (1973; Fig. 25.1), George Lucas's *American Graffiti* (1973) and *Star Wars* (1977), John Avildsen's *Rocky* (1976), and Steven Spielberg's *Jaws* (1975) and *Close Encounters of the Third Kind* (1977).

During the boom of the early and mid-1970s, most major firms had at least one top hit, so the industry as a whole maintained its stability. Studios recently threatened with bankruptcy found their profits hitting unprecedented levels. *Jaws* surpassed $100 million in domestic rentals. *Star Wars* approached $200 million domestically; by 1980 it had grossed $500 million worldwide. The industry's overall rentals from domestic and foreign release increased about $200 million per year, reaching $2 billion in 1979.

The new prosperity created changes. Now the industry's success was based on very few films. In any year, only ten or so "must-see" pictures gained the bulk of admissions, while most of the Majors' releases did not break even. The industry therefore sought to minimize the risks. Assuming that too much competition would hurt all parties, the Majors released no more than 150 films per year, often many fewer. Companies began releasing their big-budget films in the peak leisure periods, summer and Christmas. Following the lead of exploitation companies like AIP, studios filled television with advertising and released films in hundreds of theaters on the same day.

When viewers returned to *Jaws* over and over, distributors learned that it was profitable to extend runs for big films. In planning productions, studios opted for sequels and series which were based on successes, such as the *Rocky* films, the sequels to *Star Wars*, and the Indiana Jones series launched with *Raiders of the Lost Ark* (1981). Moreover, the success of *Star Wars* toys, T-shirts, and other spin-offs convinced studios to create their own merchandising divisions. By 1990, movie-related items had generated nearly $90 billion of income.

The boom years of the 1970s brought new companies to the film business. "Mini-majors" like Orion and Cannon, as well as low-budget independents, moved in. On the whole, however, the market was ruled by familiar players. The seven firms that dominated production were the companies controlling distribution as well: Warner Communications, Gulf + Western (Paramount), Disney, MCA (Universal), MGM/UA Corporation, 20th Century-Fox, and Columbia. Although several now belonged to conglomerates (see Box), these firms had controlled the industry since the 1920s. They produced only about one-third of all films released in the United States, but they garnered 90 percent of all revenues.

Fig. 25.1 *The Exorcist*, an adaptation of a best-selling horror novel, aroused controversy with its blasphemous language and its shocking special effects. Here, thanks to a life-sized puppet, the possessed Regan mockingly rotates her head.

THE VICISSITUDES OF THE HOLLYWOOD MAJORS

The decline of the studios in the 1960s made them vulnerable to absorption by conglomerates, giant firms owning companies in a wide range of industries. Kinney National Services had wide-ranging interests in parking lots, recording companies, and sports before buying Warner Bros. Gulf + Western, purchaser of Paramount, owned Madison Square Garden, financial services, and publishing houses. The recession of the late 1960s and early 1970s brought in new managers, often from other industries, and many representatives of the prime studio years withdrew: Jack Warner retired in 1967, Darryl Zanuck in 1971.

As the industry began to prosper in the 1970s, Fox and Columbia diversified their investments on the conglomerate model. They ventured into pinball games, soft-drink bottling, and skiing. Most film companies retained strong ties to the music industry as well.

In the 1980s, in the wake of unprecedented profits, a new round of acquisitions began. Fox and Columbia were purchased by financial interests lying outside the United States. Conglomerates like Warner Communications and Gulf + Western (renamed Paramount Communications Incorporated) began concentrating on leisure-time activities, with their film companies playing a central role in this strategy.

1962 Music Corporation of America (MCA) acquires Universal Pictures.

1966 Gulf + Western Industries buys Paramount Pictures.

1967 Seven Arts buys Warner Bros.
Transamerica Corporation buys United Artists.

1968 Financier Kirk Kerkorian acquires control of MGM and then sells most of its assets.

1969 Warner Bros.–Seven Arts merges with Kinney National Services to become Warner Communications, Inc.

1981 MGM buys United Artists from Transamerica Corporation.
Entrepreneur Marvin Davis buys 20th Century-Fox.

1982 Coca-Cola buys Columbia Pictures.

1984 Roy E. Disney, Walt's nephew, takes over Disney and installs new management.

1985 Cable-TV mogul Ted Turner purchases MGM; later, after failing to make loan payments, Turner resells all MGM assets except laboratory and film library.
Publishing magnate Rupert Murdoch acquires 20th Century-Fox.

1989 Sony Corporation buys Columbia Pictures from Coca-Cola.
Time, Inc., purchases Warner Communications, Inc.

1990 Matsushita Electric Industrial Company purchases MCA, which controls Universal.
Pathé Communications buys MGM.

1992 The European bank Crédit Lyonnais forecloses on loans to MGM/UA and takes over the company.

As ever, the Majors controlled domestic and international distribution of U.S. films. A film financed outside the studios could not get widely screened unless it was distributed by a top company. The standard distribution fee, 30 percent, came directly from gross rentals, thus delaying profits for investors or filmmakers. *Jaws* and *Star Wars* earned enormous distribution income for Universal and 20th Century-Fox, respectively, over and above any investments the studios made in the productions.

In the absence of a mass-production studio system, the major companies had to compete for projects initiated outside. An independent producer might assemble a package consisting of script, director, and stars. Alternatively, a director or star might set up a project. Increasingly, agents were gathering their clients into packages, a strategy developed by Michael Ovitz's Creative Artists Agency.

Filmmakers depended upon the major companies for financing, studio facilities, and distribution. Studio executives—often conglomerate employees with little experience in motion pictures—gambled that producers, directors, and stars with strong track records were worth the increasing investments. Spielberg and Lucas became powerful producers who could find financing anywhere and could even demand reductions in distribution fees.

Accordingly, the 1970s initiated an era dominated by "the deal." Agents, executives, and creative personnel devoted greater energy to the long negotiations necessary to satisfy all participants in a package. "Development deals" generated income for the agents, producers, scriptwriters, and stars, but most resulted in no completed film. "Overall deals" paid stars and directors to develop "vanity projects" for studios. Executives hoped that such "housekeeping" deals would make the beneficiaries willing to participate in other studio projects. Many filmmakers complained that shooting pictures had become secondary to making deals.

As successful filmmakers gained more control over their projects, budgets often inflated. Coppola's *Apocalypse Now* (1979) took three years to shoot, cost over $30 million, and initially ran seven and a half hours. Even highly successful directors were not immune to cost overruns, as Spielberg's *1941* (1979) showed. The most notorious failure of the system involved Michael Cimino's *Heaven's Gate* (1980), an ambitious Western. The budget rose to $40 million, the highest production cost of the 1970s. After the director's cut had a disastrous premiere, United Artists released a shortened version. It earned less than $2 million in rentals.

Despite such miscalculations, budgets continued to expand over the next decade. The average costs of producing and promoting a film rose from about $16 million in 1983 to over $40 million in 1992. Yet the industry continued to thrive. In 1990, world rentals of Hollywood movies reached an all-time high of $3.5 billion. Internationally, total admissions held steady, and in key markets, such as Japan and Australia, ticket sales for U.S. films rose. *E.T.* (1982) was the first film to surpass $200 million in rentals. Other top-grossing pictures emerged: *The Empire Strikes Back* (1980), *Return of the Jedi* (1983), *Ghostbusters* (1984), *Beverly Hills Cop* (1984), *Top Gun* (1986), *Batman* (1989), the Indiana Jones series, *Home Alone* (1990), *Terminator 2: Judgment Day* (1991), *Dances with Wolves* (1991), *The Bodyguard* (1992), and *Jurassic Park* (1993).

Producers discovered that hits could be exploited to an unprecedented extent. Sequels, which had had a spotty record before the 1970s, were proved viable with *The Godfather, Part II* (1974). *Rocky, Rambo, Star Trek*, and other "Roman-numeral movies" followed. Series, long associated with studio B pictures, were considered a good investment after the success of the James Bond films, and soon Indiana Jones, Freddy Kruger, and other protagonists were stabilizing investments in a string of pictures.

Conglomerate ownership accelerated trends toward making a film part of a product line of toys, clothes, and other spin-offs. In a process called "synergy," a film could feed the conglomerate's record label, musical artists, satellite and cable video divisions, and merchandising. Warner Communications Incorporated, for instance, revamped the image of Batman in its comic books before making the film *Batman* (1989), which in turn yielded Batman merchandise and two sound-track albums, one by Warner-contracted rock star Prince.

Outside forces continued to acquire major companies. The Japanese company Matsushita purchased MCA (Music Corporation of America) and Universal, and Sony bought Columbia. Pathé Communications acquired MGM, but after the studio ran up massive debt, the French bank Crédit

Lyonnais acquired it through foreclosure in 1992. More foreign financing flowed into American production, notably from France's pay-television channel Canal Plus.

U.S. admission income grew steadily as well, although increasing percentages demanded by distributors often limited exhibitors' profits. (As much as one-third of a theater's income derived from snack concessions.) Films were increasingly financed out of guarantees put up by exhibitors, who shouldered a greater risk to get access to the next Lucas or Spielberg success. Exhibitors also began replacing the sticky-floored mall shoeboxes with better-kept and more luxurious theaters. Cineplex Odeon, a Canadian firm emphasizing state-of-the-art technology and comfort, created a trend toward large and sumptuous "multiplexes," or multiple-screen theaters. By the end of the 1980s the number of screens in the United States had risen to almost 24,000, a postwar high. Most of these were in suburban areas; the small-town movie house was dead.

Soon conglomerates holding film production and distribution companies began to acquire theater chains. By 1991, MCA owned both Cineplex Odeon and Universal Studios. This practice bypassed the antimonopoly decrees of 1948 and signaled the return of the vertically integrated company of the studio era.

EXPANSION INTO VIDEO

The industry's 1980s prosperity was due partly to new technologies. As pay television emerged in the late 1970s, studios began selling film rights to HBO, Showtime, and other cable services. Cable showing became another phase in a film's life, coming after in-flight airline screenings and before network broadcast. Soon cable firms were financing movies and buying cable rights before production. Disney created its own channel, while other companies purchased interests in cable firms. Later, in the early 1990s, the pattern would reverse, with big cable companies buying interests in theater chains and planning to finance studio films for pay-per-view programming which would compete with first-run theatrical releases of the same titles.

The videocassette recorder also helped the film industry to new profits. Japan's Sony corporation began marketing the Betamax home machine in 1975, and Matsushita introduced its Video Home System (VHS) soon after. Home video expanded rapidly throughout the world; by 1988, most U.S. households had a VCR.

At first film companies were suspicious of the videocassette. Surely home playback would eliminate moviegoing, and taping movies would destroy future markets. Skirmishes ensued, notably in 1976 when MCA and Disney sued to stop the sale of VCRs on the grounds that taping infringed copyright. But soon, after it became clear that video did not damage U.S. theatrical attendance, the major companies realized that the videocassette could earn them still more money. The studios established divisions to make and distribute cassettes of their films. Sales to rental stores, particularly the growing national chains, proved very lucrative. This practice recast the multiple-run system of Hollywood's heyday, with a film's theatrical second or third run being replaced by its release on cassette.

Distributors also found to their delight that if a videotape was priced reasonably, many viewers would buy it. Paramount daringly offered *Flashdance* (1983) for cassette purchase while the film was still playing in theaters; the cassette version not only sold well but increased the film's theater business.

By 1986, at least half of major film companies' domestic revenues came from videocassette sales. Some industry analysts predicted that this market would soon provide the bulk of revenues. At the close of the 1980s, a hit film could earn $10 million worldwide from cassette sales, and even an average title could draw $3 or $4 million. Home video thereby helped Hollywood firms reduce the risks of production. In addition, it intensified interest in first-run films. A theatrical run generated publicity and commentary which helped a film to succeed on videocassette. More recently, popular films also spawned video games, and studios began creating their own game subsidiaries.

The industry's resurgence in the 1970s set the pattern for its conduct over the next two decades. Throughout the 1970s and 1980s, only one film in ten showed a profit, and this encouraged producers to keep banking on blockbusters. As usual, some very expensive films failed in theaters, while receipts from others, such as *Terminator 2*, justified huge budgets. The disappointing returns of such apparently presold pictures as *Dick Tracy* (1990) and *Batman Returns* (1992), alongside the huge revenues from much cheaper pictures like *Ghost* (1990), *Home Alone* (1990), and the *Naked Gun* comedies, demonstrated that predicting a film's success was as difficult as ever.

Whatever the shortfalls on a picture-by-picture basis, the overall system worked to Hollywood's benefit. Roughly half the industry's theatrical income continued to flow from foreign countries, and blockbuster successes after the mid-1970s assured U.S. dominance in offshore markets. In the late 1980s, Hollywood's share of takings increased in every European country, and the changes in eastern Europe left a new market open to American invasion (Chapter 26). Firms outside the United States rushed to invest in Hollywood films, offering private capital and government-sponsored coproduction arrangements. *Terminator 2, Dances with Wolves* (1991), and *Basic Instinct* (1992) all benefited from co-financing and presales to European firms. In the emerging global film market, Hollywood remained the principal player.

BIG AND SMALL INDEPENDENTS

The difficulties and recovery of the Majors and mini-majors were bound up with the fate of independent production in the United States during the period. The 1948 divorcement decrees and the rise of the teenage market gave independent companies like Allied Artists and American International Pictures (AIP) an entry into the low-budget market (p. 381).

During the late 1960s, the low-budget independents grew stronger, partly through the relaxing of the Production Code and partly through the

NEW PRODUCTION AND EXHIBITION TECHNOLOGIES

Between the late 1960s and the early 1990s, the photographic and mechanical medium of film was modified by means of modern electronic and computer technology.

As in most decades, there were important changes in film stocks and camera design. Agfa, Fuji, and Eastman continually introduced faster and more sensitive emulsions. In the 1980s, the super-35mm gauge permitted filmmakers to prepare excellent prints for all formats—70mm, anamorphic or flat 35mm, videocassette, and laserdisc.

Reflex viewing, which allows the cinematographer to see exactly what the lens is taking in, became widely available in the late 1960s. Reflex viewing encouraged the dissemination of the pan-and-zoom style of cinematography: since the cinematographer could now see precisely what the lens was encompassing, he or she could quickly reframe or zoom to follow the action.

As the aspect ratio of the image became standardized at 1.85:1 (nonanamorphic 35mm) and at 2.35:1 (anamorphic), the Panavision firm became the principal source of cameras. The Steadicam, first publicized on *Bound for Glory* (1976), permitted hand-held shots of unprecedented smoothness and became standard in the 1980s. Both the Steadicam and the lightweight, remote-controlled Louma crane used a video monitor for viewfinding, reflecting the increasing importance of video as an aid for shot composition and rehearsal on the set.

The 1970s also saw a revolution in sound recording and reproduction techniques. Robert Altman's *California Split* (1974) pioneered multitrack recording during production, using radio microphones on the actors to create up to fourteen distinct channels. At the same period, the "time code" designed to identify frames on videotape was modified to synchronize the film strip with one or more tape recorders. Time-coded editing made sound mixing and rerecording much easier. A modified time code also put video technology firmly into the post-production process. In the 1980s, editors began transferring film footage to videotape or videodiscs, editing the film on video with the aid of computerized random-access memory before making the final cut on film.

In sound reproduction, the principal innovations came from the laboratories of Ray Dolby. Dolby introduced digital noise-reduction techniques to the recording industry in the mid-1960s; *A Clockwork Orange* (1971) was the first film to employ them. A few films used Dolby magnetic sound for multiple-track theater reproduction, but not until Dolby's optical stereo system was proved on *Star Wars* (1977) did it become feasible. Stereo reproduction came within the reach of most exhibitors, and during the 1980s high-budget films exploited it. Experiments were also made with digital reproduction in theaters.

Special effects achieved new levels of sophistication, principally under the leadership of George Lucas's firm Industrial Light and Magic. Designers created new optical printers, blue-screen methods, and other techniques for compositing images. Computer assistance also enabled technicians to create "motion-control" systems that could repeat, frame by frame, camera movements over miniatures or models. *Tron* (1982) showed that computer-generated imagery could yield special effects. As video technology more and more assisted production and editing, improvements in digital video allowed special effects to increase in sophistication, as was seen in the digital "morphing" of *Terminator 2: Judgment Day* (1991; Color Plate 25.3) and *Jurassic Park* (1993).

decline of the Majors. Russ Meyer blazed the trail for 1970s pornography with films such as *Vixen* (1968). The youthpix craze was fed by AIP's cycle of motorcycle-gang movies and *Wild in the Streets* (1968). The films of AIP's main director, Roger Corman, had a strong influence on young directors of the late 1960s, and AIP gave opportunities to Coppola, Woody Allen, Scorsese, John Milius, De Palma, Robert De Niro, and Jack Nicholson. The low-budget independent film *Night of the Living Dead* (1968), rejected by AIP as too gory, went on to become a colossal cult hit and launched the career of director George Romero.

During most of the 1970s independent production proved a robust alternative to the Majors. As the studios cut back production, low-budget films helped fill the market. Film investments proved to be cozy tax shelters. Firms began to specialize in certain genres—martial-arts films, action pictures, erotic pictures ("sexploitation"). Films aimed at African-Americans ("blaxploitation") showcased young black performers and, sometimes, black creative personnel like directors Gordon Parks Sr. (*Shaft*, 1971) and Michael Schultz (*Cooley High*, 1975; *Car Wash*, 1976). The teenage exploitation market was tapped with horror films like Tobe Hooper's grotesquely comic *Texas Chainsaw Massacre* (1974), Wes Craven's *Last House on the Left* (1973), and John Carpenter's more sober and expensive *Halloween* (1978). These started an ongoing cycle of stalker-slasher films. Corman's New World Pictures, founded in 1970, created cycles and trained new directors (Jonathan Demme, John Sayles, James Cameron).

In some venues, the cheaper film could find an audience denied to the glossier studio product. Teenagers and college students began flocking to cult movies like those directed by John Waters. Theaters found it profitable to offer "midnight movies" that would attract a young crowd. *The Rocky Horror Picture Show* (1975) and *Eraserhead* (1978) became profitable almost solely through such shows. Sunn International discovered, to the Majors' surprise, that there was still a family audience who could be lured from the television set, while Tom Laughlin, the enterprising director-producer-star of *Billy Jack* (1971), showed that small-town viewers would still come to films which mixed sentiment, action, and populist themes.

The Majors responded by absorbing the sensational elements which had given independent films their edge. Big-budget films became more sexually explicit, and for a time Russ Meyer, exploiter of erotica, found himself working for a studio. *The Exorcist* traded on blasphemy and visceral disgust to a new degree. *Star Wars* and *Close Encounters* incorporated elements of low-budget science fiction (*Silent Running*, 1971; *Dark Star*, 1974), while *Alien* (1979) and other films reflected the new standards of gory violence established by independent directors such as Carpenter and David Cronenberg (*Shivers*, 1976; *Rabid*, 1977). Throughout the 1980s, the Majors' films continued to incorporate exploitation elements. When even the family-oriented Spielberg experimented with more shocking material in *Gremlins* (1984) and *Indiana Jones and the Temple of Doom* (1984), the MPAA rating system was revised to include a "PG-13" category. " 'Exploitation' films were so named because you made a film about something wild with a great deal of action, a little sex, and possibly some sort of strange gimmick," wrote Corman. "[Later] the majors saw they could have enormous commercial success with *big-budget* exploitation films."[1]

As a result, the independent market suffered somewhat in the late 1970s and early 1980s. Still, a great many of the emergent filmmakers of the period learned their trade in the genres of low-budget cinema: Joe Dante (*The Howling*, 1980), John Sayles (who wrote for Dante), Katherine Bigelow (*Near Dark*, 1987), and Susan Seidelman (*Smithereens*, 1982; *Desperately Seeking Susan*, 1985). Moreover, the independents regained some power with the rise of cable and home video. After 1984, when these new technologies became essential sources of funding, a low-budget production could be financed almost completely from presales to video. For many independent films, there would be no theatrical opening: the film would go straight to cable and video cassette. And most independent productions were slanted toward well-established formulas, which expanded interest in genre cinema. Young viewers became aficionados of musicals, thrillers, horror films, and science fiction—all neatly categorized at their local video outlet.

Fig. 25.2 *Illusions*: Black women struggle against racism in World War II Hollywood. Mignon, a light-skinned black woman pretending to be white, telephones her mother beneath a sign pleading for racial equality ("I am *so* an American!").

While the number of annual releases by U.S. Majors and mini-majors rose slightly above 150 at the end of the 1980s, independents released as many, largely because of the new financing and distribution available through video. This huge number of films was difficult for exhibitors to absorb and strained advertising budgets. Eventually, most of the big independent companies, such as Cannon, De Laurentiis, New World, and Island, overextended themselves by trying to become central players in both production and distribution and suffered financial setbacks.

Nevertheless, the dramatic increase in production yielded fresh opportunities for filmmakers of all generations. Director James Ivory and his producer Ismail Merchant had made small, literary films since the 1960s, but the new independent market enabled them to make prestigious adaptations of Edwardian novels (*The Europeans*, 1979; *Howards End*, 1992). The Public Broadcasting Service (PBS), through its "American Playhouse" series, supported veteran experimentalist Jon Jost in his cerebral, painterly *All the Vermeers in New York* (1990; Color Plate 25.4). African-American filmmaker Julie Dash's feature about Gullah women, *Daughters of the Dust* (1991), was also funded by PBS; her earlier short film *Illusions* (1983; Fig. 25.2) was supported by the American Film Institute and a private foundation.

Low-budget filmmakers could shoot on the new format of super-16mm and make acceptable 35mm prints. A number of regional film festivals also continued to offer venues and awards for low-budget independent work. Robert Redford's Sundance Institute in Utah encouraged off-Hollywood films through seminars and an annual film festival. Thanks largely to the Sundance Institute, low-budget work by women directors, such as Allison Anders's *Gas Food Lodging* (1992), and films by gay and lesbian filmmakers (e.g., Gregg Araki's *The Living End*, 1991) earned wide press coverage. Although hurt by recessions during the 1980s, low-budget independent filmmaking proved remarkably resilient.

TOWARD A HOLLYWOOD ART CINEMA: FROM 1968 TO THE MID-1970s

When Paramount Pictures asked Francis Ford Coppola to make a film based on the novel *The Godfather*, he went home in despair. "They want me to direct this hunk of trash," he told his father. "I don't want to do it. I want to do art films."[2]

That Coppola could harbor such hopes reflects a new trend in American filmmaking. Robert Rossen's *Lilith* (1964), Arthur Penn's *Mickey One* (1965), and Sidney Lumet's *The Pawnbroker* (1965) had drawn on the French New Wave for disjunctive cutting, fantasy and flashback inserts, and a general loosening of cause-and-effect relations. But such films were regarded as ambitious oddities. With the late 1960s recession and the search for college audiences, Hollywood cinema became more hospitable to the storytelling techniques pioneered in the European art cinema. In the early 1970s, one cure for Hollywood's slump seemed to be the "art film" dwelling on mood, characterization, and psychological ambiguity.

A case in point is Richard Lester's much-praised *Petulia* (1968). In one scene, the eccentric and abused Petulia confronts her lover Archie at his apartment. Lester interrupts their conversation with brief shots: a flashback of Archie trying to return the tuba Petulia had brought him, and a "false" flashback of Petulia stealing the tuba (Figs. 25.3–25.6). Overall, the film's

Fig. 25.3

Fig. 25.4

Fig. 25.5

Fig. 25.6

Fig. 25.3 *Petulia*: Archie explains that he tried to return the tuba Petulia had left with him . . .

Fig. 25.4 . . . and Lester intercuts a flashback of Archie doing so.

Fig. 25.5 Soon Archie learns that Petulia paid for renting the tuba . . .

Fig. 25.6 . . . and Lester inserts a shot of her breaking a pawnshop window to steal the tuba. This visualizes a lie which she told Archie earlier.

Fig. 25.7

Fig. 25.8

Figs. 25.7 and 25.8 Dennis Hopper's *Easy Rider* assimilated the jump cuts that Godard had pioneered in *À bout de souffle*.

play with character subjectivity and temporal ordering is reminiscent of Resnais.

Similarly, Stanley Kubrick's *2001: A Space Odyssey* (1968), while at one level a revival of the science-fiction genre, exploits the enigmatic symbolism of European art cinema. Lengthy scenes of antiseptic daily life on the spacecraft (including many stretches empty of dramatic values), an ironic use of music, and a teasing, allegorical ending invite the sort of thematic interpretation usually reserved for films by Fellini or Antonioni.

The youthpix also encouraged stylistic experimentation. *Easy Rider*'s rock sound track and drug-laced tour of America may have attracted young audiences, but its style was jolting to an unprecedented degree (Figs. 25.7, 25.8). Transitions are choppy: a few frames from the last shot of one scene alternate with a few frames of the first shot of the next. [Hopper, a fan of underground films, may have borrowed the device from Gregory Markopoulos (p. 584).] An enigmatic shot of a burning bike punctuates the narrative, foreshadowing the end of the drug dealers' odyssey.

Other "road movies" took a loose, open approach to narrative, as in Bob Rafelson's *Five Easy Pieces* (1970) and Monte Hellman's *Two Lane Blacktop* (1971), the latter remarkable for its sparse dialogue and minimal characterizations. Brian De Palma's *Greetings* (1968) and *Hi, Mom!* (1970) were episodic countercultural films that merged rock music, raunchy humor, and reflexive stylistic devices borrowed from Truffaut and Godard. Haskell Wexler's *Medium Cool* (1969; Fig. 25.9), Paul Williams's *The Revolutionary* (1970), and Michelangelo Antonioni's *Zabriskie Point* (1970) offered a parallel to the critical political cinema emerging in Europe (Chapter 23), and they often relied upon ambiguous narratives and open endings. Melvin Van Peebles's *Sweet Sweetback's Baadasssss Song* (1971), a frenetic call to black revolution, exploited a variety of New Wave techniques. Hopper's *The Last Movie* (1971), about a Kansas cowboy eking out a living in Peru, employed cryptic symbolic scenes and a pervasive reflexivity (including title cards reading "SCENE MISSING").

Older directors made sporadic ventures into the Americanized art cinema. Paul Mazursky's *Alex in Wonderland* (1970) paid homage to Fellini's *8½*, while Sydney Pollack's *They Shoot Horses, Don't They?* (1969) flaunted stylized flashforwards. Mike Nichols's *Catch-22* (1970) and George Roy Hill's *Slaughterhouse Five* (1972) drew upon the new time-juggling techniques in

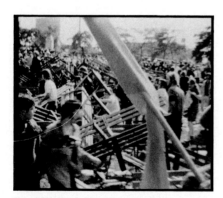

Fig. 25.9 The hand-held camera captures demonstrators building barricades against the police in sequences shot at the 1968 Democratic convention (*Medium Cool*).

Fig. 25.10 The decentered compositions and dominating architecture of *The Parallax View*.

adapting well-known novels. In *Images* (1972) and *Three Women* (1977) Robert Altman emphasized ambiguous shifts between objective reality and character subjectivity, decorated with abstract, enigmatic compositions. Woody Allen's *Interiors* (1978) was a somber chamber drama modeled on Bergman's work, while Alan J. Pakula's *The Parallax View* (1974) adorned an assassination thriller with alienating widescreen compositions reminiscent of Antonioni (Fig. 25.10).

Art-cinema conceptions of realism were revived as well. John Cassavetes, the only member of the American New Wave to enter mainstream filmmaking, harked back to his *Shadows* (1960) with a string of films featuring quasi-improvised performances and casual camerawork. *Faces* (1968) and *Husbands* (1970), with their sudden zooms to close-up and their search for revelatory detail, use Direct Cinema techniques to comment on the bleak affairs and deceptions of middle-class American couples. Characteristically, Cassavetes's "counterculture" comedy *Minnie and Moskowitz* (1971) centers on the love affair of a middle-aged hippy and a lonely museum curator. In *A Woman under the Influence* (1974), *Opening Night* (1979), and *Love Streams* (1984) Cassavetes continued to create a spasmodic rhythm that highlights the individual instants of each actor's performance. This, and his focus on the near-hysteria underlying adult love and work, made his midlife melodramas seem experimental by 1970s and 1980s Hollywood standards.

The auteur policy had become widely known in the United States (see Notes and Queries), and the "film brats" who began in the 1960s had learned of it in film school. Many harbored dreams of becoming artists like Europe's venerated auteurs and Young Cinema directors.

The most celebrated movie brat was Francis Ford Coppola. His youth comedy *You're a Big Boy Now* (1967) displays the flashy techniques of Richard Lester's Beatles films and the "swinging London" pictures (p. 555). With *The Rain People* (1969), shot on the road with a Dodge bus, minuscule financing, and a crew of friends, Coppola sought to make a film that had the stylistic richness and the dedramatization of prestigious European cinema. Natalie leaves her husband because her marriage is beginning to stifle her. On her aimless drive she picks up Killer, a brain-damaged football player. Abrupt, jagged flashbacks interrupt scenes, and Coppola's sound designer

Fig. 25.11

Fig. 25.12

Fig. 25.13

Fig. 25.11 *The Conversation*: As Harry watches the mysterious younger people leave the corporation under press scrutiny . . .

Fig. 25.12 . . . Coppola interrupts the scene with glimpses of the murder . . .

Fig. 25.13 . . . and suggests that these images are either Harry's imaginings or fragments of the real action.

Walter Murch provides a montage of environmental textures—the crackle of phone lines, the muffled rumble of high-speed trucks shaking roadside motel rooms. The glistening sidewalks of the opening credits take on significance when Killer tells Natalie of the "rain people" who disappear because "they cry themselves away."

In 1969 Coppola founded American Zoetrope, a company dedicated to personal filmmaking. Although it collapsed through mismanagement, American Zoetrope left a legacy in Coppola's *The Conversation* (1974), financed on the success of *The Godfather*. Like Altman's works, the film blends conventions of the art cinema with those of a Hollywood genre—in this case, the detective film.

Although *The Conversation* is frequently compared to *Blow-Up* (1966), Coppola probes his protagonist's mind far more deeply than Antonioni does. Harry Caul, an expert in audio surveillance, records fragments of a conversation which lead him to suspect a murder plot. As he replays and remixes the telltale dialogue (rendered in Murch's intricate sound design), Harry's growing anxiety is charted through dreams and fragmentary flashbacks. The murder is presented in disorienting shards, as Harry glimpses and overhears it. Eventually the audience discovers that parts of the original conversation have been filtered through Harry's mind. As Harry realizes the true situation, Coppola intercuts shots of him with shots of the murder, perhaps as he now imagines it to have taken place (Figs. 25.11–25.13).

A few directors sustained efforts toward Americanized art cinema. Altman protégé Alan Rudolph explored such techniques in the ambiguous fantasy/flashback sequences of *Choose Me* (1984) and the mysterious city landscape of *Trouble in Mind* (1985). David Lynch's *Eraserhead, The Elephant Man* (1980), and *Blue Velvet* (1986) pushed such tendencies toward expressionistic distortion. On the whole, however, directors shied away from the experimentation encouraged by the art-cinema vogue of the late 1960s and early 1970s. After the success of *The Godfather, American Graffiti*, and *Jaws*, most young directors aimed for accessible movies that did not challenge mainstream storytelling. In the process, they revived Hollywood while still occasionally making idiosyncratic and challenging films.

THE "NEW HOLLYWOOD": FROM THE EARLY 1970s TO THE PRESENT

The industry recession of the late 1960s coincided with the waning careers of many older directors. John Huston, Billy Wilder, Alfred Hitchcock, and William Wyler remained active, but most critics considered their major work to be behind them. Other directors gradually retired (e.g., Ford, Walsh, Hawks) or worked intermittently and garnered little praise (Cukor, Minnelli, Aldrich, Fuller). As producers cast about for "youth" pictures, art-flavored films, and blockbusters, less-entrenched directors came to the fore.

Some were emigrants who had made their name in European art cinema: the Czechs Milos Forman and Ivan Passer, the Pole Roman Polanski, and the Britishers John Schlesinger, Jack Clayton, and Ken Russell. Other directors were older Americans, often from television, whose careers were given fresh impetus by the New Hollywood, such as Altman and Paul Mazursky (*Bob & Carol & Ted & Alice*; *Next Stop, Greenwich Village*, 1976).

The directors who attracted the most attention were younger. Most were born around 1940, had some film school training, and were devoted fans of the classical Hollywood tradition. The movie-brat generation was very diverse, including critic-turned-filmmaker Peter Bogdanovich (*The Last Picture Show*, 1971; *What's Up, Doc?*, 1972), independent director George Romero (*The Night of the Living Dead*, 1968), former television director Bob Rafelson (*Five Easy Pieces*, 1970; *The King of Marvin Gardens*, 1972), and novices such as Brian De Palma (*Greetings*, 1968; *Sisters*, 1973), John Carpenter (*Dark Star*, 1974; *Assault on Precinct 17*, 1977), Terrence Malick (*Badlands*, 1973), and John Milius (*Dillinger*, 1973; *The Wind and the Lion*, 1975).

The most powerful and widely respected of the movie brats—Coppola, George Lucas, Steven Spielberg, and Martin Scorsese—established themselves as major talents in the early 1970s. Other filmmakers, about the same age, came to prominence later: the screenwriter Paul Schrader with *Blue Collar* (1978), Michael Cimino with *The Deer Hunter* (1978), David Lynch with *Eraserhead* (1978), and Jonathan Demme with *Melvin and Howard* (1980).

In the early 1980s there emerged a second generation. Born around 1950, these directors took the New Hollywood for granted. If the movie brats learned by working for television or AIP, the next generation trained with the movie brats themselves. Robert Zemeckis (*Back to the Future*, 1985) was a protégé of Steven Spielberg, while Lawrence Kasdan wrote scripts for Spielberg and Lucas before becoming a director (*Body Heat*, 1981; *The Big Chill*, 1983). After starring in *American Graffiti* and its television spin-off *Happy Days*, Ron Howard directed cheap action pictures and eventually big-budget items (*Splash*, 1984; *Parenthood*, 1989).

As the major companies began turning out more films, still more young people began directing. Some found success quickly, becoming the Coppolas and Spielbergs of the 1980s. Before the end of the decade, Tim Burton (*Pee-Wee's Big Adventure*, 1985; *Beetlejuice*, 1988) and James Cameron (*Termi-*

nator, 1984) would direct two of the industry's all-time blockbusters: *Batman* (Burton), and *Terminator 2* (Cameron). John Hughes's first feature, *16 Candles* (1984), established him as a purveyor of sentimental teenage comedy and enabled him to produce a series of successful low-budget films. As in the early 1970s, directing opportunities also arose for older talents, often former scriptwriters such as Barry Levinson (*Diner*, 1982; *Rain Man*, 1989) and Oliver Stone (*Salvador*, 1986; *Platoon*, 1986). Barbra Streisand, Robert Redford, Danny De Vito, and other actors also turned to directing.

The expansion of production helped marginal filmmakers enter the mainstream. For virtually the first time since the silent era, women directors found places in the industry. Katherine Bigelow, Susan Seidelman, Amy Heckerling (*Fast Times at Ridgemont High*, 1982; *Look Who's Talking*, 1990), Martha Coolidge (*Valley Girl*, 1983), Mira Nair (*Mississippi Masala*, 1991), and Penelope Spheeris (*Wayne's World*, 1992) established careers in the "New New Hollywood." Similarly, the independent success of Chinese-American Wayne Wang's *Chan Is Missing* (1982) and African-American Spike Lee's *She's Gotta Have It* (1986) led both to larger budgets and wider audiences. By the beginning of the 1990s, nearly two dozen African-American directors were at work, some creating intimate, oblique dramas (Dash's *Daughters of the Dust*; Charles Burnett's *To Sleep with Anger*, 1990), others working in more popular genres (Mario Van Peebles's *New Jack City*, 1991; John Singleton's *Boyz N the Hood*, 1991; Color Plate 25.5).

For both generations—those who revived Hollywood in the mid-1970s and those who owed their start to the expansion of production in the 1980s— the reference point was often the great Hollywood tradition. Many filmmakers worked in the shadow of established genres, hallowed classics, and venerated directors. In several ways, the New Hollywood defined itself by reference to the old.

Limping through 1970s Los Angeles with his bag of laundry, the elderly detective in Robert Benton's *The Late Show* (1976) sarcastically explains: "I'm on my way to the Brown Derby to meet Louis B. Mayer." The line exemplifies the extent to which many films of the 1970s and 1980s became ironic or affectionate tributes to Hollywood tradition. Exploitation science fiction is celebrated in *Strange Invaders* (1983) and *Earth Girls Are Easy* (1989), while *New Jack City* refers to 1930s gangster films as well as to De Palma's *Scarface* (1983). The New Hollywood also undertook to remake sturdy genre pictures like *DOA*, *The Invasion of the Body Snatchers*, *Cat People*, and *The Thing*.

In addition, directors began to revive stylistic devices associated with Hollywood's golden era. In *Jaws*, Spielberg borrowed Hitchcock's zoom-in/ track-out from *Vertigo*, a device that was to become common in 1980s film to show a background eerily squeezing around an unmoving figure. During the late 1960s and early 1970s, directors had become reliant on long lenses; entire scenes might be shot with the depth-flattening telephoto. By contrast, many directors of the New Hollywood, notably Spielberg and De Palma, introduced wide-angle-lens compositions reminiscent of Welles, Wyler, and *film noir*. The results were often striking depth of focus and distortion of figures (Figs. 25.14, 25.15). Yet most directors did not abandon long lenses.

Fig. 25.14 The return of wide-angle shots: *Close Encounters of the Third Kind* . . .

Fig. 25.15 . . . and *The Untouchables* (1987, De Palma).

Fig. 25.16

Fig. 25.17

Figs. 25.16 and 25.17 In *Catch-22* (1970), Mike Nichols intercuts exaggerated deep-focus shots with images taken with a much longer lens.

The dominant style of the 1970s and 1980s mixed occasional deep-focus shots with flatter telephoto images (Figs. 25.16, 25.17; Color Plates 25.6, 25.7). As the films' scripts often gave 1940s and 1950s genres a contemporary treatment, so their style became a synthesis of techniques derived from many eras.

Yet cinema of the 1970s and 1980s also sought to differentiate itself by displays of technical prowess. More powerful theater projection lamps enabled cinematographers to bathe sets in a hazy murk, virtually creating a new "soft style" (p. 176). (See Fig. 25.18.) Hard-edged, low-key lighting, influenced by techniques of music video, could coexist with a bright, saturated color scheme reminiscent of Pop Art (Color Plate 25.8). The mise-en-scene might also include pools or rays of unrealistically hued light (Color Plate 25.9). Spielberg, Lucas, and Coppola (*One from the Heart*, 1979) turned their films into displays of technical wizardry, while more experimental works like

Fig. 25.18 The new soft style in *The Last Boy Scout* (Tony Scott, 1991).

David Byrne's *True Stories* (1986) used minimal means to create almost Surrealist imagery (Color Plate 25.10). American cinema's search for an eye-catching "postmodern" look strongly influenced the young French cinema (p. 742).

The new pride in technical virtuosity was evident in the comeback of the lavish cartoon feature. *Yellow Submarine* and *Fritz the Cat* had been roughly animated, disguising low budgets with eye-catching design and countercultural attitudes. Even the Disney studio relinquished its realistically detailed look in *Robin Hood* (1973) and *The Rescuers* (1977). Some of the studio's former animators broke away under the leadership of Don Bluth to make *The Secret of NIMH* (1982) and *An American Tail* (1986), the first cartoon produced by Steven Spielberg. Bluth's success led to a proliferation of features with rich textures and fully articulated movements. Disney went further in *Beauty and the Beast* (1991), in which rotoscope techniques are applied to the sets, giving space considerable volume and solidity (Color Plate 25.11). In addition, the new animated features moved away from young-adult audiences and targeted children. Yet *Beauty and the Beast*, thanks partly to its Broadway-style songs, appealed to adults as well. Its nomination for an Oscar as Best Picture confirmed that animation was reaching a full spectrum of the audience, just as animated shorts had in the 1930s.

Across the 1970s and 1980s, two further trends stood out. For some filmmakers, the main concern was to continue the Hollywood tradition through updating genres and paying respect to venerated filmmakers. Other directors tried to create a more personal cinema; they sought to bring art-cinema conventions to mass production and popular genres. Both trends are characterized by "movie consciousness," an intense awareness of film history and its continuing influence on contemporary culture.

HOLLYWOOD CONTINUED

Most straightforwardly, many films of the era aimed to sustain Hollywood's tested genres. Directors and performers associated with *National Lampoon* magazine and television's "Saturday Night Live" revived slapstick comedy in *Animal House* (1978) and *Stripes* (1981). Musicals were updated to incorporate disco (*Saturday Night Fever*, 1977), music video (*Flashdance*, 1983), and rap and hip-hop (*House Party*, 1990). The rogue-cop film reemerged with Clint Eastwood as *Dirty Harry* (1971) and later, in a more comic vein, with Eddie Murphy vehicles (*Beverly Hills Cop*, 1984), while the interracial cop-buddy movie became a long-lasting cycle with *48 Hours* (1982) and *Lethal Weapon* (1987). The war film reappeared, with Vietnam a prominent theater of combat.

Several films of the New Hollywood revisited traditional genres. *The Godfather* revived the classic gangster film but gave the formula some fresh twists. Part I (1972) emphasizes the genre's conventional ethnic divisions (Italian/Irish/WASP) and its machismo values but adds a new stress on family unity and intergenerational succession. Michael Corleone, at first remote from the "family business," comes to take his place as his father's rightful heir

(Color Plate 25.12), at the cost of distancing himself from his wife Kay. Part II shows how Michael's father became a success, harking back to another genre formula, the emigrant gangster's rise to power (Color Plate 25.13). This earlier time period is intercut with Michael's expanding authority and ruthlessness in the present. Whereas the first *Godfather* had ended with Michael's full assimilation into the male line of the family, Part II closes with him locked in autumnal shadow, alone and brooding, unable to trust anyone (Color Plate 25.14).

The *Godfather* did not lead to a renaissance of the gangster film, but two other genres spearheaded by the New Hollywood were revived on a major scale. The horror film, long associated with low-budget exploitation, was given a new respectability in *The Exorcist* (1973) and became an industry mainstay for twenty years. Carpenter's *Halloween* spawned a long cycle of slasher films in which the victims, usually voluptuous teenagers, meet gory ends. Adaptations from best-selling novels by Stephen King yielded *Carrie* (1976, De Palma), *The Shining* (1980, Kubrick), and *The Dead Zone* (1983, Cronenberg). Eventually, dramas such as *Fatal Attraction* (1987) and *Cape Fear* (1991) began borrowing from the horror genre.

The other significant genre to be revived was science fiction. Kubrick's *2001: A Space Odyssey* (1968) was the major forerunner, but it was Lucas and Spielberg who impressed Hollywood with the profit possibilities of a genre previously identified with kiddie matinees and teenage exploitation. *Star Wars* (1977) showed that space adventure, mounted with updated special effects, could attract a new generation of moviegoers, and its unprecedented success triggered not only its own film series but one based on the television program "Star Trek." *Close Encounters of the Third Kind* (1977) turned the 1950s "invasion film" into a cozy, quasi-mystical experience of communion with extraterrestrial wisdom. *E.T.* (1982) carried the theme further, becoming the top-grossing film of the era. At around the same period, a sour, dystopian science fiction came to the fore with *Blade Runner* (1982). In such films, the genre served partly to showcase innovations in production design and special effects. As in the 1950s, some films merged science fiction with elements drawn from the horror film: *Alien* (1979), *Aliens* (1986), and *Terminator*.

For Lucas and Spielberg, continuing the Hollywood tradition was an act of nostalgia. They tried to re-create the uncomplicated fun of space opera (*Star Wars*), action-packed serials (*Raiders of the Lost Ark*, 1981), or Disney fantasy (*Close Encounters*, *E.T.*). In making *Star Wars*, Lucas assembled the most exciting portions of several air battles from war pictures, storyboarded the compiled sequence, and then shot his space dogfights to match the older footage. As producers, Lucas and Spielberg revived the family film of adventure (*Willow*, 1988), fantasy (*Gremlins*, 1984), and cartoon comedy (*Who Framed Roger Rabbit?*, 1988; Color Plate 25.15).

Spielberg divided his attention between what he called "fast-food movies" (*Jaws*, the Indiana Jones series) and more upscale directorial efforts (*The Color Purple*, 1985; *Empire of the Sun*, 1987). These dignified adaptations of best-selling novels remained committed to nostalgia as well, recalling the "prestige picture" of the 1930s and 1940s. Looking back to the great tradition, both Lucas and Spielberg filled their films with reverent allusions to the

Fig. 25.19 *Raising Arizona*: Comic-book distortion thanks to the wide-angle lens.

studio program picture (*Always*, 1989, is a remake of *A Guy Named Joe*, 1943), to Disney (in *Close Encounters* and *Hook*, 1991), and to venerated auteurs (John Ford is cited in both *Star Wars* and *E.T.*).

Other filmmakers saw themselves as continuing the studio tradition in a more complex way. "We were very much concerned with making the Hollywood film," recalled John Milius, "not to make a lot of money, but as artists."[3] Strongly influenced by the auteur theory, these directors based entire films upon ideas of authorship developed by film critics.

For example, John Carpenter's *Assault on Precinct 13* updates Hawks's *Rio Bravo*, pitting its masculine code of conduct against contemporary urban violence. Similarly, Carpenter's remake of *The Thing* gives a pessimistic turn to Hawks's original. Brian De Palma became famous for his pastiches of Hitchcock: *Obsession* (1976) is *Vertigo* with an incestuous twist; *Dressed to Kill* (1980) confronts *Psycho* with contemporary sexual mores. John Milius's attempt to revive the swashbuckling action film in *The Wind and the Lion* (1975) pays homage to Raoul Walsh. The films of Joel and Ethan Coen constitute grotesque reworkings of *film noir* (*Blood Simple*, 1984), Preston Sturges comedy (*Raising Arizona*, 1987), and the Warner Bros. gangster film (*Miller's Crossing*, 1989).

Unlike Lucas and Spielberg, these directors often cultivated a style that recognizably borrows from the masters. The wide-angle exaggeration of the Coens' imagery echoes Welles's *Touch of Evil* (Fig. 25.19), while Carpenter's rhythmic cutting in *Precinct 13* is indebted to Hawks's *Scarface*. De Palma's overhead shots, startling deep-focus imagery, and split-screen handling of action recall Hitchcock's bravura ingenuity; a bird's-eye view in *Bonfire of the Vanities* (1990) cites the assassination scene in Hitchcock's *Foreign Correspondent* (1940).

Hollywood's departed past was treated less respectfully in the satires and parodies that poured out during the 1970s and 1980s. Mel Brooks turned the Western (*Blazing Saddles*, 1973), the Universal horror film (*Young Frankenstein*, 1974), the Hitchcockian thriller (*High Anxiety*, 1977), and the historical epic (*History of the World, Part I*, 1981) into raucous, bawdy farces. Woody Allen parodied the caper film (*Take the Money and Run*, 1969), the science-fiction film (*Sleeper*, 1973), and the documentary (*Zelig*, 1983). David and Jerry Zucker, along with Jim Abrahams, savaged the disaster film in *Airplane!* (1980), the spy movie in *Top Secret!* (1984), and "flyboy" movies in *Hot Shots!* (1991). Such zany treatment of genre conventions was itself conventional in silent slapstick and in the comedies of Bob Hope and Bing Crosby or Dean Martin and Jerry Lewis. Mocking Hollywood was a Hollywood tradition.

PERSONAL CINEMA IN HOLLYWOOD

The interest in creating an American art cinema encouraged some mainstream directors to make more personal films. Often these mingled the conventions of classical narrative cinema with strategies drawn from European art cinema. In these films, genre conventions are respected but also reworked; the classical style remains in place but is inflected by momentary innovations. The overall result is taken to express the director's view of the world.

An outstanding example is the work of Robert Altman. He directed some fairly orthodox features before his career was energized by the late 1960s slump, the youthpix cycle, and the vogue for Hollywood art cinema. His films travesty their genres, from the war film *M*A*S*H* to the antimusical *Popeye* (1980). They radiate a distrust of authority, a criticism of American pieties, and a celebration of energetic, if confused, idealism.

Altman also developed an idiosyncratic style. He relied on shambling, semi-improvised performances, a restless pan-and-zoom camera style, abrupt cutting, multiple-camera shooting that kept the viewpoint resolutely outside the character action, and a sound track of unprecedented density. His long lenses crowd characters in on one another and lock them behind reflecting glass (Fig. 25.20). *Nashville* (1975), for many critics Altman's major achievement, follows twenty-four characters across a weekend, often scattering them across the widescreen frame (Fig. 25.21). In Altman's films, characters mumble, interrupt each other, talk simultaneously, or find themselves drowned out by the droning loudspeakers of official wisdom. Through his distinctive handling of theme, genre, image, and sound, Altman created a personal cinema in 1970s Hollywood.

So did Altman's contemporary Woody Allen. A television gag writer and a stand-up comedian, Allen wrote plays, starred in films, and began directing

Fig. 25.20 In *The Long Goodbye*, a dense window reflection shows the detective Philip Marlowe on the beach while inside the house novelist Roger Wade quarrels with his wife.

Fig. 25.21 Several major characters pass each other unawares in the bustling airport scene at the beginning of *Nashville*.

Fig. 25.22 Middle-class couples debate artificial insemination: Romantic satire in *Hannah and Her Sisters.*

with *Take the Money and Run.* He became one of the most noted comic directors of the early 1970s, sustaining the wisecracking absurdist tradition of the Marx Brothers and Bob Hope. Allen's early films also appealed to young audiences through their cinematic in-jokes, such as the homage to *Potemkin*'s Odessa Steps in *Bananas* (1971).

With *Annie Hall* (1977), Allen launched a series of films that blended his interest in the psychological problems of the urban professional with his love for American film traditions and for such European filmmakers as Fellini and Bergman. "When I started making pictures, I was interested in the kind of pictures I enjoyed when I was younger. Comedies, real funny comedies, and romantic comedies, sophisticated comedies. As I got a little more savvy, that part of me which responded to foreign films started to take over."[4]

Allen's most influential films have thrown his comic persona—the hypersensitive, insecure Jewish intellectual—into a tangle of psychological conflicts. Sometimes the plot centers on the Allen figure's confused love life (*Annie Hall; Manhattan*, 1979). In *Hannah and Her Sisters* (1986) and *Crimes and Misdemeanors* (1990), the plot consists of intertwined romantic relationships among several characters, played for contrasts between verbal comedy and sober drama. *Hannah*, for instance, mixes marital infidelity, a cancer scare, and satiric observation of New York intellectual life (Fig. 25.22). Allen built many of his films around the questions that preoccupied him, and he unabashedly recorded his loves (jazz, Manhattan), dislikes (rock music, drugs, California), and values (love, friendship, and trust).

A unique production arrangement allowed Allen to retain control over the script, casting, and editing; he was even permitted extensive reshooting of portions of his films. He explored a range of styles, from the pseudo-documentary realism of *Zelig* to the mock German Expressionism of *Shadows and Fog* (1992). Allen also paid homage to a number of his favorite films and auteurs. *Stardust Memories* (1980) is an overt reworking of *8½; Radio Days* (1987), in its glowing evocation of period detail, recalls *Amarcord*. *Interiors* (1978) and *September* (1987) are Bergmanesque chamber dramas, while the holiday family gatherings of *Hannah and Her Sisters* evoke *Fanny and Alexander*.

Martin Scorsese is another director whose personal concerns melded Hollywood and art-cinema qualities. Brought up on Hollywood features and "Million Dollar Movie" TV broadcasts, Scorsese went to film school at New York University. There he was strongly influenced by Andrew Sarris and the auteur theory. (See Notes and Queries.) He made an underground reputation with several shorts and two low-budget features before *Mean Streets* (1973) drew wide attention. *Alice Doesn't Live Here Any More* (1974) and *Taxi Driver* (1975) propelled Scorsese to fame. *Raging Bull* (1980), a biography of prize-fighter Jake LaMotta, won still greater notice; many critics consider it the finest American film of the 1980s. Scorsese's later films (notably *King of Comedy*, 1982; *The Last Temptation of Christ*, 1988; *Goodfellas*, 1989) cemented his reputation as the most critically acclaimed director of his generation.

As a movie brat, Scorsese was heavily indebted to the Hollywood tradition. *Cape Fear* was a remake; *Taxi Driver* was scored by Hitchcock's composer Bernard Herrmann; as preparation for shooting *New York, New*

Fig. 25.23

Fig. 25.24

Figs. 25.23 and 25.24 Two different fights in *Raging Bull*, each with a distinct cinematic texture.

York (1976) Scorsese studied 1940s Hollywood musicals. Like Altman and Allen, however, he was also influenced by European traditions. A shot change in *Raging Bull* is as likely to derive from Godard as from *Shane*.

Scorsese's film consciousness also emerges in his virtuosic displays of technique. His films alternate intense, aggressive dialogue scenes designed to highlight the skills of performers such as Robert De Niro with scenes of physical action served up with dazzling camera flourishes. The action sequences are often abstract and wordless, built out of hypnotic imagery: a yellow cab gliding through hellishly smoky streets, billiard balls ricocheting across a pool table (*The Color of Money*, 1986). Each of the boxing scenes in *Raging Bull* is staged and filmed differently (Figs. 25.23, 25.24). Whereas other movie brats create spectacle through high-technology special effects, Scorsese engages the viewer by his dynamic, florid style.

Like Allen's films, Scorsese's have strong autobiographical undercurrents. *Mean Streets* and *Goodfellas* drew upon his Italian-American youth. After years of self-destructive behavior he felt ready to tackle *Raging Bull*: "I understood then what Jake was, but only after having gone through a similar experience. I was just lucky that there happened to be a project there ready for me to express this."[5] Perhaps as a result of his emotional absorption in his stories, Scorsese's films center on driven, even obsessed protagonists, and his technique often puts us firmly in their minds. Rapid point-of-view shots, flickering glances, slow-motion imagery, and subjective sound heighten our identification with Jake LaMotta, the taxi driver Travis Bickle, and the aspiring stand-up comedian Rupert Pupkin (Fig. 25.25). The hero of *Goodfellas* provides a voice-over narration justifying his deeds, and in the final sequence he addresses the audience.

If Allen and Scorsese made a personal cinema out of the psychological dramas of their protagonists, other directors conveyed socially critical views through "problem pictures." In a series of strenuous, politically charged films (*Platoon*, 1986; *Born on the Fourth of July*, 1989; *JFK*, 1991), Oliver Stone expressed his sense that 1960s liberal idealism lost its way after the death of Kennedy. The more reflective and lyrical films of John Sayles presented a critical vision of class struggle in American history (*Matewan*, 1987) and in the present (*The Return of the Secaucus Seven*, 1980; *City of Hope*, 1991). Lizzie Borden's futurist and feminist *Born in Flames* (1986) led to projects on prostitution (*Working Girls*, 1987) and rape (*Love Crimes*, 1992).

Fig. 25.25 In his basement aspiring talk-show host Rupert Pupkin interviews cardboard cut-outs of Liza Minnelli and Jerry Lewis (*King of Comedy*).

Fig. 25.26 To-camera address in *She's Gotta Have It* (1986).

Spike Lee, the most visible proponent of mainstream African-American filmmaking of the late 1980s, created vigorous, didactic problem pictures (*School Daze*, 1988; *Do the Right Thing*, 1989; *Jungle Fever*, 1991). Lee's films pose questions to both the African-American community and the white audience. His vibrant color design and shot composition (Color Plate 25.16) and his habit of letting his characters address the camera directly (Fig. 25.26) give his films a posterlike urgency.

During the 1980s, personal cinema emerged in another guise. The quirky film that would previously have flourished in independent production slipped into the mainstream. From the cult item *Eraserhead* David Lynch moved to the more traditional *Elephant Man* before *Blue Velvet* (1986) and *Twin Peaks: Fire Walk with Me* (1992) invested small-town life with eerie, perverse passions. Gus Van Sant mixed seedy realism and *film noir* stylization in *Mala Noche* (1987), in the more mainstream *Drugstore Cowboy* (1989), and in *My Own Private Idaho* (1991), a gay/grunge road movie based on Shakespeare. Jim Jarmusch's experiments in narrative construction—the post-Punk and Beat-flavored *Stranger Than Paradise* (1984), the male melodrama *Down by Law* (1986), and *Mystery Train* (1989), with its three overlapping stories—depend upon deadpan performance styles and a rueful homor. In *Trust* (1991) and *Simple Men* (1992) Hal Hartley thrusts melodramatically convoluted plots into looming, expressionless close-ups. Flirting with narrative strategies which have their sources in art films, such directors formed an eccentric "parallel cinema."

The diversity of directorial options at the beginning of the 1990s ran parallel with American film's new saliency in contemporary life. Despite predictions that cinema would wither under the assault of cable and videocassettes, theatrical motion pictures remained central ingredients in the media mix. Television networks modeled series on successful films and invited prominent directors to create broadcast "events." More broadly, the excitement generated by American films pervaded the world's popular culture. Newspapers and television reported on the week's top-grossing films, the Academy Awards ceremony became an international ritual, and fan magazines like *Premiere* found success by catering to an apparently insatiable appetite for gossip about moviemaking.

In the early 1990s, approximately 4000 theatrical feature films were made worldwide. The U.S. Majors and independents produced only 300 to 400 of these, yet these films attracted 70 percent of global box-office revenues. As American cinema reached its centennial in 1994, it remained the most economically and culturally powerful film industry in the world.

◆ NOTES AND QUERIES

THE AMERICAN DIRECTOR AS SUPERSTAR

The auteur theory of film criticism and history made the individual director the primary source of the film's formal, stylistic, and thematic qualities. This theory, reinforced by the prominence of postwar directors in Europe and

Asia, was applied by *Cahiers du cinéma* to Hollywood directors as well (Chapter 19, Notes and Queries). In the early 1960s, the American Andrew Sarris and British critics centered around the journal *Movie* introduced the theory to English-language readers. Collections of interviews such as Sarris's *Interviews with Film Directors* (Indianapolis: Bobbs-Merrill, 1967) and Joseph Gelmis's *The Film Director as Superstar* (New York: Doubleday, 1970) reinforced the impression that the director was the central figure in the creation of a film. By the 1980s, this belief was taken for granted even in mass journalism and fan magazines.

Many of the directors who came to prominence in America during the 1970s and 1980s knew the auteur theory through its promulgation in film schools and the popular press. Young directors self-consciously sought to create personal films on the model of European art cinema or the Hollywood classics of Hitchcock, Ford, and Hawks. The results of this strategy are discussed in Noël Carroll, "The Future of Allusion," *October* **20** (Spring 1982): 51–81, and David Thomson, *Overexposures: The Crisis in American Filmmaking* (New York: Morrow, 1981), pp. 49–68.

FILM CONSCIOUSNESS AND FILM PRESERVATION

American filmmakers' new awareness of film history has a parallel in a growing sense of the need to safeguard the country's motion-picture heritage. During the 1970s and 1980s nitrate copies decomposed and 1950s to 1970s Eastman Color prints began to fade. There were new efforts to *preserve* films (that is, keep good negatives and prints in archival conditions), to *restore* films (to bring deteriorated material back to something approaching its original quality), and to *reconstruct* films (to gather lost or discarded footage so as to enable viewers to see more complete or original versions of films).

The American Film Institute, founded in 1967, took as part of its charter the preservation and restoration of films. It saved hundreds of films with the assistance of the Library of Congress, the Academy of Motion Picture Arts and Sciences, the Museum of Modern Art, and other archives. During the 1980s, the UCLA Film Archive restored *Becky Sharp* and *For Whom the Bell Tolls*, while MoMA reconstructed *Intolerance*. [See Robert Gitt and Richard Dayton, "Restoring *Becky Sharp*," *American Cinematographer* **65,** 10 (November 1984): 99–106, and Russell Merritt, "D. W. Griffith's *Intolerance*: Reconstructing an Unattainable Text," *Film History* **4,** 4 (1990): 337–375.] Individual specialists also took part. Ronald Haver found new footage for a longer version of *A Star Is Born* (1954) [*A Star Is Born: The Making of the 1954 Movie and Its 1983 Restoration* (New York: Knopf, 1988)], and Robert Harris restored *Lawrence of Arabia* and *Spartacus* ["HP Interviews Robert Harris on Film Restoration," *The Perfect Vision* **12** (Winter 1991–1992): 29–34]. Martin Scorsese supported the 1993 restoration and release of *El Cid* (1961, Anthony Mann).

The 1980s also saw a new public for older films, made available in special events or on video. Kevin Brownlow's series of silent films for Thames television led to gala theatrical showings of new prints of *The Wind, Greed,* and other classics. Brownlow and David Robinson discovered precious material from Charles Chaplin's outtakes and made them available on video formats as *The Unknown Chaplin*. Studios, recognizing the financial benefits of rereleases or video versions, have become somewhat more willing to preserve and restore their films. Ted Turner, owner of the MGM/UA library, has energetically struck new prints, many of which have become available on laserdisc.

◆ REFERENCES

1. Roger Corman and Jim Jerome, *How I Made a Hundred Movies in Hollywood and Never Lost a Dime* (New York: Random House, 1990), p. 34.
2. Quoted in Peter Cowie, *Coppola* (London: Faber and Faber, 1990), p. 61.
3. Quoted in Michael Goodwin and Naomi Wise, *On the Edge: The Life and Times of Francis Coppola* (New York: Morrow, 1989), p. 30.
4. Quoted in Eric Lax, *Woody Allen: A Biography* (New York: Knopf, 1991), p. 255.
5. Quoted in David Thompson and Ian Christie, eds., *Scorsese on Scorsese* (London: Faber and Faber, 1989), pp. 76–77.

Plate 22.1 *How Tasty Was My Little Frenchman*

Plate 22.2 An ICAIC poster for *Lucia*

Plate 23.1 *Larks on a String*

Plate 23.2 *Pirosmani*

Plate 23.3 *Viva la muerte!*

Plate 23.4 *The Lost Honor of Katherina Blum*

Plate 24.1 *Field Diary*

Plate 24.2 *The Thin Blue Line*

Plate 24.3 *Our Lady of the Sphere*

Plate 24.4 *Dimensions of Dialogue*

Plate 24.5 *Surfacing on the Thames*

Plate 24.6 *T.O.U.C.H.I.N.G*

Plate 24.7 *Meridian Transit* (Japan, 1977,

Plate 24.8   *Street of Crocodiles*

Plate 24.9   *Quasi at the Quackadero*

Plate 24.10   *Lineage*

Plate 24.11   *Journeys from Berlin / 1971*

Plate 24.12   *One Way Boogie Woogie*

Plate 24.13   *A Walk through H*

Plate 24.14   *Cinderella*

Plate 25.1   *Fritz the Cat*

Plate 25.2   *Allegro non troppo*

Plate 25.3   *Terminator 2*

Plate 25.4   *All the Vermeers in New York*

Plate 25.5   *Boyz N the Hood*

Plate 25.6   *Black Rain* (1990)

Plate 25.9 *Edward Scissorhands (1990)*

Plate 25.10 *True Stories*

Plate 25.11 *Beauty and the Beast*

Plate 25.12 *The Godfather*

Plate 25.13 *The Godfather II*

Plate 25.14 *The Godfather II*

Plate 25.15 *Who Framed Roger Rabbit?*

Plate 25.16 *Do the Right Thing*

Plate 26.1   *Mona Lisa*

Plate 26.2   *Le Bal*

Plate 26.3   *Night of the Shooting Stars*

Plate 26.4   *Pressure*

Plate 26.5   *Voyage to Cythera*

Plate 26.6   *Landscape in the Mist*

Plate 26.7   *Toute une nuit*

Plate 26.8   *Appletrees*

Plate 26.9 *The Green Room*

Plate 26.10 *Barry Lyndon*

Plate 26.11 *The Draughtsman's Contract*

Plate 26.12 *El Sur*

Plate 26.13 *Distant Voices, Still Lives*

Plate 26.14 *The Goalie's Anxiety at the Penalty Kick*

Plate 26.15 *Paris, Texas*

Plate 26.16 *Wings of Desire*

Plate 26.17 *Wings of Desire*

Plate 26.18 *Parsifal*

Plate 26.19 *Act of Spring*

Plate 26.20 *The Cannibals*

Plate 26.21 *Un Chambre en ville*

Plate 26.22 *Mauvais sang*

Plate 26.25 *The Quince Tree Sun*

Plate 26.26 *Freak Orlando*

Plate 26.27 *Passion*

Plate 26.28 *Hail Mary*

Plate 26.29 *Détective*

Plate 26.30 *Stalker*

Plate 26.31 *Nostalghia*

Plate 26.32 *The Legend of Suram Fortress*

Plate 26.33 *Taxi Blues*

Plate 26.34 *Swan Lake: The Zone*

Plate 26.35 *Picnic at Hanging Rock*

Plate 26.36 *An Angel at My Table*

Plate 26.37 *Eijanaika*

Plate 26.38 *In the Realm of the Senses*

Plate 27.1 *The Blue Eyes of Yonta*

Plate 27.2 *Tangos: The Exile of Gardel*

Plate 27.3 *Frida*

Plate 27.4 *Cantata de Chile*

Plate 27.5 *Kasba*

Plate 27.6 *Shanghai Blues*

Plate 27.7 *The Killer*

Plate 27.8 *Rouge*

Plate 27.9 *Dust in the Wind*

Plate 27.10 *The Black Cannon Incident*

Plate 27.11 *King of the Children*

Plate 27.12 *Life on a String*

Plate 27.13 *Ju Dou*

Plate 27.14 *Yol*

Plate 27.15 *Life and Nothing More*

Plate 27.16 *Yeelen*

26

NEW CINEMAS AND NEW DEVELOPMENTS: EUROPE, THE USSR, AND THE PACIFIC SINCE THE 1970s

The revival of Hollywood had complex effects on cinema in other countries. The New Hollywood was a boon for distributors and exhibitors dealing in American films, but, as ever, those films presented formidable competition for local industries.

During the 1970s and early 1980s, France, Italy, the USSR, Mexico, Hong Kong, and West Germany produced films in significant quantity, and some countries, such as India and Japan, continued to produce many more than the U.S. industry did. There were also some strong regional production centers—France for Francophone countries, Mexico for Latin America, Hong Kong for East Asia, Bombay and Madras for the Indian subcontinent. But no nation could match Hollywood's global reach. Films from Hollywood circulated in far more countries than did those of any competitors. In many countries, U.S. movies consumed 90 percent of screen time. Moreover, U.S. movie attendance had stabilized at around a billion per year, but in most other countries, attendance fell steadily. This further reduced the chance that a local film might recoup its costs in the home market.

Since the early 1970s, then, film industries outside the United States faced a familiar problem. They had to find a broad enough economic base to support steady production. One strategy was to differentiate the local product from Hollywood offerings, just as German Expressionist or Italian Neorealist cinema had created distinctive "national schools." The appearance of New Waves and New Cinemas signaled this urge for constant novelty. Throughout the 1970s and 1980s, this process brought forward several Young Cinemas in Germany, Australia, the USSR, and elsewhere.

Since a domestic release seldom returned production costs, producers tried to export their films. As Hollywood increased its domination of the international market, European producers aimed increasingly for a "global cinema." The most prestigious films would be internationally financed, made by creative personnel drawn from several countries, and designed for world-wide consumption. The government-overseen coproductions of the postwar era lessened, and more projects were funded by media conglomerates—television concerns, recording companies, and other leisure-time industries.

In eastern Europe and the Soviet Union, most filmmakers proceeded cautiously during the 1970s, working within political dictates. Only Poland saw a striking revival of filmmaking energy, born out of the political struggles of the Solidarity movement. Soviet President Mikhail Gorbachev's strategic withdrawal of support from Communist regimes in eastern Europe accelerated their collapse. In the Soviet Union, Gorbachev's policies freed filmmakers from seventy years of censorship, but his inability to cure the ailing economy confronted filmmakers with problems of privatization, a decrepit infrastructure, and audiences eager to see American films. Nations freed from Soviet domination sought to enter the global cinema market.

On the Pacific Rim, Australia exemplified how a New Cinema could be a deliberate attempt to enter the global film market. In Japan, the once-powerful studio system began to decline, another Young Cinema bore the marks of American pop music and domestic comic books, and local electronics companies entered the international film market through outright purchase of media empires.

WESTERN EUROPE

CRISIS IN THE INDUSTRY

By the mid-1970s Europe's postwar economic boom was definitely over. The 1973 oil shock, in which the Middle Eastern petroleum-producing countries began drastically raising the price of oil, created inflation, unemployment, and a recession that lasted throughout the decade. Politically, the appeal of left-wing parties waned and more conservative governments came to power. Although the left won some victories, as in the Socialist François Mitterand's 1981 election to the French presidency, all governments faced persistent inflation and recession. Even leftist regimes took austerity measures that moved them closer to the center. During the same period, however, right-wing dictatorships in Spain, Greece, and Portugal ended and democratic reforms were introduced.

On the whole western Europe's economy recovered and restabilized in the 1980s. The European Community (EC) began to plan a unified market which, with 320 million persons, could compete with the United States and Japan. A European assembly, created in 1979, started to consider the possibility of a "Single Europe," and a bill promoting this was passed by the twelve member nations in 1987. The EC sought to eliminate the continent's trade barriers and to create a common currency.

The hard times of the 1970s were also felt throughout the European film industry. Attendance continued to drop, and theaters closed. Although in some countries production increased, the figures were artificially inflated by the growing number of pornographic films. Box-office income rose or remained steady, but this was chiefly because of increasing ticket prices. Overall, television—now in color, with good image quality—was reducing film audiences. Home video made deep inroads after the late 1970s, damaging attendance and eliminating the theatrical market for erotic films. As in the United States, fewer and fewer films gained a larger portion of box-office revenues, and most titles were aimed at an audience aged fifteen to twenty-five.

What theater income there was went largely to Hollywood. Since the late 1940s, American firms owned powerful distribution companies in Europe, ensuring U.S. pictures preferred theaters and excluding imports from other countries. Moreover, the countries which had highly concentrated ownership of exhibition chains (France, West Germany, and Great Britain) welcomed the lucrative Hollywood product. Consequently, despite quotas, taxes, and other protectionist measures, American films dominated Europe. In the early 1980s, they attracted almost 50 percent of the attendance in Belgium, France, and West Germany; 60 to 70 percent of that in Denmark, Italy, and Greece; 80 percent in the Netherlands; and over 90 percent in the United Kingdom.

European film industries were not vertically integrated, so for most of the 1970s there was no coordinated response to declining audiences and increased U.S. penetration. Throughout the postwar era, for example, France had been western Europe's major film-producing country. Yet nearly half of its market was still fed by small producers. Pathé, the Union Générale Cinématographique, and Gaumont devoted most of their resources to exhibition. In the late 1970s, Gaumont struck out on an expansion program, buying theater chains abroad, building new theaters, and tripling its production output to around forty films per year. Soon, however, this strategy yielded large losses and Gaumont was forced to cut back. French production remained largely artisanal; most of the 600 companies made no films, and only 100 or so released a single film annually.

For a time, there was hope that American financing might help the more visible auteurs. Since the mid-1960s U.S. Majors had produced a few English-language films by Truffaut, Bergman, Antonioni, and others. Bertolucci and certain New German directors won such support in the 1970s. In addition, some companies established "classics" divisions to distribute foreign prestige pictures in the United States. But with the significant exception of Bertolucci's scandalous *Last Tango in Paris* (1973), most Hollywood-supported art movies proved unsuccessful. Moreover, the new entertainment conglomerates could not exploit art films through the increasingly popular "synergistic" cross-marketing of music, books, television spin-offs, and merchandise based on a film.

European filmmakers were obliged to rely chiefly upon the systems of coproductions and government assistance initiated in the postwar era. The prototypical "Eurofilm" might have stars from Italy, France, and Germany, with a director from one country, a mixed-nations crew, and location shooting in several regions. East-West coproductions increased, with the USSR and eastern European countries participating in runaway projects and joint ventures. International productions also drew upon government aid, as European states continued to promote cinema as a cultural vehicle.

New Television Support. Thanks to strategies put into place after World War II (p. 409), state subsidies carried national cinemas through hard times. Governments made funds available to producers through loans, grants, and prizes. Several countries modeled aid upon France's policy of *avance sur recettes*—giving funding before production on the expectation of repayment from a percentage of the film's earnings. In Greece, Spain, Switzerland, Italy, and Belgium, ministries and cultural bodies made funding available. In the UK, local filmmaking had suffered from a sudden decline in Hollywood investment, but producers' demands on the National Film Finance Corporation were augmented by the National Film Development Fund, created in 1976. Governments drew such funds from general revenues and from taxes on tickets or license fees for televisions and VCRs. In Finland, the national film foundation raised money from taxes on blank videocassettes.

Yet few European films repaid government investment. In Denmark, where the Film Institute covered up to 85 percent of a film's budget, the investment was seldom recouped. France, which had the most comprehensive plan for financing films, lost money on 90 percent of all projects supported through the *avance sur recettes*. In effect, the French government was subsidizing films judged to have cultural significance, many by auteurs but lacking commercial appeal.

A more practical form of government subsidy benefited from the growth ot film's chief audio-visual competitor. Up to the mid-1970s, European television was dominated by state-owned public agencies, such as the British Broadcasting Corporation, France's ORTF, and Italy's RAI. These kept out independent television companies, banned advertising, and presented themselves as showcases for national culture. Needing films for broadcast, TV agencies often supported directors. ORTF financed Bresson's *Mouchette* (1967), and RAI produced Rossellini's historical films, Fellini's *The Clowns* (1970), and films by Ermanno Olmi and the Taviani brothers.

West Germany was the first country to use national television to support filmmaking in a systematic fashion. The country had no private channels and three public ones: ARD, ZDF, and a regional chain. The Young German Film launched at the 1962 Oberhausen festival (p. 534) had suffered from cutbacks in government funding, but in 1974 a new Film and Television Agreement offered favorable terms for joint productions. Between 1974 and 1978, government television spent 34 million deutsche marks on films to be shown on television after they had completed a theatrical run. In addition, funding was allotted for script development. The agreement acknowledged the possibility that the *Autorenfilm*, or "author's cinema," could lift television above its normal programming by appeals to high art and national culture.

The 1974 agreement created a fresh burst of energy and led many New German filmmakers to international reputations and financing. (See Notes and Queries.) The new agreement and funding also gave German women directors their first significant chance to make features. The amorphousness of the New German Cinema as a film movement owes something to the fact that it is more a result of such favorable production circumstances than of aesthetic or political positions shared by the filmmakers.

As in most cases of government funding, West Germany's television-financed films did not repay their investment: the New German directors were more popular abroad than at home. Still, the films did fill airtime. And when the government-assisted *Tin Drum* (1979) won box-office success and an Academy Award for best foreign film, the investment in New German Cinema yielded international prestige.

Other nations' state-sponsored television agencies took up film financing in the German mode, supplementing coproduction arrangements with state subsidy. Soon, however, the depression of the mid-1970s and the declining income of public broadcasting forced many governments to admit commercial channels to the airwaves. France dissolved ORTF, created two public channels, and added several private channels throughout the 1970s and 1980s. Britain admitted Channel 4 in 1982. The most unregulated growth in television programming occurred in Italy, where hundreds of small local stations sprang up, some broadcasting twenty-four hours a day. With the development of cable and satellite transmission, some countries could receive programming from all over Europe.

As commercial-television outlets proliferated, film attendance plunged. Between 1976 and 1983, British audiences fell from 107 to 70 million; Spain's attendance dropped from 250 to 141 million. In Italy, where 400 local TV channels programmed a staggering 2000 films per week, theaters lost about 50 million spectators each year. West Germany's public-television system, which blocked private broadcasting the longest, began to strain under its film policy; the government continued to subsidize low-budget art films, but most never won theatrical release. Some German directors responded with hybrid works that could become "events" in either medium, such as the marathon films/series *Berlin Alexanderplatz* (1980, Fassbinder) and *Heimat* (1983, Edgar Reitz).

By the early 1980s, the crisis in European filmmaking could not be ignored. Governments tried to attract private capital to the cinema. In Italy, RAI contracted with the Cecchi Gori group to produce fifteen films annually, with RAI paying the lion's share in exchange for television rights. Mitterand's minister of culture, Jack Lang, declared that he wished French cinema to return to its international prestige. Encouraging the industry to imitate Hollywood's entrepreneurship, Lang helped create private investment companies. These Sociétés de Financement du Cinéma et de l'Audiovisuel (SOFICAs) offered tax-exempt investments to individuals, banks, and companies that bought rights to films' future earnings. By the early 1990s, 25 percent of French production funds derived from SOFICAs.

The most powerful form of private capital came, once more, from television. Caught up in intense competition, Europe's broadcasters needed recent films to program. Moreover, if a television company financed a film which recouped its costs theatrically, broadcasting it would become even more profitable. As a result, during the 1980s private television firms started funding production. Italy's Silvio Berlusconi, owner of several networks, began investing in features in 1985; his holdings sometimes comprised 40 percent of all investment in Italian production.

Fig. 26.1 Stephen Frear's *My Beautiful Launderette* was originally intended as a television film, but its depiction of racism, homosexuality, and class struggle led to a successful release in theaters. Here the young Pakistani and white lovers confront a hostile gang.

In the UK, new state policies turned producers toward television. Margaret Thatcher's Conservative government, adhering to a policy of privatization, abolished the quota in 1982 and the Eady levy three years later. Government funding for film production virtually ceased. Channel 4 was thrust into a central position, producing about twelve films a year, including such international successes as *The Draughtsman's Contract* (1982) and *My Beautiful Launderette* (1985; Fig. 26.1). Other television companies began producing films.

In France, by 1983 one-third of domestic films were being financed by independent television firms. Canal Plus, the cable company established that year, raised the stakes enormously. Like its U.S. counterparts Home Box Office and Cinemax, Canal Plus had a huge appetite, transmitting more than 300 current features per year. Canal Plus was required to commit funds to production, with half devoted to French films. In 1987, Canal Plus became the major funding source for French filmmaking.

Throughout Europe the burden of film finance shifted from individual investors and national governments to media conglomerates. Canal Plus, Berlusconi of Italy, Prisa of Spain, Britain's Thorn-EMI (which had absorbed the Rank theater chain), Polygram of the Netherlands, and Bertelsmann of West Germany began backing films made outside their own countries. The Compagnie Luxembourgeoise de Télédiffusion acquired Gaumont, while the publishing giant Bertelsmann owned Ufa Film and Television.

Along with governmental sources and private investment consortia, banking concerns also took a more active role in production. Crédit Lyonnais, an international bank, became a principal source of loans to European and American companies during the 1980s. In 1992, banking concerns in France, Germany, and Luxembourg formed a joint venture, Films Ltd., to help finance major projects.

The Return of Film Europe.   New forms of international funding also became available under the auspices of the European Community. In 1987, with its twelve member nations looking toward European integration at the end of the century, the EC founded MEDIA, a program to develop the Continent's "audio-visual industries." MEDIA funded EC production projects through loans and created the European Film Distribution Office, which offered financial incentives for national distributors to handle imported films. Another EC commission, Eurimages, offered an *avance sur recettes* for coproductions. Four years after its founding in 1988, Eurimages had backed *Cyrano de Bergerac* (1990), *Prospero's Books* (1991), *Europa* (1991), and over a hundred other films.

Since the 1950s, coproductions and internationally financed projects had been accused of being bland "Eurofilms," lacking any distinctive national qualities. This was, in the cinematic domain, the equivalent of many Europeans' worries that a Single Europe would iron out differences between cultures. Doubts about Eurofilms intensified as international investment and television participation expanded. The big international film, following the tradition of the Sam Spiegel-David Lean epics of the 1950s and 1960s, was epitomized in Bertolucci's *The Last Emperor* (1987), but diversified financing was necessary for less grandiose projects as well. Companies in London, St. Petersburg, Rome, Paris, and Amsterdam co-financed Sally Potter's

Orlando (1992). Bille August's *Best Intentions* (1992) was wryly described as a Swedish-Danish-Norwegian-Icelandic-Finnish-British-German-French-Italian film.

Now even a "first film" was likely to be an international product. Jaco Van Dormaël's *Toto le héros* ("Toto the Hero," 1991) was funded by the Belgian government's *avance sur recettes*, as well as by Germany's ZDF, French public television, Belgian public television, and Canal Plus. *Toto* also benefited from MEDIA, Eurimages, and the EC's European Script Fund. Van Dormaël spent three years conferring about where the film should be shot and what language should be used. After winning a major prize at Cannes, the film attracted audiences in Europe, Japan, and even the United States. Some observers criticized it as "Europudding" or called it *Toto l'Euro*, but others saw it as an emblem of how a small first feature could find an audience through the concerted effort of pan-European government agencies and private venture capital.

"Unless all European producers work together," prophesied one producer, "we will soon have zero percent of the market."[1] In the heyday of the Eurofilm, however, distinctive national film movements were unlikely to emerge, and some observers believed that their time had passed.

During the 1920s, producers had laid the groundwork for a Film Europe market that could compete with the United States (p. 183). In the late 1980s, something like that began to emerge out of the cooperation of national governments, television companies, investment concerns, and EC agencies. In tempo with these developments were the creation of the European Film Academy, which gave annual achievement awards modeled on the American Oscars, and the establishment of Lumière, a Lisbon-based agency coordinating the activity of European archives.

Despite these initiatives, European production remained far from healthy. Only 5 percent of all films recouped their investments in theatrical runs; 80 percent of them were never screened outside their country of origin. Even bright signs, such as a slight upsurge in attendance or the popularity of multiplex theaters, helped American films more than the local product.

By the beginning of the 1990s, U.S. films were more firmly ensconced than ever. While European films received only 1 percent of U.S. theater income, Hollywood films received 80 percent of the European box office. Hollywood companies owned major theaters and multiplexes; by early 1993, MGM's 500-screen circuit was Europe's largest. Meanwhile, both Disney-MGM and Universal were planning to open major studio complexes outside Paris. And 1993 debates on the General Agreement on Tariffs and Trade between Europe and the United States raised the prospect of ending quotas and subsidies—a step which would all but wipe out Europe's film production.

The European film industry struggled to hold its own. Roman Polanski, John Boorman, and other directors of the New Wave generation had trouble finding financing, while auteurs such as Fellini had become virtually unbankable. As Hollywood began remaking European films in English, European filmmakers designed their product with an eye to selling rights. Continental companies also invested in U.S. filmmaking. Canal Plus owned a large share of *Terminator 2* and *JFK* (1991), while Ciby 2000, a wing of a construction-company conglomerate, backed films by David Lynch and Charles Burnett.

Relics of Europe's film past remained, but the new era of multinational media transformed them, sometimes in eerie ways. Cinecittà, established by Mussolini's government in 1937, was scheduled to be sold off in 1993. In East Germany, the old Ufa studio at Neubelsberg, site of the filming of *Metropolis* and *The Blue Angel*, had housed DEFA. With the fall of the Berlin Wall in 1989, the decrepit studio was bought by a French real-estate concern and the rejuvenated Ufa, now a television conglomerate. Overseen by Volker Schlöndorff, the studio was reconstructed. "If in ten years Babelsberg does not make money," Schlöndorff vowed, "that will mean there is no European cinema any more."[2]

THE ART CINEMA REVIVED: TOWARD ACCESSIBILITY

In a climate presenting few opportunities for magnificent success, European popular genres maintained their stability. International audiences were drawn to Italian comedies, from Franco Brusatti's *Bread and Chocolate* (1973) to Maurizio Nichetti's *Icycle Thief* (1990) and Roberto Begnini's *Johnny Stecchino* (1992). French sex comedies (e.g., *Cousin Cousine*, 1975) and British eccentric humor (e.g., the Monty Python films) also kept their place in both domestic and foreign markets. French and British crime films often evoked the shadowy traditions of Poetic Realism and *film noir* (Color Plate 26.1). As censorship laws were liberalized, pornographic cinema swept Europe. The international success of *Emmanuelle* (1974) showed that sex films had a huge theatrical market, until video eliminated it in the early 1980s.

At a more self-consciously artistic level of production, a new Tradition of Quality appeared. The decline of attendance and export markets, the conservatism of investors, and competition from Hollywood drove producers and directors toward a more accessible, less challenging and disruptive cinema than had been seen during the era of political modernism. Many European directors returned to the comfortable mode of prestige pictures, literary adaptations, and the milder modernism forged in the 1950s and 1960s.

In Italy, for example, Ettore Scola was a scriptwriter and director of comedies before *We All Loved Each Other So Much* (1974) established him as an astringent commentator on the political disillusionments of postwar Italian history. With that film, *A Special Day* (1977), and *Le Bal* ("The Ball," 1983) he won international success. Each project wittily merges art-cinema modernism with accessible comedy. *Le Bal*, for example, is set entirely in a French dance hall at different eras, and the whole film is played without dialogue. Scola's close-ups heighten the caricatural performances, and he cleverly manipulates color design, as when the Popular Front sequence drains all color from the shot save that of the Communist flag (Color Plate 26.2).

Critics pointed out that literary values and elegant style seemed to be creating a new French Tradition of Quality (p. 437). For example, the success of Bertrand Blier as a novelist led him to adapt his own work in *Les Valseuses* ("The Waltzers," 1974). *Get Out Your Handkerchiefs* (1978) earned an Academy Award, while *Too Beautiful for You* (1989) won prizes both at home and abroad. Similarly, the critic-turned-director Bernard Tavernier evoked the golden years of the postwar French cinema by hiring Jean Aurenche as scenarist (see p. 438) and by making such films as *Un Dimanche à la compagne* (*Sunday in the Country*, 1984) in homage to Jean Renoir.

Established directors participated in the new Eurofilm by creating prestigious, exportable works. Andrzej Wajda, in exile from Poland, made films in France (*Danton*, 1982) and West Germany (*A Love in Germany*, 1983). Ermanno Olmi's *Tree of the Wooden Clogs* (Italy, 1978) marked a return to Neorealism, re-creating the life of nineteenth-century peasants in their original dialect but also giving them the dimension of legend. Carlos Saura's prodigious output drew on Spanish culture: *Blood Wedding* (1981), *Carmen* (1983), and *El Amor brujo* ("Love, the Magician," 1986) employed indigenous dance, while *El Dorado* (1988), a lavish coproduction with Italy, presented Spanish colonialism as a brutal political game.

Vittorio and Paolo Taviani, who had promoted a humanistic, populist political cinema during the 1960s and early 1970s, became prestigious directors with the success of *Padre padrone* (1977). They sealed their reputation with a mythic recasting of the Neorealist tradition, *Notte di San Lorenzo* (*Night of the Shooting Stars*, 1982; Color Plate 26.3), and a luxuriant adaptation of Pirandello stories, *Kaos* (1984). *Good Morning Babylon* (1987) returns in both theme and structure to the romantic simplicity of the American silent cinema. The Tavianis, along with many others, forged an international "tradition of quality" for the 1970s and 1980s.

That the new international cinema could also present political critique was demonstrated when, in the 1970s, with New German Cinema gaining respect around the world, Rainer Werner Fassbinder came onto the international stage with a series of big-budget films featuring renowned stars. When *The Marriage of Maria Braun* (1978) proved an international success, Fassbinder moved quickly to large-scale coproductions such as *Lili Marlene* (1980), *Lola* (1981), and *Querelle* (1982). In these late films, all the resources of color, costume, soft focus, and spectacle are used to stylize the characters' worlds: unrealistic strips of pink light falling across a face (*Lola*), or a tangerine glow emanating from a wharf (*Querelle*). Extreme close-ups of historically exact details interrupt the action of *Maria Braun* (Fig. 26.2). Yet Fassbinder did not wholly abandon his experimental impulses. Unlike Straub and Huillet, he preferred postdubbing, and this allowed him to make his sound tracks no less baroque than the settings. *In a Year of 13 Moons* (1978) and *The Third Generation* (1979) overlay radio broadcasts, television commentary, and conversations to create dense acoustic ambiences.

Fassbinder sought to remind viewers that their country retained close ties to its Nazi past. His late films presented an epic history of Germany, from the 1920s (*Bolweiser*, 1977; *Despair*, 1977) through the Fascist era (*Lili Marlene*) to the rise of postwar Germany (*Maria Braun*; *Veronika Voss*, 1981; *Lola*). He was also concerned with contemporary history, as in his controversial treatment of homosexual relations in *Fox and His Friends* (1974), his critique of leftists in *Mother Kusters' Journey to Happiness* (1975), and his mockery of chic terrorism in *The Third Generation*. By contrast, Maria Braun, "the Mata Hari of the Economic Miracle," survives by coolly separating her devotion to her husband from her shrewd manipulation of others. Fassbinder's

Fig. 26.2 A pack of cigarettes evokes the privations of postwar Germany in *The Marriage of Maria Braun*.

Fig. 26.3 *À nos amours*: Sandrine Bonnaire as the middle-class teenager avid for excitement.

Fig. 26.4 Jean-Pierre Léaud (Antoine Doinel of *The 400 Blows*) as the shifty and selfish protagonist of Eustache's *The Mother and the Whore*.

Fig. 26.5 The hero of *Kes* shows a flicker of interest in school: Asked to tell about his pet falcon, he writes falconry terms on the board.

last films continued, in muted form, the vein of melodrama plus social critique he had explored earlier.

As directors began to retreat from the radical extremes of politically critical modernism, several sought to reveal social conflicts in a more realistic, even naturalistic way. In France, Maurice Pialat's *Nous ne vieillirons pas ensemble* ("We Won't Grow Old Together," 1972) and *Passe ton bac d'abord* ("First Get Your Degree," 1978) harshly depicted middle-class problems such as divorce, unwanted children, and cancer. His brand of domestic realism won international acceptance in *Loulou* (1980) and *À nos amours* (1983), a story of a girl's coming of age in an era of sexual liberation (Fig. 26.3). Jean Eustache offered a withering portrait of the self-centered young male, lying and quarreling his way through women's lives, in *The Mother and the Whore* (1972; Fig. 26.4).

In Great Britain, working-class life provided a subject for realistic film-making. Ken Loach used nonprofessional actors, shooting in a quasi-documentary style on location in the industrial north for *Kes* (1969). It depicts a working-class boy who is miserable in school and whose only interest in life comes from an ill-fated fascination with training a falcon (Fig. 26.5). In the early 1970s, the British Film Institute Production Board, which had been formed in 1966 and had concentrated on independent shorts, began funding features as well. One of the first was an autobiographical trilogy by Bill Douglas: *My Childhood* (1972), *My Ain Folk* (1974), and *My Way Home* (1977). In an elliptical, unsentimental fashion, these trace a boy's impoverished, loveless life in a northern industrial town (Fig. 26.6).

The British Film Institute also supported filmmaking by members of ethnic minorities. For example, Jamaican Horace Ové directed a feature, *Pressure* (1974), in which two brothers in an immigrant family living in London deal with racism in different ways. Eschewing a radical modernist style, Ové created polished political commentary on a small budget (Color Plate 26.4).

Still, a more experimental and disruptive political modernism did not entirely vanish from the European scene. Alexander Kluge, after his more straightforward narrative *Strongman Ferdinand* (West Germany, 1975), returned to fragmented historical allegories which inquired into the continuing effects of Naziism and the war (Fig. 26.7). Jean-Marie Straub and Danièle Huillet continued to make both static, text-centered films (*Fortini/Cani*, 1976; *Too Early, Too Late*, 1981) and more narratively oriented literary adaptations (Fig. 26.8). The Chilean exile Raul Ruiz created labyrinthine modernist puzzles. *La Vocation suspendu* ("The Suspended Vocation," 1977) purports to present two unfinished films, one intercut with the other, about intrigues within a religious order. *Memory of Appearances: Life Is a Dream* (1987) drops a political agent into a dictatorship where police interrogate suspects behind the screen of a movie theater (Fig. 26.9).

Of all directors in the tradition of political modernism, the one who gained most stature during the 1980s was the Greek Theo Angelopoulos. His frescoes of Greek history such as *Traveling Players* (1975; p. 654) gave way to more intimate dramas that retained strong political resonance. *Voyage to Cythera* (1984) shows an elderly Communist exile returned to Greece (Color Plate 26.5). Angelopoulos also took up the problems of European emigration

Fig. 26.6

Fig. 26.7

Fig. 26.8

and the dissolution of national borders. In *Landscape in the Mist* (1988) children leave home in search of the father they believe to be in Germany, while *The Suspended Step of the Stork* (1991) centers on a famous novelist who abandons middle-class comforts for the precarious life of a refugee. In the 1980s Angelopoulos replaced Antonioni and Jancsó as the major representative of the long-take approach to film style. His distant camera emphasizes characters moving through landscapes, delineating the force of location on action or contrasting a milieu with the event (as when a lengthy extreme long shot intensifies the shocking rape of the adolescent girl in *Landscape in the Mist*; Color Plate 26.6).

New Women Filmmakers. The most extensive wave of politically oriented films came from women. As political commitment turned from revolutionary aspirations to micropolitics (Chapter 23), the 1970s and 1980s saw female filmmakers gain wider recognition. In the popular cinema, the Italian Lina Wertmuller, the German Doris Dörrie, and the French Diane Kurys and Colline Serreau found success with comedies on women's friendship and male-female relations.

Other women directors expressed feminine or feminist concerns through art-cinema conventions. Two major examples are Marguerite Duras and Mar-

Fig. 26.6 *My Childhood* explores the small events of youth as the hero's brother rushes to stand exultantly in the smoke above a passing train.

Fig. 26.7 In Kluge's *Female Patriot* (1979), a persistent researcher, sickle in hand, exhumes the German past.

Fig. 26.8 Characteristically static framings and a range of performance styles in Straub and Huillet's *Class Relations* (1983).

Fig. 26.9 Ruiz accentuates the cryptic narrative of *Memory of Appearances: Life Is a Dream* with colossal wide-angle shots.

MARGUERITE DURAS, MARGARETHE VON TROTTA, AND THE EUROPEAN ART CINEMA

Two of the most important women directors of the era exemplify several trends. Duras, established in the 1950s as a major novelist, also wrote film scripts, most notably for *Hiroshima mon amour* (1959). She began to direct in 1966 and made a strong impression with *Détruire dit-elle* (*Destroy, She Said*, 1969). Her fame increased considerably with *Nathalie Granger* (1973), *La Femme du Gange* ("Woman of the Ganges," 1974), *Le Camion* ("The Truck," 1977), and particularly *India Song* (1975).

Duras's writing had ties to the avant-garde Nouveau Roman ("New Novel"), and she carried literary conceptions of experimentation over to her films much as Cocteau and Robbe-Grillet had earlier. Like Germaine Dulac, Maya Deren, and Agnès Varda, though, she also explored a "feminine modernism." Her slow, laconic style, using static images and minimal dialogue, searches for a distinctively female use of language. Duras also developed a private world set in Vietnam during the 1930s. Several of her novels, plays, and films tell recurring and overlapping stories about colonial diplomats and socialites entangled in complex love affairs.

India Song remains a landmark in 1970s modernist cinema. It is set almost entirely in a French embassy in Vietnam, mostly during a long evening party. Couples dance to languid tangos, drifting through the frame or gliding out of darkness in the huge mirror that dominates the sitting room (Fig. 26.10). But there is no synchronized dialogue. We hear anonymous voices who seem to be commenting on the image, even though the voices are in the present and the action occurs in the past. Moreover, most of the dramatic action—seductions, betrayal, and a suicide—takes place offscreen or in the mirror.

India Song is an experiment in sustained tempo: Duras timed every gesture and camera movement with a stopwatch. We cannot be sure that the action we see took place or is a kind of emblematic staging of the characters' relations. Murmurs on the sound track suggest that the party is crowded, but the vacant long shots show only the principal characters. The film pulls the spectator into a hypnotic reverie while also meditating upon the insular routines of colonialist life.

Margarethe von Trotta belongs to a younger generation. Born in 1942, she worked as an actress in several Young German films. She married Schlöndorff in 1971 and collaborated with him on several films. The popular success of their codirected effort *The Lost Honor of Katherina Blum* (1975; p. 663) enabled von Trotta to direct several films herself: *The Second Awakening of Christa Klages* (1977), *The German Sisters* (1981), *Friends and Husbands* (1982), *Rosa Luxemburg* (1986), and *Three Sisters* (1988).

Not as experimental as Duras or Akerman, von Trotta exploits more accessible conventions of the art cinema. Somewhat like Varda, she poses questions of women's problems in society. Her earliest works show women breaking out of their domestic roles and becoming scandalous public figures: Katherina Blum aids a terrorist on the run; Christa Klages becomes a bank robber. Von Trotta's later films concentrate on the conflicting pulls of work roles, family ties, and sexual love. She is keenly interested in the ways in which mothers, daughters, and sisters, sharing key moments of family history, slip into situations in which they exercise power over one another.

Sisters, or the Balance of Happiness (1979), for example, contrasts two women. The crisp, efficient Maria is an executive secretary geared to career advancement. Her younger sister Anna, halfheartedly pursuing a degree in biology, lives in her imagination, lingering over memories of childhood. Anna commits suicide, partly because of Maria's demand that she succeed. Maria responds by finding a substitute sister, a typist whom she tries to mold into a professional. Eventually, however, Maria realizes that she has been too rigid: "I will attempt to dream in the course of my life. I will endeavor to be Maria and Anna."

Fassbinder would have turned *Sisters* into a sinister melodrama of sadomasochistic domination, but von Trotta presents a character study that refuses to portray Maria as a monster. Von Trotta manipulates point of view to create a gradual shift of sympathies. At first the audience enters Anna's memories and reveries (Fig. 26.11) and stays at a distance from Maria. After Anna's suicide, von Trotta takes us more into Maria's guilt-ridden mind (Fig. 26.12). At the end, the characteristic art-cinema blend of memories, fantasies, and ambiguous images suggests that Maria has gained something of her sister's imagination: she seems to envision the mysterious forest that had formed part of Anna's daydreams.

The two directors' uses of mirrors neatly encapsulate the differences in their approaches. The luxurious geometry of *India Song*'s parlor illustrates Duras's emphasis on form, with the mirror sometimes losing its surface and resembling a window to another realm (Fig. 26.13). Duras's experimental impulses led her into forbidding and esoteric explorations of sound and image relations. *Son nom de Venise dans Calcutta désert* ("Her Name, Venice, in the Desert of Calcutta," 1976) uses *India Song*'s soundtrack but shows entirely different shots of the embassy, all empty of human presence. Thirty of the forty-five minutes of *L'Homme atlantique* ("The Atlantic Man," 1981) consist of a black screen.

By contrast, Von Trotta's mirrors link and contrast characters, intensifying story issues. "If there is such a thing at all as a female form of aesthetics in film, it lies for me in the choice of themes, in the attentiveness as well, the respect, the sensitivity, the care, with which we approach the people we're presenting as well as the actors we choose."[3] The poles of rarefied formal experiment and accessible subjects and themes typified the range of feminine art cinema of the 1970s and 1980s.

Fig. 26.10 The parlor mirror in *India Song*: Class relations doubled.

Fig. 26.12 After Anna's death, von Trotta presents her "haunting" of Maria through a hallucinatory mirror vision.

Fig. 26.11 Mirrors define Anna's fantasy world in *Sisters, or the Balance of Happiness*: Here, she recalls herself and Maria putting on lipstick as children.

Fig. 26.13 Mirror as window, playing perceptual tricks (*India Song*).

garethe von Trotta. (See Box.) Another is Agnès Varda, who won a major prize at the Venice festival with *Sans toit ni loi* ("Neither Roof nor Law," aka *Vagabond*, 1985). Through the countryside tramps an enigmatic young woman, self-destructively bent on living in an unorthodox way. The film obeys the art-cinema norm of flashing back from the investigation of Mona's death to her life in the past. Varda traces Mona's breakdown with a spare, detached camera technique (Fig. 26.14) that suggests both respect for her self-reliance and a sense of a life wasted.

In line with the general move toward more accessible filmmaking, Chantal Akerman of Belgium followed her demanding *Jeanne Dielman* (1975, p. 654) with films closer to familiar models. *Les Rendez-vous d'Anna* ("Anna's Appointments," 1978) follows a filmmaker through Europe in a female

Fig. 26.14 Directorial detachment in *Vagabond*: While the yuppie researcher complains to his wife, the protagonist Mona collapses in the background.

Fig. 26.15 The road movie, filmed in Akerman's dry, rectilinear manner (*Les Rendez-vous d'Anna*).

Fig. 26.16 Akerman revises the musical: Hairdressers deflate romantic aspirations with bawdy lyrics about male duplicity (*The Golden 80s*).

Fig. 26.17 *Years of Hunger*: Older women explain menstruation to Ursula; later her mother will tell her father Ursula has a stomachache.

version of the road movie (Fig. 26.15). *Toute une nuit* ("All Night Long," 1982) is a cross-section of a single night in which nearly three dozen couples meet, wait, quarrel, make love, and part (Color Plate 26.7). *The Golden 80s* (aka *Window Shopping*, 1983) offers a high-gloss musical in the Demy manner, with romantic intrigues crisscrossing a shopping mall, bubbly song numbers, and bitter reflections on sexual stratagems and the failures of love (Fig. 26.16). *Nuit et jour* ("Night and Day," 1991) is something of a feminist rethinking of the Nouvelle Vague, as if the love triangle of *Jules and Jim* were told from the woman's point of view. In all these, the fragmented narrative of the postwar art-cinema enables Akerman to dwell on casual encounters and accidental epiphanies, as well as her consistent interest in women's work and their desire for both love and physical pleasure.

Women directors created a virtual wing of the New German Cinema, thanks partly to the ambitious funding programs launched by television and government agencies. Von Trotta was only the most visible representative of a boom in films which used art-cinema strategies to investigate women's issues. For example, Helke Sander was a student activist in 1968 and a cofounder of the German women's liberation movement. After several short films linked to the women's movement, including one on the side effects of contraception, Sander made *The All-Around Reduced Personality: Redupers* (1978), the story of a photographer who shows unofficial images of West Berlin and encounters opposition to publishing them. Helma Sanders-Brahms, who came to prominence at the same time as von Trotta, also concentrated on contemporary social controversies such as emigrant workers and women's rights. Her *Apfelbäume* (*Appletrees*, 1991) tells of an East German woman who is tempted by the Communist elite but who must remake her life when the two Germanies unite (Color Plate 26.8).

One of the most forceful recastings of art-cinema modernism was Jutta Brückner's *Hungerjahre* (*Years of Hunger*, 1979). In a voice-over from the present, a women recalls growing up in the politically and sexually repressive 1950s. Cold War ideology and a strict family life confuse Ursula as she grows to sexual maturity (Fig. 26.17). Unexpected voice-overs and an uncertain ending—in which Ursula may or may not commit suicide—create ambiguities of space and time reminiscent of Resnais and Duras. Brückner's goal recalls the fragmentation of *Hiroshima mon amour* and later art-cinema experiments; she sought a "psychoanalytic" narrative in which scenes combine "disparately, in uncoordinated juxtapositions, because memory tends to make leaps by association."[4]

The Return of Art-Cinema Modernism. Despite the work of the few political modernists and the many feminist filmmakers, most significant European films avoided the direct engagement with political issues that had characterized the 1965–1975 period. Established directors continued to produce moderately modernist films for the international market. François Truffaut, for instance, won great success with *La Nuit américain* (*Day for Night*, 1973) and *The Last Metro* (1980), but the fierce melancholy of *The Green Room* (1978) proved less popular (Color Plate 26.9). Alain Resnais became increasingly concerned with exposing the artifices of storytelling, often with a light touch seldom displayed in his official masterpieces *Hiroshima mon amour* and *Muriel*. In *Mon oncle d'Amérique* ("My American Uncle," 1980) human beings' careers illustrate theories of animal behavior (Fig. 26.18). *Providence* (1976), with its scenes halted and revised in midcourse, lays bare the arbitrariness of fictional plotting.

Two older directors, based in Britain, helped revive the European art cinema. Stanley Kubrick brought a cold detachment to his 1975 adaptation of Thackeray's *Barry Lyndon*, treating it as an occasion for technical experimentation with a lens that could capture candlelit images (Color Plate 26.10). Nicholas Roeg, a distinguished cinematographer, made his reputation with the ambiguous, aggressive *Performance* (1970) before creating Resnais-like flashes of subjectivity in *Don't Look Now* (1974; Fig. 26.19) and *Bad Timing: A Sensual Obsession* (1985).

A great many younger directors arose to sustain the new pan-European art cinema. From the experimental realm came Peter Greenaway, who moved squarely into the art cinema with *The Draughtsman's Contract* (1982), co-produced by Channel 4 and the British Film Institute. A lush seventeenth-century costume drama, *The Draughtsman's Contract* (Color Plate 26.11) retains the gamelike labyrinths of Greenaway's early films in tracing how an artist discovers the secrets of a wealthy family while preparing drawings of their estate. Elaborate conceits underlie Greenaway's later work, as when he systematically works numerals into the settings of his dark sex comedy, *Drowning by Numbers* (1988), or brings to life the twenty-four texts of *Prospero's Books* (1991), a free adaptation of Shakespeare's *The Tempest*.

Pastiche and humor offered opportunities to several younger directors. Pedro Almodóvar moved from gay underground films to more mainstream productions that fused melodrama, camp, and sex comedy. In Almodóvar's world, nuns become heroin addicts (*Sisters of Night*, aka *Dark Habits*, 1983), a downtrodden wife slays her husband with a hambone (*What Have I Done to Deserve This?*, 1984), a newscaster confesses to murder on television (*High Heels*, 1991), and a woman is attracted to a man because he slays bulls (*Matador*, 1986) or because he has abducted her (*Atame!*, aka *Tie Me Up! Tie Me Down!*, 1989). Like Fassbinder and the Kuchar brothers, Almodóvar works with plots reminiscent of Douglas Sirk, full of romantic rivalries and sudden deaths. As in some Mexican works of Buñuel, scandalous situations

Fig. 26.18 The rat race as a fight between executive mice in *Mon oncle d'Amérique.*

Fig. 26.19 The hero's glimpse of his mourning wife and two mysterious women may be a fantasy or a premonition of the future in *Don't Look Now.*

Fig. 26.20 In Almodóvar's *What Have I Done to Deserve This?* the harried housewife loans her next-door neighbor, a prostitute, a staff for a client who wants "some sophisticated sadism, like in French films."

Fig. 26.21 No one in the office notices the death of a drab London bureaucrat in Kaurismaki's *I Hired a Contract Killer.*

Fig. 26.20

Fig. 26.21

and imagery are handled with a casual, ingratiating lightness (Fig. 26.20). Almodóvar also parodies ordinary movies, often through a film within a film.

At the same time that Almodóvar achieved international notoriety (with the sex farce *Women on the Verge of a Nervous Breakdown,* 1988), Finland's Aki Kaurismaki won worldwide notice with the Wendersian *Ariel* (1989) and the Bressonian *Match Factory Girl* (1989). His cruel, deadpan mockery, born partly of a passion for hard-rock music, is most unadulterated in *Leningrad Cowboys Go America* (1989), while it is tempered with ironic sentiment in *I Hired a Contract Killer* (1990) and *Vie de bohème* ("Bohemian Life," 1991). Kaurismaki's celebration of bizarre, marginal characters, his wide-ranging film references, and his satire of middle-class values (Fig. 26.21) made him a cult director across 1990s Europe.

The Spaniard Victor Erice was far less prolific than Almodóvar or Kaurismaki, but his films attracted attention for their calm beauty and their exploration of childhood as a time of fantasy and mystery. *Spirit of the Beehive* (1972), set in 1930s Spain, follows a little girl who believes that the criminal she hides is a counterpart to the monster in her favorite film, *Frankenstein. El Sur* ("The South," 1983) is centered on an adolescent who discovers her father's love affair. Through chiaroscuro cinematography, Erice creates a twilight world between childhood and adulthood (Color Plate 26.12).

Another director working with family relationships in an art-cinema framework was Terence Davies. Davies's highly autobiographical films combine a post-1968 sense of the political implications of personal experience with a facility in art-cinema conventions. Thanks to BFI production initiatives, Davies broke through to international markets with *Distant Voices, Still Lives* (1988). Here the anguish of family life under a psychopathic, abusive father is tempered by the love shared among mother, daughters, and son. The painful material is intensified by a rigorous, rectilinear style akin to Akerman's in *Jeanne Dielman.* Davies dwells on empty hallways and thresholds and treats family encounters and sing-alongs as if they were portrait sittings (Color Plate 26.13). In *The Long Day Closes* (1992), a lusher style re-creates the bittersweet atmosphere in a family after the father's death. Slow camera movements, dissolves synchronized with lighting changes, and bridging songs slide the action imperceptibly from one time to another and between fantasy and reality.

Davies's films use complex, fragmentary flashbacks, and in this regard they typified a trend of the late 1980s. The new Eurofilm often returned to the sort of free-floating time shifts pioneered by Fellini, Buñuel, and others.

Van Dormaël's *Toto le héros*, the prototype of 1990s Eurofilm, created a Resnais-like interplay between reality, memory, and fantasy. Lars von Trier's *The Element of Crime* (Denmark, 1983) and *Europa* (aka *Zentropa*, Germany, 1991) sketch ominous, phantasmagoric landscapes hovering between history and dream. After a brief concern for social realism during the 1970s, the most ambitious new directors adopted the artifice-laden plot constructions and ambiguity of form and theme characteristic of 1960s art cinema.

THE ARRESTING IMAGE

Along with a new acknowledgment of artifice in narrative went a "return to the image." As Spielberg, Lucas, and Coppola dazzled audiences with visual pyrotechnics, many European directors also gave their films a captivating surface. Hollywood's hyperkinetic spectacle of chases, explosions, and special effects was countered by European directors' efforts to let the beautiful or startling image be the ultimate spectacle, to absorb the spectator in a rapt contemplation of the picture. Both the Europeans and the New Hollywood were offering images of a scale and intensity not to be found on television. In addition, the new pictorialism of the art cinema had local sources, many of them distinctly modernist.

Two Munich-based directors manifested this tendency in the early 1970s: Werner Herzog and Wim Wenders. Because of their concentration on the revelatory shot, they were identified as "sensibilist" directors. Trusting to the beauty of the image and the sensitivity of the viewer, they turned away from the political concerns of other New German filmmakers. Their introspective cinema was also in tune with a "new inwardness" trend in German literature of the period.

Herzog made his reputation with a string of cryptic dramas: *Signs of Life* (1968), *Even Dwarfs Started Small* (1970), *Aguirre, the Wrath of God* (1972), *Every Man for Himself and God against All* (*The Enigma of Kaspar Hauser*) (1975), and *Heart of Glass* (1976). All flaunt Herzog's highly romantic sensibility. He fastens on the heroic achiever (the conquistador Aguirre out to rule the world; Fig. 26.22), the marginal and innocent (dwarfs, the feral child Kaspar Hauser), and the mystic (the entire community in *Heart of Glass*). "That's why I want to make films. . . . I want to show things that are inexplicable somehow."[5]

Even in his documentaries, Herzog sought to capture the immediacy of experience, a purity of perception unhampered by language. He often celebrates the encounter of people with the sheer physicality of the world—the world's most determined "ski flier" (*The Great Ecstasy of the Sculptor Steiner*, 1974), blind and deaf people visiting a cactus farm or taking their first airplane trip (*Land of Silence and Darkness*, 1971). Film images, he believed, should return people to the world as it is, but as we seldom see it. "People should look straight at a film. . . . Film is not the art of scholars, but of illiterates. And film culture is not analysis, it is agitation of the mind."[6]

In order to increase this agitation, Herzog conjures up bizarre images, often suspending the narrative so that the viewer can "look straight" at them. The camera observes impassively as an empty car circles a barnyard while

Fig. 26.22 *Aquirre, the Wrath of God*: The conquistador holds his dead daughter but still vows to rule the globe.

Fig. 26.23 The final images of *Heart of Glass* illustrate a character's parable about men who set out for the edge of the world.

a little man laughs maniacally. Conquistadors floating through the Peruvian jungle stare at a ship nestled in a treetop. Slow motion far more excruciating than in any sports reportage follows the soaring arc of the skier Steiner as he launches himself into space. A door about to close mysteriously stops, and this tiny event becomes an occasion for contemplation.

Herzog's images open onto the infinite through visions of water, mists, and skies (Fig. 26.23). In the opening of *Heart of Glass*, clouds flow like boiling rivers through mountain valleys. Periodically *Aguirre* contemplates the hypnotic pulsations of the turbulent Amazon. The deserts of *Fata Morgana* (1970) dissolve into teeming speckles of film grain, flickers akin to those which interrupt *Kaspar Hauser* and invite us to share the protagonist's vision.

Herzog declared himself the heir of Murnau; he made a new version of *Nosferatu* (1978), and he recaptured Expressionist acting style by hypnotizing the cast of *Heart of Glass*. His allegiance to the silent cinema was evident in his belief that sheerly striking images could express mystical truths beyond language; but the evocative power of his cinema also depended upon the throbbing scores supplied by the art-rock group Popol Vuh. The loosening of cause and effect characteristic of the art cinema finds one apotheosis in Herzog's dedication to the rapt contemplation of the pure, timeless image.

Wim Wenders began with similar antinarrative impulses, making a series of minimalist experimental shorts during the late 1960s. When Wenders came to make features, his sensibilist side found expression in loose journey narratives that halted for contemplation of locales and objects. Strongly influenced by American culture, he found as much sensuous pleasure in pinball, rock and roll, and Hollywood movies as Herzog found in mountains and sports of nature.

Wenders praised the moments in films which are "so unexpectedly lucid, so overwhelmingly concrete, that you hold your breath or sit up or put your hand to your mouth."[7] In *The Goalie's Anxiety at the Penalty Kick* (1971), a young man drifts about, moves in with a woman, murders her, drifts some more, and waits for the police to find him. The plot, based on a novel by the "new inwardness" writer Peter Handke, crumbles into a series of "overwhelmingly concrete" moments, as when a cigarette tossed from a bus showers sparks in the road while the radio plays "The Lion Sleeps Tonight" (Color

Plate 26.14). Similarly, in Wenders's "road" trilogy—*Alice in the Cities* (1973), *The Wrong Move* (1974), and *In the Course of Time* (aka *Kings of the Road*, 1976)—the wanderings of displaced characters are punctuated by long landscape shots, silences, and images which invite intense study. Not surprisingly, Wenders declared Ozu his favorite director, making a documentary in homage to him (*Tokyo-Ga*, 1985).

"I totally reject stories," Wenders wrote in 1982, "because for me they only bring out lies, nothing but lies, and the biggest lie is that they show coherence where there is none. Then again, our need for these lies is so consuming that it's completely pointless to fight them and to put together a sequence of images without a story—without the lie of a story. Stories are impossible, but it's impossible to live without them."[8] Wenders's films enact an ongoing struggle between the demand for narrative and a search for instantaneous visual revelation. In *The American Friend* (1977), *Lightning over Water* (aka *Nick's Movie*, 1980), and *Hammett* (1982) Wenders paid his debts to American genre cinema, often subordinating the images to a thriller intrigue. *Paris, Texas* (1984) moves from a wordless, wandering opening to a gradual involvement in language, ending with a lengthy soliloquy as the hero explains to his long-separated wife why he thinks their marriage failed (Color Plate 26.15).

Himmel über Berlin ("Heavens over Berlin," aka *Wings of Desire*, 1987) again searches for the overwhelmingly concrete—this time by means of the angel Damiel, who is captivated by the transient beauty of the world. He decides to join the human race; like Dorothy entering Oz, he falls into a world of color (Color Plate 26.16). He eventually unites with a trapeze artist, while his fellow angel must watch from the celestial, black-and-white world (Color Plate 26.17). Yet this initiation into the everyday is a fall into narrative and history, emblematically represented by Homer, the elderly storyteller who links Berlin to its past. *Wings of Desire* is dedicated to "all the old angels, especially Yasujiro [Ozu], François [Truffaut], and Andrei [Tarkovsky]"—all directors who reconciled narrative significance with pictorial beauty.

The fascination with images was shared by German directors outside the sensibilist trend. For some, theater provided another way to return to the image and spectacle. Werner Schroeter, a distinguished opera director, created several stylized, baroque films (Fig. 26.24). Hans-Jürgen Syberberg followed *Hitler* with *Parsifal* (1982), which made Wagner's music drama a colossal allegory of German history and myth (Color Plate 26.18).

Further manifestations of the new pictorialism came from the Portuguese Manoel Oliveira. Born in 1908, Oliveira directed only sporadically after his 1931 city symphony, *Douro, Faina Fluvial* (Fig. 14.33). His second feature, *Act of Spring* (1963) was a quasidocumentary about a village reenactment of Christ's passion. Oliveira went on to make a string of films whose visual beauty often arose from a transformation of theatrical traditions.

Oliveira perpetuates conventions of art-cinema narration: *Act of Spring*, for instance, displays the act of filming according to then-current conventions of reflexivity and *cinéma vérité*. Once the Passion Play begins, however, he treats it as a self-contained ritual, eliminating the audience and dwelling on the tensions between theatrical conventions and the open-air space, where

Fig. 26.24 Divas freeze into histrionic poses (*Death of Maria Malibran*, 1971).

Fig. 26.25

Fig. 26.26

Fig. 26.25 The artificial image in Rohmer's *Perceval le gallois*.

Fig. 26.26 A photocopy store becomes a dizzying play of shadows, moving light, and reflections (*Boy Meets Girl*).

stylized costumes and props stand in sunlight and landscape (Color Plate 26.19). In other films Oliveira adapts plays written by himself or by other Portuguese dramatists. All his work displays a sumptuous mise-en-scene, often acknowledging theatricality through direct address to the camera or tableau shots incorporating prosceniums, backdrops, and curtains (Color Plate 26.20).

In France, the new pictorialism surfaced in an uncharacteristic film by Eric Rohmer, *Perceval le gallois* (1978; Fig. 26.25). It emerged in a glossier form in André Téchiné's *Barocco* (1976), a pastiche of *film noir*. Jacques Demy's most important 1980s contribution, the "musical tragedy" *Un Chambre en ville* ("A Room in Town," 1982), presents saturated colors and busy wallpaper patterns which frame a grim story of lovers' betrayal and a workers' strike (Color Plate 26.21).

In the early 1980s a younger generation of French filmmakers began to steer this visual manner in fresh directions. They turned away from the political modernism of the post-1968 era and the grubby realism of Eustache and Pialat toward a fast-moving, highly artificial cinema. They drew inspiration from the New Hollywood (especially Coppola's *One from the Heart* and *Rumble Fish*), late Fassbinder, television commercials, music videos, and fashion photography. Characteristic examples of the new French trend are Jean-Jacques Beineix's *Diva* (1982), *Moon in the Gutter* (1983), *37°2 le matin* (aka *Betty Blue*, 1985), and *IP5* (1992); Luc Besson's *Subway* (1985), *Big Blue* (1988), and *Nikita* (aka *La Femme Nikita*, 1990); and Leos Carax's *Boy Meets Girl* (1984), *Mauvais sang* ("Bad Blood," aka *The Night Is Young*, 1986), and *Les Amants du Pont-Neuf* ("The Lovers of the Pont-Neuf," 1992).

Parisian critics called this the *cinéma du look*. The films decorate fairly conventional plot lines with chic fashion, high-technology gadgetry, and conventions drawn from advertising photography and television commercials. The directors fill the shots with crisp edges and stark blocks of color; mirrors and polished metal create dazzling reflections (Fig. 26.26). The slick images of Beineix and Besson evoke publicity and video style, as well as *Blade Runner* and *Flashdance*. Carax, the most resourceful of the group, creates sensuous imagery through chiaroscuro lighting, unusual framings, and unexpected choices of focus (Color Plate 26.22). Several critics diagnosed this trend as a "postmodern" style which borrowed from mass-culture design in order to create an aesthetic of surfaces. In a broader perspective, the *cinéma du look* was a mannerist, youth-oriented version of that post-1968 tendency toward abstract beauty seen in less flashy form in Herzog, Wenders, and Syberberg.

For other directors inclined to return to the image, neither theater nor mass media provided as much inspiration as did painting. Derek Jarman's first mainstream feature, *Caravaggio* (1986), not only portrays the master creating his paintings (Color Plate 26.23) but also employs a painterly style in the dramatic scenes. In Raul Ruiz's *Hypothèse du tableau volé* ("Hypothesis of the Stolen Painting," 1978), the camera wends its way around figures frozen in place and representing missing paintings by an obscure artist. Alain Cuny's *Annonce fait à Marie* ("The Annunciation to Mary," 1991) creates strikingly Pre-Raphaelite images in staging Claudel's religious drama (Color Plate 26.24). Jacques Rivette's *La Belle noiseuse* ("The Beautiful Flirt," 1991) and Victor Erice's *The Quince Tree Sun* (1992) center on painters, and in each the plot is secondary to quiet observation of the meticulous process by which an image is born (Color Plate 26.25).

Ulrike Ottinger, a West German photographer and graphic artist, was a central participant in the new pictorialism. Her *Ticket of No Return* (1979) follows a rich woman alcoholic on a binge through Berlin, dogged by three sociologists who interject lectures on the dangers of drink. The unrealistic staging is interrupted by several of the woman's daydreams. *Freak Orlando* (1981) confronts Virginia Woolf's dual-gendered time traveler Orlando with "freaks" at various points in history. Ottinger's outlandish costumes intensify the fantasy (Color Plate 26.26).

Godard also took inspiration from painting. His video work had concentrated on the relation among images, dialogues, and written texts, but upon his return to cinema he was calling himself a painter who happened to work in film. Freeze-frame and jerky slow-motion shots in *Sauve qui peut (la vie)* ("Let One Who Can Save His Life," aka *Every Man for Himself*, 1978) signaled a new attention to the static image.

However much Wenders believed he gave up the story for the sake of the singular image, Godard went much further. *Passion* (1982), one of the most pictorially rich films of his career, centers on an east European filmmaker who replicates famous paintings on video by shooting tableaux of actors. As Godard's camera coasts over these groupings, a two-dimensional image becomes voluminous, as if the cinema had the power to revivify clichéd masterpieces (Color Plate 26.27).

Godard's films of the decade—*First Name Carmen* (1983), *Hail Mary* (1985), *Détective* (1985), *King Lear* (1987), *Soigne ta droite* ("Keep Up Your Right," 1987), *Nouvelle Vague* ("New Wave," 1990)—do not relax his usual demands on the viewer. Though sometimes based on familiar texts (the Bible, Shakespeare), the plots are oblique and often incomprehensible. Shots and sounds are broken to bits and reassembled for maximum disorientation, an effect enhanced by a jolting use of Dolby stereo. Late Godard remains faithful to the aesthetic of fragmentation he launched thirty years earlier.

Yet the films also suggest a new serenity. There is a lyrical treatment of foliage, water, and sunlight. Instead of the flat, frontal, posterlike shots of the late 1960s and early 1970s, Godard builds his scenes out of oblique, close views of the human body and its surroundings. He uses available light, without fill, to create rich shadow areas. His angles split the scene into planes of sharp detail and out-of-focus action (Color Plates 26.28, 26.29). In all, the "painterly" Godard has a calm radiance that softens the abrasiveness of the narrative construction. In his characteristically radical way, he shows the rewards of a return to the arresting image. Along with directors as old as Oliveira and as young as Van Dormaël, he demonstrated that the art cinema continued to offer a modernist meditation on cinema, history, and psychological experience.

EASTERN EUROPE AND THE USSR

EASTERN EUROPE: FROM REFORM TO REVOLUTION

"It is time to relegate to the archives the postulates of the cold war, when Europe was viewed as an arena of confrontation divided into 'spheres of influence.' . . . Any interference in internal affairs and any attempts to restrict the sovereignty of states—either friends and allies or anyone else—are inadmissible."[9] These remarks, made by Soviet President Mikhail Gorbachev in June 1989, went beyond the Soviet platitudes about the independence of its satellites. Gorbachev's *glasnost* ("openness") policy included a greater degree of self-determination for the eastern European countries.

In the months before and after Gorbachev's speech, these countries astonished the world—and Gorbachev himself—by throwing off their governments. Throughout 1989 East Germany, Hungary, Poland, Czechoslovakia, Bulgaria, and Romania cast out their Communist leaders and demanded democracy and economic reform along capitalist lines. Joyous crowds, gathering from all over Europe, smashed the Berlin Wall. Less than two years later an aborted coup against Gorbachev triggered the collapse of the Communist party in the Soviet Union itself.

Twenty years before, few would have predicted such a dramatic death for eastern European communism. The 1968 Prague Spring had been aborted by an invasion of Soviet troops (p. 634), and all hopes of democracy seemed stilled. Poland, Hungary, and some other eastern countries pacified their citizens with economic reforms and boosts in the standard of living that suggested that "socialist consumerism" had finally arrived.

Yet the prosperity of eastern Europe was artificial, sustained by price controls. OPEC's 1973 oil-price increase, along with domestic shortfalls in agriculture and consumer goods, led to the beginning of discontent. "A spectre is haunting Eastern Europe," wrote Václav Havel in 1979, "the spectre of what is called in the west 'dissent.' "[10] New forces for change—labor unions, nationalist groups, and even religious bodies—began to chip away at the Communist regimes.

The most decisive events took place in Poland. In 1976–1977, the government's attempt to raise fixed prices was met by a rash of strikes. In 1980, more strikes erupted when thousands of workers occupied the shipyards of Gdansk. With the aid of the Catholic Church Lech Walesa and other workers founded a new union, Solidarity. Solidarity rapidly became a kind of popular front, claiming that it was working to turn Poland into a "self-governing republic." The regime responded by outlawing Solidarity and declaring martial law. Leaders of Solidarity were arrested, and the organization went underground. When Gorbachev announced in 1985 that the Soviet government would not sponsor an invasion of a sovereign nation, the Polish government began negotiations with Solidarity. Eventually, in the summer of 1989, in open elections Solidarity won a stunning victory over Communist incumbents and Walesa became president of the new Poland.

Popular movements toward liberalization emerged in Hungary and Czechoslovakia as well. In Yugoslavia and other Balkan States, the collapse of communism was accelerated by new leaders who played on nationalistic feelings. The failures of eastern Europe's planned economies made people eager to move toward democracy, free- or mixed-market economies, and access to agricultural produce, modern housing, and up-to-date consumer goods. The "velvet revolutions" of 1989 were partly responses to the inability of communism to deliver social services and to guarantee citizens a modern lifestyle.

Political freedom, however, eventually proved damaging to film production. East European cinema, galvanized by growing dissent after the mid-1970s, was battered by the economic crises and political upheavals of the late 1980s.

In the staunch Soviet ally East Germany, for example, Socialist Realism held on, counterbalanced by more progressive trends toward "youth films" and "outsider films" centering on nonconformist women. The end of Erich Honecker's regime in 1989, followed by reunification with West Germany the following year, left old-line Communist filmmakers stranded. After reunification German films claimed only 10 percent of the national box office.

In Bulgaria, expensive historical spectacles made in the late 1970s and early 1980s ate up the nation's film funds, just before the economic crisis in all Communist satellites led to massive cutbacks in state industries. In Yugoslavia, an emergent independent film movement, strongly decentralized production aided by television funding, and a move toward privatization were cut short by the country's economic collapse in the mid-1980s. After the fall of communism, an ethnic war started in 1991 and destroyed the nation's civil society. Yugoslavian cinema came to an end, leaving questions about how filmmakers would fare in Serbia, Bosnia-Herzegovina, and the other new states.

Events in Hungary, Czechoslovakia, and Poland illustrate further how eastern European film moved from the stagnant years of the mid-1970s to the bleak conditions of the 1990s. Hungarian cinema suffered the least radical changes. In the 1970s Hungary became a crucible for reform within a socialist economy, and the state's "New Economic Mechanism" successfully raised living standards through a mixture of centralized control, private busi-

Fig. 26.27 In a memoir as cinéphiliac as any offered by the French New Wave, Márta Mészarós recalls sharing her mother's love at a village movie show (*Diary for My Children*).

nesses, and joint ventures with the capitalist West. The Communist party, though firmly in control, had tolerated multicandidate elections, and censorship was relatively relaxed.

Accordingly, Hungarian cinema consistently made between twelve and twenty features per year, many of them signed by major directors. After working in Italy, Miklós Jancsó returned to make *Hungarian Rhapsody* (1978) and *Allegro Barbaro* (1978) as parts of an uncompleted trilogy. Throughout the 1980s and 1990s, he made films regularly, but none aroused the acclaim that had greeted his earlier work, and some, such as *Private Vices, Public Virtues* (1976), struck critics as verging on sexploitation. Karoly Makk seemed a similarly spent force, except for *Another Way* (1982). Far more successful on the international scene was István Szabó. His Hungarian *Confidence* (1979) led him to the high-budget and high-profile *Mephisto* (1981) and *Colonel Redl* (1983; both West German).

Arguably the most consistent and accomplished senior director in Hungary was Márta Mészarós. "I tell my own life story in most of my films. The search for Mother and Father is a determining experience in my own life."[11] Mészarós dramatized her quest in *Anna* (1981) and the fictionalized series of her memoirs of growing up under Stalinism, *Diary for My Children* (1984; Fig. 26.27), *Diary for My Loves* (1987), and *Diary for My Father and Mother* (1991). Thanks to Mészarós, Szabó, Pal Gábor (*Angi Vera*, 1978), and others, Hungary maintained a modicum of prestige on the art-cinema and festival circuit through the 1970s and 1980s.

Czechoslovakian filmmakers had a less equable time during these decades. The crackdown after the Prague Spring of 1968 kept pressure firm. The government tightened control over film units, where byzantine bureaucracies and corps of "literary advisers" steered production away from political subjects and toward popular entertainment. Many directors emigrated to the United States, Canada, and western Europe.

Of the New Wave directors who stayed, Jiří Menzel did not make a film until 1976, and thereafter turned out several characteristically bittersweet comedies, notably *Seclusion Near a Forest* (1976); *Cutting It Short* (1980); and *My Sweet Little Village* (1986), which was a popular triumph at home and a foreign art-house success. Vera Chytilová, after campaigning for years against the sexism of the regime's film policy (p. 635), returned to directing with *The Apple Game* (1976), a farce about sexual relations that earned official disapproval but was marketed abroad. She followed this with films that mixed commercial narrative forms with eroticism and social satire.

After the 1989 revolts, major banned films came off the shelf. Audiences around the world saw what the censors had forbidden, and the vivacity of the Prague Spring was recaptured. Menzel's *Larks on a String* (1969; p. 634), taken out of the vaults, won the main prize at the Berlin Film Festival twenty years after it was finished. More recently banned works, such as Dušan Hanák's *I Love, You Love* (1980), also received international notice.

The most energetic eastern European cinema of the period was to be found in Poland. Neither as liberated as Hungary nor as repressive as Czechoslovakia, Poland offered filmmakers some latitude for social criticism. Although production units had been dissolved in the wake of the 1968 demonstrations (p. 636), they were soon reconstituted, and filmmakers won even greater freedom. Each production unit consisted of an artistic director (usually a major filmmaker) and a literary director (usually a screenwriter). During the early 1970s, filmmakers adhered to safe literary and historical subjects. Midway through the decade, in synchronization with popular discontent with economic policy, there arose the "cinema of moral concern."

A prime example was Andrzej Wajda's *Man of Marble* (1976), a fictionalized investigation of a "model worker" from the 1950s. The filmmaker Agnieszka tries to find out why Birkut, a loyal bricklayer, was erased from history. In a knowing echo of *Citizen Kane,* her interviews with people who knew Birkut frame extensive flashbacks. Wajda's exposure of Stalinist and post-Stalinist political intrigue reflexively invokes cinema's ability to create ideology (Fig. 26.28). At first, Agnieszka trusts the camera as a documentary tool (Fig. 26.29), but by the end of the film, denied raw stock and a camera, she must discover the truth directly, through human contact with Birkut's son.

Fig. 26.28 *Man of Marble:* Birkut's triumphs as a bricklayer staged for the "documentary" camera.

Along with Krzysztof Zanussi's *Camouflage* (1976), a depiction of conformity and idealism at a summer camp for college students, *Man of Marble* signaled a new disaffection with the regime. A harder-line vice-minister of culture for films came to power, and the filmmaking community protested. Directors pointed out that the public was treating film as the conscience of Poland, the only witness to the conditions of social life. Feliks Falk's *Top Dog* (1977), Zanussi's *Spiral* (1978), and other films of "moral concern" countered the regime's boasts about improved living standards with charges that Poles had sacrificed their honor and conscience. Many of the younger directors, born after the war, grew up in Stalinist culture and were alert for its signs in contemporary life.

Fig. 26.29 *Man of Marble:* Agnieszka discovers the statue glorifying Birkut.

When Solidarity's strikes galvanized the nation in 1980, film workers immediately rallied to the cause. As Solidarity won initial concessions from the government, the annual national film festival in Gdansk announced a new socially critical cinema. The filmmaker, Wajda declared in 1980, "can succeed only if he makes an honest scrutiny of contemporary realities and the scale of the human effort and suffering they contain . . . and explores them for the chances they offer of man's spiritual victory."[12]

From the production units supervised by Wajda and Zanussi came several films reflecting the new realism. The most celebrated was Wajda's *Man of Iron* (1980), a sequel to *Man of Marble* in which Agnieszka and Birkut's son press their investigation into the 1960s and 1970s. It was shot during the Solidarity strike and incorporated documentary footage of contemporary events. Attacking the government with unprecedented audacity, *Man of Iron* quickly became the most widely seen Polish film in history.

When the gains of Solidarity were overturned by the government, the outspoken filmmakers felt the counterblows. The declaration of martial law closed all the theaters for two months, banned several films, shut down Wajda's production unit, and encouraged filmmakers to turn out diverting musicals, comedies, sex films, and costume pictures. Some directors emigrated. Gradually, however, the constraints relaxed. In 1983, the filmmakers were allowed to reshape their professional association (on the condition that Wajda would step down as president). Soon several films criticized the imposition of martial law.

As Gorbachev's new policies toward eastern Europe led the government to open negotiations with Solidarity, Polish filmmakers returned to the cinema of moral urgency. The most significant director from an international perspective was Krzysztof Kieslowski. He had made his name during the 1970s with barbed television documentaries and *The Scar* (1976), an acerbic study of an ineffectual factory foreman. In *Camera Buff* (1979), a worker tries to make an amateur film about his factory but runs into problems of honesty and bad faith. *Chance* (1981) presents three hypothetical plots, tracing out the life choices available to a man: becoming a party leader, an opposition fighter, or an apolitical bystander. *No End* (1984) was the boldest film about martial law. In a pungent mixture of the religious and the secular, Kieslowski's series of television films "The Decalogue" (1988) offered a story for each of the Ten Commandments; two of these grim tales were expanded into features (*A Short Film about Killing* and *A Short Film about Love*, 1988). By the time Solidarity was voted into office in 1989, Kieslowski had become one of the most famous directors in Europe.

Just before the 1989 revolutions, reform was brewing in several film industries. Yugoslavia made its regional studios autonomous. Hungary and Poland abolished the state monopoly on film and gave the production units their independence, urging them to pursue financing and create joint productions with capitalist nations. After the 1989 events, Czechoslovakia dissolved its central film bureau. Throughout eastern Europe, film companies were privatized, and western money was welcomed. Censorship was virtually abolished. Hungary made a distribution arrangement with American companies in 1989, and soon other countries opened their markets.

The new conditions created a fresh barrage of problems. Under Communist regimes ticket prices had been absurdly low (usually less than a dollar), but open-market conditions required a price rise, which drove audiences away. Theaters had lacked maintenance for years, but without state subsidy there was no money for renovations. Home video, late in penetrating eastern Europe but offering unrestrained (often pirated) access to popular western films, further cut theater attendance.

Worst of all, post-1989 freedom put filmmakers head to head with Hollywood. The results were predictable. American films, long barred from eastern Europe, flooded the market much as they had deluged western Europe after 1945. In 1991, 95 percent of the films playing in Poland were from U.S. companies, and Czechoslovakian films attracted less than one-fourth of domestic box-office revenues. In the same year, the audience for Hungarian films was only one-seventh what it had been two years before. The local product played in small art theaters and barely broke even.

Eastern European governments sought to imitate western Europe by offering loans, subsidies, and prizes, but funds remained pitifully small. With eastern countries struggling to heal fractured economies and inflation running high, art cinema could no longer expect much help. Filmmakers had little choice but to pursue global cinema. "We want to make films for viewers in Paris, New York, Tokyo," announced one Polish director. "We cannot make films only for Poland."[13] Doubtless most directors dreamed of a success such as that of Kieslowski's *Double Life of Véronique* (1991). Its art-cinema plot, involving two apparently identical women living in different countries, found a ready audience around the world. Shot in Poland and France, it was funded by Kieslowski's own company, a private French production firm, and Canal Plus.

Such benefits were given to few. After dissolving the Warsaw Pact in 1991, eastern Europe sought to join the European community. Some filmmakers began to win funds from Eurimages, but most would take many years just to achieve the defensive, beleaguered position of most of their western European counterparts.

THE USSR: THE FINAL THAW

During the years 1964–1982, Leonid Brezhnev served as Secretary of the Communist Party of the Soviet Union. Opposed to reform, favoring rule by elderly officials, Brezhnev's regime presented an image of solidity and apparent growth. During the 1970s citizens acquired televisions, refrigerators, and cars. At the same time, Brezhnev committed himself to a policy of military intervention, assisting revolts in Angola and Ethiopia and invading Afghanistan.

Although consumer comforts increased, culture suffered another "freeze." Aleksandr Solzhenitsyn, Andrei Sakharov, and other dissidents were silenced by exile or imprisonment. Sergei Paradzhanov, the director of *Shadows of Forgotten Ancestors* and *The Color of Pomegranates*, was released from prison in 1977, but he was forbidden to emigrate or to work in cinema. Goskino had become a bloated bureaucracy, encouraging popular entertainment in tune with the new "socialist consumerism." The strategy was rewarded by the international success of *Moscow Does Not Believe in Tears* (1980), the first Soviet film to win an Academy Award. As in Hollywood during the same period, the bulk of box-office income was supplied by relatively few films.

Despite the conservatism of the Brezhnev era, some slice-of-life films gave voice to the problems of daily existence, especially among Soviet youth. Dinara Asanova (*The Restricted Boy*, 1977), Lana Gogoberidze (*Some Interviews on Personal Matters*, 1979), and other women directors created distinctive psychological studies. The lyrical or "poetic" tendencies associated with the republics' studios continued in the work of Tengiz Abuladze (e.g., the banned *Repentance*, 1984).

In addition, several directors created idiosyncratic, self-consciously artistic works that reflected both European art cinema and Russian traditions. In the massive *Siberiade* (1979; banned), Andrei Mikhalkov-Konchalovsky offered a personalized historical epic, while in *A Slave of Love* (1976) and *Unfinished Piece for Player Piano* (1977) his brother Nikita Mikhalkov experimented with reflexivity in the manner of Fellini and other European directors. Larissa Shepitko's films emphasize individual conscience and moral choice in the vein of Dostoyevsky and contemporary anti-Stalinist literature. Her World War II film *The Ascent* (1977) shows two partisan soldiers captured by the Germans and forced to decide between collaboration and execution. The intellectual Sotnikov, having conquered his fear of death

Fig. 26.30 In the course of *The Ascent*, Sotnikov becomes paralleled to Christ in his willingness to sacrifice himself for other Russians captured by the Germans.

Fig. 26.31 The hard, westernized Soviet teenagers of *Scarecrow*.

Fig. 26.32 To-camera address intensifies the brutality of *Come and See*. Here the young hero returns to his village to be told that his family has been massacred.

in an earlier skirmish, bears up under torture and accepts death with an eerie, Christ-like gentleness (Fig. 26.30).

The most visible exponent of an artistic cinema opposed to mass genres and propaganda films remained Andrei Tarkovsky. *Solaris* (1972) had somewhat mitigated the scandal of *Andrei Roublev* (1966; p. 538), but the obscure, dreamlike *The Mirror* (1975) confirmed that he worked in a mystical vein fiercely opposed to the mainstream.

Considered a "reactionary," Tarkovsky insisted on the family, poetry, and religion as central forces in social life. He declared himself against cinema with a political message, arguing for a cinema of direct, evocative impressions—a position that put him close to the sensibilist German directors. But his somber films seek to engage the spectator in a more weighty way than do those of Herzog and Wenders. *Stalker* (1979) presents an allegorical expedition through a wrecked postindustrial landscape into "the Zone," a region where human life can be fundamentally changed. Filmed in a blue murk, *Stalker* uses hypnotic, achingly slow camera movements to create what the director called "the pressure of the time" running through the shots (Color Plate 26.30).[14]

Tarkovsky went to Italy to make *Nostalghia* (1983), a melancholy, virtually nonnarrative meditation on memory and exile (Color Plate 26.31). He decided not to return to the USSR. He directed some stage productions, and in Sweden he filmed the Bergmanesque *The Sacrifice* (1986), which won the special jury prize at Cannes. By the time of his death in 1986, Tarkovsky had become an emblem of the cinema of artistic conscience. His prominence abroad had saved his films from shelving, and even if they went unseen in the USSR, they were salable foreign exports. He influenced the pictorialist strain of European cinema during the 1970s and 1980s, and his Soviet contemporaries gathered courage from his resistance to official policies. A self-conscious auteur on the European model, Tarkovsky demanded that art be a moral quest: "Masterpieces are born of the artist's struggle to express his ethical ideals."[15]

During Tarkovsky's silence and exile, Soviet cinema was changing. Rolan Bykov's *Scarecrow* (1983), a film about a village girl despised by her classmates, quietly celebrates indigenous tradition and historical memory over the harsh selfishness of the new consumerist Russia (Fig. 26.31). Alexei German's *My Friend Ivan Lapshin* (1983; banned) eclectically mixes newsreels and abstractly staged footage in order to criticize Stalinist conceptions of political crimes. The World War II movie was given a new savagery in Elem Klimov's *Come and See* (1985), a harrowing portrayal of the German occupation of Byelorussia (Fig. 26.32). Based on an idea of Klimov's wife, the deceased Larissa Shepitko, *Come and See* presented the naive young hero as something less than the Socialist Realist ideal. During the same period, Paradzhanov returned to feature filmmaking. *The Legend of Suram Fortress* (1984) recalls *The Color of Pomegranates* in its stylized simplicity and vibrant textures (Color Plate 26.32). Even a "parallel cinema" shot on 16mm and super 8mm was beginning to lurk in students' apartments and artists' basements (p. 688).

Behind the façade of Brezhnev's regime, the USSR had stagnated. Agricultural and industrial production had declined, and so had health and living standards. Corruption, inefficiency, and overextended military commitments were draining the state's resources. Neither Brezhnev nor the two elderly General Secretaries who succeeded him faced up to the challenge. A younger politician, Mikhail Gorbachev, assumed leadership in 1985, and he revealed that the USSR was on the verge of financial collapse. His announcement that the USSR would no longer sustain its satellites in eastern Europe led to the overthrow of Communist regimes there. Gorbachev also called for a policy of *glasnost* which was to initiate a long-overdue rebuilding of Soviet institutions, or *perestroika* ("restructuring"). Another "thaw" had begun.

At first Gorbachev sought to implement reforms through the chain of party command, but in 1987 he began to call for more fundamental changes. *Glasnost* meant confronting the errors of the past. Stalin's regime was excoriated, and citizens were encouraged to discuss the failures of the economy, the rise of crime and drug use, and the sense that the Soviet system bred people to be hard and selfish.

Glasnost gave filmmakers an unprecedented freedom. Stalin's policies were attacked in *The Cold Summer of '53* (1987), a sort of Soviet Western which shows a village terrorized by a gang of released political prisoners. Valery Ogorodnikov's *Prishvin's Paper Eyes* (1989) portrays the early days of Soviet television, with jabs at propaganda filming and a remarkable sequence which mixes newsreels and Eisenstein's Odessa Steps massacre in ways which suggest that Stalin is selecting the victims from a balcony.

Youth films dwelt upon student rebellion, often laced with rock music and a post-Punk anomie (e.g., Sergei Solvyev's *Assa*, 1988). *Chernukha*, or "black cinema," rubbed audiences' noses in the sordidness of daily life and predatory politics. Satiric films mocked party tradition and current fashions. Even mass entertainment exploited the new attitudes, as when the enormously successful gangster film *King of Crime* (1988) showed the KGB, the state, and criminals conspiring to defraud the public. Internationally, the hallmark of *glasnost* cinema was Vasily Pichul's *Little Vera* (1988). Vera's cynical amorality and casual promiscuity once and for all deflated the myth of the virtuous heroine who could sacrifice all for the collective.

Most of these films would not have been made had not *perestroika* opened up the film industry. In May 1986, at the Congress of Soviet Filmmakers, Elem Klimov, director of *Come and See* and a friend of Gorbachev's, was elected head of the union. The same congress set in motion the restructuring of Goskino, the state agency overseeing all film activity. Under the new policy, Goskino would serve principally as a conduit for funds and a source of facilities. Filmmaking would be in the hands of free creative production units on the eastern European model. In addition, censorship was markedly liberalized.

One of Klimov's major reforms was the establishment of the Conflict Commission, aimed at the review and release of banned films. Soon critical works such as the humanistic war dramas *My Friend Ivan Lapshin* (1984) and *Commissar* (1967) and the surreal Ukrainian satire *Repentance* (1984) were unshelved. In the year after Tarkovsky's death, he was honored with a complete retrospective in his homeland.

Glasnost and *perestroika* gave more autonomy to the republics as well. In Kazakhstan, quasi-Punk directors offered films like *The Needle* (1988,

Rashid Nugmanov), a drug movie bearing the influence of Hollywood melodrama, Fassbinder, and Wenders' road sagas. In Georgia, Alexander Rekhviashvili made *The Step* (1986), a structurally adventurous, wryly absurd film about the meaningless routines of Soviet life. Before Paradzhanov's death in 1990, he directed *Ashik Kerib* (1989), a literary adaptation transformed by his ritualized treatment of Georgian legend and ethnic custom.

While international circles grew interested in the "New Soviet Cinema," Gorbachev's attempt to reform communism from the top down was proving unworkable. He pressed for a more rapid shift to individual initiative and a market system. In 1989, the government demanded that film studios become profitable and encouraged filmmakers to form private companies and independent cooperatives. Formerly Goskino had sole distribution power, but now independent producers could distribute their own products. Plans were made for Goskino to act as a clearinghouse for funds, but in late 1990, Goskino was dismantled. For the first time since the Revolution, filmmaking was a fully private enterprise.

The decline in state funding came at a bad time. Not only were cinema's economic agencies vulnerable, but technology was in disrepair. The thirty-nine Soviet studios badly needed renovation. Only one had Dolby sound equipment, a necessity for western markets, and Soviet film stock was still the world's worst. In addition, the studio complexes, burdened with overhead and staff, were competing with hundreds of independent producers and with "studios" consisting of filmmakers who had banded together.

The free market was an anarchic one. No legislation regulated film activity. Video piracy flourished. Clandestine companies churned out pornography, often as diversions for black-market funds. Before *glasnost*, national production averaged 150 features per year; in 1991, 400 features were made. A year later, there were fewer than 100.

As in India and other countries of unpredictable, highly fragmented production, film distribution and exhibition proved to be a bottleneck. Very few completed films found their way into theaters. Attendance dropped to around one-tenth of theater capacity, and most of the upstart entrepreneurs were decimated. The devaluation of the ruble increased production costs tenfold. Top directors could not get their films released; in 1992 the head of Lenfilm complained that no Russian film could recoup its costs on the domestic market.

The local product also had new competition. The former Soviet empire boasted an annual audience of over 700 million, and this was a tempting target for U.S. firms. Although the MPEAA refused to release new major films until the USSR took antipiracy measures, old or cheap Hollywood pictures dominated the market, capturing 70 percent of audiences.

The final years of Soviet cinema were nevertheless prestigious ones. Filmmakers joined writers and composers as representatives of a vigorous, eclectic culture. Not since the 1960s had so many Soviet films won praise in the West. *Taxi Blues* (1990, Pavel Loungine), a Soviet-French effort, portrays a decaying urbanism and amoral, rudderless characters (Color Plate 26.33). Vitaly Kanevsky's *Freeze, Die, Come to Life!* (1990), a "black film," suggests the savagery and spite pervading contemporary Soviet life by means of a story about children's corruption in a village during World War II (Fig. 26.33). The Ukrainian-Canadian production *Swan Lake: The Zone* (1990), directed

Fig. 26.33 Ramshackle structures and a sea of mud: The landscape of Soviet life in *Freeze, Die, Come to Life!*

by the veteran Yuri Ilienko from a story by Paradzhanov, renders a political fable with Bressonian asceticism. An escapee from a prison camp hides in a gigantic, hollow hammer-and-sickle sign (Color Plate 26.34). The ponderous symbolism of the looming, rusting emblem is counterbalanced by a rich sonic texture and a painstaking rendering of the man's cramped, dank shelter.

An aborted coup against Gorbachev in August 1991 triggered the dissolution of the Communist party. Boris Yeltsin ascended to leadership, and the USSR was replaced by the Commonwealth of Independent States (CIS). Now Russia, the Ukraine, Armenia, and other former Soviet republics would function as separate nations. The bipolar model that had ruled world political strategy since World War II was ended.

Like their counterparts in eastern Europe, CIS filmmakers were eager for productions with the West. Yet the "common European home" envisaged by Gorbachev, a huge market stretching from the Atlantic to the Ural Mountains, was not taking shape. The CIS had a collapsed economy, a steeply declining standard of living, and modern problems of crime and drug addiction. The European Community proved reluctant to aid or assimilate CIS nations.

Desperate, the former Soviet nations threw their resources and markets open to western exploitation. The major U.S. companies set up distribution offices and began building multiplex theaters. British, French, and Italian film companies launched "international" pictures featuring prominent western stars in CIS locales. Mosfilm, Lenfilm, and other studios became service facilities for runaway productions. Western producers would find exotic locales and eager personnel, and the former land of proletarian liberation would set no restraints on foreign capitalists' investment.

THE PACIFIC RIM: NATIONAL INDUSTRIES AND THE NEW INTERNATIONAL FILM

Australia and New Zealand entered the international scene thanks in part to government subsidies akin to those supporting western European cinema. Each was able to create a New Cinema for the festival circuit. In addition,

Australian film won some successes in mainstream popular film. By contrast, the Japanese government offered virtually no funding for filmmaking, and the studio system declined as independent production rose and quotas on foreign imports were abolished. The Japanese penetrated the international film market through a few successful exports but, more importantly, through conglomerates' investments in Hollywood and European companies.

AUSTRALIA

Australian production reached a low ebb in the 1950s and early 1960s. One of the first indications that the country could again make commercially viable films came when Michael Powell, forced to work in television after the scandal resulting from *Peeping Tom* (p. 553), made an Australian feature film. *They're a Weird Mob* (1966), a low-budget comedy about an immigrant worker, proved hugely popular. In 1971, Canadian director Ted Kotcheff made *Wake in Fright* (aka *Outback*).

When the Liberal party took power in the early 1970s, Australia sought to establish a distinctive national identity. The arts enjoyed a new period of support. In 1970, the government formed the Australian Film Development Corporation, which funded Bruce Beresford's comedy *The Adventures of Barry McKenzie* (1972), Peter Weir's *The Cars That Ate Paris* (1974), and other films by directors who would soon create a New Wave. The government also created the Australian Film and Television School. In 1975, the Film Development Corp. was replaced by the Australian Film Commission (AFC), which helped finance about fifty features in its first five years of existence. The AFC outperformed some of its European counterparts, recovering about 38 percent of its investments.

Television had come to Australia in 1956, siphoning off cinema audiences but also fostering a generation of young filmmakers who longed to make theatrical features. Australian film critics of the 1970s favored films of the French New Wave and of auteurs like Ingmar Bergman and Luis Buñuel. This combination of government support and interest in European-style art cinema led Australian directors toward international elite audiences. The breakthrough film was Peter Weir's *Picnic at Hanging Rock* (1976), based on a 1900 incident in which a group of schoolgirls mysteriously disappeared during an outing. The film proceeds at a leisurely pace, creating intense atmosphere through actual locations, haunting music, and luminous cinematography (Color Plate 26.35).

Although the "New Australian Cinema" included several genres, including low-budget exploitation films, historical films became the most visible internationally. Bruce Beresford made another film set in a Victorian girls' school, *The Getting of Wisdom* (1977), and a World War I story about an absurd court-martial, *"Breaker" Morant* (1980). Weir's World War I drama *Gallipoli* (1981) and *The Year of Living Dangerously* (1982), re-creating the overthrow of Sukarno in Indonesia, construct a comparably rich historical context. One of the rare historical films devoted to the plight of Aborigines, *The Chant of Jimmie Blacksmith* (1978, Fred Schepisi) shows a young black man striving to succeed in a white world, only to be driven to murderous

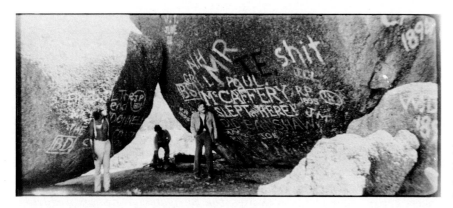

Fig. 26.34 The hero and his Aborigine friends find a sacred spot covered with graffiti left by white tourists (*The Chant of Jimmie Blacksmith*).

Fig. 26.35 In a shot reminiscent of the wide-angle images of Spielberg and De Palma, *The Road Warrior* uses a bold depth composition to show the wounded Max flown into the besieged camp.

rebellion (Fig. 26.34). Gillian Armstrong used the Victorian era to make a feminist study in *My Brilliant Career* (1979), and Philip Noyce admiringly portrayed newsreel filmmakers of the 1930s in his *Newsfront* (1978). Weir, Beresford, Schepisi, Noyce, and other major directors were eventually lured to Hollywood.

Aside from its prestige pictures, the Australian industry also had some international popular successes. Independently of government funding, a small production firm called Kennedy-Miller made a pair of violent futuristic road movies, *Mad Max* (1978) and *Mad Max II* (aka *The Road Warrior*, 1982). Producer-director George Miller, influenced by the spaghetti Westerns of Sergio Leone and by Spielberg's Indiana Jones films, peopled a savage, postnuclear Australian outback with bizarre warriors. Miller's aggressive, visceral style owed a good deal to the New Hollywood (Fig. 26.35). Somewhat later *Crocodile Dundee* (1986), a simple action comedy featuring Australian star Paul Hogan, became a surprise hit around the world.

The successes of both art films and popular movies led to a concentration on more foreign investment, coproductions, and export. *Mad Max beyond Thunderdome* (1985) was financed by Warner Bros., distributor of *The Road Warrior*, and *Crocodile Dundee 2* (1988) was also a foreign production. By the late 1980s, Australian cinema had moved heavily into an international mode, often depending on foreign stars [e.g., Meryl Streep in Fred Schepisi's *Evil Angels* (aka *A Cry in the Dark*), 1990].

NEW ZEALAND

New Zealand followed a similar, though shorter, path to national film production. Sporadic filmmaking had gone on since the early silent era, but there was no organized industry until the 1970s. In 1978, the government established the New Zealand Film Commission to support films at the preproduction stage and to help them find private investment. By the 1980s, a low, if fluctuating, level of production had been established.

Because the population of New Zealand numbered only about 3 million people during the 1980s, films had to be exported in order to recoup their costs. As usual, directors' best opportunities often lay with art-house audiences. For example, Vincent Ward's *The Navigator: A Mediaeval Odyssey* (1988) transports its characters from England in the Middle Ages to a modern Australian city.

Another major director, Jane Campion, was born in New Zealand but studied at the Australian Film and Television School. Her first feature, *Sweetie* (1989), was produced in Australia. By contrasting two sisters with differing mental problems, the film explores the boundaries between madness and sanity and between art cinema and melodrama. *An Angel at My Table* (1990) was planned as a three-part miniseries for New Zealand television but was released to theaters internationally. Based on the autobiographical works of poet Jane Frame, it attracted art-cinema audiences through its subtle performances depicting the heroine's struggle against being labeled "insane." Campion uses many close shots to emphasize her grubby daily existence, punctuating the scenes with breathtaking landscapes that suggest her lyrical vision (Color Plate 26.36). Campion's third feature, *The Piano*, a French-Australian-New Zealand coproduction, won the Grand Prize at the 1993 Cannes Festival.

JAPAN

Japan's vertically integrated film industry was much stronger than Australia's or New Zealand's. Yet while Japan was becoming one of the world's great economic powers, its film companies were falling on hard times.

As in western countries, the problems began with slumping attendance. In 1958, the peak year for the Japanese box office, 1.2 billion tickets were sold; in 1972, fewer than 200 million were. The studios cut production to around 350 features per year. Toei, Toho, and Shochiku ruled the domestic market, but the latter two put little money into filmmaking, preferring to invest in other leisure-time industries.

Consequently, during the 1970s independent production and distribution gained ground (p. 550). Smaller firms financed nonstudio projects and became strong presences in international export. The most artistically oriented independent group was the Art Theater Guild (ATG), founded in 1961 and throughout the 1970s still funding a few films by Oshima, Hani, Yoshida, Shindo, and other New Wave directors. The ATG also owned a circuit of arthouse theaters for showcasing its product. Bigger independent companies founded by department stores, television companies, and publishing concerns also began producing films, and these firms gave the studios stiff competition.

The studios' most dependable in-house projects came to be their endless series, such as Toho's monster movies and Shochiku's sentimental Tora-San dramas. Like their Hollywood counterparts, most of the studios built their release schedules out of independent projects which they had helped finance. The Big Three dominated distribution and exhibition, so they still controlled the market. The most profitable genres were martial-arts films, *yakuza* (gangster) tales, science-fiction movies (based on the success of *Star Wars*), disaster films, and soft-core pornography (the so-called *roman porno*).

Most of the well-established auteurs were able to work by acquiring financing from both the studios and independent sources. Ichikawa had a hit with a *Godfather*-type gangster story, *The Inugami Family* (1976), financed by Toho and a publishing house specializing in crime fiction. Shohei Imamura's own company joined with Shochiku for a characteristic tale of rape and revenge, *Vengeance Is Mine* (1979), and for *Eijanaika* (1981), a story about the clash of cultures in the modernizing Japan of 1866 (Color Plate 26.37). Imamura's *Ballad of Narayama* (1983), a Toei production, won worldwide notice for its presentation of the rural custom of abandoning the old to die.

The most renowned big-budget directors moved toward internationally financed productions. Akira Kurosawa's *Dersu Uzala* (1975) was a Russian project; *Kagemusha* (1980) and *Ran* (1985) were assisted by French and U.S. backing. *Dreams* (1990) was partially financed by Warner Bros.

Nagisa Oshima's international coproductions *Empire of Passion* (1978), *Merry Christmas, Mr. Lawrence* (1982), and *Max mon amour* (1986), the latter made without any Japanese participation, represented a retreat from the disjunctive experimentation of his works of the 1960s. None of these productions matched the scandalous success of his first French-Japanese vehicle, *In the Realm of the Senses* (1976). Based on a famous 1936 incident, it centers on a man and woman who withdraw from the political upheavals of their day into a world of erotic experimentation. At the climax, the man languidly succumbs to murder and mutilation. The film relinquishes virtually all the modernist experimentation that had made Oshima famous, presenting its erotic encounters in sumptuous imagery (Color Plate 26.38). Although shot in Japan, *In the Realm of the Senses* was heavily censored there; flying to Paris to see the complete version became a fad among wealthy Japanese.

Imamura, Kurosawa, and Oshima slowed their pace to a film every four or five years. While they struggled to find backing for their ambitious projects, a younger generation was glad to work quickly and cheaply. The super-8mm underground, often Punk-flavored, carried several directors to mainstream production.

Born around 1960, the new generation found political modernism as alien as the New Wave directors had found the great tradition of Ozu and Mizoguchi. The young directors of the late 1970s and early 1980s reveled in the anarchic vulgarity of violent comic books (*manga*) and heavy-metal rock music. Financed by the Art Theater Guild and some major studios, they attacked the stereotypes of Japanese harmony and prosperity with a raucous humor.

Not surprisingly, they often concentrated on youth culture, with such rocker-biker films as *Crazy Thunder Road* (1980, Sogo Ishii). Hitoshi Yazaki's

Fig. 26.36 *To Sleep, So As to Dream*: A pastiche of a silent-era swordfight movie (*chambara*), remarkably accurate in both its technique and its simulation of aging film stock.

Afternoon Breezes (1980) offered youthful lesbian fantasies. Domestic tradition formed another target. In Yoshimitsu Morita's *The Family Game* (1983), a college student tutoring a boy winds up seducing an entire family. Sogo Ishii offered *The Crazy Family* (1984), in which household hatreds escalate into a desperate chainsaw battle. The same absurd violence permeates Shinya Tsukamoto's *Tetsuo* (1989). Tsukamoto, who started shooting super-8 movies at age fourteen, worked in an advertising agency and directed television commercials before he produced this raw fantasy about ordinary citizens becoming robots as a result of their macabre erotic impulses.

Other films by young directors were less grotesque in their experimentation. Among the most remarkable was Kaizo Hayashi's *To Sleep, So As to Dream* (1986). A meditation on the history of Japanese cinema, the film plunges two detectives into a search for a kidnapped woman who is enigmatically linked to an unfinished silent film. Scenes from the 1920s movie, filmed by Hayashi in a pastiche of Japanese silent style, interrupt the plot (Fig. 26.36). Moreover, *To Sleep, So As to Dream* is itself constructed as a silent film. It includes music and noise, but the dialogue is presented as intertitles; the only spoken language is a *benshi*'s commentary. Hayashi offers a complex play with fantasy and memory characteristic of the international art cinema.

Parallel to the new generation of live-action directors there emerged a group of animators specializing in feature-length science-fiction and fantasy cartoons known as *anime*. Derived from *manga*, these energetic films featured robots, astronauts, and superheroic teenagers (even schoolgirls, as in *Project A-Ko*, 1986). Several domestic box-office hits of the 1980s were animated features, and one, Katsuhiro Otomo's bloody, postapocalyptic *Akira* (1987), became a cult success in other countries. Working under low budgets, *anime* artists gave up much of the complex movement of classic animation in favor of canted angles, rapid editing, computer-generated imagery, and a striking command of gradual shading and translucent surfaces (Color Plate 26.39). *Anime* of all types yielded profitable foreign television and videocassette sales.

Another hope of the mainstream industry was Juzo Itami. Son of a distinguished director, he had been an actor, a screenwriter, and an author since the 1960s. Itami's *The Funeral* (1985), *Tampopo* (1986), and *A Taxing Woman* (1987) are mordant satires of contemporary Japanese life (Fig. 26.37). Full of physical comedy and mockery of the new consumerist Japan, they became highly exportable items and made Itami the most visible Japanese director of the 1980s.

The success of the "New Japanese Cinema" was undergirded by industrial factors. As in the United States, the decline in attendance leveled off; by the late 1970s, it stabilized at around 150 million annually. The market could support about 250 films per year, although at least half of these would be low-budget soft-core pornography. Producers sought filmmakers willing to turn out inexpensive films attuned to the free-spending younger audience.

Yet even offbeat films faced increasingly stiff competition from U.S. firms. In 1976, for the first time, receipts from foreign films surpassed those from Japanese films. By the end of the 1980s, most of each year's top-grossing films were American, and Japanese films comprised only about one-third of

Fig. 26.37 *The Funeral*: A family member takes a snapshot: "Get a little closer to the coffin. Look sad."

all features released. Japan replaced Britain as Hollywood's biggest foreign market.

The film industry, facing few export prospects and sharper competition at home, drew some hope from its new directors and from favorable tax laws which encouraged motion-picture investments. In addition, the studios' control of exhibition guaranteed them a share of Hollywood's income. Yet even this security was shaken in 1993, when Time Warner, in partnership with a Japanese supermarket chain, opened a chain of multiplex theaters. This new penetration of the market threatened to weaken the Big Three still further.

Outside the film industry, though, Japanese business was coming to terms with Hollywood. This took place in the context of the stunning success of the nation's industry, which by 1980 was supreme in manufacturing automobiles, watches, motorcycles, cameras, and electronic goods. Japan replaced the United States as the world's major creditor, holding the largest banks and insurance companies and investing billions of dollars in foreign companies and real estate.

Major Japanese media concerns participated in foreign film production. During the 1980s investment companies began funneling hundreds of millions of dollars to Hollywood firms. With the launching of pay television and high-definition television, Japanese media companies needed attractive material of the sort that Hollywood could provide. On a less prodigal scale, JVC invested in films by Luc Besson and Jim Jarmusch, while an advertising agency financed Wenders's *Until the End of the World* (1990). A company supported by the *Nippon Herald* newspaper partially funded the British film *The Crying Game* (1992). Japanese investment was also expanding to films made in Hong Kong and Taiwan.

More spectacularly, Japanese manufacturers of consumer electronics were buying Hollywood studios. Sony purchased Columbia Pictures Entertainment for $3.4 billion in 1989, while Matsushita Electric Industrial Company paid $6 billion for Music Corporation of America, the parent company of Universal Pictures. The latter was the largest investment any Japanese company had ever made in a U.S. firm. Sony and Matsushita joined Time Warner and Rupert Murdoch's News Corporation as the most powerful global entertainment conglomerates. Despite the reduced stature of the industry at home, the scale of Japanese investments ensured the nation a central place in international film commerce.

As video recorders became common household appliances, as cable and satellite television spread through the West, and as new technologies such as high-definition television were in development, the market for U.S. films expanded. Hollywood's competitors were forced to rely on export markets and cross-national financing. During the postwar decades, governmentally overseen coproductions had become normal filmmaking practice. In the 1970s and 1980s, coproductions, with their strict requirements as to staffing, became less important than international "cooperative" and runaway productions. The growth of Japan's economy, the strengthening of European unity, and the collapse of communism further intensified the trend toward a global film market. Aesthetically, this tendency encouraged filmmakers to woo audiences through accessible variants upon the popular genres and art-cinema conventions pioneered in earlier eras.

◆ NOTES AND QUERIES

THE NEW GERMAN CINEMA

French Impressionist or Italian Neorealist cinema can be discussed as a group of filmmakers sharing broad assumptions about film form, style, and subject. After the early 1960s, however, most New Cinemas in both West and East were not clear-cut stylistic movements. During this era, a New Cinema often consisted of younger filmmakers who happened to make films that won international recognition.

The New German Cinema offers an example. Most historians consider it to be a development out of Young German Film (p. 534). It includes several diverse trends: the political wing we discussed in Chapter 23 (pp. 660–665), the sensibilist trend (pp. 739–741), and diverse works of female, gay, and lesbian directors (pp. 687–690). By the late 1980s, New German Cinema had become a broad term for all independent filmmaking in West Germany since the 1960s, and many historians believed it continued into the 1990s.

The term itself played a concrete historical role. In the 1970s international film culture took young filmmakers as representatives of a "new German cinema" as yet unacknowledged in their homeland. The New York Film Festival, the Cannes festival, the Museum of Modern Art, and other institutions helped build up the sense of a new trend in international art cinema. After directors such as Fassbinder, Herzog, and Wenders won recognition outside Germany, their reputations became elevated at home. State support of production was accompanied by initiatives from cultural agencies such as the Goethe Institute, which helped promote the director-based *Autorenfilm* (the "author's cinema," in a literary sense of authorship) in other countries by circulating films and subsidizing filmmakers to tour with their works.

For some historians, the radical edge of the 1960s and 1970s films was blunted as the films became absorbed into the European art cinema. By 1979, when Schlöndorff's *Tin Drum*, Fassbinder's *Marriage of Maria Braun*, Herzog's *Nosferatu*, and von Trotta's *Sisters* won international acclaim, the process of assimilation had become evident. During the 1980s new directors—particularly women—won government and television funding, and several of them gained international recognition. Once in place, the idea of a "new" national cinema could be developed and exploited by the nation as a sign of cultural prestige.

For extensive discussions of how the New German Cinema came to be treated as a distinctive trend in film history, see Eric Rentschler, *West German Film in the Course of Time* (Bedford Hills, N.Y.: Redgrave, 1984), and Thomas Elsaesser, *New German Cinema: A History* (New Brunswick, N.J.: Rutgers University Press, 1989).

◆ REFERENCES

1. René Cleitman, director of Hachette Premiere Films, quoted in Peter Bart, "Too Little or Too Much?" *Variety* (24 May 1993): 5.
2. Quoted in Philippe Boulet-Gercourt, "Berlin's Hollywood," *World Press Review* (December 1992): 52.
3. Margarethe von Trotta, "Female Film Aesthetics," in Eric Rentschler, ed., *West German Filmmakers on Film: Visions and Voices* (New York: Holmes & Meier, 1988), p. 89.
4. Quoted in Marc Silberman, "Women Filmmakers in West Germany: A Catalog," *Camera Obscura* no. 6 (Fall 1980): 128.
5. Quoted in Timothy Corrigan, *New German Film: The Displaced Image* (Austin: University of Texas Press, 1983), p. 146.
6. Quoted in Alan Greenberg, *Heart of Glass* (Munich: Skellig, 1976), p. 174.
7. Wim Wenders, "Three LPs by Van Morrison," in Jan Dawson, ed., *Wim Wenders* (New York: Zoetrope, 1976), p. 30.
8. Wim Wenders, "Impossible Stories," in *The Logic of Images: Essays and Conversations,* trans. Michael Hofmann (London: Faber, 1991), p. 59.
9. Mikhail Gorbachev, "A Common European Home," in Gale Stokes, ed., *From Stalinism to Pluralism: A Documentary History of Eastern Europe since 1945* (New York: Oxford University Press, 1991), p. 266.
10. Quoted in Vladimir Tismaneau, *Reinventing Politics: Eastern Europe from Stalin to Havel* (New York: Free Press, 1992), p. 134.
11. Quoted in Barbara Koenig Quart, *Women Directors: The Emergence of a New Cinema* (New York: Praeger, 1988), p. 193.
12. Andrzej Wajda, "The Artist's Responsibility," in David W. Paul, ed., *Politics, Art and Commitment in the East European Cinema* (New York: St. Martins, 1983), p. 299.
13. Waldemar Dziki, quoted in Andrew Nagorski, "Sleeping without the Enemy," *Newsweek* (19 August 1991): 56.
14. Andrei Tarkovsky, *Sculpting in Time: Reflections on the Cinema,* trans. Kitty Hunter-Blair (London: Faber, 1989), p. 117.
15. Ibid., p. 27.

27

NEW CINEMAS IN DEVELOPING COUNTRIES SINCE THE 1970s

As radicals' hopes for social change faded, belief in the Third World as a distinct political force came to seem less plausible. Economists began to describe the regions as the "developing world," pointing out that life expectancy and literacy had increased, employees' earnings were growing, and the "green revolution" in agricultural practices had expanded food productivity. South Korea, Hong Kong, Singapore, and Taiwan became vigorous manufacturing and investment centers.

Overall, however, prospects for the developing world were even more grim than they had been in the period before 1975. Many nations were ruled by military juntas or charismatic dictators. The gap between rich and poor countries widened catastrophically: by 1989, the top fifth of the world's population had become sixty times richer than the bottom fifth. Mechanized farming increased rural unemployment, forcing families to migrate to urban areas. The developing countries had fifteen of the world's biggest cities, usually ringed by shantytowns and squatters' camps.

Most countries failed to substitute new products for the exports they had relied on in the colonial era, and their debt to the West rose dizzyingly. This occurred just when the industrial countries, shaken by the oil shocks of 1973 and 1979, began to cut foreign aid. A world recession in the early 1980s only intensified developing nations' financial problems. As the International Monetary Fund (IMF) imposed austerity measures on debtor nations, hunger riots erupted in Brazil, Tunisia, Algeria, and Venezuela.

The underdeveloped nations were also wracked by wars—conflicts with neighbors, as in the Middle East and Southeast Asia, or civil struggles, as in the guerrilla wars of Latin America and the ethnic and religious strife of Africa. Disease began to spread; in 1988, one out of thirteen people in Zaire carried the HIV virus. Perhaps most alarmingly, population was expanding unchecked. In 1977, three-quarters of the world's population lived in the developing nations. At the same rate of increase, by 2026 these countries would be home to nearly 90 percent of the human race.

Huge as these social problems were, the developing world continued to play an important role in world cinema. Audiences remained large—200 million per year in Africa, nearly 800 million in Latin America, nearly 5 billion in India—and U.S. and European film companies targeted them. After the mid-1970s, the New Hollywood penetrated markets even more thoroughly than it had previously. In Cairo and Mexico City, Brazzaville and Taipei, the U.S. product consumed up to 80 percent of screen time.

Yet some markets proved resistant to imports. Strong national industries such as India's and Hong Kong's were able to keep foreign competition at bay. Communist regimes blocked the entry of American cinema; China, where annual attendance was said to be a staggering 2.7 billion, was a closed market to the major American companies. Moreover, as American films became more popular worldwide, a brisk video piracy cut into the studios' profits. In any country, illicit copies of Hollywood pictures were rented, sold, and bartered—often saturating the local market well before the official premieres. There sprang up "video parlors" where friends could gather in a cubicle to watch a recent release while eating and drinking. In Burma, storefront "theaterettes" reminiscent of early cinema showed VHS tapes on video projectors. Bootleg videocassettes also penetrated markets to which Hollywood had little access, such as Saudi Arabia and other Islamic states which banned movie theaters on religious grounds.

The U.S. industry used all its might to smash these barriers to its product. Beginning in 1976, when Thailand sharply raised taxes on imported films, the MPEAA boycotted the country for four years until the government capitulated. In 1985, Congress and the U.S. embassy demanded that South Korea allow Hollywood to install its own distribution companies; soon the country became the second-largest Asian market for American films. The MPEAA fought vigorously against video piracy. In 1992, it forced Taiwan to shut down all its cities' video parlors.

Still, despite Hollywood's increasing power, the developing world continued to produce many films of its own. At the end of the 1980s, global film output remained at approximately 4000 features. The nations in the developing world produced about half of them. After the early 1970s, production slackened in Egypt, Mexico, Brazil, Pakistan, Turkey, the Philippines, and other major producing countries, but this downturn was offset by the emergence of new industries in Bangladesh, Indonesia, Thailand, and elsewhere. Hong Kong maintained a steady output, and India even expanded production. In 1987, these two countries and Thailand accounted for half of the Third World's output.

These totals do not convey the conditions of distribution and exhibition in the developing countries. In India, Indonesia, and South Korea, many films never received theatrical release, passing straight to videocassette. Moreover, regardless of the number of films produced locally, imports garnered most countries' box-office takings. Some industries were devastated by economic problems; national debt drove Brazilian and Argentine cinema to virtual oblivion in the early 1990s. Video also took a toll in Malaysia, where attendance dropped from 1 million to less than one-third of that, and in Turkey, where the number of theaters fell from 3000 to about 350.

Nevertheless, cinema remained an important aspect of national cultures throughout the developing world. In Asia, Latin America, and Africa, filmmakers gave voice to indigenous conceptions of national history, social life, and personal conduct. Cinema displayed a sense of regional, cross-national identity as well, as when some directors sought to express pan-African themes. In addition, some films from developing countries commanded the attention of international audiences. The global film market, set up for the benefit of the West, made room for both popular entertainment and more unusual fare from its former colonies.

As in Europe, governments discovered that if they wanted a national cinema, they would have to help pay for it. Most New Cinemas were the result of state funding. Filmmakers also relied on coproduction arrangements with neighboring countries or with European firms—often countries which had been colonial rulers. Euzhan Palcy's *Rue cases nègres* (*Sugar Cane Alley*, Antilles, 1983) was financed by French concerns, while *The Blue Eyes of Yonta* (1992; Color Plate 27.1), directed by Flora Gomes, was a coproduction between Guinea-Bissau and Portugal, with other funding from a French firm and England's Channel 4.

The New Cinemas which emerged from the developing world had virtually none of the stylistic or thematic coherence that characterized silent-film movements or Italian Neorealism. The New Argentine Cinema, India's Parallel Cinema, the Hong Kong New Wave, China's Fifth Generation—each rubric often lumped together very different directors.

Still, there were a few common features. Because of the problems of developing nations, New Cinemas often proposed political critiques. The heritage of revolutionary cinema lived on in films about dictators' abuse of power, the plight of families, ethnic conflicts, and other sensitive issues. One of the most important realms of human rights involved women, long oppressed in developing countries. The UN's designation of 1975–1985 as the international "Decade of the Woman" helped groups address day care, abortion, rape, and other issues. In the same period, female filmmakers began to enter production, often focusing on women's concerns.

Even when directors took on political subjects or themes, most continued the movement of the early 1970s away from radical experimentation. Politically critical films from the developing world tended to rely on conventions of classical narrative or of art-cinema modernism (particularly the interplay between objective realism, subjective realism, and authorial commentary). These strategies enabled filmmakers to reach wider audiences. By abandoning extreme political modernism, they gained some access to festivals and distributors in the First World.

LATIN AMERICA:
ACCESSIBILITY AND DECLINE

During the 1970s, military governments took power in much of South and Central America. Brazil, Bolivia, Uruguay, Chile, and Argentina all fell under military dictatorships. After 1978, pluralist democracy returned to most Latin American countries, but the new governments faced colossal inflation rates, declining productivity, and huge foreign indebtedness. Since 1982, no major debtor country in South and Central America has been able to pay any of the principal on its loan. The IMF imposed austerity measures on Mexico, Brazil, and Argentina.

Latin America's screens had been dominated by Hollywood cinema since World War I. The region's film output had grown significantly during 1965–1975, but because most right-wing governments provided little protection against U.S. imports, productivity declined steadily over the next decade. Occasionally, however, local industries gained strength, and some filmmakers won a place on the international art-cinema circuit.

BRAZIL

By 1973, guerrillas had definitively lost their struggle against Brazil's military government. A year later General Ernesto Geisel assumed the presidency and made promises of greater openness. In 1975, Embrafilme, originally a state distribution agency, was reorganized to create a vertically integrated monopoly over Brazilian cinema. The government also increased the screen quota, thereby cutting down imports and creating a demand for domestic films.

Embrafilme worked with independent producers and courted television and foreign countries for coproductions. Embrafilme's efforts helped double attendance and raise production to a level of sixty to eighty films per year. The agency's powers increased under the transition to democratic constitutional rule. Embrafilme was even able to support the controversial *Pixote* (1980), which presented an unflattering portrait of life in Brazil's cities.

The veterans of Cinema Nôvo (p. 606) retained their central roles in Brazilian film culture. Embrafilme was headed by two Cinema Nôvo directors, Roberto Farias and Carlos Diegues. Like their peers elsewhere, Brazil's directors relinquished political militancy and formal experimentation in the name of more accessible strategies. Many directors, from Brazil and elsewhere on the continent, affiliated their works with the Latin American literature of "Magical Realism." (See Box.)

Other directors adapted to an international market. Carlos Diegues's *Bye Bye Brazil* (1980), dedicated "To the Brazilian people of the 21st Century," found success abroad. A tale of an itinerant sideshow troupe drifting through a poverty-stricken country full of discos, brothels, boomtowns, and TV antennas, the film has a boisterousness and sentiment reminiscent of the

LATIN AMERICAN LITERATURE AND CINEMA

During the 1960s, Latin American writing became renowned throughout the world. The Mexican Carlos Fuentes (*The Death of Artemio Cruz*, 1962), the Argentine Julio Cortázar (*Hopscotch*, 1963), the Peruvian Mario Vargas Llosa (*The Green House*, 1966), and the Colombian Gabriel García Marquez (*One Hundred Years of Solitude*, 1967) were recognized as masters of a literature that mingled European influences with indigenous cultural sources.

Working in a vein of Magical Realism (*lo real maravilloso*), these writers spiced social realism with myth, fantasy, and fairy tales taken from popular culture. Episodic, folktale plots might turn suddenly into symbolic labyrinths, full of images as disconcerting as those of European Surrealism. But whereas the Surrealists sought the liberation of the individual psyche, the fantastic imagery of Magical Realism sought to reflect the collective imagination of colonized peoples, for whom everyday reality was only one step away from the supernatural.

Latin American filmmaking had already been influenced by this strain in literature, as when Brazilian films took inspiration from the "Tropicalism" of the prewar period (p. 609). During the 1980s, filmmakers began to develop the Magical Realist trend further. Often this involved adapting literary works, as in the six-part series "Difficult Loves" (1988); each film was derived from a story by García Marquez and signed by a major director from a different country. Other directors opted for more original mixtures of realism and fantasy, as in Eliseo Subiela's Borgesian *Conquest of Paradise* (Argentina, 1981) and *Man Looking Southeast* (1986).

A key example of Magical Realist film is Ruy Guerra's *Erendira* (Mexico, 1982), with a script by García Marquez. The beautiful Erendira undergoes a series of grotesque adventures, mostly involving the efforts of her Gorgon-like grandmother to gain money from prostituting the girl. They travel

Fig. 27.1 Senator Onesimo's campaign is adorned by a huge billboard ship that mysteriously spouts smoke (*Erendira*).

across a vaguely modern Latin America, teeming with smugglers, corrupt police, and cynical politicians. Their home is a vast circus tent, housing statues, a huge boat, and a labyrinth of veiled and curtained corridors. The film leaps from the brutality of Erendira's exploitation to lyrical fantasy: handbills turn into birds, blue fish swim through the air, a political rally becomes a fairy-tale spectacle (Fig. 27.1).

The dynamic relations between film and fiction were also seen in the ways in which Latin American writers absorbed the lessons of popular cinema. Gabriel Cabrera Infante's novels sought to capture the raucous vulgarity of movies. Manuel Puig's novel *Kiss of the Spider Woman* (1976) drew plots from Hollywood B pictures; the process of appropriation came full circle when the novel was filmed in 1984. Latin American cinema won a place in world film markets partly through its ties with a prestigious literary trend.

Fig. 27.2 Salomé in *Bye Bye Brazil* examines the Indians' totem, which suspiciously resembles a TV set.

early Fellini (Fig. 27.2). Another lucrative export was Bruno Barretto's *Dona Flor and Her Two Husbands* (1976), in which a man who returns from the dead shares his wife's bed with her second husband. After the success of *Pixote*, Hector Babenco won U.S. backing for *Kiss of the Spider Woman* (1984). Also gaining access to international screens were the women directors Area Carolina (*Sea of Roses*, 1977), Tizuki Yamasaki (*Gaijin, The Roads of Freedom*, 1980), and Suzana Amaral (*The Hour of the Star*, 1985).

ARGENTINA AND ELSEWHERE

During Argentina's military dictatorship (1976–1983), thousands of citizens were arrested and secretly killed. The regime privatized state industries and cut tariffs, opening the country to U.S. films and encouraging cheap local production. What came to be known as the "dirty war" pursued artists, killing, blacklisting, or exiling them. The ill-judged campaign to capture the Malvinas Islands (aka the Falkland Islands, held by Britain) helped topple the regime and led to the election of a civilian government in 1984.

With the emergence of democracy, censorship was abolished and filmmaker Manuel Antín became a director of the National Film Institute (INC). The industry faced 400 percent inflation, but it attracted attention with several films, notably Luis Puenzo's *The Official Story* (1985). The film's highly emotional drama—a woman discovers that her adopted child's mother "disappeared" at the hands of death squads—employs traditional plotting highlighted by symbolic incidents (Fig. 27.3). *The Official Story* won the 1986 Academy Award for the Best Foreign Film.

Soon the "New Argentine Cinema" was announced. María Luisa Bemberg explored women's roles in *Camila* (1984) and *Miss Mary* (1986). Most widely seen internationally, apart from *The Official Story*, was Fernando Solanas's *Tangos: The Exile of Gardel* (1985). Argentine exiles in Paris stage a *tanguedia*, a comedy/tragedy presented through dance. Alternately amusing and mournful, the film celebrates the tango's place in Argentine culture. Solanas, collaborator on the militant *Hour of the Furnaces* (p. 621), exploits art-cinema shifts into fantasy, wrapping his exiles in a cheerful, unexplained cloud of yellow smoke (Color Plate 27.2). Started in France during the "dirty war," *Tangos* was completed in Argentina and became a box-office hit.

Many countries underwent comparable shifts from free-market dictatorship to uneasy and economically precarious democracy. In Bolivia, after a period of repression in the 1970s, the populist Ukamau directors Jorge Sanjinés and Antonio Eguino returned to filmmaking. In Chile, the military coup that ousted Salvador Allende in 1973 installed Augusto Pinochet in power for almost twenty years. His government sold off businesses to multinational corporations, bequeathing the country the largest per capita foreign debt in the world. During Pinochet's reign, over fifty "Chilean" features were made in exile by Raul Ruiz, Miguel Littín, and other New Cinema veterans. Littín even returned in disguise to make a film. (See Notes and Queries.)

Fig. 27.3 Boys disrupt a birthday party by mimicking a police raid, suggesting that military brutality has warped Argentina's children (*The Official Story*).

MEXICO

For decades the Mexican government controlled the film industry (p. 489), but during the 1970s and 1980s, the state's attitude oscillated wildly from one regime to another.

In 1975, the liberal government bought the principal studio facilities and founded several production companies. It also took over distribution. These measures encouraged production and fostered an auteur cinema. During the late 1960s and early 1970s several young directors had called for a political cinema. Paul Leduc's reenacted biography of the journalist John Reed, *Reed: Insurgent Mexico* (1970), marked the official emergence of this group, which included Arturo Ripstein (*The Inquisition*, 1973) and Jaime Humberto Hermosillo (*The Passion According to Berenice*, 1976). The older director Felipe Cazals caused a sensation with *Canoa* (1975), the reconstruction of a 1968 lynching in a village.

Mexico was not ruled by the sort of military government that dominated Brazil, Argentina, and Chile, but it did move to the right in the late 1970s. A new president took steps to privatize the economy and oversaw the liquidation of the National Film Bank, the closing of a major production agency, and the return to private production. The state invested in only a handful of prestigious projects. Film output fell steeply, and only a few genres found success—chiefly fantasy films featuring the masked wrestler Santo.

Mexico depended on oil revenues, and soon a slump in prices forced the government to borrow from abroad. The results were hyperinflation, mass unemployment, and debt. Film culture suffered several blows. In 1979 police attacked the Churubusco studios and, charging the staff with mismanagement, jailed and tortured several people. In 1982 a fire at the nation's archive, the Cineteca Nacional, destroyed thousands of prints and documents.

The pendulum swung slightly back when, under a new president in the early 1980s, Mexico began an economic reconstruction that included more intervention in the film trade. A national agency was created to finance quality production and lure coproductions from abroad. Mexico became a popular spot for U.S. runaway productions, and the *sexycomedia*, a new genre derived from popular comic strips, began to attract audiences.

Many of the directors favored by state policy in the early 1970s became the mainstays of quality production in the 1980s. In *Doña Herlinda and Her Son* (1984), Hermosillo made the first explicitly gay Mexican film. Leduc attracted worldwide notice with *Frida* (1984), a biography of the Mexican painter Frida Kahlo. Leduc daringly omits dialogue and offers virtually no plot. Episodes from Frida's life, jumbled out of chronological order, present rich tableaux which recall motifs from her paintings (Color Plate 27.3).

CUBA AND OTHER LEFT-WING CINEMAS

As a Communist state, Cuba had a more centralized and stable film industry during this period, but here too formal experimentation largely vanished. Julio García Espinosa explained that Cuban directors were not yet the masters of their film theaters because "one cannot show only revolutionary films in them."[1] Humberto Solas's *Cantata de Chile* (1976) was a stirring musical pageant projecting theatrical techniques on an epic scale (Color Plate 27.4), but even it was less daring than the works of the late 1960s and early 1970s. Tomás Guttiérez Alea's *The Last Supper* (1977), a critique of the slaveholding aristocracy, was far more "transparent" and linear in construction than *Memories of Underdevelopment*. Directors sought a more accessible style, and genre films, such as spy and *film noir* intrigues, came to the fore. Like the Soviet Union, Cuba was turning toward more accessible entertainment.

Cuba made only eight to ten features annually, guaranteeing that the films could cover their costs at home. The local films were outnumbered by features from Japan, the Soviet bloc, and other Latin American countries. Yet the domestic product garnered a substantial share of exhibition income, not least because the typical Cuban went to the movies nine to ten times per year—the highest average in the western hemisphere.

Cuba also remained the center of Latin American Third Worldism.

Havana hosted the annual International Festival of Latin American Cinema (established 1979), which grew to include hundreds of films from the region. In 1985, Cuba established the Foundation for Latin American Cinema, which created the International School of Film and Television, directed by the esteemed Argentine pioneer of left cinema, Fernando Birrí.

Cuba's economic position was precarious, depending on the sugar trade and the bounty of the USSR. The United States pressured western countries to avoid trading with Castro. Crop failures in the late 1970s, along with the massive emigration of 1980, created a new ideological and economic tightening. In the early 1980s, the state film agency ICAIC reduced budgets, and in 1987 it was reorganized along the lines of the production-unit system of eastern Europe, with each team headed by a major director.

Other countries became identified with a politicized Latin American cinema. In El Salvador, where an oppressive military government terrorized the populace and fought to quell opposition guerrillas, there appeared clandestine film collectives. Nicaragua, long ruled by Anastasio Somoza, was taken over in 1979 by the Sandinistas, a moderate guerrilla faction. President Reagan's embargo on the new regime, as well as struggles by the U.S.-backed Contras, pushed Nicaragua closer to Cuba. A new film culture was launched with the founding of the Nicaragua Film Institute (1979) and was brought to prominence with *Alsino and the Condor* (1982), made by the Chilean exile Miguel Littín.

1980s TRENDS

Nicaragua coproduced *Alsino* with Mexico, Cuba, and Costa Rica, and in this respect the film typifies a tendency that was as significant in Latin America as elsewhere in the world. Cuba successfully gathered funding within Latin America, but elsewhere producers turned to Europe for capital. Guerra's *Erendira* was a French-German-Mexican coproduction, while Spanish television funded many features, most notably the "Difficult Loves" series. Such internationalist efforts were also aided by the appearance of new film festivals: at Bogotá, Colombia (1984); at San Juan, Puerto Rico (1991); and at Viña del Mar, Chile (reestablished in 1990).

As in Europe and the United States, women directors became more prominent. In Brazil, a feminist group made *Mulheres de boca* ("Women of the Street," 1983). A Mexican film collective, Grupo Cine Mujer, also produced works oriented toward the women's movement. More mainstream female filmmakers emerged; those in Argentina and Cuba were joined by the Venezuelan Marianela Alas, whose *Oriana* (1985) draws upon art-cinema conventions to convey a woman's half-fantasized childhood memories.

As Latin American countries sank into debt, the obstacles to filmmaking intensified. By 1992 the most important industries had all but ceased to function. The Argentine industry, plagued by steeply declining attendance and colossal inflation, heaved to a virtual halt, producing only fifteen features in 1991. In response the National Film Institute stimulated production by taxing admissions and home video, and it held out hopes of new import markets in Europe.

In Mexico, a plan to support "quality cinema" dissolved as inflation ate up government funding. In 1988 the new government began liquidating its production companies, studios, and theater circuits. Películas Nacionales, the major private company, collapsed soon after. In 1991 Mexican output shriveled to fewer than forty films. In Brazil, Embrafilme went bankrupt in 1988 and was closed in 1990. A mere nine features were released the following year. At Cannes, Hector Babenco declared Brazilian cinema dead.

Most smaller countries suffered as well. In the first half of the 1980s the government of Colombia encouraged the growth of a modest industry that produced about ten films per year. But these were financed by a tax on tickets, and as attendance declined, exhibitors withheld revenues in protest. At the same time, the government was plunged into a war with the cartels producing illicit drugs for North America. In 1990, drug chieftains kidnapped the head of the state film agency; the government soon abandoned film production.

In the late 1980s new Cuban directors began turning out youth movies and satiric comedies (e.g., Juan Carlos Tabío's *Plaff,* 1988). But when the Soviet bloc crumbled and the USSR dissolved, Cuba was left more isolated than ever. No longer subsidized by the Soviets, Castro had only North Korea and China as allies. In 1991, ICAIC, heavily in debt, released a mere five features; a year later, it was absorbed into the film sector of the armed forces and the radio-television institute. Cuba's international film school foundered, and Birrí resigned and left the country. Censorship became harsher: *Alice in Wonderland* (1991), a mild satire, was pulled from distribution and attacked as counterrevolutionary. Some film workers, most notably director Sergio Giral, went into exile. Film stock and equipment, normally supplied by eastern Europe, became scarce. With Castro requiring that his citizens conserve gasoline by riding bicycles, still more difficult times lay ahead.

The continent's economic crises strengthened the role of imports. The end of quotas in Brazil gave Hollywood a free rein; in Argentina, 90 percent of all films screened came from the United States. Even in Cuba, pirated prints of American films began to dominate theaters. Hollywood's conquest of eastern Europe and the former Soviet Union was accompanied by an undisputed sway over America's southern neighbors.

INDIA: A PARALLEL CINEMA

By contrast with Latin America, India maintained a strong indigenous industry. Thanks to firm government controls on imports, the local product ruled the market; Hollywood had little foothold. The basic genres, revamped to incorporate new musical styles or to imitate foreign hits, remained in place. The most popular film of the era, *Sholay* ("Flames of the Sun," 1975, Ramesh Sippy), blended the tradition of rural outlaw films with the spaghetti Western to create what came to be called a "curry-Western."

Nevertheless, production remained the chaotic, risky business it had been since World War II. As many as 800 films per year vied for screens. Distributors, exhibitors, and stars controlled the trade, and filmmaking continued to serve as a way to launder black-market money. The international market for Indian films expanded during the 1970s, drawing audiences in Moscow, Cairo, Buenos Aires, and Hong Kong. Within the country, film stars became parliamentary representatives and even heads of states. Cinema was India's ninth-largest industry and its main form of popular culture.

Hindi was the official national language, a state of affairs which strengthened Bombay's "all-India" film. At the same time, though, regional cinemas expanded. By 1980, the states of Tamil Nadu, Anam Pradesh, and Kerala were each making over a hundred films per year. Madras, the southern production center, became the most prolific filmmaking capital in the world. In addition, because of India's many languages, territorial distribution was the norm, with producers financing films through presale to regional distributors.

The cutthroat competition of the commercial industry, with its romance plots, established genres, and its song-and-dance formulas, left little room for alternative filmmaking. In the late 1960s the government created a "parallel" cinema by encouraging the Film Finance Corporation to shift its support from commercial fare toward low-budget, art-cinema efforts. When Mrinal Sen's *Bhuvan Shome* (1969; p. 611) proved successful with audiences, other directors' projects won loans. The Bombay-based Parallel Cinema overshadowed the Bengali cinema, long associated with the prestigious productions of Satyajit Ray. In addition, some state governments aided low-budget filmmakers; for example, Kerala's Communist government encouraged political films. A sense of "quality" film culture also emerged from new film festivals and screenings at the National Film Archive at Pune.

Although many New Cinema films were made in Hindi, they offered none of the spectacle and flamboyant music of the mainstream cinema. Most represented quiet social commentary, influenced by Ray's humanistic realism, Italian Neorealism, and European New Cinemas. Basu Chatterji's *The Whole Sky* (1969), for example, recalls the wry poignancy of Czech cinema.

Other New Cinema directors used their films for political critique. In Sen's *The Interview* (1971), a hero looking for a job is played by an unemployed worker; *Calcutta '71* (1972) samples five cases of poverty drawn from forty years of the city's history; and *Chorus* (1974) attacks multinational corporations. Sen experimented with stylized performance, Brechtian reflexivity, direct address to the audience, and other tactics of political modernism. Similarly self-conscious was Ritwik Ghatak's final film, *Reason, Argument, and Tale* (1974). In this rambling, disjunctive work, the aging pioneer of political cinema plays an alcoholic intellectual killed by young revolutionaries. Shyam Benegal contributed to the political orientation of the New Cinema with *The Seedling* (1974), a social drama of a young landlord who exploits a servant and his wife, and *The Churning* (1976), a tale of a rural milk cooperative; the latter film was financed by 50,000 members of such cooperatives.

Not all New Cinema films stressed political comment. Although both Kumar Shahani and Mani Kaul studied with Ghatak at the Pune Film Institute, neither embraced radical critique. Shahani studied at IDHEC in Paris as well, and he served as assistant director for Bresson on *Une Femme douce* (1969). In India, Shahani made *The Mirror of Illusion* (1972), about an aristocratic woman who dreams of escape from her father's crumbling mansion

Fig. 27.4 *The Mirror of Illusion*: In the deserted villa, Taran lives with her father and yearns for a life outside (production still).

in the countryside (Fig. 27.4). *The Mirror of Illusion* uses subtle color progressions and solemn long takes; Bresson called it the most slowly paced film he had ever seen. The film won praise abroad but had no screenings in India.

Mani Kaul, an admirer of Bresson, Tarkovsky, and Ozu, also created a sparse, demanding film in *A Day's Bread* (1970). A study of a few hours in the life of a village woman oppressed by a callous husband, the film's minimal gestures, uninflected performance, and long-held "empty" shots convey her endless waiting for her husband's bus. Although Kaul's work recalls European films, he strove for the cinematic equivalent of Indian classical music, in which time is felt as suspended.

Openly refusing the formulas of popular cinema, the new films depended upon government financing, and problems arose fairly soon. Censors clamped down on many directors; M. S. Sathyu's *Hot Winds* (1975), which revived the memories of the wrenching division of India from Pakistan, was suppressed for a year. Moreover, the Film Finance Corporation (FFC) had failed to create an alternative distribution and exhibition network. With no art theaters in the country, there were no venues for experimental or political films, and most failed to pay off their government loans. In 1975 a government inquiry into the FFC decided that many of the New Cinema films were self-indulgent exercises and should not have been funded. The commission also suggested that in future all sponsored films would have to have commercial potential.

In 1975 as well, Indian politics was rocked by the announcement that the election of Indira Gandhi had been found invalid because of campaign irregularities. She immediately declared a nationwide state of emergency and ordered mass arrests of her critics, including nearly all the leaders of opposition parties. The emergency lasted until 1977, when Gandhi was voted out of power by the non-Communist opposition; but a 1980 election returned her to power.

Under the emergency, the Parallel Cinema's difficulties with censorship and finance intensified. Political dissent was discouraged, and controversial films sent to the censors sometimes simply vanished. A business leader was put in charge of the FFC to stem the growing drain on loan money. The state, reaping profits from high exhibition taxes and its monopoly on film import, favored the commercial industry. After the 1977 elections, however, a burst of politically critical cinema appeared in Bengal. The more mainstream Shyam Benegal became identified with a blend of social criticism and entertainment values. *The Role* (1977) studies a 1940s film actress, and *The Obsession* (1978), financed by its star Shashi Kapoor, was a major commercial success. Benegal's cameraman, Govind Nihalani, directed *Cry of the Wounded* (1980), a denunciation of the government's oppression of a tribe denied any caste.

Fig. 27.5 Brother and sister visit their captured rat, unaware that the man's refusal to adapt will eventually trap him as well (*Rat Trap*).

In 1980, the government recast the FFC as the National Film Development Corporation (NFDC). It aimed to develop a quality cinema distinct from the commercial fare. It sponsored screenwriting competitions, promoted Indian films abroad, and helped fund films through loans and co-financing agreements. During its first decade, the NFDC supported almost 200 films. The NFDC was able to pay for such risks by its monopoly powers: only it could import foreign films, bring in raw film and equipment, and distribute foreign films on video. Costs were also defrayed by the NFDC's participation in international coproductions, most notably *Gandhi* (1984).

A new generation of directors, most trained at the national film academy in Pune, emerged under the auspices of government patronage. Some pushed further in the intimist tradition of Ray. Aparna Sen, India's best-known woman director, won comparison with Ray in her English-language feature *36 Chowringhee Lane* (1981). Asha Dutta, the only woman to concentrate on camerawork at the Pune Film Institute, made *My Story* (1984), a seriocomic tale of spoiled youth. In Kerala, Pune graduates founded a film cooperative to help back independent features. An example was Adoor Gopalakrishnan's *Rat Trap* (1981), which uses symbolic devices reminiscent of the art cinema to show a man's obliviousness to social change (Fig. 27.5).

More experimental was the work of Ketan Mehta, who drew stylized techniques from popular theater and early Bombay talkies. *A Folk Tale* (1980) employs a narrator familiar from folk drama and offers the audience alternative endings. Mehta's *Mirch Masala* (1986) synthesizes popular musical genres, and *Hero Hiralal* (1988) satirizes the film industry.

Older directors found new energy under the NFDC policy. Ray, Sen, and Benegal won NFDC financing throughout the 1980s. Shahani, who had not made a film for twelve years, reentered production with *Tarang* (1984), a three-hour study of the industrial bourgeoisie, and went on to *Kasba* (1990), a Chekhovian dissection of a struggling family in the countryside (Color Plate 27.5). Significantly, *Kasba* relied on stars—one of many signs that the art cinema had to make itself more mainstream.

As television grew during the 1980s, the central government, which had a monopoly on the new medium, asked important directors to make telefilms. The network also broadcast award-winning films. At the same time, the expansion of videocassettes and cable lured away the middle-class audience and made the film industry even more volatile and precarious. Bombay films vied for popularity with southern products. Blockbusters and top stars began failing; in 1989, 95 percent of all theatrical films failed to earn back their costs. Directors began preparing features for direct release to cassette shops and video parlors.

Astonishingly, production did not abate. A burst of new investment led producers to churn out almost 950 films in 1990, probably an all-time high. As everywhere, international coproductions promised new markets. "Quality" directors were working with firms in the Netherlands, the USSR, France, and the United States; Britain's Channel 4, for instance, participated in the financing of *Kasba* and Mira Nair's *Salaam Bombay!* (1988).

At the beginning of the 1990s, there were signs that the West was at last making inroads into the Indian market. For a decade the MPEAA had held back its strongest exports, offering only low-budget or outdated items. In 1992, the strategy paid off. The Indian government ended the NFDC's monopoly on film import, and current foreign titles poured in. Although Indian audiences were loyal to their nation's product, the emergence of cable television and the availability of recent Hollywood cinema suggested that the film industry would face new crises in the decade.

NEW CINEMAS IN EAST ASIA

By 1975, of the 4000 or so feature films made worldwide, half came from Asia. Although the bulk of these were produced in India and Japan, smaller countries contributed a surprising number. Malaysia, for instance, developed a significant film industry thanks to government encouragement. Similarly, Indonesian cinema benefited from protectionist legislation, allowing companies to produce an average of seventy films a year, many in a distinctive horror genre featuring "were-crocodiles." Thailand became another major force, producing over 600 films between 1983 and 1987. Although most of these countries' output dropped when the video boom decimated Asian attendance in the mid-1980s, they produced some significant works, such as Teguh Karya's *Mementos* (Indonesia, 1986) and Cherd Songsi's *The Scar* (Thailand, 1978). South Korea, site of a flourishing industry in the late 1960s, eventually attracted festival notice with such meditative films as *Why Has Bodhi-Dharma Left for the East?* (1989, Bae Yong-kyun).

THE PHILIPPINES

The Philippines established a small, vertically integrated studio system during the 1930s, but the companies declined in the postwar era and most production was done by independents. Under the rule of Fernando Marcos and his wife Imelda production rose, leveling off at about 150 features per year in the mid-1970s. Most of these were in the popular genres of romantic melodrama, musicals (*zarzuela*), comedies, religious films, and soft-core eroticism (*bomba*). A star system was firmly in place, and many plots were derived from action- or romance-based comic books. The audience was, proportionately, very large: 1300 theaters lured in over 66 million viewers per year.

Fig. 27.6

Fig. 27.7

In the early 1970s a new generation of Filipino filmmakers began to tackle social subjects. Their films retained the rapes, beatings, and other lurid conventions of mainstream genres, but framed these as part of social criticism. Ishmal Bernal's *Speck in the Water* (1976), Eddie Romero's *We Were Like This Yesterday, How Is It Today?* (1976), and Mike De Leon's *Black* (1977) dwell on poverty, crime, and corruption in a manner reminiscent of American *film noir.*

One of the most noteworthy efforts was *Maynila: In the Claws of Neon* (1975). Lino Brocka had begun making films in 1970, most of them exploiting the conventional love triangles, rapes, and violent action in order to make points about contemporary Filipino life. In *Maynila,* Ligaya is lured to the city by a procuress, who sells her to a Chinese. When Ligaya's fiancé Julio finds her, the Chinese kills Ligaya, and Julio murders him before being slain by a mob. Alongside the passion-driven plot line, however, runs an indictment of economic exploitation. Julio's search for Ligaya becomes a cross-section of Manila's unemployed men and women, and collateral scenes, such as some dockers' brutal attack on bourgeois men in a movie theater, define the city as a class battleground. Brocka underlines the suffering of slum dwellers with symbolic compositions (Fig. 27.6).

Just as the "New Filipino Cinema" was emerging, President Marcos's government installed much stricter censorship. Scripts were reviewed before production, and completed films could be cut or banned. De Leon, Brocka, and others aroused censors' ire: not particularly popular at home, their films were winning praise abroad and calling attention to the seamy side of Marcos's regime. Brocka, the most outspoken of the group, spent time in prison for fighting censorship and participating in strikes. Yet he and his peers were still allowed to make films merging social criticism and entertainment conventions. One of the most stinging is Brocka's *My Country: Clinging to a Knife Edge* (1982), which criticizes the regime's inequities with remarkable bluntness (Fig. 27.7).

In 1986, an urban insurrection overthrew Marcos's regime and installed

Fig. 27.6 The slum dwellers' plight emphasized by the name of the street (*Maynila: In the Claws of Neon*).

Fig. 27.7 *My Country: Clinging to a Knife Edge*: A worker forced into a robbery meets a gang member under portraits of the Philippines' First Family.

President Corazon Aquino, widow of an assassinated opposition leader. The revolution raised hopes for a new, dynamic cinema, but as of the late 1980s one had not yet emerged. Mass entertainment ruled the market as intensely as before, Aquino's government passed no measures to protect the industry, and the Marcos censorship apparatus remained in place. Many filmmakers expressed bitter disappointment with Aquino's policies; Brocka's *Fight for Us* (1989), produced by Pathé, suggested that repression and militarism had not left the islands.

In other respects, however, the Philippines' commercial industry prospered. Attendance and feature output rose sharply, and several local productions proved to be huge successes. New laws gave more rights to women, and several female directors began careers. Aquino's daughter Kris found stardom in a series of romantic comedies in 1991—the same year that an auto accident killed Brocka, who was planning another film critical of the post-Marcos era. Some international money flowed in; a German television network commissioned Raymond Red's *Heroes* (1991), a feature-length reflection on the failure of the Filipino revolt against Spain in the 1890s. As Aquino's former defense chief Fidel Ramos assumed the presidency, popular film stars were elected vice-president and senators. The industry, geared to producing over 125 low-budget features per year, hoped to win from Ramos's regime favors which Aquino had failed to deliver.

HONG KONG

Despite the expansion of output in small Asian countries, Hong Kong films continued to dominate the region. In the colony, the local product overwhelmed imports at the box office. The genres and stars were hugely popular throughout Asia, as well as in Africa, Latin America, and Asian communities in Europe and North America.

Hong Kong retained its place on the market by virtue of several factors. Vertically integrated companies like Shaw Brothers and Raymond Chow's Golden Harvest kept production costs down while supplying their own theaters with a staple product. Benefiting from the most relaxed censorship standards in the region, the films could offer Hollywoodian appeals at lower costs.

Hong Kong firms also sought novelty by creating fresh genres and cycles. Some directors, such as Lin Jialing, sustained the martial-arts genre in *Spiritual Boxer* (1975) and *The Eight-Diagram Pole Fighter* (1984), but on the whole swordplay and kung-fu films declined. Police thrillers, contemporary comedies, and underworld action films became the major genres of the 1980s. For many critics and audiences, the new genres embodied a modern, urban culture. Even the language of the films, the Cantonese dialect spoken in Hong Kong, marked a change from the films of the 1970s, in which the Mandarin dialect of mainland China had been supreme.

Emerging stars also emblematized the brash energy of a region on the rise. The television comedian Michael Hui formed his own company with Golden Harvest for a string of successful slapstick films (*Games Gamblers Play,* 1974; *The Private Eyes,* 1976; *Security Unlimited,* 1981; *Chicken and Duck Talk,* 1988). Hui played grasping merchants and boorish professionals, types readily associated with the new mercantile Hong Kong.

Fig. 27.8 In *Snake in the Eagle's Shadow*, Jackie Chan practices his "snake" attack on unsuspecting eggs.

The success of Hui's comedies accelerated the rise of another performer, Jackie Chan. Chan began his career as a Bruce Lee imitator before mixing acrobatic kung fu with breakneck comedy in *Snake in the Eagle's Shadow* (1978; Fig. 27.8), *Fearless Hyena* (1979), and *Young Master* (1980). Chan soon became the biggest star in Asia. Refusing to use a double, he executed astonishingly risky stunts while giving himself a screen persona reminiscent of Keaton and Harold Lloyd—the diminutive, resourceful, never-say-die average man. Chan also shifted genres rapidly. Sensing that pure martial art was waning in popularity, he combined it and physical comedy with historical intrigue (*Project A*, 1983), the cop thriller (*Police Story*, 1985), and swashbuckling adventure modeled on *Raiders of the Lost Ark* (*Armour of God*, 1986; Fig. 27.9).

Fig. 27.9 Jackie Chan in an awkward defensive position (*Armour of God*).

The sense of a cosmopolitan Hong Kong identity was an important ingredient in the New Wave of the late 1970s. A new film culture emerged with the establishment of the Hong Kong Film Festival (1977), serious magazines, and college courses. Several directors, often trained abroad and starting out in local television production, won international recognition. Some remained independent filmmakers, while others quickly became central forces in the industry—the Hong Kong equivalents of the Hollywood movie brats of the 1970s.

After directing in television, Ann Hui entered feature production with *The Secret* (1979), a murder mystery using an unprecedented number of women in production roles. Her *The Spooky Bunch* (1980) helped revive the ghost-story genre, and *The Story of Woo Viet* (1981) looked forward to the "hero" crime films. Hui's international reputation rested upon more somber dramas reflecting on postwar Asian history. *Boat People* (1982) explains the political oppression that drives Vietnamese to emigrate to Hong Kong. *Song of the Exile* (1990) traces how a young woman comes to understand the complex past of her mother, a Japanese woman sent to become a prostitute in China during the war.

Fig. 27.10 In an echo of *The 400 Blows*, boys play truant to see *City Lights* (*Father and Son*, Allen Fong, 1981).

Other filmmakers contributed to the New Wave. Shu Kei's *Sealed with a Kiss* (1981) detailed a love affair between two handicapped adolescents. Allen Fong, who studied filmmaking at the University of Southern California, also specialized in intimate human dramas. Rejecting the flamboyant spectacle of commercial cinema and often obliged to shoot in 16mm, Fong worked in a bittersweet vein reminiscent of Truffaut (Fig. 27.10).

Fig. 27.11 Chow Yun-Fat as a prosperous counterfeiter in Woo's *A Better Tomorrow.*

Fig. 27.12 Chow Yun-Fat and Danny Lee discuss matters in *The Killer.*

The sobriety of such works identified the Hong Kong New Wave with social commentary and psychological nuance. But this side of the trend was quickly overwhelmed by a rapid-fire revamping of popular genres. Central to this development was Tsui Hark, the Steven Spielberg of Hong Kong.

Hark, a Vietnamese who emigrated to the colony as an adolescent, studied film in the United States before getting directing jobs in television. Like Ann Hui, he entered filmmaking with a crime film, *The Butterfly Murders* (1979). After some violent satires, Hark turned abruptly toward family entertainment. He helped create the cycle of "supernatural kung fu" with *Zu: Warriors of the Magic Mountain* (1982), and he soon gained prominence with *Shanghai Blues* (1984) and *Peking Opera Blues* (1986). These dazzling, frantic mixtures of martial arts, comedy, and sentimental romance borrow openly from the New Hollywood. Hark's scenes are busy to the point of exhaustion: the camera rushes up to the actors, wide-angle setups multiply rapidly, and fighters soar endlessly through space. A characteristic scene of *Shanghai Blues* shows several characters dodging one another, popping up in unexpected crannies of the frame (Color Plate 27.6).

Like Spielberg and Lucas, Hark became a powerful producer. His company, Film Workshop, encouraged directors to cultivate a personal style while still aiming at the mass audience. Hark produced several of the all-time successes of the Hong Kong cinema. John Woo's gory *A Better Tomorrow* (1986) made television star Chow Yun-Fat sensationally popular and founded a cycle of "hero" films featuring sensitive, romanticized gangsters. Woo invoked Jean-Pierre Melville's films in celebrating an underworld code of trust and honor, but his characters are far more boyish and narcissistic than their French counterparts (Fig. 27.11). Hark also produced Ching Siu-Tung's *A Chinese Ghost Story* (1987), an extravaganza of supernatural martial arts. Both *A Better Tomorrow* and *A Chinese Ghost Story* spawned sequels, some directed by Hark.

Hark's success with spectacle-centered entertainment signaled the end of the New Wave. Young directors were encouraged to make crowd-pleasing comedies and action pictures that would sustain the concentrated, vertically integrated industry. Shaw Brothers withdrew from production in 1984, but Chow's Golden Harvest remained a central force. Aggressive new companies took over old exhibition circuits, sought fresh talent, and nurtured rapidly changing fads. Chow and others began establishing financial bases in Canada, a likely site for emigrant production after Hong Kong reverts to the control of the People's Republic of China in 1997.

Despite deep inroads made by cable television and home video, Hong Kong audiences remained heavy moviegoers and supported the colony's product. *Boat People* outgrossed *E. T.*; Hark's *Chinese Ghost Story II* surpassed *Batman*; John Woo's *Once a Thief* (1991) ran ahead of *Terminator 2*. Perhaps more surprising, in the late 1980s western intellectuals and film fans made Hong Kong cinema something of a cult object. Its flamboyant style and its unapologetic appeal to emotion made American movies seem pallid. European and North American distributors circulated Woo's *The Killer* (1989), in which the gangster-hero cycle reaches delirious heights. Amid almost unremitting carnage and sentimental scenes of manly devotion, conversations are conducted at gunpoint (Fig. 27.12) and memories are rendered in bursts of semiabstract imagery (Color Plate 27.7). By 1993, Woo had won the admiration of young American directors, and he began directing Hollywood action pictures with *Hard Target*. Along with the manic energy of Chan, Hark, and Woo, western art-house audiences also discovered the more muted productions of Fong and Ann Hui, as well as Stanley Kwan's graceful ghost romance *Rouge* (1988; Color Plate 27.8). The end of the New Wave coincided with growing worldwide appreciation of Hong Kong's cinema.

TAIWAN

In 1982, Taiwan was an unlikely source of innovative filmmaking. Its products were notorious for being either stultifyingly propagandistic or rudimentary, low-budget entertainment. Yet by 1986 Taiwanese cinema had become one of the most exciting areas of international film culture.

Taiwan had long been occupied by Japanese forces before World War II drove them out. In 1949 Jiang Jie-shi's Guomindong troops fled Mao's revolution, bringing 2 million mainland Chinese to the island. Taiwan quickly became an authoritarian state. Martial law was declared for the indefinite future. Initially, filmmaking was under the control of the government, principally through the Central Motion Picture Corporation (CMPC). The CMPC and other agencies concentrated on anti-Communist documentaries. Commercial firms copied the costume operas, comedies, and love stories brought in from Hong Kong.

During the 1960s, the success of imported martial-arts films spurred Taiwanese producers to imitate them, sometimes by bringing over Hong Kong directors such as King Hu (p. 603). Hong Kong companies also set up studios in Taiwan. The CMPC, now obliged to support itself, moved toward fictional films no less didactic than its earlier documentaries had been. Production soared, reaching over 200 features per year, and moviegoing increased dramatically.

But the boom was followed by a crash. The new Hong Kong stars and genres attracted Taiwanese audiences, and profits from the domestic product plummeted. At the same time, Taiwan was shifting from a rural economy to one based on manufacturing and modern technology. For many young people Jiang's promise to recapture the mainland was dead; like Hong Kong youth, they sought a distinct cultural identity. College-educated and urban white-collar workers disdained the action pictures and romances that were the staples of Taiwanese production.

During this period a new film culture emerged. The government created a national archive in 1979, and three years later an annual film festival began showcasing new works. Film magazines appeared, and European classics were screened in universities and small theaters. As with many New Waves—in 1950s France, in 1960s eastern Europe, in 1970s Germany—an educated, affluent audience was ready for a national art cinema.

So, too, was the industry. By 1982, the box-office decline pressed the CMPC and commercial producers to recruit young, largely western-trained directors. The success of the anthology films *In Our Times* (1982) and *The Sandwich Man* (1983) and of a host of new features proved that low-budget

Fig. 27.13 The Eurasian woman in *The Terrorizers* discovers that a photographer has obsessively blown up her image.

films could attract audiences and win prestige at festivals. Like many other Young Cinemas, the Taiwanese New Wave benefited from a crisis in the industry that encouraged cheap, quickly made films by newcomers.

Most of the New Wave films reacted against the studio-bound spectacle characteristic of Taiwanese cinema. Like the Neorealists, the Nouvelle Vague, and other movements before them, the directors took their cameras on location to film loose, episodic narratives, often enacted by nonprofessional performers. Many of the films were autobiographical stories or psychological studies. Since government policy banned overt political comment, social criticism was left implicit. Directors cultivated an elliptical approach to storytelling, using flashbacks, fantasy sequences, and dedramatized situations—all owing something to European art cinema of the 1960s. Two very different directors stood out: Edward Yang and Hou Hsiao-Hsien.

Yang had studied filmmaking briefly in the United States, but he returned to Taiwan with few prospects. After doing some scriptwriting and television directing, he won a chance to direct an episode of *In Our Times*, which led to his first feature, *That Day, on the Beach* (1983). The success of the film led him to make *Taipei Story* (1985) and *The Terrorizers* (1986).

With these films Yang established his area of concern as the anomie and frustration of young urban professionals. Wearing chic fashions and living in modern apartments, his characters fall prey to mysterious forces rippling through the metropolis. *The Terrorizers*, for instance, intercuts two stories: that of a Eurasian woman involved with terrorists and that of a young novelist who eventually separates from her husband. Yang presents the story in abrupt, static shots (Fig. 27.13). A fan of comic books, Yang relies on striking imagery, staccato cutting, and a minimum of dialogue.

Hou Hsiao-Hsien cultivated a more tranquil style. Hou had made some pop-music features in the early 1980s, but his episode in *The Sandwich Man* turned him toward a more personal and contemplative cinema. His major New Wave films—*A Summer at Grandpa's* (1984), *The Time to Live and the Time to Die* (1985), and *Dust in the Wind* (1986)—dedramatize the narrative. Coming-of-age stories, usually taking place in a rural milieu, the films recall Ray's Apu trilogy in building up a rich texture of daily life through dwelling on mundane routines. The story emerges not out of dramatic climaxes but out of details, observed in a painstaking, slow rhythm. Hou also obliquely evokes the history of Taiwan through the interplay among generations.

In *Dust in the Wind* and *City of Sadness* (1990) Hou applied this dedramatizing strategy to film technique through extreme long shots, long takes, static framing, and almost no shot/reverse-shot cutting. Like Mizoguchi and Tati, he subordinates character action to a large-scale visual field. The viewer's eye roams around the frame, led into depth and often to the very limits of visibility (Color Plate 27.9). Hou punctuates these long-take scenes with Ozu-like shots of landscapes or objects.

Hou and Yang, who collaborated on several projects, won worldwide fame with their mid-1980s works. They tried to form a cooperative production company and an alternative distribution network. But the troubles of the domestic industry blocked their efforts to consolidate the gains of the New Wave. The colossal success of video entertainment in Taiwan (a center of videocassette piracy) drove production to abysmal lows, and Hong Kong imports ruled the market. By 1987 the New Cinema had ended.

At the same moment, however, martial law was lifted, censorship relaxed, and those filmmakers still practicing could frankly broach sensitive issues of Taiwanese history and identity. Hou's *City of Sadness,* which won the main prize at the Venice Film Festival, portrays in muted form how the events of 1945–1949 tear a family apart—a topic filmmakers could not have treated only a few years earlier. Yang's *A Brighter Summer Day* (1991), made with Japanese financing, follows eighty characters through a tale of juvenile delinquency in the 1960s. Filmmakers from an even younger generation were starting to explore new ways of defining Taiwanese culture.

MAINLAND CHINA: THE FIFTH GENERATION

Chinese film historians have typically slotted filmmakers into generations associated with major political events. The Fourth Generation of filmmakers began their careers following the Revolution of 1949. Their most prominent member was Xie Jin, who directed *Two Stage Sisters* (p. 480). The Fifth Generation did not begin working until 1982. The long gap is explained by the Cultural Revolution (1966–1976), during which very few films were made (p. 629) and the Beijing Film Academy was closed.

The academy's reopening in 1978 admitted a new class into the four-year program. The graduates, along with a few directors who worked their way up the studio ranks, formed the Fifth Generation. Several of these became the first Chinese filmmakers whose work was widely known abroad.

Once the Cultural Revolution ended, Deng Xiaoping and other Chinese leaders returned to a policy of mild reform. Marketing of privately grown agricultural produce, joint ventures with foreign companies, and other types of free enterprise were introduced. Yet China's leadership tried to promote these economic reforms with little liberalization of individual rights.

The Chinese cinema took several years to recover from the Cultural Revolution. To supply the theaters while production was geared up, hundreds of banned pre-1966 films were rereleased. Foreign films were again imported, and Chinese filmmakers could see works from the European art cinema of the 1960s and 1970s.

Production climbed steadily, from 19 features (1977) to 125 (1986). Most films made soon after the Cultural Revolution tended to revert to the polished studio style. *Rickshaw Boy* (1982, Ling Zifeng), a melodrama set in the prerevolutionary period, concerns a man who loses his rickshaw and must rent one from his boss, whose daughter pressures him into marrying her. Meanwhile, a young woman living in the same courtyard has to beome a prostitute in order to support her brothers. All the characters in the film end unhappily. This glossy studio picture recalled *The New Year's Sacrifice* and other 1950s works.

A few films, however, began to imitate European models. Yang Yanjin and Deng Yimin's *Bitter Laughter* (1979), set during the Cultural Revolution, centers on a journalist forced to write inaccurate stories. *Bitter Laughter*'s style reflects art-cinema influences, using flashbacks, vision scenes, and many special effects to convey subjectivity. Yang, who had graduated just before the Beijing Film Academy closed in 1968, went on to make *The Alley* (1981), a film which offers three alternative endings. Wu Yigong's *My Memories of Old Beijing* (1980) consists of three stories in flashback, filtered through a little girl. While Cultural Revolution policies had favored films with simple character types and unambiguous meanings, these films utilized psychological depth, symbolism, and ambiguity.

In 1982, the Beijing Film Academy graduated its first class since reopening. These students had had unusual training. During the Cultural Revolution, education had emphasized rote learning, mostly based on Mao's writings. Fifth Generation filmmakers, however, were not taught exactly what to think. Chen Kaige, one of the most famous members of the group, recalled his education:

> I really appreciated my teachers because they didn't know how to teach us. They hadn't taught anybody for ten years. They were very openminded. They said they would not teach the old way they used to, the old-fashioned way. We would see films, work nights, and have discussions.[2]

These students saw many imported films, and proved susceptible to their influence. By 1983, the works of these Fifth Generation filmmakers were being released. (See Box.)

Traditionally, each academy graduate was permanently assigned to a studio in Beijing, Shanghai, or the provinces. Several Fifth Generation filmmakers broke this pattern, moving about to find interesting work. Chen Kaige, for example, was assigned to the Beijing Film Studio, but he went instead to join a fellow graduate, cinematographer Zhang Yimou, at the Guangxi studio, where they made *Yellow Earth* and *The Big Parade*. Tian Zhuangzhuang, also delegated to the Beijing Film Studio, could get no directorial work, and so he went to the tiny Inner Mongolia Film Studio to make *On the Hunting Ground*.

Virtually all the Fifth Generation films were made at such provincial studios. The most significant was the Xi'an Film Studio, a medium-size facility in central China. It had had a poor record before Wu Tianming took over as its head in 1983. Wu, an actor who had begun directing in 1979, became a patron to the Fifth Generation, hiring young filmmakers and giving them artistic freedom. As the Chronology indicates, over a third of the Fifth Generation films were made at Xi'an. Wu also asked cinematographer Zhang

CHRONOLOGY OF CHINA'S FIFTH GENERATION

1978	Beijing Film Academy reopens after Cultural Revolution.
1982	First class of students graduates.
1983	*One and Eight,* Zhang Junzha; cinematography, Zhang Yimou
	The Candidate, Wu Ziniu
1984	*Yellow Earth,* Chen Kaige; cin., Zhang Yimou
	Secret Decree, Wu Ziniu
	Life, Wu Tianming (Xi'an Film Studio)
	The Big Parade, Chen Kaige; cin., Zhang Yimou
1985	*In the Wild Mountains,* Yan Xueshu (Xi'an Film Studio)
	Army Nurse, Hu Mei
	Swan Song, Zhang Zeming
	The Black Cannon Incident, Huang Jianxin (Xi'an Film Studio)
	On the Hunting Ground, Tian Zhuangzhuang
	The Dove Tree (banned), Wu Ziniu

1986	*Old Well,* Wu Tianming; cin., Zhang Yimou (Xi'an Film Studio)
	The Stand-In (aka *Dislocation*), Huang Jianxin (Xi'an Film Studio)
	The Horse Thief, Tian Zhuangzhuang (Xi'an Film Studio)
	The Last Day of Winter, Wu Ziniu
1987	*Far from War,* Hu Mei
	The Drum Singers (aka *The Street Players*), Tian Zhuangzhuang
	Red Sorghum, Zhang Yimou (Xi'an Film Studio)
	King of the Children, Chen Kaige (Xi'an Film Studio)
	The Sun and the Rain, Zhang Zeming
1988	*Evening Bell,* Wu Ziniu
1989	April: Pro-democracy demonstrations begin in and around Tiananmen Square.
	June 3–4: The demonstrations are forcibly put down by the government.

Yimou to come from Guangxi to photograph *Old Well.* Zhang agreed on condition that he then be allowed to direct. His film, *Red Sorghum,* became the most popular Fifth Generation work, both in China and abroad.

The Fifth Generation filmmakers, influenced by European art films, reacted against the Cultural Revolution. While Cultural Revolution films used character types, the younger directors favored psychological depth. Instead of presenting simple tales with clear-cut meanings, they adopted complex narratives, ambiguous symbolism, and vivid, evocative imagery. Their films remained political, but they aimed at exploring issues rather than restating approved policy.

Huang Jianxin's *The Black Cannon Incident* is a bitter satire on bureaucracy. A German adviser supervising the assembly of heavy equipment in China needs a translator with technical expertise. The best translator happens to send a telegram concerning a "black cannon," a game piece. Mistaking the phrase for a code, party officials remove him from the job and launch an elaborate inquiry which eventually damages expensive equipment. Huang uses a series of flashbacks to follow the investigation. His color design aids the satire, as in a stylized white-on-white set where the officials meet (Color Plate 27.10).

King of the Children, by Chen Kaige, also exemplifies how some of the Fifth Generation filmmakers emphasized narrative subtlety and striking visual design. A young man, sent to work in the countryside during the Cultural Revolution, is suddenly assigned to teach at a rural school. Trying to inspire the students to think for themselves rather than learn by rote, he runs afoul of his superiors and is dismissed. At the end, his departure from the village is interrupted by imagery of a fire sweeping over the countryside—perhaps symbolizing the devastation of the Cultural Revolution or the purifying effects of ending it. Such an ambiguous scene suggests the influence of European art cinema. Motifs of setting and color in *King of the Children* contrast the enclosed world of the school and the vast terrain surrounding it. In Color Plate 27.11, filters create an unnatural tint in the looming clouds, demonstrating Chen's concern with immense landscapes.

Some Fifth Generation films make even fewer concessions to popular entertainment. Tian Zhuangzhuang's *The Horse Thief*, for example, simply follows a horse thief and his family as they roam Tibet for a year. Tian does not explain Tibetan rituals and customs. The film's interest lies in its very exoticism and in its handsome shots of barren plains, mountains, and temples.

Most Fifth Generation films were criticized for being too obscure for peasants, who made up 80 percent of the Chinese population. China had no tradition of art theaters where specialized audiences could see such films. Whereas a popular film might circulate in a hundred or more copies, only six prints of *The Horse Thief* were made. Few Fifth Generation films did well financially, so Wu Tianming produced more popularly oriented films at Xi'an to balance the losses. In addition, because these films drew on foreign influences, they could be appreciated abroad more easily than most other Chinese films. The money earned by exporting Fifth Generation films helped the group to keep working.

Even as it was gaining fame abroad, however, the group began encountering more difficulties at home. During late 1986, a series of student protests for greater political reforms led the government to tighten control. It conducted a campaign against "bourgeois liberalization," including foreign influences. In cinema, officials demanded accessible, profitable films. As a result, during 1987 and 1988, some Fifth Generation filmmakers undertook more commercial projects. Tian Zhuangzhuang switched from the austere style of *The Horse Thief* and made a slick film called *Rock Kids.* Huang Jianxin and others worked in television. In 1987, Chen Kaige left for New York.

The government's violent suppression of the pro-democracy movement of 1989 brought an end to the Fifth Generation. Some directors went into exile. Wu Tianming emigrated to the United States, trying to find backing to direct a film. Huang Jianxin went to teach in Australia. Most of those who remained in China worked in popularly oriented film and television.

Directors who managed to keep working in their own styles depended on foreign financing. Chen Kaige's *Life on a String* (1991) was produced with German, British, and Chinese backing. A legendlike story of a wandering blind musician and his apprentice, the film contains even more symbolism and ambiguities than Chen's earlier films. Filmed in China, it continues his reliance on expressionistic, overpowering landscape (Color Plate 27.12). Zhang Yimou stayed in China and made *Ju Dou* (1990) with Japanese financing. Its yellow-suffused cinematography evokes the dye shop in which the action is set (Color Plate 27.13). *Raise the Red Lantern* (1991), a Taiwanese-Chinese coproduction, was initially banned in China and eventually released in 1992. Zhang's sumptuous explorations of eroticism and the repression of women carried his films into art theaters abroad. In 1992 his

Hong Kong-financed *Story of Qiu Ju* won a prize at the Venice festival and caused Chinese authorities to claim it as a coproduction.

By the beginning of the 1990s, a regional Chinese cinema was emerging—an Asian equivalent of Europe's "international film market." Taiwanese producers set up companies in Hong Kong to invest in mainland projects. *Raise the Red Lantern* was produced by Hou Hsiao-Hsien's firm, and Hou became one of the first Taiwanese directors to film in China. Yang's *A Brighter Summer Day* was a Taiwan-Japan-U.S. coproduction, while Hong Kong director Ann Hui made *Song of the Exile* as a Taiwanese film. Chen Kaige, now settled in New York, filmed *Farewell My Concubine* (1993) in Beijing; the project was financed by Hsu Feng, a Taiwanese producer who had starred in King Hu's swordplay films of the 1970s (p. 604). Perhaps most significantly, Hong Kong films were starting to flow into China. Their popularity in theaters and on video raised the possibility that the mainland Chinese film industry would be dominated by Hong Kong talent when the colony was taken over by the People's Republic in 1997.

FILMMAKING IN THE MIDDLE EAST

Throughout the 1970s and 1980s, Middle Eastern politics were pervaded by the friction between Israel and the Arab states. Hostilities intensified after Israel's victory in a 1967 war with Egypt, Syria, and Jordan. In 1973, Egypt and Syria launched a new attack. This Yom Kippur War triggered a fourfold increase in oil prices set by the oil-producing countries, and the United States and the USSR began to supply arms to the combatants. President Jimmy Carter coaxed Egypt and Israel to accept a peace plan in 1979, but the 1991 assassination of Egypt's President Anwar Sadat, as well as Israel's refusal to cede captured territory, ensured continued conflict in the region. Arabs in territories under Israeli occupation carried on the struggle begun in the 1960s by the Palestine Liberation Organization, which sought an autonomous homeland for Palestinians. The heirs of Arab nationalism, Palestinian militants took refuge in Lebanon and triggered a civil war that continued into the 1990s.

The cinemas of the region were very diverse. Egypt, Iran, and Turkey had large-scale industries, exporting comedies, musicals, action pictures, and melodramas. Other nations' governments created film production which would promote indigenous cultural traditions. Some filmmakers aligned themselves with Third Cinema developments (p. 611), but after the mid-1970s many filmmakers undertook to broaden their audiences, participating in the international art cinema of the West.

ISRAEL

Israel was not an underdeveloped country, but it had a very small film industry. In the 1960s Menahem Golan and his cousin Yoram Globus began producing musicals, spy films, melodramas, and the ethnic romantic comedies known as *bourekas*. During the 1970s Israel also hosted a Young Cinema which focused on psychological problems of the middle classes. Then, in 1979, the Ministry of Education and Culture offered financial support for "quality film," thus stimulating low-budget films of personal reflection (e.g., Dan Wolman's *Hide and Seek*, 1980) or political inquiry (Daniel Wachsmann's *Transit*, 1980). Soon the quality fund was supporting about half of the fifteen or so features produced annually. The subsidy dwindled in the early 1980s but was revived and increased later in the decade.

As the Middle Eastern country most closely aligned with the West, Israel became part of that international market. The films of Moshe Mizrahi and the teenage nostalgia comedy *Lemon Popsicle* (1978) proved successful abroad. There were coproductions with European countries, and several films were nominated for Academy Awards. Israeli directors shot English-language films with U.S. stars, and Warner Bros. distributed Uri Barbash's *Beyond the Walls* (1984), a story of Arabs and Israelis in prison. The quality fund encouraged foreign companies to invest in internationally oriented projects.

Golan and Globus made a bid for international prominence in 1979 by acquiring control of Cannon Pictures, an independent production company. The pair produced both international entertainment movies (e.g., *Delta Force*, 1985) and art films by Altman, Cassavetes, Konchalovsky, and Godard. Cannon also bought theaters and gained control over half of Israeli film distribution. In addition, Cannon helped bring runaway productions to Israel, bolstering the local industry as a service sector. Although Globus left Cannon in 1989 to found his own company, the Israeli industry continued to have strong western affiliations.

EGYPT

Other Middle Eastern countries were more closely tied to the Third World circuits of film export and personnel flow. In the early 1970s, Syria had a robust industry, sending films to Lebanon, Kuwait, and Jordan. There was a "new Syrian cinema" of social protest, as well as the biannual Damascus Film Festival showcasing Third World products. Lebanon also had a vigorous film industry before the outbreak of civil war in 1975 forced most personnel to emigrate.

Cairo had once been the Hollywood of Arab cinema, but in the 1970s Egyptian production declined. Major directors went into exile; after making *The Betrayed* (1972) in Syria, Tewfik Saleh became head of the Iraqi film institute. The Egyptian industry's output rose during the 1980s, chiefly because of hospitable Arab Gulf markets and the popularity of Egyptian films on video. Yet soon the industry fell on hard times. Video piracy ran rampant, and the government withdrew all financial assistance to producers. U.S. films conquered the market, leaving the local product to fend for itself.

While some new Egyptian directors (including women) emerged during the period, the most famous filmmaker remained the veteran Youssef Chahine. An early proponent of Nasser's pan-Arab nationalism, Chahine later examined Egyptian history from a critical perspective. *The Sparrow* (1973) interrogates the causes of Egypt's defeat in the 1967 war. Later, his films became at once more personal and more transnational. *Alexandria, Why?*

(1978) intercuts events of 1942 with Hollywood films of the era; in *Memory* (1982), a filmmaker facing a heart operation recalls his career over thirty years. Both films are autobiographical, but Chahine joined many political filmmakers of the era in seeking a broader audience by means of more intimate dramas. "I would like to be able to communicate with all of humanity and not only with the narrow parents-children-country group."[3]

TURKEY

Turkish cinema came to international notice in the late 1960s with such films as Yilmaz Güney's *Umut* ("Hope," 1970; p. 610). Turkey already boasted the highest output in the region. Erotic films, comedies, historical epics, melodramas, and even Westerns drew in an audience of over 100 million per year. But production and attendance were already declining when a military contingent seized power in 1980.

The government's oppression of suspect directors was little short of terroristic. Güney became the most visible target. A popular actor who had become a left-wing sympathizer, he fell under suspicion in the mid-1970s. When the military took power, Güney was already serving a twenty-four-year prison sentence. During his prison stay, he wrote scripts which were filmed by others. The most famous of these, *Yol* (*The Way*, 1982) follows five prisoners given a week's release to visit their families, and its forlorn landscapes hint at the oppressiveness of contemporary Turkey (Color Plate 27.14). In 1981 Güney escaped to France, where he made his last film. *The Wall* (1983) is a bitter, dispirited indictment of a prison system that oppresses men, women, and children alike. The prison wall, filmed in different sorts of light and weather, becomes an ominous presence throughout. When Güney died in 1984, the Turkish government sought to erase every trace of him. Police burned all his films and arrested anyone who possessed his photo.

Despite stifling censorship, the film industry gradually rebuilt itself, and production grew to almost 200 films. Only half of these, however, would get released to theaters; the rest were destined for the increasingly powerful video market. At the same time, the government sought to attract western capital, and U.S. companies reappeared on the scene in the late 1980s. Their expanding hold on the market drove production to a mere twenty-five films in 1992, most made with European co-financing.

IRAQ AND IRAN

Filmmakers fell under comparable constraints in two nearby states on the Arabian Peninsula. In 1979, a revolt drove the shah of the Pahlavi dynasty out of Iran, and the Ayatollah Khomeini took over the government. While Khomeini was consolidating a fundamentalist Islamic state, his country was attacked by Iraq, led by Saddam Hussein. The war proved costly for Iran. At the cease-fire of 1988, Khomeini's leadership was shaken and Saddam had gained stature.

Iraq's cinema had long been inconsequential; Iraqi dialect was incom-

Fig. 27.14 The regional realism of *Gav*: Hassan returns to his village, unaware that his beloved cow has died.

prehensible in other Middle Eastern countries, and no stars or genres were worth exporting. But as Saddam bid for leadership of the Arab community, his government launched a patriotic film program. It established a monopoly on production and began inviting Arab filmmakers to work on big-budget features. The $15 million battle epic *Al-Qadissa* (1981) was the most expensive film ever made in the Arab world. Directed by the Egyptian veteran Salah Abou Seif, it utilized a crew drawn from all over the Middle East. In celebrating a seventh-century Iraqi victory over Persian forces, *Al-Qadissa* suggests parallels to Saddam's war with Iran.

Iran's cinema, much more significant than Iraq's, underwent more severe fluctuations. Under the shah, Tehran boasted a major film festival and a commercial industry releasing up to seventy films a year. In the early 1970s the mass-entertainment cinema was counterbalanced by the "New Iranian Cinema" (*cinema motefävet*), exemplified by films such as Dariush Mehrjui's *Gav* ("The Cow," 1970; Fig. 27.14). Some directors left the film workers' union to establish the New Film Group, which received limited government funding. Mehrjui's *The Cycle* (1976) and Bahman Farmanara's *Tall Shadows of the Wind* (1978) were among several films criticizing social conditions, including the shah's secret police.

After Khomeini's 1979 revolution, many filmmakers went into exile, and film production slackened. Only about a hundred features were made between 1979 and 1985. Censorship, confined largely to political topics under the shah, now also focused on sexual display and western influences. Foreign films were drastically cut and shown with dubbed commentary. Soon Khomeini's regime drove out foreign cinema altogether.

Iran's theocracy condemned many western traditions, but government officials soon recognized that film could mobilize citizens to support the regime. Movies were powerful in a nation in which nearly half the population was under the age of fifteen. Khomeini's government created a film industry that reflected his interpretation of Iranian culture and the Shi'ite Muslim tradition. The Farabi Cinema Foundation, established in 1983, offered government financial aid to producers willing to back directors' first films. Although the war with Iraq was depleting the country's resources, the regime encouraged a new generation of filmmakers, and production rose steadily. Even women directors entered the industry.

The strategy also gave Iranian cinema an international identity. Festivals in Europe and North America welcomed several postrevolutionary directors. The most acclaimed was Abbas Kiarostami. His unpretentious story of a child searching for his classmate in a distant village, *Where Is My Friend's Home?* (1986), brought attention to the New Iranian Cinema. In *Close-Up* (1990), Kiarostami investigates a bizarre crime in which a film buff impersonated a famous director and swindled people by promising to put them in movies. Kiarostami intercuts documentary footage of the culprit's trial with restaged scenes in which the participants reenact the events. Another semidocumentary, *Life and Nothing More* (aka *Life Goes On,* 1992) shows the devastation of the 1991 earthquake as a filmmaker and his son search remote mountain villages for the boy who performed in *Where Is My Friend's Home?* Kiarostami uses imaginative framings to dedramatize the quake's horror, as when the son pours a drink for an offscreen mother in an adjacent vehicle (Color Plate 27.15).

Iranian leaders after Khomeini pursued less militant policies and opened avenues to the European Community, and some of the nation's film-makers won praise and distribution in the West. Israeli, Egyptian, and Turk-ish directors were already coming to worldwide notice. *Yol* won the major prize at the Cannes Film Festival, and the Israeli director Mizrahi's French production *Madame Rosa* (1977) captured an Academy Award. Chahine became an "international" director with *Adieu Bonaparte* (1985), a French-Egyptian coproduction. The Palestinian Michel Khleifi returned from exile to make the Franco-Belgian coproduction *Wedding in Galilee* (1987). As U.S. companies penetrated Middle Eastern markets, trying to curb video piracy and gaining power in weakened distribution and exhibition circumstances, filmmakers from the region fed into the West's international art cinema.

AFRICAN CINEMA

Of all Third World regions, Africa remained the most underdeveloped. Al-though about 10 percent of the world's population lived there, the continent represented only 1 percent of world productivity and trade. After 1980, Africa's external debt was as large as its total gross product. Already poor in arable land, the region suffered from devastating droughts. As people fled the villages, the cities became the fastest-growing in the Third World. Of the thirty poorest countries in the world, twenty-five were in Africa.

Because of this poverty, most African countries did not produce a fea-ture-length film before the mid-1970s. Many nations had small populations, few theaters, and virtually no technical facilities. Distribution was controlled by foreign companies, and they had little to gain from promoting competition within Africa. And governments living on IMF austerity measures were un-likely to support much domestic production.

As a result, African filmmakers moved toward international cooperation. In 1970, they created the Fédération Pan-Africaine des Cinéastes (FEPACI), an association of over thirty countries which aimed to solve common prob-lems. In 1980 the United Nations helped film workers found a continent-wide distribution network, the Consortium Interafricain de Distribution

Cinematographique (CIDC), to assist the dissemination of African films. To the festivals of Carthage, Tunisia (established in 1966) and Ouagadougou, Burkina Faso (1969) was added another in Mogadishu, Somalia (1981).

Such initiatives generated a little state support. Senegal, Algeria, and Tunisia nationalized film import and distribution. Some countries also nationalized production. Burkina Faso, despite its tiny size, became an administrative center of black African film, increasing the importance of the annual Ouagadougou festival and creating a film school and a well-equipped production facility. New directors emerged, including Senegal's Safi Faye, the first black African woman filmmaker (*Letter from My Village*, 1976).

On the whole, however, continental associations and state support failed to raise production or enhance distribution possibilities. The CIDC halted its work in 1984; of the 1200 titles it distributed, only about 60 were African. The Cinafric studio in Burkina Faso remained the only indigenous production facility. Filmmaking was still an artisanal activity, with the director forced to raise funds, arrange publicity, and negotiate distribution. Few filmmakers completed second films, and those who did waited many years between projects.

The late 1980s saw little cooperation among African states. The continent's production outside Egypt and South Africa amounted to fewer than twenty features annually. Senegal, the leader of Francophone filmmaking on the continent, had produced around two dozen features, most notably the works of Ousmane Sembene (p. 626). Most countries had made fewer than ten features since achieving independence. The production of short films and documentaries was more robust, however, especially in Anglophone countries like Ghana and Nigeria, which were bequeathed documentary film units by the British colonists.

NORTH AFRICA

The Francophone North African countries known as the Maghreb were in a position to develop filmmaking somewhat. In Morocco, private producers made a few popular entertainments on the model of Egyptian melodramas and musicals. One Moroccan filmmaker, Souhel Ben Barka, attracted attention with accessible dramas of social criticism, such as *A Thousand and One Hands* (1972), about the carpet industry, and *Amok* (1982), a treatment of South African apartheid filmed on a big budget and starring singer Miriam Makeba. In Tunisia, a mixture of government funding and private investment turned out a few coproductions.

The most significant film industry in the Maghreb was Algeria's. After winning its independence from France in 1962, Algeria nationalized all aspects of its film industry and successfully resisted a Hollywood boycott. The government also established a national film archive. Throughout the late 1960s and the early 1970s, the most influential films were dramas of the revolutionary struggle, such as Mohamed Lakhdar Hamina's *Wind of Aurès* (1965).

In the early 1970s, Algeria's government shifted to the left, and social criticism emerged in a New Cinema (*Cinema djidid*), seen in Mohamed

Bouamari's *The Charcoal Maker* (1973) and other works. Within two years, however, the New Cinema declined as the government began subsidizing big-budget historical dramas. The most famous of these, Hamina's *Chronicle of the Years of Embers* (1975), treats the history of the country between 1939 and 1954. Hamina's saga of village life under colonialism cost $2 million and became the first African film to win the Grand Prize at the Cannes Film Festival. Much criticized for his mainstream style, Hamina echoed Youssef Chahine in asserting that political modernism could not reach large audiences: "I believe that good films are distinctive by their universality."[4]

Algeria had the second-highest film output in the Arab-African world, and its 300 theaters gave it a fairly strong audience base. Popular cinema underwent a revival with satiric comedies and political thrillers reminiscent of Costa-Gavras, while some directors explored the everyday life of ordinary Algerians. In the early 1980s, filmmakers took up new themes, notably women's emancipation and workers' emigration to Europe. At the same time, however, the government relinquished central control of filmmaking. As private companies began producing mass-market films, Algerian filmmakers pursued projects abroad and embarked on Francophone coproductions featuring European actors. Even militant members of the New Cinema generation found themselves, like Latin American and European proponents of critical political cinema, making more mainstream and accessible works. Some emigrants from Algeria found commercial success in French cinema, and during the mid-1980s a genre of *beur* (a colloquial anagram for "Arab") dramas and comedies featuring Algerian-French teenagers became popular.

SUB-SAHARAN AFRICA

By contrast, comparatively little black African production was in a mass-market vein. The Nigerian director Ola Balogun produced musical films based on Yoruba theater (Fig. 27.15). Cameroun turned out police thrillers as well as very successful comedies by Danial Kamwa (*Boubou cravate*, 1972; *Pousse-pousse*, 1975) and Jean-Pierre Dikongue-Pipa (*Muna moto*, 1975; *The Price of Liberty*, 1978). Ghana generated commercial action pictures, while in Zaire *La Vie est belle* (*Life Is Beautiful*, 1986) became a box-office hit by capitalizing on the charisma of music star Papa Wemba.

Less mass-oriented films, principally from Francophone countries, claimed worldwide attention. Shown at festivals during the 1970s and 1980s, black African films suggested avenues for a postcolonial cinema. International audiences might miss indigenous details and specific references, but the films' recurrent thematic oppositions—tradition versus modernity, country versus city, native lore versus westernized education, collective values versus individuality—were evident. They posed questions of authorship and Third Cinema with particular acuteness. And because most directors had been trained in Europe and had grown up watching American films, their works displayed a dynamic interaction between western filmmaking conventions and explorations of African aesthetic traditions.

One of the most significant traditions was that of oral storytelling. (See Notes and Queries.) Sometimes a film includes a storyteller as part of its

Fig. 27.15 Balogun's *Ajani Ogun* (1976) exemplifies his popular adaptations of Nigerian theater and dance.

Fig. 27.16 In *Jom,* the *griot* moves through history, appearing at various moments of crisis to aid his people; here he joins women on their way to force their husbands to join a strike.

Fig. 27.17 Women storytellers in *Faces of Women.*

Fig. 27.18 In a single instant, a mute boy discovers death, remembers his mother, and regains speech (*Wend Kuuni*).

action, as when Fadiko Kramo-Lancine makes the *griot* a main character in *Djeli* ("Blood," Ivory Coast, 1981). A film might also employ the storyteller as an omniscient narrator, as in Ababakar Samb's *Jom* ("Dignity," 1981; Fig. 27.16). Or a film might draw from folklore character types such as the trickster or plot action such as the initiation or quest. Oumarou Ganda's *The Exiled* (Niger, 1980) links an ambassador's adventures in an episodic folktale pattern. More recently, Jean-Pierre Bekolo's *Quartier Mozart* (Cameroon, 1992) combines elements of folk magic with music-video editing.

For the most part, black African filmmaking since the mid-1970s followed the trends of political commentary and social criticism characteristic of Third World cinema of the late 1960s. There were comparatively few films of exile, but films dramatizing colonial conflict continued to be made. In *West Indies* (1979) Med Hondo staged an operatic treatment of the slave trade within a vast set, built in an abandoned Paris auto factory. Hondo returned to Africa to film *Sourraouina* (1987), an epic of anticolonial rebellion. After a ten-year hiatus, Sembene resumed filmmaking with *Campe de Thiaroye* (Senegal, 1987; co-directed by Thiemo Faty Sow), a drama treating the clash between French and Senegalese infantrymen at the end of World War II.

Studies of contemporary conditions continued as well. Souleymane Cissé's *Finye* (*The Wind,* 1982) criticizes a military regime by dramatizing the growth of student protest. At the climax of the action, a young man's grandfather, committed to ancestral magic, joins the political struggle. Cissé's sumptuous images—the product of his belief that too many African films were technically awkward—enhance the drama's mixture of politics and supernatural forces.

One of the most widely seen films portraying contemporary African life was Désiré Écaré's *Visages de femmes* (*Faces of Women,* Ivory Coast, 1985). Although his earlier films (p. 626) had won prestigious festival prizes, Écaré took twelve years to finance and film *Faces of Women.* The film's first story centers on two village women's attempts to outwit their husbands. The film then shifts to present a prosperous, middle-aged city woman seeking to expand her business while taking care of her lazy husband, spoiled daughters, and demanding rural kinfolk.

Écaré emphasizes the tension between tradition and modernization through contrasting film styles—a rough Direct Cinema approach for the village story, a more polished technique for the urban tale. The first story is interrupted by shots of women at a festival reciting it and commenting on it (Fig. 27.17), in the manner of oral performance, while in the second story voice-over commentary is supplied by the heroine herself. This narrational contrast neatly expresses the conflict between collective commitments and modernizing individualism that is central to much Third World filmmaking. A witty and ambivalent comment on the contradictions of a developing economy, *Faces of Women* won festival prizes and proved itself commercially viable in Africa and Europe.

Sembene's *Ceddo* (1977; p. 626) had helped initiate a "return to the sources" in African film. In the years that followed, several directors sought to portray the distinctive roots of African culture. In Gaston Kaboré's *Wend Kuuni* ("God's Gift," Burkina Faso, 1982), a mute boy is brought back to speech by recalling his traumatic past (Fig. 27.18). The most significant

Fig. 27.19 *Yeelen*: Nianankoro uses his magic to freeze his attackers in place.

instance of the back-to-the-sources trend, and arguably the most internationally important black African film since *Ceddo*, is Cissé's *Yeelen* (*Brightness,* aka *The Light,* 1989).

Even more than in *Finye,* a supernatural dimension comes to the fore. *Yeelen* presents an initiation, a quest, and a battle which determines the fate of history. A young man steals secret knowledge from the elite caste of magicians to which his father belongs. The old man pursues him. Cissé creates a world in which magic is a powerful natural force (Fig. 27.19). At the climax, the old magician who uses knowledge for personal gain and the youth who wants to share knowledge with others confront each other in a duel of dazzling light.

The plot's elemental symbolism—fire and water, earth and sky, milk and light—creates a filmic equivalent of African oral myth. As in *Finye,* a yellow-orange motif suggests peace and rebirth. Cissé shot most scenes in *Yeelen* in the light of morning, creating golden hues and glowing earth tones which correspond to the central image of "brightness" (Color Plate 27.16). As with many films dealing with precolonial history, however, *Yeelen* refuses to ratify the conservatism of many folk traditions, calling for a radical transformation of myth and knowledge in order to create a new society.

Throughout the 1980s black African production remained limited to around ten features per year, and the films did not find the wide international audience won by African popular music. Nevertheless, Cissé, Sembene, and several other directors created films that presented social issues within accessible storytelling forms. Despite the continent's economic and political problems, its filmmakers reaffirmed the possibility that cinema might forge pan-African solidarity while also engaging viewers in distant countries.

Outside the few remaining Communist countries, the Third World came under increasing domination by western cinema. At the same time, however, regional cinemas in Asia, Africa, and Latin America emerged to create transnational trends. Moreover, international film culture absorbed films from a wider range of "marginal" countries than ever before. A Hong Kong thriller or an Indian romance could be seen in the Middle East or in a New York neighborhood. Film festivals would routinely include features from countries whose cinemas had been unknown in the early 1970s. New and Young Cinemas would continue to appear, with directors coming forward with distinctive works. And video circulation ensured a market for films from Indonesia, Thailand, South Korea, and other regional industries. Well into the 1990s, the filmmaking of the developing countries played a part in the system of world cinema.

◆ NOTES AND QUERIES

Pinning the Tail on Pinochet

Miguel Littín, director of *The Jackal of Nahueltoro* (1969; p. 623), was one of 5000 exiles whom Pinochet's dictatorship forbade on pain of death to return to Chile. In 1985, posing as a Uruguayan businessman, Littín returned. His goal was to make a secret film documenting life under the regime, with the hope, as his children put it, of "pinning a great long donkey's tail on Pinochet."

Littín oversaw three European film crews, each working unknown to the others, and several young Chilean teams. They shot twenty-five hours of documentary footage, including scenes in Pinochet's palace. After several narrow brushes with the authorities, Littín escaped and produced a four-hour television film and a two-hour documentary, both called *Acta general de Chile* (1986). His state of disguised exile—unable to visit friends and relatives, fearing that a passerby would recognize his identity—is engrossingly told in Gabriel García Marquez, *Clandestine in Chile: The Adventures of Miguel Littín*, trans. Asa Zatz (New York: Holt, 1986). Pinochet's forces seized 15,000 copies of the Spanish edition and burned them.

Storytelling in Third World Cinema

During the 1980s "narratology" led many film scholars to reflect on how cinema mobilized basic patterns and strategies of storytelling. For overviews of these developments see David Bordwell, *Narration in the Fiction Film* (Madison: University of Wisconsin Press, 1985), and Robert Stam et al., *New Vocabularies for Film Semiotics* (New York: Routledge, 1992).

The issue of narrative organization had a particular pertinence for cinemas in the developing world, where rural populations still recited or sang folktales. Filmmakers in Latin America, the Middle East, and Africa explored ways in which films might appeal to audiences through an integration of film technique and oral narrative. As yet there exists no broad study of how oral storytelling techniques have been applied to cinema, but some critics have made valuable forays into the area. Karl G. Heider studies folklore plots in *Indonesian Cinema: National Culture on Screen* (Honolulu: University of Hawaii Press, 1991). Lizbeth Malkmus and Roy Armes offer useful discussions of oral strategies in their *Arab and African Film Making* (London: Zed, 1991). As our chapter indicates, African cinema has made extensive use of oral techniques. Some significant studies are André Gardiès and Pierre Hafner, *Regards sur le cinéma négro-africain* (Brussels: OCIC, 1987); Manthia Diawara, "Oral Literature and African Film: Narratology in *Wend Kuuni,*" in Jim Pines and Paul Willemen, eds., *Questions of Third Cinema* (London: British Film Institute, 1989), pp. 199–212; and several essays in "Cinémas noirs d'Afrique," *CinémAction* no. 26 (1983).

◆ REFERENCES

1. Quoted in Michael Chanan, *The Cuban Image* (London: British Film Institute, 1985), p. 275.
2. Chen Kaige, "Breaking the Circle: The Cinema and Cultural Change in China," *Cinéaste* **17,** 3 (1990): 28.
3. Quoted in Magda Wassef, "La Mémoire," in Christian Bosséno, ed., "Youssef Chahine l'Alexandrin," *CinémAction* no. 33 (1985): 99.
4. Guy Hennebelle et al., "Mohamed Lakhdar-Hamina: 'Écouter l'histoire aux portes de la légende,'" *CinémAction* no. 14 (Spring 1981): 67.

CONCLUSION

At the beginning of this book we suggested that three principal questions have shaped our narrative history of world cinema. In framing answers to each of these questions, we have tried to indicate not only the "how"—the process by which stability or change occurred—but also something of the "why," the causal forces at work in the situation.

1. *How have uses of the film medium changed or become normalized over time?*

This is essentially a question about form, style, and genres. Within mainstream entertainment cinema, we have seen that the fictional narrative film of "feature" length became the dominant form in the middle 1910s. There was nothing inevitable about this: audience preference and production flexibility combined to make documentaries (topicals, scenics, and the like) secondary items on most theater programs.

Film technique initially emphasized mise-en-scene, the staging of material for the camera, which was often placed at a considerable distance from the action. Méliès and other directors found ingenious ways to use these conventions. In the early 1900s filmmakers also developed editing as a means to connect scenes, to suggest adjacent locales (as in chase films), and to enlarge details of the action. Intercutting actions taking place in different locales at the same time, a technique developed by filmmakers in several countries and brought to great complexity by Griffith, enabled narrative films to generate tension and to expand plots beyond simple anecdotes. With the new prominence of fictional story films, techniques which would intensify films' appeal to customers were sought after.

Several of these techniques combined to create a system of filming and editing which emphasized breakdown of the action into separate shots, each clearly presenting a piece of narrative information. This "continuity" system, accompanied by three-point lighting and tight adherence to a narrative line, became normal practice in Hollywood and was taken up with minor modifications in other major film-producing countries. American studio directors standardized an approach to cinematic storytelling that became the basis of commercial film style.

Hollywood's use of film technique was not absolutely unchanging. The hard-edged, rapidly cut style of the late 1910s and early 1920s was followed by a "softer" look in the late 1920s and the 1930s. A tendency toward chiaroscuro and depth staging, amplified by deep-focus cinematography, grew in the 1930s and found its most famous expression in Welles's *Citizen Kane*, one of the most influential films of all time. For over a decade thereafter, American films displayed exaggerated foregrounds and somber lighting, enhanced by long takes and complex camera movements. By the beginning of the 1960s, however, a new vogue for flatter, more shallow images with softer focus had come in from documentary filming and European Young Cinemas. In the 1970s and 1980s, "film brat" directors who had themselves studied the history of cinema were combining both options, mixing long takes and rapid cutting, deep-focus and telephoto images. *Citizen Kane* also intensified the use of flashback narration, a tendency which reached its apogee in the U.S. "art films" of the late 1960s.

Hollywood developed popular genres as well, from the silent comedies, Westerns, and melodramas to gangster films, musicals, and widescreen epics of later eras. The animated cartoon, inheritor of slapstick comedy, was a showcase for the polished production values of the Hollywood studios. These genres remained central to the popularity of U.S. films. Hollywood's most skillful directors blended their own artistic interests with the demands of the genres, working comfortably within them (Harold Lloyd, Hawks, Minnelli) or innovating within them (Chaplin, Keaton, Lubitsch, Ford, Sirk, Hitchcock). Those directors of the 1960s and 1970s who wished to make more personal or artistic films were usually obliged to work within genres to some extent.

National film movements offered a more concerted attempt to differentiate a group of films from the Hollywood product. In the silent era, German Expressionism, French Impressionism, Soviet Montage, and international trends fusing these styles were the primary alternatives to Hollywood within mainstream filmmaking. These brought experimental tendencies of modernist art—Expressionist painting and theater, Art Deco settings, Constructivist graphic design—to filmmaking. Rather than simply apply these ideas in a superficial way, many filmmakers rethought cinematic problems in modernist terms. The subjectivity of *The Cabinet of Dr. Caligari* and *The Smiling Madame Beudet*, the compositional design of *Siegfried* and *Nosferatu*, and the experiments in disjunctive editing of Eisenstein, Gance, and Kinugasa all showed that cinema could extend and enrich the possibilities already broached in other media.

Later, France's Poetic Realist trend and the USSR's Socialist Realism offered important variations on the Hollywood model. It was, however, Italian Neorealism, taking shape in the war years and coming to full expression in the late 1940s, which proved the most vivid and influential later alternative to what was perceived as Hollywood's artificiality. Directors around the world were impressed by the authenticity of Neorealism's images, its use of non-actors and locations, its unhappy or unresolved endings, its powerful social criticism. Filmmakers throughout Latin America and Africa saw that one could make films about contemporary life without the professional finish of the Hollywood product.

Neorealism's narrative strategies also gave an impetus to the revival of modernist tendencies. With the end of the war, films could circulate among different countries, and a larger public was prepared to accept stories and styles that were more challenging than the American norm. The development of an international art cinema was partly predicated upon an attempt to mix greater realism of *what* was portrayed with a more self-conscious recognition of *how* it was represented: the modern world, but seen through the filter of the artist's consciousness. The rise of the idea of the film director as *auteur* contributed to the belief that even in mainstream filmmaking a director could function as an artist and express a personal vision of the world.

Accordingly, a host of New Cinemas, Young Film movements, and New Waves emerged throughout Europe, Asia, the Pacific Rim, and Latin America over the period 1958–1980. The Nouvelle Vague was the prototype, with its critics-turned-directors and its triumph in international markets, but there were many other groups, even in the USSR. Animated cinema shared in this return to modernism, with Surrealism and other tendencies surfacing in eastern Europe and elsewhere. Virtually no group displayed the unity of form and style that one could find in the national film movements of the 1920s, or even in Neorealism, but all stirred the sense of art cinema as a continuing process of renewal and novelty, with New Cinemas emerging on the festival scene periodically from all over the globe.

The sense of a new generation probing the limits of the medium was intensified during the 1960s when political commitment came to be a powerful force in film culture. Some Third World revolutionary directors, such as Brazil's Cinema Nôvo group, were already committed to social criticism and formal experimentation early in the decade, but as political struggles grew more intense between the mid-1960s and the mid-1970s, a Third Cinema developed in Latin America and Africa. Soon after, filmmakers in the developed countries adopted left-wing political stances in unprecedented numbers. They made "engaged" films, modified popular genres to carry political baggage, and, most radically, proposed a "political modernism" which merged social critique and formal experimentation.

With the decline of leftist movements in the 1970s, a milder and more moderate art-cinema experimentation reappeared, and even rather stringent political modernists (Godard, Oshima, Kluge) returned to more accessible fare. The New German Cinema and parallel developments in France, India, Japan, Latin America, Taiwan, mainland China, and the USSR carried the stylistic and formal conventions of ambiguity and symbolic narrative into the 1980s and 1990s. In Africa, Hong Kong, and other locales of the developing world, however, there seemed the possibility that indigenous narrative impulses could merge with widely accepted conventions of filmic construction to make the films at once regionally significant and internationally accessible.

Periodically the fiction film has renewed itself by returning to documentary impulses, as in the Soviet cinema of the 1920s, the Poetic Realist films of the 1930s, the Neorealist movement, and the use of Direct Cinema equipment and technique in various New Waves. But the documentary film, largely relegated to a realm outside mass entertainment with the rise of feature narratives, saw substantial new developments in its own domain.

Flaherty made the documentary feature a distinct attraction and bent the recording of reality to his own conception of picturesque adventure, while Vertov gathered "cine-facts" and assembled them in ways which would lead to the "Communist deciphering of the visible." During the 1930s and 1940s, as governments mobilized documentary to promote state policies, individuals and groups used the documentary mode to criticize social conditions and debate social policy. With the end of World War II, many documentarists turned inward, using documentary as a means of personal expression and poetic or essayistic statement. But the development of lightweight sound and camera equipment, along with more sensitive films and magnetic tape recording, provided a new means of capturing reality on film. Direct Cinema, whether quietly observational or vigorously confrontational, changed viewers' notions of how cinema could record the immediate instant. From Rouch and Leacock to Wiseman, documentarists sought the revelatory power of the unstaged instant.

Direct Cinema seldom stayed in a pure state, mixing on-the-fly shots with talking heads, stock footage, and staged scenes, but this synthetic format, soon to become a staple of television journalism, retained its power in the political cinema of De Antonio, Kopple, and the Newsreel groups. At the same time, documentarists returned to the issues of reflexivity and personal statement which had marked the art cinema, probing the forms and styles of documentary for their conventions and taken-for-granted ideologies. There nonetheless remained documentarists who believed that cinema could pick out important truths about the world in powerful images and sounds.

The experimental cinema was usually even more marginal to the film industry than was documentary. Still, it also furnished provocative explorations of film form and style, usually under the aegis of tendencies within modern art. The abstract film, from the "cine-paintings" of the 1910s to the computer-generated imagery of the 1980s, remained a perennial genre, while the assemblage film continued to hold out strong collage possibilities. Dada and Surrealism, given strong visibility in the silent era by Duchamp, Buñuel, and others, remained central to the avant-garde film in the postwar era as well, as much in animation as in other domains.

The psychodrama, the film lyric, the Pop-flavored underground film, the Structural Film, and the Punk film emerged as distinct formal and stylistic alternatives, often cued by parallel developments in music, painting, and poetry. Deren, Brakhage, Kren, Warhol, Snow, Frampton, Rainer, and many other innovators demonstrated that the cinema could be "composed" as much as any other art and that a film artist need not be only a director but could also be a "film-maker," a creator who manipulates the medium directly, as other artists do theirs.

2. *How have the conditions of film production, distribution, and exhibition affected the uses of the medium?*

When films were a minute or less long, the exhibitor controlled presentation, creating programs tailored to particular audiences. As films became longer and narrative fiction won the field, most of the power was taken away from the exhibition end and was put in the hands of producers, directors, and other production personnel. The intended reaction to the film was "built into" the design of the movie itself, and this facilitated the development of linear storytelling and continuity techniques.

The power of Hollywood's approach to narrative and style went along with the rise of its film industry. An early attempt at a trust, the Motion Picture Patents Company, was defeated in the courts, leaving the way clear for independent film companies to build a vertically integrated oligopoly. Production companies acquired distribution outlets and theater chains, while theater owners established production firms. Working together, the studios—MGM, Paramount, Fox, First National, and later Warner Bros. and RKO—were able to control the high-income theaters.

Not until 1948, when a Supreme Court decision found vertical integration monopolistic, was Hollywood's power curtailed somewhat. At that point, with film attendance in a downturn that scarcely ceased until the mid-1960s, the studios relinquished their theaters.

A few national cinemas developed Hollywood-like vertical integration. Communist countries and Nazi Germany centralized control of their film industries by force. In Japan, Hong Kong, and other Asian countries, the industries were able to keep U.S. films at bay through the studios' massive theater ownership. Other countries had virtually no vertical integration. By the 1920s large French producers held only small exhibition chains; most theaters were individually owned. India, with a huge and relatively untapped market, was dominated by western films until after independence, when it gradually built up its industry to an unparalleled scale of output. Yet India's industry, like most outside the Communist bloc, consisted of small, artisanal production companies competing for distribution and screen time. At the end of World War II, even the once-mighty German industry had splintered into small production and distribution companies. This left it and other European industries prey to the Hollywood invasion.

Outside the United States, producers sought either to imitate the popular Hollywood product or to develop a distinctive national cinema. Throughout the 1920s several film industries sought to differentiate their product through film movements such as French Impressionism and German Expressionism. The same impulse resurfaced in the 1940s with Neorealism and in the late 1950s with Young Cinemas aimed at new generations of ticket buyers.

More commonly, producers banked on indigenous genres, which had a local appeal Hollywood could not match. Italy developed historical spectacles, particularly the "strongman" subgenre, and ingratiating comedies. Germany specialized in the fantasy, the historical drama, and the *Heimatfilm*. France pioneered the intimate psychological drama and the fatalistic thriller of Poetic Realism. Soviet films celebrated revolutionary triumphs and World War II heroics. Mexico had its *ranchero* Westerns, Argentina its tango films. There were carnival spectacles in Brazil, *jidai-geki* swordfight films in Japan, "devotionals" and "mythologicals" in India, kung-fu and gangster movies in Hong Kong. Most national cinemas also drew on national literature for adaptations of plays and fiction.

World War II allowed many nations even greater room for indigenous development, since enmity or occupation blocked the flow of the U.S. product. With the war's end, however, most nations returned to the policy of targeting the local market. Occasional films for the expanded international trade in art cinema led to transnational forms and styles, familiar from modern literature and drama and aimed at an educated audience. At the same time, governments began to realize that they would have to protect and subsidize cinema as a wing of "national culture." The filmmaker—even the auteur—was obliged to present a film at once deeply national and aesthetically universal. These conditions intensified as television, both state-run and private, became a major source of film finance.

Elsewhere other conditions prevailed. The USSR and its eastern satellites could count on a fixed internal market for their films; thus film policy was dictated by changing political winds, alternating freezes and thaws. Middle Eastern and African governments often financed films on social problems or national history, sometimes in alliance with former colonizing countries. In Latin America, the strongest alternatives were at first within the well-developed film industries of Mexico, Brazil, and Argentina, but soon Cuba and smaller nations began to develop modest national industries—again, typically under the protection of the state.

Hollywood's mass-production system was dismantled in the early 1950s, and eventually every producer was an independent packager and every actor a free agent. Companies experimented with targeting specific markets—notably teenagers, children, or college-educated adults. The Majors kept control of distribution, which saw them through the difficult 1960s recession. With the success of films in the wake of *The Godfather* and *Jaws*, Hollywood's strengths renewed. And in the 1980s, with film conglomerates buying theaters with the permission of the Reagan administration, the divorcement decrees were de facto outdated.

Faced with new competition from Hollywood and recognizing the dissolution of radical political modernism, many directors returned to the art-cinema conventions of objective realism, subjective realism, and authorial commentary that had crystallized in the 1950s, heightening them with a new emphasis on the gorgeous image. Even Third World filmmakers moved toward more accessible forms and styles, seeking regional audiences but also aiming for the international festival market.

It became clear that isolated film industries could no longer ward off the Americans. National cinemas were collapsing in Brazil, Argentina, the USSR, and all through eastern Europe. Germany, Britain, and France were starting to flag. In response the European Community began to unite, a Hong Kong–Taiwan–China axis started to form, and the nations of the former USSR began to seek outside investment. Now any film aiming at a large audience was forced to be international, and either popular genres or an accessible version of art-cinema form and style would be the basis of export.

Documentary cinema moved further to the edges of the film industry. In the studio era, newsreel shorts were financed by some companies and shown as part of theater programs, but longer documentaries, such as those made by Esfir Shub and Pare Lorentz, depended upon government patronage. The occasional independent documentary, such as *Spanish Earth*, would have to be funded by marginal groups. In the postwar era, national governments began to subsidize personal documentaries, such as those by Resnais, Franju, and Marker. Private, often television-based, companies underwrote Direct Cinema journalism. Up to the present, foundations, government agencies, and television concerns remain the principal sources of funding for documentaries.

The same is true of avant-garde cinema. The filmmaker typically plays the role of an artist, but one without much chance of selling the finished work to a collector or a gallery. Thus foundations, grants, and personal income become the chief source of funding. In some countries experimentalists could find support within commercial structures: Fischinger and the Alexieff-Parker team survived by making advertising films, while in eastern Europe, Trnka, Švankmajer, and many other animators were employed by studios. In the West, experimentalists found employment teaching or working in commercial cinema. Yet their marginality also allowed them freedom. They still labored within constraints, notably the institutional pressures of the "art world" and avant-garde film culture, but they continued to mount open-ended investigations of film form and style.

3. *How have international trends emerged in the uses of the film medium and in the film market?*

The first twenty years of cinema saw a free flow of films among countries. No quotas blocked the passage of a film around the world. An audience might not know a film's national origin. World War I, however, broke up the international film market. It fostered nation-based film industries, but it also required the major European countries to divert energy and capital to the war effort. The U.S. firms seized this moment to expand, first by breaking into markets previously supplied by Europe (such as South America). By 1920 Hollywood film was the dominant force in world film trade.

Central to the industry's international expansion was the fact that the United States was a large, highly modern country. Most European countries were modern but small; most large countries, such as the USSR and China, were underdeveloped. A Hollywood film could cover its costs simply by playing in the United States. Since any foreign income would be pure profit, companies could offer their films to other countries at reduced rates and undercut foreign competition.

This phase of Hollywood's dominance lasted for about two decades. In the meantime, members of alternative film movements, experimentalists, and documentarists established strong international networks. Independent documentaries and avant-garde efforts were hand-carried from country to country and played in film societies and workers' clubs. Left-wing filmmakers assimilated the influence of Soviet Montage films. Experimental trends such as Surrealism and abstract cinema expanded their influence. Joris Ivens, Jay Leyda, and other cosmopolitan travelers linked film trends in distant countries, while journals such as *Close Up* spread information about international developments.

The migration of filmmakers increased as another global war began in the late 1930s, but the hostilities blocked the international flow of films. While film export did not cease, some national industries benefited from lessened U.S. competition and audiences eager for news and distraction. Even Nazi-occupied countries, such as France and Denmark, saw their film industries strengthen in the early war years. As the war turned in favor of the Allies, the Axis nations' film industries slumped.

The international market came back more strongly after the war, as new institutions were created to facilitate alternatives to U.S. filmmaking. Governments erected quotas and other protectionist policies, helped subsidize "quality" films, and established agencies to promote their films abroad. International film festivals served as showcases and markets. Ideas of authorship and artistic cinema migrated across countries, and film schools were started to train young talent. In Europe, the Common Market nations entered into formal coproduction arrangements, while elsewhere national film industries launched joint productions and runaway ventures. Ironically, however, U.S. companies also benefited from such protectionist and nationalist initiatives.

In the broadest perspective, the pattern since 1945 has been a two-tiered system: most films stay within a nation and cater to its population, while a small number of films are designed to travel abroad, marked either as widely appealing—comedies, spy films, melodramas with international casts—or as prestigious art films, of erotic or aesthetic interest. More and more, the mass-audience films suffered by comparison with the Hollywood product. Art films, needing bigger budgets to compete with Hollywood, also required more financing and broader audiences. Hence the growth of joint productions, the increasing investment of television companies and international media conglomerates, and the demand that national governments and regional associations like the EC coordinate efforts to combat U.S. encroachment. In Europe, Asia, Latin America, and Africa, significant film projects would increasingly require international funding.

Accessibility came to the fore. Hollywood focused on blockbuster pictures of universal appeal and with the cachet of a "special event." Art cinema retreated from the extremes of political modernism. Documentarists and experimentalists began emphasizing pleasure, either for a broad public (e.g., *The Thin Blue Line, Daughters of the Dust*) or for subcultures (e.g., films for lesbian and gay audiences).

Throughout the 1980s, video was touted as the savior of film industries outside the United States. Cable, satellite, and eventually high-definition television (HDTV) were expected to sustain even higher levels of production and revive international markets. Early in the 1990s, the promise of video had not paid off, and investments in European, Asian, and Latin American cable were looking more and more risky. HDTV, the dream of appliance manufacturers in the face of a VCR-saturated market, seemed far off. The videocassette had created more profits for the biggest industries—chiefly Hollywood—but it had also created an enormous web of piracy. At the beginning of the 1990s, the global film industry looked to be almost completely an extension of the U.S. market.

Yet recent decades have also seen contrary signs. Talented young filmmakers have come to light throughout the world. "Marginal" industries, notably those in Hong Kong and India, have created some competition for the U.S. product. Hollywood has broadened its talent base by recruiting directors of color, and countries around the world are bringing women filmmakers into the industry. And while film on video is not a substitute for film on film, it does give access to a wider range of movies, old and new, famous and obscure, than viewers could see in earlier eras. Archives, more numerous and conscious of their mission, are disseminating classics, and national governments tour packages of films. Whatever cinema's future, at this moment we have an unprecedented access to its past and its present.

BIBLIOGRAPHY

This is a select bibliography, emphasizing book-length studies and special issues of journals. Most of the works listed are comprehensible to the nonspecialist. Each chapter's Notes and Queries section supplies additional bibliographical information about particular topics.

GENERAL REFERENCE WORKS

Under the editorship of Michael Singer, Lone Eagle Publishing (Los Angeles, California) publishes a series of reference books compiling information on directors, screenwriters, film composers, and other creative personnel. The directors volume is updated annually.

The American Film Institute Catalogue: Feature Films, 1911–1920. 2 vols. Berkeley: University of California Press, 1988.

The American Film Institute Catalogue: Feature Films, 1921–1930. 2 vols. New York: Bowker, 1971.

Atkins, Robert. *Artspeak: A Guide to Contemporary Ideas, Movements, and Buzzwords.* New York: Abbeville, 1989.

Cowie, Peter, ed. *International Film Guide.* London: Tantivy; later, Variety, Inc., 1964–present.

The Film Daily Yearbook of Motion Pictures. New York: Film Daily, 1928–1969.

The Film/Literature Index. Albany: Filmdex, 1973–present.

Gerlach, John C., and Lana Gerlach. *The Critical Index: A Bibliography of Articles on Film in English, 1946–1973, Arranged by Names and Topics.* New York: Teachers College Press, 1974.

Gifford, Denis. *The British Film Catalogue 1895–1985: A Reference Guide.* Newton Abbott, England: David & Charles, 1986.

The International Index of Film Periodicals. Brussels: International Federation of Film Archives, 1972–present.

Katz, Ephriam. *The Film Encyclopedia.* New York: Crowell, 1979.

Konigsberg, Ira. *The Complete Film Dictionary.* New York: New American Library, 1987.

Lauritzen, Einar, and Gunnar Lundquist. *American Film-Index 1908–1915.* Stockholm: Film-Index, 1976.

———. *American Film-Index 1916–1920.* Stockholm: Film-Index, 1984.

Lyon, Christopher. *The International Dictionary of Films and Filmmakers.* 4 vols. Chicago: St. James Press, 1984.

MacCann, Richard Dyer, and Edward S. Perry. *The New Film Index: A Bibliography of Magazine Articles in English, 1930–1970.* New York: Dutton, 1975.

The Motion Picture Almanac. New York: Quigley, 1933–present.

Passek, Jean-Loup, ed. *Dictionnaire du cinéma.* 2d ed. Paris: Larousse, 1991.

Plazola, Luis Trelles. *South American Cinema: Dictionary of Film Makers.* Rio Pideras: University of Puerto Rico, 1989.

Spottiswoode, Raymond, et al. *The Focal Encyclopedia of Film and Television Techniques.* London: Focal Press, 1969.

UNESCO. *Statistical Yearbook.* Paris: UNESCO, 1964–present.

United Nations Development Program. *Human Development Report.* New York: Oxford University Press, 1992.

Vincent, Carl. *General Bibliography of Motion Pictures.* Rome: Ateneo, 1953.

Wid's Year Book (later *Film Year Book*). New York: Wid's, 1918–1927.

Workers of the Writers' Program of the Work Projects Administration in the City of New York. *The Film Index: A Bibliography.* Vol. 1: *The Film as Art.* New York: Museum of Modern Art, 1941. Vol. 2: *The Film as Industry.* White Plains, N.Y.: Kraus, 1985. Vol. 3: *Film in Society.* White Plains, N.Y.: Kraus, 1985.

HISTORIOGRAPHY

Allen, Robert C., and Douglas Gomery. *Film History: Theory and Practice.* New York: Random House, 1985.

Cherchi Usai, Paolo. *Burning Passions: An Introduction to the Study of Silent Film.* Trans., Elizabeth Sansone. London: British Film Institute, 1994.

Lagny, Michèle. *De l'histoire: Méthode historique et histoire du cinéma.* Paris: Colin, 1992.

Sadoul, Georges. "Materiaux, méthodes et problèmes de l'histoire du cinéma." In his *Histoire du cinéma mondial des origines à nos jours.* 9th ed. Paris: Flammarion, 1972, pp. v-xxix.

Sklar, Robert, and Charles Musser, eds. *Resisting Images: Essays on Cinema and History.* Philadelphia: Temple University Press, 1990.

WORLD CINEMA SURVEYS

Bernardo, Mario. *La Macchina del cinematografico.* Turin: Gruppo Editoriale Forma, 1983.

Luhr, William, ed. *World Cinema since 1945.* New York: Ungar, 1987.

Pratt, George, ed. *Spellbound in Darkness: A History of the Silent Film.* Rev. ed. Greenwich, Conn.: New York Graphic Society, 1973.

Sadoul, Georges. *Histoire du cinéma mondial des origines à nos jours.* 9th ed. Paris: Flammarion, 1972.

———. *Histoire générale du cinéma.* Vols. 1–4, 6. Paris: Denoël, 1946–1975.

Thompson, Kristin. *Exporting Entertainment: America in the World Film Market, 1907–1934.* London: British Film Institute, 1985.

REGIONAL AND NATIONAL CINEMA SURVEYS

Apart from the works listed below, an excellent set of national cinema histories has been published in the French series "Cinéma/pluriel" by the Pompidou Center under the general editorship of Jean-Loup Passek. As of 1993, volumes have been devoted to Australia, Brazil, Canada, Soviet Central Asia, China, Cuba, Denmark, the Republic of Georgia, Germany (1913–1933), Hungary, India, Italy (1905–1945), Mexico, Poland, Portugal, Scandinavia, the USSR, and Yugoslavia.

Anderson, Joseph, and Donald Richie. *The Japanese Film: Art and Industry.* Expanded ed. Princeton, N.J.: Princeton University Press, 1982.

Armes, Roy. *Third World Filmmaking and the West.* Berkeley: University of California Press, 1987.

Bachy, Victor. *Pour une histoire du cinéma africain.* Brussels: OCIC, 1987.

Balio, Tino, ed. *The American Film Industry.* 2d ed. Madison: University of Wisconsin Press, 1985.

———. *Hollywood in the Age of Television.* Boston: Unwin Hyman, 1990.

Balski, Grzegorz. *Directory of Eastern European Film-Makers and Films, 1945–1991.* London: Flicks, 1992.

Banerjee, Shampa, and Anil Srivastava. *One Hundred Indian Feature Films: An Annotated Filmography.* New York: Garland, 1988.

Barnouw, Erik, and S. Krishnaswamy. *Indian Film.* 2d ed. New York: Oxford University Press, 1980.

Barr, Charles, ed. *All Our Yesterdays: 40 Years of British Cinema.* London: British Film Institute, 1986.

Bergan, Ronald. *The United Artists Story.* New York: Crown, 1986.

Bock, Audie. *Japanese Film Directors.* New York: Kodansha, 1978.

Bondanella, Peter. *Italian Cinema from Neorealism to the Present.* New York: Ungar, 1983.

Bonnell, René. *Le Cinéma exploité.* Paris: Seuil, 1978.

Bordwell, David, Janet Staiger, and Kristin Thompson. *The Classical Hollywood Cinema: Film Style and Mode of Production to 1960.* New York: Columbia University Press, 1985.

Boughedir, Ferid. *Le Cinéma africain de A à Z.* Brussels: OCIC, 1987.

Brunet, Patrick J. *Les Outils de l'image: Du cinématographe au caméscope.* Montreal: Université de Montréal, 1992.

Buehrer, Beverly Bare. *Japanese Films: A Filmography and Commentary, 1921–1989.* Jefferson, N.C.: McFarland, 1990.

Burch, Noël. *To the Distant Observer: Form and Meaning in the Japanese Cinema.* Berkeley: University of California Press, 1978.

Chanan, Michael. *Chilean Cinema.* London: British Film Institute, 1974.

———. *The Cuban Image.* London: British Film Institute, 1985.

"Les Cinémas arabes et Grand Maghreb." *CinémAction* no. 43 (1987).

Clark, Paul. *Chinese Cinema: Culture and Politics since 1949.* Cambridge, England: Cambridge University Press, 1987.

Cluny, Claude Michel. *Dictionnaire des nouveaux cinémas arabes.* Paris: Sindbad, 1978.

Courtade, Françis. *Les Malèdictions du cinéma français: Une Histoire du cinéma français parlant (1928–1978).* Paris: Moreau, 1978.

Cowie, Peter. *Swedish Cinema.* London: Tantivy, 1966.

Curran, James, and Vincent Porter, eds. *British Cinema History.* London: Weidenfeld and Nicolson, 1983.

Davay, Paul. *Cinéma de Belgique.* Gembloux: Duculot, 1973.

Dennis, Jonathan, and Jan Beringa, eds. *Film in Aotearoa New Zealand.* Wellington, New Zealand: Victoria University Press, 1992.

Dickinson, Margaret, and Sarah Street. *Cinema and State: The Film Industry and the British Government 1927–1984.* London: British Film Institute, 1985.

Dermody, Susan, and Elizabeth Jacka. *The Screening of Australia: Anatomy of a National Cinema.* 2 vols. Sydney: Currency, 1988.

Dyer, Richard, and Ginette Vincendeau, eds. *Popular European Cinema.* London: Routledge, 1992.

Eames, John Douglas. *The MGM Story*. New York: Crown, 1976.
———. *The Paramount Story*. New York: Crown, 1985.

Elsaesser, Thomas. *New German Cinema: A History*. New Brunswick, N.J.: Rutgers University Press, 1989.

Feldman, Seth. *Take Two: A Tribute to Film in Canada*. Toronto: Irwin, 1984.

Feldman, Seth, and Joyce Nelson, eds. *Canadian Film Reader*. Toronto: Peter Mastin, 1977.

Finler, Joel W. *The Hollywood Story*. New York: Crown, 1988.

Gomery, Douglas. *The Hollywood Studio System*. New York: St. Martin's, 1986.
———. *Shared Pleasures: A History of Movie Presentation in the United States*. Madison: University of Wisconsin Press, 1992.

Hayward, Susan, and Ginette Vincendeau, eds. *French Film: Texts and Contexts*. London: Routledge, 1990.

Hennebelle, Guy, and Alfonso Gumicio-Dagron, eds. *Les Cinémas de l'Amérique Latine*. Paris: Lherminier, 1981.

Hibon, Danièle, ed. *Cinémas d'Israël*. Paris: Galerie Nationale du Jeu de Paume, 1992.

Higginbotham, Virginia. *Spanish Film under Franco*. Austin: University of Texas Press, 1988.

Hirschorn, Clive. *The Columbia Story*. New York: Crown, 1990.
———. *The Universal Story*. New York: Crown, 1983.
———. *The Warner Bros. Story*. New York: Crown, 1979.

Holliss, Richard, and Brian Sibley. *The Disney Studio Story*. New York: Crown, 1988.

Issari, M. Ali. *Cinema in Iran, 1900–1979*. Metuchen, N.J.: Scarecrow, 1989.

Jarvie, Ian. *Hollywood's Overseas Campaign: The North Atlantic Movie Trade, 1920–1950*. Cambridge, England: Cambridge University Press, 1992.
———. *Window on Hong Kong: A Sociological Study of the Hong Kong Film Industry and Its Audience*. Hong Kong: University of Hong Kong Centre of Asian Studies, 1977.

Jewell, Richard B., and Vernon Harbin. *The RKO Story*. New York: Arlington House, 1982.

Johnson, Randal. *The Film Industry in Brazil: Culture and the State*. Pittsburgh: University of Pittsburgh Press, 1987.

Johnson, Randal, and Robert Stam, eds. *Brazilian Cinema*. Austin: University of Texas Press, 1982.

Kenez, Peter. *Cinema and Soviet Society 1917–1953*. Cambridge, England: Cambridge University Press, 1992.

King, John. *Magical Reels: A History of Cinema in Latin America*. London: Verso, 1990.

King, John, and Nissa Torrents, eds. *The Garden of Forking Paths: Argentine Cinema*. London: British Film Institute, 1987.

Larraz, Emmanuel. *Le Cinéma espagnol des origines à nos jours*. Paris: Cerf, 1986.

"Latin American Cinema." *Iris* no. 13 (Summer 1991).

Lawton, Anna, ed. *The Red Screen: Politics, Society, Art in Soviet Cinema*. New York: Routledge, 1992.

Lent, John A., ed. *The Asian Film Industry*. London: Helm, 1990.

Leprohon, Pierre. *The Italian Cinema*. Trans., Roger Greaves and Oliver Stallybrass. New York: Praeger, 1972.

Lever, Yves. *Histoire générale du cinéma au Québec*. Montreal: Boréal, 1988.

Leyda, Jay. *Kino: A History of the Russian and Soviet Film*. 3rd ed. Princeton, N.J.: Princeton University Press, 1983.

Liehm, Mira. *Passion and Defiance: Film in Italy from 1942 to the Present*. Berkeley: University of California Press, 1984.

Liehm, Mira, and Antonin J. Liehm. *The Most Important Art: Soviet and Eastern European Film after 1945*. Berkeley: University of California Press, 1977.

Low, Rachel. *The History of the British Film*. 6 vols. London: George Allen & Unwin, 1948–1979.

Marcus, Millicent. *Italian Film in the Light of Neorealism*. Princeton, N.J.: Princeton University Press, 1986.

Michalek, Boleslaw, and Frank Turaj. *The Modern Cinema of Poland*. Bloomington: Indiana University Press, 1988.

Mora, Carl J. *Mexican Cinema: Reflections of a Society 1896–1988*. Berkeley: University of California Press, 1989.

Neergaard, Ebbe. *The Story of Danish Film*. Copenhagen: The Danish Institute, 1963.

Nemeskurty, István. *A Short History of the Hungarian Cinema*. Budapest: Corvina, 1980.

Noletti, Arthur, and David Desser, eds. *Reframing Japanese Cinema: Authorship, Genre, History*. Bloomington: Indiana University Press, 1992.

"Other Cinemas, Other Criticisms." *Screen* **26,** 3–4 (May–August 1985).

Park, James. *British Cinema: The Lights That Failed*. London: Batsford, 1990.

Pfaff, Françoise. *Twenty-Five Black African Filmmakers: A Critical Study, with Filmography and Bio-Bibliography*. New York: Greenwood, 1988.

Prédal, René. *Le Cinéma français depuis 1945*. Paris: Nathan, 1991.
———. *La Photo de cinéma*. Paris: Cerf, 1985.

Ramachandran, T. M., ed. *Seventy Years of Indian Cinema (1913–1983)*. Bombay: Cinema India, 1983.

Rayns, Tony, ed. *Eiga: 25 Years of Japanese Cinema*. Edinburgh: Film Festival, 1984.

Rayns, Tony, and Scott Meek, eds. *Electric Shadows: 45 Years of Chinese Cinema*. London: British Film Institute, 1980.

Reid, Nicholas. *A Decade of New Zealand Film: **Sleeping Dogs** to **Came a Hot Friday***. Dunedin: John McIndoe, 1986.

Rimberg, John David. *The Motion Picture in the Soviet Union: 1918–1952*. New York: Arno, 1973.

Rockett, Kevin, Luke Gibbons, and John Hill. *Cinema and Ireland*. Syracuse: Syracuse University Press, 1988.

Roy, Rajat. *Filmography of Sixty Eminent Indian Movie-Makers*. Singhbhum, Bihar: Cine Society Mosaboni, 1983.

Sabria, Jean-Charles. *Cinéma français: Les Années 50*. Paris: Pompidou Center, 1987.

Sadoul, Georges. *The Cinema in the Arab Countries*. Beirut: Interarab Centre of Cinema and Television, 1966.

Schmidt, Nancy J. *Sub-Saharan African Films and Filmmakers*. Bloomington: Indiana University African Studies Program, 1986.

Schnitman, Jorge A. *Film Industries in Latin America: Dependency and Development*. Norwood, N.J.: Ablex, 1984.

Shiri, Keith, ed. *Directory of African Film-Makers and Films*. London: Flicks, 1992.

Shirley, Graham, and Brian Adams. *Australian Cinema: The First Eighty Years*. Sydney: Angus and Robertson, 1983.

Shohat, Ella. *Israeli Cinema: East/West and the Politics of Representation*. Austin: University of Texas Press, 1989.

Slater, Thomas J. *Handbook of Soviet and East European Films and Filmmakers*. New York: Greenwood, 1992.

Slattery, Margaret, ed. *Modern Days, Ancient Nights: Thirty Years of African Filmmaking*. New York: Film Society of Lincoln Center, 1993.

Sobański, Oscar. *Polish Feature Films: A Reference Guide 1945–1985*. West Cornwall, Conn.: Locust Hill, 1987.

Stites, Richard. *Russian Popular Culture: Entertainment and Society since 1900*. Cambridge, England: Cambridge University Press, 1992.

Stoil, Michael Jon. *Cinema beyond the Danube: The Camera and Politics*. Metuchen, N.J.: Scarecrow, 1974.

Taylor, Richard, and Ian Christie, eds. *The Film Factory: Russian and Soviet Cinema in Documents 1896–1939*. Cambridge, Mass.: Harvard University Press, 1988.

Tessier, Max. *Le Cinéma japonais au présent 1959–1984*. Paris: Lherminier, 1984.

Thomas, Tony, and Aubrey Solomon. *The Films of 20th Century-Fox*. Secaucus, N.J.: Citadel, 1979.

Thoraval, Yves. *Regards sur le cinéma égyptien*. Paris: L'Harmattan, 1988.

"Le Tiers monde en films." *CinémAction* special number (1981).

Vasudev, Aruna, and Philippe Leuglet, eds. *Indian Cinema Superbazaar*. Delhi: Vikas, 1983.

Véronneau, Pierre, ed. *Les Cinémas canadiens*. Paris: Lherminier, 1978.

Willemen, Paul, and Behroze Gardhy, eds. *Indian Cinema*. London: British Film Institute, 1982.

Williams, Alan. *Republic of Images: A History of French Filmmaking*. Cambridge, Mass.: Harvard University Press, 1992.

Zglinicki, F. V. *Der weg des Films*. 2 vols. Rep., Hildesheim: Olms Press, 1979.

Zorkaya, Neya. *The Illustrated History of the Soviet Cinema*. New York: Hippocrene, 1989.

FIGURES AND PERSONALITIES

These sources pertain to individuals whose activities are discussed in several chapters of this book. For other major figures, see the bibliographic entries for specific chapters.

G. K. Hall (Boston) publishes a useful series of annotated reference guides to major filmmakers.

Annenkov, Georges. *Max Ophüls*. Paris: Le Terrain Vague, 1962.

Aranda, Francisco. *Luis Buñuel: A Critical Biography*. Trans. and ed., David Robinson. London: Secker and Warburg, 1975.

Bellour, Raymond, ed. *Jean-Luc Godard: Son + Image*. New York: Museum of Modern Art, 1992.

Bertin, Celia. *Jean Renoir: A Life in Pictures*. Trans., Mireille Muellner and Leonard Muellner. Baltimore: Johns Hopkins University Press, 1991.

Bordwell, David. *The Cinema of Eisenstein*. Cambridge, Mass.: Harvard University Press, 1993.

———. *The Films of Carl-Theodor Dreyer*. Berkeley: University of California Press, 1981.

———. *Ozu and the Poetics of Cinema*. Princeton, N.J.: Princeton University Press, 1988.

Brakhage, Stan. *Film at Wit's End: Eight Avant-Garde Filmmakers*. Kingston, N.Y.: McPherson, 1989.

Cazals, Patrick. *Serguei Paradjanov*. Paris: Cahiers du Cinéma, 1993.

Cerisuelo, Marc. *Jean-Luc Godard*. Paris: Lherminier, 1989.

Danvers, Louis, and Charles Tatum, Jr. *Nagisa Oshima*. Paris: Cahiers du Cinéma, 1986.

Dumont, Hervé. *Frank Borzage: Sarastro à Hollywood*. Milan: Mazzotta, 1993.

Durgnat, Raymond, and Scott Simmon. *King Vidor, American*. Berkeley: University of California Press, 1988.

Fraigneau, André. *Cocteau on the Film: Conversations with Jean Cocteau*. Trans., Vera Traill. New York: Dover, 1972.

Gallagher, Tag. *John Ford: The Man and His Films*. Berkeley: University of California Press, 1986.

Goodwin, James. *Eisenstein, Cinema, and History*. Urbana: University of Illinois Press, 1993.

Insdorf, Annette. *François Truffaut*. New York: Morrow, 1979.

McDonald, Keiko. *Mizoguchi*. Boston: Twayne, 1984.

Pfaff, Françoise. *The Cinema of Ousmane Sembene, a Pioneer of African Film*. Westport, Conn.: Greenwood, 1984.

Prinzler, Hans Helmut, and Enno Patalas, eds. *Lubitsch*. Munich: C. J. Bucher, 1984.

Rabinovitz, Lauren. *Points of Resistance: Women, Power and Politics in the New York Avant-Garde Cinema, 1943–71*. Urbana: University of Illinois Press, 1991.

Renoir, Jean. *My Life and My Films*. Trans., Norman Denny. New York: Atheneum, 1974.

Richie, Donald. *Ozu: His Life and Films*. Berkeley: University of California Press, 1974.

Robinson, David. *Chaplin: His Life and Art*. New York: McGraw-Hill, 1985.

Rotha, Paul. *Robert J. Flaherty: A Biography*. Philadelphia: University of Pennsylvania Press, 1983.

Sarris, Andrew, ed. *Interviews with Film Directors*. Indianapolis: Bobbs-Merrill, 1967.

Seton, Marie. *Sergei M. Eisenstein*. London: John Lane, The Bodley Head, 1952.

Spoto, Donald. *The Art of Alfred Hitchcock*. Garden City: Doubleday, 1979.

Tarkovsky, Andrey. *Sculpting in Time: Reflections on the Cinema*. Trans., Kitty Hunter-Blair. London: Faber, 1989.

Turovskaya, Maya. *Tarkovsky: Cinema as Poetry*. London: Faber, 1989.

Van Cauwenberge, Geneviève. "Chris. Marker and French Documentary Filmmaking: 1962–1982." Ph.D. dissertation, New York University, 1992.

"Youssef Chahine, l'Alexandrin." *CinémAction* no. 33 (1985).

GENRES, MOVEMENTS, AND OTHER TRENDS

The Aurum Film Encyclopedia (London: 1985–present), edited by Phil Hardy, has published reference volumes on horror, science fiction, and the Western.

Altman, Rick. *The American Film Musical*. Bloomington: Indiana University Press, 1987.

Barsam, Richard M. *Nonfiction Film: A Critical History*. Rev. ed. Bloomington: Indiana University Press, 1992.

Bendazzi, Giannalberto. *Cartoons: Il Cinema d'animazione 1888–1988*. Venice: Marsilio, 1988.

Coe, Brian. *The History of Movie Photography*. London: Ash and Grant, 1981.

Cornwell, Regina. *The Other Side: European Avant-Garde Cinema 1960–1980*. New York: American Federation of the Arts, 1983.

Crafton, Donald. *Before Mickey: The Animated Film 1898–1928*. Cambridge, Mass.: MIT Press, 1982.

Crawford, Peter Ian, and David Turton, eds. *Film as Ethnography*. Manchester, England: Manchester University Press, 1992.

Cripps, Thomas. *Making Movies Black: The Hollywood Message Movie from World War II to the Civil Rights Era*. New York: Oxford University Press, 1993.

———. *Slow Fade to Black: The Negro in American Film, 1900–1942*. New York: Oxford University Press, 1977.

Drummond, Philip, et al. *Film as Film: Formal Experiment in Film, 1910–1975*. London: Hayward Gallery, 1979.

Dyer, Richard. *Now You See It: Studies on Lesbian and Gay Film*. New York: Routledge, 1990.

Flitterman-Lewis, Sandy. *To Desire Differently: Feminism and the French Cinema*. Urbana: University of Illinois Press, 1990.

Fordin, Hugh. *Hollywood's Greatest Musicals: The World of Entertainment*. New York: Avon, 1975.

Frayling, Christopher. *Spaghetti Westerns: Cowboys and Europeans from Karl May to Sergio Leone*. London: Routledge, 1981.

German Experimental Films from the Beginnings to the 1970s. Munich: Goethe Institute, 1981.

Gili, Jean A. *La Comédie italienne*. Paris: Veyrier, 1983.

Gledhill, Christine, ed. *Home Is Where the Heart Is: Studies in Melodrama and the Woman's Film*. London: British Film Institute, 1987.

Green, Stanley. *Encyclopedia of the Musical Film*. New York: Oxford University Press, 1981.

Heider, Karl G. *Ethnographic Film*. Austin: University of Texas Press, 1976.

Hennebelle, Guy, and Raphael Bassan. *Cinémas d'avant-garde: Expérimental et militant*. CinémAction no. 10–11 (Spring–Summer 1980).

"The History of Black Film." *Black Film Review* **7**, 4 (1993).

"The Hollywood Cartoon." *Film Comment* **11**, 1 (January–February 1975).

James, David. *Allegories of Cinema: American Film in the Sixties*. Princeton, N.J.: Princeton University Press, 1989.

Jones, G. William. *Black Cinema Treasures: Lost and Found*. Denton: University of North Texas Press, 1991.

Kallinak, Kay. *Settling the Score: Music and the Classical Hollywood Film*. Madison: University of Wisconsin Press, 1992.

Kuhn, Annette, and Susannah Radstone, eds. *Women in Film: An International Guide*. New York: Fawcett Columbine, 1990.

Lamartine, Thérèse. *Elles: Cinéastes ad lib 1895–1981*. Paris: Remne-Ménage, 1985.

Lovell, Alan, and Jim Hillier. *Studies in Documentary*. New York: Viking, 1972.

Maltin, Leonard. *Of Mice and Magic: A History of American Animated Cartoons*. New York: New American Library, 1980.

McCarthy, Helen. *Manga Manga Manga: A Celebration of Japanese Animation at the ICA Cinema*. London: Institute for Contemporary Art, 1992.

Noguez, Dominique. *Éloge du cinéma expérimental: Définitions, jalons*. Paris: Pompidou Center, 1979.

Quart, Barbara Koenig. *Women Directors: The Emergence of a New Cinema*. New York: Praeger, 1988.

Rollwagen, Jack R., ed. *Anthropological Filmmaking*. Chur, Switzerland: Harwood, 1988.

Russett, Robert, and Cecile Starr. *Experimental Animation: An Illustrated Anthology*. New York: Van Nostrand Reinhold, 1976.

Russo, Vito. *The Celluloid Closet: Homosexuality in the Movies*. Rev. ed. New York: Harper & Row, 1981.

Scheugl, Hans, and Ernst Schmidt Jr. *Eine Subgeschichte des Films Lexikon des Avantgarde-, Experimental- und Undergroundfilms*. 2 vols. Frankfurt: Suhrkamp, 1974.

Silver, Alain. *The Samurai Film*. South Brunswick, N.J.: Barnes, 1977.

Silver, Alain, and Elizabeth Ward. *Film Noir: An Encyclopedic Reference to the American Style*. Woodstock, N.Y.: Overlook, 1979.

Sitney, P. Adams. *Visionary Film: The American Avant-Garde 1943–1978*. 2d ed. New York: Oxford University Press, 1979.

Sobchak, Vivian. *Screening Space: The American Science Fiction Film*. 2d ed. New York: Ungar, 1987.

Stauffacher, Frank, ed. *Art in Cinema: A Symposium on the Avant-Garde Film together with Program Notes and References for*

Series One of Art in Cinema. San Francisco: San Francisco Museum of Art, 1947.

Swedish Avantgarde Film 1924–1990. New York: Anthology Film Archives, 1991.

Tudor, Andrew. *Monsters and Mad Scientists: A Cultural History of the Horror Movie.* Oxford: Blackwell, 1989.

Waugh, Thomas, ed. *"Show Us Life": Toward a History and Aesthetics of the Committed Documentary.* Metuchen, N.J.: Scarecrow, 1984.

Wees, William. *Recycled Images: The Art and Politics of Found Footage Films.* New York: Anthology Film Archives, 1993.

Weis, Elisabeth, and John Belton, eds. *Film Sound: Theory and Practice.* New York: Columbia University Press, 1985.

Weiss, Andrea. *Vampires and Violets: Lesbians in the Cinema.* London: Jonathan Cape, 1992.

Weisser, Thomas. *Spaghetti Westerns—The Good, the Bad, and the Violent: 558 Eurowesterns and Their Personnel, 1961–1977.* Jefferson, N.C.: McFarland, 1992.

CHAPTER 1

Barnes, John. *The Beginnings of the Cinema in England 1894–1901.* Vol. 1: *The Beginnings of the Cinema in England.* New York: Barnes & Noble, 1976. Vol. 2: *Pioneers of the British Film.* London: Bishopsgate Press, 1983. Vol. 3: *The Rise of the Cinema in Great Britain.* London: Bishopsgate Press, 1983. Vol. 4: *Filming the Boer War.* London: Bishopsgate Press, 1992.

Cook, Olive. *Movement in Two Dimensions: A Study of the Animated and Projected Pictures Which Preceded the Invention of Cinematography.* London: Hutchinson, 1963.

Elsaesser, Thomas, with Adam Barker, eds. *Early Cinema: Space, Frame, Narrative.* London: British Film Institute, 1990.

Fell, John L., ed. *Film before Griffith.* Berkeley: University of California Press, 1983.

Guibbert, Pierre, ed. *Les Premiers ans de cinéma français.* Perpignon: Institut Jean Vigo, 1985.

Hammond, Paul. *Marvelous Méliès.* New York: St. Martin's, 1975.

Hendricks, Gordon. *Beginnings of the Biograph: The Story of the Invention of the Mutoscope and Biograph and Their Supplying Camera.* New York: The Beginnings of the American Film, 1964.

———. *The Edison Motion Picture Myth.* Berkeley: University of California Press, 1961.

Holman, Roger, ed. *Cinema 1900/1906.* 2 vols. Brussels: FIAF, 1982.

Leyda, Jay, and Charles Musser, eds. *Before Hollywood: Turn-of-the-Century Film from American Archives.* New York: American Federation of the Arts, 1986.

Musser, Charles. *Before the Nickelodeon: Edwin S. Porter and the Edison Manufacturing Company.* Berkeley: University of California Press, 1991.

———. *The Emergence of Cinema: The American Screen to 1907.* New York: Scribners, 1990.

Pinel, Vincent. "Chronologie commentée de l'invention du cinéma." *1895* (1992).

CHAPTER 2

Bernardini, Aldo. "An Industry in Recession: The Italian Film Industry 1908–1909." *Film History* **3,** 4 (1989): 341–368.

Bowser, Eileen. *The Transformation of Cinema: 1907–1915.* New York: Scribners, 1990.

Crafton, Donald. *Emile Cohl, Caricature and Film.* Princeton, N.J.: Princeton University Press, 1990.

Gunning, Tom. *D. W. Griffith and the Origins of American Narrative Film.* Urbana: University of Illinois Press, 1991.

High, Peter B. "The Dawn of Cinema in Japan." *Journal of Contemporary History* **19,** 1 (1984): 23–57.

Mottram, Ron. *The Danish Cinema before Dreyer.* Metuchen, N.J.: Scarecrow, 1988.

Musser, Charles. "Pre-Classical American Cinema: Its Changing Modes of Film Production." *Persistence of Vision* no. 9 (1991): 46–65.

Slide, Anthony. *The Big V: A History of the Vitagraph Company.* Rev. ed. Metuchen, N.J.: Scarecrow, 1987.

CHAPTER 3

Brewster, Ben. "*Traffic in Souls:* An Experiment in Feature-Length Narrative Construction." *Cinema Journal* **31,** 1 (Fall 1991): 37–56.

Brownlow, Kevin. *The Parade's Gone By . . .* New York: Knopf, 1969.

Cherchi Usai, Paolo, et al., eds. *Silent Witnesses: Russian Films 1908–1919.* London: British Film Institute, 1989.

Cherchi Usai, Paolo, and Lorenzo Codelli, eds. *Before **Caligari:** German Cinema, 1895–1920.* Madison: University of Wisconsin Press, 1990.

———. *The DeMille Legacy.* Pordenone: Biblioteca dell'Immagine, 1991.

———. *Sulla via di Hollywood.* Pordenone: Biblioteca dell'Immagine, 1988.

Forslund, Bengt. *Victor Sjöström: His Life and His Work.* Trans., Peter Cowie. New York: New York Zoetrope, 1988.

Koszarski, Richard, ed. *The Rivals of D. W. Griffith: Alternate Auteurs 1913–1918.* Minneapolis: Walker Art Center, 1976.

Lahue, Kalton C. *Continued Next Week: A History of the Moving Picture Serial.* Norman: University of Oklahoma Press, 1964.

Quaresima, Leonardo. "*Dichter, heraus!* The Autorenfilm and German Cinema of the 1910's." *Griffithiana* no. 38/39 (October 1990): 101–120.

Robinson, David. "The Italian Comedy." *Sight and Sound* **55,** 2 (Spring 1986): 105–112.

Singer, Ben. "Female Power in the Serial-Queen Melodrama: The

Etiology of an Anomaly." *Camera Obscura* no. 22 (January 1990): 90–129.

CHAPTER 4

Abel, Richard. *French Cinema: The First Wave, 1915–1929.* Princeton, N.J.: Princeton University Press, 1984.

———. *French Film Theory and Criticism: A History/Anthology 1907–1939.* Vol. 1: *1907–1929.* Princeton, N.J.: Princeton University Press, 1988.

Bordwell, David. *French Impressionist Cinema: Film Culture, Film Theory, Film Style.* New York: Arno, 1980.

Icart, Roger. *Abel Gance.* Lausanne: L'Age d'Homme, 1983.

Thompson, Kristin. "The Ermolieff Group in Paris: Exile, Impressionism, Internationalism." *Griffithiana* no. 35/36 (October 1989): 48–57.

CHAPTER 5

Barlow, John D. *German Expressionist Film.* Boston: Twayne, 1987.

Budd, Mike, ed. **The Cabinet of Dr. Caligari:** *Texts, Contexts, Histories.* New Brunswick, N.J.: Rutgers University Press, 1990.

Courtade, Francis. *Cinéma expressioniste.* Paris: Beyrier, 1984.

Eisner, Lotte H. *The Haunted Screen: Expressionism in the Cinema and the Influence of Max Reinhardt.* Berkeley: University of California Press, 1969.

———. *Murnau.* Berkeley: University of California Press, 1973.

Jacobson, Wolfgang. *Erich Pommer: Ein Produzent macht Filmgeschichte.* Berlin: Argon, 1989.

Kracauer, Siegfried. *From Caligari to Hitler: A Psychological History of the German Film.* Princeton, N.J.: Princeton University Press, 1947.

Kurtz, Rudolf. *Expressionismus und Film.* Berlin: Lichtbildbühne, 1926; rep., Zurich: Rohr, 1965.

Plummer, Thomas G., et al., eds. *Film and Politics in the Weimar Republic.* Minneapolis: University of Minnesota Press, 1982.

CHAPTER 6

Kepley, Vance. *In the Service of the State: The Cinema of Alexander Dovzhenko.* Madison: University of Wisconsin Press, 1986.

Kuleshov, Lev. *Selected Works: Fifty Years in Films.* Moscow: Raduga, 1987.

Michelson, Annette, ed. *Kino-Eye: The Writings of Dziga Vertov.* Berkeley: University of California Press, 1984.

Schnitzer, Luda, and Jean Schnitzer, eds. *Cinema and Revolution.* New York: Hill and Wang, 1973.

Taylor, Richard. *The Politics of the Soviet Cinema 1917–1929.* Cambridge, England: Cambridge University Press, 1979.

Taylor, Richard, and Ian Christie, eds. *Inside the Film Factory: New Approaches to Russian and Soviet Cinema.* London: Routledge, 1991.

Youngblood, Denise J. *Movies for the Masses: Popular Cinema and Soviet Society in the 1920s.* Cambridge, England: Cambridge University Press, 1992.

———. *Soviet Cinema in the Silent Era, 1918–1935.* Ann Arbor: UMI Research Press, 1985.

CHAPTER 7

Blesh, Rudi. *Keaton.* New York: Collier, 1966.

Canemaker, John. *Felix: The Twisted Tale of the World's Most Famous Cat.* New York: Pantheon, 1991.

"Frank Borzage: Hollywood's Lucky Star." *Griffithiana* no. 46 (December 1992).

Koszarski, Richard. *An Evening's Entertainment: The Age of the Silent Feature Picture, 1915–1928.* New York: Scribners, 1990.

———. *The Man You Loved to Hate: Erich von Stroheim and Hollywood.* New York: Oxford University Press, 1983.

O'Leary, Liam. *Rex Ingram: Master of the Silent Cinema.* New York: Barnes & Noble, 1980.

Reilly, Adam. *Harold Lloyd: The King of Daredevil Comedy.* New York: Collier, 1977.

CHAPTER 8

Komatsu, Hiroshi. "The Fundamental Change: Japanese Cinema before and after the earthquake of 1923." *Griffithiana* no. 38/39 (October 1990): 186–196.

Kuenzli, Rudolf E., ed. *Dada and Surrealist Film.* New York: Willis Laker and Owens, 1987.

Lawder, Standish D. *The Cubist Cinema.* New York: New York University Press, 1975.

Leitner, Angelika, and Uwe Nitschke, eds. *The German Avant-Garde Film of the 1920s.* Munich: Goethe-Institut, 1989.

Peterson, James. "A War of Utter Rebellion: *Page of Madness* and the Japanese Avant-Garde of the 1920s." *Cinema Journal* **29,** 1 (Fall 1989): 36–53.

Thompson, Kristin. "(Re)Discovering Charles Dekeukeleire." *Millennium Film Journal* no. 7/8/9 (Fall–Winter 1980–1981): 115–129.

CHAPTER 9

Andrew, Dudley. "Sound in Focus: The Origins of a Native School." In Mary Lea Bandy, ed., *Rediscovering French Film.* New York: Museum of Modern Art, 1983, pp. 57–65.

Bandy, Mary Lea, ed. *The Dawn of Sound.* New York: Museum of Modern Art, 1989.

Belaygue, Christien, ed. *Le Passage du muet au parlant.* Toulouse: Cinémathèque de Toulouse, 1988.

Gomery, J. Douglas. "The Coming of Sound to the American Cinema: A History of the Transformation of an Industry." Ph.D. dissertation, University of Wisconsin—Madison, 1975.

Jossé, Harald. *Die Entstehung des Tonfilms.* Munich: Freiburg, 1984.

Murphy, Robert. "Coming of Sound to the Cinema in Britain." *Historical Journal of Film, Radio and Television* **4,** 2 (1984): 143–160.

Thompson, Kristin. "Early Sound Counterpoint." *Yale French Studies* no. 60 (1980): 115–140.

Walker, Alexander. *The Shattered Silents: How the Talkies Came to Stay.* New York: Morrow, 1979.

CHAPTER 10

Balio, Tino. *Grand Design: Hollywood as a Modern Business Enterprise, 1930–1939.* New York: Scribners, 1993.

Borde, R., and E. Chaumeton. *Panorama du film noir américain.* 1953; rep., Paris: Editions d'Aujourd'hjui, 1976.

Hoberman, J. *Bridge of Light: Yiddish Film between Two Worlds.* New York: Museum of Modern Art/Schocken, 1991.

Jacobs, Lea. *The Wages of Sin: Censorship and the Fallen Woman Film, 1928–1942.* Madison: University of Wisconsin Press, 1991.

Jenkins, Henry. *What Made Pistachio Nuts? Early Sound Comedy and the Vaudeville Aesthetic.* New York: Columbia University Press, 1992.

Maltby, Richard. " 'Baby Face' or How Joe Breen Made Barbara Stanwyck Atone for Causing the Wall Street Crash." *Screen* **27,** 2 (March–April 1986): 22–45.

Schrader, Paul. "Notes on *Film Noir.*" In Kevin Jackson, ed., *Schrader on Schrader and Other Writings.* London: Faber, 1990, pp. 80–94.

Sikov, Ed. *Screwball: Hollywood's Madcap Romantic Comedies.* New York: Crown, 1989.

Sturges, Sandy, ed. *Preston Sturges by Preston Sturges: His Life in His Hands.* New York: Simon and Schuster, 1990.

CHAPTER 11

Bock, Audie E. *Mikio Naruse.* Locarno: Editions de Festival International du Film, 1983.

"Challenge of Sound: The Indian Talkie (I)." *Cinema Vision India* **1,** 2 (April 1980).

Kirihara, Donald. *Patterns of Time: Mizoguchi in the 1930s.* Madison: University of Wisconsin Press, 1992.

König, Regula, and Marianne Lewinsky, eds. *Keisuke Kinoshita.* Locarno: Editions de Festival International du Film, 1986.

Low, Rachel. *Film Making in 1930s Britain.* London: Allen and Unwin, 1985.

Murphy, Robert. *Realism and Tinsel: Cinema and Society in Britain 1939–48.* London: Routledge, 1989.

———. "A Rival to Hollywood? The British Film Industry in the Thirties." *Screen* **24,** 4/5 (July–December 1983): 96–106.

Ryall, Tom. *Alfred Hitchcock and the British Cinema.* London: Croom Helm, 1986.

Shah, Panna. *The Indian Film.* Bombay: Motion Picture Society of India, 1950.

CHAPTER 12

Aprà, Adriano, and Patrizio Pistagneri, eds. *The Fabulous Thirties: Italian Cinema 1929–1944.* Milan: Electra, 1979.

Forgacs, David. *Italian Culture in the Industrial Era 1886–1980.* Manchester, England: Manchester University Press, 1990.

Gili, Jean A. *L'Italie de Mussolini et son cinéma.* Paris: Veyrier, 1985.

Hay, James. *Popular Film Culture in Fascist Italy: The Passing of the Rex.* Bloomington: Indiana University Press, 1987.

Hull, David Stewart. *Film in the Third Reich.* Berkeley: University of California Press, 1969.

Landy, Marcia. *Fascism in Film: The Italian Commercial Cinema, 1931–1943.* Princeton, N.J.: Princeton University Press, 1986.

Mancini, Elaine. *Struggles of the Italian Film Industry under Fascism.* Ann Arbor: UMI Research Press, 1985.

Taylor, Richard. "Boris Shumyatsky and the Soviet Cinema in the 1930s: Ideology in Mass Entertainment." *Historical Journal of Film, Radio and Television* **6,** 1 (1986): 43–64.

———. "A 'Cinema for the Millions': Soviet Socialist Realism and the Problem of Film Comedy." *Journal of Contemporary History* **18,** 3 (July 1983): 439–461.

Welch, David. *Propaganda and the German Cinema 1933–1945.* Oxford: Clarendon Press, 1983.

CHAPTER 13

Bertin-Maghit, Jean-Pierre. *Le Cinéma sous l'Occupation: Le Monde du cinéma français de 1940 à 1946.* Paris: Orban,1989.

Buchsbaum, Jonathan. ***Cinéma Engagé:*** *Film in the Popular Front.* Urbana: University of Illinois Press, 1988.

Chirat, Raymond. *Le Cinéma français des années de guerre.* Renan, Switzerland: Five Continents/Hatier, 1983.

Clair, René. *Cinema Yesterday and Today.* Ed. and trans., Stanley Appelbaum. New York: Dover, 1972.

Ehrlich, Evelyn. *Cinema of Paradox: French Filmmaking under the German Occupation.* New York: Columbia University Press, 1985.

Garçon, François. *De Blum à Pétain: Cinéma et société française (1936–1944).* Paris: Cerf, 1984.

Guillaume-Grimart, Geneviève. *Le Cinéma de Front Populaire.* Paris: Lherminier, 1986.

Siclier, Jacques. *La France de Pétain et son cinéma.* Bourges, France: Veyrier, 1981.

CHAPTER 14

Campbell, Russell. *Cinema Strikes Back: Radical Filmmaking in the United States 1930–1942.* Ann Arbor: UMI Research Press, 1982.

Curnow, Wystan, and Roger Horrocks, eds. *Figures of Motion: Len Lye's Selected Writings.* Auckland: Auckland University Press, 1984.

Evans, Gary. *John Grierson and the National Film Board: The Politics of Wartime Propaganda.* Toronto: University of Toronto Press, 1984.

Hodgkinson, Anthony W., and Rodney E. Sheratsky. *Humphrey Jennings: More Than a Maker of Films.* Hanover, N.H.: University Press of New England, 1982.

Hogencamp, Bert. *Deadly Parallels: Film and the Left in Britain 1929–39.* London: Lawrence and Wishart, 1986.

Kuhn, Annette. "*Desert Victory* and the People's War." *Screen* **22**, 2 (1981): 45–68.

Moritz, William. "The Films of Oskar Fischinger." *Film Culture* no. 58/59/60 (1974): 37–188.

Sitney, P. Adams. "The Cinematic Gaze of Joseph Cornell." In Kynastan McShine, ed., *Joseph Cornell.* New York: Museum of Modern Art, 1980.

Swann, Paul. *The British Documentary Film Movement, 1926–1946.* Cambridge, England: Cambridge University Press, 1989.

CHAPTER 15

Balio, Tino. "When Is an Independent Producer Independent? The Case of United Artists after 1948." *The Velvet Light Trap* no. 22 (1986): 53–64.

Belton, John. *Widescreen Cinema.* Cambridge, Mass.: Harvard University Press, 1992.

Benayoun, Robert. *Bonjour Monsieur Lewis.* Paris: Losfeld, 1972.

Bragg, Herbert. "The Development of CinemaScope." *Film History* **2**, 4 (1988): 359–372.

Carr, Robert E., and R. M. Hayes. *Wide Screen Movies: A History and Filmography of Wide Gauge Filmmaking.* Jefferson, N.C.: McFarland, 1988.

Ceplair, Larry, and Steven Englund. *The Inquisition in Hollywood: Politics in the Film Community, 1930–1960.* Garden City, N.Y.: Anchor Press/Doubleday, 1980.

Ciment, Michel. *Kazan on Kazan.* New York: Viking, 1970.

Doherty, Thomas. *Teenagers and Teenpics: The Juvenilization of American Movies in the 1950s.* Boston: Unwin Hyman, 1988.

Finler, Joel W. *Alfred Hitchcock: The Hollywood Years.* London: Batsford, 1992.

Halliday, Jon. *Sirk on Sirk.* New York: Viking, 1972.

Hardy, Phil. *Sam Fuller.* New York: Praeger, 1970.

Hayes, R. M. *3-D Movies: A History and Filmography of Stereoscopic Cinema.* Jefferson, N.C.: McFarland, 1989.

Johnston, Claire, and Paul Willemen, eds. *Frank Tashlin.* Edinburgh: Film Festival, 1973.

Kindem, Gorham A. "Hollywood's Conversion to Color: The Technological, Economic, and Aesthetic Factors." *Journal of the University Film Association* **31**, 2 (Spring 1979): 29–36.

McCarthy, Todd, and Charles Flynn, eds. *Kings of the Bs: Working within the Hollywood System.* New York: Dutton, 1975.

Segrave, Kerry. *Drive-In Theaters: A History from Their Inception in 1933.* Jefferson, N.C.: McFarland, 1992.

"United States of America v. Paramount Pictures, Inc. et al." Special issue of *Film History* **4**, 1 (1992).

Ward, Melinda, and Bruce Jenkins, eds. *The American New Wave: 1958–1967.* Minneapolis: Walker Art Center, 1982.

Wilson, Michael and Deborah Silverton Rosenfelt. *Salt of the Earth.* New York: Feminist Press, 1978.

CHAPTER 16

Armes, Roy. *Patterns of Realism: A Study of Italian Neo-Realist Cinema.* South Brunswick, N.J.: Barnes, 1971.

Bernardini, Aldo, and Jean A. Gili, eds. *Cesare Zavattini.* Paris: Pompidou Center, 1990.

Brunette, Peter. *Roberto Rossellini.* New York: Oxford University Press, 1987.

Guback, Thomas H. *The International Film Industry.* Bloomington: Indiana University Press, 1969.

"Le Néo-réalisme italien." *Études cinématographiques* no. 32–35 (1964).

Overbey, David, ed. *Springtime in Italy: A Reader on Neo-Realism.* London: Talisman, 1978.

Rossellini, Roberto. *My Method: Writings and Interviews.* Ed., Adriano Aprà. New York: Marsilio, 1992.

Servadio, Gaia. *Luchino Visconti: A Biography.* New York: Watts, 1983.

CHAPTER 17

Barrot, Jean-Pierre. "Une Tradition de la qualité." In H. Agel et al., *Sept ans de cinéma français.* Paris: Cerf, 1953, pp. 26–37.

Bazin, André. *The Cinema of Cruelty: From Buñuel to Hitchcock.* Ed., François Truffaut. New York: Seaver, 1982.

Bellour, Raymond. *Alexandre Astruc.* Paris: Seghers, 1963.

Braucourt, Guy. *André Cayatte.* Paris: Seghers, 1969.

Farwagi, André. *René Clement.* Paris: Seghers, 1967.

Hirano, Kyoko. *Mr. Smith Goes to Tokyo: Japanese Cinema under the American Occupation 1945–1952*. Washington: Smithsonian Institution Press, 1992.

Jarvie, Ian. "The Postwar Economic Policy of the American Film Industry: Europe 1945–1950." *Film History* **4,** 4 (1990): 277–288.

Jeancolas, Jean-Pierre. "L'Arrangement. Blum-Byrnes à l'épreuve des faits. Les relations (cinématographiques) franco-américaines de 1944 à 1948." *1895* no. 13 (December 1992): 3–49.

Nogueira, Ruy, ed. *Melville on Melville*. New York: Viking, 1971.

Roud, Richard. *A Passion for Films: Henri Langlois and the Cinémathèque Française*. New York: Viking, 1983.

Turk, Edward Baron. *Child of Paradise: Marcel Carné and the Golden Age of French Cinema*. Cambridge, Mass.: Harvard University Press, 1989.

Willemen, Paul, ed. *Ophuls*. London: British Film Institute, 1978.

Zimmer, Jacques, and Chantal de Béchade. *Jean-Pierre Melville*. Paris: Edilig, 1983.

CHAPTER 18

Babitsky, Paul, and John Rimberg. *The Soviet Film Industry*. New York: Praeger, 1955.

Banerjee, Haimanti. *Ritwik Kumar Ghatak: A Monograph*. Poona: National Film Archive of India, 1985.

Dissanayake, Wimal, and Malti Sahai. *Raj Kapoor's Films: Harmony of Discourses*. New Delhi: Vikas, 1988.

Franco, Jean. *The Modern Culture of Latin America: Society and the Artist*. Harmondsworth, England: Penguin, 1970.

Ghatak, Ritwik. *Arguments/Stories*. Ed., Ashish Rajadhyaksha and Amrit Gangar. Bombay: Screen Unit, 1987.

"Indian Cinema." *Quarterly Review of Film Studies* **11,** 3 (1989).

Michalek, Boleslaw. *The Cinema of Andrzej Wajda*. Trans., Edward Rothert. London: Tantivy, 1973.

Oms, Marcel. *Leopoldo Torre Nilsson*. Paris: Première Plan, 1962.

Rajadhyaksha, Ashish. *Ritwik Ghatak: A Return to the Epic*. Bombay: Screen Unit, 1982.

Rangoonwalla, Fironze. *Guru Dutt: 1925–1965*. Poona: National Film Archive of India, 1973.

Wajda, Andrzej. *Double Vision: My Life in Film*. Trans., Rose Medina. New York: Holt, 1989.

CHAPTER 19

Bergman, Ingmar. *The Magic Lantern: An Autobiography*. Trans., Joan Tate. New York: Viking, 1988.

Bondanella, Peter, ed. *Federico Fellini: Essays in Criticism*. New York: Oxford University Press, 1978.

Bresson, Robert. *Notes on Cinematography*. Trans., Jonathan Griffin. New York: Urizen, 1977.

Buñuel, Luis. *My Last Sigh*. Trans., Abigail Israel. New York: Knopf, 1983.

Cameron, Ian, and Robin Wood. *Antonioni*. New York: Praeger, 1968.

Chatman, Seymour. *Antonioni; or, The Surface of the World*. Berkeley: University of California Press, 1985.

Das Gupta, Chidananda. *The Cinema of Satyajit Ray*. New Delhi: Vikas, 1980.

Durgnat, Raymond. *Luis Buñuel*. Berkeley: University of California Press, 1968.

Gado, Frank. *The Passion of Ingmar Bergman*. Durham, N.C.: Duke University Press, 1986.

Hanlon, Lindley. *Fragments: Bresson's Film Style*. Rutherford, N.J.: Associated University Presses, 1986.

Hardy, James. *Jacques Tati: Frame by Frame*. London: Secker and Warburg, 1984.

Hillier, Jim, ed. **Cahiers du cinéma:** *The 1950s: Neo-Realism, Hollywood, New Wave*. Cambridge, Mass.: Harvard University Press, 1985.

Kaminsky, Stuart M., and Joseph F. Hill, eds. *Ingmar Bergman: Essays in Criticism*. New York: Oxford University Press, 1975.

Kurosawa, Akira. *Something Like an Autobiography*. Trans., Audie E. Bock. New York: Knopf, 1982.

Kyrou, Ado. *Luis Buñuel: An Introduction*. New York: Simon and Schuster, 1963.

Leprohon, Pierre. *Michelangelo Antonioni: An Introduction*. New York: Simon and Schuster, 1963.

Ray, Satyajit. *Our Films, Their Films*. Bombay: Orient Ltd., 1976.

Richie, Donald. *The Films of Akira Kurosawa*. 2d ed. Berkeley: University of California Press, 1984.

Robinson, Andrew. *Satyajit Ray: The Inner Eye*. Berkeley: University of California Press, 1989.

Salachas, Gilbert. *Federico Fellini: An Investigation into His Films and Philosophy*. Trans., Rosalie Siegel. New York: Crown, 1969.

Sandro, Paul. *Diversions of Pleasure: Luis Buñuel and the Crises of Desire*. Columbus: Ohio State University Press, 1987.

Seton, Marie. *Portrait of a Director: Satyajit Ray*. Bloomington: Indiana University Press, 1971.

Wood, Robin. *The Apu Trilogy*. New York: Praeger, 1971.

———. *Ingmar Bergman*. New York: Praeger, 1969.

CHAPTER 20

"Agnès Varda." *Études cinématographiques* nos. 179–186 (1991).

"Alexander Kluge." *October* no. 46 (Fall 1988).

Armes, Roy. *The Films of Alain Robbe-Grillet*. Amsterdam: John Benjamins, 1981.

Benayoun, Robert. *Alain Resnais: Arpenteur de l'imaginaire*. Paris: Stock, 1980.

Björkman, Stig. *Film in Sweden: The New Directors*. London: Barnes, 1977.

Brown, Royal S., ed. *Focus on Godard.* Englewood Cliffs, N.J.: Prentice-Hall, 1972.

Desser, David. *Eros Plus Massacre: An Introduction to the Japanese New Wave Cinema.* Bloomington: Indiana University Press, 1988.

Gerber, Jacques, ed. *Pierre Braunberger: Producteur; Cinémémoire.* Paris: Pompidou Center, 1987.

Godard on Godard. Trans. and commentary, Tom Milne. New York: Viking, 1972.

Goulding, Daniel J. *Liberated Cinema: The Yugoslav Experience.* Bloomington: Indiana University Press, 1985.

Graham, Peter, ed. *The New Wave.* Garden City, N.Y.: Doubleday, 1968.

Greene, Naomi. *Pier Paolo Pasolini: Cinema as History.* Princeton, N.J.: Princeton University Press, 1990.

Hames, Peter. *The Czechoslovak New Wave.* Berkeley: University of California Press, 1985.

Hill, John. *Sex, Class and Realism: British Cinema 1956–1963.* London: British Film Institute, 1986.

Murphy, Robert. *Sixties British Cinema.* London: British Film Institute, 1992.

Petrie, Graham. *History Must Answer to Man: The Contemporary Hungarian Cinema.* Budapest: Corvina, 1978.

Rohmer, Eric. *The Taste for Beauty.* Trans., Carol Volk. Cambridge, England: Cambridge University Press, 1989.

Siclier, Jacques. *Nouvelle vague?* Paris: Cerf, 1961.

Stoil, Michael J. *Balkan Cinema: Evolution after the Revolution.* Ann Arbor: UMI Research Press, 1982.

Truffaut, François. *The Films in My Life.* Trans., Leonard Mayhew. New York: Simon and Schuster, 1975.

Van Wert, William F. *The Film Career of Alain Robbe-Grillet.* Pleasantville, N.Y.: Redgrave, 1977.

CHAPTER 21

Banes, Sally. *Greenwich Village 1963: Avant-Garde Performance and the Effervescent Body.* Durham, NC: Duke University Press, 1993.

Battcock, Gregory, ed. *The New American Cinema: A Critical Anthology.* New York: Dutton, 1967.

Blistene, Bernard, et al. *Andy Warhol, cinéma.* Paris: Pompidou Center, 1990.

Brakhage, Stan. *Brakhage Scrapbook: Collected Writings 1964–1980.* Ed., Robert A. Haller. New Paltz, N.Y.: Documentext, 1982.

"The Cinema of Jean Rouch." *Visual Anthropology* **2**, 3–4 (1989).

Clark, Vèvè A., Millicent Hodson, and Catrina Neiman. *The Legend of Maya Deren: A Documentary Biography and Collected Works.* 2 vols. New York: Anthology Film Archives and Film Culture, 1984, 1988.

Devaux, Frédérique. *Le Cinéma lettriste (1951–1991).* Paris: Experimental Editions, 1992.

Eaton, Mick, ed. *Anthropology—Reality—Cinema: The Films of Jean Rouch.* London: British Film Institute, 1979.

Jaffe, Patricia. "Editing *Cinéma Vérité.*" *Film Comment* **3**, 3 (Summer 1965): 43–47.

James, David E., ed. *To Free the Cinema: Jonas Mekas and the New York Underground.* Princeton, N.J.: Princeton University Press, 1992.

Koch, Stephen. *Star-Gazer: Andy Warhol's World and His Films.* New York: Praeger, 1973.

Lauf, Cornelia, and Susan Hapgood, eds. *Flux Attitudes.* Ghent: Imschoot Uitgevers, 1991.

Lebrat, Christian, ed. *Peter Kubelka.* Paris: Experimental Editions, 1990.

Levin, Thomas Y. "Dismantling the Spectacle: The Cinema of Guy Debord." In Elisabeth Sussman, ed., *On the Passage of a Few People through a Rather Brief Moment in Time: The Situationist International 1957–1972.* Boston: ICA, 1989, pp. 72–123.

Mamber, Stephen. **Cinéma Vérité** *in America: Studies in Uncontrolled Documentary.* Cambridge, Mass.: MIT Press, 1974.

Marcorelles, Louis. *Living Cinema: New Directions in Contemporary Film-Making.* Trans., Isabel Quigley. New York: Praeger, 1973.

Markopoulos, Gregory. "Towards a New Narrative Film Form." *Film Culture* no. 31 (Winter 1963–1964): 11–12.

Marsolais, Gilles. *L'Aventure du cinéma direct.* Paris: Seghers, 1974.

Mekas, Jonas. *Movie Journal: The Rise of a New American Cinema, 1959–1971.* New York: Macmillan, 1972.

———. "Notes after Reseeing the Movies of Andy Warhol." In John Coplans, ed., *Andy Warhol.* New York: New York Graphic Society, 1968, pp. 139–195.

O'Pray, Michael, ed. *Andy Warhol: Film Factory.* London: British Film Institute, 1989.

Renan, Sheldon. *An Introduction to the American Underground Film.* New York: Dutton, 1967.

Rouch, Jean. "The Camera and Man." In Paul Hockings, ed., *Principles of Visual Anthropology.* Paris: Mouton, 1975, pp. 83–102.

Ruby, Jay, ed. *The Cinema of John Marshall.* Chur, Switzerland: Harwood, 1993.

Stan Brakhage: An American Independent Film-Maker. London: Arts Council of Great Britain, 1980.

VanDerBeek, Stan. "The Cinema Delimina: Films from the Underground." *Film Quarterly* **14**, 4 (Summer 1961): 5–15.

Youngblood, Gene. *Expanded Cinema.* New York: Dutton, 1970.

CHAPTER 22

Baddeley, Oriana, and Valerie Fraser. *Drawing the Line: Art and Cultural Identity in Contemporary Latin America.* New York: Verso, 1989.

Burton, Julianne, ed. *Cinema and Social Change in Latin America: Conversations with Filmmakers.* Austin: University of Texas Press, 1986.

Chanan, Michael, ed. *Twenty-Five Years of New Latin American Cinema.* London: British Film Institute/Channel 4, 1983.

Diawara, Manthia. *African Cinema: Politics and Culture.* Bloomington: Indiana University Press, 1992.

Downing, John H., ed. *Film and Politics in the Third World.* New York: Autonomedia, 1987.

Fusco, Coco, ed. *Reviewing Histories: Selections from New Latin American Cinema.* Buffalo: Hallwalls Contemporary Art Center, 1987.

Jarvie, Ian. *Window on Hong Kong: A Sociological Study of the Hong Kong Film Industry and Its Audience.* Hong Kong: University of Hong Kong, 1977.

Johnson, Randal. *Cinema Novo × 5: Masters of Contemporary Brazilian Film.* Austin: University of Texas Press, 1984.

Pierre, Sylvie. *Glauber Rocha.* Paris: Cahiers du Cinéma, 1987.

A Study of Hong Kong Cinema in the Seventies. Hong Kong: Urban Council, 1984.

Vieyra, Paulin Soumanou. *Le Cinéma africain des origines à 1973.* Paris: Présence Africaine, 1975.

CHAPTER 23

Browne, Nick, ed. **Cahiers du cinéma** *1969–1972: The Politics of Representation.* Cambridge, Mass.: Harvard University Press, 1990.

Clouzot, Claire. *Le Cinéma français depuis la nouvelle vague.* Paris: Nathan, 1972.

Cockburn, Alexander, and Robin Blackburn, eds. *Student Power: Problems, Diagnosis, Action.* Baltimore: Penguin, 1969.

"The Estates General of the French Cinema." *Screen* **13**, 4 (Winter 1972–1973): 58–88.

Fassbinder, Rainer Werner. *The Anarchy of the Imagination: Interviews, Essays, Notes.* Ed., Michael Töteberg and Leo A. Lensing. Trans., Krishna Winston. Baltimore: Johns Hopkins University Press, 1992.

"Groupe 5: Portrait d'une expérience." *Cinéma* [Zurich] no. 1 (January 1974).

Harvey, Sylvia. *May '68 and Film Culture.* London: British Film Institute, 1978.

Kay, Karyn, and Gerald Peary, eds. *Women and the Cinema: A Critical Anthology.* New York: Dutton, 1977.

Lesage, Julia. "Feminist Film Criticism: Theory and Practice." *Women and Film* **1**, 5–6 (1974): 12–18.

"New German Cinema." *New German Critique* no. 24–25 (Fall–Winter 1981–1982).

Olson, Ray. "Gay Film Work (1972–1977)." *Jump Cut* no. 20 (May 1979): 9–12.

"Une Phénomenon nouveau . . . " *Cinéma 70* no. 151 (December 1970): 81–104. (On radical filmmaking groups.)

Phillips, Klaus, ed. *New German Filmmakers: From Oberhausen through the 1970s.* New York: Ungar, 1984.

Randall, Vicky. *Women and Politics: An International Perspective.* 2d ed. Chicago: University of Chicago, 1987.

Rayns, Tony. *Fassbinder.* Rev. ed. London: British Film Institute, 1980.

Sandford, John. *The New German Cinema.* London: Eyre Methuen, 1980.

Turkle, Sherry. *Psychoanalytic Politics: Freud's French Revolution.* Cambridge, Mass.: MIT Press, 1978.

Walsh, Martin. *The Brechtian Aspect of Radical Cinema.* Ed., Keith M. Griffiths. London: British Film Institute, 1981.

"West German Film in the 1970s." *Quarterly Review of Film Studies* **5**, 2 (Spring 1980).

CHAPTER 24

"Avant-Garde Film in England and Europe." *Studio International* no. 978 (November–December 1975).

Benson, Thomas W., and Carolyn Anderson. *Reality Fictions: The Films of Frederick Wiseman.* Carbondale: Southern Illinois University Press, 1989.

Canemaker, John. "Susan Pitt." *Funnyworld* no. 21 (Fall 1979): 15–19.

Caux, Daniel, et al. *Peter Greenaway.* Paris: Dis, Voir, 1987.

Curtis, David, ed. *The Elusive Sign: British Avant-Garde Film and Video, 1977–1987.* London: Arts Council, 1987.

Curtis, David, and Deke Dusinberre. *A Perspective on English Avant-Garde Film.* London: Arts Council, 1978.

Ehrenstein, David. *Film: The Front Line 1984.* Denver: Arden, 1984.

Gregor, Ulrich. *The German Experimental Film of the Seventies.* Munich: Goethe Institute, 1980.

Grenier, Vincent, ed. *Ten Years of Living Cinema.* New York: Collective for Living Cinema, 1982.

Hall, Doug, and Sally Jo Fifer, eds. *Illuminating Video: An Essential Guide to Video Art.* New York: Aperture, 1990.

Hoberman, J. *Home Made Movies: Twenty Years of American 8mm and Super-8mm Films.* New York: Anthology Film Archives, 1981.

"Hollis Frampton." Special issue of *October* no. 32 (Spring 1985).

Jenkins, Bruce. "CB: Cinema Broodthaers." In *Marcel Broodthaers.* Minneapolis: Walker Art Center, 1989, pp. 93–109.

Jenkins, Bruce, and Susan Krane, eds. *Hollis Frampton: Recollections, Recreations.* Cambridge, Mass.: MIT Press, 1984.

MacDonald, Scott. *Avant-Garde Film: Motion Studies.* Cambridge, England: Cambridge University Press, 1993.

———. *A Critical Cinema: Interviews with Independent Filmmakers.* Berkeley: University of California Press, 1988.

———. *A Critical Cinema 2: Interviews with Independent Filmmakers.* Berkeley: University of California Press, 1992.

Mercer, Kobena, ed. *Black Film, British Cinema.* London: Institute for Contemporary Art, 1988.

Minh-Ha, Trinh T. *Framer Framed.* New York: Routledge, 1992.

"The New Talkies: A Special Issue." *October* no. 17 (Summer 1981).

A Passage Illuminated: The American Avant-Garde Film 1980–1990. Amsterdam: Mecano, 1991.

Peterson, James. *Dreams of Chaos, Visions of Order: Understanding the American Avant-Garde Cinema.* Detroit: Wayne State University Press, 1993.

Rainer, Yvonne. *The Films of Yvonne Rainer.* Bloomington: Indiana University Press, 1989.

Rosenbaum, Jonathan. *Film: The Front Line 1983.* Denver: Arden, 1983.

"The State of (Some) Things: New Film and Video." *Motion Picture* **3,** 1/2 (Winter 1989–1990).

CHAPTER 25

Cones, John W. *Film Finance and Distribution: A Dictionary of Terms.* Los Angeles: Silman-James Press, 1992.

Donahue, Suzanne Mary. *American Film Distribution: The Changing Marketplace.* Ann Arbor: UMI Research Press, 1987.

Gomery, Douglas. "The American Film Industry of the 1970s: Stasis in the 'New Hollywood.'" *Wide Angle* **5,** 4 (1983): 52–59.

————. "Corporate Ownership and Control in the Contemporary US Film Industry." *Screen* **25,** 4–5 (July–October 1984): 60–69.

Goodwin, Michael, and Naomi Wise. *On the Edge: The Life and Times of Francis Coppola.* New York: Morrow, 1989.

Hoberman, J., and Jonathan Rosenbaum. *Midnight Movies.* New York: Harper & Row, 1983.

Kellner, Douglas, and Michael Ryan. *Camera Politica: The Politics and Ideology of Contemporary Hollywood Film.* Bloomington: Indiana University Press, 1988.

Levin, Lear. "Robert Altman's Innovative Sound Techniques." *American Cinematographer* **61,** 4 (April 1980): 336–339, 368, 384.

McGilligan, Patrick. *Robert Altman: Jumping Off the Cliff.* New York: St. Martin's, 1989.

Monaco, James. *American Film Now: The People, the Power, the Money, the Movies.* New York: New American Library, 1979.

Mott, Donald R., and Cheryl McAllister Saunders. *Steven Spielberg.* Boston: Twayne, 1986.

"New Queer Cinema." *Sight and Sound* new series **2,** 5 (September 1992): 14–35.

Noriega, Chon A. *Chicanos and Film: Representation and Resistance.* Minneapolis: University of Minnesota Press, 1992.

Patterson, Richard. "The Preservation of Color Films." *American Cinematographer* **62,** 7 (July 1981): 694–697, 714–729; **62,** 8 (August 1981): 792–799, 816–822.

Pye, Michael, and Lynda Myles. *The Movie Brats: How the Film Generation Took over Hollywood.* New York: Holt, Rinehart and Winston, 1979.

Reid, Mark A. *Redefining Black Film.* Berkeley: University of California Press, 1993.

Squires, Jason E. *The Movie Business Book.* 2d ed. New York: Simon & Schuster, 1992.

Welbon, Yvonne. "Calling the Shots: Black Women Directors Take the Helm." *The Independent* **15,** 2 (March 1992): 18–22.

CHAPTER 26

Bonnell, René. *La Vingt-cinquième image: Une Économie de l'audio-visuel.* Paris: Gallimard, 1989.

Cieri, Marie, and Igor Aleinikov, eds. *Red Fish in America: New Independent Film and Video from the Soviet Union.* Cambridge, Mass.: The Arts Company, 1990.

"Contemporary Soviet Cinema." *Wide Angle* **12,** 4 (1990).

Corrigan, Timothy. *New German Film: The Displaced Image.* Austin: University of Texas Press, 1983.

————, ed. *The Films of Werner Herzog: Between Mirage and History.* New York: Methuen, 1986.

Dawson, Jan. *Wim Wenders.* New York: New York Zoetrope, 1976.

Dibié, Jean Noël. *Les Mécanismes de financement du cinéma et de l'audiovisuel en Europe.* Paris: Dixit, 1992.

Fassbinder, Rainer Werner. *The Marriage of Maria Braun.* Ed., Joyce Rheuban. New Brunswick, N.J.: Rutgers University Press, 1986.

Forbes, Gill. *The Cinema in France after the New Wave.* London: Macmillan, 1992.

Goulding, Daniel J., ed. *Post New Wave Cinema in the Soviet Union and Eastern Europe.* Bloomington: Indiana University Press, 1989.

Halberstam, Judith. "Some Like It Hot: The New Sapphic Cinema." *The Independent* **15,** 9 (November 1992): 26–29, 43.

Horton, Andrew, and Michael Brashinsky. *The Zero Hour: Glasnost and Soviet Cinema in Transition.* Princeton, N.J.: Princeton University Press, 1992.

"Il était une fois en Europe . . . " *Cahiers du cinéma* no. 455/456 (May 1992).

"L'influence de la télévision sur le cinéma." *CinémAction* no. 44 (1987).

Jeancolas, Jean-Pierre. *Cinéma hongrois 1963–1988.* Paris: CNRS, 1984.

Landeau, Yann, et al. *Manoel de Oliveira.* Paris: Dis, Voir, 1988.

Lawton, Anna. *Kinoglasnost: Soviet Cinema in Our Time.* Cambridge, England: Cambridge University Press, 1992.

Magny, Joël. *Maurice Pialat.* Paris: Cahiers du Cinéma, 1992.

Michalet, Charles-Albert. *Le Drôle de drame du cinéma mondiale: Une Industrie culturelle menacée.* Paris: Editions la Découverte, 1987.

Park, James. *Learning to Dream: The New British Cinema.* London: Faber, 1984.

Paul, David W., ed. *Politics, Art and Commitment in the East European Cinema.* New York: St. Martin's, 1983.

Portuges, Catherine. *Screen Memories: The Hungarian Cinema of Márta Mészáros.* Bloomington: Indiana University Press, 1993.

Prédal, René. *Le Cinéma français contemporain*. Paris: Cerf, 1984.

Pym, John. *Film on Four: A Survey 1982/1991*. London: British Film Institute, 1992.

Rayns, Tony, and Simon Field, eds. *Young Japanese Cinema*. London: Institute for Contemporary Art, 1990.

Reader, Keith. *Intellectuals and the Left in France since 1968*. New York: St. Martin's, 1987.

Rentschler, Eric. *West German Films in the Course of Time: Reflections on the Twenty Years since Oberhausen*. Bedford Hills, N.Y.: Redgrave, 1984.

Silberman, Marc. "Women Filmmakers in West Germany: A Catalog." *Camera Obscura* no. 6 (Fall 1980): 123–151; no. 11 (Fall 1983): 133–145.

"Special URSS." *Cahiers du cinéma* supplement to no. 427 (January 1990).

Stratton, David. *The Last New Wave: The Australian Film Revival*. London: Angus and Robertson, 1980.

Tavenas, Stéphane, and François Volard. *Guide of European Cinema*. Trans., David Clougher. Paris: Ramsaye, 1989.

Vidal, Nuria. *The Films of Pedro Almodóvar*. Madrid: Ministry of Culture, 1988.

Wildman, Steven S., and Stephen E. Siwek. *International Trade in Films and Television Programs*. Cambridge, Mass.: Ballinger, 1988.

CHAPTER 27

Armes, Roy. "Black African Cinema in the Eighties: A Survey." *Screen* **26,** 3–4 (May–August 1985): 60–73.

Berg, Charles Ramírez. *Cinema of Solitude: A Critical Study of Mexican Film, 1967–1983*. Austin: University of Texas Press, 1992.

Centre d'Étude sur la Communication en Afrique. *Camera Nigra: Le Discours du film africain*. Brussels: L'Harmattan, n.d.

Cham, Mbye, ed. *Ex-Iles: Essays on Caribbean Cinema*. Trenton, N.J.: Africa World Press, 1992.

"Cinema Special." *Koreana* **3,** 4 (1989).

"Cinémas du Maghreb." *CinémAction* no. 14 (Spring 1981).

"Contemporary Latin American Film." *Review: Latin American Literature and Arts* no. 46 (Fall 1992).

Diawara, Manthia. "African Cinema Today." *Framework* no. 37 (1989): 110–128.

Fusco, Coco. "The Tango of Esthetics and Politics: An Interview with Fernando Solanas." *Cineaste* **16,** 1–2 (1987–1988): 57–59.

Hennebelle, Guy, and Khemais Khayati, eds. *La Palestine et le cinéma*. Paris: E.100, 1977.

Hong Kong Cinema in the Eighties. Hong Kong: International Film Festival, 1991.

Huang, Vivian. "Taiwan's Social Realism." *The Independent* **13,** 1 (January–February 1990): 24–27.

Indian Cinema 1980–1985. Bombay: Directorate of Film Festivals, 1985.

Kaige, Chen, and Tony Rayns. ***King of the Children*** and the *New Chinese Cinema*. London: Faber, 1989.

Lopez, Ana. "An 'Other' History: The New Latin American Cinema." *Radical History Review* no. 41 (April 1988): 93–116.

"Made in Hong-Kong." *Cahiers du cinéma* no. 362–363 (September 1984).

Malkmus, Lizbeth, and Roy Armes. *Arab and African Film Making*. London: Zed, 1991.

Mattelart, Armand, et al. *International Image Markets: In Search of an Alternative Perspective*. London: Comedia, 1984.

Salmane, Hala, Simon Hartog, and David Wilson, eds. *Algerian Cinema*. London: British Film Institute, 1976.

"Southeast Asian Cinema." *East-West Film Journal* **6,** 2 (July 1992).

Stanbrook, Allan. "The Worlds of Hou Hsiao-hsien." *Sight and Sound* **59,** 2 (1990): 120–124.

Tomaselli, Keyan G. *The Cinema of Apartheid: Race and Class in South African Film*. New York: Smyrna/Lake Press, 1988.

Vasudev, Aruna. *The New Indian Cinema*. Delhi: Macmillan, 1986.

"Voice of Vietnam." *Cinemaya* no. 16 (Summer 1992): 46–72.

GLOSSARY

Academy ratio In the silent era, the film frame was customarily 1⅓ times as wide as it was high (1.33:1). When a sound track was added, however, the image became nearly square. The 1.33:1 silent *aspect ratio* was standardized by the Academy of Motion Picture Arts and Sciences in 1932. (In practice, the sound-film ratio was closer to 1.37:1.)

actualities An early term for documentary films.

anamorphic lens A lens for making widescreen films using regular *Academy ratio* frame size. The camera lens takes in a wide field of view and squeezes it onto the frame, and a similar projector lens unsqueezes the image onto a wide theater screen. The most famous anamorphic widescreen processes are CinemaScope and Panavision.

animation Any process whereby artificial movement is created by photographing a series of drawings (see *cel animation*), objects, or computer images one by one. Small changes in position, recorded frame by frame, create the illusion of movement.

art cinema (1) Critical term used to describe films, which, while made within commercial circumstances, take an approach to form and style influenced by modernist trends (see *modernism*) within "high art" and which offer an alternative to mainstream entertainment. (2) Term used by U.S. film industry to describe imported films of interest principally to upper-middle-class, college-educated audiences.

artisanal production The process in which a filmmaker, producer, and crew devote their energy to making a single film, often with no expectation that they will collaborate on another project in the future. This is in contrast to the mass production and division of labor of *studio production*.

aspect ratio The relationship of the frame's width to its height. The standard international ratio was 1.33:1 until the early 1950s, when *widescreen formats* became more common.

auteur The presumed or actual "author" of a film, usually identified as the director. The term is also sometimes used in an evaluative sense to distinguish good filmmakers (auteurs) from bad ones. Identifying the director as the film's "author" and evaluating the film as the work of an auteur has a long history,

but it became a prominent issue after the 1940s, particularly in French and English-language film criticism.

avance sur recettes ("advance on receipts") A government policy of loaning money to a film project on the basis of anticipated ticket sales. The system came into use in France after World War II and provided a model for other countries' film-financing policies.

axis of action In the *continuity editing* system, the imaginary line that passes from side to side through the main actors, defining the spatial relations of all the elements of the scene as being to the right or left. The camera is not supposed to cross the axis at a cut and thus reverse those spatial relations. The axis is also called the "180-degree line." See also *180-degree system*.

backlighting Illumination cast onto the figures in the scene from the side opposite the camera, usually creating a thin outline of light on the figures' edge.

block booking An arrangement in which the distributor forces exhibitors to rent several films in order to get the most desirable ones. Common in the U.S. film industry after the 1910s, the practice was declared illegal in the "Paramount decision" of 1948.

camera angle The position of the frame in relation to the subject it shows: above it, looking down (a high angle); horizontal, on the same level (a straight-on angle); looking up (a low angle).

camera movement The onscreen impression that the framing is changing with respect to the scene being photographed. This is usually caused by the camera's being physically moved, but it may also be caused by a *zoom lens* or certain *special effects*. See also *crane shot, pan, tilt, tracking shot*.

canted framing A view in which the frame is not level; either the right or the left side is lower, causing objects in the scene to appear tipped.

cel animation Animation that uses a series of drawings on pieces of celluloid, called "cels" for short. Slight changes between the drawings combine to create an illusion of movement.

cinematography A general term for all the manipulations of the film strip by the camera in the shooting phase and by the laboratory in the developing phase.

close-up A framing in which the scale of the object shown is relatively large. Most commonly, a close-up shows a person's head from the neck up, or a medium-size object.

closure The degree to which the ending of a narrative film reveals the effects of all the causal events and resolves (or "closes off") all lines of action.

collage A film style which assembles footage from widely disparate sources, often juxtaposing staged fictional scenes with newsreel, animation, or other sorts of material. Explored by experimental filmmakers such as Joseph Cornell in the 1930s, it became a major resource for the avant-garde and political filmmaking of the 1960s.

compilation film A genre of documentary cinema which draws together news footage from various sources in order to convey a large-scale process, such as a war or a social change. Widely used in government and public-affairs documentaries of the sound era, the compilation film was also subjected to experimental treatment by the French Lettrists and Bruce Conner.

continuity editing A system of cutting to maintain continuous and clear narrative action. Continuity editing relies upon matching action, screen direction, and figures' positions from shot to shot. For specific techniques of continuity editing, see *axis of action, cut-in, establishing shot, eyeline match, intercutting, match on action, reestablishing shot, screen direction, shot/reverse shot.*

crane shot A shot in which a change of framing is accomplished by having the camera above the ground and moving up, down, or laterally through the air.

crosscutting. See *intercutting.*

cut (1) In filmmaking, the joining of two strips of film together with a splice. (2) In the finished film, an instantaneous change from one framing to another. See also *jump cut.*

cut-in An instantaneous shift from a distant framing to a closer view of some portion of the same space.

cycle A relatively short-lived fashion for certain subgenres within a genre: e.g., the "adult" Westerns in Hollywood during the 1950s or the films about heroic gangsters in the 1980s Hong Kong cinema.

dedramatization In narrative filmmaking, the strategy of minimizing suspense, emotional high points, and physical action in favor of low-key character portrayal, *temps morts,* and an emphasis on surroundings. Commonly used in European *art cinema* of the post-World War II era, often to explore character psychology, evoke mood, or bring out environmental details.

deep focus A use of the camera lens and lighting that keeps both the close and distant planes in sharp focus.

deep space An arrangement of mise-en-scene elements so that there is a considerable distance between the plane closest to the camera and the one farthest away. Any or all of these planes may be in focus.

depth of field The measurements of the closest and farthest planes in front of the camera lens between which everything will be in sharp focus. A depth of field from 5 to 16 feet, e.g., would mean everything closer than 5 feet and farther than 16 feet would be out of focus.

diegetic sound Any voice, musical passage, or sound effect presented as originating from a source within the film's world. See also *nondiegetic sound.*

diorama An entertainment in which the spectators sat in a circular room and viewed long transparent paintings that seemed to move as the lighting changed.

direct sound Music, noise, and speech recorded from the event at the moment of filming; the opposite of *postsynchronization.* Early sound films and Direct Cinema documentaries emphasized direct sound.

dissolve A transition between two shots during which the first image gradually disappears while the second image gradually appears. For a moment the two images blend briefly in superimposition.

distance of framing The apparent distance of the frame from the mise-en-scene elements; also called "camera distance" and "shot scale." See also *close-up, extreme close-up, medium shot.*

distribution One of the three branches of the film industry; the process of supplying films to the places where they will be shown. See also *exhibition, production.*

dolly A camera support with wheels, used in making *tracking shots.*

dubbing The process of replacing part or all of the voices on the sound track in order to correct mistakes or rerecord dialogue. See also *postsynchronization.*

editing (1) In filmmaking, the task of selecting and joining camera *takes.* (2) In the finished film, the set of techniques that governs the relations among *shots.*

ellipsis In narrative, the omission of certain scenes or portions of the action.

elliptical editing Editing which omits portions of the action, often with the purpose of startling the viewer or creating questions about what occurred in the missing stretches.

establishing shot A shot, usually involving a distant framing, that shows the spatial relations among the important figures, objects, and setting in a scene.

exhibition One of the three branches of the film industry; the process of showing the finished film to audiences. See also *distribution, production.*

experimental cinema Filmmaking which avoids the conventions of mass-entertainment film and seeks to explore unusual aspects of the medium and/or suppressed or taboo subject matter. When experimental films present plots, these are frequently predicated upon dreams or symbolic journeys, but often experimental films avoid narrative form altogether, exploring lyric, associational, descriptive, or other formal means.

extreme close-up A framing which enlarges a small detail, such as an eye or a line of newsprint.

eyeline match A cut obeying the *axis of action* principle, in which the first shot shows a person looking off in one direction and the second shows a nearby space containing what he or she sees. If the person looks to the left, the following shot should imply that the looker is offscreen right.

fade (1) Fade-in: A dark screen that gradually brightens as a shot appears. (2) Fade-out: A shot that gradually darkens as the screen goes black. Occasionally fade-outs brighten to pure white or to a color.

fill light Illumination from a source less bright than the *key light,* used to soften deep shadows in a scene. See also *three-point lighting.*

film noir ("dark film") A term applied by French critics to a type of American film, usually in the detective and thriller genres, with low-key lighting and a somber mood. *Film noir* was most prevalent in the 1940s and 1950s, though it was revived occasionally later.

film stock The strip of material upon which a series of film frames is registered. It consists of a clear base coated on one side with a light-sensitive emulsion.

filter A piece of glass or gelatin placed in front of the camera or printer lens to alter the light striking the film in the aperture.

flashback An alteration of story order in which events occurring in the present are interrupted by the showing of events which took place earlier.

flashforward An alteration of story order in which the plot presentation moves forward to future events and then returns to the present.

focal length The distance from the center of the lens to the point at which the light rays meet in sharp focus. The focal length determines the perspective relations of the space represented on the flat screen. See also *normal lens, telephoto lens, wide-angle lens.*

focus The degree to which light rays coming from the same part of an object through different parts of the lens converge at the same point on the film frame, creating sharp outlines and distinct textures.

frame A single image on the strip of film. When a series of frames is projected onto a screen in quick succession, the spectator sees an illusory movement.

framing The use of the edges of the film frame to select and to compose what will be visible onscreen.

front projection A composite process whereby footage meant to appear as the background of a shot is projected from the front onto a screen. Figures in the foreground are filmed in front of the screen as well. See also *rear projection.*

frontality In staging, the positioning of figures so that they face the viewer.

gauge The width of the film strip, measured in millimeters. The standard gauges in film history are 8mm, 16mm, 35mm, and 70mm.

genres Various types of films which audiences and filmmakers recognize by their recurring conventions. Common genres are horror films, gangster films, and Westerns.

graphic match Two successive shots joined so as to create a strong similarity of compositional elements, such as color or shape.

hand-held camera The use of the camera operator's body as a camera support, either holding it by hand or using a harness. Seen in some silent films, such as Abel Gance's *Napoléon,* but more common in Direct Cinema documentaries and fiction films from the 1960s on.

hard lighting Illumination that creates sharp-edged shadows.

height of framing The distance of the camera above the ground, regardless of its angle to the horizontal.

high-key lighting Illumination that creates comparatively little contrast between light and dark areas of the shot. Shadows are fairly transparent and brightened by *fill light.*

horizontal integration A practice in which a company in one sector of the motion-picture industry acquires or gains control over other companies in that sector. For example, a production company may expand by purchasing other production firms.

intellectual montage The juxtaposition of a series of images to create an abstract idea not suggested by any one image. Pioneered by Soviet Montage directors, particularly Eisenstein, it returned to widespread use in *experimental cinema* and left-wing cinema of the 1960s.

intercutting Editing that alternates shots of two or more lines of action occurring in different places, usually simultaneously. Used synonymously with "crosscutting."

iris A round, moving *mask* that can (1) close down to end a scene (iris-out) or emphasize a detail; or (2) open to begin a scene (iris-in) or reveal more space around a detail.

jump cut An elliptical cut that appears to be an interruption of a single shot. Either the figures seem to change instantly against a constant background or the background changes instantly while the figures remain constant. See also *elliptical editing.*

key light In the *three-point lighting* system, the brightest illumination coming into the scene. See also *backlighting, fill light.*

linearity In a narrative, the clear motivation of a series of causes and effects that progress without significant digressions, delays, or irrelevant interpolations.

long shot A framing in which the scale of the object shown is small. A standing human figure would appear nearly the height of the screen.

long take A shot that continues for an unusually lengthy time. Rare in silent cinema, the long take became more significant in the 1930s and 1940s, especially as used by Jean Renoir and Orson Welles. It soon became a common technique in films throughout the world. See also *plan-séquence.*

low-key lighting Illumination that creates strong contrast between light and dark areas of the shot, with deep shadows and little *fill light.*

Majors A term for the most powerful film companies in the U.S. industry. In the 1920s, the Majors were also known as the "Big Three" and consisted of Paramount-Publix, Loew's (MGM), and First National. During the 1930s, the Majors (now the "Big Five") were MGM, Paramount, 20th Century-Fox, Warner Bros., and RKO. Before 1948, the Majors achieved their status because they had a high degree of *vertical integration.* Today the Majors consist of several production-distribution companies, such as MCA/Universal, Warner Communications, Disney, and Columbia.

mask An opaque screen placed in the camera or printer which blocks part of the frame and changes the shape of the image. As seen on the screen, most masks are black, although they can be white or colored.

masking In exhibition, stretches of black fabric that frame the theater screen. Masking may be adjusted according to the *aspect ratio* of the film to be projected.

match on action A continuity cut which joins two shots of the same gesture, making it appear to continue uninterrupted.

matte shot A type of *process shot* in which different areas of the image (usually actors and setting) are photographed separately and combined in laboratory work.

medium shot A framing in which the scale of the object shown is of moderate size. A human figure seen from the waist up would fill most of the screen.

Minors During the 1920s–1950s, significant Hollywood production companies which did not own theaters. Also known as the "Little Three," the Minors consisted of Universal, Columbia, and United Artists. See also *Majors*.

mise-en-scene All the elements placed in front of the camera to be photographed: the settings and props, lighting, costumes and make-up, and figure behavior.

mixing Combining two or more sound tracks by rerecording them onto a single track.

modernism A broad trend in twentieth-century art and literature emphasizing aesthetic innovation and themes which comment upon contemporary life. Modernist art flaunts difficult, often aggressive or disruptive, forms and styles; it frequently challenges traditional "realistic" art and criticizes mass popular entertainment. Thematically, modernism displays a fascination with technology, city life, and problems of personal identity. It embraces both political critique and spiritual exploration. Expressionism, Surrealism, and atonal music are some typical manifestations of modernism. Modernism's impact has been felt in *experimental cinema, art cinema*, and some mainstream commercial filmmaking.

montage (1) A synonym for *editing*. (2) An approach to editing developed by the Soviet filmmakers of the 1920s. Soviet Montage emphasizes dynamic, often discontinuous, relationships between shots. It also emphasizes *intellectual montage*.

montage sequence A segment of a film that summarizes a topic or compresses a passage of time into brief symbolic or typical images. Frequently *dissolves, fades, superimpositions*, and *wipes* are used to link the shots in a montage sequence.

motif An element in a film that is repeated in a significant way.

movement A group of filmmakers working in a common period and place who share some distinctive presumptions about how films should be made. Typically, the films of a movement share formal, stylistic, and thematic features. Some movements, such as French Surrealism of the 1920s, can be seen as fairly unified; others, such as the French New Wave of the late 1950s, are comparatively loose.

nickelodeon boom Beginning in 1905, a period of rapid expansion in the number of small, inexpensive store-front theaters showing programs of short films. During the 1910s, nickelodeons disappeared as larger theaters were built.

nondiegetic sound Sound, such as mood music or a narrator's commentary, represented as coming from a source outside the world of the narrative (the "diegesis").

normal lens A lens that shows objects without severely exaggerating or reducing the depth of the scene's planes. In theatrical filmmaking, a normal lens is 35mm to 50mm. See also *telephoto lens, wide-angle lens*.

oligopoly An economic situation in which a few companies control a market, often cooperating with each other to keep out new firms. In the U.S. film industry after the 1920s, the *Majors* and the *Minors* constituted an oligopoly.

180-degree system In the continuity approach to editing, the dictate that the camera should stay on one side of the action to ensure consistent spatial relations between objects to the right and left of the frame. The 180-degree line is the same as the *axis of action*. See also *continuity editing, screen direction*.

overlapping editing Cuts that repeat part or all of an action, thus expanding the duration of the action on screen.

pan A *camera movement* in which the camera body swivels to the right or left. The onscreen effect is of scanning the space horizontally.

pan-and-zoom technique A way of substituting for cutting into and out of a scene; continuous *pans* and zooms concentrate attention on significant aspects of a scene. Rossellini pioneered this technique in the late 1950s, and it became widespread during the 1960s. Often the pan-and-zoom technique enables the director to create a *long take*. See also *zoom lens*.

pixillation A form of animation in which three-dimensional objects, often people, are made to move in staccato bursts through the use of stop-action cinematography.

plan-séquence ("sequence shot") French term for a scene handled in a single shot, usually a *long take*.

point-of-view (POV) shot A shot taken with the camera placed approximately where a character's eyes would be, showing what the character would see. A POV shot is usually preceded or followed by a shot of the character looking.

postsynchronization The process of adding sound to images after they have been shot and assembled. This can include *dubbing* of voices, as well as inserting *diegetic* music or sound effects. Contemporary fiction films are often postsynchronized. The technique is the opposite of *direct sound*.

process shot Any shot involving rephotography to combine two or more images into one or to create a special effect; also called "composite shot." See also *front projection, matte shot, rear projection, special effects*.

production One of the three branches of the film industry; the process of creating a film. See also *distribution, exhibition*.

protectionism Government policy which defends national filmmaking from competition by foreign imports. Typical protectionist policies are quotas on the number of films which may be imported or shown, requirements that theater time be set aside for the domestic product, and forms of financial aid to domestic production.

racking focus Shifting the area of sharp focus from one plane to another during a shot. The effect on the screen is called "rack focus."

rear projection A technique for combining a foreground action with a background action filmed earlier. The foreground is filmed in a studio, against a screen; the background imagery is projected from behind the screen. The technique is the opposite of *front projection.*

reestablishing shot A return to a view of an entire space after a series of closer shots following the *establishing shot.*

reflexivity A tendency, characteristic of cinematic modernism, to call attention to the fact that the film is an artifact or an illusion. Advocates of reflexivity often suggest that while mainstream cinema encourages the viewer to take the world on screen as real, a more self-conscious cinema will expose the ways in which movie makers create this effect of reality.

reframing Using short *pan* or *tilt* movements of the camera to keep figures onscreen or centered.

rotoscope A machine that projects live-action motion-picture film frames one by one onto a drawing pad or *cel* so that an animator can trace the figures in each frame. The aim is to achieve more realistic movement in an animated cartoon.

run A distinct period during which a film is exhibited during its release. In Hollywood's studio era, a film's "first run" in major urban theaters would be followed by subsequent runs in neighborhoods or small towns. Today, after a film's first theatrical run, later runs include screenings in budget theaters, 16mm nontheatrical screenings, cable television premieres, and videocassette release.

runaway production The practice of Hollywood film companies shooting their films abroad after World War II. This was done partly to save money and partly to utilize the rental income ("frozen funds") which European governments had forbidden U.S. companies to withdraw from the country.

scenics Early nonfiction short films that displayed picturesque or exotic locales.

screen direction The right-left relationships in a scene, set up in an establishing shot and determined by the position of characters and objects in the frame, the directions of movement, and the characters' eyelines. *Continuity editing* attempts to keep screen direction consistent between shots. See also *axis of action, eyeline match, 180-degree system.*

sequence shot See *plan-séquence.*

shallow focus A restricted *depth of field,* which keeps only those planes close to the camera in sharp focus; the opposite of *deep focus.*

shallow space An arrangement in which the action is staged with relatively little depth; the opposite of *deep space.*

shot (1) In shooting, one uninterrupted run of the camera to expose a series of frames. Also called a *take.* (2) In the finished film, one uninterrupted image with a single static or mobile framing.

shot/reverse shot Two or more shots edited together that alternate characters, typically in a conversation situation. In *continuity editing,* characters in one framing usually look left, in the other framing, right. Over-the-shoulder framings are common in shot/reverse-shot editing.

side lighting Lighting coming from one side of a person or object, usually in order to create a sense of volume, to bring out surface textures, or to fill in areas left shadowed by light from another source.

soft lighting Illumination that avoids harsh bright and dark areas, creating a gradual transition from highlights to shadows.

sound-over Any sound that is not represented as being directly audible within the space and time of the images on the screen. A spoken narration (called "voice-over") is a common example.

sound perspective The sense of a sound's position in space, yielded by volume, timbre, pitch, and, in multichannel reproduction systems, binaural information.

special effects A general term for various photographic manipulations that create illusory spatial relations in the shot, such as *superimposition,* a *matte shot,* and *rear projection.*

storyboard A tool used in planning film production, consisting of comic-strip-like drawings of individual shots, with descriptions written below each drawing.

studio production A manner of filmmaking in which an enterprise creates motion pictures on a mass scale. Usually labor is divided on the basis of extensive preparation, guided by the shooting script and other written plans. Typically, some personnel, such as directors and cinematographers, work on one film at a time, while other staff, such as screenwriters or specialized technicians, work on several films more or less simultaneously. The Hollywood companies between the 1920s and 1950s exemplify studio production.

style The systematic and salient uses of film *techniques* characteristic of a film or a group of films (e.g., a filmmaker's work or a film *movement*).

superimposition The exposure of more than one image on the same film strip.

synchronous sound Sound that is matched temporally with the movements occurring in the images, as when dialogue corresponds to lip movements.

take In filmmaking, the *shot* produced by one uninterrupted run of the camera. One shot in the final film may be chosen from among several takes of the same action.

technique Any aspect of the film medium that can be manipulated in making a film.

telephoto lens A lens of long focal length that affects a scene's perspective by enlarging distant planes and making them seem close to the foreground planes. In 35mm filming, a telephoto lens is 75mm or more in length. See also *normal lens, wide-angle lens.*

temps morts ("dead moments") French phrase used to describe a manner of staging and filming which stresses long intervals between actions or lines of dialogue in which no major narrative development takes place. A *temps mort* might be a lengthy pause in a dialogue scene or an extended sequence showing a character walking through a landscape. Usually *temps morts* are used to suggest realism, characterization, or mood. The device, seen occasionally in silent films and exploited by Italian Neorealism after World War II, has become widely used in the European *art cinema* since the 1950s.

three-point lighting A common arrangement using three directions of light on a scene: from behind the subjects (*backlighting*), from one bright source (*key light*), and from a less bright source (*fill light*).

tilt A *camera movement* in which the camera body swivels upward or downward on a stationary support. It produces a mobile framing that scans the space vertically.

top lighting Lighting coming from above a person or object, usually in order to outline the upper areas of the figure or to separate it more clearly from the background.

topicals Early short films showing current events, such as parades, disasters, government ceremonies, and military maneuvers. Most topicals recorded the action as it was occurring, but many restaged the event.

tracking shot A *camera movement* in which the camera body moves through space in a horizontal path. On the screen, it produces a mobile framing that travels through space forward, backward, or to one side.

typage A performance technique of Soviet Montage cinema in which an actor is given features believed to characterize a social group, often an economic class.

underlighting Illumination from a point below the figures in the scene.

vertical integration A practice in which a single company engages in two or more of the activities of the film industry (*production, distribution,* and *exhibition*). In the U.S. film industry, the *Majors* were vertically integrated from the 1920s on, owning production facilities, distribution companies, and theaters. The industry's vertical integration was judged monopolistic by the Supreme Court in the "Paramount decree" of 1948. In the 1980s the practice reemerged when production and distribution companies began acquiring interests in theater chains and cable television concerns.

whip pan An extremely fast movement of the camera from side to side, which causes the image to blur briefly into a set of indistinct horizontal lines. Often an imperceptible cut will join two whip pans to create a transition between scenes.

wide-angle lens A lens of short focal length that affects a scene's perspective by bulging straight lines near the edges of the frame and exaggerating the distance between foreground and background planes. In 35mm filming, a wide-angle lens is 30mm or less. See also *normal lens, telephoto lens.*

widescreen formats Screen ratios wider than the *Academy ratio,* which is standardized at 1.37:1 in the United States. Important widescreen formats are the U.S. standard of 1.85:1, the CinemaScope and anamorphic Panavision ratio of 2.35:1, and the 70mm ratio of 2.2:1. See also *anamorphic lens, aspect ratio.*

wipe A transition between shots in which a line passes across the screen, gradually eliminating the first shot and replacing it with the next one.

zoom lens A lens with a *focal length* that can be changed during a shot. A shift toward the telephoto range (zoom-in) enlarges the central portions of the image and flattens its planes together. A shift toward the wide-angle range (zoom-out) de-enlarges the central portions of the image and separates planes more. See also *telephoto lens, wide-angle lens.*

PHOTO CREDITS

Most of the illustrations in this book are from the authors' personal collection. Others have come from various sources, as listed below. The boldface numbers are figure references.

Academy of Motion Picture Arts and Sciences, Beverly Hills: **3.29**

Anthology Film Archives, New York: **21.35, 21.37, 21.38, 24.29** (original photo by Michael Chakiris)

Art Resource: **21.66**

Bakhrushin State Central Theatrical Museum, Moscow: **6.14**

BFI Stills, Posters and Designs, London: **1.19, 11.1, 11.2, 17.1, 18.40, 18.41, 22.12, 24.24, 24.39**

Bison 101 Archive, Beverly Hills: **3.30, 9.3**

From the collection of Ben Brewster and Lea Jacobs: **1.32**

From the collection of Donald Crafton: **1.4**

Det Danske Filmmuseum, Copenhagen: **2.7**

Lenin Library, Moscow: **6.7**

Sophie Lissitsky-Kuppers, *El Lissitsky* (Thames & Hudson, 1968): **Color Plate 6.1**

Milwaukee Museum of Art: **Color Plate 5.1** (Gift of Mrs. Harry L. Bradley)

Motion Picture Division, George Eastman International Museum of Photography, Rochester: **1.1, 1.3, 1.5, 1.8, 1.9, 1.12, 1.28, 1.29, 1.30, 2.10, 2.11, 9.1, 9.2, 9.12, 10.2, 10.3, 10.4**

Museum of Modern Art Film Stills Library, New York: **1.14, 3.1, 4.22, 4.41, 7.1, 15.4, 17.5, 18.39**

Michael Patterson, *The Revolution in German Theatre 1900–1933* (London: Routledge & Kegan Paul, 1981): **5.4**

Staatliche Museen Preussischer Kulturbesitz, Nationalgalerie, Berlin: **5.26**

Theatermuseen, Munich: **5.3**

University of Iowa, Museum of Art, Iowa City: **Color Plate 5.2**

Wisconsin Center for Film and Theater Research: **1.6, 15.1, 15.2, 15.8, 15.9, 15.10, 15.29**

We are grateful to these sources for supplying illustrative material.

INDEX